Rick Steves'
BEST OF
EUROPE
2004

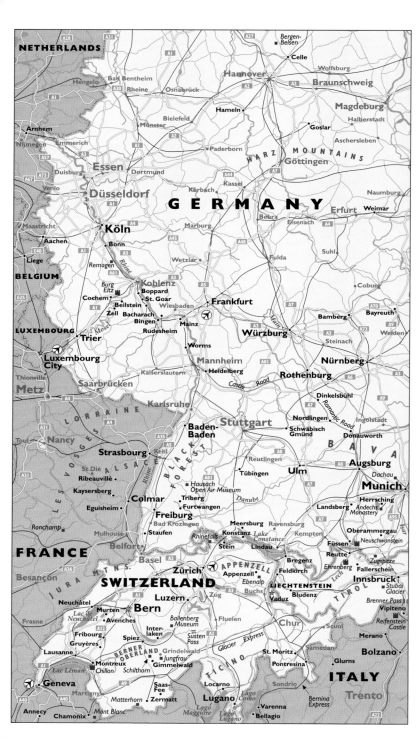

GERMANY, AUSTRIA & SWITZERLAND

![A24]	Freeway/Motorway
	Major Roads
	Major Rail Line
✈	Airport
St. Goar	Recommended Location*
Bebra	Just passing through**
■	Ruin, Museum, Other Point of Interest
⌂	Castle/Monument/Palace

* Black locations are places of interest to tourists, sized by importance.

** Gray locations are not places of interest to tourists and are sized by population.

0 km   50   100 km

0 miles   50 miles

Tegel ✈ **Berlin** Frankfurt an der Oder

Brandenburg • Potsdam
Sanssouci Palace

POLAND

Rzepin

Zielona Góra

• **Wittenberg**

Cottbus

Zary

Lauchhammer

Elbe

Halle

Leipzig Moritzburg

Boleslawiec

Meissen

Zgorzelec Görlitz

SAXONY

Dresden

Bad Schandau

Zittau

Glauchau

Chemnitz

Seiffen

Decin

Plauen

Ústí nad Labem
• **Litoměřice**
Terezín

Ruzyně ✈

Karlovy Vary

Prague

Kutná Hora •

Štramberk

Cheb

Mariánské Lázně

Karlstejn Castle

CZECH REPUBLIC

Olomouc

Marktredwitz

E50

Plzeň •

MORAVIA

Kromeriz •

BOHEMIA

E50   E65

Zlín

Český Kubice

Tabor

Veselí nad Lužnicí

• Telc

Brno •

Furth

Breclav

Regensburg

Ober-traubling

A3

Summerau

Český Budějovice

Český Velenice

Gmund

Slavonice

Kuty

SLOVAKIA

Passau

Danube

WACHAU

Durnstein

Krems

• **Vienna** ✈

Český Krumlov

Grinzing •

A92

✈

Linz

• Mauthausen

Melk

Schönbrunn Palace

Bratislava

RIA

Attnang Puchheim

A1

St. Valentin

Puchberg

Eisenstadt

M1

Salzach

Herrenchiemsee Chiemsee

A8

Salzburg

• Bad Ischl

Schneeberg

Sopron •

Esterhazy Palace

Rosenheim •

Hallstatt

AUSTRIA

Selzthal

Berchtesgaden

Kufstein

Hallein

SALZKAMMERGUT

Bruck an der Mur

Szombathely

Wörgl

• Hinterhornalm

Zell am See

Stainach Irdning

Leoben

• Hall

Kitzbühel

Piber •

Graz •

HUNGARY

Badgastein

Grossglockner Pass

Spittal

A10

Spielfeld

A2

Nagykanizsa

Dobbiaco

Lienz

Klagenfurt •

Maribor

ALPE DI SIUSI

• Cortina

Tarvisio

Jesenice

Vršič Pass

Bled/Lesce

Koprivnica

Castelrotto

Calalzo

A23

Lake Bohinj

Lake Bled

✈ Brnik

CROATIA

DOLOMITES

Belluno

FRIULI

Udine

JULIAN ALPS

Ljubljana

Zagreb

✈

VENETO

Pordenone

Palmanova •

SLOVENIA

■ Postojna Caves

A27

A4

■ Škocjan Caves

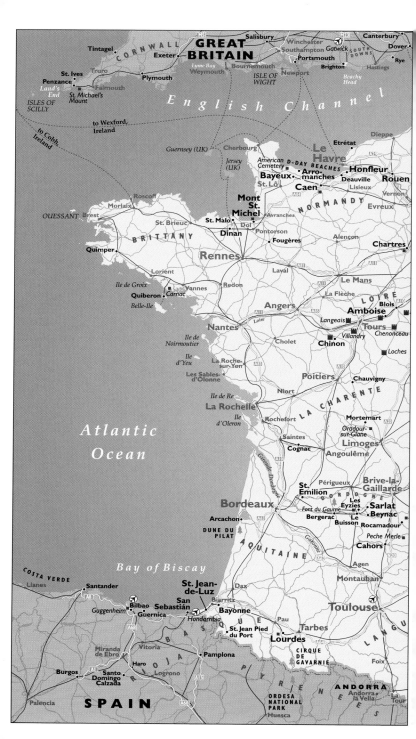

FRANCE

0 km   50 km   100 km

0 miles   50 miles

Channel Tunnel
Ostende
Bruges • Antwerp
Dunkerque
Calais
Boulogne
St. Omer
Ghent
Brussels ✈
Waterloo
Aachen
BELGIUM
Lille
FLANDERS
Arras
Abbeville
Cambrai
Aulnoye
Amiens
Namur
WALLONIE
Liège
Cochem
Wetzlar
Rhine
St. Goar
Bacharach
Frankfurt ✈
Beauvais
Chantilly
Senlis
Soissons
Laon
St. Quentin
Charleville-Mézières
ARDENNES
Charles de Gaulle ✈
Reims
Verdun Battlefield
LUXEMBOURG
Longwy
Thionville
Luxembourg City
Trier
Zell
Rudesheim
GERMANY
Kaiserslautern
Mannheim
Heidelberg
Giverny
Paris ✈
Seine
Disneyland Paris
Epernay
CHAMPAGNE
Châlons
Metz
Saarbrücken
Karlsruhe
Stuttgart ✈
Versailles ✈ Orly
Vaux-le-Vicomte
Fontainebleau
St. Dizier
Toul
Nancy
Chaumont
LORRAINE
Strasbourg ✈
ALSACE
Ribeauvillé
Baden-Baden
BLACK FOREST
Freudenstadt
Orléans
Cheverny
Chambord
Loire
Troyes
Chablis
Auxerre
Laroche
Avallon
Vézelay
Guedelon
Sancerre
Seine
Rhine
Kaysersberg
Colmar
Eguisheim
Ronchamp
Mulhouse
Freiburg
Triberg
Meersburg
Staufen
Vierzon
Bourges
Châteauroux
Autun
BURGUNDY
Semur-en-Auxois
Culmont
Belfort
JURA MTNS.
Zurich ✈
Nevers
Le Creusot
Châteauneuf-en-Auxois
Dijon
Besançon
Dol
SWITZERLAND
Neuchâtel
Lac de Neuchâtel
Luzern
Lake Luzern
Moulins
Montluçon
FRANCE
Guéret
Clermont-Ferrand
AUVERGNE
Vichy
Brançion
Cluny
Mâcon
Châlon-sur-Saône
Beaune
Frasne
Avenches
Fribourg
Bern
Gruyères
Lausanne
Interlaken
BERNER OBERLAND
Gimmelwald
Roanne
BEAUJOLAIS
Tournus
Bourg-en-Bresse ✈
Rhône
Geneva ✈
Montreux
Locarno
Lago Maggiore
Lugano
St. Etienne
Vienne
Lyon ✈
SAVOIE
Chambéry
Martigny
Annecy
Chamonix
Mont Blanc
Mont Blanc Tunnel
Aosta
Lago di Orta
Malpensa ✈
Milan
Loire
Bourg S.M.
PIEDMONT
Po
Le Puy-en-Velay
Modane
Grenoble
Briançon
Clelles
Gap
Torino
ITALY
Gouffre Padirac
Lot
St. Cirq Lapopie
Rodez
Mende
Montélimar
Valence
Rhône
Pinerolo
Cuneo
LE LANGHE
Barolo
Savona
Genoa
GORGES DU TARN
Cordes
Millau
GORGE DE L'ARDÈCHE
PROVENCE
Vaison la Romaine
Digne
Finale
Albi
Castres
Tarn
Caunes-Minervois
Minerve
LANGUEDOC
Orange
Pont du Gard
Uzès
Châteauneuf-du-Pape
Avignon
Isle sur la Sorgue
Les Baux
Nîmes
St. Rémy
Roussillon
LUBERON
St. Paul
Vence
Grasse
Menton
MONACO
Villefranche
Ligurian Sea
to Bastia, Corsica
Carcassonne
Béziers
Montpellier
Arles
CAMARGUE
Aix-en-Provence
GRAND CANYON DU VERDON
Antibes
Cannes
COTE D'AZUR
Nice ✈
Queribus & Peyrepertuse
Narbonne
Marseille ✈
Cassis
St. Tropez
Toulon
Perpignan
Collioure
Port Bou
Figueres
Cadaques
Mediterranean Sea
to Ajaccio, Corsica
to Porto Torres, Sardinia
L'Île Rousse
CORSICA (France)

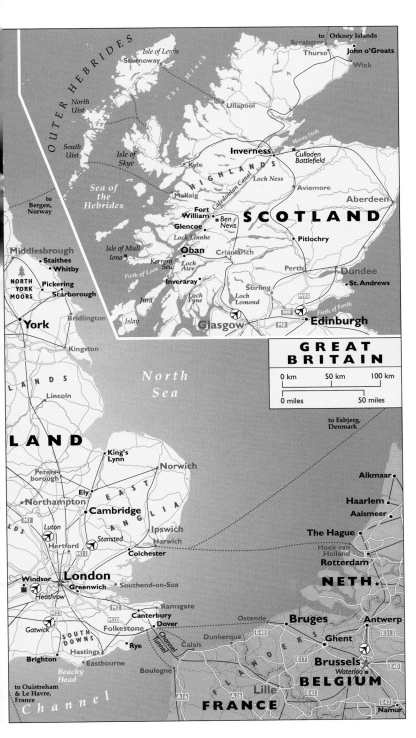

to Orkney Islands
Scrabster
Thurso
John o'Groats
Wick

OUTER HEBRIDES
Isle of Lewis
Stornoway
The Minch
North Uist
Ullapool
South Uist
Isle of Skye
Kyle
Inverness
Culloden Battlefield
Moray Firth
HIGHLANDS
Loch Ness
Aviemore
Mallaig
Caledonian Canal
Aberdeen
to Bergen, Norway
Sea of the Hebrides
Fort William
Glencoe
Ben Nevis
SCOTLAND
Loch Linnhe
Isle of Mull
Oban
Iona
Kerrera
Seil
Loch Awe
Crianlarich
Pitlochry
Perth
Dundee
Middlesbrough
Staithes
Whitby
NORTH YORK MOORS
Pickering
Scarborough
Bridlington
York
Kingston
Jura
Islay
Loch Fyne
Inveraray
Loch Lomond
Stirling
M90
St. Andrews
Firth of Lorn
Firth of Forth
Glasgow
M9
Edinburgh
M8

North Sea

GREAT BRITAIN

0 km   50 km   100 km

0 miles   50 miles

Lincoln

LANDS

LAND

King's Lynn
Peters-borough
Northampton
Ely
EAST ANGLIA
Norwich
Alkmaar
Haarlem
Aalsmeer
The Hague
M1
Luton
Hertford
Stansted
Cambridge
Ipswich
Harwich
Colchester
Hoek van Holland
Rotterdam
NETH.
M11
Windsor
Heathrow
Greenwich
London
Southend-on-Sea
Gatwick
M23
SOUTH DOWNS
Brighton
Hastings
Eastbourne
Beachy Head
to Ouistreham & Le Havre, France
Ramsgate
M2
Canterbury
M20
Folkestone
Dover
Rye
Channel tunnel
Ostende
Dunkerque
Calais
Boulogne
Bruges
Ghent
Antwerp
E313
E40
FLANDERS
E17
Brussels
Waterloo
BELGIUM
Lille
A16
A26
E42
FRANCE
E40
Namur
E42
Channel
to Esbjerg, Denmark

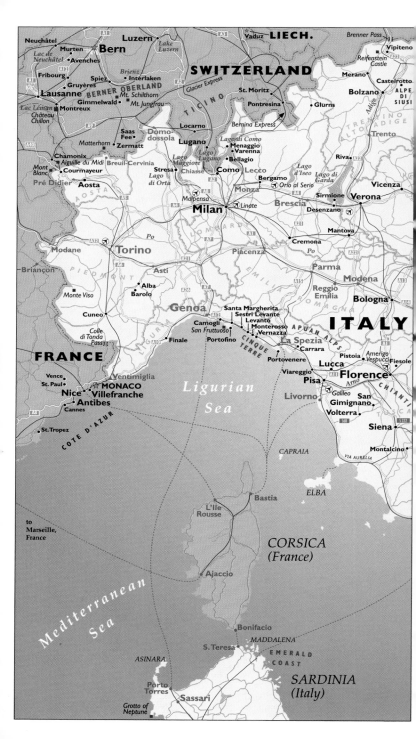

SPAIN &
PORTUGAL

0 km   50 km   100 km

0 mi   50 mi   100 mi

Atlantic Ocean

Coruña
San Martin
Ribadeo
Canero
Avilés
Gijón
COSTA VERDE
Santander
Santillana del Mar
Altamira Caves
La Espina
Oviedo
Cangas
Llanes
Potes
Cabo Finisterre
Santiago de Compostela
Lugo
Piedrafita
PICOS DE EUROPA
G A L I C I A
A S T U R I A S
Pontevedra
Ponferrada
León
Aguilar
Cillervel
Vigo
Gullarei
Orense
Valencia
S. Maria
Becilla
Benevente
Palencia
Burgos
Lerma
Viana do Castelo
Braga
Bragança
Zamora
Valladolid
Aranda
Amarante
DOURO
Mirandela
Medina del Campo
S P A
Porto
Vila Nova
Vila Real
Pocinho
CASTILE-LEON
Douro
Regua
P O R T U G A L
Aveiro
Viseu
Salamanca
Peñaranda
Segovia
La Granja
Figueira da Foz
Conimbriga
Coimbra
Guarda
Vilar
Valley of the Fallen
Ávila
Barajas
Mondego
Ciudad Rodrigo
Piedrahita
El Escorial
Madrid
Batalha
Leiria
Castelo Branco
Plasencia
Toledo
Aranjue
Nazaré
Valado
Tomar
Fátima
Tajo
Talavera de la Reina
Tajo
Alcobaça
Caldas da Rainha
Entroncamento
Valencia de Alcantara
CASTILE-
Óbidos
Santarém
Cáceres
La Nava
Almoncid
Cabo da Roca
Sintra
Portalegre
Trujillo
Consuegra
LA
Estoril
Lisbon
Elvas
Badajoz
Zorita
Puerto Lapice
Cascais
Cromlech dos Almendres
Évora
Mérida
Tomelloso
Setúbal
Escoural
Anta do Zambujeiro
La Albuera
Don Benito
Ciudad Real
Manza-nares
Cabo Espichel
Casa Branca
EXTREMA-DURA
Valde-peñas
Sines
ALENTEJO
Beja
Llerena
Alcarecejos
AVE High Speed Rail
Puertollano
Cercal
Galaroza
Odemira
Vila do Bispo
Funcheira
Córdoba
Linares
Sagres
ALGARVE
Vila Real
Ayamonte
Italica
Carmona
Úbeda
Lagos
Tunes
Faro
Huelva
Sevilla
Ecija
Jaén
Salema
Loule
Cacela Velha
Utrera
A N D A L U C I A
Albufeira
Tavira
Sanlucar
WHITE HILL TOWNS
Bobadilla
Alhambra
Jerez
Arcos
Zahara
Antequera
Granada
Rota
Grazalema
Málaga
SIERRA NEVADA
Cádiz
Benaojan
Ronda
Frigiliana
Nerja Caves
Medina-Sidonia
Pileta Caves
Torremolinos
Nerja
Motril
Marbella
Fuengirola
Salobreña
Vejer
San Pedro
COSTA DEL SOL
Atlantic Ocean
Cabo Trafalgar
Algeciras
La Linea
Tarifa
GIBRALTAR (UK)
Tangier
Strait of Gibraltar
CEUTA (Spain)
MOROCCO
Tétouan
COSTA DE LA LUZ

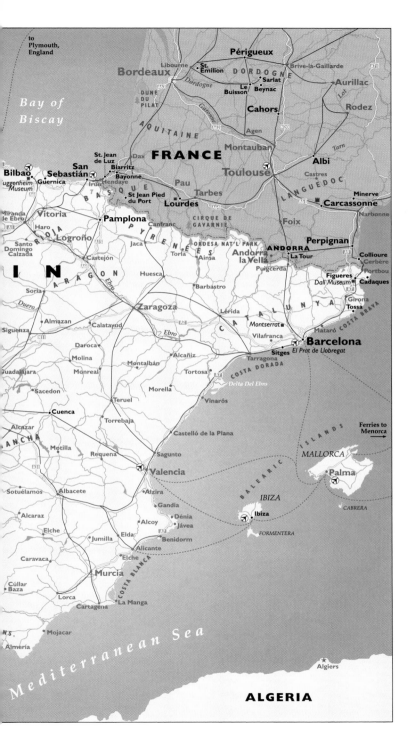

LOW COUNTRIES

0 km	50 km	100 km

0 miles	50 miles

North

Sea

Wadden Islands

Waddenzee

Emden

Groningen

Leeuwarden

A7

A28

Den Helder

Afsluitdijk

Hindeloopen

A31

NETHERLANDS

IJsselmeer

A7

■ *Open-Air Museum*

Enkhuizen

Alkmaar ●

Hoorn

Zaanse Schans ■

Edam ●

Lelystad

Flevoland

Bad Bentheim

Haarlem ●

Keukenhof ■

★ Amsterdam

Aalsmeer ●

✈ *Schiphol*

Hengelo

A30

A1

Scheveningen ●

Leiden

Utrecht

Kröller-Müller Museum

The Hague ●

A2

A12

Delft ●

Open-Air Museum

Hoek van Holland

Arnhem ●

A15

Waal

to Harwich, England

Rotterdam ●

A16

A27

Nijmegen ●

Emmerich

Essen

Delta Expo ■

Maas

A2

A57

Rhine

A3

Eindhoven ●

to Dover, England

Zeebrugge

Middelburg ●

A58

A67

A73

Duisburg ✈

Ostende

Venlo ●

Düsseldorf

E40

Bruges ●

Antwerp ●

F L A N D E R S

E313

GERMANY

Flanders Fields Museum ■

Ghent ●

✈

Köln ●

● Ieper

E17

Brussels ★

Hasselt

Maastricht ●

Waterloo ■

Leuven

Tournai ●

E40

Aachen ●

Lille

E42

BELGIUM

A1

E40

Remagen ■

A26

E42

Namur

Meuse

Liège ●

Arras

Cambrai

Mons ●

W A L L O N I E

Meuse

Cochem ●

Aulnoye

Dinant ●

La Roche ●

A1

Ze

FRANCE

Bastogne

A R D E N N E S

Vianden ●

St. Quentin

LUXEMBOURG

Mosel

Laon ●

Charleville-Mézières

Trier ●

Soissons

A26

Longwy

Thionville

Luxembourg City ★ ✈

● Senlis

✈ *Charles de Gaulle*

A4

Reims ●

Verdun Battlefield

Saarbrücken

A4

A4

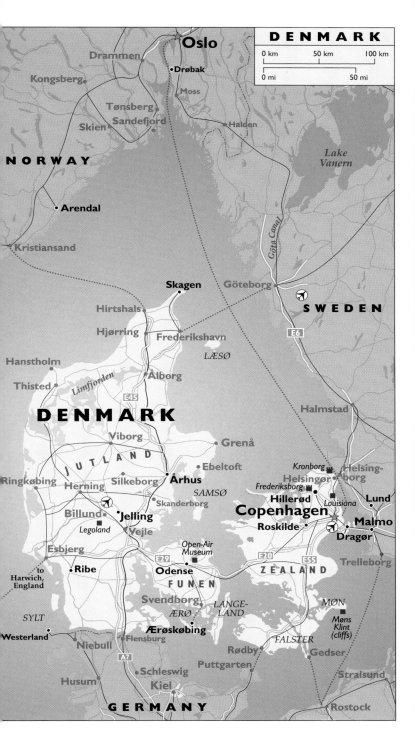

Rick Steves'
BEST OF
EUROPE
2004

AVALON
TRAVEL

For a complete listing of Rick Steves' books, see page 9.

Avalon Travel Publishing
1400 65th Street, Suite 250
Emeryville, CA 94608
Avalon Travel Publishing is a division of Avalon Publishing Group.

Printed in the United States of America by Worzalla
First printing February 2004

For the latest on Rick Steves' lectures, guidebooks, tours, and public television series,
contact Europe Through the Back Door, Box 2009, Edmonds, WA 98020, 425/771-8303,
fax 425/771-0833, www.ricksteves.com, rick@ricksteves.com.

ISBN: 1-56691-532-5 • ISSN: 1096-7702

Europe Through the Back Door Managing Editor: Risa Laib
Europe Through the Back Door Editors: Cameron Hewitt, Jill Hodges
Avalon Travel Publishing Editor and Series Manager: Laura Mazer
Avalon Travel Publishing Project Editor: Patrick Collins
Research Assistance: Rolinka Bloeming, Carlos Galvin, Cameron Hewitt,
    Jill Hodges, Kristen Kusnic, Susana Minich, Sarah Murdoch, Pat O'Connor,
    Heidi Sewell, Steve Smith
Production & Typesetting: PDBD
Interior Design: Laura Mazer, Jane Musser, Amber Pirker
Cover Design: Kari Gim, Laura Mazer
Maps and Graphics: David C. Hoerlein, Rhonda Pelikan, Zoey Platt,
    Mike Morgenfeld
Front Matter Color Photos: Page i: Neuschwanstein Castle, Germany © Dominic
    Bonuccelli; page xvi: Koln Cathedral, Germany © Andrea Johnson
Cover Photos: Front image: Dosset, England © Guy Edwardes; back image: Zell,
    Italy © Dominic Bonuccelli
Avalon Travel Publishing Graphics Coordinator: Justin Marler

Distributed to the book trade by Publishers Group West, Berkeley, California

CONTENTS

Europe's Best Destinations

INTRODUCTION

This book breaks Europe into its top big-city, small-town, and rural destinations. It then gives you all the information and opinions necessary to wring the maximum value out of your limited time and money in each of them. If you plan to stay for two months or less in Europe, this lean and mean book is all you need.

Experiencing Europe's culture, people, and natural wonders economically and hassle-free has been my goal for more than 25 years of traveling, tour guiding, and travel writing. With this book, I pass on to you the lessons I've learned, updated for 2004.

Rick Steves' Best of Europe is the crème de la crème of places featured in my Country Guides. This book is balanced to include a comfortable mix of exciting big cities and cozy small towns: from Paris, London, and Rome to traffic-free Italian Riviera ports, alpine villages, and mom-and-pop châteaux. It covers the predictable biggies and mixes in a healthy dose of Back Door intimacy. Along with Leonardo in the Louvre, you'll enjoy Caterina in her Cantina. I've been selective. For example, rather than listing countless castles and hill towns, I recommend the best three or four of each.

The best is, of course, only my opinion. But after more than two decades of travel research, I've developed a sixth sense for what travelers enjoy.

This Information Is Accurate and Up-to-Date

This book is updated every year. Most publishers of guidebooks that cover Europe from top to bottom can afford an update only every two or three years, and rarely is the research done in person. Since this book covers only my favorite places, my research partners and I are able to update it in person each year. Even with an annual update, things change. But if you're traveling with the current edition of this book, I guarantee you're using the most up-to-date information available in print. For the latest, see www.ricksteves.com/update. Also at my Web site, check my Graffiti Wall (select "Rick Steves' Guidebooks," then the destination you're visiting) for a huge, valuable list of reports and experiences—good and bad—from fellow travelers.

Use this year's edition. People who try to save a few bucks by traveling with an old book are not smart. They learn the seriousness of their mistake...in Europe. Your trip costs about $10 per waking hour. Your time is valuable. This guidebook saves lots of time.

Planning Your Trip

This book is organized by destinations. Each destination is covered as a mini-vacation on its own, filled with exciting sights and homey, affordable places to stay. In each chapter, you'll find the following:

Planning Your Time contains a suggested schedule, with thoughts on how to best use your limited time.

Orientation includes tourist information, city transportation, and an easy-to-read map designed to make the text clear and your arrival smooth.

Sights are rated: ▲▲▲—Don't miss; ▲▲—Try hard to see; ▲—Worthwhile if you can make it; No rating—Worth knowing about.

Sleeping and Eating includes addresses and phone numbers of my favorite budget hotels and restaurants.

Transportation Connections covers how to reach nearby destinations by train or bus.

The **appendix** is a traveler's tool kit, with telephone tips, a climate chart, and a list of national tourist offices.

Browse through this book, choose your favorite destinations, and link them up. Then have a great trip! You'll travel like a temporary local, getting the most out of every mile, minute, and dollar.

You won't waste time on mediocre sights because this guidebook, unlike others, covers only the best. Since your major financial pitfalls are lousy, expensive hotels, I've worked hard to assemble good-value accommodations for each stop. And as you travel the route I know and love, I'm happy you'll be meeting some of my favorite Europeans.

Trip Costs

Five components make up your trip cost: airfare, surface transportation, room and board, sightseeing/entertainment, and shopping/miscellany.

Airfare: Don't try to sort through the mess yourself. Get and use a good travel agent. A basic round-trip U.S.A.-to-Europe flight should cost $700 to $1,000 (even cheaper in winter), depending on where you fly from and when. Always consider saving time and money in Europe by flying "open-jaw" (flying into one city and out of another, such as flying into London and out of Rome).

EXCHANGE RATES

I've priced things in local currencies throughout this book. Most countries in this book have adopted the euro currency: Austria, Belgium, France, Germany, Ireland, Italy, Spain, and the Netherlands.

1 euro € = $1.10.

One euro is broken down into 100 cents. You'll find coins ranging from 1 cent to 2 euros, and bills from 5 euros to 500 euros. To roughly convert prices in euros to dollars, add 10 percent: €20 is about $22, €45 is about $50, and so on.

Britain, Denmark, Switzerland, and the Czech Republic have kept their traditional currencies:

1 British pound (£) = about $1.60, and £0.60 = about $1.

1 Danish kroner (kr) = about 14 cents, and 7 kr = about $1.

1 Swiss franc (SF) = about 70 cents, and 1.40 SF = about $1.

1 Czech koruna (kč) = about 3 cents, and 30 kč = about $1.

To roughly convert British pounds to dollars, add 50 percent to British prices: £6 is about $9 (actually $9.60). To translate Danish prices into U.S. dollars, divide by 7 (e.g., 100 kr = about $14, actually $14.30). To estimate the dollar equivalent of prices in Swiss francs, subtract one-third (e.g., 60 SF = about $40, actually $43). To convert Czech prices into dollars, drop the last digit and divide by three (2,000 kč = about $65).

Surface Transportation: Your best mode depends upon the time you have and the scope of your trip. For many it's a Eurailpass (for prices, see sidebar on pages 14–15). Train passes are normally available only outside of Europe. You may save money by simply buying tickets as you go (for more information, see "Transportation," below).

Drivers can figure $200 per person per week (based on 2 people splitting the cost of the car, tolls, gas, and insurance). Car rental is cheapest to arrange from the United States. Leasing, for trips over three weeks, is even cheaper.

Room and Board: You can thrive in Europe in 2004 on an overall average of $80 a day per person for room and board (more for cities, less for towns). An $80 a day budget allows $10 for lunch, $5 for snacks, $15 for dinner, and $50 for lodging (based on 2 people splitting the cost of a $100 double room that includes breakfast). That's doable. Students and tightwads will do it on $35 or $40 ($15-20 per bed, $20 for meals and snacks). But budget sleeping and eating require the skills and information covered below (or much more extensively in *Rick Steves' Europe Through the Back Door*).

Sightseeing and Entertainment: In big cities, figure $5 to $10 per major sight, $2 for minor ones, and $25 for splurge experiences (e.g., tours, concerts, gelato binges). An overall average of $15 a day works for most. Don't skimp here. After all, this category directly powers most of the experiences all the other expenses are designed to make possible.

Shopping and Miscellany: Figure $1 per postcard and $2 per coffee, beer, and ice-cream cone. Shopping can vary in cost from nearly nothing to a small fortune. Good budget travelers find that this category has little to do with assembling a trip full of lifelong and wonderful memories.

Prices, Times, and Discounts

The prices in this book, as well as the hours and telephone numbers, are accurate as of mid-2003. Europe is always changing, and I know you'll understand that this, like any other guidebook, starts to yellow even before it's printed.

In Europe—and in this book—you'll be using the 24-hour clock. After 12:00 noon, keep going—13:00, 14:00, and so on. For anything over 12, subtract 12 and add p.m. (14:00 is 2 p.m.).

While discounts for sights and transportation are not listed in this book, seniors (60 and over), students (with International Student Identity Cards), and youths (under 18) may snare discounts—but only by asking. Some discounts (particularly for sights) are granted only to European residents.

When to Go

May, June, September, and October are the best travel months. Peak season (July and August) offers the sunniest weather and the most exciting slate of activities—but the worst crowds. During this busy time, it's best to reserve rooms well in advance, particularly for the big cities (see "Making Reservations," below).

Off-season, October through April, expect generally shorter hours at attractions, more lunchtime breaks, fewer activities, and fewer guided tours in English. If you're traveling off-season, be careful to confirm opening times.

As a general rule of thumb any time of year, the climate north of the Alps is mild (like Seattle), and south of the Alps it's like Arizona. For specifics, check the Climate Chart in the appendix. If you wilt in the heat, avoid the Mediterranean in summer. If you want blue skies in the Alps, Britain, and Scandinavia, travel in the height of summer. Plan your itinerary to beat the heat (for a spring trip, start in the south and work north) but also to moderate culture shock (start in mild Britain and work south and east) and minimize crowds. Touristy places in the core of Europe (Germany, the Alps, France, Italy, and Greece) suffer most from crowds.

Sightseeing Priorities

Depending on the length of your trip, here are my recommended priorities. Assuming you're traveling by train, I've taken geographical proximity into account.

5 days:	London, Paris
7 days, add:	Amsterdam, Haarlem
10 days, add:	Rhine, Rothenburg
14 days, add:	Salzburg, Swiss Alps
17 days, add:	Venice, Florence
21 days, add:	Rome, Cinque Terre
24 days, add:	Siena, Bavarian sights
30 days, add:	Arles (Provence), Barcelona, Madrid
36 days, add:	Vienna, Prague, Berlin
40 days, add:	Copenhagen, Bath

Red Tape, News, and Electricity

Red Tape: Americans need a passport but no visa and no shots to travel throughout Europe. Canadians need a visa to enter the Czech Republic. Crossing borders is easy. Sometimes you won't even realize it's happened. When you do change countries, however, you change phone cards, postage stamps, gas prices, ways to flush a toilet, words for "hello," figurehead monarchs, and breakfast breads. Plan ahead for these changes (use up stamps and phone cards, brush up on the new language).

Twelve European countries have adopted the euro currency, but some haven't, including Denmark, Britain, Switzerland, and the Czech Republic. If you're about to cross a border with spare coins you won't be able to use anywhere else, spend them on candy, souvenirs, gas, or a telephone call home.

News: Americans keep in touch with the *International Herald Tribune* (published almost daily via satellite throughout Europe). Every Tuesday, the European editions of *Time* and *Newsweek* hit the stands with articles of particular interest to European travelers. Sports addicts can get their fix from *USA Today*. News in English will only be sold where there's enough demand: in big cities and tourist centers. Good Web sites include www.europeantimes.com and http://news.bbc.co.uk.

If you're concerned about how some event might affect your safety as an American traveling abroad, call the U.S. consulate or embassy in the nearest big city for advice (see appendix for list).

Watt's up? If you're bringing electrical gear, you'll need an adapter plug (two round prongs for the Continent, three square ones for Britain and Ireland; sold cheap at travel stores like mine, www.ricksteves.com). Travel appliances often have convenient, built-in converters; look for a voltage switch marked 120V (U.S.) and 240V (Europe). If yours doesn't have a built-in converter, you'll have to buy an external one.

Banking

Bring plastic (ATM, credit, or debit cards) along with a couple hundred dollars as a backup. Traveler's checks are a waste of time and money.

To withdraw cash from a bank machine, you'll need a PIN code (numbers only, no letters) and your bankcard. Before you go, verify with your bank that your card will work and alert them that you'll be making withdrawals in Europe; otherwise, the bank may not approve transactions if it perceives unusual spending patterns. Bring two cards in case one gets demagnetized or eaten by a machine. If you plan on getting cash advances with your regular credit card, be sure to ask the card company about fees before you leave.

Visa and MasterCard are more commonly accepted than American Express. Just like at home, credit or debit cards work easily at larger hotels, restaurants, and shops, but smaller businesses prefer payment in local currency.

Regular banks have the best rates for changing money and traveler's checks. For a large exchange, it pays to compare rates and fees. Post offices and train stations usually change money if you can't get to a bank.

If you lose your credit, debit, or ATM card, you can stop people from using your card by reporting the loss immediately to the respective global customer assistance centers. Call these 24-hour U.S. numbers collect: VISA—410/581-9994, MasterCard—636/722-7111, and American Express—336/393-1111.

You should use a money belt (sold at travel stores or call 425/771-8303 for our free newsletter/catalog). Thieves target tourists. A money belt provides peace of mind. You can carry lots of cash safely in a money belt.

Don't be petty about changing money. You don't need to waste time every few days returning to a bank or tracking down a cash machine. Change a week's worth of money, get big bills, stuff them in your money belt, and travel!

VAT Refunds and Customs Regulations

VAT Refunds for Shoppers: Wrapped into the purchase price of your souvenirs is a Value-Added Tax (VAT) ranging from seven to 22 percent. If you make a purchase that meets your host country's minimum purchase requirement (an average of $100; see chart in appendix) at a store that participates in the VAT refund scheme, you're entitled to get most of that tax back. Personally, I've never felt that VAT refunds are worth the hassle, but if you do, here's the scoop.

If you're lucky, the merchant will subtract the tax when you make your purchase (this is more likely if the store ships the goods to your home). Otherwise, you'll need to:

Get the paperwork. Have the merchant completely fill out the necessary refund document, typically called a "cheque." You'll have to present your passport at the store.

Have your cheque(s) stamped at the border by the customs agent who deals with VAT refunds. If you're in a European Union country, then you get the stamp at your last stop in the European Union. Otherwise, get your cheque stamped when you leave the country.

It's best to keep your purchases in your carry-on for viewing, but if they're too large or considered too dangerous (such as knives) to carry on, then track down the proper customs agent to inspect them before you check your bag. You're not supposed to use your purchased goods before you leave. If you show up at customs wearing your new sweater, officials might look the other way—or deny you a refund.

To collect your refund, you'll need to return your stamped documents to the retailer or its representative. Many merchants work with a service that has offices at major airports, ports, and border crossings, such as Easy Tax-Free (www.easytaxfree.com), Global Refund (www.globalrefund.com) or Cashback (www.cashback.it). These services, which extract a four percent fee, usually can refund your money immediately in your currency of choice or credit your card (within two billing cycles). If you have to deal directly with the retailer, mail the store your stamped documents and then wait. It could take months.

Customs Regulations: You can take home $800 in souvenirs per person duty-free. The next $1,000 is taxed at a flat 3 percent. After that, you pay the individual item's duty rate. You can also bring in duty-free a liter of alcohol (slightly more than a standard-sized bottle of wine), a carton of cigarettes, and up to 100 cigars. To check customs rules and duty rates, visit www.customs.gov.

Travel Smart

Your trip to Europe is like a complex play—easier to follow and really appreciate on a second viewing. While no one does the same trip twice to gain that advantage, reading this book's chapters on your intended destinations before your trip accomplishes much the same thing.

Reread this book as you travel and visit local tourist information offices. Upon arrival in a new town, lay the groundwork for a smooth departure. Buy a phone card and use it for reservations, reconfirmations, and double-checking hours. Enjoy the friendliness of the local people.

Slow down and ask questions. Most locals are eager to point you in their idea of the right direction. Wear your money belt, learn the local currency, and develop a simple formula to quickly estimate rough prices in dollars. Keep a notepad in your pocket for organizing your thoughts. Those who expect to travel smart, do.

As you read this book, note the days of markets and festivals and when sights are closed. Anticipate problem days: Mondays are bad in Florence, Tuesdays are bad in Paris. Museums and sights, especially large ones, usually stop admitting people 30 to 60 minutes before closing time.

Sundays have the same pros and cons as they do for travelers in the United States. Sightseeing attractions are generally open, shops and banks are closed, and city traffic is light. Rowdy evenings are rare on Sundays. Saturdays in Europe are virtually weekdays with earlier closing hours. Hotels in tourist areas are most crowded on Fridays and Saturdays.

Plan ahead for banking, laundry, post office chores, and picnics. Mix intense and relaxed periods. Every trip (and every traveler) needs at least a few slack days. Pace yourself. Assume you will return.

Tourist Information

The tourist information office is your best first stop in any new city. Try to arrive, or at least telephone, before it closes. In this book, I'll refer to a tourist information office as a TI. Throughout Europe, you'll find TIs are usually well organized and English speaking.

As national budgets tighten, many TIs have been privatized. This means they become sales agents for big tours and hotels, and their "information" becomes unavoidably colored. While the TI has listings of all the rooms and is eager to book you one, use their room-finding service only as a last resort. Across Europe, room-finding services are charging commissions from hotels, taking fees from travelers, blacklisting establishments that buck their materialistic rules, and are unable to give hard opinions on the relative value of one place over another. The accommodations stakes are too high to go potluck through the TI. By using the listings in this book, you can avoid that kind of "help."

Tourist Offices, U.S.A. Addresses: Each country has a national tourist office in the U.S.A. (see the appendix for addresses). Before your trip, you can ask for the free general information packet and for specific information (such as city maps and schedules of upcoming festivals).

Rick Steves' Books, Videos, and DVDs

Rick Steves' Europe Through the Back Door 2004 gives you budget-travel skills, such as minimizing jet lag, packing light, planning your itinerary, traveling by car or train, finding rooms, changing money, avoiding rip-offs, buying mobile phones, hurdling the language barrier, staying healthy, taking great photographs, using a bidet, and much more. The

RICK STEVES' GUIDEBOOKS

Country Guides
  Rick Steves' Best of Europe
  Rick Steves' Best of Eastern Europe
  Rick Steves' France
  Rick Steves' Germany, Austria & Switzerland
  Rick Steves' Great Britain
  Rick Steves' Ireland
  Rick Steves' Italy
  Rick Steves' Scandinavia
  Rick Steves' Spain & Portugal
City and Regional Guides
  Rick Steves' Amsterdam, Bruges & Brussels
  Rick Steves' Florence & Tuscany
  Rick Steves' London
  Rick Steves' Paris
  Rick Steves' Provence & the French Riviera
  Rick Steves' Rome
  Rick Steves' Venice
  Rick Steves' Easy Access Europe
      (with a focus on London, Paris, Bruges, Amsterdam,
      and the Rhine)

(Avalon Travel Publishing)

book also includes chapters on 38 of my favorite "Back Doors."

Rick Steves' Country Guides, an annually-updated series that covers Europe, offer you the latest on the top sights and destinations, with tips on how to make your trip efficient and fun. You'll learn the best places to stay, eat, enjoy, and explore. If you wish this book covered more of any particular country, my Country Guides are for you.

My **City and Regional Guides,** freshly updated every year, focus on Europe's most compelling destinations. Along with specifics on sights, restaurants, hotels, and nightlife, you'll get self-guided, illustrated tours of the outstanding museums and most characteristic neighborhoods.

New for 2004, *Rick Steves' Easy Access Europe,* written for travelers with limited mobility, covers London, Paris, Bruges, Amsterdam, and the Rhine River.

Rick Steves' Europe 101: History and Art for the Traveler (with Gene Openshaw) gives you the story of Europe's people, history, and art.

Written for smart people who were sleeping in their history and art classes before they knew they were going to Europe, *101* helps Europe's sights come alive.

Rick Steves' Mona Winks (with Gene Openshaw) gives you fun, easy-to-follow self-guided tours of the major museums and historic highlights in cities covered in this book, including **Amsterdam** (Rijksmuseum and Van Gogh Museum), **London** (British Museum, British Library, National Gallery, Tate Britain, Westminster Abbey, and a Westminster Walk), **Paris** (Louvre, Orsay Museum, Rodin Museum, Notre-Dame, Sainte-Chapelle, and Versailles), **Madrid** (Prado), **Venice** (St. Mark's, Doge's Palace, and Accademia Gallery), **Florence** (Uffizi Gallery, Bargello, Michelangelo's *David,* and a Renaissance Walk), and **Rome** (Colosseum, Forum, Pantheon, National Museum of Rome, Borghese Gallery, Vatican Museum, and St. Peter's Basilica). If you're planning on touring these sights, *Mona* will be a valued friend.

Rick Steves' Phrase Books: After more than 25 years as an English-only traveler struggling with other phrase books, I've designed a series of practical, fun, and budget-oriented phrase books to help you ask the gelato man for a free little taste and the hotel receptionist for a room with no street noise. If you want to chat with your cabbie and make hotel reservations over the phone, my pocket-sized Rick Steves' Phrase Books (French, German, Italian, Portuguese, Spanish, and French/Italian/German) will come in handy.

My new public television series, *Rick Steves' Europe,* keeps churning out shows. Many of the 82 episodes (from the new series and from *Travels in Europe with Rick Steves*) explore the destinations featured in this book. These air nationally on public television and on the Travel Channel. They're also available in information-packed home videos and seven- or eight-episode DVDs (available online at www.ricksteves.com or call us at 425/771-8303 for our free newsletter/catalog).

Rick Steves' Postcards from Europe, my autobiographical book, packs 25 years of travel anecdotes and insights into the ultimate 2,000-mile European adventure. Through my guidebooks, I share my favorite European discoveries with you. *Postcards* introduces you to my favorite European friends.

All of my books are published by Avalon Travel Publishing (www.travelmatters.com).

Other Guidebooks

You may want some supplemental information, especially if you'll be traveling beyond my recommended destinations. When you consider the improvements they'll make in your $3,000 vacation, $25 or $35 for extra maps and books is money well spent. Especially for several people traveling by car, the weight and expense are negligible.

The Lonely Planet guides to various European countries are thorough, well-researched (though not updated annually), and packed with good maps and hotel recommendations for low- to moderate-budget travelers. The hip, insightful Rough Guide series (by British researchers, not updated annually) and the highly opinionated Let's Go series (annually updated by Harvard students) are great for students and vagabonds. If you're a backpacker with a train pass and interested in the youth and night scene, get Let's Go. The popular, skinny green Michelin guides (covering most southern countries and French regions) are excellent, especially if you're driving. They're known for their city and sightseeing maps, dry but concise and helpful information on all major sights, and good cultural and historical background. English editions are sold locally at tourist shops and gas stations.

Maps

The black-and-white maps in this book, drawn by Dave Hoerlein, are concise and simple. Dave, who is well-traveled in Europe, has designed the maps to help you locate recommended places and get to the tourist offices, where you can pick up a more in-depth map (usually free) of the city or region.

For an overall map of Europe, consider my Rick Steves' Europe Planning Map—geared to travelers' needs—with sightseeing destinations listed prominently (available online at www.ricksteves.com).

European bookstores, especially in tourist areas, have good selections of maps. For drivers, I'd recommend a 1:200,000- or 1:300,000-scale map for each country. Train travelers can usually manage fine with the freebies they get with their train pass and at the local tourist offices.

Tours of Europe

Travel agents will tell you about mainstream tours of Europe, but they won't tell about ours. At Europe Through the Back Door, we run 21-day tours of Europe featuring most of the highlights in this book (departures April-October, 26-28 people on a big roomy bus with a great guide). We also offer regional tours of Britain, Ireland, France, Spain/Portugal, Italy, Germany/Austria/Switzerland, Scandinavia, Turkey, and Eastern Europe (with groups of 26-28 people). And we lead week-long, in-depth getaways to seven of the most magical cities in Europe: London, Paris, Rome, Florence, Venice, Prague, and Barcelona (departures Jan-Dec, 22-24 travelers). For details, call us at 425/771-8303, ext. 217, or visit www.ricksteves.com.

Transportation in Europe
By Car or Train?

Each has pros and cons. Cars are an expensive headache in big cities but give you more control for delving deep into the countryside. Groups of

Europe by Rail: Dollars and Time

This map can help you determine if a railpass is right for you. Add up the ticket prices for your route. If your total is about the same or more than the cost of a pass, buy the pass (unless you like waiting in lines at train stations).

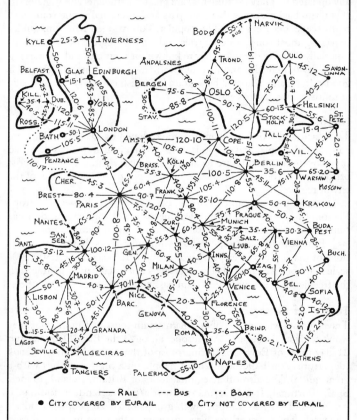

The first number between cities = approximate cost in $US for a 1-way, 2nd class ticket. The second number = number of hours the trip takes.

Important: These fares and times are based on the Eurail Tariff Guide. Actual prices may vary due to currency fluctuations and local promotions. Local competition can cut the actual price of some boat crossings (from Italy to Greece, for example) by 50% or more. For approximate 1st class rail prices, multiply the prices shown by 1.5. Travel times and fares are for express trains where applicable.

three or more go cheaper by car. If you're packing heavy (with kids), go by car. Trains are best for city-to-city travel and give you the convenience of doing long stretches overnight. By train, I arrive relaxed and well rested—not so by car. A rail 'n' drive pass allows you to mix train and car travel. When thoughtfully used, this pass economically gives you the best of both transportation worlds.

Traveling by Train

A major mistake Americans make is relating public transportation in Europe to the pathetic public transportation they're used to at home. By rail you'll have the Continent by the tail. While many simply buy tickets as they go ("point to point"), the various train passes give you the simplicity of ticket-free, unlimited travel, and depending on how much traveling you do, often offer a tremendous savings over regular point-to-point tickets. The Eurailpass gives you several options (explained in the sidebar on page 14).

For a summary of railpass deals and point-to-point ticket options (available in the U.S. and in Europe), check our free Railpass Guide at www.ricksteves.com. If you decide to get a railpass, this guide will help you know you're getting the right one for your trip. To study train schedules in advance on the Web, look up http://bahn.hafas.de/english .html (Germany's excellent all-Europe timetable).

Eurailpass and Eurail Selectpass

The granddaddy of European railpasses, Eurail, gives you unlimited rail travel on the national trains of 17 European countries. That's 100,000 miles of track through all of western Europe, including Ireland, Greece, and Hungary (but excluding Great Britain and most of Eastern Europe). The pass includes many bonuses, such as free boat rides on the Rhine, Mosel, and lakes of Switzerland; several international ferries (Sweden-Finland and Italy-Greece, plus a 50 percent discount on the Ireland-France route); and a 60 percent discount on the Romantic Road bus tour through Germany.

The Eurail Selectpass covers any three, four, or five Eurail countries connected by rail or ferry (e.g., a three-country Selectpass could cover France, Italy, and Greece). Selectpasses are fine for a focused trip, but to see the Best of Europe, you'd do best with a Eurailpass. Either pass gives a 15 percent Saverpass discount to two or more companions traveling together.

Eurail Analysis

Break-even point? For an at-a-glance break-even point, remember that a one-month Eurailpass pays for itself if your route is Amsterdam-Rome-Madrid-Paris on first class or Copenhagen-Rome-Madrid-Copenhagen on second class. A one-month Eurail Youthpass saves you

Rail Passes

Prices listed are for 2003. *Rick Steves' Guide to European Railpasses* has the latest and can be found at www.ricksteves.com/rail. Prices subject to change.

EURAILPASSES

These passes cover all 17 Eurail countries: Austria, Belgium, Denmark, Finland, France, Germany, Greece, Hungary, Ireland, Italy, Luxembourg, Netherlands, Norway, Portugal, Spain, Sweden, and Switzerland.

	1st class	1st class Saver	2nd class Youth
10 days in 2 months flexi	$694	$592	$488
15 days in 2 months flexi	914	778	642
15 consecutive days	588	498	414
21 consecutive days	762	648	534
1 month consec. days	946	804	664
2 months consec. days	1338	1138	938
3 months consec. days	1654	1408	1160

To order Rail and Drive passes, call your travel agent or Rail Europe at 800-438-7245.

FIRST CLASS EURAILDRIVE PASSES

4 first class rail days and 2 car days in a 2 month period.

Car categories	2 adults	1 adult	Extra car day	Extra rail day
Economy	$409	$452	$49	$45
Compact	423	481	64	45
Intermediate	431	496	75	45
Small Automatic	447	531	95	45

Prices are per person. Third and fourth persons sharing car get a 4-day out of 2-month railpass for approx. $365 (kids 4-11 $182.50). You can add rail days (max. 5) and car days (no limit). Rail and car travel in all 17 Eurail countries.

FIRST CLASS SELECTPASS DRIVE

Any 3 days of rail travel + 2 days of Hertz or Avis car rental in 2 months within 3 adjoining countries.

Car Categories	2 adults	1 adult	Extra car day	Extra rail day
Economy	$291	$335	$49	$39
Compact	305	365	64	39
Intermediate	315	392	75	39
Small Automatic	331	429	95	39

Prices are per person. You can add rail days (max. 7) and car days (no limit). Rail travel and car rental in three connecting Eurail countries (a fourth or fifth country each adds about $35 to these prices). Third and fourth adults sharing the car pay $246 (kids 4-11 $123).

SELECTPASSES

This pass covers travel in three, four, or five adjacent countries. For details check out www.ricksteves.com/rail.

3 Countries	1st class Selectpass	1st class Saverpass	2nd class Youthpass
5 days in 2 months	$356	$304	$249
6 days in 2 months	394	336	276
8 days in 2 months	470	400	329
10 days in 2 months	542	460	379

4 Countries	1st class Selectpass	1st class Saverpass	2nd class Youthpass
5 days in 2 months	$398	$340	$279
6 days in 2 months	436	372	306
8 days in 2 months	512	436	359
10 days in 2 months	584	496	409

5 Countries	1st class Selectpass	1st class Saverpass	2nd class Youthpass
5 days in 2 months	$438	$374	$307
6 days in 2 months	476	406	334
8 days in 2 months	552	470	387
10 days in 2 months	624	530	437
15 days in 2 months	794	674	556

Saverpass prices are per person for 2 or more people traveling together at all times. Youthpasses: Under age 26 only. Kids 4-11 pay half adult or saver fare; under 4: free.

Eurailpass/Selectpass diagram key:

*Every **Eurailpass** includes travel in every country shown here. A **Selectpass** can be designed to connect a "chain" of any three, four, or five countries in this diagram linked by direct lines. (Examples that qualify: Norway-Sweden-Germany; Spain-France-Italy; Austria-Italy-Greece.) "Benelux" is considered one country.*

NORWAY
DENMARK SWEDEN
IRELAND BENELUX FINLAND
FRANCE GERMANY
HUNG.
SPAIN SWITZ. AUSTRIA
PORTUGAL ITALY
GREECE

money if you're traveling from Amsterdam to Rome to Madrid and back to Amsterdam. Passes pay for themselves quicker in the north, where the cost per mile is higher. Check the "Europe by Rail: Dollars and Time" map on page 12 to see if your planned travels merit purchasing a train pass. If it's about even, go with the pass for the convenience of not having to wait in line to buy tickets and for the fun and freedom to travel "free."

Using one Eurailpass versus a series of country passes: While nearly every country has its own mini-version of the Eurailpass, trips covering several countries are usually cheapest with the budget whirl-wind traveler's old standby, the Eurailpass, or its budget cousin, the Eurail Selectpass. This is because the more rail days included in a pass, the cheaper your per-day cost is. A group of country passes with a few rail days apiece will have a high per-day cost, while a Eurailpass with a longer life span offers a better deal overall. However, if you're traveling in a single country, an individual country railpass (such as Francerail or Germanrail) is often a better value than any of the Eurail passes.

EurailDrive Pass: The EurailDrive Pass is for those who want to combine train travel with the freedom of having a car a day here and a day there. Great areas for a day of joyriding include the Dutch country-side; Germany's Rhine, Mosel, or Bavaria; France's Provence; Italy's Tuscany and Umbria; or the Alps (for "car hiking"). When comparing prices, remember that each day of car rental comes with about $30 of extra expenses (CDW insurance, gas, parking), which you can divide among the people in your party.

Car Rental

It's cheaper to arrange European car rentals in the United States, so check rates with your travel agent or directly with the companies. Rent by the week with unlimited mileage. If you'll be renting for three weeks or more, ask your agent about leasing, which is a scheme to save on insurance and taxes. I normally rent the smallest, least expensive model. Explore your drop-off options (and costs).

For peace of mind, I spring for the Collision Damage Waiver insurance (CDW, about $15 per day), which has a zero- or low-deductible rather than the standard value-of-the-car "deductible." Ask your travel agent about money-saving alternatives to CDW. A few gold credit cards cover CDW insurance; quiz your credit card company on the worst-case scenario. Or consider Travel Guard, which offers CDW insurance for $7 a day (U.S. tel. 800/826-1300, www.travelguard.com); it'll cover you throughout Europe but is not honored in Scotland, Ireland, and Italy.

Note that if you'll be driving in Italy, theft insurance (separate from CDW insurance) is mandatory. The insurance usually costs about $10 to $15 a day, payable when you pick up the car.

If you plan to drive your rental car into the Czech Republic, keep these tips in mind: State your travel plans up front to the rental com-pany. Some won't allow any of their rental cars to enter Eastern European countries due to the high theft rate. Some won't allow certain types of cars: BMWs, Mercedes, and convertibles. Ask about extra fees—some companies automatically tack on theft and collision cover-age for a Czech excursion. To avoid hassles at the Czech border, ask the rental agent to mark your contract with the company's permission to cross.

Driving

For much of Europe, all you need is your valid U.S. driver's license and a car. Confirm with your rental company if an international license is required in the countries you plan to visit. Those traveling in Austria, Germany, Italy, Portugal, Spain, and Eastern Europe should probably get an international driver's license (at your local AAA office—$10 plus the cost of two passport-type photos).

While gas is expensive, if you keep an eye on the big picture, paying $4 per gallon is more a psychological trauma than a financial one. I use

STOP AND LEARN THESE ROAD SIGNS

Speed Limit (km/hr)

Yield

No Passing

End of No Passing Zone

One Way

Intersection

Main Road

Freeway

Danger

No Entry

No Entry for cars

All Vehicles Prohibited

Parking

No Parking

Customs

Peace

the freeways whenever possible. They are free in the Netherlands and Germany. You'll pay a one-time road fee of about $25 as you enter Switzerland, about $7 for Austria, and about $3 for the Czech Republic. The Italian autostradas and French autoroutes are punctuated by toll-booths (charging about $1 for every 10 minutes). The alternative to these superfreeways often is being marooned in rural traffic. The autostrada/autoroute usually saves enough time, gas, and nausea to justify its expense. Mix scenic country-road rambling with high-speed autobahning, but don't forget that in Europe, the shortest distance between two points is the autobahn.

Metric: Outside of Britain, get used to metric. A liter is about a quart, four to a gallon. A kilometer is six-tenths of a mile. I figure kilometers to miles by cutting them in half and adding back 10 percent of the original (120 km: 60 + 12 = 72 miles, 300 km: 150 + 30 = 180 miles).

Parking: Parking is a costly headache in big cities. You'll pay about $20 a day to park safely. Ask at your hotel for advice. I keep a pile of coins in my ashtray for parking meters, public phones, launderettes, and wishing wells.

Telephones, Mail, and E-mail

Smart travelers learn the phone system and use it daily to reserve or reconfirm rooms, find tourist information, or phone home. Many European phone booths take insertable phone cards rather than coins.

Phone Cards: There are two kinds of phone cards: official phone cards that you insert into the phone (which can only be used in phone booths), and long-distance scratch-off PIN cards that can be used from virtually any phone (you dial a toll-free number and enter your PIN code). Both kinds of cards work only in the country where you bought them (for example, a Swiss phone card works when you're making calls in Switzerland, but is worthless in France).

You can buy **insertable phone cards** from post offices, newsstands, or tobacco shops. Insert the card into the phone, make your call, and the value is deducted from your card. These are a good deal for calling within Europe, but it's cheaper to make international calls with a PIN card.

PIN cards, which have a scratch-off Personal Identification Number, allow you to call home at the rate of about a dime a minute. To use a PIN card, dial the toll-free access number listed on the card; then, at the prompt, enter your Personal Identification Number (also listed on card) and dial the number you want to call. These are sold at newsstands, exchange bureaus, souvenir shops, and mini-marts. There are many different brands. Ask for a "cheap international telephone card." Make sure you get a card that allows you to make international calls (some types permit only local calls). Buy a lower denomination in case the card is a dud.

If you use **coins** to make your calls, have a bunch handy. Or look for a **metered phone** ("talk now, pay later") in the bigger post offices. Avoid using hotel-room phones for anything other than local calls and PIN card calls.

Making Calls within a European Country: You'll save money by dialing direct. You just need to learn to break the codes. About half of all European countries use area codes; the other half uses a direct-dial system without area codes.

In countries that use area codes (such as Austria, Britain, Germany, Ireland, and the Netherlands), you dial the local number when calling within a city, and you add the area code if calling long-distance within the country. For example, Berlin's area code is 030, and the number of one of my recommended Berlin hotels is 3150-3944. To call it from Frankfurt, dial 030/3150-3944.

To make calls within a country that uses a direct-dial system (Belgium, the Czech Republic, Denmark, France, Italy, Spain, and Switzerland), you dial the same number whether you're calling across the country or across the street.

Making International Calls: You always start with the international access code (011 if you're calling from America or Canada, or 00 from Europe), then dial the country code of the country you're calling (see chart in appendix).

What you dial next depends on the phone system of the country you're calling. If the country uses area codes, drop the initial zero of the area code, then dial the rest of the number. To call the Berlin hotel from Copenhagen, dial 00, 49 (Germany's country code), 30/3150-3944 (omitting the initial zero in the area code).

Countries that use direct-dial systems (no area codes) vary in how they're accessed internationally by phone. For instance, if you're making an international call to Denmark, Italy, Spain, or the Czech Republic, simply dial the international access code, country code, and phone number. But if you're calling Belgium, France, or Switzerland, drop the initial zero of the phone number. Example: To call a Paris hotel (tel. 01 47 05 49 15) from London, dial 00, 33 (France's country code), then 1 47 05 49 15 (phone number without the initial zero).

To call my office from Europe, I dial 00 (Europe's international access code), 1 (U.S.A.'s country code), 425 (Edmonds' area code), and 771-8303.

European time is six/nine hours ahead of the east/west coast of the U.S.A.

U.S. Calling Cards: Calling home from Europe is easy but expensive with AT&T, MCI, or Sprint calling cards. Since direct-dial rates have dropped, U.S. calling cards are no longer a good value. It's also outrageously expensive to use your calling card to make calls between European countries. It's much cheaper to make your calls using a phone card or PIN card purchased in Europe.

Mobile Phones: Many travelers now buy cheap mobile phones in Europe to make both local and international calls. (Typical American mobile phones don't work in Europe, and those that do, have horrendous per-minute costs.) For about $75, you can get a phone with $20 worth of calls that will work in the country where you purchased it. (You can buy more time at newsstands or mobile phone shops.) For about $100, you can get a phone that will work in most countries once you pick up the necessary chip per country. If you're interested, stop by any European shop that sells mobile phones (you'll see prominent store window displays). Depending on your trip and budget, ask for a phone that works only in that country or one that can be used throughout Europe. If you're on a budget, skip mobile phones and use PIN cards instead.

Mail: To arrange for mail delivery, reserve a few hotels along your route in advance and give their addresses to friends or use American Express Company's mail services (free for AmEx cardholders and available at a minimal fee for others). Allow 10 days for a letter to arrive. Federal Express makes two-day deliveries—for a price. Phoning is so easy that I've dispensed with mail stops all together.

E-mail: More and more hotels have e-mail addresses and Web sites (included in this book). I've listed some Internet cafés, but your hotelier or TI can steer you to the nearest Internet access point.

Sleeping

In the interest of smart use of your time, I favor hotels and restaurants handy to your sightseeing activities. Rather than list hotels scattered throughout a city, I describe my favorite two or three neighborhoods and recommend the best accommodations values in each.

Now that hotels are so expensive and tourist information offices' room-finding services are so greedy, it's more important than ever for budget travelers to have a good listing of rooms and call directly to make reservations. This book gives you a wide range of budget accommodations to choose from: hostels, bed-and-breakfasts, guest houses, pensions, small hotels, and splurges. I like places that are quiet, clean, small, central, traditional, friendly, and not listed in other guidebooks. Most places I list are a good value, having at least five of these seven virtues.

Rooms with private bathrooms are often bigger and renovated, while the cheaper rooms without bathrooms often will be on the top floor or not yet refurbished. Any room without a bathroom has access to a bathroom in the corridor (free unless otherwise noted). Rooms with tubs often cost more than rooms with showers. All rooms have a sink. Unless I note a difference, the cost of a room includes a continental breakfast. When breakfast is not included, the price is usually posted in your hotel room.

SLEEP CODE

I've divided the rooms into three categories, based on the price for a standard double room with bath:

$$$ **Higher Priced**
$$ **Moderately Priced**
$ **Lower Priced**

To give maximum information in a minimum of space, I use this code to describe accommodations listed in this book. Prices listed are per room, not per person. When there is a range of prices in one category, the price will fluctuate with the season, size of room, or length of stay.

S = Single room (or price for one person in a double).
D = Double or twin. Double beds are usually big enough for non-romantic couples.
T = Triple (often a double bed with a single bed moved in).
Q = Quad (an extra child's bed is usually less).
b = Private bathroom with toilet and shower or tub.
s = Private shower or tub only (the toilet is down the hall).
no CC = Does not accept credit cards; you'll need to pay with the local currency.
SE = Speaks English. This code is used only when it seems predictable that you'll encounter English-speaking staff.
NSE = Does not speak English. Used only when it's unlikely you'll encounter English-speaking staff.

According to this code, a couple staying at a "Db-€90, SE" hotel in Spain would pay a total of 90 euros (about $100) for a double room with a private bathroom. The staff speaks English. The hotel accepts credit cards or cash in payment; you can assume a hotel takes credit cards unless you see "no CC" in the listing.

Before accepting a room, confirm your understanding of the complete price. The only tip my recommended hotels would like is a friendly, easygoing guest. I appreciate feedback on your hotel experiences.

TIPS ON TIPPING

Tipping in Europe isn't as automatic and generous as it is in the U.S., but for special service, tips are appreciated, if not expected. As in the U.S., the proper amount depends on your resources, tipping philosophy, and the circumstance, but some general guidelines apply.

Restaurants: Tipping is an issue only at restaurants that have waiters and waitresses. If you order your food at a counter, don't tip.

At restaurants with wait staff, the service charge (10-15 percent) is usually listed on the menu and included in your bill. When the service is included, there's no need to tip beyond that, but if you like to tip and you're pleased with the service, you can round up the bill (but not more than five percent).

If the service is not included, tip up to 10 percent by rounding up or leaving the change from your bill. Leave the tip on the table or hand it to your server. It's best to tip in cash even if you pay with your credit card. Otherwise the tip may never reach your waitress.

Taxis: To tip the cabbie, round up. For a typical ride, round up to the next euro on the fare (to pay a €13 fare, give €14); for a long ride, to the nearest 10 (for a €75 fare, give €80). If the cabbie hauls your bags and zips you to the airport to help you catch your flight, you might want to toss in a little more. But if you feel like you're being driven in circles or otherwise ripped off, skip the tip.

Special services: It's thoughtful to tip a couple of euros to someone who shows you a special sight and who is paid in no other way (such as the man who shows you an Etruscan tomb in his backyard). Tour guides at public sites often hold out their hands for tips after they give their spiel; if I've already paid for the tour, I don't tip extra, though some tourists do give a euro or two, particularly for a job well done. I don't tip at hotels, but if you do, give the porter a euro for carrying bags and leave a couple of euros in your room at the end of your stay for the maid if the room was kept clean. In general, if someone in the service industry does a super job for you, a tip of a couple of euros is appropriate...but not required.

When in doubt, ask. If you're not sure whether (or how much) to tip for a service, ask your hotelier or the TI; they'll fill you in on how it's done on their turf.

Hotels

While most hotels listed in this book cluster around $70 to $100 per double, they range from $10 bunks to $200+ (maximum plumbing and more) per double. The cost is higher in big cities and heavily-touristed cities and lower off the beaten track. Three or four people can save money by requesting one big room. Traveling alone can get expensive: A single room is often only 20 percent cheaper than a double. If you'll accept a room with twin beds and you ask for a double, you may be turned away. Ask for "a room for two people" if you'll take a twin or a double.

Rooms are generally safe, but don't leave valuables lying around. More (or different) pillows and blankets are usually in the closet or available on request. Remember, in Europe towels and linen aren't always replaced every day. Drip-dry and conserve.

A very simple continental breakfast is almost always included. (Breakfasts in Europe, like towels and people, get smaller as you go south.) If you like juice and protein for breakfast, supply it yourself. I enjoy a box of juice in my hotel room and often supplement the skimpy breakfast with a piece of fruit and cheese.

Pay your bill the evening before you leave to avoid the time-wasting crowd at the reception desk in the morning.

Making Reservations

It's possible to travel at any time of year without reservations (especially if you arrive early in the day), but given the high stakes, erratic accommodations values, and the quality of the gems I've found for this book, I'd highly recommend calling for rooms at least a day or two in advance as you travel (your fluent receptionist will likely help you call your next hotel if you pay for the call). Even if a hotel clerk says the hotel is fully booked, you can try calling between 9:00 and 10:00 on the day you plan to arrive. That's when the hotel clerk knows who'll be checking out and just which rooms will be available. I've taken great pains to list telephone numbers with long-distance instructions (see "Telephones," above and the appendix). Use the telephone and the convenient phone cards. Most hotels listed are accustomed to English-only speakers. A hotel receptionist will trust you and hold a room until 16:00 (4:00 p.m.) without a deposit, though some will ask for a credit-card number. Honor (or cancel by phone) your reservations. Long distance is cheap and easy from public phone booths. Don't let these people down—I promised you'd call and cancel if for some reason you won't show up. Don't needlessly confirm rooms through the tourist office; they'll take a commission.

If you know exactly which dates you need and really want a particular place, reserve a room well in advance before you leave home. To reserve from home, e-mail, call, or fax the hotel. Phone and fax costs are reasonable, e-mail is a steal, and simple English is usually fine. To fax, use the form in the appendix (or find it online at www.ricksteves.com/reservation). A two-night stay in August would be "2 nights, 16/8/04 to 18/8/04" (Europeans write the date in this order—day/month/year—and hotel jargon counts your stay from your day of arrival through your day of departure).

If you e-mail or fax a reservation request and receive a response with rates stating that rooms are available, this is not a confirmation. You must confirm that the rates are fine and that indeed you want the room. You'll often receive a response requesting one night's deposit. A credit card number and expiration date will usually work. If you use your credit card for the deposit, you can pay with your card or cash when you arrive; if you don't show up, you'll be billed for one night. Ask about the cancellation policy when you reserve; sometimes you may have to cancel as much as two weeks ahead to avoid paying a penalty. Reconfirm your reservations several days in advance for safety.

Bed-and-Breakfasts

You can stay in private homes throughout Europe and enjoy double the cultural intimacy for about half the cost of hotels. You'll find them mainly in smaller towns and in the countryside (so they are most handy for those with a car). In Germany, look for *Zimmer* signs. For Italian *affitta camere* and French *chambre d'hôte* (CH), ask at local tourist offices. Doubles cost about $50, and you'll often share a bathroom with the family. While your European hosts will rarely speak English (except in Switzerland, the Netherlands, Belgium, and Scandinavia), they will almost always be enthusiastic, delightful hosts.

Hostels

For $10 to $20 a night, you can stay at one of Europe's 2,000 youth hostels. While most hostels admit nonmembers for an extra fee, it's best to join the club and buy a youth hostel card before you go (call Hostelling International at 202/783-6161 or order online at www.hiayh.org). Except in Bavaria (where you must be under 27 to stay in a hostel), travelers of any age are welcome as long as they don't mind dorm-style accommodations and making lots of traveling friends. Cheap meals are sometimes available, and kitchen facilities are usually provided for do-it-yourselfers. Expect crowds in the summer, snoring, and lots of youth groups giggling and making rude noises while you try to sleep. Family rooms and doubles are often available on request, but it's basically boys' dorms and girls' dorms. Many hostels are locked up from about 10:00 until 17:00, and a 23:00 curfew is often enforced. Hostelling is ideal for those traveling single: prices are per bed, not per room, and you'll have an instant circle of friends. More and more hostels are getting their business acts together, taking credit card reservations over the phone and

leaving sign-in forms on the door for each available room. If you're serious about traveling cheaply, get a card, carry your own sheets, and cook
in the members' kitchens.

Camping

For $5 to $10 per person per night, you can camp your way through
Europe. "Camping" is an international word, and you'll see signs everywhere. All you need is a tent and a sleeping bag. Good campground
guides are published, and camping information is also readily available at
local tourist information offices. Europeans love to holiday camp. It's a
social rather than a nature experience and a great way for traveling
Americans to make local friends. Camping is ideal for families traveling by car on a tight budget.

Eating European

Europeans are masters at the art of fine living. That means eating long
and eating well. Two-hour lunches, three-hour dinners, and endless
hours sitting in outdoor cafés are the norm. Americans eat on their way
to an evening event and complain if the check is slow in coming. For
Europeans, the meal is an end in itself, and only rude waiters rush you.

Even those of us who liked dorm food will find that the local cafés,
cuisine, and wines become a highlight of our European adventure. This
is sightseeing for your palate, and even if the rest of you is sleeping in
cheap hotels, your taste buds will want an occasional first-class splurge.
You can eat well without going broke. But be careful: You're just as
likely to blow a small fortune on a mediocre meal as you are to dine
wonderfully for $15.

Restaurants

When restaurant hunting, choose a place filled with locals, not the place
with the big neon signs boasting "We Speak English and Accept Credit
Cards." Look for menus posted outside; if you don't see one, move
along.

For a no-stress meal in France and Italy, look for set-price *menus*
(called the tourist menu, *menu del giorno, prix-fixe,* or simply *le menu*)
that give you several choices of courses. At some restaurants, the *menu* is
cheaper at lunch than dinner. Combination plates (*le plat* in France,
plato combinado in Spain) provide house specialties at reasonable prices.

Galloping gourmets bring a menu translator. The *Marling Menu
Master,* available in French, Italian, and German editions, is excellent.

When you're in the mood for something halfway between a restaurant and a picnic meal, look for take-out food stands, bakeries (with
sandwiches and small pizzas to go), delis with stools or a table, a department store cafeteria, or simple little eateries for fast and easy sit-down
restaurant food.

Picnics

So that I can afford the occasional splurge in a nice restaurant, I like to picnic. In addition to the savings, picnicking is a great way to sample local specialties. And, in the process of assembling your meal, you get to plunge into local markets like a European.

Gather supplies early. Many shops close for a lunch break. While it's fun to visit the small specialty shops, a *supermarché* gives you more efficiency with less color for less cost.

When driving, I organize a backseat pantry in a cardboard box: plastic cups, paper towels, a water bottle (the standard disposable European half-liter plastic mineral water bottle works fine), a damp cloth in a Zip-loc baggie, a Swiss army knife, and a petite tablecloth. To take care of juice once and for all, stow a rack of liter boxes of orange juice in the trunk. (Look for "100%" on the label or you'll get a sickly sweet orange drink.)

Picnics (especially French ones) can be an adventure in high cuisine. Be daring: Try the smelly cheeses, midget pickles, ugly pâtés, and minuscule yogurts. Local shopkeepers sell small quantities of produce and even slice and stuff a sandwich for you.

A typical picnic for two might be fresh bread (half loaves on request), two tomatoes, three carrots, 100 grams of cheese (about a quarter-pound, called an *etto* in Italy), 100 grams of meat, two apples, a liter box of orange juice, and yogurt. Total cost for two: about $10.

Stranger in a Strange Land

We travel all the way to Europe to enjoy differences—to become temporary locals. You'll experience frustrations. Certain truths that we find "God-given" or "self-evident," like cold beer, ice in drinks, bottomless cups of coffee, hot showers, body odor smelling bad, and bigger being better, are suddenly not so true. One of the benefits of travel is the eye-opening realization that there are logical, civil, and even better alternatives. A willingness to go local ensures that you'll enjoy a full dose of local hospitality.

If there is a negative aspect to the European image of Americans, we can appear loud, aggressive, impolite, rich, and a bit naive. While Europeans look bemusedly at some of our Yankee excesses—and worriedly at others—they nearly always afford us individual travelers all the warmth we deserve.

Back Door Manners

While updating this book, I heard over and over again that my readers are considerate and fun to have as guests. Thank you for traveling as temporary locals who are sensitive to the culture. It's fun to follow you in my travels.

Send Me a Postcard, Drop Me a Line

If you enjoy a successful trip with the help of this book and would like to share your discoveries, please fill out the survey at the end of this book (or find it online at www.ricksteves.com/feedback) and send it to me at Europe Through the Back Door, Box 2009, Edmonds, WA 98020. I personally read and value all feedback.

For our latest travel information, tap into our Web site: www.ricksteves.com. To check on updates for this book, visit www.ricksteves.com/update. My e-mail address is rick@ricksteves.com. Anyone is welcome to request a free issue of our *Back Door* travel newsletter.

Judging from all the positive feedback I receive from travelers who have used this book, it's safe to assume you'll enjoy a great, affordable vacation—with the finesse of an experienced, independent traveler. Thanks, and happy travels!

BACK DOOR TRAVEL PHILOSOPHY
From Rick Steves' *Europe Through the Back Door*

Travel is intensified living—maximum thrills per minute and one of the last great sources of legal adventure. Travel is freedom. It's recess, and we need it.

Experiencing the real Europe requires catching it by surprise, going casual... "Through the Back Door."

Affording travel is a matter of priorities. (Make do with the old car.) You can travel—simply, safely, and comfortably—anywhere in Europe for $80 a day ($90 in bigger cities) plus transportation costs. In many ways, spending more money only builds a thicker wall between you and what you came to see. Europe is a cultural carnival and, time after time, you'll find that its best acts are free and the best seats are the cheap ones.

A tight budget forces you to travel close to the ground, meeting and communicating with the people, not relying on service with a purchased smile. Never sacrifice sleep, nutrition, safety, or cleanliness in the name of budget. Simply enjoy the local-style alternatives to expensive hotels and restaurants.

Extroverts have more fun. If your trip is low on magic moments, kick yourself and make things happen. If you don't enjoy a place, maybe you don't know enough about it. Seek the truth. Recognize tourist traps. Give a culture the benefit of your open mind. See things as different but not better or worse. Any culture has much to share.

Of course, travel, like the world, is a series of hills and valleys. Be fanatically positive and militantly optimistic. If something's not to your liking, change your liking. Travel is addicting. It can make you a happier American as well as a citizen of the world. Our Earth is home to six billion equally important people. It's humbling to travel and find that people don't envy Americans. They like us, but with all due respect, they wouldn't trade passports.

Globetrotting destroys ethnocentricity. It helps you understand and appreciate different cultures. Travel changes people. It broadens perspectives and teaches new ways to measure quality of life. Many travelers toss aside their hometown blinders. Their prized souvenirs are the strands of different cultures they decide to knit into their own character. The world is a cultural yarn shop. And Back Door travelers are weaving the ultimate tapestry. Come on, join in!

VIENNA
(Wien)

Vienna is a head without a body. For 640 years the capital of the once-grand Hapsburg empire, she started and lost World War I, and with it her far-flung holdings. Today, you'll find an elegant capital of 1.6 million people (20 percent of Austria's population) ruling a small, relatively insignificant country. Culturally, historically, and from a sightseeing point of view, this city is the sum of its illustrious past. The city of Freud, Brahms, Maria Theresa's many children, a gaggle of Strausses, and a dynasty of Holy Roman Emperors ranks right up there with Paris, London, and Rome.

Vienna has always been the easternmost city of the West. In Roman times, it was Vindobona, on the Danube facing the Germanic barbarians. In medieval times, Vienna was Europe's bastion against the Ottoman Turks (a horde of 200,000 was repelled in 1683). Though the ancient walls held out the Turks, World War II bombs destroyed nearly a quarter of the city's buildings. In modern times, Vienna took a big bite out of the USSR's Warsaw Pact buffer zone.

The truly Viennese person is not Austrian, but a second-generation Hapsburg cocktail, with grandparents from the distant corners of the old empire—Poland, Serbia, Hungary, Romania, the Czech Republic, Slovakia, and Italy. Vienna is the melting-pot capital of a now-collapsed empire that, in its heyday, consisted of 60 million people—only 8 million of whom were Austrian.

In 1900, Vienna's 2.2 million inhabitants made it the world's fifth-largest city (after New York, London, Paris, and Berlin). But the average Viennese mother today has 1.3 children, and the population is down to 1.6 million. (Dogs are the preferred "child.")

Some ad agency has convinced Vienna to make Elisabeth, wife of Emperor Franz Josef, with her narcissism and difficulties with royal life, the darling of the local tourist scene. You'll see "Sissy" all over town. But stay focused on the Hapsburgs who mattered.

Vienna Overview

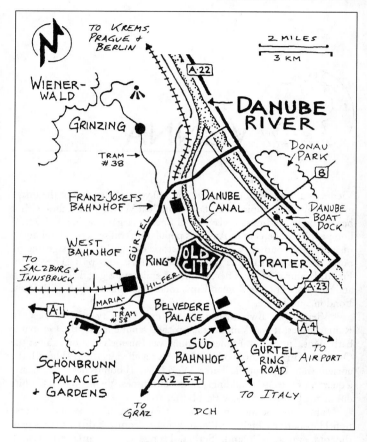

Of the Hapsburgs who ruled Austria from 1273 to 1918, Maria Theresa (ruled 1740–1780) and Franz Josef (ruled 1848–1916) are the most famous. People are quick to remember Maria Theresa as the mother of 16 children (10 survived). This was actually no big deal back then (one of her daughters had 18 kids, and a son fathered 16). Maria Theresa's reign followed the Austrian defeat of the Turks, when Europe recognized Austria as a great power. She was a strong and effective queen. (Her rival, the Prussian emperor, said, "When at last the Hapsburgs get a great man, it's a woman.")

Maria Theresa was a great social reformer. During her reign, she avoided wars and expanded her empire by skillfully marrying her children into the right families. After daughter Marie Antoinette's marriage into the French Bourbon family (to Louis XVI), for instance, a country that had been an enemy became an ally. (Unfortunately for Marie, she arrived in time for the Revolution, and she lost her head.)

A great reformer and in tune with her era, Maria Theresa employed "Robin Hood" policies to help Austria glide through the "age of revolution" without turmoil. She taxed the Church and the nobility, provided six years of obligatory education to all children, and granted free health care to all in her realm. She also welcomed the boy genius Mozart into her court.

As far back as the 12th century, Vienna was a mecca for musicians—both sacred and secular (troubadours). The Hapsburg emperors of the 17th and 18th centuries were not only generous supporters of music but fine musicians and composers themselves. (Maria Theresa played a mean double bass.) Composers like Haydn, Mozart, Beethoven, Schubert, Brahms, and Mahler gravitated to this music-friendly environment. They taught each other, jammed together, and spent a lot of time in Hapsburg palaces. Beethoven was a famous figure, walking—lost in musical thought—through Vienna's woods.

After the defeat of Napoleon and the Congress of Vienna in 1815 (which shaped 19th-century Europe), Vienna enjoyed its violin-filled belle époque, which shaped our romantic image of the city—fine wine, chocolates, cafés, and waltzes. "Waltz King" Johann Strauss and his brothers kept Vienna's 300 ballrooms spinning.

This musical tradition continues into modern times, leaving some prestigious Viennese institutions for today's tourists to enjoy: the Opera, the Boys' Choir, and the great Baroque halls and churches, all busy with classical and waltz concerts.

ORIENTATION

(area code: 01)

Vienna—Wien in German (veen)—sits between the Vienna Woods (Wienerwald) and the Danube (Donau). To the southeast is industrial sprawl. The Alps, which arc across Europe from Marseille, end at Vienna's wooded hills. These provide a popular playground for walking and new-wine–drinking. This greenery's momentum carries on into the city. More than half of Vienna is parkland, filled with ponds, gardens, trees, and statue-maker memories of Austria's glory days.

Think of the city map as a target. The bull's-eye is the cathedral, the first circle is the Ring, and the second is the Gürtel. The old town—snuggling around towering St. Stephan's Cathedral south of the Danube—is bound tightly by the Ringstrasse. The Ring, marking what was the city wall, circles the first district (or *Bezirk*). The Gürtel, a broader ring road, contains the rest of downtown (*Bezirkes* 2–9).

Addresses start with the *Bezirk,* followed by street and building number. Any address higher than the ninth *Bezirk* is beyond the Gürtel, far from the center. The middle two digits of Vienna's postal codes show the *Bezirk.* The address "7, Lindengasse 4" is in the seventh district, #4 on Linden Street. Its postal code would be 1070. Nearly all your sight-seeing will be done in the core first district or along the Ringstrasse. As a tourist, concern yourself only with this compact old center. When you do, sprawling Vienna suddenly becomes manageable.

Planning Your Time

For a big city, Vienna is pleasant and laid-back. Packed with sights, it's worth two days and two nights on the speediest trip. It seems like Vienna was designed to help people just meander through a day. To be grand-tour efficient, you could sleep in and sleep out on the train (Berlin, Venice, Rome, the Swiss Alps, Paris, and the Rhine are each handy night trains away). I'd spend two days this way:

Day 1: 9:00–Circle the Ring by tram, following the self-guided tour (see "Do-It-Yourself Bus Orientation Tour," below), 10:00–Drop by TI for any planning and ticket needs, then see the sights in Vienna's old center (described below): Monument against War and Fascism, Kaisergruft crypt, Kärntner Strasse, St. Stephan's Cathedral, and Graben, 12:00–Finger sandwiches for lunch at Buffet Trzesniewski, 13:00–Tour the Hofburg and treasury, 16:00–Time to hit one more museum or shop, or browse and people-watch, 19:30–Choose classical music (concert or opera), House of Music museum, or *Heurige* wine garden.

Day 2: 9:00–Schönbrunn Palace (drivers: This is conveniently on the way out of town toward Salzburg; horse-lovers: You'll need to rearrange—or rush the palace—to see the Lipizzaner stallions' morning practice), 12:00–Lunch at Rosenberger Markt, 13:00–Tour the Opera, 14:00–Kunsthistorisches Museum, 16:00–Your choice of the many sights left to see in Vienna, Evening–See Day 1 evening options.

Tourist Information

Vienna has one real tourist office, a block behind the Opera House at Albertinaplatz (daily 9:00–19:00, tel. 01/24555, www.info.wien.at). Confirm your sightseeing plans and pick up the free and essential city map with a list of museums and hours (also available at most hotels), the monthly program of concerts (called *Wien-Programm*), and the youth guide *(Ten Good Reasons for Vienna).* The TI also books rooms (for a €2.90 fee). While hotel and ticket booking agencies answer ques-tions and give out maps and brochures at the train stations and airport, I'd rely on the TI if possible.

Consider the TI's handy €3.60 *Vienna from A to Z* booklet. Every important building sports a numbered flag banner that keys into this guidebook. A to Z numbers are keyed into the TI's city map. When lost, find one of the "famous-building flags" and match its number to your map. If you're at a famous building, check the map to see what other key numbers are nearby, then check the A to Z book description to see if you want to go in. This system is especially helpful for those just wandering aimlessly among Vienna's historic charms.

The much-promoted €17 Vienna Card might save the busy sightseer a few euros. It gives you a 72-hour transit pass (worth €12) and discounts of 10–50 percent at the city's museums.

Arrival in Vienna

By Train at the West Station (Westbahnhof): Train travelers arriving from Munich, Salzburg, and Melk land at the Westbahnhof. The *Reisebüro am Bahnhof* books hotels (for a €4 fee), has maps, answers questions, and has a train info desk (daily 7:30–21:00). To get to the city center (and most likely, your hotel), catch the U-3 metro (buy your ticket or transit pass—described below—from a *Tabak* shop in the station or from a machine—good on all city transit). U-3 signs lead down to the metro tracks. If your hotel is along Mariahilfer Strasse, your stop is on this line (direction Simmering; see "Sleeping," below). If you're sleeping in the center or just sightseeing, ride five stops to Stephansplatz, escalate in the exit direction Stephansplatz, and you'll hit the cathedral. The TI is a five-minute stroll down the busy Kärntner Strasse pedestrian street.

The Westbahnhof has a grocery store (daily 5:30–23:00), ATMs, Internet access, change offices, and storage facilities. Airport buses and taxis wait in front of the station.

By Train at the South Station (Südbahnhof): Those arriving from Italy and Prague land here. The Südbahnhof has all the services, left luggage, and a TI (daily 9:00–19:00). To reach Vienna's center, follow the S *(Schnellbahn)* signs to the right and down the stairs, and take any train in the direction Floridsdorf; transfer in two stops (at Landsstrasse/Wien Mitte) to the U-3 line, direction Ottakring, which goes directly to Stephansplatz and Mariahilfer Strasse hotels. Also, tram D goes to the Ring, and bus #13A goes to Mariahilfer Strasse.

By Train at Franz Josefs Station: If you're coming from Krems (in the Danube Valley), you'll arrive at Vienna's Franz Josefs station. From here, take tram D into town. Better yet, get off at Spittelau (the stop before Josefs) and use its handy U-Bahn station.

By Plane: Vienna's airport (12 miles from town, tel. 01/7007-22233 for info and to connect with various airlines, www.viennaairport.com) is connected by S-Bahn to the very central Wien-Mitte station (€3, 2/hr, 24 min). Beginning in 2004, an even speedier new train connects the airport to Wien-Mitte (€8, 16 min). With these new, faster options now available, the express airport bus (€6, 3/hr, 20 min) will likely be phased out. Taxis into town cost about €35 (including €10 airport sur-charge). Hotels arrange for fixed-rate car service to the airport (€30, 30-min ride).

Getting around Vienna

By Bus, Tram, and Metro: Take full advantage of Vienna's simple, cheap, and super-efficient transit system. Buses, trams, and the metro all use the same tickets. Buy your tickets from *Tabak* shops, station machines, or *Vorverkauf* offices in the station. You have lots of choices:

• single tickets (€1.50, €2 if bought on tram, good for 1 journey with necessary transfers)
• 24-hour pass (€5)
• 72-hour pass (€12)
• 7-day pass (€12.50, pass always starts on Mon)
• *Acht Tage Karte:* eight all-day trips for €24 (can be shared, for example, 4 people for 2 days each). With a per-person cost of €3/day (compared to €5/day for a 24-hour pass) this can be a real saver for groups. Kids under 15 travel free on Sundays and holidays.

Take a moment to study the eye-friendly city-center map on metro station walls to internalize how the metro and tram system can help you (metro routes are designated by the end-of-the-line stop). I use the tram mostly to zip along the Ring (tram #1 or #2) and take the metro to out-lying sights or hotels. The free tourist map has essentially all the lines marked, making the too-big €1.50 transit map unnecessary. Numbered lines (such as #38) are trams, numbers followed by an *A* (such as #38A) are buses. Lines that begin with *U* (e.g., U-3) are subways, or *U-Bahnen.* And blue lines are the speedier S-Bahns *(Schnellbahnen).*

Stamp a time on your ticket as you enter the system or tram (stamp it only the first time for a multiple-use pass). Cheaters pay a stiff €44 fine if caught—and then they make you buy a ticket. Rookies miss stops because they fail to open the door. Push buttons, pull latches—do whatever it takes. Study the excellent wall-mounted street map before you exit the metro. Choosing the right exit—signposted from the moment you step off the train—saves lots of walking (for information call 01/790-9105).

By Taxi: Vienna's comfortable, civilized, and easy-to-flag-down taxis start at €2. You'll pay about €8 to go from the Opera to the West Train Station (Westbahnhof). Consider the luxury of having your own car and driver. Johann (John) Lichtl is a kind, honest, English-speak-ing cabbie who can take up to four passengers in his car (€25/1 hr, €20/hr for 2 or more hours, mobile 0676/670-6750).

By Bike: Handy as you'll find the city's transit system, you may want to rent a bike (list of rental places at the TI). If the tram's not your style, you can circle the Ring on a convenient bike path.

By Buggy: Rich romantics get around by traditional horse and buggy. You'll see the horse buggies, called *Fiakers,* clip-clopping tourists on tours lasting 20 minutes (€40—old town), 40 minutes (€65—old town and the Ring), or one hour (€95—all of the above, but more thorough). You can share the ride and cost with up to five people. Because it's a kind of guided tour, before settling on a carriage, talk to a few drivers and pick one who's fun and speaks English.

Helpful Hints

Banking: ATMs are everywhere. Banks are open weekdays roughly from 8:00 to 15:00 and until 17:30 on Thursday. After-hours, you can change money at train stations, the airport, post offices, or the American Express office (Mon–Fri 9:00–17:30, Sat 9:00–12:00, closed Sun, Kärntner Strasse 21-23, tel. 01/5154-0456).

Post Offices: Choose from the main post office (Postgasse in center, open 24 hrs daily, handy metered phones), West Train Station (daily 6:00–23:00), South Train Station (daily 7:00-22:00), or near the Opera (Mon–Fri 7:00–19:00, closed Sat–Sun, Krugerstrasse 13).

English Bookstores: Consider the **British Bookshop** (Mon–Fri 9:30–18:30, Sat 9:30–17:00, closed Sun, at corner of Weihburggasse and Seilerstätte, tel. 01/512-1945; same hours at branch at Mariahilferstrasse 4, tel. 01/522-6730) or **Shakespeare & Co.** (Mon–Sat 9:00–19:00, closed Sun, north of Höher Markt square, Sterngasse 2, tel. 01/535-5053).

Internet Access: The TI has a list of Internet cafés. BigNet is the dominant outfit (about €3/hr, cheaper if you buy snack or drink, www.bignet.at), with lots of stations at Kärntner Strasse 61 (daily 10:00–24:00), Mariahilfer Strasse 27 (daily 8:00–2:00), and Hoher Markt 8–9 (daily 10:00–24:00). Surfland Internet Café is near the Opera (€1.40 to start, then €0.08/min, daily 10:00–23:00, Krugerstrasse 10, tel. 01/512-7701).

TOURS

Walks—The *Walks in Vienna* brochure at the TI describes Vienna's guided walks. The basic 90-minute Vienna First Glance introductory walk is given daily throughout the summer (€11, 14:00 from TI, in English and German, tel. 01/894-5363, www.wienguide.at).

Local Guides—The tourist board Web site (www.info.wien.at) has a long list of local guides with specialties and contact information. Lisa Zeiler is a good English-speaking guide (2-hr walks for €120—if she's booked, she can set you up with another guide, tel. 01/402-3688, lisa.zeiler@gmx.at).

Bus Tours—The Yellow Cab Sightseeing company offers a one-hour, €12, quickie double-decker bus tour with a tape-recorded narration, departing at the top of each hour (10:00–17:00) from in front of the Opera (corner of Operngasse). Vienna Sightseeing offers hop-on, hop-off tours covering the 13 predictable sightseeing stops. Given Vienna's excellent public transportation and this outfit's meager one-bus-per-hour frequency, I'd take this not to hop on and off, but only to get the narrated orientation drive through town (recorded narration in 8 languages, €20 for 24-hr ticket, or €12 if you stay on for the 60-minute circular ride). Their basic Vienna city sights tour includes a visit to the Schönbrunn Palace and a bus tour around town (€33, 3/day April–Nov, 2/day Dec–March, 3.5 hrs; to book this or get info on other tours, call 01/7124-6830).

DO-IT-YOURSELF TRAM ORIENTATION TOUR

In the 1860s, Emperor Franz Josef had the city's ingrown medieval wall torn down and replaced with a grand boulevard 190 feet wide. The road, arcing nearly three miles around the city's core, predates all the buildings that line it—so what you'll see is neoclassical, neo-Gothic, and neo-Renaissance. One of Europe's great streets, it's lined with many of the city's top sights. Trams #1 and #2 and a great bike path circle the whole route—and so should you.

This self-service tram tour, rated ▲▲, gives you a fun orientation and a ridiculously quick glimpse of the major sights as you glide by (€1.50, 30-min circular tour). Tram #1 goes clockwise; tram #2, counterclockwise. Most sights are on the outside, so use tram #2 (sit on the right, ideally in the front seat of the front car; or—for maximum view and minimum air—sit in the bubble-front seat of the second car). Start immediately across the street from the Opera House.

You can jump on and off as you go (trams come every 5 min). Read ahead and pay attention—these sights can fly by. Let's go:

☛ Immediately on the left: The city's main pedestrian drag, Kärntner Strasse, leads to the zigzag roof of **St. Stephan's Cathedral.** This tram tour makes a 360-degree circle around the cathedral, staying about this same distance from it.

☛ At first bend (before first stop): Look right toward the tall fountain and the guy on a horse. Schwartzenberg Platz shows off its **equestrian statue** of Prince Charles Schwartzenberg, who fought Napoleon. Behind that is the Russian monument (behind the fountain), which was built in 1945 as a forced thanks to the Soviets for liberating Austria from the Nazis. Formerly a sore point, now it's just ignored.

☛ Going down Schubertring, you reach the huge **Stadtpark** (city park) on the right, which honors many great Viennese musicians and composers with statues. At the beginning of the park, the gold-and-cream concert hall behind the trees is the **Kursalon,** opened in 1867 by the Strauss brothers, who directed many waltzes here. The touristy Strauss concerts are held here (see "Summer Music Scene," below).

☛ Immediately after next stop, look right: In the same park, the gilded statue of Waltz King **Johann Strauss** holds a violin as he did when he

Vienna

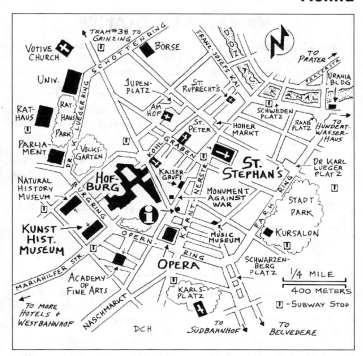

conducted his orchestra, whipping his fans into a two-stepping frenzy.

☞ At next stop at end of park: On the left, a green statue of Dr. Karl Lueger honors the popular man who was mayor of Vienna until 1910.

☞ At next bend: On the right, the quaint white building with military helmets decorating the windows was the Austrian ministry of war—back when that was a big operation. Field Marshal Radetzky, a military big shot in the 19th century under Franz Josef, still sits on his high horse. He's pointing toward the post office, the only art nouveau building facing the Ring. Locals call the architecture along the Ring "**historicism**" because it's all neo-this and neo-that—generally fitting the purpose of the particular building (for example, farther along the Ring, we'll see a neo-Gothic city hall—recalling when medieval burghers ran the city government in Gothic days, a neoclassical parliament building—celebrating ancient Greek notions of democracy, and a neo-Renaissance opera house—venerating the high culture filling it).

☞ At next corner: The white-domed building over your right shoulder as you turn is the Urania, Franz Josef's 1910 **observatory.** Lean forward

VIENNA AT A GLANCE

▲▲▲**Opera** Dazzling, world-famous opera house. **Hours:** Visit by 35-min tour only, daily in English, July–Aug at 11:00, 13:00, 14:00, 15:00, and often at 10:00 and 16:00; Sept–June fewer tours, afternoon only, confirm tour times by calling.

▲▲▲**Hofburg Treasury** The Hapsburgs' collection of jewels, crowns, and other valuables—the best on the Continent. **Hours:** Wed–Mon 10:00–18:00, closed Tue.

▲▲▲**Schönbrunn Palace** Spectacular summer residence of the Hapsburgs, similar in grandeur to Versailles. **Hours:** April–Oct daily 8:30–17:00, July–Aug until 18:00, Nov–March daily 8:30–16:30, reservations recommended.

▲▲▲**Kunsthistorisches Museum** World-class exhibit of the Hapsburgs' art collection, including Raphael, Titian, Caravaggio, Bosch, and Brueghel. **Hours:** Tue–Sun 10:00–18:00, Thu until 21:00, closed Mon.

▲▲**St. Stephan's Cathedral** Beautiful, enormous Gothic cathedral in the center of Vienna. **Hours:** Church doors open Mon–Sat 6:00–22:00, Sun 7:00–22:00, officially only open for tourists Mon-Sat 8:30-11:30 & 13:00-16:30, Sun 13:00-16:30.

▲▲**Stephansplatz, Graben, and Kohlmarkt** Atmospheric pedestrian squares and streets around the cathedral. **Hours:** Always open.

▲▲**Hofburg Imperial Apartments** Lavish main residence of the Hapsburgs. **Hours:** Daily 9:00–17:00.

▲▲**Hofburg New Palace Museums** Uncrowded collection of armor, musical instruments, and ancient Greek statues, in the elegant halls of a Hapsburg palace. **Hours:** Wed–Mon 10:00–18:00, closed Tue.

▲▲**Kaisergruft** Crypt for the Hapsburg royalty. **Hours:** Daily 9:30–16:00.

▲▲**KunstHausWien** Modern art museum dedicated to zany local artist/environmentalist Hundertwasser. **Hours:** Daily 10:00–19:00.

▲▲**Haus der Musik** Modern musuem with interactive exhibits on Vienna's favorite pastime. **Hours:** Daily 10:00–22:00.

▲**Monument against War and Fascism** Powerful four-part statue remembering victims of the Nazis. **Hours:** Always open.

▲**Albertina Museum** Newly opened Hapsburg residence with ho-hum apartments and world-class permanent and temporary exhibits. **Hours:** Daily 10:00–18:00, Wed until 21:00.

▲**Kärntner Strasse** Vienna's lively main pedestrian drag, connecting the Opera with the cathedral. **Hours:** Always open.

▲**Lipizzaner Museum** Displays dedicated to the regal Lipizzaner Stallions; horse-lovers should check out their practice sessions. **Hours:** Museum open daily 9:00–18:00, stallions practice across the street roughly Feb–June and Sept–Oct, Tue–Sat 10:00–12:00 when the horses are in town, call to confirm.

▲**Augustinian Church** Hapsburg marriage church, now hosting an 11:00 Sunday Mass with wonderful music.

▲**Imperial Furniture Collection** Eclectic collection of Hapsburg furniture. **Hours:** Tue–Sun 10:00–18:00, closed Mon.

▲▲**Academy of Fine Arts** Small but exciting collection with works by Bosch, Botticelli, Rubens, Guardi, and Van Dyck. **Hours:** Tue–Sun 10:00–16:00, closed Mon.

▲**Belvedere Palace** Elegant palace of Prince Eugene of Savoy, with a collection of 19th- and 20th-century Austrian art (including Klimt). **Hours:** Tue–Sun 10:00–18:00, closed Mon.

▲**Dorotheum** Vienna's highbrow auction house. **Hours:** Mon–Fri 10:00–18:00, Sat 9:00–17:00, closed Sun.

and look behind it for a peek at the huge red cars of the giant 100-year-old Ferris wheel in Vienna's Prater Park (fun for families, described in "Top People-Watching and Strolling Sights," below).

☛ Now you're rolling along the **Danube Canal.** This "Baby Danube" is one of the many small arms of the river that once made up the Danube at this location. The rest have been gathered together in a mightier modern-day Danube, farther away. This neighborhood was thoroughly bombed in World War II. The buildings across the canal are typical of postwar architecture (1960s). This was the site of the original Roman town, Vindobona. In three long blocks, on the left (opposite the BP station, be ready—it passes fast), you'll see the ivy-covered walls and round Romanesque arches of St. Ruprechts, the oldest church in Vienna (built in the 11th century on a bit of Roman ruins). Remember, medieval Vienna was defined by that long-gone wall which you're tracing on this tour. Relax for a few stops until the corner.

☛ Leaving the canal, turning left up Schottenring, at first stop: On the left, the orange-and-white, neo-Renaissance temple of money, the **Börse,** is Vienna's stock exchange.

☛ Next stop, at corner: The huge, frilly, neo-Gothic church on the right is a "votive church," built as a thanks to God when an 1853 assassination attempt on Emperor Franz Josef failed. Ahead on the right (in front of tram stop) is the Vienna University building (established in 1365, it has no real campus as the buildings are scattered around town). It faces (on the left, behind a gilded angel) a chunk of the old city wall.

☛ At next stop on right: The neo-Gothic city hall, flying the flag of Europe, towers over **Rathaus Platz,** a festive site in summer with a huge screen showing outdoor movies, operas, and concerts. Immediately across the street (on left) is the **Hofburg Theater,** Austria's national theater.

☛ At next stop on right: The neo-Greek temple of democracy houses the **Austrian Parliament.** The lady with the golden helmet is Athena, goddess of wisdom. Across the street (on left) is the royal park called the "Volksgarten."

☛ After the next stop on the right is the **Natural History Museum,** the first of Vienna's huge twin museums. It faces the **Kunsthistorisches Museum,** containing the city's greatest collection of paintings. The **MuseumsQuartier** behind them completes the ensemble with a collection of mostly modern-art museums. A hefty statue of Empress Maria Theresa sits between the museums, facing the grand gate to the **Hofburg,** the emperor's palace (on left). Of the five arches, only the center one was used by the emperor. (Your tour is essentially finished. If you want to jump out here, you're at many of Vienna's top sights.)

☛ Fifty yards after the next stop, on the left through a gate in the black iron fence, is the statue of Mozart. It's one of many charms in the **Burggarten,** which until 1880 was the private garden of the emperor. Vienna had more than its share of intellectual and creative geniuses. A hundred yards farther (on left, just out of the park), the German philosopher Goethe sits in a big, thought-provoking chair playing trivia with Schiller (across the street on your right). Behind the statue of Schiller is the Academy of Fine Arts.

☛ Hey, there's the **Opera** again. Jump off the tram and see the rest of the city.

SIGHTS

Vienna's Old Center

▲▲▲**Opera (Staatsoper)**—The Opera, facing the Ring and near the TI, is a central point for any visitor. While the critical reception of the building 130 years ago led the architect to commit suicide, and though it's been rebuilt since the WWII bombings, it's still a dazzling place (€4.50, by guided 35-min tour only, daily in English, July–Aug at 11:00, 13:00, 14:00, 15:00, and often at 10:00 and 16:00; Sept–June fewer tours, afternoon only). Tours are often canceled for rehearsals and shows, so check the posted schedule or call 01/514-442-613.

The Vienna State Opera—with musicians provided by the Vienna Philharmonic Orchestra in the pit—is one of the world's top opera houses. There are 300 performances a year, except in July and August, when the singers rest their voices. Since there are different operas nearly nightly, you'll see big trucks out back and constant action backstage—all the sets need to be switched each day. Even though the expensive seats normally sell out long in advance, the opera is perpetually in the red and subsidized by the state.

Tickets for seats: For ticket information, call 01/513-1513 (phone answered daily 10:00–21:00, www.culturall.com or www.wiener-staatsoper.at). If seats aren't sold out, last-minute tickets (for pricey seats—up to €100) are sold for €30 from 9:00 to 14:00 only the day before the show.

Standing room: Unless Pavarotti is in town, it's easy to get one of 567 *Stehplätze* (standing-room spots, €2 at the top or €3.50 downstairs). While the front doors open 60 minutes early, a side door (on the Operngasse side, the door under the portico nearest the fountain) is open 80 minutes before curtain time, giving those in the know an early grab at standing-room tickets. Just walk in straight, then head right until you see the ticket booth marked *Stehplätze* (tel. 01/5144-42419). If fewer than 567 people are in line, there's no need to line up early. You can even buy standing-room tickets after the show has started—in case you want only a little taste of opera (see "Rick's crude tip" below). Dress is casual (but do your best) at the standing-room bar. Locals save their spot along the rail by tying a scarf to it.

Rick's crude tip: For me, three hours is a lot of opera. But just to see and hear the Opera House in action for half an hour is a treat. You can buy a standing-room spot and just drop in for part of the show. Ushers don't mind letting tourists with standing-room tickets in for a short look. Ending time is posted in the lobby—you could stop by for just the finale. If you go at the start or finish, you'll see Vienna dressed up. With all the time you save, consider stopping by...

Sacher Café, home of every chocoholic's fantasy, the Sacher torte, faces the rear of the Opera. While locals complain that the cakes have gone downhill, a coffee and slice of cake here is €8 well invested. For maximum elegance, sit inside (daily 8:00–23:30, Philharmoniker Strasse 4, tel. 01/51456). The adjacent Café Mozart is better for a meal.

The U-Bahn station in front of the Opera is actually a huge under-ground shopping mall with fast food, newsstands, lots of pickpockets, and even an Opera Toilet Vienna experience (€0.50, *mit Musik*).

▲**Monument against War and Fascism**—A powerful four-part statue stands behind the Opera House on Albertinaplatz. The split white mon-ument, *The Gates of Violence,* remembers victims of the 1938–1945 Nazi rule of Austria. A montage of wartime images—clubs and gas masks, a dying woman birthing a future soldier, slave laborers—sits on a pedestal of granite cut from the infamous quarry at Mauthausen, a nearby con-centration camp. The hunched-over figure on the ground behind is a Jew forced to wash anti-Nazi graffiti off a street with a toothbrush. The statue with its head buried in the stone reminds Austrians of the consequences of not keeping their government on track. Behind that, the 1945 decla-ration of Austria's second republic is cut into the stone. This monument stands on the spot where several hundred people were buried alive while hiding in the cellar of a building demolished in a WWII bombing attack.

Austria was pulled into World War II by Germany, which annexed the country in 1938, saying Austrians were wannabe Germans, anyway. But Austrians are not Germans—never were...never will be. They're quick to tell you that while Austria was founded in 976, Germany wasn't born until 1870. For seven years during World War II (1938–1945), there was no Austria. In 1955, after 10 years of joint occupation by the victorious Allies, Austria regained total independence.

Across the square from the TI, you'll see what looks like a big ter-race overlooking the street. This was actually part of Vienna's original defensive rampart. Next to it is the...

▲**Albertina Museum**—For years, this building—the oldest of the Hapsburgs' Vienna residences—was closed for reconstruction. Now it has re-opened its doors so that commoners like you and me can wander its regal halls and enjoy some world-class artwork.

The Albertina consists of various components. First, you can stroll through the Hapsburg state rooms (French classicism—lots of white marble—but pretty ho-hum stuff compared to the apartments in the Hofburg up the street). Second, the Albertina routinely borrows world-famous artwork for special exhibitions; in 2004, you'll see Paul Klee

(Feb–April), Rembrandt (April–June), and Piet Mondrian (mid-Oct 2004 through Feb 2005). Finally, the Albertina also has its own spectacular collection of works by Michelangelo, Rubens, Rembrandt, and Raphael, plus a huge sampling of precise drawings by Albrecht Dürer. They're still experimenting with how to exhibit these masterpieces—so ask if your favorite artist is on display (state rooms only-€4, more for other exhibitions, audioguide also available for both permanent and temporary exhibits, daily 10:00–18:00, Wed until 21:00, overlooking Albertinaplatz across from TI and Opera House, tel. 01/534-830).

▲▲**Kaisergruft (Remains of the Hapsburgs)**—The crypt for the Hapsburg royalty, a block down the street from the Monument against War and Fascism, is covered in detail under "More Hofburg Sights," below.

▲**Kärntner Strasse**—This grand, mall-like street (traffic-free since 1974) is the people-watching delight of this in-love-with-life city. It points south in the direction of the southern Austrian state of Kärnten (for which it's named). Starting from the Opera, you'll find lots of action—shops, street music, the city casino (at #41), American Express (#21–23), and then, finally, the cathedral.

▲▲**St. Stephan's Cathedral**—Stephansdom is the Gothic needle around which Vienna spins. It has survived Vienna's many wars and symbolizes the city's freedom (church doors open Mon–Sat 6:00–22:00, Sun 7:00–22:00, officially only open for tourists Mon–Sat 8:30–11:30 & 13:00–16:30, Sun 13:00–16:30, otherwise closed for services; during services, you can enter back of church and get to north tower elevator, but unless you're attending Mass, you cannot enter main nave; entertaining English tours daily April–Oct at 15:45, €4, information board inside entry has tour schedules).

This is the third church to stand on this spot. (In fact, an older Romanesque chapel—the Virgilkapelle—is on display in the adjacent metro station.) The last bit of the 13th-century Romanesque church, the portal, round windows of the towers, and fascinating carvings in the tympanum, can be seen on the west end (above the entrance). The church survived the bombs of World War II, but, in the last days of the war, fires from the street fighting between Russian and Nazi troops leapt to the rooftop; the original timbered Gothic rooftop burned, and the cathedral's huge bell crashed to the ground. With a financial outpouring of civic pride, the roof of this symbol of Austria was rebuilt in its original splendor by 1952. The ceramic tiles are purely decorative (locals who contributed to the postwar reconstruction each "own" one for their donation).

Inside, find the Gothic sandstone **pulpit** in the middle of the nave (on left). A spiral stairway winds up to the lectern, surrounded and supported by the four Latin Church fathers: Saints Ambrose, Jerome, Gregory, and Augustine. The railing leading up swarms with symbolism: lizards (animals of light), battle toads (animals of darkness), and the "Dog of the Lord" standing at the top to be sure none of those toads pollutes the sermon. Below the toads, wheels with three parts (the Trinity) roll up, while wheels with four parts (standing for the four seasons, symbolizing mortal life) roll down. This work, by Anton Pilgram, has all the elements of flamboyant Gothic in miniature. But this was around 1500, and the Renaissance was going strong in Italy. While Gothic persisted in the North, the Renaissance spirit had already arrived. Pilgram included what's thought to be a rare self-portrait bust in his work (the guy with sculptor's tools, looking out a window under the stairs). Gothic art was done for the glory of God. Artists were anonymous. In the more humanist Renaissance, man was allowed to shine—and artists became famous.

You can ascend both towers, the north (via crowded elevator inside on the left) and the south (outside right transept, by spiral staircase). The north shows you a big **bell** (the 21-ton Pummerin, cast from the cannon captured from the Turks in 1683, supposedly the second biggest bell in the world that rings by swinging) but a mediocre view (€4, daily 8:30–17:30, July–Aug until 18:00, Nov–March until 17:00). The 450-foot-high **south tower,** called St. Stephan's Tower, offers a great view—343 tightly wound steps up the spiral staircase (€3, daily 9:00–17:30, this hike burns about 1 Sacher torte of calories). From the top, use your *Vienna from A to Z* to locate the famous sights.

The forlorn **Cathedral Museum** (Dom Museum, outside left transept past horses) gives a close-up look at piles of religious paintings, statues, and a treasury (€5, Tue–Sat 10:00–17:00, closed Sun–Mon, Stephansplatz 6, tel. 01/515-523-560).

▲▲**Stephansplatz, Graben, and Kohlmarkt**—The atmosphere of the church square, Stephansplatz, is colorful and lively. At nearby Graben Street (which was once a *Graben,* or ditch—originally the moat for the Roman military camp), top-notch street entertainers dance around an exotic **plague monument** (at Bräuner Strasse). In medieval times, people did not understand the causes of plagues and figured they were a punishment from God. It was common for survivors to thank God with a monument like this one from the 1600s. Find Emperor Leopold, who ruled during the plague and made this statue in gratitude. (Hint: The typical inbreeding of royal families left him with a gaping underbite.) Below Leopold, Faith (with the help of a disgusting little cupid) tosses old naked women—symbolizing the plague—into the abyss.

Just before the plague monument is Dorotheergasse, leading to the Dorotheum auction house (see "More Sights in Vienna," below). Just beyond the monument, you'll pass a fine set of public WCs before dead-ending at the recommended restaurant Julius Meinl am Graben (see "Eating," below). Turning left on **Kohlmarkt,** you enter Vienna's most elegant shopping street (except for "American Catalog Shopping," at #5, second floor) with the emperor's palace at the end. Strolling Kohlmarkt, daydream about the edible window displays at **Demel** (#14). These delectable displays change about weekly, reflecting current happenings in Vienna. Drool through the interior (coffee and cake—€7.50). Shops like this boast "K. u. K."—good enough for the *König und Kaiser* (king and emperor—same guy). Just beyond Demel and across the street, at #1152, you can pop into a charming little Baroque carriage courtyard, with the surviving original carriage garages.

Kohlmarkt ends at Michaelerplatz, with a scant bit of Roman Vienna exposed at its center. On the left are the fancy Laden Plankl shop, with traditional formal wear, and the stables of the Spanish Riding School. Study the grand entry facade to the Hofburg Palace—it's neo-Baroque from around 1900. The four heroic giants are Hercules wrestling with his great challenges (much like the Hapsburgs, I'm sure). Opposite the facade, notice the modern Loos House, which was built at about the same time. It was nicknamed the "house without eyebrows" for the simplicity of its windows. This anti-art nouveau statement was actually shocking at the time. To quell some of the outrage, the architect added flower boxes. Enter the Hofburg Palace by walking through the gate, under the dome, and into the first square (In der Burg).

Vienna's Hofburg Palace

▲▲**Hofburg**—The complex, confusing, and imposing Imperial Palace, with 640 years of architecture, demands your attention. This first Hapsburg residence grew with the family empire from the 13th century until 1913, when the last "new wing" opened. The winter residence of the Hapsburg rulers until 1918, it's still the home of the Spanish Riding School, the Vienna Boys' Choir, the Austrian president's office, 5,000 government workers, and several important museums.

Rather than lose yourself in its myriad halls and courtyards, focus on three sections: the Imperial Apartments, Treasury, and Neue Burg (New Palace).

Hofburg orientation from In der Burg Square: The statue is of Emperor Franz II, grandson of Maria Theresa, grandfather of Franz Josef, and father-in-law of Napoleon. Behind him is a tower with three kinds of clocks (the yellow disk shows the stage of the moon tonight). On the right, a door leads to the Imperial Apartments. Franz faces the oldest part of the palace. The colorful gate, which used to have a draw-bridge, leads to the 13th-century Swiss Court (named for the Swiss mercenary guards once stationed here), the Schatzkammer (treasury), and the Hofburgkapelle (palace chapel, where the Boys' Choir sings the Mass). For the Heroes' Square and the New Palace, continue opposite the way you entered In der Burg, passing through the left-most tunnel (with a tiny but handy sandwich bar—Hofburg Stüberl, Mon–Fri 7:00–18:00, Sat 9:00–15:00, Sun 10:00–15:00—your best bet if you need a bite or drink before touring the Imperial Apartments).

Vienna's Hofburg Palace

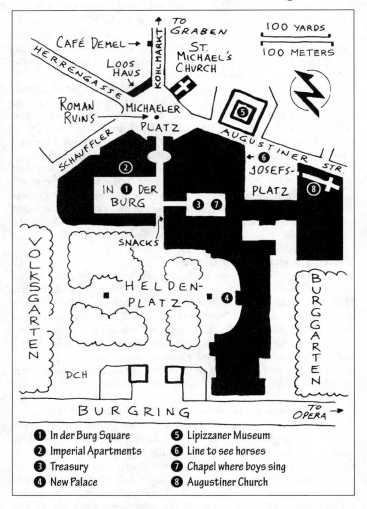

1. In der Burg Square
2. Imperial Apartments
3. Treasury
4. New Palace
5. Lipizzaner Museum
6. Line to see horses
7. Chapel where boys sing
8. Augustiner Church

▲▲**Imperial Apartments (Kaiserappartements)**—These lavish, Versailles-type, "wish-I-were-God" royal rooms are the downtown version of the grander Schönbrunn Palace. If you're rushed and have time for only one palace, do this (€7.50, daily 9:00–17:00, last entry 16:30, from courtyard through St. Michael's Gate, just off Michaelerplatz, tel. 01/533-7570). Palace visits are a one-way romp through 20 rooms.

EMPEROR FRANZ JOSEF

Franz Josef I—who ruled for 68 years (1848–1916)—was the embodiment of the Hapsburg Empire as it finished its six-century-long ride. Born in 1830, Franz Josef had a stern upbringing that instilled in him a powerful sense of duty and—like so many men of power—a love of things military. His uncle, Ferdinand I, was a dimwit, and, as the revolutions of 1848 were rattling royal families throughout Europe, the Hapsburgs replaced him, putting 18-year old Franz Josef on the throne. FJ was very conservative. But worse, he figured he was a talented military tactician, leading Austria into disastrous battles against Italy (which was fighting for its unification and independence) in the 1860s. His army endured severe, avoidable casualties. It was clear: FJ was a disaster as a general. Wearing his uniform to the end, he never saw what a dinosaur his monarchy was becoming, and never thought it strange that the majority of his subjects didn't even speak German. He had no interest in democracy and pointedly never set foot in Austria's parliament building. But, like his contemporary Queen Victoria, he was the embodiment of his empire—old-fashioned but sacrosanct. His passion for low-grade paperwork earned him the nickname "Joe bureaucrat." Mired in these petty details, he missed the big picture. He helped start a world war that ultimately ended the age of monarchs. The year 1918 marked the end of Europe's big royal families: Hohenzollerns (Prussia), Romanovs (Russia), and Hapsburgs (Austria).

You'll find some helpful English information within, and, with that and the following description, you won't need the €6.90 Hofburg guidebook. The €3.20 audioguide is only worthwhile for a Hapsburg history buff. Tickets include the royal silver and porcelain collection *(Silberkammer)* near the turnstile. If touring the silver and porcelain, do it first to save walking.

Get your ticket, study the big model of the palace complex, and (just after the turnstile) notice the family tree tracing the Hapsburgs from 1273 to their messy WWI demise. The first two rooms give an overview (in English) of Empress Elisabeth's fancy world—her luxury homes and fairy-tale existence. Throughout the tour, banners describe royal life.

Amble through the first several furnished rooms to the...

Waiting room for the audience room: A map and mannequins

SISSY

Empress Elisabeth, Emperor Franz Josef's mysterious, narcissistic, and beautiful wife, is in vogue. She was mostly silent, worked out frantically to maintain her Barbie Doll figure, and spent hours each day tending to her ankle-length hair. Sissy's main goals in life seem to have been preserving her reputation as a beautiful empress and maintaining her fairy-tale hair. In spite of severe dieting and fanatic exercise, age took its toll. After turning 30, she allowed no more portraits to be painted and was generally seen in public with a delicate fan covering her face (and bad teeth). Complex and influential, she was adored by Franz Josef, whom she respected. Her personal mission and political cause was promoting Hungary's bid for nationalism. Her personal tragedy was the death of her son Rudolf, the crown prince, by suicide. Disliking Vienna and the confines of the court, she traveled more and more frequently. Over the years, the restless Sissy and her hardworking husband became estranged. In 1898, while visiting Geneva, Switzerland, she was murdered by an Italian anarchist. Sissy has been compared to Princess Diana because of her beauty, bittersweet life, and tragic death.

from the many corners of the Hapsburg realm illustrate the multi-ethnicity of the empire. Every citizen had the right to meet privately with the emperor. Three huge paintings entertained guests while they waited. They were propaganda, showing crowds of commoners enthusiastic about their Hapsburg royalty. On the right: An 1809 scene of the emperor returning to Vienna, celebrating news that Napoleon had begun his retreat. Left: The return of the emperor from the 1814 Peace of Paris, the treaty that ended the Napoleonic wars. (The 1815 Congress of Vienna that followed was the greatest assembly of diplomats in European history. Its goal: to establish peace through a "balance of power" among nations. While rulers ignored nationalism in favor of continued dynastic rule, this worked for about 100 years, until a colossal war—World War I—wiped out Europe's royal families.) Center: Less important, the emperor makes his first public appearance to adoring crowds after recovering from a life-threatening illness (1826). The chandelier—considered the best in the palace—is Baroque, made of Bohemian crystal.

Audience room: Suddenly, you were face-to-face with the emp. The portrait on the easel shows Franz Josef in 1915, when he was over 80 years old. Famously energetic, he lived a spartan life dedicated to duty. He'd stand at the high table here to meet with commoners, who came to show gratitude or make a request. (Standing kept things moving.) On the table, you can read a partial list of 56 appointments he had on January 3, 1910 (family name and topic of meeting).

Conference room: The emperor presided here over the equivalent of cabinet meetings. Remember, after 1867, he ruled the Austro-Hungarian Empire, so Hungarians sat at these meetings. The paintings on the wall show the military defeat of a popular Hungarian uprising...subtle.

Emperor Franz Josef's study: The desk was originally between the windows. Franz Josef could look up from his work and see his lovely, long-haired empress Elisabeth's reflection in the mirror. Notice the trompe l'oeil paintings above each door, giving the believable illusion of marble relief.

The walls between the rooms are wide enough to hide servants' corridors (the door to his valet's room is in the back left corner). The emperor lived with a personal staff of 14: three valets, four lackeys, two doormen, two manservants, and three chambermaids.

Emperor's bedroom: This features his famous spartan iron bed and portable washstand (necessary until 1880, when the palace got running water). A small painted porcelain portrait of the newlywed royal couple sits on the dresser. Franz Josef lived here after his estrangement from Sissy. An etching shows the empress—an avid hunter—riding sidesaddle while jumping a hedge. The big ornate stove in the corner was fed from behind. Through the 19th century, this was a standard form of heating.

Great salon: See the paintings of the emperor and empress in grand gala ballroom outfits from 1865.

Small salon: This is dedicated to the memory of the assassinated Emperor Maximilian of Mexico (bearded portrait, Franz Josef's brother, killed in 1867). This was also a smoking room—necessary in the early 19th century, when smoking was newly fashionable (but only for men—never in the presence of women).

Empress' bedroom and drawing room: This was Sissy's, refurbished neo-rococo in 1854. She lived here—the bed was rolled in and out daily—until her death in 1898.

Sissy's dressing/exercise room: Servants worked two hours a day on Sissy's famous hair here. She'd exercise on the wooden structure. While she had a tough time with people, she did fine with animals. Her favorite circus horses, Flick and Flock, prance on the wall.

Sissy's bathroom: Detour into the behind-the-scenes palace. In the narrow passageway, you'll walk by Sissy's hand-painted porcelain WC (on the right). In the main bathroom, you'll see her huge copper tub (with the original wall coverings behind it). Sissy was the first Hapsburg to have running water in her bathroom. From here, you can wander (over the first linoleum ever used in Vienna—from around 1880) through the servants' quarters, with tropical scenes painted by Bergl in 1766. As you leave these rooms and re-enter the imperial world, look back to the room on the left.

Empress' great salon: The room is painted with Mediterranean escapes, the 19th-century equivalent of travel posters. The statue is of Elisa, Napoleon's oldest sister (by the neoclassical master, Canova). In the next room, at the end of the hall, admire the empress' hard-earned thin waist (20 inches at age 16, 21 inches at age 50...after giving birth to 4 children). Turn the corner and pass through the anterooms of Alexander's apartments.

Red salon: The Gobelin wall hangings were a 1776 gift from Marie Antoinette and Louis XVI in Paris to their Viennese counterparts.

Dining room: It's dinnertime, and Franz Josef has called his extended family together. The settings are modest...just silver. Gold was saved for formal state dinners. Next to each name card was a menu with the chef responsible for each dish. (Talk about pressure.) While the Hofburg had tableware for 4,000, feeding 3,000 was a typical day. The cellar was stocked with 60,000 bottles of wine. The kitchen was huge—50 birds could be roasted on the hand-driven spits at once.

After a few more rooms and the shop, you're back on the street. Two quick lefts take you back to the palace square (In der Burg), where you can pass through the black, red, and gold gate and to the treasury.

▲▲▲**Treasury (Weltliche und Geistliche Schatzkammer)**—This Secular and Religious Treasure Room contains the best jewels on the Continent. Slip through the vault doors and reflect on the glitter of 21 rooms filled with scepters, swords, crowns, orbs, weighty robes, double-headed eagles, gowns, gem-studded bangles, and an eight-foot-tall, 500-year-old unicorn horn (or maybe the tusk of a narwhal)—which was considered incredibly powerful in the old days, giving its owner the grace of God. These were owned by the Holy Roman Emperor—a divine monarch. The well-produced, included audioguide provides a wealth of information (€7.50, Wed–Mon 10:00–18:00, closed Tue, follow Schatzkammer signs to the Schweizerhof, tel. 01/52524).

Room 2: The personal crown of Rudolf II has survived since 1602—it was considered too well-crafted to cannibalize for other crowns. This crown is a big deal because it's the adopted crown of the Austrian Empire, established in 1806 after Napoleon dissolved the Holy Roman Empire (so named because it tried to be the grand continuation of the Roman Empire). Pressured by Napoleon, the Austrian Francis II—who had been Holy Roman Emperor—became Francis I, Emperor of Austria. Francis I/II (the stern guy on the wall) ruled from 1792 to 1835. Look at the crown. Its design symbolically merges the typical medieval king's crown and a bishop's miter.

Rooms 3 and 4: These contain some of the coronation vestments and regalia needed for the new Austrian emperor.

Room 5: Ponder the Throne Cradle. Napoleon's son was born in 1811 and made king of Rome. The little eagle at the foot is symbolically not yet able to fly, but glory-bound. Glory is symbolized by the star, with dad's big *N* raised high.

Room 11: The collection's highlight is the 10th-century crown of the Holy Roman Emperor. The imperial crown swirls with symbolism "proving" that the emperor was both holy and Roman. The jeweled arch over the top is reminiscent of the parade helmet of ancient Roman emperors whose successors the HRE claimed to be. The cross on top says the HRE ruled as Christ's representative on earth. King Solomon's portrait (on the crown, right of cross) is Old Testament proof that kings can be wise and good. King David (next panel) is similar proof that they can be just. The crown's eight sides represent the celestial city of Jerusalem's eight gates. The jewels on the front panel symbolize the Twelve Apostles.

The nearby 11th-century Imperial Cross preceded the emperor in ceremonies. Encrusted with jewels, it carried a substantial chunk of *the* cross and *the* holy lance (supposedly used to pierce the side of Jesus while on the cross; both items displayed in the same glass case). Look behind the cross to see how it was actually a box that could be clipped open and shut. You can see bits of the "true cross" anywhere, but this is a prime piece—with the actual nail hole.

The other case has jewels from the reign of Karl der Grosse (Charlemagne), the greatest ruler of medieval Europe. Notice Charlemagne modeling the crown (which was made a hundred years after he died) in the tall painting adjacent.

Room 12: The painting shows the coronation of Josef II in 1764. He's wearing the same crown and royal garb you've just seen.

Room 16: Most tourists walk right by perhaps the most exquisite workmanship in the entire treasury, the royal vestments (15th century). Look closely—they are painted with gold and silver threads.

▲**Heroes' Square and the New Palace (Heldenplatz and the Neue Burg)**—This last grand addition to the palace, from just before World War I, was built for Franz Ferdinand but never used. (It was tradition for rulers not to move into their predecessor's quarters.) Its grand facade arches around Heldenplatz, or Heroes' Square. Notice statues of the two great Austrian heroes on horseback: Prince Eugene of Savoy (who beat the Turks that had earlier threatened Vienna) and Archduke Charles (first to beat Napoleon in a battle, breaking Nappy's image of invincibility and heralding the end of the Napoleonic age). The frilly spires of Vienna's neo-Gothic city hall break the horizon, and a line of horse-drawn carriages await their customers.

▲▲**New Palace Museums: Armor, Music, and Ancient Greek Statues**—The Neue Burg—technically part of the Kunsthistorisches Museum across the way—houses three fine museums (same ticket): an armory (with a killer collection of medieval weapons), historical musical instruments, and classical statuary from ancient Ephesus. The included audioguide brings the exhibits to life and lets you actually hear the fascinating old instruments in the collection being played. An added bonus is the chance to wander all alone among those royal Hapsburg halls, stairways, and painted ceilings (€7.50, Wed–Mon 10:00–18:00, closed Tue, almost no tourists, tel. 01/5252-4484).

More Hofburg Sights

These sights are near—and associated with—the palace.

▲Lipizzaner Museum—A must for horse-lovers, this tidy museum in the Renaissance Stallburg Palace shows (and tells in English) the 400-year history of the famous riding school. Lipizzaner fans have a warm spot in their hearts for General Patton, who, at the end of World War II—knowing that the Soviets were about to take control of Vienna—ordered a raid on the stable to save the horses and ensure the survival of their fine old bloodlines. Videos show the horses in action on TVs throughout the museum. The "dancing" originated as battle moves: *pirouette* (quick turns) and *courbette* (on hind legs to make a living shield for the knight). The 45-minute movie in the basement theater also has great horse footage (showings alternate between German and English).

A highlight for many is the opportunity to view the stable from a museum window and actually see the famous white horses just sitting there looking common. Don't bother waving...it's a one-way mirror (€5, daily 9:00–18:00, Reitschulgasse 2 between Josefsplatz and Michaelerplatz, tel. 01/533-8658).

Seeing the Lipizzaner Stallions: Seats for performances by Vienna's prestigious Spanish Riding School book up months in advance, but standing room is often available the same day (tickets-€35–105, standing room-€24–28, March–June and Sept–Oct Sun at 11:00, sometimes also Fri at 18:00). Lucky for the masses, training sessions (with music) in a chandeliered Baroque hall are open to the public (€11.50 at the door, roughly Feb–June and Sept–Oct, Tue–Sat 10:00–12:00 when the horses are in town, tel. 01/533-9031, www.srs.at). Tourists line up early at Josefsplatz, gate 2. Save money and avoid the wait by buying the €14.50 combo-ticket that covers both the museum and the training session (and lets you avoid that ticket line). Or, better yet, simply show up late. Tourists line up for hours to get in at 10:00, but almost no one stays for the full two hours—except for the horses. As people leave, new tickets are printed continuously, so you can just waltz in with no wait at all. If you arrive at 10:45, you'll see one group of horses finish and two more perform before they quit at noon.

▲Augustinian Church—The Augustinerkirche (on Josefsplatz) is the Gothic and neo-Gothic church where the Hapsburgs latched, then buried, their hearts (weddings took place here and the royal hearts are in the vault). Don't miss the exquisite, tomb-like Canova memorial (neo-classical, 1805) to Maria Theresa's favorite daughter, Maria Christina, with its incredibly sad white-marble procession. The church's 11:00 Sunday Mass is a hit with music-lovers—both a Mass and a concert, often with an orchestra accompanying the choir. To pay, contribute to the offering plate and buy a CD afterwards. (Programs are available at the table by the entry all week.)

▲▲**Kaisergruft, the Remains of the Hapsburgs**—Visiting the imperial remains is not as easy as you might imagine. These original organ donors left their bodies—about 150 in all—in the unassuming Kaisergruft (Capuchin Crypt), their hearts in the Augustinian Church (church open daily, but to see the goods you'll have to talk to a priest; Augustinerstrasse 3), and their entrails in the crypt below St. Stephan's Cathedral. Don't tripe.

Upon entering the Kaisergruft (€4, daily 9:30–16:00, last entry 15:40, behind Opera on Neuer Markt), buy the €0.50 map with a Hapsburg family tree and a chart locating each coffin.

The double coffin of Maria Theresa and her husband is worth a close look for its artwork. Maria Theresa outlived her husband by 15 years—which she spent in mourning. Old and fat, she installed a special lift enabling her to get down into the crypt to be with her dead husband (even though he had been far from faithful). The couple recline—Etruscan style—atop their fancy lead coffin. At each corner are the crowns of the Hapsburgs—the Holy Roman Empire, Hungary, Bohemia, and Jerusalem. Notice the contrast between the rococo splendor of Maria Theresa's tomb and the simple box holding her more modest son, Josef II (at his parents' feet). An enlightened monarch, Josef mothballed the too-extravagant Schönbrunn, secularized the monasteries, established religious tolerance within his realm, and freed the serfs. Josef was a model of practicality (he even invented a reusable coffin)—and very unpopular with other royals.

Franz Josef (1830–1916) is nearby in an appropriately austere military tomb. Flanking Franz Josef are the tombs of his son, Rudolf II, and Empress Elizabeth. Rudolf committed suicide in 1898 and—since the Church wouldn't allow such a burial for someone who took his own life—it took considerable legal hair-splitting to win Rudolf this spot (after examining his brain, it was determined that he was physically retarded and therefore incapable of knowingly killing himself). *Kaiserin* Elisabeth (1837–1898), a.k.a. Sissy, always gets the "Most Flowers" award.

In front of those three is the most recent Hapsburg tomb. Empress Zita was buried in 1989. Her burial procession was probably the last such Old Regime event in European history. The monarchy died hard in Austria.

Rather than chasing down all these body parts, remember that the magnificence of this city is the real remains of the Hapsburgs. Pan up. Watch the clouds glide by the ornate gables of Vienna.

▲**Imperial Furniture Collection (Kaiserliches Hofmobiliendepot)**— Bizarre, sensuous, eccentric, or precious, this is your peek at the Hapsburgs' furniture—from grandma's wheelchair to the emperor's spittoon—all thoughtfully described in English. The Hapsburgs had many palaces, but only the Hofburg was permanently furnished. The rest were furnished on the fly—set up and taken down by a gang of royal roadies called the "Depot of Court Movables" (Hofmobiliendepot). When the monarchy was dissolved in 1918, the state of Austria took possession of the Hofmobiliendepot's inventory—165,000 items. Now this royal storehouse is open to the public in a fine, new, sprawling museum. Don't go here for the Biedermeier or *Jugendstil* furnishings. The older Baroque and rococo pieces are the most impressive and tied most intimately to the royals. Combine a visit to this museum with a stroll down the lively shopping boulevard, Mariahilfer Strasse (€7, Tue–Sun 10:00–18:00, closed Mon, Mariahilfer Strasse 88, tel. 01/5243-3570).

Schönbrunn Palace

▲▲▲**Schönbrunn Palace**—Among Europe's palaces, only Schloss Schönbrunn rivals Versailles. Located four miles from the center, it was the Hapsburgs' summer residence. It's big (1,441 rooms), but don't worry—only 40 rooms are shown to the public. (The families of 260 civil servants actually rent simple apartments in the rest of the palace.)

While the exterior is Baroque, the interior was finished under Maria Theresa in let-them-eat-cake rococo. The chandeliers are either of hand-carved wood with gold-leaf gilding or of Bohemian crystal. Thick walls hid the servants as they ran around stoking the ceramic stoves from the back, and so on. Most of the public rooms are decorated in neo-Baroque, as they were under Franz Josef (ruled 1848–1916). When WWII bombs rained on the city and the palace grounds, the palace itself took only one direct hit. Thankfully, that bomb, which crashed through three floors—including the sumptuous central ballroom—was a dud.

Reservations and Hours: Schönbrunn suffers from crowds. To avoid the long delays in July and August (mornings are worst), make a reservation by telephone (tel. 01/8111-3239, answered daily 8:00–17:00). You'll get an appointment time and a ticket number. Check in at least 30 minutes early. Upon arrival, go to the group desk, give your number, pick up your ticket, and jump in ahead of the masses. If you show up in peak season without calling first, you deserve the frustration. Wait in line, buy your ticket, and wait until the listed time to enter (which could be tomorrow). Kill time in the gardens or coach museum (palace open April–Oct daily 8:30–17:00, July–Aug until 18:00, Nov–March daily

8:30–16:30). Crowds are worst from 9:30 to 11:30, especially on weekends and in July and August; it's least crowded from 12:00 to 14:00 and after 16:00.

Cost and Tours: The admission price is the price of the tour you select. Choose between two recorded audioguide tours: the Imperial Tour (22 rooms, €8, 35 min, Grand Palace rooms plus apartments of Franz Josef and Elisabeth) or the Grand Tour (40 rooms, €10.50, 50 min, adds apartments of Maria Theresa). The Schönbrunn Pass Classic includes the Grand Tour, Gloriette viewing terrace, maze, court bakery, and privy garden (€18, available April–Oct only; more info: www.schoenbrunn.at). I'd go for the Grand Tour.

Getting to Palace: Take tram #58 from Westbahnhof directly to the palace, or ride U-4 to Schönbrunn and walk 400 yards. The main entrance is in the left side of the palace as you face it.

Coach Museum Wagenburg—The Schönbrunn coach museum is a 19th-century traffic jam of 50 impressive royal carriages and sleighs. Highlights include silly sedan chairs, the death-black hearse carriage (used for Franz Josef in 1916, and most recently for Empress Zita in 1989), and an extravagantly gilded imperial carriage pulled by eight Cinderella horses. This was rarely used other than for the coronation of Holy Roman Emperors, when it was disassembled and taken to Frankfurt for the big event (€4.50, April–Oct daily 9:00–18:00, Nov–March daily 10:00–16:00, last entry 30 min before closing time, closed Mon in winter, 200 yards from palace, walk through right arch as you face palace, tel. 01/877-3244).

Palace Gardens—After strolling through all the Hapsburgs tucked neatly into their crypts, a stroll through the emperor's garden with countless commoners is a celebration of the natural evolution of civilization from autocracy into real democracy. As a civilization, we're doing well.

The sculpted **gardens** (with a palm house, €3.50, May–Sept daily 9:30–18:00, Oct–April daily 9:30–17:00) lead past Europe's oldest **zoo** *(Tiergarten,* built by Maria Theresa's husband for the entertainment and education of the court in 1752; €12, May–Sept daily 9:00–18:30, less off-season, tel. 01/877-9294) up to the **Gloriette,** a purely decorative monument celebrating an obscure Austrian military victory and offering a fine city view (viewing terrace-€2.30, included in €18 Schönbrunn Pass Classic, April–Sept daily 9:00–18:00, July–Aug until 19:00, Oct until 17:00, closed Nov–March). The park itself is free (daily sunrise to dusk, entrance on either side of the palace). A touristy choo-choo train makes the rounds all day, connecting Schönbrunn's many attractions.

More Sights in Vienna

▲▲▲**Kunsthistorisches Museum**—This exciting museum, across the Ring from the Hofburg Palace, showcases the grandeur and opulence of the Hapsburgs' collected artwork. There are European masterpieces galore, all well hung on one glorious floor, plus a fine display of Egyptian, classical, and applied arts.

Starting with the Italian wing of the museum, you get an immediate sense of the richness of this collection—you've walked right into the High Renaissance. Here, you'll see Raphael's graceful *Madonna of the Meadow* and Correggio's voluptuous *Jupiter and Io*. Meander through the Venetian Renaissance rooms to spend time with Titian, and land (with a thud) in the heart of Realism. (Caravaggio's still-shocking *David with the Head of Goliath* shows the artist was distinctly ahead of his time.)

The Baroque rooms offer pudgy winged babies galore—quite a contrast to the simple, direct, and down-to-earth Northern paintings by Dutch and Flemish artists only steps away. Enjoy Hieronymus Bosch's bizarrely crowded work and linger at the paintings by Peter Brueghel, the undisputed master of the slice-of-life village scene. Giuseppe Arcimboldo's *Summer* and *Water* (with faces made of produce and fish, respectively) are always crowd-pleasers. Try the helpful, included audio-guide for the full picture (€9, Tue–Sun 10:00–18:00, Thu until 21:00, closed Mon, tel. 01/525-240).

Sadly, one of the jewels in the museum's crown is now missing. Cellini's *Salt Cellar,* a divine golden salt bowl valued at €50 million, was stolen (to the anguish of the Vienna art world) in 2003 by expert thieves.

▲**Natural History Museum**—In the twin building facing the art museum, you'll find moon rocks, dinosaur stuff, and the fist-sized *Venus of Willendorf*—at 30,000 years old, the world's oldest sex symbol, found in the Danube Valley (€6.50, Wed–Mon 9:00–18:30, Wed until 21:00, closed Tue, tel. 01/521-770).

MuseumsQuartier—This sprawling collection of blocky, modernist museums is housed within the Baroque facade of the former imperial stables. The centerpiece is the **Leopold Museum,** which features modern Austrian art, including the best collection of works by Egon Schiele (1890–1918) and a few works by Kokoschka and Klimt (€9, Wed–Mon 10:00–19:00, Fri 10:00–21:00, closed Tue, behind Kunsthistorisches Museum, U-2 or U-3: Volkstheater/Museumsplatz, Museumsplatz 1–5, tel. 01/525-700).

The new **Museum of Modern Art** (Museum Moderner Kunst Stiftung Ludwig, a.k.a. Mumok), also in the MuseumsQuartier, is Austria's leading modern-art gallery. Its huge, state-of-the-art building displays revolving exhibits showing off art of the last generation—including Klee, Picasso, and Pop (€8, Tue–Sun 10:00–18:00, Thu until 21:00, closed Mon, tel. 01/525-001-440, www.mumok.at). Rounding out the sprawling MuseumsQuartier are an architecture museum, Transeuropa, Electronic Avenue, children's museum, and the Kunsthalle Wien—an exhibition center for contemporary art. Various combo-tickets are available for those interested in more than just the Leopold Museum (visit www.mqw.at). Walk into the center from the Hofburg side, where the main entrance (with visitor center and info room) leads to a big courtyard with cafés, fountains, and huge lounging sponges surrounded by the quarter's various museums.

▲**Academy of Fine Arts**—This small but exciting collection includes works by Bosch, Botticelli, and Rubens; a Venice series by Guardi; and a self-portrait by 15-year-old Van Dyck (€5, Tue–Sun 10:00–16:00, closed Mon, 3 blocks from Opera at Schillerplatz 3, tel. 01/5881-6225). As you wander the halls of this academy, ponder how history might have been different if Hitler—who applied to study architecture here but was rejected—had been accepted as a student.

▲▲**KunstHausWien: Hundertwasser Museum**—This "make yourself at home" museum is a hit with lovers of modern art. It mixes the work and philosophy of local painter/environmentalist Hundertwasser. Stand in front of the colorful checkerboard building and consider Hundert-wasser's style. He was against "window racism." Neighboring houses allow only one kind of window. But 100H_2O's windows are each dif-ferent—and he encouraged residents to personalize them. He recognized tree tenants as well as human tenants. His buildings are spritzed with a forest and topped with dirt and grassy little parks—close to nature, good for the soul. Floors and sidewalks are irregular—to "stimulate the brain" (although current residents complain it just causes wobbly furniture and sprained ankles). Thus 100H_2O waged a one-man fight—during the 1950s and 1960s, when concrete and glass ruled—to save the human soul from the city. (Hundertwasser claimed that "straight lines are god-less.") Inside the museum, start with his interesting biography (which ends in 2000). His fun-loving paintings are half *Jugendstil* ("youth style") and half just kids' stuff. Notice the photographs from his 1950s days as part of Vienna's bohemian scene. Throughout the museum, notice the fun philosophical quotes from an artist who believed, "If man is creative, he comes nearer to his creator" (€8 for Hundertwasser Museum, €14 combo-ticket includes special exhibitions, half price on Mon, daily 10:00–19:00, extremely fragrant and colorful garden café, U-3: Landstrasse, Weissgerberstrasse 13, tel. 01/712-0491).

The KunstHausWien provides by far the best look at Hundert-wasser. For an actual lived-in apartment complex by the green master, walk five minutes to the one-with-nature **Hundertwasserhaus** (free, at Löwengasse and Kegelgasse). This complex of 50 apartments, subsidized by the government to provide affordable housing, was built in the 1980s as a breath of architectural fresh air in a city of boring, blocky apartment complexes. While not open to visitors, it's worth visiting for its fun-loving and colorful patchwork exterior and the Hundertwasser festival of shops across the street. Don't miss the view from Kegelgasse to see the "tree tenants" and the internal winter garden residents enjoy.

▲**Belvedere Palace**—This is the elegant palace of Prince Eugene of Savoy—the still-much-appreciated conqueror of the Turks. Eugene, a

Frenchman considered too short and too ugly to be in the service of Louis XIV, offered his services to the Hapsburgs. While he was short and ugly indeed, he became the greatest military genius of his age. Today, his palace houses the Austrian gallery of 19th- and 20th-century art. Skip the lower palace and focus on the garden and the upper palace *(Oberes Belvedere)* for a winning view of the city, a fine collection of *Jugendstil* art, and Vienna's best look at the dreamy work of Gustav Klimt (€7.50, Tue–Sun 10:00–18:00, closed Mon, entrance at Prinz Eugen Strasse 27, tel. 01/7955-7134). Your ticket includes the Austrian Baroque and Gothic art in the Lower Palace.

▲▲**Haus der Musik**—Vienna's House of Music has a small first-floor exhibit on the Vienna Philharmonic, and upstairs you'll enjoy fine audiovisual exhibits on each of the famous hometown boys (Haydn, Mozart, Beethoven, Strauss, and Mahler). But the museum is unique for its effective use of interactive touch-screen computers and headphones to actually explore the physics of sound. You can twist, dissect, and bend sounds to make your own musical language, merging your voice with a duck's quack or a city's traffic roar. Wander through the "sonosphere" and marvel at the amazing acoustics—I could actually hear what I thought only a piano tuner could hear. Pick up a virtual baton to conduct the Vienna Philharmonic Orchestra (each time you screw up, the orchestra stops and ridicules you). A computer will help you compose your own waltz by throwing dice. Really seeing the place takes time. It's open late and makes a good evening activity (€10, daily 10:00–22:00, 2 blocks from Opera at Seilerstatte 30, tel. 01/51648, www.hdm.at).

Judenplatz Memorial and Museum—Judenplatz marks the location of Vienna's 15th-century Jewish community, one of Europe's largest at the time. The square, once filled with a long-gone synagogue, is now dominated by a blocky memorial to the 65,000 Austrian Jews killed by the Nazis. The memorial—a library turned inside out—symbolizes Jews as "people of the book" and causes one to ponder the huge loss of culture, knowledge, and humanity that took place during 1938 to 1945.

The Judenplatz Museum, while sparse, has displays on medieval Jewish life and a well-done video re-creating community scenes from five centuries ago. Wander the scant remains of the medieval synagogue below street level—discovered during the construction of the Holocaust memorial. This was the scene of a medieval massacre. Since Christians weren't allowed to lend money, Jews were Europe's moneylenders. As so often happened in Europe, when Christian locals fell too deeply into debt, they found a convenient excuse to wipe out the local ghetto—and their debts at the same time. In 1421, 200 of Vienna's Jews were burned at the stake. Others who refused a forced conversion committed mass suicide in the synagogue (€3, €7 combo-ticket includes a synagogue and Jewish Museum of the City of Vienna, Sun–Thu 10:00–18:00, Fri

JUGENDSTIL

Vienna gave birth to its own curvaceous brand of art nouveau around the early 1900s: *Jugendstil* ("youth style"). The TI has a brochure laying out Vienna's 20th-century architecture. The best of Vienna's scattered *Jugendstil* sights: the Belvedere Palace collection, the clock on Hoher Markt (which does a musical act at noon), and the gilded, cabbage-domed building at the Ring end of the Naschmarkt (U-1, U-2, or U-4: Karlsplatz, and follow signs to Secession). This gallery (housing a huge Beethoven frieze by Klimt) proclaims the movement's slogan: "To each century its art, and to art its liberty." Klimt, Wagner, and friends (who called themselves the Vienna Secession) first exhibited their "liberty-style" art here in 1897.

10:00–14:00, closed Sat, Judenplatz 8, tel. 01/535-0431).

▲**Vienna's Auction House, the Dorotheum**—For an aristocrat's flea market, drop by Austria's answer to Sotheby's, the Dorotheum. Its five floors of antique furniture and fancy knickknacks have been put up either for immediate sale or auction, often by people who inherited old things they don't have room for (Mon–Fri 10:00–18:00, Sat 9:00–17:00, closed Sun, classy little café on second floor, between Graben and Hofburg at Dorotheergasse 17, tel. 01/515-600). Fliers show schedules for actual auctions, which you are welcome to attend.

Honorable Mention—There's much, much more. The city map lists everything. If you're into butterflies, Esperanto, undertakers, tobacco, clowns, firefighting, Freud, or the homes of dead composers, you'll find them all in Vienna. Several good museums that try very hard but are submerged in the greatness of Vienna include: **Jewish Museum of the City of Vienna** (€5, or €7 combo-ticket includes synagogue and Judenplatz Museum—listed above, Sun–Fri 10:00–18:00, Thu until 20:00, closed Sat, Dorotheergasse 11, tel. 01/535-0431, www.jmw.at), **Historical Museum of the City of Vienna** (Tue–Sun 9:00–18:00, closed Mon, Karlsplatz), **Folkloric Museum of Austria** (Tue–Sun 10:00–17:00, closed Mon, Laudongasse 15, tel. 01/406-8905), and **Museum of Military History**, one of Europe's best if you like swords and shields (Heeresgeschichtliches Museum, Sat–Thu 9:00–17:00, closed Fri, Arsenal district, Objekt 18, tel. 01/795-610). The vast **Austrian Museum of Applied Arts** (Österreichisches Museum für Angewandte Kunst, or MAK) is Vienna's answer to London's Victoria & Albert collection. The museum shows off the fancies of local aristocratic society, including a fine *Jugendstil* collection (€8, free Sat, open Tue–Sun

10:00–18:00, Tue until 24:00, closed Mon, Stubenring 5, tel. 01/711-360, www.mak.at).

For a walk in the **Vienna Woods,** catch the U-4 metro to Heiligenstadt, then bus #38A to Kahlenberg, for great views and a café overlooking the city. From there, it's a peaceful 45-minute downhill hike to the *Heurigen* of Nussdorf or Grinzing to enjoy some wine (see "Vienna's Wine Gardens," below).

Top People-Watching and Strolling Sights

▲**City Park**—Vienna's Stadtpark is a waltzing world of gardens, memorials to local musicians, ponds, peacocks, music in bandstands, and locals escaping the city. Notice the *Jugendstil* entrance at the Stadtpark metro station. The Kursalon, where Strauss was the violin-toting master of waltzing ceremonies, hosts daily touristy concerts in 3/4 time.

▲**Prater**—Vienna's sprawling amusement park tempts many visitors with its huge 220-foot-tall, famous, and lazy Ferris wheel *(Riesenrad),* roller coaster, bumper cars, lilliputian railroad, and endless eateries. Especially if you're traveling with kids, this is a fun, goofy place to share the evening with thousands of Viennese (daily 9:00–24:00 in summer, but quiet after 22:00, U-1: Praterstern). For a local-style family dinner, eat at Schweizerhaus (good food, great beer) or Wieselburger Bierinsel.

Sunbathing—Like most Europeans, the Austrians worship the sun. Their lavish swimming centers are as much for tanning as swimming. To find the scene, follow the locals to their "Danube Sea" and a 20-mile, skinny, man-made beach along Danube Island. It's traffic-free concrete and grass, packed with in-line skaters and bikers, with rocky river access and a fun park (easy U-Bahn access on U-1 to Donauinsel).

▲**Naschmarkt**—Vienna's ye olde produce market bustles daily near the Opera along Wienzeile Street. It's likeably seedy and surrounded by sausage stands, Turkish *döner kebab* stalls, cafés, and theaters. Each Saturday, it's infested by a huge flea market where, in olden days, locals would come to hire a monkey to pick little critters out of their hair (Mon–Fri 7:00–18:00, Sat 6:00–18:00, closed Sun, closes earlier in winter, U-4: Kettenbruckengasse). For a picnic park, walk a block down Schleifmuhlgasse.

SUMMER MUSIC SCENE

Vienna is Europe's music capital. It's music *con brio* from October through June, reaching a symphonic climax during the Vienna Festival each May and June. Sadly, in July and August, the Boys' Choir, the Opera, and many more music companies are—like you—on vacation. But Vienna hums year-round with live classical music. In the summer, you have these basic choices:

Touristy Mozart and Strauss Concerts—If the music comes to you, it's touristy—designed for flash-in-the-pan Mozart fans. Powdered-wig orchestra performances are given almost nightly in grand traditional settings (€25–50). Pesky wigged-and-powdered Mozarts peddle tickets in the streets with slick sales pitches about the magic of the venue and the quality of the musicians. Second-rate orchestras, clad in historic costumes, perform the greatest hits of Mozart and Strauss. While there's not a local person in the audience, the tourists generally enjoy the evening. To sort through all your options, check with the ticket office in the TI (same price as on the street but with all venues to choose from).

Strauss Concerts in the Kursalon—For years, Strauss concerts have been held in the Kursalon, where the Waltz King himself directed wildly popular concerts 100 years ago (€32–49, 4 concerts nightly April–Oct, 1 concert nightly other months, tel. 01/512-5790). Shows are a touristy mix of ballet, waltzes, and a 15-piece orchestra in wigs and old outfits. For the cheap option, enjoy a summer afternoon coffee concert (free if you buy a drink weekends and maybe also weekdays July–Aug 15:00–17:00).

Serious Concerts—These events, including the Opera, are listed in the monthly *Wien-Programm* (available at TI). Tickets run from €36 to €75 (plus a stiff 22 percent booking fee when booked in advance or through a box office like the one at the TI). If you call a concert hall directly, they can advise you on the availability of (cheaper) tickets at the door. Vienna takes care of its starving artists (and tourists) by offering cheap standing-room tickets to top-notch music and opera (1 hour before show time).

Vienna's **Summer of Music Festival** assures that even from June through September, you'll find lots of great concerts, choirs, and symphonies (special *Klang Bogen* brochure at TI; get tickets at Wien Ticket pavilion off Kärntner Strasse next to Opera House or go directly to location of particular event; Summer of Music tel. 01/42717).

Musicals—The Wien Ticket pavilion sells tickets to contemporary American and British musicals (€10–95 with €2.50 standing room) and offers these tickets at half price from 14:00 until 17:00 the day of the show. Or you can reserve (full-price) tickets for the musicals by calling up to one day ahead (call combined office of the 3 big theaters at tel. 01/58885).

Vienna Boys' Choir—The boys sing (heard but not seen, from a high balcony) at Mass in the Imperial Chapel *(Hofburgkapelle)* of the Hofburg (entrance at Schweizerhof, from Josefs Platz go through tunnel) 9:15–10:30 on Sundays, except in July and August. While seats must be reserved two months in advance (€5–29, reserve by fax, e-mail, or mail: fax 011-431-533-992-775 from the U.S., hmk@aon.at, or write Hofmusikkapelle, Hofburg-Schweizerhof, 1010 Wien; tel. for information only—cannot book tickets—01/533-9927), standing room inside is free and open to the first 60 who line up. Rather than line up early, you can simply swing by and stand in the narthex just outside, where you can hear the boys and see the Mass on a TV monitor. Boys' Choir concerts (on stage at the Musikverein) are also given Fridays at 16:00 in May, June, September, and October (€35–48, standing room goes on sale at 15:30 for €15, Karlsplatz 6, U-1, U-2, or U-4: Karlsplatz, tel. 01/5880-4141). They're nice kids, but, for my taste, not worth all the commotion. Remember, many churches have great music during Sunday Mass. Just 200 yards from the Boys' Choir chapel, Augustinian Church has a glorious 11:00 service each Sunday.

VIENNA'S CAFÉS

In Vienna, the living room is down the street at the neighborhood coffeehouse. This tradition is just another example of Viennese expertise in good living. Each of Vienna's many long-established (and sometimes even legendary) coffeehouses has its individual character (and characters). They offer newspapers, pastries, sofas, elegance, smoky ambience, and "take all the time you want" charm for the price of a cup of coffee. Order it *melange* (with a little milk) or *schwarzer* (black). Rather than buy the *Herald Tribune* ahead of time, buy a cup of coffee and read it for free, Vienna-style.

These are my favorites: **Café Hawelka,** with a dark, "brooding Trotsky" atmosphere, paintings by struggling artists who couldn't pay for coffee, a saloon-wood flavor, chalkboard menu, smoked velvet couches, an international selection of newspapers, and a phone that rings for regulars (Wed–Mon 8:00–2:00, Sun from 16:00, closed Tue, just off Graben, Dorotheergasse 6); **Café Central,** with *Jugendstil* decor and great *Apfelstrudel* (high prices and stiff staff, Mon–Sat 8:00–22:00, Sun 10:00-18:00, Herrengasse 14, tel. 01/533-376-326); the **Café Sperl,** dating from 1880 with furnishings identical to the day it opened, from the coat tree to the chairs (Mon–Sat 7:00–23:00, Sun 11:00–20:00 except closed Sun July–Aug, just off Naschmarkt near Mariahilfer Strasse, Gumpendorfer 11, tel. 01/586-4158); and the basic, untouristy **Café Ritter** (daily 7:30–23:30, Mariahilfer Strasse 73, U-3: Neubaugasse, near several recommended hotels, tel. 01/587-8237).

VIENNA'S WINE GARDENS

The *Heurige* is a uniquely Viennese institution celebrating the *Heurige,* or new wine. When the Hapsburgs let Vienna's vintners sell their own wine tax-free, several hundred families opened *Heurigen* (wine-garden restaurants clustered around the edge of town), and a tradition was born. Today, they do their best to maintain the old-village atmosphere, serving the homemade new wine (the last vintage, until November 11, when a new vintage year begins) with light meals and strolling musicians.

Most *Heurigen* are decorated with enormous antique presses from their vineyards. Wine gardens might be closed on any given day; always call ahead to confirm, if you have your heart set on a particular place. (For a near-*Heurige* experience right downtown, drop by Gigerl Stadtheuriger; see "Eating," below.)

At any *Heurige*, fill your plate at a self-serve cold-cut buffet (€6–9 for dinner). Dishes to look out for: *Stelze* (grilled knuckle of pork), *Fleischlaberln* (fried ground meat patties), *Schinkenfleckerln* (pasta with cheese and ham), *Schmalz* (a spread made with pig fat), *Blunzen* (black pudding...sausage made from blood), *Presskopf* (jellied brains and innards), *Liptauer* (spicy cheese spread), *Kornspitz* (whole-meal bread roll), and *Kummelbraten* (crispy roast pork with caraway). Waitresses will then take your wine order (€2.20 per quarter liter, about 8 oz). Many locals claim it takes several years of practice to distinguish between *Heurige* and vinegar.

There are more than 1,700 acres of vineyards within Vienna's city limits, and countless *Heurige* taverns. For a *Heurige* evening, rather than go to a particular place, take a tram to the wine-garden district of your choice and wander around, choosing the place with the best ambience.

Getting to the *Heurigen:* You have three options: trams and buses, a 15-minute taxi ride, or a goofy tourist train.

Trams make a trip to the Vienna Woods quick and affordable. The fastest way is to ride U-4 to its last stop, Heiligenstadt, where trams and buses in front of the station fan out to the various neighborhoods. Ride tram D to its end point for Nussdorf. Ride bus #38A for Grinzing and on to the Kahlenberg viewpoint—#38A's end station (note that tram #38—different from bus #38A—starts at the Ring and finishes at Grinzing). To get to Neustift am Walde, ride U-6 to Nussdorfer Strasse and catch bus #35A. Connect Grinzing and Nussdorf with bus #38A and tram D (transfer at Grinzingerstrasse).

The **Heuriger Express** train is tacky but handy and relaxing, chugging you on a hop-on, hop-off circle from Nussdorf through Grinzing and around the Vienna Woods (€7.30, 50 min, daily April–Oct 12:00–19:00, departs from end station of tram D in Nussdorf at the top of every hr, tel. 01/479-2808).

Here are four good *Heurige* neighborhoods:

Grinzing: Of the many *Heurige* suburbs, Grinzing is the most famous, lively...and touristy. Many people precede their visit to Grinzing by riding bus #38A to its end (up to Kahlenberg for a grand Vienna view) and then ride 20 minutes back into the *Heurige* action. From the Grinzing tram stop, follow Himmelgasse uphill toward the onion-top dome. You'll pass plenty of wine gardens—and tour buses—on your way up. Just past the dome, you'll find the heart of the *Heurige*.

Pfarrplatz: Between Grinzing and Nussdorf, this area features several decent spots, including the famous and touristy **Beethovenhaus**

Hotels and Restaurants in Central Vienna

1 Pension Pertschy
2 Pension Neuer Markt
3 Pension Aviano
4 To Hotel Schweizerhof & Pension Dr. Geissler
5 Hotel zur Wiener Staatsoper
6 Pension Nossek
7 Pension Suzanne
8 To Schweizer Pension Solderer
9 Restaurant Rosenberger Markt
10 Restaurant Gigerl Stadtheuriger
11 To Restaurants Brezel-Gwölb, Ofenloch & Beisl Zum Scherer
12 To Restaurant zu den Drei Hacken
13 Wrenkh Vegetarian Restaurant
14 Buffet Trzesniewski
15 Café Restaurant Palmenhaus
16 Julius Meinl am Graben Deli
17 Café Hawelka
18 Rest. Esterhazykeller
19 To Café Central & Restaurant Melker Stiftskeller
20 Sacher Café
21 Zanoni & Zanoni Ice Cream

(Mon–Sat 16:00–24:00, Sun 11:00–24:00, bus #38A stop: Fernsprechamt/Heiligenstadt, walk 5 min uphill on Dübling Nestelbachgasse to Pfarrplatz 2, tel. 01/370-3361). Beethoven lived—and composed his Sixth Symphony—here in 1817. He hoped the local spa would cure his worsening deafness. **Weingut and Heuriger Werner Welser,** a block uphill from Beethoven's place, is lots of fun, with music nightly from 19:00 (daily 15:30–24:00, Probusgasse 12, tel. 01/318-9797).

Nussdorf: A less-touristy district—characteristic and popular with locals—Nussdorf has plenty of *Heurige* ambience. Right at the end station of tram D, you'll find three long and skinny places side by side: **Heuriger Kierlinger** (daily 15:30–24:00, Kahlenbergerstrasse 20, tel. 01/370-2264), **Steinschaden** (daily 15:00–24:00, Kahlenbergerstrasse 18, tel. 01/370-1375), and **Schübel-Auer Heuriger** (Tue–Sat 16:00–24:00, closed Sun–Mon, Kahlenbergerstrasse 22, tel. 01/370-2222). Walk through any of these and you pop out on Kahlenbergerstrasse, where a walk uphill takes you to some more eating and drinking fun: **Bamkraxler** (the tree jumper), the only beer garden amid all these vineyards. It's a fun-loving, youthful place with fine keg beer and a regular menu, rather than the *Heurige* cafeteria line (€6–10 meals, veggie options, Tue–Sat 16:00–24:00, Sun 11:00–24:00, closed Mon, Kahlenbergerstrasse 17, tel. 01/318-8800).

Neustift am Walde: This neighborhood has lots of *Heurigen,* plenty of charm, and the fewest tourists of all (U-6: Nussdorferstrasse, then bus #35A stop: Neustift am Walde). A line of big, venerable places invite you through welcoming arches that lead up terraced backyards filled with rough tables until you hit the actual vineyards. Pop into **Weingut Wolff** (Wed–Sun 16:00–24:00, closed Mon–Tue, Rathstrasse 50, tel. 01/440-3727) and **Fuhrgassl Huber Weingut** (daily 14:00–24:00, live music Tue–Sat 19:00–24:00, Neustift am Walde 68, tel. 01/440-1405) and take your choice. If you want to really be rural—surrounded by vineyards—hike 10 minutes from there to **Weinhof Zimmermann** (Mon–Fri 15:00–23:00, Sat–Sun 12:00–23:00, Mitterwurzergasse 20, tel. 01/440-1207). Find Mitterwurzergasse—the lane behind the two places listed above—and hike to the right. Look for the sign taking you uphill into a farm. There you'll see 50 rough picnic tables between the farmhouse and the vines.

NIGHTLIFE

If old music and new wine aren't your thing, Vienna has plenty of alternatives. For an up-to-date rundown on fun after dark, get the TI's free *Ten Good Reasons for Vienna* booklet. An area known as the "Bermuda Dreieck" (Triangle), north of the cathedral between Rotenturmstrasse and Judengasse, is the hot local nightspot, with lots of classy pubs, or *Beisl* (such as Krah Krah, Salzamt, Slammer, and Bermuda Bräu), and music spots. On balmy summer evenings, the liveliest scene is at Danube Island (especially during the Summer Stage festival). If you just want a good movie, the English Cinema Haydn plays three different English-language movies nightly (Mariahilfer Strasse 57, tel. 01/587-2262).

SLEEPING

Sleeping within the Ring, in the Old City Center

You'll pay extra to sleep in the atmospheric old center, but if you can afford it, staying here gives you the best classy Vienna experience.

$$$ **Pension Pertschy** circles an old courtyard and is bigger and more hotelesque than the others listed here. Its 50 rooms are huge, but well-worn and a bit musty. Those on the courtyard are quietest (Sb-€77, Db-€112–162 depending on size, cheaper off-season, extra bed-€30, non-smoking rooms, elevator, U-1 or U-3: Stephensplatz, Hapsburger-gasse 5, tel. 01/534-490, fax 01/534-4949, www.pertschy.com, pertschy @pertschy.com).

$$$ **Pension Neuer Markt** is a four-star place that feels family-run, with 37 quiet, comfy, old-feeling rooms in a perfectly central locale (Ss-€81, Sb-€95, Ds-€88, Db-€112, prices can vary with season and room size, extra bed-€20, elevator, Seilergasse 9, tel. 01/512-2316, fax 01/513-9105, www.hotelpension.at/neuermarkt, neuermarkt@hotelpension.at).

$$$ **Pension Aviano** is another peaceful four-star place, with 17 comfortable rooms on the fourth floor above lots of old center action (Sb-€82, Db-€122–142 depending on size, 15 percent cheaper Nov–March, extra bed-€30, elevator, non-smoking rooms, between Neuer Markt and Kärntner Strasse at Marco d'Avianogasse 1, tel. 01/512-8330, fax 01/5128-3306, aviano@pertschy.com).

$$$ **Hotel Schweizerhof** is a classy 55-room place with big rooms, three-star comforts, and a more formal ambience. It's centrally located midway between St. Stephan's Cathedral and the Danube canal, with all its rooms at least four floors above any street noise (Sb-€84–88, Db-€109–131, Tb-€131–146, low prices are for July–Aug and slow times, with cash and this book get your best price and then claim a 10 percent discount, elevator, Bauernmarkt 22, U-1 or U-3: Stephansplatz, tel. 01/533-1931, fax 01/533-0214, www.schweizerhof.at, office@schweizerhof.at).

$$$ **Hotel zur Wiener Staatsoper** (the Schweizerhof's sister hotel) is quiet and rich. Its 22 tight rooms come with high ceilings, chandeliers, and fancy carpets on parquet floors—ideal for people whose hotel tastes are a cut above mine. The singles are tiny, with beds too short for anyone over six feet tall (Sb-€76–88, Db-€109–131, Tb-€131–146, extra bed-€22, prices depend on season, July–Aug and Dec–March are cheaper, elevator, U-1, U-2, or U-4: Karlsplatz, a block from Opera at Krugerstrasse 11, tel. 01/513-1274, fax 01/513-127-415, www .zurwienerstaatsoper.at, office@zurwienerstaatsoper.at).

SLEEP CODE

(€1 = about $1.10, country code: 43, area code: 01)
Sleep Code: **S** = Single, **D** = Double/Twin, **T** = Triple, **Q** = Quad, **b** = bathroom, **s** = shower only, **no CC** = Credit Cards not accepted. English is spoken at each place. Unless otherwise noted, credit cards are accepted and breakfast is included.

To help you sort easily through these listings, I've divided the rooms into three categories, based on the price for a standard double room with bath:

$$$ **Higher Priced**—Most rooms €110 or more.
$$ **Moderately Priced**—Most rooms between €75–110.
$ **Lower Priced**—Most rooms €75 or less.

Book accommodations by phone a few days in advance. Most places will hold a room without a deposit if you promise to arrive before 17:00. My recommendations stretch mainly from the center, and along the likeable Mariahilfer Strasse, to the Westbahnhof (West Station). Even places with elevators often have a few stairs to climb, too.

$$ At **Pension Nossek,** an elevator takes you above any street noise into Frau Bernad's and Frau Gundolf's world, where the children seem to be placed among the lace and flowers by an interior designer. Right on the wonderful Graben, this is a particularly good value (26 rooms, S-€46–54, Ss-€58, Sb-€66–88, Db-€105, €25 extra for sprawling suites, extra bed-€35, no CC, elevator, U-1 or U-3: Stephansplatz, Graben 17, tel. 01/5337-0410, fax 01/535-3646, www.pension-nossek.at, reservation@pension-nossek.at).

$$ **Pension Suzanne,** as Baroque and doily as you'll find in this price range, is wonderfully located a few yards from the Opera. It's small, but run with the class of a bigger hotel; the 26 rooms are packed with properly Viennese antique furnishings. Streetside rooms come with some noise (Sb-€72, Db-€90–111 depending on size, extra bed-€30, spacious apartment for up to 6 also available, discounts in winter, elevator, a block from Opera, U-1, U-2, or U-4: Karlsplatz, follow signs for the Opera exit, Walfischgasse 4, tel. 01/513-2507, fax 01/513-2500, www.pension-suzanne.at, info@pension-suzanne.at).

$$ **Schweizer Pension Solderer,** family-owned for three generations, is run by Anita. She runs an extremely tight ship (lots of rules), but offers 11 homey rooms, parquet floors, and lots of tourist info

(S-€35–42, Ss-€51–55, Sb-€58–62, D-€55–62, Ds-€65–75, Db-€80-85, Tb-€95–105, Qb-€120–125, prices depend on season and room size, no CC, non-smoking, elevator, laundry-€11/load, U-2 and U-4: Schottenring, Heinrichsgasse 2, tel. 01/533-8156, fax 01/535-6469, www.schweizerpension.com, schweizer.pension@chello.at).

$$ Pension Dr. Geissler has 23 comfortable rooms on the eighth floor of a modern building about 10 blocks northeast of St. Stephan's, near the canal (S-€43, Ss-€63, Sb-€72, D-€60, Ds-€72, Db-€90, 20 percent less in winter, elevator, U-1 and U-4: Schwedenplatz, Postgasse 14, tel. 01/533-2803, fax 01/533-2635, www.hotelpension.at/dr-geissler, dr.geissler@hotelpension.at).

Hotels and Pensions along Mariahilfer Strasse

Lively Mariahilfer Strasse connects the West Station and the city center. The U-3 metro line, starting at the Westbahnhof, goes down Mariahilfer Strasse to the cathedral. This very Viennese street is a tourist-friendly and vibrant area filled with local shops and cafés. Most hotels are within a few steps of a metro stop, just one or two stops from the West Train Station (direction from the station: Simmering).

$$$ NH Hoteles, a Spanish chain, runs two stern, passionless business hotels a few blocks apart on Mariahilfer Strasse. Both rent ideal-for-families suites, each with a living room, two TVs, bathroom, desk, and kitchenette (rack rate: Db suite-€170, going rate usually closer to €105, plus €13 per person for optional breakfast, cheaper Sat–Sun, apartments for 2–3 adults, kids under 12 free, non-smoking rooms, elevator). The 78-room **NH Atterseehaus** is at Mariahilfer Strasse 78 (U-3: Zieglergasse, tel. 01/5245-6000, fax 01/524-560-015, nhattersee-haus@nh-hotels.com), and the **NH Wien** has 106 rooms at Mariahilfer Strasse 32 (U-3: Neubaugasse, tel. 01/521-720, fax 01/521-7215, nhwien@nh-hotels.com). The Web site for both is www.nh-hotels.com.

$$ Pension Corvinus is bright, modern, and warmly run by a Hungarian family: Miklos, Judit, and Zoltan. Its eight comfortable rooms are spacious with small yacht-type bathrooms (Sb-€58, Db-€91, Tb-€105, extra bed-€26, non-smoking rooms, portable air-con-€10, elevator, free Internet access, parking garage-€11/day, on the third floor at Mariahilfer Strasse 57–59, tel. 01/587-7239, fax 01/587-723-920, www.corvinus.at, hotel@corvinus.at). If heading for the Corvinus, don't be pirated by the people in the Haydn Hotel (below).

$$ Pension Mariahilf is a four-star place offering a clean, aristocratic air in an affordable and cozy pension package. Its 12 rooms are spacious but outmoded, with an art deco flair. You'll find the latest American magazines and even free Mozart balls at the reception desk (Sb-€59–66, Db-€95–102, Tb-€124, lower prices are for longer stays, elevator, U-3: Neubaugasse, Mariahilfer Strasse 49, tel. 01/586-1781, fax 01/586-178-122, penma@atnet.at, warmly run by Frau and Herr Ender).

$$ Haydn Hotel, in the same building the Pension Corvinus (listed above), is a big, fancy, dark place with 40 spacious rooms that have seen better days (Sb-€58–70, Db-€72–100, suites and family apartments, extra bed-€30, portable air-con-€12, elevator, free Internet access, Mariahilfer Strasse 57–59, tel. 01/587-4414, fax 01/586-1950, www.haydn-hotel.at, info@haydn-hotel.at).

$$ Hotel Admiral is a huge, quiet, family-run hotel with 80 large, comfortable rooms. Alexandra works hard to keep her guests happy, though others on the staff are less friendly (Sb-€66, Db-€91, extra bed-€23, prices promised through 2004 with this book, cheaper in winter, breakfast-€5 per person, free parking, U-2 or U-3: Volkstheater, a block off Mariahilfer Strasse at Karl Schweighofer Gasse 7, tel. 01/521-410, fax 01/521-4116, www.admiral.co.at, hoteladmiralwien@aon.at).

$ Pension Hargita rents 24 generally small, bright, and tidy rooms (mostly twins) with Hungarian decor. This spick-and-span, well-run, well-located place is an excellent value (S-€31, Ss-€35, Sb-€50, D-€45, Ds-€52, Db-€60, Ts-€63, Tb-€71, Qb-€87, breakfast-€3 per person, credit card adds 3 percent to cost and not for 1-night stays, U-3: Zieglergasse, corner of Mariahilfer Strasse and Andreasgasse, Andreasgasse 1, tel. 01/526-1928, fax 01/526-0492, www.hargita.at, pension @hargita.at, classy Amalia SE).

$ Pension Lindenhof rents 19 worn but clean rooms and is filled with plants (S-€29, Sb-€36, D-€49, Db-€65, no CC, elevator, U-3: Neubaugasse, Lindengasse 4, tel. 01/523-0498, fax 01/523-7362, pensionlindenhof@yahoo.com, Gebrael family, Zara and Keram SE).

$ K&T Boardinghouse rents four big, comfortable rooms facing the bustling Mariahilfer Strasse above a sex shop (S-€40, D-€50, Db-€60, Tb-€80, Qb-€100, 2-night minimum, no breakfast, no CC, non-smoking, free Internet access, 3 flights up, no elevator, Mariahilfer Strasse 72, tel. 01/523-2989, fax 01/522-0345, www.kaled.at, kaled @chello.at, Tina SE).

Two women rent rooms out of their dark and homey apartments in the same building at Lindengasse 39 (classic old elevator). Each has high ceilings and Old World furnishings, with two cavernous rooms sleeping two to four and a skinny twin room, all sharing one bathroom. These places are great if you're on a tight budget and wish you had a grandmother to visit in Vienna: **$ Budai Ildiko** lives on the mezzanine level and speaks English (S-€29, D-€44, T-€64, Q-€82, no breakfast but free coffee, no CC, laundry, apt. #5, tel. 01/523-1058, tel. & fax 01/526-2595, budai@hotmail.com). **$ Maria Pribojszki** lives on the first floor (D-€48, D for 2 nights-€44, T-€69, Q-€88, breakfast-€4 per person, no CC, no clothes-washing in room, smoky place, apt. #7, tel. 01/523-9006, b&b@aon.at).

$ Hilde Wolf, with the help of her grandson, Patrick, shares her homey apartment with travelers. Her four huge but stuffy rooms are like

Vienna: Hotels Outside the Ring

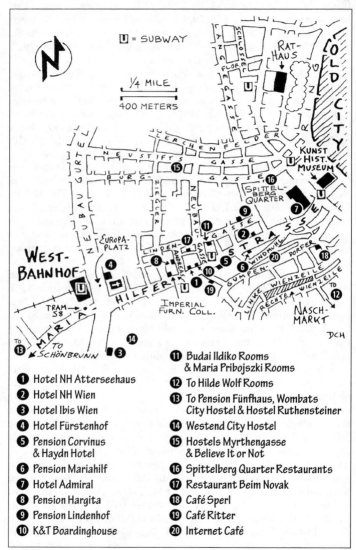

1 Hotel NH Atterseehaus
2 Hotel NH Wien
3 Hotel Ibis Wien
4 Hotel Fürstenhof
5 Pension Corvinus
   & Haydn Hotel
6 Pension Mariahilf
7 Hotel Admiral
8 Pension Hargita
9 Pension Lindenhof
10 K&T Boardinghouse

11 Budai Ildiko Rooms
   & Maria Pribojszki Rooms
12 To Hilde Wolf Rooms
13 To Pension Fünfhaus, Wombats
   City Hostel & Hostel Ruthensteiner
14 Westend City Hostel
15 Hostels Myrthengasse
   & Believe It or Not
16 Spittelberg Quarter Restaurants
17 Restaurant Beim Novak
18 Café Sperl
19 Café Ritter
20 Internet Café

old libraries (S-€33, D-€48, T-€70, Q-€90, breakfast-€4, no CC, U-2: Karlsplatz, 3 blocks below Naschmarkt at Schleifmühlgasse 7, tel. 01/586-5103, fax 01/689-3505, www.schoolpool.at/bb, santa.claus@aon.at).

Near the Westbahnhof Train Station

$$ **Hotel Ibis Wien,** a modern high-rise hotel with American charm, is ideal for anyone tired of quaint old Europe. Its 340 cookie-cutter rooms are bright, comfortable, and modern and have all the conveniences (Sb-€64, Db-€79, Tb-€94, prices €5 more per room May–June, Aug, and Sept–Oct, breakfast-€9 per person extra, non-smoking rooms, elevator, parking garage-€10/day, exit Westbahnhof to the right and walk 400 yards, Mariahilfer Gürtel 22-24, tel. 01/59998, fax 01/597-9090, h0796@accor-hotels.com).

$$ **Hotel Fürstenhof,** right across from the station, charges top euro for its 58 spacious but borderline-musty rooms. This venerable hotel has an Old World maroon-velvet feel (S-€44, Sb-€67–92, D-€62, Db-€108, Tb-€114, Qb-€120, elevator, Internet access-€6/hr, Europaplatz 4, tel. 01/523-3267, fax 01/523-326-726, www.hotel-fuerstenhof.com, reception@hotel-fuerstenhof.com).

$ **Pension Fünfhaus** is big, clean, stark, and quiet—almost institutional. Although the neighborhood is run-down and comes with a few ladies loitering late at night, this 47-room place is a good value (S-€30, Sb-€38, D-€44, Db-€51, T-€66, Tb-€72, apartments for 4 people-€90, prices promised through 2004 with this book, no CC, closed mid-Nov–Feb, Sperrgasse 12, tel. 01/892-3545 or 01/892-0286, fax 01/892-0460, Frau Susi Tersch). Half the rooms are in the fine main building and half are in the annex, which has good rooms but is near the train tracks and a bit scary on the street at night. From the station, ride tram #52 or #58 two stops down Mariahilfer Strasse to Kranzgasse stop, then backtrack two blocks to Sperrgasse.

Cheap Dorms and Hostels near Mariahilfer Strasse

$ **Believe It or Not** is a tiny, basic place with two coed rooms for up to 10 travelers and the cheapest beds in town. Hardworking and friendly Gosha warns that this place is appropriate only for the young at heart. It's locked up from 10:00 to 12:30, has kitchen facilities, and has no curfew (bed-€13.50, €10 Nov–Easter, no CC, Myrthengasse 10, ring apt. #14, tel. 01/526-4658, www.believe-it-or-not-vienna.at, believe_it_or_not_vienna@hotmail.com, SE).

$ **Jugendherberge Myrthengasse** is a well-run youth hostel (260 beds-€16–18 each in 3- to 6-bed rooms, includes sheets and breakfast, non-members pay €3.50 extra, some private rooms for couples and families, Myrthengasse 7, tel. 01/523-6316, fax 01/523-5849, hostel@chello.at).

$ **Westend City Hostel,** just a block from the West Station and

Mariahilfer Strasse, is new, with 180 beds in 4- to 12-bed dorms (€16–18 per bed including sheets, breakfast, and a locker, no CC, laundry, Internet access-€4.40/hr, Fügergasse 3, tel. 01/597-6729, fax 01/597-672-927, www.westendhostel.at, westendcityhostel@aon.at, SE).

$ Other hostels with €14 beds near Mariahilfer Strasse are **Wombats City Hostel** (Grangasse 6, tel. 01/897-2336, wombats@chello.at) and **Hostel Ruthensteiner** (also has doubles for €20 per person, Robert-Hamerling-Gasse 24, tel. 01/893-4202, info@hostelruthensteiner.com).

EATING

The Viennese appreciate the fine points of life, and right up there with waltzing is eating. The city has many atmospheric restaurants. As you ponder the Slavic and Eastern European specialties on menus, remember that Vienna's diverse empire may be gone, but its flavor lingers.

While cuisines are routinely named for countries, Vienna claims to be the only *city* with a cuisine of its own: Vienna soups come with fillings (semolina dumpling, liver dumpling, or pancake slices). *Gulasch* is a beef ragout of Hungarian origin (spiced with onion and paprika). Of course, Viennese schnitzel (Wiener schnitzel) is a breaded and fried veal cutlet. Another meat specialty is boiled beef *(Tafelspitz)*. While you're sure to have *Apfelstrudel*, try the sweet cheese strudel, too *(Topfenstrudel,* wafer-thin strudel pastry filled with sweet cheese and raisins).

On nearly every corner, you can find a colorful *Beisl* (Viennese tavern) filled with poetry teachers and their students, couples loving without touching, housewives on their way home from cello lessons, and waiters who enjoy serving hearty food and good drink at an affordable price. Ask at your hotel for a good *Beisl*.

Wherever you're eating, some vocabulary will help. Try the *grüner Veltliner* (dry white wine), *Traubenmost* (a heavenly grape juice—alcohol-free but on the verge of wine), *Most* (the same thing but lightly alcoholic), and *Sturm* (stronger than *Most,* autumn only). The local red wine (called *Portugieser)* is pretty good. Since the Austrian wine is often sweet, remember the word *trocken* (dry). You can order your wine by the *Viertel* (quarter liter, 8 oz) or *Achtel* (eighth liter, 4 oz). Beer comes in a *Krügel* (half liter, 17 oz) or *Seidel* (0.3 liter, 10 oz).

Near St. Stephan's Cathedral
All of these places are within a five-minute walk of the cathedral.

Gigerl Stadtheuriger offers a near-*Heurige* experience (à la Grinzing, see "Vienna's Wine Gardens," above), often with accordion or live music—without leaving the city center. Just point to what looks good. Food is sold by the weight; 200 grams is about a quarter of a pound (cheese and cold meats cost about €2.50–5 per 100 grams, salads are about €2 per 100 grams; price sheet is posted on the wall to right of buffet line, 10 *dag* equals 100 grams). They also have menu entrées, along with spinach strudel, quiche, *Apfelstrudel,* and, of course, casks of new and local wines. Meals run €7–11 (daily 15:00–24:00, indoor/outdoor seating, behind cathedral, a block off Kärntner Strasse, a few cobbles off Rauhensteingasse on Blumenstock, tel. 01/513-4431).

Am Hof square (U-3: Herrengasse) is surrounded by a maze of atmospheric medieval lanes; the following places are all within a block of the square. **Restaurant Ofenloch** serves good, old-fashioned Viennese cuisine with friendly service, both indoors and out. This 300-year-old eatery, with great traditional ambience, is central, but not overrun with tourists (main dishes €15–22, Tue–Sat 11:30–24:00, Mon 18:00–24:00, closed Sun, Kurrentgasse 8, tel. 01/533-8844). **Brezel-Gwölb,** a wonderfully atmospheric wine cellar with outdoor dining on a quiet square, serves delicious light meals, fine *Krautsuppe,* and old-fashioned local dishes. It's ideal for a romantic late-night glass of wine (daily 11:30–1:00, leave Am Hof on Drahtgasse, then take first left to Ledererhof 9, tel. 01/533-8811). Around the corner, **Beisl "Zum Scherer"** is just as untouristy, with indoor or outdoor seating, a soothing woody atmosphere, intriguing decor, and local specialties (Mon–Sat 11:00–24:00, closed Sun, Judenplatz 7, tel. 01/533-5164). Just below Am Hof, the ancient and popular **Esterhazykeller** has traditional fare deep underground or outside on a delightful square (Mon–Fri 11:00–23:00, Sat–Sun 16:00–23:00, self-service buffet in lowest cellar or from menu, Haarhof 1, tel. 01/533-2614).

These wine cellars are fun and touristy but typical, in the old center, with reasonable prices and plenty of smoke: **Melker Stiftskeller,** less touristy, is a *Stadtheurige* in a deep and rustic cellar with hearty, inexpensive meals and new wine (Tue–Sat 17:00–24:00, closed Sun–Mon, between Am Hof and Schottentor metro stop at Schottengasse 3, tel. 01/533-5530). **Zu den Drei Hacken** is famous for its local specialties (Mon–Sat 11:00–23:00, closed Sun, indoor/outdoor seating, Singerstrasse 28, tel. 01/512-5895).

Wrenkh Vegetarian Restaurant and Bar is popular for its high vegetarian cuisine. Chef Wrenkh offers daily lunch menus (€8–10) and dinner plates (€8–13) in a bright, mod bar or in a dark, smoke-free, fancier restaurant (daily 11:30–24:00, Bauernmarkt 10, tel. 01/533-1526).

Buffet Trzesniewski is an institution—justly famous for its elegant and cheap finger sandwiches and small beers (€0.70 each). Three different sandwiches and a *kleines Bier (Pfiff)* make a fun, light lunch. Point to whichever delights look tasty and pay for them and a drink. Take your drink tokens to the lady on the right. Sit on the bench and scoot over to a tiny table when a spot opens up (Mon–Fri 8:30–19:30, Sat 9:00–17:00, closed Sun, 50 yards off Graben, nearly across from brooding Café Hawelka, Dorotheergasse 2, tel. 01/512-3291). This is a good opportunity to try the fancy grape juices—*Most* or *Traubenmost* (see above).

Julius Meinl am Graben has been famous since 1862 as a top-end delicatessen with all the gourmet fancies (including a highly rated restaurant upstairs, shop open Mon–Fri 8:00–19:30, Sat 8:30–17:00, closed Sun, restaurant Mon–Sat until 24:00, closed Sun, Am Graben 19, tel. 01/532-3334).

Akakiko Sushi: If you're just schnitzeled out, this small chain of Japanese restaurants with an easy sushi menu may suit you. The bento box meals are tasty. Three locations are very convenient (all open daily 10:00–24:00): Singerstrasse 4 (a block off Kärntner Strasse near the cathedral), Heidenschuss 3 (near other recommended eateries just off Am Hof), and Mariahilfer Strasse 42–48 (fifth floor of Kaufhaus Gerngross, near many recommended hotels).

Ice Cream! For a gelato treat or fancy dessert with a mob of happy Viennese, stop by the thriving **Zanoni & Zanoni** (daily 7:00–24:00, 2 blocks up Rotenturmstrasse from cathedral at Lugeck 7, tel. 01/512-7979).

Near the Opera

Café Restaurant Palmenhaus, overlooking the palace garden *(Burggarten)*, tucked away in a green and peaceful corner two blocks behind the Opera in the Hofburg's backyard, is a world apart. If you want to eat modern Austrian cuisine with palm trees rather than tourists, this is it. And at the edge of a huge park, it's great for families (€11 lunches, €15 dinners, daily 10:00–2:00, serious vegetarian dishes, fish, and an extensive wine list, indoors in greenhouse or outdoors, at Burggarten, tel. 01/533-1033). While nobody goes to the Palmenhaus for good prices, the **Palmenhaus BBQ**—a cool parkside outdoor pub just below that uses the same kitchen—is a wonderful value with more casual service (summer Wed–Sat from 20:00, closed Sun–Tue, open in good weather only, informal with €8 BBQ and meals posted on chalkboard).

Rosenberger Markt Restaurant is my favorite for a fast, light, and central lunch. Just a block toward the cathedral from the Opera, this place—while not cheap—is brilliant. Friendly and efficient, with special theme rooms for dining, it offers a fresh, smoke-free, and healthy cornucopia of food and drink (daily 10:30–23:00, lots of fruits, veggies, fresh-squeezed juices, addictive banana milk, ride the glass elevator downstairs, Maysedergasse 2, tel. 01/512-3458). You can stack a small salad or veggie plate into a tower of gobble for €2.50.

Spittelberg Quarter

A charming cobbled grid of traffic-free lanes and Biedermeier apartments has become a favorite place for Viennese wanting a little dining charm between the MuseumsQuartier and Mariahilfer Strasse (handy to many recommended hotels; take Stiftgasse from Mariahilfer Strasse, or wander over here after you close down the Kunsthistorisches or Leopold Museum). Tables tumble down sidewalks and into breezy courtyards filled with appreciative locals enjoying dinner or a relaxing drink. Stroll Spittelberggasse, Schrankgasse, and Gutenberggasse and pick your favorite place. Check out the courtyard inside Spittelberggasse 3, and don't miss the vine-strewn wine garden inside Schrankgasse 1. I ate well and cheaply at **Plutzer Bräu** (daily 11:00–2:00, good daily specials and beer from the keg, Schrankgasse 4, tel. 01/526-1215). For traditional Viennese cuisine with tablecloths, consider the classier **Witwe Bolte** (Mon–Fri 11:30–15:00 & 17:30–23:30, Sat–Sun 11:30–23:20, Gutenberggasse 13, tel. 01/523-1450).

Mariahilfer Strasse

Mariahilfer Strasse is filled with reasonable cafés serving all types of cuisine. **Restaurant Beim Novak** serves good local cuisine away from the modern rush (Mon–Fri 11:30–15:00 & 18:00–22:00, open Sat for dinner Sept–March, closed Sun, a block down Andreasgasse from Mariahilfer Strasse at Richtergasse 12, tel. 01/523-3244).

Naschmarkt is Vienna's best Old World market, with plenty of fresh produce, cheap local-style eateries, cafés, and *döner kebab* and sausage stands (Mon–Fri 7:00–18:00, Sat 6:00–18:00, closed Sun, closes earlier in winter, U-4: Kettenbrückengasse).

TRANSPORTATION CONNECTIONS

Vienna has two main train stations: the Westbahnhof (West Train Station), serving Munich, Salzburg, Melk, and Budapest; and the Südbahnhof (South Train Station), serving Italy, Budapest, Prague, Poland, Slovenia, and Croatia. A third station, Franz Josefs, serves Krems and the Danube Valley (but Melk is served by the Westbahnhof). Metro line U-3 connects the Westbahnhof with the center, tram D takes you from the Südbahnhof and the Franz Josefs station to downtown, and tram #18 connects West and South stations. Train info: tel. 051717 (wait through long German recording for operator).

By train to: Melk (hrly, 75 min, sometimes change in St. Pölten), **Krems** (hrly, 1 hr), **Salzburg** (hrly, 3 hrs), **Innsbruck** (every 2 hrs, 5.5 hrs), **Budapest** (6/day, 3 hrs), **Prague** (4/day, 4.5 hrs), **Český Krumlov** (5/day, 6–7 hrs, up to 3 changes), **Munich** (hrly, 5.25 hrs, change in Salzburg, a few direct trains), **Berlin** (2/day, 10 hrs, longer on night train), **Zürich** (3/day, 9 hrs), **Ljubljana** (7/day, 6–7 hrs, convenient early-morning direct train, others change in Villach or Maribor), **Zagreb** (8/day, 6.5–10.5 hrs, 3 direct, others with up to 3 changes including Villach and Ljubljana), **Kraków** (4/day, 6.5–9 hrs, 2 direct including a night train), **Warsaw** (4/day, 7.5–10 hrs, 2 direct including a night train), **Rome** (1/day, 13.5 hrs), **Venice** (3/day, 7.5 hrs, longer on night train), **Frankfurt** (4/day, 7.5 hrs), **Amsterdam** (1/day, 14.5 hrs).

SALZBURG

Salzburg is forever smiling to the tunes of Mozart and *The Sound of Music*. Thanks to its charmingly preserved old town, splendid gardens, Baroque churches, and Europe's largest intact medieval fortress, Salzburg feels made for tourism. It's a museum city with class. Vagabonds wish they had nicer clothes.

But even without Mozart and the von Trapps, Salzburg is steeped in history. In about A.D. 700, Bavaria gave Salzburg to Bishop Rupert for his promise to Christianize the area. Salzburg remained an independent state until Napoleon came (around 1800). Thanks in part to its formidable fortress, Salzburg managed to avoid the ravages of war for 1,200 years...until World War II. Half the city was destroyed by WWII bombs, but the historic old town survived.

Eight million tourists crawl its cobbles each year. That's a lot of Mozart balls—and all that popularity has led to a glut of businesses hoping to catch the tourist dollar. Still, Salzburg is a must.

ORIENTATION

(area code: 0662)

Salzburg, a city of 150,000 (Austria's fourth largest), is divided into old and new. The old town, sitting between the Salzach River and the 1,600-foot-high hill called Mönchsberg, holds nearly all the charm and most of the tourists.

Tourist Information: Salzburg's TIs are helpful. There are three branches: at the **train station** (April–Sept daily 9:00–18:30, July–Aug until 19:30, Oct–March until 17:45, tel. 0662/8898-7340), on **Mozartplatz** in the old center (daily 9:00–18:00, July–Aug until 19:00, sometimes closed Sun in winter, tel. 0662/8898-7330), and at the **Salzburg Süd park-and-ride** (July–Aug daily 9:00–19:00, Easter–June and Sept–Oct Mon–Sat 10:00–18:00, closed Sun, closed Nov–Easter, tel.

0662/8898-7360; central office: tel. 0662/889-870, www.salzburg.info).
At any TI, you can pick up a free city center map (the €0.70 map, with
more information on sights, probably isn't necessary), a brochure of
sights with current hours and prices, and a bimonthly schedule of events.
Book a concert upon arrival. The TIs also book rooms (€2.20 fee for up
to 2 people, or €4.40 for 3 people or more).

Salzburg Card: The TI sells the Salzburg Card, which covers all
your public transportation (including elevator and funicular) and admission to all the city sights (including Hellbrunn Palace). The card is
pricey (€20/24 hrs, €28/48 hrs, €1 less Oct–May), but if you'd like to
pop into all the sights without concern for the cost, this can save money
and enhance your experience.

Planning Your Time

While Vienna measures much higher on the Richter scale of sightseeing
thrills, Salzburg is simply a touristy, stroller's delight. You'll probably
need two nights here—nights are important for swilling beer in atmospheric local gardens and attending concerts in Baroque halls and chapels.
Seriously consider one of Salzburg's many evening musical events (about
€30–40). While the sights are mediocre, the town is an enjoyable
Baroque museum of cobbled streets and elegant buildings.

Arrival in Salzburg

By Train: The little Salzburg station is user-friendly. The TI is at track
2A. Downstairs at street level, you'll find a place to store your luggage,
buy tickets, and get train information. Bike rental is nearby (see below).
The bus station is across the street (where buses #1, #5, #6, #51, and
#55 go to the old center; get off at the first stop after you cross the river
for most sights and city center hotels, or just before the bridge for
Linzergasse hotels). Figure €6.50 for a taxi to the center. To walk downtown (15 min), leave the station ticket hall to the left and walk straight
down Rainerstrasse, which leads under the tracks past Mirabellplatz,
turning into Dreialtigkeitsgasse. From here, you can turn left onto
Linzergasse for many of the recommended hotels or cross the
Staatsbrücke (bridge) for the old town (and more hotels). For a more
dramatic approach, leave the station the same way but follow the tracks
to the river, turn left, and walk the riverside path toward the fortress.

By Car: Follow *Zentrum* signs to the center and park short-
term on the street or longer under Mirabellplatz. Ask at your hotel for
suggestions.

Getting around Salzburg

By Bus: Single-ride tickets are sold on the bus for €1.70. At machines
and *Tabak* shops, you can buy a €3.20 day pass (*Tageskarte,* good for 24
hrs) and cheaper single tickets (€1.40 each, but you must buy 5 at a

time). To signal the driver you want to get off, press the buzzer on the pole. Bus info: tel. 0662/4480-6262.

By Bike: Salzburg is a biker's delight. Top Bike rents bikes from two outlets (at the river side of the train station and on the old town side of the Staatsbrücke, €3.70/hr, €13/24 hrs, tel. 06272/4656, mobile 0676-476-7259, www.topbike.at, Sabina SE). Velo-Active rents bikes on Residenzplatz under the *Glockenspiel* in the old town (€4.50/hr, €15/24 hrs, mountain bikes-€6/hr, €18/24 hrs, daily 9:00–18:00 but hours unreliable—often you'll have to call, shorter hours off-season and in bad weather, passport number for security deposit, tel. 0662/435-595, mobile 0676/435-5950). Thanks to a promotional deal they have with the train station, both companies offer 20 percent off with a valid train ticket or Eurailpass—ask for it.

By Funicular and Elevator: The old town is connected to Mönchsberg (and great views) via funicular and elevator. The **funicular** (FestungsBahn) whisks you up to the imposing Hohensalzburg fortress (€8.50 round-trip includes admission to fortress grounds, €5.50 one-way; funicular runs May–Aug daily 9:00–22:00, Sept until 21:30, Oct–Dec and mid-March–April until 17:00, closed for maintenance Jan–mid-March, www.festungsbahn.at). You can't take the funicular up without paying for entrance to the fortress grounds—unless you have a concert ticket and it's within an hour before the performance (see "Music Scene," below).

The **elevator** (MönchsbergAufzug) on the east side of the old town propels you to the recommended Naturfreundehaus (see "Sleeping in the Old Town," below), the Modern Art Museum, and lots of wooded paths (€1.60 one-way, €2.60 round-trip, summer daily 9:00–21:00, off-season until 18:00, www.moenchsbergaufzug.at).

By Taxi: Salzburg is a fine taxi town. Meters start around €3 (from train station to your hotel, allow about €6.50). As always, small groups can taxi for about the same price as riding the bus.

By Boat: Salzburg's first attempt at a Salzach River Cruise sank to the bottom—literally—when someone moored the boat with too short a rope during the August 2002 floods. Now the boat is back up and running (€10 for basic 40-min roundtrip cruise, April–Sept 8/day, more June–Aug, €13 to Hellbrunn with return on bus, April–Sept 3/day, more June–Aug, boat leaves from old-town side of river just west—downstream—of Staatsbrücke, tel. 0662/8257-6912, www.salzburgschifffahrt.at).

By Buggy: The horse buggies *(Fiaker)* that congregate at the Residenz Platz charge €35 for a 25-minute trot around the old town (www.fiaker-salzburg.at).

Helpful Hints

Internet Access: BigNet, a block off Mozartplatz at Judengasse 5, has 33 terminals (about €6/hr, daily 9:00–22:00, tel. 0662/841-470).

The Internet Café is on Mozartplatz next to the TI (€9/hr, daily 9:00–24:00, off-season until 22:00, 11 terminals, Mozartplatz 5, tel. 0662/844-822).

Laundry: The launderette near recommended Linzergasse hotels at the corner of Paris-Lodron Strasse and Wolf-Dietrich Strasse is handy (€10 self-service, €15 same-day full-service, Mon–Fri 7:30–18:00, Sat 8:00–12:00, closed Sun, tel. 0662/876-381).

Guide Association: Salzburg's many guides can give you a good three-hour walk through town for €125 (tel. 0662/840-406). Barbel Schalber, who enjoys leaving the touristy places, offers my readers a two-hour walk packed with information and spicy opinions for €75 per family or group (tel. 0662/632-225, baxguide@utanet.at).

American Express: AmEx has travel agency services, but doesn't sell train tickets—and it charges no commission to cash AmEx checks (Mon–Fri 9:00–17:30, Sat 9:00–12:00, closed Sun, Mozartplatz 5, tel. 0662/8080).

SELF-GUIDED OLD TOWN WALKING TOUR

The tourist office offers two-language, one-hour guided walks of the old town. They are informative and worthwhile if you don't mind listening to a half hour of German (€8, daily at 12:15, not on Sun in winter, start at TI on Mozartplatz, tel. 0662/8898-7330—just show up and pay the guide). But you can easily do it on your own.

Here's a basic old-town orientation walk, worth ▲▲▲.

Mozartplatz—This square features a statue of Mozart erected in 1842. Mozart spent much of his first 20 years (1756–1777) in Salzburg, the greatest Baroque city north of the Alps. But the city's much older. The Mozart statue actually sits on bits of Roman Salzburg. And the pink church of St. Michael overlooking the square is from A.D. 800. The first Salzburgers settled right around here. Surrounding you are Café Glockenspiel, the Internet Café, the American Express office, and the tourist information office with a concert box office. Just around the downhill corner is a pedestrian bridge leading over the Salzach River to the quiet, most medieval street in town, Steingasse (see "Across the River," below). Walk toward the cathedral and into the big square with the huge fountain.

Residenz Platz—Salzburg's energetic Prince-Archbishop Wolf Dietrich (who ruled from 1587–1612) was raised in Rome, counted the Medicis as his buddies, and had grandiose Italian ambitions for Salzburg. After a convenient fire destroyed the cathedral, he set about building "the Rome of the North." This square, with his new cathedral and palace, was the centerpiece of his Baroque dream city. A series of interconnecting squares—like you'll see nowhere else—lead from here through the old town.

Salzburg

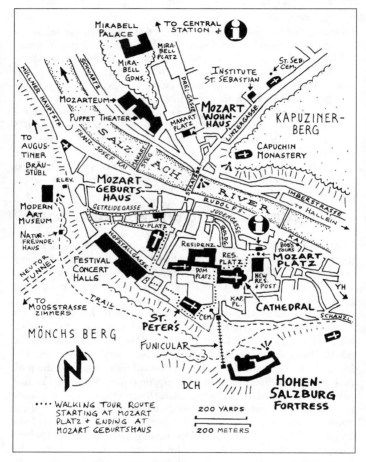

MIRABELL PALACE

TO CENTRAL STATION

MIRA-BELL PLATZ

MIRA-BELL GDNS.

INSTITUTE ST. SEBASTIAN

ST. SEB. CEM.

MOZARTEUM→

MOZART WOHN-HAUS

KAPUZINER-BERG

PUPPET THEATER→

MAKART PLATZ

LINZERGASSE

SCHWARZ

DREI-GASSE

TO AUGUS-TINER BRÄU-STÜBL

FRANZ JOSEF KAI

MAKART STEG

SALZACH

RIVER

CAPUCHIN MONASTERY

ELEV.

MODERN ART MUSEUM

MOZART GEBURTS-HAUS

GETREIDEGASSE

RUDOLFS

STAATSBR.

IMBERSTRASSE

TO HALLEIN

NATUR-FREUNDE-HAUS

U-PLATZ

JUDENGASSE

GOLDG.

BOB'S TOURS

MOZART PLATZ

NEUTOR TUNNEL

HOFSTALLGASSE

RESIDENZ

RES. PLATZ

FESTIVAL CONCERT HALLS

DOM PLATZ

NEW RES. & POST

YH

TO MOOSSTRASSE ZIMMERS

TRAIL

KAP. PL.

CATHEDRAL

SCHANZL.

MÖNCHS BERG

ST. PETER'S

CEM.

FUNICULAR→

DCH

HOHEN-SALZBURG FORTRESS

•••• WALKING TOUR ROUTE STARTING AT MOZART PLATZ & ENDING AT MOZART GEBURTSHAUS

200 YARDS

200 METERS

For centuries, Salzburg's leaders were both important church officials and princes of the Holy Roman Empire, hence the title "Prince-Archbishop"—mixing sacred and secular authority. Wolf Dietrich misplayed his power and spent his last five years imprisoned in the Salzburg castle.

The fountain is as Italian as can be, with a Triton matching Bernini's famous Triton Fountain in Rome. Lying on a busy trade route to the south, Salzburg was well aware of the exciting things going on in Italy. Things Italian were respected (as in colonial America, when a bumpkin would "stick a feather in his cap and call it macaroni"). Local artists even Italianized their names in order to raise their rates.

Residenz—Dietrich's skippable palace is connected to the cathedral by a skyway. A series of ornately decorated rooms and an art gallery are open to visitors with time to kill (€7.30 includes both palace and gallery with audioguide, €5 each for palace or picture gallery, daily 10:00–17:00, gallery closed Mon except July–Aug, entire complex closed one month around Easter, tel. 0662/8042-2690).

Opposite the old Residenz is the new Residenz, which has long been a government administration building. Today it houses the central post office and the Heimatwerk, a fine shop showing off all the best local handicrafts (Mon–Fri 9:00–18:00, Sat 9:00–13:00, closed Sun). Atop the new Residenz is the famous...

Glockenspiel—This bell tower has a carillon of 35 17th-century bells (cast in Antwerp) that chimes throughout the day and plays tunes (appropriate to the month) at 7:00, 11:00, and 18:00. There was a time when Salzburg could afford to take tourists to the top of the tower to actually see the big barrel with adjustable tabs turn (like a giant music box mechanism)...pulling the right bells in the right rhythm. Notice the ornamental top: an upside-down heart in flames surrounding the solar system (symbolizing that God loves all of creation).

Look back, past Mozart's statue, to the 4,220-foot-high Gaisberg— the forested hill with the television tower. A road leads to the top for a commanding view. Its summit is a favorite destination for local nature-lovers (by city bus or bike). Walk under the Prince-Archbishop's skyway and step into Domplatz, the cathedral square.

Salzburg Cathedral—Built in the 17th century, this was one of the first Baroque buildings north of the Alps. It was built during the Thirty Years' War to emphasize Salzburg's commitment to the Roman Catholic cause and the power of the Church here. Salzburg's archbishop was technically the top papal official north of the Alps (donation requested, May–Oct Mon–Sat 9:00–18:30, Sun 13:00–18:30, Nov–April Mon–Sat 10:00–17:00, Sun 13:00–17:00). The dates on the iron gates refer to milestones in the church's history: In 774, the previous church (long since destroyed) was founded by St. Virgil, to be replaced in 1628 by the church you see today. In 1959, the reconstruction was completed after a WWII bomb blew through the dome.

Wander inside. Built in just 14 years (1614–1628), the church boasts harmonious architecture. When the pope visited in 1998, 5,000 people filled the cathedral (dimensions: 330 feet long and 230 feet tall). The baptismal font (dark bronze, left of the entry) is from the previous cathedral (c. 1320). Mozart was baptized here (Amadeus means "beloved by God"). Gape up. The interior—with its five independent organs—is marvelous. Concert and Mass schedules are posted at the entrance; the Sunday Masses at 10:00 and 11:30 are famous for their music. Mozart, who worked here as the organist for two years, would advise you that the acoustics are best in pews immediately under the dome.

Under the skyway, a stairway leads down to the *Domgrabungen*—an **excavation site** under the church with a few second-century Christian Roman mosaics and the foundation stones of the previous Romanesque and Gothic churches (€2, May–Sept Wed–Sun 9:00–17:00, closed Mon–Tue, closed Oct–April, 0662/845-295). The **Cathedral Museum** (Dom Museum) has a rich collection of church art (entry at portico, €4.50, mid-May–Oct Mon–Sat 10:00–17:00, Sun 13:00–18:00, closed Nov–mid-May, tel. 0662/844-189).

From Cathedral Square to St. Peter's: The cathedral square is surrounded by "ecclesiastical palaces." The statue of Mary (1771) is looking away from the church, but, if you stand in the rear of the square immediately under the middle arch, you'll see how she's positioned to be crowned by the two angels on the church facade.

From the cathedral, walk toward the fortress into the next square (passing the free underground public WCs and the giant chessboard) to the pond. This was a horse bath, the 18th-century equivalent of a car wash. Notice the puzzle above it—the artist wove the date of the structure into a phrase. It says, "Leopold the Ruler Built Me," using the letters LLDVICMXVXI, which total 1732—the year it was built. A small road (back by the chessboard) leads uphill to the fortress (and fortress lift). The stage is set up for the many visiting choirs who are unable to line up a gig. They are welcome to sing here anytime at all. Leave the square through a gate on the right that reads St. Peter. It leads to a waterfall and St. Peter's Cemetery.

The **waterfall** is part of a canal system that has brought water into Salzburg from Berchtesgaden, 16 miles away, since 1150. The stream, divided from here into smaller canals, was channeled through town to power factories (more than 100 water-mill–powered firms as late as the 19th century), provide fire protection, and flush out the streets (Sat morning was flood-the-streets day). Drop into the traditional **bakery** at the waterfall. It's hard to beat their rocklike *Roggenbrot* (sold Thu–Tue 7:00–17:30, Sat until 12:00, closed Wed). Then step into the cemetery *(Katakomben)*.

St. Peter's Cemetery—This collection of lovingly tended mini-gardens abuts the Mönchberg's rock wall (April–Sept daily 6:30–19:00, Oct–March daily 6:30–18:00). Iron crosses were much cheaper than stone tombstones. The graves are cared for by relatives. (In Austria, grave sites are rented, not owned. Rent bills are sent out every 10 years. If no one cares enough to make the payment, you're gone.) Look up the cliff. Medieval hermit monks lived in the hillside—but "catacombs" they're not. For €1, you can climb lots of steps to see a few old caves, a chapel, and some fine views (May–Sept Tue–Sun 10:30–17:00, closed Mon, Oct–April Wed–Thu 10:30–15:30, Fri–Sun 10:30–16:00, closed

Mon–Tue). While the cemetery the von Trapp family hid out in was actually in Hollywood, it was inspired by this one. Walk through the cemetery (silence is requested) and out the opposite end. Drop into St. Peter's Church, a Romanesque basilica done up beautifully Baroque. Continue through the arch opposite the church entry and through a modern courtyard (past dorms for student monks).

Toscanini Hof faces the 1925 Festival Hall. Its three halls seat 5,000. This is where the nervous Captain von Trapp waited before walking onstage to sing "Edelweiss" just before he escaped with Maria and his family to Switzerland. On the left is the city's 1,500-space, inside-the-mountain parking lot; ahead behind the *Felsenkeller* sign is a tunnel (generally closed) leading to the actual concert hall; and to the right is the backstage of a smaller hall where carpenters are often building stage sets (open on hot days). Walk downhill through Max Reinhardt Platz, to the right of the church and past the public WC to...

Universitätsplatz—This square comes with a busy open-air produce market—Salzburg's liveliest (mornings Mon–Sat, best on Sat). Locals are happy to pay more here for the reliably fresh and top-quality produce (half of Austria's produce is now grown organically). The market really bustles on Saturday mornings, when the farmers are in town. Public marketplaces have fountains for washing fruit and vegetables. The fountain here (notice the little ones for smaller dogs and bigger dogs)—a part of the medieval water system—plummets down a hole and to the river. The sundial is accurate (except for the daylight savings hour), showing both the time (obvious) and the date (less obvious). Continue to the end of the square (opposite cathedral), passing several characteristic and nicely arcaded medieval tunnel passages (on right) connecting the square to Getreidegasse. At the big road (across from the giant horse troughs), take two right turns and you're at the start of...

Getreidegasse—This street was old Salzburg's busy, colorful main drag. (*Schmuck* means jewelry.) Famous for its old wrought-iron signs, the street still looks much as it did in Mozart's day. On the right at #39, Sporer is known for its homemade spirits (Mon–Fri 9:00–12:30 & 14:30–19:00, Sat 8:30–17:00, closed Sun, tel. 0662/845-431). At #40, Eisgrotte serves good ice cream. Across from Eisgrotte, a tunnel leads to Bosna Grill, the local choice for the very best sausage in town (see "Eating Cheap in the Old Town," below). Farther along you'll see the Nordsee Restaurant, which was a more controversial addition to this street than the McDonald's—notice the medieval golden arches street sign. Wolfgang was born on this street. Find his very gold house at #9 (follow the crowds).

Mozart's Birthplace (Geburtshaus)—Mozart was born here in 1756. It was in this building—the most popular Mozart sight in town—that he composed most of his boy-genius works. Filled with scores of scores, portraits, his first violin (picked up at age 5), the clavichord (a predecessor to the piano with simple teeter-totter keys that played very softly) on which he composed *The Magic Flute* and the *Requiem,* a relaxing video concert hall, and exhibits about the life of Wolfgang on the road and Salzburg in Mozart's day, including a furnished middle-class apartment (all well-described in English), it's almost a pilgrimage (€5.50, or €9 for combo-ticket to Mozart's *Wohnhaus*—see "Sights—Across the River," below, July–Aug daily 9:00–19:00, Sept–June daily 9:00–18:00, last entry 30 min before closing, Getreidegasse 9, tel. 0662/844-313). Note that Mozart's *Wohnhaus* provides a more informative visit than this more-visited site.

SOUND OF MUSIC DEBUNKED

Rather than visit the real-life sights from the life of Maria von Trapp and family, most tourists want to see the places where Hollywood chose to film this fanciful story. Local guides are happy not to burst any *S.O.M.* pilgrim's bubble, but keep these points in mind:

- "Edelweiss" is not a cherished Austrian folk tune or national anthem. Like all the "Austrian" music in the *S.O.M.*, it was composed for Broadway by Rodgers and Hammerstein. It was, however, the last composition that the famed team wrote together, as Hammerstein died in 1960—nine months after the musical opened.
- The *S.O.M.* implies that Maria was devoutly religious throughout her life, but Maria's foster parents raised her as a socialist and atheist. Maria discovered her religious calling while studying to be a teacher. After completing school, she joined the convent as a novitiate.
- Maria's position was not as governess to all the children, as portrayed in the musical, but specifically as governess and teacher for the Captain's second-oldest daughter, Maria, who was bedridden with rheumatic fever.
- The Captain didn't run a tight domestic ship. In fact, his seven children were as unruly as most. But he did use a whistle to call them—each kid was trained to respond to a certain pitch.
- Though the von Trapp family did have seven children, the show changed all their names and even their genders. Rupert, the eldest child, responded to the often-asked tourist question, "Which one are you?" with a simple, "I'm Leisl!"
- The family never escaped by hiking to Switzerland (which is a 5-hour drive away). Rather, they pretended to go on one of their

SIGHTS

Above the Old Town

▲**Hohensalzburg Fortress**—Built on a rock 400 feet above the Salzach River, this fortress was never really used. That's the idea. It was a good investment—so foreboding, nobody attacked the town for a thousand years. One of Europe's mightiest, it dominates Salzburg's skyline and offers incredible views. You can hike up or ride the *Festungsbahn* (funicular, €8.50 round-trip includes fortress courtyard entry, €5.50 one-way, pleasant to walk down). The fortress visit has two parts—a relatively dull courtyard with some fine views (€3.60 or included in €8.50 funicular

frequent mountain hikes. With only the possessions in their backpacks, they "hiked" all the way to the train station (it was at the edge of their estate) and took a train to Italy. Hitler immediately closed the Austrian borders when he learned of this. The movie scene showing them climbing into Switzerland was actually filmed near Berchtesgaden, Germany...home to Hitler's Eagle's Nest, and certainly not a smart place to flee.

- The actual von Trapp family house exists...but it's not the one in the film. The mansion in the movie is actually two different buildings, one used for the front, the other for the back. The interiors were all filmed on Hollywood sets.
- For the film, Boris Levin designed a reproduction of Nonnberg Abbey courtyard so faithful to the original (down to its cobblestones and stained-glass windows) that many still believe the cloister scenes were really shot at the abbey. And no matter what you hear in Salzburg, the graveyard scene (in which the von Trapps hide from the Nazis) was also filmed on the Fox lot.
- In 1956, a German film producer offered Maria $10,000 for the rights to her book. She asked for royalties, too, and a share of the profits. The agent explained that German law forbids film companies from paying royalties to foreigners (Maria had by then become a U.S. citizen). She agreed to the contract and unknowingly signed away all film rights to her story. Only a few weeks later, he offered to pay immediately if she would accept $9,000 in cash. Because it was more money than the family had seen in all of their years of singing, she accepted the deal. Later, she discovered the agent had swindled them—no such law existed.

fare) and the palatial interior (worth the €3.60 extra admission). Tourists are allowed inside only with an escort, so you'll go one room at a time, listening to the entire 50-minute audioguide narration (included).

The decorations are from around 1500—fantastic animals and plants inspired by tales of New World discoveries. While the interior furnishings are mostly gone—to the museums of Vienna, Paris, London, and Munich—the rooms survived as well as they did because no one wanted to live there after 1500, so it was never modernized. Your tour includes the obligatory room dedicated to the art of "intensive questioning"—filled with tools of that gruesome trade—and a sneak preview of the room used for the nightly fortress concerts. The last rooms show music, daily life in the castle, and an exhibit dedicated to the Salzburg regiment in World War I and World War II. The highlight is the commanding city view from the top of a tower (fortress open daily year-round; mid-March–mid-June: grounds 9:00–18:00, interior 9:30–17:30; mid-June–mid-Sept: grounds 9:00–19:00, interior 9:30–18:00; mid-Sept–mid-March: grounds 9:00–17:00, interior 9:30–17:00; last entry 30 min before closing, tel. 0662/8424-3011). Warning: The one-room marionette exhibit in the fortress courtyard is a bad value—you'll see more for free in its lobby than by paying to go inside.

▲The Hills Are Alive Walk—For a great little hike, exit the fortress by taking the trail across Salzburg's little mountain, Mönchsberg. The trail leads through the woods high above the city (stick to the high lanes, or you'll end up back in town), taking you to the Naturfreundehaus (café, light meals, cheap beds, elevator nearby for a quick descent to Neumayr Platz in the old town) and eventually to the church that marks the rollicking Augustiner Bräustübl (described in "Eating Away from the Center," below).

Museum of Modern Art on Mönchsberg (Museum der Moderne auf dem Mönchsberg)—New for the summer of 2004 is a modern-art museum on top of Mönchsberg, housing Salzburg's Rupertinum Gallery, plus special exhibitions. While the collection is so-so, the restaurant has some of the best views in town (www.museumdermoderne.at).

Across the River

▲▲Mozart's *Wohnhaus*—This reconstruction of Mozart's second home (his family moved here when he was 17) is the most informative Mozart sight in town. The English-language audioguide (free with admission, keep it carefully pointed at the ceiling transmitters and don't move while listening) provides a fascinating insight into Mozart's life and music, with the usual scores, old pianos, and an interesting 30-minute-long film that runs continuously, all in English (€5.50, or €9 for combo-ticket to birthplace, guidebook-€4.50, daily 9:00–18:00, July–Aug until 19:00, last tickets sold 30 min before closing, allow 1 hr for visit, across river from old town, Makartplatz 8, tel. 0662/8742-2740).

Greater Salzburg

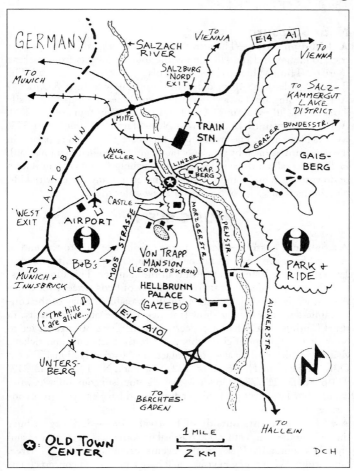

GERMANY

← SALZACH RIVER

TO VIENNA

E·14 A1

TO VIENNA

TO MUNICH

SALZBURG 'NORD' EXIT

TO SALZ- KAMMERGUT LAKE DISTRICT

MITTE

TRAIN STN.

GRAZER BUNDESSTR.

AUG. KELLER →

LINZER.

KAP. BERG

GAIS- BERG

A U T O B A H N

'WEST' EXIT

AIRPORT

CASTLE →

MÖZGERSTR.

ALPENSTR.

B+B's

VON TRAPP MANSION (LEOPOLDSKRON)

TO MUNICH & INNSBRUCK

MOOS STRASSE

HELLBRUNN PALACE (GAZEBO)

PARK + RIDE

AIGNERSTR.

"The hills are alive..."

E·14 A10

UNTERS- BERG

N

TO BERCHTES- GADEN

TO HALLEIN

OLD TOWN CENTER

1 MILE

2 KM

DCH

▲**Mirabell Gardens and Palace** *(Schloss)*—The bubbly gardens, laid out in 1730, are always open and free. You may recognize the statues and the arbor featured in the *S.O.M.* A brass band plays free park concerts (May–Aug Sun 10:30 and Wed 20:30). To properly enjoy the lavish Mirabell Palace—once the prince bishop's summer palace and now the seat of the mayor—get a ticket to a *Schlosskonzert* (my favorite venue for a classical concert). Baroque music flying around a Baroque hall is a happy bird in the right cage. Tickets (€26–31, student-€14) are rarely sold out (tel. 0662/848-586). The nearby **Café Bazar** is a great place for a break (see "Eating," below).

Near Salzburg

▲**Hellbrunn Castle**—The attractions here are a garden full of clever trick fountains and the sadistic joy the tour guide gets from soaking tourists. (Hint: When you see a wet place, cover your camera.) The Baroque garden, one of the oldest in Europe, now features *S.O.M.*'s "I Am 16, Going on 17" gazebo (€7.50, includes 35-min tour, daily 9:00–17:30, July–Aug until 18:00 and €7 fountain tours until 22:00, April and Oct until 16:30, closed Nov–March, tel. 0662/820-372, www.hellbrunn.at). The archbishop's mediocre 17th-century palace, in the courtyard, is open by tour only (audioguide included in admission). Hellbrunn is about three miles south of Salzburg (bus #55 from station or downtown, 2/hr, 20 min). It's most fun on a sunny day or with kids, but, for many, it's a lot of trouble for a few water tricks.

MUSIC SCENE

▲▲**Salzburg Festival**—Each summer, from late July to the end of August, Salzburg hosts its famous Salzburger Festspiele, founded in 1920 to employ Vienna's musicians in the summer. This fun and festive time is crowded, but there are plenty of beds (except for a few August weekends). Tickets are normally available the day of the concert unless it's a really big show (the ticket office on Mozartplatz, in the TI, prints a daily list of concerts and charges a 30 percent fee to book them). For specifics on this year's festival schedule and tickets, visit www.salzburgfestival.at, or contact the Austrian National Tourist Office in the United States (Box 1142, New York, NY 10108-1142, 212/944-6880, fax 212/730-4568, www.austria-tourism.com, info@oewnyc.com)—but I've never planned in advance and have enjoyed great concerts with every visit.

▲▲**Musical Events outside of Festival Time**—Salzburg is busy throughout the year, with 2,000 classical performances in its palaces and churches annually. Pick up the events calendar at the TI (free, bimonthly). Whenever you visit, you'll have a number of concerts (generally small chamber groups) to choose from. There are nearly nightly concerts at the fortress (for beginners—Mozart's greatest hits) and at the Mirabell Palace (with more sophisticated programs). Both feature small chamber groups, have open seating, and charge roughly €30–36 for tickets (concerts at 19:30, 20:00, or 20:30, doors open 30 min early). The *Schlosskonzerte* at the Mirabell Palace offer a fine Baroque setting for your music (tel. 0662/848-586). The fortress concerts, called *Festungskonzerte,* are held in the "prince's chamber" (tel. 0662/825-858 to reserve, you can pick up tickets at the door). This medieval-feeling room atop the fortress has windows overlooking the city, and the concert gives you a chance to enjoy the grand city view and a stroll through the castle courtyard. (The €8.50 round-trip funicular is discounted to €3.20 within an hour of the show if you have a concert ticket.)

The **"5:00 Concert"** next to St. Peter's is cheaper, since it features young artists (€10, July–Sept daily except Wed, 45 min, tel. 0662/8445-7619, www.sbg.ac.at/mus/5.htm). While the series is formally named after the brother of Joseph Haydn, it offers music from various masters.

Salzburg's impressive **Marionette Theater** performs operas with remarkable marionettes and recorded music (€22–35, nearly nightly June–Sept except Sun, also some in May, tel. 0662/872-406, www.marionetten.at).

For those who'd like some classical music but would rather not sit through a concert, Stiftskeller St. Peter offers a **Mozart Dinner Concert,** with a traditional candlelit meal and Mozart's greatest hits performed by a string quartet and singers in historic costumes gavotting among the tables. In this elegant Baroque setting, you'll enjoy three courses of food mixed with three 20-minute courses of top-quality music (€45, almost nightly at 20:00, see "Eating," below, call to reserve at 0662/828-6950).

The *S.O.M.* dinner show at the Sternbräu Inn (see "Eating," below) is Broadway in a dirndl with tired food. But it's a good show, and *S.O.M.* fans are mesmerized by the evening. A piano player and a hardworking quartet of singers perform an entertaining mix of *Sound of Music* hits and traditional folk songs (€43 includes a schnitzel and crisp apple strudel dinner at 19:30, €29 for 20:30 show only, those booking direct get a 10 percent discount with this book, reserve ahead, fun for families, daily mid-May–mid-Oct, Griesgasse 23, tel. 0662/826-617, www.soundofmusicshow.com).

SLEEPING

Linzergasse and Rupertgasse

These listings are between the train station and the old town in a pleasant neighborhood (with easy parking), a 15-minute walk from the train station (for directions, see "Arrival in Salzburg/By Train," above) and a 10- to 15-minute walk to the old town. If you're coming from the old town, simply cross the main bridge (Staatsbrücke) to the mostly traffic-free Linzergasse.

$$$ **Altstadthotel Wolf Dietrich,** around the corner from Linzergasse on Wolf-Dietrich Strasse, is well located and a reasonable big-hotel option, if that's what you want. Their main hotel, at Wolf-Dietrich Strasse 7, has 27 rooms and an elevator (Sb-€54–109, Db-€100–154, family deals, €40 more during festival time, complex pricing but readers of this book get a 10 percent discount on prevailing price, garage-€12/day, pool, sauna). Their annex—the **Hotel Residenz** across

SLEEP CODE

(€1 = about $1.10, country code: 43, area code: 0662)

Sleep Code: **S** = Single, **D** = Double/Twin, **T** = Triple, **Q** = Quad, **b** = bathroom, **s** = shower only, **no CC** = Credit Cards not accepted, **SE** = Speaks English, **NSE** = No English. Unless otherwise noted, credit cards are accepted, English is spoken, and breakfast is included.

To help you sort easily through these listings, I've divided the rooms into three categories, based on the price for a standard double room with bath:

$$$ **Higher Priced**—Most rooms €90 or more.
  $$ **Moderately Priced**—Most rooms between €60–90.
    $ **Lower Priced**—Most rooms €60 or less.

Finding a room in Salzburg, even during the music festival, is usually easy. Rates rise significantly (20–30 percent) during the music festival (mid-July through Aug) and sometimes also around Easter and Christmas; these higher prices do not appear in the price ranges included in hotel listings below.

the street, at #4—has 14 very similar rooms, cheaper prices, and no elevator (Db-€99–149; contact for both hotels: tel. 0662/871-275, fax 0662/882-320, www.salzburg-hotel.at, office@salzburg-hotel.at).

$$$ **Hotel Trumer Stube,** a few blocks from the river just off Linzergasse, has 20 clean, cozy rooms and a friendly, can-do owner (Sb-€56–70, Db-€89–103, Tb-€89–125, Qb-€132–140, prices depend on room size, some taller guests consider ceilings low in top-floor rooms, no CC except to hold reservation, non-smoking, elevator, small breakfast in small breakfast room, Internet access-€4/hr, Bergstrasse 6, tel. 0662/874-776, fax 0662/874-326, www.trumer-stube.at, info@trumer-stube.at, pleasant Silvia SE).

$$ **Hotel Goldene Krone,** about five blocks from the river, is big, quiet, and creaky-traditional but modern, with comforts rare in this price range (25 rooms, Sb-€55, Db-€80, Tb-€115, claim your 10 percent discount with this book, closed in March, elevator, relaxing backyard garden, Linzergasse 48, tel. 0662/872-300, fax 0662/8723-0066, www.hotel-goldenekrone.com, Claudia and Günther SE). Guests can watch *The Sound of Music* and other Salzburg videos in the lounge when they like. Every night at 18:00, Günther offers a free orientation talk on Salzburg. He also guides a just-for-fun, low-key, four-hour walking and

Salzburg Center Hotels

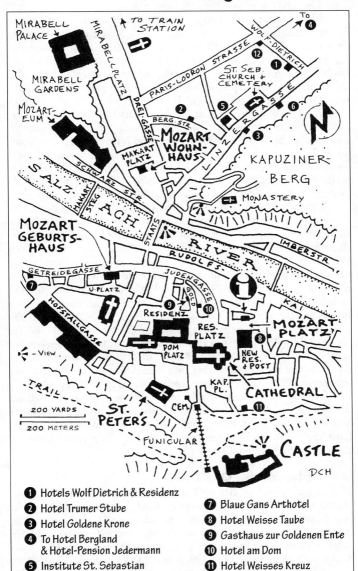

1 Hotels Wolf Dietrich & Residenz

2 Hotel Trumer Stube

3 Hotel Goldene Krone

4 To Hotel Bergland
& Hotel-Pension Jedermann

5 Institute St. Sebastian

6 Pension zum Jungen Fuchs

7 Blaue Gans Arthotel

8 Hotel Weisse Taube

9 Gasthaus zur Goldenen Ente

10 Hotel am Dom

11 Hotel Weisses Kreuz

12 Launderette

biking tour of untouristy Salzburg (€5, May–Sept in good weather only, Tue, Thu, and Sat at 14:00, must reserve ahead).

$$ Pensions on Rupertgasse: These two hotels are about five blocks farther from the river up Paris-Lodron Strasse to Rupertgasse, a breeze for drivers but with more street noise than the places on Linzergasse. They're both modern and well-run—excellent values if you don't mind being a bit away from the old town. **Bergland Hotel** is charming and classy, with comfortable neo-rustic rooms (Sb-€55, Db-€85, Tb-€95, Qb-€115, elevator, Internet access-€0.15/min, English library, bike rental, Rupertgasse 15, tel. 0662/872-318, fax 0662/872-3188, www.berglandhotel.at, kuhn@berglandhotel.at, Kuhn family). The similar, boutique-like **Hotel-Pension Jedermann,** a few doors down, is also tastefully done and comfortable, with artsy decor and a backyard garden (Sb-€55, Db-€75–85, Tb-€105, Qb-€135, Internet access-€0.15/min, Rupertgasse 25, tel. 0662/873-241, fax 0662/873-2419, www.hotel-jedermann.com, office@hotel-jedermann.com).

$ Institute St. Sebastian—a somewhat sterile but very clean, historic building—houses female students from various Salzburg colleges, and rents some rooms, October through June. From July through September, they rent all 50 rooms to travelers. The building has spacious public areas, a roof garden, and some of the best rooms and dorm beds in town for the money. The immaculate doubles come with modern baths and head-to-toe twin beds (Sb-€33, Db-€54, Tb-€69, Qb-€84, elevator, includes small breakfast, self-service laundry-€3/load, reception open July–Sept 7:30–12:00 & 13:00–22:00, Oct–June 8:00–12:00 & 16:00–21:00, Linzergasse 41, enter through arch at #37, tel. 0662/871-386, fax 0662/8713-8685, www.st-sebastian-salzburg.at, office@st-sebastian-salzburg.at). Students like the €17 bunks in 4- to 10-bed dorms (€2 less if you have sheets, no lockout time, free lockers, free showers). You'll find self-service kitchens on each floor (fridge space is free; request a key).

$ Pension zum Jungen Fuchs terrifies claustrophobes and titillates troglodytes. It's plain and sometimes smelly, but sleepable and wonderfully located in a funky, dumpy old building (16 rooms, S-€27, D-€38, Db-€65, T-€50, no breakfast, no CC, just up from Hotel Krone at Linzergasse 54, tel. 0662/875-496).

In (or above) the Old Town

$$$ The ultramodern **Blaue Gans Arthotel** gives you a break from charming old Salzburg—with artsy public spaces and 40 sleek, Scandinavian-style rooms beautifully located right on Getreidegasse. The standard rooms are supposedly smaller than the €20-more-expensive superior rooms—but there's really not much difference (Sb-€99, standard Db-€109, superior Db-€129, deluxe Db-€159, junior suite-€169, non-smoking rooms, elevator, Getreidegasse 41–43, tel. 0662/842-4910, fax 0662/842-4919, www.blauegans.at, office@blauegans.at).

$$$ **Hotel Weisse Taube** is a big, quiet, old-feeling 30-room place with more comfort than character, well-located about a block off Mozartplatz (Sb-€59–67, Db-€93–122, prices depend on room size, elevator, tel. 0662/842-404, fax 0662/841-783, Kaigasse 9, www.weissetaube.at, hotel @weissetaube.at).

$$ **Gasthaus zur Goldenen Ente** is in a 600-year-old building with medieval stone arches and narrow stairs. Located above a good restaurant, it's as central as you can be on a pedestrian street in old Salzburg. The 17 rooms are modern yet worn, and the service is uneven—from friendly to brusque to nonexistent (Sb-€53, Db-€79 with this book, extra person-€29, in July–Aug and Dec: Sb-€61, Db-€98 with this book, elevator, parking-€6/day, Goldgasse 10, tel. 0662/845-622, fax 0662/845-6229, www.ente.at, hotel@ente.at, Robert and family Steinwender SE).

$$ **Hotel am Dom** is just up Goldgasse from the Goldenen Ente—and equally well-located. The 14 rooms are old, basic, but well-maintained (Sb-€76–79, Db-€79–117, extra bed-€33, prices slightly lower Nov–mid-June, non-smoking rooms, Goldgasse 17, tel. 0662/872-765, fax 0662/8727-6555, www.amdom.at, bach@salzburg.co.at, family Bachleitner).

$$ **Hotel Restaurant Weisses Kreuz** is a Tolkienesque little family-run place on a cobbled backstreet under the fortress. It's away from the crowds and offers a fine restaurant, four rooms, and a peaceful roof garden (Sb-€55–73, Db-€66–90, Tb-€120, prices depend on room size, garage, Bierjodlgasse 6, tel. 0662/845-641, fax 0662/845-6419, weisses.kreuz@eunet.at).

$ **Naturfreundehaus,** also called "Gasthaus Stadtalm," is a local version of a mountaineer's hut and a great budget alternative. In a forest guarded by singing birds, it's snuggled in the remains of a 15th-century castle wall atop the little mountain overlooking Salzburg, with magnificent town and mountain views (€13.50/person in 2-, 4-, and 6-bed dorms, includes breakfast and shower, no CC, €6 bike rental, open mid-April–Oct, 2 min from top of €2.60 round-trip Mönchsberg elevator, Mönchsberg 19-C, tel. & fax 0662/841-729, www.stadtalm.com, Peter SE).

Away from the Center

$$$ **Hotel am Nussdorferhof** is a creatively run, 29-room place, located about halfway between the old town and the *Zimmer* on Moosstrasse (listed below). Run enthusiastically by Herbert and Ilse, the hotel has all the amenities including a sauna, whirlpool, and Internet access. It's a 15-minute walk or short bus ride from the old town (Sb-€68, Db-€98, big Db-€115, 1–2 kids sleep free, claim a 10 percent discount with this book when you reserve, some waterbeds, some theme rooms, elevator, 1 free 24-hr bus pass per person per stay, attached Italian restaurant, shuttle to/from train station or airport for a

fee, Moosstrasse 36, bus stop Nussdorferstrasse, tel. 0662/824-838, fax 0662/824-8389, www.nussdorferhof.at, info@nussdorferhof.at).

$ Pension Bloberger Hof is comfortable and friendly, with a rural location and 20 modern, good-value rooms. It's just beyond the *Zimmer* on Moosstrasse (listed below), and reached by the same bus #60 from the center (Sb-€32–46, Db-€51–55, big new Db with balcony-€79–85, extra bed-€15, family apartment, non-smoking rooms, free loaner bikes, will pick up at station, Hammerauerstrasse 4, bus stop: Hammerauerstrasse, tel. 0662/830-227, fax 0662/827-061, www.blobergerhof.at, office@blobergerhof.at).

Zimmer (Private Rooms)

These are generally roomy and comfortable and come with a good breakfast, easy parking, and tourist information. Off-season, competition softens prices. They are a bus ride from town, but, with a day pass and the frequent service, this shouldn't keep you away. In fact, most will happily pick you up at the train station if you simply telephone them and ask. Most will also do laundry for a small fee for those staying at least two nights. Unsavory *Zimmer* skimmers lurk at the station. Ignore them. I've listed prices for two nights or more. If staying only one night, expect a 10 percent surcharge.

Beyond the Train Station

$ Brigitte Lenglachner fills her big, traditional home with a warm welcome (S-€24, D-€37, Db-€44, T-€50, Tb-€64, Qb-€88, apartment with kitchen for up to 5, Scheibenweg 8, tel. & fax 0662/438-044, bedandbreakfast4u@yahoo.de). It's a 10-minute walk northeast of the station (cross pedestrian Pioneer Bridge, turn right, walk along the river to the third street—Scheibenweg—turn left, and it's halfway down on the right).

$ Trude Poppenberger's three pleasant rooms share a long, mountain-view balcony (S-€24, D-€37, T-€55; Wachtelgasse 9, tel. & fax 0662/430-094, www.trudeshome.com, mail@trudeshome.com). Call for a pick-up or walk 30 minutes northwest of the station (cross pedestrian Pioneer Bridge, turn right, walk along river 300 yards, cross canal, left on Linke Glanzeile for 3 min, right onto Wachtelgasse).

On Moosstrasse

The busy street called Moosstrasse, southwest of Mönchsberg, is lined with *Zimmer*. Those farther out are farmhouses. Handy bus #60 connects Moosstrasse to the center frequently (Mon–Fri 4/hr until 17:00, then 2/hr, Sat 4/hr until 12:00, then 2/hr)—but service drops to a frustrating once per hour on Sundays. To get to these from the train station, take bus #1, #5, #6, #51, or #55 to Makartplatz, where you'll change to #60. If you are coming from the old town, catch bus #60 from Hanuschplatz, just downstream of the Staatsbrücke near the *Tabak* kiosk. Buy a €1.70 *Einzelkarte-Kernzone* ticket (for 1 trip) or a €3.20 *Tageskarte* (for the entire day) from the streetside machine and punch it when you board the bus. If you're driving from the center, go through the tunnel, straight on Neutorstrasse, and take the fourth left onto Moosstrasse.

$ **Frau Ballwein** offers cozy, charming, fresh rooms in two buildings—one of them a 160-year-old farmhouse that feels new (S-€23, D-€40, Db-€48–50, Tb-€65–70, family deals, farm-fresh breakfasts, no CC, non-smoking, Moosstrasse 69-A, bus stop: Gsengerweg, tel. & fax 0662/824-029, www.privatvermieter.com/haus-ballwein, haus.ballwein @gmx.net).

$ **Helga Bankhammer** rents four old-feeling but pleasant rooms in a farmhouse, with a real dairy farm out back (D-€40, Db-€45, no surcharge for one-nighters, family deals, non-smoking, laundry-about €5/load, Moosstrasse 77, bus stop: Marienbad, tel. & fax 0662/830-067, www .privatzimmer.at/helga.bankhammer, helga.bankhammer@telering.at).

$ **Haus Reichl,** with three good rooms ranging from fresh to musty, feels the most remote (Db-€48, Tb-€66, Qb with balcony and view-€80, non-smoking, between Ballwein and Bankhammer B&Bs, 200 yards down Reiterweg to #52, bus stop: Gsengerweg, tel. & fax 0662/826-248, www.privatzimmer.at/haus-reichl, haus.reichl@telering.at).

Near the Train Station

$$ **Pension Adlerhof,** a plain and decent old place, is two blocks in front of the train station (left off Kaiserschutzenstrasse), but a 15-minute walk from the sightseeing action. It has a quirky staff and 35 well-maintained rooms (Sb-€55–60, D-€52–64, Db-€78–88, Tb-€90–102, Qb-€112–120, 10 percent cheaper off-season and during slow times, no CC, Internet access-€7/hr, elevator, Elisabethstrasse 25, tel. 0662/875-236, fax 0662/873-6636, www.pension-adlerhof.com, adlerhof@pension -adlerhof.at, Kurt and Inge Pregartbauer).

$ **International Youth Hotel,** a.k.a. the "Yo-Ho," is the most lively, handy, and American of Salzburg's hostels (€15 in 6- to 8-bed dorms, €18 in dorms with b, D-€20/person, Db-€23/person, Q-€17/person, Qb-€20/person, prices lower for 2- or 3-night stays, sheets included, breakfast cheap, 6 blocks from station toward Linzergasse and 6 blocks from river at Paracelsusstrasse 9, tel. 0662/879-649, fax 0662/878-810, www.yoho.at, office@yoho.at). This easygoing place speaks English first; has cheap meals, 160 beds, lockers, Internet access, laundry, tour discounts, and no curfew; plays *The Sound of Music* free daily at 13:30; runs a lively bar; and welcomes anyone of any age. The noisy atmosphere and lack of a curfew can make it hard to sleep.

EATING

Salzburg boasts many inexpensive, fun, and atmospheric places to eat. I'm a sucker for big cellars with their smoky, Old World atmosphere, heavy medieval arches, time-darkened paintings, antlers, hearty meals, and plump patrons. These places, all centrally located in the old town, are famous with visitors but are also enjoyed by the locals.

Gasthaus zum Wilder Mann is the place if the weather's bad and you're in the mood for *Hofbräu* atmosphere and a hearty, cheap meal at a shared table in one small, well-antlered room (€6–8 daily specials, Mon–Sat 11:00–21:00, closed Sun, smoky, 2 min from Mozart's birthplace, enter from Getreidegasse 22 or Griesgasse 17, tel. 0662/841-787). For a quick lunch, get the *Bauernschmaus,* a mountain of dumplings, kraut, and peasant's meats (€8).

Stiftskeller St. Peter has been in business for more than 1,000 years—it was mentioned in the biography of Charlemagne. It's classy (with strolling musicians) and central as can be, serving uninspired traditional Austrian cuisine (meals €15–25, daily 11:00–24:00, indoor/outdoor seating, next to St. Peter's church at foot of Mönchsberg, restaurant tel. 0662/841-268). They host the Mozart Dinner Concert described in "Music Scene," above (€45, nearly nightly at 20:00, call 0662/828-6950 to reserve).

Gasthaus zur Goldenen Ente (see "Sleeping," above) serves great food in an elegant, subdued hotel dining room or on a quiet pedestrian lane. The chef, Robert, specializes in roast duck *(Ente)* and Tirolean traditions. But he'll happily replace your kraut and dumplings with a wonderful selection of steamed green and orange vegetables for no extra charge. Their *Salzburger Nockerl,* the mountainous sweet soufflé served all over town, is big enough for four—try it (Tue–Sat 11:30–21:00, closed Sun–Mon, Goldgasse 10, tel. 0662/845-622).

Stieglkeller is a huge, atmospheric institution that has several rustic rooms and outdoor garden seating with a great rooftop view of the old town (May–Sept daily 10:00–23:00, closed Oct–April, 50 yards uphill from the lift to the fortress, Festungsgasse 10, tel. 0662/842-681).

Sternbräu Inn is a sprawling complex of popular eateries (traditional, Italian, self-serve, and vegetarian) in a cheery garden setting—explore both courtyards before choosing a seat (most restaurants open daily 9:00–24:00). One fancy, air-conditioned room hosts the *Sound of Music* dinner show (see "Music Scene," above).

Resch & Lieblich, wedged between the cliffside and the back of the big concert hall, is a rough and characteristic place popular with locals for salads, goulash, and light meals (daily 10:00–23:00, closed Sun off-season, indoor/outdoor seating in rustic little cellar or under umbrellas on square, Toscaninihof, tel. 0662/843-675).

Salzburg Center Restaurants

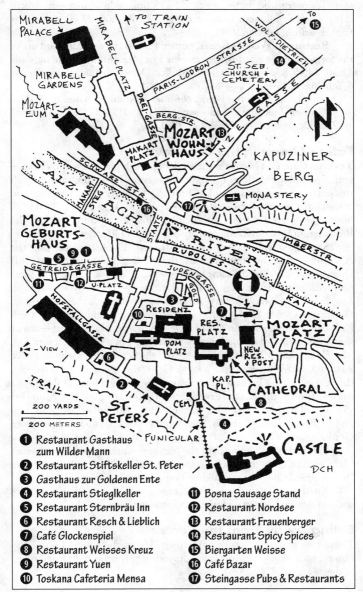

1. Restaurant Gasthaus zum Wilder Mann
2. Restaurant Stiftskeller St. Peter
3. Gasthaus zur Goldenen Ente
4. Restaurant Stieglkeller
5. Restaurant Sternbräu Inn
6. Restaurant Resch & Lieblich
7. Café Glockenspiel
8. Restaurant Weisses Kreuz
9. Restaurant Yuen
10. Toskana Cafeteria Mensa
11. Bosna Sausage Stand
12. Restaurant Nordsee
13. Restaurant Frauenberger
14. Restaurant Spicy Spices
15. Biergarten Weisse
16. Café Bazar
17. Steingasse Pubs & Restaurants

Café Glockenspiel, on Mozartplatz 2, is the place to see and be seen. It's overpriced, but—like St. Mark's Square in Venice—it's worth it if you want to linger and enjoy the spot (daily 9:00–23:00, closes earlier off-season, tel. 0662/841-403).

Restaurant Weisses Kreuz, nestled behind the cathedral and under the fortress, serves good Balkan cuisine in a pleasant dining room (daily 11:30–14:45 & 17:00–22:45, closed Tue Oct–mid-June, Bierjodlgasse 6, tel. 0662/845-641).

For a break from the *Wurst,* consider **Restaurant Yuen,** with darn good Chinese food and friendly service (daily 11:30–23:00, in courtyard at Getreidegasse 24, tel. 0662/843-770).

Eating Cheap in the Old Town

Toskana Cafeteria Mensa is the students' lunch place, fast and cheap—with fine indoor seating and a great courtyard for sitting outside with students and teachers instead of tourists. They serve a daily soup and main course special for €3.50 (Mon–Thu 8:30–17:00, Fri 8:30–15:00, hot meals served 11:00–13:30 only, closed Sat–Sun, behind the Residenz, in the courtyard opposite Sigmund-Haffnergasse 16).

Sausage stands serve the local fast food. The best places (like the Altstadt-Imbiss on the side of the Collegiate Church just off Universitätsplatz) use the same boiling water all day, which fills the weenies with more flavor. Key words: *Weisswurst*—boiled white sausage, *Bosna*—with onions and curry, *Käsekrainer*—with melted cheese inside, *Debreziner*—spicy Hungarian, *Frankfurter*—our weenie, *frische*—fresh ("eat before the noon bells"), and *Senf*—mustard (ask for sweet—*süss* or sharp—*scharf).* Only a tourist puts the sausage in a bun like a hot dog. Munch alternately between the meat and the bread (that's why you have 2 hands), and you'll look like a local. Generally, the darker the weenie, the spicier it is. The best spicy sausage is at the 54-year-old **Bosna Stand,** run by the chatty Frau Ebner (€2.40, to go only, Mon–Fri 11:00–19:00, May–Dec also Sat 11:00–17:00, July–Dec also Sun 16:00–20:00, hiding down the tunnel marked #33 across from Getriedegasse 40).

Picnickers will appreciate the bustling morning **produce market** (daily except Sun) on Universitätsplatz, behind Mozart's house (see "Self-Guided Old Town Walking Tour," above).

Nordsee, a popular chain, serves good, fast, and inexpensive seafood next to Mozart's House on Getreidegasse.

Eating Away from the Center

These two places are on the old-town side of the river, about a 15-minute walk along the river (river on your right) from the Staatsbrücke bridge.

Augustiner Bräustübl, a monk-run brewery, is rustic and crude. It's closed for lunch, but on busy nights, it's like a Munich beer hall with no music but the volume turned up. When it's cool, you'll enjoy a historic setting with beer-sloshed and smoke-stained halls. On balmy evenings, it's a Monet painting with beer breath under chestnut trees in the garden. Local students mix with tourists eating hearty slabs of schnitzel with their fingers or cold meals from the self-serve picnic counter, while children frolic on the playground kegs. Waiters only bring drinks. For food, go up the stairs, survey the hallway of deli counters, and assemble your meal (or, as long as you buy a drink, you can bring in your own picnic, open daily 15:00–23:00, Augustinergasse 4, tel. 0662/431-246; head up Müllner Hauptstrasse northwest along the river and ask for "Müllnerbräu," its local nickname). Don't be fooled by second-rate gardens serving the same beer nearby. Augustiner Bräustübl is a huge, 1,000-seat place within the Augustiner brewery. For your beer: Pick up a half-liter or full-liter mug (*shank* means self-serve price, *bedienung* is the price with waiter service), pay the lady, wash your mug, give Mr. Keg your receipt and empty mug, and you will be made happy.

For dessert—after a visit to the strudel kiosk—enjoy the incomparable floodlit view of old Salzburg from the nearby Müllnersteg pedestrian bridge and a riverside stroll home.

Krimplestätter employs 450 years of experience serving authentic old-Salzburger food in its authentic old-Austrian interior or its cheery garden (Tue–Sun 11:00–24:00, closed Mon all year and Sun Sept–April, Müllner Hauptstrasse 31, tel. 0662/432-274). For fine food with a wild finale, eat here and drink at the nearby Augustiner Bräustübl.

Eating on or near Linzergasse

These cheaper places are near the recommended hotels on Linzergasse.

Frauenberger is friendly, picnic-ready, and inexpensive, with indoor or outdoor seating (Mon 8:00–14:00, Tue–Fri 8:00–18:00, Sat 8:00–12:30, closed Sun, *Wurst* grill open longer hours and on Sun, across from Linzergasse 16).

Spicy Spices is a trippy vegetarian-Indian restaurant serving tasty curry and rice take-out, samosas, organic salads, vegan soups, and fresh juices (€5 lunch specials, Mon–Sat 10:00–22:00, Sun 12:00–21:00, Wolf-Dietrich Strasse 1, tel. 0662/870-712).

The very local **Biergarten Weisse** is closer to the hotels on Rupertgasse and away from the tourists (Mon–Sat 10:30–2:00, Sun 16:00–24:00, on Rupertgasse east of Bayerhamerstrasse, tel. 0662/872-246).

The copper-topped **Café Bazar,** overlooking the river between the Mirabell Gardens and the Staatsbrücke, is a great place for a classy drink with an old-town and castle view (Mon–Sat 7:30–24:00, closed Sun, Schwarzstrasse 3, tel. 0662/874-278).

TRANSPORTATION CONNECTIONS

By train, Salzburg is the first stop over the German–Austrian border. This means that if Salzburg is your only stop in Austria, and you're using a Eurail Selectpass that does not include Austria, you don't have to pay extra or add Austria to your pass to get here.

By train to: Innsbruck (direct every 2 hrs, 2 hrs), **Vienna** (2/hr, 3.5 hrs), **Hallstatt** (hrly, 50 min to Attnang Puchheim, 20-min wait, then 90 min to Hallstatt), **Reutte** (every 2 hrs, 4 hrs, transfer to a bus in Innsbruck), **Munich** (2/hr, 1.5–2). Train info: tel. 051717 (wait through long German recording for operator).

HALLSTATT AND THE SALZKAMMERGUT: AUSTRIA'S LAKE DISTRICT

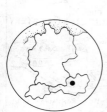

Commune with nature in Austria's Lake District. "The hills are alive," and you're surrounded by the loveliness that has turned on everyone from Emperor Franz Josef to Julie Andrews. This is *Sound of Music* country. Idyllic and majestic, but not rugged, it's a gentle land of lakes, forested mountains, and storybook villages, rich in hiking opportunities and inexpensive lodging. Settle down in the postcard-pretty, lake-cuddling town of Hallstatt.

ORIENTATION

(area code: 06134)

Lovable Hallstatt is a tiny town bullied onto a ledge between a selfish mountain and a swan-ruled lake, with a waterfall ripping furiously through its middle. It can be toured on foot in about 15 minutes. The town is one of Europe's oldest, going back centuries before Christ. The symbol of Hallstatt, which you'll see all over town, is two adjacent spirals—a design based on jewelry found in Bronze Age Celtic graves high in the nearby mountains.

The charms of Hallstatt are the village and its lakeside setting. Go there to relax, nibble, wander, and paddle. While tourist crowds can trample much of Hallstatt's charm in August, the place is almost dead in the off-season. The lake is famous for its good fishing and pure water.

Tourist Information: The friendly and helpful TI, on the main drag, can explain hikes and excursions, arrange private tours of Hallstatt (€65), and find you a room (April–Oct Mon–Fri 9:00–12:00 & 14:00–17:00, in July–Aug also Sat–Sun 10:00–14:00, Nov–March Mon–Fri 9:00–13:00, closed Sat–Sun, a block from Marktplatz toward lakefront parking, above post office, Seestrasse 169, tel. 06134/8208, www.hallstatt.net or www.inneres-salzkammergut.at). On Saturdays in July and August, the TI offers a €5 tour of the town in English (check with TI for details).

Hallstatt

NOT TO SCALE—
BUS STOP TO MARKTPLATZ
IS A 10 MINUTE WALK

SALT MINE

TO ECHERNTAL VALLEY

FUNICULAR

SMALL UPPER PARKING LOT #1 IN TUNNEL

CATHOLIC CHURCH & CEMETERY

BONE CHAPEL

TUNNEL

TO BAD ISCHL & SALZBURG

MAIN ROAD

DR. MORTON WEG

MUSEUM

MARKT PLATZ

GOSAUMUHL

GROC ROAD

TO MAIN

BUS STOP W.C. + PARKING LOT #2

BOAT RENTAL

PROT CHURCH

MARKT DOCK

BOAT RENTAL

TO OBERTRAUN

LAHN DOCK

POST

TO HALLSTATT TRAIN STATION

BOAT RENTAL

BADE-INSEL

HALLSTATTERSEE

❶ Gasthof Zauner
❷ Pension Hallberg
❸ Gasthof Simony
❹ Hotel/Restaurant Bräugasthof
❺ To Gasthof Grüner Anger & Launderette
❻ Helga Lenz Rooms
❼ Haus Trausner Rooms
❽ Herta Höll Rooms
❾ Gasthaus zur Mühle Hostel
❿ Pension Seethaler
⓫ Pension Sarstein
⓬ Rest. Grüner Baum
⓭ Strand Café

Planning Your Time

While there are plenty of lakes and charming villages, Hallstatt is really the only one that matters. One night and a few hours to browse are all you'll need to fall in love. To relax or take a hike in the surroundings, give it two nights and a day. It's a relaxing break between Salzburg and Vienna.

Arrival in Hallstatt

By Train: Hallstatt's train station is a wide spot on the tracks across the lake. *Stefanie* (a boat) meets you at the station and glides scenically across the lake into town (€1.90, meets each train until about 18:30—don't arrive after that). The last departing boat-train connection leaves Hallstatt around 18:15, and the first boat goes in the morning at 6:50 (9:20 on Sun). Walk left from the boat dock for the TI and most hotels. Since there's no train station in town, the TI can help you find schedule information, or check www.oebb.at.

By Car: The main road skirts Hallstatt via a long tunnel above the town. Parking is tight mid-June through mid-October. Hallstatt has several numbered parking areas outside the town center. Parking lot #1 is in the tunnel above the town (swing through to check for a spot, free with guest card). Otherwise, several numbered lots are just after the tunnel. If you have a hotel reservation, the guard will let you drive into town to drop your bags (ask if your hotel has any in-town parking). It's a lovely 10- to 20-minute lakeside walk to the center of town from the lots. Without a guest card, you'll pay €4.20 per day for parking. Off-season parking in town is easy and free.

Helpful Hints

Bike Rental: Hotel Grüner Baum, facing the market square, rents bikes (€6/half-day, €11/full day).

Parks and Swimming: Green and peaceful lakeside parks line the south end of Lake Hallstatt. If you walk 10 minutes south of town to Hallstatt-Lahn, you'll find a grassy public park, playground, and swimming area *(Badestrand)* with a fun man-made play island *(Bade-Insel)*.

Views: For a great view over Hallstatt, hike above Helga Lenz's *Zimmer* as far as you like (see "Sleeping," below), or climb any path leading up the hill. The 40-minute steep hike down from the salt-mine tour gives the best views (see "Sights," below).

Internet: Try Hallstatt Umbrella Bar (€4/hr, summers only, weather permitting—since it's literally under a big umbrella, halfway between Lahn boat dock and Museum Square at Seestrasse 145).

Laundry: A small full-service launderette is at the campground up from the *Bade-Insel,* just off the main road (about €8/load, mid-April–mid-Oct daily 7:00–12:00 & 15:00–22:00, closed off-season, tel. 06134/83224). In the center, Hotel Grüner Baum does laundry for non-guests (€11/load, facing Market Square).

HALLSTATT HISTORIC TOWN WALK

This short walk starts at the dock.

Boat Landing—There was a Hallstatt before there was a Rome. In fact, because of the importance of salt mining here, an entire epoch—the Hallstatt era, from 800 to 400 B.C.—is named for this important spot. Through the centuries, salt was traded and people came and went by boat. You'll still see the traditional *Fuhr* boats, designed to carry heavy loads in shallow water.

Towering above the town is the Catholic church. Its faded St. Christopher—patron saint of travelers with his cane and baby Jesus on his shoulder—watched over those sailing in and out. Until 1875, the only way into town was by boat. Then came the train and the road. The good ship *Stefanie* shuttles travelers back and forth from here to the Hallstatt train station immediately across the lake. The *Bootverleih* sign advertises boat rentals (see "Lake Trip," below).

Notice the one-lane road out of town (with the waiting time, width, and height posted). Until 1966, when a bigger tunnel was built above Hallstatt, all the traffic crept single file right through the town.

Look down the shore at the huge homes. Several families lived in each of these houses back when Hallstatt's population was about double its present 1,000; today, many of them rent rooms to visitors.

Parking is tight here in the tourist season. Locals and hotels have cards getting them into the prime town-center lot. From October through May, the barricade is lifted and anyone can park here. Hallstatt has snow for about three months each winter, but the lake hasn't frozen over since 1981.

See any swans? They've patrolled the lake like they own it since the 1860s, when Emperor Franz Josef and Empress Sissy—the Princess Di of her day—made this region their annual holiday retreat. Sissy loved swans, so locals made sure she'd see them here. During this period, the Romantics discovered Hallstatt, many top painters worked here, and the town got its first hotel.

Tiny Hallstatt has two big churches—Protestant (you can step into its grassy lakeside playground) and Catholic up above (described below, with its fascinating bone chapel). After the Reformation, most of Hallstatt was Protestant. Then, under Hapsburg rule, it was mostly Catholic. Today, 60 percent of the town is Catholic. Walk over the town's stream, past the Protestant church, one block to the...

Market Square—In 1750, a fire leveled this part of town. The buildings you see now are all late-18th-century and built of stone rather than burnable wood. Take a close look at the two-dimensional, up-against-the-wall pear tree (it likes the sun-warmed wall). The statue features the Holy Trinity. Continue a block past Gasthof Simony to the pair of phone booths and step into the...

Museum Square—Because 20th-century Hallstatt was of no industrial importance, it was untouched by World War II. But once upon a time, its salt was worth defending. High above, peeking out of the trees, is Rudolf's Tower (Rudolfsturm). Originally a 13th-century watchtower protecting the salt mines, and later the mansion of a salt-mine boss, it's now a restaurant with a great view. A zigzag trail connects the town with Rudolfsturm and the salt mines just beyond. The big white houses by the waterfall were water-powered mills that once ground Hallstatt's grain. If you hike up a few blocks, you'll see the river raging through town. Around you are the town's TI, post office, a museum, city hall, and the Dachstein Sport shop (with a prehistoric basement, described below). The statue on the square is of the mine manager who excavated prehistoric graves around 1850. Much of the *Schmuck* (jewelry) sold locally is inspired by the jewelry found in the area's Bronze Age tombs.

For thousands of years, people have been leaching salt out of this mountain. A brine spring sprung here, attracting Bronze Age people around 1500 B.C. Later, they dug tunnels to mine the rock, which was 70 percent salt, dissolved it into a brine, and distilled out salt—precious for preserving meat (and making french fries so tasty). For a look at early salt-mining implements, visit the museum.

SIGHTS

▲▲Hallstatt's Catholic Church and Bone Chapel—The Catholic church overlooks the town from above. From near the boat dock, hike up the covered stone stairway and follow signs to *Kath. Kirche*. The lovely church has 500-year-old altars and frescoes dedicated to St. Barbara (patron of miners) and St. Catherine (patron of foresters—lots of wood was needed to fortify the many miles of tunnels and boil the brine to distill out the salt). The last priest modernized parts of the church, but since Hallstatt is a UNESCO World Heritage Site, now they're changing it all back to its original state.

Behind the church, in the well-tended graveyard, is the 12th-century Chapel of St. Michael (even older than the church). Its bone chapel—or charnel house *(Beinhaus)*—contains more than 600 painted skulls. Each skull has been lovingly named, dated, and decorated (skulls with dark, thick garlands are oldest—18th century, those with flowers more recent—19th century). Space was so limited in this cemetery that bones had only 12 peaceful, buried years here before making way for the freshly dead. Many of the dug-up bones and skulls ended up in this chapel. They stopped this practice in the 1960s, about the same time the Catholic Church began permitting cremation (€1, mid-May–Sept daily 10:00–18:00, Easter–mid-May daily 11:00–16:00 and Oct daily 10:00–17:00 weather permitting, closed Nov–Easter).

▲World Heritage Hallstatt Museum—This newly redone museum tells the story of Hallstatt—with a special focus on the Hallstatt period (800–400 B.C.), when this little village was the crucial salt-mining hub of a culture that spread from France to the Balkans. Back then, Celtic tribes dug for precious salt, and Hallstatt was, as its name means, the "place of salt."

First you'll watch a video that takes you back in time 7,000 years. Then you'll walk through exhibits tracing the town's evolution to the present day. This fun museum—though pricey—is well organized into meaningful, bite-sized chunks. There are displays on everything from the region's flora and fauna to local artists and the surge in Hallstatt tourism during the Romantic age—and lots and lots of salt-mining artifacts. Everything's in German, but the €2 English guide explains most of it (€6, July–Aug daily 10:00–19:00, May–June and Sept–Oct daily

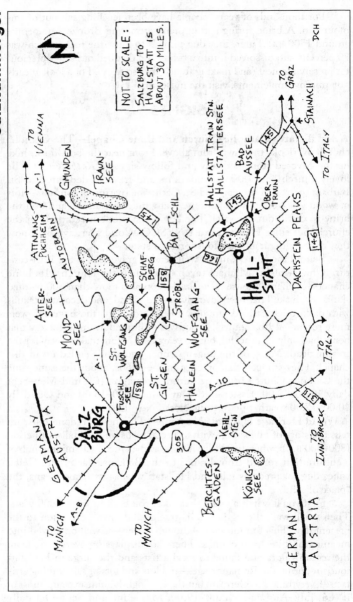

Salzkammergut

NOT TO SCALE:
SALZBURG TO
HALLSTATT IS
ABOUT 30 MILES.

9:00–18:00, Nov–April Tue–Sun 10:00–16:00, closed Mon, Seestrasse 56, adjacent to TI, tel. 06134/828-015). The Dachstein Sport shop across from the TI dug into a prehistoric site, and now its basement is another small museum (free).

▲**Lake Trip**—For a quick boat trip, you can ride *Stefanie* across the lake and back for €3.80. It stops at the tiny Hallstatt train station for 30 minutes, giving you time to walk to a hanging bridge and enjoy the peaceful, deep part of the lake. Longer lake tours are also available (€6.50/50 min, €8/75 min, www.hallstatt.net/schiffahrt, sporadic schedules—especially off-season—so check chalkboards by boat docks for today's times). Those into relaxation can rent a sleepy electric motorboat to enjoy town views from the water (two rental places: Riedler, next to ferry dock or near the Bräugasthof, tel. 06134/8320, or Hemetsberger, near Gasthof Simony, tel. 06134/8228; both daily in-season and in good weather until 19:00; boats have 2 speeds: slow and stop; €9/hr, spend an extra €3/hr for faster 500-watt boats).

▲▲**Salt Mine Tour**—If you have yet to pay a visit to a salt mine, Hallstatt's—which claims to be the oldest in the world—is a good one. You'll ride a steep funicular high above the town (funicular-€7.90 round-trip, €4.70 one-way, May–Sept daily 9:00–18:00, Oct until 16:30, closed Nov–April), take a 10-minute hike, check your bag and put on old miners' clothes, hike 650 feet higher in your funny outfit to meet your guide, load onto the train, and ride into the mountain through a tunnel actually made by prehistoric miners. Inside, you'll watch a great video (English headsets), slide down two banisters, and follow your guide. While the tour is mostly in German, the guide is required to speak English if you ask—so ask (salt mine tour-€14.50, €19.90 combo-ticket includes entrance and round-trip funicular, can buy mine tickets at cable car station, May–Sept daily 9:30–16:30, Oct daily 9:30–15:00, the 16:00 funicular departure catches the last tour at 16:30, no children under age 4, rarely a long wait but arrive after 15:00 and you'll find no lines and a smaller group, tel. 06132/200-2400). The well-publicized ancient Celtic graveyard excavation sites nearby are really dead (precious little to see). If you skip the funicular, the scenic 40-minute hike back into town is (with strong knees) a joy.

At the base of the funicular, notice train tracks leading to the Erbstollen tunnel entrance. This lowest of the salt tunnels goes many miles into the mountain, where a shaft connects it to the tunnels you just explored. Today, the salty brine from these tunnels flows 25 miles through the world's oldest pipeline to the huge modern salt works (next to the highway) at Ebensee. You'll pass a stack of the original 120-year-old wooden pipes between the lift and the mine.

SLEEPING

$$$ Gasthof Zauner is a business machine offering 12 pricey, modern, pine-flavored rooms on the main square (Sb-€46–53, Db-€84–98, prices depend on season and view, closed mid-Nov–mid-Dec, Marktplatz 51, tel. 06134/8246, fax 06134/82468, www.zauner.hallstatt.net, zauner @hallstatt.at).

$$$ Pension Hallberg-Tauchergasthof (Diver's Inn), across from the TI, has six big rooms and a funky mini-museum of WWII artifacts found in the lake (Sb-€40–75, Db-€60–110, rooms for up to 5 also available, price depends on size, cash preferred, tel. 06134/8709, fax 06134/82865, www.pension-hallberg.at.tf, hallberg@aon.at, Gerda the "Salt Witch" and Eckbert Winkelmann).

$$ Gasthof Simony, my 500-year-old favorite, is on the square, with a lake view, balconies, creaky wood floors, slippery rag rugs, antique furniture, a lakefront garden for swimming, and a huge breakfast. Reserve in advance. For safety, reconfirm your room and price a day or two before you arrive and call again if arriving late (S-€35, D-€45, Ds-€55, Db-€75, third person-€30 extra, cash preferred, Markt 105, tel. & fax 06134/8231, Susanna Scheutz SE).

$$ Bräugasthof Hallstatt is another creaky, friendly old place—a former brewery—with eight cozy, mostly lakeview rooms run by Susanna's sister and her family (Sb-€42, Db-€76, Tb-€110, Db/Tb cheaper for 3-night stays, just past TI on the main drag at Seestrasse 120, tel. 06134/8221, fax 06134/82214, braugasthof-fam.lobisser@aon.at, Lobisser family).

$$ Gasthof Pension Grüner Anger is a practical, modern 11-room place away from the medieval town center—the only place in town that doesn't squeak and creak. It's big and quiet, a few blocks from the base of the salt mine lift, and a 10-minute walk from Market Square (Sb-€30, Db-€63, €3 more per room July–Aug, more for 1-night stays July–Aug, third person-€15, non-smoking, free parking, Lahn 10, tel. 06134/8397, fax 06134/83974, www.hallstatt.net/gruener.anger, anger @aon.at, Sulzbacher family).

$ Helga Lenz is a five-minute climb above the Pension Seethaler (look for the green *Zimmer* sign). This big, sprawling, woodsy house has a nifty garden perch, wins the Best View award, and is ideal for those who sleep well in tree houses (S-€17—only available April–June & Oct, D-€30, Db-€36, T-€44, Tb-€51, 1-night stays-€2 per person extra, family room, no CC, closed Nov–March, Hallberg 17, tel. & fax 06134/8508, www.demregio.at/lenz, haus-lenz@aon.at).

$ Two *Zimmers* are a few minutes' stroll south of the center, just past the bus stop/parking lot and over the bridge: **Haus Trausner** has four clean, bright, new-feeling rooms (Ds-€35, Db-€38, Ts-€52.50, less for more than 1 night, no CC, Lahnstrasse 27, tel. 06134/8710,

SLEEP CODE

(€1 = about $1.10, country code: 43, area code: 06134)
Sleep Code: **S** = Single, **D** = Double/Twin, **T** = Triple, **Q** = Quad, **b** = bathroom, **s** = shower only, **no CC** = Credit Cards not accepted, **SE** = Speaks English, **NSE** = No English. Unless otherwise noted, credit cards are accepted, English is spoken, and breakfast is included.

To help you sort easily through these listings, I've divided the rooms into three categories, based on the price for a standard double room with bath:

$$$ **Higher Priced**—Most rooms €80 or more.
$$ **Moderately Priced**—Most rooms between €50–80.
$ **Lower Priced**—Most rooms €50 or less.

Hallstatt's TI can almost always find you a room (either in town or at B&Bs and small hotels outside of town—which are more likely to have rooms available and come with easy parking). Mid-July and August can be tight. Early August is worst. Hallstatt is not the place to splurge—some of the best rooms are in *Zimmers,* just as nice and modern as the bigger hotels, at half the cost. A bed in a private home costs about €20 with breakfast. It's hard to get a one-night advance reservation. But if you drop in and they have a spot, one-nighters are welcome. Prices include breakfast, lots of stairs, and a silent night. *"Zimmer mit Aussicht?"* means "Room with view?"—worth asking for. Only a few of my listings accept plastic, which goes for most businesses here.

trausner1@utanet.at, Maria Trausner SE), while **Herta Höll** rents out three rooms in a riverside house crawling with kids (Db-€40, apartment-€60, no CC, Malerweg 45, tel. 06134/8531, fax 06134/825-533, frank .hoell@aon.at).

$ **Gasthaus zur Mühle Jugendherberge,** below the waterfall, with the cheapest good beds in town, is popular for its great pizzas and cheap grub (21 rooms, bed in 3- to 20-bed coed dorms-€11, D-€24, sheets-€3 extra, family quads, breakfast-€3, big lockers with a €20 deposit, closed Nov, reception closed Tue Sept–mid-May—so arrange in advance if arriving on Tue, below tunnel car park, Kirchenweg 36, tel. & fax 06134/8318, toeroe.f@magnet.at, run by Ferdinand Törö).

$ **Pension Seethaler** is a dark, homey old lodge with 45 beds and a breakfast room mossy with antlers, perched above the lake. The confusing floor plan is like an M. C. Escher house with more fire hazards, and the staff won't win any awards for congeniality—*Zimmer* are friendlier and cheaper—but this place is a reasonable last resort (€18/person in S, D, T, or Q , €26/person in Db, Tb, or Qb, no CC, coin-op showers downstairs-€1/8 min, Dr. Morton Weg 22, find the stairs to the left of Seestrasse 116, at top of stairs turn left, tel. 06134/8421, pension .seethaler@kronline.at).

$ Ancient-feeling **Pension Sarstein** has 25 beds in basic, dusty rooms with flower-bedecked, lakeview balconies, in a charming building run by friendly Frau Fischer. You can swim from her lakeside garden (S-€18, D-€32, Ds-€44, Db-€50 with this book, Ds and Db have balconies, 1-night stays-€1.50 per person extra, no CC, leave the boat dock to the right and walk 200 meters to Gosaumühlstrasse 83, tel. 06134/8217, NSE).

EATING

You can enjoy good food inexpensively, with delightful lakeside settings. While everyone cooks the typical Austrian fare, your best bet here is trout. *Reinanke* trout is from Lake Hallstatt. Restaurants in Hallstatt tend to have unreliable hours and close early on slow nights, so don't wait too long to get dinner.

Feed the swans while your trout is being cooked at **Restaurant Bräugasthof** (fun menu and tasty food, May–Oct daily 10:00–21:00, closed Nov–April, tel. 06134/20012, see "Sleeping," above). Other lakefront options include **Restaurant Simony** (see "Sleeping," above) and **Hotel Grüner Baum** (May–Oct Tue–Sun 11:30–22:00, closed Mon and Nov–April, at bottom of Market Square, tel. 06134/8263).

While it lacks a lakeside setting, **Gasthof Zauner's** classy restaurant is well respected for its grilled meat and fish; the interior of its dining room is covered in real ivy that grows in through the windows (daily 11:30–14:30 & 17:30–22:00, closed Mon Feb–April, reservations smart, see "Sleeping," above).

For the best pizza in town with a fun-loving local crowd, chow down cheap and hearty at **Gasthaus zur Mühle** (daily 11:00–14:00 & 17:00–21:00, closed Tue and no lunch mid-Oct–mid-May, see "Sleeping," above).

Locals like the smoky **Strand Café,** a 10-minute lakeside hike away, near the town beach (April–Oct Tue–Sun 10:00–21:00, closed Mon and Nov–March, great garden setting on the lake, Seelande 102, tel. 06134/8234).

For your late-night drink, savor the market square from the trendy little pub called **Ruth Zimmermann** (June–Oct daily 9:00–2:00, Nov–May daily 12:00–2:00, tel. 06134/8306).

TRANSPORTATION CONNECTIONS

By train to: Salzburg (hrly, 90 min to Attnang Puchheim, short wait, 50 min to Salzburg), **Vienna** (hrly, 90 min to Attnang Puchheim, short wait, 2.5 hrs to Vienna). Day-trippers to Hallstatt can check bags at the Attnang Puchheim station. (Note: Connections there and back can be very fast—about 5 min; have coins ready for the lockers at track 1.) Train info: tel. 051717 (wait through long German recording for operator).

BRUGES
(Brugge)

With Renoir canals, pointy gilded architecture, vivid time-tunnel art, and stay-awhile cafés, Bruges is a heavyweight sightseeing destination as well as a joy. Where else can you ride a bike along a canal, munch mussels, wash them down with the world's best beer, savor heavenly chocolate, and see Flemish Primitives and a Michelangelo, all within 300 yards of a bell tower that jingles every 15 minutes? And there's no language barrier.

The town is Brugge (BROO-ghah) in Flemish, or Bruges (broozh) in French and English. Its name comes from the Viking word for wharf. Right from the start, Bruges was a trading center. In the 11th century, the city grew wealthy on the cloth trade.

By the 14th century, Bruges' population was 35,000, as large as London's. As the middleman in sea trade between Northern and Southern Europe, it was one of the biggest cities in the world and an economic powerhouse. In addition, Bruges had become the most important cloth market in Northern Europe.

In the 15th century, while England and France were slogging it out in a 100-year-long war, Bruges was the favored residence of the powerful Dukes of Burgundy—and at peace. Commerce and the arts boomed. The artists Jan van Eyck and Hans Memling had studios here.

But by the 16th century, the harbor had silted up and the economy had collapsed. The Burgundian court left, Belgium became a minor Hapsburg possession, and Bruges' Golden Age abruptly ended. For generations, Bruges was known as a mysterious and dead city. In the 19th century, a new port, Zeebrugge, brought renewed vitality to the area. And in the 20th century, tourists discovered the town.

Today Bruges prospers because of tourism: It's a uniquely well-preserved Gothic city and a handy gateway to Europe. It's no secret, but even with the crowds, it's the kind of city where you don't mind being a tourist.

Bruges' ultimate sight is the town itself, and the best way to enjoy that is to get lost on the back streets, away from the lace shops and ice-cream stands.

Planning Your Time

Bruges needs at least two nights and a full, well-organized day. Even non-shoppers enjoy browsing here, and the Belgian love of life makes a hectic itinerary seem a little senseless. With one day (other than a Monday, when all the museums are closed), the speedy visitor could do the Bruges town walk described below:

9:30	Climb the bell tower on the Market Square.
10:00	Tour the sights on the Burg Square.
11:00	Tour the Groeninge Museum.
12:00	Tour the Gruuthuse Museum.
13:00	Eat lunch and buy chocolates.
14:00	Take a short canal cruise (discount dock).
14:30	Visit the Church of Our Lady and see the Michelangelo Madonna.
15:00	Tour the Memling Museum.
16:00	Catch the Straffe Hendrik Brewery tour.
17:00	Calm down in the Begijnhof.
18:00	Ride a bike around the quiet back streets of town or take a horse-and-buggy tour.
20:00	Lose the tourists and find a dinner.

(If this schedule seems insane, skip the bell tower and the brewery—or stay another day.)

ORIENTATION

The tourist's Bruges (you'll be sharing it) is one square kilometer contained within a canal, or moat. Nearly everything of interest and importance is within a convenient cobbled swath between the train station and Market Square (a 15-min walk). Many of my quiet and charming recommended accommodations lie just beyond Market Square.

Tourist Information

The main office is on Burg Square (April–Sept Mon–Fri 9:30–18:30, Sat–Sun 10:00–12:30 & 14:00–18:30, Oct–March Mon–Fri 9:30–17:00, Sat–Sun 9:30–13:00 & 14:00–17:30, lockers, money-exchange desk, WC in courtyard, tel. 050-448-686, www.brugge.be). The other TI is at the train station (generally Tue–Sat 10:00–13:00 & 14:00–18:00, closed Sun–Mon).

The TIs sell a great €1 Bruges visitor's guide with a map and listings of all of the sights and services. You can also pick up a bimonthly English-language program called *events@brugge*. The TIs have information on

Bruges

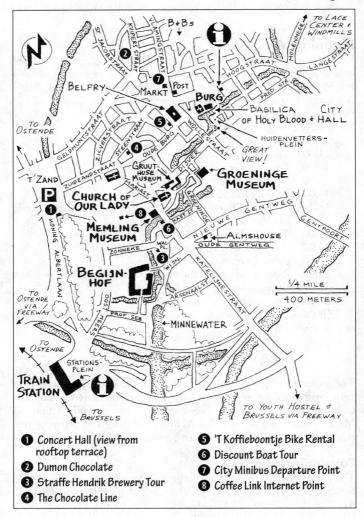

1. Concert Hall (view from rooftop terrace)
2. Dumon Chocolate
3. Straffe Hendrik Brewery Tour
4. The Chocolate Line
5. 'T Koffieboontje Bike Rental
6. Discount Boat Tour
7. City Minibus Departure Point
8. Coffee Link Internet Point

train schedules and on the many tours available (see "Tours," below). Bikers will want the "5X on the Bike around Bruges" map/guide (€1.25) that shows five routes through the countryside. Many hotels give free maps with more detail than the map the TIs sell.

Arrival in Bruges

By Train: Coming in by train you'll see the square bell tower marking the main square. Upon arrival, stop by the station TI to pick up the €1 Bruges visitor's guide (map in centerfold). The station lacks ATMs but has lockers (from €2, daily 6:00–24:00).

Your best way to get to the town center is by bus. All buses go directly to the Market Square. Simply hop on any bus, pay €1, and in four minutes you're there. The €1 tickets are good for an hour. A day pass costs €3. Buses #4 and #8 go farther, to the northeast part of town (to the windmills and recommended places on Carmersstraat).

Note that nearly all city buses go directly from the station to the Market Square and fan out from there. They then return to Market Square (bus #2 stops at post office on square; other buses stop at library on nearby Kuiperstraat) and go directly back to the station.

The **taxi** fare from the train station to most hotels is around €6 (tel. 050-334-444).

It's a 20-minute **walk** from the station to the center—no fun with your luggage. If you want to walk, cross the busy street and canal in front of the station, head up Oostmeers, and turn right on Zwidzandstraat to reach Market Square.

You can rent a **bike** at the station for the duration of your stay, but other bike-rental shops are closer to the center (see "Helpful Hints," below).

By Car: Park at the train station for just €2.50 per day; show your parking receipt for a free bus ride into town. There are pricier (€9/day) underground parking garages at 't Zand and around town, and these garages are well-marked. Driving in Bruges is very complicated because of the one-way system.

Helpful Hints

Bike Rental: 'T Koffieboontje, just under the bell tower, is extremely well organized and the handiest. They take a credit-card imprint for a deposit, and you're on your way with a nearly new bike (€3/1 hr, €6/4 hrs, or €9/24-hr day, €6/day with an ISIC student card, free city maps and child seats, daily 9:00–22:00, the €15 "bike plus any 3 museums" deal could save enough to pay for lunch, Hallestraat 4, tel. 050-338-027).

Other rental places include the following: **Fietsen Popelier** (€6/4 hrs, €9/24 hrs, new bikes, no deposit, 50 yards from Church of Our Lady at Mariastraat 26, tel. 050-343-262), the less central **De Ketting** (cheap at €5/day, daily 9:00–20:00, Gentpoortstraat 23, tel. 050-344-196), and the **train station** (ticket window #3, daily 8:00–20:00, €9/day, €6.50/half day after 14:00, €20 deposit).

Internet Access: The relaxing **Coffee Link,** with mellow music and pleasant art, is centrally located across from the Church of Our

Lady (€2.20/30 min, daily 10:00–20:00, 16 terminals, Mariastraat 38, tel. 050-349-973).

Laundry: Bruges' most convenient place to do laundry is **Belfort Auto Wash** (daily 8:30–22:00, just off Market Square in an arcade at Sint Jakobsstraat 51, tel. 050-335-902). A less central launderette is at Gentpoortstraat 28 (daily 7:00–22:00).

Shopping: Shops are open from 9:00 to 18:00, a little later on Friday. Grocery stores are usually closed on Sunday. The main shopping street, Steenstraat, stretches from Market Square to the square called 't Zand. The Hema department store is at Steenstraat 73 (Mon–Sat 9:00–18:00).

Market Days: Wednesday morning (Market Square) and Saturday morning ('t Zand) are market days. On Saturday and Sunday afternoons, a flea market hops along Dijver in front of the Groeninge Museum.

Festival of Canals: In 2004, Bruges' famous festival will be held from Aug 20–28 (nightly 21:00–24:00).

Post Office: It's on Market Square near the bell tower (Mon–Fri 9:00–19:00, Sat 9:30–12:30, closed Sun, tel. 050-331-411).

Best Town View: The bell tower overlooking the Market Square rewards those who climb it with the ultimate town view. The best view without a climb is from the rooftop terrace of Bruges' concert hall (Concertgebouw). This seven-story building, built in 2002, is the city's only modern highrise (daily 11:00–23:00, free elevator, on edge of old town on 't Zand).

TOURS

Bruges by Boat—The most relaxing and scenic (though not informative) way to see this city of canals is by boat, with the captain narrating. Boats leave from all over town (€5.50, 4/hr, 10:00–17:00, copycat 30-min rides). Boten Stael offers an €0.80 discount with this book (just over the canal from Memling Museum at Katelijnestraat 4, tel. 050-332-771).

City Minibus Tour—City Tour Bruges gives a rolling overview of the town in an 18-seat, two-skylight minibus with dial-a-language headsets and video support (€9.50, 50 min). The tour leaves hourly from Market Square (10:00–19:00 in summer, until 18:00 in spring and fall, less in winter, tel. 050-355-024). The narration, while clear, is slow-moving and boring. But the tour is a lazy way to cruise past virtually every sight in Bruges.

Walking Tour—Local guides walk small groups through the core of town (€5, daily July–Aug, Sat–Sun only in June and Sept, depart from TI at 15:00, 2 hrs, no tours off-season). Though earnest, the tours are heavy on history and in two languages, so they may be less than peppy. Still, to propel you beyond the pretty gables and canal swans of Bruges, they're good medicine. A private two-hour guided tour costs €40

MUSEUM TIPS

Admission prices are steep but include great audioguides—so plan on spending some time and getting into it. The information number for all museums is 050-448-711.

Combo-Ticket: The TIs and participating museums sell a museum combo-ticket (any 5 museums for €15). Since the Groeninge and Memling museums cost €8 each, anyone interested in art will save money with this pass.

Dark Monday: In Bruges, nearly all sights are open Tuesday through Sunday year-round from 9:30 to 17:00 and closed on Monday. If you're in Bruges on a Monday, consider a boat, bus, or walking tour (see "Tours," above).

(reserve at least 3 days in advance through TI, tel. 050-448-685); consider Christian Scharle (mobile 0476-493-203, tmb@skynet.be).

Horse-and-Buggy Tour—You'll see buggies around town ready to take you for a clip-clop tour (€28/30 min, price is per carriage, not per person).

SIGHTS

These sights are listed in walking order from Market Square to Burg Square to the cluster of museums around the Church of our Lady to the Begijnhof (10-min walk from beginning to end).

▲**Market Square (Markt)**—Ringed by banks, the post office, lots of restaurant terraces, great old gabled buildings, and the bell tower, this is the modern heart of the city (most city buses run from here to the train station). Under the bell tower are two great Belgian french-fry stands, a quadrilingual Braille description of the old town, and a metal model of the tower. In Bruges' heyday as a trading center, a canal came right up to this square.

Geldmuntstraat, just off the square, is a delightful street with many fun and practical shops and eateries.

▲▲**Bell Tower (Belfort)**—Most of this bell tower has presided over Market Square since 1300. The octagonal lantern was added in 1486, making it 290 feet high—that's 366 steps (daily 9:30–17:00, ticket window closes 45 min early, WC in courtyard). The view is worth the climb and the €5. Just before you reach the top, peek into the carillon room. The 47 bells can be played mechanically with the giant barrel and movable tabs (as they are on each quarter hour) or with a manual keyboard (as they are during concerts). The carillon player uses his fists and feet rather than fingers. Be there on the quarter hour, when things ring. It's *bellissimo* at the top of the hour.

BRUGES AT A GLANCE

▲▲▲**Groeninge Museum** World-class collection of mainly Flemish art. **Hours:** Tue–Sun 9:30–17:00, closed Mon.

▲▲**Bell Tower** 366 steps to a worthwhile view and a carillon close-up. **Hours:** Daily 9:30–17:00.

▲▲**Burg Square** Historic square with TI, sights, and impressive architecture. **Hours:** Always open.

▲▲**St. Jans Hospital/Memling Museum** Art by the greatest of the Flemish Primitives. **Hours:** Tue–Sun 9:30–17:00, closed Mon.

▲▲**Church of Our Lady** Tombs and church art, including Michelangelo's Madonna and Child. **Hours:** Tue–Sun 9:00–12:30 & 13:30–17:00, closed Mon.

▲▲**Begijnhof** Benedictine nuns' peaceful courtyard and Begijn's House museum. **Hours:** Courtyard always open, museum open daily 10:00–12:00 & 13:45–17:30, off-season closes at 17:00.

▲▲**Straffe Hendrik Brewery Tour** Fun and handy tour, includes beer. **Hours:** Daily on the hour 11:00–16:00, Oct–March 11:00 and 15:00 only.

Atop the tower, survey the town. On the horizon you can see the towns along the North Sea coast. Back on the square, facing the bell tower, turn left (east) onto the pedestrian-only Breidelstraat and thread yourself through the lace and *wafels* to Burg Square.

▲▲**Burg Square**—The opulent square called Burg is Bruges' civic center, historically the birthplace of Bruges and the site of the ninth-century castle of the first Count of Flanders. Today it's the scene of outdoor concerts and home of the TI (with a €0.25 WC). It's surrounded by six centuries of architecture.

▲**Basilica of the Holy Blood**—Originally the Chapel of Saint Basil, the church is famous for its relic of the blood of Christ which, according to tradition, was brought to Bruges in 1150 after the Second Crusade. The lower chapel is dark and solid—a fine example of Romanesque style. The upper chapel (separate entrance, climb the stairs) is decorated Gothic (museum is next to upper chapel, €1.25, April–Sept daily 9:30–12:00 & 14:00–18:00, Oct–March Thu–Tue 10:00–12:00 & 14:00–16:00, Wed 10:00–12:00 only, tel. 050-336-792).

▲▲**Biking** Explore the countryside and pedal to nearby Damme. **Hours** of 'T Koffieboontje bike rental: Daily 9:00–22:00.

▲**Market Square** Main square that is the modern heart of the city, with carillon bell tower. **Hours:** Always open.

▲**Basilica of the Holy Blood** Romanesque and Gothic church housing relic of the blood of Christ. **Hours:** April–Sept daily 9:30–12:00 & 14:00–18:00, Oct–March Thu–Tue 10:00–12:00 & 14:00–16:00, Wed 10:00–12:00.

▲**City Hall's Gothic Room** Beautifully restored hall from 1400. **Hours:** Daily 9:30–17:00.

▲**Gruuthuse Museum** 15th-century mansion with furniture, tapestries, even a guillotine. **Hours:** Tue–Sun 9:30–17:00, closed Mon.

▲**Chocolate** Sample Bruges' specialty: try Dumon, The Chocolate Line, Sweertvaegher, and on and on. **Hours:** Shops generally open 10:00–18:00.

▲**City Hall's Gothic Room**—Your ticket gives you a room full of old town maps and paintings and a grand, beautifully restored "Gothic Hall" from 1400. Its painted and carved wooden ceiling features hanging arches (€2.50, includes audioguide and admission to Renaissance Hall, daily 9:30–17:00, Burg 12).

Renaissance Hall (Brugse Vrije)—This elaborately-decorated room with a grand Renaissance chimney carved from oak by Bruges' Renaissance man, Lancelot Blondeel in 1531. If you're into heraldry, the symbolism (explained in the free English flier) makes this room worth a five-minute stop. If you're not, you'll wonder where the rest of the museum is (€2.50, includes audioguide and admission to City Hall's Gothic Room, Tue–Sun 9:30–12:30 & 13:30–17:00, closed Mon, entrance in corner of square at Burg 11a).

▲▲▲**Groeninge Museum**—This museum houses a world-class collection of mostly Flemish art, from van Eyck to Memling to Magritte, including some fine Flemish works from the 1400s. Early Flemish art is less appreciated and understood today than the Italian Renaissance art produced a century later. But by focusing on a few masterpieces, you can get a sense of this subtle, technically advanced, and beautiful style (€8, Tue–Sun 9:30–17:00, closed Mon, Dijver 12, tel. 050-448-751).

▲**Gruuthuse Museum**—The 15th-century mansion of a wealthy Bruges merchant displays period furniture, tapestries, coins, and musical instruments. Nowhere in the city do you get such an intimate look at the materialistic revolution of Bruges' glory days. With the help of the excellent and included audioguide, just browse through rooms of secular objects that are both functional and beautiful (€6, Tue–Sun 9:30–17:00, closed Mon, Dijver 17).

▲▲**Church of Our Lady**—The church stands as a memorial to the power and wealth of Bruges in its heyday. A delicate *Madonna and Child* by Michelangelo is near the apse (to the right if you're facing the altar). It's said to be the only Michelangelo statue to leave Italy in his lifetime (thanks to the wealth generated by Bruges' cloth trade). If you like tombs and church art, pay to wander through the apse (Michelangelo free, art-filled apse €2.50, Tue–Sun 9:00–12:30 & 13:30–17:00, closed Mon, Mariastraat).

▲▲**St. Jans Hospital/Memling Museum**—The former monastery/hospital complex has two entrances—one is to a welcoming Visitors Center (free), the other to the Memling Museum. The Memling Museum, in the monastery's former church, was once a medieval hospital and now contains six much-loved paintings by the greatest of the Flemish Primitives, Hans Memling (€8 includes fine audioguide, Tue–Sun 9:30–17:00, closed Mon, across the street from the Church of Our Lady, Mariastraat 38).

▲▲**Begijnhof**—*Begijnhofs* (pron. gutturally: buh-HHHINE-hof) were built to house women of the lay order called beguines, who spent their lives in piety and service (without having to take the same vows a nun would). For military or other reasons, there were more women than men in the medieval Low Countries. The order of beguines offered women (often single or widowed) a dignified place to live and work. When the order died out, many *begihnhofs* were taken over by towns for subsidized housing, but some became homes for nuns.

Bruges' begijnhof—now inhabited by Benedictine nuns—almost makes you want to don a habit and fold your hands as you walk under its wispy trees and whisper past its frugal little homes. For a good slice of Begijnhof life, walk through the simple museum (Begijn's House, left of entry gate, €2, has English explanations, daily 10:00–12:00 & 13:45–17:30, off-season closes at 17:00).

Minnewater—Just south of the Begijnhof is Minnewater, an idyllic world of flower boxes, canals, and swans.

Almshouses—Walking from the Begijnhof back to the town center, you might detour along Nieuwe Gentweg to visit one of about 20 almshouses in the city. At #8, go through the door marked "Godshuis de

Meulenaere 1613" (free) into the peaceful courtyard. This was a medieval form of housing for the poor. The rich would pay for someone's tiny room here in return for lots of prayers.

Bruges Experiences: Beer, Chocolate, Lace, and Biking

▲▲Straffe Hendrik Brewery Tour—Belgians are Europe's beer connoisseurs. This fun and handy tour is a great way to pay your respects. The happy gang at this working family brewery gives entertaining and informative 45-minute, three-language tours (often by friendly Inge, €4 including a beer, lots of very steep steps, great rooftop panorama, daily on the hour 11:00–16:00, 11:00 and 15:00 are your best times to avoid groups, Oct–March 11:00 and 15:00 only, 1 block past church and canal, take a right down skinny Stoofstraat to #26 on Walplein, tel. 050-332-697).

At Straffe Hendrik (Strong Henry), they remind their drinkers: "The components of the beer are vitally necessary and contribute to a well-balanced life pattern. Nerves, muscles, visual sentience, and a healthy skin are stimulated by these in a positive manner. For longevity and lifelong equilibrium, drink Straffe Hendrik in moderation!"

Their bistro, where you'll be given your beer (included with the tour), serves quick and hearty lunch plates. You can eat indoors with the smell of hops or outdoors with the smell of hops. This is a great place to wait for your tour or to linger afterward.

▲Chocolate—Bruggians are connoisseurs of fine chocolate. You'll be tempted by chocolate-filled display windows all over town. While Godiva is the best big-factory/high-price/high-quality brand, there are plenty of smaller, family-run places in Bruges that offer exquisite handmade chocolates.

Perhaps Bruges' smoothest and creamiest chocolates are at **Dumon** (€1.70/100 grams). Madam Dumon and her children (Stefaan and Christophe) make their top-notch chocolate daily and sell it fresh just off Market Square (Thu–Tue 10:00–18:00, closed Wed, old chocolate molds on display in basement, Eiermarkt 6, tel. 050-346-282, www.chocolatierdumon.com). Their *ganache,* a dark creamy combo, wows chocoholics. The Dumons don't provide English labels because they believe it's best to describe their chocolates in person.

Locals and tourists alike flock to **The Chocolate Line** (€3.20/100 grams) for their *"gastronomique"* varieties—unique concoctions such as Havana cigar (marinated in rum, cognac, and Cuban tobacco leaves—so therefore technically illegal in the United States), lemon grass, ginger (shaped like a Buddha), saffron curry (a white elephant), and a spicy chili. My fave: the sheets of chocolate with crunchy roasted cocoa beans. The kitchen—busy whipping up their 80 varieties—is on display in the back (Mon–Sat 9:30–18:00, Sun from 10:30, Simon Stevinplein 19, between Church of Our Lady and Market Square, tel. 050-341-090).

The smaller **Sweertvaegher,** near Burg Square, features top-quality chocolate (€2.60/100 grams) that's darker rather than sweeter, made with fresh ingredients and no preservatives (Tue–Sun 9:30–18:15, closed Mon, Philipstockstraat 29, tel. 050-338-367).

For a different experience, try chocolate fondue as a dessert at **'t Fonduehuisje** (€19-cheese or *bourguignonne* fondue, €6.50-chocolate fondue, Fri–Wed 18:00–22:00, closed Thu, Wijngaardstraat 20, tel. 050-335-557).

Lace and Windmills by the Moat—A 10-minute walk from the center to the northeast end of town brings you to four windmills strung along a pleasant grassy setting on the "big moat" canal (between Kruispoort and Dampoort, on Bruges side of the moat). One windmill (St. Janshuismolen) is open to visitors (€2, daily 9:30–12:30 & 13:30–17:00, closed Oct–April, at the end of Carmersstraat).

To actually see lace being made, drop by the nearby **Lace Centre,** where ladies toss bobbins madly while their eyes go bad (€2 includes afternoon demonstrations and a small lace museum called Kantcentrum, as well as the adjacent Jeruzalem Church; Mon–Fri 10:00–12:00 & 14:00–18:00, until 17:00 on Sat, closed Sun, Peperstraat 3, tel. 050-330-072). The **Folklore Museum,** in the same neighborhood, is cute but forgettable (€3, daily 9:30–17:00, closed Mon, Rolweg 40, tel. 050-330-044). To find either place, ask for the Jeruzalem Church.

Two lace shops with good reputations are **'t Apostelientje** (Mon–Fri 9:30–18:00, Sat 9:30–17:00, Sun 10:00–13:00, tel. 050-337-860, Balstraat 11, near the Lace Centre) and the little **Lace Shop,** which has been run by the Muylle family for four generations and can offer lace-making demonstrations (daily 9:30–18:00, Wijngaardstraat 32, near Begijnhof, tel. 050-336-406).

▲▲**Biking**—The Flemish word for bike is *fiets* (pron. feets). While the sights are close enough for easy walking, the town is a treat to bike through. And a bike quickly gets you into the dreamy back lanes without a hint of tourism. Take a peaceful evening ride through the back streets and around the outer canal. Consider keeping a bike for the duration of your stay. It's the way the locals get around in Bruges.

Rental shops have maps and ideas. The TI sells a handy "5X on the Bike around Bruges" map/guide (€1.25) describing five different bike routes (10–18 miles) through the idyllic countryside nearby. The best trip is 30 minutes along the canal out to Damme and back (described below). The Belgium/Netherlands border is a 40-minute pedal beyond Damme.

SLEEPING

Hotels

$$$ **Hotel Heritage** offers 24 rooms in a completely modernized old building. It's tastefully decorated and has all the amenities. It's a great splurge (standard Db-€135, superior Db-€177, deluxe Db-€218, singles take a double for nearly the same cost, extra bed-€40, suites available, air-con, non-smoking, elevator, free Internet access, sauna, tanning bed, fitness room, bike rental for €6.50/half day, €10/day, Niklaas Despars-straat 11, a block north of Market Square, tel. 050-444-444, fax 050-444-440, www.hotel-heritage.com, info@hotel-heritage.com, run by cheery and hardworking Johan and Isabelle).

$$$ **Hotel Egmond** is quietly located in the middle of the melancholy Minnewater. Its eight 18th-century rooms have all the comforts (Sb-€92, Db-€120, Tb-€150, no CC, for longer stays ask about their apartments a few blocks away, free parking, Minnewater 15, tel. 050-341-445, fax 050-342-940, www.egmond.be, info@egmond.be).

$$$ **Crowne Plaza Hotel Brugge** is the most modern, comfortable, and central hotel option. It's just like a fancy American hotel, each of its 96 air-conditioned rooms equipped with a magnifying mirror and trouser press (Db-€225-240, prices drop as low as €180 on weekdays and off-season, elevator, pool, Burg 10, tel. 050-446-844, fax 050-446-868, www.crowneplaza.com).

$$ **Hotel Adornes** is small and classy—a great value. It has 20 comfy rooms with full, modern bathrooms in a 17th-century canalside house, and offers free parking, free loaner bikes, and a cellar lounge with games and videos (Db-€90-110 depending upon size, singles take a double for nearly the same cost, Tb-€125, Qb-€135, elevator, near Van Nevel B&B, mentioned below, and Carmersstraat at St. Annarei 26, tel. 050-341-336, fax 050-342-085, www.adornes.be, hotel.adornes @proximedia.be, Nathalie runs the family business, Britt provides a warm welcome).

$$ **Hotel Patritius,** family-run and centrally located, is a grand circa-1830 neoclassical mansion with 16 stately rooms, a plush lounge and breakfast room, and a courtyard garden (small Db-€85, Db-€90-99, Tb-€130, free parking, Riddersstraat 11, tel. 050-338-454, fax 050-339-634, www.hotelpatritius.be, hotel.patritius@proximedia.be, Garrett and Elvi Spaey).

$$ **Hotel Botaniek** has three stars, nine rooms, and a quiet location a block from Astrid Park (Db-€92, big Db-€96, Tb-€105, Qb-€115, eight percent discount for 3 nights, elevator, Waalsestraat 23, tel. 050-341-424, fax 050-345-939, hotel.botaniek@pi.be).

In a jam you might try these large, well-located hotels of lesser value: $$ **Hotel ter Reien** (26 rooms, Db-€90, Langestraat 1, tel. 050-349-100, hotel.ter.reien@online.be) and $$ **Hotel Sablon** (the "oldest

SLEEP CODE

(€1 = about $1.10, country code: 32)
Sleep Code: **S** = Single, **D** = Double/Twin, **T** = Triple, **Q** = Quad, **b** = bathroom, **s** = shower only, **no CC** = Credit Cards not accepted. Unless otherwise noted, credit cards are accepted. Everyone speaks English.

To help you sort easily through these listings, I've divided the rooms into three categories based on the price for a standard double room with bath:

$$$ **Higher Priced**—Most rooms €110 or more.
$$ **Moderately Priced**—Most rooms between €75–110.
$ **Lower Priced**—Most rooms €75 or less.

Most places are located between the train station and the old center, with the most distant (and best) being a few blocks beyond Market Square to the north and east. B&Bs offer the best value (listed after "Hotels"). All include breakfast, are on quiet streets, and (with a few exceptions) keep the same prices throughout the year. Bruges is most crowded Friday and Saturday evenings Easter through October—with July and August weekends being worst.

Bruges is a great place to sleep, with Gothic spires out your window, no traffic noise, and the cheerily out-of-tune carillon heralding each new day at 8:00 sharp. (Thankfully the bell tower is silent from 22:00 to 8:00.)

hotel in town" with 36 rooms, Sb-€89, Db-€110, Tb-€126, Noordzandstraat 21, tel. 050-333-902, info@sablon.be).

$ Hotel Cavalier, which has more stairs than character, rents 8 decent rooms and serves a hearty buffet breakfast in a royal setting (Sb-€50-52, Db-€59-64, Tb-€73-78, Qb-€80-85, 2 lofty "backpackers' doubles" on fourth floor-€42 or €47, Kuipersstraat 25, tel. 050-330-207, fax 050-347-199, hotel.cavalier@skynet.be, run by friendly Viviane de Clerck).

$ Hotel Cordoeanier, a family-run place, rents 22 bright, simple, modern rooms on a quiet street two blocks off Market Square (Sb-€52-65, Db-€65-70, Tb-€72-80, Qb-€85, Quint/b-€97, higher prices are for bigger rooms, small groups should ask about holiday house across the street, Internet access, Cordoeanierstraat 16, tel. 050-339-051, fax 050-346-111, www.cordoeanier.be, Kris, Veerle, Guy, and family).

Bruges Hotels

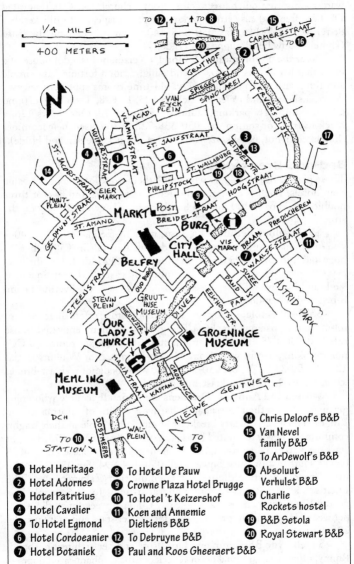

1/4 MILE

400 METERS

Chris Deloof's B&B
Van Nevel family B&B
To ArDewolf's B&B
Absoluut Verhulst B&B
Charlie Rockets hostel
B&B Setola
Royal Stewart B&B

1 Hotel Heritage
2 Hotel Adornes
3 Hotel Patritius
4 Hotel Cavalier
5 To Hotel Egmond
6 Hotel Cordoeanier
7 Hotel Botaniek

8 To Hotel De Pauw
9 Crowne Plaza Hotel Brugge
10 To Hotel 't Keizershof
11 Koen and Annemie Dieltiens B&B
12 To Debruyne B&B
13 Paul and Roos Gheeraert B&B

$ Hotel de Pauw is tall, skinny, and family-run, with straightforward rooms on a quiet street across from a church (Sb-€60, renovated Db-€75, free and easy street parking or pay garage, Sint Gilliskerkhof 8, tel. 050-337-118, fax 050-345-140, www.hoteldepauw.be, info @hoteldepauw.be, Philippe and Hilde).

Near the Train Station: $ Hotel 't Keizershof is a dollhouse of a hotel that lives by its motto, "Spend a night, not a fortune." It's simple and tidy, with seven small, cheery, old-time rooms split between two floors, a shower and toilet on each (S-€25, D-€38, T-€60, Q-€70, no CC, free and easy parking, laundry service-€7.50, Oostmeers 126, a block in front of station, tel. 050-338-728, http://users.belgacom.net /hotel.keizershof, hotel.keizershof@belgacom.net, Stefaan and Hilde).

Bed-and-Breakfasts

These places, run by people who enjoy their work, offer a better value than hotels. Each is central and offers lots of stairs and two or three doubles you'd pay €100 for in a hotel. Parking is generally easy on the street.

$$ Absoluut Verhulst is a great, modern-feeling B&B in a 400-year-old house, run by friendly Frieda and Benno (Sb-€50, Db-€75, huge and lofty suite-€95 for 2, €115 for 3, and €125 for 4, 1-night stays pay €10 extra per room, no CC, 5-min walk east of Market Square at Verbrand Nieuwland 1, tel. & fax 050-334-515, www.b-bverhulst.com, b-b.verhulst@pandora.be).

$$ B&B Setola, run by Lut and Bruno Setola, offers three modern rooms and a spacious breakfast/living room in their renovated house (Sb-€50, Db-€75, Tb-€75, 1-night stay-€10 extra per room, no CC, non-smoking, 6-min walk from Market Square, Sint Walburgastraat 12, tel. 050-334-977, fax 050-332-551, www.bedandbreakfast-bruges .com, setola@bedandbreakfast-bruges.com).

$ Koen and Annemie Dieltiens are a friendly couple who enjoy getting to know their guests and sharing a wealth of information on Bruges. You'll eat a hearty breakfast around a big table in their bright, comfortable, newly renovated house (Sb-€50, Db-€55, Tb-€75, 1-night stays pay €10 extra per room, no CC, non-smoking, Waalse Straat 40, 3 blocks southeast of Burg Square, tel. 050-334-294, fax 050-335-230, http://users.skynet.be/dieltiens, koen.dieltiens@skynet.be). The Dieltiens also rent a cozy studio and apartment for 2-6 people in a nearby 17th-century house (2 people pay €350 per week for studio, €400 per week for apartment, prices higher for shorter stays and more people, 20 percent cheaper off-season).

$ Debruyne B&B, run by Marie-Rose and her architect husband, Ronny, offers artsy, original decor (check out the elephant-sized doors—Ronny's design) and genuine warmth. If the Gothic is getting medieval, this is refreshingly modern (Sb-€50, Db-€55, Tb-€75, 1-night stay-€10 extra per room, no CC, non-smoking, free Internet, 7-min walk north of Market Square, Lange Raamstraat 18, tel. 050-347-606, fax 050-340-285, www.bedandbreakfastbruges.com).

$ **Paul and Roos Gheeraert** live on the first floor, while their guests take the second. This neoclassical mansion with big, bright, comfy rooms is another fine value (Sb-€50, Db-€55, Tb-€75, no CC, strictly non-smoking; rooms have coffeemakers, TVs, and fridges; Riddersstraat 9, 4-min walk east of Market Square, tel. 050-335-627, fax 050-345-201, http://users.skynet.be/brugge-gheeraert, gheeraert .brugge@skynet.be). They also rent three modern, fully equipped apartments and a large loft nearby (3-night minimum).

$ **Chris Deloof's** big, homey rooms are a good bet in the old center. Check out the fun, lofty A-frame room upstairs (Sb-€50, Ds/Db-€55, pleasant breakfast room and a royal lounge, no CC, non-smoking, Geerwijnstraat 14, tel. 050-340-544, fax 050-343-721, www .sin.be/chrisdeloof, chris.deloof@pi.be). Chris also rents a nearby apartment (Qb-€70-80) and a holiday house for a family or group of up to five (€100-150).

$ The **Van Nevel family** rents three attractive top-floor rooms with built-in beds in a 16th-century house (D-€45-55, Db-€60, third person pays €17, no CC, non-smoking, 10-min walk from Market Square, or bus #4 or #8 from train station or Market Square to Carmersbridge, Carmersstraat 13, tel. 050-346-860, fax 050-347-616, www.brugesbb .com, Robert.VanNevel@advalvas.be). Robert, who works at the Memling Museum, enthusiastically shares the culture and history of Bruges with his guests.

$ **ArDewolf's B&B** is a family-friendly place warmly run by Nicole and Arnold in a stately, quiet neighborhood at the edge of the old town near the windmills and moat (S-€30, D-€35-37, T-€50, Q-€60, Quint-€70, no CC, Oostproosse 9, tel. 050-338-366, www.ardewolf.be). From the train station, take bus #4 to Sasplein. Walk to the path behind the first windmill and turn left on Oostproosse.

$ **Royal Stewart B & B,** run by Scottish Maggie, has three thoughtfully-decorated rooms in a 17th-century house which was inhabited by nuns until 1953 (D/Db-€57, no CC, pleasant breakfast rooms, non-smoking, Genthof 25-27, 5-min walk from Market Square, tel. & fax 050-337-918, r.stewart@pandora.be).

Hostels

Bruges has several good hostels offering beds for around €10-12 in two- to eight-bed rooms (singles go for about €15). Breakfast is about €3 extra. The American-style **Charlie Rockets** bar and hostel is the liveliest and most central (56 beds, €14 per bed, 2-6 per room, no CC, Hoogstraat 19, tel. 050-330-660, fax 050-343-630, www.charlierockets.com). The dull **Snuffel Travelers Inn** (Ezelstraat 47, tel. 050-333-133) and

Bruges Restaurants

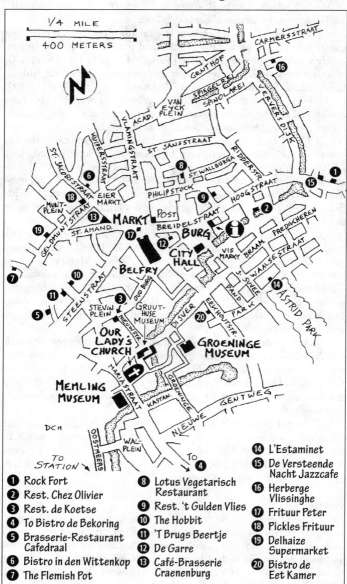

1 Rock Fort
2 Rest. Chez Olivier
3 Rest. de Koetse
4 To Bistro de Bekoring
5 Brasserie-Restaurant Cafedraal
6 Bistro in den Wittenkop
7 The Flemish Pot
8 Lotus Vegetarisch Restaurant
9 Rest. 't Gulden Vlies
10 The Hobbit
11 'T Brugs Beertje
12 De Garre
13 Café-Brasserie Craenenburg
14 L'Estaminet
15 De Versteende Nacht Jazzcafe
16 Herberge Vlissinghe
17 Frituur Peter
18 Pickles Frituur
19 Delhaize Supermarket
20 Bistro de Eet Kamer

the funky **Passage** (Dweerstraat 26, tel. 050-340-232; its hotel next door rents €40 doubles) are both small, loose, and central.

EATING

Bruges' specialties include mussels cooked a variety of ways (one order can feed two), fish dishes, grilled meats, and french fries. Don't eat before 19:30 unless you like eating alone. Tax and service are always included.

You'll find plenty of affordable, touristy restaurants on flood-lit squares and along dreamy canals. Bruges feeds 3.5 million tourists a year, and most are seduced by a high-profile location. These can be fine experiences for the magical setting and views, but the quality of food and service is low. I wouldn't blame you for eating at one of these places, but I won't recommend any. I prefer the candle-cool bistros that flicker on back streets.

Rock Fort is a chic new eight-table place with a modern, fresh coziness and a high-powered respect for good food. Two young chefs (Peter and Hermes) give their French cuisine a creative twist, and after just a few months in business became the talk of the town (€10 Mon–Fri lunch special with coffee, €15–20 beautifully presented dinner plates, Thu–Tue 12:00–14:30 & 18:00–23:00, closed Wed and at lunch on Sun, great pastas and salads, reservations smart for dinner, Langestraat 15, tel. 050-334-113).

Restaurant Chez Olivier—a classy, white-tablecloth, 10-table place—is considered the best fancy French cuisine splurge in town. While delicate Anne serves, her French husband, Olivier, is busy cooking up whatever he found freshest that day. While you can order à la carte, it's wise to go with the recommended daily *menu* (3-course lunch €35, 4-course dinner-€55, wine adds €20, 12:00–13:30 & 19:00–21:30, closed Sun and Thu, reserve for dinner, Meestraat 9, tel. 050-333-659).

Restaurant de Koetse is a good bet for central, affordable, quality local-style food. The ambience is traditional, yet fun and kid-friendly. The cuisine is Belgian and French with a stress on grilled meat, seafood, and mussels (3-course meals for €25, €20 plates include vegetables and a salad, Fri–Wed 12:00–15:00 & 18:00–22:00, closed Thu, smoke-free section, wheelchair accessible, Oude Burg 31, tel. 050-337-680).

Bistro de Eetkamer (the Living Room) is an intimate eight-table place offering stay-awhile elegance, uppity service, and fine French/Italian cuisine—but only to those with a reservation (fine 4-course €42 menu, Thu–Mon 12:00–14:00 & 18:30–22:00, closed Tue–Wed, just south of Market Square, Eekhout 6, tel. 050-337-886).

Bistro de Bekoring—a cute, candlelit Gothic place—is tucked within two almshouses that were joined together. Rotund and friendly Chef Roland and his wife Gerda love serving traditional Flemish food from a small menu (€30 dinners, Wed–Sat open from 12:00 and from 18:30, closed Sun–Tue, out past Begijnhof at Arsenaalstraat 53, tel. 050-344-157).

Brasserie-Restaurant Cafedraal is boisterous and fun-loving, serving a local crowd good-quality modern European cuisine with the accent on French and fish. The high-ceilinged room is rustic but elegantly candlelit and the back bar sparkles in a brown way (€10 2-course lunches, €24 dinner plates, Tue–Sat 12:00–15:00 & 18:00–23:00, closed Sun–Mon, Zilverstraat 38, tel. 050-340-845).

Bistro in den Wittenkop, very Flemish, is a cluttered, laid-back, old-time place specializing in the beer-soaked equivalent of beef Bourguignon (€15–19 main courses, Tue–Sat 12:00–14:00 & 18:00–24:00, closed Sun–Mon, terrace in back, Sint Jakobsstraat 14, tel. 050-332-059).

The Flemish Pot (a.k.a. The Little Pancake House) is a cute restaurant serving delicious, inexpensive pancake meals (savory and sweet) and homemade *wafels* for lunch. Then at 18:00, enthusiastic chefs Mario and Rik stow their waffle irons and pull out a traditional menu of vintage Flemish plates (good €15 dinner menu, daily 10:00–22:00, just off Geldmuntstraat at Helmstraat 3, tel. 050-340-086).

Lotus Vegetarisch Restaurant serves good vegetarian lunch plates (€9 *plat du jour* offered daily), salads, and homemade chocolate cake in a smoke-free, pastel-elegant setting without a trace of tie-dye (Mon–Sat 11:45–14:00, closed Sun, just off Burg at Wapenmakersstraat 5, tel. 050-331-078).

Restaurant 't Gulden Vlies—romantic and candlelit, quiet and less "ye olde" than the other places—serves when the others are closed. The *menu* is Belgian and French with a creative twist (€16 plates, €25 monthly menu, Wed–Sun 19:00–03:00, closed Mon–Tue, Mallebergplaats 17, tel. 050-334-709).

The Hobbit is a popular grill house across the street from the recommended bar 't Brugs Berrtje (listed below). It features an entertaining menu, including all-you-can-eat spareribs with salad for €13—nothing fancy, just good basic food in a fun traditional setting (daily 18:00–24:00, Kemelstraat 8-10, tel. 050-335-520).

Bars Offering Light Meals, Beer, and Ambience

Stop into one of the city's atmospheric bars for a light meal or a drink with great Bruges ambience. Straffe Hendrik (Strong Henry), a potent and refreshing local brew, is—even to a Bud Lite kind of guy—obviously great beer. Among the more unusual to try: Dentergems (with coriander and orange peel) and Trappist (a malty, usually dark, monk-made beer). Non-beer drinkers enjoy Kriek (a cherry-flavored beer) and Frambozen Bier (raspberry-flavored beer).

Any pub or restaurant carries the basic beers, but for a selection of more than 300 types, including brews to suit any season, drink at **'t Brugs Beertje.** For a light meal, consider their traditional cheese plate (Thu–Tue 16:00–24:00, closed Wed, Kemelstraat 5, tel. 050-339-616).

Another good place to gain an appreciation of the Belgian beer culture is **de Garre.** Rather than a noisy pub scene, it has a more dressy sit-down-and-focus-on-your-friend-and-the-fine-beer ambience (huge selection, off Breidelstraat, between Burg and Markt, on tiny Garre alley, daily 12:00–24:00, tel. 050-341-029).

Cafe-Brasserie Craenenburg is one of the few decent places on Markt Square, good for a coffee or beer in a historic setting (daily 8:00–23:00, Markt 16, tel. 050-333-402).

L'Estaminet is a youthful, trendy, jazz-filled eatery. Away from the tourists, it's popular with local students who come for hearty €7 spaghetti (11:30–24:00, closed Mon afternoon and all day Thu, facing peaceful Astrid Park at Park 5, tel. 050-330-916).

De Versteende Nacht Jazzcafe is another popular young hangout serving vegetarian dishes, salads, and pastas on Langestraat 11 (€12.50 meals, Tue–Thu 19:00–24:00, Fri–Sat 18:00–24:00, closed Sun–Mon, live jazz on Wed from 21:00, tel. 050-343-293).

Herberge Vlissinghe, the oldest pub in town (1515), serves hot snacks in a great atmosphere (Wed–Sun open from 11:00 on, closed Mon–Tue, Blekersstraat 2, tel. 050-343-737).

Fries, Fast Food, and Picnics

Local french fries *(frites)* are a treat. Proud and traditional *frituurs* serve tubs of fries and various local-style shish kebabs. Belgians dip their *frites* in mayonnaise, but ketchup is there for the Yankees (along with spicier sauces). For a quick, cheap, and scenic meal, hit a *frituur* and sit on the steps or benches overlooking Market Square, about 50 yards past the post office. The best fries in town are from **Frituur Peter**—twin takeaway carts on the Market Square at the base of the bell tower (daily 10:00–24:00).

Pickles Frituur, a block off Market Square, is handy for sit-down fries. Run by Marleen, its forte is greasy, fast, deep-fried Flemish corn dogs. The "menu 2" comes with three traditional gut bombs (Mon–Sat 11:00–24:00, at the corner of Geldmuntstraat and Sint Jakobstraat, tel. 050-337-957).

Delhaize Supermarket is great for picnics (push-button produce pricer lets you buy as little as one mushroom, Mon–Sat 9:00–18:00, Fri until 18:30, closed Sun, 3 blocks off the Market Square on Geldmuntstraat). The small **Delhaize grocery** is on Market Square opposite the bell tower (Mon–Sat 9:00–12:00 & 14:00–18:00, Sun 14:00–18:00). For midnight munchies, you'll find Indian-run corner grocery stores.

Belgian Waffles

While Americans think of "Belgian" waffles for breakfast, the Belgians (who don't eat waffles or pancakes for breakfast) think of *wafels* as Liège-style (dense, sweet, eaten plain, and heated up) and Brussels-style (lighter, often with powdered sugar or whipped cream and fruit, served in teahouses only in the afternoons from 14:00–18:00). You'll see waffles sold at restaurants and take-away stands.

For good €1.50 Liège-style *wafels,* stop by **Tea-Room Laurent** (Steenstraat 79) or **Restaurant Hennon** (between Market Square and Burg at Breidelstraat 16).

TRANSPORTATION CONNECTIONS

From Brussels, an hour away by train, all of Europe is at your fingertips. Train info: tel. 050-302-424.

By train to: Brussels (2/hr, usually at :33 and :59, 1 hr, €10), **Ghent** (4/hr, 40 min), **Ostende** (3/hr, 15 min), **Köln** (6/day, 4 hrs), **Paris** (hrly via Brussels, 2.5 hrs, must pay supplement of €10.50 second class,€21 first class, even with a railpass), **Amsterdam** (hrly, 3.5 hrs, transfer in Antwerp or Brussels), **Amsterdam's Schiphol Airport** (hrly, 3.5 hrs, transfer in Antwerp or Brussels, €35).

Trains from England: Bruges is an ideal "welcome to Europe" stop after London. Take the Eurostar train from London to Brussels under the English Channel (8/day, 2.5 hrs), then transfer, backtracking to Bruges (2/hr, 1 hr).

PRAGUE

It's amazing what 14 years of freedom can do. Prague has always been historic. Now it's fun, too. No place in Europe has become so popular so quickly. And for good reason: The capital of the Czech Republic—the only major city of central Europe to escape the bombs of the last century's wars—is one of Europe's best-preserved cities. It's filled with sumptuous Art Nouveau facades, offers tons of cheap Mozart and Vivaldi, and brews the best beer in Europe. But even beyond its architecture and traditional culture, it's an explosion of pent-up entrepreneurial energy jumping for joy after 40 years of Communist rule. And its low prices will make your visit enjoyable and nearly stress-free.

Planning Your Time

Two days (with 3 nights, or 2 nights and a night train) make the long train ride in and out worthwhile and give you time to get beyond the sightseeing and enjoy Prague's fun-loving ambience. Many wish they'd scheduled three days for Prague. From Munich, Berlin, and Vienna, it's about a five-hour train ride. Also from Munich, you could take a longer night train.

With two days in Prague, I'd spend a morning seeing the castle and a morning in the Jewish Quarter—the only two chunks of sightseeing that demand any brainpower. Spend your afternoons loitering around the Old Town, Charles Bridge, and the Little Quarter and your nights split between beer halls and live music. Keep in mind that Jewish sites close on Saturday.

ORIENTATION

Locals call their town "Praha." It's big, with 1.2 million people, but focus on its small old-town core during a quick visit. I will refer to the tourist landmarks in English (with the Czech name in parentheses). Study the map and learn these key places:

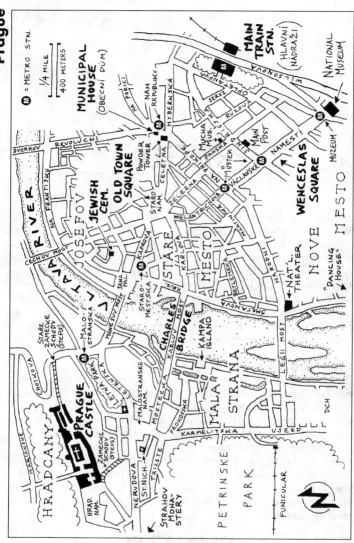

Main Train Station:	*Hlavní Nádraží* (hlav-nee nah-dra-shzee)
Old Town:	*Staré Město* (sta-rey min-yes-toh)
Old Town Square:	*Staroměstské Náměstí* (star-roh-min-yes-ststi-keh nah-min-yes-tee)
New Town:	*Nové Město* (no-vay min-yes-toh)

Little Quarter:	*Malá Strana* (mah-lah strah-nah)
Jewish Quarter:	*Josefov* (yoo-zef-fohf)
Castle Area:	*Hradčany* (hrad-chah-nee)
Charles Bridge:	*Karluv Most* (kar-loov most)
Wenceslas Square:	*Václavske Náměstí* (vah-slawf-skeh nah-min-yes-tee)
The River:	*Vltava* (vul-tah-vah)

The Vltava River divides the west side (castle and Little Quarter) from the east side (train station, Old Town, New Town, and nearly all of the recommended hotels). Prague addresses come with a general zone. Praha 1 is in the old center on either side of the river. Praha 2 is in the new city south of Wenceslas Square. Praha 3 and higher indicate a location farther from the center.

Tourist Information

TIs are at four key locations: **main train station** (Easter–Oct Mon–Fri 9:00–19:00, Sat–Sun 9:00–16:00; Nov–Easter Mon–Fri 9:00–18:00, Sat 9:00–15:00, closed Sun), **Old Town Square** (Easter–Oct Mon–Fri 9:00–19:00, Sat–Sun 9:00–18:00; Nov–Easter Mon–Fri 9:00–18:00, Sat–Sun 9:00–17:00, tel. 224-482-018), **below Wenceslas Square** at Na Príkope 20 (Easter–Oct Mon–Fri 9:00–19:00, Sat–Sun 9:00–17:00; Nov–Easter Mon–Fri 9:00–18:00, Sat 9:00–15:00, closed Sun, tel. 224-226-088), and the castle side of **Charles Bridge** (Easter–Oct daily 10:00–18:00, closed Nov–Easter). They offer maps, phone cards, information on guided walks and bus tours, and bookings for concerts, hotel rooms, and rooms in private homes. There are several monthly events guides—all of them packed with ads—including *Prague Guide* (29 kč), *Prague This Month* (free), and *Heart of Europe* (free, summer only). The English-language *Prague Post* is handy for entertainment listings and current events.

Helpful Hints

Formalities: Travel in Prague is like travel in western Europe—15 years ago and for half the price. Americans don't need a visa, but because of a recent reciprocation flap, Canadians do need a visa. Just flash your passport at the border. The U.S. Embassy in Prague is near the Little Quarter Square, or Malostranske Náměstí (Trziste 15, tel. 257-530-663). Since Eurailpasses don't cover the Czech Republic, you'll need to buy train tickets or a Prague Excursion pass for your travels to and from Prague (see "Transportation Connections—Prague," below).

Rip-offs: Prague's new freedom comes with new scams. There's no particular risk of violent crime—but green, rich tourists do get taken by con artists. Simply be on guard: traveling on trains (thieves thrive on overnight trains), changing money (tellers anywhere with bad arithmetic and inexplicable pauses while counting back your change), dealing with taxis (see "Getting around Prague," below), and in restaurants (see "Eating in Prague," below).

Anytime you pay for something, make a careful note of how much it costs, how much you're giving them, and—most importantly—how much you expect back. Don't let them get away with giving you any less. Remember how Czechs—and all Europeans— write their numbers: 1's have a long tail (which makes them look like 7's to American eyes), and 7's are crossed. Someone selling you a phone card marked 190 kč might first tell you it's 790 kč, hoping to pocket the difference. Call the bluff and they'll pretend it never happened.

Plainclothes policemen "looking for counterfeit money" are con artists. Don't show them your cash. If you are threatened with a fine by a "policeman," conductor, or other official, ask for the receipt that they are legally required to provide. Pickpockets (who can be little children or adults dressed as professionals, or even as tourists) target Western tourists. Many thieves drape jackets over their arms to disguise busy fingers. Be careful if anyone creates a commotion at the door of a metro or tram car (especially the made-for-tourists trams #22 and 23)—it's a smokescreen for theft. Car theft is also a big problem in Prague (many western European car-rental companies don't allow their rentals to cross the Czech border). Never leave anything valuable in your car—not even in broad daylight in the middle of Old Town Square.

Telephoning: Czech phones work like any in Europe. For international calls, buy a phone card at a kiosk or your hotel (various prices). If you call the United States directly (dial 00-1, the area code, and the number) from a public phone booth with the local phone card, you'll get about three minutes for $1. If you start with 0521 instead of 001, the connection won't be as good but you'll save about 30 percent (since the connection is carried over the Internet). The Czech Republic doesn't use area codes, so you'll dial the same number whether you're calling across the street or across the country. To call Prague from abroad, dial the international code (00 in Europe or 011 in the U.S.), the Czech Republic code (420), then the local number. For cheap calls to America, get a PIN card; ask for an international calling card (cards differ in cost per minute; compare rates before you buy, or ask the clerk for advice).

Money: 30 crowns (kč, *koruna* in Czech) = about U.S. $1. ATMs are everywhere and offer the best way to change money. Don't exchange too much; Czech money is tough to change in the West.

There is no black market. Assume anyone trying to sell money on the streets is peddling obsolete (or Bulgarian) currency. Buy and sell easily at the station (5 percent fees), banks, or hotels. Change bureaus advertise no commission and decent but deceptive rates.

These rates are for selling dollars. Their rates for buying your dollars are worse. Hidden fees abound; ask exactly how many crowns you'll walk away with before you agree to the transaction.

American Express: Václavske Náměstí 56, Praha 1 (foreign exchange daily 9:00–19:00, travel service Mon–Fri 9:00–18:00, Sat 9:00–12:00, closed Sun, tel. 222-211-136).

Internet Access: Internet cafés—which beg for business all along Karlova Street on the city side of the Charles Bridge—are commonplace. Consider Bohemia Bagel (see "Eating," below).

Laundry: The launderette nearest most recommended hotels is at Karolíny Světlé 10 (200 kč/load, Mon–Sat 7:30–19:00, closed Sun, 200 yards from Charles Bridge on Old Town side).

Medical Help: For English-speaking help, contact the American Medical Center (open 24 hrs, Janovskeho 48, Praha 7, tel. 220-807-756). A 24-hour pharmacy is at Palackeho 5 (Praha 1, tel. 224-946-982).

Local Help: Athos Travel books rooms (see "Sleeping," below); rents cars; has guides for hire (1–5 people-700 kč/hr, see "Tours," below); and perhaps best of all, provides stress-free taxi transfers to and from your hotel and airport (1–4 people-550 kč) or either train station (1–4 people-200 kč, see "Arrival in Prague," below; tel. 241-440-571, fax 241-441-697). Readers of this book get a discount for booking online (2 percent discount on rooms or car rental, 10 percent discount on local guide or airport and train station transfers); to get the discount, log on to www.athos.cz with Username: Rick, Password: Steves.

Magic Praha is a tiny travel service run by hardworking, English-speaking Lida Steflova. A charming Jill-of-all-trades who takes her clients' needs seriously, she's particularly helpful with accommodations, private tours, side trips to historic towns, and airport or train station transfers anywhere in the Czech Republic (Národní 17, Praha 1, 5th floor, tel. 224-232-755, mobile 604-207-225, emergency home tel. & fax 235-325-170, magicpraha@magicpraha.cz).

Best Views: Enjoy "the golden city of a hundred spires" during the early evening, when the light is warm and the colors are rich. Good viewpoints include the restaurant terrace at the Strahov Monastery (above the castle), the top of St. Vitus Cathedral at the castle, Petřín Tower (Eiffel's little brother—take funicular up from Malá Strana south of castle), the top of the east tower of Charles Bridge, the Old Town Square clock tower, and the steps of the National Museum overlooking Wenceslas Square.

Language: Czech, a Slavic language, has little resemblance to western European languages. These days, English is "modern," and you'll find the language barrier minimal. If you speak German, it's helpful. An acute accent means you linger on that vowel. The little accent above the c, s, or z makes it ch, sh, or zh.

Learn these key Czech words:

Hello/Goodbye (familiar)	*Ahoj* (ah-hoi)
Good day, Hello (formal)	*Dobrý den* (DOH-bree den)
Yes/No	*Ano* (AH-no)/*Ne* (neh)
Please	*Prosím* (proh-zeem)
Thank you	*Děkuji* (dyack-quee)
You're welcome	*Prosím* (proh-zeem)
Where is...?	*Kde je...?* (gday yeh)
Do you speak English?	*Mluvíte anglicky?* (MLOO-vit-eh ANG-litz-key)
crown (the money)	*koruna* (koh-roo-nah)

Arrival in Prague

Prague unnerves many travelers—it's relatively run-down, it's behind the former Iron Curtain, and you've heard stories of rip-offs and sky-high hotel prices. But in reality, Prague is charming, safe, and ready to show you a good time.

By Train: Most travelers coming from and going to the West use the main station (Hlavní Nádraží) or the secondary station (Nádraží Holešovice). Trains to other points within the country use Masarykovo or Smíchov stations. (For information on getting to Prague, see "Transportation Connections—Prague," below.)

Upon arrival, change money. The stations have ATMs (at the main station, a cash machine is near the subway entrance). Exchange bureau rates vary—compare by asking at two windows what you'll get for $100 (but keep in mind that many of the windows are run by the same company). Count carefully. At an exchange window or the tobacco stand, buy a city map with trams and metro lines marked and tiny sketches of the sights for ease in navigating (many different brands, 40–69 kč). It's a mistake to try doing Prague without a good map—you'll refer to it constantly. Confirm your departure plans at the train information window. Consider arranging a room or tour at the TI or AVE travel agency (AVE has branches in both stations). The left-luggage counter is reportedly safer than the lockers.

At Prague's train stations, anyone arriving on an international train will be met at the tracks by room hustlers (snaring tourists for cheap rooms).

At Prague's main station, **Hlavní Nádraží,** the orange, low-ceilinged hall is a fascinating mix of travelers, kiosks, gamblers, loitering teenagers, and older riffraff. The creepy station ambience is the work of Communist architects, who took a classy building and made it just big. If you're killing time here (or for a glimpse of a more genteel age), go upstairs into the Art Nouveau hall. The station was originally named

Prague Metro

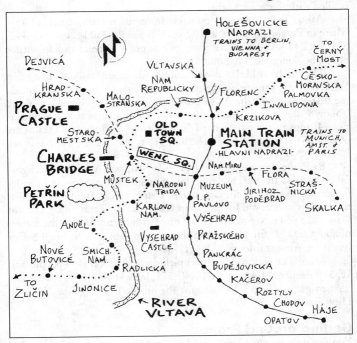

for Emperor Franz Josef, later named for President Woodrow Wilson (his promotion of self-determination led to the creation of the free state of Czechoslovakia in 1918), and then called simply the Main Station by the Communists (who weren't big fans of Wilson). Here, under an elegant dome, you can trace this history as you sip coffee, enjoy music from the 1920s, and watch new arrivals spilling into the city.

From the main station, it's a 10-minute walk to Wenceslas Square (turn left out of the station and follow Washingtonova to the huge Narodni Museum and you're there). You can also catch tram #9 (or, at night, tram #55 or #58; to find the stop, walk into park, head 2 min to right) or take the metro (inside station, look for the red M with 2 directions: Muzeum or Florenc; take Muzeum, then transfer to the green line—direction Dejvická—and get off at either Můstek or Staroměstska; these stops straddle the Old Town).

The courageous and savvy get a cabby to treat them fairly and get to their hotel fast and sweat-free for no more than 150 kč (see "Getting around Prague," below; to avoid the train station taxi stand, call AAA Taxi (tel. 233-113-311) or ride the metro a stop and catch one on the street. The park in front of the station—nicknamed Sherwood Forest—is filled with thieves at night.

Athos Travel provides transfers from either train station to anywhere in Prague (1–4 people-200 kč, 5–8 people-350 kč, tel. 241-440-571, fax 241-441-697, www.athos.cz); to get a 10 percent discount for online booking, see "Helpful Hints," above.

The **Nádraží Holešovice** station is suburban mellow. The main hall has all the services of the main station in a compact area. Outside the first glass doors, the ATM is on the left, the metro is straight ahead (follow *Vstup*, which means "entrance," take it 3 stops to the main station, 4 stops to the city center Muzeum stop), and taxis and trams are outside to the right (allow 200 kč for a cab to the center). Train info tel. 224-224-200.

By Plane: Prague's new, tidy, low-key **Ruzyně Airport**—a delightful contrast to the old, hulking, dreary main train station—is 12 miles (about 30 min) west of the city center. Your hotel can arrange for a shuttle minibus to take you to the airport economically. Taxis called "Airport Cars" take you into town at a fixed rate (without turning on the meter) of about 600 kč; firmly establish the price to your specific hotel before boarding. Airport info: tel. 220-113-314.

Athos Travel provides airport pick-up or drop-off (1–4 people-550 kč, 5–8 people-900 kč, tel. 241-440-571, fax 241-441-697, www.athos.cz); to get a 10 percent discount for online booking, see "Helpful Hints," above.

Getting around Prague

You can walk nearly everywhere. But the Metro is slick, the trams fun, and the taxis quick and easy once you're initiated. For details, pick up the handy transit guide at the TI.

Public Transport: The trams and metro work on the same cheap tickets. Buy from machines (select ticket price, then insert coins) at kiosks or purchase at hotels. For convenience, buy all the tickets you think you'll need: 15-minute ticket—8 kč, 60-minute ticket—12 kč, 24-hour ticket—70 kč, three-day pass—200 kč. Estimate conservatively. Remember, Prague is a great walking town, so unless you're commuting from a hotel far outside the center, you will likely find that individual tickets work best. You technically have to pay an additional 6 kč to transport luggage, but the rule is rarely enforced. The metro closes at midnight, but some trams keep running all night (identified with white numbers on blue backgrounds at tram stops).

City maps show the tram/bus/metro lines. The three-line metro system is handy and simple, but doesn't serve many hotels and sights. Although it seems that all metro doors lead to the neighborhood of *Výstup*, that's simply the Czech word for "exit." Trams are also easy to use; track your route with your city map. They run every 5 to 10 minutes

Central Prague

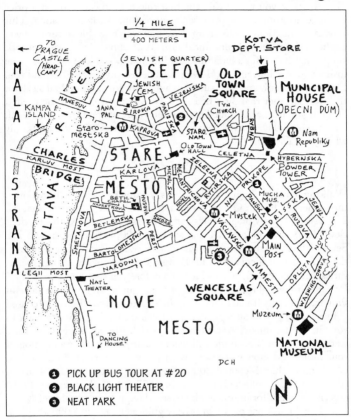

1 PICK UP BUS TOUR AT #20
2 BLACK LIGHT THEATER
3 NEAT PARK

in the daytime (a schedule is posted at each stop). Get used to hopping on and off. Be sure to always validate your ticket on the tram/bus/metro by sticking it in the machine (which stamps a time on it). Cheaters—including those who don't stamp their tickets—are fined 800 kč, or 400 kč if the fine is paid on the spot.

Taxis: Prague's taxis—notorious for meters that spin for tourists like pinwheels—are being tamed. Still, many cabbies are no-neck mafia types who consider one sucker a good day's work. While most hotel receptionists and guidebooks advise avoiding taxis, I find Prague is a great taxi town and use them routinely. With the local rate, they're cheap (read the rates on the door: drop charge—30 kč, per-kilometer charge—22 kč, and wait time per min—5 kč). Unfortunately, the meter isn't always reliable; some crooked cabbies use "turbo boxes" to speed it up.

Anytime you take a cab, the first rule is to always request a price estimate up front. If the price seems unreasonable, keep looking. This way, even the tricky turbo-charged cabbies won't be able to surprise you at the end with an astronomical fare. If a cabby tries to rip you off, simply pay 200 kč for a long ride. Let him follow you into the hotel if he insists you owe him more. (He won't.) The receptionist will defend you. Don't bother with any taxi parked in a touristy zone. If you hail a cab on the street (rather than at a taxi rank), you're most likely to be treated fairly. If you have a cab called from a hotel or restaurant (try AAA Taxi, tel. 233-113-311), you're likely to get a fair meter rate (which starts only when you take off).

TOURS

Walking Tours—Prague Walks offers walking tours of the Old Town, the castle, the Jewish Quarter, and more (all 300 kč, 90 min-3 hrs, tel. 261-214-603, www.praguewalks.com, pwalks@comp.cz). Consider their clever Good Morning Walk that starts at 8:00, before the crowds hit. Several other decent companies give guided walks. For the latest, pick up the walking tour fliers at the TI. Beware that the quality of these walks varies; find out exactly what's included before you sign on.

Private Guides—Hiring your own personal guide can be a great value in Prague, especially if you're traveling in a group. Athos Travel's licensed guides can lead you on a general sightseeing tour or tailor the walk to your interests: music, Art Nouveau, Jewish life, architecture, Franz Kafka, and more. The guide will meet you at your hotel or a location of your choice and show you exactly what you want to see (1–5 people-700 kč/hr, more than 5 people-800 kč/hr, arrange tour at least 24 hrs in advance, tel. 241-440-571, fax 241-441-697, info@athos.cz; to get a 10 percent discount for online booking, see "Helpful Hints," above).

The TI also has plenty of private guides (1 person-1,000 kč/3 hrs, 2 people-1,200 kč/3 hrs, 3 people-1,500 kč/3 hrs, 4 people-1,600 kč/3 hrs, desk at Old Town Square TI, arrange in person at least 2 hrs in advance, fax 224-482-380, guides.pis@volny.cz). For a listing of private guides, see www.guide-prague.cz.

Bus Tours—Cheap big-bus orientation tours provide an efficient once-over-lightly look at Prague and a convenient way to see the castle. But in a city as walkable as Prague, bus tours should be used only in case of rain, laziness, or both. Premiant City Tours—the best, yet still unexceptional—offers 20 different tours, including several overview tours of the city (1 hr-220 kč, 2 hrs-380 kč, 3.5 hrs-750 kč), the Jewish Quarter (700 kč, 2 hrs), Prague by night, Bohemian glass, Terezín Concentration Camp memorial, Karlštejn Castle, Český Krumlov (1,750 kč, 10 hrs), and a river cruise. The tours feature live guides (English and some-

PRAGUE AT A GLANCE

▲▲▲**Old Town Square** Magical main square of Old World Prague. **Hours:** Always open.

▲▲▲**Jewish Quarter** The most fascinating Jewish site in Europe, featuring various synagogues and an evocative cemetery. **Hours:** Sun–Fri 9:00–17:30, closed Sat.

▲▲▲**Charles Bridge** Atmospheric statue-lined bridge connecting the Old Town to the castle. **Hours:** Always open.

▲▲**Mucha Museum** Likeable collection of Art Nouveau works by Alfons Mucha. **Hours:** Daily 10:00–18:00.

▲▲**Wenceslas Square** Lively boulevard at the heart of modern Prague. **Hours:** Always open.

▲▲**Prague Castle** Traditional seat of Czech rulers, with St. Vitus Cathedral (listed below), the Old Royal Palace, the Basilica of St. George, and the shop-lined Golden Lane. **Hours:** April–Oct daily 9:00–17:00, Nov–March 9:00–16:00.

▲**St. Vitus Cathedral** The Czech Republic's most important church, featuring a climbable tower and a striking stained-glass window by Art Nouveau artist Alfons Mucha. **Hours:** April–Oct daily except Sunday morning, 9:00–17:00.

▲**Old Town Hall Astronomical Clock** Intricate landmark clock attracting throngs of gawking tourists. **Hours:** Always open.

Strahov Monastery and Library Baroque center of learning with ornate reading rooms and old-fashioned science exhibits. **Hours:** Daily 9:00–11:45 & 13:00–16:45.

times also German) and depart from near the bottom of Wenceslas Square at Na Príkope 23. Get tickets at an AVE travel agency, hotel, on the bus, or at Na Príkope 23 (tel. 224-946-922, mobile 606-600-123, www.premiant.cz).

Tram Joyride—Trams #22 and #23 (following the same route) both make a fine joyride through town. Consider it a scenic lead-up to touring the castle. Catch it at metro: Náměstí Míru, roll through a bit of new town, the old town, across the river, and hop out just above the castle (at Hotel Savoy, stop: Pohorelec, and hike down the hill into castle area).

Self-Guided Walking Tour

The King's Walk *(Královská cesta)*, the ancient way of coronation processions, is touristy but great. Pedestrian-friendly and full of playful diversions, it connects the essential Prague sites. The king would be crowned in St. Vitus Cathedral in the Prague Castle, walk through the Little Quarter to the Church of St. Nicholas, cross Charles Bridge, and finish at the Old Town Square. If he hurried, he'd be done in 20 minutes. Like the main drag in Venice between St. Mark's and the Rialto Bridge, this walk mesmerizes tourists. Use it as a spine, but venture off it—especially to eat.

While you could cover this route in the same direction as the king, he's long gone and it's a new morning in Prague. Here are Prague's essential sights in walking order, starting at Wenceslas Square, where modern independence was proclaimed, proceeding through the Old Town and across the bridge, and finishing at the castle. This walk laces together all the following recommended sights except the Jewish Quarter.

▲▲**Wenceslas Square (Václavske Náměstí)**—More a broad boulevard than a square (until recently, trams rattled up and down its park-like median strip), it's named for the equestrian statue of King Wenceslas that stands at the top of the boulevard.

The square is a stage for modern Czech history: The Czechoslovak state was proclaimed here in 1918. In 1968, the Soviets put down huge popular demonstrations here. Starting at the top (Metro: Muzeum), stroll down the square:

The **National Museum** (Národní Muzeum) stands grandly at the top. The only exciting thing about it is the view (80 kč, summer daily 10:00–18:00, winter daily 9:00–17:00, free first Mon of each month, closed first Tue of each month, halls of Czech fossils and animals).

The metro stop (Muzeum) is the cross point of two metro lines. From here, you could roll a ball straight down the boulevard and through the heart of Prague to Charles Bridge.

Stand behind the statue facing the museum (uphill). The light-colored patches in the columns are from the very recent repair of bullet holes from the Russian crackdown in 1968. Look left (about 10:00 on an imaginary clock) at the ugly Communist-era building—it housed the Parliament back when they voted with Moscow. A social-realism statue showing workers triumphing still stands at its base. It's now home to Radio Free Europe. After Communism fell, RFE lost its funding and could no longer afford its Munich headquarters. As gratitude for how its broadcasts kept their people in touch with real news, the current Czech government now rents the building to RFE for one crown a year.

As you wander down this great square, notice the fun mix of **architectural styles,** all post-1850: Romantic neo-Gothic, neo-Renaissance, neo-Baroque from the 19th century, Art Nouveau from 1900, ugly functionalism from the mid-20th century (the "form follows function," "ornamentation is a crime" answer to Art Nouveau), Stalin Gothic from the 1950s "Communist epoch" (a good example is the Jalta building—a block downhill on the right), and glass-and-steel buildings of the 1970s.

St. Wenceslas (Václav), commemorated by the statue, is the "good king" of Christmas-carol fame. He was never really a king, but the wise and benevolent 10th-century duke of Bohemia. A rare example of a well-educated and literate ruler, he was credited by his people for Christianizing his nation and lifting up the culture. Wenceslas astutely allied the Czechs with Saxony rather than Bavaria, giving the Czechs a vote when the Holy Roman Emperor was selected (and therefore more political importance). After being assassinated in 929, he became a symbol of Czech nationalism and statehood. Study the statue. Wenceslas is surrounded by the four other Czech patron saints. Notice the focus on books. A small nation without great military power, the Czech Republic chose national heroes who enriched the culture by thinking, rather than fighting. This statue is a popular meeting point. Locals say, "I'll see you under the horse's tail."

Thirty yards below the big horse is a small, round garden with a low-key **memorial** "to the victims of Communism"—such as Jan Palach. In 1969, a group of patriots decided that a self-immolation would stoke the fires of independence. They drew straws, and Jan Palach got the short one. He set himself on fire for the cause of Czech independence and died on this place. Czechs are keen on anniversaries. On the 20th anniversary of Palach's death, demonstrations stoked the popular fire which, 10 months later, led to the overthrow of the Czech Communist government.

Walk a couple of blocks downhill through the real people of Prague (not tourists) to the Grand Hotel Europa, with its hard-to-miss, dazzling, Art Nouveau exterior and plush café interior.

In November 1989, this huge square was filled with hundreds of thousands of ecstatic Czechs believing freedom was at hand. Assembled on the balcony of the Melantrich building (opposite the Grand Hotel Europa; look for the KNIHY sign) was a priest, a rock star (famous for his kick-ass-for-freedom lyrics), Alexander Dubček (hero of the 1968 revolt), and Václav Havel (the charismatic playwright, newly released from prison, and every freedom-loving Czech's Mandela). Through a sound system provided by the rock star, Havel's voice boomed over the gathered masses, announcing the resignation of the Czech politburo and saying the Republic of Czechoslovakia's freedom was imminent. Picture the cold November evening with thousands of Czechs jingling their key chains for solidarity, chanting, "It's time to go now!" (While the revolt stirred, government tanks could have given it the Tiananmen Square treatment—which spilled lots of patriotic blood in China just six months earlier. Locals figure Gorbachev must have made a phone call saying, "Let's not shed blood over this.")

Havel ended his second (and, constitutionally, last) five-year term early in 2003. He is still popular among Czechs, but his popularity took a hit when he got married for the second time—to an actress 17 years his junior. (Some say his brain dropped about three feet.)

Immediately opposite the Grand Hotel Europa is the **Lucerna Gallery** (use entry marked Divadlo Rokoko and work your way back to Lucerna). This is a classic mall from the 1920s and 1930s with shops, theaters, a ballroom in the basement, and the fine Lucerna café upstairs. Curiously, the place was built and is owned by the Havel family.

If you're ready for a coffee with a grand Wenceslas Square view (and if the building's renovation is completed), ride the elevator at the foot of Wenceslas Square (at Na Príkope 9, under cover near top of metro station) to the **Blue Terrace** restaurant (described below).

▲**Na Príkope**—The bottom of Wenceslas Square meets a spacious pedestrian mall lined with stylish shops. Na Príkope (meaning "the moat") follows the line of the old town wall, leading from Wenceslas Square right to a former gate in that wall, the Powder Tower (Prasná Brána, not worth touring). While the tower area is probably not worth the detour on this walk, consider these reasons to explore it later: City tour buses leave from along this street. And, next to the Powder Tower, the dazzling **Municipal House** (Obecní Dům), with a great Art Nouveau facade, contains three recommended restaurants (see "Eating," below).

Before you venture on, consider a stop at the **Museum of Communism** (turn right on Na Príkope, nestled between a McDonald's and a casino—somewhere, Stalin spins in his grave). The museum is a hodgepodge of artifacts from the Czech Republic's 40-year stint with Soviet economics. You'll find propaganda posters, busts of Communist All-Stars (Marx, Lenin, Stalin), and re-created slices of Communist life, from a bland store counter to a typical classroom (with a poem on the chalkboard extolling the virtues of the tractor). It's fun and described in English but lacks the cheeky spunk of other such museums in Eastern Europe (180 kč, daily 9:00–21:00, upstairs at Na Príkope 10, tel. 224-212-966, www.muzeumkomunismu.cz).

▲**Havelská Market**—Central Prague's best open-air flower and pro-duce market scene is a block toward the Old Town Square from the bottom of Wenceslas Square. Laid out in the 13th century for the German trading community, it still keeps hungry locals and vagabonds fed cheaply. Since only those who produce their goods personally are allowed to have a stall, you'll be dealing with the actual farmer or craftsperson.

Czech Sex—The strip between the base of Wenceslas Square and the market is notorious for its sex clubs, filled mostly with Russian girls and German and Asian guys. Be warned: These routinely rip off naive tourists and can be dangerous.

▲▲▲**Old Town Square (Staroměstské Náměstí)**—The focal point for most visits, this has been a market square since the 11th century. It became the nucleus of a town (Staré Město) in the 13th century when its city hall was built. Today, the old-time market stalls have been replaced by cafés, touristy horse buggies, and souvenir hawkers.

The **Hus Memorial**—erected in 1915, 500 years after his burning—marks the center of the square and symbolizes the long struggle for Czech freedom. Walk around the memorial. The Czech reformer Jan Hus stands tall between two groups of people: victorious Hussite patriots and Protestants defeated by the Hapsburgs. One of the patriots holds a cup—in the medieval Church, only priests could drink the wine at Communion. Hussites fought for the right to take both the wine and the bread. Behind Hus, a mother with her children represents the ultimate rebirth of the Czech nation. Hus was excommunicated and burned in Germany a century before the age of Martin Luther.

Do a **spin tour** in the center of the square to get a look at architectural styles: Gothic, Renaissance, Baroque, rococo, and Art Nouveau.

Spin clockwise, starting with the green domes of the Baroque Church of St. Nicholas. A Hussite church, it's a popular venue for concerts. (There's another green-domed Church of St. Nicholas across the Charles Bridge in Malá Strana.) The Jewish Quarter (Josefov) is a few blocks behind it, down the uniquely tree-lined Paris Street (Parizska)—a cancan of mostly Art Nouveau facades. On the horizon, at the end of Paris Street, a giant metronome ticks where an imposing statue of Stalin once stood. Spin to the right past the Hus Memorial and the fine golden and mosaic Art Nouveau facade of the Ministry of the Economy. Notice the Goth-ic Tyn Church (described below), with its fanciful spires flanking a solid gold effigy of the Virgin Mary. Lining the uphill side of the square is an interesting row of pastel houses with Gothic, Renaissance, and Baroque facades. The pointed 250-foot-tall spire marks the 14th-century Old Town Hall, famous for its astronomical clock (described below). In front of the city hall, 27 white inlaid crosses mark the spot where 27 Protestant nobles, merchants, and intellectuals were beheaded in 1621 after rebelling against the Catholic Hapsburgs.

Tyn Church—The towering Tyn (pronounced "teen") Church facing the Old Town Square was rebuilt fancier than the original—but enjoy it. For 200 years after Hus' death, this was Prague's leading Hussite church.

The lane leading to the church from the Old Town Square has a public WC and the most convenient box office in town (see "Entertainment," below).

▲**Old Town Hall Astronomical Clock**—Ignore the ridiculous human sales racks, and join the gang for the striking of the hour (daily 8:00-21:00, until 20:00 in winter) on the 15th-century town hall clock. As you wait, see if you can figure out how the clock works.

With revolving disks, celestial symbols, and sweeping hands, this clock keeps several versions of time. Two outer rings show the hour: Bohemian time (Gothic numbers, counts from sunset—find the zero, next to 23...supposedly the time of tonight's sunset) and modern time (24 Roman numerals, XII at the top being noon, XII at the bottom being midnight). Five hundred years ago, everything revolved around the earth (the fixed middle background).

To indicate the times of sunrise and sunset, arcing lines and moving spheres combine with the big hand (a sweeping golden sun) and the little hand (the moon showing various stages). Look for the orbits of the sun and moon as they rise through day (the blue zone) and night (the black zone).

If this seems complex today, it must have been a marvel 500 years ago. The circle below (added in the 19th century) shows the zodiac, scenes from the seasons of a rural peasant's life, and a ring of saints' names—one for each day of the year, with a marker showing today's special saint (out of order).

Four statues flanking the clock represent 15th-century Prague's four biggest worries: invasion (a Turkish conqueror, his hedonism symbolized by a mandolin), death (a skeleton), greed (a miserly moneylender, which used to have "Jewish" features until after World War II, when anti-Semitism became politically incorrect), and vanity (enjoying the mirror). Another interpretation: earthly pleasures brought on by vanity, greed, and hedonism are fleeting because we are all mortal.

At the top of the hour (don't blink—the show is pretty quick): (1) Death tips his hourglass and pulls the cord, ringing the bell; (2) the windows open and the Twelve Apostles parade by, acknowledging the gang of onlookers; (3) the rooster crows; and (4) the hour is rung. The hour is often off because of daylight saving time (completely senseless to 15th-century clock makers). At the top of the next hour, stand under the tower—protected by a line of banner-wielding, powdered-wigged concert salespeople—and watch the tourists.

Old Town Hall Tower, Hall, and Chapel—The main TI, left of the astronomical clock, contains a guides' desk and these sights: the tower climb (30 kč, long hike, fine view) and a tour of the town hall and Gothic chapel (40 kč, only interesting for a close-up of Twelve Apostles and clock mechanism).

Torture Museum—This gimmicky moneymaker is similar to other European torture museums, but is nevertheless interesting, showing models of gruesome medieval tortures with well-written English descriptions (100 kč, daily 10:00–22:00, on the Old Town Square at Staroměstské Náměstí 20, tel. 224-215-581).

To reach the bridge, turn your back to the fancy Tyn Church and march with the crowds.

Karlova Street—This street winds through medieval old Prague from the City Hall Square to the Charles Bridge (it zigzags...just follow the crowds). This is a commercial gauntlet, and it's here that the touristy feeding frenzy of Prague is most ugly. Street signs keep you on track, and *Karluv Most* signs point to the bridge. Obviously, you'll find great people-watching, but no good values, on this drag.

For a detour from this hyper-capitalistic orgy—every good Communist's worst nightmare—take a left on Husova to reach one of Prague's most important medieval buildings, the Bethlehem Chapel.

Bethlehem Chapel (Betlémská Kaple)—Emperor Charles IV founded the first university north of the Alps, and this was its chapel. The room is plain, with a focus on the pulpit and the message of the sermon. Around 1400, priest and professor Jan Hus preached his reformist ideas from this pulpit. While meant primarily for students and faculty, the Mass was open to the public. Soon, huge crowds were drawn by Hus' empowering Luther-like ideas: such as that people should be more involved in worship (e.g., actually drinking the wine at Communion) and have better access to the word of God through services and scriptures written in the people's language rather than Latin. Standing-room-only crowds of more than 3,000 were the norm when Hus preached. The stimulating and controversial ideas debated at the university spread throughout the city (30 kč, April–Oct daily 9:00–18:00, Nov–March daily 9:00–17:00, cellular 602-664-079).

▲▲▲Charles Bridge (Karluv Most)—This much-loved bridge, commissioned by the Holy Roman Emperor Charles IV in 1357, offers one of the most pleasant and entertaining 500-yard strolls in Europe. Until 1850, it was the only bridge crossing the river here. Be on the bridge when the sun is low for the best light, people-watching, and photo opportunities.

Before crossing the bridge, step into the little square on the right with the statue of the Holy Roman Emperor Charles IV (Karlo Quatro). Charles ruled his vast empire from Prague in the 14th century. He's holding a contract establishing Prague's university—the first in central Europe. The women around his pedestal symbolize the university's four faculties: medicine, law, theology, and the arts. The statue was erected in 1848 to celebrate the university's 500th birthday. Enjoy the view across the river. The bridge tower—once a tollbooth—is considered one of the finest Gothic gates anywhere. Climb it for a fine view but nothing else (30 kč, daily 10:00–19:00, last entry 18:30).

Charles Bridge is famous for its statues. But most of those you see today are replicas—the originals are in city museums and out of the polluted air.

Two statues on the bridge are worth a comment: the crucifix (facing the castle, near the start on the right) is the spot where convicts would pause to pray on their way to execution on the Old Town Square. Farther on (midstream, on right) the statue of John Nepomuk—a saint of the Czech people—draws a crowd (look for the guy with the five golden stars and the shiny dog). Back in the 14th century, he was the priest to whom the queen confessed all her sins. The king wanted to know her secrets, but Father John dutifully refused to tell. He was tortured, eventually killed, and tossed off the bridge. When he hit the water, five stars appeared. The shiny spot on the base of the statue shows the heave-ho. Locals touch it to help wishes come true. The shiny dog killed the queen...but that's another story. From the end of the bridge (TI in tower on castle side), the street leads two blocks to the Little Quarter Square at the base of the huge St. Nicholas church.

Kampa Island and Lennon Wall—One hundred yards from the castle end of Charles Bridge, stairs lead down to the Kampa Island and its relaxing, pub-lined square, breezy park, new art gallery, and river access.

From the square, a lane on the right leads past a water mill (many of which once lined the canal here) to the Lennon Wall (Lennonova zed').

While the ideas of Lenin sat like a water-soaked trench coat upon the Czech people, the ideas of John Lennon gave many locals hope and a vision. When Lennon was killed in 1980, a memorial wall filled with graffiti spontaneously appeared. Night after night, the police would paint over the "all you need is love" and "imagine" graffiti. And day after day, it would reappear. Until independence came in 1989, travelers, freedom-lovers, and local hippies gathered here. Even today, while the tension and danger associated with this wall is gone, the message stays fresh.

▲▲**Little Quarter (Malá Strana)**—This is the most characteristic, fun-to-wander old section of town. It's one of four medieval towns (along with Hradčany, Staré Město, and Nové Město) that united in the late 1700s to make modern Prague. It centers on the Little Quarter Square (Malostranské Náměstí) with the huge St. Nicholas church standing in the middle and a plague monument facing the church entry (uphill side).

Church of St. Nicholas (Kostel Sv. Mikuláše)—When the Jesuits came, they found the perfect piece of real estate for their church and associated school—the Little Quarter Square. Imagine this square without the big church in its middle—a real square. The Church of St. Nicholas (built 1703–1760) is the best example of High Baroque in town. It's a Jesuit church, giddy with curves and illusions. The altar features a lavish gold-plated Nicholas flanked by the two top Jesuits: St. Ignatius Loyola and St. Francis Xavier. For a good look at the city and the church's 250-foot dome, climb the tower for 30 kč; the entrance is outside the right transept (church entry-50 kč, but free for prayer daily 8:30–9:00, open daily April–Nov 9:00–16:45, Dec–March 9:00–15:45, tower open daily 10:00–18:00, church used as a concert venue in evenings). From here, hike 10 minutes uphill to the castle.

SIGHTS

Prague's Castle Area

▲▲**Prague Castle (Prazský Hrad)**—For over a thousand years, Czech rulers have ruled from the Prague Castle. It's huge (by some measures, the biggest castle on earth) and confusing—with plenty of sights not worth seeing. Rather than worry about rumors that you should spend all day here with long lists of museums to see, keep things simple. Five stops matter and are explained here: Castle Square, St. Vitus Cathedral, Old Royal Palace, Basilica of St. George, and the Golden Lane.

You can choose from three ticket routes: Route A includes the cathedral, Old Royal Palace, Basilica, Powder Tower, Golden Lane, and sometimes also temporary exhibitions for 220 kč. Route B includes the cathedral, Old Royal Palace, and the Golden Lane for 180 kč. Route C covers only the Golden Lane for 40 kč (castle hours: April–Oct daily 9:00–17:00, Nov–March 9:00–16:00, last entry 15 min before closing, tel. 224-373-368 or 224-372-434). For most people (and for the purposes of this tour), Route B is best. If you rent the worthwhile audioguide (200-kč/2 hrs or 250-kč/3 hrs), you won't be able to exit the castle area from the bottom since you need to return the audioguide where you got it.

Hour-long **tours** in English depart from main ticket office about three times a day, but cover only the cathedral and Old Royal Palace (80 kč, reserve a week in advance if you want a private guide-400 kč for up to 5 people, then 80 kč per additional person, tel. 224-373-368).

Getting to the Castle: You can ride a taxi, catch a tram, or hike. Those hiking follow the main cobbled road from Charles Bridge through Malá Strana, the Little Quarter (the nearest subway stop is Malostranska). From the big church, hike uphill along Nerudova Street. After about 10 minutes, a steep lane on the right leads to the castle. (If you continue straight, Nerudova becomes Úvoz and heads past two recommended restaurants to the Strahov Monastery and Library.)

Trams #22 and #23 go from the National Theater or Malostranska to the castle. You have two options: Get off at the stop Královský Letohrádek for the castle, or stay on farther to Pohore-lec to visit the Strahov Monastery (go uphill and through the gate toward the twin spires) and then hike down to the castle.

If you get off the tram at Královský Letohrádek, you'll see the royal summer palace across the street. This love gift—a Czech Taj Mahal—from Emperor Ferdinand I, who really did love his Queen Anne, is the finest Renaissance building in town. Notice the fine reliefs, featuring classical rather than Christian stories. From here, walk through the park with fine views of the cathedral to the gate taking you over the moat and into the castle grounds. This garden—once the private grounds and residence (you'll see the building) of the Communist president—was

Prague's Castle Area

200 YARDS
200 METERS

TO TRAM #22 & #23

TO MALOSTRANSKA METRO

CAFE

PRASNY MOST

LORETÁNSKÁ

ÚVOZ

KE HRADU

DCH

JANSKY VRSEK

NERUDOVA

BRETISLAVOVA

VLASSKA

S. MIKULAS

TRZISTE

ZAMECKE SCHODY STEPS

THUNOVSKA

RAMPART GARDENS

STARE ZAMECKE STEPS

TO CHARLES BRIDGE →

LITTLE QUARTER SQUARE

MALA STRANA

❶ ARMORY MUSEUM
❷ PLAGUE MONUMENT
❸ NATIONAL GALLERY
❹ GATE TO CASTLE
❺ CAFE
❻ INFO & TICKETS
❼ ST. VITUS CATHEDRAL
❽ OLD PALACE
❾ ST. GEORGE'S BASILICA
❿ GOLDEN LANE
⓫ TO DOMUS HENRICI HOTEL & STRAHOV MONASTERY
⓬ USA EMBASSY
⓭ MALY BUDDHA TEA HOUSE
⓮ FORMER GARDENS OF COMMUNIST PRESIDENT

opened to the public with the coming of freedom under Václav Havel.
Castle Square (Hradčanske Náměstí)—The big square facing the castle
feels like the castle's entry, but it's actually the central square of the
Castle Town. Enjoy the awesome city view and the two string quartets
that play regularly at the gate (their CD is terrific; say hello to friendly,
mustachioed Josef). A tranquil café (Espresso Kajetánka—see "Eating,"
below) hides a few steps down immediately to the right as you face the
castle. From here, stairs lead into the Little Quarter.

The Castle Square was a kind of Czech Pennsylvania Avenue.
Look uphill from the gate. The Renaissance Schwarzenberg Palace
(Svarcenberskě palác, on the left, with the fake big stones scratched on
the wall) is now a museum of military history. The statue marked

"TGM" honors Thomáš Masaryk, Czechoslovakia's George Washington. At the end of World War I, this pal of Woodrow Wilson united the Czechs and the Slovaks into one nation, and became its first president. A plague monument stands in the center (built by the city in thanks for surviving the Black Plague). On the right, find the archbishop's rococo yellow palace. Through the portal on the left-hand side, a lane leads to the Sternberg Palace *(Sternberský palác)*, filled with the National Gallery's skippable collection of European paintings—mostly minor works by Dürer, Rubens, Rembrandt, and El Greco (90 kč, Tue–Sun 10:00–18:00, closed Mon).

Survey the castle from this square—the tip of a 1,500-foot-long series of courtyards, churches, and palaces. Huge throngs of tourists make the castle grounds one sea of people during peak times; late afternoon is least crowded. The guard changes on the hour, with the most ceremony at noon. Walk under the fighting giants, under an arch, into the second courtyard. The mod green awning with the golden winged cat (just past the ticket office) marks the offices of the Czech president. You can walk through the castle and enter the cathedral without a ticket, but you'll need a ticket to see the castle properly (see ticket options above).

▲St. Vitus Cathedral (Katedrála Sv. Víta)—This Roman Catholic cathedral—containing the tombs and relics of the most important local saints and kings, including the first three Hapsburg kings—symbolizes the Czech spirit. What's up with the guys in suits carved into the facade below the big round window? They're the architects and builders who finished the church. Started in 1344, construction was stalled by wars and plagues. But, fueled by the 19th-century rise of Czech nationalism, Prague's top church was finished in 1929 for the 1,000th anniversary of the death of St. Wenceslas. It looks all Gothic, but it's two distinct halves: modern neo-Gothic and the original 14th-century Gothic. For 400 years, a temporary wall sealed off the unfinished cathedral.

Go inside and find the third stained-glass window on the left. This masterful 1931 Art Nouveau window is by Czech artist Alfons Mucha (if you like this, you'll love the Mucha museum downtown—described below under "Art Nouveau"). Notice Mucha's stirring nationalism: Methodious and Cyril top and center (leaders in Slavic-style Christianity). Cyril is baptizing the mythic, lanky, long-haired Czech man. Lower, you'll see two Czech flappers and the classic Czech patriarch in the lower right. Notice also Mucha's novel use of color: your eyes are drawn from blue (symbolizing the past) to the golden center (where the boy and the seer look into the future).

Show your ticket and circulate around the **apse** past a carved wood relief of Prague in 1630 (before Charles Bridge had any statues), lots of faded Gothic paintings, and tombs of local saints. A fancy roped-off chapel (right transept) houses the **tomb of Prince Wenceslas,** surrounded by precious 14th-century murals showing scenes of his life, and a locked door leading to the crown jewels. More kings are buried in the royal mausoleum in front of the high altar and in the crypt underneath. You can climb 287 steps up the **spire** for a fine view (included in Route A or B ticket, or pay 20 kč at the cathedral ticket window, April–Oct daily except Sunday morning, 9:00–17:00, last entry 16:15).

Leaving the cathedral, turn left (past the public WC). The **obelisk** was erected in 1919—a single piece of granite celebrating the establishment of Czechoslovakia. (It was originally much taller but broke in transit—an inauspicious start for a nation destined to last only 70 years.) Find the 14th-century mosaic of the *Last Judgment* outside on the right transept. It was built Italian-style by the modern-and-cosmopolitan-for-his-era King Charles IV. Jesus oversees the action, as some go to heaven and some go to hell. The Czech king and queen kneel directly below Jesus and the six patron saints. On coronation day, they would walk under this arch, which would remind them (and their subjects) that even those holding great power are not above God's judgment. The royal crown and national jewels are kept in a chamber (see the grilled windows) above this entryway, which was the cathedral's main entry for centuries while the church was incomplete. Twenty yards to the right, a door leads to the...

Old Royal Palace (Starý Královský Palác)—This was the seat of the Bohemian princes in the 12th century. While extensively rebuilt, the large hall is late Gothic. It was a multipurpose hall for the old nobility. It's big enough for jousts—even the staircase was designed to let a mounted soldier gallop in. It was filled with market stalls, giving nobles a chance to shop without actually going into town. In the 1400s, the nobility met here to elect their king. This tradition survives today, as the parliament crowds into this room every five years to elect the Czech president. Look up at the impressive vaulted ceiling, look down on the chapel from the end, and go out on the balcony for a fine Prague view. Is that Paris in the distance? No, it's Petřín Tower, built for an exhibition in 1891 (200 feet tall, a quarter of the height of the Parisian big brother built in 1889). The spiral stairs on the left lead up to several rooms with painted coats of arms and no English explanations. The downstairs of the palace sometimes houses special exhibitions. Across from the palace exit is the basilica.

Basilica of St. George and Convent (Bazilika Sv. Jiří)—Step into the beautifully lit Basilica of St. George to see Prague's best-preserved Romanesque church. St. Ludmila was buried here in 973. The first Bohemian convent was established here near the palace. To visit the basilica in addition to the other castle sights described here, you'll pay an extra 40 kč for the Route A ticket—worth it if you're interested in Romanesque.

Today, the convent next door houses the National Gallery's Collection of Old Masters (best Czech paintings from Gothic,

Renaissance, and Baroque periods, 50 kč, Tue–Sun 10:00–18:00, closed Mon). Continue walking downhill through the castle grounds. Turn left on the first street, which leads into a cute lane.

Golden Lane (Zlatá Ulička)—This street of old buildings, which originally housed goldsmiths, is now jammed with tourists and lined with expensive gift shops, boutiques, galleries, and cafés. The Czech writer Franz Kafka lived at #22. There's a deli/bistro at the top and a convenient public WC at the bottom (Golden Lane-40 kč for "Route C" ticket, also included in Routes A and B). Beyond that, at the end of the castle, are fortifications beefed up in anticipation of the Turkish attack— the cause for most medieval arms buildups in Europe—and steps funneling the mobs of tourists back into town. At the bottom of the castle, continue down into the Little Quarter (Malá Strana) or follow the garden along the castle back to the castle square and on to the monastery.

Strahov Monastery and Library (Strahovský Kláster a Knihovna)— Twin Baroque domes standing high above the castle (a 10-min hike uphill) mark the Strahov Monastery. If you want to visit this sight and the castle, take tram #22 or #23 (from the National Theater or Malostranska) to the Pohorelec stop, visit the monastery (go uphill and through the gate toward the twin spires), then hike down to the castle.

The monastery is a Romanesque structure decorated in textbook Baroque (look through the window inside the front door to see its interior). The adjacent library (50 kč, daily 9:00–11:45 & 13:00–16:45, last entry 15 min before closing) offers a peek at how enlightened thinkers in the 18th century impacted learning. Two rooms are filled with 17th-century books under ceilings decorated with appropriate themes. Because the Czechs were a rural people with almost no high culture at this time, there were few books in the Czech language. The theme of the first and bigger hall is philosophy, with the history of man's pursuit of knowledge painted on its ceiling. The other is theology. Notice the gilded locked case containing the *"libri prohibiti"* (prohibited books) at the end of the room. Only the abbot had the key, and you could read these books—like Copernicus, Jan Hus, even the French encyclopedia— only with the abbot's blessing. As the Age of Enlightenment took hold in Europe, monasteries still controlled the books. With the Enlightenment, the hallway connecting these two library rooms was filled with cases illustrating the new practical approach to natural sciences. Find the baby dodo bird (which went extinct in the 17th century).

Prague's Jewish Quarter

▲▲▲**Jewish Quarter (Josefov)**—The Jewish people were dispersed by the Romans 2,000 years ago. Over the centuries, their culture survived in enclaves throughout the Western world: "The Torah was their sanctuary which no army could destroy." Jews first came to Prague in the 10th

Prague's Jewish Quarter

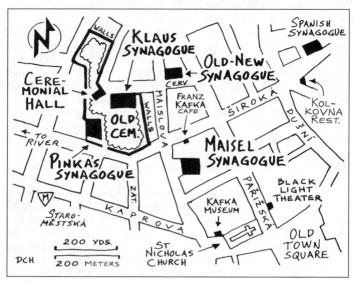

century. The main intersection of Josefov (Maiselova and Siroka Streets) was the meeting point of two medieval trade routes.

When the pope declared that Jews and Christians should not live together, Jews had to wear yellow badges, and their quarter was walled in so that it became a ghetto. In the 16th and 17th centuries, Prague had one of the biggest ghettos in Europe, with 11,000 inhabitants. Within its six gates, Prague's Jewish Quarter was a gaggle of 200 wooden buildings. Someone wrote: "Jews nested rather than dwelled."

The "outcasts" of Christianity relied mainly on profits from money-lending (forbidden to Christians) and community solidarity to survive. While their money protected them, it was often also a curse. Throughout Europe, when times got tough and Christian debts to the Jewish community mounted, entire Jewish communities were evicted or killed.

In the 1780s, Emperor Joseph II eased much of the discrimination against Jews. In 1848, the walls were torn down and the neighborhood, named Josefov in honor of the emperor who was less anti-Semitic than the norm, was incorporated as a district of Prague.

In 1897, ramshackle Josefov was razed and replaced with a new modern town—the original 31 streets and 220 buildings became 10 streets and 83 buildings. This is what you'll see today: an attractive neighborhood of fine, mostly Art Nouveau buildings, with a few surviving historic Jewish buildings. In the 1930s, some 50,000 Jews lived in

Prague. Today, only a couple of thousand remain.

As the Nazis decimated Jewish communities in the region, Prague's Jews were allowed to collect and archive their treasures in this museum. While the archivists ultimately died in concentration camps, their work survives. Seven sites scattered over a three-block area make up the tourists' Jewish Quarter. Six of the sites, called "the Museum," are treated as one admission. Your ticket comes with a map locating the sights and admission appointments: times you'll be let in if it's very crowded. (Without crowds, ignore the times.)

For all seven sights, you'll pay 500 kč (300 kč for "the Museum" and 200 kč for the Old-New Synagogue, all sites open Sun–Fri 9:00–17:30, closed Sat—the Jewish Sabbath). There are occasional guided walks in English (often at 14:00, 40 kč, 2.5 hrs, start at Maisel Synagogue, tel. 222-317-191). Most stops are described in English. This museum is well-presented and profoundly moving: It tells the story of the Jews of this region and, for me, is the most interesting Jewish site in Europe.

Maisel Synagogue (Maiselova Synagóga)—This shows a thousand years of Jewish history in Bohemia and Moravia. Exhibit topics include the origin of the Star of David, Jewish mysticism, discrimination, and the creation of Prague's ghetto.

Spanish Synagogue (Spanělská Synagóga)—This 19th-century, ornate, Moorish-style synagogue continues the history of the Maisel Synagogue, covering the 18th, 19th, and tumultuous 20th centuries. The upstairs is particularly intriguing (with c. 1900 photos of Josefov).

Pinkas Synagogue (Pinkasova Synagóga)—A site of Jewish worship for 400 years, today this is a poignant memorial to the victims of the Nazis. Of the 120,000 Jews living in the area in 1939, only 10,000 lived to see liberation in 1945. The walls are covered with the handwritten names of 77,297 Czech Jews who were sent from here to the gas chambers of Auschwitz and other camps. Hometowns are in gold, family names are in red, followed in black by the individual's first name, birthday, and last date known to be alive. Notice that families generally perished together. Climb six steps into the women's gallery. The names in poor condition near the ceiling are from 1953. When the Communists moved in, they closed the synagogue and erased everything. With freedom, in 1989, the Pinkas Synagogue was reopened and all the names rewritten.

Upstairs is the **Terezín Children's Art Exhibit.** Terezín, near Prague, was a fortified town of 7,000 Czechs. The Nazis moved these people out and moved in 60,000 Jews, creating Theresienstadt, their model "Jewish town," a concentration camp dolled up for propaganda purposes. The town's medieval walls, originally to keep people from getting in, were used by Nazis to prevent people from getting out. Jewish culture seemed to thrive in Terezín, as "citizens" put on plays and concerts, published a magazine, and raised their families in ways impressive to Red Cross inspectors. But virtually all of the Jews ended up dying at concentration camps in the East, such as Auschwitz. The art of the children of Terezín survives as a striking testimony to the horror of the Holocaust. While the Communists kept the art away from the public, it is now well-displayed and described in English.

Terezín is a powerful day trip from Prague for those interested in touring the concentration camp memorial/museum. You can either take a public bus (6/day, 60 min, leaves from Prague's Florenc bus station) or a tour bus (see "Tours," above).

Old Jewish Cemetery (Starý Zidovský Hřbitov)—As you wander among 12,000 evocative tombstones, remember that from 1439 until 1787, this was the only burial ground allowed for the Jews of Prague. With limited space and about 12,000 graves, tombs were piled atop each other. With its many layers, the cemetery became a small plateau. The Jewish word for cemetery means "House of Life"; like Christians, Jews believe that death is the gateway into the next world. Pebbles on the tombstones are "flowers of the desert," reminiscent of the old days when a rock was placed upon the sand gravesite to keep the body covered. Often a scrap of paper with a prayer on it is under a pebble.

Ceremonial Hall (Obradní Sín)—Leaving the cemetery, you'll find a neo-Romanesque mortuary house built in 1911 for the purification of the dead (on left). It's filled with a worthwhile exhibition, described in English, on Jewish burial traditions with historic paintings of the cemetery.

Klaus Synagogue (Klauzová Synagóga)—This 17th-century synagogue (also at the exit of the cemetery) is the final wing of this museum, devoted to Jewish religious practices. On the ground floor, exhibits explain the festive Jewish calendar. Upstairs features the ritual stages of Jewish life.

Old-New Synagogue (Staronová Synagóga)—For over 700 years, this has been the most important synagogue and central building in Josefov. Standing like a bomb-hardened bunker, it feels like it's survived plenty of hard times. Stairs take you down to the street level of the 13th century and into the Gothic interior. Built in 1270, it's the oldest synagogue in Europe. The Shrine of the Ark in front is the focus of worship. The holiest place in the synagogue, it holds the sacred scrolls of the Torah. The old rabbi's chair to the right remains empty out of respect. Twelve is a popular number (e.g., windows) because it symbolizes the 12 tribes of Israel. The slit-like windows on the left are an 18th-century addition allowing women to view the men-only services (separate 200 kč admission, Sun–Thu 9:30–18:00, Fri 9:30–17:00, closed Sat).

Art Nouveau

Prague is the best Art Nouveau town in Europe, with fun-loving facades gracing streets all over town. The streets of Josefov, the Mucha window in the St. Vitus Cathedral, and Hotel Europa and its sisters on Wenceslas Square are just a few highlights. The top two places for Art Nouveau fans are the Mucha Museum and the Municipal House.

▲▲**Mucha Museum (Muchovo Muzeum)**—This is one of Europe's most enjoyable little museums. I find the art of Alfons Mucha (MOO-kah, 1860–1939) insistently likeable. See the crucifixion scene he painted as an eight-year-old boy. Read how this popular Czech artist's posters, filled with Czech symbols and expressing his people's ideals and aspirations, were patriotic banners arousing the national spirit. And check out the photographs of his models. With the help of this abundant supply of slinky models, Mucha was a founding father of the Art Nouveau movement. Prague isn't much on museums, but, if you're into Art Nouveau, this one is great. Run by Mucha's grandson, it's two blocks off Wenceslas Square and wonderfully displayed on one comfortable floor (120 kč, daily 10:00–18:00, Panska 7, tel. 224-233-355, www.mucha .cz). While the exhibit is well described in English, the 40-kč English brochure on the art is a good supplement. The video is also worthwhile (30 min, at least once hourly in English, ask upon entry).

Municipal House (Obecní Dům)—The Municipal House (built 1905–1911, near Powder Tower) features Prague's largest concert hall, a great Art Nouveau café, and two other restaurants. Look for the *Homage to Prague* mosaic—with a goddess-like Praha presiding over a land of peace and high culture—on the building's striking facade; it stoked cultural pride and nationalist sentiment. Then choose your place for a meal or drink (see "Eating," below).

The Dancing House (Tancici Dům)—Prague also has some delightful modern architecture. If ever a building could get your toes tapping, check out the building nicknamed Fred and Ginger. This metallic samba was designed by Frank Gehry (who designed the equally striking Guggenheim Museum in Bilbao, Spain, and Seattle's Experience Music Project). It's easy to spot (2 bridges down from Charles Bridge where Jiraskuv bridge hits Nové Město, tram #17). A pleasant riverside walk from Charles Bridge to the Dancing House takes you by a famous riverside ballroom and the grand National Theater. Across the street from the theater is the venerable haunt of Prague's intelligentsia, **Kavarna Slavia,** a Vienna-style coffeehouse fine for a meal or drink with a view of the river.

ENTERTAINMENT

Prague booms with live (and inexpensive) theater, classical, jazz, and pop entertainment. Everything's listed in several monthly cultural events programs (free at TI) and in the *Prague News*.

Black Light Theater, a kind of mime/modern dance variety show, has no language barrier and is, for many, more entertaining than a classical concert. Unique to Prague, this originated in the 1960s as a playful and almost mystifying theater of the absurd.

Six or eight classical "tourist" **concerts** daily fill delightful Old Town halls and churches with music of the crowd-pleasing sort: Vivaldi, Best of Mozart, Most Famous Arias, and works by local boy Anton Dvořák. Leafleteers are everywhere announcing the evening's events. Concerts typically cost 400–1,000 kč, start anywhere from 13:00 to 21:00, and last one hour.

Common venues are in the Little Quarter Square—Malostranské Náměstí (at the St. Nicholas church and the Prague Academy of Music in Liechtenstein Palace), at the city end of Charles Bridge (St. Francis Church), and on the Old Town Square (another St. Nicholas church).

To really understand all your options (the street Mozarts are pushing only their concert), drop by the **Týnská Galerie** box office at the Tyn Church. The wall display clearly shows what's playing today and tomorrow (concerts, Black Light Theater, marionette shows, photos of each venue, and a map locating everything, daily 10:00–19:00, tel. 224-826-969).

Young locals keep countless "music clubs" in business. A favorite with a handy locale, **Malostranská Beseda** offers live music nightly (on the downhill side of the Little Quarter's main square). Many of the best local rock and jazz groups perform here (nightly from 20:30, generally about 100 kč cover).

Prague isn't great for a boat tour. Still, the hour-long **Vltava River cruises,** which leave from near the Malá Strana end of Charles Bridge about hourly (100 kč), are scenic and relaxing, though not informative.

Prague's top **sports** are soccer (that's "football" here) and hockey (they are a world power, routinely beating even Canada). Think about it: there are over a hundred Czech players in America's NHL. Tickets are normally easy to get (soccer—usually late Sat or Sun afternoon Feb-May and Aug-Nov; hockey—weeknights Sept-April; see *Prague News*). The two big Czech hockey rivals are Sparta and Slavia. Near the top of Castle Hill is the enormous 200,000-seat Strahov Stadium. This was built during Communist times as a venue for *Spartakiade,* sort of a synchronized calisthenics encouraged by the regime. Now it's used for soccer and other sports.

SLEEPING

Room-Booking Services

Prague is awash with fancy rooms on the push list; private, small-time operators with rooms to rent in their apartments; and roving agents eager to book you a bed and earn a commission. You can save about 30 percent by showing up in Prague without a reservation and finding accommodations upon arrival. If driving, you'll see booking agencies as you enter town. Generally, book here and your host can come and lead you to their place.

Athos Travel, run by friendly entrepreneur Filip Antoš, will find the right room for you from among 140 properties (from hostels to five-star hotels), 90 percent of which are in the historical center. Its handy Web site allows you to search based on various criteria to find the right room (best to arrange in advance during peak season, can also help with last-minute booking off-season, tel. 241-440-571, fax 241-441-697, www.athos.cz, info@athos.cz); to get a 2 percent discount for online booking, see "Helpful Hints," above.

AVE, at the main train station **(Hlavní Nádraží),** is a less friendly but helpful booking service (daily 6:00–23:00, tel. 251-551-011, fax 251-555-156, www.avetravel.cz, ave@avetravel.cz). With the tracks at your back, walk down to the orange ceiling and past the "meeting point" (don't go downstairs)—their office is in the left corner by the exit to the rip-off taxis. AVE has several other offices—at Holešovice station, the airport, Wenceslas Square, and Old Town Square. Their display board shows discounted hotels. They have a slew of hotels and small pensions available ($70 pension doubles in old center, $35 doubles a metro ride away). You can reserve by e-mail (using your credit card as a deposit) or just show up at the office and request a room. Many of AVE's rooms are not very convenient to the center; be clear on the location before you make your choice.

For a more personal touch, contact Lida at **Magic Praha** for help with accommodations (tel. 224-232-755, magicpraha@magicpraha.cz, see "Helpful Hints," above).

Old Town

You'll pay higher prices to stay in the Old Town, but for many travelers, the convenience is worth the expense. These places are all within a 10-minute walk of the Old Town Square.

$$$ Hotel Central is a sentimental favorite—I stayed there in the Communist days. Now it's changing with the times, like the rest of Prague—its 69 rooms have recently been renovated, leaving it fresh and bright. The place is well-run and the location, three blocks east of the Old Town Square, is excellent (Sb-3,600 kč, Db-4,200 kč, deluxe Db-4,900 kč, Tb-4,700 kč, low season-30-40 percent less, elevator, Rybná 8, Praha 1, Metro: Náměstí Republiky, tel. 224-812-041, fax 222-328-404, central@orfea.cz).

$$$ Cloister Inn is a well-located, modern place with 75 rooms. The exterior is more concrete than charm—the building used to be shared by a convent and a secret police prison—but inside, it's newly renovated and plenty comfortable (Sb-3,000-3,600 kč, Db-3,300-4,200 kč, Tb-3,800-5,000 kč, elevator, free Internet access, Konviktska 14, Praha 1, tel. 224-211-020, fax 224-210-800, www.cloister-inn.com, cloister@cloister-inn.com).

SLEEP CODE

(30 kč = about $1, country code: 420)
Sleep Code: **S** = Single, **D** = Double/Twin, **T** = Triple, **Q** = Quad, **b** = bathroom, **s** = shower only, **no CC** = Credit Cards not accepted. Unless otherwise noted, credit cards are accepted.

To help you sort easily through these listings, I've divided the rooms into three categories based on the price for a standard double room with bath:

$$$ **Higher Priced**—Most rooms 4,000 kč or more.
$$ **Moderately Priced**—Most rooms between 3,000–4,000 kč.
$ **Lower Priced**—Most rooms 3,000 kč or less.

Finding a bed in Prague worries Western tourists. It shouldn't. You have several options. Capitalism is working as Adam Smith promised: With a huge demand, the supply is increasing and the price is going up. Peak time is May, June, September, October, Christmas, and Easter. July and August are not too bad. Expect crowds on weekends. I've listed peak-time prices. If you're traveling in July or August, you'll find slightly lower rates. Prices tend to go up even more on holidays (especially German ones). English is generally spoken. Reserve by phone or e-mail. Generally, you simply promise to come and need no deposit.

Prague's hotels, plenty professional and comfortable, are often beholden to agencies that have a lock on rooms (generally until 6 weeks in advance). Agencies get a 30 percent discount and can sell the rooms at whatever price they like between that and the "rack rate." Consequently, Prague has a reputation of being perpetually booked up. But because the agencies rarely use up their allotment, the "crowds" are only an illusion. You need to make reservations either long in advance, when the few rooms not reserved for agencies are still available, or a few weeks in advance, after the agencies have released their rooms.

To call Prague from outside the country, dial the international access code (00 for Europe or 011 for U.S./Canada), the Czech Republic's country code (420), then the local number.

$$ Betlem Club, a shiny jewel of comfort, is on a pleasant medieval square in the heart of the Old Town, across from the Bethlehem Chapel (where Jan Hus preached his troublemaking sermons). Its 22 modern and comfy rooms face a quiet inner courtyard, and breakfast is served in a Gothic cellar (Sb-2,700 kč, Db-3,900 kč, extra bed-1,000 kč, prices flex with season, elevator, Internet access, airport pickup-800 kč, airport drop-off-650 kč, Betlémské Náměstí 9, Praha 1, tel. 222-221-575, fax 222-220-580, www.betlemclub.cz, betlem.club @login.cz).

$$ Pension u Medvídků has 31 comfortably renovated rooms in a big, rustic, medieval shell with dark wood furniture. Upstairs, you'll find lots of beams to run into (Sb-2,300 kč, Db-3,500 kč, Tb-4,500 kč, extra bed-500 kč, "historical" rooms 10 percent more, apartment 20 percent more, prices flex with season, Internet access-70 kč/hr, Na Perštýně 7, Praha 1, tel. 224-211-916, fax 224-220-930, www.umedvidku.cz, info @umedvidku.cz). The pension runs a popular restaurant that has live music most Fri-Sat until 23:00.

$$ Hotel u Klenotníka, with 10 modern and comfortable rooms in a plain building, is three blocks off the Old Town Square (Sb-2,500 kč, Db-3,800 kč, Tb-4,500 kč, 10 percent off when booking direct with this book, Rytiřska 3, Praha 1, tel. 224-211-699, fax 224-221-025, www.uklenotnika.cz, info@uklenotnika.cz). They run a good restaurant.

$ Pension Unitas rents 35 small, tidy, youth hostel-type rooms with plain, minimalist furnishings and no sinks (S-1,100–1,400 kč, D-1,400–2,000 kč, T-1,750–2,350 kč, Q-2,000–2,700 kč, T and Q are cramped with bunks in D-sized rooms, non-smoking, quiet hours 22:00–7:00, Bartolomejská 9, Praha 1, tel. 224-211-020, fax 224-210-800, www.cloister-inn.com/unitas, unitas@cloister-inn.com).

$ Hotel Expres rents 26 simple rooms and brings a decent continental breakfast to your room (S-1,000 kč, Sb-2,600 kč, D-1,200 kč, Db-2,800 kč, Tb-3,200 kč, 5 percent more if you pay with credit card, elevator, Skořepka 5, Praha 1, tel. 224-211-801, fax 224-223-309, www.hotelexpres.wz.cz, expres@zero.cz).

Wenceslas Square

$$$ Hotel Adria, with a prime Wenceslas Square location, cool Art Nouveau facade, 88 rooms, and completely modern and business-class interior, is your big-time, four-star central splurge (Db-5,250 kč, air-con, elevator, Internet access-400 kč/hr, minibars...the works, Václavske Náměstí 26, tel. 221-081-111, fax 221-081-300, www.hoteladria.cz, mailbox@hoteladria.cz).

$$ Hotel Europa is in a class by itself. This landmark place, famous for its wonderful 1903 Art Nouveau facade, is the centerpiece of Wenceslas Square. But someone pulled the plug on the hotel about 50 years ago, and it's a mess. It offers haunting beauty in all the public spaces, 92 dreary, ramshackle rooms, and a weary staff. They're waiting for a billion-crown investor to come along and rescue the place, but for now they offer some of the cheapest rooms on Wenceslas Square (S-1,600 kč, Sb-3,000 kč, D-2,600 kč, Db-4,000 kč, T-3,100 kč, Tb-5,000 kč, some rooms have been very slightly refurbished, some remain in unrefurbished old style, they cost the same either way, every room is different, elevator, Václavské Náměstí 25, Praha 1, tel. 224-228-117, fax 224-224-544, www.europahotel.cz).

Away from the Center

Moving just outside the Old Town saves you money—and gets you away from the tourists and into some fun residential neighborhoods. These listings (great values compared to Old Town hotels) are all within a five- to 15-minute tram or metro ride from the center.

$$ Hotel Julian—an oasis of professional, predictable decency in a quiet, untouristy neighborhood—is a five-minute taxi or tram ride from the action on the castle side of the river. Its 32 spacious, fresh, well-furnished rooms and big, homey public spaces hide behind a noble neoclassical facade. The staff is friendly and helpful (Sb-3,280 kč, Db-3,580 kč, suite Db-4,280 kč, extra bed-900 kč, family room, 5 percent discount off best quoted rate with this book, velvety elevator, Internet access, parking lot, Elišky Peškové 11, Praha 5, tel. 257-311-150, reception tel. 257-311-144, fax 257-311-149, www.julian.cz, casjul@vol.cz). Free lockers and a shower are available for those needing to check out early but stay until late (e.g., for an overnight train). Mike's Chauffeur Service, based here, is reliable and affordable (see "Transportation Connections," below).

$$ Hotel Anna, bright, pastel, and classically charming, is in an upscale residential neighborhood (near former royal vineyards, or Vinohrady) 10 minutes by foot east of Wenceslas Square (Sb-2,300 kč, Db-3,100 kč, Tb-3,900 kč, cheaper off-season, non-smoking rooms, elevator, Budečská 17, Praha 2, Metro: Náměstí Míru, tel. 222-513-111, fax 222-515-158, www.hotelanna.cz). The hotel runs a cheaper but similarly pleasant annex, the **Dependance,** two blocks away (Sb-1,650 kč, Db-2,300 kč, cheaper off-season, no elevator but all rooms on first floor, reception and breakfast at main hotel).

$$ Hotel 16, a stately little place with an intriguing Art Nouveau facade, high ceilings, and a clean, sleek interior, rents 14 fine rooms (Sb-2,500–2,700 kč, Db-3,400–3,900 kč, Tb-4,600 kč, 10 percent lower off-season, back/quiet rooms face the garden, front/noisier rooms face the street, air-con, elevator, a 10-min walk south of Wenceslas Square, Metro: I. P. Pavlova, Kateřinská 16, Praha 2, tel. 224-920-636, fax 224-920-626, www.hotel16.cz, hotel16@hotel16.cz).

$$ Hotel Union is a grand 1906 Art Nouveau building, filling its street corner with 57 rooms. It's away from the touristy center in a more

Prague Hotels and Restaurants

❶ Pick up bus tour at #20	⓫ Hotel Europa	㉑ Plzenska Rest. u Dovu Kocek
❷ Black Light Theater	⓬ Pension Unitas	
❸ Neat Park	⓭ Hotel Expres	㉒ Cloister Inn
❹ Hotel Julian	⓮ To Hotel 16	㉓ To Dum u Semíka & Guest House Lída
❺ Hotel Central	⓯ Hotel Adria	
❻ Betlem Club & Rest. u Plebána	⓰ Dobrá Cajovna	㉔ To Hotel Sax & Henrici
❼ Pension U Medvídku	⓱ Czech Kitchen	㉕ To Hotel Anna & Depandance
❽ Pension U Klenotníka	⓲ Rest. Mucha	
❾ Hotel Luník	⓳ Country Life	㉖ Launderette
❿ To Hotel Union	⓴ Mlejnice	

laid-back neighborhood a direct 10-minute ride to Wenceslas Square on tram #24, or to Charles Bridge on tram #18 (Sb-2,815 kč, Db-3,380 kč, Db deluxe-4,050 kč, Tb-4,495 kč, extra bed-1,115 kč, all rates at least 1,000 kč cheaper Jan-Feb, rates higher during several holidays, elevator, Ostrčilovo Náměstí 4, Praha 2-Nusle, tel. 261-214-812, fax 261-214-820, www.hotelunion.cz, hotelunion@hotelunion.cz).

$ Dům u Šemíka, a friendly hotel named for a heroic mythical horse, is in a residential neighborhood just below Vyšehrad castle, a 10-minute tram ride from the center (Sb-1,700 kč, Db-2,100–2,650 kč, apartment-2,800–4,850 kč depending on size, extra bed-700 kč, from the center take tram #18 to Albertov then walk 2 blocks uphill, or take tram #7 to Výtoň, go under rail bridge, and walk 3 blocks uphill to Vratislavova 36, Praha 2, tel. 224-920-736, fax 224-911-602, www .usemika.cz).

$ Hotel Luník, with 35 rooms, is a stately but friendly, no-non-sense place out of the medieval faux-rustic world in a normal, pleasant business district. It's two metro stops from the main station (Metro: I. P. Pavlova) or a 10-minute walk from Wenceslas Square (Sb-2,050 kč, Db-2,900 kč, Tb-3,350 kč, elevator, Londýnská 50, Praha 2, tel. 224-253-974, fax 224-253-986, www.hotel-lunik.cz, recepce@hotel-lunik.cz).

$ Guest House Lída, with 12 homey and spacious rooms, fills a big house in a quiet residential area a 30-minute walk or 15-minute tram ride from the center. Jan and Jiří Prouza, who run the place, are a wealth of information and know how to make people feel at home (small Db-1,350 kč, Db-1,650 kč, Tb-1,980 kč, 10 percent off Nov-March, no CC, family rooms, top-floor family suite with kitchenette, parking in garage-150 kč/day, Metro: Pražského Pov-stání, exit metro and turn left on Lomnicka between the metro station and big blue glass ČSOB build-ing, follow Lomnicka for 500 yards, then turn left on Lopatecka, go uphill and ring bell at Lopatecka #26, no sign outside, Praha 4, tel. & fax 261-214-766, lida@login.cz). The Prouza brothers also rent four apart-ments across the river (Db-1,500 kč, Tb-1,920 kč, Qb-2,100 kč).

Across the River, near the Castle

$$$ Hotel Sax, on a quiet corner a block below the Malá Strana action, will delight the artsy yuppie with its 22 rooms, fruity atrium, and modern, stylish decor (Sb-3,700 kč, Db-4,400 kč, Db suite-5,100 kč, extra bed-1,000 kč, cheaper off-season, elevator, near St. Nicholas church, 1 block below Nerudova at Jánský Vršek 3, Praha 1, reserve long in advance, tel. 257-531-268, fax 257-534-101, www.sax.cz, hotelsax@bon.cz).

$$$ Residence Domus Henrici, just above the castle square, is a quiet retreat that charges—and gets—top prices for its eight smartly appointed rooms, some of which include good views (Ds-4,650 kč, Db-5,400–5,700 kč depending on size, extra bed-810 kč, less off-season, pleasant terrace, Loretánská 11, Praha 1, tel. 220-511-369, fax 220-511-502, www.domus-henrici.cz, reception@domus-henrici.cz). This is a five-minute walk above the castle gate in a stately and quiet area.

EATING

The beauty of Prague is wandering aimlessly through the winding old quarters marveling at the architecture, watching the people, and sniffing out fun restaurants. You can eat well for very little money. What you'd pay for a basic meal in Vienna or Munich will get you an elegant meal in Prague. Choose between traditional, dark Czech beer hall-type ambience, elegant *Jugendstil*/early-20th-century atmosphere, ethnic, or hip and modern.

Watch out for scams. Many restaurants put more care into ripping off green tourists (and even locals) than in their cooking. Tourists are routinely served cheaper meals than what they ordered, given a menu with a "personalized" price list, charged extra for things they didn't get, or shortchanged. Avoid any menu without clear and explicit prices. Carefully examine your itemized bill and understand each line (a 10 percent service is sometimes added—no need to tip beyond that). Be careful of waiters padding the tab: tax is always included in the price, so it shouldn't be tacked on later. Deliberately count your change, parting with very large bills only if necessary. Never let your credit card out of your sight and check the numbers carefully. Make it a habit to get cash from an ATM to pay for your meals. Remember, there are two parallel worlds in Prague: the tourist town and the real city. Generally, if you walk two minutes away from the tourist flow, you'll find much better value, ambience, and service.

Art Nouveau Restaurants

The sumptuous Art Nouveau concert hall—**Municipal House**—has three special restaurants: a café, a French restaurant, and a beer cellar (Náměstí Republiky 5). The dressy café, **Kavarna Obecní Dům,** is drenched in chandeliered Art Nouveau elegance (light meals, 1 hot meal special daily, daily 7:30–23:00, live piano or jazz trio 17:00–21:00, tel. 222-002-763). **Francouzska Restaurace,** the fine and formal French restaurant, is in the next wing (700-kč meals, daily 12:00–16:00 & 18:00–23:00, tel. 222-002-777). **Plzeňská Restaurace,** downstairs, brags it's the most beautiful Art Nouveau pub in Europe (cheap meals, great atmosphere, daily 11:30–23:00, tel. 222-002-780).

Restaurant Mucha is touristy, with decent Czech food in a formal Art Nouveau dining room (300-kč meals, daily 12:00–24:00, Melantrichova 5, tel. 224-225-045).

Uniquely Czech Places near the Old Town Square

Prices go way down when you get away from the tourist areas. At least once, eat in a restaurant with no English menu.

Plzeňská Restaurace U Dvou Koček is a typical Czech pub with cheap, no-nonsense, hearty Czech food, great beer, and—once upon a time—a local crowd (250 kč for 3 courses and beer, serving original Pilsner Urquell with accordion music nightly until 23:00, under an arcade, facing the tiny square between Perlova and Skořepka Streets).

Restaurace Mlejnice is a fun little pub strewn with farm implements and happy eaters, tucked away just out of the tourist crush two blocks from the Old Town Square (order carefully and understand your itemized bill, daily 11:00–24:00, between Melantrichova and Zelezna at Kožná 14, reservations smart in evening, tel. 224-228-635).

Restaurant U Plebána is a quiet little place with good service, Czech cuisine, and a modern yet elegant setting (daily 12:00–24:00, live piano music nightly 19:00–23:00, Betlémské Náměstí 10, tel. 222-221-568).

Country Life Vegetarian Restaurant is a bright, easy, and smoke-free cafeteria that has a well-displayed buffet of salads and veggie hot dishes. It's midway between the Old Town Square and the bottom of Wenceslas Square. They are serious about their vegetarianism, serving only plant-based, unprocessed, and unrefined food (Mon–Thu 9:00–20:30, Fri 9:00–18:00, Sun 11:00–20:30, closed Sat, through courtyard at Melantrichova 15/Michalska 18, tel. 224-213-366).

Czech Kitchen (Ceská Kuchyně) is a blue-collar cafeteria serving steamy old Czech cuisine to a local clientele. There's no English. Just pick up your tally sheet at the door, grab a tray, and point liberally to whatever you'd like. It's extremely cheap (daily 9:00–20:00, across from Havelská Market at Havelská 23, tel. 224-235-574).

Bohemia Bagel is hardly authentic Czech—exasperated locals insist that bagels have nothing to do with Bohemia. Owned by an American, this trendy place caters mostly to youthful tourists (and advertises heavily along the tourist drag), but has good sandwiches (125–150 kč) and Internet access close to the Old Town Square (daily 24 hrs, locations at Újezd 16, tel. 257-310-529, and Masná 2, tel. 224-812-560, www.bohemiabagel.cz).

Above the Castle

Oživlé Dřevo, a stately yet traditional restaurant, feels like a country farmhouse and comes with perhaps the most commanding view terrace in all of Prague. It serves good quality traditional cuisine. Hiking up the Nerudova/Úvoz road, bypass the castle and carry on five minutes more to the Strahov Monastery (daily 11:00–23:00, Strahovske Nadvori 1, tel. 220-517-274).

Maly Buddha ("Little Buddha") serves delightful food—especially vegetarian—and takes its theme seriously. You'll step into a mellow, low-lit escape of bamboo and peace to be served by people with perfect complexions and almost no pulse. Ethnic eateries like this are trendy with young Czechs (Tue–Sun 13:00–22:30, closed Mon, smoke-free, continue on road to castle, bypassing castle turnoff about 100 yards to Úvoz 46, tel. 220-513-894).

U Hrocha ("By the Hippo") is a very local little pub packed with beer drinkers and smoke. Just below the castle near Malá Strana's main square, it's actually the haunt of many members of Parliament—located just around the corner (daily 12:00–23:00, chalkboard lists daily meals, Thunovska 10).

Espresso Kajetánka, just off of Castle Square, is a pricey café worth considering for the view and convenience (tel. 257-533-735).

Near the Jewish Quarter

Kolkovna is a big, new, woody yet modern place catering to locals and serving a fun mix of Czech and international cuisine (ribs, salads, cheese plates, great beer, daily 11:00–24:00, across from Spanish Synagogue at U Kolkovna 8, tel. 224-819-701).

The **Franz Kafka Café** is pleasant for a snack or drink (daily 10:00–21:00, Siroká 12, a block from the cemetery).

Eating with a View at Wenceslas Square

The **Modra Terasa (Blue Terrace) Restaurant** may still be closed for renovation. When open, it serves good food, uniquely perched for those wanting to survey Prague's grandest square while eating without a tourist in sight (smoky interior, fun terrace on sunny days, ride elevator at Na Mustku 9—from top of metro station at the base of Wenceslas Square, tel. 224-226-288).

Czech Beer

For many, *pivo* (beer) is the top Czech tourist attraction. After all, the Czechs invented lager in nearby Pilsen. This is the famous Pilsner Urquell, a great lager on tap everywhere. Budvar is the local Budweiser, but it's not related to the American brew. Czechs are among the world's biggest beer drinkers—adults drink about 80 gallons a year. The big degree symbol on bottles and menus marks the beer's heaviness, not its alcohol content (12 degrees is darker, 10 degrees lighter). The smaller figure shows alcohol content. Order beer from the tap *(sudove pivo)* in either small (0.3 liter, or 10 oz, *male pivo*) or large (0.5 liter, or 17 oz, *pivo*). In many restaurants, a beer hits your table like a glass of water in the United States. *Pivo* for lunch has me sightseeing for the rest of the day on Czech knees. Be sure to venture beyond the Pilsner Urquell. There are plenty of other good Czech beers.

Teahouses

Many Czech people prefer the mellow, smoke-free environs of a teahouse to the smoky, traditional beer hall. While there are teahouses all over town, one fine example in a handy locale is **Dobrá Čajovna** (Mon–Sat

10:00–23:00, Sun 14:00–23:00, near the base of Wenceslas Square at Václavske Náměstí 14). This teahouse, just a few steps off the bustle of the main square, takes you into a very peaceful world that elevates tea to an almost religious ritual. Ask for the English menu, which lovingly describes each tea (www.cajovna.com).

TRANSPORTATION CONNECTIONS

Getting to Prague: Those with railpasses need to purchase tickets to cover the portion of their journey from the border of the Czech Republic to Prague (buy at station before you board train for Prague). Or supplement your pass with a Prague Excursion pass, giving you passage from any Czech border station into Prague and back to any border station within seven days. Ask about this pass (and get reservations) at the EurAide offices in Munich or Berlin (first class-€50, second class-€40, youth second class-€35). EurAide's U.S. office sells these passes for a bit less (U.S. tel. 941/480-1555, fax 941/480-1522). Direct night trains leave Munich for Prague daily around 23:00 (8.5-hr trip). Tickets cost about €60 from Munich or, if you have a railpass covering Germany, €20 from the border.

For Czech train and bus schedules, see www.vlak-bus.cz.

By train to: Český Krumlov (8/day, 4 hrs, verify departing station), **Berlin** (5/day, 5 hrs), **Munich** (3/day, 5 hrs), **Frankfurt** (3/day, 6 hrs), **Vienna** (3/day, 5 hrs), **Budapest** (6/day, 9 hrs). Train info: tel. 224-224-200.

By car, with a driver: Mike's Chauffeur Service is a reliable little company with fair and fixed rates around town and beyond. Friendly Mike's motto is, "we go the extra mile for you" (round-trip fares with waiting time included: Český Krumlov-3,500 kč, Terezín-1,700 kč, Karlštejn-1,500 kč, up to 4 people, tel. 241-768-231, mobile 602-224-893, www.mike-chauffeur.cz, mike.chauffeur@cmail.cz). On the way to Krumlov, Mike will stop at no extra charge at Hluboka Castle or České Budějovice, where the original Bud beer is made.

COPENHAGEN
(København)

Copenhagen, Denmark's capital, is the gateway to Scandinavia. And now, with the bridge connecting Sweden and Denmark (creating the region's largest metropolitan area), Copenhagen is energized and ready to dethrone Stockholm as Scandinavia's powerhouse city. A busy day cruising the canals, wandering through the palace, and taking an old-town walk will give you your historical bearings. Then, after another day strolling the Strøget (Europe's first and greatest pedestrian shopping mall), biking the canals, and sampling the Danish good life, you'll feel right at home. Copenhagen is Scandinavia's cheapest and most fun-loving capital. So live it up.

Planning Your Time
A first visit deserves a minimum of two days.

Day 1: Catch the 10:30 or 11:00 city walking tour (see "Tours," below). After a Riz-Raz lunch, visit the Use It information center and catch the relaxing canal-boat tour out to *The Little Mermaid* and back. Enjoy the rest of the afternoon tracing Denmark's cultural roots in the National Museum (touring the Victorian Apartment if possible) and visiting the Ny Carlsberg Glyptotek art gallery. Spend the evening strolling Strøget (follow "Heart and Soul" walk described below) and/or dipping into Christiania.

Day 2: At 10:00, go neoclassical at Thorvaldsen's Museum. At 11:00, take the 50-minute guided tour of Denmark's royal Christiansborg Palace. After a *smørrebrød* lunch in a park, spend the afternoon seeing the Rosenborg Castle/crown jewels and the Nazi Resistance museum. Spend the evening at Tivoli Gardens.

ORIENTATION

Nearly all of your sightseeing is in Copenhagen's compact old town. By doing things by bike or on foot, you'll stumble into some charming bits of Copenhagen that many miss.

I rent a bike for my entire visit (for the cost of about a single cab ride per day) and park it safely in my hotel courtyard. I get anywhere in the town center literally faster than by taxi. The city is a joyride by bike.

For most visitors, the core of the town is the axis formed by the train station, Tivoli Gardens, Rådhus (City Hall) Square, and the Strøget pedestrian street. Bubbling with street life and colorful pedestrian zones, this main drag is fun. But be sure to get off Strøget.

You need to remember one character in Copenhagen's history: Christian IV. Ruling from 1588 to 1648, he was Denmark's Renaissance king and a royal party animal. The personal energy of this "Builder King" sparked a golden age when Copenhagen prospered and many of the city's grandest buildings were erected. Locals love to tell stories of everyone's favorite king, whose drinking was legendary.

Tourist Information

Copenhagen This Week is a free, handy, and misnamed monthly guide to the city, worth reading for its good maps, museum hours with telephone numbers, sightseeing tour ideas, shopping suggestions, and calendar of events, including free English tours and concerts (online at www.ctw.dk). This is *the* essential listing of everything in town, and it's always the most up-to-date information in print. While the "TIs" are really just an advertising agency (see below), with a map and *Copenhagen This Week*—both free and available at TIs and most hotels—you should be ready to roll. The Danish Tourist Board's Web site is also a wealth of information on activities and events in Copenhagen (www.visitdenmark.com).

Wonderful Copenhagen, as the tourist office is called, is a for-profit company. This colors the advice and information it provides. Mindful of this, drop by to get a city map and *Copenhagen This Week,* browse the racks of brochures, and get your questions answered (July–August Mon–Sat 9:00–20:00, Sun 9:00–18:00, May–June and Sept Mon–Sat 9:00–18:00, closed Sun, Oct–April Mon–Sat 10:00–16:00, closed Sun; across from train station on Bernstorffsgade, tel. 70 22 24 42, www.visitcopenhagen.dk). They also book rooms for a 60-kr fee. The TI only posts information from outfits that pay for the shelf space. This week's entertainment program for Tivoli is posted on posts outside Tivoli's main entrance (around the corner from the TI).

Use It is a better information service (10-min walk from train station). Government-sponsored and student-run, it caters to Copenhagen's young but welcomes travelers of any age. It's a friendly, driven-to-help, energetic, no-nonsense source of budget travel information, offering a

Copenhagen Overview

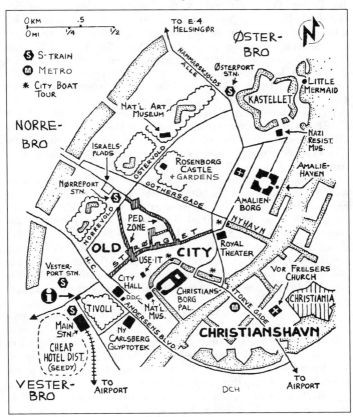

0 KM   .5
0 MI   1/4   1/2

🅢 S-TRAIN
Ⓜ METRO
✳ CITY BOAT TOUR

TO E·4
HELSINGØR

ØSTER-BRO

NORRE-BRO

NAMMARSKJOLDS ALLE

ØSTERPORT STN.

KASTELLET

• LITTLE MERMAID

HAT'L. ART MUSEUM

ISRAELS-PLADS

ROSENBORG CASTLE & GARDENS

NAZI RESIST. MUS.

AMALIE-HAVEN

NØRREPORT STN.

GOTHERSGADE

AMALIEN-BORG

OSTERVOLD

PED. ZONE

NYHAVN

OLD   CITY

ROYAL THEATER

USE IT

VESTER-PORT STN.

NORREVOLD

H.C.

STRØGET

CITY HALL

DDC.

CHRISTIANS BORG PAL.

VOR FRELSERS CHURCH

CHRISTIANIA

TIVOLI

HAT'L MUS.

ANDERSENS BLVD.

TORVE GADE

CHRISTIANSHAVN

MAIN STN.

NY CARLSBERG GLYPTOTEK

CHEAP HOTEL DIST. (SEEDY)

VESTER-BRO

TO AIRPORT

DCH

TO AIRPORT

free room-finding service, free Internet access, candy bowls of free condoms, and free luggage lockers. Their free annual *Playtime* publication
has Back Door-style articles on Copenhagen and the Danish culture,
special budget tips, and self-guided tours. Read it! They book private
rooms (350-kr doubles, no booking fee). From the station, head down
Strøget, then turn right on Rådhustræde for three blocks to #13 (mid-
June–mid-Sept daily 9:00–19:00; otherwise Mon–Wed 11:00–16:00,
Thu 11:00–18:00, Fri 11:00–14:00, closed Sat–Sun; tel. 33 73 06 20).

The Copenhagen Card, which includes free entry to many of the
city's sights, can save you some money if you're sightseeing like crazy
(160 kr for 24 hours; the 72-hour version for 400 kr also covers outlying
sights and public transportation).

Arrival in Copenhagen

By Train: The main train station is called Hovedbanegården (HOETH-bahn-gorn; learn that word—you'll need to recognize it). It's a temple of travel and a hive of travel-related activity, offering lockers (35 kr/day), a checkroom (*garderobe*, Mon–Sat 5:30–24:00, Sun 6:00–24:00, 40 kr/day per backpack), a post office (Mon–Fri 8:00–21:00, Sat 9:00–16:00, Sun 10:00–16:00), a grocery store (daily 8:00–24:00), 24-hour thievery, and the best bike rental shop in town (see "Getting around Copenhagen: By Bike," below). The station has ATMs and long-hour FOREX exchange desks (daily 8:00–21:00; FOREX is the least expensive place in town to change money). Showers (10 kr) are available at the public rest rooms at the back of the station. The Wonderful Copenhagen TI also has a hotel/room-finding office here (60 kr, Mon–Wed 10:00–20:00, Thu–Sat 9:00–20:00, closed Sun).

While you're in the station, reserve your overnight train seat or *couchette* out at the Rejse-bureau (Mon–Fri 10:00–17:00, closed Sat–Sun, tel. 33 54 55 10). International rides and all IC (fast) trains require reservations (usually 20 kr). If you have a railpass, you must make your reservations at the *Billetsalg* (Mon–Fri 8:00–19:00, Sat 9:30–16:00, closed Sun). The *Kviksalg* office sells tickets within Denmark (plus the regional train to Malmö, Sweden). This "quick sale" office will also help you with reservations for international trips if the *Billetsalg* office is closed and you're departing by train within one hour or early the next day (daily 5:45–23:30).

To get to the recommended Christianshavn B&Bs from the train station, catch bus #2A or #48 (15 kr, 4/hr, in front of station on near side of Bernstorffsgade, with back to the station heading to right, get off at stop just after *Knippelsbro*—Knippels bridge). Note the time the bus departs, then stop by the TI (across the street) and pick up a free Copenhagen city map that shows bus routes.

By Plane: Kastrup, Copenhagen's international airport, is a traveler's dream, with a TI, baggage check, bank, post office, shopping mall, grocery store, and bakery. You can use dollars or euros at the airport—but you'll get change back in kroner (airport info tel. 32 47 47 47, SAS info tel. 70 10 20 00). Need to kill a night at the airport? The Transfer Hotel, under the Transit Hall, rents fetal rest cabins. Called *hvilekabiner,* they are especially handy for early flights, but you must have a ticket and you're stuck in the transit area (Sb-400 kr, Db-600 kr for 8 hrs, prices vary for 2- to 16-hr periods, reception open daily 5:30–23:30, easy telephone reservations, sauna and showers available, tel. 32 31 24 55, fax 32 31 31 09, transferhotel@cph.dk).

Getting Downtown from the Airport: Taxis are fast and civil, accept credit cards, and, at about 200 kr to the town center, are a reasonable deal for foursomes. The slick and easy Air Rail train (23 kr, 3/hr, 12 min) links the airport with the train station, as well as the

Nørreport stations. City bus #250S gets you downtown (City Hall Square, train station) in 30 minutes for 23 kr (6/hr, across the street and to the right as you exit airport).

If you're going from the airport to Christianshavn, you can take the Air Rail shuttle to Nørreport, then change to the Metro for Christianshavn (same 23-kr ticket works for the entire trip). Or, simpler, from the airport just hop on bus #2A, which takes you right through the middle of Christianshavn (30 min). In a few years, the Metro will connect the airport and Christianshavn directly in 10 minutes.

Helpful Hints

Jazz Festival: The Copenhagen Jazz Festival—10 days starting the first Friday in July (July 2–11 in 2004)—puts the town in a rollicking slide-trombone mood. The Danes are Europe's jazz enthusiasts, and this music festival fills the town with happiness. The TI prints up an extensive listing of each year's festival events, or get the latest at www.jazzfestival.dk. There's also an autumn jazz festival the first week of November.

Telephones: Use the telephone liberally. Everyone speaks English, and *This Week* and this book list phone numbers for everything you'll be doing. All telephone numbers in Denmark are eight digits, and there are no area codes. Calls anywhere in Denmark are cheap; calls to Norway and Sweden cost 6 kr per minute from a booth (half that from a private home). Get a phone card (at newsstands, starting at 30 kr). To call the USA or make international calls, buy an international PIN card (with a scratch-off personal identity number). The "Go Bananas" card is particularly reliable (sold at kiosks for 100 kr—giving you more than 100 minutes of talk time to the USA, same card good in Germany, Denmark, Sweden, and Norway).

Emergencies: Dial 112 and specify fire, police, or ambulance. Emergency calls from public phones are free.

Pharmacy: Steno Apotek is across from the train station (open 24 hrs daily, Vesterbrogade 6c, tel. 33 14 82 66).

U.S. Embassy: It's at Dag Hammerskjolds Alle 24, tel. 35 55 31 44.

Getting around Copenhagen

By Bus, S-tog, and Metro: It's easy to navigate Copenhagen with its fine buses, new Metro, and S-tog, a suburban train system with stops in the city (Eurail valid on S-tog). A 15-kr two-zone ticket (pay as you board buses, buy from station ticket offices or vending machines for the Metro) gets you an hour's travel within the center. Consider the blue two-zone *klippekort* (95 kr for 10 1-hr "rides") and the 24-hour pass (90 kr, validate day pass in yellow machine on bus or at station, both sold at stations and the TI). Assume you'll be within the middle two zones. Buses go every three to six minutes. Bus drivers are patient, have change, and speak English. City maps list bus and subway routes. Locals are friendly and helpful. The HUR Kundecenter (big black building) on the Rådhus Square is very helpful and has a fine, free map showing all the bus routes (tel. 36 13 14 15).

Copenhagen's super-futuristic Metro line connects Christianshavn and Nørreport (2 stops on S-tog from main train station). Eventually the Metro will run from Copenhagen to the airport and on to Ørestad, the industrial and business center created after the new Øresund Bridge was built between Denmark and Sweden (for the latest, see www.m.dk).

By Bus Tour: Open Top Tour buses do a hop-on, hop-off 60-minute circle connecting the city's top sights; for details, see "Tours," below.

By Taxi: Taxis are plentiful and easy to call or flag down but pricey (24-kr drop charge, then 10 kr per km, credit cards accepted). For a short ride, four people spend about the same by taxi as by bus (e.g., 50 kr from train station to recommended Christianshavn B&Bs). Calling 35 35 35 35 will get you a taxi within minutes...with the meter already way up there.

Free Bikes: From May through November, 2,000 clunky but practical little bikes are scattered around the old-town center (basically the terrain covered in the Copenhagen map in this chapter). Simply locate one of the 150 racks, unlock a bike by popping a 20-kr coin into the handlebar, and pedal away. When you're done, plug your bike back into any other rack and your deposit coin will pop back out (if you can't find a rack, just abandon your bike and a bum will take it back and pocket your coin). These simple bikes come with theft-proof parts (unusable on regular bikes) and—they claim—computer tracer chips embedded in them so bike patrols can retrieve strays. These are funded by advertisements painted on the wheels and by a progressive electorate.

Copenhagen's radical city bike program is a clever idea. But in practice, it doesn't work great for sightseers. It's hard to find bikes in working order, and when you get to the sight and park your bike, it'll be gone by the time you're ready to pedal on. (There's a 20-kr deposit coin as an incentive for any kid to pick up city bikes not plugged back into their special racks.) Use the free bikes for a one-way pedal here and there. But if you really want to bike efficiently, pay to rent one.

Good Bikes: For a comfortable bike that's yours for the duration and in great working order, rent one at the main train station's Cykelcenter (75 kr/24 hrs, cheaper for longer if paid in advance, Mon–Fri 8:00–17:30, Sat 9:00–13:00, July–Aug open Sun 9:00–13:00, otherwise closed Sun; no helmets, tel. 33 33 86 13). Bikers see more, save time and money, and really feel like locals.

Copenhagen

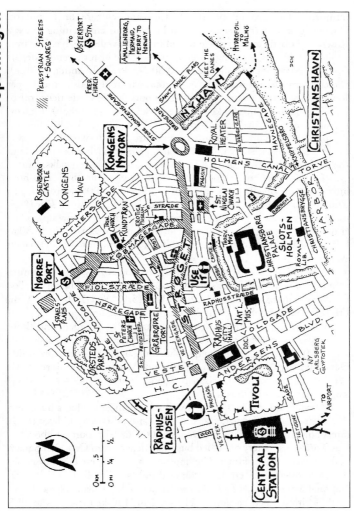

TOURS

▲▲▲**Walking Tours**—Once upon a time, American **Richard Karpen** visited Copenhagen and fell in love with the city (and one of its women). Now, dressed as Hans Christian Andersen he leads daily 90-minute tours that wander in and out of buildings, courtyards, backstreets, and unusual parts of the old town. Along the way, he gives insightful and humorous background on the history and culture of Denmark, Copenhagen, and the Danes. Richard offers four entertaining tours: a Rosenborg Castle tour (see below) and three city walks (each a little over a mile with breaks, covering different parts of the historic center; depart from TI May–Sept Mon–Sat at 10:30, 75 kr, kids under 12 free). Richard's excellent Rosenborg Castle tour, which he leads as the dapper Renaissance "Sir Richard," departs from outside the castle ticket office (13:30 Mon and Thu, 50 kr plus the 60-kr castle admission). Richard has an infectious love of Copenhagen. His tours, while all different, complement each other and are of equal introduction value. No reservations needed—just show up. For details, pick up Richard's schedule in *Copenhagen This Week*, at the TI, or see www.copenhagenwalks.com.

Go with the Danes: These Danish guides give a fine basic two-hour intro walk to Copenhagen (75 kr, Sat and Sun at 11:00 year-round, also Thu and Fri in June–Aug, confirm schedule in *Copenhagen This Week*, tours start outside TI across from train station, simply show up). They also give Rosenborg Castle tours (50 kr, 60 min, Sun and Tue at 13:30 in July and Aug, www.copenhagen-walkingtours.dk, info@copenhagen -walkingtours.dk).

Copenhagen History Tours: Christian Donatzky, a charming young Dane with a Master's in history, gives a series of history walks. Each day features a different century (Tue-15th, Wed-16th, Thu-17th, Fri-18th, Sat-19th, Sun-20th). While the tours are light on actual visual connections to his lectures, they are thoughtfully designed, and those with a serious interest in Danish history find them time well spent (70 kr, 60–90 min each, small groups, Tue–Sun at 11:00, mid-April–mid-Oct only, depart from statue of Bishop Absalon on Hojbro Plads between Strøget and Christiansborg Palace, tel. 28 49 44 35, www .copenhagenhistorytours.dk).

Local Guides: The Danish tour guide organization has a huge staff of well-trained guides ready to show you around (www.guides.dk). Or hire a guide from Go with the Danes (1,000 kr/2-hr tour; see above).

Bus Tours—A variety of guided bus tours depart from City Hall Square in front of the Palace Hotel. The hop-on, hop-off **Open Top Tour** does the basic 60-minute circle of the city sights—Tivoli, Royal Palace, National Museum, *The Little Mermaid,* Rosenborg Castle, Nyhavn, and more—with a taped narration (110 kr, 2/hr, 140 kr for access to all 3 tour lines, ticket good for 48 hrs, April–Oct daily 9:30–17:00; you can get off, see a sight, and catch a later bus; bus departs City Hall below the *Lur Blowers* statue—to the left of City Hall—or at many other stops throughout city, pay driver, tel. 32 54 06 06, run by Copenhagen Excursions). The same company also runs jaunts into the countryside, with themes such as Vikings, castles, and Hamlet.

▲▲**Harbor Cruise and Canal Tours**—Two companies offer essentially the same live, three-language, 50-minute tours through the city canals.

Both boats leave at least twice an hour from near Christiansborg Palace, cruise around the palace and Christianshavn area, and then proceed into the wide-open harbor. It's a relaxing way to see *The Little Mermaid* and munch a lazy picnic during the slow-moving narration.

The low-overhead **Netto-Bådene** tour boats leave from Holmen's Bridge in front of the palace and from Nyhavn (25 kr, late April–Sept daily 10:00–17:00, later in summer, sign at dock shows next departure, 2–5/hr, dress warmly—boats are open-top until Sept, tel. 32 54 41 02, www.havnerundfart.dk). Don't mix up the boats—this cheaper line advertises less. Its Nyhavn dock is midway down the canal (on the city side), while the expensive boat is at the head of the canal.

The expensive option, **DFDS Canal Tours,** does the same tour for 50 kr (departs from Gammel Strand, 200 yards away; and from Nyhavn, April–mid-Oct daily 10:00–17:00). They also offer unguided "water bus" hop-on, hop-off tours for 30 kr (mid-May–early Sept 10:15–16:45, tel. 33 93 42 60).

Go with Netto. There's no reason to pay double.

Bike Tours—City Safari offers 2.5-hour guided bike tours of Copenhagen, a general city intro including Christiania (June–Aug daily 10:00 and 13:00, 150 kr includes bike, in English and Danish as needed, no reservation needed, show up 10 min in advance at Danish Center for Architecture, Gammel Dok Storehouse, Strandgade 27B, tel. 33 23 94 90, www.citysafari.dk, or ask at Use It; energetic Steen is a one-man show and speaks fine English).

Do-It-Yourself Orientation Walk: Strøget and Copenhagen's Heart and Soul

Start from **Rådhuspladsen (City Hall Square),** the bustling heart of Copenhagen, dominated by the tower of city hall. This was Copenhagen's fortified west end. For 700 years, Copenhagen was contained within its walls. In the mid-1800s, 140,000 people were packed inside. The over-crowding led to hygiene problems. (A cholera outbreak killed 5,000.) It was clear: the walls needed to come down...and they did.

In 1843, magazine publisher Georg Carstensen convinced the king to let him build a pleasure garden outside the walls of crowded Copenhagen. The king quickly agreed, knowing that people, when well entertained, care less about fighting for democracy. **Tivoli** became Europe's first great public amusement park. When the train lines came, the station was placed just beyond Tivoli. Those formidable walls faded away, surviving only in echoes—a circular series of roads and remnants of moats, now people-friendly city lakes.

The City Hall, or **Rådhus,** is worth a visit (Mon–Fri 8:00–17:00, closed Sat–Sun—described under "Sights," below). Old **Hans Christian Andersen** sits to the right of city hall, almost begging to be in another photo (as he used to in real life). Climb onto his well-worn knee. (While

COPENHAGEN AT A GLANCE

▲▲▲**Tivoli** Copenhagen's classic amusement park, with rides, music, food, and other fun. **Hours:** Mid-April–mid-Sept daily 11:00–23:00, later on Fri, Sat, and in summer.

▲▲▲**National Museum** History of Danish civilization with tourable 19th-century Victorian Apartment. **Hours:** Museum: Tue–Sun 10:00–17:00, closed Mon; Apartment: tours Sat and Sun (likely also Thu and Fri) at 12:00, 13:00, 14:00, and 15:00.

▲▲▲**Rosenborg Castle and Treasury** Renaissance castle of larger-than-life "warrior king" Christian IV. **Hours:** Daily June–Aug 10:00–17:00, May and Sept 10:00–16:00, Oct 11:00–15:00, Nov–April Tue–Sun 11:00–14:00, closed Mon.

▲▲▲**Christiania** Colorful counterculture squatters' colony where marijuana is sold and smoked openly. **Hours:** Always open.

▲▲**Christiansborg Palace** Royal reception rooms with dazzling tapestries. **Hours:** Visit only with tour: May–Sept daily at 11:00, 13:00, and 15:00; Oct–April Tue, Thu, Sat, and Sun at 15:00.

▲▲**Denmark's Resistance Museum** Chronicle of Denmark's struggle against the Nazis. **Hours:** May–mid-Sept Tue–Sat 10:00–16:00, Sun

up there, you might take off your shirt for a racy photo, as many Danes enjoy doing.) In 2005, Copenhagen will be celebrating H.C.A.'s 200th birthday—and party plans are already underway. On a pedestal left of city hall, note the *Lur Blowers* sculpture honoring the earliest warrior Danes. The *lur* is a horn that was used 3,500 years ago. The ancient originals (which still play) are displayed in the National Museum. (City tour buses leave from below these Vikings.)

The golden **weather girls** high up on the tower (marked "Philips" in blue) opposite the Strøget's entrance tell the weather: on a bike (fair) or with an umbrella. These two have been called the only women in Copenhagen you can trust. But for years, they've been stuck on the almost-sunny mode...with the bike just peeking out. Notice that the red temperature dots only go to 28 degrees (that's 82 Fahrenheit).

Here in the traffic hub of this huge city, you'll notice...not many cars. Denmark's 180 percent tax on car purchases makes the bus or bike a sweeter option.

The **SAS building** is Copenhagen's only skyscraper. Locals say it

10:00–17:00, closed Mon; off-season Tue–Sat 11:00–15:00, Sun 11:00–16:00, closed Mon.

▲**City Hall** Impressive building packed with Danish history and symbolism. **Hours:** Mon–Fri 8:00–17:00, open Sat only for tours, closed Sun.

▲**Thorvaldsen's Museum** Works of the Danish neoclassical sculptor. **Hours:** Tue–Sun 10:00–17:00, closed Mon.

▲**Ny Carlsberg Glyptotek** Scandinavia's top art gallery, featuring Egyptians, Greeks, Etruscans, French, and Danes. **Hours:** Tue–Sun 10:00–16:00, closed Mon.

▲**National Art Museum** Good Danish and Impressionist collections. **Hours:** Tue–Sun 10:00–17:00, Wed until 20:00, closed Mon.

▲**Amalienborg Palace Museum** Quick and intimate look at Denmark's royal family. **Hours:** May–Oct daily 10:00–16:00, Nov–April Tue–Sun 11:00–16:00.

▲**Our Savior's Church** Spiral-spired church with bright Baroque interior. **Hours:** April–Aug Mon–Sat 11:00–16:30, Sun 12:00–16:30, closes off-season at 15:30.

seems so tall because the clouds hang so low. When it was built in 1960, Copenhageners took one look and decided—that's enough of a skyline.

The American trio of Burger King, 7-Eleven, and KFC marks the start of the otherwise charming **Strøget.** Finished in 1962, Copenhagen's experimental, tremendously successful, and most-copied pedestrian shopping mall is a string of lively (and individually named) streets and lovely squares that bunny-hop through the old town from city hall to Nyhavn, a 20-minute stroll away.

As you wander down this street, remember that the commercial focus of a historic street like Strøget drives up the land value, which generally trashes the charm and tears down the old buildings. Look above the modern window displays and street-level advertising to discover bits of 19th-century character surviving. While Strøget has become hamburgerized, historic bits and charming pieces of old Copenhagen are just off this commercial cancan.

Copenhagen was fortified around large mansions with expansive **courtyards.** As the population grew, the city's physical size was constricted

Strøget

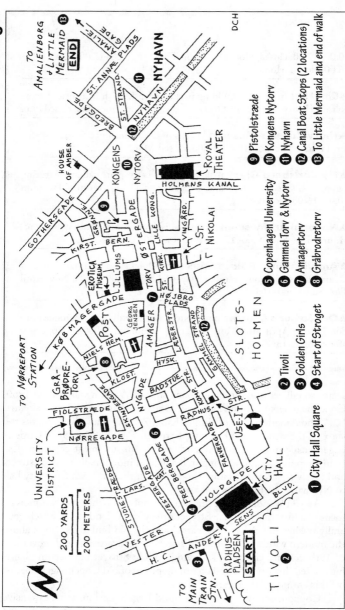

1. City Hall Square
2. Tivoli
3. Golden Girls
4. Start of Strøget
5. Copenhagen University
6. Gammel Torv & Nytorv
7. Amagertorv
8. Gråbrødretorv
9. Pistolstræde
10. Kongens Nytorv
11. Nyhavn
12. Canal Boat Stops (2 locations)
13. To Little Mermaid and end of walk

by its walls. Therefore, these courtyards were gradually filled with hig-gledy-piggledy secondary buildings. Today throughout the old center, you can step off a busy pedestrian mall and back in time into these characteristic half-timbered time-warps. Replace the parked car with a tired horse, replace the bikes with a line of outhouses, and you are in 19th-century Copenhagen. If you see an open door, you're welcome to discreetly wander in and look around. Don't miss the courtyards of Copenhagen.

After one block (at Kattesundet), make a side-trip three blocks left into Copenhagen's colorful **university district.** Formerly the old brothel neighborhood, then ground zero for Copenhagen's hippies in the 1960s, today this "Latin Quarter" is Soho chic.

At Sankt Peders Stræde, turn right and walk to the end of the street. On your right is the big neoclassical **Cathedral of Our Lady.** Stand across the street from its facade. The Reformation Memorial celebrates the date Denmark broke from the Roman Catholic Church and became Lutheran (1536). Walk around and study the reliefs of great Danish reformers protesting from their pulpits. The relief facing the church shows King Christian III, who, after being influenced by Luther in his German travels (and realizing the advantages of being the head of his own state church), oversees the town council meeting that decided on this break. Because of 1536, there's no Mary in the Cathedral of Our Lady.

The cathedral's **facade** is a Greek temple. (To the right in the distance, notice more neoclassicism—the law courts.) You can see why golden-age Copenhagen (early 1800s) fancied itself a Nordic Athens. Old Testament figures (King David and Moses) flank the cathedral's entryway. Above, John the Baptist stands where you'd expect to see Greek gods. He invites you in...to the New Testament.

Enter the cathedral—a world of neoclassical serenity (free, open daily 7:30–17:00). This pagan temple now houses Christianity. The nave is lined by the 12 Apostles (each clad in Roman togas)—masterpieces by the great Danish sculptor Bertel Thorvaldsen. They lead to a statue of the risen Christ—standing where the statue of Caesar would have been. Rather than wearing an imperial toga, Jesus wears his burial shroud and says, "Come to me." The marvelous acoustics are demonstrated in free organ concerts each Saturday at noon. This is where Copenhagen gathers for extraordinary events. After 9/11, the queen, her government, and the entire diplomatic core held a memorial service here.

Head back outside. If you face the facade and look to the left, you'll see **Copenhagen University**—home of 30,000 students. The king began the university in the 17th century to stop the Danish brain drain to Paris. Today tuition is free (but room, board & beer are not). Locals say it's easy to get in...but (given the lovely lifestyle) very hard to get out.

Step up the middle steps of the university's big building and enter a colorful lobby starring Athena and Apollo. The frescoes celebrate high thinking, with themes such as the triumph of wisdom over barbarism. Notice how harmoniously the architecture, sculpture, and painting work together. Outside, busts honor great minds from the faculty, including (at the end) Neils Bohr—a professor who won the 1922 Nobel Prize for theoretical physics. He evaded the clutches of the Nazi science labs by fleeing to America in 1943, where he helped develop the atomic bomb.

Rejoin Strøget (down where you saw the law courts) at **Gammel Torv** and **Nytorv** (Old Square and New Square). This was the old town center. In Gammel Torv, the Fountain of Charity (Caritas) is named for the figure of charity on top. It has provided drinking water to locals since the early 1600s. Featuring a pregnant woman squirting water from her breasts next to a boy urinating, this was just too much for people of the Victorian age. They corked both figures and raised the statue to what they hoped would be out of eyesight. The Oriental-looking kiosk was one of the city's first community telephone centers before phones were privately owned. Look at the reliefs ringing its top: an airplane with bird wings (c. 1900) and two women talking on the newfangled phone. (It was thought business would popularize the telephone, but actually it was women.... Now, 100 years later, look at the mobile phones.)

While Gammel Torv was a place of happiness and merriment, Nytorv was a place of severity and judgment. Walk to the small raised area in front of the old ancient-Greek-style city hall. Do a 360. The entire square is neoclassical. Read the old Danish on the city hall facade: With Law Shall Man Land Build. Look down at the pavement and read the plaque: "Here stood the town's Kag (whipping post) until 1780."

Next, walk down **Amagertorv,** prime real estate for talented street entertainers and pickpockets (past the Gad Bookstore—excellent selection of English-language guidebooks and cookbooks) to the stately brick Holy Ghost church. The fine spire is typical of old Danish churches. Under the stepped gable was a medieval hospital run by monks. A block behind the church (walk down Valkendorfsgade and through a passage under a rust-colored building) is the leafy and caffeine-stained **Gråbrødretorv** (Grey Friars' Square)—a popular place for an outdoor meal or drink in the summer—surrounded by fine old buildings. At the end of the square, the street Niels Hemmingsens Gade returns (past the Copenhagen Jazz House, a good place for live music nightly) to Strøget. Continue down the pedestrian street—with its fine inlaid Italian granite stonework—to the next square with the stork fountain (actually a heron). The Victorian WCs here (steps down from fountain, 2 kr) are a delight.

Amagertorv—the next stretch of Stroget—is a highlight for shoppers. A line of Royal Copenhagen stores here sell porcelain (with demos), glassware, jewelry and silverware. Illums Bolighus is known for modern design (Mon–Sat 10:00–18:00, Sun 12:00–17:00). From here you can see the imposing Parliament building, Christiansborg Palace, and an equestrian statue of Bishop Absalon, the city's founder (canal boat tours from nearby). A block toward the canal, running parallel to Strøget, starts Strædet, a second Strøget with cafés, antique shops, and no fast food. North of Amagertorv, a broad pedestrian mall, Købmagergade, leads past the Museum of Erotica to Christian IV's Round Tower and the Latin Quarter (university district). Café Norden overlooks the fountain—a smoky but good place for a coffee with a view. The second floor offers the best vantage point.

The final stretch of Strøget leads to **Pistolstræde** (leading off Strøget to the left from Østergade at #24), a cute lane of shops in restored 18th-century buildings. Wander back into the half-timbered section. The Kransekagehuset bakery (see "Eating," below) has a rack of tourist fliers including the very handy-for-shoppers "Local Life," which highlights small specialty shops in the area.

Continuing along Strøget, you'll pass McDonald's (good view from top floor) and major department stores (Illum and Magasin—see "Shopping," below) to Kongens Nytorv.

Kongens Nytorv, the biggest square in town, is home to the Royal Theater, French Embassy, and venerable Hotel D'Angleterre. The statue in the middle of the square celebrates Christian V who, in the 1670s, enlarged Copenhagen by adding this "King's New Square" (Kongens Nytorv). The entire center is a happy skating rink for three months each winter.

On the right (just before the new Metro station, at #19), Hviids Vinstue, the town's oldest wine cellar (from 1723), is a colorful if smoky spot for an open-face sandwich and a beer (3 sandwiches and a beer for 50 kr at lunchtime). Wander around inside, if only to see the old photos. Just off Knogens Nytorv (30 yards from Hviids Vinstue) is the entry to the futuristic new Metro. Ride the escalators down and up to see the latest in Metro design (automated cars, no driver...sit in front to watch the tracks coming at you).

Head back up to ground level. Across the square is the trendy harbor of Nyhavn.

Nyhavn is a recently gentrified sailors' quarter. (Hong Kong is the last of the nasty bars from the rough old days.) With its trendy cafés, jazz clubs, and tattoo shops (pop into Tattoo Ole at #17—fun photos, very traditional), Nyhavn is a wonderful place to hang out. The canal is filled with glamorous old sailboats of all sizes. Any historic sloop is welcome to moor here in Copenhagen's ever-changing boat museum. Hans Christian Andersen lived and wrote his first stories here (in the red double-gabled building on the right at #20). Wander the quai, enjoying the frat party parade of tattoos (hotter weather reveals more tattoos). Celtic and Nordic mythological designs are in (as is bodybuilding, by the looks of things). The place thrives—with the cheap-beer drinkers dockside and the richer and older ones looking on from comfier cafes.

A note about all this public beer-drinking: There's no more beer consumption here than in the U.S.; it's just out in public. Many young Danes can't afford to drink in a bar. So they "picnic drink" their beers in squares and along canals, spending a quarter the bar price for a bottle from a nearby kiosk (just past the bridge on the right).

Just past the first bridge, a line of people wait for the best ice cream around—packed into fresh-baked waffles (look through the window to see the waffle iron in action).

Continuing north along the harborside (from end of Nyhavn canal, turn left), you'll stroll a delightful waterfront promenade to the modern fountain of Amaliehave Park (immediately across the harbor from the new opera house).

The orderly **Amalienborg Palace and Square** is a block inland, behind the fountain. Queen Margrethe II and her family live in the mansion to your immediate left as you enter the square from the harborside. Her son and heir to the throne, Crown Prince Frederik, recently moved into the mansion directly opposite his mother's. While the guards change with royal fanfare at noon only when the queen is in residence, they shower every morning. The small Amalienborg Palace Museum offers an intimate look at royal living (see "Sights—Near *The Little Mermaid*," below). If in need of a very traditional cheap lunch, head inland two blocks just past the Marble Church, to Svend Larsen's Smørrebrød (fine little 8-kr open-face sandwiches to go, St. Kongensgade 83, Mon–Fri 8:00–14:00, closed Sat–Sun).

From the square, Amaliegade leads north to Kastellet (Citadel) Park and Denmark's fascinating WWII Resistance Museum (see "Sights—Near *The Little Mermaid*," below). A short stroll past the Gefion fountain (illustrating the myth of the goddess who was given one night to carve a chunk out of Sweden to make into Denmark's main island, Zealand—which you're on) and an Anglican church built of flint brings you to the overrated, overfondled, and overphotographed symbol of Copenhagen, *Den Lille Havfrue—The Little Mermaid.*

You can get back downtown on foot, by taxi, or on bus #1A, #15, or #19 from Store Kongensgade on the other side of Kastellet Park, or bus #29 from behind the Nazi Resistance museum on Langelinie Street.

Tivoli

The world's grand old amusement park—since 1843—is 20 acres, 110,000 lanterns, and countless ice-cream cones of fun. You pay one admission price and find yourself lost in a Hans Christian Andersen wonderland of rides, restaurants, games, marching bands, roulette wheels, and funny mirrors. Tivoli doesn't try to be Disney. It's wonderfully and happily Danish.

Cost, Hours, and Location: The park is open every day—but only from about April 10 to September 20 (11:00–23:00, later on Fri, Sat, and in summer, 60 kr gets you in, tel. 33 15 10 01, www.tivoli.dk). Rides range in price from 10 to 50 kr (180 kr for all-day pass). All children's amusements are in full swing by 11:30; the rest of the amusements open by 14:00. Tivoli is across from the train station. If you're catching an overnight train, this is *the* place to spend your last Copenhagen hours. Tivoli also opens for a Christmas Market (mid-Nov–Christmas daily 11:00–22:00—with ice skating on Tivoli Lake).

Entertainment in Tivoli: Upon arrival (through main entry, on right in shop), pick up a map and events schedule. Take a moment to sit down and plan your entertainment for the evening. Events are spread between 15:00 and 23:00; the 19:30 concert in the concert hall can be free or may cost up to 500 kr, depending on the performer (box office tel. 33 15 10 12). If the Tivoli Symphony is playing, it's worth paying for. The Ticket Box Office is outside, just to the left of the main entry (daily 11:00–20:00, if you buy a concert ticket you get into Tivoli for free). The daily events schedule is also posted on the posts outside the main entry.

Free concerts, pantomime theater, ballet, acrobats, puppets, and other shows pop up all over the park, and a well-organized visitor can enjoy an exciting evening of entertainment without spending a single kroner. The children's theater, Valmuen, plays excellent traditional fairy tales daily at 12:00, 13:00, and 14:00. Friday evenings feature a (usually free) rock or pop show at 22:00. On Saturday from late April through late September, fireworks light up the sky at 23:45. The park is particularly romantic at dusk, when the lights go on.

Eating at Tivoli: Inside the park, expect to pay amusement-park prices for amusement-park-quality food. **Søcafeen,** by the lake, allows picnics if you buy a drink. The *pølse* (sausage) stands are cheap. **Færgekroen** is a good lakeside place for typical Danish food, beer, and an impromptu sing-along with a bunch of drunk Danes. The Croatian restaurant, **Hercegovina,** overlooks a leafy section of the amusement park and serves a 129-kr lunch buffet (mostly cold, 12:00–16:00) and a 169-kr dinner buffet (salads, veggies and lots and lots of meat; daily 17:00–22:00, music nightly after 19:00—see "Eating," below). For a cake and coffee, consider the **Viften** café. **Georg,** to the left of the concert hall, has tasty 45-kr sandwiches and 150-kr dinners (which include a glass of wine).

More Sights near the Train Station

▲**City Hall (Rådhus)**—This city landmark, between the train station/Tivoli/TI and Strøget pedestrian mall, offers private tours and trips up its 345-foot-tall tower. It's draped, inside and out, in Danish symbolism. The city's founder, Bishop Absalon, stands over the door. The polar bears climbing on the rooftop symbolize the giant Danish protectorate of Greenland.

Step inside. The lobby has racks of tourist information (city maps and *This Week*). The building was inspired by the city hall in Siena, Italy (with the necessary addition of a glass roof). Huge functions fill this grand hall (the iron grill in the center of the floor is an elevator for bringing up 1,200 chairs) while the busts of four illustrious local boys—the fairy-tale writer Hans Christian Andersen, the sculptor Bertel Thorvaldsen, the physicist Niels Bohr, and the building's architect Martin Nyrop—look on. Underneath the floor are national archives dating back to 1275, popular with Danes researching their family roots. The city hall is free and open to the public (Mon–Fri 8:00–17:00, open on Sat only for tours—see below). You can wander throughout the building and into the peaceful garden out back. Guided English-language **tours** get you into more private, official rooms (30 kr, 45 min, year-round Mon–Fri at 15:00, Sat at 10:00 and 11:00).

Tourists romp (in groups with an escort) up the **tower**'s 300 steps for the best aerial view of Copenhagen (20 kr, June–Sept: Mon–Fri 10:00, 12:00, and 14:00, Sat 12:00, Oct–May: Mon–Sat 12:00, tel. 33 66 25 82).

▲▲**Christiansborg Palace**—A complex of government buildings stands on the ruins of Copenhagen's original 12th-century fortress: the Parliament, Supreme Court, prime minister's office, royal reception rooms, royal library, several museums, and the royal stables.

While the current palace dates only from 1928 and the royal family moved out 200 years ago, the building is the sixth to stand here in 800 years and is rich with tradition. The information-packed 50-minute English-language tours of the royal reception rooms are excellent. As you slip-slide on protect-the-floor slippers through 22 rooms, you'll gain a good feel for Danish history, royalty, and politics. (For instance, the family portrait of King Christian IX shows why he's called the "father-in-law of Europe"—with children eventually becoming or marrying royalty in Denmark, Russia, Greece, Britain, France, Germany, and Norway.) The highlight is the dazzling set of modern tapestries—Danish-designed but Gobelin-made in Paris. This gift, given to the queen on her 60th birthday in 2000, celebrates 1,000 years of Danish history with wild wall-hangings from the Viking age to our chaotic times (admission by tour only, 40 kr, May–Sept daily at 11:00, 13:00, and 15:00; Oct–April Tue, Thu, Sat, and Sun at 15:00; from equestrian statue in front, go through wooden door, past entrance to Christiansborg Castle ruins, into courtyard, and up stairs on right; tel. 33 92 64 92).

Christiansborg Castle Ruins—An exhibit in the scant remains of the first fortress built by Bishop Absalon—the 12th-century founder of Copenhagen—lies under the palace. There's precious little to see, but it's old and well-described (20 kr; May–Sept daily 9:30–15:30; Oct–April Tue, Thu, Sat, and Sun 9:30–15:30, closed Mon, Wed, and

Fri; good 1-kr guide). Early birds note that this sight opens 30 minutes before other nearby sights.

▲**Thorvaldsen's Museum**—This museum—with some of the best swoon art you'll see anywhere—tells the story and shows the monumental work of the great Danish neoclassical sculptor Bertel Thorvaldsen (1770–1844). Considered Canova's equal among neoclassical sculptors, Thorvaldsen spent 40 years in Rome. He was lured home to Copenhagen with the promise to showcase his work in a fine museum—which opened in the revolutionary year of 1848 as Denmark's first public art gallery. The ground floor showcases his statues (pull open the little black "information" cases for descriptions). Upstairs, get into the mind of the artist by perusing his personal possessions and private collection of paintings—from which he drew inspiration (20 kr, free Wed, open Tue–Sun 10:00–17:00, closed Mon, well-described, located in neoclassical building with colorful walls next to Christiansborg Palace, tel. 33 32 15 32).

Royal Library—Copenhagen's "Black Diamond" library is a striking building made of shiny black granite, leaning over the harbor at the edge of the palace complex. Wander through the old and new sections, read a magazine, and enjoy a classy—and pricey—lunch (restaurant, café; library hours: Sept–mid-June Mon–Fri 10:00–21:00, Sat 10:00–14:00, closed Sun, mid-June–Aug until 17:00, tel. 33 47 47 47).

▲▲▲**National Museum**—Focus on the excellent and curiously enjoyable Danish collection, which traces this civilization from its ancient beginnings. Exhibits are laid out chronologically and described in English. Pick up the museum map. The audioguide (25 kr) describes the highlights but adds little to the printed descriptions you'll find inside. Start with "Denmark's Old Tide" at room #1 (right of entrance, through glass tunnel), and follow the numbers through the "prehistory" section circling the ground floor—oak coffins with still-clothed and armed skeletons from 1300 B.C., ancient and still-playable *lur* horns, the 2,000-year-old Gundestrup Cauldron of art-textbook fame, lots of Viking stuff, and an bitchin' collection of well-translated rune stones. Then go upstairs, find room 101, and carry on to find fascinating material on the Reformation, an exhibit on everyday town life in the 16th and 17th centuries, and, in room 126, a unique "cylinder perspective" of the noble family (from 1656) and two peep shows. The next floor takes you into modern times, with historic toys and a slice-of-Danish-life 1600-to-2000 gallery where you'll see everything from rifles and old bras to early jukeboxes (50 kr, free Wed, Tue–Sun 10:00–17:00, closed Mon, mandatory bag check—10 kr coin deposit, cafeteria, enter at Ny Vestergade 10, tel. 33 13 44 11).

▲**National Museum's Victorian Apartment**—The museum inherited an incredible Victorian apartment just around the corner, a tour of which is included with your admission. The wealthy Christensen family managed to keep its plush living quarters a 19th-century time-capsule until the granddaughters passed away in 1963. Since then, it's been part of the National Museum with all but two of its room looking like they did around 1890. Visit it if the tour schedule works for you (45-min tours leave from museum ticket desk Sat and Sun at 12:00, 13:00, 14:00, and 15:00; tours also likely at those times on Thu and Fri).

▲Ny Carlsberg Glyptotek—Scandinavia's top art gallery is an impressive example of what beer money can do. Enjoy the intoxicating Egyptian, Greek, and Etruscan collections; a fine sample of Danish golden age (early-19th-century) painting; and a heady, if small, exhibit of 19th-century French paintings (in the new "French Wing," including Géricault, Delacroix, Manet, Impressionists, and Gauguin before and after Tahiti). Linger with marble gods under the palm leaves and glass dome of the very soothing winter garden. Designers, figuring Danes would be more interested in a lush garden than classical art, used this wonderful space as leafy bait to cleverly introduce locals to a few Greek and Roman statues. (It works for tourists, too.) One of the original Rodin *Thinker*s (wondering how to scale the Tivoli fence?) is in the museum's backyard. This collection is artfully displayed and thoughtfully described (40 kr, free Wed and Sun, Tue–Sun 10:00–16:00, closed Mon, 2-kr English brochure/guide, classy cafeteria under palms, behind Tivoli, Dantes Plads 7, tel. 33 41 81 41, www.glyptoteket.dk). This is likely to be at least partly closed for part of 2004 as they add a new wing.

Danish Design Center—This center, with its building a masterpiece in itself, shows off the best in Danish design as well as top examples from around the world, from architecture to fashion and graphic arts. A visit to this low-key display case for sleek Scandinavian design offers an interesting glimpse into the culture. The basement showcases the Industrial Design prizewinners from 1965 through 1999. Here's a sample English description: "He taught the materials to do things not even they realized they were able to do" (40 kr, Mon–Fri 10:00–17:00, Wed until 21:00, Sat–Sun 13:00–16:00, across from Tivoli at H. C. Andersens Boulevard 27, tel. 33 69 33 69, www.ddc.dk). The boutique next to the ticket counter features three themes: travel light (chic travel accessories and gadgets), modern Danish classics, and books and posters. The café on the main level, under the atrium, serves light lunches (60–70 kr).

Hovedbanegården—Copenhagen's great train station is a fascinating mesh of Scandinavian culture and transportation efficiency. Even if you're not a train traveler, check it out (see "Arrival in Copenhagen," above). Notice how the classical music effectively keeps the junkies away from the back door.

Rosenborg Castle

▲▲▲Rosenborg Castle and Treasury—This finely furnished Dutch Renaissance- style castle was built by Christian IV in the early 1600s as a summer castle. Open to the public since 1838, it houses the Danish crown jewels and 500 years of royal knickknacks, including some great Christian IV memorabilia, such as the shrapnel (removed from his eye and forehead after a naval battle) that he had made into earrings for his girlfriend. Because nothing is explained in English, a tour—or the following self-guided tour—is essential.

Cost, Hours, and Location: 60 kr, daily June–Aug 10:00–17:00, May and Sept 10:00–16:00, Oct 11:00–15:00, Nov–April Tue–Sun 11:00–14:00, closed Mon. S-tog: Nørreport, tel. 33 15 32 86.

Tours: Richard Karpen leads fascinating 90-minute tours (Mon and Thu at 13:30, 50 kr plus your palace entrance, see "Tours," above). **Go with the Danes** offers similar tours (60 min, Sun and Tue at 13:30 in July and Aug). If these don't work for you, follow this self-guided tour through the castle and treasury I've woven together from highlights of Richard's walk.

Self-Guided Tour: You'll tour the first floor room-by-room, then climb to the third floor for the big throne room. After a quick sweep of the middle floor, finish in the basement for the jewels. Begin the tour on the ground floor, in the Audience Room.

Ground floor: Here in the **Audience Room,** all eyes were on Christian IV. Today, your eyes should be on him, too. Take a close look at his bust by the fireplace. Check this guy out—earring and fashionable braid, a hard drinker, hard lover, energetic statesman, and warrior king. Christian IV was dynamism in the flesh, wearing a toga: a true Renaissance guy. During his reign, the size of Copenhagen doubled. Rosenborg was his favorite residence, and where he chose to die. You're surrounded by Dutch paintings (the Dutch had a huge influence on 17th-century Denmark). Note the smaller statue of the 19-year-old king, showing him jousting jauntily on his coronation day. The astronomical clock—with musical works and moving figures—did everything you can imagine.

The **study** (nearest where you entered) was small (and easy to heat). Kings did a lot of corresponding. We know a lot about Christian because 3,000 of his handwritten letters survive. The painting shows eight-year-old Christian—after his father died, but still too young to rule. A portrait of his mother hangs above the boy, and opposite is a portrait of Christian in his prime.

In the **bedroom,** paintings show the king as an old man...and as a dead man. In the case are the clothes he wore when wounded in battle. Riddled with shrapnel, he lost an eye. No problem for the warrior king with a knack for heroic publicity stunts: He had the shrapnel bits taken out of his eye and forehead made into earrings. (They hang in the case above the blood-stained cloth.) Christian lived to be 70 and fathered 26 children.

The next room displays **wax casts** of royal figures. This was the way famous and important people were portrayed back then. The **chair** is a forerunner of the whoopee cushion. When you sat on it, metal cuffs pinned your arms down, allowing the prankster to pour water down the back of the chair (see hole)—making you "wet your pants." When you stood up, the chair made embarrassing tooting sounds.

The next room has a particularly impressive inlaid **marble floor.** Imagine Christian meeting emissaries here in the center, with the emblems of Norway (right), Denmark (center), and Sweden (left) behind him.

The end room was a **dining room.** Study the box made of amber (petrified tree resin, 30 to 50 million years old). The tiny figures show a healthy interest in sex. (You might want to shield children from the more graphic art—the case next to the door you just passed.) By the window (opposite where you entered), a hole in the wall let the music performed by the band in the basement waft in. (Who wants the actual musicians in the dining room?) The audio hole was also used to call servants.

The **long hall** leading to the staircase exhibits an intriguing painting of Frederick III being installed as the absolute monarch. Study it closely for slice-of-life details. Next, a sprawling family tree makes it perfectly clear that Christian IV comes from good stock. Note the tree is labeled in German—the second language of the realm.

The queen had a hand-pulled elevator, but you'll need to hike up two flights of stairs to the top-floor throne room.

Throne room (top floor): The **Long Hall**—considered one of the best-preserved Baroque rooms in Europe—was great for banquets. The decor trumpets the great accomplishments of Denmark's great kings. The four corners of the ceiling feature the four continents known at the time (America was still considered pretty untamed—notice the decapitated head with the arrow sticking out of it). In the center, of course, is the proud seal of Denmark. The tapestries are from the late 1600s, designed for this room. Effective propaganda, they show the Danes defeating their Swedish rivals on land and at sea. The king's throne was made of "unicorn horn" (actually narwhal tusk from Greenland)—believed to bring protection from evil and poison. It was about the most precious material in its day. The queen's throne is of hammered silver. The 150-pound hammered-silver lions are 300 years old.

The small room to the left holds a delightful **royal porcelain** display with Chinese, French, German, and Danish examples of the "white gold." For five centuries, Europeans couldn't figure out how the Chinese made this stuff. The difficulty in just getting it back to Europe in one piece made it precious. The Danish pieces, called "Flora Danica" (on the left as you enter) are from a huge royal set showing off the herbs and vegetables of the realm.

On your way back down, the **middle floor** is worth a look: Circling counter-clockwise, you'll see more fine clocks, fancy furniture, and royal portraits. In the first room, notice the fancy double portrait of the king and his sister. The queen enjoyed her royal lathe (with candleholders for lighting and pedals to spin it hidden away below). The small mirror room (on the side) was where the king played Hugh Hefner—using mirrors on the floor to see what was under those hoop skirts. In hidden cupboards, he had a fold-out bed and a handy escape staircase.

Back outside, find the stairs leading down to the...

Royal Danish Treasury (castle basement): The palace was a royal residence for a century and has been the royal vault right up until today. As you enter, peek into the royal **wine cellar,** with thousand-liter barrels, to right of ticket checker. Then continue into the treasury.

The diamond- and pearl-studded **saddles** were Christian IV's—the first for his coronation, the second for his son's wedding. When his kingdom was nearly bankrupt, Christian had these constructed lavishly—complete with solid-gold spurs—to impress visiting dignitaries and bolster Denmark's credit rating.

Next case: **tankards.** Danes were always big drinkers, and to drink in the top style, a king had narwhal steins (#4030 and #4031). Note the fancy Greenland Eskimo on the lid. The case is filled with exquisitely-carved ivory.

Next case: What's with the mooning snuffbox (#4063)? Also, check out the amorous whistle (#4064).

Case in corner: The 18th century was the age of **brooches.** Many of these are made of freshwater pearls. Find the fancy combination toothpick and ear spoon (#1140). A queen was caught having an affair after 22 years of royal marriage. Her king gave her a special present: a golden ring—showing the hand of his promiscuous queen shaking hands with a penis (#4146).

Step downstairs, away from all this silliness. Passing through the serious vault door, you come face to face with a big, jeweled **sword.** The tall, two-handed, 16th-century coronation sword was drawn by the new king, who cut crosses into the air in four directions, symbolically promising to defend the realm from all attacks. The cases surrounding the sword contain everyday items used by the king (all solid gold, of course). What looks like a trophy case of gold records is actually a collection of dinner plates with amber centers (#5032).

Go down the steps. In the center case is Christian IV's **coronation crown** (from 1596, 7 pounds of gold and precious stones, #1524), which some consider to be the finest Renaissance crown in Europe. Its 12 gables radiate symbolism. Find the symbols of justice (sword and scales); fortitude (a woman on a lion with a sword); and charity (a woman nursing—meaning the king will love God and his people as a mother loves her child). The pelican (which famously pecks its own flesh to feed its children) symbolizes how God sacrificed his son, just as the king would make great sacrifices for his people. Climb the footstool to look inside—it's as exquisite as the outside. The shields of various Danish provinces remind the king that he's surrounded by his realms.

Circling the cases along the wall (right to left), notice: the fine enameled lady's goblet with traits of a good woman spelled out in Latin (#5128); above that, an exquisite prayer book (with handwritten favorite prayers, #5134); the big solid-gold baptismal basin (#5262) hanging above tiny boxes that contained the royal children's umbilical chords (handy for protection later in life, #5272); and royal writing sets with wax, seals, pens, and ink (#5320).

Go down a few more steps into the lowest level of the treasury and last room. The two **crowns** in the center cases are more modern (from 1670), lighter, and more practical—just gold and diamonds without all the symbolism. The king's is only four pounds, and the queen's is a mere two.

The cases along the walls show off the **crown jewels.** These were made in 1840 of diamonds, emeralds, rubies, and pearls from earlier royal jewelry. The saber (#5540) shows emblems of the 19 provinces of the realm. The sumptuous pendant features a 19-carat diamond cut (like its neighbors) in the 58-facet "brilliant" style for maximum reflection. Imagine these on the dance floor. The painting shows the coronation of Christian VIII at Frederiksborg Chapel in 1840. The crown jewels are still worn on special occasions several times a year by the queen.

▲**Rosenborg Gardens**—The Rosenborg Castle is surrounded by the royal pleasure gardens and, on sunny days, a minefield of sunbathing Danish beauties and picnickers. While "ethnic Danes" grab the shade, the rest of the Danes worship the sun. When the royal family is in residence, there's a daily changing-of-the-guard mini-parade from the Royal Guard's barracks adjoining Rosenborg Castle (at 11:30) to Amalienborg Castle (at 12:00). The Queen's Rose Garden (across the moat from the palace) is a royal place for a picnic (cheap open-face sandwiches to go at Sos's Smørrebrød, nearby at the corner of Borgergade and Dronningens Tværgade, Mon–Fri 8:00–14:00, closed Sat–Sun). The fine statue of Hans Christian (H. C.) Andersen in the park, actually erected in his lifetime (and approved by H. C., pronounced HOH see), is meant to symbolize how his stories had a message even for adults.

▲**National Art Museum (Statens Museum for Kunst)**—The museum fills an impressive building with Danish and European paintings from the 14th century through today. Of most interest is the Danish golden age of paintings and those from the late 19th and early 20th centuries. Its Impressionist collection is impressive (with works by Manet, Monet, Renois, Cézanne, Gaugin, and van Gogh). It's complemented with works by Danish artists, who, inspired by the Impressionists, introduced that breezy movement to Scandinavia. Make a point to meet the "Skagen" artists. They gathered in the fishing village of Skagen on the north tip of Denmark, surrounded by the sea and strong light, and painted heroic folk fishermen themes in the late 1800s (50 kr, Tue–Sun 10:00–17:00, Wed until 20:00, closed Mon, excellent 20-kr audioguide, Sølvgade 48, tel. 33 74 84 94).

Near Strøget

Museum of Erotica—This museum's focus: The love life of *Homo sapiens*. Better than the Amsterdam equivalent, it offers a chance to visit a porno shop and call it a museum. It took some digging, but they've put together a history of sex from Pompeii to present day. Visitors get a peep into the world of 19th-century Copenhagen prostitutes and a chance to read up on the sex lives of Mussolini, Queen Elizabeth, Charlie Chaplin, and Casanova. After reviewing a lifetime of *Playboy* centerfolds and an entire room filled with Marilyn Monroe, visitors sit down for the arguably artistic experience of watching the "electric *tabernakel*," a dozen silently slamming screens of porn (worth the 79 kr entry fee only if fascinated by sex, they'll try to charge you 99 kr with optional graphic booklet, daily May–Sept 10:00–23:00, Oct–April 11:00–20:00, a block north of Strøget at Købmagergade 24, tel. 33 12 03 11). Copenhagen's dreary little red light district along Istedgade behind the train station has withered away to almost nothing. If you came to Copenhagen to sightsee sex...it's in the museum.

Round Tower—Built in 1642 by Christian IV, the tower connects a church, library, and observatory (the oldest functioning observatory in Europe) with a ramp that spirals up to a fine view of Copenhagen (20 kr, June–Aug Mon–Sat 10:00–20:00, Sun 12:00–20:00; Sept–May Mon–Sat 10:00–17:00, Sun 12:00–17:00; nothing to see inside but the ramp and the view, just off Strøget on Købmagergade).

Near *The Little Mermaid*

▲▲**Denmark's Resistance Museum (Frihedsmuseet)**—The compelling story of Denmark's heroic Nazi resistance struggle (1940–1945) is well-explained in English, from Himmler's eyepatch to fascinating tricks of creative sabotage (40 kr, free on Wed; open May–mid-Sept Tue–Sat 10:00–16:00, Sun 10:00–17:00, closed Mon; off-season Tue–Sat 11:00–15:00, Sun 11:00–16:00, closed Mon; guided tours at 14:00 Tue, Thu, and Sun in the summer; on Churchillparken between Queen's Palace and *The Little Mermaid*, bus #26 from Langelinie, bus #1, #6, #19, or #29 from farther away, tel. 33 13 77 14).

▲**Amalienborg Palace Museum**—While Queen Margrethe II and her family live quite privately in one of the four mansions that make up the palace complex, another mansion has been open to the public since 1994. It displays the private studies of four kings of the House of Glucksborg, who ruled from 1863 through 1972. Your visit is short—six or eight rooms on one floor. But it affords an intimate and unique peek into Denmark's royal family (45 kr, May–Oct daily 10:00–16:00, Nov–April Tue–Sun 11:00–16:00, enter on side of palace square farthest from the harbor, tel. 33 12 08 08).

Amalienborg Palace Changing of the Guard—This noontime event is boring in the summer when the queen is not in residence—the guards just change places. For more information about the palace and Amalienborg Square, see page 186.

Christianshavn

▲**Our Savior's Church (Vor Frelsers Kirke)**—The church's bright Baroque interior (1696), with the pipe organ supported by the royal elephants, is worth a look (free, helpful English flier, April–Aug Mon–Sat 11:00–16:30, Sun 12:00–16:30, off-season closes 1 hr earlier, bus #2A, #8, #19, or Metro: Christianshavn, Sankt Annægade 29, tel. 32 57 27 98). The unique spiral spire that you'll admire from afar can be climbed for great views of the city and of the Christiania commune below (20 kr, 400 steps, 311 feet high, closed in bad weather and Nov–March).

▲▲▲**Christiania**—In 1971, the original 700 Christianians established squatters' rights in an abandoned military barracks just a 10-minute walk from the Danish parliament building. A generation later, this "free city"—an ultra-human mishmash of idealists, hippies, potheads, non-materialists, and happy children—not only survives, it thrives (600 adults, 250 kids, and 250 dogs). Now that it's been around for so long, there are a handful of Willie Nelson-type seniors among the 180 remaining here from the original takeover. And an amazing thing has happened: the place has become the third-most-visited sight among tourists in Copenhagen. Move over, *Little Mermaid*.

Pusher Street is Christiania's main drag. Get beyond this touristy side of Christiania, and you'll find a fascinating ramshackle world of moats and earthen ramparts, alternative housing, cozy tea houses, carpenter shops, hippie villas, children's playgrounds, peaceful lanes, and people who believe that "to be normal is to be in a straightjacket." Be careful to distinguish between real Christianians and Christiania's motley guests—druggies (mostly from other countries) who hang out here in the summer for the freedom. Part of the original charter guaranteed that the community would stay open to the public.

The Community: Christiania is broken into 14 administrative neighborhoods on a former military base. The land is still owned by Denmark's Ministry of Defense. Locals build their homes but don't own the land. There's no buying or selling of property. When someone moves out, the community decides who will be invited in to replace that person. A third of the adult population works on the outside, a third works on the inside, and a third doesn't work much at all. There are nine rules: no cars, no hard drugs, no guns, no explosives, and so on. The Christiania flag—red with three yellow dots—is heavy with symbolism.

Christiania

- **1** Carl Madsens Place
- **2** Nemoland
- **3** Green Hall
- **4** Månefiskeren Café
- **5** Morgenstedet Vegetarian Restaurant
- **6** Spiseloppen Restaurant
- **7** Old Entrance

When the original hippies took over, they found a lot of red and yellow paint. The three dots are from the three "i"s in Christiania.

The community pays the city about $1 million a year for utilities and has about $1 million a year more to run its local affairs. A few "luxury hippies" have oil heat, but most use wood or gas. The ground here was poisoned by its days as a military base, so nothing is grown in Christiania. The community has one mailing address (for 25 kr/month, you can receive mail here). A phone chain provides a system of communal security (they have had "bad experiences calling the police"). Each September 26, the day those first squatters took over the barracks here in 1971, Christiania has a big birthday bash.

Tourists are entirely welcome here, because they've become a major part of the economy. Visitors react in very different ways to the place. Some see dogs, dirt, drugs, and dazed people. Others see a haven of peace, freedom, and no taboos. Locals will remind judgmental Americans (whose country incarcerates over a quarter of the world's prison inmates) that a society must make the choice: Allow for alternative lifestyles...or build more prisons.

For 25 years, Christiania has been a political hot potato. No one in the Danish establishment wanted it. And no one had the nerve to mash it. In the last decade, Christiania has connected better with the rest of society—paying its utilities and taxes, and so on. Today Denmark's conservative government (with pressure from the U.S.) is threatening the community, but "save Christiania" banners fly everywhere, and locals are confident that their free way of life will survive.

Orientation Tour: Passing under the gate, take Pusher Street directly into the community. The first square—a kind of market square (souvenirs and marijuana-related stuff)—is named Carl Madsens Place, honoring the lawyer who took the squatters' case to the Danish supreme court in 1976 and won. Beyond that is Nemoland (a food circus, on the right). A huge warehouse (Den Gronne Hal, "the green hall") is a recycling center (where people get most of their building material) that does double duty at night as a concert hall and place where children work on crafts. On the left, a lane leads to the Manefiskeren café, and beyond that, to the Morgenstedet vegetarian restaurant. Going straight on Pusher Street takes you to the ramparts that overlook the lake. A walk or bike ride through Christiania is a great way to see how this community lives. As you leave, look up—the sign above the gate says, "You are entering the EU."

Smoking Marijuana: Beefy marijuana plants stand on proud pedestals at the market square. While hard drugs are out, marijuana is sold openly (cheap, in joints or loose, bars have bongs) and smoked happily. The open-air food circus (or the canal-view perch above it, on the earthen ramparts) creates just the right ambience to lose track of time. Local dealers are friendly, talkative, and helpful to Americans who suddenly feel like fish no longer out of water. They claim you're safe within Christiania. But they warn that it's risky to take pot out. At the risk of losing its favored trade status with America, Denmark is required by Uncle Sam to make an occasional arrest of someone leaving the "free city" with pot.

About hard drugs: For the first few years, junkies were tolerated. But that led to violence and polluted the mellow ambience residents envisioned. In 1979, the junkies were expelled—an epic confrontation in the community's folk history now—and since then, a fist breaking a syringe is as prevalent as the leafy marijuana symbol. Hard drugs are emphatically forbidden in Christiania.

Eating in Christiania: The people of Christiania appreciate good food and count on tourism as a big part of their economy. Consequently, there are plenty of decent eating options. Most of the restaurants are closed on Monday (the community's weekly holiday). **Pusher Street** has a few grungy but tasty falafel stands. **Nemoland** is a fun food circus with Thai food, fast hippie food, and great tented outdoor seating. Its stay-a-while ambience comes with backgammon, foosball, bakery goods, and fine views from the ramparts. **Morgenstedet** is a good, cheap vegetarian café (60-kr meals, Tue–Sun 12:00–21:00, closed Mon, left after Pusher Street). **Månefiskeren** ("Moonfisher Bar") looks like a Breughel painting—from 2004—with billiards, chess, light meals, and drinks. **Spiseloppen** is *the* classy, good-enough-for-Republicans restaurant in the community (closed Mon, described in "Eating," below).

Hours and Tours: Christiania is open all the time (main entrance is down Prinsessegade behind Vor Frelsers' spiral church spire in Christianshavn). Photography is absolutely forbidden on Pusher Street. Otherwise, you're welcome to snap photos, but ask residents before you photograph them. Guided tours leave from the front entrance of Christiania at 15:00 (just show up, 30 kr, 90 min, daily late June–Aug, Sat–Sun rest of year, in English and Danish, tel. 32 57 96 70). For a private tour, contact Nina Pontoppidan. Nina and her husband have been part of the community since its early days, and she charges 180 kr for a 90-minute tour (tel. 32 57 69 51, pontoppidan@mail.mira.dk).

Greater Copenhagen

Carlsberg Brewery—Denmark's beloved source of legal intoxicants, Carlsberg, welcomes you to its Visitors Center for a self-guided tour and a half-liter of beer (free, Tue–Sun 10:00–16:00, closed Mon, bus #18, enter at Gamle Carlsbergvej 11, around corner from brewery entrance, tel. 33 27 13 14).

Open-Air Folk Museum (Frilandsmuseet)—This park is filled with traditional Danish architecture and folk culture (50 kr, free Wed, open April–Sept Tue–Sun 10:00–17:00, closed Mon and off-season, outside of town in the suburb of Lyngby, S-tog: Sorgenfri and 10-min walk to Kongevejen 100, tel. 33 13 44 11).

Bakken—Danes gather at Copenhagen's other great amusement park, Bakken (free, April–Aug daily 12:00–24:00, S-tog: Klampenborg, then walk 10 min through the woods, tel. 39 63 73 00, www.bakken.dk).

Dragør—Consider a trip a few minutes out of Copenhagen to the fishing village of Dragør (bus #250S or #5A from station 5 stops at Sundbyvesterplads, change to #350A).

SHOPPING

Shops are generally open Monday through Friday from 10:00 to 19:00 and Saturday from 9:00 to 16:00. While the big department stores dominate the scene, many locals favor the characteristic, small artisan shops and boutiques that are listed in the "Local Life" flier. You can't get this flier at the TI, but keep your eyes peeled for it (for example, at the bus info center on Rådhus Square and at the bakery on Pistol Street).

For a street's worth of shops selling "**Scantiques**," wander down Ravnsborggade from Nørrebrogade.

Copenhagen's colorful **flea markets** are small but feisty and surprisingly cheap (Sat May–Nov 8:00–14:00 at Israels Plads; Fri and Sat May–Sept 8:00–17:00 along Gammel Strand and on Kongens Nytorv). For other street markets, ask at the TI.

The city's top **department stores** (Illum at Østergade 52, tel. 33 14 40 02; and Magasin at Kongens Nytorv 13, tel. 33 11 44 33) offer a good, if expensive, look at today's Denmark. Both are on Strøget and have fine cafeterias on their top floors. The department stores and the Politiken Bookstore on the Rådhus Square have a good selection of maps and English travel guides.

Shoppers who like jewelry look for amber, known as "gold of the North." Globs of this petrified sap wash up on the shores of all the Baltic countries. **House of Amber** has a shop and tiny two-room museum with about fifty examples of prehistoric insects trapped in the amber under magnifying glasses (remember *Jurassic Park?*, 25 kr, daily 10:00–20:00, 50 yards off Nyhavn at Kongens Nytorv 2).

If you buy anything substantial (over 300 kr, about $40) from a shop displaying the **Danish Tax-Free Shopping** emblem, you can get a refund of the Value Added Tax, roughly 20 percent of the purchase price (VAT is MOMS in Danish). If you have your purchase mailed, the tax can be deducted from your bill. For details, call 32 52 55 66, and see "VAT Refunds and Customs Regulations" in the Introduction.

NIGHTLIFE

For the latest on the city's hopping jazz scene, inquire at the TI, study your *Copenhagen This Week* booklet, or pick up the "alternative" *Playtime* magazine at Use It. The **Copenhagen Jazz House** is a good bet for live jazz (around 90 kr, Tue–Thu and Sun at 20:30, Fri–Sat at 21:30, closed Mon, Niels Hemmingsensgade 10, tel. 33 15 26 00 for the schedule in Danish, www.jazzhouse.dk). For blues, try the **Mojo Blues Bar** (50 kr on Fri and Sat, otherwise no cover, nightly 20:00–5:00, music starts at 22:00, Løngangsstræde 21c, tel. 33 11 64 53, www.mojo.dk). Christiania always seems to have something musical going on after dark.

If you'd rather dance, join Denmark's salsa-wave at **Sabor Latino Salsa Club.** Located one block south of Rådhus Square, it offers free salsa lessons in English. Salsa dancing is surprisingly easy to learn in this friendly environment, and you'll get a chance to know the fun-loving Danes (free on Thu, 50 kr Fri-Sat, Thu-Sun 21:00-3:00, free lesson 22:00-23:00, closed Mon-Wed, no reservation required, wear comfortable shoes, Vestervoldgade 85, tel. 33 11 97 66 or 26 16 46 96).

SLEEPING

Central Copenhagen

Prices include breakfast unless noted otherwise. All are big and modern places with elevators and non-smoking rooms upon request, and all accept credit cards. Beware, many hotels have rip-off phone rates even for local calls. The first four are big, expensive, and soul-less. The rest are smaller, cheaper, and more characteristic.

$$$ **Hotel Excelsior** is a comfortable but sterile place on a quiet street behind the station (Sb-1,075 kr, Db-1,275 kr rack rate but Db often go for 800 or 900 kr, a block from station and a block off busy Vesterbrogade at Colbjørnsensgade 6, tel. 33 24 50 85, fax 33 24 50 87, www.choicehotels.dk).

$$$ **Webers Scandic Hotel** faces busy Vesterbrogade (some noisy rooms), but has a peaceful garden courtyard and a modern, inviting interior (high-season rack rates: small Sb-1,145 kr, Sb-1,395 kr, Db-1,545 kr, but ask about summer/weekend rates June-Aug and Fri-Sun all year—you can save 20-30 percent; 10 percent discount when you show this book; sauna, exercise room, particularly expensive phone rates, Vesterbrogade 11B, tel. 33 31 14 32, fax 33 31 14 41, www.scandic-hotels .com, webers@scandic-hotels.com).

$$$ **Sophie Amalie Hotel** is a classy and modern Danish-style hotel a block from the big cruise-ship harbor and a block from trendy Nyhavn (134 rooms, Sb-875/1,075/1,275 kr, Db-1,075/1,175/1,275 kr, prices vary with size of room from pretty tight to very spacious, breakfast-115 kr, Sankt Annae Plads 21, tel. 33 13 34 00, fax 33 11 77 07, www.remmen.dk, booking.has@remmen.dk).

$$$ **Ibis Copenhagen,** a big chain, has several hotels with cookie-cutter rooms at reasonable prices in the center (May-Oct: Sb-745 kr, Db-900 kr; Nov-April: Sb or Db-600 kr; breakfast 60 kr extra, elevator). Two identical hotels a block behind the station are **Ibis Triton Hotel** (Helgolandsgade 7, tel. 33 31 32 66, triton@accorhotel.dk) and **Ibis Star** Hotel (Colbjornsensgade 13, tel. 33 22 11 00, star@accorhotel.dk).

$$ **Ibsens Hotel** is an elegant 118-room hotel in a charming neighborhood away from the main train station commotion and a short walk from the old center (Db-880 kr promised with this book through 2004, Tb-1,320 kr, Vendersgade 23, S-tog: Nørreport, tel. 33 13 19 13, fax 33 13 19 16, www.ibsenshotel.dk, hotel@ibsenshotel.dk).

$$ **Hotel Nebo,** a secure-feeling refuge with a friendly welcome and comfy, spacious rooms, is half a block from the station on the edge of Copenhagen's red light district (S-510 kr, Sb-850 kr, D-730 kr, older Db-950 kr, newly-renovated Db-1,230 kr, cheaper Oct-April, extra bed-250 kr, Istedgade 6, tel. 33 21 12 17, fax 33 23 47 74, www.nebo .dk, nebo@email.dk).

Copenhagen Hotels

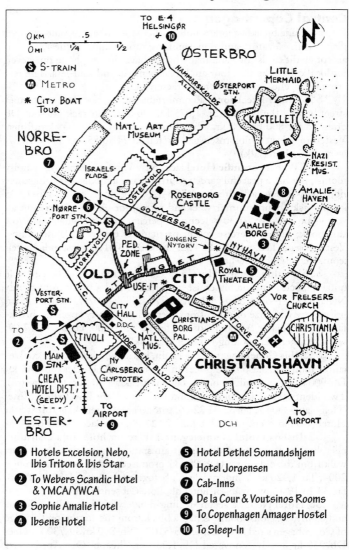

0 KM .5
0 MI 1/4 1/2

S S-TRAIN
M METRO
* CITY BOAT TOUR

TO E·4 HELSINGØR 🔟

ØSTERBRO

LITTLE MERMAID

ØSTERPORT STN.

HAMMARSKJOLDS ALLE

KASTELLET

NAT'L. ART MUSEUM

NAZI RESIST. MUS.

NORRE-BRO 🔼

ISRAELS-PLADS

ROSENBORG CASTLE

AMALIE-HAVEN

🔢

NØRRE-PORT STN. 🔼 🔼

OSTERVOLD

GOTHERSGADE

AMALIEN-BORG 🔼

KONGENS NYTORV

NYHAVN

NORREVOLD

PED. ZONE

OLD STRØGET CITY

USE·IT

ROYAL THEATER 🔼

VESTER-PORT STN. 🔼

H.C.

CITY HALL

D.D.C.

CHRISTIANS-BORG PAL.

VOR FRELSERS CHURCH

CHRISTIANIA

TO 🔢

ℹ️ 🔼

TIVOLI

NAT'L MUS.

ANDERSENS BLVD.

TORVE GADE

🔼

CHRISTIANSHAVN

MAIN STN. 🔼

NY CARLSBERG GLYPTOTEK

CHEAP HOTEL DIST. (SEEDY)

VESTER-BRO

TO AIRPORT 🔢

DCH

TO AIRPORT

🔼 Hotels Excelsior, Nebo, Ibis Triton & Ibis Star

🔼 To Webers Scandic Hotel & YMCA/YWCA

🔼 Sophie Amalie Hotel

🔼 Ibsens Hotel

🔼 Hotel Bethel Somandshjem

🔼 Hotel Jorgensen

🔼 Cab-Inns

🔼 De la Cour & Voutsinos Rooms

🔼 To Copenhagen Amager Hostel

🔟 To Sleep-In

SLEEP CODE

(7.5 kr = about $1, country code: 45)
Sleep Code: **S** = Single, **D** = Double/Twin, **T** = Triple, **Q** = Quad, **b** = bathroom, **s** = shower only, **no CC** = Credit Cards not accepted. Breakfast is generally included at hotels but not at private rooms or hostels. Unless otherwise noted, credit cards are accepted. Everybody speaks English.

To help you sort easily through these listings, I've divided the rooms into three categories based on the price for a standard double room with bath during high season:

$$$ **Higher Priced**—Most rooms 1,000 kr. or more.

  $$ **Moderately Priced**—Most rooms between 450–1,000 kr.

    $ **Lower Priced**—Most rooms 450 kr. or less.

I've listed a few big business-class hotels (see below), the best budget hotels in the center, cheap rooms in private homes in great neighborhoods an easy bus ride from the station, and a few backpacker dorm options.

Big Copenhagen hotels have an exasperating pricing policy. Their high rack rates are actually charged only about 20 or 30 days a year (unless you book in advance and don't know better). Hotels are swamped at certain times and need to keep their gouging options open. Therefore, you need to check their Web site for deals or be bold enough to simply show up and let the TI (for a 60-kr fee) find you a room on their push list. The TI swears that, except for maybe 10 days a year, they can land you a deeply-discounted room in a three- or four-star business-class hotel in the center. That means a 1,400-kr American-style comfort double for around 800 kr, including a big buffet breakfast.

$$ Hotel Bethel Somandshjem is a calm and stately former seamen's hotel facing the boisterous Nyhavn canal and offering 30 fine rooms at the most reasonable rack rates in town. It's an old-fashioned place—no e-mail, but it's easy to reserve a room with a phone call and a promise to show up. A third of their rooms are non-smoking and newly-renovated, but the older rooms are a bit more spacious (Sb-595 kr, Db-745 kr, harborview Db-795 kr, big Db on corner-895 kr, extra bed-150 kr, includes breakfast, bus #650S from station or Metro to Kongens Nytorv, facing bridge over the canal at Nyhavn 22, tel. 33 13 03 70, fax 33 15 85 70).

$$ **Hotel Jorgensen** is a friendly little 30-room hotel beautifully located just off Nørreport with some cheap, depressing rooms and some good-value, nicer rooms. While the lounge is classy and welcoming, the halls are a narrow, tangled maze (basic S-474 kr, Sb-575 kr, very basic D-575 kr, more elegant Db-700 kr, includes breakfast, Romersgade 11, tel. 33 13 81 86, fax 33 15 51 05, www.hoteljoergensen.dk, hoteljoergensen @mail.dk). They also rent dorm beds to those under 35 (6 to 14 beds per room, 160 kr, includes sheets and breakfast).

The Danish Motel-6

Cab-Inn is a radical innovation: identical, mostly collapsible, tiny but comfy, cruise ship-type staterooms, all bright, molded, and shiny with TV, coffeepot, shower, and toilet. Each room has a single bed that expands into a twin with one or two fold-down bunks on the walls. The staff will hardly give you the time of day, but it's tough to argue with this efficiency (Sb-510 kr, Db-630 kr, Tb-750 kr, Qb-870 kr, break-fast-50 kr, easy parking-60 kr, www.cabinn.dk). There are two virtually identical Cab-Inns in the same neighborhood (a 15-min walk northwest of the station): **Cab-Inn Copenhagen** (86 rooms, Danasvej 32-34, tel. 33 21 04 00, fax 33 21 74 09) and **Cab-Inn Scandinavia** (201 rooms, "Commodore" rooms have a real double bed for 100 kr extra, Vodroffsvej 55, tel. 35 36 11 11, fax 35 36 11 14). A third location opens in spring of 2004, just south of Tivoli: **Cab-Inn City** (350 rooms, check Web site for details on this and other new locations).

Rooms in Private Homes

Lots of travelers seem shy about rooms in private homes. Don't be. I almost always sleep in a private home. And, at 450 kr or so per double, they are a great value. The experience is as private or social as you want it to be, offering a great "at home in Denmark" opportunity in good neighborhoods (in Christianshavn and near Amalienborg Palace) for a third of the price of hotels. You'll get a key and come and go as you like. Always call ahead—they book in advance. All speak English and afford a fine peek into Danish domestic life. Rooms generally have no sink. While they usually don't include breakfast, you'll have access to the kitchen. If their rooms are booked up, they can often find you a place with a neighbor. You can trust the quality of their referrals. If you still can't snare a place, remember that the TI or Use It would love to send you to one from their stable of locals renting out rooms. For more listings, visit www.bbdk.dk.

Private Rooms in Christianshavn

This area is a never-a-dull-moment hodgepodge of the chic, artistic, hippie, and hobo, with historic fixed-up warehouses in the shadow of government ministries. Colorful with shops, cafés, and canals,

Christianshavn

1. Hollender House
2. Esben Juhl Rooms
3. Chicken's Private Pension
4. To Gitte Kongstad Rooms
5. Færge Cafeen
6. Ravelin Restaurant
7. Bastionen & Løven Restaurant
8. Lagkagehuset Baker
9. Spicy Kitchen Indian
10. Spiseloppen Restaurant

Christianshavn is an easy 10-minute walk to the center and has good bus connections to the airport and downtown. The bus stop is just outside the 7-Eleven on Torvegade. Take bus #2A or #48 to City Hall or the main train station and #2A to the airport. The new Metro connects Christianshavn and Nørreport (2 stops on S-tog from main train station).

$ Annette and Rudy Hollender enjoy sharing their 300-year-old home with my readers. Even with a long and skinny staircase, sinkless rooms, and two rooms sharing one toilet/shower, it's a comfortable and cheery place to call home (S-350 kr, D-450 kr, T-625 kr, no CC, closed Nov-April, half a block off Torvegade at Wildersgade 19, Metro: Christianshavntorv, tel. 32 95 96 22, hollender@adr.dk).

$ Esben Juhl, a soft-spoken gentleman, rents two double rooms out of his modern apartment in a quiet neighborhood. This elegant apartment complex affords a fine slice of today's life in Copenhagen

(S-350 kr, D-425 kr, with breakfast, David Balfours Gade 5, 4th floor, elevator, tel. 32 57 39 08, mobile 22 82 75 08, magreb125@mail.dk).

$ **Chicken's Private Pension** rents five playful rooms and two four-bed suites in a mod-funky-pleasant old house. The stairs are steep, and the furniture is old-time rustic but with a modern feel. It's right on Christianshavn's main drag (S-350 kr, D-450 kr, T-625 kr, Q-800 kr, extra bed-125 kr, kitchen available for breakfast on your own, no CC, Torvegade 36, Metro: Christianshavntorv, tel. 32 95 32 73, mobile 20 41 32 73, www.chickens.dk, morten@chickens.dk, Morton Frederiksen).

$ South of Christianshavn, **Gitte Kongstad** rents two apartments, each taking up an entire spacious floor in her 100-year-old house. You'll have a kitchen, little garden, Internet connection, and your own bike as you settle comfortably far from the big-city intensity (Sb-400 kr, Db-450 kr, extra bed-150 kr, no CC, family-friendly, bus #2A from airport, bus #12 or #13 from station, and just 75 yards from the new Metro stop: Lergravsparken at Badensgade 2, tel. & fax 32 97 71 97, mobile 21 65 75 22, www.gittes-guesthouse.dk, g.kongstad@post.tele.dk). You'll feel at home here, and the bike ride into town (or to the beach) is a snap.

Lower-Priced Private Rooms a Block from Amalienborg Palace

Amaliegade is a stately cobbled street in a quiet neighborhood (a 10-min walk north of Nyhavn and Strøget). You can look out your window and see the palace guards changing. Catch bus #1A or #15 from the station to Fredericiagade.

Puk (pook) and Line (LEE-nuh) are artistic and professional women who each rent out two rooms in their utilitarian, mod, and very Danish flats: **Holger and Puk de la Cour** (S-350 kr, D-425 kr with breakfast, extra bed-150 kr, no CC, kitchen/lounge available, Amaliegade 34, 4th floor, tel. 33 12 04 68, mobile 23 72 96 45, holgerdelacour@private.dk) and **Line Voutsinos** (May-Sept only, 2 double rooms, 1 with queen bed, 1 with 2 large single beds, D-425 kr including breakfast, extra bed-150 kr, family deals, no CC, Amaliegade 34, 3rd floor, tel. & fax 33 14 71 42, line.voutsinos@privat.dk).

Hostels

Copenhagen energetically accommodates the young vagabond on a shoestring. The Use It office is your best source of information. Each of these places charges about 100 kr per person for a bed and breakfast. Some don't allow sleeping bags, and if you don't have your own hostel bedsheet, you'll usually have to rent one for around 30 kr. IYHF hostels normally sell non-cardholders a guest pass for 25 kr.

$ The modern **Copenhagen Amager Hostel** (IYHF) is huge (528 beds), with 300-kr doubles, 390-kr triples, 460-kr quads, and five-bed dorms at 95 kr per bed (membership required, sheets-35 kr, no curfew, excellent facilities, breakfast-45 kr, dinner-65 kr, Internet access, self-serve laundry). It's on the edge of town, but the new Metro now gets you within a 10-minute walk (Metro: Balla Center). By bus, it's 30 minutes from the center (#250S with change to #100S, direction Svanmøllen S, Vejlands Alle 200, tel. 32 52 29 08, fax 32 52 27 08, www.danhostel.dk).

$ The following two big, grungy, central crash pads are open in July and August only: **Danish YMCA/YWCA** (dorm bed-90 kr, 4- to 10-bed rooms, breakfast-25 kr, sheets-15 kr, Valdemarsgade 15, 10-min walk from train station or bus #6, tel. 33 31 15 74) and **Sleep-In** (dorm bed-95 kr, sheets-30 kr, 4- or 6-bed cubicles in a huge 286-bed room, no curfew, breakfast-20 kr, lockers, always has room and free condoms, Blegdamsvej 132, bus #1, #6, or #14 to Triangle stop and look for sign, tel. 35 26 50 59, www.sleep-in.dk).

$ **Sleep-in Green**, the "ecological hostel," is very young, cool, and open mid-April through October (100-kr bunks, organic breakfast-30 kr, in a quiet spot a 15-min walk from center or catch bus 5A from station to Ravnsborggade, off Nørrebrogade at Ravnsborggade 18, tel. 35 37 77 77, www.sleep-in-green.dk).

EATING

Cheap Meals

For a quick lunch, try a *smørrebrød*, a *pølse*, or a picnic. Finish it off with a pastry.

Smørrebrød

Denmark's 300-year-old tradition of open-face sandwiches survives. Find a *smørrebrød* take-out shop and choose two or three that look good (around 10 kr each). You'll get them wrapped and ready for a park bench. Add a cold drink, and you have a fine, quick, and very Danish lunch. Tradition calls for three sandwich courses: herring first, then meat, then cheese. Downtown, you'll find these handy local alternatives to Yankee fast-food chains:

Near Kongens Nytorv: Try Tria Cafe (Mon–Fri 8:00–14:00, closed Sat–Sun, Gothersgade 12).

Near the Round Tower: Café Halvvejen is good for sit-down *smørrebrød* (lunch only, on Krystalgade).

Near Gammeltorv/Nytorv: Sorgenfri offers a local experience in a dark, woody spot just off Strøget (Brolæggerstræde 8, Mon–Sat 11:00–21:00, Sun 12:00–21:00, tel. 33 11 58 80). Or consider Domhusets Smørrebrød (Mon–Fri 7:00–14:30, closed Sat–Sun, Kattesundet 18, tel. 33 15 98 98).

Near Amalienborg Palace: Head inland two blocks just past the Marble Church to Svend Larsen's Smørrebrød (8-kr sandwiches to go,

St. Kongensgade 83, Mon–Fri 8:00–14:00, closed Sat–Sun).

Near Rosenborg Palace: Sos's Smørrebrød delights local office workers (Mon–Fri 8:00–14:00, closed Sat–Sun, at corner of Borgergade and Dronningens Tværgade). The nearby Rosenborg Gardens are perfect for your picnic.

The Pølse

The famous Danish hot dog, sold in *pølsevogn* (sausage wagons) throughout the city, is another typically Danish institution that has resisted the onslaught of our global, Styrofoam-packaged, fast-food culture. Study the photo menu for variations. These are fast, cheap, tasty, and—like their American cousins—almost worthless nutritionally. Even so, what the locals call the "dead man's finger" is the dog Danish kids love to bite.

There's more to getting a *pølse* than simply ordering a hot dog. Employ these handy phrases: *rød* (red, the basic weenie); *medister* (spicy, better quality); *knæk* (short, stubby, tastier than rød); *ristet* (fried); *brød* (a bun, usually smaller than the sausage); *svøb* ("swaddled" in bacon); *Fransk* (French style, buried in a long skinny hole in the bun with sauce); and *flottenheimer* (a fat one with onions and sauce). *Sennep* is mustard and *ristet løg* are crispy, fried onions. Wash everything down with a *soda-vand* (soda pop).

By hanging around a *pølsevogn*, you can study this institution. Denmark's "cold feet cafés" are a form of social care: People who have difficulty finding jobs are licensed to run these wiener-mobiles. As they gain seniority, they are promoted to work at more central locations. Danes like to gather here for munchies and *pølsesnak*—the local slang for empty chatter (literally, "sausage talk").

Picnics

Throughout Copenhagen, small delis *(viktualiehandler)* sell fresh bread, tasty pastries, juice, milk, cheese, and yogurt (drinkable, in tall liter boxes). Two of the largest supermarket chains are **Irma** (in arcade on Vesterbrogade next to Tivoli) and **Super Brugsen. Netto** is a cut-rate outfit with the cheapest prices. The little grocery store in the main train station is expensive but handy (daily 8:00–24:00).

Pastry

Bakeries have a golden pretzel sign hanging over the door or windows. The pastry we call a Danish is called a *wienerbrød* (Vienna bread) in Denmark. It's named for the Viennese bakers who brought the art of pastry-making to Denmark, where the Danes say they perfected it. Try these bakeries: **Nansens** (on corner of Nansensgade and Ahlefeldtsgade, near Ibsens Hotel), **Kransekagehuset** (on Pilestræde—Pistol Street, just off Strøget, near Kongens Nytorv, for their cheaper takeout, go around the corner at Ny Ostergade 9), and **Lagekagehuset** (on Torvegade in Christianshavn). For a gentile bit of high class 1870s Copenhagen, pay a lot for a coffee and a fresh danish at **Conditori La Glace,** just off Stroget at Skoubogade 3.

Dining with Danes

For a unique experience and a great opportunity to meet locals in their homes, consider dining with a Danish family. You get a homey two-course meal with lots of conversation. Some effort is made to match your age and interests (but not occupations). Try to book in advance so the families can prepare. You can book these dinners through two of the city's TIs. The Wonderful Copenhagen TI offers **Dine with the Danes** for 350 kr (reserve at least a day in advance, tel. 26 85 39 61, www .dinewiththedanes.dk). **Meet the Danes** does the same thing (720 kr per couple, tel. 33 46 46 46, www.meetthedanes.dk). For information on the TIs, see "Tourist Information," page 172.

Restaurants
Eating in the Center

Det Lille Apotek ("the little pharmacy") is a reasonable, candlelit place. It's been popular with locals for 200 years, and now it's also quite touristy (sandwich lunches, traditional dinners for 120–170 kr nightly from 17:30, just off Strøget, between Frue Church and Round Tower at St. Kannikestræde 15, tel. 33 12 56 06). Their specialty is "Stone Beef," a big slab of tender, raw steak plopped down in front of you on a scalding-hot lava stone. Flip it over a few times and it's cooked within minutes.

Riz-Raz Vegetarian Buffet has two locations in Copenhagen: around the corner from the canal boat rides at Kompagnistræde 20 (tel. 33 15 05 75) and across from Det Lille Apotek at Store Kannikestræde 19 (tel. 33 32 33 45). At both places, you'll find a healthy all-you-can-eat 59-kr Mediterranean/vegetarian buffet lunch (daily 11:30–16:00) and an even bigger 69-kr dinner buffet (16:00–24:00). The dinner has to be the best deal in town. And they're happy to serve free water with your meal.

Cafe Norden, smoky and very Danish with fine pastries, overlooks Amagertorv by the swan fountain. They have good light meals and salads and great people-watching from window seats on the second floor (order at the bar upstairs).

Bryggeriet Apollo, just outside the main entrance to Tivoli, offers pub atmosphere Danish-style. Beer is brewed on the premises while the kitchen cranks out generous portions of meat-and-potatoes dishes for reasonable prices (140-kr dinners, Mon–Sat 11:30–24:00, Sun 15:00–24:00, Vesterbrogade 3, tel. 33 12 33 13). Order a one-liter mug of beer and they take a surprising security deposit.

The Bistro, the train station's dressy restaurant, has long been famous for its big traditional buffet. For 149 kr, you get all you want from the various herring and fish courses to salads, cooked veggies and meat, and dessert. Tap water is free, or pay extra for drinks (daily 11:30–22:30, at the train station, tel. 33 69 21 12).

Hercegovina, a Croatian restaurant with folksy seating overlooking a leafy section of Tivoli, serves a 129-kr lunch buffet (mostly cold, 12:00–16:00) and a 169-kr dinner buffet (salads, veggies and lots and lots of meat, including a lamb on a spit; daily 17:00–22:00, music nightly after 19:00). While this is technically in Tivoli, diners can get in from the outside by going through the restaurant's office (facing the train station, next to the TI). You can eat here without a Tivoli ticket, but you will not be allowed into the park.

Gråbrødretorv is perhaps the most popular square in the old center for a meal. It's a food circus—especially in good weather. Choose from Greek, Mexican, Danish, or a meal in the old streetcar #14.

Department stores serving cheery, reasonable meals in their cafeterias include **Illum** (head to the elegant glass-domed top floor, Østergade 52) and **Magasin** (Kongens Nytorv 13), which also has a great grocery and deli in the basement.

Gammel Strand serves "Danish-inspired French cuisine" and is ideal for a dressy splurge in the old center (3-course menu-300 kr, Mon–Sat 12:00–15:00 & 17:30–22:00, closed Sun, reservations wise, across from Canal Tours Copenhagen tour boats at Gammel Strand 42, tel. 33 91 21 21). Outdoor tables enjoy a canal and strolling people scene. Indoor tables are white-tablecloth elegant.

Eating in Christianshavn

This neighborhood is so cool, it's worth combining an evening wander with dinner even if you're not staying here. It's a 10-minute walk across the bridge from the old center (or a 3-min ride on the Metro); map on page 205.

Færge Cafeen is a fun-loving pub with a local following. They serve inexpensive traditional Danish specialties indoors or along the canal (daily specials about 70 kr, daily 12:00–16:00 & 17:00–21:00, Strandgade 50, tel. 32 54 46 24).

Ravelin Restaurant, on a tiny island on the big road 100 yards south of Christianshavn, serves good, traditional Danish food at reasonable prices to happy local crowds. Dine indoors or on the lovely lakeside terrace (*smørrebrød* lunches 40–100 kr, dinners 100–200 kr, daily mid-April through mid-Sept, Torvegade 79, tel. 32 96 20 45).

Bastionen & Løven, at the little windmill (Lille Mølle), serves gourmet Danish: nouveau cuisine from a small but fresh menu on a Renoir terrace or in its Rembrandt interior (95-kr lunch specials; 145–190-kr dinners; 310-kr 3-course *menu;* 125-kr weekend brunch; daily 10:00–24:00, brunch Sat–Sun 10:00–14:00, Voldgade 50, walk to end of Torvegade and follow ramparts up to restaurant, at south end of

Christianshavn, tel. 32 95 09 40 for reservations indoors). The inside feels like a colonial mansion—but smoky.

Lagkagehuset, with a big selection of pastries, sandwiches, and excellent fresh-baked bread, is a great place for breakfast (take-out coffee and pastries for 15 kr, Torvegade 45). **Spicy Kitchen** serves cheap and good Indian food (Torvegade 56).

Spiseloppen ("the flea eats") is a wonderfully classy place in Christiania. They serve great 140-kr vegetarian meals and 160- to 220-kr meaty ones by candlelight. It's gourmet anarchy—a good fit for Christiania, the free city/squatter town (restaurant open Tue–Sun 17:00–22:00, closed Mon, live music Fri and Sat, 3 blocks behind spiral spire of Vor Frelser's church, on top floor of old brick warehouse; turn right just inside Christiania's gate, enter the wildly empty warehouse, and climb the graffiti-riddled stairs, reservations often necessary on weekends, tel. 32 57 95 58). Beware, the people at the next table are likely to light up a joint while waiting for their ribs. Other, less-expensive Christiania eateries are listed above (see "Sights—Christianshavn," above).

Eating near Nørreport

These places—near the recommended Ibsens and Jorgensens Hotels— are all close enough to survey before making a choice.

Kost Bar serves good-sized portions of pub fare, indoors or outdoors (60-kr salads, 50-75 kr for lunch, 75-120 kr for dinner, daily 11:00–24:00, Vendersgade 16, tel. 33 33 00 35).

Café Klimt, which draws a young, hip, heavy-smoking crowd, offers omelettes, sandwiches, and mod world cuisine (50–100 kr, Frederickborggade 29, tel. 33 11 76 70).

Café Marius, with a jazzy elegance and dressy indoor tables with casual sidewalk seating is popular for its homemade pasta, hearty burgers, and big salads. Marius is from Chicago, so don't expect traditional Danish here (90-kr plates, daily 12:00–23:00, Norre Farimagsgade 55, tel. 33 11 83 83).

TRANSPORTATION CONNECTIONS

By train to: Hillerød/Frederiksborg (6/hr, 40 min), **Roskilde** (1–3/hr, 30 min), **Odense** (2/hr, 1.75 hrs), **Helsingør** (3/hr, 50 min), **Malmö** (3/hr, 35 min), **Stockholm** (11/day, 5 hrs on X2000 high-speed train, night service via Malmö 23:10–6:10; take regional train to Malmö first, but if you get off at Malmö Syd, you'll miss your connection—wait for Malmö C, for Central), **Växjö** (5/day, 3 hrs), **Kalmar** (5/day, 4 hrs), **Oslo** (2/day departing 8:20 and 13:36, 8–9 hrs, you must change in Göteborg, Sweden; no night train), **Berlin** (4/day, 9 hrs, via Hamburg),

Amsterdam (2/day, 11 hrs), and **Frankfurt/Rhine** (4/day, 8 hrs). Convenient overnight trains from Copenhagen run to Stockholm, Amsterdam, and Frankfurt, some with one connection. National train info tel. 70 13 14 15. International train info tel. 70 13 14 16. Cheaper bus trips are listed at Use It.

PARIS

Paris offers sweeping boulevards, sleepy parks, world-class art galleries, chatty crêpe stands, Napoleon's body, sleek shopping malls, the Eiffel Tower, and people-watching from outdoor cafés. Climb Notre-Dame and the Eiffel Tower, cruise the Seine and the avenue des Champs-Elysées, and master the Louvre and Orsay museums. Save some after-dark energy for one of the world's most romantic cities. Many people fall in love with Paris. Some see the essentials and flee, overwhelmed by the huge city. With the proper approach and a good orientation, you'll fall head over heels for Europe's capital.

Planning Your Time:
Paris in One, Two, or Three Days

Day 1

Morning: Follow "Historic Core of Paris" Walk (see "Sights," below), featuring Ile de la Cité, Notre-Dame, Latin Quarter, and Sainte-Chapelle.

Afternoon: Visit the Pompidou Center (at least from the outside), then walk to the Marais neighborhood, visit the place des Vosges, and consider touring any of three museums nearby: Carnavalet Museum (city history), Jewish Art and History Museum, or Picasso Museum.

Evening: Cruise the Seine River or take the "Paris Illumination" nighttime bus tour.

Day 2

Morning: Visit Arc de Triomphe, then saunter down the Champs-Elysées.

Afternoon: Have lunch in the Tuileries (several lunch cafés in the park), then tour the Louvre.

Evening: Enjoy the Trocadéro scene and a twilight ride up the Eiffel Tower.

DAILY REMINDER

Monday: These sights are closed today—Orsay, Rodin, Marmottan, Montmartre, Carnavalet, Catacombs, Giverny, and Versailles; the Louvre is more crowded because of this, but the Denon wing (with *Mona Lisa, Venus de Milo,* and more highlights) stays open until 21:45. Napoleon's Tomb is closed the first Monday of the month. Some small stores don't open until 14:00. Street markets such as rue Cler and rue Mouffetard are dead today. Some banks are closed. It's discount night at most cinemas.

Tuesday: Many museums are closed today, including the Louvre, Picasso, Cluny, and Pompidou Center, as well as the châteaux of Chantilly (except July–Aug) and Fontaine-bleau. The Eiffel Tower, Orsay, and Versailles are particularly busy today.

Wednesday: All sights are open (Louvre until 21:45). The weekly *Pariscope* magazine comes out today. Most schools are closed, so many kids' sights are busy. Some cinemas offer discounts.

Thursday: All sights are open except the Sewer Tour. The Orsay is open until 21:45. Department stores are open late.

Friday: All sights are open except the Sewer Tour. Afternoon trains and roads leaving Paris are crowded; TGV reservation fees are higher.

Saturday: All sights are open (except the Jewish Art and History Museum). The fountains run at Versailles (July–Sept) and Vaux-le-Vicomte hosts candlelight visits (May–Oct); otherwise avoid weekend crowds at area châteaux. Department stores are busy. The Jewish Quarter is quiet.

Sunday: Some museums are two-thirds price all day and/or free the first Sunday of the month, thus extremely more crowded (e.g., Louvre, Orsay, Rodin, Cluny, Pompidou, and Picasso). The fountains run at Versailles (early April–early Oct). Most of Paris' stores are closed on Sunday, but shoppers will find relief in the Marais neighborhood's lively Jewish Quarter and in Bercy Village, where many stores are open. Look for organ concerts at St. Sulpice and possibly other churches. The American Church sometimes hosts a free evening concert at 18:00 (Sept–May only). Most recommended restaurants in the rue Cler neighborhood are closed for dinner.

Day 3
Morning: Tour the Orsay Museum.
Afternoon: Either tour the nearby Rodin Museum and Napoleon's Tomb or visit Versailles (take RER-C train direct from Orsay).
Evening: Visit Montmartre and the Sacré-Cœur basilica.

ORIENTATION

Paris is split in half by the Seine River, divided into 20 *arrondissements* (proud and independent governmental jurisdictions), and circled by a ring-road freeway (the *périphérique*). You'll find Paris easier to navigate if you know which side of the river you're on, which *arrondissement* you're in, and which subway (Métro) stop you're closest to. If you're north of the river (the top half of any city map), you're on the Right Bank *(rive droite)*. If you're south of it, you're on the Left Bank *(rive gauche)*. Most of your sightseeing will take place within five blocks of the river.

Arrondissements are numbered, starting at Notre-Dame (ground zero) and moving in a clockwise spiral out to the ring road. The last two digits in a Parisian zip code are the *arrondissement* number. The notation for the Métro stop is "Mo." In Parisian jargon, Napoleon's tomb is on *la rive gauche* (the Left Bank) in the *7ème* (7th *arrondissement*), zip code 75007, Mo: Invalides. Paris Métro stops are used as a standard aid in giving directions, even for those not using the Métro. As you're tracking down addresses, these words will help: *place* (plahs, square), *rue* (roo, road), and *pont* (phon, bridge).

Tourist Information

Avoid the Paris tourist offices (abbreviated as "TI" in this book) because of their long lines, short information, and charge for maps. This book, the *Pariscope* magazine (described below), and one of the freebie maps available at any hotel (or in the front of this book) are all you need. Paris TIs share a single phone number: 08 36 68 31 12 (from the States, dial 011 33 8 36 68 31 12). The main TI is at 127 avenue des **Champs-Elysées** (daily 9:00–20:00), but the other TIs are less crowded: at **Gare de Lyon** (daily 8:00–20:00), at the **Eiffel Tower** (May–Sept daily 11:00–18:40, closed Oct–April), and at the **Louvre** (Wed–Mon 10:00–19:00, closed Tue). Both **airports** have handy TIs (called ADP) with long hours and short lines (see "Transportation Connections," below).

Paris' TIs have an official Web site (www.paris-touristoffice.com) offering practical information on hotels, special events, museums, children's activities, fashion, nightlife, and more. Two other Web sites that are entertaining and at times useful are www.bonjourparis.com (which claims to offer a virtual trip to Paris with interactive French lessons, tips on wine and food, and news on the latest Parisian trends) and the similar www.paris-anglo.com (with informative stories on visiting Paris, plus a directory of over 2,500 English-speaking businesses).

For a complete schedule of museum hours and English-language museum tours, pick up the free *Musées, Monuments Historiques, et Expositions* booklet from any museum.

Pariscope: The *Pariscope* weekly magazine (or one of its clones, €0.40 at any newsstand) lists museum hours, art exhibits, concerts, music festivals, plays, movies, and nightclubs. Smart tour guides and sightseers rely on this for all the latest listings.

Maps: While Paris is littered with free maps, they don't show all the streets. You may want the huge Michelin #10 map of Paris. For an extended stay, I prefer the pocket-size, street-indexed *Paris Pratique* (about €6) with an easy-to-use Métro map.

Bookstores: There are many English-language bookstores in Paris where you can pick up guidebooks, for nearly double their American prices. Most carry this book. My favorite is the friendly Red Wheelbarrow, run by charming Penelope and Abigail, in the Marais neighborhood (13 rue Charles V, Mo: St. Paul, tel. 01 42 77 42 17). Others include: Shakespeare and Company (daily 12:00–24:00, some used travel books, 37 rue de la Bûcherie, across the river from Notre-Dame, Mo: St. Michel, tel. 01 43 26 96 50), W. H. Smith (248 rue de Rivoli, Mo: Concorde, tel. 01 44 77 88 99), and Brentanos (37 avenue de L'Opéra, Mo: Opéra, tel. 01 42 61 52 50).

American Church: The American Church is a nerve center for the American émigré community. It distributes a free, handy, and insightful monthly English-language newspaper called the *Paris Voice,* which as useful reviews of concerts, plays, and current events; find it at about 200 locations in Paris (http://parisvoice.com). Also available is an advertisement paper called *France—U.S.A. Contacts,* which is full of useful information for those seeking work or long-term housing. The church faces the river between the Eiffel Tower and Orsay Museum (reception open Mon–Sat 9:30–22:30, Sun 9:00–19:30, 65 quai d'Orsay, Mo: Invalides, tel. 01 40 62 05 00).

Arrival in Paris

By Train: Paris has six train stations, all connected by Métro, bus, and taxi (see map on page 217). All have ATMs, banks or change offices, information desks, telephones, cafés, lockers *(consigne automatique)*, newsstands, and clever pickpockets. Hop the Métro to your hotel (see "Getting around Paris," below).

By Plane: For detailed information on getting from Paris' airports to downtown Paris (and vice versa), see "Transportation Connections" at the end of this chapter.

Paris Overview

Paris train stations & destinations

1 Gare St. Lazare: To Normandy (also Giverny)

2 Gare Nord: To London & Brussels via Eurostar,
to northern Europe (some trips via pricey Thalys trains)

3 Gare L'Est: To eastern France, southern Germany,
Switzerland & Austria

4 Gare du Lyon: To southeast France & Italy,
also Fontainebleau & Melun (for Vaux-le-Vicomte)

5 Gare d' Austerlitz: To southwest France, Loire & Spain

6 Gare Montparnasse: To Normandy, Brittany, Chartres,
TGV trains to Loire & southwest France

Paris

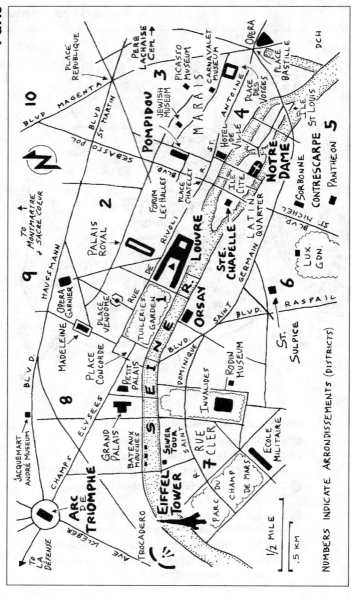

NUMBERS INDICATE ARRONDISSEMENTS (DISTRICTS)

Helpful Hints

Paris Museum Pass: This worthwhile pass, covering most sights in
Paris, is available at major Métro stations, TIs, and museums. For
information, see page 220.

Theft Alert: Pickpockets seem more numerous and determined than
ever. Métro and RER lines that serve popular sights are infested
with thieves. Wear a money belt, put your wallet in your front
pocket, loop your day bag over your shoulders (consider wearing it
in front), and keep a tight grip on a purse or shopping bag.
Muggings are rare, but they do occur. If you're out late, avoid the
dark riverfront quays and anywhere the lighting is dim and pedestrian activity minimal.

Useful Telephone Numbers: American Hospital—01 46 41 25 25;
English-speaking pharmacy—01 45 62 02 41 (Pharmacie les
Champs, open 24 hrs, 84 avenue des Champs-Elysées, Mo: George
V); Police—17; U.S. Embassy—01 43 12 22 22; Paris and France
directory assistance—12.

Street Safety: Be careful on foot! Parisian drivers are notorious for ignoring pedestrians. Look both ways, as many streets are one-way, and
be careful of seemingly quiet bus/taxi lanes. Don't assume you have
the right of way, even in a crosswalk. When crossing a street, keep
your pace constant and don't stop suddenly. By law, drivers must
miss pedestrians by three feet (five feet in the countryside). Drivers
carefully calculate your speed and won't hit you, provided you don't
alter your route or pace.

Toilets: Carry small change for pay toilets, or walk into any sidewalk
café like you own the place and find the toilet in the back. The
toilets in museums are free and generally the best you'll find, and

---

KEY WORDS FOR THE MÉTRO AND RER

- *direction* (dee-rek-see-ohn): direction
- *ligne* (leen-yuh): line
- *correspondance* (kor-res-pohn-dahns): transfer
- *sortie* (sor-tee): exit
- *carnet* (kar-nay): cheap set of 10 tickets
- *Pardon, madame/monsieur* (par-dohn, mah-dahm/mes-yur): Excuse me, lady/sir.
- *Je descend* (juh day-sahn): I'm getting off.
- *Donnez-moi mon porte-feuille!* (doh-nay mwah mohn port-foo-ay): Give me my wallet!

THE PARIS MUSEUM PASS

In Paris, there are two classes of sightseers—those with a Paris museum pass and those who stand in line. Serious sightseers save time and money by getting this pass.

Most of the sights listed in this chapter are covered by the Paris museum pass, except for the Eiffel Tower, Montparnasse Tower, Marmottan Museum, Opéra Garnier, Notre-Dame treasury, Jacquemart-André Museum, Jewish Art and History Museum, Grande Arche de La Défense, Jeu de Paume Exhibition Hall, Catacombs, *Paris Story* film, and the ladies of Pigalle. Outside Paris, the pass covers the châteaux of Versailles, Chantilly, and Fontainebleau.

The pass pays for itself in two admissions and gets you into most sights with no lining up to buy tickets (1one day–€15, three consecutive days–€30, five consecutive days–€45, no youth or senior discount). It's sold at museums, main Métro stations (including Ecole Militaire and Bastille), and TIs (even at airports). Try to avoid buying the pass at a major museum (such as the Louvre), where supply can be spotty and the lines long.

The pass isn't activated until the first time you use it (you enter the date on the pass). Think and read ahead to make the most of your pass, since some museums are free (e.g., Carnavalet and Victor Hugo's house), many sights are discounted on Sundays, and your pass must be used on consecutive days.

The pass isn't worth buying for children, as most museums are free for those under 18. Note that kids can skip the lines with their passholder parents.

The free museum-and-monuments directory that comes with your pass lists the latest hours, phone numbers, and specifics on what kids pay. The cutoff age for free entry varies from 5 to 18. Most major art museums let young people under 18 in for free, but anyone over age 5 has to pay to tour the sewers—go figure.

if you have a museum pass, you can drop into almost any museum for the clean toilets. Modern, super-sanitary, street-booth toilets provide both relief and a memory (coins required, don't leave small children inside unattended). Keep some toilet paper or tissues with you, as some toilets are poorly supplied.

Getting around Paris

By Métro: In Paris, you're never more than a 10-minute walk from a Métro station. Europe's best subway (open daily from 5:30 until 00:30) allows you to hop from sight to sight quickly and cheaply. Learn to use it.

Pickpockets and Panhandlers: Thieves spend their days in the Métro. Be on guard. For example, if your pocket is picked as you pass through

Included sights you're likely to visit (and admission prices without the pass): Louvre (€7.50), Orsay Museum (€7), Sainte-Chapelle (€5.50), Arc de Triomphe (€7), Les Invalides/Napoleon's Tomb (€6), Conciergerie (€5.50), Panthéon (€5.50), Sewer Tour (€4), Cluny Museum (€7), Pompidou Center (€5.50), Notre-Dame towers (€5.50) and crypt (€3.50), Picasso Museum (€5.50), and the Rodin Museum (€5). Outside Paris, the pass covers the Palace of Versailles (€7.50, plus its Trianon châteaux—€5), Château of Fontainebleau (€5.50), and Château of Chantilly (€7).

Tally up what you want to see—and remember, an advantage of the pass is that you skip to the front of some lines, which saves hours of waiting, especially in summer (though everyone must pass through the slow-moving metal-detector lines at some sights, and a few places, such as Notre-Dame's tower, can't accommodate a bypass lane). With the pass, you'll pop freely into sights that you're walking by (even for a few minutes) that otherwise might not be worth the expense (e.g., Notre-Dame crypt, Conciergerie, and the Panthéon).

Museum Tips: The Louvre and many other museums are closed on Tuesday. The Orsay, Rodin, Marmottan, and Carnavalet museums and Versailles are closed Monday. Most museums offer reduced prices on Sunday. Most sights stop admitting people 30–60 minutes before they close, and many begin closing rooms 45 minutes before the actual closing time.

For the fewest crowds, visit very early, at lunch, or very late. Most museums have slightly shorter hours October through March. French holidays can really mess up your sightseeing plans on Jan 1, May 1, May 8, July 14, Nov 1, Nov 11, and Dec 25.

a turnstile, you end up stuck on the wrong side while the thief strolls away. Stand away from Métro doors to avoid being a target for a pickpocket who grabs your things and runs as the doors close. Any jostling or commotion, especially when boarding or leaving trains, is likely the sign of a thief or team of thieves in action. Ask any fare inspector for proof of identity (ask locals for help if you're not certain).

Paris has a huge homeless population and higher than 11 percent unemployment; expect a warm Métro welcome by pan-handlers, musicians, and those selling magazines produced by the homeless community.

Tickets and Passes: One ticket (€1.40) takes you anywhere in the system with unlimited transfers. Tickets are also good on the RER suburban trains (see below) and on city buses, although one ticket cannot be used as a transfer between subway and bus. Save 40 percent by buying a *carnet* (car-nay) of 10 tickets for €10 (a single ticket is €1.40, kids 4–10 pay €5 for a *carnet*). Buy tickets at any Métro station from a human or a machine (some machines also accept credit cards).

If you're staying in Paris for a week or more, consider the **Carte Orange** (kart oh-rahnzh) for about €15, which gives you free run of the bus and Métro system for one week, starting Monday and ending Sunday; ask for the Carte Orange *coupon vert* and supply a passport-size photo. The month-long version costs about €50; request a Carte Orange *coupon orange* (good from the first day of the month to the last). These passes cover only central Paris; you can pay more for passes covering regional destinations (like Versailles). All passes can be purchased at any Métro station, most of which have photo booths where you can get the photo required for the pass. While some Métro agents may hesitate to sell you Carte Orange passes because you're not a resident, Carte Orange passes are definitely not limited to residents; if you're refused, simply go to another station to buy your pass. The overpriced **Paris Visite** passes were designed for tourists and offer minor reductions at minor sights (1 day–€9, 2 days–€14, 3 days–€19, 5 days–€28), but you'll get a better value with a cheaper *carnet* of 10 tickets or a Carte Orange.

How the Métro works: To get to your destination, determine the closest "Mo" stop and which line or lines will get you there. The lines have numbers, but they're best known by their direction or end-of-the-line stop. (For example, the La Défense/Château de Vincennes line runs between La Défense in the west and Vincennes in the east.) Once in the Métro station, you'll see blue-and-white signs directing you to the train going in your direction (e.g., "*direction:* La Défense"). Insert your ticket in the automatic turnstile (brown stripe down), pass through, and reclaim your ticket, and keep it until you exit the system. Fare inspectors regularly check for cheaters and accept absolutely no excuses from anyone. I repeat, keep that ticket until you leave the Métro system.

Transfers are free and can be made wherever lines cross. When you transfer, look for the orange *correspondance* (connections) signs when you exit your first train, then follow the proper direction sign.

While the Métro whisks you quickly from one point to another, be prepared to walk significant distances within stations to reach your platform (most noticeable when you transfer). Escalators are usually available for vertical movement, but they're not always in working order. To limit excessive walking, avoid transferring at these sprawling stations: Montparnasse-Bienvenüe, Chatelet-Les Halles, Charles de Gaulle-Etoile, Gare du Nord, and Bastille.

Before taking the *sortie* (exit) to leave the Métro, check the helpful *plan du quartier* (map of the neighborhood) to get your bearings, locate your destination, and decide which *sortie* you want. At stops with several *sorties*, you can save lots of walking by choosing the best exit.

After you exit the system, toss or tear your used ticket so you don't confuse it with your unused ticket—they look virtually identical.

By RER: The RER (Réseau Express Régionale; air-ay-air) is the suburban train system serving destinations such as Versailles, Disneyland Paris, and the airports. These routes are indicated by thick lines on your subway map and identified by letters A, B, C, and so on.

Within the city center, the RER works like the Métro but can be speedier (if it serves your destination directly) because it makes only a few stops within the city. Métro tickets are good on the RER when traveling in the city center. (You can transfer between the Métro and RER systems with the same ticket.) But to travel outside the city (to Versailles or the airport, for example), you'll need to buy a separate, more expensive ticket at the station window before boarding. Unlike in the Métro, you need to insert your ticket in a turnstile to exit the RER system. Also unlike the Métro, not every train stops at every station along the way; check the sign over the platform to see if your destination is listed as a stop (*toutes les gares* means it makes all stops along the way) or confirm with a local before you board.

By City Bus: The trickier bus system is worth figuring out. Métro tickets are good on both bus and Métro, though you can't use the same ticket to transfer between the two systems. One ticket gets you anywhere in central Paris, but if you leave the city center (shown as *zone 1* on the diagram on board the bus), you must validate a second ticket. While the Métro shuts down about 00:30, some buses continue much later.

Enter through the front doors. Punch your Métro ticket in the machine behind the driver, or pay the higher cash fare. Get off the bus using the rear door. Even if you're not certain you've figured it out, do some joyriding (outside of rush hour). Lines #24, #63, and #69 are Paris' most scenic routes and make a great introduction to the city. Bus #69 is particularly handy, running east-west between the Eiffel Tower and the Père Lachaise Cemetery by way of rue Cler (recommended hotels), the quai d'Orsay, the Louvre, and the Marais (recommended hotels).

Schedules are posted at bus stops. Handy bus-system maps *(plan des autobus)* are available in any Métro station and are provided in your *Paris Pratique* map book if you invest €6. Big system maps, posted at each bus and Métro stop, display the routes. Individual route diagrams show the exact routes of the lines serving that stop. Major stops are displayed on the side of each bus. The handiest bus routes are listed for each recommended hotel neighborhood.

By Taxi: Parisian taxis are reasonable—especially for couples and families. The meters are tamper-proof. Fares and supplements (described in English on the back windows) are straightforward. There's a €5 minimum. A 10-minute ride costs about €8 (versus €1 to get anywhere in town using a *carnet* ticket on the Métro). You can try waving down a taxi, but it's easier to ask for the nearest taxi stand (*Où est une*

PARIS AT A GLANCE

▲▲▲**Louvre** Europe's oldest and greatest museum, starring Mona Lisa and Venus di Milo. **Hours:** Wed–Mon 9:00–18:00, closed Tue. Denon wing open Mon until 21:45; all wings open Wed until 21:45.

▲▲▲**Orsay Museum** Nineteenth-century art, including Europe's greatest Impressionist collection. **Hours:** June 20–Sept 20 Tue–Sun 9:00–18:00; Sept 21–June 19 Tue–Sat 10:00–18:00, Sun 9:00–18:00; Thu until 21:45 year-round, closed Mon.

▲▲▲**Eiffel Tower** Paris' soaring exclamation point. **Hours:** March–Sept daily 9:00–24:00, Oct–Feb 9:30–23:00.

▲▲▲**Arc de Triomphe** Triumphal arch with viewpoint, marking start of Champs-Elysées. **Hours:** Outside always open; inside April–Sept daily 10:00–23:00, Oct–March daily 10:00–22:30.

▲▲▲**Sainte-Chapelle** Gothic cathedral with peerless stained glass. **Hours:** Daily 9:30–18:00.

▲▲▲**Versailles** The ultimate royal palace, with Hall of Mirrors, vast gardens, a grand canal, and smaller palaces. **Hours:** May–Sept Tue–Sun 9:00–18:30, Oct–April Tue–Sun 9:00–17:30, closed Mon. Gardens open early (7:00) and smaller palaces open late (12:00).

▲▲**Notre-Dame Cathedral** Paris' most beloved church, with towers and gargoyles. **Hours:** Church daily 8:00–18:45; tower April–Sept daily 9:30–19:30, Oct–March daily 10:00–17:30.

▲▲**Sacré-Cœur** White basilica atop Montmartre with spectacular views. **Hours:** Daily until 23:00.

▲▲**Napoleon's Tomb** The emperor's imposing tomb, flanked by army museums. **Hours:** April–Sept daily 10:00–18:00, Oct–March daily 10:00–17:00, closed first Mon of month.

▲▲**Rodin Museum** Works by the greatest sculptor since Michelangelo. **Hours:** April–Sept Tue–Sun 9:30–17:45; Oct–March Tue–Sun 9:30–17:00, closed Mon.

▲▲**Marmottan Museum** Untouristy art museum focusing on Monet. **Hours:** Tue–Sun 10:00–18:00, closed Mon.

▲▲**Pompidou Center** Modern art in colorful building with city views. **Hours:** Wed–Mon 11:00–21:00, closed Tue.

▲▲**Jacquemart-André Museum** Art-strewn mansion. **Hours:** Daily 10:00–18:00.

▲▲**Cluny Museum** Medieval art with unicorn tapestries. **Hours:** Wed–Mon 9:15–17:45, closed Tue.

▲▲**Carnavalet Museum** Paris' history wrapped up in a 16th-century mansion. **Hours:** Tue–Sun 10:00–18:00, closed Mon.

▲▲**Jewish Art and History Museum** Displays history of Judaism in Europe. **Hours:** Mon–Fri 11:00–18:00, Sun 10:00–18:00, closed Sat.

▲▲**Deportation Memorial** Memorial to Holocaust victims, near Notre-Dame. **Hours:** April–Sept daily 10:00–12:00 & 14:00–19:00; Oct–March daily 10:00–12:00 & 14:00–17:00.

▲▲**Champs-Elysées** Paris' grand boulevard. **Hours:** Always open.

▲▲**Luxembourg Garden** Paris' most beautiful and enjoyable park—rent a toy sailboat. **Hours:** Daily dawn until dusk.

▲**Old Opera (Opéra Garnier)** 19th-century opera house open for tours. **Hours:** Daily 10:00–17:00 except during performances.

▲**La Défense and La Grande Arche** Paris' modern arch on outskirts of city. **Hours:** Elevator daily 10:00–19:00.

▲**Picasso Museum** World's largest collection of Picasso's works. **Hours:** April-Sept Wed–Mon 9:30–18:00; Oct-March 9:30-17:30, closed Tue.

▲**Catacombs** Underground tunnels lined with bones. **Hours:** Tue–Sun 10:00–17:00, closed Mon.

▲**Paris Sewer Tour** The lowdown on Paris plumbing. **Hours:** May-Sept Sat–Wed 11:00–17:00, Oct-April 11:00-16:00, closed Thu–Fri.

▲**St. Sulpice Organ Concert** Opportunity to get intimate with a 7,000-pipe organ. **Hours:** 11:40 recital every Sun, followed by visit with organist.

station de taxi?; oo ay oon stah-see-ohn duh taxi). Taxi stands are indicated by a circled T on many city maps, including Michelin's #10 Paris.
A typical taxi takes three people (maybe four if you're polite and pay
€2.60 extra); groups of up to five can use a *grand taxi,* which must be
booked in advance—ask your hotel to call. If a taxi is summoned by
phone, the meter starts as soon as the call is received, adding €3-4 to
the bill. Higher rates are charged at night from 19:00 to 7:00, all day
Sunday, and to either airport. There's a €1 charge for each piece of baggage and for train station pick-ups. To tip, round up to the next euro
(minimum €0.50). Taxis are tough to find on Friday and Saturday
nights, especially after the Métro closes (around 00:30). If you need to
catch a train or flight early in the morning, book *un normal taxi* the day
before.

TOURS

Bus Tours—Paris Vision offers handy bus tours of Paris, day and night
(advertised in hotel lobbies); their "Paris Illumination" tour is much more
interesting (see "Nightlife," below). Far better daytime bus tours are the
hop-on, hop-off double-decker bus services connecting Paris' main sights
while providing running commentary (ideal in good weather when you
can sit on top; see also Batobus under "Boat Tours" below).

Two companies provide hop-on, hop-off bus service: **L'Open
Tours** and **Les Cars Rouges** (pick up their brochures showing routes
and stops from any TI or on their buses).

L'Open Tours, which uses yellow buses, provides more extensive
coverage and offers three different routes, which roll by most of the
important sights in Paris. Their Paris Grand Tour offers the best introduction. Tickets are good for any route. Buy your tickets from the driver (1-day ticket-€25, 2-day ticket-€27, kids 4–11 pay €13 for one or two
days, 20 percent less if you have a *Carte Orange* Métro pass, allow two
hours per tour). Two or three buses depart hourly from about 10:00 to
18:00; expect to wait 10–20 minutes at each stop (stops can be tricky to
find). You can hop off at any stop, then catch a later bus. You'll see these
bright-yellow, topless double-decker buses all over town; pick one up at
the first important sight you visit, or start your tour at the Eiffel Tower
stop (on avenue Joseph Bouvard, tel. 01 42 66 56 56).

Les Cars Rouges' bright red buses offer largely the same service
with fewer stops on a single Grand Tour Route, for less money (2-day
tickets, adult-€23, kids 4–12-€12, tel. 01 53 95 39 53).

Boat Tours—Several companies offer one-hour boat cruises on the Seine
(by far best at night). The huge, mass-production **Bateaux-Mouches**
boats, which depart every 20–30 minutes from the pont de l'Alma's right
bank and right in front of the Eiffel Tower, are convenient to rue Cler
hotels (€7, €4 for ages 4–12, daily 10:00–22:30, useless taped explanations

Core of Paris

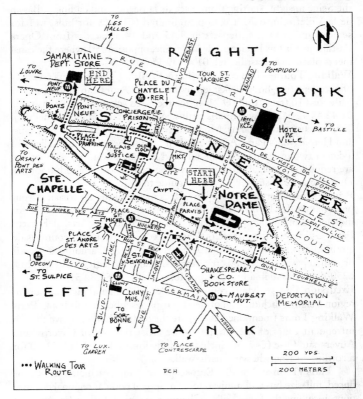

in six languages and tour groups by the dozens, tel. 01 40 76 99 99). The smaller and more intimate **Vedettes du Pont-Neuf** depart only once an hour from the center of pont Neuf (twice an hour after dark), but they come with a live guide giving explanations in French and English and are convenient to Marais and Contrescarpe hotels (€9, €4.50 for ages 4–12, tel. 01 46 33 98 38).

From April through October, the **Batobus** hop-on, hop-off boats on the Seine connect eight popular stops every 15–25 minutes: Eiffel Tower, Champs-Elysées, Orsay/place de la Concorde, Louvre, Notre-Dame, St. Germain-des-Prés, Hôtel de Ville, and Jardin des Plantes. Pick up a schedule at any stop (or TI) and use the boats as a scenic alternative to the Métro. (€ 2.50 per trip, €10 for 1 day, €5.50 under 12; €12.50 for 2 days, €6.50 under 12). Boats run from 10:00 to 19:00, or until 21:00 June through September.

Canauxrama offers a 2.5-hour cruise on a peaceful canal without the Seine in sight, starting from place de la Bastille and ending at Bassin de la Villette, near Métro stop Stalingrad (€14, €9 for kids, €11 for seniors and students, departs at 9:45 and 14:30 across from Opéra Bastille, just below boulevard de la Bastille, opposite #50, where the canal meets place de la Bastille, tel. 01 42 39 15 00).

Walking Tours—The company **Paris Walking Tours** offers a variety of excellent two-hour walks, led by British or American guides, nearly daily for €10 (tel. 01 48 09 21 40 for recorded schedule in English, fax 01 42 43 75 51, see www.paris-walks.com for their complete schedule). Tours focus on the Marais, Montmartre, Ile de la Cité and Ile St. Louis, and Hemingway's Paris. Ask about their family-friendly tours. Call ahead a day or two to learn their schedule and starting point. No reservations are required. These are thoughtfully prepared, relaxing, and humorous. Don't hesitate to stand close to the guide to hear.

Private Guide Service—For many, Paris merits hiring a Parisian as your personal guide. Two excellent licensed local guides who freelance for individuals and families are Arnaud Servignat, who runs Accueil-France-Paris-Guide (€170/4 hrs, €260/day, also does car tours of countryside around Paris, tel. 06 72 77 94 50, fax 01 42 57 00 38, arnotour@noos.fr or franceparisguide@noos.fr), and Marianne Siegler (€150/4 hrs, €250/day, reserve in advance if possible, tel. 01 42 52 32 51).

Excursion Tours—Many companies offer minivan and big bus tours to regional sights, including all of the day trips described in this book. **Paris Walking Tours** (mentioned above) are the best, with informative though infrequent tours of the Impressionist artist retreats of Giverny and Auvers-sur-Oise (€47–56, includes admissions, tel. 01 48 09 21 40 for recording in English, www.paris-walks.com).

Paris Vision and smaller **Euroscope** companies each offer mass-produced, full-size bus and minivan tours to several popular regional destinations, including the Loire Valley, Champagne region, D-Day beaches, and Mont St. Michel. Their minivan tours are more expensive but more personal, given in English, and offer pick-up at your hotel (€130–200/person). Their full-size bus tours are multilingual and cost about half the price of a minivan tour—worth it for some simply for the ease of transportation to the sights (full-size buses depart from 214 rue de Rivoli, Mo: Tuileries, tel. 01 42 60 30 01, fax 01 42 86 95 36, www.parisvision.com).Euroscop leaves from II boulevard Houssman (Mo: Opéra or Chausée d'Antin, tel. 01 53 34 11 94, www.euroscope.com

THE "HISTORIC CORE OF PARIS" WALK

(This information is distilled from the Historic Paris Walk chapter in *Rick Steves' Mona Winks*, by Gene Openshaw and Rick Steves.)

Allow four hours for this self-guided tour, including sightseeing.

Start where the city did—on the Ile de la Cité. Face Notre-Dame and follow the dotted line on the "Core of Paris" map (see page 227). To get to Notre-Dame, ride the Métro to Cité, Hôtel de Ville, or St. Michel and walk to the big square facing the...

▲▲Notre-Dame Cathedral—This 700-year-old cathedral is packed with history and tourists. Study its sculpture and windows, take in a Mass, eavesdrop on guides, and walk all around the outside (free, daily 8:00–18:45; treasury-€2.50, not covered by museum pass, daily 9:30–17:30; ask about free English tours, normally Wed and Thu at 12:00 and Sat at 14:30; Mo: Cité, Hôtel de Ville, or St. Michel). Climb to the top for a great view of the city; you get 400 steps for only €5.50 (April–Sept daily 9:30–19:30, Oct–March daily 10:00–18:00, last entry 45 min before closing, covered by museum pass though you can't bypass line, arrive early to avoid long lines). There are clean €0.50 toilets in front of the church near Charlemagne's statue.

The **cathedral facade** is worth a close look. The church is dedicated to "Our Lady" (Notre-Dame). Mary is center stage—cradling Jesus, surrounded by the halo of the rose window. Adam is on the left and Eve is on the right.

Below Mary and above the arches is a row of 28 statues known as the Kings of Judah. During the French Revolution, these biblical kings were mistaken for the hated French kings. The citizens stormed the church, crying, "Off with their heads!" All were decapitated, but have since been recapitated.

Speaking of decapitation, look at the carving above the doorway on the left. The man with his head in his hands is St. Denis. Back when there was a Roman temple on this spot, Christianity began making converts. The fourth-century bishop of Roman Paris, Denis, was beheaded. But these early Christians were hard to keep down. The man who would become St. Denis got up, tucked his head under his arm, and headed north until he found just the right place to meet his maker: Montmartre. (Although the name "Montmartre" comes from the Roman "Mount of Mars," later generations—thinking of their beheaded patron St. Denis— preferred a less pagan version, "Mount of Martyrs.") The Parisians were convinced of this miracle, Christianity gained ground, and a church soon replaced the pagan temple.

Medieval art was OK if it embellished the house of God and told Bible stories. For a fine example, move to the base of the central column (at the foot of Mary, about where the head of St. Denis could spit if he were really good). Working around from the left, find God telling a barely created Eve, "Have fun, but no apples." Next, the sexiest serpent I've ever seen makes apples à la mode. Finally, Adam and Eve, now ashamed of their nakedness, are expelled by an angel. This is a tiny example in a church covered with meaning.

Now move to the right and study the carving above the **central portal**. It's the end of the world, and Christ sits on the throne of Judgment (just under the arches, holding his hands up). Below him an angel and a demon weigh souls in the balance. The "good" stand to the left, looking up to heaven. The "bad" ones to the right are chained up and led off to...Versailles on a Tuesday. The "ugly" ones must be the crazy, sculpted demons to the right, at the base of the arch.

Wander through the interior. You'll be routed around the ambulatory, much as medieval pilgrims would have been. Don't miss the rose windows filling each of the transepts. Back outside, walk around the church through the park on the riverside for a close look at the flying buttresses.

The neo-Gothic, 300-foot **spire** is a product of the 1860 reconstruction. Around its base are apostles and evangelists (the green men) as well as Eugène-Emmanuel Viollet-le-Duc, the architect in charge of the work. Notice how the apostles look outward, blessing the city, while the architect (at top, seen from behind the church) looks up, admiring his spire.

The archaeological **crypt** is a worthwhile 15-minute stop with your museum pass (€3.50, Tue–Sun 10:00–18:00, closed Mon, enter 100 yards feet in front of church). You'll see Roman ruins, trace the street plan of the medieval village, and see diagrams of how the earliest Paris grew and grew, all thoughtfully explained in English.

If you're hungry near Notre-Dame, the nearby Ile St. Louis has inexpensive *crêperies* and grocery stores open daily on its main drag. Plan a picnic for the quiet, bench-filled park immediately behind the church (public WC available).

Behind Notre-Dame, squeeze through the tourist buses, cross the street, and enter the iron gate into the park at the tip of the island. Look for the stairs and head down to reach the...

▲▲**Deportation Memorial (Mémorial de la Déportation)**—This memorial to the 200,000 French victims of the Nazi concentration camps draws you into their experience. As you descend the steps, the city around you disappears. Surrounded by walls, you have become a prisoner. Your only freedom is your view of the sky and the tantalizing glimpse of the river below.

Enter the single-file chamber ahead. Inside, the circular plaque in the floor reads, "They descended into the mouth of the earth and they did not return." A hallway stretches in front of you, lined with 200,000 lighted crystals, one for each French citizen that died. Flickering at the far end is the eternal flame of hope. The tomb of the unknown deportee lies at your feet. Above, the inscription reads, "Dedicated to the living memory of the 200,000 French deportees sleeping in the night and the fog, exterminated in the Nazi concentration camps."

Ile St. Louis

● 1 Hotel Jeu de Paume
● 2 Hotel de Lutèce
● 3 Hotel des Deux Iles
● 4 La Tastevin
● 5 Auberge de la Reine Blanche
● 6 Café Med
● 7 La Brasserie de l'Isle St. Louis
● 8 Rests. Nos Ancêtres les Gaulois & La Taverne du Sergeant Recruteur
● 9 Grocery Store
● 10 Les Glaces Berthillon Ice Cream
● 11 Amorino Gelati
● 12 Le Cave du Franc Pinot (Jazz Club)
● 13 Good Picnic Spot

Above the exit as you leave is the message you'll find at all Nazi sights: "Forgive, but never forget." (Free, April–Sept daily 10:00–12:00 & 14:00–19:00, Oct–March daily 10:00–12:00 & 14:00–17:00, east tip of the island Ile de la Cité, behind Notre-Dame and near Ile St. Louis, Mo: Cité.)

Ile St. Louis—Look across the river to the Ile St. Louis. If the Ile de la Cité is a tug laden with the history of Paris, it's towing this classy little residential dinghy laden only with boutiques, famous sorbet shops, and restaurants (see "Eating," below). This island wasn't developed until much later (18th century). What was a swampy mess is now harmonious Parisian architecture. The pedestrian bridge, pont St. Louis, connects the two islands, leading right to rue St. Louis-en-l'Ile. This spine of the island is lined with interesting shops. A short stroll takes you to the famous Berthillon ice-cream parlor (#31). Loop back to the pedestrian bridge along the parklike quays (walk north to the river and turn left). This walk is about as peaceful and romantic as Paris gets.

Before walking to the opposite end of the Ile de la Cité, loop through the Latin Quarter (as indicated on the map in this book). From the Deportation Memorial, cross the bridge onto the Left Bank and enjoy the riverside view of Notre-Dame and window-shop among the green book stalls, browsing through used books, vintage posters, and souvenirs. At the little park and church (over the bridge from the front of Notre-Dame), venture inland a few blocks, basically arcing through the Latin Quarter and returning to the island two bridges down at place St. Michel.

▲Latin Quarter—The neighborhood's touristic fame relates to its intriguing artsy, bohemian character. This was perhaps Europe's leading university district in the Middle Ages—home, since the 13th century, to the prestigious Sorbonne University. Back then, Latin was the language of higher education. And, since students here came from all over Europe, Latin served as their linguistic common denominator. Locals referred to the quarter by its language: Latin.

The neighborhood's main boulevards (St. Michel and St. Germain) are lined with far-out bookshops, street singers, and jazz clubs. While still youthful and artsy, the area has become a tourist ghetto filled with cheap North African eateries. The cafés that were once the haunts of great poets and philosophers are now the hangout of tired tourists. For colorful wandering or café sitting, afternoons and evenings are best (Mo: St. Michel).

Walking along rue St. Séverin, you can still see the shadow of the medieval sewer system (the street slopes into a central channel of bricks). In the days before plumbing and toilets, when people still went to the river or neighborhood wells for their water, "flushing" meant throwing it out the window. Certain times of day were flushing times. Maids on the fourth floor would holler, "*Garde de l'eau!*" ("Look out for the water!") and heave it into the streets, where it would eventually be washed down into the Seine.

Consider a visit to the Cluny Museum for its medieval art and unicorn tapestries (listed under "Sights—Southeast Paris," below).

Place St. Michel (facing the St. Michel bridge) is the traditional core of the Left Bank's artsy, liberal, hippie, bohemian district of poets, philosophers, winos, and tourists. In less-commercial times, place St. Michel was a gathering point for the city's malcontents and misfits. Here, in 1871, the citizens took the streets from the government troops, set up barricades *Les Miz*–style, and established the Paris Commune. During World War II, the locals rose up against their Nazi oppressors (read the plaques by St. Michel fountain). And in the spring of 1968, a time of social upheaval all over the world, young students—battling riot batons and tear gas—took over the square and demanded change.

From place St. Michel, look across the river and find the spire of Sainte-Chapelle church and its weathervane angel (below). Cross the river on pont St. Michel and continue along boulevard du Palais. On your left, you'll see the high-security doorway to Sainte-Chapelle. But first, continue another 30 yards and turn right at a wide pedestrian street, the rue de Lutèce.

Cité "Métropolitain" Stop—Of the 141 original turn-of-the-19th-century subway entrances, this is one of 17 survivors preserved as national art treasures. The curvy, plantlike ironwork is a textbook example of Art Nouveau, the style that rebelled against the erector-set squareness of the Industrial Age (e.g., Mr. Eiffel's tower).

The flower market here on place Louis Lépine is a pleasant detour. On Sundays, this square chirps with a busy bird market. And across the way is the Prefecture de Police, where Inspector Clouseau of *Pink Panther* fame used to work, and where the local resistance fighters took the first building from the Nazis in August 1944, leading to the Allied liberation of Paris a week later.

Pause here to admire the view. Sainte-Chapelle is a pearl in an ugly architectural oyster, part of a complex of buildings that includes the Palace of Justice (to the right of Sainte-Chapelle, behind the fancy gates). Return to the entrance of Sainte-Chapelle. Everyone needs to pass through a metal detector to get in. Free toilets are ahead on the left. The line into the church may be long. (Museum passholders can go directly in; pick up the excellent English info sheet.) Enter the humble ground floor of the...

▲▲▲Sainte-Chapelle—This triumph of Gothic church architecture is a cathedral of glass like no other. It was speedily built from 1242 to 1248 for Louis IX (the only French king who is now a saint) to house the supposed Crown of Thorns. Its architectural harmony is due to the fact that it was completed under the direction of one architect in only six years—unheard of in Gothic times. (Notre-Dame took more than 200 years to build.)

The design clearly shows an Old Regime approach to worship. The basement was for staff and other common folk. Royal Christians worshiped upstairs. The ground-floor paint job, a 19th-century restoration, is a reasonably accurate copy of the original.

Climb the spiral staircase to the **Chapelle Haute.** Fill the place with choral music, crank up the sunshine, face the top of the altar, and really believe that the Crown of Thorns was there, and this becomes one awesome space.

"Let there be light." In the Bible, it's clear: Light is divine. Light shining through stained glass was a symbol of God's grace shining down to earth. Gothic architects used their new technology to turn dark stone buildings into lanterns of light. The glory of Gothic shines brighter here than in any other church.

There are 15 separate panels of stained glass (6,500 square feet—two-thirds of it 13th-century original), with more than 1,100 different scenes, mostly from the Bible.

Sainte-Chapelle

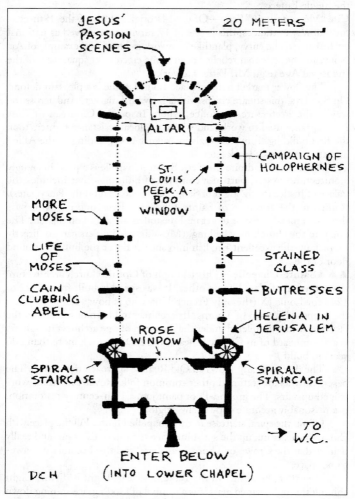

JESUS' PASSION SCENES

20 METERS

ALTAR

CAMPAIGN OF HOLOPHERNES

ST. LOUIS PEEK-A-BOO WINDOW

MORE MOSES

LIFE OF MOSES

STAINED GLASS

CAIN CLUBBING ABEL

BUTTRESSES

HELENA IN JERUSALEM

ROSE WINDOW

SPIRAL STAIRCASE

SPIRAL STAIRCASE

TO W.C.

ENTER BELOW (INTO LOWER CHAPEL)

DCH

The altar was raised up high to better display the relic—the Crown of Thorns—around which this chapel was built. The supposed crown cost King Louis three times as much as this church. Today, it is kept in the Notre-Dame treasury and shown only on Fridays during Lent.

Louis IX's little private viewing window is in the wall to the right of the altar. Louis IX, both saintly and shy, liked to go to church without dealing with the rigors of public royal life. Here, he could worship while still dressed in his jammies.

Lay your camera on the ground and shoot the ceiling. Those ribs growing out of the slender columns are the essence of Gothic.

Books in the gift shop explain the stained glass in English. There are concerts (€16–25) almost every summer evening (€5.50, €8 combo-ticket covers Conciergerie, both covered by museum pass, daily 9:30–18:00, Mo: Cité, tel. 01 44 07 12 38 for concert information).

Palais de Justice—Back outside, as you walk around the church exterior, look down and notice how much Paris has risen in the 800 years since Sainte-Chapelle was built. You're in a huge complex of buildings that has housed the local government since ancient Roman times. It was the site of the original Gothic palace of the early kings of France. The only surviving medieval parts are the Sainte-Chapelle church and the Conciergerie prison.

Most of the site is now covered by the giant Palais de Justice, home of France's supreme court (built in 1776). "*Liberté, Egalité, Fraternité*," emblazoned over the doors, is a reminder that this was also the head-quarters of the Revolutionary government.

As you face the Palais de Justice, the building to the right is the...

Conciergerie—This former prison is a gloomy place. Kings used it to torture and execute failed assassins. The leaders of the Revolution put it to similar good use. A tower along the river, called "the babbler," was named for the painful sounds that leaked from it.

Step inside; Marie-Antoinette was imprisoned here. During a busy eight-month period in the Revolution, she was one of 2,600 prisoners kept here on the way to the guillotine. The interior, with its huge vaulted and pillared rooms, echoes with history but is pretty barren (€5.50, €8 combo-ticket covers Sainte-Chapelle, both covered by museum pass, April–Sept daily 9:30–18:30, Oct–March daily 10:00–17:00, good English descriptions). You can see Marie-Antoinette's cell, which houses a collection of her mementos. In another room, a list of those made "a foot shorter at the top" by the "national razor" includes ex-King Louis XVI, Charlotte Corday (who murdered Jean-Paul Marat in his bathtub), and the chief revolutionary who got a taste of his own medicine, Maximilien de Robespierre.

Back outside, turn left (toward the Right Bank). On the corner is the site of the oldest public clock in the city (built in 1334). While the present clock is said to be Baroque, it somehow still manages to keep accurate time.

Staying on the island, take a left and walk along the river. Across the river you can see the venerable Samaritaine department store. At the first corner, veer left past France's supreme-court building and into a sleepy triangular square called place Dauphine. Marvel at how such quaintness could be lodged in the midst of such greatness as you walk through the park to the end of the island (one of the departure points for Seine river cruises). At the equestrian statue of Henry IV, turn right onto the bridge and take refuge in one of the nooks on the Eiffel Tower side.

Pont Neuf—This "new bridge" is now Paris' oldest. Built during Henry IV's reign (around 1600), its 12 arches span the widest part of the river. The fine view includes the park on the tip of the island (note Seine tour boats), the Orsay Museum, and the Louvre. These turrets were originally for vendors and street entertainers. In the days of Henry IV, who originated the promise of "a chicken in every pot," this would have been a lively scene.

Near here, you can tour the Seine by boat (see Vedettes de Pont-Neuf, listed above in "Tours"), shop at the Samaritaine (across the bridge), or continue to the Louvre.

SIGHTS

Paris Museums near the Tuileries Garden

The newly renovated Tuileries Garden was once private property of kings and queens. Paris' grandest public park links these museums.

▲▲▲**Louvre**—This is Europe's oldest, biggest, greatest, and maybe most crowded museum. There is no grander entry than through the pyramid, but metal detectors create a long line at times.

There are several ways to avoid the line. Museum passholders can use the group entrance in the pedestrian passageway between the pyramid and rue de Rivoli (facing the pyramid with your back to the Tuileries Garden, go to your left, which is north; under the arches, you'll find the entrance and escalator down). Otherwise, you can enter the Louvre underground directly from the Métro stop Palais Royal-Musée du Louvre (exit following signs to *Musée du Louvre*) or from the Carrousel shopping mall, which is connected to the museum. Enter the mall at 99 rue de Rivoli (the door with the red awning, daily 8:30–23:00). The taxi stand is across rue de Rivoli next to the Métro station.

Pick up the free "Louvre Handbook" in English at the information desk under the pyramid as you enter. Don't try to cover the entire museum. Consider taking a tour (see "Tours," page 240).

Self-Guided Tour: Start in the Denon wing and visit the highlights, in the following order (thanks to Gene Openshaw for his help with this).

Wander through the **ancient Greek and Roman works** to see the Parthenon frieze, Pompeii mosaics, Etruscan sarcophagi, and Roman portrait busts. You can't miss lovely *Venus de Milo (Aphrodite)*. This goddess of love (c. 100 B.C., from the Greek island of Melos) created a sensation when she was discovered in 1820. Most "Greek" statues are actually later Roman copies, but Venus is a rare Greek original. She, like

Paris Museums near the Tuileries Garden

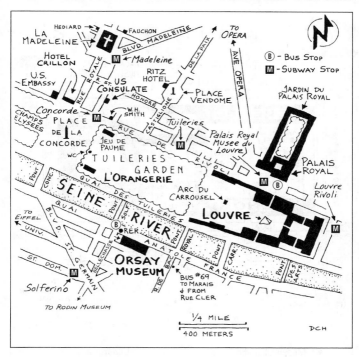

Golden Age Greeks, epitomizes stability, beauty, and balance. Later Greek art was Hellenistic, adding motion and drama. For a good example, see the exciting *Winged Victory of Samothrace (Victoire de Samothrace,* on the landing). This statue of a woman with wings, poised on the prow of a ship, once stood on a hilltop to commemorate a great naval victory. This is the *Venus de Milo* gone Hellenistic.

The **Italian collection** is on the other side of the Winged Victory. The key to Renaissance painting was realism, and for the Italians "realism" was spelled "3-D." Painters were inspired by the realism and balanced beauty of Greek sculpture. Painting a 3-D world on a 2-D surface is tough, and after a millennium of Dark Ages, artists were rusty. Living in a religious age, they painted mostly altarpieces full of saints, angels, Madonnas-and-bambinos, and crucifixes floating in an ethereal gold-leaf heaven. Gradually, though, they brought these otherworldly scenes down to earth. The Italian collection—including the *Mona Lisa*—is scattered throughout rooms *(salles)* 3 and 4, in the long Grand Gallery, and in adjoining rooms.

The Louvre

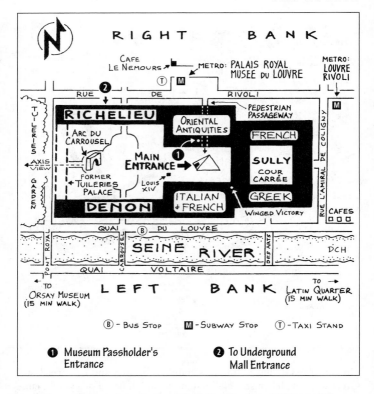

● Museum Passholder's Entrance

❷ To Underground Mall Entrance

Two masters of the Italian High Renaissance (1500–1600) were Raphael (see his *La Belle Jardinière,* showing the Madonna, Child, and John the Baptist) and Leonardo da Vinci. The Louvre has the greatest collection of Leonardos in the world—five of them, including the exquisite *Virgin, Child, and St. Anne,* the neighboring *Madonna of the Rocks,* and the androgynous *John the Baptist.* His most famous, of course, is the *Mona Lisa.*

Leonardo was already an old man when François I invited him to France. Determined to pack light, he took only a few paintings. One was a portrait of a Lisa del Giocondo, the wife of a wealthy Florentine merchant. When Leonardo arrived, François I immediately fell in love with the painting and made it the centerpiece of the small collection of Italian masterpieces that would, in three centuries, become the Louvre museum. He called it *La Gioconda.* We know it as a contraction of the Italian for "my lady Lisa"—*Mona Lisa.* Warning: François I was impressed, but

Mona may disappoint you. She's smaller and darker than you'd expect, engulfed in a huge room, and hidden behind a glaring pane of glass.

Mona's overall mood is one of balance and serenity, but there's also an element of mystery. Her smile and long-distance beauty are subtle and elusive, tempting but always just out of reach, like strands of a street singer's melody drifting through the Métro tunnel. *Mona* doesn't knock your socks off, but she winks at the patient viewer.

Now for something **neoclassical**. Notice the fine work, such as *The Coronation of Napoleon* by Jacques-Louis David, near *Mona* in the Salle Daru. Neoclassicism, once the rage in France (1780–1850), usually features Greek subjects, patriotic sentiment, and a clean, simple style. After Napoleon quickly conquered most of Europe, he insisted on being made emperor (not merely king) of this "New Rome." He staged an elaborate coronation ceremony in Paris, and rather than let the pope crown him, he crowned himself. The setting is the Notre-Dame cathedral, with Greek columns and Roman arches thrown in for effect. Napoleon's mom was also added, since she couldn't make it to the ceremony. A key on the frame describes who's who in the picture.

The **Romantic** collection, in an adjacent room (Salle Mollien), has works by Théodore Géricault *(The Raft of the Medusa)* and Eugène Delacroix *(Liberty Leading the People)*. Romanticism, with an emphasis on motion and emotion, is the complete flip side of neoclassicism, though they both flourished in the early 1800s. Delacroix's *Liberty,* commemorating the stirrings of democracy in France, is also a fitting tribute to the Louvre, the first museum opened to the common rabble of humanity. The good things in life don't belong only to a small wealthy part of society, but to all. The motto of France is *"Liberté, Egalité, Fraternité"*—liberty, equality, and brotherhood.

Exit the room at the far end (past the café) and go downstairs, where you'll bump into the bum of a large, twisting male nude who looks like he's just waking up after a thousand-year nap. The two *Slaves* (1513–1515) by Michelangelo are a fitting end to this museum—works that bridge the ancient and modern worlds. Michelangelo, like his fellow Renaissance artists, learned from the Greeks. The perfect anatomy, twisting poses, and idealized faces look like they could have been done 2,000 years earlier. Michelangelo said that his purpose was to carve away the marble to reveal the figures God put inside. The *Rebellious Slave,* fighting against his bondage, shows the agony of that process and the ecstasy of the result.

Cost: €7.50, €5 after 15:00 and on Sunday, free on first Sunday of month and for those under 18, covered by museum pass. Tickets good all day. Reentry allowed. Tel. 01 40 20 51 51, recorded info tel. 01 40 20 53 17 (www.louvre.fr).

Hours: Wed–Mon 9:00–18:00, closed Tue. All wings open Wed until 21:45. On Mon, only the Denon wing is open until 21:45, but it contains the biggies: *Mona Lisa, Venus de Milo,* and more. Galleries start closing 30 minutes early. Closed Jan 1, Easter, May 1, Nov 1, and Dec 25. Crowds are worst on Sun, Mon, Wed, and mornings. Save money by visiting after 15:00.

Tours: The 90-minute English-language tours, which leave six times daily except Tuesday, when the museum is closed, and Sunday, boil this overwhelming museum down to size (normally at 11:00, 14:00, and 15:45, €3 plus your entry ticket, tour tel. 01 40 20 52 63). Clever €5 digital audioguides (after ticket booths, at top of stairs) give you a receiver and a directory of about 130 masterpieces, allowing you to dial a (rather dull) commentary on included works as you stumble upon them. Rick Steves' and Gene Openshaw's museum guidebook, *Rick Steves' Mona Winks* (buy in United States), includes a self-guided tour of the Louvre.

Underground Louvre: To explore the subterranean shopping mall, enter through the pyramid, walk toward the inverted pyramid, and uncover a post office, a handy TI and SNCF (train tickets) office, glittering boutiques and a dizzying assortment of good-value eateries (up the escalator), and the Palais Royal-Musée du Louvre Métro entrance. Stairs at the far end take you right into the Tuileries Garden, a perfect antidote to the stuffy, crowded rooms of the Louvre.

▲▲▲**Orsay Museum**—The Musée d'Orsay (mew-zay dor-say) houses French art of the 1800s (specifically, art from 1848 to 1914), picking up where the Louvre leaves off. For us, that means Impressionism. The Orsay houses the best general collection anywhere of Edouard Manet, Claude Monet, Pierre-Auguste Renoir, Edgar Degas, Vincent van Gogh, Paul Cézanne, and Paul Gauguin.

The museum shows art that is also both old and new, conservative and revolutionary. You'll start on the ground floor with the Conservatives and the early rebels who paved the way for the Impressionists, then head upstairs to see how a few visionary young artists bucked the system, revolutionized the art world, and paved the way for the 20th century.

For most visitors, the most important part of the museum is the Impressionist collection upstairs. Here, you can study many pictures you've probably seen in books, such as Manet's *Luncheon on the Grass,* Renoir's *Dance at the Moulin de la Galette,* Monet's *Gare St. Lazare,* James Abbott McNeill Whistler's *Portrait of the Artist's Mother,* van Gogh's *The Church at Auvers-sur-Oise,* and Cezanne's *The Card Players.* As you approach these beautiful, easy-to-enjoy paintings, remember that there is more to this art than meets the eye.

Impressionism 101: The camera threatened to make artists obsolete. A painter's original function was to record reality faithfully, like a journalist. Now a machine could capture a better likeness faster than you could say Etch-A-Sketch.

But true art is more than just painted reality. It gives us reality from the artist's point of view, putting a personal stamp on the work. It records

Orsay Ground Floor—Overview

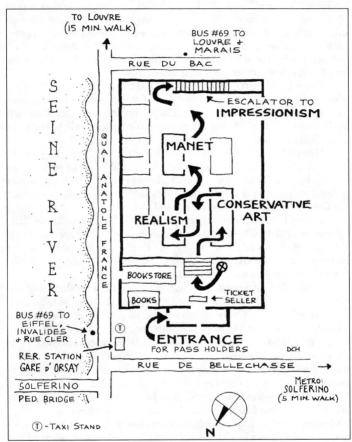

not only a scene—a camera can do that—but the artist's impressions of that scene. Impressions are often fleeting, so the artist has to work quickly.

The Impressionist painters rejected camera-like detail for a quick style more suited to capturing the passing moment. Feeling stifled by the rigid rules and stuffy atmosphere of the Academy, the Impressionists took as their motto, "out of the studio, into the open air." They grabbed their berets and scarves and took excursions to the country, where they set up their easels on riverbanks and hillsides, or they sketched in cafés and dance halls. Gods, goddesses, nymphs, and fantasy scenes were out; common people and rural landscapes were in.

The quick style and simple subjects were ridiculed and called child-ish by the "experts." Rejected by the Salon, the Impressionists staged their own exhibition in 1874. They brashly took their name from an insult thrown at them by a critic, who laughed at one of Monet's impres-sions of a sunrise. During the next decade, they exhibited their own work independently. The public, opposed at first, was slowly drawn in by the simplicity, color, and vibrancy of Impressionist art.

Cost: €7; €5 after 16:15, on Sun, and for ages 18 to 25; free for youth under 18 and for anyone first Sun of month; covered by museum pass. Tickets are good all day. Museum passholders can enter to the left of the main entrance (during the renovation, they can walk to the front of the line and show their passes).

Hours: June 20–Sept 20 Tue–Sun 9:00–18:00; Sept 21–June 19 Tue–Sat 10:00–18:00, Sun 9:00–18:00; Thu until 21:45 all year, always closed Mon. Last entrance is 45 minutes before closing. The Impressionist galleries start closing at 17:15, frustrating many unwary visitors. Note that the Orsay is crowded on Tue, when the Louvre is closed.

Tours: Live English-language tours of the Orsay usually run daily (except Sun) at 11:30. The 90-minute tours cost €6 and are also avail-able on audioguide (€5). Tours in English that focus on the Impressionists are offered Tuesdays at 14:30 and Thursdays at 18:30 (sometimes also on other days, €6).

Cafés: The museum has a cheap café on the fourth floor, and the elegant Salon de Thé du Musée is on the second floor (good salad bar).

Location: The Orsay sits above the RER-C stop called Musée d'Orsay. The nearest Métro stop is Solférino, three blocks south of the Orsay. Bus #69 from the Marais and rue Cler neighborhoods stops at the museum on the river side (quai Anatole France).

Jeu de Paume—The Jeu de Paume hosts rotating exhibits of top contem-porary artists (€6, not covered by museum pass, Tue 12:00–21:30, Wed–Fri 12:00–19:00, Sat–Sun 10:00–19:00, closed Mon, on place de la Concorde, just inside Tuileries Garden on rue de Rivoli side, Mo: Concorde).

L'Orangerie—This Impressionist museum, lovely as a water lily, is due to reopen sometime late in 2004 after renovation (for the latest, ask at a Paris TI or any Paris museum). When it opens, you can step out of the tree-lined, sun-dappled Impressionist painting that is the Tuileries Garden, and into L'Orangerie (loh-rahn-zheh-ree), a little *bijou* of select works by Maurice Utrillo, Cézanne, Renoir, Henri Matisse, and Pablo Picasso. On the ground floor, you'll find a line of eight rooms dedicated to these artists. Downstairs is the finale: Monet's water lilies. The museum's collection is small enough to enjoy in a short visit, but complete enough to see the tran-sition from Impressionism to the Moderns. Plus, it's all beautiful (located in Tuileries Garden near place de la Concorde, Mo: Concorde).

Southwest Paris: The Eiffel Tower Neighborhood

▲▲▲**Eiffel Tower (La Tour Eiffel)**—It's crowded and expensive, but worth the trouble. To avoid most crowds, go early (by 9:00) or late in the day (after 18:00, after 20:00 in summer, last entry one hour before closing); weekends are worst. A TI/ticket booth is between the Pilier Nord (north pillar) and Pilier Est (east pillar). The stairs (yes, you can walk up partway) are next to the Jules Verne restaurant entrance (allow $125 per person for the restaurant at lunch, double for dinner, reserve 3 months in advance). A sign in the cheek-to-jowl elevator tells you to beware of pickpockets.

The tower is a 1,000-foot-tall ornament. In hot weather, it's six inches taller. It covers 2.5 acres and requires 50 tons of paint. Its 7,000 tons of metal are spread out so well at the base that it's no heavier per square inch than a linebacker on tiptoes. Visitors to Paris may find *Mona Lisa* to be less than expected, but the Eiffel Tower rarely disappoints, even in an era of skyscrapers.

Built a hundred years after the French Revolution (and in the midst of an Industrial one), the tower served no function but to impress.

Eiffel Tower Neighborhood

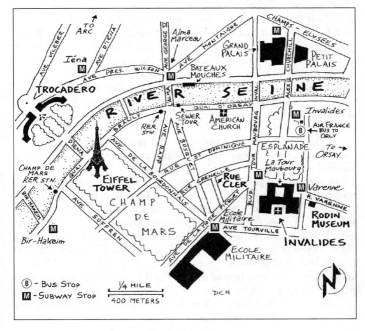

Bridge-builder Gustave Eiffel won the contest for the 1889 Centennial World's Fair by beating out such rival proposals as a giant guillotine. To a generation hooked on technology, the tower was the marvel of the age, a symbol of progress and of man's ingenuity. To others it was a cloned-sheep monstrosity. The writer Guy de Maupassant routinely ate lunch in the tower just so he wouldn't have to look at it.

Delicate and graceful when seen from afar, it's massive—even a bit scary—from close up. You don't appreciate the size until you walk toward it; like a mountain, it seems so close but takes forever to reach. There are three observation platforms, at 200, 400, and 900 feet; the higher you go, the more you pay. Each requires a separate elevator (and line), so plan on at least 90 minutes if you want to go to the top and back. For most, the view from the second level is plenty. As you ascend through the metal beams, imagine being a worker, perched high above nothing, riveting this giant erector set together. On top, all of Paris lies before you, with a panorama guide. On a good day, you can see for 40 miles.

The **first level** has exhibits, a post office (daily 10:00–19:00, cancellation stamp will read Eiffel Tower), a snack bar, WCs, and souvenirs. Read the informative signs (in English) describing the major monuments, see the entertaining free movie on the history of the tower, and don't miss a century of fireworks—including the entire millennium blast—on video. Then consider a drink or a sandwich as you overlook all of Paris at the snack café (outdoor tables in summer) or at the city's best view bar/restaurant, **Altitude 95** (€21–31 lunches, €55 dinners, dinner seatings at 19:00 and 21:00, reserve well ahead for a view table; before you ascend to dine, drop by the booth between the north/*nord* and east/*est* pillars to buy your Eiffel Tower ticket and pick up a pass that enables you to skip the line; tel. 01 45 55 20 04, fax 01 47 05 94 40).

The **second level** has the best views (walk up the stairway to get above the netting), a small cafeteria, WCs, Internet stations, and various exhibits.

While you'll save no money, you can easily save time and enjoy a fun and different perspective on the Eiffel Tower by climbing down (from the lower two levels only) via the stairway. The hike takes only about five minutes per level and is punctuated by English-language factoid boards. Fit travelers could ride the lift up and hike the stairs down.

Cost and Hours: It costs €4 to go to the first level, €7.50 to the second, and €11 to go all the way (not covered by museum pass). On a budget? You can climb the stairs to the second level for only €3.50 (March–Sept daily 9:00–24:00, Oct–Feb daily 9:30–23:00, last entry one hour before closing, shorter lines at night, can catch Bateaux-Mouches boat for Seine cruise at base of tower, Mo: Trocadéro, RER: Champ de Mars-Tour Eiffel, tel. 01 44 11 23 23).

Views: The best place to view the tower is from **Trocadéro Square** to the north (a 10-min walk across the river, and a happening scene at night). Consider arriving at the Trocadéro Métro stop for the view, then walk toward the tower. Another great viewpoint is the long, grassy field, le parc du Champ de Mars, to the south (after about 20:00, the *gendarmes* look the other way as Parisians stretch out or picnic on the grass). However impressive it may be by day, the tower is an awesome thing to see at twilight, when it becomes engorged with light and virile Paris lies back and lets night be on top.

▲**Paris Sewer Tour (Egouts)**—This quick and easy visit takes you along a few hundred yards of underground water tunnel lined with interesting displays, well-described in English, that explain the evolution of the world's longest sewer system. (If you straightened out Paris' sewers, they would reach beyond Istanbul.) Don't miss the slideshow, the fine WCs just beyond the gift shop, and the occasional tour in English (€4, covered by museum pass, May-Sept Sat-Wed 11:00-17:00, closes at 16:00 Oct-April, always closed Thu-Fri, where pont de l'Alma greets the Left Bank, Mo: Alma-Marceau, RER: Pont de l'Alma, tel. 01 47 05 10 29).

▲▲**Napoleon's Tomb and Army Museum (Les Invalides)**—The emperor lies majestically dead inside several coffins under a grand dome— a goose-bumping pilgrimage for historians. Napoleon is surrounded by the tombs of other French war heroes and a fine military museum in Hôtel des Invalides. Check out the interesting World War II wing. Follow signs to the "crypt" to find Roman Empire–style reliefs that list the accomplishments of Napoleon's administration. The restored dome glitters with 26 pounds of gold (€6, students-€5, under 18 free, covered by museum pass, April–Sept daily 9:00–18:00, Oct–March daily 10:00–17:00; closed first Mon of month, Mo: La Tour Maubourg, Varenne or Invalides, tel. 01 44 42 37 72).

▲▲**Rodin Museum (Musée Rodin)**—This user-friendly museum is filled with passionate works by the greatest sculptor since Michelangelo. See *The Kiss, The Thinker, The Gates of Hell,* and many more. Don't miss the room full of work by Rodin's student and mistress, Camille Claudel (€5, €3 on Sun and for students, free for youth under 18 and for anyone first Sun of month; covered by museum pass; €1 for gardens only, which may be Paris' best deal as many works are well displayed in the beautiful gardens; April–Sept Tue–Sun 9:30–17:45, closed Mon, gardens close 18:45, Oct–March Tue–Sun 9:30–17:00, closed Mon, gardens close 16:45; near Napoleon's Tomb, 77 rue de Varenne, Mo: Varenne, tel. 01 44 18 61 10). There's a good self-serve cafeteria as well as idyllic picnic spots in the family-friendly back garden.

▲▲**Marmottan Museum (Musée Marmottan Monet)**—In this private, intimate, less-visited museum, you'll find more than 100 paintings by Claude Monet (thanks to his son Michel), including the *Impression: Sunrise* painting that gave the movement its start—and name (€6.50, not covered by museum pass, Tue–Sun 10:00–18:00, closed Mon, 2 rue Louis Boilly, Mo: La Muette, follow museum signs six blocks through a delightful

kid-filled park, tel. 01 44 96 50 33). Nearby is one of Paris' most pleasant shopping streets, the rue de Passy (from La Muette Métro stop).

Southeast Paris: The Latin Quarter

This Left Bank neighborhood, just opposite Notre-Dame, is the Latin
Quarter. (For more information and a walking tour, see the "Historic
Core of Paris Walk," above.)

▲▲Cluny Museum (Musée National du Moyen Age)—This treasure
trove of medieval art fills the old Roman baths, offering close-up looks
at stained glass, Notre-Dame carvings, fine goldsmithing and jewelry,
and rooms of tapestries—the best of which is the exquisite *Lady with the
Unicorn.* In five panels, a delicate-as-medieval-can-be noble lady introduces a delighted unicorn to the senses of taste, hearing, sight, smell, and
touch (€7, €5.50 on Sun, free first Sun of month, covered by museum
pass, Wed–Mon 9:15–17:45, closed Tue, near corner of boulevard St.
Michel and boulevard St. Germain, Mo: Cluny-La Sorbonne, St.
Michel, or Odéon, tel. 01 53 73 78 00).

St. Germain-des-Prés—A church was first built on this site in A.D. 452.
The church you see today was constructed in 1163. The area around the
church hops at night with fire eaters, mimes, and scads of artists (Mo:
St. Germain-des-Prés).

▲St. Sulpice Organ Concert—For pipe-organ enthusiasts, this is a
delight. The Grand-Orgue at St. Sulpice has a rich history, with a succession of 12 world-class organists (including Charles-Marie Widor and
Marcel Dupré) going back 300 years. Widor started the tradition of
opening the loft to visitors after the 10:30 service on Sundays. Daniel
Roth continues to welcome guests in three languages while playing five
keyboards at once. The 10:30 Sunday Mass is followed by a high-powered 25-minute recital at 11:40. Then, just after noon, the small,
unmarked door is opened (left of entry as you face the rear). Visitors
scamper like 16th notes up spiral stairs, past the 18th-century
StairMasters that were used to fill the bellows, into a world of 7,000
pipes, where they can watch the master play during the next Mass. You'll
generally have 30 minutes to kill (there's a plush lounge) before the organ
plays; visitors can leave at any time. If late or rushed, show up around
12:30 and wait at the little door. As someone leaves, you can slip in (Mo:
St. Sulpice or Mabillon). The Luxembourg Garden and St. Germain
market are both nearby and open daily (the St. Germain market is
between St. Sulpice and Métro stop Mabillon on rue Clément).

▲▲Luxembourg Garden (Jardin du Luxembourg)—Paris' most beautiful, interesting, and enjoyable garden/park/recreational area is a great
place to watch Parisians at rest and play (open daily until dusk, Mo:
Odéon, RER: Luxembourg). These private gardens are property of the
French Senate (housed in the château) and have special rules governing
their use (e.g., where cards can be played, where dogs can be walked,

Latin Quarter

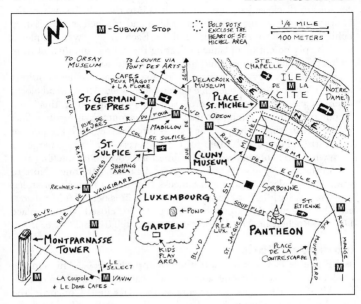

where joggers can run, when and where music can be played). The brilliant flower beds are completely changed three times a year, and the boxed trees are brought out of the orangery in May. Challenge the card and chess players to a game (near the tennis courts), rent a toy sailboat, or find a free chair near the main pond and take a breather. Notice any pigeons? The story goes that a poor Ernest Hemingway used to hand-hunt (read: strangle) them here. Paris Walking Tours offers a good tour of the park (see "Tours," page 226).

The grand, neoclassical-domed Panthéon, now a mausoleum housing the tombs of several great Frenchmen, is a block away and only worth entering if you have a museum pass.

If you enjoy the Luxembourg Garden and want to see more, visit the nearby, colorful Jardin des Plantes (Mo: Jussieu or Gare d'Austerlitz, RER: Gare d'Austerlitz) and the more elegant Parc Monceau (Mo: Monceau).

▲Catacombs—These underground tunnels contain the anonymous bones of six million permanent Parisians. In 1785, the Revolutionary Government of Paris decided to relieve congestion and improve sanitary conditions by emptying the city cemeteries (which traditionally surrounded churches) into an official ossuary. The perfect locale was the many miles of underground tunnels from limestone quarries, which were, at that time, just outside the city. For decades, priests led ceremonial processions of black-veiled, bone-laden carts into the quarries, where the bones were stacked into piles five feet high and as much as 80 feet deep behind neat walls of skull-studded tibiae. Each transfer was completed with the placement of a plaque indicating the church and district from which that stack of bones came and the date they arrived.

From the entry of the catacombs, a spiral staircase leads 60 feet down. Then you begin a one-mile subterranean walk. After several blocks of empty passageways, you ignore a sign announcing: "Halt, this is the empire of the dead." Along the way, plaques encourage visitors to reflect upon their destiny: "Happy is he who is forever faced with the hour of his death and prepares himself for the end every day." You emerge far from where you entered, with white limestone-covered toes, telling anyone in the know you've been underground gawking at bones. Note to wannabe Hamlets: An attendant checks your bag at the exit for stolen souvenirs. A flashlight is handy. Being under 6'2" is helpful (€5, not covered by museum pass, Tue–Sun 10:00–17:00, closed Mon, 1 place Denfert-Rochereau, Mo: Denfert-Rochereau, tel. 01 43 22 47 63).

Northwest Paris

▲▲Place de la Concorde and the Champs-Elysées—This famous boulevard is Paris' backbone, and has the greatest concentration of traffic. All of France seems to converge on the place de la Concorde, the city's largest square. It was here that the guillotine took the lives of thousands—including King Louis XVI and Marie-Antoinette. Back then it was called the place de la Revolution.

Catherine de Médicis wanted a place to drive her carriage, so she started draining the swamp that would become the avenue des Champs-Elysées. Napoleon put on the final touches, and it's been the place to be seen ever since. The Tour de France bicycle race ends here, as do all parades (French or foe) of any significance. While the boulevard has become a bit hamburgerized, a walk here is a must. Take the Métro to the Arc de Triomphe (Mo: Charles de Gaulle-Etoile) and saunter down the Champs-Elysées (Métro stops every few blocks: Franklin D. Roosevelt, George V, and Charles de Gaulle-Etoile).

▲▲▲Arc de Triomphe—Napoleon had the magnificent Arc de Triomphe commissioned to commemorate his victory at the Battle of Austerlitz. There's no triumphal arch bigger (165 feet high, 130 feet wide). And, with 12 converging boulevards, there's no traffic circle more thrilling to experience—either behind the wheel or on foot (take the underpass). An elevator or a spiral staircase leads to a cute museum about the arch and a grand view from the top, even after dark.

Ponder the Tomb of the Unknown Soldier (from World War I, at base of arch) wehre the flame is rekindled daily at 18:30. Find François

Northwest Paris: Champs-Elysées, Arc de Triomphe, and Beyond

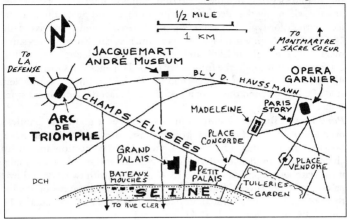

Rude's famous relief, La Marseillaise (on the right piller), showing a shouting Lady Liberty rallying weary troops. Climb the arch (284 steps) for an eye-opening view of *toute* Paris.

Cost and Hours: €7 for climb and elevator, covered by museum pass (April–Sept daily 10:00–23:00, Oct–March daily 10:00–22:30, Mo: Charles de Gaulle-Etoile, use underpass to reach arch, tel. 01 55 37 73 77).

▲**Old Opera House (Opéra Garnier)**—This grand palace of the belle époque was built for Napoleon III and finished in 1875. (After completing this project, the architect—Charles Garnier—went south to do the casino in Monte Carlo.) From the grand avenue de l'Opéra, once lined with Paris' most fashionable haunts, the newly restored facade seems to say "all power to the wealthy." While huge, the actual theater seats only 2,000. The real show was before and after, when the elite of Paris—out to see and be seen—strutted their elegant stuff in the extravagant lobbies. Think of the grand marble stairway as a theater itself. As you wander the halls and gawk at the decor, imagine the place filled with the beautiful people of the day. The massive foundations straddle an underground lake (creating the mysterious world of the *Phantom of the Opera*). Tourists can peek from two boxes into the actual red velvet theater, where they see Marc Chagall's colorful ceiling (1964) playfully dancing around the eight-ton chandelier. Note the box seats next to the stage—the most expensive in the house, with an obstructed view of the stage but just right if you're there only to be seen. The elitism of this place prompted President François Mitterand to have a people's opera house built in the 1980s (symbolically, on place de la Bastille, where the

French Revolution started in 1789). This left the Opéra Garnier home only to ballet and occasional concerts (usually no performances from mid-July to mid-Sept). While the library/museum is of interest to opera buffs, anyone will enjoy the second-floor grand foyer and Salon du Glacier, iced with decor typical of 1900 (€6, not covered by museum pass, daily 10:00–17:00 except when in use for performance, €10 English tours summers only, normally at 12:00 and 14:00, 90 min, includes entry, call to confirm; enter through the front off place de l'Opéra, Mo: Opéra, tel. 01 40 01 22 53). American Express and the *Paris Story* film are on the left side of the opera, and the venerable Galeries Lafayette department store is just behind.

***Paris Story* Film**—The entertaining film gives a good and painless overview of Paris' turbulent and brilliant past, covering 2,000 years in 45 fast-moving minutes. The theater's wide-screen projection and cushy chairs provide an ideal break from bad weather and sore feet and make it fun with kids (€8, kids ages 6 to 18-€5, families with two kids and two parents-€21, not covered by museum pass, get a 20 percent discount with this book, shows are on the hour daily 9:00–19:00, next to opera at 11 rue Scribe, Mo: Opéra, tel. 01 42 66 62 06).

▲▲**Jacquemart-André Museum (Musée Jacquemart-André)**—This thoroughly enjoyable museum showcases the lavish home of a wealthy, art-loving, 19th-century Parisian couple. After wandering the grand boulevards, you now get inside for an intimate look at the lifestyles of the Parisian rich and fabulous. Edouard André and his wife, Nélie Jacquemart—who had no children—spent their lives and fortunes designing, building, and then decorating a sumptuous mansion. What makes this visit so rewarding is the fine audioguide tour (in English, free with admission). The place is strewn with paintings by Rembrandt, Sandro Botticelli, Paolo Uccello, Andrea Mantegna, Giovanni Bellini, François Boucher, and Honoré Fragonard—enough to make a painting gallery famous. Plan on spending an hour with the audioguide (€8, not covered by museum pass, daily 10:00–18:00, elegant café, 158 boulevard Haussmann, Mo: Miromesnil, tel. 01 42 89 04 91).

▲**View from Hôtel Concorde-Lafayette**—For a remarkable (and free unless you buy a drink) Parisian panorama, take the Métro to the Porte Maillot stop, then find the unappealing concrete tower that houses this luxury hotel. Take the elevator in the rear of the lobby to floor 34 and enter a world of €8 beers, €6 espresso, and jaw-dropping views. If it's clear or the sun's about to set, spring for a drink (the ride was free).

▲**Grande Arche de la Défense**—On the outskirts of Paris, the centerpiece of Paris' ambitious skyscraper complex (La Défense) is the Grande Arche. Inaugurated in 1989 on the 200th anniversary of the French Revolution, it was dedicated to human rights and brotherhood. The place is big—38 floors holding offices for 30,000 people on more than 200 acres. Notre-Dame Cathedral could fit under its arch. The complex at La Défense is an interesting study in 1960s land-use planning. More than 100,000 workers commute here daily, directing lots of business and development away from downtown and allowing central Paris to retain its more elegant feel. This makes sense to most Parisians, regardless of whatever else they feel about this controversial complex. You will enjoy city views from the Grande Arche elevator (€8, under 18-€6, not covered by museum pass, daily 10:00–19:00, includes a film on its construction and art exhibits, RER or Mo: La Défense, follow signs to Grande Arche or get off one stop earlier at Esplanade de la Défense and walk through the interesting business complex, tel. 01 49 07 27 57).

North Paris: Montmartre

▲▲Sacré-Cœur and Montmartre—This Byzantine-looking church, while only 130 years old, is impressive (church free: daily 7:00-23:00; €5 to climb dome: June–Sept daily 9:00–19:00, Oct–May daily 10:00–18:00). One block from the church, the place du Tertre was the haunt of Henri de Toulouse-Lautrec and the original bohemians. Today, it's mobbed with tourists and unoriginal bohemians, but it's still fun (go early in the morning to beat the crowds). Take the Métro to the Anvers stop (one more Métro ticket buys your way up the funicular and avoids the stairs) or the closer but less scenic Abbesses stop. A taxi to the top of the hill saves time and avoids sweat. For restaurant recommendations, see "Eating," below.

Pigalle—Paris' red-light district, the infamous "Pig Alley," is at the foot of butte Montmartre. *Oo la la.* It's more shocking than dangerous. Walk from place Pigalle to place Blanche, teasing desperate barkers and fast-talking temptresses. In bars, a €150 bottle of cheap champagne comes with a friend. Stick to the bigger streets, hang on to your wallet, and exercise good judgment. Cancan can cost a fortune, as can con artists in topless bars. After dark, countless tour buses line the streets—a reminder that tour guides make big bucks by bringing their groups to touristy nightclubs like the famous Moulin Rouge (Mo: Pigalle or Abbesses).

Northeast Paris: Marais Neighborhood and More

The Marais neighborhood extends along the Right Bank of the Seine from the Pompidou Center to the Bastille. It contains more pre-revolutionary lanes and buildings than anywhere else in town and is more atmospheric than touristy. It's medieval Paris. This is how much of the city looked until, in the mid-1800s, Napoleon III had Baron Haussmann blast out the narrow streets to construct broad boulevards (wide enough for the guns and ranks of the army, too wide for revolutionary barricades), thus creating modern Paris. Originally a swamp *(marais)* during the reign of Henry IV, this area became the hometown of the French aristocracy. In the 17th century, big shots built their private mansions *(hôtels),* close

Marais Sights

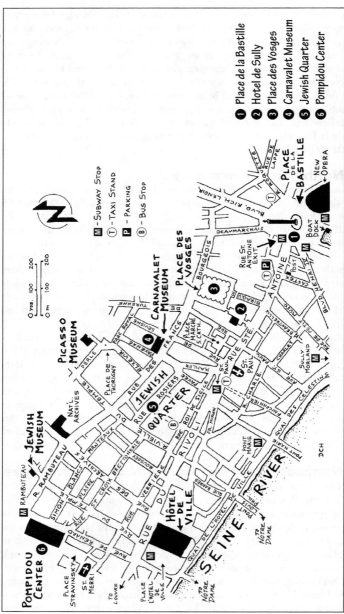

- **1** Place de la Bastille
- **2** Hotel de Sully
- **3** Place des Vosges
- **4** Carnavalet Museum
- **5** Jewish Quarter
- **6** Pompidou Center

to Henry IV's place des Vosges. When strolling the Marais, stick to the west-east axis formed by rue Sainte-Croix de la Bretonnerie, rue des Rosiers (heart of Paris' Jewish community), and rue St. Antoine. On Sunday afternoons, this trendy area pulses with shoppers and café crowds.

▲**Place des Vosges**—Study the architecture in this grand square: nine pavilions per side. Some of the brickwork is real, some is fake. Walk to the center, where Louis XIII sits on a horse surrounded by locals enjoying their community park. Children frolic in the sandbox, lovers warm benches, and pigeons guard their fountains while trees shade this retreat from the glare of the big city. Henry IV built this centerpiece of the Marais in 1605. As hoped, this turned the Marais into Paris' most exclusive neighborhood. As the nobility flocked to Versailles in a later age, this too was a magnet for the rich and powerful of France. With the Revolution, the aristocratic elegance of this quarter became working-class, filled with gritty shops, artisans, immigrants, and Jews. **Victor Hugo** lived at #6, and you can visit his house (free, Tue–Sun 10:00–17:40, closed Mon, 6 place des Vosges, tel. 01 42 72 10 16). Leave the place des Vosges through the doorway at southwest corner of the square (near the three-star Michelin restaurant, l'Ambrosie) and pass through the elegant **Hôtel de Sully** (great example of a Marais mansion) to rue St. Antoine.

▲▲**Pompidou Center**—Europe's greatest collection of far-out modern art, the Musée National d'Art Moderne, is housed on the fourth and fifth floors of this newly renovated and colorful exoskeletal building. Once ahead of its time, this 20th-century (remember that century?) art has been waiting for the world to catch up with it. After so many Madonnas-and-Children, a piano smashed to bits and glued to the wall is refreshing (€5.50, free on first Sun of the month, covered by museum pass, audioguide-€4, Wed–Mon 11:00–21:00, closed Tue and May 1; to use escalator you need museum ticket or museum pass, good Café La Mezzanine on Level 1 is cheaper than cafés outside, Mo: Rambuteau, tel. 01 44 78 12 33).

The Pompidou Center and its square are lively, with lots of people, street theater, and activity inside and out—a perpetual street fair. Kids of any age enjoy the fun, colorful fountains (called *Homage to Stravinsky*) on the square.

▲▲**Jewish Art and History Museum (Musée d'Art et Histoire du Judaïsme)**—This fascinating museum is located in a beautifully restored Marais mansion and tells the story of Judaism throughout Europe, from the Roman destruction of Jerusalem to the theft of famous artworks during World War II. Helpful, free audioguides and many English explanations make this an enjoyable history lesson (red numbers on small signs indicate the number you should press on your audioguide). Move along at your own speed. The museum illustrates the cultural unity maintained by this continually dispersed population. You'll learn about the history of

Jewish traditions from bar mitzvahs to menorahs, and see exquisite traditional costumes and objects around which daily life revolved. Don't miss
the explanation of "the Dreyfus affair," a major event in early 1900s French
politics. You'll also see photographs of and paintings by famous Jewish
artists, including Marc Chagall, Amedeo Modigliani, and Chaim Soutine.
A small but moving section is devoted to the deportation of Jews from
Paris (€6.50, ages 18 to 26-€4, under 18 free, not covered by museum pass,
Mon–Fri 11:00–18:00, Sun 10:00–18:00, closed Sat, 71 rue du Temple,
Mo: Rambuteau or Hôtel de Ville a few blocks away, tel. 01 53 01 86 60).

▲Picasso Museum (Musée Picasso)—Tucked into a corner of the
Marais and worth ▲▲▲ if you're a Picasso fan, this museum contains
the world's largest collection of Picasso's paintings, sculptures, sketches,
and ceramics, and includes his small collection of Impressionist art. The
art is well-displayed in a fine old mansion with a peaceful garden café.
The room-by-room English introductions help make sense of Picasso's
work—from the Toulouse-Lautrec–like portraits at the beginning of his
career, to his gray-brown Cubist period, to his Salvador Dalí–like finish.
The well-done €3 English guidebook helps Picassophiles appreciate the
context of his art and learn more about his interesting life. Most will be
happy reading the posted English explanations while moving at a steady
pace through the museum—the ground and first floors satisfied my
curiosity (€5.50, free first Sun of month, covered by museum pass,
Wed–Mon 9:30–18:00, Oct–March Wed-Mon 9:30-17:30, closed Tue,
5 rue Thorigny, Mo: St. Paul or Chemin Vert, tel. 01 42 71 25 21).

▲▲Carnavalet Museum—The tumultuous history of Paris is well-displayed in this converted Marais mansion. Unfortunately, explanations
are in French only, but many displays are fairly self-explanatory. You'll
see paintings of Parisian scenes, French Revolution paraphernalia, old
Parisian store signs, a small guillotine, a model of 16th-century Ile de la
Cité (notice the bridge houses), and rooms full of 17th-century Parisian
furniture (free, Tue–Sun 10:00–18:00, closed Mon, 23 rue de Sévigné,
Mo: St. Paul, tel. 01 44 59 58 58).

▲Promenade Plantée Park—This two-mile-long, narrow garden walk
on a viaduct was once a railroad and is now a joy. It runs from place de
la Bastille (Mo: Bastille) along avenue Daumesnil to St. Mandé (Mo:
Michel Bizot). Part of the park is elevated. At times, you'll walk along
the street until you pick up the next segment. To reach the park from
place de la Bastille, take avenue Daumesnil (past opera building) to
the intersection with avenue Ledru Rollin; walk up the stairs and
through the gate (free, opens Mon–Fri at 8:00, Sat–Sun at 9:00, closes
at sunset). The shops below the viaduct's arches make for entertaining
window-shopping.

▲Père Lachaise Cemetery (Cimetière Père Lachaise)—Littered with
the tombstones of many of the city's most illustrious dead, this is your
best one-stop look at the fascinating, romantic world of "permanent

Parisians." More like a small city, the place is confusing, but maps will direct you to the graves of Frédéric Chopin, Molière, Edith Piaf, Oscar Wilde, Gertrude Stein, Jim Morrison, and Héloïse and Abelard. In section 92, a series of statues memorializing World War II makes the French war experience a bit more real (helpful €1.50 maps at flower store near entry, closes at dusk, across street from Métro stop, Mo: Père Lachaise or bus #69).

Disappointments de Paris

Here are a few negatives to help you manage your limited time:

La Madeleine is a big, neoclassical church with a postcard facade and a postbox interior. The famous aristocratic deli behind the church, Fauchon, is elegant, but so are many others handier to your hotel.

Paris' **Panthéon** (nothing like Rome's) is another stark neoclassical edifice, filled with the mortal remains of great Frenchmen who mean little to the average American tourist.

The **Bastille** is Paris' most famous non-sight. The square is there, but confused tourists look everywhere and can't find the famous prison of Revolution fame. The building's gone and the square is good only as a jumping-off point for Promenade Plantée Park (see "Sights—Northeast Paris," above).

Finally, the **Latin Quarter** is a frail shadow of its characteristic self. The blocks nearest the river are more Tunisian, Greek, and Woolworth's than old-time Paris. The neighborhood is worth a wander, but focus on boulevard St. Germain, rue de Buci, and the streets around the Maubert-Mutualité Metro stop.

PALACE OF VERSAILLES

Every king's dream, Versailles was the residence of the French king and the cultural heartbeat of Europe for about 100 years—until the Revolution of 1789 ended the notion that God deputized some people to rule for Him on Earth. Louis XIV spent half a year's income of Europe's richest country turning his dad's hunting lodge into a palace fit for a divine monarch. Louis XV and Louis XVI spent much of the 18th century gilding Louis XIV's lily. In 1837, about 50 years after the royal family was evicted, King Louis Philippe opened the palace as a museum. Europe's next-best palaces are Versailles wannabes.

Information: A helpful TI is just past Sofitel Hôtel on your walk from the station to the palace (May–Sept daily 9:00–19:00, Oct–April daily 9:00–18:00, tel. 01 39 24 88 88, www.chateauversailles.fr). You'll also find information booths inside the château (doors A, B-2, and C) and, in peak season, kiosks scattered around the courtyard. The useful brochure "Versailles Orientation Guide" explains your sightseeing options. A baggage check is available at door A.

Versailles

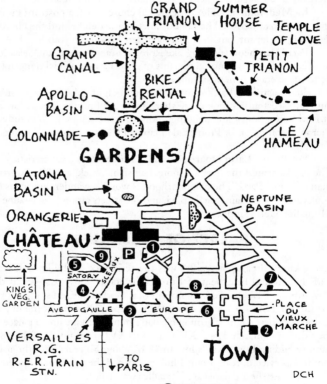

WALKING TIMES
Train Station to Chateau = 10 min.
Chateau to Grand Trianon = 30 min.
Grand Trianon to Le Hameau = 20 min.
Le Hameau to Chateau = 30 min.

GRAND TRIANON
SUMMER HOUSE
TEMPLE OF LOVE
PETIT TRIANON
GRAND CANAL
BIKE RENTAL
APOLLO BASIN
COLONNADE
GARDENS
LE HAMEAU
LATONA BASIN
NEPTUNE BASIN
ORANGERIE
CHÂTEAU
KING'S VEG. GARDEN
SATORY
AVE DE GAULLE
L'EUROPE
PLACE DU VIEUX MARCHÉ
VERSAILLES R.G. R.E.R. TRAIN STN.
TO PARIS
TOWN

DCH

❶ Hôtel de France
❷ Hôtel le Cheval Rouge
❸ Hôtel Ibis Versailles
❹ Hôtel du Palais
❺ Hôtel d'Angleterre
❻ Rest. La Boeuf á la Mode
❼ Rest. Fenêtres sur Cour
❽ Rest. A la Côte Bretonne
❾ Rest. Le Limousin

Cost: €7.50 (main palace and both Trianon palaces are covered by museum pass); €5.50 after 15:30, under 18 free (the palace is also theoretically free for all teachers, professors, and architecture students). Admission is payable at entrances A, C, and D. Tours cost extra (see "Touring Versailles from A to D"). The Grand and Petit Trianons cost €5 together, €3 after 15:30 (both covered by museum pass). The gardens, which usually cost €3, are €5.50 on fountain "spray days" on summer weekends (gardens not covered by museum pass, see "Fountain Spectacles," below).

If you don't have a museum pass, consider getting the Versailles Pass, which covers your entrance, gives you priority access (no lines) to everything, and includes an audioguide (€21, sold at Versailles train station, RER stations that serve Versailles, and at FNAC department stores).

Hours: The **palace** is open May–Sept Tue–Sun 9:00–18:30, Oct–April Tue–Sun 9:00–17:30, closed Mon (last entry 30 min before closing). The **Grand and Petit Trianon Palaces** are open daily April–Oct 12:00–18:00, Nov–March 12:00–17:00, closed Mon. The **garden** is open daily from 7:00 (8:00 in winter) to sunset (as late as 21:30 or as early as 17:30).

In summer, Versailles is especially crowded around 10:00 and 13:00, and all day Tue and Sun. Remember, the crowds gave Marie-Antoinette a pain in the neck, too, so relax and let them eat cake. For fewer crowds, go early or late: Either arrive by 9:00 (when the palace opens, touring the palace first, then the gardens) or after 15:30 (you'll get a reduced entry ticket, but you'll miss the last guided tours of the day, which generally depart at 15:00). If you arrive midday, see the gardens first and the palace later, at 15:00. The gardens and palace are great late. On my last visit, I was the only tourist in the Hall of Mirrors at 18:00...even on a Tuesday.

Palace: To tour the palace on your own, join the line at entrance A if you need to pay admission. Those with a museum pass are allowed in through entrance B-2 without a wait. Enter the palace and take a one-way walk through the State Apartments from the King's Wing, through the Hall of Mirrors, and out via the Queen's and Nobles' Wing.

The Hall of Mirrors was the ultimate hall of the day—250 feet long, with 17 arched mirrors matching 17 windows with royal garden views, 24 gilded candelabra, eight busts of Roman emperors, and eight classical-style statues (seven are ancient originals). The ceiling is decorated with stories of Louis' triumphs. Imagine this place filled with silk gowns and powdered wigs, lit by thousands of candles. The mirrors—a luxurious rarity at the time—were a reflection of a time when aristocrats felt good about their looks and their fortunes. In another age altogether, this was the room in which the Treaty of Versailles was signed, ending World War I.

Before going downstairs at the end, take a stroll clockwise around the long room filled with the great battles of France murals. If you don't

TOURING VERSAILLES
FROM A TO D

Versailles' highlights are the State Apartments (including the magnificent Hall of Mirrors) and the gardens, dotted with the Trianon Palaces. Versailles aficionados should spend extra time and money to see the lavish King's Private Apartments, the Opera House, and more, which can be visited only with an audioguide or live guide.

The price of any tour is added to the €7.50 entry fee to Versailles (entry covered by Paris museum pass, but tours are not). If you don't have a pass, keep your ticket as proof you've paid for admission, in case you decide to take a guided tour after you've wandered through the palace by yourself.

• *Stand in the courtyard to orient yourself to Versailles' entrances.*

Entrance A: State Apartments, Self-Guided Tour—To tour the palace on your own (by following my tour, below, or a €4 audioguide), join the line at entrance A if you need to pay admission. Those with a museum pass are allowed in through entrance B-2 without a wait. Enter the palace and take a one-way walk through the State Apartments from the King's Wing, through the Hall of Mirrors, and out via the Queen's and Nobles' Wing.

Entrance B-2—Museum passholders can avoid the line to buy

have *Rick Steves' Paris* or *Rick Steves' Mona Winks*, the guidebook called *The Châteaux, The Gardens, and Trianon* gives a room-by-room rundown.

Fountain Spectacles: Classical music fills the king's backyard, and the garden's fountains are in full squirt, July–Sept Sat and early April–early Oct Sun (schedule for both days: 11:00–12:00 & 15:30–17:00 & 17:20–17:30). On these "spray days," the gardens cost €5.50 (not covered by museum pass, ask for a map of fountains). Louis had his engineers literally reroute a river to fuel these fountains. Even by today's standards, they are impressive. Pick up the helpful brochure of the fountain show ("Les Grandes Eaux Musicales") at any information booth for a guide to the fountains. Also ask about the impressive *Les Fêtes de Nuit* nighttime spectacle (July–mid-Sept some Sat).

Getting around the Gardens: It's a 30-minute hike from the palace, down the canal, past the two mini-palaces to the Hamlet. You can rent bikes (€6/hr). The fast-looking, slow-moving tourist train leaves from behind the château and serves the Grand Canal and the Trianon Palaces (€5, 4/hr, four stops, you can hop on and off as you like; nearly worthless commentary).

tickets at Entrance by using this entrance to get into the State Apartments.

Entrance C: King's Private Apartments—Using a dry but informative audioguide, you tour Louis XIV's private bedroom, some other rooms, and the Hall of Mirrors.

Entrance D: Various Guided Tours—You can select a one-hour guided tour from a variety of themes, such as the daily life of a king or the lives of such lesser-known nobles as the well-coiffed Madame de Pompadour (€4, join first English tour available). Or consider the 90-minute tour (€6) of the King's Private Apartments (Louis XV, Louis XVI, and Marie-Antoinette) and the chapel. This tour, which is the only way visitors can see the sumptuous Opera House, can be long depending on the quality of your guide.

For a live tour, make reservations immediately upon arrival, as tours can sell out by 13:00 (first tours generally begin at 10:00, last tours depart usually at 15:00 but as late as 16:00).

The Gardens—If you want to visit these first, go around the left side of the palace. The spacious gardens stretch for miles behind the palace, featuring landscaped plots, statues, bubbling fountains, a Grand Canal, and several smaller palaces, interesting both outside and in.

Palace Gardens: The gardens offer a world of royal amusements. Outside the palace is *l'orangerie*. Louis, the only person who could grow oranges in Paris, had a mobile orange grove that could be wheeled in and out of his greenhouses according to the weather. A promenade leads from the palace to the Grand Canal, an artificial lake that, in Louis' day, was a mini-sea with nine ships, including a 32-cannon warship. France's royalty used to float up and down the canal in Venetian gondolas.

While Louis cleverly used palace life at Versailles to "domesticate" his nobility, turning otherwise meddlesome nobles into groveling socialites, all this pomp and ceremony hampered the royal family as well. For an escape from the public life at Versailles, they built more intimate palaces as retreats in their garden. Before the Revolution there was plenty of space to retreat—the grounds were enclosed by a 25-mile-long fence.

The beautifully restored **Grand Trianon Palace** is as sumptuous as the main palace, but much smaller. With its pastel-pink colonnade and more human scale, this is a place you'd like to call home. The nearby **Petit Trianon**, which has a fine neoclassical exterior and an interior that can be skipped, was Marie-Antoinette's favorite residence (see "Cost"

Entrances to Versailles

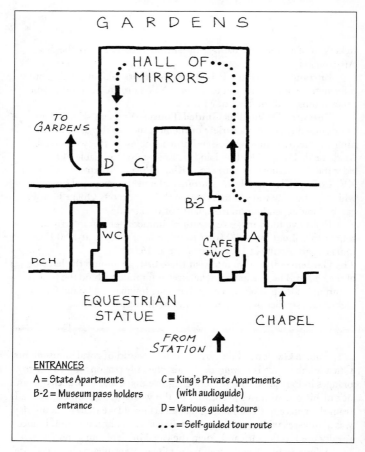

GARDENS

HALL OF MIRRORS

TO GARDENS

D C

B-2

WC

DCH

CAFE & WC   A

EQUESTRIAN STATUE ■

CHAPEL

FROM STATION

ENTRANCES

A = State Apartments
B-2 = Museum pass holders entrance

C = King's Private Apartments (with audioguide)
D = Various guided tours

• • • = Self-guided tour route

and "Hours," above).

You can almost see princesses bobbing gaily in the branches as you walk through the enchanting forest, past the white marble temple of love (1778) to the queen's fake-peasant **Hamlet** (*le Hameau;* interior not tourable). Palace life really got to Marie-Antoinette. Sort of a back-to-basics queen, she retreated further and further from her blue-blooded reality. Her happiest days were spent at the Hamlet, under a bonnet, tending her perfumed sheep and her manicured gardens in a thatch-happy wonderland.

Cafés: The cafeteria and WCs are next to door A. You'll find a sandwich kiosk and a decent restaurant are at the canal in the garden. For more recommendations, see "Eating in Versailles," below. A handy McDonald's is immediately across from the train station (WC without crowds).

Trip Length: Allow two hours for the palace and two for the gardens. Including two hours to cover your round-trip transit time, it's a six-hour day trip from Paris.

Getting There: Take the **RER-C train** (€5 round-trip, 5/hr 30 min one-way) from any of these RER stops: Gare d'Austerlitz, St. Michel, Musée d'Orsay, Invalides, Pont de l'Alma, and Champ de Mars. Any train whose name starts with a V (e.g., "Vick") goes to Versailles; don't board other trains. Get off at the last stop (Versailles R.G. or "Rive Gauche"—not Versailles C.H., which is farther from the palace), and exit through the turnstiles by inserting your ticket. To reach the château, turn right out of the station, then left at the first boulevard. It's a 10-minute walk to the palace.

Your Eurailpass covers this inexpensive trip, but it uses up a valuable "flexi" day. If you really want to use your railpass, consider seeing Versailles on your way in to or out of Paris. To get free passage, show your railpass at an SNCF ticket window—for example, at the Les Invalides or Musée d'Orsay RER stops—and get a *contremarque de passage*. Keep this ticket to exit the system.

When returning from Versailles, look through the windows past the turnstiles for the departure board. Any train leaving Versailles serves all downtown Paris RER-C stops (they're marked on the schedule as stopping at *"toutes les gares jusqu'à Austerlitz,"* meaning "all stations until Austerlitz").

Taxis for the 30-minute ride between Versailles and Paris cost about €25.

To reach Versailles from Paris by **car,** get on the *périphérique* freeway that circles Paris and take the toll-free autoroute A-13 toward Rouen. Follow signs into Versailles, then look for *Château* signs and park in the huge lot in front of the palace (pay lot). The drive takes about 30 minutes one-way.

Town of Versailles: After the palace closes and the tourists go, the prosperous, wholesome town of Versailles feels a long way from Paris. The central market thrives on place du Marché on Sunday, Tuesday, and Friday until 13:00 (leaving the RER station, turn right and walk 10 min). Consider the wisdom of picking up or dropping your rental car in Versailles rather than in Paris. In Versailles, the Hertz and Avis offices are at Gare des Chantiers (Versailles C.H., served by Paris' Montparnasse station). Versailles makes a fine home base; see Versailles accommodations and recommended restaurants under "Sleeping" and "Eating," below.

SHOPPING, PARISIAN-STYLE

Even staunch anti-shoppers may be tempted to partake of chic Paris. Wandering among the elegant and outrageous boutiques provides a break from the heavy halls of the Louvre, and, if you approach it right, a little cultural enlightenment.

Here are some tips for avoiding *faux pas* and making the most of the experience.

French Etiquette: Before you enter a Parisian store, remember the following points.

- In small stores, always greet the clerk by saying *Bonjour,* plus the appropriate title *(Madame, Mademoiselle,* or *Monsieur).* When leaving, say, *Au revoir, Madame/Mademoiselle/Monsieur.*
- The customer is not always right. In fact, figure the clerk is doing you a favor by waiting on you.
- Except for in department stores, it's not normal for the customer to handle clothing. Ask first.
- Observe French shoppers. Then imitate.

Department Stores: Like cafés, department stores were invented here (surprisingly, not in America). Parisian department stores, monuments to a more relaxed and elegant era, begin with their spectacular perfume sections. Helpful information desks are usually nearby (pick up the handy store floor plan in English). Most stores have a good selection of souvenirs and toys at fair prices and reasonable restaurants; some have great view terraces. Choose from these four great Parisian department stores: Galeries Lafayette (behind old Opéra Garnier, Mo: Opéra), Printemps (next door to Galeries Lafayette), Bon Marché (Mo: Sèvres-Babylone), and Samaritaine (near pont Neuf, Mo: Pont Neuf). Forum des Halles is a huge subterranean shopping center (Mo: Les Halles).

Boutiques: I enjoy window-shopping, pausing at cafés, and observing the rhythm of neighborhood life. While the shops are more intimate, sales clerks are more formal—mind your manners.

Here are four very different areas to explore:

A stroll from Sèvres-Babylone to St. Sulpice allows you to sample smart, classic clothing boutiques while enjoying one of Paris' prettier neighborhoods—for sustenance along the way, there's La Maison du Chocolat at 19 rue de Sèvres, selling handmade chocolates in exquisitely wrapped boxes.

The ritzy streets connecting place de la Madeleine and place Vendôme form a miracle mile of gourmet food shops, jewelry stores, four-star hotels, perfumeries, and exclusive clothing boutiques. Fauchon, on place de la Madeleine, is a bastion of over-the-top food products, hawking €7,000 bottles of Cognac (who buys this stuff?). Hediard, across the square from Fauchon, is an older, more appealing, and accessible gourmet food shop. Next door, La Maison des Truffes sells black mushrooms for about €180 a pound, and white truffles from Italy for €2,500 a pound.

For more eclectic, avant-garde stores, peruse the artsy shops between the Pompidou Center and place des Vosges in the Marais.

For a contemporary, more casual, and less frenetic shopping experience, and to see Paris' latest urban renewal project, take the Métro to Bercy Village, a once-thriving wine warehouse district that has been transformed into an outdoor shopping mall (Mo: Cour St. Emilion).

Flea Markets: Paris hosts several sprawling weekend flea markets (*marché aux puces,* mar-shay oh poos; literally translated, since *puce* is French for flea). These oversized garage sales date back to the Middle Ages, when middlemen would sell old, flea-infested clothes and discarded possessions of the wealthy at bargain prices to eager peasants. Today, some travelers find them claustrophobic, crowded, monster versions of those back home, though others find their French diamonds-in-the-rough and return happy.

The Puces St. Ouen (poos sahn-wahn) is the biggest and oldest of them all, with more than 2,000 vendors selling everything from flamingos to faucets (Sat 9:00–18:30, Sun–Mon 10:00–18:30, Mo: Porte de Clingancourt).

Street Markets: Several traffic-free street markets overflow with flowers, produce, fish vendors, and butchers, illustrating how most Parisians shopped before there were supermarkets and department stores. Good market streets include the rue Cler (Mo: Ecole Militaire), rue Montorgueil (Mo: Etienne Marcel), rue Mouffetard (Mo: Cardinal Lemoine or Censier-Daubenton), and rue Daguerre (Mo: Denfert-Rochereau). Browse these markets to collect a classy picnic (open daily except Sun afternoons and Mon, also closed for lunch 13:00–15:00).

Souvenir Shops: Avoid souvenir carts in front of famous monuments. Prices and selection are better in shops and department stores. The riverfront stalls near Notre-Dame sell a variety of used books, magazines, and tourist paraphernalia in the most romantic setting.

Whether you indulge in a new wardrobe, an artsy poster, or just one luscious pastry, you'll find that a shopping excursion provides a priceless slice of Parisian life.

NIGHTLIFE

Paris is brilliant after dark. Save energy from your day's sightseeing and get out at night. Whether it's a concert at Sainte-Chapelle, an elevator up the Arc de Triomphe, or a late-night café, experience the city of light lit up. If a **Seine River cruise** appeals, see "Tours," page 226.

Pariscope magazine (see "Tourist Information," above), offers a complete weekly listing of music, cinema, theater, opera, and other special events. *Paris Voice* newspaper, in English, has a monthly review of Paris entertainment (available at any English-language bookstore, French-American establishments, or the American Church, www.parisvoice.com).

Music

Jazz Clubs: With a lively mix of American, French, and international musicians, Paris has been an internationally acclaimed jazz capital since World War II. You'll pay €7–25 to enter a jazz club (a drink may be included; if not, expect to pay €5–9 per drink; beer is cheapest). See *Pariscope* magazine under "Musique" for listings; or, better yet, check out the American Church's *Paris Voice* paper for a good monthly review, or drop by the clubs to check out their calendars posted on the front door. Music starts after 21:00 in most clubs. Some offer dinner concerts from about 20:30 on. Here are several good bets:

Caveau de la Huchette, a characteristic old jazz club, fills an ancient Latin Quarter cellar with live jazz and frenzied dancing every night (€9 weekday, €12 weekend admission, €5 drinks, Tue–Sun 21:30–2:30 or later, closed Mon, 5 rue de la Huchette, Mo: St. Michel, recorded info tel. 01 43 26 65 05).

For a hotbed of late-night activity and jazz, go to the two-block-long rue des Lombards, at boulevard Sébastopol, midway between the river and the Pompidou Center (Mo: Châtelet). **Au Duc des Lombards,** right at the corner, is one of the most popular and respected jazz clubs in Paris, with concerts generally at 21:00 (42 rue des Lombards, tel. 01 42 33 22 88). **Le Sunside** offers more traditional jazz—Dixieland and big band—and fewer crowds, with concerts generally at 21:00 (60 rue des Lombards, tel. 01 40 26 21 25).

At the more down-to-earth and mellow **Le Cave du Franc Pinot,** you can enjoy a glass of chardonnay at the main-floor wine bar, then drop downstairs for a cool jazz scene (good dinner-and-jazz values as well, located on Ile St. Louis where pont Marie meets the island, 1 quai de Bourbon, Mo: Pont Marie, tel. 01 46 33 60 64).

If it's a blues band you seek, join Parisian lovers of mostly American bands at **The Front Page** (58 rue St. Denis, Mo: Etienne Marcel).

Classical Concerts: For classical music on any night, consult *Pariscope* magazine; the "Musique" section under "Concerts Classiques" lists concerts (free and fee). Look for posters at the churches. Churches that regularly host concerts (usually March–Nov) include St. Sulpice, St. Germain-des-Prés, Ste. Madeleine, St. Eustache, St. Julien-le-Pauvre, and Sainte-Chapelle. It's worth the €15–23 entry for the pleasure of hearing Mozart while surrounded by the stained glass of the tiny Sainte-Chapelle (it's unheated—bring a sweater). Look also for daytime concerts in parks, such as the Luxembourg Garden. Even the Galeries Lafayette department store offers concerts. Many concerts are free *(entrée libre)*, such as the Sunday atelier concert sponsored by the American

Church (18:00, not every week, Sept–May, 65 quai d'Orsay, Mo: Invalides, RER: Pont de l'Alma, tel. 01 40 62 05 00).

Opera: Paris is home to two well-respected opera venues. The Opéra Bastille is the massive, modern opera house that dominates place de la Bastille. Come here for state-of-the-art special effects and modern interpretations of classic ballets and operas. In the spirit of this everyman's opera, unsold seats are available at a big discount to seniors and students 15 minutes before the show (Mo: Bastille, tel. 01 43 43 96 96). The Opéra Garnier, Paris' first opera house, hosts opera and ballet performances. Come here for less expensive tickets and grand belle époque decor (Mo: Opéra, tel. 01 44 73 13 99). For tickets, call 01 44 73 13 00, go to the opera ticket offices (open 11:00–18:00), or best, reserve on the Web at www.opera-de-paris.fr (for both opera houses).

Bus Tours

Several companies offer after-dark tours of Paris. I've described two here. These trips are sold through your hotel (brochures in lobby) or directly at the offices listed below. You save no money by buying direct.

Paris Illumination Tours, run by Paris Vision, connect all the great illuminated sights of Paris with a 100-minute bus tour in 12 languages. Double-decker buses have huge windows, but customers continuing to the overrated Moulin Rouge get the most desirable front seats.

You'll stampede on with a United Nations of tourists, get an audioguide, and listen to a tape-recorded spiel (interesting but occasionally hard to hear). Uninspired as it is, this provides an entertaining first-night overview of the city at its floodlit and scenic best (bring your city map to stay oriented as you go). Left-side seats are marginally better. Visibility is fine in the rain. You're always on the bus except for one five-minute cigarette break at the Eiffel Tower viewpoint (adults-€26, kids under 11 ride free, departures at 20:30 nightly all year, also at 21:30 April–Oct only, departs from Paris Vision office at 214 rue de Rivoli, across the street from Mo: Tuileries, tel. 01 42 60 30 01, fax 01 42 86 95 36, www.parisvision.com).

Euroscope offers the same kind of bus tour but with live guides (they try to keep the different languages to no more than three). This smaller, "we try harder" company offers better service and if their big buses don't fill up, they'll send you in a more personal minivan (buses depart from 11 boulevard Haussmann, Mo: Opéra or Chaussée d'Antin-La Fayette, tel. 01 53 34 11 94, www.euroscope.com).

SLEEPING

I've focused on three safe, handy, and colorful neighborhoods: rue Cler, Marais, and Luxembourg/Contrescarpe. For each, I list good hotels, helpful hints, and restaurants (see "Eating," below). Before reserving, read the descriptions of the three neighborhoods closely. Each offers

SLEEP CODE

(€1 = about $1.10, country code: 33)
Sleep Code: **S** = Single, **D** = Double/Twin, **T** = Triple, **Q** = Quad, **b** = bathroom, **s** = shower only, **no CC** = Credit Cards not accepted, ***** = French hotel rating system (0–4 stars). For more information on the rating system, see "Sleeping" in this book's introduction. Hotels with two or more stars are required to have an English-speaking staff. Nearly all hotels listed here will have someone who speaks English. You can assume a hotel takes credit cards unless you see "no CC" in the listing.

To help you sort easily through these listings, I've divided the rooms into three categories based on the price for a standard double room with bath:

$$$ **Higher Priced**—Most rooms €140 or more.
$$ **Moderately Priced**—Most rooms between €100-150.
$ **Lower Priced**—Most rooms €100 or less.

---

different pros and cons, and your neighborhood is as important as your hotel for the success of your trip.

Reserve ahead for Paris, the sooner the better. Conventions clog Paris in September (worst), October, May, and June (very tough). In August, when Paris is quiet, some hotels offer lower rates to fill their rooms (if you're planning to visit Paris in the summer, the extra expense of an air-conditioned room can be money well spent). For advice on booking rooms, see "Making Reservations" in this book's introduction.

Old, characteristic, budget Parisian hotels have always been cramped. Retrofitted with elevators, toilets, and private showers (as most are today), they are even more cramped. Even three-star hotel rooms are small and often not worth the extra expense in Paris. Some hotels include the hotel tax (*taxe du séjour,* about €0.50–1 per person per day), though most will add this to your bill.

Recommended hotels have an elevator unless otherwise noted. Quad rooms usually have two double beds. Because rooms with double beds and showers are cheaper than rooms with twin beds and baths, room prices vary within each hotel.

Continental breakfasts average €6, buffet breakfasts (baked goods, cereal, yogurt, and fruit) cost about €12. Café or picnic breakfasts are cheaper, but hotels usually give unlimited coffee.

Get advice from your hotel for safe parking (consider longterm parking at Orly Airport and taxi in). Meters are free in August. Garages are plentiful (€14–23/day, with special rates through some hotels). Self-serve launderettes are common; ask your hotelier for the nearest one (*Où est un laverie automatique?*; ooh ay uh lah-vay-ree auto-mah-teek).

If you have any trouble finding a room using our listings, try this Web site: www.parishotel.com. You can select from various neighborhood areas (e.g., Eiffel Tower area), give the dates of your visit and preferred price range, and presto—they'll list options with rates. You'll find the hotels listed in this book to be better located and objectively reviewed, though as a last resort, this online service is handy.

Rue Cler

Rue Cler is a safe, tidy, village-like pedestrian street. It's so French that when I step out of my hotel in the morning, I feel like I must have been a poodle in a previous life. How such coziness lodged itself between the high-powered government district and the wealthy Eiffel Tower and Invalides areas, I'll never know. This is a neighborhood of wide, tree-lined boulevards, stately apartment buildings, and lots of Americans. The American Church, American Library, American University, and many of my readers call this area home.

Become a local at a rue Cler café for breakfast or join the afternoon crowd for *une bière pression* (a draft beer). On rue Cler, you can eat and browse your way through a street full of tart shops, delis, cheese shops, and colorful outdoor produce stalls. Afternoon *boules* (lawn bowling) on the Esplanade des Invalides is a relaxing spectator sport (look for the dirt area to the upper right as you face Les Invalides. The manicured gardens behind the golden dome of Les Invalides are free, peaceful, and filled with flowers (close at about 19:00). Take an evening stroll above the river through the parkway between pont de l'Alma and pont des Invalides.

For an after-dinner cruise on the Seine, it's a 15-minute walk to the river and the Bateaux-Mouches. For a post-dinner cruise on foot, saunter into Champ de Mars park to admire the glowing Eiffel Tower.

Cross the Champ de Mars park to mix it up with bargain-hunters at the twice-weekly open-air market, **Marché Boulevard de Grenelle,** under the Métro a few blocks southwest of Champ de Mars park (Wed and Sun until 12:30, between Mo: Dupleix and Mo: La Motte Picquet-Grenelle). The Epicerie de la Tour **grocery** is open until midnight (197 rue de Grenelle). Rue St. Dominique is the area's boutique-browsing street. **Cyber World Café** is at 20 rue de l'Exposition (open daily, tel. 01 53 59 96 54).

Your neighborhood **TI** is at the Eiffel Tower (May–Sept daily 11:00–18:40, closed Oct-April, all-Paris TI tel. 08 36 68 31 12). There's a **post office** at the end of rue Cler on avenue de la Motte Picquet, and a handy **SNCF train office** at 78 rue St. Dominique (Mon–Fri 9:00–19:00, Sat 10:00–12:30 & 14:00–18:00, closed Sun).

The **American Church and Franco-American Center** is the community center for Americans living in Paris and should be one of your first stops if you're planning to stay awhile (reception open Mon–Sat 9:00–22:00, Sun 9:00–19:30, 65 quai d'Orsay, tel. 01 40 62 05 00). Pick up copies of the *Paris Voice* for a monthly review of Paris entertainment, and *France-U.S.A. Contacts* for information on housing and employment through the community of 30,000 Americans living in Paris. The interdenominational services at 11:00 on Sunday, the coffee hour after church, and the free Sunday concerts (Sept–May 18:00, not every week) are a great way to make some friends and get a taste of émigré life in Paris.

Key **Métro** stops are Ecole Militaire, La Tour Maubourg, and Invalides. The **RER-C** line runs from the Pont de l'Alma and Invalides stations, serving Versailles to the west; Auvers-sur-Oise to the north; and the Orsay Museum, Latin Quarter (St. Michel stop), and Austerlitz train station to the east.

Smart travelers take advantage of these helpful **bus routes** (see Rue Cler Hotels map for stop locations): Line #69 runs along rue St. Dominique and serves Les Invalides, Orsay, Louvre, Marais, and Père Lachaise cemetery. Line #63 runs along the river (the quai d'Orsay); it serves the Latin Quarter along boulevard St. Germain to the east, and Trocadéro and the Musée Marmottan Monet to the west. Line #92 runs along avenue Bosquet north to the Champs-Elysées and Arc de Triomphe and south to the Montparnasse Tower. Line #87 runs on avenue de la Bourdonnais and serves St. Sulpice, Luxembourg Garden, and the Sèvres-Babylone shopping area. Line #28 runs on boulevard La Tour Maubourg and serves Gare St. Lazare.

Sleeping in the Rue Cler Neighborhood
(7th *arrondissement*, Mo: Ecole Militaire or La Tour Maubourg)
Rue Cler is the glue that holds this handsome neighborhood together. From here you can walk to the Eiffel Tower, Napoleon's Tomb, the Seine River, and the Orsay and Rodin Museums. Hotels here are relatively spacious and a great value, considering the elegance of the neighborhood and the high prices of the more cramped hotels of the trendy Marais.

Many of my readers stay in this neighborhood. If you want to disappear into Paris, choose a hotel away from the rue Cler, or in the other neighborhoods I list. And if nightlife matters, sleep elsewhere. The first five hotels listed below are within Camembert-smelling distance of rue Cler; the others are within a 5- to 10-minute stroll.

Sleeping in the Heart of Rue Cler
$$$ **Hôtel Relais Bosquet***** is modern, spacious, and a bit upscale, with snazzy, air-conditioned rooms, electric darkness blinds, and big beds. Gerard and his staff are politely formal and friendly (Sb-€125–150, standard Db-€145, spacious Db-€165, extra bed-€30,

Rue Cler Hotels

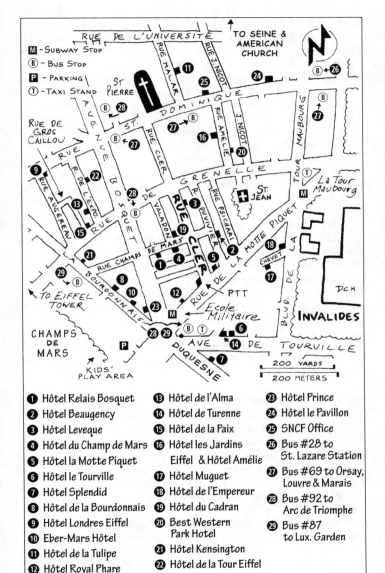

M – Subway Stop
B – Bus Stop
P – Parking
T – Taxi Stand

RUE DE L'UNIVERSITÉ

TO SEINE & AMERICAN CHURCH

RUE DE GROS CAILLOU

ST PIERRE

DOMINIQUE

GRENELLE

ST. JEAN

La Tour Maubourg

RUE DE MARS

RUE CHAMPS

RUE CLER

BOURDONNAIS

PTT

Ecole Militaire

TO EIFFEL TOWER

CHAMPS DE MARS

KIDS' PLAY AREA

DUQUESNE

AVE. DE TOURVILLE

INVALIDES

DCH

200 YARDS
200 METERS

❶ Hôtel Relais Bosquet
❷ Hôtel Beaugency
❸ Hôtel Leveque
❹ Hôtel du Champ de Mars
❺ Hôtel la Motte Piquet
❻ Hôtel le Tourville
❼ Hôtel Splendid
❽ Hôtel de la Bourdonnais
❾ Hôtel Londres Eiffel
❿ Eber-Mars Hôtel
⓫ Hôtel de la Tulipe
⓬ Hôtel Royal Phare

⓭ Hôtel de l'Alma
⓮ Hôtel de Turenne
⓯ Hôtel de la Paix
⓰ Hôtel les Jardins Eiffel & Hôtel Amélie
⓱ Hôtel Muguet
⓲ Hôtel de l'Empereur
⓳ Hôtel du Cadran
⓴ Best Western Park Hotel
㉑ Hôtel Kensington
㉒ Hôtel de la Tour Eiffel

㉓ Hôtel Prince
㉔ Hôtel le Pavillon
㉕ SNCF Office
㉖ Bus #28 to St. Lazare Station
㉗ Bus #69 to Orsay, Louvre & Marais
㉘ Bus #92 to Arc de Triomphe
㉙ Bus #87 to Lux. Garden

parking-€14, 19 rue du Champ de Mars, tel. 01 47 05 25 45, fax 01 45 55 08 24, www.relaisbosquet.com).

$$$ Hôtel la Motte Picquet****, at the end of rue Cler, is like staying in an antique dollhouse. Most of its 18 adorable, spendy rooms face a busy street, but the twins are on the quieter rue Cler (Sb-€105-121, Db-€129-165, 30 avenue de la Motte Picquet, tel. 01 47 05 09 57, fax 01 47 05 74 36, www.paris-hotel-mottepicquet.com).

$$ Hôtel Beaugency****, on a quieter street a short block off rue Cler, has 30 small, cookie-cutter rooms, and a lobby you can stretch out in. Rooms have automated air-conditioning that shuts off once you go to bed (Sb-€106, Db-€118, Tb-€140, buffet breakfast, 21 rue Duvivier, tel. 01 47 05 01 63, fax 01 45 51 04 96, www.hotel-beaugency.com).

Warning: The next two hotels listed here—while good values—are busy with my readers (reserve long in advance).

$ Grand Hôtel Lévêque**** is ideally located, with a helpful staff (Christophe and female Pascale SE), a singing maid, and a Starship *Enterprise* elevator. It's a classic old hotel with well-designed rooms that have all the comforts, including air-conditioning and ceiling fans. It feels a bit frayed at the edges but remains a solid value (S–€53, Db–€84–91, Tb–€114 for two adults and one child only, breakfast-€7, first breakfast free for readers of this book, 29 rue Cler, tel. 01 47 05 49 15, fax 01 45 50 49 36, www.hotel-leveque.com, info@hotelleveque.com).

$ Hôtel du Champ de Mars**** , with charming pastel rooms and helpful English-speaking owners Françoise and Stephane, is a homier rue Cler option. This plush little hotel has a Provence-style, small-town feel from top to bottom. Rooms are small, but comfortable and an excellent value. Single rooms can work as tiny doubles (Sb-€68, Db-€72–78, Tb-€94, 30 yards off rue Cler at 7 rue du Champ de Mars, tel. 01 45 51 52 30, fax 01 45 51 64 36, www.hotel-du-champ-de-mars.com, stg@club-internet.fr).

Sleeping near Rue Cler

The following listings are a five- to 10-minute walk from rue Cler, near Métro stop École Militaire or RER stop Pont de l'Alma.

$$$ Hôtel le Tourville***** is the most classy and expensive of my rue Cler listings. This four-star place is surprisingly intimate and friendly, from its designer lobby and vaulted breakfast area to its pretty but small pastel rooms (small standard Db-€145, superior Db-€215, Db with private terrace-€240, junior suite for 3–4 people-€310, air-con, 16 avenue de Tourville, tel. 01 47 05 62 62, fax 01 47 05 43 90, hotel@tourville.com).

$$$ Hôtel Splendid**** is Art Deco modern, professional, and worth your while if you land one of its three suites with great Eiffel Tower views. Fifth-floor rooms have small terraces (Db-€126–150, Db suite-€200-225, 29 avenue de Tourville, tel. 01 45 51 24 77, fax 01 44 18 94 60, www.hotels-exclusive.com/hotels/splendid).

$$$ Hôtel de la Bourdonnais*** is a *très* Parisian place, mixing slightly faded Old World elegance with professional service, comfortable public spaces, and mostly spacious, traditionally decorated rooms (avoid the few *petite* rooms, Sb-€120, Db-€150, Tb-€160, Qb-€180, five-person suite-€210, air-con, 111 avenue de la Bourdonnais, tel. 01 47 05 45 42, fax 01 45 55 75 54, www.hotellabourdonnais.fr).

$$ Hôtel Londres Eiffel*** is my closest listing to the Eiffel Tower and Champ de Mars park. It offers immaculate, warmly decorated rooms, cozy public spaces, Internet access, and air-conditioning. The helpful staff takes good care of their guests. It's less convenient to the Métro (10-min walk); handy bus #69 and the RER stop Pont de l'Alma stop are better options (Sb-€95-99, Db-€110-140, Tb-€150-165, extra bed-€17, 1 rue Augerau, tel. 01 45 51 63 02, fax 01 47 05 28 96, www.londres-eiffel.com, info@londres-eiffel.com).

$$ Eber-Mars Hôtel,** with helpful owner Jean-Marc, is a good midrange value with larger-than-average rooms and a beam-me-up-Jacques, coffin-sized elevator (small Db-€75, large Db-€90-110, Tb-€135, extra bed-€25, pricey €10 breakfast, 117 avenue de la Bourdonnais, tel. 01 47 05 42 30, fax 01 47 05 45 91).

$$ Hôtel de la Tulipe*** is a unique place three blocks from rue Cler toward the river, with friendly Bernhard behind the desk. The smallish but artistically decorated rooms—each one different—come with little, stylish bathrooms and surround a seductive wood-beamed lounge and a peaceful, leafy courtyard (Db-€110-140, Tb-€170, two-room suite-€220-250, no elevator, 33 rue Malar, tel. 01 45 51 67 21, fax 01 47 53 96 37 www.hoteldelatulipe.com).

$ Hôtel Royal Phare** is a simple yet reasonable value facing the busy Ecole Militaire Métro stop. Rooms are unimaginative but pink-pastel-comfortable; those on the courtyard are far quieter (Sb-€62, Db-€72-77, Tb-€92, 40 avenue de la Motte Picquet, tel. 01 47 05 57 30, fax 01 45 51 64 41, www.hotel-royalphare-paris.com).

$ Hôtel de l'Alma*** is well-located on "restaurant row," with cheery rooms, small bathrooms, a nice little courtyard, and very reasonable rates only with this book (Sb-€72, Db-€79, includes breakfast, 32 rue de l'Exposition, tel. 01 47 05 45 70, fax 01 45 51 84 47, www.alma-paris -hotel.com, Carine SE).

Hôtel de Turenne,** with sufficiently comfortable, air-conditioned rooms and so-so bed quality, is a good value particularly when it's hot. It also has five truly single rooms and several connecting rooms (Sb-€61, Db-€71–83, Tb-€98, extra bed-€10, 20 avenue de Tourville, tel. 01 47 05 99 92, fax 01 45 56 06 04, hotel.turenne.paris7@wanadoo.fr).

$ Hôtel de la Paix **, a smart hotel located away from the fray on a quiet little street, offers 23 plush, well-designed rooms and is a good value (Sb-€61, Db-€91-100, Tb-€110-120, fine buffet breakfast, 19 rue du Gros-Caillou, tel. 01 45 51 86 17, fax 01 45 55 93 28, hotel.de.la.paix @wanadoo.fr).

Sleeping near Métro: La Tour Maubourg

The next three listings are within two blocks of the intersection of avenue de la Motte Picquet and boulevard de la Tour Maubourg.

$$$ **Hôtel les Jardins Eiffel*****, on a quiet street, feels like a modern motel, but earns its three stars with professional service, its own parking garage, a spacious lobby, and 80 comfortable, air-conditioned rooms—some with private balconies (ask for a room *avec petit balcon*). Even better: Readers of this book get free buffet breakfasts (Db-€130–€160, extra bed-€21 or free for a child, parking-€20/day, 8 rue Amélie, tel. 01 47 05 46 21, fax 01 45 55 28 08, www.hoteljardinseiffel.com, Marie SE).

$$ **Hôtel Muguet****, a peaceful, stylish and immaculate hotel, gives you three-star comfort for a two-star price. This delightful hotel offers 48 tasteful, air-conditioned rooms, a greenhouse lounge, and a small garden courtyard. The hands-on owner, Catherine, gives her guests a restful and secure home in Paris (Sb-€87, Db-€97–105, Tb-€135, 11 rue Chevert, tel. 01 47 05 05 93, fax 01 45 50 25 37, www.hotelmuguet.com).

$ **Hôtel de l'Empereur**** lacks intimacy but is roomy and another fair value. Its 38 pleasant, woody rooms come with sturdy furniture and all the comforts except air-conditioning. Streetside rooms have views but some noise; fifth-floor rooms have small balconies and Napoleonic views (Sb-€70–80, Db-€80-100, Tb-€120, Qb-€140, 2 rue Chevert, tel. 01 45 55 88 02, fax 01 45 51 88 54, www.hotelempereur.com, Alba SE).

Sleeping on the Other Side Of Champs de Mars Park

To stay in a peaceful neighborhood with many qualities of the rue Cler area (in the 7th *arrondissement*), cross Champs de Mars park and enter the 15th *arrondissement*. While it's a 10- to 15-minute walk to rue Cler, you get more space for your money and fewer fellow Americans.

$$ **Hôtel Ares***** is a handsome hotel situated on a quiet street a block toward the river from avenue de le Motte Picquet. The hotel has a classy lobby with elbow room, and comfortable rooms you can stretch out in (Sb-€105, Db-€122, Tb-€155, Qb-€180, between avenue de Suffren and avenue de Grenelle—not to be confused with rue de Grenelle that crosses rue Cler—at 7 rue du Général de Larminat, Mo: La Motte Picquet-Grenelle, tel. 01 47 34 74 04, fax 01 47 34 48 56, aresotel@easynet.fr).

Lesser Values in the Rue Cler Area

Given this fine area, these are acceptable last choices.

$$$ **Hôtel du Cadran*****, while perfectly located, has a shiny lobby but no charm and tight, narrow, pricey rooms (Db-€152–170, 10 rue du Champ de Mars, air-con, tel. 01 40 62 67 00, fax 01 40 62 67 13, www.hotelducadran.com).

$$$ **Best Western Park Hotel***** is a dead-quiet, concrete business hotel with all the comforts, a friendly staff, pleasant if unexceptional rooms,

and a nifty and spacious rooftop terrace (Db-€135-185, 17 bis rue Amélie, tel. 01 45 55 10 01, fax 01 47 05 28, 68, reservation@eiffelpark.com).

$$ Hôtel Prince,** just across avenue Bosquet from the Ecole Militaire Métro stop, has good-enough rooms, many overlooking a busy street (Sb-€73, Db-€87-113, 66 avenue Bosquet, tel. 01 47 05 40 90, fax 01 47 53 06 62, www.hotel-paris-prince.com).

$ Hôtel Amélie** is another midrange possibility (Db-€95-105, 5 rue Amélie, tel. 01 45 51 74 75, fax 01 45 56 93 55, hotelamelie @wanadoo.fr).

$ Hôtel Kensington** is impersonal with miniscule rooms, but is a fair value (Sb-€53, Db-€67-82, 79 avenue de la Bourdonnais, tel. 01 47 05 74 00, fax 01 47 05 25 81, www.hotel-kensington.com).

$ Hôtel de la Tour Eiffel** is a modest little place with fairly priced rooms, but cheap furnishings and foam mattresses (Sb-€65, Db-€80, Tb-€100, 17 rue de l'Exposition, tel. 01 47 05 14 75, fax 01 47 53 99 46, Muriel SE).

$ Hôtel le Pavillon** is quiet, with basic rooms, no elevator, and cramped halls in a charming location (Sb-€72, Db-€80, Tb, Qb, or Quint/b-€105, 54 rue St. Dominique, tel. 01 45 51 42 87, fax 01 45 51 32 79, patrickpavillon@aol.com).

Marais

Those interested in a more Soho/Greenwich Village locale should make the Marais their Parisian home. Only 15 years ago, it was a forgotten Parisian backwater, but now the Marais is one of Paris' most popular residential, tourist, and shopping areas. This is jumbled, medieval Paris at its finest, where classy stone mansions sit alongside trendy bars, antique shops, and fashion-conscious boutiques. The streets are a fascinating parade of artists, students, tourists, immigrants, and babies in strollers munching baguettes. The Marais is also known as a hub of the Parisian gay and lesbian scene. This area is *sans* doubt livelier (and louder) than the rue Cler area.

In the Marais, you have these sights close at hand: Picasso Museum, Carnavalet Museum, Victor Hugo's House, Jewish Art and History Museum, and the Pompidou Center. You're also a manageable walk from Paris' two islands (Ile St. Louis and Ile de la Cité), home to Notre-Dame and the Sainte-Chapelle. The Opéra Bastille, Promenade Plantée park, place des Vosges (Paris' oldest square), Jewish Quarter (rue des Rosiers), and nightlife-packed rue de Lappe are also walkable. (Sight descriptions are listed in "Sights," above.)

The Marais has two good open-air markets: the sprawling Marché de la Bastille on place de la Bastille (Thu and Sun until 12:30) and the more intimate Marché de la place d'Aligre (daily 9:00–12:00, a few blocks behind Opéra on place d'Aligre). Two little grocery shops are open until 23:00 on rue St. Antoine (near intersection with rue Castex).

The nearest **TIs** are in the Louvre (Wed–Mon 10:00–19:00, closed Tue) and Gare de Lyon (daily 8:00–20:00, all-Paris TI tel. 08 36 68 31 12). Most banks and other services are on the main drag, rue de Rivoli, which becomes rue St. Antoine. For your Parisian Sears, find the **BHV** next to the Hôtel de Ville. Marais **post offices** are on rue Castex and on the corner of rue Pavée and rue des Francs Bourgeois. A rare **Internet café**, @aron, is at 3 rue des Ecouffes (tel. 01 42 71 05 07).

Métro service to the Marais neighborhood is excellent, with direct service to the Louvre, Champs-Elysées, Arc de Triomphe, La Défense (all on line 1), rue Cler area (line 8 from Bastille stop) and four major train stations: Gare de Lyon, Gare du Nord, Gare de l'Est, and Gare d'Austerlitz. Key Métro stops in the Marais are, from east to west: Bastille, St. Paul, and Hôtel de Ville (Sully-Morland, Pont Marie, and Rambuteau stops are also handy). There are also several helpful **bus routes:** Line #69 on rue St. Antoine takes you to the Louvre, Orsay, and Rodin museums, plus Napoleon's Tomb, and ends at the Eiffel Tower. Line #86 runs down boulevard Henri IV, crosses Ile St. Louis, and serves the Latin Quarter along boulevard St. Germain. Line #96 runs on rue Turenne and rue François Miron, and it serves the Louvre and boulevard St. Germain (near Luxembourg Garden), ending at the Gare Montparnasse. Line #65 gets you to the Gare d'Austerlitz, Gare de l'Est, and Gare du Nord train stations from place de la Bastille.

You'll find **taxi stands** on place de la Bastille, on the north side of rue St. Antoine (where it meets rue Castex), and on the south side of rue St. Antoine (in front of St. Paul church).

Sleeping in the Marais Neighborhood
(4th *arrondissement*, Mo: St. Paul or Bastille)

The Marais runs from the Pompidou Center to the Bastille (a 15-min walk), with most hotels located a few blocks north of the main east–west drag, the rue de Rivoli/rue St. Antoine. It's about 15 minutes on foot from any hotel in this area to Notre-Dame, Ile St. Louis, and the Latin Quarter. Strolling home (day or night) from Notre-Dame along the Ile St. Louis is marvelous.

$$$ Hôtel de la Place des Vosges** is so well-located—in a medieval building on a quiet street just off place des Vosges—that the staff can take or leave your business (Sb-€90, Db-€140, 16 rooms, one flight of stairs then elevator, 12 rue de Birague, Mo: St. Paul, tel. 01 42 72 60 46, fax 01 42 72 02 64, hotel.place.des.vosges@gofornet.com).

$$ Hôtel Castex***, newly-renovated and on a quiet street near the place de la Bastille, feels Spanish from the formal entry to the red-tiled floors and dark wood accents. A clever system of connecting rooms allows families total privacy between two rooms. Rooms are slender but sharp and air-conditioned, and the new elevator is big (Sb-€100, Db-€120, Tb-€140, good buffet breakfast-€8, just off place de la Bastille and

Marais Hotels

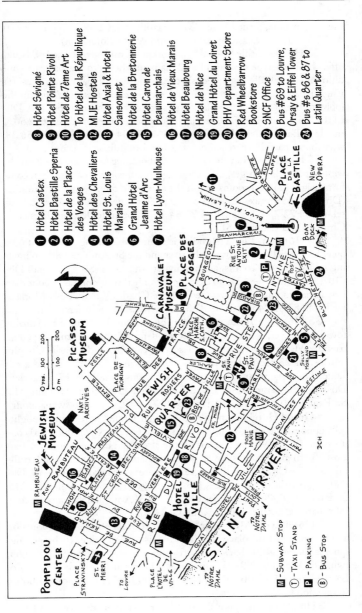

1. Hôtel Castex
2. Hôtel Bastille Speria
3. Hôtel de la Place des Vosges
4. Hôtel des Chevaliers
5. Hôtel St. Louis Marais
6. Grand Hôtel Jeanne d'Arc
7. Hôtel Lyon-Mulhouse
8. Hôtel Sévigné
9. Hôtel Pointe Rivoli
10. Hôtel de 7ème Art
11. To Hôtel de la République
12. MIJE Hostels
13. Hôtel Axial & Hôtel Sansonnet
14. Hôtel de la Bretonnerie
15. Hôtel Caron de Beaumarchais
16. Hôtel de Vieux Marais
17. Hôtel Beaubourg
18. Hôtel de Nice
19. Grand Hôtel du Loiret
20. BHV Department Store
21. Red Wheelbarrow Bookstore
22. SNCF Office
23. Bus #69 to Louvre, Orsay & Eiffel Tower
24. Bus #s 86 & 87 to Latin Quarter

M – Subway Stop
T – Taxi Stand
P – Parking
B – Bus Stop

rue St. Antoine, 5 rue Castex, Mo: Bastille, tel. 01 42 72 31 52, fax 01 42 72 57 91, www.castexhotel.com, info@castexhotel.com).

$$ Hôtel Bastille Spéria***, a short block off the place de la Bastille, offers business-type service. The 42 plain but cheery rooms have air-conditioning, thin walls, and curiously cheap and sweaty foam mattresses. It's English-language-friendly, from the *International Herald Tribunes* in the lobby to the history of the Bastille posted in the elevator (Sb–€100, Db–€110–135, child's bed–€20, excellent but pricey buffet breakfast–€12.50, 1 rue de la Bastille, Mo: Bastille, tel. 01 42 72 04 01, fax 01 42 72 56 38, www.hotel-bastille-speria.com, info@hotel-bastille-speria.com).

$$ Hôtel des Chevaliers***, a little boutique hotel one block northwest of place des Vosges, offers small, pleasant rooms with modern comforts. Eight of its 24 rooms are off the street and quiet—worth requesting (Db–€120–135, prices depend on season, 30 rue de Turenne, Mo: St. Paul, tel. 01 42 72 73 47, fax 01 42 72 54 10, info@hoteldeschevaliers.com, Christele and Laurence SE).

$$ Hôtel St. Louis Marais** is a tiny, welcoming place, lost on a quiet residential street between the river and rue St. Antoine, with an inviting lobby, 16 cozy rooms, and an owner who cares (Sb–€91, small Db–€107, standard Db–€125, no elevator but only three floors, ask about their new annex rooms, all at street level, 1 rue Charles V, Mo: Sully Morland tel. 01 48 87 87 04, fax 01 48 87 33 26, www.saintlouismarais.com).

$$ Hôtel de 7ème Art**, two blocks south of rue St. Antoine toward the river, is a relaxed, Hollywood-nostalgia place, run by young, friendly Marais types, with a full-service café-bar and Charlie Chaplin murals. Its 23 rooms lack imagination, but are comfortable and a fair value. The large rooms are American-spacious (small Db–€77, standard Db–€88–100, large Db–€115–135, extra bed–€20, 20 rue St. Paul, Mo: St. Paul, tel. 01 44 54 85 00, fax 01 42 77 69 10, hotel7art@wanadoo.fr).

$ Grand Hôtel Jeanne d'Arc**, a well-tended hotel with thoughtfully appointed rooms, is ideally located for (and very popular with) connoisseurs of the Marais. Rooms on the street can be noisy until the bars close. Sixth-floor rooms have a view, and corner rooms are wonderfully bright in the City of Light. Reserve this place way ahead (Sb–€55-70, Db–€80, larger twin Db–€95, Tb–€113, good Qb–€130, 3 rue de Jarente, Mo: St. Paul, tel. 01 48 87 62 11, fax 01 48 87 37 31, www.hoteljeannedarc.com, information@hoteljeannedarc.com, Gail SE).

$ Hôtel Lyon-Mulhouse**, with half of its 40 pleasant rooms on a busy street just off place de la Bastille, is a good value. Its bigger and quieter rooms on the back are worth the extra euros (Sb–€55, Db–€66, twin Db–€85, Tb–€90–95, Qb–€115, 8 boulevard Beaumarchais, Mo: Bastille, tel. 01 47 00 91 50, fax 01 47 00 06 31, hotelyonmulhouse @wanadoo.fr).

$ Hôtel Sévigné**, is a sharp little air-conditioned place with lavender halls, tidy, comfortable rooms at fair prices, and a dour owner (Sb–

€64, Db-€74-86, Tb-€10, 2 rue Malher, Mo: St. Paul, tel. 01 42 72 76 17, fax 01 42 78 68 26, www.le-sevigne.com).

$ Hotel Pointe Rivoli*, across from the St. Paul Métro stop, is a jumbled treehouse of rooms in the thick of the Marais, with Paris' steepest stairs (no elevator) and modest rooms at reasonable rates (Sb-€60, Db-€70, Tb-€100, 125 rue St. Antoine, tel. 01 42 72 14 23, fax 01 42 72 51 11, pointerivoli@libertysurf.fr).

$ Hôtel de la République**, owned by the people who run the Castex (see above), is in a less appealing, out-of-the-way location, compared to other listed Marais hotels, but it often has rooms when others don't (Sb-€53, Db-€61, near place de la République, 31 rue Albert Thomas, 75010 Paris, Mo: République, Mo: St. Paul, tel. 01 42 39 19 03, fax 01 42 39 22 66, www.republiquehotel.com).

$ MIJE Youth Hostels: The Maison Internationale de la Jeunesse et des Etudiants (MIJE) runs three classy old residences clustered a few blocks south of rue St. Antoine. Each offers simple, clean, single-sex, one- to four-bed rooms for travelers under the age of 30 (exceptions are made for families). None has an elevator or double beds, each has an Internet station, and all rooms have showers. You can stay seven days maximum and prices given are per person and favor single travelers (two people can find a double in a very simple hotel for similar rates). You can pay more to have your own room, or pay less and room with as many as three others (Sb-€48, Db-€38, Tb-€32, Qb-€26, no CC, includes breakfast but not towels, which you can get from a machine; required membership card-€2.50 extra/person; rooms locked 12:00–15:00 and at 1:00). The hostels are: **MIJE Fourcy** (€10 dinners available to anyone with a membership card, 6 rue de Fourcy, just south of rue de Rivoli), **MIJE Fauconnier** (11 rue du Fauconnier), and the best, **MIJE Maubisson** (12 rue des Barres). They all share the same contact information (tel. 01 42 74 23 45, fax 01 40 27 81 64, www.mije.com) and Métro stop (St. Paul). Reservations are accepted, though you must arrive by noon.

Sleeping near the Pompidou Center

These hotels are farther west and closer to the Pompidou Center than to place de la Bastille.

$$$ Hôtel Axial Beaubourg***, a block from Hôtel de Ville toward the Pompidou Center, has a minimalist lobby and 28 pricey but plush rooms, many with wood beams. If you cancel with less than seven days' notice, you'll lose your one-night deposit (standard Db-€145, big Db-€185, air-con, 11 rue du Temple, Mo: Hôtel de Ville, tel. 01 42 72 72 22, fax 02 42 72 03 53, www.axialbeaubourg.com).

$$$ Hôtel Caron de Beaumarchais*** feels like a folk-museum, with its 20 sweet little rooms and a lobby cluttered with bits from an elegant 18th-century Marais house. Short antique collectors love this place (small back-side Db-€145, larger Db on the front-€160, air-con, 12 rue

Vielle du Temple, Mo: Hôtel de Ville, tel. 01 42 72 34 12, fax 01 42 72 34 63, www.carondebeaumarchais.com).

$$$ Hôtel de la Bretonnerie*,** three blocks from the Hôtel de Ville, is a fine Marais splurge. It has an on-the-ball staff, a big, welcoming lobby, elegant decor, and tastefully-appointed rooms with an antique, open-beam warmth (perfectly good standard "classic" Db-€114, bigger "charming" Db-€148, Db suite-€190, Tb suite-€215, Qb suite-€245, between rue Vielle du Temple and rue des Archives at 22 rue Ste. Croix de la Bretonnerie, Mo: Hôtel de Ville, tel. 01 48 87 77 63, fax 01 42 77 26 78, www.bretonnerie.com, Francoise SE).

$$ Hôtel de Vieux Marais** is tucked away on a quiet street two blocks east of the Pompidou Center with bright, spacious, and well-designed rooms. The we-try-harder owner, Marie-Hélène, loves her work and gives this place its charm. Greet Leeloo, the hotel hound (Db-€110-140, extra bed-€23, air-con, just off rue des Archives at 8 rue du Plâtre, Mo: Rambuteau or Hôtel de Ville, tel. 01 42 78 47 22, fax 01 42 78 34 32, www.vieuxmarais.com).

$$ Hôtel Beaubourg* is a good three-star value on a quiet street in the shadow of the Pompidou Center. Its 28 rooms are wood-beam comfy, and the inviting lounge is warm and pleasant (Db-€115, some with balconies-€135, twins are considerably larger than doubles, includes breakfast, 11 rue Simon Le Franc, Mo: Rambuteau, tel. 01 42 74 34 24, fax 01 42 78 68 11, htlbeaubourg@hotellerie.net).

$$ Hôtel de Nice,** on the Marais' busy main drag, is a turquoise-and-rose, "Marie-Antoinette does tie-dye" place. Its narrow halls are littered with paintings, and its 23 rooms are filled with thoughtful touches and include tight bathrooms. Twin rooms, which cost the same as doubles, are larger and on the street side—but have effective double-paned windows (Sb-€68, Db-€105, Tb-€125, Qb-€135, extra bed-€20, 42 bis rue de Rivoli, Mo: Hôtel de Ville, tel. 01 42 78 55 29, fax 01 42 78 36 07).

$ Hotel Sansonnet,** a block from Hôtel de Ville toward the Pompidou Center, is a spotless, homey and unassuming oasis with no elevator but with 26 comfortable, well-maintained, and top-value rooms (Sb-€48-68, Db-€60–80, 48 rue de la Verrerie, Mo: Hôtel de Ville, tel. 01 48 87 96 14, fax 01 48 87 30 46, www.hotel-sansonnet.com, info @hotel-sansonnet.com).

$ Grand Hôtel du Loiret** is a bare-bones and basic place where you get what you pay for (S-€37, Sb-€47–62, D-€42, Db-€56–72, Tb-€72–84, 8 rue des Mauvais Garçons, Mo: Hôtel de Ville, tel. 01 48 87 77 00, fax 01 48 04 96 56, hotelduloiret@hotmail.com).

Sleeping near the Marais on Ile St. Louis

The peaceful, residential character of this river-wrapped island, its brilliant location, and homemade ice cream have drawn Americans for decades, allowing hotels to charge top euro for their rooms. There are no budget values here, but the island's coziness and proximity to the Marais, Notre-Dame, and the Latin Quarter compensate for higher rates. The hotels listed below are shown on the map on page 231. All are on the island's main drag, the rue St. Louis-en-l'Ile, where I list several restaurants (see "Eating," below). Use Mo: Pont Marie or Sully Morland.

$$$ **Hôtel du Jeu de Paume******, located in a 17th-century tennis center, is the most expensive hotel I list in Paris. When you enter its magnificent lobby, you'll understand why. Greet Scoop, the hotel dog, then ride the glass elevator for a half-timbered-treehouse experience, and marvel at the cozy lounges. The 30 quite comfortable rooms are carefully designed and *très* tasteful, though small for the price (you're paying for the location and public spaces). Most face a small garden and all are pin-drop peaceful (Sb-€160, standard Db-€220, larger Db-€230–260, deluxe Db-€285, Db suite-€460, 54 rue St. Louis-en-l'Ile, tel. 01 43 26 14 18, fax 01 40 46 02 76, www.jeudepaumehotel.com).

The following two hotels are owned by the same person. For both, if you must cancel, do so a week in advance or pay fees:

$$$ **Hôtel de Lutèce***** is the better, cozier value on the island, with a sit-a-while wood-paneled lobby, a fireplace, and warmly designed air-conditioned rooms. Twin rooms are larger and the same price as double rooms (Sb-€127, Db-€152, Tb-€170, 65 rue St. Louis-en-l'Ile, tel. 01 43 26 23 52, fax 01 43 29 60 25, www.hotel-ile-saintlouis.com).

$$$ **Hôtel des Deux Iles***** is brighter and more colorful with marginally smaller rooms and the same rates (59 rue St. Louis-en-l'Ile, tel. 01 43 26 13 35, fax 01 43 29 60 25).

Luxembourg and Contrescarpe

I've patched together three small neighborhoods (St. Sulpice, Panthéon, and rue Mouffetard) to construct this diverse hotel area. St. Sulpice has a picturesque, pleasing square and Paris' best window-shopping. The Panthéon is stately and reserved, and the rue Mouffetard is light-hearted and youthful.

Sleeping in the Luxembourg/Contrescarpe area puts the Latin Quarter, Luxembourg Garden, boulevard St. Germain, Cluny Museum, Latin Quarter, and the Jardin des Plantes within easy walking distance. Here you get the best of many worlds—two lively areas (Latin Quarter and rue Mouffetard), two fine parks, and the classy trappings that surround the monumental Panthéon and St. Sulpice church. To walk from one end of this area to the other (from St. Sulpice church to the bottom of rue Mouffetard) takes about 25 minutes.

Having the Luxembourg Garden at your back door allows strolls through meticulously cared-for flowers, a great kids' play area, and a purifying escape from city traffic. Place St. Sulpice offers an elegant, pedestrian-friendly square and some of Paris' best boutiques. The rue Mouffetard is the bohemian soul of this area, running south from its

Luxembourg and Contrescarpe
Hotels and Restaurants

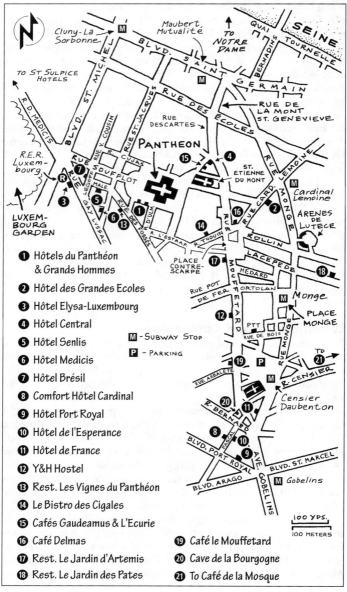

① Hôtels du Panthéon
   & Grands Hommes

② Hôtel des Grandes Ecoles

③ Hôtel Elysa-Luxembourg

④ Hôtel Central

⑤ Hôtel Senlis

⑥ Hôtel Medicis

⑦ Hôtel Brésil

⑧ Comfort Hôtel Cardinal

⑨ Hôtel Port Royal

⑩ Hôtel de l'Esperance

⑪ Hôtel de France

⑫ Y&H Hostel

⑬ Rest. Les Vignes du Panthéon

⑭ Le Bistro des Cigales

⑮ Cafés Gaudeamus & L'Ecurie

⑯ Café Delmas

⑰ Rest. Le Jardin d'Artemis

⑱ Rest. Le Jardin des Pates

⑲ Café le Mouffetard

⑳ Cave de la Bourgogne

㉑ To Café de la Mosque

heart, place de la Contrescarpe, to rue de Bazeilles. Two thousand years ago, it was the principal Roman road south to Italy. Today, this small, meandering street has a split personality. The lower part thrives in the daytime as a pedestrian market street. The upper part sleeps during the day but comes alive after dark, teeming with bars, restaurants, and nightlife.

The flowery Jardin des Plantes park, just east of rue Mouffetard, is ideal for afternoon walks, picnics, naps, and kids. The doorway at 49 rue Monge leads to a hidden **Roman arena** (Arènes de Lutèce). Today, *boules* players occupy the stage while couples cuddle on the seats. Admire the Panthéon from the outside (it's not worth paying to enter, though it's free with a museum pass), and peek inside the exquisitely beautiful St. Etienne-du-Mont church.

Place Monge hosts a good **outdoor market** on Wednesday, Friday, and Sunday mornings until 13:00. The **street market** at the bottom of rue Mouffetard bustles daily except Monday (Tue–Sat 8:00–12:00 & 15:30–19:00, Sun 8:00–12:00, five blocks south of place de la Contrescarpe). Lively cafés at place de la Contrescarpe hop with action from the afternoon into the wee hours.

The nearest **TI** is at the Louvre museum. To get wired, try Edmicro **Internet Access**, two blocks from place Contrescarpe toward the Seine (Tue–Fri 11:00–20:00, Sat and Mon 14:00–20:00, closed Sun, 29 rue Descartes, tel. 01 43 25 35 47). The **post offices** (PTT) are between rue Mouffetard and rue Monge at 10 rue de l'Epée-de-Bois, and at the corner of rue des Ecoles and rue du Cardinal Lemoine. **Bus** #47 runs along rue Monge north to Notre-Dame, the Pompidou Center, Gare de l'Est, and Gare du Nord.

Sleeping near St. Sulpice Church (6th arrondissement)

These three are all within a block of St. Sulpice and Luxembourg Garden, and two blocks from the famous boulevard St. Germain. Métro stops St. Sulpice and Mabillon are equally close.

$$$ Hôtel Relais St. Sulpice***, on the small street just behind St. Sulpice church, feels like a cozy bar with a melt-in-your-chair lounge and beautifully-designed rooms, most of which surround a leafy atrium court-yard. The dazzling breakfast room sits below the glass atrium near the sauna (Db-€165-205, good buffet breakfast-€12, air-con, 3 rue Garancière, tel. 01 46 33 99 00, fax 01 46 33 00 10, relaisstsulpice@wanadoo.fr).

$$$ Hôtel Bonaparte** sits between boutiques a few steps from place St. Sulpice on the smart rue Bonaparte. While the rooms don't live up to the handsome entry, they are homey, comfortable, and generally spacious with big bathrooms, molded ceilings, and clashing bedspreads (Sb-€90-135, Db-€118-150, Tb-€155, air-con, 61 rue Bonaparte, tel. 01 43 26 97 37, fax 01 46 33 57 67).

$$ Hotel le Récamier**, which feels like grandma's house, is an overlooked prize tucked in the corner of place St. Sulpice. Flowery wall-paper, dark halls, and spotless, just-what-you-need rooms (with no TV!)—some with views of the square—make this an ideal Paris refuge. How such a low-key place escaped the trendy style of other hotels in this chic area, I'll never know (S-€90, Sb-€110, Db-€115-130, Tb-€155, Qb-€200, includes breakfast, 3 bis place St. Sulpice, tel. 01 43 26 04 89, fax 01 46 33 27 73).

Sleeping near the Panthéon (5th arrondissement)

The following two wannabe-four-star hotels face the Panthéon's right transept and are owned by the same family (ask about their promotional rates, which can be offered anytime, even during some summer weeks). The rates are sky-high and the rooms aren't big, but the quality is tops. I prefer the first hotel.

Use Métro stops Cardinal Lemoine or Maubert-Mutualité, or RER stop Luxembourg for these hotels.

$$$ **Hôtel du Panthéon***** welcomes you with a cushy lobby and 32 country-French-cute rooms with air-conditioning and every possible comfort. Fifth-floor rooms have sliver balconies, but sixth-floor rooms have the best views (Sb-€188, Db-€218, Tb-€235, 19 place du Panthéon, tel. 01 43 54 32 95, fax 01 43 26 64 65, www.hoteldupantheon.com).

$$$ **Hôtel des Grands Hommes***** was built to look good—and it does. The lobby is to be admired but not enjoyed, and the 31 rooms reflect an interior designer's dream. They're generally tight but adorable, with great attention to detail and little expense spared. Fifth- and sixth-floor rooms have balconies (sixth-floor balconies, with grand views, are big enough to use). For more luxury, splurge for a suite (Sb-€188, standard Db-€218, Db suite-€390, air-con, 17 place du Panthéon, tel. 01 46 34 19 60, fax 01 43 26 67 32, www.hoteldesgrandshommes.com).

$$ **Hôtel des Grandes Ecoles***** is simply idyllic. A short alley leads to three buildings protecting a flower-filled garden courtyard, preserving a sense of tranquility that is rare in a city this size. Its 51 rooms are reasonably spacious and comfortable, with large beds. This romantic place is deservedly popular, so call well in advance, though reservations are not accepted more than four months ahead (Db-€105–115, a few bigger rooms-€130, extra bed-€20, parking-€30, 75 rue du Cardinal Lemoine, Mo: Cardinal Lemoine, tel. 01 43 26 79 23, fax 01 43 25 28 15, www.hotel-grandes-ecoles.com, mellow Marie speaks some English, Maman does not).

$$ **Hôtel Elysa-Luxembourg***** sits on a busy street and is my closest listing to Luxembourg Garden. It has plush, air-conditioned rooms, but little personality (Db-€125-140, 6 rue Gay Lussac, tel. 01 43 25 31 74, fax 01 46 34 56 27, www.elysa-luxembourg.fr).

$ **Hôtel Central***, wedged between two cafés, has a smoky, dingy reception, a steep, slippery stairway, so-so beds, and basic-but-cheery-

if-somewhat-mildewed rooms. To an optimist, this hotel defines unpre-
tentiousness; to a pessimist, it's a dive with a charming location.
Regardless, it's cheap (all rooms with showers, though toilets are down
the hall, Ss-€29–37, Ds-€39–45, no CC, no elevator, 6 rue Descartes,
Mo: Cardinal Lemoine, tel. 01 46 33 57 93, sweet Pilar NSE).

$ **Hôtel de Senlis**** is a fair deal hiding quietly two blocks from
Luxembourg Garden, with modest rooms, carpeted walls, and metal
closets. Most rooms have beamed ceilings, and all rooms could use a dec-
orator with taste (Sb-€67, Db-€72–87, Tb-€95, Qb-€110, 7 rue
Malebranche, Mo: Cluny-La Sorbonne, tel. 01 43 29 93 10, fax 01 43
29 00 24, www.hoteldesenlis.fr).

$ **Hôtel Médicis** is as cheap, stripped-down, and basic as it gets, with
a soiled-linoleum charm, a happy owner, and a great location (S-€16, D-
€31, 214 rue St. Jacques, tel. 01 43 54 14 66, hotelmedecis@aol.com, Denis
speaks English).

$ **Hôtel du Brésil****, one block from Luxembourg Garden, has lit-
tle character and some smoky rooms, but reasonable rates, making it an
acceptable last resort (Sb-€64, Db-€68–85, 10 rue le Goff, tel. 01 43 54
76 11, fax 01 46 33 45 78, hoteldubresil@wanadoo.fr).

Sleeping at the Bottom of Rue Mouffetard

Of my recommended accommodations in this area, these are farthest
from the Seine and other tourists, in an appealing workaday area. They
require a longer walk or Métro ride to sights but may have rooms when
others don't. Use Métro stops Censier-Daubenton or Les Gobelins.

$$ **Comfort Hôtel Cardinal**** is a well-designed hotel with less
character but agreeable decor and modern comforts like air-conditioning.
Room prices vary enormously depending on demand, so the low-end prices
listed could be available anytime—it's worth a call to check their rates (Sb-
€68-100, standard Db-€88-138, large Db-€135-185, 20 rue Pascal, tel.
01 47 07 41 92, fax 01 47 07 43 80, hotelcardinal@aol.com).

$ Don't let **Port-Royal-Hôtel**'s* lone star fool you—this 46-room
place is polished bottom to top and has been well-run by the same proud
family for 66 years. You could eat off the floors of its spotless, comfy
rooms. Ask for a room off the street (S-€39-50, D-€66, big hall showers-
€2.50, Db-€76, deluxe Db-€89, no CC, requires cash deposit, climb stairs
from rue Pascal to busy boulevard de Port Royal, 8 boulevard de Port
Royal, tel. 01 43 31 70 06, fax 01 43 31 33 67, www.portroyalhotel.fr.st).

$ **Hôtel de l'Espérance**** is a solid two-star value. It's quiet, pink,
fluffy, and comfortable, with thoughtfully appointed rooms complete
with canopy beds and a flamboyant owner (Sb-€70, Db-€73–86, small
Tb-€101, 15 rue Pascal, Mo: Censier-Daubenton, tel. 01 47 07 10 99,
fax 01 43 37 56 19, hotel.esperance@wanadoo.fr).

$ **Hôtel de France**** is set on a busy street, with adequately com-
fortable rooms, fair prices, and charming owner, Madame Margo. The

best and quietest rooms are *sur le cour* (on the courtyard), though street-side rooms are OK (Sb-€66, Db-€76–80, requires one-night non-refundable deposit, 108 rue Monge, tel. 01 47 07 19 04, fax 01 43 36 62 34, hotel.de.fce@wanadoo.fr).

$ Y&H Hostel is easygoing and English-speaking, with Internet access, kitchen facilities, and basic but acceptable hostel conditions (beds in four-bed rooms-€23, beds in double rooms-€26, sheets-€2.50, no CC, rooms closed 11:00–16:00 but reception stays open, 2:00 curfew, reservations require deposit, 80 rue Mouffetard, Mo: Cardinal Lemoine, tel. 01 47 07 47 07, fax 01 47 07 22 24, smile@youngandhappy.fr).

Sleeping in Versailles

For a laid-back alternative to Paris within easy reach of the big city by RER train (5/hr, 30 min), Versailles, with easy, safe parking and reasonably priced hotels, can be a good overnight stop. Park in the château's main lot while looking for a hotel, or leave your car there overnight (free 19:30–8:00). Get a map of Versailles at your hotel or at the TI.

$$$ Hôtel de France*, in an 18th-century townhouse, offers four-star value, with air-conditioned, appropriately royal rooms, a pleasant courtyard, comfy public spaces, a bar, and a restaurant (Db-€145, Tb-€180, Qb-€240, just off parking lot across from château, 5 rue Colbert, tel. 01 30 83 92 23, fax 01 30 83 92 24, www.hotelfrance-versailles.com).

$ Hôtel le Cheval Rouge,** built in 1676 as Louis XIV's stables, now houses tourists. It's a block behind the place du Marché in a quaint corner of town on a large, quiet courtyard with free parking and sufficiently comfortable rooms (Ds-€51, Db-€68–80, Tb-€90, Qb-€95, 18 rue André Chenier, tel. 01 39 50 03 03, fax 01 39 50 61 27, www.chevalrouge.fr.st).

$ Ibis Versailles** offers fair value and modern comfort, but no air-conditioning (Db-€71, cheaper weekend rates can't be reserved ahead, across from RER station, 4 avenue du Général de Gaulle, tel. 01 39 53 03 30, fax 01 39 50 06 31).

$ Hôtel du Palais, facing the RER station, has clean, sharp rooms—the cheapest I list in this area. Ask for a quiet room off the street (Ds-€45, Db-€52, extra person-€11, piles of stairs, 6 place Lyautey, tel. 01 39 50 39 29, fax 01 39 50 80 41, hotelpalais@ifrance.com).

$ Hôtel d'Angleterre** away from the frenzy, is a tranquil old place with smiling, Polish Madame Kutyla in control. Rooms are comfortable and spacious. Park nearby in the château lot (Db-€58–88, extra bed-€15, just below palace to the right as you exit, 2 rue de Fontenay, tel. 01 39 51 43 50, fax 01 39 51 45 63, hotel.angleterre@voila.fr).

EATING

Paris is France's wine and cuisine melting pot. While it lacks a style of its own (only French onion soup is truly Parisian), it draws from the best

RESTAURANTS

To help you choose among these listings, I've divided the restaurants into three categories, based on the price for a typical meal without wine.

\$\$\$ Higher Priced—Most meals €34 or more.
\$\$ Moderately Priced—Most meals between €20–34.
\$ Lower Priced—Most meals under €20.

of France. Paris could hold a gourmet's Olympics and import nothing.

Picnic or go to bakeries for quick take-out lunches, or stop at a café for a lunch salad or *plat du jour,* but linger longer over dinner. Cafés are happy to serve a *plat du jour* (garnished plate of the day, about €11) or a chef-like salad (about €9) day or night, while restaurants expect you to enjoy a full dinner. Restaurants open for dinner around 19:00, and small local favorites get crowded after 21:00. Most of the restaurants listed below accept credit cards.

To save piles of euros, review the budget eating tips in this book's introduction and consider dinner picnics (great take-out dishes available at charcuteries). My recommendations are centered around the same three great neighborhoods I list accommodations for (above); you can come home exhausted after a busy day of sightseeing and have a good selection of restaurants right around the corner. And evening is a fine time to explore any of these delightful neighborhoods, even if you're sleeping elsewhere.

Restaurants

If you are traveling outside of Paris, save your splurges for the countryside, where you'll enjoy regional cooking for less money. Many Parisian department stores have huge supermarkets hiding in the basement and top-floor cafeterias that offer affordable, low-risk, low-stress, what-you-see-is-what-you-get meals. The three neighborhoods highlighted in this book for sleeping in Paris are also pleasant areas to window-shop for just the right restaurant, as is the Ile St. Louis. Most restaurants we've listed in these areas have set-price *menus* between €15 and €30. In most cases, the few extra euros you pay for not choosing the least-expensive option is money well spent, as it opens up a variety of better choices. You decide.

Good Picnic Spots: For great people-watching, try the Pompidou Center (by the *Homage to Stravinsky* fountains), the elegant place des Vosges (closes at dusk), the gardens at the Rodin Museum, and Luxembourg Garden. The Palais Royal (across the street from the Louvre) is a good spot for a peaceful, royal picnic.

For a romantic picnic place, try the pedestrian bridge (pont des Arts) across from the Louvre, with its unmatched views and plentiful benches; the Champ de Mars park under the Eiffel Tower; and the western tip of Ile St. Louis, overlooking Ile de la Cité. Bring your own dinner feast, and then watch the riverboats and the Eiffel Tower light up the city for you.

Eating in the Rue Cler Neighborhood

The rue Cler neighborhood caters to its residents. Its eateries, while not destination places, have an intimate charm. My favorites are small mom-and-pop places that love to serve traditional French food at good prices to a local clientele. You'll generally find great dinner *menus* for €20–30 and *plats du jour* for around €12-15. Eat early with tourists or late with locals.

$$$ **Le Bourdonnais,** boasting one Michelin star, is the neighborhood's intimate gourmet splurge. You'll find friendly but formal service in a plush and very subdued 10-table room. Micheline Coat, your hostess, will treat you well (lunch *menu*-€43, dinner *menu*-€66, daily, 113 avenue de la Bourdonnais, tel. 01 47 05 47 96).

$$$ **Café de l'Esplanade,** the latest buzz, is your opportunity to be surrounded by chic, yet older and sophisticated Parisians enjoying top-notch traditional cuisine as foreplay. There's not a tourist in sight. It's a sprawling place—half its tables with well-stuffed chairs fill a plush, living-room–like interior, and the other half are lined up outside under its elegant awning facing the street, valet boys, and car park. Dress competitively, as this is *the* place to be seen in the 7th *arrondissement* (*plats du jour*-€20, plan on €45 plus wine for dinner, open daily, reserve—especially if you want a curbside table, smoke-free room in the back, bordering Les Invalides at 52 rue Fabert, tel. 01 47 05 38 80).

$$ **Léo le Lion,** a warm, charming souvenir of old Paris, is popular with locals. Expect to spend €25 per person for fine à la carte choices (closed Sun, 23 rue Duvivier, tel. 01 45 51 41 77).

$$ Save **Le Florimond** for a special occasion. Locals come for classic French cuisine like grandma used to make, served with care in an intimate, warm setting—and so should you. Since it's a neighborhood favorite, it's best to reserve ahead. Friendly English-speaking Laurent will take good care of you (*menu*-€30, closed Sun, good and reasonable wine selection, 19 avenue de la Motte Picquet, tel. 01 45 55 40 38).

$$ At **L'Affriolé,** you'll compete with young professionals for a table. This small and trendy place is well-deserving of its rave reviews. Item selections change daily and the wine list is extensive, with some good bargains (*menu*-€32, closed Sun, 17 rue Malar, tel. 01 44 18 31 33).

$$ **Au Petit Tonneau** is a purely Parisian experience. Fun-loving owner-chef Madame Boyer prepares everything herself, wearing her tall chef's hat like a crown as she rules from her family-style kitchen. The

Rue Cler Restaurants

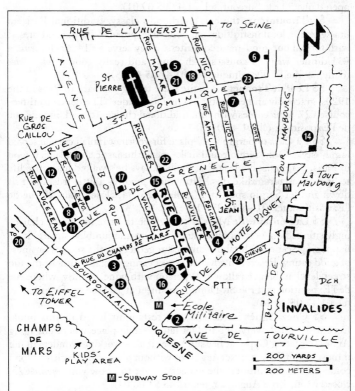

M – Subway Stop

1. Café du Marche
2. Le Comptoir du Septième
3. Café le Bosquet
4. Leo le Lion
5. L'Affriole
6. Au Petit Tonneau
7. Brasserie Thoumieux
8. P'tit Troquet & Casa Sergio
9. Restaurant la Serre
10. La Fontaine de Mars
11. La Varangue
12. Chez Agnes
13. Le Bourdonnais
14. Café de l'Esplanade
15. Tarte Julie
16. Flo Prestige
17. Real McCoy
18. Pourjauran bakery
19. Petite Brasserie PTT
20. To Le Sancerre
21. Le Toulouse
22. Café la Roussillon
23. O'Brien's Pub
24. Le Florimond

small dining room is plain and a bit smoky (allow €35/person with wine, open daily, 20 rue Surcouf, tel. 01 47 05 09 01).

$$ Thoumieux, the neighborhood's classy, traditional Parisian brasserie, is a local institution and deservedly popular. It's big and dressy, with formal but good-natured waiters. They serve a €14 lunch *menu,* a €31 dinner *menu* (3 courses with wine), and really good *crème brulée* (daily, 79 rue St. Dominique, tel. 01 47 05 49 75).

$$ Le P'tit Troquet is a petite place taking you back to Paris in the 1920s, gracefully and earnestly run by Dominique. The delicious three-course €27 *menu* comes with fun, traditional choices (closed Sun, 28 rue de l'Exposition, tel. 01 47 05 80 39).

$$ La Casa di Sergio is *the* place for gourmet Italian cuisine served family-style. Only Sergio could make me enthusiastic about Italian food in Paris. Sergio, a people-loving Sicilian, says he's waited his entire life to open a restaurant like this. Eating here involves a little trust...just sit down and let Sergio spoil you (*menus*-€26–34, closed Sun, 20 rue de l'Exposition, tel. 01 45 51 37 71).

$$ La Fontaine de Mars is a longtime favorite for locals, charmingly situated on a classic tiny Parisian street and jumbled square. It's a happening scene, with tables jammed together for the serious business of good eating. Reserve in advance or risk eating upstairs without the fun street-level ambience (allow €40/person with wine, nightly, where rue de l'Exposition and rue St. Dominique meet at 129 rue St. Dominique, tel. 01 47 05 46 44).

$$ Chez Agnès is the smallest restaurant listed in this book. Eccentric and flowery, it's truly a family-style place where engaging Agnès (with dog Gypsy at her side) does it all—working wonders in her minuscule kitchen, and serving, too, without a word of English. Don't come for a quick dinner; she expects to get to know you (*menu*-€23, closed Mon, 1 rue Augereau, tel. 01 45 51 06 04).

$ Café du Marché, with the best seats, coffee, and prices on rue Cler, serves hearty €9 salads and good €10 *plats du jour* for lunch or dinner to a trendy, smoky, mainly French crowd. This easygoing café is ideal if you want a light dinner (good dinner salads) or a more substantial but simple meal. Arrive before 19:30; it's packed at 21:00. A chalkboard lists the plates of the day—each a meal (Mon–Sat 11:00–23:00, close at 17:00 on Sun, at the corner of rue Cler and rue du Champ de Mars at 38 rue Cler, tel. 01 47 05 51 27, well-run by Frank, Jack, and Bruno). You'll find similar dishes and prices with better (but smoky) indoor seating at, **Le Comptoir du Septième,** two blocks away on a busy street at the Ecole Militaire Métro stop (daily, 39 avenue de la Motte Picquet, tel. 01 45 55 90 20).

$ Petite Brasserie PTT is popular with postal workers, offering traditional café fare at reasonable prices next to the PTT on rue Cler (closed Mon, opposite 53 rue Cler).

$ **Café le Bosquet** is a vintage Parisian brasserie with dressy wait-
ers and classic indoor or sidewalk tables on a busy street. Come here for
a bowl of French onion soup, a salad, or a three-course set *menu* for €16
(closed Sun, many choices from a fun menu, the house red wine is plenty
good, corner of rue du Champs de Mars and avenue Bosquet at 46
avenue Bosquet, tel. 01 45 51 38 13).

$ **La Varangue** is an entertaining one-man show featuring English-
speaking Phillipe, who ran a French catering shop in Pennsylvania for
three years, then returned to Paris to open his own place. He lives
upstairs, and clearly has found his niche serving a Franco-American
clientele who are all on a first-name basis. The food is cheap and good
(try his snails and chocolate cake—but not together), the tables are few,
and he opens early, at 17:30. Norman Rockwell would dig his tiny dining room (*plats du jour*-€10, *menu*-€14.50, closed Sun, always a veggie
option, 27 rue Augereau, tel. 01 47 05 51 22).

$ **Le Toulouse** is a friendly, easygoing boutique/restaurant that serves
southwest French cuisine featuring duck, *cassoulet,* and hearty salads at very
fair prices (closed Sun, 86 rue St Dominique, tel. 01 45 56 04 31).

$ **Restaurant la Serre** is also worth considering and reasonable
(*plats du jour*-€11–15, closed Sun-Mon, good onion soup and duck specialties, 29 rue de l'Exposition tel. 01 45 55 20 96, Margot).

$ **Le Sancerre** wine bar-café is wood-beam warm and ideal for a
light lunch or dinner, or just a glass of wine after a long day of sightseeing. The owner's cheeks are the same color as his wine (open Mon-Fri
until 21:30, closed Sat night and Sun, great omelets, 22 avenue Rapp,
tel. 01 45 51 75 91).

Picnicking in Rue Cler
The rue Cler is a moveable feast that gives "fast food" a good name. The
entire street is clogged with connoisseurs of good eating. Only the
health-food store goes unnoticed. A festival of food, the street is lined
with people whose lives seem to be devoted to their specialty: polished
produce, rotisserie chicken, crêpes, or cheese.

For a magical picnic dinner at the Eiffel Tower, assemble it in no
fewer than five shops on rue Cler and lounge on the best grass in Paris
(the police don't mind after dusk), with the dogs, Frisbees, a floodlit
tower, and a cool breeze in the parc du Champ de Mars.

The **crêpe stand** next to Café du Marché does a wonderful top-end
dinner crêpe for €4. **Asian delis** (generically called *Traiteur Asie*) provide
tasty, low-stress, low-price, take-out treats (€6 dinner plates, two delis
have tables on the rue Cler—one across from Grand Hôtel Lévêque, and
the other near the rue du Champ de Mars). For a variety of savory
quiches or a tasty pear-and-chocolate tart, try **Tarte Julie** (closed Mon,
take-out or stools, 28 rue Cler). The elegant **Flo Prestige** *charcuterie* is
open daily until 23:00 and offers mouthwatering meals to go (at the

Ecole Militaire Métro stop). **Real McCoy** is a little shop selling American food and sandwiches (closed Sun, 194 rue de Grenelle). There are small, **late-night groceries** at 186 and 197 rue de Grenelle (open nightly until midnight).

Breakfast in Rue Cler

Café la Roussillon (daily, at corner of rue de Grenelle and rue Cler) serves American breakfasts and a dynamite Sunday brunch at fair prices. The **Pourjauran** bakery offers great baguettes and hasn't changed in 70 years (at 20 rue Jean Nicot). The **bakery** at 112 rue St. Dominique is worth the detour, with classic decor and tables where you can enjoy your *café au lait* and croissant.

Nightlife in Rue Cler

This sleepy neighborhood is not the place for night owls, but there are a few notable exceptions. **Café du Marché** and its brother, **Le Comptoir du Septième** (both listed above), hop with a Franco-American crowd until about midnight, as does the flashier **Café la Roussillon** (nightly, at corner of rue de Grenelle and rue Cler). **O'Brien's Pub** is a relaxed, Parisian rendition of an Irish pub (77 avenue St. Dominique).

Eating in the Marais Neighborhood

The trendy Marais is filled with locals enjoying good food in colorful and atmospheric eateries. The scene is competitive and changes all the time. Here is an assortment of places—all handy to recommended hotels— that offer good food at reasonable prices, plus a memorable experience. For maximum ambience, go to the place des Vosges or place du Marché Ste. Catherine (several places listed below in each of these squares).

$$$ **Ma Bourgogne** is a good match for the classy place des Vosges with a certain snob appeal. You'll sit under arcades in a whirlpool of Frenchness as bow-tied and black-aproned waiters serve traditional Burgundian specialties: steak, *coq au vin*, lots of French fries, escargot, and great red wine. Service at this institution comes with food but few smiles (allow €38/person with wine, open daily, dinner reservations smart, no CC, #19 at northwest corner, tel. 01 42 78 44 64).

$$$ **L'Excuse,** one of the neighborhood's top restaurants, is a good splurge for a romantic, dressy evening in a hushed atmosphere, with lounge-lizard music and elegant Mediterranean nouveau cuisine. The plates are petite but creative and presented with panache (*menu*-€37, closed Sun, reserve ahead, request downstairs—ideally by the window, 14 rue Charles V, tel. 01 42 77 98 97).

$$ *Restaurants on place du Marché Ste. Catherine:* This tiny square just off rue St. Antoine is an international food festival cloaked in extremely Parisian, leafy-square ambience. On a balmy evening, this is clearly a neighborhood favorite, with five popular restaurants offering

Marais Restaurants

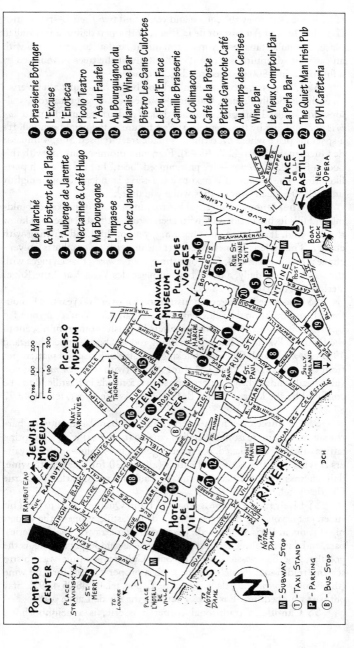

1. Le Marché & Au Bistrot de la Place
2. L'Auberge de Jarente
3. Nectarine & Café Hugo
4. Ma Bourgogne
5. L'Impasse
6. To Chez Janou

7. Brasserie Bofinger
8. L'Excuse
9. L'Enoteca
10. Picolo Teatro
11. L'As du Falafel
12. Au Bourguignon du Marais Wine Bar
13. Bistro Les Sans Culottes
14. Le Fou d'En Face
15. Camille Brasserie
16. Le Colimacon
17. Café de la Poste
18. Petite Gavroche Café
19. Au Temps des Cerises Wine Bar
20. Le Vieux Comptoir Bar
21. La Perla Bar
22. The Quiet Man Irish Pub
23. BVH Cafeteria

€20–30 meals. Survey the square and you'll find two French-style bistros (**Le Marché** and **Au Bistrot de la Place,** both open daily), a fun Italian place, a popular Japanese/Korean restaurant, and a Russian eatery with an easy but adventurous menu. You'll eat under the trees surrounded by a futuristic-in-1800 planned residential quarter.

$$ L'Impasse, a cozy, neighborhood bistro on a quiet alley, serves an enthusiastically French, €26 three-course *menu* (great escargots, scallops, and steak). Françoise, a former dancer and artist, runs the place *con brio* and, judging by the clientele, she's a fixture in the neighborhood. It's a spacious place where everything is made fresh (closed Sun, 4 impasse de Guéménée, tel. 01 42 72 08 45). Françoise promises anyone with this book a free glass of *byrrh*—it's pronounced "beer," but it's a French portlike drink. The restaurant is next to a self-serve launderette (open nightly until 21:30—clean your clothes while you dine).

$$ Chez Janou, a Provençal bistro, tumbles out of its corner building and fills its broad sidewalk with keen eaters. At first glance, you know this is a find. It's relaxed and charming, yet youthful and bustling with energy. The style is French Mediterranean, with an emphasis on vegetables (*plats du jour*-€14, €27 for a three-course *menu* that changes with the season, open daily, a block beyond place des Vosges at 2 rue Roger Verlomme, tel. 01 42 72 28 41).

$$ Brasserie Bofinger, an institution for over 100 years, is famous for fish and traditional cuisine with an Alsatian flair. You're surrounded by brisk, black-and-white attired waiters in plush rooms reminiscent of the Roaring Twenties. The non-smoking room is best—under the grand 1919 *coupole.* Watch the boys shucking and stacking seafood platters out front before going in. Their €31 three-course (with wine) *menu* is a good value (daily and nightly, reservations smart, 5 rue de la Bastille, don't be confused by the lesser "Petite" Bofinger across the street, tel. 01 42 72 87 82).

$$ L'Enoteca is a high-energy, half-timbered Italian wine barrestaurant serving reasonable Italian cuisine (no pizza) with a tempting antipasti bar. It's a relaxed, open setting with busy, blue-aproned waiters serving two floors of local eaters (allow €30 for meals with wine, daily, across from L'Excuse at rue St. Paul and rue Charles V, 25 rue Charles V tel. 01 42 78 91 44).

$$ Lively rue de Lappe is what the Latin Quarter wants to be. This street, just beyond the more stately place de la Bastille, is one of the wildest night spots in Paris. You'll walk past a dizzying array of wacky eateries, bars, and dance halls. Then, sitting there like a van Gogh painting, is the popular, zinc-bar-classic **Bistrot les Sans Culottes**—a time-warp bistro serving traditional French cuisine with a proper respect for fine wine (three-course *menu*-€20, daily, 27 rue de Lappe, tel. 01 48 05 42 92). Stay out past your bedtime. Eat here. Then join the rue de Lappe party.

$$ Camille, a traditional corner brasserie, is a neighborhood favorite with great indoor and sidewalk seating. White-aproned waiters serve €9 salads and very French *plats du jour* for €15 to a down-to-earth but sophisticated clientele (daily, 24 rue des Francs Bourgeois at corner of rue Elzévir, tel. 01 42 72 29 50).

You can dine cheaply on the elegant place des Vosges at the mod and pastel **$ Nectarine,** a teahouse serving healthy salads, quiches, and inexpensive *plats du jour* both day and night. Its fun menu lets you mix and match omelets and crêpes (daily, 16 place des Vosges, tel. 01 42 77 23 78). **$ Café Hugo,** next door (open daily, named for the square's most famous resident), is a typical bistro serving good traditional favorites such as onion soup (€6) and crêpes (€5).

$ Café de la Poste is a tight little place serving good €11 *plats du jour* from a small but reliable menu (closed Sun, near place de la Bastille at 13 rue Castex, tel. 01 42 72 95 35).

$ Au Temps des Cerises, a *très* local wine bar, is relaxed and amiably run by the incredibly mustachioed Monsieur Vimard. This place is great for a colorful lunch or a very light dinner of cheese or cold meats with good wine (Mon–Fri until 20:00, closed Sat–Sun, at rue du Petit-Musc and rue de la Cerisaie).

$ L'Auberge de Jarente, is just off the charming place du Marché Ste. Catherine and offers a reliable, rainy-day, budget option, where a hard-working father-and-son team serve good Basque food (€18 for three-course *menu* with wine, closed Sun–Mon, just off the square at 7 rue de Jarente, tel. 01 42 77 49 35).

$ Piccolo Teatro is where vegetarians should go for a fine meal (closed Mon, near rue des Rosiers, 6 rue des Ecouffes, tel. 01 42 72 17 79).

$ L'As du Falafel serves inexpensive Jewish cuisine with bustling ambience (closed Sat, tasty falafels for €5, 34 rue des Rosiers).

$ Several hard-working **Chinese fast food** places are along rue St. Antoine, great for a €6 meal.

Eating Nearer the Pompidou Center and Hôtel de Ville

$$$ Au Bourguignon du Marais, a small wine bar south of rue de Rivoli, is a place that wine-lovers shouldn't miss. Gentle English-speaking Jacques offers excellent Burgundy wines that blend well with his fine, though limited, selection of *plats du jour* (allow €45 with wine, closed Sat–Sun, call by 19:00 to reserve, 52 rue Francois Miron, tel. 01 48 87 15 40).

$$ Le Fou d'En Face, with dynamite ambience inside and out, is a wine-focused restaurant run by an amiable fellow who loves his lot in life. It's on a small square barely off rue de Rivoli near the recommended Hôtel de Nice. Try the *pot-au-feu* (beef stew-€16), and test the superb wine selection (closed Sun, 3 rue du Bourg-Tibourg, tel. 01 48 87 03 75).

$$ Le Colimacon, at #44, rue Vieille du Temple, is a romantic little place twirled around its spiral stairs *(colimacon),* offering two-course

(€18) or three-course (€23) *menus* of traditional cuisine including *magret de canard aux fruits de saison*—duck breast with a sauce of seasonal fruit (closed Tue, reservations required, tel. 01 48 87 12 01).

$ **BHV Department Store**'s fifth-floor cafeteria provides an escape from the busy streets below, nice views, and no-brainer, point-and-shoot cafeteria cuisine (Mon-Sat 11:30-18:00, closed Sun, at intersection of rue du Temple and rue de la Verrerie, one block from Hôtel de Ville).

$ **Petite Gavroche** is a charmingly basic place offering dirt-cheap French cooking (€8 *plats du jour*, 15 rue Ste. Croix de la Bretonnerie, tel. 01 48 87 74 26).

Picnicking in the Marais Neighborhood

Picnic at peaceful place des Vosges (closes at dusk) or on the Ile St. Louis *quais* (see below). Stretch your euros at the basement supermarket of the **Monoprix** department store (closed Sun, near place des Vosges on rue St. Antoine). Two small grocery shops are open until 23:00 on rue St. Antoine (near intersection with rue Castex). For a cheap breakfast, try the tiny *boulangerie-pâtisserie* where the hotels buy their croissants (coffee machine-€0.70, baby quiche-€1.50, one block off place de la Bastille, corner of rue St. Antoine and rue de Lesdiguières).

Nightlife in the Marais Neighborhood

The best scene is the bars and dance halls of rue de Lappe (beyond place de la Bastille, see above). Trendy cafés and bars also cluster on rue Vielle du Temple, rue des Archives, and rue Ste. Croix de la Bretonnerie (close about 2:00), and are popular with gay men. **Le Vieux Comptoir** is tiny, lively, and just hip enough (off place des Vosges at 8 rue de Birague). **La Perla** is full of Parisian yuppies in search of the perfect margarita (26 rue François Miron). **The Quiet Man** is a traditional Irish pub with happy hour from 16:00 to 20:00 (5 rue des Haudriettes).

Eating on Ile St. Louis

The Ile St. Louis is a romantic and peaceful place to window-shop for plenty of promising dinner possibilities. Cruise the island's main street for a variety of options, from cozy *crêperies* to Italian (intimate pizzeria and upscale) to typical brasseries (several with fine outdoor seating facing the bridge to Ile de la Cité). After dinner, sample Paris' best sorbet. Then stroll across to the Ile de la Cité to see an illuminated Notre-Dame. All listings below line the island's main drag, the rue St. Louis-en-l'Ile. Consider skipping dessert to enjoy a stroll licking the best ice cream in Paris.

$$ **Le Tastevin** and **Auberge de la Reine Blanche** are two little family-run places that serve top-notch traditional French cuisine with white-tablecloth, candlelit elegance in small, 10-table rooms under heavy wooden beams. Their *menus* start with three courses at about €29 and

offer plenty of classic choices that change with the season for freshness. Le Tastevin at #46, run by Madame Puisieux, is a little more intimate (daily, tel. 01 43 54 17 31). Auberge de la Reine Blanche is a bit more touristy—but in the best sense—with friendly Françoise and her crew working hard to please in a characteristic little place with dollhouse furniture on the walls and a two-dove welcoming committee at the door (closed Wed, #30, tel. 01 46 33 07 87). Reservations are smart for each.

$$ **La Brasserie de l'Ile St. Louis** is situated at the prow of the island's ship as it faces Ile de la Cité, offering fine Alsatian cuisine (try the *choucroute garni* for €16), served in Franco-Germanic ambience with no-nonsense, brasserie service (closed Wed, no reservations, 55 quai de Bourbon, tel. 01 43 54 02 59).

$$ **Nos Ancêtres les Gaulois** and **La Taverne du Sergeant Recruteur,** next door to each other, are famous for their rowdy, medieval cellar atmosphere. They serve all-you-can-eat buffets with straw baskets of raw veggies (cut whatever you like with your dagger), massive plates of pâté, a meat course, and all the wine you can stomach for €36. The food is just food; burping is encouraged. If you want to eat a lot, drink a lot of wine, and holler at your friends while receiving smart-aleck buccaneer service, these food fests can be fun. Nos Ancêtres les Gaulois, or "Our Ancestors the Gauls," has bigger tables and seems made-to-order for local stag parties (daily from 19:00, at #39, tel. 01 46 33 66 07). If you'd rather be surrounded by drunk tourists than locals, pick La Taverne du Sergeant Recruteur. The "Sergeant Recruteur" used to get young Parisians drunk and stuffed here, then sign them into the army (daily from 19:00, #41, tel. 01 43 54 75 42).

$ **Café Med,** closest to Notre-Dame at #77, is best for inexpensive salads, crêpes, and lighter *menus* in a tight but cheery setting (daily, very limited wine list, tel. 01 43 29 73 17, charming Eva SE). There's a similar *crêperie* just across the street.

Riverside Picnic

On sunny lunchtimes and balmy evenings, the *quais* on the Left Bank side of Ile St. Louis is lined with locals who have more class than money, spreading out tablecloths and even lighting candles for elegant picnics. The grocery store on the main drag, at 67 rue St. Louis-en-l'Ile, is open daily until midnight if you'd like to join them. Otherwise, it's a great walk for people-watching.

Ice Cream Dessert

Half the people strolling Ile St. Louis are licking an ice cream cone, because this is the home of *les glaces Berthillon*. The original **Berthillon** shop, at 31 rue St. Louis-en-l'Ile, is marked by the line of salivating customers (closed Mon-Tue). It's so popular that the wealthy people who can afford to live on this fancy island complain about the congestion it causes. For a less famous but at least as tasty treat, the homemade Italian gelato a block away at **Amorino Gelati** is giving Berthillon competition (no line, bigger portions, easier to see what you want, and they offer little tastes—Berthillon doesn't need to, 47 rue St. Louis-en-l'Ile, tel. 01 44 07 48 08). Having some of each is a fine option.

Eating in the Luxembourg and Contrescarpe Neighborhood

There are a few diamonds for fine dining in this otherwise rough, but appealing restaurant area. Most come here for the lively and cheap eateries that line rue Mouffetard and rue du Pot-de-Fer. Study the many menus, compare crowds, then plunge in and have fun (see map on page 280).

$$ **Les Vignes du Panthéon,** near the Panthéon, is a homey, traditional place with a zinc bar and original flooring. It serves a mostly local clientele and will make you feel you're truly in Paris (allow €26 for à la carte, closed Sat–Sun, 4 rue des Fossés St. Jacques, tel. 01 43 54 80 81).

$$ Sprawling **Café Delmas,** on place de la Contrescarpe, is the place to see and be seen with a broad outdoor terrace, tasty salads (€12), and good *plats du jour* from €14 (open daily).

$$ **Le Jardin d'Artemis** is one of the better values on rue Mouffetard, at #34 (*menus*-€17–26, closed Tue).

$ **Le Bistro des Cigales,** between the Panthéon and place de la Contrescarpe, offers an escape to Provence, with deep yellow-and-blue decor and a purely Provençal *menu,* helpful staff, and air-conditioned rooms (*menus*-€17–24, daily, 12 rue Thouin, tel. 01 40 46 03 76).

$ **Gaudeamus,** with a low-profile café on one side and a pleasant bistro on the other, has friendly owners and cheap, €15 *menus* with good vegetarian options (daily, behind the Panthéon, 47 rue de la Montagne Ste. Geneviève, tel. 01 40 46 93 40).

$ **L'Ecurie** is for those who prefer ambience and setting over top cuisine. They serve inexpensive, acceptable meals on small, wood tables around a zinc bar in an unpretentious atmosphere with a few outdoor tables (*menus* from €16, daily, 58 rue de la Montagne Ste. Geneviève, tel. 01 46 33 68 49).

$ **Le Jardin des Pâtes** is popular with less strict vegetarians, serving pastas and salads at fair prices (daily, near Jardin des Plantes, 4 rue Lacépède, tel. 01 43 31 50 71).

$ **Café le Mouffetard** is in the thick of the street-market hustle and bustle (daily, at corner of rue Mouffetard and rue de l'Arbalète).

$ At **Cave de la Bourgogne,** the outdoor tables are picture-perfect (at the bottom of rue Mouffetard on rue de Bazeilles).

$ **Café de la Mosque** makes you feel like you've been beamed to Morocco. At this purely Arab café, order a mint tea, pour in the sugar, and enjoy the authentic interior and peaceful outdoor terrace (behind mosque, 2 rue Daubenton).

Eating in Montmartre

Montmartre is extremely touristy, with many mindless mobs following guides to cancan shows. But the ambience is undeniable, and an evening up here overlooking Paris is a quintessential experience in the City of Light. Along the touristy main drag and just off it, several fun piano bars serve reasonable crêpes with great people-watching.

$$ **Restaurant Chez Plumeau,** just off the jam-packed place du Tertre, is a touristy yet cheery, reasonably priced place with great seating on a tiny characteristic square (*menu*–€25, daily, place du Calvaire, tel. 01 46 06 26 29).

$ **L'Eté en Pente Douce,** away from the crowds on a classic neighborhood corner, offers fine indoor and outdoor seating, €10 *plats du jour* and salads, veggie options, and good wines (daily, 23 rue Muller, hike from Sacré-Cœur basilica away from tourist zone and down the stairs, tel. 01 42 64 02 67).

Eating in Versailles

In the pleasant town center, around place du Marché Notre-Dame, you'll find a variety of reasonable restaurants, cafés, and a few cobbled lanes (market days Sun, Tue, and Fri until 13:00; see map on page 256). The square is a 15-minute walk from the château (veer left when you leave château). From the place du Marché Notre-Dame, consider shortcutting to Versailles' gardens by walking 10 minutes west down rue de la Paroisse. The château will be to your left after entering, the main gardens, Trianon palaces, and Hameau straight ahead. The quickest way to the château's front door is along avenue de St. Cloud and rue Colbert.

These places are on or near place du Marché Notre-Dame, and all are good for lunch or dinner. **La Bœuf à la Mode** is a bistro with traditional cuisine right on the square (*menu*–€25, daily, 4 rue au Pain, tel. 01 39 50 31 99). **Fenêtres sur Cour** is the romantic's choice, where you dine in a glass gazebo surrounded by antique shops, just below the square in the "antique village," on place de la Geôle (closed all day Mon and Tue–Wed eves, tel. 01 39 51 97 77). **À la Côte Bretonne** is the place to go for crêpes in a cozy setting (daily, a few steps off the square on traffic-free rue des Deux Ponts, at #12).

Rue Satory is a pedestrian-friendly street lined with restaurants, on the south side of the château near Hôtel d'Angleterre (10-min walk, angle right out of the château). **Le Limousin** is a warm, traditional restaurant on the corner nearest the château, with mostly meat dishes (allow €35 with wine, daily, lamb is a specialty, 4 rue de Satory, tel. 01 39 50 21 50).

TRANSPORTATION CONNECTIONS

Paris is Europe's rail hub, with six major train stations, each serving different regions: Gare de l'Est (eastbound trains), Gare du Nord (northern France and Europe), Gare St. Lazare (northwestern France), Gare d'Austerlitz (southwestern France and Europe), Gare de Lyon (southeastern France and Italy), and Gare Montparnasse (northwestern France and TGV service to France's southwest). Any train station can give you schedule information, make reservations, and sell tickets for any destination. Buying tickets is handier from an SNCF neighborhood office (e.g., Louvre, Invalides, Orsay, Versailles, airports) or at your neighborhood travel agency—worth the small fee (SNCF signs in their window indicate they sell train tickets). For schedule information, call 08 36 35 35 35 (€0.50/min, English sometimes available).

All six train stations have Métro, bus, and taxi service. All have banks or change offices, ATMs, information desks, telephones, cafés, baggage storage (*consigne automatique,* none at Gare St. Lazare), newsstands, and clever pickpockets. Each station offers two types of rail service: long distance to other cities, called *Grandes Lignes* (major lines); and suburban service to outlying areas, called *banlieue* or RER. Both *banlieue* and RER trains serve outlying areas and the airports; the only difference is that *banlieue* lines are operated by SNCF (France's train system) and RER lines are operated by RATP (Paris' Métro and bus system). Paris train stations can be intimidating, but if you slow down, take a deep breath, and ask for help, you'll find them manageable and efficient. Bring a pad of paper for clear communication at ticket/info windows. All stations have helpful *accueil* (information) booths; the bigger stations have roving helpers, usually in red vests.

Station Overview

Here's an overview of Paris' major train stations. Métro, RER, buses, and taxis are well-signposted at every station. When arriving by Métro, follow signs for *Grandes Lignes*-SNCF to find the main tracks.

Gare du Nord: This vast station serves cities in northern France and international destinations north of Paris, including Copenhagen, Amsterdam (see "To Brussels and Amsterdam by Thalys Train," below), and the Eurostar to London as well as two of the day trips described in this book (Auvers-sur-Oise and Chantilly).

Arrive early to allow time to navigate this station. From the Métro, follow *Grandes Lignes* signs (main lines) and keep going up until you reach the tracks at street level. *Grandes Lignes* depart from tracks 3–21, suburban *(banlieue)* lines from tracks 30–36, and RER trains depart from tracks 37–44 (tracks 41–44 are one floor below). Glass train information booths *(accueil)* are scattered throughout the station and information staff circulate to help (all rail staff are required to speak English).

The tourist information kiosk opposite track 16 is a hotel reservation service for Accor chain hotels (they also have free Paris maps). Information booths for the **Thalys** (high-speed trains to Brussels and Amsterdam) are opposite track 8. All non-Eurostar ticket sales are opposite tracks 3–8. Passengers departing on **Eurostar** (London via Chunnel) must buy tickets and check in on the second level, opposite track 6. (Note: Britain's time zone is one hour earlier; times listed on Eurostar tickets are local times.) Monet-esque views over the trains and peaceful, air-conditioned cafés hide on the upper level, past the Eurostar ticket windows. Lockers, baggage check, taxis, and rental cars are at the far end, opposite track 3 and down the steps.

Key destinations served by Gare du Nord *Grandes Lignes*: **Brussels** (12/day, 1.5 hrs, see "To Brussels and Amsterdam by Thalys Train," below), **Bruges** (18/day, 2 hrs, change in Brussels, one direct), **Amsterdam** (10/day, 4 hrs; see "To Brussels and Amsterdam by Thalys Train," below), **Copenhagen** (1/day, 16 hrs, two night trains), **Koblenz** (6/day, 5 hrs, change in Köln), **London** Eurostar via Chunnel (17/day, 3 hrs, tel. 08 36 35 35 39.

By *banlieue*/**RER lines**: **Chantilly-Gouvieux** (hrly, fewer on weekends, 35 min), **Charles de Gaulle Airport** (2/hr, 30 min, runs 5:30–23:00, track 4), **Auvers-sur-Oise** (2/hr, 1 hr, transfer at Pontoise).

Gare Montparnasse: This big and modern station covers three floors, serves lower Normandy and Brittany, and offers TGV service to the Loire Valley and southwestern France, as well as suburban service to Chartres. At street level, you'll find a bank, *banlieue* trains (serving Chartres; you can also reach the *banlieue* trains from the second level), and ticket windows in the center, just past the escalators. Lockers *(consigne automatique)* are on the mezzanine level between levels 1 and 2. Most services are provided on the second level, where the *Grandes Lignes* arrive and depart (ticket windows to the far left with your back to glass exterior). *Banlieue* trains depart from *Grandes Lignes* tracks 10 through 19. The main rail information office is opposite track 15. Taxis are to the far left as you leave the tracks.

Key destinations served by Gare Montparnasse: Chartres (20/day, 1 hr, *banlieue* lines), **Pontorson-Mont St. Michel** (5/day, 4.5 hrs, via Rennes, then take bus; or take train to Pontorson via Caen, then bus from Pontorson), **Dinan** (7/day, 4 hrs, change in Rennes and Dol), **Bordeaux** (14/day, 3.5 hrs), **Sarlat** (5/day, 6 hrs, change in Bordeaux, Libourne, or Souillac), **Toulouse** (11/day, 5 hrs, most require change, usually in Bordeaux), **Albi** (7/day, 6–7.5 hrs, change in Toulouse, also night train), **Carcassonne** (8/day, 6.5 hrs, most require changes in Toulouse and Bordeaux, direct trains take 10 hrs), **Tours** (14/day, 1 hr).

Gare de Lyon: This huge and bewildering station offers TGV and regular service to southeastern France, Italy, and other international destinations (for more trains to Italy, see "Gare de Bercy," below). Frequent *banlieue* trains serve Melun (near Vaux-le-Vicomte) and Fontainebleau (some depart from the main *Grandes Lignes* level, more frequent departures are from one level down, follow RER-D signs, and ask at any *accueil* or ticket window where the next departure leaves from). Don't leave this station without checking out Le Train Bleu Restaurant, up the stairs opposite track G (€45 menu, open daily, up the stairs opposite track L, tel. 01 43 43 09 06, www.le-train-bleu.com).

Grande Ligne trains arrive and depart from one level but are divided into two areas (tracks A-N and 5-23). They are connected by the long platform along tracks A and 5, and by the hallway adjacent to track A and opposite track 9. This hallway has all the services, ticket windows, ticket information, banks, shops, and access to car rental. *Banlieue* ticket windows are just inside the hall adjacent to track A *(billets Ile de France)*. *Grandes Lignes* and *banlieue* lines share the same tracks. A helpful tourist office (Mon–Sat 8:00–20:00, closed Sun) and a train information office are both opposite track L. From the RER or Métro, follow signs for *Grandes Lignes Arrivées* and take the escalator up to reach the platforms. Train information booths *(accueil)* are opposite tracks G and 11. Baggage check is down the stairs opposite track 13. Taxi stands are in front of the station and one floor below.

Key destinations served by Gare de Lyon: Vaux-le-Vicomte (train to Melun, hrly, 30 min), **Fontainebleau** (nearly hrly, 45 min), **Beaune** (12/day, 2.5 hrs, most require change in Dijon), **Dijon** (15/day, 1.5 hrs), **Chamonix** (9/day, 9 hrs, change in Lyon and St. Gervais, direct night train), **Annecy** (8/day, 4–7 hrs), **Lyon** (16/day, 2.5 hrs), **Avignon** (9/day in 2.5 hrs, 6/day in four hours with change), **Arles** (14/day, 5 hrs, most with change in Marseille, Avignon, or Nîmes), **Nice** (14/day, 5.5–7 hrs, many with change in Marseille), **Venice** (3/day, 3/night, 11–15 hrs, most require changes), **Rome** (2/day, 5/night, 15–18 hrs, most require changes), **Bern** (9/day, 5–11 hrs, most require changes, night train).

Gare de Bercy: This smaller station handles some night train service to Italy during renovation work at the Gare de Lyon (Mo: Bercy, one stop east of Gare de Lyon on line 14).

Gare de l'Est: This single-floor station (with underground Métro) serves eastern France and European points east of Paris. Train information booths are at tracks 1, 18 and 26; ticket windows are in the big hall opposite track 8; luggage storage is through the hall opposite track 12.

Key destinations served by Gare de l'Est: Colmar (12/day, 5.5 hrs, change in Strasbourg, Dijon, or Mulhouse), **Strasbourg** (14/day, 4.5 hrs, many require changes), **Reims** (12/day, 1.5 hrs), **Verdun** (5/day, 3 hrs, change in Metz or Chalon), **Munich** (5/day, 9 hrs, some require changes, night train), **Vienna** (7/day, 13–18 hrs, most require changes, night train), **Zürich** (10/day, 7 hrs, most require changes, night train), **Prague** (2/day, 14 hrs, night train).

Gare St. Lazare: This relatively small station serves upper Normandy, including Rouen and Giverny. All trains arrive and depart one floor above street level. Follow signs to Grandes Lignes from the Métro to reach the tracks. Ticket windows are in the first hall on the second floor. Grandes Lignes (main lines) depart from tracks 17–27; banlieue (suburban) trains depart from 1–16. The train information office (accueil) is opposite track 15. There's a post office along track 27, and WCs are opposite track 19. There is no baggage check.

Key destinations served by Gare St. Lazare: **Giverny** (train to Vernon, 5/day, 45 min; then bus or taxi 10 min to Giverny), **Rouen** (15/day, 75 min), **Honfleur** (6/day, 3 hrs, via Lisieux, then bus), **Bayeux** (9/day, 2.5 hrs, some with change in Caen), **Caen** (12/day, 2 hrs).

Gare d'Austerlitz: This small station provides non-TGV service to the Loire Valley, southwestern France, and Spain. All tracks are at street level. The information booth is opposite track 17, and all ticket sales are in the hall opposite track 10. Baggage consignment (if open) and car rental are near porte 27 (along the side, opposite track 21).

Key destinations served by Gare d'Austerlitz: **Amboise** (8/day in 2 hrs, 12/day in 1.5 hrs with change in St. Pierre-des-Corps), **Cahors** (7/day, 5–7 hrs, most with changes), **Barcelona** (1/day, 9 hrs, change in Montpellier, night trains), **Madrid** (two night trains only, 13–16 hrs), **Lisbon** (1/day, 24 hrs).

Buses
The main bus station is the Gare Routière du Paris-Gallieni (28 avenue du Général de Gaulle, in suburb of Bagnolet, Mo: Gallieni, tel. 01 49 72 51 51). Buses provide cheaper—if less comfortable and more time-consuming—transportation to major European cities. Eurolines' buses depart from here (tel. 08 36 69 52 52, www.eurolines.com). Eurolines has a couple of neighborhood offices: in the Latin Quarter (55 rue St. Jacques, tel. 01 43 54 11 99) and in Versailles (4 avenue des Sceaux, tel. 01 39 02 03 73).

Airports
Charles de Gaulle Airport
Paris' primary airport has two main terminals, T-1 and T-2, and two lesser terminals, T-3 and T-9. British Airways, SAS, United, US Airways, KLM, Northwest, and Lufthansa all normally use T-1. Air

France dominates T-2, though you'll also find Delta, Continental, American, and Air Canada. Smaller airlines use T-3 and charter flights leave from T-9. Airlines sometimes switch terminals, so verify your terminal before flying. Terminals are connected every few minutes by a free *navette* (shuttle bus, line #1). The RER (Paris subway) stops at T-2 and T-3 terminals, and the TGV (stands for *train à grande vitesse;* tay-zhay-vay) station is at T-2. There is no bag storage at the airport. Beware of pickpockets on *navettes* between terminals and (worse) on RER trains. Do not take an unauthorized taxi from the men greeting you on arrival (official taxi stands are well signed).

Those flying to or from the United States will almost certainly use T-1 or T-2. Below is information for each terminal. For flight information, call 01 48 62 22 80.

TERMINAL 1 (T-1): This circular terminal covers three floors—arrival (*arrivées*, top floor), departure (*départs*, one floor down) and shops/boutiques (basement level). For information on getting to Paris, see "Transportation between Charles de Gaulle Airport and Paris," below.

On the **arrival** level you'll find a variety of services at these gates.

Gate 36 (called *Meeting Point*): ADP, a quasi–tourist office, sells museum passes, offers free maps, and provides tourist/hotel information (daily 7:00–22:00). A nearby *Relay* store sells phone cards. To find the shuttle buses *(navettes)* for Terminal 2 and the RER trains to Paris, take the elevator down to level *(niveau)* 2, then walk outside (line #1 serves T-2 including the TGV station; line #2 goes directly to the RER station).

Gate 34: Outside are Air France buses to Paris and Orly Airport.

Gate 32: ATMs. Outside are Roissy Buses to Paris (buy tickets inside at gate 30 or from driver) and Disneyland Express buses.

Gate 22: SNCF train ticket office.

Gate 20: Taxis outside.

Gate 16: A bank with lousy rates for currency exchange.

Gates 10-24: Car-rental offices.

The **departure level** (*niveau* 3) is limited to flight check-in, though you will find ADP information desks here. Those departing from T-1 will find restaurants, a PTT (post office), a pharmacy, boutiques, and a handy grocery store one floor below the ticketing desks (level 2 on the elevator).

TERMINAL 2 (T-2): This long, horseshoe-shaped terminal is divided into several sub-terminals (or Halls), each identified by a letter. Halls are connected with each other, the RER, the TGV station, and T-1 every five minutes with free *navettes* (shuttle buses, line #1 runs to T-1). Here is where you should find these key carriers: in Hall A—Air France, Air Canada, and American Airlines; in Hall C—Delta, Continental, and more Air France. The RER and TGV stations are below the Sheraton Hotel (access by *navettes* or on foot). Stops for *navettes,* Air France buses, and Roissy Buses are all well-marked and near each Hall (see "Transportation between Charles de Gaulle Airport and Paris," below). ADP information desks are located near gate 5 in each Hall. Car-rental offices, post offices, pharmacies, and ATMs *(point d'argent)* are also well-signed.

Transportation between Charles de Gaulle Airport and Paris: Three efficient public-transportation routes, taxis, and airport shuttle vans link the airport's terminals with central Paris. All are well-marked and stops are centrally located at all terminals. (If you're carrying lots of baggage or just plain tired, airport shuttle vans or taxis are well worth the extra cost). The Roissy bus and Métro combination is the most convenient public transport route to rue Cler area hotels; the Air France bus to Gare de Lyon (then Métro line 1) is the easier route to hotels in the Marais (both described below).

RER trains, with stops near T-1 and at T-2 (€8), run every 15 minutes and stop at Gare du Nord, Châtelet-Les Halles, St. Michel, and Luxembourg in central Paris. When coming from Paris to the airport, T-1 is the first RER stop at Charles de Gaulle; T-2 is the second stop. Beware of pickpockets preying on jet-lagged tourists on these trains; wear your moneybelt. The other transportation options described below have far fewer theft problems.

Roissy Buses run every 15 minutes to Paris' Opéra Garnier (€8, 40-60 min). You'll arrive (and also depart) from a bus stop on rue Scribe at the American Express office on the left side of the Opéra. To reach rue Cler and Marais hotels, turn left out of the bus and find the Métro entrance in front of the Opéra. Take the Métro (direction Balard) to Ecole Militaire or La Tour Maubourg.

Air France bus routes serve central Paris about every 15 minutes (Arc de Triomphe and Porte Maillot-€10, 40 min; Montparnasse Tower/train station-€11.50, 60 min; or the Gare de Lyon station-€11.50, 40 min). To reach Marais hotels from Gare de Lyon, take Métro line 1 (direction La Défense) to the Bastille, St. Paul, or Hôtel de Ville stops.

Taxis with luggage will run €40–55 with bags. If taking a cab to the airport, ask your hotel to call for you (the night before if you must leave early) and specify that you want a real taxi *(un taxi normal)* and not an illegal limo-service that costs €30 more.

Airport shuttles offer a less stressful trip between either of Paris' airports and downtown, ideal for single travelers or families of four or more (taxis are limited to three). Reserve from home and they'll meet you at the airport (€23 for one person, €27 for two people, €41 for three people, €55 for four people, plan on a 30-min wait if you ask them to pick you up at the airport). Be clear on where and how you are to meet your driver. Choose between **Airport Connection** (tel. 01 44 18 36 02, fax 01 45 55 85 19, www.airport-connection.com) and **Paris Airports Service** (tel. 01 55 98 10 80, fax 01 55 98 10 89, www.parisairportservice.com).

Sleeping at or near Charles de Gaulle Airport: Hôtel Ibis**, outside the RER Roissy Rail station at T-3 (the first RER stop coming from Paris), offers standard and predictable accommodations (Db-€90, near *navette* stop, free shuttle bus to all terminals, tel. 01 49 19 19 19, fax 01 49 19 19 21, h1404sb@accor-hotels.com). **Novotel***** is next door and the next step up (Db-€155–170, tel. 01 49 19 27 27, fax 01 49 19 27 99, h1014@accor-hotels.com).

To avoid rush-hour traffic, drivers may consider sleeping in the pleasant medieval town of **Senlis** (15 min north of airport) at **Hostellerie de la Porte Bellon** (Db-€55-75, in the center at 51 rue Bellon, near rue de la République, tel. 03 44 53 03 05, fax 03 44 53 29 94).

Orly Airport

This airport feels small. Orly has two terminals: Sud and Ouest. International flights arrive at Sud. After exiting Sud's baggage claim (near gate H), you'll see signs directing you to city transportation, car rental, and so on. Turn left to enter the main terminal area, and you'll find exchange offices with bad rates, an ATM, the ADP (a quasi–tourist office that offers free city maps and basic sightseeing information, open until 23:00), and an SNCF French rail desk (closes at 18:00, sells train tickets and even Eurailpasses, next to ADP). Downstairs is a sandwich bar, WCs, a bank (same bad rates), a newsstand (buy a phone card), and a post office (great rates for cash or American Express traveler's checks). Car-rental offices are located in the parking lot in front of the terminal. For flight info on any airline serving Orly, call 01 49 75 15 15.

Transportation between Orly Airport and Paris: Several efficient public-transportation routes, taxis, and a couple of airport shuttle services link Orly with central Paris. The gate locations listed below apply to Orly Sud, but the same transportation services are available from both terminals.

The **Air France bus** (outside gate K) runs to Paris' Invalides Métro stop (€8, 4/hr, 30 min) and is handy for those staying in or near the rue Cler neighborhood (from Invalides bus stop, take the Métro two stops to Ecole Militaire to reach recommended hotels, see also RER Trains below).

Bus #285 (also called Jetbus, outside gate H, €5, 4/hr) is the quickest way to the Paris subway and the best way to the Marais and Contrescarpe neighborhoods. Take Jetbus to Villejuif Métro stop, buy a *carnet* of 10 Métro tickets, then take the Métro to the Sully-Morland stop for the Marais area, or the Censier-Daubenton or Monge stops for the Contrescarpe area. If you're going to the airport, make sure your train serves Villejuif, as the route splits at the end of the line. The **Orlybus** (outside gate H, €6, 4/hr) takes you to the Denfert-Rochereau RER-B line and the Métro, offering subway access to central Paris.

These routes provide access to Paris via **RER trains:** an ADP shuttle bus takes you to RER line C, with connections to Gare d'Austerlitz, St. Michel, Musée d'Orsay, Invalides, and Pont de l'Alma stations (outside gate G, 4/hr, €5.50). The **Orlyval trains** are overpriced (€9) and require a transfer at the Antony stop to reach RER line B (serving Luxembourg, Châtelet-Les Halles, St. Michel, and Gare du Nord stations in central Paris).

Taxis are to the far right as you leave the terminal, at gate M. Allow €26–35 with bags for a taxi into central Paris.

Airport shuttle minivans are ideal for single travelers or families of four or more (see "Charles de Gaulle Airport," above, for the companies to contact; from Orly, figure about €18 for one person, €12/person for two people, less for larger groups and kids).

Sleeping near Orly Airport: Hôtel Ibis** is reasonable, basic, and close by (Db-€60, tel. 01 56 70 50 60, fax 01 56 70 50 70, h1413@accor-hotels.com). **Hôtel Mercure***** provides more comfort for a price (Db-€120–135, tel. 01 49 75 15 50, fax 01 49 75 15 51, h1246@accor-hotels.com). Both have free shuttles to the terminal.

PROVENCE

This magnificent region is shaped like a giant wedge of quiche. From its sunburned crust, fanning out along the Mediterranean coast from Nîmes to Nice, it stretches north along the Rhône Valley to Orange. The Romans were here in force and left many ruins—some of the best anywhere. Seven popes; great artists, such as Vincent van Gogh, Paul Cézanne, and Pablo Picasso; and author Peter Mayle all enjoyed their years in Provence. The region offers a splendid recipe of arid climate (except for occasional vicious winds known as the mistral), captivating cities, exciting hill towns, dramatic scenery, and oceans of vineyards.For more indepth coverage, see *Rick Steves' Provence & the French Riviera*.

Explore the ghost town that is ancient Les Baux and see France's greatest Roman ruin, Pont du Gard. Spend your starry, starry nights where van Gogh did, in Arles. Uncover its Roman past, then find the linger-longer squares and café corners that inspired van Gogh. Youthful but classy Avignon bustles in the shadow of its brooding pope's palace.

Planning Your Time

Make Arles or Avignon your sightseeing base, particularly if you have no car. Arles has an undeniably scruffy quality and good-value hotels, while Avignon (three times larger than Arles) feels sophisticated and offers more nightlife and shopping. Italophiles prefer smaller Arles, while poodles pick urban Avignon.

You'll want a full day for sightseeing in Arles (best on Wed or Sat, when the morning market rages), a half-day for Avignon, and a day or two for the villages and sights in the countryside.

Getting around Provence

By Car: The yellow Michelin map of this region is essential for drivers. Avignon (population 100,000) is a headache for drivers; Arles (population 35,000) is easier, though it still requires go-cart driving skills. Park

Provence

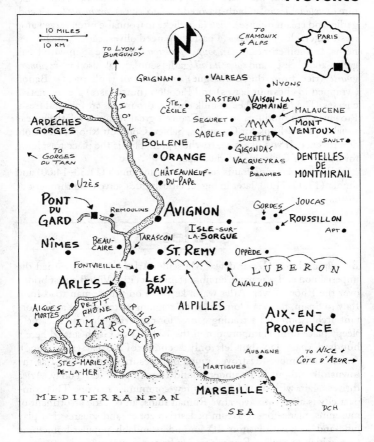

only in well-watched spaces and leave nothing in your car.

By Train or Bus: Frequent trains link Avignon and Arles (about 30 min between each). Les Baux is accessible by bus from Arles. Pont du Gard and St. Rémy—and to a lesser extent, Vaison-la-Romaine and some Côtes du Rhône villages. The TIs in Arles and Avignon have information on bus excursions to regional sights that are hard to reach *sans car* (half day-€20, full day-€36).

Cuisine Scene—Provence

The almost extravagant use of garlic, olive oil, herbs, and tomatoes makes Provence's cuisine France's liveliest. To sample it, order anything *à la provençale*. Among the area's spicy specialties are *ratatouille* (a thick mixture of vegetables in an herb-flavored tomato sauce), *brandade* (a salt cod, garlic, and cream mousse), *aioli* (a garlicky mayonnaise often served atop fresh vegetables), *tapenade* (a paste of pureed olives, capers, anchovies, herbs, and sometimes tuna), *soupe au pistou* (vegetable soup with basil, garlic, and cheese), and *soupe à l'ail* (garlic soup). Look also for *riz camarguaise* (rice from the Camargue) and *taureau* (bull meat). Banon (wrapped in chestnut leaves) and Picodon (nutty taste) are the native cheeses. The region's sheep's milk cheese, Brousse, is creamy and fresh. Provence also produces some of France's great wines at relatively reasonable prices. Look for Gigondas, Sablet, Côtes du Rhône, and Côte de Provence. If you like rosé, try the Tavel. This is the place to splurge for a bottle of Châteauneuf-du-Pape.

Remember, restaurants serve only during lunch (11:30–14:00) and dinner (19:00–21:00, later in bigger cities); cafés serve food throughout the day.

Arles

By helping Julius Caesar defeat Marseille, Arles (pron. arl) earned the imperial nod and was made an important port city. With the first bridge over the Rhône River, Arles was a key stop on the Roman road from Italy to Spain, the Via Domitia. After reigning as the seat of an important archbishop and a trading center for centuries, the city became a sleepy place of little importance in the 1700s. Van Gogh settled here a hundred years ago, but left only a chunk of his ear (now gone). American bombers destroyed much of Arles in World War II as the townsfolk hid out in its underground Roman galleries. Today, Arles thrives again with one of France's few communist mayors. This compact city is alive with evocative Roman ruins, an eclectic assortment of museums, made-for-ice-cream pedestrian zones, and squares that play hide-and-seek with visitors. It's an understandably popular home base from which to explore France's trendy Provence region.

ORIENTATION

Arles faces the Mediterranean and turns its back on Paris. Though on the Rhône River, the town completely ignores the river (the part of Arles most damaged by Allied bombers in World War II, and therefore the least charming today).

Landmarks hide in Arles' medieval tangle of narrow, winding streets. Everything is close—but first-time visitors can walk forever to get there. Hotels have good, free city maps, and Arles provides helpful street-corner signs that point you toward sights and hotels. Racing cars

LE MISTRAL

Provence lives with its vicious mistral winds, which blow 30 to 60 miles per hour, about 100 days out of the year. Locals say it blows in multiples of threes: three, six, or nine days in a row. *Le mistral* clears people off the streets and turns lively cities into virtual ghost towns. You'll likely spend a few hours taking refuge—or searching for cover.

When *le mistral* blows, it's everywhere, and you can't escape. Peter Mayle said it could blow the ears off a donkey. Locals say it ruins crops, shutters, and roofs (look for the stones holding tiles in place on many homes). They'll also tell you that this pernicious wind has driven many crazy (including young Vincent van Gogh). A weak version of the wind is called a *mistralet*.

The mistral starts above the Alps and Massif Central Mountains and gathers steam as it heads south, gaining momentum as it screams over the Rhône Valley (which acts like a funnel between the Alps and Pyrenees) before exhausting itself as it hits the Mediterranean. While this wind rattles shutters throughout the Riviera and Provence, it's strongest over the Rhône Valley...so Avignon, Arles, and the Côtes du Rhône villages bear its brunt. While wiping the dust from your eyes, remember the good news: The mistral brings clear skies.

enjoy Arles' medieval lanes, turning sidewalks into tightropes and pedestrians into leaping targets.

The elevated riverside walk provides a direct route to the excellent Ancient History Museum, an easy return to the train station, and fertile ground for dogs with poorly-trained owners.

The free "Starlette" minibus-shuttle circles the town's major sights every 15 minutes, but does not serve the Ancient History Museum, so it isn't very helpful (just wave at the driver and hop in; Mon–Sat 7:30–19:30, never on Sun). It does serve the train station, the only stop you pay for (€0.80). A tourist choo-choo takes tired visitors around town with a 30-minute English recorded spiel (€4, 2/hr, stops include train station, TI, and Ancient History Museum).

Tourist Information: The main TI is on the ring road, esplanade Charles de Gaulle (April–Sept daily 9:00–18:45, Oct–March Mon–Sat 9:00–17:45, Sun 10:30–14:30, tel. 04 90 18 41 20). There's also a TI at the train station (open year-round, Mon–Sat 9:00–13:00, closed Sun). Both charge €1 to reserve hotel rooms. Pick up the good city map, note the bus schedule to Les Baux and other destinations, and get English information on the Camargue wildlife area. Ask about bullfights and bus excursions to regional sights.

Arles

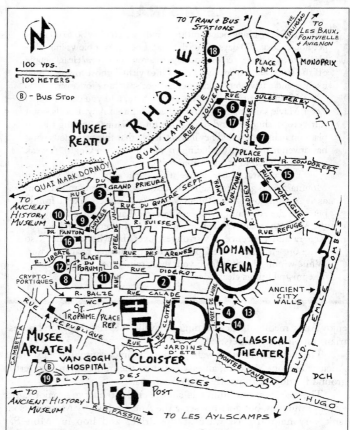

1. Hôtel d'Arlatan
2. Hôtel de l'Amphithéâtre
3. Hôtel du Musée
4. Hôtel Calendal
5. Hôtel Régence
6. Hôtel Acacias
7. Hôtel Voltaire & Hôtel le Rhone
8. Restaurant l'Estaminet
9. Restaurant la Vitamine
10. Restaurant Au Bryn du Thym
11. Restaurant la Boeheme
12. Restaurant le 6
13. Restaurant le Pistou
14. Restaurant Lou Caleu
15. Restaurant la Giraudière
16. Soleilei's Ice Cream
17. Launderettes (2 locations)
18. "Starry Night" view
19. Bus stop for Les Baux (also stops at station)

Arrival in Arles

By Train and Bus: The stations are next to each other on the river, a 10-minute walk from the center (baggage storage not available). Get what you need at the train station TI before leaving (see above). To reach the old town, turn left out of the station or take bus #1 (€0.80, 2/hr, buy ticket from driver). Taxis generally do not wait at the station, but you can summon one by calling 04 90 96 90 03 (allow €8-10 to any hotel I list).

By Car: Follow signs to *Centre-ville*, then follow signs toward *Gare SNCF* (train station). You'll come to a huge roundabout (place Lamartine) with a Monoprix department store to the right. Park along the city wall or in nearby lots; pay attention to No Parking signs on Wednesday and Saturday until 13:00 (violators will be cleared out to make way for Arles' huge outdoor produce markets). Some hotels have limited parking. Theft is a big problem; leave nothing in your car. From place Lamartine, walk into the city between the two stumpy towers.

Helpful Hints

Laundry: A launderette is at 12 rue Portagnel; another is nearby at 6 rue Cavalerie, near place Voltaire (both daily 7:00–21:00, later once you're in, English instructions).

Public Pools: Arles has three public pools (indoor and outdoor). Ask at the TI or your hotel.

Taxis: Arles' taxis charge a minimum fee of about €8. Nothing in town is worth a taxi ride (figure €40-45 to Les Baux or St. Rémy, tel. 04 90 96 90 03).

Bike Rental: Try the Peugeot store (15 rue du Pont, tel. 04 90 96 03 77). While Vaison-la-Romaine and Isle-sur-la-Sorgue make better biking bases, rides to Les Baux (very steep climb) or into the Camargue work from Arles, provided you're in great shape (forget it in the wind).

Car Rental: Avis is at the train station (tel. 04 90 96 82 42), Europcar is downtown (2 bis avenue Victor Hugo, tel. 04 90 93 23 24), and National is just off place Lamartine toward the station (4 avenue Paulin Talabot, tel. 04 90 93 02 17).

Local Guide: Jacqueline Neujean, an excellent guide, knows Arles like the back of her hand (€90/2 hrs, tel. 04 90 98 47 51).

SIGHTS

The worthwhile **monument pass** *(le pass monuments)* covers Arles' many sights and is valid for one week (€12, €10 under 18, sold at each sight). Otherwise, it's €3–4 per sight and €5 for the Ancient History Museum. While any sight is worth a few minutes, many aren't worth the individual admission. Many sights begin closing rooms 30 minutes early. Start at the Ancient History Museum for a helpful overview, then dive into the sights (ideally in the order described below).

▲▲▲**Ancient History Museum (Musée de l'Arles Antique)**—Begin your town visit here—it's Roman Arles 101. Models and original sculptures (with the meager help of the English flier) re-create the Roman city, making workaday life and culture easier to imagine.

You're greeted by an impressive row of pagan and early-Christian sarcophagi (second through fifth centuries). These would have lined the Via Aurelia outside the town wall. Pagan sarcophagi show simple slice-of-Roman-life scenes, while the Christian ones feature Bible stories. In the early days of the Church, Jesus was often portrayed beardless and as the good shepherd—with a lamb over his shoulder.

The city model helps you visualize Roman Arles, complete with wall, pontoon bridge (over the widest and therefore slowest part of the river), theater, amphitheater, and chariot racecourse (where you are now). Models of Arles' Arena even illustrate the moveable stadium cover, good for shade and rain. While virtually nothing is left of Arles' chariot racecourse (a.k.a. circus), the model shows that it must have rivaled Rome's Circus Maximus. Looking at the model, one see clearly that an emphasis on sports—with huge stadiums at the edge of town—is not unique to modern America.

Other models bring each of Arles' famous Roman buildings to life. All of the statues are original, except for the greatest—the Venus of Arles—who Louis XIV took a liking to and had moved to Versailles. It's now in the Louvre (and, as locals say, "When it's in Paris...bye-bye"). Jewelry, fine metal and glass artifacts, and well-crafted mosaic floors make it clear that Roman Arles was a city of art and culture.

Built at the site of the chariot racecourse (the arc of which is built into the parking lot), this air-conditioned, all-on-one-floor museum is a 20-minute walk from Arles along the river (€5, March–Oct daily 9:00–19:00, Nov–Feb daily 10:00–17:00, tel. 04 90 18 88 88, www.arles-antique.org). By foot from the center, turn left at the river and take the riverside path to the big modern building just past the new bridge. Or take bus #1 from boulevard des Lices and the TI (€0.80, pay driver, no buses Sun).

▲▲**Forum Square (Place du Forum)**—Named for the Roman forum that once stood here, this square was the political and religious center of Roman Arles. Still lively, this café-crammed square is popular for a *pastis* (see "Eating," below). The bistros on the square, while no place for a fine dinner, can put together a good salad—and when you sprinkle in the ambience, that's €10 well spent.

At the corner of Grand Hôtel Nord-Pinus, a plaque shows how the Romans built a foundation of galleries to make the main square level. The two columns are all that survive of a temple. Steps leading to the entrance are buried (the Roman street level was about 20 feet below you).

The statue on the square is of Frédéric Mistral. This popular poet, who wrote in the local dialect rather than French, was a champion of Provençal culture. After receiving the Nobel Prize for literature in 1904, he used his prize money to preserve and display the folk identity of Provence. He founded the Arlaten folk museum at a time when France was rapidly centralizing. (The famous local mistral wind—literally "master"—has nothing to do with his name.)

The bright-yellow café is famous as the subject of one of Vincent van Gogh's first works in Arles. While his painting showed the café in a brilliant yellow from the glow of gas lamps, the facade was bare limestone, just like the other cafés on this square. The café's current owners have painted it to match van Gogh's version...and cash in on the Vincent-crazed hordes who pay too much to eat or drink here.

Cryptoportiques du Forum—The only Baroque church in Arles (admire the wood ceiling) provides a dramatic entry to this underground system of arches and vaults that supported the southern end of the Roman Forum (and hid resistance fighters during World War II). The galleries of arches demonstrate the extent to which Roman engineers would go to follow standard city plans: If the land doesn't suit the blueprint, change the land. While remarkable, there's not much to it beyond the initial "Oh, wow!" (€3.50, May–Sept daily 9:00–11:30 & 14:00–18:30, April and Oct daily 9:00–11:30 & 14:00–17:30, Nov–March daily 10:00–11:30 & 14:00–16:30; leave place du Forum with Grand Hôtel Nord-Pinus on your right and turn right on rue Balze).

▲▲St. Trophime Church, Cloisters, and Place de la République—This church, named after a third-century bishop of Arles and located on a fun-loving square, sports the finest Romanesque main entrance (west portal) I've seen anywhere. Get a good view of it from...

Place de la République: This square used to be called "place Royale"... until the French Revolution. The obelisk was the centerpiece of Arles' Roman Circus. The playful lions at its base are the symbol of the city, whose slogan is "far from the anger of the lion." This is a popular gathering place for young Arlesians at night. Sit on the steps opposite the church and watch the peasants—pilgrims, locals, and street musicians. There's nothing new about this scene.

Tympanum (on church facade): Like a Roman triumphal arch, the church trumpets the promise of Judgment Day. The tympanum (the semicircular area above the door) is filled with Christian symbolism. Christ sits in majesty, surrounded by symbols of the four evangelists: Matthew—the winged man, Mark—the winged lion, Luke—the ox, and John—the eagle. The 12 apostles are lined up below Jesus. It's Judgment Day...some are saved and others aren't. Notice the condemned (on the right)—a chain gang doing a sad bunny-hop over the fires of hell. For them, the tune trumpeted by the three angels at the very top is not a happy one. Below the chain gang, St. Stephen is being stoned to death, with his soul leaving through his mouth and instantly being welcomed by angels. Ride the exquisite detail back to a simpler age. In an illiterate medieval world, long before the vivid images of our Technicolor time, this was a neon billboard over the town square. (A chart just inside the church—on the right—helps explain the carvings.)

Inside St. Trophime: The tall, 12th-century Romanesque nave is decorated by a set of tapestries showing scenes from the life of Mary (17th-century, from French town of Aubusson). Immediately to the left of entry, a chapel is built on an early-Christian sarcophagus from Roman Arles (from around A.D. 300). On its right side, the three Magi give gifts to baby Jesus, and a frieze below shows the flight to Egypt. Farther down the ambulatory, another Roman sarcophagus shows Jews hopping over the Red Sea as they leave Egypt. Amble around the Gothic apse and check out the relic chapel. This church is a stop on the ancient pilgrimage route to Santiago de Compostela in northwest Spain. For 800 years, pilgrims on their way to Santiago have paused here. Even today, modern pilgrim trips are advertised near the church's entry (church entry free, May–Sept daily 9:00–18:30, March-April and Oct daily 9:00–17:30, Nov–Feb daily 10:00–16:30).

The adjacent **cloisters** are the best in Provence (enter from square, 65 feet to right of church). Enjoy the sculpted capitals of the rounded 12th-century Romanesque columns and the pointed 14th-century Gothic columns. The second floor offers only a view of the cloisters from above (€4, same hours as church).

To get to the next sight, the Classical Theater, face the church, walk left, then take the first right on rue de la Calade.

Classical Theater (Théâtre Antique)—Precious little survives from this Roman theater, which served as a handy town quarry throughout the Middle Ages. Walk to a center aisle and pull up a stone seat. Built in the first century B.C., this theater seated 10,000. To appreciate its original size, look to the upper left side of the tower and find the protrusion that supported the highest of three seating levels. Today, 3,000 can attend events in this restored facility. Two lonely Corinthian columns look out from the stage over the audience. The orchestra section is defined by a semicircular pattern in the stone. Stepping up onto the left side of the stage, look down to the narrow channel that allowed the curtain to disappear below. Take a stroll backstage through broken bits of Rome, and loop back to the entry behind the grass (€3, you can see much of the theater by peeking through the fence for free, May–Sept daily 9:00–11:30 & 14:00–18:30, April and Oct daily 9:00–11:30 & 14:00–17:30, Nov–March daily 10:00–11:30 & 14:00–16:30). For more on Roman theaters, see "Orange," below. A block uphill is the...

▲▲▲**Roman Arena (Amphithéâtre)**—Nearly 2,000 years ago, gladiators fought wild animals here to the delight of 20,000 screaming fans. Today, local daredevils fight wild bulls. In Roman times, games were free (sponsored by city bigwigs) and fans were seated by social class. The many exits allowed for rapid dispersal after the games—fights would break out among frenzied fans if they couldn't exit quickly. Through medieval times and until the early 1800s, the arches were bricked up and the stadium became a fortified town—with 200 humble homes crammed within its circular defenses. Three of the medieval towers survive (the one above the ticket booth is open and rewards those who climb it with a good view). To see two still-sealed arches, complete with cute medieval window frames, turn right as you leave, walk to the Andaluz restaurant, and look back (€4, May–Sept daily 9:00–18:30, March-April and Oct daily 9:00–17:30, and Nov–Feb daily 10:00–16:30). Bullfight posters around the Arena advertise upcoming spectacles.

Turn left out of the Arena and find the...

▲▲**Fondation Van Gogh**—Refreshing to any art-lover and especially interesting to van Gogh fans, this small gallery features works by major contemporary artists paying homage to Vincent through their thought-provoking interpretations of his works. Many pieces are explained in English by the artists. The black-and-white photographs (both art and shots of places Vincent painted) complements the paintings (€7, not covered by monument pass, great collection of van Gogh prints and postcards for sale in free entry area, April–mid-Oct daily 10:00–19:00, mid-Oct–March Tue–Sun 9:30–12:00 & 14:00–17:30, closed Mon, facing Roman Arena at 24 bis rond-point des Arènes).

▲**Musée Arlaten**—Built on the remains of the Roman forum (see the courtyard), this museum houses the treasures of daily Provençal life. It was given to Arles by Nobel Prize winner Frédéric Mistral (see "Forum Square," above). Mistral's vision was to give locals an appreciation of their cultural roots, presented in tableaux that illiterates could understand—"a veritable poem for the ordinary people who cannot read." Even though there are no English descriptions, the museum offers a unique and intimate look at local folk culture from the 18th and 19th centuries.

A one-way course takes you through 30 rooms. The first rooms display folk costumes presented chronologically until about 1900, when the traditional Provençal dress was replaced by the modern nondescript norm. You'll then see fine freestanding wedding armoires (given to brides by parents and filled with the essentials to begin a new home). Finely crafted wooden cages—called *Panetière*—hung from the walls and kept bread away from the mice. *Santons* were popular figurines giving manger scenes a Provençal flavor. The second floor shows local history and a large room covering lifestyles of the marshy Camargue. A fascinating case shows antique *Coursa Provanciale* bullfighting memorabilia, including a champion bull named Lion, who died of old age.

The last two rooms are the collection's pride and joy. In one, a rich mom is shown with her newborn. Four friends visit with gifts representing four physical and moral qualities one hopes a new baby will have—

VAN GOGH IN ARLES

"The whole future of art is to be found in the south of France."
—*Vincent van Gogh, 1888*

Vincent was 35 years old when he arrived in Arles in 1888, and it was here that he discovered the light that would forever change him. Coming from the gray skies and flatlands of the Netherlands and Paris, he was bowled over by everything Provençal—jagged peaks, gnarled olive trees, brilliant sunflowers, and the furious wind. Van Gogh painted in a flurry in Arles, producing more paintings than at any other period of his too-brief career—over 200 in just a few months. (The fact that locals pronounced his name "vahn-saw van gog" had nothing to do with his psychological struggles here.)

Sadly, none of van Gogh's paintings remain in Arles—but you can still visit the places that inspired him. Around downtown Arles, you'll find 17 steel-and-concrete van Gogh "**easels**" that mark places Vincent painted, including the *Café at Night* on place du Forum. Each comes with a photo of the actual painting and provides fans with a fun opportunity to compare the scene then and now. The TI has a €1 brochure that locates all the easels.

The **hospital** where Vincent was sent to treat his self-inflicted ear wound is today a cultural center (called *Espace Van Gogh* and *Mediathèque*). It surrounds a garden that the artist loved. Only the courtyard is open to public; find the "easel" to see what Vincent painted here (free, near Musée Arlaten on rue President Wilson). He was sent from here to the mental institution in nearby St. Rémy (below) before Dr. Paul Gachet invited him to Auvers-sur-Oise, near Paris.

From place Lamartine, walk to the river, then look toward the town to find where Vincent set his easel for this famous *Starry Night* painting, where stars boil above the skyline of Arles. Riverfront cafés that once stood here were destroyed by bridge-seeking bombs in World War II, as was the bridge whose remains you see on your right.

good as bread, full as an egg, wise as salt, and straight as a match. The cradle is fully stocked with everything you needed to raise a baby in 1888.

The next room shows "the great supper"—a traditional feast served before the Christmas Mass. It's 1860, and everything on the table is locally produced. Traditionally 13 sweets—for Jesus and the 12 apostles—were served. Grandma and grandpa warm themselves in front of the fireplace; grandpa pours wine on a log for good luck in the coming year (€4, pick up excellent English brochure, April–Sept daily 9:30–12:30 & 14:00–18:00, Oct–March daily until 17:00, 29 rue de la République, tel. 04 90 96 08 23).

Musée Réattu—Housed in a beautiful 15th-century mansion, this mildly interesting, mostly modern art collection includes 57 Picasso drawings (some two-sided and all done in a flurry of creativity—I liked the bullfights best), a room of Henri Rousseau's Camargue watercolors, and an unfinished painting by the neoclassical artist Jacques Réattu, none with English explanations (€3, plus €1.50 for special exhibits, April–Sept daily 9:00–12:00 & 14:00–18:30, Oct and March daily until 17:00, Nov–Feb daily until 16:00, 10 rue du Grand Prieuré, tel. 04 90 96 37 68).

Events in Arles

▲▲**Wednesday and Saturday Markets**—Twice a week, Arles' ring road erupts into an open-air market of fish, flowers, produce, and you-name-it (boulevard Émile Combes on Wed, boulevard des Lices on Sat, both until 12:00). Join in, buy flowers, try the olives, sample some wine, and swat a pickpocket. On the first Wednesday of the month, it's a grand flea market.

Much of the market has a North African feel, thanks to the number of Algerians and Moroccans who live in Arles. They came to do the lowly city jobs that locals didn't want, and now mostly do the region's labor-intensive agricultural jobs (picking olives, harvesting fruit, and working in local greenhouses).

▲▲**Bullfights (Courses Camarguaise)**—Occupy the same seats fans have used for nearly 2,000 years, and take in Arles' most memorable experience—a bullfight *à la provençale* in the ancient Arena. These are more sporting than bloody Spanish bullfights—the names of Arles' bulls (who, locals stress, "die of old age") are listed even bolder than their human foes in the posters. The bulls have a ribbon *(cocarde)* on their forehead laced to their horns. The fighter, with a special hook, has 15 minutes to snare the ribbon. Local businessmen encourage the fighters by hollering out how much money they'll pay for the *cocarde*. If the bull pulls a good stunt, the band plays the famous song from *Carmen*. The following day, newspapers have reports on the fight, including how many *Carmens* the bull earned.

Three classes of bullfights—determined by the experience of the fighters—are advertised in posters: The *course de protection* is for rookie bullfighters. The *trophée de l'Avenir* comes with better fighters. And the *trophée des As* features the top professionals. During Easter and the fall rice harvest festival *(Féria du Riz)*, the Arena hosts actual Spanish bullfights (look for *corrida*) with outfits, swords, spikes, and the whole gory shebang (tickets €5–10; Easter–Oct Sat, Sun, and holidays, skip the "rodeo" spectacle, get more details at TI). There are nearby village bull-fights in small wooden bullrings nearly every weekend (TI has schedule).

SLEEPING

Hotels are a great value here; many are air-conditioned, though few have elevators.

$$$ Hôtel d'Arlatan***, built over the site of a Roman basilica, is classy in every sense of the word. It has sumptuous public spaces, a tranquil terrace, a designer pool, and antique-filled rooms, most with high, wood-beamed ceilings and stone walls. In the lobby of this 15th-century building, a glass floor looks down into Roman ruins (Db-€90–160, Db/Qb suites-€180–250, great buffet breakfast-€10, air-con, elevator, parking-€11, 26 rue Sauvage, one block off place du Forum, tel. 04 90 93 56 66, fax 04 90 49 68 45, www.hotel-arlatan.fr, hotel-arlatan@provnet.fr, SE).

The next three hotels are worthy of three stars; each offers exceptional value:

$$ Hôtel de l'Amphithéâtre**, a carefully decorated boutique hotel, is just off the Roman Arena. Public spaces are very sharp with a museum quality, and the owners pay attention to every detail of your stay. All rooms have air-conditioning, and the Belvedere room (€140) has the best view over Arles I've seen (Db-€52–72, superior Db-€82, Tb-€92, Qb-€120, parking-€4, 5 rue Diderot, one block from Arena, tel. 04 90 96 10 30, fax 04 90 93 98 69, www.hotelamphitheatre.fr, contact@hotelamphitheatre.fr, SE).

$$ Hôtel du Musée** is a quiet, delightful manor-home hideaway with 20 comfortable, air-conditioned rooms, a flowery two-tiered court-yard, and a snazzy art-gallery lounge. The rooms in the new section are worth the few extra euros and steps. Laurence speaks some English (Sb-€41–48, Db-€48–63, Tb-€60–72, Qb-€80, buffet breakfast-€7, parking-€7, 11 rue du Grand Prieuré, follow signs to Musée Réattu, tel. 04 90 93 88 88, fax 04 90 49 98 15, www.hoteldumusee.com.fr, contact @hoteldumusee.com.fr).

$$ Hôtel Calendal**, located between the Roman Arena and Classical Theater, is Provençal chic and does everything right, with smartly appointed rooms—some with views overlooking the Arena—surrounding a large, palm-shaded courtyard. Enjoy the great buffet breakfast (€8), the salad-and-pasta bar lunch buffet (€14), and the seductive ambience (Db facing street-€47–70, Db facing garden-€70–85, Db with balcony-€90-100, air-con, Internet access, reserve ahead for parking-€10, 5 rue Porte de Laure, just above Arena, tel. 04 90 96 11 89, fax 04 90 96 05 84, www.lecalendal.com, contact@lecalendal.com, SE).

$ Hôtel Régence**, which sits on the river, is one of the best deals in Arles, with immaculate and comfortable rooms, good beds, safe parking, and easy access to the train station (Db-€30–35, bigger Db-€42-48,

SLEEP CODE

(€1 = about $1.10, country code: 33)

Sleep Code: **S** = Single, **D** = Double/Twin, **T** = Triple, **Q** = Quad, **b** = bathroom, **s** = shower only, **no CC** = Credit Cards not accepted, **SE** = Speaks English, **NSE** = No English, ***** = French hotel rating system (0–4 stars). For more information on the rating system, see "Sleeping" in this book's introduction. Hotels with two or more stars are required to have an English-speaking staff. Nearly all hotels listed here will have someone who speaks English. You can assume a hotel takes credit cards unless you see "no CC" in the listing.

To help you sort easily through these listings, I've divided the rooms into three categories based on the price for a standard double room with bath:

$$$ **Higher Priced**—Most rooms €140 or more.
 $$ **Moderately Priced**—Most rooms between €100-150.
  $ **Lower Priced**—Most rooms €100 or less.

Tb-€40–57, Qb-€60-65, choose river-view or quiet air-con courtyard rooms, 5 rue Marius Jouveau, from place Lamartine turn right immediately after passing between towers, tel. 04 90 96 39 85, fax 04 90 96 67 64, www.hotel-regence.com, contact@hotel-regence.com, the gentle Nouvions speak a little English).

$ Hôtel Acacias**, just off place Lamartine and inside the old city walls, is a modern new hotel. It's a pastel paradise, with smallish rooms that have all the comforts, including cable TV, hairdryers, and air-conditioning (Db-€48–55, Tb-€62–80, Qb-€80-87, buffet breakfast-€6, elevator, 1 rue Marius Jouveau, tel. 04 90 96 37 88, fax 04 90 96 32 51, www.hotel-acacias.com, contact@hotel-acacias.com, Christophe and Sylvie SE).

$ Hôtel Voltaire* rents 12 small and spartan rooms with ceiling fans and nifty balconies overlooking a caffeine-stained square. It's perfect for starving artists, a block below the Arena. Smiling owner Mr. Ferrin loves the States (his dream is to travel there) and hopes you'll support his postcard collection (D-€25, Ds-€28, Db-€36, third or fourth person-€8 each, 1 place Voltaire, tel. 04 90 96 49 18, fax 04 90 96 45 49).

$ Hôtel le Rhône*, with hardworking owners from the north, provides another good value on place Voltaire with cute, spotless little rooms in cheery colors (D-€26, Ds-€31, Db-€38-40, some rooms have balconies, 11 place Voltaire, tel. 04 90 96 43 70, fax 04 90 93 87 03, hotellerhone@wanadoo.fr).

EATING

You can dine well in Arles on a modest budget—in fact, it's hard to blow a lot on dinner here (all my listings have *menus* for €22 or less). All restaurants listed have outdoor seating except La Bohème. Before dinner, go local on the place du Forum and enjoy a *pastis*. This anise-based aperitif is served straight in a glass with ice, plus a carafe of water—dilute to taste.

For **picnics,** a big, handy Monoprix supermarket/department store is on place Lamartine (Mon–Sat 8:30–19:25, closed Sun).

Place du Forum

Great atmosphere and mediocre food at fair prices awaits on place du Forum. **L'Estaminet** probably does the best dinner (I like the *salade Estaminet*).

A half-block below the forum on rue du Dr. Fanton lies a tempting lineup of good places. **La Vitamine** has decent salads, *assiettes* (a mixed plate of several foods), and pastas; show this book and enjoy a free *kir*—champagne with cassis (closed Sun, just below place du Forum on 16 rue du Dr. Fanton, tel. 04 90 93 77 36). **Au Brin du Thym,** almost next door, is always crowded and specializes in traditional Provençal cuisine. Arrive early for an outdoor table (*menu*-€18, closed Tue, 22 rue du Dr. Fanton, tel. 04 90 49 95 96).

La Bohème, a block above the Forum, has a beer-hall feel, with a long, vaulted room and sometimes-raucous clients. It's a good budget option (vegetarian *menu*-€14, Provençal *menu*-€18, closed Sun-Mon, 6 rue Balze, tel. 04 90 18 58 92).

Le 6 offers the best quality I could find in this area. Gentle owner Pierre changes his menu regularly, offering a fresh blend of classic and regional cuisine. The vine-covered terrace is peaceful and the non-Provençal decor is crisp (€20 *menu*, closed Tue, 6 rue du Forum, a block off the Forum down rue de la Liberté, tel. 04 90 96 02 58).

Near the Roman Arena

For about the same price as on place du Forum, you can enjoy regional cuisine with a point-blank view of the Arena at **Le Pistou.** Arrive early to get an outdoor table with a view, though the interior is also cozy (*menus* from €16, open daily, at top of Arena, 30 rond-point des Arènes).

On the same block as the recommended Hôtel Calendal lies a mini-restaurant row, with several reasonable options. **Lou Caleu** is the best (though not cheapest), with very Provençal cuisine and *menus* from €17 (closed Mon, 27 rue Porte de Laure, tel. 04 90 49 71 77). **La**

Giraudière, a few blocks below the Arena on place Voltaire, offers reliable regional cuisine with mauve tablecloths under a heavy beamed ceiling. Come here to dine inside, and show this book to get a free *kir* (*menu*—€22, closed Tue, air-con, tel. 04 90 93 27 52). The recommended **Hôtel Calendal** hosts a daily, all-you-can-eat salad-and-pasta bar, open to anyone from 12:00-16:00 for €14; the selection is as good as the quality. Retreat from the city and enjoy a healthy lunch in the hotel's palm-shaded garden.

Dessert
For the best ice cream in Arles, find **Soleilei,** with all-natural ingredients and unusual flavors such as *fadoli*—olive-oil-flavored ice cream (open daily, across from recommended La Vitamine restaurant at 9 rue du Dr. Fanton).

TRANSPORTATION CONNECTIONS

By bus to: Les Baux (4/day Mon-Sat, 1/day Sun, fewer Nov–March, first departure 8:30, last at 14:30, ideal departure is 8:30 with a return from Les Baux around 11:45 or 13:15, trip takes 30 min), **Camargue/Stes-Maries-de-la-Mer** (5/day Mon-Sat, 4/day Sun, 1 hr). There are two bus stops in Arles: the *Centre-ville* stop is at 16 boulevard Cléemenceau (two blocks below main TI, next to Café le Wilson); the other is at the train station. Bus info: tel. 04 90 49 38 01.

By train to: Paris (17/day, 2 direct TGVs in 4 hrs, 15 with transfer in Avignon in 5 hrs), **Avignon Centre-ville** (12/day, 20 min, afternoon gaps), **Nîmes** (9/day, 25 min), **Orange** (4/day direct, 35 min, more with transfer in Avignon), **Aix-en-Provence Centre-ville** (10/day, 2 hrs, requires at least one transfer, in Marseille), **Marseille** (20/day, 1 hr), **Carcassonne** (6/day, 3 hrs, three with transfer in Narbonne), **Beaune** (10/day, 4.5 hrs, nine with transfer in Nîmes or Avignon and Lyon), **Nice** (11/day, 4 hrs, 10 with transfer in Marseille), **Barcelona** (2/day, 6 hrs, transfer in Montpellier), **Italy** (3/day, transfer in Marseille and Nice; from Arles, it's 4.5 hrs to Ventimiglia on the border, 8 hrs to Milan, 9.5 hrs to Cinque Terre, 11 hrs to Florence, and 13 hrs to Venice or Rome).

Avignon

Famous for its nursery rhyme, medieval bridge, and brooding Palace of the Popes, contemporary Avignon (ah-veen-yohn) bustles and prospers behind its mighty walls. During the 68 years (1309–1377) that Avignon starred as the *Franco Vaticano,* it grew from a quiet village to the thriving city it remains. With its large student population and fashionable shops, today's Avignon is an intriguing blend of youthful spirit and urban sophistication. Street performers entertain the international crowds who fill Avignon's ubiquitous cafés and trendy boutiques. If you're here in July, be prepared for the rollicking theater festival and reserve your hotel months in advance. Clean, sharp, and popular, Avignon is more impressive for its outdoor ambience than for its museums and monuments. See the Palace of the Popes, then explore the city's thriving streets and beautiful vistas from the parc de Rochers des Doms.

ORIENTATION

The cours Jean Jaurès (which turns into rue de la République) runs straight from the train station to place de l'Horloge and the Palace of the Popes, thus splitting Avignon in two. The larger eastern half is where the action is. Climb to the parc des Rochers des Doms for a fine view, enjoy the people scene on place de l'Horloge, meander the backstreets (see "Discovering Avignon's Backstreets," below), and lose yourself in a quiet square. Avignon's shopping district fills the traffic-free streets where rue de la République meets place de l'Horloge.

Tourist Information

The main TI is between the train station and the old town at 41 cours Jean Jaurès (April–Oct Mon–Sat 9:00–18:00, Sun 9:00–17:00, Nov–March Mon–Fri 9:00–18:00, Sat 9:00–17:00, Sun 10:00–12:00, longer hours during July festival, tel. 04 32 74 32 74). Other branch offices may be open at either the pont St. Bénézet or in the Palace of the Popes. Get the good tear-off map and pick up the free, handy *Guide Pratique* (info on car and bike rental, hotels, and museums) as well as their Avignon discovery guide, which includes several good (but tricky-to-follow) walking tours. Get the free **"Avignon Passion" Pass**—you'll get the card stamped when you pay full price at your first sight, then get reductions at the others (e.g., €2 less at Palace of the Popes, €3 less at Petit Palais). The TI offers informative English-language **walking tours** of Avignon (€8, €5 with "Avignon Passion" Pass, Apr-Oct Tue, Thu, and Sat at 10:00, Nov–March Sat only, depart from the main TI). They also have information on bus excursions to popular regional sights (including the wine route, Luberon, and Camargue).

Arrival in Avignon

By Train: TGV passengers take the shuttle bus (*navette,* €1.10, 4/hr, 10 min) from the TGV station (*gare TGV,* see below) to near the central train station in downtown Avignon (car rental at both stations, easier at TGV). All non-TGV trains serve the central station *(Avignon Centre).* Baggage check is available at the central station, but not at the TGV station. From the central station, walk through the city walls onto cours Jean Jaurès (TI is three blocks down at #41). The bus station *(gare* *routière)* is 100 yards to the right of the central train station (beyond and below Ibis Hôtel).

Avignon's space-age TGV train station—located away from the center—is big news. While it makes Paris a zippy three-hour ride away, locals say it benefits rich Parisians the most. As Provence is now within easy weekend striking distance of the French capital, rural homes are being gobbled up by urbanites at inflated prices that locals can't afford.

By Car: Drivers enter Avignon following *Centre-ville* signs. Park either near the wall or in the big structure just inside the walls (where there's a TI in season). Figure half-day-€3 and full day-€6 for pay lots. Hotels have advice for smart overnight parking. Leave nothing in your car.

Helpful Hints

Closed Day: Many of Avignon's sights are closed on Tuesdays, though the Palace of the Popes is open.

Book Ahead for July: During the July theater festival, rooms are rare—reserve very early or stay in Arles or St. Rémy.

Laundry: Handy to most hotels is the launderette at 66 place des Corps-Saints, where rue Agricol Perdiguier ends (daily 7:00–20:00).

Internet Access: Consider Webzone (daily 14:00–24:00, 25 rue Carnot) or ask your hotelier for the nearest Internet café.

English Bookstore: Try Shakespeare Bookshop (Tue–Sat 9:30–12:30 & 14:00–18:30, closed Mon, 155 rue Carreterie, in Avignon's northeast corner, tel. 04 90 27 38 50).

Car Rental: The TGV station has the most options, with long hours daily; you'll find fewer near the central station, with shorter hours.

Tourist Trains: Two little trains, designed for tired tourists, leave regularly from the Palace of the Popes. One does a town tour (€6, 2/hr, 30 min, English commentary) and the other choo-choos you sweat-free to the top of the park, high above the river (€2, schedule depends on demand, no commentary).

Commanding City Views: Walk or drive across pont Daladier (bridge) for a great view of Avignon and the Rhône River. Other top views are from the top of the park and from the end of the broken bridge.

SIGHTS

I've listed sights in the best order to visit, and have added a short walking tour of Avignon's backstreets to get you beyond the surface. Entries are listed at full price and with discount card (the "Avignon Passion" Pass). Start your tour where the Romans did, on place de l'Horloge, and find a seat on a stone bench in front of city hall (Hôtel de Ville).

Place de l'Horloge—This square, which was the town forum during Roman times and the market square through the Middle Ages, is Avignon's café square, with a fun ambience (but high prices and low food

Avignon

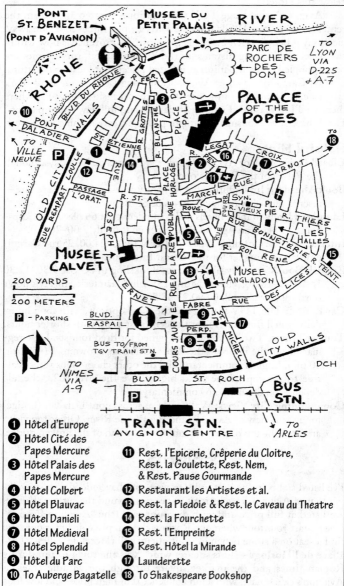

1. Hôtel d'Europe
2. Hôtel Cité des Papes Mercure
3. Hôtel Palais des Papes Mercure
4. Hôtel Colbert
5. Hôtel Blauvac
6. Hôtel Danieli
7. Hôtel Medieval
8. Hôtel Splendid
9. Hôtel du Parc
10. To Auberge Bagatelle
11. Rest. l'Epicerie, Crêperie du Cloitre, Rest. la Goulette, Rest. Nem, & Rest. Pause Gourmande
12. Restaurant les Artistes et al.
13. Rest. la Piedoie & Rest. le Caveau du Theatre
14. Rest. la Fourchette
15. Rest. l'Empreinte
16. Rest. Hôtel la Mirande
17. Launderette
18. To Shakespeare Bookshop

quality). Named for a medieval clock tower that the city hall now hides, this square's present popularity arrived with the trains in 1854. Walk a few steps to the center, and look down the main drag, rue de la République. When trains arrived in Avignon, proud city fathers wanted a direct, impressive way to link the new station to the heart of the city (just like in Paris)—so they plowed over homes to create the rue de la République and widened place de l'Horloge.

Walk past the merry-go-round, veer right uphill past the Palace of the Popes, and enter...

Palace Square (Place du Palais)—You'll see the forbidding Palace of the Popes, Petit Palace, and cathedral surrounding this grand square.

In the 1300s, the Vatican moved the entire headquarters of the Catholic Church to Avignon. The Church bought Avignon and gave it a complete facelift. Along with clearing out vast spaces like this square and building this three-acre palace, the Church built more than three miles of protective wall with 39 towers, "appropriate" housing for cardinals (read: mansions), and residences for the entire Vatican bureaucracy. The city was Europe's largest construction zone. Avignon's population grew from 6,000 to 25,000 in short order (today 13,000 people live within the walls). The limits of pre-pope Avignon are outlined on the TI map. Rue Joseph Vernet, rue Henri Fabre, rue des Lices, and rue Philonarde follow the route of the city's earlier defensive wall.

The Petit Palais (little palace) seals the uphill end of the end of the square and was built for a cardinal; today, it houses medieval paintings (described below). The church to the left of the Palace of the Popes is Avignon's cathedral. It predates the Church's purchase of Avignon by 200 years. Its small size reflects Avignon's modest, pre-pope population. The gilded Mary was added in 1859.

Notice the stumps in front of the Conservatoire National de Musique. Nicknamed *"bites,"* slang for the male anatomy, they effectively keep cars from double-parking in areas designed for people. Many slide up and down by remote control to let privileged cars come and go.

Musée du Petit Palais—This palace displays the Church's collection of medieval Italian painting and sculpture. All 350 paintings deal with Christian themes. A visit here before going to the Palace of the Popes helps furnish and people that otherwise barren building (€6, €3 with Avignon Passion Pass, Wed–Mon 9:30–13:00 & 14:00–17:30, closed Tue, at north end of place du Palais).

▲▲**Parc des Rochers des Doms, the Ramparts, and Pont St. Bénézet**— With a short loop, you can enjoy a park, hike to a commanding river view, walk a bit of the wall, and visit Avignon's famous broken bridge.

The Park (Parc des Rochers des Doms): Hike (or catch the tourist train) from the Palace of the Popes to the rock top where Avignon was first settled. While the park itself is a delight, don't miss the climax—a grand view of the Rhône River Valley and the broken bridge. A tableau explains the view and provides a little history in English. St. André Fortress (in the distance, on the right) was built by the French in 1360 (shortly after the Pope moved in) to counter the papal incursion into this part of Europe. The castle was in the kingdom of France. Avignon's famous bridge was a key border crossing, with towers on either end—one French and one Vatican.

The Ramparts: From the viewpoint, stairs lead down onto the only bit of the rampart you can walk on. When the pope came in the 1360s, small Avignon had no town wall...so he built one (restored in the 19th century).

The Bridge (Pont St. Bénézet): This bridge, whose construction and location were inspired by a shepherd's religious vision, is the "pont d'Avignon" of nursery-rhyme fame. The ditty (which you've probably been humming all day) dates back to the 15th century: *Sur la pont d'Avignon, on y danse, on y danse, sur la pont d'Avignon, on y danse tout en rond* ("On the bridge of Avignon, we will dance, we will dance, on the bridge of Avignon, we will dance in a circle").

But the bridge is a big deal even outside of its kiddie-tune fame. This was the only bridge crossing the mighty Rhône in the Middle Ages until it was knocked down by a flood. While only four arches survive today, the bridge was huge: Imagine a 22-arch, 3,000-foot-long bridge extending from Vatican territory to the lonely Tower of Philip the Fair, which marked the beginning of France. A Romanesque chapel on the bridge is dedicated to St. Bénézet. While there's not much to actually see on the bridge, the audioguide included in the €3.50 admission tells a good story...and it's fun to just be in the breezy middle of the river with a fine city view (daily 9:00-18:00). Dip into the tiny and free Musée du Pont for some bridge history (daily 9:00-22:00, next to the bridge).

▲**Palace of the Popes (Palais des Papes)**—In 1309, a French pope was elected (Pope Clement V). At the urging of the French king, His Holiness decided he'd had enough of unholy Italy. So he loaded up his carts and moved to Avignon for a steady rule under a supportive king. The Catholic Church literally bought Avignon (then a two-bit town), and popes resided here until 1403. From 1378 on, there were twin popes, one in Rome and one in Avignon, causing a schism in the Catholic Church that wasn't fully resolved until 1417.

The papal palace is tourable. The included audioguide leads you through the one-way route and does a decent job of overcoming the lack of furnishings and teaching the basic history while allowing you to tour this largely empty palace at your own pace. As you wander, remember that this palace—the biggest surviving Gothic palace in Europe—was built to accommodate 500 people as the administrative center of the Vatican and home of the pope (you'll walk through his personal quarters frescoed with happy hunting scenes). In the Napoleonic age, the palace was a barracks, housing 1,800 soldiers. You can see cuts in the wall where high ceilings gave way to floor beams.

The film auditorium shows a continuous 20-minute video in French, featuring images of the papal court both in the Vatican and in Avignon. Nearby, a staircase leads to the tower for a view and windswept café.

A room at the end of the tour is dedicated to the region's wines, of which the pope was a fan. Sniff Le Nez du Vin (54 tiny bottles designed to develop your "nose"). Châteauneuf-du-Pape is a nearby village where the pope summered in the 1320s. Its famous wine is a direct descendant of his wine. You're welcome to taste some here (free, or split the €6 tasters deal, which comes with a souvenir tasting cup).

You'll exit to the rear of the palace, where my backstreets walking tour begins (below). To return to the palace square, make two rights after exiting (€9.50, €7.50 with "Avignon Passion" Pass, April–Nov daily 9:00–19:00, July daily until 21:00, Aug and Sept daily until 20:00, Dec–March daily 9:30–17:45, last entry one hour before closing, tel. 04 90 27 50 74).

▲▲**Discovering Avignon's Backstreets**—Use the map in this book or the TI map to navigate this easy, level 30-minute walk. This self-guided tour begins in the small square behind the Palace of the Popes, where visitors exit. (If you skipped the palace interior, walk down the Palace Square with the palace to your left and take the first left down the narrow, cobbled rue Peyrolerie; notice how it was cut through the rock. You'll pop out into a small square behind the Palace of the Popes. Veer left and you're ready to go.)

Hôtel la Mirande: Located on the square, Avignon's finest hotel welcomes visitors. Find the atrium lounge and consider a coffee break amid the understated luxury (afternoon tea with a pastry, €14, is served 15:00–18:00). Inspect the royal lounge and dining room (recommended in "Eating," below); cooking courses are offered in the basement below. Rooms start at €300.

Turn left out of the hotel and left again on rue Peyrolerie ("street of the coppersmiths"), then take your first right on rue des Ciseaux d'Or and find the...

Church of St. Pierre: The original chestnut doors were carved in 1551, when tales of New World discoveries raced across Europe (notice the Indian headdress). The fine Annunciation (lower left) shows Gabriel giving Mary the exciting news in impressive Renaissance 3-D.

The alley to the left—which turned into a tunnel when it was covered with housing as the town's population grew—leads into what was the cloister of St. Pierre (place des Châtaignes—named for chestnut trees, now replaced by plane trees). See "Eating" for good places to eat on both sides of the church.

With the church on your right, cross busy rue Carnot to the Banque Chaix. The building opposite, with its beams showing, is a rare vestige from the Middle Ages. Notice how the building widens the higher it gets. A medieval loophole based taxes on ground-floor area—everything above was tax-free. Walking down the rue des Fourbisseurs ("street of animal furriers"), notice how the top floors almost meet. Fire was a constant danger in the Middle Ages, as flames leapt easily from one home to the next. In fact, the lookout guard's primary responsibility was watching for fires, not the enemy. Virtually all of Avignon's medieval homes have been replaced by safer structures.

Turn left on the traffic-free rue du Vieux Sextier ("street of the balance," for weighing items); another left under the first arch leads to...

Avignon's Synagogue: Jews first came to Avignon with the Diaspora of the first century. Avignon's Jews were nicknamed "the Pope's Jews" because of the protection that the Pope offered to Jews expelled from France. While this synagogue dates from 1220s, it was completely rebuilt in a neoclassical Greek-temple style by a non-Jewish architect in Revolutionary times. This is the only synagogue under a rotunda that you'll see anywhere. The arc holding the Torah is in the east, next to a list of Jews deported from here to Auschwitz in 1942, after Vichy France was gobbled up by the Nazis. To visit the synagogue, press the buzzer and friendly Rabbi Moshe Aman will be your guide (Mon–Fri 10:00–12:00 & 15:00–17:00, closed Sat–Sun).

From here, retrace your steps to rue du Vieux Sextier. Cross it, then go through the arch and down the yellow alley. Turn left on rue de la Bonneterie ("street of bonnets"), which leads to the big, boxy...

Market (Les Halles): In 1970, the open-air market was replaced by this modern one, which may be ugly, but it provides plenty of parking upstairs. Step inside for a sensual experience of organic breads, olives, and festival-of-mold cheeses. The rue de Temptations cuts down the center. The cafés and cheese shops are on the left—as far as possible from the stinky fish stall on the right (Tue-Sun until 13:00, closed Mon).

Continuing on, rue de la Bonneterie becomes...

Rue des Teinturiers: This "street of the dyers" is Avignon's headquarters for all that's hip. You'll pass the Gray Penitents chapel. The facade shows the GPs, who dressed up in robes and pointy hoods to do their anonymous good deeds back in the 13th century (long before the KKK dressed this way).

Limestone car barriers are carved whimsically by amateur sculptors. Earthy cafés, galleries, and a small stream (a branch of the Sorgue River) with waterwheels line this tie-dyed street. This was the cloth industry's dyeing and textile center in the 1800s. Those stylish Provençal fabrics and patterns you see for sale everywhere started here (after a pattern imported from China).

Waterwheel: At the waterwheel, imagine the Sorgue River, which hits the mighty Rhône here in Avignon, being broken into several canals in order to turn 23 such wheels, thus powering the town's industries around 1800. The little cogwheel above the big one could be shoved into place and kick another machine into gear behind the wall.

Across from the wheel, **La Cave Breysse** would love to serve you a fragrant glass of regional wine (€2.50 per glass); choose from the blackboard by the bar listing all the bottles open today. You're welcome to take it out and sit by the canal (wine with salads and lunch plates Tue-Sat 11:00-15:00, wine only Tue-Sat 18:00-22:30, closed Sun-Mon, Christine Savory and Tim Sweet SE).

To get back to the real world, double back on rue des Teinturiers, turning left on rue des Lices, which traces the first medieval wall (*lices* is the no-man's-land along a wall). You'll pass a four-story arcaded building (which was a home for the poor in the 1600s, an army barracks in the 1800s, a fine arts school in the 1900s, and a deluxe condominium today—much of this neighborhood is going high-class residential). Eventually you'll return to rue de la République, Avignon's main drag.

More Sights in Avignon

Fondation Angladon-Dubrujeaud—This museum mixes a small but enjoyable collection of art from Post-Impressionists (including Cézanne, van Gogh, Honoré Daumier, Edgar Degas, and Picasso) with re-created art studios and furnishings from many periods. It's a quiet place with a few superb paintings (€5, €3 with "Avignon Passion" Pass, Tue–Sun 13:00–18:00, closed Mon, 5 rue Laboureur).

Musée Calvet—This fine-arts museum impressively displays its good collection without a word of English explanation (€6, €3 with "Avignon Passion" Pass, Wed–Mon 10:00–12:00 & 14:00–18:00, closed Tue, on quieter west half of town at 65 rue Joseph Vernet; its antiquities collection is a few blocks away at 27 rue de la République, same hours and ticket).

Sights near Avignon, in Villeneuve-lès-Avignon

▲**Tower of Philip the Fair (Tour Philippe-le-Bel)**—Built to protect access to pont St. Bénézet in 1307, this massive tower offers the best view over Avignon and the Rhône basin. It's best late in the day (€1.60, €0.90 with "Avignon Passion" Pass, April–Sept daily 10:00–12:00 & 15:00–19:00, Oct–March Tue–Sun 10:00–12:00 & 15:00–17:30, closed Mon). To reach the tower from Avignon, you can drive (5 min, cross pont Daladier bridge, follow signs to Villeneuve-lès-Avignon); take a boat (Bateau-Bus departs from Mireio Embarcadère near pont Daladier); or take bus #11 (2/hr, catch bus across from central train station, in front of post office, on cours Président Kennedy).

SLEEPING

(€1 = about $1.10, country code: 33)

Hotel values are distinctly better in Arles, though these are all solid values. Only the first three have elevators.

At $$$ **Hôtel d'Europe****, you can be a Gypsy in the palace at Avignon's most prestigious address—if you get one of the 15 surprisingly reasonable "standard rooms." Enter into a fountain-filled courtyard, and linger in every lounge. The hotel is located on the handsome place Crillon near the river (standard Db-€130, spacious Db standard-€160, first-class Db-€220, deluxe Db-€300, deluxe Db-€400, breakfast-€20, elevator, every comfort, garage-€14, 12 place Crillon, near pont Daladier, tel. 04 90 14 76 76, fax 04 90 14 76 71, www.hotel-d-europe.fr.

$$$ **Cité des Papes Mercure***, a modern hotel chain within spitting distance of the Palace of the Popes, has 73 smartly designed, smallish rooms, musty halls, air-conditioning, elevators, and all the comforts (Db-€113, extra bed-€14, many rooms have views over place de l'Horloge, 1 rue Jean Vilar, tel. 04 90 80 93 00, fax 04 90 80 93 01, h1952@accor-hotels.com, SE). The **Palais des Papes Mercure*** (87 rooms, same chain, same price) is nearby, just inside the walls, near pont St. Bénézet (rue Ferruce, tel. 04 90 80 93 93, fax 04 90 80 93 94, h0549@accor-hotels.com, SE).

$$ **Hôtel Colbert**** is a fine midrange bet. Parisian refugees Patrice (SE) and Sylvie (NSE) are your hosts, and their care for this restored manor house shows in the attention to detail, from the peaceful patio to the warm room decor throughout (Sb-€43-53, Db-€60-70, Tb-€70-90, air-con, 7 rue Agricol Perdiguier, tel. 04 90 86 20 20, fax 04 90 85 97 00, www.lecolbert-hotel.com, colbert.hotel@wanadoo.fr).

$$ **Hôtel de Blauvac**** offers 16 mostly spacious, high-ceilinged rooms (many with an upstairs loft) and a sky-high atrium in a grand old manor home near the pedestrian zone (Sb-€56-66, small Db-€60, Db loft-€65-73, Tb/Qb-€80-90, 11 rue de la Bancasse, one block off rue de la République, tel. 04 90 86 34 11, fax 04 90 86 27 41, www.hotel-blauvac.com, info@hotel-blauvac.com, friendly Nathalie SE like an American).

$$ **Hôtel Danieli**** is a Hello-Dolly fluffball of a place, renting 29 colorful and comfortable rooms on the main drag with air-conditioning and lots of tour groups (Sb-€60-65, Db-€70-85, Tb-€80-100, Qb-€92-110, elevator, 17 rue de la République, tel. 04 90 86 46 82, fax 04 90 27 09 24, www.hotel-danieli-avignon.com, contact@hotel-danieli-avignon.com, owner Madame Shogol SE).

$$ **Hôtel Mediéval**** is burrowed deep a few blocks from the St. Pierre church in a massive stone mansion with a small flower-filled garden and friendly managers. The unimaginative yet adequate rooms have firm beds (Db-€55-68, Tb-€77, kitchenettes available but require three-day minimum stay, 15 rue Petite Saunerie, five blocks east of place de

l'Horloge, behind Church of St. Pierre, tel. 04 90 86 11 06, fax 04 90 82 08 64, hotel.medieval@wanadoo.fr).

The next three listings are a 10-minute walk from the station; turn right off cours Jean Jaurès on rue Agricol Perdiguier.

At **$ Hôtel le Splendid***, ever-smiling Madame Prel-Lemoine rents 17 cheery rooms with good beds, ceiling fans, and small bathrooms (Sb-€42-45, Db-€53-60, 17 rue Agricol Perdiguier, tel. 04 90 86 14 46, fax 04 90 85 38 55, www.avignon-splendid-hotel.com, contact@avignon -splendid-hotel.com).

$ Hôtel du Parc*, across the street, is a similar value—a little less sharp, but cheaper, with entertaining Avignon native Madame Rous thrown in for free. Rooms have pretty stone walls; the best overlook the park (D-€35, Ds-€44, Db-€48, 18 rue Agricol Perdiguier tel. 04 90 82 71 55, fax 04 90 85 64 86, hotelduparc84@wanadoo.fr).

$ Auberge Bagatelle's hostel/campground offers dirt-cheap beds, a lively atmosphere, busy pool, café, grocery store, launderette, great views of Avignon, and campers for neighbors (D-€24, dorm bed-€11, across pont Daladier on the island Ile de la Barthelasse, bus #10 from main post office, tel. 04 90 86 30 39, fax 04 90 27 16 23).

EATING

Skip the overpriced places on the place de l'Horloge (Les Domaines and La Civette near the carousel are the least of evils here) and find a more intimate location for your dinner. Avignon has many delightful squares filled with tables ready to seat you.

Near the Church of St. Pierre

This church has enclosed squares on both sides, offering outdoor yet intimate ambience.

L'Épicerie is charmingly located and popular, with the highest-quality cuisine around the Church of St. Pierre, including a good selection of à la carte items (cozy interior good for bad weather, closed Sun, 10 place St. Pierre, tel. 04 90 82 74 22).

Pass under the arch by L'Épicerie restaurant and enter enchanting place des Châtaignes, filled with the tables of four restaurants: **Crêperie du Cloître** (big salad and main-course crêpe for about €12, closed Sun–Mon); **Restaurant la Goulette** (Tunisian specialties, *tagine* or couscous-€16, closed Mon); **Restaurant Nem** (Vietnamese, family-run, *menus* from €10); and **Pause Gourmande** (lunch only, *plats du jour*-€7, always a veggie choice).

Place Crillon

This large, open square just off the river provides more ambience than quality. Several cafés offer inexpensive bistro fare with *menus* from €14, *plats* from €12, and many tables to choose from. **Restaurant les Artistes** is one of several (daily, 21 place Crillon, tel. 04 90 82 23 54).

Elsewhere in Avignon

At **La Piedoie,** a few blocks northeast of the TI, eager-to-please owner-chef Thierry Piedoie serves fine traditional and Provençal dishes in an intimate, elegant setting (interior seating only, *menu*–€27, 26 rue des Trois Faucons, tel. 04 90 86 51 52).

Le Caveau du Théâtre is the antithesis of its neighbor, La Piedoie, with wild posters decorating a carefree interior. Wine and good-value dishes are the specialties (*plats*–€13, *menus*–€18, fun ambience for free, closed Sun, 16 rue des Trois Faucons, tel. 04 90 82 60 91).

La Fourchette is cozy, indoor-only, traditional, and well-respected. It's a block from place de l'Horloge toward the river (*menus* from €27, closed Sat-Sun, 17 rue Racine, tel. 04 90 85 20 93).

L'Empreinte is good for North African cuisine in a trendy location (copious couscous for €11–16, daily, 33 rue des Teinturiers, tel. 04 32 76 36 35).

Hôtel la Mirande is the ultimate Avignon splurge. Reserve ahead here for understated elegance and Avignon's top cuisine (lunch *menu*–€28, dinner *menu*–€50, tasting *menu*–€85, closed Tue-Wed, behind Palace of the Popes, 4 place de la Mirande, tel. 04 90 86 93 93, fax 04 90 86 26 85, www.la-mirande.fr).

TRANSPORTATION CONNECTIONS

Trains

Remember, there are two train stations in Avignon: the new suburban TGV station and the Centre-ville station in the city center (€1.10 shuttle buses connect both stations, 4/hr, 10 min). Only the Centre-ville station has baggage check. Car rental is available at both stations (better at TGV). Some cities are served both by slower local trains from the Centre-ville station and by faster TGV trains from the TGV station; I've listed the most convenient stations for each trip.

By train from Avignon's Centre-ville station to: Arles (12/day, 20 min), **Orange** (10/day, 15 min), **Nîmes** (14/day, 30 min), **Isle-sur-la-Sorgue** (6/day, 30 min), **Lyon** (10/day, 2 hrs, also from TGV station—see below), **Carcassonne** (8/day, 7 with transfer in Narbonne, 3 hrs), **Barcelona** (2/day, 6 hrs, transfer in Montpellier).

By train from Avignon's TGV station to: Nice (10/day, 4 hrs, a few direct, most require transfer in Marseille), **Marseille** (10/day, 70 min), **Aix-en-Provence TGV** (10/day, 75 min), **Lyon** (12/day, 1.5 hrs, also from Centre-ville station—see above), **Paris'** Gare de Lyon (14/day, three with transfer in Lyon, 2.5 hrs), **Paris'** Charles de Gaulle Airport (7/day, 3 hrs).

Buses

The bus station (*halte routière,* tel. 04 90 82 07 35) is just past and below the Ibis Hôtel to the right as you exit the train station (information desk open Mon–Fri 8:00–12:00 & 13:00-18:00, Sat 8:00–12:00, closed Sun). Nearly all buses leave from this station. The biggest exception is the SNCF bus service that runs from the Avignon TGV station to Arles (10/day, 30 min). The Avignon TI has schedules. Service is reduced or nonexistent on Sunday and holidays.

By bus to: **Pont du Gard** (5/day in summer, 3/day off-season, 40 min, see details under "Pont du Gard," below). **St. Rémy** (7/day, 45 min, handy way to visit its Wed market).

Pont du Gard

Throughout the ancient world, aqueducts were flags of stone that heralded the greatness of Rome. A visit to this sight still works to proclaim the wonders of that age. This perfectly preserved Roman aqueduct was built as *the* critical link of a 30-mile canal that, by dropping one inch for every 350 feet, supplied nine million gallons of water per day (about 100 gallons per second) to Nîmes—one of ancient Europe's largest cities. Though most of the aqueduct is on or below the ground, at the Pont du Gard it spans a canyon on a massive bridge—one of the most remarkable surviving Roman ruins anywhere.

ORIENTATION

There are two riversides to the Pont du Gard: the left and right banks *(Rive Gauche* and *Rive Droite).* Park on the *Rive Gauche,* where you'll find the museums, ticket booth, cafeteria, WC, and shops, all built into a modern plaza. You'll see the aqueduct in two parts: first, a fine new museum complex, then the actual river gorge spanned by the ancient bridge.

Cost: While seeing the aqueduct itself is free, the various optional activities each have a cost: parking (€5), museum (€6), silly 23-minute film (€3, see below), a kid's space called *Ludo* (€3, scratch-and-sniff experience in English of various aspects of Roman life and the importance of water), and the new extensive outdoor *garrigue* natural area, featuring historic crops and landscapes of the Mediterranean (€4, includes well-done English audioguide). All are designed to give the sight more meaning—and they do—but for most visitors, only the museum is worth paying for. The €10 combo-ticket—which covers all sights and parking—is often your best bet. If you go for the combo-ticket, check the movie schedule—the 23-minute film offers good information delivered in a flirtatious French style...and a cool, entertaining, and cushy break.

During summer months, a nighttime sound and light show plays against the Pont du Gard.

Hours: The complex is open Easter–Nov daily 9:30–19:00, mid-June–Aug daily until 21:30, Dec–Easter daily until 18:00 (tel. 04 66 37 50 99). The aqueduct itself is open until 22:00.

Canoe Rental: Consider seeing the Pont du Gard by canoe. Collias Canoes will pick you up at the Pont du Gard (or elsewhere, if pre-arranged) and shuttle you to the town of Collias. You'll float down the river to the nearby town of Remoulins, where they'll pick you up and take you back to the Pont du Gard (€27 per two-person canoe; usually 2 hrs, though you can take as long as you like, tel. 04 66 22 85 54, SE).

SIGHTS

▲▲**Museum**—The state-of-the-art museum's multimedia approach (well-described in English) shows how water was an essential part of the Roman "art of living." You'll see examples of lead pipes, faucets, and siphons; walk through a rock quarry; and learn how they moved those huge rocks into place and how those massive arches were made. The exhibit shows the immensity of the undertaking as well as the payoff. Imagine the excitement as this extravagant supply of water finally tumbled into Nîmes. A relaxing highlight is the scenic video helicopter ride along the entire 30-mile course of the structure from its start at Uzès all the way to the Castellum in Nîmes.

▲▲▲**Viewing the Aqueduct**—A park-like path leads to the aqueduct. Until a few years ago, this was an actual road—adjacent to the aqueduct—that has spanned the river since 1743. Before you cross the bridge, pass under it and hike 350 feet along the riverbank for a grand viewpoint from which to study the second-highest standing Roman structure (Rome's Colosseum is two yards taller).

This was the biggest bridge in the whole 30-mile-long aqueduct. It seems exceptional because it is: The arches are twice the width of standard aqueducts, and the main arch is the largest the Romans ever built—80 feet (so it wouldn't get its feet wet). The bridge is about 160 feet high, and was originally about 1,100 feet long (today 12 arches are missing, reducing the length to 792 feet.)

While the distance from the source (in Uzès) to Nîmes was only 12 miles as the eagle flew, engineers chose the most economical route, winding and zigzagging 30 miles. The water made the trip in 24 hours with a drop of only 40 feet. While 90 percent of the aqueduct is on or under the ground, a few river canyons like this required bridges. A stone lid hides a four-foot-wide, six-foot-tall chamber lined with waterproof mortar that carried a stream for over 400 years. For 150 years, this system provided Nîmes with good drinking water. Expert as the Romans were, they miscalculated the backup caused by a downstream corner, and had to add the thin extra layer you can see just under the lid to make the channel deeper.

The bridge and the river below provide great fun for holiday-goers. While parents suntan on inviting rocks, kids splash into the gorge from under the aqueduct. Some daredevils actually jump from the aqueduct itself—not knowing that crazy winds scrambled by the structure cause painful belly flops and sometimes even accidental deaths. For the most refreshing view, float flat on your back under the structure (bring a swimsuit and sandals for the rocks).

The appearance of the entire gorge changed in 2002, when a huge flood flushed lots of greenery downstream. Those floodwaters put Roman provisions to the test. Notice the triangular-shaped buttresses at the lower level—designed to split and divert the force of any flood *around* the feet of the arches rather than *into* them. The 2002 floodwaters reached the top of those buttresses. Anxious park rangers winced at the sounds of trees crashing onto the ancient stones...but the arches stood strong.

The stones that jut out—giving the aqueduct a rough, unfinished appearance—supported the original scaffolding. The protuberances were left, rather than cut off, in anticipation of future repair needs. The lips under the arches supported the wooden templates that allowed the stones of the round arches to rest on something until the all-important keystone was dropped into place. Each stone weighs four to six tons. The structure stands with no mortar—taking full advantage of the innovative Roman arch, made strong by gravity.

Hike over the bridge for a closer look. Across the river, a high trail (marked *panorama*) leads upstream and offers commanding views. On the exhibit side of the structure, a trail marked *Accès l'Aqueduc* leads up to surviving stretches of the aqueduct. For a peaceful walk alongside the top of the aqueduct (where it's on land and no longer a bridge), follow the red-and-yellow markings. Remains of this part are scant because of medieval cannibalization—frugal builders couldn't resist the pre-cut stones as they constructed local churches. The ancient quarry (about a third of a mile downstream on the exhibit side) may open in 2004.

TRANSPORTATION CONNECTIONS

By car: Pont du Gard is an easy 25-minute drive due west of Avignon (follow signs to Nîmes) and 45 minutes northwest of Arles (via Tarascon). The *Rive Gauche* parking is off D-981, which leads from Remoulins to Uzès. (Parking is also available on the *Rive Droite* side, but it's farther away from the museum.)

By bus: Buses run to Pont du Gard *(Rive Gauche)* from Avignon (5/day summer, 3/day off-season, 40 min). Bus stops are at the traffic roundabout 300 yards from the Pont du Gard. The stop from Avignon is on the opposite side of the roundabout from the Pont du Gard; the stop to Avignon is on the same side as the Pont du Gard, just to the left as you enter the traffic circle. Make sure you're waiting for the bus on the correct side of the traffic circle.

Les Baux

Crowning the rugged Alpilles Mountains, this rock-capping castle town is a striking, memorable place to visit. Even with the tourist crowds, the place evokes a strong community that lived a rugged life—thankful more for their top-notch fortifications than their dramatic views. While mobbed with tour groups through most of the day, those arriving by 9:00 or after 17:00 enjoy a more peaceful scene. Sunsets are dramatic, and nights in Les Baux are pin-drop peaceful. After dark, the castle is closed—but beautifully illuminated.

Les Baux is actually two visits in one: castle ruins on an almost lunar landscape and, below, a medieval town packed with shops, cafés, and tourist knickknacks. See the castle, then savor or blitz the lower town on your way out. There's no free parking; get as close to the top as you can and pay €4. One cobbled street leads into town, where you're greeted first by the **TI** (April–Sept daily 9:00–19:00, Oct–March daily 9:00–18:00, in Hôtel de Ville, tel. 04 90 54 34 39). The main drag leads directly to the castle.

The Castle Ruins

The old olive-mill room (where you buy your ticket) has a few museum exhibits (models of the town in the 13th and 16th centuries, interesting photos showing the town before tourism and today). Pick up the good included audioguide in the next building.

A 12th-century regional powerhouse, Les Baux was razed in 1632 by a paranoid Louis XIII, who was afraid of these troublemaking upstarts. The sun-bleached "dead city" ruins are carved into, out of, and on top of a rock 650 feet above the valley floor. As you wander out on the wind-blown field past kid-thrilling medieval weaponry, try to imagine 6,000 people living behind stone walls on this rock. Notice the water-catchment system (a slanted field that caught rain water and drained it into a cistern—necessary during a siege). In the little chapel across from the museum, the slideshow ("Van Gogh, Gauguin, and Cézanne: Painting in the Land of the Olive Trees") provides a relaxing 10-minute interlude. Early July through late August, costumed knights on horses and sword-wielding peasants reenact battle techniques (several 20-min shows daily, check at TI as you enter; castle entry-€7, Easter–Oct daily 9:00–19:00, July–Aug daily until 20:00, Nov–Easter daily 9:30–17:00).

Les Baux

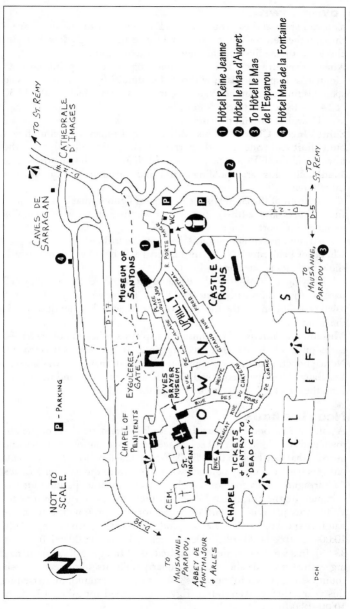

1 Hôtel Reine Jeanne
2 Hôtel le Mas d'Aigret
3 To Hôtel le Mas de l'Esparou
4 Hôtel Mas de la Fontaine

P — PARKING

NOT TO SCALE

Lower Town

You can shop and eat your way back to your car or the bus station through the new town. Or you can take your first left, go downhill, and check out these minor but fun sights as you descend:

Musée Yves Brayer—This is an appealing exhibit of paintings (van Gogh-like Expressionism, without the tumult) by Yves Brayer, who spent his final years in the 1970s here in Les Baux (€4, daily 10:00–12:30 & 14:00–18:30, in Hôtel des Porcelet).

Downhill, around the corner, is…

Saint Vincent Church—This 12th-century Romanesque church was built short and wide to fit the terrain. Inside, on the far right, is the town's traditional Provençal processional chariot. Each Christmas Eve, a ram pulled this cart—holding a lamb and surrounded by candles—to this church.

In front of the church is the old-town "Laundromat"—with a pig-snout faucet and 14th-century stone washing surfaces with drains designed for short women.

Around the corner, towards a great view, is the…

Chapel of Penitents—Notice the nativity painted by Yves Brayer, which shows how Jesus was born in Les Baux.

Staying left as you round the Laundromat and head downhill, you'll pass plenty of cafés with wonderful views. Just downhill, you'll see the town wall and one of the fortified wall's two gates. Farther downhill is the…

Museum of *Santons*—This museum displays a collection of *santons*—the popular folk figures that decorated local manger scenes (free entry). Notice how the manger scene proves once again that Jesus was born in Les Baux. These painted clay dolls show off local dress and traditions. Find the old couple leaning into the mistral wind.

Near Les Baux

A half-mile beyond Les Baux, D-27 leads to dramatic views of the hill town and two sights that fill cool, cavernous caves in former limestone quarries that date back to the Middle Ages. (The limestone is easy to cut, but gets hard and nicely polished when exposed to the weather.) **Caves de Sarragan**—with the best Les Baux views from its parking lot—is occupied by the Sarragnan Winery, which invites you in for a taste. While this place is big and designed for tour groups, the friendly, English-speaking staff welcomes individuals (free, April–Sept daily 10:00–12:00 & 14:00–19:00, Oct–March daily until 18:00, tel. 04 90 54 33 58). In a similar cave nearby, **Cathédrale d'Images** sells a mesmerizing sound-and-slide show. On the quarry walls, its 48 projectors flash countless images set to music, as visitors wander around, immersed in this year's theme: Alexandria, Egypt is planned for 2004 (€7, daily 10:00–18:00).

Speaking of quarries, in 1821 the red rocks and soil of the area were discovered to contain an important mineral for the making of aluminum. It was named after the town—bauxite.

SLEEPING IN AND NEAR LES BAUX

(€1 = about $1.10, country code: 33)

$$$ The appealing **Le Mas d'Aigret***** crouches barely past Les Baux on the road to St. Rémy. Lie on your back and stare up at the castle walls rising beyond your swimming pool in this mini-oasis. Many of the smartly designed rooms have private terraces and views over the valley, and the restaurant is troglodyte-chic (smaller Db-€100, larger Db with terrace-€135, Tb-€175–200, air-con, some daytime road noise, tel. 04 90 54 20 00, fax 04 90 54 44 00, www.masdaigret.com, contact@masdaigret.com, SE).

$$ **Le Mas de L'Esparou** *chambre d'hôte,* a few minutes below Les Baux, is welcoming and kid-friendly, with spacious rooms, squishy mattresses, a swimming pool, table tennis, and distant views of Les Baux. Jacqueline loves her job, and her lack of English only makes her more animated. Monsieur Roux painted the artwork in your room and has a gallery in Les Baux (Db-€62, extra person-about €16, no CC, between Les Baux and Maussane on D-5, look for white sign with green lettering, tel. & fax 04 90 54 41 32, NSE).

$ **Hôtel Reine Jeanne**** is 150 feet to your right after the main entry to the live city (standard Db-€51, Db with deck-€63, great family suite-€90, most air-con, ask for *chambre avec terrasse,* good *menus* from €20, tel. 04 90 54 32 06, fax 04 90 54 32 33, www.la-reinejeanne.com, reine.jeanne@wanadoo.fr).

$ **Mas de la Fontaine,** right below Les Baux behind the Gendarmerie, is a throwback to the past, with simple, fair-priced rooms, a pool (when there is water), and an impersonal owner (closed Nov-March, Db-€50-58, Tb-€67, no CC, tel. 04 90 54 34 13).

$ **Le Mazet des Alpilles** is a small home with three tidy air-conditioned rooms just outside the unspoiled village of Paradou, five minutes below Les Baux. It may have space when others don't (Db-€52, ask for largest room, child's bed available, no CC, follow signs from D-17, in Paradou look for route de Brunelly, tel. 04 90 54 45 89, fax 04 90 54 44 66, lemazet@wanadoo.fr, Annick NSE).

TRANSPORTATION CONNECTIONS

By car: Les Baux is a 20-minute drive from Arles. Follow signs to Avignon, then Les Baux. Drivers can combine Les Baux with St. Rémy (15 minutes away, see below) and the Pont du Gard (see above).

By bus: Four convenient daily buses serve Les Baux from the Arles bus station (30 min, Les Baux TI has schedule, see "Transportation Connections—Arles," above). There is no bus from Les Baux to St. Rémy—figure €15 for a taxi (tel. 06 80 27 60 92).

St. Rémy-de-Provence

Circular and sophisticated St. Rémy gave birth to Nostradamus, sprouted a once-thriving Roman city (Glanum), and cared for a distraught artist. Today you can visit the Roman city called Glanum and the mental ward where Vincent van Gogh was sent after slicing off his ear. Best of all, elbow your way through its raucous Wednesday market (until 12:30). The ring road hems in a pedestrian-friendly center, well-stocked with the latest Provençal fashions.

The **TI** is two blocks toward Les Baux from the ring road (Mon-Sat 9:30-12:30 & 14:00-19:00, Sun 10:00-12:00 & 15:00-17:00, tel. 04 90 92 05 22). It's a 20-minute walk from St. Rémy's center to Glanum and the Clinique St. Paul (van Gogh's mental hospital).

SIGHTS

▲**Glanum**—These crumbling stones are the foundations of a Roman market town, located at the crossroads of two ancient trade routes between Italy and Spain. A massive Roman arch and tower stand proud and lonely near the ruins' parking lot. The arch marked the entry into Glanum, and the tower is a memorial to the grandsons of Emperor Caesar Augustus. The setting is stunning, though shadeless, and the small museum at the entry sets the stage well. While the ruins are, well, ruined, they remind us of the range and prosperity of the Roman Empire. Along with other Roman monuments in Provence, they allow us to paint a more complete picture of Roman life. The English handout is helpful, but consider buying one of the two English booklets (one has better photos, the other provides much better background). Inside the ruins, signs give basic English explanations at key locations, and the view from the belvedere justifies the effort (€6, April–Sept daily 9:00–12:00 & 14:00–19:00, Oct–March daily 9:30–12:00 & 14:00–17:00).

Cloître St. Paul de Mausole—Just below Glanum is the still-functioning mental hospital (Clinique St. Paul) that treated Vincent van Gogh from 1889 to 1890. Pay €3.50 and enter Vincent's temporarily peaceful world: a small chapel, intimate cloisters, and a re-creation of his room. You'll find limited information in English about Vincent's life. Amazingly, he painted 150 works in his 53 weeks here—none of which remain anywhere nearby today. The contrast between the utter simplicity of his room (and his life) and the multimillion-dollar value of his paintings today is jarring. The site is managed by Valetudo, a center

St. Rémy

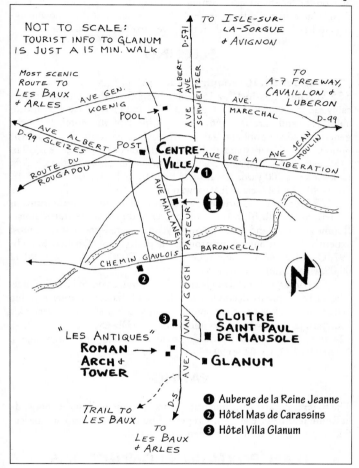

NOT TO SCALE:
TOURIST INFO TO GLANUM
IS JUST A 15 MIN. WALK

TO ISLE-SUR-
LA-SORGUE
& AVIGNON

D-571

MOST SCENIC
ROUTE TO
LES BAUX
& ARLES

AVE GEN.
KOENIG

ALBERT AVE.

AVE SCHWEITZER

TO
A-7 FREEWAY,
CAVAILLON &
LUBERON

POOL

AVE.
MARECHAL

D-99

D-99
AVE. ALBERT
GLEIZES

POST

ROUTE DU
ROUGADOU

CENTRE-
VILLE ❶

AVE MAILLANE

AVE DE LA
LIBERATION

AVE JEAN
MOULIN

AVE PASTEUR

ℹ

CHEMIN GAULOIS

BARONCELLI

❷

N

❸

AVE. VAN GOGH

CLOITRE
SAINT PAUL
DE MAUSOLE

"LES ANTIQUES"
ROMAN ➔
ARCH &
TOWER

■ GLANUM

D-5

TRAIL TO
LES BAUX

TO
LES BAUX
& ARLES

❶ Auberge de la Reine Jeanne
❷ Hôtel Mas de Carassins
❸ Hôtel Villa Glanum

specializing in art therapy (April–Oct daily 9:30–19:00, Nov–March daily 10:15–16:45). Outside the complex, dirt paths lead to Vincent's favorite footpaths with (sometimes vandalized) copies of his paintings from where he painted them.

Hike to Les Baux—These directions will help you find your way on the beautiful three-hour hike from St. Rémy to Les Baux (for more details, ask at TI). Start from the signposted slope opposite the Glanum entry. Follow the goat path up into the mountain and arrive at the chimney.

Go down the iron ladder, and you'll come to a lake. Walk around the lake on the left-hand side, turning left along the *Mas de Gros* cart track. A mile later, turn right on *Sentier des Crêtes,* and follow the yellow markings to Les Baux. You'll end on the paved road in the Val d'Enfer.

SLEEPING

(€1 = about $1.10, country code: 33)

$$$ **Mas de Carassins*****, a 15-minute walk from the center, is impeccably run by friendly Paris refugees, Michel and Pierre. Luxury is affordable here, and care is given to every aspect of the hotel, from the generously sized pool and gardens to the muted room decor and the optional €25 dinner (standard Db-€95–110, deluxe Db-€120, large Tb-€155, extra bed-€15, air-con, table tennis, bike rental, 1 Chemin Gaulois, look for signs 200 yards toward Les Baux from TI, tel. 04 90 92 15 48, fax 04 90 92 63 47, carassin@pacwan.fr).

$$ **Hotel Villa Glanum****, right across from the Glanum ruins, is a 15-minute walk from the town center and gets some traffic noise. Rooms are small and unimaginative, yet adequate—the best (and most expensive) are in bungalows around the pretty pool (Db-€60-82, Tb-€97, Qb-€120, 46 avenue van Gogh, tel. 04 90 92 03 59, fax 04 90 92 00 08, villa.glanum@wanadoo.fr).

$$ **Auberge de la Reine Jeanne**** is central, cozy, and a solid value. The 11 traditionally decorated, spotless, and spacious rooms with big beds take a backseat to the popular restaurant. Some rooms overlook a courtyard jammed with tables and umbrellas (Db-€58-66, Tb/Qb-€74, €24 *menu* in fine restaurant, on ring road at 12 boulevard Mirabeau, tel. 04 90 92 15 33, fax 04 90 92 49 65).

EATING

The town is packed with fine restaurants. To dine well, try **Auberge de la Reine Jeanne** (see above). **Crêperie Lou Planet** is cheap and peaceful, on pleasant place Favier (open until 20:00).

TRANSPORTATION CONNECTIONS

St. Rémy is a spectacular 15-minute drive (or three-hour walk, described above) over the hills and through the woods from Les Baux. The town is probably too close to Avignon for its own good (6 buses/day between here and Avignon, 45 min, no buses to Arles).

THE FRENCH RIVIERA

A hundred years ago, celebrities from London to Moscow flocked here to socialize, gamble, and escape the dreary weather at home. The belle époque is today's tourist craze, as this most sought-after, fun-in-the-sun destination now caters to budget travelers as well. Some of the Continent's most stunning scenery and intriguing museums lie along this strip of land—as do millions of heat-seeking tourists. Nice has world-class museums, a grand beachfront promenade, a seductive old town, and all the drawbacks of a major city (traffic, crime, pollution, etc.). But the day trips possible from Nice are easy and exciting: Monte Carlo welcomes everyone with cash registers open; Antibes has a romantic port and silky-sandy beaches; and the hill towns present a breezy and photogenic alternative to the beach scene. Evenings on the Riviera, a.k.a. the Côte d'Azur, were made for a promenade and outdoor dining.

Choose a Home Base

For most, the best home base is Nice, Antibes, or Villefranche-sur-Mer. **Nice** is the region's capital and France's fifth-largest city. With great train and bus connections to most regional sights, this is the most practical base for train travelers. Urban Nice also has a full palette of museums, a beach scene that rocks, the best selection of hotels in all price ranges, and good nightlife options. A car is a headache in Nice, though it's easily stored at one of the many parking garages.

Nearby **Antibes** is smaller, with a bustling center, the best sandy beaches I found, good walking trails, and the Picasso Museum. It has frequent train service to Nice and Monaco, and it's easy for drivers.

Villefranche-sur-Mer is the romantic's choice, with a serene setting and small-town warmth. It has finely-ground pebble beaches, good public transportation to Nice and Monaco, easy parking, and hotels in most price ranges.

The French Riviera

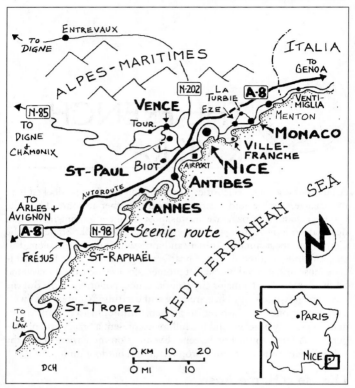

Planning Your Time

Most should plan a full day for Nice and at least a half-day each for Monaco and Antibes. Monaco is best at night (sights are closed but crowds are few; consider dinner here), and Antibes during the day (good beaches and Picasso Museum). The Riviera is infamous for staging major events—it's best to avoid the craziness and room shortage if you can (unless, of course, you're a fan). Here are the three biggies in 2004: Nice Carnival (Feb 13-25), Grand Prix of Monaco (May 20-23), and the Cannes Film Festival (May 12-23).

To save money, consider the *Carte Musées* discount card, which includes admission to many major Riviera museums, including four museums in Nice (Chagall, Matisse, Fine Arts, and Modern and Contemporary Art), plus the Picasso Museum and Fort Carré in Antibes. It's a great value for those planning to visit more than one museum in a day, or several museums over a few days (one day-€10, three days-€17, seven days-€27). Note that it does not cover the casino and aquarium in Monaco, or the Rothschild Villa Ephrussi near Villefranche-sur-Mer.

Getting around the Riviera

Getting around the Côte d'Azur by train or bus is easy (park your car and leave the driving to others). Drivers who want to see some of the Riviera's best scenery should take the short drive along the Middle Corniche from Nice to Monaco.

Nice is perfectly located for exploring the Riviera by public transport. Villefranche, Antibes, St-Paul, and Vence are all within a 60-minute bus or train ride of each other. The TI and most hotels have information on minivan excursions from Nice (half day-€50-60/, full day-€80–110). **Tour Azur** is one of many (tel. 04 93 44 88 77, www.tourazur.com); **Med Tour** is a bit cheaper (tel. 04 93 82 92 58, www.med-tour.com).

At Nice's efficient bus station on boulevard Jean Jaurès, you'll find a baggage check (called *messagerie*, €2.50/bag, Mon–Sat 7:30–18:00, closed Sun), clean WCs (€0.50), and several bus companies. Get schedules and prices from the helpful English-speaking clerk at the information desk in the bus station (tel. 04 93 85 61 81). Buy tickets in the station or on the bus.

Two bus companies, RCA and Cars Broch, provide service on the same route between Nice, Villefranche, Eze, and Monaco (RCA buses run more frequently).

Nice

Nice (sounds like niece), with its spectacular Alps-to-Mediterranean surroundings, eternally entertaining seafront promenade, and fine museums, is an enjoyable big-city highlight of the Riviera. In its traffic-free old city, Italian and French flavors mix to create a spicy Mediterranean dressing. Nice may be nice, but it's hot and jammed in July and August (reserve ahead). Get a room with air-conditioning *(une chambre avec climatisation)*. Everything you'll want to see in Nice is walkable or a short bus ride away.

ORIENTATION

Most sights and hotels recommended in this book are near avenue Jean Médecin, between the train station and the beach. It's a 20-minute walk from the train station to the beach (or an €8 taxi ride), and a 20-minute walk along the promenade from the fancy Hôtel Negresco to the heart of Old Nice.

Nice

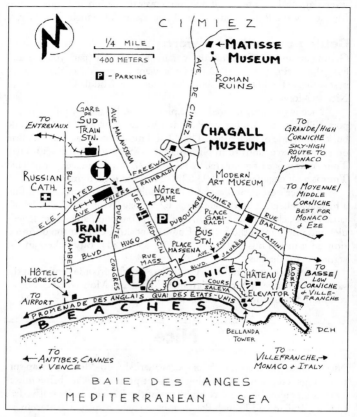

Tourist Information: Nice has four helpful TIs: terminal 1 at the airport (Mon–Sat 8:00–22:00, Sun 8:00–20:00); next to the train station (Mon–Sat 8:00–19:00, Sun 9:00–18:00); on RN-7 after the airport on the right (summers only, 8:00–20:00); and facing the beach at 5 promenade des Anglais (Mon–Sat 9:00–19:00, Sun 10:00–18:00, tel. 08 92 70 74 07, www.nicetourisme.com). Pick up the excellent free Nice map (which lists all the sights and hours), the extensive *Practical Guide to Nice*, information on regional day trips (such as city maps), and the museums booklet.

Consider buying a **museum pass,** sold at any participating sight. The seven-day Nice Municipal Museums Pass is €6. If you're traveling beyond Nice, and visiting several museums, the regional *Carte Musées* is a good value (see "Planning Your Time," above).

Arrival in Nice

By Train: All trains stop at Nice's one main station (*Nice-Ville*, bag check available but closes at 17:45 and all day Sun). Avoid the suburban stations, and never leave your bags unattended. The TI is next door to the left as you exit the station; car rental and taxis are to the right. To reach most of my recommended hotels, turn left out of the station, then right on avenue Jean Médecin. To get to the beach and the promenade des Anglais from the station, continue on foot for 20 minutes down avenue Jean Médecin or take bus #12 (catch bus on avenue Jean Médecin). To get to the old city and the bus station *(gare routière)*, catch bus #5 from avenue Jean Médecin.

By Car: Follow signs for *Nice Centre/Promenade des Anglais*. Try to avoid arriving at rush hour, when the promenade des Anglais grinds to a halt (Mon–Fri 17:00–19:30). Hoteliers know where to park (allow €10–17/day). The parking garage at the Nice Étoile shopping center on avenue Jean Médecin is handy to many of my hotel listings (ticket booth on third floor, about €17/day, €10 from 20:00-8:00). All on-street parking is metered.

By Plane: Nice's easy-to-navigate little airport is on the Mediterranean, about 20 minutes west of the city center. International flights use terminal 1; domestic flights use terminal 2 (airport tel. 04 93 21 30 30, TI and banks at terminal 1). Taxis are expensive, charging €30 to Nice hotels and €45 to Villefranche.

To reach the bus information office, turn left after passing customs and exit the doors at the far end. Three bus lines run from the airport to Nice: #99 runs nonstop to the main train station (stall #1, €3.50, 2/hr until 21:00, 20 min, drops you within a 10-min walk of many recommended hotels); local bus #23 serves stops between the airport and train station (stall #6, €1.40, 4/hr, 40 min, direction: St. Maurice); and the yellow "NICE" bus goes to the bus station *(gare routière*, stall #1, €3.50, 3/hr, 25 min). Buy tickets in the office or from the driver. To get to Villefranche from the airport, take the yellow "NICE" bus to the bus station *(gare routière)* and transfer to the Villefranche bus (€1.40, 4/hr). Buses also run hourly from the airport to Antibes (€7, 20 min), and to Monaco (€14, 50 min).

Helpful Hints

Theft Alert: Nice is notorious for pickpockets. Have nothing important on or around your waist, unless it's in a money belt tucked out of sight (thieves target fanny packs); don't leave anything visible in your car; be wary of scooters when standing at intersections; don't leave things unattended on the beach while swimming; and stick to main streets in Old Nice after dark.

Museums: Most Nice museums are closed Tuesdays, and free the first Sunday of the month. For information on museum passes, see

"Orientation," above.

U.S. Consulate: You'll find it at 7 avenue Gustave V (tel. 04 93 88 89 55, fax 04 93 87 07 38).

Canadian Consulate: It's at 10 rue Lamartine (tel. 04 93 92 93 22).

Medical Help: Riviera Medical Services has a list of English-speaking physicians. They can help you make an appointment or call an ambulance (tel. 04 93 26 12 70).

Rocky Beaches: To make life tolerable on the rocks, swimmers should buy a pair of the cheap plastic beach shoes (flip-flops fall off in the water) sold at many shops.

American Express: AmEx faces the beach at 11 promenade des Anglais (tel. 04 93 16 53 53).

English Bookstore: The Cat's Whiskers has a great selection (closed Sun, 26 rue Lamartine, near Hôtel Star).

Local Guide: Pascale Rucker, Nice's only "singing guide," does fine tours with or without a performance (half day-€135, full day-€203, tel. 04 93 87 77 89, mobile 06 16 24 29 52).

Launderettes and Internet Cafés: These abound. Your hotelier can direct you to ones near your hotel.

Renting a Bike (and Other Wheels): Roller Station rents bikes, skates (*rollers*), and mini-scooters (*trotinettes*) for the same price (€5/1 hr, €10/4 hr, €15/day, open daily, across from seaside promenade at 49 quai des États-Unis, tel. 04 93 62 99 05).

English Radio: Tune into Riviera-Radio at FM 106.5.

Getting around Nice

While walking gets you to most places, you'll want to ride the bus to the Chagall and Matisse museums. Bus fare is €1.40, and an all-day pass is €4.

Taxis are expensive but handy for the Chagall and Matisse museums and the Russian Church (figure €8-10 from promenade des Anglais). They normally only pick up at taxi stands *(tête de station)* or if you call (tel. 04 93 13 78 78).

For €6, you can spend 40 embarrassing minutes on the **tourist train** tooting through town and up to the castle with a taped English narration. This is a sweat-free way to get to the castle (departures at the top of the hour, load up opposite Albert I park).

NICE IN THE BUFF:
A WALK THROUGH OLD NICE (VIEUX NICE)

This fun and informative self-guided walking tour gives a helpful introduction to Nice's bicultural heritage and most interesting neighborhoods. It's best done early in the morning (while the outdoor market still thrives). Allow about two hours at a leisurely pace, with a stop for coffee and *socca* (chickpea crêpe). Our tour begins on promenade des Anglais (near the landmark Hôtel Negresco) and ends in the heart of Old Nice.

Promenade des Anglais: There's something for everyone along this four-mile-long seafront circus. Stroll like the belle époque English aristocrats for whom the promenade was built. The broad sidewalks of the promenade des Anglais (literally "Walkway of the English") were financed by wealthy English tourists who wanted a "safe" place to stroll and admire the view. The walk was paved in marble in 1822 for aristocrats who didn't want to dirty their shoes or smell the fishy gravel. This grand promenade leads to the old town and Castle Hill.

Hôtel Negresco: Start at this pink-domed hotel—Nice's finest, and a historic monument. The hotel offers the city's most expensive beds and a free "museum" interior (free, always open—provided you're dressed decently). March straight through the lobby into the exquisite Salon Royal. The chandelier hanging from the Eiffel-built dome is made of 16,000 pieces of crystal. It was built in France for the Russian czar's Moscow palace...but, because of the Bolshevik Revolution in 1918, he couldn't take delivery. Read the explanation of the dome and saunter around counterclockwise: The bucolic scene, painted in 1913 for the hotel, sets the tone. Nip into the toilets for either a belle époque powder room or a Battle of Waterloo experience. The chairs nearby were typical of the age (cones of silence for an afternoon nap sitting up).

On your way out, pop into the Salon Louis XIV (right of entry lobby as you leave), where the embarrassingly short Sun King models his red platform boots (English descriptions explain the room).

Walk around the back to see the hotel's original entrance (grander than today's)—a reminder that, in the 19th century, classy people stayed out of the sun, and any posh hotel that cared about its clientele would design its entry on the shady north side.

Cross the big street, turn left, and, before you begin your seaside promenade, grab a bench at the...

Bay of Angels (Baie des Anges): The body of Nice's patron saint, Réparate, was supposedly escorted into this bay by angels in the fourth century. Face the water. To your right is the airport, built on a landfill. On that tip of land way beyond the runway is Cap d'Antibes. Until 1860, Antibes and Nice were in different countries—Antibes was French, but Nice was a protectorate of the Italian kingdom of Savoy-Piedmont. (During that period, the Var River—just west of Nice—was the geographic border between these two peoples.) In 1850, the people here spoke Italian and ate pasta. As Italy was uniting, the region was given a choice: join the new country of Italy or join France (which was enjoying good times under the rule of Napoleon III). The vast majority voted to go French...and *voilà!*

To the far left lies Villefranche-sur-Mer (marked by the tower at land's end—and home to lots of millionaires), then Monaco, then Italy.

Behind you are the foothills of the Alps (les Alpes Maritimes), which gather threatening clouds but leave alone the Côte d'Azur to enjoy the sunshine more than 300 days each year. While half a million people live here, pollution is carefully treated—the water is routinely tested and very clean.

Now head to the left and begin...

Strolling the Promenade: The block next to Hôtel Negresco has a lush park and the Masséna Museum (closed for renovation). Nearby sit two other belle époque establishments: the West End and Westminster hotels—English names to help those original guests feel at home. These hotels represent Nice's arrival as a tourist mecca a century ago, when the combination of leisure time and a stable economy allowed tourists to find the sun even in winter.

Even a hundred years ago, there was already sufficient tourism in Nice to justify building its first casino (a leisure activity imported from Venice). An elegant casino stood on pilings in the sea until the Germans destroyed it during World War II. While that's gone, you can see the striking 1920s Art Nouveau facade of the Palais de la Mediterranean—a grand casino and theater. Only the facade survives, and today it fronts a luxury condominium. The less charming Casino Ruhl is farther along (just before the park). Anyone can drop in for some one-armed-bandit fun, but for the tables at night you'll need to dress up and bring your passport.

Albert I Park is named for the Belgian king who enjoyed wintering here. While the English came first, the Belgians and Russians were also huge fans of 19th-century Nice. The 1960 statue in the park commemorates Nice's being part of France for 100 years.

Walk into the park and continue down the center of the grassy strip between the two boulevards all the way to place Masséna. The mod sculpture you pass is an answer to a prayer for local skateboarders. Walk to the fountains and face them. (To save water, they get high pressure only after 17:00.)

Place Masséna: You're standing on Nice's river, the Paillon (covered since the 1800s). Turn around. You can track the river's route under the green parkway you just walked up (it meets the sea at the Casino Ruhl). For centuries, this river was Nice's natural defense. A fortified wall ran along its length to the sea. With the arrival of tourism in the 1800s, Nice expanded over and beyond the river. The rich red coloring of the buildings around you was the preference of Nice's Italian rulers.

Cross the square and follow the steps that lead past the three palm trees and to rue de l'Opéra between the curved buildings. Walk down rue de l'Opéra and turn left on...

Rue St. François de Paule: You've entered Old Nice. Peer into the Alziari olive oil shop at #14 (opposite the city hall). Dating from 1868, it produces top-quality, stone-ground olive oil. The proud owner, Gilles Piot, claims that stone wheels create less acidity (since metal grinding builds up heat). Locals fill their own containers from the huge vats (the cheapest one is peanut oil, not olive oil). Consider a gift for the olive-oil lover on your list. A block down on the left (#7), Pâtisserie Auer's belle époque storefront has changed little since the pastry shop opened in 1820. The writing on the window says "For over 170 years from father to son." The royal medallions on the back wall remind shoppers that Queen Victoria fed her sweet tooth here. Across the street is Nice's grand opera house, from the same era. Imagine this opulent jewel buried deep in the old town of Nice back in the 19th century. With all the fancy big-city folks wintering here, the rough-edged town needed some high-class entertainment. The four statues on top represent theater, dance, music, and singing.

Continue on, sifting your way through tacky souvenirs to the cours Saleya (coor sah-lay-yuh).

Cours Saleya: Named for its broad exposure to the sun (*soleil*), this cacophony of color, sights, smells, and people has been Nice's main market square since the Middle Ages (produce market held daily until 13:00—except on Monday, when an antique market takes over the square). Amazingly, the square was a parking lot until 1980, when the mayor of Nice had an underground parking garage built.

The first section is devoted to freshly cut flowers that seem to grow effortlessly and everywhere in this ideal climate. Carnations, roses, and jasmine are local favorites in what has been the Riviera's biggest flower market since the 19th century. Fresh flowers are perhaps the best value in this otherwise pricey city.

The boisterous produce section trumpets the season with mushrooms, strawberries, white asparagus, zucchini flowers—whatever's fresh gets top billing.

Place Pierre Gautier (also called Plassa dou Gouvernou—bilingual street signs include the old Niçoise language) is where the actual farmers set up stalls to sell their produce and herbs directly. For a good overall view, climb the steps closest to the water (stepping over the trash sacks) above the Grand Bleu restaurant.

From your perch, look up to the hill that dominates to the east. The city of Nice was first settled there by Greeks circa 400 B.C. In the Middle Ages, a massive castle stood there, with turrets, high walls, and soldiers at the ready. With the river guarding one side and the sea the other, this mountain fortress seemed strong—until Louis XIV leveled it in 1706. Nice's medieval seawall ran along the lineup of two-story buildings where you're standing. Now, look across place Pierre Gautier to the large "palace." This Ducal Palace was where the kings of Savoy-Piedmont (Nice's Italian rulers until about 1860) would reside when in Nice. Today it's police headquarters.

Resume your stroll down the center of cours Saleya, stopping when you see La Cambuse restaurant on your left. In front, hovering over the black barrel fire with the paella-like pan on top, is the self-proclaimed Queen of the Market, Thérèse (tehr-ehz). When she's not looking for a husband, Thérèse is cooking *socca*, Nice's chickpea crêpe specialty. Spend €2 for wad of *socca* (careful—it's hot, but good).

Continue down cours Saleya. The fine golden building at the end is where Henri Matisse lived for 17 years. Turn left at the Civette du Cours café, and head down...

Rue de la Poissonnière: Look up at #4. Adam and Eve are squaring off, each holding a zucchini-like gourd. This scene (post-apple) represents the annual rapprochement in Nice to make up for the sins of a too-much-fun Carnival (Mardi Gras). Nice residents have partied hard during Carnival for more than 700 years. The iron grill above the door allows cooling air to enter the building, but keeps out uninvited guests. You'll see lots of these open grills in Old Nice. They were part of an ingenious system of sucking in cool air from the sea, through the homes, and out through the vents in the roof. Across the street, check out the small Baroque church dedicated to St. Rita, the patron saint of desperate causes. She holds a special place in locals' hearts, and this church is the most popular in Nice.

Turn right on the next street, then left on "Right" Street (rue Droite), into a world that feels like Naples.

Rue Droite: In the Middle Ages, this straight, skinny street provided the most direct route from wall to wall, or river to sea. Stop at Esipuno's bakery (#38). Thirty years ago, this baker was voted the best in France, and his son now runs the place. Notice the firewood stacked by the oven. Farther along, at #28, Thérèse (who you met earlier) cooks her *socca* in the wood-fired oven before she carts it to her barrel on cours Saleya. The balconies of the mansion in the next block mark the Palais Lascaris (1647), a rare souvenir from one of Nice's most prestigious families (free, 10:00-18:00, worth touring for a peek at 1700s Baroque Italy high life, look up and make faces back at the guys under the balconies).

Turn left on the rue de la Loge, then left again on rue Centrale to reach...

Place Rossetti: The most Italian of Nice's piazzas, place Rossetti feels more like Rome than Nice. This square comes alive after dark. Fennochio is popular for its many gelato flavors. Walk to the fountain and stare back at the church. This is the Cathedral of St. Réparate—an unassuming building for a major city's cathedral. The cathedral was relocated here in the 1500s, when Castle Hill was temporarily converted to military-only. The name comes from Nice's patron saint, a teenage virgin named Réparate whose martyred body was floated to Nice in the fourth century, accompanied by angels (remember the Bay of Angels?). The interior is overwhelmingly Baroque. Remember that Baroque was a response to the Protestant Reformation. With the Catholic Church's "Counter-Reformation," the theatrical energy of churches was cranked up—with reenergized, high-powered saints and eye-popping decor.

Back outside the cathedral, the steps leading up rue Rossetti are the most direct path from here to Castle Hill (15 min straight up). If you're pooped, wander back down to quai des États-Unis near the beach and ride the elevator (next to Hôtel Suisse, where bayfront road curves right, one way-€0.70, round-trip-€1).

Castle Hill (Colline du Château): This hill—in an otherwise flat city center—offers good views over Nice, the port (to the east), the foothills of the Alps, and the Mediterranean. The views are best at sunset or whenever the weather's really clear (park closes at 20:00 in summer, earlier off-season). Until the 1100s, the city of Nice was crammed onto this hilltop, as it was too risky to live in the flatlands below. Today, you'll find a waterfall, a playground, two cafés (fair prices), and a cemetery—but no castle—on Castle Hill.

To walk back downtown, follow signs from just below the upper café to Vieille Ville (not Le Port), and turn right at the cemetery, then look for the walkway down on your left.

MUSEUMS

▲▲▲Chagall Museum (Musée National Marc Chagall)—Even if you're suspicious of modern art, this museum—with the largest collection of Chagall's work in captivity anywhere—is a delight. After World War II, Chagall returned from the United States to settle in nearby Vence. Between 1954 and 1967, he painted a cycle of 17 large murals designed for, and donated to, this museum. These paintings, inspired by the biblical books of Genesis, Exodus, and the Song of Songs, make up the "nave," or core, of what Chagall called the "House of Brotherhood."

Each painting is a lighter-than-air collage of images that draw from Chagall's Russian-folk-village youth, his Jewish heritage, biblical themes, and his feeling that he existed somewhere between heaven and earth. He believed that the Bible was a synonym for nature, and that color and biblical themes were key ingredients for understanding God's love for his creation. Chagall's brilliant blues and reds celebrate nature, as do his spiritual and folk themes.

Notice the focus on couples. To Chagall, humans loving each other mirrored God's love of creation. Chagall enjoyed the love of two women in his long life—his first wife Bella, then Valentina, who gave him a second wind as he was painting these late works. Chagall was one of the few "serious" 20th-century artists to portray unabashed love. Where the Bible uses the metaphor of earthly, physical, sexual love to describe God's love for humans, Chagall uses unearthly colors and a mystical ambience to celebrate human love. Chagall's canvases are hard to interpret on a literal level, but they capture the rosy spirit of a man in love with life.

On your way out, be sure to visit the three Chagall stained-glass windows in the auditorium (depicting God's creation of the universe).

Cost, Hours, and Information: €5.50, covered by Riviera *Carte Musées* pass, Wed–Mon 10:00–17:00, until 18:00 July–Aug, closed Tue, tel. 04 93 53 87 31, www.musee-chagall.fr. While Chagall would suggest that you explore his works without help, the €3 museum guidebook is useful in explaining the symbolism.

Getting to the Chagall and Matisse Museums: The museums are at the top of town. Chagall is a confusing but manageable 15-minute walk from the top of avenue Jean Médecin (and the train station); Matisse is another 30 minutes above that. You can get to either musuem by bus or on foot. **Buses** #15 and #17 serve the museums from the eastern side of avenue Jean Médecin (both run 6/hr, €1.40). The bus stops are on avenue de Cimiez (use stop Musée Chagall for you-know-where, or stop Arènes for Matisse). To **walk,** go to the train-station end of avenue Jean Médecin and turn right onto boulevard Raimbaldi along the overpasses, then turn left under the overpasses onto avenue Raymond Comboul. When you emerge from the overpass, angle to the right up avenue de l'Olivetto to the alley (with the big wall on your right). A pedestrian path soon emerges, leading up and up to signs for both museums.

▲**Matisse Museum (Musée Matisse)**—This museum, worth a ▲▲▲ rating for his fans, contains the world's largest collection of Matisse paintings. It offers a painless introduction to the artist, whose style was shaped by Mediterranean light and by fellow Côte d'Azur artists Picasso and Renoir.

Henri Matisse, the master of leaving things out, could suggest a woman's body with a single curvy line—leaving it to the viewer's mind to fill in the rest. Ignoring traditional 3-D perspective, he used simple dark outlines saturated with bright blocks of color to create recognizable but simplified scenes composed into a decorative pattern to express nature's serene beauty. You don't look "through" a Matisse canvas, like a window; you look "at" it, like wallpaper.

Matisse understood how colors and shapes affect us emotionally. He could create either shocking, clashing works (Fauvism) or geometrical, balanced, harmonious ones (later works). While other modern artists reveled in purely abstract design, Matisse (almost) always kept the subject matter at least vaguely recognizable. He used unreal colors and distorted lines not just to portray what an object looks like, but to express the object's inner nature (even inanimate objects). Meditating on his paintings helps you connect with nature—or so Matisse hoped.

As you wander the museum, look for motifs including fruit, flowers, wallpaper, and interiors of sunny rooms—often with a window opening onto a sunny landscape. Another favorite subject is the odalisque (harem concubine)—usually shown sprawled in seductive poses, with a simplified mask-like face.

Notice works from his different periods. Room 9 houses paintings from his formative years as a student. In Room 10, his work evolves through many stages, becoming simpler with time. Upstairs, in and around Room 17, you'll find sketches and models of his famous Chapel of the Rosary in nearby Vence and related religious work. On the same floor, there are rooms dedicated to his paper cutouts and his *Jazz* series. Throughout the building are souvenirs from his travels, which inspired much of his work.

The museum is in a 17th-century Genoese villa, set in an olive grove amid the ruins of the Roman city of Cemenelum. Part of the ancient Roman city of Nice, Cemenelum was a military camp that housed as many as 20,000 people.

Cost, Hours, and Location: €4, covered by Riviera *Carte Musées* pass, Wed–Mon 10:00–18:00, closed Tue, tel. 04 93 81 08 08, www .musee-matisse-nice.org. To reach the museum, see "Getting to the Chagall and Matisse Museums," above.

Modern and Contemporary Art Museum (Musée d'Art Moderne et d'Art Contemporain)—This ultramodern museum features an enjoyable collection of art from the 1960s and 1970s, including works by Andy Warhol and Roy Lichtenstein, and offers frequent special exhibits (€4, covered by Riviera *Carte Musées* pass, Wed–Mon 10:00–18:00, closed Tue, on promenade des Arts near bus station, tel. 04 93 62 61 62).

Molinard Perfume Museum—The Molinard family has been making perfume in Grasse (about an hours' drive from Nice) since 1849. Their Nice store has a small museum in the back which illustrates the story of their industry. Back when people believed water spread cholera and the plague (Louis XIV is said to have bathed less than once a year), doctors advised people to rub fragrances into their skin and then powder their body. Back then, perfume was a necessity of everyday life.

Room 1 shows photos of the local flowers used in perfume production. Room 2 shows the earliest (18th-century) production method. Petals would be laid on a bed of animal fat. After baking in the sun, the fat would absorb the essence of the flowers. Petals would be replaced daily for two months until the fat was saturated. Models and old photos show the later distillation process (300 kilos of lavender would produce one liter of essence). Perfume is "distilled like cognac and then aged like wine." Room 3 shows the desk of a "nose." Of the 150 real "noses" (top perfume creators) in the world, more than 100 are French. You are welcome to enjoy the testing bottles before heading into the shop (museum free, daily 10:00-19:00, just between beach and place Masséna at 20 rue St. François de Paule, tel. 04 93 62 90 50).

Other Nice Museums—These museums are decent rainy-day options (generally open Tue–Sun 10:00–12:00 & 14:00–18:00, closed Mon). The

Fine Arts Museum (Musée des Beaux-Arts), with 6,000 works from the 17th to 20th centuries, will satisfy your need for a fine-arts fix (€4, covered by Riviera *Carte Musées* pass, 3 avenue des Baumettes, western end of Nice, tel. 04 92 15 28 28). The **Naval Museum** (Musée de la Marine) is interesting and relevant (€2.50, closed Mon–Tue, in Bellanda Tower, or *Tour Bellanda,* halfway up Castle Hill, tel. 04 93 80 47 61). The **Archaeological Museum** (Musée Archeologique) displays Roman ruins and various objects from the Romans' occupation of this region (€4, near Matisse Museum at 160 avenue des Arènes, tel. 04 93 81 59 57). Nice's city museum, **Museum Masséna** (Musée Masséna), is closed until at least 2004.

▲**Russian Cathedral (Cathédrale Russe)**—Nice's Russian Orthodox church—which claims to be the finest outside Russia—is worth a visit. Five hundred rich Russian families wintered in Nice. Since they couldn't pray in a Catholic church, the community needed a worthy Orthodox house of worship. Czar Nicholas I's widow saw the need and provided the land (which required tearing down her house). Czar Nicholas II gave this church to the Russian community in 1912. (A few years later, Russian comrades—who didn't winter on the Riviera—assassinated him.) Here in the land of olives and anchovies, these proud onion domes seem odd. But, I imagine, so did those old Russians.

Step inside (pick up English info sheet). The one-room interior is filled with icons and candles, and the old Russian music adds to the ambience. The icon wall divides things between the spiritual world and the temporal world of the worshippers. Only the priest can walk between the two worlds, by using the "Royal Door." Take a close look at items lining the front (starting in the left corner). The angel with red boots and wings—the protector of the Romanov family—stands over a symbolic tomb of Christ. The tall, black, hammered-copper cross commemorates the massacre of Nicholas II and his family in 1918. Notice the Jesus icon near the Royal Door. According to a priest here, as the worshipper meditates, staring deep into the eyes of Jesus, he enters a lake where he finds his soul. Surrounded by incense, chanting, and your entire community…it could happen. Farther to the right, the icon of the Virgin and Child is decorated with semi-precious stones from the Ural Mountains. Artists worked a triangle into each iconic face—symbolic of the Trinity (€2.50, daily 9:00–12:00 & 14:30–18:00, chanted services Sat at 17:30 or 18:00, Sun at 10:00, no shorts, 10-min walk behind station at 17 boulevard du Tzarewitch, tel. 04 93 96 88 02).

SLEEPING

Near the Train Station

Most hotels near the station are overrun, overpriced, and loud. Here are the pleasant exceptions (most are between Old Nice and the train station,

SLEEP CODE

(€1 = about $1.10, country code: 33)
Sleep Code: **S** = Single, **D** = Double/Twin, **T** = Triple, **Q** = Quad, **b** = bathroom, **s** = shower only, **no CC** = Credit Cards not accepted, **SE** = Speaks English, **NSE** = No English, * = French hotel rating (0–4 stars). Hotels have elevators and accept credit cards unless otherwise noted.

To help you sort easily through these listings, I've divided the rooms into three categories based on the price for a standard double room with bath:

$$$ **Higher Priced**—Most rooms €100 or more.
$$ **Moderately Priced**—Most rooms between €65-100.
$ **Lower Priced**—Most rooms €65 or less.

Don't look for charm in Nice. Go for modern and clean, with a central location and, in summer, air-conditioning. I've divided my sleeping recommendations into three areas: between the train station and Nice Étoile Shopping Center, near Old Nice and the beaches, and in a more stately area between the station and promenade des Anglais (by boulevard Victor Hugo).

Reserve early for summer visits. The rates listed here are for April through October. Prices generally drop €10-20 from November through March, and can increase dramatically during the Nice Carnival (Feb 13–25 in 2004) and Monaco's Grand Prix (May 20-23 in 2004). June is convention month, and Nice is Europe's top convention city—so book ahead.

near avenue Jean Médecin and boulevard Victor Hugo). For parking, ask your hotelier, or see "Arrival in Nice: By Car," above.

$$$ **Hôtel Vendôme*****, a mansion set off the street, gives you a whiff of the belle époque, with pink pastels, high ceilings, and grand staircases. Rooms are modern and come in all sizes. The best have balconies—request *une chambre avec balcon* (Sb-€85–92, Db-€105-125, Tb-€120-140, buffet breakfast-€10, air-con, parking-€9/day, 26 rue Pastorelli, tel. 04 93 62 00 77, fax 04 93 13 40 78, www.vendome-hotel-nice.com, contact@vendome-hotel-nice.com).

$$ **Hôtel Excelsior*****, one block below the station, is a diamond in the rough. You'll find turn-of-the-century decor, a small but lush garden courtyard, and pleasant rooms with real wood furnishings. Rooms on the garden are best in the summer; streetside rooms have balconies

Nice Hotels

1. Hôtel Excelsior
2. Hôtel Vendome
3. Hôtel Clemenceau & Hôtel St. Georges
4. Hôtel du Petit Louvre
5. Hôtel Aria
6. Hôtel Masséna & Hôtel le Guitry
7. Hôtel Suisse
8. Hôtel Lafayette
9. Hôtel Mercure
10. Hôtel le Royal
11. Hôtel Lorrain
12. Hôtel Windsor
13. Hôtel les Cigales
14. Hôtel Splendid & Hôtel Gounod
15. Hôtel l'Oasis

and get winter sun (Db-€76-105, includes breakfast, air-con, 19 avenue Durante, tel. 04 93 88 18 05, fax 04 93 88 38 69, www.excelsiornice.com, excelsior.hotel@wanadoo.fr).

$ **Hôtel Clémenceau****, run by the charming La Serres, is an exceptional value with a simple, homey feel. Rooms—some with balconies, some without closets, all air-conditioned—are mostly spacious and traditional (S-€31, Sb-€43, D-€43, Db-€46, Tb-€69, Qb-€84, kitchenette-€8 extra and only for stays of at least three nights, no elevator, 3 avenue Georges Clémenceau, one block west of avenue Jean Médecin, tel. 04 93 88 61 19, fax 04 93 16 88 96, hotel-clemenceau@wanadoo.fr, Marianne SE).

$ **Hôtel St. Georges****, a block away, is big and bright, with a backyard garden, reasonably clean and comfortable rooms, and happy Jacques at the reception (Sb-€55, Db-€65, Tb with three separate beds-€82, extra bed-€16, air-con, 7 avenue Georges Clémenceau, tel. 04 93 88 79 21, fax 04 93 16 22 85, nicefrance.hotelstgeorges@wanadoo.fr).

$ **Hôtel du Petit Louvre*** is basic, but a good budget bet, with playful owners (the Vilas), art-festooned walls, and adequate rooms (S-€36, Ds-€42, Db-€47, Tb-€55, pay on arrival, 10 rue Emma Tiranty, tel. 04 93 80 15 54, fax 04 93 62 45 08, petilouvr@wanadoo.com).

Near Old Nice

$$$ **Hôtel Masséna******, in an elegant building a few blocks from place Masséna, is a consummate business hotel that offers 100 four-star rooms with all the comforts at reasonable rates (small Db-€105, larger Db-€140, still larger Db-€200, extra bed-€30, Internet access, reserve parking ahead-€16/day, 58 rue Giofreddo, tel. 04 92 47 88 88, fax 04 92 47 88 89, www.hotel-massena-nice.com).

$$$ **Hôtel Suisse***** has Nice's best ocean views for the money, and is surprisingly quiet given the busy street below. Rooms are comfortable, with air-conditioning and modern conveniences. There's no reason to sleep here if you don't land a view, so I've listed prices only for view rooms—many of which have balconies (Db-€135-145, 15 quai Rauba Capeu, tel. 04 92 17 39 00, fax 04 93 85 30 70, hotelsuisse.nice@wanadoo.fr).

$$$ **Hôtel Mercure*****, wonderfully situated on the water behind cours Saleya, offers tastefully designed rooms at good rates for the location (Sb-€94, Db-€105-112, buffet breakfast-€12, air-con, 91 quai des États-Unis, tel. 04 93 85 74 19, fax 04 93 13 90 94, h0962@accor-hotels.com).

$$ **Hôtel Lafayette***** looks big and average from the outside, but inside it's a cozy, good value that offers 18 sharp, spacious, three-star rooms at two-star rates, all one floor up from the street. Sweet Sandrine will take good care of you (standard Db-€70–85, spacious Db-€88-104, extra bed-€18, no elevator, central air-con, 32 rue de l'Hôtel des Postes, tel. 04 93 85 17 84, fax 04 93 80 47 56, lafayette@nouvel-hotel.com).

$$ **Hôtel le Guitry***** is a small place with 16 rooms: Half are traditional, half are just renovated and *très* plush, and a few have little

natural light (Db-€88, big family room-€120, central air-con, 6 rue Sacha Guitry, tel. 04 93 80 83 83, fax 04 93 13 02 91, dynamo Geraldine S enough E).

$ Hôtel Lorrain** offers kitchenettes in all of its large, modern, linoleum-floored rooms. It's conveniently located one block from the bus station and Old Nice (Db-€46, extra person-€23, 6 rue Gubernatis, push top buzzer to release door, tel. 04 93 85 42 90, fax 04 93 85 55 54, hotellorrain@aol.com).

Uptown, between the Station and Promenade des Anglais

$$$ Hôtel Windsor** is a well-run and snazzy garden retreat with contemporary rooms designed by modern artists. It has a swimming pool and gym (both free for guests), and a €10 sauna (Db-€135-150, extra bed-€20, rooms over garden worth the higher price, 11 rue Dalpozzo, tel. 04 93 88 59 35, fax 04 93 88 94 57, www.hotelwindsornice.com, contact@hotelwindsornice.com).

$$$ Hôtel les Cigales** is a smart little pastel place with tasteful decor, air-conditioning, and a slick upstairs terrace (standard Db-€115, big Db-€135, 16 rue Dalpozzo, tel. 04 97 03 10 70, fax 04 97 03 10 71, www.hotel-lescigales.com, infos@hotel-lescigales.com).

$$$ Hôtel Splendid*** is a worthwhile splurge if you miss your Hilton. The rooftop pool, Jacuzzi, and panoramic breakfast room alone almost justify the cost...but throw in luxurious rooms, a free gym, Internet access, and air-conditioning, and you're as good as home (Db-€215, deluxe Db with terrace-€250, suites-€325, parking-€19/day, 50 boulevard Victor Hugo, tel. 04 93 16 41 00, fax 04 93 16 42 70, www.splendid-nice.com).

$$$ Hôtel Gounod** is behind Hôtel Splendid and shares the same owners, so it allows its clients free access to Hôtel Splendid's pool, Jacuzzi, and other amenities. Don't let the lackluster lobby fool you. Its fine rooms are big, air-conditioned, and richly decorated, with high ceilings (Db-€125–140, palatial four-person suites-€215, parking-€16/day, 3 rue Gounod, tel. 04 93 16 42 00, fax 04 93 88 23 84, www.gounod-nice.com).

$$$ Hôtel Aria** is a soft-yellow, very sharp big-city refuge with comfortable rooms, half of which overlook a small park (Db-€95-110, extra bed-€20, buffet breakfast-€9, 15 avenue Auber, tel. 04 93 88 30 69, fax 04 93 88 11 35, www.aria-nice.com, contact@aria-nice.com).

$$ Hôtel le Royal** stands shoulder-to-shoulder on the promenade des Anglais with the big boys (hôtels Negresco and New Westminster). It feels like a retirement home-turned-hotel, but offers solid comfort with air-conditioning at €100-200 less than its more famous neighbors (seaview rooms: Sb-€70, Db-€105; city-facing rooms: Sb-€60, Db-€85; 23 promenade des Anglais, tel. 04 93 16 43 00, fax 04 93 16 43 02, royal@vacancesbleues.com).

$$ Hôtel l'Oasis*** is just that. This orange-pastel hotel sits away from the street, surrounding a large, flowery courtyard. Its 40 rooms are also calming, with air-conditioning, earth tones, pleasing fabrics, sharp bathrooms, and reasonable rates (Sb-€75, Db-€95, Tb-€115, 23 rue Gounod, tel. 04 93 88 12 29, fax 04 93 16 14 40, www.hotel-oasis -nice.com.fr, mail@hotel-oasis-nice.com.fr).

EATING

My recommended restaurants are concentrated in the same neighbor-hoods as my favorite hotels. The promenade des Anglais is ideal for pic-nic dinners on warm, languid evenings, and the old town is perfect for restaurant-shopping. Gelato-lovers should save room for **Fenocchio** (on place Rossetti in Old Nice, 86 flavors from tomato to lavender, daily until 23:30). Ice cream cone in hand, you can join the evening parade along the Mediterranean (best view at night is from east end of quai des États-Unis, on tip below Castle Hill).

In Old Nice, on or near Cours Saleya

Nice's dinner scene converges on cours Saleya—entertaining enough in itself to make the generally mediocre food of its restaurants a good value. It's a fun, festive place to compare tans and mussels. Even if you're eat-ing elsewhere, wander through here in the evening.

La Cambuse offers a refined setting and fine cuisine for those who want to eat on cours Saleya without sacrificing quality (allow €30-40 per person, daily, at #5, tel. 04 93 80 82 40).

Le Safari—a good budget option for Italian fare—has the best "eat-ing energy" on the cours Saleya (daily, at Castle Hill end at #1, tel. 04 93 80 18 44).

Nissa Socca offers good, cheap Italian cuisine and a lively atmos-phere a few blocks from cours Saleya (Mon-Sat from 19:00, closed Sun, arrive early, a block off place Rossetti on rue Ste. Réparate, tel. 04 93 80 18 35).

L'Acchiardo, deeper in the old city, is a budget traveler's friend, with simple, hearty, traditional cuisine at bargain prices in a homey setting (dinner *plats*-€12, closed Sat–Sun, 38 rue Droite, tel. 04 93 85 51 16).

Lou Pilha Leva offers a fun, *très* cheap dinner option with Niçoise specialties and outdoor-only benches. Order your food from one side and drinks from the other (daily, located where rue de la Loge and rue Centrale meet in Old Nice).

L'Univers, a block off place Masséna, has earned a Michelin star while maintaining a warm ambience. This Riviera-elegant place is as relaxed as a "top" restaurant can be, from its casual decor to the tasteful dinnerware. But when the artfully-presented food arrives, you know this is high cuisine (*menus* from €40, closed Sun, 53 boulevard Jean Jaurès,

Nice Restaurants

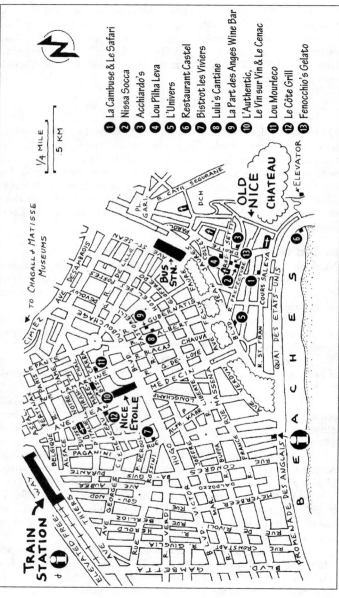

1/4 MILE
.5 KM

1 La Cambuse & Le Safari
2 Nissa Socca
3 Acchiardo's
4 Lou Pilha Leva
5 L'Univers
6 Restaurant Castel
7 Bistrot les Viviers
8 Lulu's Cantine
9 La Part des Anges Wine Bar
10 L'Authentic,
   Le Vin sur Vin & Le Cenac
11 Lou Mourleco
12 Le Côte Grill
13 Fenocchio's Gelato

tel. 04 93 62 32 22, plumailunivers@aol.com).

Restaurant Castel is your best beach option. Eating here, you almost expect Don Ho to grab a mic. You're right on the beach below Castle Hill, perfectly positioned to watch evening swimmers get in their last laps as the sky turns pink and city lights flicker on. Arrive before sunset and linger long enough to merit the few extra euros the place charges (daily, salads and pastas-€11-14, main courses-€22, *Panaché de la Mer* is a good sampling of seafood and vegetables, tel. 04 93 85 22 66).

Close to Recommended Hotels near the Station

These restaurants lie closer to most of the recommended hotels, within a few blocks of avenue Jean Médecin near the Nice Étoile shopping center.

Reserve ahead at enchanting little **Bistrot les Viviers** for the most authentic Niçoise cuisine in this book (allow €35 per person for dinner, closed Sun, 22 rue Alphonse Karr, 5-min walk west of avenue Jean Médecin, tel. 04 93 16 00 48). Make sure to reserve for the *bistrot*, not their classier restaurant next door.

Charming **Lulu's Cantine** is a fine value, wonderfully small, and Czech-owned, with homemade recipes from Nice to Prague (closed Sat-Mon, 26 rue Alberti, tel. 04 93 62 15 33).

La Part des Anges, an atmospheric wine shop with a few tables in the rear, serves a limited, mouthwatering menu with a large selection of wines (open daily for lunch, Fri–Sat only for dinner, reserve ahead, 17 rue Gubernatis, tel. 04 93 62 69 80).

Laid-back cafés line up along the broad sidewalk on rue Biscarra (just east of avenue Jean Médecin behind Nice Étoile, all closed Sun). **L'Authentic, Le Vin sur Vin,** and **Le Cenac** are all reasonable (L'Authentic is best, Le Cenac is cheapest).

Lou Mourleco is *niçoise traditionnel*. Because it serves only what's fresh, the menu changes constantly (*menus* from €18, closed Sun-Mon, 15 rue Biscarra, tel. 04 93 80 80 11).

Le Côte Grill, a block from Nice Étoile, is bright, cool, and easy, with a salad bar, air-conditioned rooms, and a large selection at reasonable prices (daily, 1 avenue Georges Clemenceau, tel. 04 93 82 45 53).

NIGHTLIFE

Nice's bars play host to the Riviera's most happening late-night scene, full of jazz and rock 'n' roll. Most activity focuses on Old Nice, near place Rossetti. Plan on a cover charge or expensive drinks. If you're out very late, avoid walking alone. The plush and smoky bar at Hôtel Negresco is fancy-cigar old English.

TRANSPORTATION CONNECTIONS

By train to: Marseille (19/day, 2.75 hrs), **Cassis** (7/day, 3 hrs, transfer in Toulon or Marseille), **Arles** (11/day, 3.5 hrs, 10 with transfer in Marseille), **Avignon** (10/day, 4 hrs, a few direct, most require transfer in Marseille), **Paris'** Gare de Lyon (14/day, 5.5–7 hrs, six with transfer in Marseille), **Aix-en-Provence TGV station** (10/day, 3.5 hrs, transfer in Marseille probable), **Chamonix** (4/day, 11 hrs, 2–3 transfers), **Beaune** (7/day, 7 hrs, transfer in Lyon), **Munich** (2/day, 12 hrs with two transfers, one night train with a transfer in Verona), **Interlaken,** Switzerland (1/day, 12 hrs), **Florence** (4/day, 7 hrs, transfers in Pisa and/or Genoa, night train), **Milan** (4/day, 5–6 hrs, 3 with transfers), **Monterosso/Cinque Terre** (12/day, 6hrs, change in Ventimiglia and Genoa or La Spezia) **Venice** (3/day, 3/night, 11–15 hrs, 5 require transfers), **Barcelona** (3/day, 11 hrs, long transfer in Montpellier, or a direct night train).

By plane to: Paris (hrly, 1 hr, about the same price as train ticket).

Villefranche-sur-Mer

Villefranche-sur-Mer offers travelers an easygoing slice of small-town Mediterranean life just 15 minutes from more high-powered Nice and Monaco. This town feels Italian—with soft orange buildings, steep, narrow streets spilling into the sea, and pasta with pesto. Luxury yachts glisten in the bay, a reminder to those lazing along the harborfront that Monaco is just down the coast. Sand-pebble beaches, a handful of interesting sights, and quick access to Cap Ferrat keep visitors just busy enough.

Originally a Roman port, Villefranche was overtaken by fifth-century barbarians. Villagers fled into the hills, where they stayed and farmed their olives. In 1295, the Duke of Provence—like much of Europe—was threatened by the Saracen Turks. He asked the hillside olive farmers to move down to the water and establish a front line against the invaders—denying them a base from which to attack Nice. In return for tax-free status, they stopped farming, took up fishing, and established *Ville-* (town) *franche* (without taxes). Since there were many such towns, this one was specifically "Tax-free town on the sea" (*sur Mer*). Around 1560, the Duke of Savoy built the town an immense citadel (which you can still tour). Today—because two-thirds of its 8,000 people call this their primary residence—Villefranche feels more like a real community than neighboring Riviera towns.

Villefranche-sur-Mer

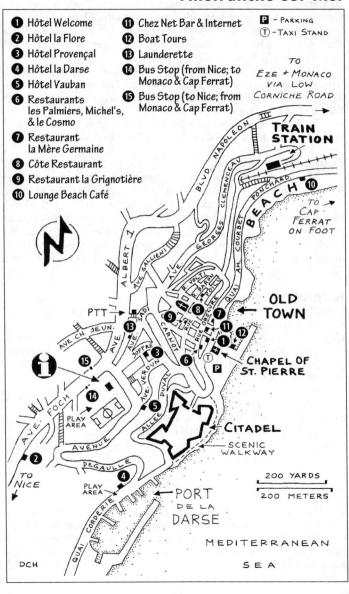

1 Hôtel Welcome
2 Hôtel la Flore
3 Hôtel Provençal
4 Hôtel la Darse
5 Hôtel Vauban
6 Restaurants les Palmiers, Michel's, & le Cosmo
7 Restaurant la Mère Germaine
8 Côte Restaurant
9 Restaurant la Grignotière
10 Lounge Beach Café

11 Chez Net Bar & Internet
12 Boat Tours
13 Launderette
14 Bus Stop (from Nice; to Monaco & Cap Ferrat)
15 Bus Stop (to Nice; from Monaco & Cap Ferrat)

P – PARKING
T – TAXI STAND

TO EZE + MONACO VIA LOW CORNICHE ROAD

TRAIN STATION

BEACH

TO CAP FERRAT ON FOOT

OLD TOWN

PTT

CHAPEL OF ST. PIERRE

CITADEL

SCENIC WALKWAY

PLAY AREA

TO NICE

PLAY AREA

PORT DE LA DARSE

200 YARDS
200 METERS

MEDITERRANEAN SEA

DCH

Arrival in Villefranche

By Car: From Nice's port, follow signs for Menton, Monaco, and Basse Corniche. In Villefranche, take the road next to the TI into the city. For a quick visit to the TI, park at the nearby pay lot. You'll find the free *Parking Fossés* a bit farther down—better for longer visits (well-signed from main road). Some hotels have parking.

By Bus: Buses from Nice and Monaco drop you just above the TI. The old town and most hotels are downhill. The stop back to Nice is across the street from where you were left (buses run every 10-15 min). Bus #111 to Cap Ferrat uses the same Villefranche stops.

By Train: Villefranche's train station is a level 15-minute walk along the water from the old town (taxi-€8, see below).

Tourist Information

The **TI** is in Jardin François Binon, below the main bus stop (July–Aug daily 9:00–19:00, Sept–June Mon–Sat 9:00–12:00 & 14:00–18:30, closed Sun, a 20-min walk or €8 taxi from train station, tel. 04 93 01 73 68). Pick up the brochure detailing a self-guided walking tour of Villefranche and information on boat rides. If you plan to visit Cap Ferrat, ask for the simple brochure-map showing the walks around this peninsula and information on the Rothschild Villa Ephrussi's gardens (see "The Three Corniches," below).

Helpful Hints

Laundry: The self-service launderette is just below the main road, opposite 6 avenue Sadi Carnot (daily 7:30-20:00).

Internet: Chez Net, an "Australian International Sports Bar Internet Café," is a fun place to get a late-night drink or check your e-mail (open daily, place du Marché).

Taxi: Beware of taxi drivers who overcharge—the normal weekday, daytime rate to central Nice is about €28; to the airport, figure about €45 (tel. 06 09 33 36 12 or 06 39 32 54 09).

Market Day: An antiques market enlivens Villefranche on Sundays (place Amélie Pollonnais by Hôtel le Welcome).

Sports Fans: Lively *boules* action takes place each evening just below the TI and the huge soccer field.

SIGHTS

The Harbor—Browse Villefranche's miniscule harbor. Only eight families still fish to make money. Gaze out to sea and marvel at the huge yachts that call this bay home. Local guides keep a list of the world's 100 biggest yachts and talk about some of them like they're part of the neighborhood. Parallel to the beach and about a block inland, you can walk the mysterious rue Obscura—a covered lane running 400 feet along the medieval rampart.

Chapel of St. Pierre (Chapelle Cocteau)—This chapel, decorated by artist, poet and filmmaker Jean Cocteau, is the town's cultural highlight. A mean fisherwoman collects a €2 donation for the fishermen's charity, then sets you free to enjoy the chapel's small but delightful interior. In 1955, Jean Cocteau covered the barrel-vaulted chapel with heavy black lines and pastels. Each of the Cocteau scenes—the Gypsies of Stes-Maries-de-la-Mer who dance and sing to honor the Virgin, girls wearing traditional outfits, and three scenes from the life of St. Peter—are explained in English (€2, daily 9:30–12:00 & 15:00–19:00, closed Mon, below Hôtel Welcome).

Citadel—The town's immense castle was built by the Duke of Savoy to defend against the French in the 1500s. When the region joined France in 1860, it became just a barracks. In the 20th century, with no military use, the city started using the citadel to house its police station, city hall, and two art galleries.

Church—The town church features a fine crucifix—carved, they say, from a fig tree by a galley slave in the 1600s.

Boat Rides (Promenades en Mer)—These little cruises, with English handouts, are offered several days a week (June–mid-Sept, one hour–€11, two hours–€15, across from Hôtel Welcome, tel. 04 93 76 65 65).

Beachwalk—A delightful walk under the citadel, along a nearly beach-level rampart, connects the yacht harbor with the old town and beach. Stroll Villefranche's waterfront beyond the train station away from the town for postcard views back to Villefranche and a quieter beach (ideal picnic benches), then consider extending your walk to Cap Ferrat (see "The Three Corniches," below). Even if you're sleeping elsewhere, consider an ice cream–licking village stroll here.

SLEEPING

(€1 = about $1.10, country code: 33)

There's a handful of hotels to choose from in Villefranche. The ones I list have at least half of their rooms with sea views—well worth paying extra for. The rooms at both of my first two listings, while different in cost, are about the same in comfort. Hôtel Welcome sits on the harbor in the center; Hôtel de la Flore is a 10-minute walk from the old town, but has a pool and free parking.

$$$ **Hôtel Welcome***** is right on the water in the old town—all 36 balconied rooms overlook the harbor. You'll pay top price for all the comforts in a very smart, professional hotel that seems to do everything right and couldn't be better located ("comfort" Db-€120–155, bigger "superior" Db-€184, suites-€220-333, extra person-€35, buffet breakfast-€12, air-con, garage-€16/day, 1 quai Amiral Courbet, tel. 04 93 76 27 62, fax 04 93 76 27 66, www.welcomehotel.com, resa@welcomehotel.com, SE).

If your idea of sightseeing is to enjoy the view from your bedroom deck, the dining room, or the pool, stay at **$$$ Hôtel la Flore***,** where most rooms have great views (Db with no view-€90, Db with view-€122, Db with view and deck-€140, extra person-€34, Qb loft with huge terrace-€210, prices 10-15 percent cheaper Oct-March, air-con, elevator, free parking, fine restaurant, just off main road high above harbor, 5 boulevard Princess Grace de Monaco, two blocks from TI toward Nice, tel. 04 93 76 30 30, fax 04 93 76 99 99, www.hotel-la-flore.fr, hotel-la-flore@wanadoo.fr, SE).

$$ Hôtel Provençal** is a big place crying out for an interior designer right below the main road. The uninspired yet comfortable-enough rooms are a fair value, with some fine views and balconies (Db-€63–95, most around €75, Tb-€76–88, extra bed-€10, skip cheaper no-view rooms, 10 percent off with this book and a two-night stay, air-con, a block from TI at 4 avenue Maréchal Joffre, tel. 04 93 76 53 53, fax 04 93 76 96 00, www.hotelprovencal.com, provencal@riviera.fr).

$ Hôtel la Darse,** a shy and unassuming little hotel sitting in the shadow of its highbrow brothers, offers a low-key alternative right on the water in Villefranche's old port. The dull hallways disguise rooms that are quiet and sharp; those facing the sea have million-dollar-view balconies (non-view Db-€50–60, view Db -€64–76, extra person-€10, from TI walk or drive down avenue Général de Gaulle to the old Port de la Darse, tel. 04 93 01 72 54, fax 04 93 01 84 37, hoteldeladarse@wanadoo.fr, SE).

$ Hôtel Vauban*, two blocks down from the TI, is a curious place with 15 basic rooms and decor as Old World as the owner (non-view Db-€45, view Db-€70, no CC, 11 avenue Général de Gaulle, tel. 04 93 76 62 18, no fax, e-what?, NSE).

EATING

Comparison-shopping is half the fun of dining in Villefranche. Make an event out of a pre-dinner stroll through the old city. Check what looks good on the lively place Amélie Pollonnais above the Hôtel Welcome, saunter the string of candle-lit places lining the waterfront, and consider the smaller, cheaper eateries embedded in the old city's walking streets.

Les Palmiers is a beachy place buzzing with cheery diners (hearty salads and pizza-€9, open daily, on place Amélie Pollonnais).

You'll dine more romantically and in style on the other side of the fountain at **Michel's** (allow €35-40 per person, closed Tue, tel. 04 93 76 73 24).

Le Cosmo Restaurant is nearby, with great tables overlooking the harbor and the Cocteau chapel's facade (floodlit after some wine,

Cocteau pops). It serves nicely-presented gourmet dishes with less fun but better quality than Les Palmiers (fine salads and pastas-€10, great Bandol red wine, open daily, place Amélie Pollonnais, tel. 04 93 01 84 05).

La Mère Germaine, right on the harborfront, is the only place in town classy enough to lure a yachter ashore. It's dressy, with fine service and a perfect harborside setting (*menu*-€34, open daily, tel. 04 93 01 71 39).

Disappear into Villefranche's walking streets and find little Italy at the reasonable and characteristic **Côte Restaurant** (cheap pizza and pastas, closed Wed, rue Poliu). A block down, cute little **La Grignotière** serves a reliable €23 *menu* (3 rue Poilu, tel. 04 93 76 79 83).

For the best view of Villefranche and decent food at reasonable prices, consider **Lounge Beach Café** on the beach below the train station. This place also works well for lunch or a drink with a view (salads, pastas, and à la carte, open daily, tel. 04 93 01 72 57).

Souris Gourmande ("Gourmet Mouse") is handy for a sandwich, to-go or to-sit (Thu-Wed 11:30-19:30, closed Fri, behind Hôtel Welcome, €4 made-to-order sandwiches…be patient and get to know your chef, Albert). Sandwich in hand, there are plenty of great places to enjoy a harborside sit.

TRANSPORTATION CONNECTIONS

By train to: Nice (2/hr, 10 min), **Monaco** (2/hr, 10 min); **Antibes** (2/hr, 40 min).

By bus to: Monaco (4/hr, 25 min), **Cap Ferrat** (6/day, 10 min), **Nice** (4/hr, 15 min). The last bus leaves Nice for Villefranche at about 19:45; the last bus from Villefranche to Nice leaves at about 21:00; and one train runs later (24:00).

The Three Corniches: Villefranche-sur-Mer to Monaco

Nice, Villefranche-sur-Mer, and Monaco are linked with three coastal routes—the Low, Middle, and High Corniches. The roads are nicknamed for the decorative frieze that runs along the top of a building (cornice). Each Corniche offers sensational views and a different perspective on this exotic slice of real estate:

Low Corniche: The *Basse Corniche* (also called *Corniche Inférieure*) strings ports, beaches, and villages together for a traffic-filled ground-floor view. It was built in the 1860s (along with the new train line) to bring people to the casino in Monte Carlo. When this Low Corniche was finished, many hill-town villagers came down and started the

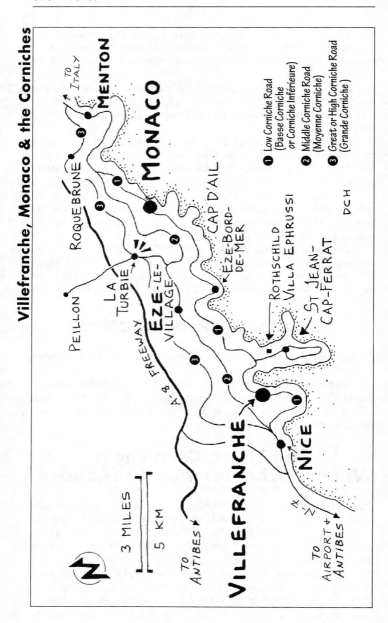

Villefranche, Monaco & the Corniches

1 Low Corniche Road (Basse Corniche or Corniche Inférieure)
2 Middle Corniche Road (Moyenne Corniche)
3 Great or High Corniche Road (Grande Corniche)

DCH

communities that line the sea today. Before 1860, the population of the coast between Villefranche and Monte Carlo was zero.

Middle Corniche: The *Moyenne Corniche* is higher, quieter, and far more impressive. It runs through Eze-le-Village and provides breath-taking views over the Mediterranean, with several scenic pullouts (the pullout above Villefranche-sur-Mer is particularly breathtaking).

High Corniche: Napoleon's crowning road-construction achieve-ment, the *Grande Corniche* caps the cliffs with staggering views from almost 1,600 feet above the sea. It is actually the Via Aurelia, used by Romans to conquer the West.

For a ▲▲▲ route, drivers should take the Middle Corniche from Nice to Eze-le-Village, follow signs to the High Corniche (*Grande Corniche/La Turbie*) from there, and after La Turbie, drop down into Monaco. Buses travel each route; the higher the Corniche, the less fre-quent the buses (roughly 5/day on Middle and High, 2/hr on Low; get details at Nice's bus station).

▲**Cap Ferrat**—This peninsula decorates Villefranche's sea views. An exclusive, largely residential community, it's a peaceful eddy off the busy Nice–Monaco route (Low Corniche). Visit the extravagant gardens of the **Rothschild Villa Ephrussi,** offering stunning views east to Villefranche and west toward Monaco. You will see seven lush, varied gardens and several lavishly decorated rooms (palace and gardens entry-€8.50, you can skip the tour of upstairs-€2 extra, Feb–Oct daily 10:00–18:00, until 19:00 in July–Aug, Nov–Jan Mon–Fri 14:00–18:00, Sat–Sun 10:00–18:00, tel. 04 93 01 45 90).

Getting to Cap Ferrat from Villefranche-sur-Mer: You can go by **car** (Low Corniche) or **taxi** (allow €12 one-way); ride the **bus** (#111 from main stop in Villefranche, 6/day, 10 min; bus from Nice to Monaco also drops you at edge of the Cap, 15-min walk to Rothschild Villa, 4/ hr, 5 min); or **walk** (50 min from Villefranche). Walkers from Villefranche go past the train station along the beach and climb the steps at the far end. Continue straight past the mansions (with gates more expensive than my house) and make the first right. You'll see signs to the Rothschild Villa Ephrussi, then to Cap Ferrat's port.

Monaco

Despite overdevelopment, high prices, and wall-to-wall daytime tourists, Monaco (mah-nah-koh) is a Riviera must. Monaco is on the go. Since 1929, cars have raced around the port and in front of the casino in one of the world's most famous auto races, the Grand Prix of Monaco (May 20-23 in 2004). The new breakwater—constructed elsewhere and towed in by sea—enables big cruise ships to actually dock here. The district of Fontvieille, reclaimed from the sea, bristles with luxury high-rise condos. But don't look for anything too deep in this glittering tax haven. Two-thirds of its 30,000 residents live here because there is no income tax—leaving fewer than 10,000 true Monegasques.

This miniscule principality (0.75 square miles) borders only France and the Mediterranean. The country has always been tiny, but it used to be...less tiny. In an 1860 plebiscite, Monaco lost two-thirds of its territory as the region of Menton voted to join France. To compensate, France suggested Monaco build a fancy casino and promised to connect it to the world with a road (the Low Corniche) and a train line. This opened the way for a high-class tourist boom that has yet to let up.

While "independent," Monaco is run as a piece of France. A French civil servant appointed by the French president—with the blessing of Monaco's Prince Rainier—serves as state minister and manages the place. Monaco's phone system, electricity, water, and so on, are all French.

Monaco is a business, and Prince Rainier is its CEO. While its famous casino provides only 5 percent of the state's revenue, its 43 banks—which offer an attractive way to hide your money—are hugely profitable. The prince also makes money with a value-added tax (19.6 percent, the same as in France) and corporate taxes.

The glamorous romance and marriage of the American actress Grace Kelly to Prince Rainier added to Monaco's fairy-tale mystique. Grace Kelly first came to Monaco to star in the 1955 Hitchcock film *To Catch a Thief*, in which she was filmed racing along the Corniches. Later, she married her prince and adopted the country. Tragically, Monaco's much-loved Princess Grace died in a car wreck on that same Corniche in 1982.

It's a special place...there are more people in Prince Rainier's philharmonic orchestra (about 100) than in his army (about 80 guards). His princedom is well-guarded, with police and cameras on every corner. (They say you could win a million dollars at the casino and walk through the wee hours to the train station without a worry.) Stamps are so few, they increase in value almost as soon as they're printed. And collectors snapped up the rare Monaco versions of euro coins (with Prince Ranier's portrait) so quickly that many locals have never even seen one.

ORIENTATION

The principality of Monaco consists of three distinct tourist areas: Monaco-Ville, Monte Carlo, and La Condamine. Monaco-Ville fills the rock high above everything else. This is the oldest section, home to Prince Rainier's palace and all the sights except the casino. Monte Carlo is the area around the casino. And La Condamine is the port (which divides Monaco-Ville and Monte Carlo). Buses #1 and #2 link all areas (10/hr, €1.40, or €3.50 for four tickets). From the port (and train station), you'll walk 15 minutes to Prince Rainier's palace or to the casino

Monaco

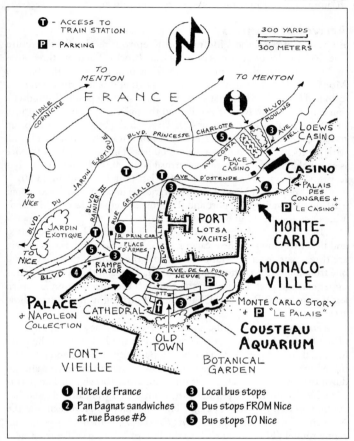

- **T** – ACCESS TO TRAIN STATION
- **P** – PARKING

300 YARDS
300 METERS

TO MENTON

TO MENTON

F R A N C E

MIDDLE CORNICHE

BLVD. PRINCESSE CHARLOTTE

JARDIN EXOTIQUE

BLVD. DU

BLVD. RAINIER III

RUE GRIMALDI

TO NICE

JARDIN EXOTIQUE

TO NICE

TO NICE

BLVD.

AVE. COSTA

PLACE DU CASINO

AVE. D'OSTENDE

BLVD. MOULINS

AVE. 3 PEL

LOEWS CASINO

CASINO

PALAIS DES CONGRES & **P** "LE CASINO"

MONTE-CARLO

PORT LOTSA YACHTS!

R. PRIN CAR.

PLACE D'ARMES

RAMPE MAJOR

AVE. DE LA PORTE NEUVE

P

PTT

MONACO-VILLE

MONTE CARLO STORY & **P** "LE PALAIS"

PALACE & NAPOLEON COLLECTION

CATHEDRAL

OLD TOWN

COUSTEAU AQUARIUM

BOTANICAL GARDEN

FONT-VIEILLE

1. Hôtel de France
2. Pan Bagnat sandwiches at rue Basse #8
3. Local bus stops
4. Bus stops FROM Nice
5. Bus stops TO Nice

(40 min from palace to casino).

Tourist Information: The main TI is near the casino (2 boulevard des Moulins), but there's a handier branch in the train station (pick up city map; both TIs open daily 9:00–19:00, tel. 00-377/92 16 61 66). From June to September, you'll find information kiosks in the Monaco-Ville parking garage and on the port.

Telephone Tip: To call Monaco from France, dial 00, then 377 (Monaco's country code) and the eight-digit number. Within Monaco, simply dial the eight-digit number.

Tourist Train: "Azur Express" tourist trains begin at the aquarium and pass by the port, casino, and palace (€6, 30 min, 2/hr 10:30-18:00 in summer, fewer in winter, taped English commentary).

Arrival in Monaco

By Bus from Nice and Villefranche: Keep your receipt for the return ride (RCA buses run twice as often as Cars Broch). There are three stops in Monaco, in order from Nice: in front of a tunnel at the base of Monaco-Ville (place d'Armes), on the port, and below the casino (on avenue d'Ostende). The first stop is the best starting point. From there, you can walk up to Monaco-Ville and the palace (10 min straight up), or catch a local bus (lines #1 or #2). To reach the bus stop and steps up to Monaco-Ville, cross the street right in front of the tunnel and walk with the rock on your right for about 200 feet. The bus stop back to Nice is across the major road from your arrival point, at the light. The last bus leaves Monaco for Nice at about 19:00 (last train leaves about 23:30).

By Train from Nice: The train station is in central Monaco, about a 10-minute walk to the port and 25 minutes to the palace in Monaco-Ville or to the casino in Monte Carlo.

In this long underground station, you'll find the TI, baggage check, and ticket windows up the escalator at the Italy-end of the tracks. There are three exits from the station: two from the train platform level and one from above the platforms, past the TI. To reach the casino, use this upper exit (go past TI, and up the elevator, then exit station and turn left on boulevard Princesse Charlotte and turn right on rue Iris; allow 10 min).

To reach Monaco-Ville and the palace from the station, take one of the two platform level exits. The exit near the Italy-end of the platform leads to the port and to the bus stop for city buses #1 and #2, serving Monaco-Ville and the casino (follow *Sortie la Condamine* and go down two escalators, then go left following *Accès Port* signs). The port is a few blocks downhill from this exit, from which you can walk another 20 minutes to the palace or casino. The other platform level exit is at the Nice-end of the tracks (signed *Sortie Fontvieille*), which takes you along a long tunnel (TI annex at end) to the foot of Monaco-Ville; from here it's a 15-minute walk to the palace.

To take the short-but-sweet coastal **walking path** into Monaco's Fontvieille district, get off the train one station before Monaco, in Cap d'Ail. Turn left out of the little station and walk 50 yards up the road, then turn left, going downstairs and under the tracks. Turn left onto the coastal trail, and hike the 20 minutes to Fontvieille. Once you reach Fontvieille, it's a 15-minute uphill hike to Monaco's sights.

By Car: Follow *Centre-Ville* signs into Monaco, then follow the red-letter signs to parking garages at *Le Casino* (for Monte Carlo) or *Le Palais* (for Monaco-Ville). The first hour of parking is free; the next costs €3.50.

SIGHTS

Monaco-Ville

All of Monaco's sights (except for the casino) are in Monaco-Ville, packed within a few Disney-esque blocks. To get to the palace square (Monaco-Ville's sightseeing ground zero), take bus #1 or #2 to place de la Visitation (leave bus to the right and walk straight 5 min, passing a fountain). If you're walking up from the port, the well-marked lane leads directly to the *Palais*.

Palace Square—This square is the best place to get oriented to Monaco, as it offers views on both sides of the rock. Facing the palace, go to the right and look out over the city. This little, pastel Hong Kong look-alike was born on this rock in 1215 and has managed to remain an independent country for most of its nearly 800 years. Looking beyond the glitzy port, notice the faded green roof above and to the right: the casino that put Monaco on the map.

Now walk to the statue of the monk grasping a sword near the palace. Meet **François Grimaldi,** a renegade Italian who, dressed as a monk, captured Monaco in 1297, and so began the dynasty that still rules the principality. Prince Rainier is his great, great, great...grandson, which makes Monaco Europe's longest-lasting monarchy.

Walk to the opposite side of the square and the Louis XIV **cannonballs.** Down below is Monaco's newest area, Fontvieille, where much of its post–WWII growth has been. Prince Rainier has continued (some say, been obsessed with) Monaco's economic growth, creating landfills (topped with homes, such as Fontvieille), flashy ports, new beaches, and the new rail station. Today, thanks to Prince Rainier's efforts, tiny Monaco is a member of the United Nations. The current buzz is about how soon he'll hand over the reign of the principality to his son, Albert.

You can buy Monaco stamps (popular collectibles, or mail from here) at the post office (PTT) a few blocks down rue Comte Félix Gastaldi.

Prince's Palace (Palais Princier)—A medieval castle sat where Monaco's palace is today. Its strategic setting has had a lot to do with Monaco's ability to resist attackers. Today Prince Rainier and his son Albert live in the palace; princesses Stephanie and Caroline live just down the main street. The palace guards protect the prince 24/7, and still change guard the old-fashioned way (11:55 daily, fun to watch but jam-packed). Automated and uninspired tours (in English) take you through part of the prince's lavish palace in 30 minutes. The rooms are well-furnished and impressive, but interesting only if you haven't seen a château lately (€6, June–Sept daily 9:30–18:00, Oct daily 10:00–17:00, closed Nov-May).

Napoleon Collection—Napoleon occupied Monaco after the French Revolution. This is the prince's private collection of what Napoleon left behind: military medals, swords, guns, letters, and, most interesting, his hat. I found this collection more appealing than the palace (€4, June–Sept daily 9:30–18:00, Oct 10:00–17:00, Nov-May 10:30–12:30 & 14:00-17:00, next to palace entry).

Cathédrale de Monaco—This somber cathedral, rebuilt in 1878 to show Monaco cared for more than just its new casino, is where centuries of Grimaldis are buried. Circle behind the altar (counter-clockwise). The last tomb—Gratia Patricia, MCMLXXXII—is where Princess Grace was buried in 1982.

As you leave the cathedral, step across the street and look down on the newly-reclaimed Fontvieille district and the fancy condos that contribute to the incredible population density of this miniscule country. The adjacent—and immaculately maintained—Jardins Botanique offer more fine views and a good place to picnic.

Cousteau Aquarium (Musée Océanographique)—Prince Albert I built this impressive cliff-hanging aquarium in 1910 to house his enthusiasm for things from the sea. One wing features Mediterranean fish; tropical species swim around the other (all well-described in English). Jacques Cousteau directed the aquarium for years. The fancy Albert I Hall upstairs houses the museum (no English), featuring models of Albert and his beachcombers hard at work (aquarium and museum-€11, ages 6–18-€5.35, April–Sept daily 9:00–19:00, July–Aug daily 9:00-20:00, Oct-March daily 10:00–18:00, at opposite end of Monaco-Ville from palace, down the steps from Monaco-Ville bus stop).

Monte Carlo Story—This informative 35-minute film gives a helpful account of Monaco's history and offers a comfortable soft-chair break from all that walking (€6.50, usually on the hour 14:00–17:00, until 18:00 July–Aug, you can join frequent extra showings for groups, English headphones; from aquarium, take escalator into parking garage, then take elevator down and follow signs).

Monte Carlo

▲Casino—Monte Carlo, which means "Charles' Hill" in Spanish, is named for the local prince who presided over Monaco's 19th-century makeover. Begin your visit to Europe's most famous casino in the park above the traffic circle. In the mid-1800s, olive groves stood here. Then, with the construction of this casino, spas, and easy road and train access, one of Europe's poorest countries was on the Grand Tour map—*the* place for the vacationing aristocracy to play. Today, Monaco has the world's highest per-capita income.

The casino is designed to make the wealthy feel comfortable while losing money. Charles Garnier designed this Casino (with an Opera House inside) in 1878, in part to thank the prince for his financial help in completing Paris' Opéra Garnier (which Garnier also designed). The central doors provide access to slot machines, private gaming rooms, and the Opera House. The private gaming rooms occupy the left wing of the building.

Count the counts and Rolls-Royces in front of Hôtel de Paris (built at the same time), then strut inside past the slots to the sumptuous atrium. This is the lobby for the Opera House (open only for performances). There's a model of the opera at the end of the room, and marble WCs on the right. Anyone over 21 (even in shorts, if before 20:00) can get as far as the one-armed bandits (push button on slot machines to claim your winnings),though you'll need decent attire to go any further. After 20:00, shorts are off-limits anywhere.

The scene is great at night and downright James Bond–like in the private rooms. The park behind the casino offers a peaceful café and a good view of the casino's rear facade and of Monaco-Ville. If paying an entrance fee to lose money is not your idea of fun, access to all games in the new, plebeian, American-style Loews Casino, adjacent to the old casino, is free.

Cost and Hours: The first rooms, Salons Européens, open at 12:00 and cost €10 to enter. The glamorous private game rooms—where you can rub elbows with high rollers—open at 16:00, others not until 21:00, and cost an additional €10 (and you must show your passport). A tie and jacket (necessary in the evening) can be rented at the bag check for €30 plus a €40 deposit. Dress standards for women are far more relaxed (only tennis shoes are a definite no-no).

Take the Money and Run: The return bus stop to Nice is at the top of the park above the casino on avenue de la Costa. To return to the train station from the casino, walk up the parkway in front of the casino, turn left on boulevard des Moulins, turn right on impasse de la Fontaine, climb the steps, and turn left on boulevard Princesse Charlotte (entrance to train station is next to Parking de la Gare).

SLEEPING AND EATING

(€1 = about $1.10, country code: 377)
For many, Monaco is best after dark. The perfectly pleasant **$$ Hôtel de France**** is reasonable (Sb-€70, Db-€90, includes breakfast, 6 rue de la Turbie, near west exit from train station, tel. 00-377/93 30 24 64, fax 00-377/92 16 13 34, hotel-france@monte-carlo.mc).

Several cafés serve basic fare at reasonable prices (day and night) on the port, along the traffic-free rue Princesse Caroline. In Monaco-Ville, you'll find good *pan bagnat* and other sandwiches at 8 rue Basse, just off the palace square.

TRANSPORTATION CONNECTIONS

By train to: Nice (2/hr, 20 min), **Villefranche** (2/hr, 10 min), **Antibes** (2/hr, 45 min).

By bus to: Nice (4/hr, 40 min), **Villefranche** (4/hr, 25 min). The last bus leaves Monaco for Villefranche and Nice at about 19:00; the last train leaves Monaco for Villefranche and Nice at about 23:30.

Antibes

Antibes has a down-to-earth, easygoing ambience that's rare for this area. Its old town is postcard-perfect: a cluster of red-tiled roofs rising above the blue Mediterranean, watched over by twin medieval lookout towers and wrapped in a rampart. Visitors making the 30-minute trip from Nice browse Europe's biggest yacht harbor, snooze on a sandy beach, loiter through an enjoyable old town, stumble upon characteristic markets, and climb to a castle filled with Picassos.

Though it's much smaller than Nice, Antibes has a history that goes back just as far. Both towns were founded by Greek traders in the fifth century B.C. To the Greeks, Antibes was "Antipolis"—the town (*polis*) opposite (*anti*) Nice. For the next several centuries, Antibes remained in the shadow of its neighbor. By the turn of the 20th century, the town was a military base—so the rich and famous partied elsewhere. But when the army checked out after World War I, Antibes was "discovered" and enjoyed a particularly roaring '20s—with the help of party animals like Rudolph Valentino and the rowdy-yet-very-silent Charlie Chaplin. Fun-seekers even invented water skiing right here in the 1920s.

ORIENTATION

Antibes' old town lies between the port and boulevard Albert 1er and avenue Robert Soleau. Place Nationale is the old town's hub of activity. Lively rue Aubernon connects the port and the old town. Stroll along the sea between the Picasso Museum and square Albert 1er (where boulevard Albert 1er meets the water); the best beaches lie just beyond square Albert 1er, and the path is beautiful. Good play areas for children are on place des Martyrs de la Résistance (close to recommended Hôtel Relais du Postillon).

Tourist Information: There are two TIs. The most convenient is located in the old town, just inside the walls at 21 boulevard d'Aguillon (Sept–May Mon–Fri 10:00–12:00 & 14:00-17:00, closed Sat-Sun, June–Aug daily 8:30–21:00). The big *Maison de Tourisme* is in the newer city, east of the old town where boulevard Albert 1er and rue de la

Antibes

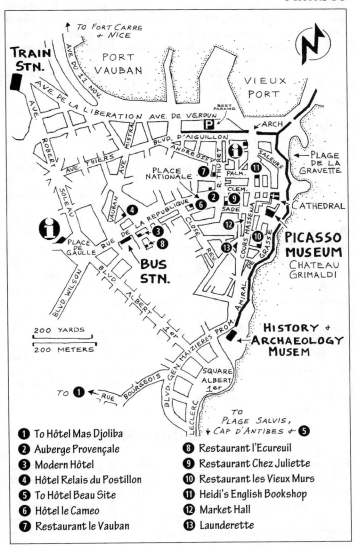

1. To Hôtel Mas Djoliba
2. Auberge Provençale
3. Modern Hôtel
4. Hôtel Relais du Postillon
5. To Hôtel Beau Site
6. Hôtel le Cameo
7. Restaurant le Vauban
8. Restaurant l'Ecureuil
9. Restaurant Chez Juliette
10. Restaurant les Vieux Murs
11. Heidi's English Bookshop
12. Market Hall
13. Launderette

République meet at 11 place Général de Gaulle (Sept–June Mon–Sat 9:00–12:30 & 13:30–18:30, closed Sun, July–Aug Mon–Sat 9:00–19:00, Sun 9:00–13:00, tel. 04 92 90 53 00). At either TI, pick up the excellent city map and the interesting brochure with a walking tour of old Antibes (in English), and get details on the hikes described below. The Nice TI has Antibes maps; plan ahead.

Getting around Antibes: A free minibus *(Minibus Gratuit)* circles Antibes, serving the train station, square Albert 1er, the old town, and the port (4/hr). To call a taxi, call tel. 04 93 67 67 67.

Helpful Hints

Laundry: A full-service launderette is near the market hall on rue de la Pompe (Mon–Sat 9:00-12:00 & 14:00-19:00).

Bookstore: Heidi's English Bookshop has a great selection of new and used books (daily 10:00–19:00, 24 rue Aubernon).

Local Guide: For a good guide, contact Madame Claude le Merdy (around €40/hr in and around Antibes, tel 04 93 34 58 14).

Arrival in Antibes

By Train: To get to the port (5-min walk), cross the street in front of the station and follow avenue de la Libération downhill. To reach the main TI in the modern city (15-min walk), exit right from the station on avenue Robert Soleau; follow *Maison du Tourisme* signs to place Général de Gaulle. Or hop on the free minibus (see above).

By Bus: The bus station is on the edge of the old town on place Guynemer, a block below the TI (info desk open Mon–Sat 8:00-12:00 & 14:00-17:30, closed Sun).

By Car: Day-trippers should follow *Centre-ville* and *Vieux Port* signs, and park near the old town walls—as close to the beach as you can (first 30 min free, then about €4 for three hours, €8 for a day). Enter the old town through the last arch on the right. If you're sleeping here, hotels are signed; get advice from your hotelier on where to park.

ANTIBES ORIENTATION STROLL

This quick walk will help you get your bearings. Begin at the train station (or harborside car park), and stroll the **harbor** along avenue de Verdun. Locals claim that this is Europe's biggest yacht harbor, with 1,600 stalls. At the end of the yachts (quai des Pêcheurs) you'll see the pathetic remains of a once-hearty fishing fleet. The Mediterranean is getting fished out. Most of the seafood you'll eat here comes from fish farms or the Atlantic.

Cross through the old gate under the ramparts to enter the **old town.** Because Antibes was the last fort before the Italian border, the French king made sure the ramparts were strong and well-defended.

Today the town is the haunt of a large community of English, Irish, and Aussie boaters who help crew giant yachts of the rich and famous. (That explains the Irish pubs and English bookstores.) Drop by the cute shell-shaped **plage de la Gravette,** an adorable public beach tucked right in the middle of old Antibes.

Continue following the ramparts to the 16th-century white stone **Château Grimaldi.** The castle stands on prime real estate: This site has been home to the acropolis of the Greek city of Antipolis, a Roman fort, and a medieval bishop's palace. This château was the home of the Grimaldi family (who still rule Monaco), and today it houses the Picasso Museum (see below). The neighboring **cathedral** is built over a Greek temple.

Notice the two **towers.** They symbolized society's two dominant land-owning classes: the church and the nobility. (In 1789, the Revolution changed all that.) From the bluff below the castle, you can see **Cap d'Antibes** crowned by its lighthouse and studded with mansions (see "Cap d'Antibes Hike," below).

The ramparts lead to the **History and Archeology Museum** (see below). Just before that (at rue du Haut Castelet), hook inland and explore the painfully charming, cobbled **pedestrian zone** around rue du Haut Castelet and rue du Bas Castelet. Poking around Antibes' peaceful back lanes, gradually work your way back to the entertaining covered **market hall** on cours Masséna.

SIGHTS

▲▲**Picasso Museum (Musée Picasso)**—In the early 20th century, Antibes' castle (Château Grimaldi) was home to an obscure little museum that nobody cared about. Then its director had a brainstorm: offer the castle to Pablo Picasso as a studio. Picasso lived in the castle for four months in 1946, where he cranked out an amazing amount of art—and the resulting collection put Antibes on the tourist map.

Sitting serenely where the old town meets the sea, this museum offers a remarkable collection of Picasso's work: paintings, sketches, and ceramics. Picasso said that if you want to see work from his Antibes period, you'll have to see it in Antibes. You'll understand why Picasso liked working here. Several photos of the artist and a movie of him hard at work (when making art, he said he was "working" rather than "painting") make this already intimate museum even more so. In his famous *La Joie de Vivre* (the museum's highlight), there's a new love in Picasso's life, and he's feelin' groovy.

The museum also displays works by Nicolas de Stael (1914-1955), who spent his final lonely winter in Antibes near the château, where he committed suicide by jumping out a window. There's also a sculpture terrace overlooking the Bay of Antibes, featuring works by local artists (such as Germaine Richier), as well as by Picasso's friend Joan Miró (*Sea Goddess*).

Cost, Hours, Location: €5, covered by Riviera *Carte Musées* pass, June–Sept Tue–Sun 10:00–18:00, July–Aug Tue–Sun 10:00–18:00 & until 20:00 on Wed and Fri; Oct–May Tue–Sun 10:00–12:00 & 14:00–18:00, closed Mon, tel. 04 92 90 54 20. It's in Château Grimaldi, just inside the rampart in Antibes' old town. To reach the museum from the train station or harborside parking lot, walk along the harborfront on avenue de Verdun. Enter the old gate under the rampart, and follow the rampart to the white stone château.

History and Archaeology Museum (Musée d'Histoire et d'Archéologie)—Featuring Greek, Roman, and Etruscan odds and ends, this is the only place to get a sense of this city's ancient roots. I liked the 2,000-year-old lead anchors (€3, no English explanations, June–Sept daily 10:00–18:00, Oct–May daily 10:00–12:00 & 14:00–18:00, closed Mon, on the water between Picasso Museum and square Albert 1er).

▲**Market Hall (Marché Provençal)**—The daily market bustles under a 19th-century canopy, with flowers, produce, Provençal products, and beach accessories (in old town behind Picasso Museum on cours Masséna). The market wears many appealing hats: produce daily except Monday until 13:00; handicrafts Thursday through Sunday in the afternoon; and romantic outdoor dining in the evenings. It's surrounded by cute tourist shops, including one that serves absinthe and features a poster proclaiming, "After 85 years of prohibition, the great-great-great grandfather of *pastis* is once again legal" (€15 for a reportedly hallucinogenic shot).

Fort Carré—This impressively situated citadel, dating from 1487, was the last fort inside France. It protected Antibes from Nice, which until 1860 was part of Italy. You can tour this unusual four-pointed fort—at its height, it held 200 soldiers—but there's precious little to see inside. People visit for the stunning views (€3, includes tour, covered by Riviera *Carte Musées* pass, June–Sept daily 10:15–17:30, Oct–May daily 10:15-16:00). Scenic footpaths link the fort to the port along the sea. It's a 30-minute portside walk from the old town to the fort (or taxi there and walk back). By foot or car, follow avenue du 11 Novembre around the port, stay on the main road (walkers can follow path by sports fields), then park on the beach just after the soccer field. A signed dirt path leads to Le Fort Carré. Keep following green-lettered signs to *Le Fort/Sens de la Visite*.

Beaches (Plages)—The best beaches stretch between Antibes' port and Cap d'Antibes, and the very best (plage de la Salis and plage du Ponteil) are just south of square Albert 1er. All are golden and sandy. Plage de la Salis is busy in summer, but it's manageable, with snack stands every so often and views to the old town. The closest beach to the old town is at the port (plage de la Gravette) and remains relatively calm in any season.

Juan-les-Pins—This village, across the Cap d'Antibes isthmus from Antibes, is where the action is in the evenings. It's a modern beach resort with good beaches, plenty of lively bars and restaurants, and a popular jazz festival in July. Buses and trains make the 10-minute connection to and from Antibes constantly.

SLEEPING

(€1 = about $1.10, country code: 33)

The best hotels require a car or taxi—central pickings are slim in this city, where most hoteliers seem more interested in their restaurants.

$$$ **Mas Djoliba***** is a good splurge, but best for drivers (since it's a 15-minute walk from the beach and old Antibes, and a 25-minute walk from the train station). Reserve early for this tranquil, bird-chirping, flower-filled manor house where no two rooms are the same. After a busy day of sightseeing, dinner by the pool is a treat (they request that you dine here May-Sept). You'll be in good hands with sweet Stephanie serving and Sylvan cooking with market-fresh products (Db with breakfast and dinner-€80-90 per person, Db room only-€85–125; several good family rooms-€160-170, breakfast-€9, 29 avenue de Provence, from boulevard Albert 1er, look for blue signs and turn right up avenue Gaston Bourgeois, tel. 04 93 34 02 48, fax 04 93 34 05 81, www.hotel-djoliba.com, hotel .djoliba@wanadoo.fr).

$$ **Auberge Provençale***, on charming place Nationale, has a popular restaurant and seven Old World rooms (those on the square get all the noise, day and night), but nonexistent management (Db-€63–85, Tb-€72–94, Qb-€108, reception in restaurant, 61 place Nationale, tel. 04 93 34 13 24, fax 04 93 34 89 88). Their huge loft room, named "Céline," faces the back and comes with a royal canopy bed and a dramatic open-timbered ceiling for no extra charge.

$$ **Modern Hôtel**** is a spick-and-span, well-run place in the pedestrian zone with 17 standard-size rooms, each with air-conditioning and pleasing decor (Db-€62-70, €10 more in summer, 1 rue Fourmillière, tel. 04 92 90 59 05, fax 04 92 90 59 06).

$$ **Hôtel Relais du Postillon****, on a thriving square, offers 15 small, tastefully designed rooms, accordion bathrooms, and helpful owners who take more pride in their well-respected restaurant (Db-€46–82, *menus* from €32, 8 rue Championnet, tel. 04 93 34 20 77, fax 04 93 34 61 24, SE).

$$ **Hôtel Beau-Site***** is my only listing on Cap d'Antibes and a 10-minute drive from the old town. It's a fine value if you want to get away, but not *too* far away. This place is a sanctuary, with friendly owners (Nathalie SE), a pool, a big patio, and easy parking. The 30 plush and well-cared-for rooms are fairly-priced (standard Db-€65-75, bigger Db-€85-90, extra bed-€25, bikes available, 141 boulevard Kennedy, tel.

04 93 61 53 43, fax 04 93 67 78 16, www.hotelbeausite.net, hbeausit
@club-internet.fr). From the hotel, it's a 10-minute walk down to the
crowded plage de la Garoupe and a nearby hiking trail (see above).

$ Hôtel le Cameo** is a rambling, refreshingly unaggressive old
place above a bustling bar (where you'll find what reception there is).
The public areas are dark, but the nine very simple, linoleum-lined
rooms are almost huggable. All open onto the charming place Nationale,
which means you don't sleep until the restaurants close (Ds-€47, Db-
€58, Ts-€55, Tb-€66, 5 place Nationale, tel. 04 93 34 24 17, fax 04 93
34 35 80, NSE).

EATING

The old town is crawling with possibilities. Lively place Nationale is
filled with tables and tourists (great ambience), while locals seem to prefer the restaurants along the market hall. Take a walk and judge for
yourself, considering these suggestions. Romantics and those on a budget should buy a picnic dinner and head for the beach.

Le Vauban is near the port, with an appealing interior and reasonably-priced salads and *plats* (closed Wed, 7 rue Thuret, tel. 04 93
34 33 05).

L' Écureuil is a fun, inexpensive place to try paella in the traffic-
free zone (closed Sun-Mon, 17 rue Fourmillière, tel. 04 93 34 07 97).

The recommended hotels **Relais du Postillon** and **Auberge
Provençale,** with cozier decor and an interior courtyard, each offer well-
respected cuisine with *menus* from €30-35 (both open daily).

Chez Juliette, just off place Nationale, offers budget meals (*menus*
from €14, closed for lunch and on Mon, rue Sade).

Les Vieux Murs is the place to splurge in Antibes for regional specialties. Its candlelit, red-tone interior is *très romantique* and overlooks
the sea (*menu-*€40, along ramparts beyond Picasso Museum at 25 promenade Amiral de Grasse, tel. 04 93 34 66 73).

TRANSPORTATION CONNECTIONS

TGV and local trains serve Antibes' little station.

By train to: Nice (2/hr, 25 min), **Villefranche** (2/hr, 40 min),
Monaco (2/hr, 60 min), **Marseille** (16/day, 2.25 hrs), **Cannes** (2/hr, 15
min).

By bus to: Cannes (3/hr, 25 min), **Nice Airport** (1/hr, 40 min),
Biot (2/hr, 20 min).

BAVARIA AND TIROL

Two hours south of Munich, between Germany's Bavaria and Austria's Tirol, is a timeless land of fairy-tale castles, painted buildings shared by cows and farmers, and locals who still yodel when they're happy.

In Germany's Bavaria, tour Mad King Ludwig's ornate Neuschwanstein Castle, Europe's most spectacular. Stop by the Wieskirche, a textbook example of Bavarian rococo bursting with curly curlicues, and browse through Oberammergau, Germany's woodcarving capital and home of the famous Passion play.

In Austria's Tirol, hike to the ruined Ehrenberg castle, scream down a ski slope on an oversized skateboard, and then catch your breath for an evening of yodeling and slap dancing.

In this chapter, I'll cover Bavaria first, then Tirol. Austria's Tirol is easier and cheaper than touristy Bavaria. My favorite home base for exploring Bavaria's castles is actually in Austria, in the town of Reutte. Füssen, in Germany, is a handier home base for train travelers.

Planning Your Time

While Germans and Austrians vacation here for a week or two at a time, the typical speedy American traveler will find two days' worth of sightseeing. With a car and more time, you could enjoy three or four days. If the weather's good and you're not going to Switzerland, be sure to ride a lift to an alpine peak.

By Car: A good schedule for a one-day circular drive from Reutte is 7:30-Breakfast, 8:00-Depart hotel, 8:30-Arrive at Neuschwanstein to pick up tickets for two castles (which you reserved by telephone several days earlier), 9:00-Tour Hohenschwangau, 11:00-Tour Neuschwanstein, 13:00-Drive to the Wieskirche (20-min stop) and on to Linderhof, 14:30-Tour Linderhof, 16:30-Drive along scenic Plansee back into Austria, 17:30-Back at hotel, 19:00-Dinner at hotel and perhaps a folk evening (or the Ludwig II musical). In peak season, you

Highlights of Bavaria and Tirol

might arrive later at Linderhof to avoid the crowds. The next morning, you could stroll through Reutte, hike to the Ehrenberg ruins, and ride the luge on your way to Innsbruck, Munich, Switzerland, Venice, or wherever.

By Public Transportation: Train travelers can use Füssen as a base and bus or bike the three miles to Neuschwanstein. Reutte is connected by bus with Füssen (except Sun; taxi €28 one-way). If you're based in Reutte, you can bike to the Ehrenberg ruins (just outside Reutte) and to Neuschwanstein Castle/Tegelberg luge (90 min). A one-way taxi from Reutte to Neuschwanstein costs about €32. Or, if you stay at the recommended Gutshof zum Schluxen hotel, you can hike through the woods to Neuschwanstein (60 min).

Getting around Bavaria and Tirol

By Car: This region is ideal by car. All the sights are within an easy 60-mile loop from Reutte or Füssen. Even if you're doing the rest of your trip by train, consider renting a car for the day here (as cheap as €50/day; see "Car Rental," below).

By Public Transportation: It can be frustrating. Local bus service in the region is spotty for sightseeing. If you're rushed and without wheels, Reutte, the Wieskirche, Linderhof, and the luge rides are probably not worth the trouble, but the Tegelberg luge near Neuschwanstein is within walking distance of the castle.

Füssen (with a 2-hr train ride to/from Munich every hour, some with a transfer in Buchloe) is three miles from Neuschwanstein Castle with easy bus and bike connections (see "Getting to the Castles from Füssen or Reutte," page 393). Reutte is a 30-minute bus ride from Füssen (Mon–Fri 6/day, Sat 2/day, none Sun, €3.20; taxis from Reutte to the castles are €32 one-way; to Füssen, €28).

Buses also run from Füssen to Oberammergau (4–5/day, less off-season, 1.5 hr, some with transfer in Echelsbacher Brücke; bus often marked Garmisch, confirm with driver that bus will stop in Oberammergau). From Munich, visiting Oberammergau directly by train is easier (hrly, 1.75 hrs, change in Murnau) than going to Füssen to catch the bus.

Füssen to Linderhof by public transportation will burn most of a valuable sightseeing day; you'll spend more time on the bus (or waiting for it) than you will at the castle. Skip Linderhof—or rent a car for the day. If you must go, take an early bus to Oberammergau, which has direct bus connections to Linderhof (4/day in summer, less off-season, 30 min).

Confirm all bus schedules in Füssen by checking the big board at the bus stop across from the train station, buying a bus timetable (€0.30) at the TI or train station, or calling 08362/939-0505. For longer-distance bus trips (such as to Garmisch or Linderhof), you'll save money if you by a *Tagesticket* (day pass).

By Tour: If you're interested only in Bavarian castles, consider an all-day organized bus tour of the Bavarian biggies as a side trip from Munich (see Munich chapter).

By Bike: This is great biking country. Shops in or near train stations rent bikes for €8–15 per day. The ride from Reutte to Neuschwanstein and the Tegelberg luge (90 min) is great for those with the time and energy.

By Thumb: Hitchhiking, always risky, is a slow-but-possible way to connect the public transportation gaps.

Füssen

Füssen has been a strategic stop since ancient times. Its main street sits on the Via Claudia Augusta, which crossed the Alps (over Brenner Pass) in Roman times. The town was the southern terminus of a medieval trade route now known among modern tourists as the "Romantic Road." Dramatically situated under a renovated castle on the lively Lech River, Füssen just celebrated its 700th birthday.

Unfortunately, Füssen is overrun by tourists in the summer. Traffic can be exasperating. Apart from Füssen's cobbled and arcaded town center, there's little real sightseeing here. The striking-from-a-distance **castle** houses a boring picture gallery. The mediocre **city museum** in the monastery below the castle exhibits lifestyles of 200 years ago and the story of the monastery, and offers displays on the development of the violin, for which Füssen is famous (€2.50, €3 includes castle gallery, April–Oct Tue–Sun 10:00–17:00, closed Mon, Nov–March Tue–Sun 13:00–16:00, closed Mon, English descriptions, tel. 08362/903-145).

Füssen's newest attraction, the **Model Railroad Museum** (Modelleisenbahn-Museum ZeitscHieneN), is small and overpriced but interesting, featuring model trains of all types—including, probably, the one you rode to town. The collection, gathered over a lifetime by brothers Ulf and Falk Haase, was donated by their mom to the town under the condition that this museum would be built (€4.50, Tue–Sun 10:00–18:00, closed Mon, Kemptener Strasse 7, tel. 08362/929-678).

Halfway between Füssen and the border (as you drive, or a woodsy walk from the town) is the **Lechfall,** a thunderous waterfall (with a handy WC).

ORIENTATION

(area code: 08362)
Füssen's train station is a few blocks from the TI, the town center (a cobbled shopping mall), and all my hotel listings (see "Sleeping in Füssen," below). If necessary, the TI can help you find a room (June–mid-Sept Mon–Sat 8:30–18:30, Sun 10:00–12:00, less off-season, 3 blocks down Bahnhofstrasse from station, tel. 08362/93850, fax 08362/938-520, www.fuessen.de). After hours, the little self-service info pavilion (7:00–24:30) near the front of the TI features an automated room-finding service.

Arrival in Füssen: Exit left as you leave the train station (lockers available) and walk a few straight blocks to the center of town and the TI. To get to Neuschwanstein or Reutte, catch a bus from in front of the station.

Helpful Hints

Bike Rental: Rent from friendly Christian at Preisschranke next to the train station (€8/24 hrs, May–Sept Mon–Sat 9:00–20:00, Oct–April Mon–Fri 10:00–18:00, Sat 10:00-15:00, closed Sun, tel. 08362/921-544; if Christian is not there during opening hours, call his mobile: 0178-374-0219). Rad Zacherl has a bigger selection but less convenient location (€8/24 hrs, mountain bikes-€15/24 hrs, passport number for deposit, May–Sept Mon–Fri 9:00–18:00, Sat 9:00–13:00, closed Sun, Oct–April Mon–Fri 9:00–12:00 & 14:00–18:00, Sat 9:00–13:00, closed Sun, 1.25 miles out of town at Kemptener Strasse 119, tel. 08362/3292, www.rad-zacherl.de).

Car Rental: Peter Schlichtling (€50/24 hrs, includes insurance, Kemptener Strasse 26, tel. 08362/922-122, www.schlichtling.de) is cheaper and more central than Hertz (Füssenerstrasse 112, tel. 08362/986-580).

Laundry: Pfronter Reinigung Wäscherei does full-service wash and dry in three hours (€11/load, Mon–Fri 9:00–12:00 & 14:00–17:00, Sat 10:00–12:30, closed Wed afternoon and Sun, in parking lot of Hotel Hirsch, 2 blocks past TI on the way out of town, Sebastianstrasse 3, tel. 08362/4529).

Internet: Try Videoland (€2/30 min, €3/hr, Mon–Sat 16:00–22:00, Sun 16:00–20:00, Luitpoldstrasse 11, tel. 08362/38300).

SIGHTS

Neuschwanstein and Hohenschwangau Castles

The most popular tourist destination in Bavaria is the "King's Castles" *(Königsschlösser).* With fairy-tale turrets in a fairy-tale alpine setting built by a fairy-tale king, they are understandably popular. The well-organized visitor can have a great four-hour visit. Others will just stand in line and perhaps not even see the castles. The key: Phone ahead for a reservation (details below) or arrive by 8:00 (you'll have time to see both castles, consider fun options nearby—mountain lift, luge course, Füssen town—and get out by early afternoon). Off-season (Oct–June), you have a little more flexibility—but it's still a good idea to get an early start (try to arrive by 9:00).

▲▲▲**Neuschwanstein Castle**—Imagine Mad King Ludwig as a boy, climbing the hills above his dad's castle, Hohenschwangau (see below), dreaming up the ultimate fairy-tale castle. He had the power to make his dream concrete and stucco. Neuschwanstein was designed by a painter first...then an architect. It looks medieval, but it's only about as old as the Eiffel Tower. It feels like something you'd see at a home show for 19th-century royalty. Built from 1869 to 1886, it's the epitome of the Romanticism popular in 19th-century Europe. Construction stopped

Neuschwanstein and Hohenschwangau

(MARIENBRÜCKE) **MARY'S BRIDGE**

SCHLOSS NEUSCHWAN-STEIN CASTLE

WUNDERBAR VIEW!

TEGELBERG 5,500 FT.

UPPER BUS STOP

PRIVATE ROAD

PÖLLAT GORGE
TRAIL IS SLIPPERY WHEN WET

STEEP TRAIL!

HANG GLIDERS

LUGE

VIEW

HORSE CART ENDS

WC

PAVED ROAD

LOWER BUS STOP

PICNIC SPOT

BOAT RENTAL

COLOMAN STRASSE

P

P

VILLAGE

HORSE CART STARTS

ALPSEE

TO MUNICH & ROTHENBURG

ROMANTISCHE

POST PHONE

②

③ ①

CASTLE TICKET CENTER

HOHEN-SCHWANGAU CASTLE

P

TO PINSWANG 1 HOUR

SCHWAN-GAU

STRASSE

PARK-STRASSE

①

LAKE FORGGEN SEE

B-17

CASTLE

GERMANY AUSTRIA

TO KAUFBEUREN ON MUNICH-LINDAU LINE

FÜSSEN

10 MILES TO REUTTE

DCH

NOTE: MAP NOT TO SCALE
BORDER TO ALPSEE PARKING = 3 MI. DRIVE
ALPSEE PARKING TO NEUSCH. = 30 MIN. WALK

① Beim "Landhannes" Rooms
② Alpenhotel Meier
③ Sonnenhof Rooms

with Ludwig's death (only a third of the interior was finished), and within six weeks, tourists were paying to go through it.

Today, guides herd groups of 60 through the castle, giving an interesting—if rushed—30-minute tour. You'll go up and down more than 300 steps, through lavish Wagnerian dream rooms, a royal state-of-the-19th-century-art kitchen, the king's gilded-lily bedroom, and his extravagant throne room. You'll visit 15 rooms with their original furnishings and fanciful wall paintings. After the tour, you'll see a room lined with fascinating drawings (described in English) of the castle plans, construction, and drawings from 1883 of Falkenstein—a whimsical, over-the-top, never-built castle that makes Neuschwanstein look stubby. Falkenstein occupied Ludwig's fantasies the year he died. Following the tour, a 20-minute slide show (alternating German and English) plays

"MAD" KING LUDWIG

Ludwig II (a.k.a. "Mad" King Ludwig), a tragic figure, ruled Bavaria for 23 years until his death in 1886 at the age of 41. Politically, his reality was to "rule" either as a pawn of Prussia or a pawn of Austria. Rather than deal with politics in Bavaria's capital, Munich, Ludwig frittered away most of his time at his family's hunting palace, Hohenschwangau. He spent much of his adult life constructing his fanciful Neuschwanstein Castle—like a kid builds a tree house—on a neighboring hill upon the scant ruins of a medieval castle. Although Ludwig spent 17 years building Neuschwanstein, he lived in it only 172 days. Ludwig was a true Romantic living in a Romantic age. His best friends were artists, poets, and composers such as Richard Wagner. His palaces are wallpapered with misty medieval themes—especially those from Wagnerian operas. Eventually he was declared mentally unfit to rule Bavaria and taken away from Neuschwanstein. Two days after this eviction, Ludwig was found dead in a lake. To this day, people debate whether the king was murdered or committed suicide.

continuously. If English is on, pop in. If not, it's not worth waiting for.

Mary's Bridge (Marienbrücke)—Before or after the Neuschwanstein tour, climb up to Mary's Bridge to marvel at Ludwig's castle, just as Ludwig did. This bridge was quite an engineering accomplishment 100 years ago. From the bridge, the frisky can hike even higher to the "Beware—Danger of Death" signs and an even more glorious castle view. (Access to the bridge is closed in bad winter weather, but many travelers walk around the barriers to get there—at their own risk, of course.) For the most interesting descent from Neuschwanstein (15 min longer and extremely slippery when wet), follow signs to the Pöllat Gorge.

▲▲**Hohenschwangau Castle**—Standing quietly below Neuschwanstein, the big yellow Hohenschwangau Castle was Ludwig's boyhood home. Originally built in the 12th century, it was ruined by Napoleon. Ludwig's father, Maximilian, rebuilt it, and you'll see it as it looked in 1836. It's more lived-in and historic, and excellent 30-minute tours actually give a better glimpse of Ludwig's life than the more-visited and famous Neuschwanstein Castle tour.

Cost and Hours: Each castle costs €8, a *Königsticket* for both castles costs €15, and children under 18 are admitted free (castles open April–Sept daily from 9:00 with last tour departing at 18:00, Oct–March daily from 10:00 with last tour at 16:00).

Getting Tickets for the Castles: Every tour bus in Bavaria converges on Neuschwanstein, and tourists flush in each morning from Munich. A handy reservation system (see below) sorts out the chaos for smart travelers. Tickets come with admission times. (Miss this time and you don't get in.) To tour both castles, you must do Hohenschwangau first (logical, since this gives a better introduction to Ludwig's short life). You'll get two tour times: Hohenschwangau and then, two hours later, Neuschwanstein.

If you arrive late and without a reservation, you'll spend two hours in the ticket line and may find all tours for the day booked. A **ticket center** for both Neuschwanstein and Hohenschwangau is located at street level between the two castles, a few blocks from the TI toward the Alpsee (April–Sept daily 7:30–18:00, Oct–March daily 8:30–16:00, last tickets sold for Neuschwanstein 60 min before closing, for Hohenschwangau 30 min before closing). First tours start around 9:00. Arrive by 8:00 and you'll likely be touring by 9:00. Warning: During the summer, tickets for English tours can run out by 16:00.

It's best to reserve ahead in peak season (July–Sept, especially Aug). You can make reservations a minimum of 24 hours in advance by contacting the ticket office by phone (tel. 08362/930-830) or e-mail (info@ticket-center-hohenschwangau.de), or booking online (www.ticket-center-hohenschwangau.de). Tickets reserved in advance cost €1.60 extra (per person, per castle), and ticket holders must be at the ticket office well before the appointed entry time (30 min for Hohenschwangau, 60 min for Neuschwanstein, allowing time to make your way up to the castle). Remember that many of the businesses are owned by the old royal family, so they encourage you to space the two tours longer than necessary in hopes that you'll spend a little more money. Insist on the tightest schedule—with no lunchtime—if you don't want too much down time.

Services: The helpful TI, bus stop, ATM, and telephones cluster around the main intersection (TI open April–June daily 9:00–17:00, July–Sept daily 9:00–18:00, Oct–March daily 9:00–16:00, tel. 08362/819-840, www.schwangau.de).

The "village" at the foot of Europe's Disney castle feeds off the droves of hungry, shop-happy tourists. The Bräustüberl cafeteria serves the cheapest grub (often with live folk music). The Alpsee is ideal for a picnic, but there are no grocery shops in the area. Your best bet is getting food to go from one of the many bratwurst stands (between the ticket center and TI) for a lazy lunch at the lakeside park or in one of the old-fashioned rowboats (rented by the hour in summer).

Getting to the Castles: From the ticket booth, Hohenschwangau is an easy 10-minute climb. Neuschwanstein is a steep 30-minute hike. To minimize hiking to Neuschwanstein, you can take a shuttle bus (from in front of Hotel Lisl, just above ticket office and to the left) or horse-drawn carriage (from in front of Hotel Müller, just above ticket office and to the right), but neither gets you to the castle doorstep. The frequent shuttle buses drop you off at Mary's Bridge, leaving you a steep 10-minute downhill walk from the castle—be sure to see the view from Mary's Bridge before hiking down to the castle (€1.80 up; €2.60 round-trip not worth it since you have to hike up to bus stop for return trip). Carriages (€5 up, €2.50 down) are slower than walking and they stop below Neuschwanstein, leaving you a five-minute uphill hike. Note: If it's less than an hour until your Neuschwanstein tour time, you'll need to hike—even at a brisk pace, it still takes 30 minutes. For a lazy, varied, and economical plan, ride the bus to Mary's Bridge for the view, hike down to the castle, and then catch the carriage from there back down.

Getting to the Castles from Füssen or Reutte: If arriving by **car,** note that road signs in the region refer to the sight as *Königsschlösser,* not Neuschwanstein. There's plenty of parking (all lots-€4). Get there early, and you'll park where you like. Lot E—past the ticket center and next to the lake—is my favorite.

From **Füssen,** those without cars can catch the roughly hourly **bus** (€1.50 one-way, €3 round-trip, 10 min, note times carefully on the meager schedule, catch bus at train station), take a **taxi** (€8.50 one-way), or ride a rental **bike** (3 miles).

From **Reutte,** take the bus to Füssen (Mon–Fri 6/day, Sat 2/day, none Sun, €3.20, 30 min), then hop a city bus to the castle.

For a Romantic twist, hike or mountain-bike from the trailhead at the recommended hotel **Gutshof zum Schluxen** in Pinswang (see page 410). When the dirt road forks at the top of the hill, go right (downhill), cross the Austria–Germany border (marked by a sign and deserted hut), and follow the narrow paved road to the castles. It's a 60- to 90-minute hike or a great circular bike trip (allow 30 min; cyclists can return to Schluxen from the castles on a different 30-min bike route via Füssen).

Near Neuschwanstein Castle

▲**Tegelberg Gondola**—Just north of Neuschwanstein is a fun play zone around the mighty Tegelberg gondola. Hang gliders circle like vultures. Their pilots jump from the top of the Tegelberg Gondola. For €15, you can ride the lift to the 5,500-foot summit and back down (May–Oct daily 9:00–17:00, Dec–April daily 9:00–16:30, closed Nov, frequency depends on demand, last lift goes up 10 min before closing time, in bad weather call first to confirm, tel. 08362/98360). On a clear day you get great views of the Alps and Bavaria and the vicarious thrill of watching hang gliders and parasailors leap into airborne ecstasy. Weather permitting, scores of adventurous Germans line up and leap from the launch ramp at the top of the lift. With one leaving every two or three minutes, it's great spec-tating. Thrill seekers with exceptional social skills may talk themselves into a tandem ride with a parasailor. From the top of Tegelberg, it's a steep 2.5-hour hike down to Ludwig's castle. Avoid the treacherous trail directly below the gondola. At the base of the gondola, you'll find a playground, a cheery eatery, and a very good luge ride (below).

▲Tegelberg Luge—Next to the lift is a luge course. A luge is like a bobsled on wheels (for more details, see "Sights near Reutte," below). This stainless-steel track is heated, so it's often dry and open when drizzly weather shuts down the concrete luges. It's not as scenic as Bichlbach and Biberwier (see below), but it's handy (€2.50/ride, 6-ride sharable card-€10, July–Sept daily 9:00–18:00, otherwise same hours as gondola, in winter sometimes opens later due to wet track, in bad weather call first to confirm, tel. 08362/98360). A funky cable system pulls riders (in their sleds) to the top without a ski lift.

▲Ludwig II Musical—A spectacular opera/musical based on the Romantic life and troubled times of Ludwig plays in a grand lakeside theater. While billed as a musical, *Ludwig II: Longing for Paradise* felt like opera to me—with an orchestra in the pit, creative stage sets, fine singing, wonderful acoustics, and an easy-to-follow story line about Ludwig abandoning the normal, guy-thing rush of political power to pal around with his muses (3 vampy women dressed in purple). It's Bismarck the realistic politician on one side versus Wagner the Romantic composer on the other, as art triumphs (and Ludwig disappears into the lake).

The music is wonderful and the show's a hit with Germans. It's clearly top classical quality, but the superscripts in English are tough to read and tickets are pricey. The state-of-the-art theater is romantically set on a lake (Forgensee) with a view of floodlit Neuschwanstein in the distance (€50–105 per seat, nightly all year Tue–Sun 19:30 plus a matinee Sat–Sun at 14:30, no shows Mon, 3 hrs including intermission, plenty of chances to eat a good light meal, parking-€3, about 1 mile north of Füssen—follow signs for Musical, book in advance, for tickets call 01805/583-944, www.ludwigmusical.com). It's possible to book directly at the TI in Füssen. If you're staying in Füssen, catch the shuttle bus that conveniently runs to and from the play.

More Sights

These are listed in driving order from Füssen.

▲▲Wies Church (Wieskirche)—Germany's greatest rococo-style church, this "church in the meadow" is newly restored and looking as brilliant as the day it floated down from heaven. Overripe with decoration but bright and bursting with beauty, this church is a divine droplet, a curly curlicue, the final flowering of the Baroque movement (donation requested, summer daily 8:00–19:00, winter daily 8:00–17:00, parking-€1, tel. 08862/932-930, www.wieskirche.de).

This pilgrimage church is built around the much-venerated statue of a scourged (or whipped) Christ, which supposedly wept in 1738. The carving—too graphic to be accepted by that generation's church—was the focus of worship in a peasant's barn. Miraculously, it wept—empathizing with all those who suffer. Pilgrims came from all around. A tiny and humble chapel was built to house the statue in 1739. (You can see it where the lane to the church leaves the parking lot.) Bigger and bigger crowds came. Two of Bavaria's top rococo architects, the Zimmermann brothers, were commissioned to build the Wieskirche that stands here today.

Follow the theological sweep from the altar to the ceiling: Jesus whipped, chained, and then killed (notice the pelican above the altar—recalling a pre-Christian story of a bird that opened its breast to feed its young with its own blood); the painting of a baby Jesus posed as if on the cross; the sacrificial lamb; and finally, high on the ceiling, the resurrected Christ before the Last Judgment. This is the most positive depiction of the Last Judgment around. Jesus, rather than sitting on the throne to judge, rides high on a rainbow—a symbol of forgiveness—giving any sinner the feeling that there is still time to repent, and there's plenty of mercy on hand. In the back, above the pipe organ, notice the empty throne—waiting for Judgment Day—and the closed door to paradise.

Above the entrances to both side aisles are murky glass cases with 18th-century handkerchiefs. People wept, came here, were healed, and no longer needed their hankies. Walk up either aisle flanking the high altar to see votives—requests and thanks to God (for happy, healthy babies, and so on). Notice how the kneelers are positioned so that worshipers can meditate on scenes of biblical miracles painted high on the ceiling and visible through the ornate tunnel frames. A priest here once told me that faith, architecture, light, and music all combine to create the harmony of the Wieskirche.

Two paintings flank the door at the rear of the church. One shows the ceremonial parade in 1749 when the white-clad monks of Steingaden carried the carved statue of Christ from the tiny church to its new big one. The second painting, from 1757, is a votive from one of the Zimmermann brothers, the artists and architects who built this church. He is giving thanks for the successful construction of the new church.

The Wieskirche is 30 minutes north of Neuschwanstein. The northbound Romantic Road bus tour stops here for 15 minutes. You can take a bus from Füssen to the Wieskirche, but you'll spend more time waiting for the bus back than you will seeing the church. By car, head north from Füssen, turn right at Steingaden, and follow the signs. Take a commune-with-nature-and-smell-the-farm detour back through the meadow to the car park.

If you can't visit Wieskirche, visit one of the other churches that came out of the same heavenly spray can: Oberammergau's church, Munich's Asam Church, Würzburg's Residenz Chapel, the splendid Ettal Monastery (free and near Oberammergau), and, on a lesser scale,

Füssen's cathedral.

▲Oberammergau—The Shirley Temple of Bavarian villages, exploited to the hilt by the tourist trade, Oberammergau wears way too much makeup. If you're passing through anyway, it's worth a wander among the half-timbered *Lüftlmalerei* houses frescoed (in a style popular throughout the town in the 18th century) with Bible scenes and famous fairy-tale characters. Browse through woodcarvers' shops—small art galleries filled with very expensive whittled works. The beautifully frescoed Pilat's House on Ludwig-Thomas-Strasse is a living workshop full of woodcarvers and painters in action (free, May–Oct, Dec, and Feb Mon–Fri 13:00–18:00, closed Sat-Sun; closed Nov, Jan, and March–April). Or see folk art at the town's Heimatmuseum (Tue–Sun 14:00–18:00, closed Mon; **TI** Mon–Fri 8:30–18:00, Sat 8:30-12:00, closed Sun, tel. 08822/92310, www.oberammergau.de).

Oberammergau Church: Visit the church, a poor cousin of the one at Wies. This church looks richer than it is. Put your hand on the "marble" columns. If they warm up, they're fakes—"stucco marble." Wander through the graveyard. Ponder the deaths that two wars dealt Germany. Behind the church are the photos of three Schneller brothers, all killed within two years in World War II.

Passion Play: Still making good on a deal the townspeople struck with God when they were spared devastation by the Black Plague several centuries ago, once each decade Oberammergau presents its Passion play. For 100 summer days in a row, the town performs an all-day dramatic story of Christ's crucifixion (in 2000, 5,000 people attended per day). Until the next performance in 2010, you'll have to settle for reading the book, seeing Nicodemus tool around town in his VW, or browsing through the theater's exhibition hall (€2.50, German tours daily 10:00–17:00, tel. 08822/945-8833 or 08822/32278). English speakers get little respect here, with only two theater tours a day scheduled (often at 11:00 and 14:00). They may do others if you pay the €25 or gather 10 needy English speakers.

Sleeping in Oberammergau: $ Hotel Bayerischer Löwe is central, with a good restaurant and 18 comfortable rooms (Db-€56, no CC, Dedlerstrasse 2, tel. 08822/1365, fax 08822/882, www.bayerischerloewe .com, gasthof.loewe@freenet.de, family Reinhofer). **$ Gasthof zur Rose** is a big, central, family-run place with 21 rooms (Sb-€33, Db-€56, Tb-€71, Qb-€82, Dedlerstrasse 9, tel. 08822/4706, fax 08822/6753, gasthof-rose@t-online.de). **$ Frau Magold's** three bright and spacious rooms are twice as nice as the cheap hotel rooms for much less money (Db-€37–43, no CC, immediately behind Gasthof Zur Rose at Kleppergasse 1, tel. & fax 08822/4340, NSE). **$ Frau Maderspacher** rents three cozy, old-time rooms in her very characteristic 160-year-old home (D-€30, no CC, July–Sept only, a block past Gasthof zur Rose at Daisenbergerstrasse 11, tel. 08822/3978, NSE). Oberammergau's modern $ **youth hostel** is on the river a short walk from the center (€13 beds, tel. 08822/4114, fax 08822/1695).

Getting to Oberammergau: From Füssen to Oberammergau, four to five buses run daily (fewer in winter, 1.5 hrs). Trains run from Munich to Oberammergau (hrly, 1.75 hrs, change in Murnau). Drivers entering the town from the north should cross the bridge, take the second right, and park in the free lot a block beyond the TI. Leaving town, head out past the church and turn toward Ettal on Road 23. You're 20 miles from Reutte via the scenic Plansee. If heading to Munich, Road 23 takes you to the autobahn, which gets you there in less than an hour.

▲▲**Linderhof Castle**—This homiest of Mad King Ludwig's castles is small and comfortably exquisite—good enough for a minor god. Set in the woods 15 minutes from Oberammergau and surrounded by fountains and sculpted, Italian-style gardens, it's the only palace I've toured that actually had me feeling envious. Don't miss the grotto, which is located outside and uphill from the palace; 15-minute tours are included with the palace ticket (€6, April–Sept daily 9:00–18:00, Oct–March daily 10:00–16:00, parking-€2, fountains often erupt on the hour, English tours every 30 min or when 15 gather—sparse off-season, so you may have to wait, tel. 08822/92030). Plan for lots of walking and a two-hour stop to fully enjoy this royal park. Pay at the entrance and get an admission time. Visit outlying sights in the garden to pass any wait time. The outside of the palace is undergoing a long-term renovation, with lots of scaffolding. But the interior, freshly refurbished, is glorious. Without a car, getting to (and home from) Linderhof is a huge headache—skip it (but diehards can find details in "Getting around Bavaria and Tirol," above).

▲▲**Zugspitze**—The tallest point in Germany is a border crossing. Lifts from Austria and Germany travel to the 10,000-foot summit of the Zugspitze. You can straddle the border between two great nations while enjoying an incredible view. Restaurants, shops, and telescopes await you at the summit.

On the German side, the 75-minute trip from Garmisch costs €43 round-trip; family discounts are available (buy a combo-ticket for cogwheel train to Eibsee and cable-car ride to summit, drivers can park for free at cable-car station at Eibsee, tel. 08821/7970). Allow plenty of time for afternoon descents: If bad weather hits in the late afternoon, cable cars can be delayed at the summit, causing tourists to miss their train from Eibsee back to Garmisch. Hikers enjoy the easy 6-mile walk around the lovely Eibsee (German side, 5 min downhill from cable car *Seilbahn*).

On the Austrian side, from the less-crowded Talstation Obermoos above the village of Erwald, the tram zips you to the top in 10 minutes (€31 round-trip, cash only, goes every 20 min, late May–Oct daily 8:40–16:40, tel. in Austria 05673/2309, www.zugspitze.com).

The German ascent from Garmisch is easier for those without a car, but buses do connect the Erwald train station and the Austrian lift nearly every hour.

SLEEPING IN BAVARIA

Füssen

Though I prefer sleeping in Reutte (see "Sleeping in Tirol" below), convenient Füssen is just three miles from Ludwig's castles and offers a cobbled, riverside retreat. It's very touristy, but it has plenty of rooms. All recommended places are within a few blocks of the train station and the town center. Parking is easy at the station.

$$$ **Hotel Kurcafé** is deluxe, with 30 spacious rooms and all of the amenities. The standard rooms are comfortable, and the newer, bigger rooms have elegant touches and fun decor—like canopy drapes and cherubic frescoes over the bed (Sb-€82, standard Db-€99, bigger Db-€113–139 depending on size, Tb-€123, Qb-€139, 4-person suite-€159, €10 more for weekends and holidays, cheaper off-season, non-smoking rooms, elevator, parking-€5/day, on tiny traffic circle a block in front of station at Bahnhofstrasse 4, tel. 08362/930-180, fax 08362/930-1850, www.kurcafe.com, info@kurcafe.com, Schöll family).

$$$ **Hotel Hirsch** is a big, romantic, old tour-class hotel with 53 rooms on the main street in the center of town. Their standard rooms are fine, and their theme rooms are a fun splurge (Sb-€56–82, standard Db-€87–133, theme Db-€118–162, prices depend on room size and demand, cheaper Nov–March and during slow times, only the expensive theme rooms are non-smoking, family rooms, elevator, free parking, Kaiser-Maximilian Platz 7, tel. 08362/93980, fax 08362/939-877, www.hotelhirsch.de, info@hotelhirsch.de).

$$$ **Hotel Sonne,** in the heart of town, rents 32 mod, institutional, yet comfy rooms (Sb-€85, Db-€105, Tb-€129, cheaper Oct–mid-June, non-smoking rooms, elevator, free parking, kitty-corner from TI at Reichenstrasse 37, tel. 08362/9080, fax 08362/908-100, www.hotel-sonne.de, info@hotel-sonne.de).

$$ **Altstadthotel zum Hechten** offers all the modern comforts in a friendly, traditional shell right under Füssen Castle in the old-town pedestrian zone (35 rooms, S-€30, Sb-€45, D-€60, Db-€75–80, Tb-€100, Qb-€112, free parking, cheaper off-season and for longer stays, non-smoking rooms, fun mini–bowling alley in basement, nearby church bells ring hourly at night; from TI, walk down pedestrian street, take second right to Ritterstrasse 6, tel. 08362/91600, fax 08362/916-099, www.hotel-hechten.com, hotel.hechten@t-online.de, Pfeiffer and Tramp families).

$$ **Suzanne's B&B** is run by a plain-spoken, no-nonsense American woman who strikes some travelers as brusque. Suzanne runs a tight ship, offering lots of local travel advice, backyard-fresh eggs, local

SLEEP CODE

(€1 = about $1.10, country code: 49, area code: 08362)
Sleep Code: **S** = Single, **D** = Double/Twin, **T** = Triple, **Q** = Quad, **b** = bathroom, **s** = shower only, **no CC** = Credit Cards not accepted, **SE** = English spoken, **NSE** = No English spoken. Unless otherwise noted, credit cards are accepted, English is spoken, and breakfast is included.

To help you sort easily through these listings, I've divided the rooms into three categories, based on the price for a standard double room with bath:

$$$ **Higher Priced**—Most rooms €85 or more.
$$ **Moderately Priced**—Most rooms between €55–85.
$ **Lower Priced**—Most rooms €55 or less.

Prices listed are for one-night stays. Most places give about 10 percent off for two-night stays—always request this discount. Competition is fierce, and off-season prices are soft. High season is mid-June through September. Rooms are generally about 12 percent less in shoulder season and much cheaper in off-season.

cheese, a children's yard, laundry (€20/load), and bright, woody, spacious rooms (Db-€80, Tb-€115, Qb-€145, Db suite-€100, Tb suite-€140, Qb suite-€160, attic special: €70 for 2, €100 for 3, €120 for 4; another room holds up to 6—ask for details, no CC, non-smoking, exit station right and backtrack 2 blocks along tracks, cross tracks at Venetianerwinkel to #3, tel. 08362/38485, fax 08362/921-396, www.suzannes.de, svorbrugg @t-online.de). Her kid-friendly loft has very low ceilings (you'll crouch), a private bathroom (you'll crouch), and up to six beds.

$$ Hotel Bräustüberl has 16 decent rooms at fair rates attached to a gruff, musty, old beer hall–type place. Don't expect much service (S-€25, Sb-€47, D-€50, Db-€64–74, no CC, Rupprechtstrasse 5, a block from station, tel. 08362/7843, fax 08362/923-951, brauereigasthof-fuessen @t-online.de).

$ Gasthof Krone, a rare bit of pre-glitz Füssen in the pedestrian zone, has dumpy halls and stairs and big, time-warp rooms at good prices (S-€28, D/Ds-€52, extra bed-€29, €3 more per person for 1-night stays, reception in restaurant, from TI head down pedestrian street, take first left to Schrannengasse 17, tel. 08362/7824, fax 08362/37505, www.krone-fuessen.de).

Füssen

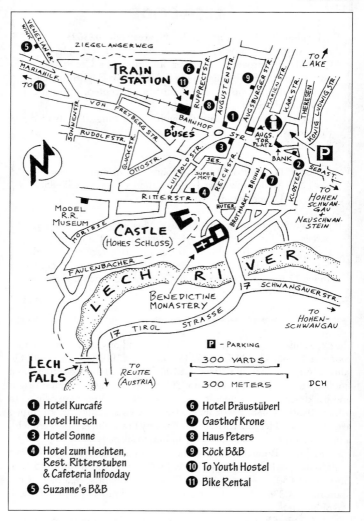

- ❶ Hotel Kurcafé
- ❷ Hotel Hirsch
- ❸ Hotel Sonne
- ❹ Hotel zum Hechten, Rest. Ritterstuben & Cafeteria Infooday
- ❺ Suzanne's B&B
- ❻ Hotel Bräustüberl
- ❼ Gasthof Krone
- ❽ Haus Peters
- ❾ Röck B&B
- ❿ To Youth Hostel
- ⓫ Bike Rental

$ **Haus Peters** is comfy, smoke-free, and friendly. But Frau Peters takes reservations only a short time in advance and shuts down in May, July, and when she's out of town (4 rooms, Ds/Db-€50, Tb-€60, no CC, Augustenstrasse 5 1/2, tel. 08362/7171).

$ **Wilhelm and Elisabeth Röck,** a sweet old couple, rent out two rooms in their home a block from the TI (D-€51, Db-€52, no CC, non-smoking, Augsburgerstrasse 7, tel. 08362/6353, just enough English spoken).

$ Füssen Youth Hostel, a fine, German-run place, welcomes travelers under 27 (€15-dorm beds in 2- to 6-bed rooms, D-€36, €3 more for non-members, includes breakfast and sheets, non-smoking, laundry-€3.50/load, dinner-€5, office open 7:00–12:00 & 17:00–23:00, from station backtrack 10 min along tracks, Mariahilferstrasse 5, tel. 08362/7754, fax 08362/2770, jhfuessen@djh-bayern.de).

Hohenschwangau, near Neuschwanstein Castle

Inexpensive farmhouse *Zimmer* (B&Bs) abound in the Bavarian countryside around Neuschwanstein, offering drivers a decent value. Look for *Zimmer Frei* signs ("room free," or vacancy). The going rate is about €50–65 for a double, including breakfast.

$$ Beim "Landhannes" is a hundred-year-old working dairy farm run by Johann and Traudl Mayr. They rent six creaky, well-antlered rooms and keep flowers on the balconies, big bells in the halls, and cows in the yard (Sb-€30, Ds-€50, Db-€60, 10 percent discount for 2 nights, no CC, poorly signed in the village of Horn on the Füssen side of Schwangau, look for the farm 100 yards in front of Hotel Kleiner König, Am Lechrain 22, tel. 08362/8349, fax 08362/819-646, www.landhannes.de, mayr@landhannes.de).

$$ Sonnenhof is a big, woody, old house with four spacious, traditionally decorated rooms and a cheery garden. It's a 15-minute walk through the fields to the castles (S-€20, D-€45, Db-€55, no CC, at Pension Schwansee on the Füssen–Neuschwanstein road, follow the small lane 100 yards to Sonnenweg 11, tel. 08362/8420, Frau Görlich SE).

$$ Alpenhotel Meier is a small, family-run hotel with 15 rooms in a bucolic setting within walking distance of the castles, just beyond the lower parking lot (Sb-€46, Db-€77, plus €1.20 tourist tax per person, 5 percent discount with cash and this book, non-smoking rooms, all rooms have porches or balconies, family rooms, sauna, easy parking, just before tennis courts at Schwangauerstrasse 37, tel. 08362/81152, fax 08362/987-028, www.alpenhotel-allgaeu.de, alpenhotelmeier@web.de, Frau Meier SE).

EATING

Füssen's old town and main pedestrian drag are lined with a variety of eateries. Three good places cluster on Ritterstrasse, just under the castle, off the top of the main street:

Ritterstuben offers reasonable and delicious fish, salads, veggie plates, and a fun kids' menu (Tue–Sun 11:30–14:30 & 17:30–23:00, closed Mon, Ritterstrasse 4, tel. 08362/7759). Demure, English-speaking Gabi serves while her husband cooks.

Zum Hechten Restaurant serves hearty, traditional Bavarian fare and specializes in pike *(Hecht)* pulled from the Lech River (€8–12 meals, Thu–Tue 11:30–14:30 & 17:30–21:00, closed Wed, Ritterstrasse 6).

Infooday is a clever and modern self-service eatery that sells its hot meals and salad bar by weight and offers English newspapers (filling salad–€3, meals–€5, Mon–Fri 10:30–18:30, Sat 10:30–14:30, closed Sun, Ritterstrasse 6).

Hotel Kurcafé's fine restaurant, right on Füssen's main traffic circle, has good and reasonable weekly specials, plus a tempting bakery (daily 11:30–14:30 & 17:30–22:00, choose between a traditional dining room and a pastel "winter garden," live Bavarian zither music most Fri–Sat during dinner, tel. 08362/930-180).

TRANSPORTATION CONNECTIONS

To: Neuschwanstein (hrly buses, 10 min, €1.50 one-way, €3 round-trip; taxis cost €8.50 one-way), **Reutte** (by bus, Mon–Fri 6/day, Sat 2/day, none Sun, 30 min, €3.20 one-way; taxis cost €28 one-way), **Munich** (hrly trains, 2 hrs, some change in Buchloe). Train info: tel. 01805-996-633.

Romantic Road Buses: The northbound Romantic Road bus departs Füssen at 8:00; the southbound bus arrives at Füssen at 20:15 (bus stops at train station). Railpasses get you a 60 percent discount on the Romantic Road bus (and the ride does not use up a day of a Flexipass). For more information, see the Rothenburg chapter.

Reutte, Austria

(€1 = about $1.10)
Reutte (ROY-teh, with a rolled "r"), a relaxed town of 5,700, is located 20 minutes across the border from Füssen. It's far from the international tourist crowd, but popular with Germans and Austrians for its climate. Doctors recommend its "grade 1" air. Reutte's one claim to fame with Americans: As Nazi Germany was falling in 1945, Hitler's top rocket scientist, Werner von Braun, joined the Americans (rather than the Russians) in Reutte. You could say the American space program began here.

Reutte isn't featured in any other American guidebook. While its generous sidewalks are filled with smart boutiques and lazy coffeehouses, its charms are subtle. It was never rich or important. Its castle is ruined, its buildings have painted-on "carvings," its churches are full, its men

Reutte

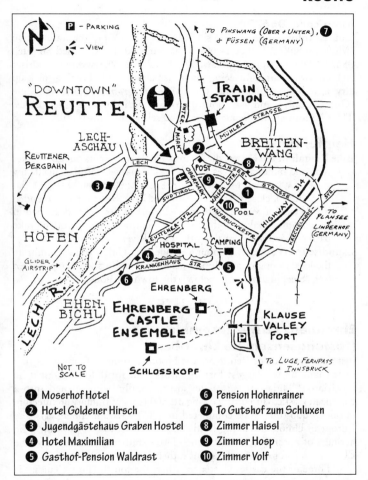

P – PARKING
◀ – VIEW

TO PINSWANG (OBER & UNTER), **7**
& FÜSSEN (GERMANY)

"DOWNTOWN"
REUTTE

TRAIN
STATION

LECH-
ASCHAU

BREITEN-
WANG

REUTTENER
BERGBAHN

MÜHLER STRASSE

UNTER-MARKT

LECH

PLANSEE

POST

OBERMARKT

KAILER LIZH

STRASSE

2

8

9

1

10 POOL

SÜDTIROL

INNSBRUCKERSTR.

REUTTENER STR.

KRECKELMOOS STR.

314

TO
PLANSEE
&
LINDERHOF
(GERMANY)

HÖFEN

GLIDER
AIRSTRIP

HOSPITAL

CAMPING

4

KRANKENHAUS STR.

5

6

EHRENBERG

EHEN-
BICHL

EHRENBERG
CASTLE
ENSEMBLE

KLAUSE
VALLEY
FORT

P

TO LUGE, FERNPASS
& INNSBRUCK

NOT TO
SCALE

SCHLOSSKOPF

LECH R.

1 Moserhof Hotel
2 Hotel Goldener Hirsch
3 Jugendgästehaus Graben Hostel
4 Hotel Maximilian
5 Gasthof-Pension Waldrast

6 Pension Hohenrainer
7 To Gutshof zum Schluxen
8 Zimmer Haissl
9 Zimmer Hosp
10 Zimmer Volf

yodel for each other on birthdays, and lately, its energy is spent soaking its Austrian and German guests in *Gemütlichkeit*. Most guests stay for a week, so the town's attractions are more time-consuming than thrilling. If the weather's good, hike to the mysterious Ehrenberg ruins, ride the luge, or rent a bike. For a slap-dancing bang, enjoy a Tirolean folk evening. For accommodations, see "Sleeping in Tirol," below.

ORIENTATION

(area code: 05672)
Tourist Information: Reutte's TI is a block in front of the train station (Mon–Fri 8:00–12:00 & 14:00–17:00, Sat 8:30–12:00, closed Sun, tel. 05672/62336 or, from Germany, 00-43-5672/62336, www.reuttetourism .at). Go over your sightseeing plans, ask about a folk evening, pick up city and biking maps and the *Sommerprogramm* events schedule (German only), and ask about discounts with the hotel guest cards. Their "Information" booklet has a good self-guided town walk.

Helpful Hints

Bike Rental: In the center, the Heinz Glätzle shop rents out good bikes (city and mountain bikes–€15/day, kids' bikes–€7.50/day, inside toy store at Obermarkt 61, Mon–Fri 8:15–12:00 & 14:00–18:00, Sat 8:15–12:00, closed Sun, tel. 05672/62752). Several recommended hotels loan or rent bikes to guests. Most of the sights described in this chapter make good biking destinations. Ask about the bike path (*Radwanderweg*) along the Lech River.

Laundry: Don't ask the TI about a launderette. Unless you can infiltrate the local campground, Hotel Maximilian, or Gutshof zum Schluxen (see "Sleeping in Tirol," below), the town has none.

SIGHTS

Ehrenberg Castle Ensemble
(Festungsensemble Ehrenberg)

Just a mile outside of Reutte are the brooding ruins of four castles that once made up the largest fort in Tirol (built for defense against he Bavarians). Today, these castles are gradually being turned into a European Castle Museum, showing off 500 years of military architecture in one swoop (due to be completed in 2007, www.ehrenberg.at). The European Union is helping fund the project because it promotes the heritage of a multinational region—Tirol—rather than a country (the EU's vision is for a zone of regions rather than nations).

Three of the castles cluster together; the fourth (Fort Claudia) is across the valley, though all four used to be connected by walls. The first three—the easiest and most interesting to visit—are described below, from lowest to highest. New signage throughout the castle complex will help you find your way and explain some background on the region's history, geology, geography, culture, flora, and fauna.

Getting to the Castle Ensemble: The Klause, Ehrenberg, and Schlosskopf castles are on the road to Lermoos and Innsbruck. These are a pleasant walk or a short bike ride from Reutte; bikers can use the *Radwanderweg* along the Lech River (the TI has a good map).

▲**Klause Valley Fort**—At the parking lot at the base of the ruin-topped hill, you'll find the recently modernized remains of a Gothic fortification. It was located on the medieval salt road (which used to be the ancient Roman road, Via Claudia). Beginning in the 14th century, this fort controlled traffic and levied tolls on all that passed through this strategic valley. Today it houses a new 60-minute **sound-and-light show** (*son et lumière*) about the castles (€10). You'll sit inside the shell of the old castle while the 2,000-year history of this valley's fortresses is projected on the old stone walls and modern screens around you. By early 2005, this will also be the home to an extensive museum about the "castle ensemble." If you're hungry, drop by the nearby café/guest house, Gasthof Klause (closed Wed), which offers a German-language flier and a wall painting of the intact castle.

▲▲**Ehrenberg Ruins**—Ehrenberg, a 13th-century rock pile, provides a great contrast to King Ludwig's "modern" castles and a super opportunity to let your imagination off its leash. Hike up 20 minutes from the parking lot for a great view from your own private ruins. Facing the hill from the parking lot, find the gravelly road at the Klaus sign. Follow the road to the saddle between the two hills. From the saddle, notice how the castle stands high on the horizon. This is Ehrenberg (which means "mountain of honor"), the first of the four ensemble castles, built in 1296. Thirteenth-century castles were designed to stand boastfully tall. With the advent of gunpowder, castles dug in. Notice the **ramparts** around you. They are from the 18th century. Approaching Ehrenberg castle, look for the small door to the left. It's the night entrance (tight and awkward, therefore safer against a surprise invasion). While hiking up the hill, you go through two doors. Castles allowed step-by-step retreat, giving defenders time to regroup and fight back against invading forces.

Before making the final and steepest ascent, follow the path around to the right to a big, grassy courtyard with commanding views and a fat, newly restored **turret.** This stored gunpowder and held a big cannon that enjoyed a clear view of the valley below. In medieval times, all the trees approaching the castle were cleared to keep an unobstructed view.

Look out over the valley. The pointy spire marks **Breitenwang,** which was a stop on the ancient Via Claudia. In A.D. 46, there was a Roman camp there. In 1489, after the Reutte bridge crossed the Lech River, Reutte (marked by the onion-domed church) was made a market town and eclipsed Breitenwang in importance. Any gliders circling? They launch from just over the river in Höfen (see "Flying and Gliding," next page).

For centuries, this castle was the seat of government—ruling an area called the "judgment of Ehrenberg" (roughly the same as today's "district of Reutte"). When the emperor came by, he stayed here. In 1604, the ruler moved downtown into more comfortable quarters and the castle was no longer a palace.

Climb the steep hill to the top of the castle. Take the high ground. There was no water supply here, just kegs of wine, beer, and a cistern to collect rain.

Ehrenberg repelled 16,000 Swedish soldiers in the defense of Catholicism in 1632. Ehrenberg saw three or four other battles, but its end was not glorious. In the 1780s, a local businessman bought the castle in order to sell off its parts. Later, when vagabonds moved in, the roof was removed to make squatting miserable. With the roof gone, deterioration quickened, leaving this evocative shell and a whiff of history.

▲**Schlosskopf**—If you have energy left after conquering Ehrenberg, hike up to the mighty Schlosskopf (literally "castle head"). When the Bavarians captured Ehrenberg in 1703, the Tiroleans climbed up to the bluff above it to rain cannonballs down on their former fortress. In 1740, a mighty new castle—designed to defend against modern artillery—was built on this same sky-high strategic location. By 2001, the castle was completely overgrown with trees—you couldn't see it from Reutte. But today the trees are shaved away, and the castle has been excavated. Beginning in 2005, the Castle Ensemble project will reconstruct the original equipment used to build this fortress (such as wooden cranes)—and then use those same means to restore parts of it. By 2007, Schloss-kopf will be partially rebuilt, and the 18th-century construction equipment will retire and become part of the exhibit.

More Sights in Reutte

Folk Museum (Heimatsmuseum)—Reutte's Heimatmuseum, offering a quick look at the local folk culture and the story of the castles, is more cute than impressive. Ask to borrow the packet of information in English (€2, May–Oct Tue–Sun 10:00–17:00, closed Mon and Nov–April, in the bright green building on Untermarkt, around corner from Hotel Goldener Hirsch, tel. 05672/72304).

▲▲**Tirolean Folk Evening**—Ask the TI or your hotel if there's a Tirolean folk evening scheduled. Usually on Thursdays in the summer (July–mid-Sept), Reutte or a nearby town puts on an evening of yodeling, slap dancing, and Tirolean frolic worth the €8–10 and short drive. Off-season, you'll have to do your own yodeling. There are also weekly folk concerts in the park (July–Aug only, ask at TI). For listings of these and other local events, pick up a copy of the German-only *Sommer-programm* schedule at the TI.

▲**Flying and Gliding**—For a major thrill on a sunny day, drop by the tiny airport in Höfen across the river, and fly. A small single-prop plane can buzz the Zugspitze and Ludwig's castles and give you a bird's-eye peek at Reutte's Ehrenberg ruins (2 people for 30 min-€110, 1 hr-€220, tel. 05672/62827, phone rarely answered, and then not in English, so your best bet is to show up at Höfen airport on good-weather afternoons). Or, for something more angelic, how about *Segelfliegen*? For €36, you get 30 minutes in a glider for two (you and the pilot). Just watching the towrope launch the graceful glider like a giant, slow-motion rubber-band gun is exhilarating (May–mid-Sept 12:00–19:00, in good but breezy weather only, find someone in the know at the "Thermic Ranch," tel. 05672/71550 or 05672/64010, or mobile 0676/711-0100).

Swimming—Plunge into Reutte's Olympic-size Alpenbad swimming pool to cool off after your castle hikes (€6, June–mid-Sept daily 10:00–21:00, mid-Nov–May Tue–Sun 14:00–21:00, closed Mon and mid-Sept–mid-Nov; indoor/outdoor pools, big water slide, mini-golf, playground on-site, 5 min on foot from Reutte center, head out Obermarkt and turn left on Kaiser Lothar Strasse, tel. 05672/62666).

Reuttener Bergbahn—This mountain lift swoops you high above the treeline to a starting point for several hikes and an alpine flower park with special paths leading you past countless local varieties (€9 one-way, €13 round-trip, flowers best in late July, lift usually mid-May–Oct daily 9:00–11:50 & 13:00–17:00, tel. 05672/62420, www.reuttener -seilbahnen.at).

Sights near Reutte

▲▲**The Luge** *(Sommerrodelbahn)*—Near Lermoos, on the road from Reutte to Innsbruck, you'll find two exciting luge courses, or *Sommerrodelbahn*. To try one of Europe's great €6 thrills, take the lift up, grab a sled-like go-cart, and luge down. The concrete course banks on the corners, and even a novice can go very, very fast. Most are cautious on their first run, speed demons on their second...and bruised and bloody on their third. A woman once showed me her journal illustrated with her husband's dried five-inch-long luge scab. He disobeyed the only essential rule of luging: Keep both hands on your stick. To avoid getting into a bumper-to-bumper traffic jam, let the person in front of you get way ahead before you start. No one emerges from the course without a windblown hairdo and a smile-creased face. Both places charge the same price (€6 per run, 5- and 10-trip discount cards) and shut down at the least hint of rain (call ahead to make sure they're open; you're more likely to get luge info in English if you call the TIs, listed below). If you're without a car, these are not worth the trouble (consider the luge near Neuschwanstein instead—see "Tegelberg Luge," above).

   The short and steep luge: Bichlbach, the first course (330-foot drop, over a 2,600-foot course), is four miles beyond Reutte's castle ruins. Look for a chairlift on the right, and exit on the tiny road at the Almkopfbahn Rosthof sign (June–Sept daily 10:00–17:00, sometimes opens in spring and fall—especially weekends—depending on weather, call first, tel. 05674/5350, or contact the local TI at tel. 05674/5354).

   The longest luge: The Biberwier *Sommerrodelbahn* is a better luge and, at 4,250 feet, the longest in Austria (15 min farther from Reutte than Bichlbach, just past Lermoos in Biberwier—the first exit after a long tunnel). The only drawbacks are its short season and hours (open late-May–June Sat–Sun 9:00–16:30 only, closed Mon–Fri, July–Sept daily 9:00–16:30, call first, tel. 05673/2323 or 05673/2111, TI tel. 05673/2922).

SLEEPING

Reutte

$$$ **Moserhof Hotel** is a plush Tirolean splurge with 30 new-feeling rooms and polished service and facilities, including an elegant dining room (Sb-€47, Db-€84, extra bed-€35, these special prices only if you reserve ahead and ask for Rick Steves rates, almost all rooms have balconies, free parking, elevator, Internet access-€3/hr; from downtown Reutte, follow signs to village Breitenwang, it's just after church at Planseestrasse 44, tel. 05672/62020, fax 05672/620-2040, www.hotel -moserhof.at, info@hotel-moserhof.at, Hosp family).

$$ **Hotel Goldener Hirsch,** located in the center of Reutte just two blocks from the station, is a grand old hotel renovated with Tirolean *Jugendstil* flair. It boasts 56 rooms and one lonely set of antlers (Sb-€56, Db-€80, Tb-€110, Qb-€124–131, 2-night discounts, family rooms, elevator, quality food in their restaurant, tel. 05672/62508, fax 05672/625-087, www.goldener-hirsch.at, info@goldener-hirsch.at, Monika, Helmut, and daughters Vanessa and Nina all SE).

$ The homey **Jugendgästehaus Graben** hostel has two to six beds per room and includes breakfast and sheets. Frau Reyman and her son Rudy keep the place traditional, clean, and friendly, and serve a great €6.50 dinner for guests only. This is a super value. If you've never hostelled and are curious (and have a car or don't mind a bus ride), try it. They accept non-members of any age (dorm bed-€19, Db-€45, no CC, non-smoking rooms, Internet access, laundry service, no curfew, less than 2 miles from Reutte, bus connection to Neuschwanstein via Reutte; from downtown Reutte, cross bridge and follow main road left along river, or take the bus—1 bus/hr until 19:30, ask for Graben stop, no buses Sun; Graben 1, tel. 05672/626-440, fax 05672/626-444, www .hoefen.at, jgh-hoefen@tirol.com).

Ehenbichl, near Reutte

The next two listings are a couple miles upriver from Reutte in the village of Ehenbichl, under the Ehrenberg ruins. From central Reutte, go south on Obermarkt and turn right on Reuttenerstrasse, following signs to Ehenbichl.

$$ **Hotel Maximilian** is a great value. It includes free bicycles, table tennis, a children's playroom, and the friendly service of the Koch

SLEEP CODE

(€1 = about $1.10, country code: 43, area code: 05672)
Sleep Code: **S** = Single, **D** = Double/Twin, **T** = Triple, **Q** = Quad, **b** = bathroom, **s** = shower only, **no CC** = Credit Cards not accepted, **SE** = Speaks English, **NSE** = No English, * = French hotel rating system (0–4 stars). Unless otherwise noted, credit cards are accepted.

To help you sort easily through these listings, I've divided the rooms into three categories, based on the price for a standard double room with bath:

$$$ Higher Priced—Most rooms €80 or more.
  $$ Moderately Priced—Most rooms €50–80.
   $ Lower Priced—Most rooms €50 or less.

Reutte is a mellow Füssen with fewer crowds and easygoing locals with a contagious love of life. Come here for a good dose of Austrian ambience and lower prices. Those with a car should make their home base here; those without should consider it. (To call Reutte from Germany, dial 00-43-5672, then the local number.) You'll drive across the border without stopping. Reutte is popular with Austrians and Germans, who come here year after year for one- or two-week vacations. The hotels are big, elegant, and full of comfy, carved furnishings and creative ways to spend lots of time in one spot. They take great pride in their restaurants, and the owners send their children away to hotel management schools. All include a great breakfast, but few accept credit cards. Most places give about a 5 percent discount for stays of two nights or longer.

family. Daughter Gabi speaks flawless English. The Kochs host many special events, and their hotel has lots of wonderful extras such as a sauna, a masseuse, and a beauty salon (Sb-€35–40, Db-€70–80, family deals, fast Internet access, laundry service-€7/load even for non-guests, good restaurant, tel. 05672/62585, fax 05672/625-8554, www.maxihotel .com, maxhotel@netway.at). They rent cars to guests only (1 VW Golf, 1 VW van, book in advance).

$$ Gasthof-Pension Waldrast, separating a forest and a meadow, is run by the farming Huter family and their huge, friendly dog, Bari. The place feels hauntingly quiet and has no restaurant, but it does offer 10 nice rooms with sitting areas and castle-view balconies (Sb-€30, Db-

€51–55, Tb-€66, Qb-€88, 10 percent discount with this book and 2 nights, no CC, non-smoking, less than 1 mile from Reutte, just off main drag toward Innsbruck, past campground and under castle ruins on Ehrenbergstrasse, tel. & fax 05672/62443, www.waldrasttirol.com, info@waldrasttirol.com).

$ **Pension Hohenrainer** is a big, no-frills alternative to Hotel Maximilian—a quiet, good value with 12 modern rooms and some castle-view balconies (Sb-€23–28, Db-€41–50, cheaper for longer stays, free Internet access, follow signs up the road behind Hotel Maximilian into village of Ehenbichl, tel. 05672/62544 or 05672/63262, fax 05672/62052, www.hohenrainer.at, hohenrainer@aon.at).

Pinswang

The village of Pinswang is closer to Füssen (and Ludwig's castles), but still in Austria.

$$$ **Gutshof zum Schluxen,** run by helpful Hermann, gets the Remote Old Hotel in an Idyllic Setting award. This family-friendly working farm offers modern rustic elegance draped in goose down and pastels, and a chance to pet a rabbit and feed the deer. Its picturesque meadow setting will turn you into a dandelion picker, and its proximity to Neuschwanstein will turn you into a hiker. King Ludwig II himself is said to have slept here (Sb-€41, Db-€82, extra person-€22, 10 percent discount for 4 nights or more, Internet access, self-service laundry, free pickup from Reutte and Füssen, good restaurant, fun bar, mountain bike rental, between Reutte and Füssen in village of Pinswang, tel. 05677/8903, fax 05677/890-323, www.schluxen.com, welcome@schluxen.com).

Private Homes in Breitenwang, near Reutte

The Reutte TI has a list of 50 private homes that rent out generally good rooms *(Zimmer)* with facilities down the hall, pleasant communal living rooms, and breakfast. Most charge €15 per person per night and speak little or no English. Reservations are nearly impossible for one- or two-night stays, but short stops are welcome if you just drop in and fill available gaps. Most *Zimmer* charge around €1.50 extra for heat in winter (worth it). The TI can always find you a room when you arrive.

Right next door to Reutte is the older and quieter village of Breitenwang. It has all the best *Zimmer,* the recommended Moserhof Hotel (above), and a bakery (a 20-min walk from Reutte train station—at post office roundabout, follow Planseestrasse past onion dome to pointy straight dome; unmarked Kaiser Lothar Strasse is first right past this church).

The following *Zimmer* (all reasonably priced, rated $) are comfortable and quiet, have few stairs, and are within two blocks of the Breitenwang church steeple: **Helene Haissl** (the best of the bunch, D-€30, 2-night discounts, no CC, children's loft room available, beautiful troll-filled garden, free bikes, laundry service, across from big Alpenhotel Ernberg at Planseestrasse 63, tel. 05672/67913); **Walter and Emilie Hosp** (3 rooms in a modern house, D-€40, D-€36 for 2 nights or more, extra person-€15, no CC, Kaiser Lothar Strasse 29, tel. 05672/65377); and **Irene and Rudolf Volf** (3 rooms closer to Reutte's main drag, D-€40, D-€30 for 2 nights, no CC, Kaiser Lothar Strasse 2, tel. 05672/65066).

EATING

The hotels here take great pride in serving local cuisine at reasonable prices to their guests and the public. Rather than go to a cheap restaurant, try a hotel. Most offer €8–14 dinners from 18:00 to 21:00 and are closed one night a week. Reutte itself has plenty of inviting eateries—traditional, ethnic, fast food, grocery stores, and delis.

TRANSPORTATION CONNECTIONS

By train to: Innsbruck (7/day, 2.5 hrs, change in Garmisch and sometimes also in Mittenwald), **Munich** (hrly, 2.5–3 hrs, change in Garmisch, Pfronten-Steinach, or Kempten), **Garmisch** (every 2 hrs, 1 hr).

By bus to: Füssen (Mon–Fri 6/day, Sat 2/day, none Sun, 30 min, €3.20, buses depart from in front of the train station, pay driver). Taxis cost €28 one-way.

By car into Reutte from Germany: Skip the north *(Nord)* exit and take the south *(Süd)* exit into town. While Austria requires a toll sticker for driving on its highways (€8/10 days, buy at the border, gas stations, car rental agencies, or *Tabak* shops), those just dipping into Tirol from Bavaria do not need one.

ROTHENBURG AND THE ROMANTIC ROAD

From Munich or Füssen to Frankfurt, the Romantic Road takes you through Bavaria's medieval heartland, a route strewn with picturesque villages, farmhouses, onion-domed churches, Baroque palaces, and walled cities.

Linger in Rothenburg (ROE-ten-burg), Germany's best-preserved walled town. Countless travelers have searched for the elusive "untouristy Rothenburg." There are many contenders (such as Michelstadt, Miltenberg, Bamberg, Bad Windsheim, and Dinkelsbühl), but none holds a candle to the king of medieval German cuteness. Even with crowds, overpriced souvenirs, Japanese-speaking night watchmen, and, yes, even *Schneebälle*, Rothenburg is best. Save time and mileage and be satisfied with the winner.

Planning Your Time

The best one-day drive through the heartland of Germany is the Romantic Road. The road is marked for drivers, and well described in the free brochure available at any TI. Those without wheels can take the bus tour; see the end of this chapter for details (railpass holders get a 60 percent discount, so the entire Frankfurt–Munich trip costs €29). Apart from Würzburg, with its Prince Bishop's Residenz, the only stop worth more than a few minutes is Rothenburg. Twenty-four hours is ideal for this town. With two nights and a day, you'll be able to see the essentials and actually relax a little.

Rothenburg

In the Middle Ages, when Frankfurt and Munich were just wide spots on the road, Rothenburg ob der Tauber was Germany's second-largest free imperial city, with a whopping population of 6,000. Today it's her

Rothenburg

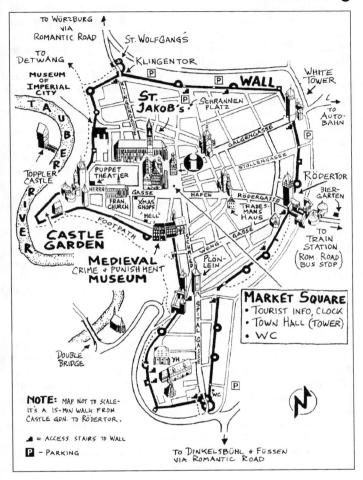

TO WÜRZBURG
VIA
ROMANTIC ROAD

ST. WOLFGANG'S

TO
DETWANG

KLINGENTOR

MUSEUM
OF
IMPERIAL
CITY

WHITE
TOWER

WALL

ST.
JAKOB'S

SCHRANNEN
PLATZ

T
A
U
B
E
R

TO
AUTO-
BAHN

GALGENGASSE

STOLLENGASSE

RÖDERTOR

TOPPLER
CASTLE

PUPPET
THEATER

HERRN   GASSE

FRAN.
CHURCH

XMAS
SHOPS

HELL

HAFEN

RÖDERGASSE

TRADES-
MANS
HAUS

BIER-
GARTEN

R
I
V
E
R

CASTLE
GARDEN

FOOTPATH

GASSE

TO
TRAIN
STATION
(ROM. ROAD
BUS STOP)

MEDIEVAL
CRIME & PUNISHMENT
MUSEUM

WENG

PLÖN-
LEIN

MARKET SQUARE
• TOURIST INFO, CLOCK
• TOWN HALL (TOWER)
• WC

S
P
I
T
A
L

G
A
S
S
E

DOUBLE
BRIDGE

YH

N

WC

NOTE: MAP NOT TO SCALE-
IT'S A 15-MIN WALK FROM
CASTLE GDN. TO RÖDERTOR.

= ACCESS STAIRS TO WALL

P - PARKING

TO DINKELSBÜHL & FÜSSEN
VIA ROMANTIC ROAD

best-preserved medieval walled town, enjoying tremendous tourist popularity without losing its charm. Get medievaled in Rothenburg.

During Rothenburg's heyday, from 1150 to 1400, it was the crossing point of two major trade routes: Tashkent–Paris and Hamburg–Venice. Today the great trade is tourism; two-thirds of the townspeople are employed to serve you. Too often, Rothenburg brings out the shopper in visitors before they've had a chance to see the historic city. True, this is a great place to do your German shopping, but appreciate the town's great history and sights first. While 2.5 million people visit each year, a mere 500,000 spend the night. Rothenburg is most enjoyable early and late, when the tour groups are gone. Rothenburg is very busy through the summer and in the Christmas Market month of December. Spring and fall are great, but it's pretty bleak from January through March—when most locals are hibernating or on vacation.

Rothenburg in a day is easy, with five essential experiences: the Medieval Crime and Punishment Museum, the Riemenschneider wood carving in St. Jakob's Church, the city walking tour, a walk along the wall, and the entertaining Night Watchman's Tour. With more time, there are several mediocre but entertaining museums, walking and biking in the nearby countryside, and lots of cafés and shops. Make a point to spend at least one night. The town is yours after dark, when the groups vacate and the town's floodlit cobbles wring some romance out of any travel partner.

ORIENTATION

(area code: 09861)

To orient yourself in Rothenburg, think of the town map as a human head. Its nose—the castle garden—sticks out to the left, and the neck is the skinny lower part, with the hostel and some of the best hotels in the Adam's apple. The town is a joy on foot. No sight or hotel is more than a 15-minute walk from the train station or each other.

Most of the buildings you'll see were built by 1400. The city was born around its long-gone castle—built in 1142, destroyed in 1356—which was located on the present-day site of the castle garden. You can see the shadow of the first town wall, which defines the oldest part of Rothenburg, in its contemporary street plan. A few gates from this wall still survive. The richest and biggest houses were in this central part. The commoners built higgledy-piggledy (read: picturesquely) farther from the center near the present walls.

Tourist Information: The TI is on Market Square (April–Oct Mon–Fri 9:00–12:00 & 13:00–18:00, Sat-Sun 10:00–15:00, Nov–March shorter hours and closed Sun, tel. 09861/40492, www.rothenburg.de). If there's a long line, just raid the rack where they keep all the free pamphlets. The map and guide comes with a virtual walking guide to the town. The "Information" monthly lists all the events and entertainment. Ask about the daily 14:00 English walking tour (April–Oct). There's free Internet access in the TI lobby (1 terminal). Visitors who arrive late can check the handy map with all hotels—highlighting which ones still have rooms available, with a free direct phone connection to them—just outside the door. The best town map is available free with this book at the Friese shop, two doors west from the TI (toward St. Jakob's Church; see "Shopping," below).

Arrival in Rothenburg

By Train: It's a 10-minute walk from the station to Rothenburg's Market Square (following the brown *Altstadt* signs, exit left from station, turn right on Ansbacher Strasse, and head straight into the Middle Ages). Day-trippers can leave luggage in station lockers (€2, on platform) or at the Friese shop on Market Square. Arrange train and *couchette*/sleeper reservations at the travel agency in the station (no charge for quick questions, Mon–Fri 9:00–18:00, Sat 9:00–13:00, closed Sun, tel. 09861/4611). The nearest WCs are at the snack bar next door to the station. Taxis wait at the station (€5 to any hotel).

By Car: Driving in town can be a nightmare, with many narrow, one-way streets. Park outside the walls and walk five minutes to the center. Parking lots line the town walls, ranging from free (the P5 parking lot just outside Klingentor) to €4 per day. Only those with a hotel reservation can park within the walls after hours (but not during festivals; easiest entry often via Spittaltor).

Helpful Hints

Laundry: A handy launderette is near the station off Ansbacher Strasse (€5.50/load, includes soap, English instructions, opens at 8:00, last load in Mon–Fri at 18:00, Sat at 14:00, closed Sun, Johannitergasse 8, tel. 09861/2775).

Swimming: Rothenburg has a fine modern recreation center with an indoor/outdoor pool and sauna. It's just a few minutes' walk down the Dinkelsbühl Road (*Hallenbad*, adult-€3, child-€1.50, swimsuit and towel rental-€2 each, Mon 14:00–21:00, Tue–Thu 9:00–21:00, Fri–Sun 9:00–18:00, Nordlingerstrasse 20, tel. 09861/4565).

Festivals

Rothenburgers dress up in medieval costumes and beer gardens spill out into the street to celebrate Mayor Nusch's Meistertrunk victory (Whitsun weekend, May 28–31 in 2004, see story below under "Rothenburg Town Walk—Meistertrunk Show") and 700 years of history in the Imperial City Festival (Sept 3–5 in 2004, with fireworks).

Christmas Market: Rothenburg is dead in November, January, and February, but December is its busiest month—the entire town cranks up the medieval cuteness with concerts and costumes, shops with schnapps, stalls filling squares, hot spiced wine, giddy nutcrackers, and mobs of earmuffed Germans. Christmas markets are big all over Germany, and Rothenburg's is considered one of the best. The festival takes place each year in the four weeks leading up to the last Sunday before Christmas (Nov 26–Dec 22 in 2004). Virtually all sights listed in this chapter are open longer hours during these four weeks. Try to avoid Saturdays and Sundays, when big-city day-trippers really clog the grog.

TOURS

▲▲**Night Watchman's Tour**—This tour is flat-out the most entertaining hour of medieval wonder anywhere in Europe. The Night Watchman (a.k.a. Hans Georg Baumgartner) lights his lamp and takes tourists on his one-hour rounds, telling slice-of-gritty-life tales of medieval Rothenburg (€4, April–Dec nightly at 20:00, in English, meet at Market Square, www.nightwatchman.de). This is the best evening activity in town.

Old Town Historic Walk—The TI on Market Square offers 90-minute guided walking tours in English (€4, April–Oct daily at 14:00 from Market Square). Take this for the serious history of Rothenburg and to make sense of its architecture. Alternatively, you can hire your own **private guide**—a local historian can really bring the ramparts alive. Gisela Vogl (€50/90 min, €70/2 hr, tel. 09861/4957, werner.vogl @t-online.de) and Anita Weinzierl (tel. 09868/7993) are both good. Martin Kamphans, a potter, also works as a guide (tel. 09861/7941, kamphans@t-online.de)

Horse-and-Buggy Rides—These give you a relaxing 30-minute clip-clop through the old town, starting from Market Square or Schrannenplatz (private buggy for €30, or wait for one to fill up for €5 per person).

SIGHTS

Rothenburg Town Walk

This one-hour walk weaves together Rothenburg's top sights. Start the walk on Market Square.

Market Square Spin Tour—Stand at the bottom of Market Square (10 feet below the wooden post on the corner) and—ignoring the little white arrow—spin 360 degrees clockwise, starting with the city hall tower. Now do it again slower, following these notes:

   Town Hall and Tower: The city's tallest spire is the **town hall tower.** At 200 feet, it stands atop the old city hall, a white, Gothic, 13th-century building. Notice the tourists enjoying the best view in town from the black top of the tower (€1 and a rigorous but interesting climb, 214 steps, narrow and steep near the top—watch your head, April–Oct daily 9:30–12:30 & 13:00–17:00, Nov–March Sat–Sun 12:00–15:00 only, enter on Market Square through middle arch of new town hall). After a fire burned down part of the original building, a **new town hall** was built alongside what survived of the old one (fronting the square). This is in Renaissance style from 1570.

   Meistertrunk Show: At the top of Market Square stands the proud **Councillors' Tavern** (clock tower from 1466). In its day, the city council drank here. Today, it's the TI and the focus of most tourists' attention when the little doors on either side of the clock flip open and the

Rothenburg Town Walk

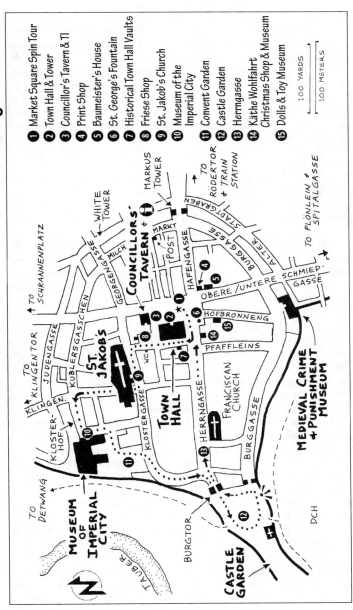

1. Market Square Spin Tour
2. Town Hall & Tower
3. Councillor's Tavern & TI
4. Print Shop
5. Baumeister's House
6. St. George's Fountain
7. Historical Town Hall Vaults
8. Friese Shop
9. St. Jakob's Church
10. Museum of the Imperial City
11. Convent Garden
12. Castle Garden
13. Herrngasse
14. Käthe Wohlfahrt Christmas Shop & Museum
15. Dolls & Toy Museum

100 YARDS
100 METERS

TO SCHRANNENPLATZ

WHITE TOWER

GEORGENGASSE

MILCH

MARKUS TOWER

TO RÖDERTOR & TRAIN STATION

STADTGRABEN

COUNCILLORS' TAVERN & TI

MARKT

POST

HAFENGASSE

OBERE/UNTERE SCHMIEDGASSE

BURGGASSE

ALTER

TO PLÖNLEIN & SPITALGASSE

ST. JAKOBS

TO KLINGENTOR

JUDENGASSE

KLINGEN.

KÜBLERSGÄSSCHEN

KLOSTERGASSE

WC

TOWN HALL

HOFBRONNENG

PFÄFFLEINS

HERRNGASSE

FRANCISCAN CHURCH

MEDIEVAL CRIME + PUNISHMENT MUSEUM

KLOSTER-HOF

MUSEUM OF IMPERIAL CITY

TO DETWANG

TAUBER

BURGTOR

BURGGASSE

CASTLE GARDEN

DCH

N

wooden figures (from 1910) do their thing. Be on Market Square at 11:00, 12:00, 13:00, 14:00, 15:00, 20:00, 21:00, or 22:00 for the ritual gathering of the tourists to see the less-than-breathtaking reenactment of the Meistertrunk story. In 1631, the Catholic army took the Protestant town and was about to do its rape, pillage, and plunder thing when, as the story goes, the mayor said, "Hey, if I can drink this entire three-liter tankard of wine in one gulp, will you leave us alone?" The invading commander, sensing he was dealing with an unbalanced person, said, "Sure." Mayor Nusch drank the whole thing, the town was saved, and he slept for three days.

While this is a nice story, it was dreamed up in the late 1800s for a theatrical play designed to promote a romantic image of the town. In actuality, Rothenburg was occupied and ransacked several times in the Thirty Years' War, and it never recovered—which is why it's such a well-preserved time capsule today. Hint: For the best show, don't watch the clock; watch the open-mouthed tourists gasp as the old windows flip open. At the late shows, the square flickers with camera flashes.

Bottom of Market Square: On the bottom end of the square, the cream-colored building has a fine **print shop** (upstairs—see "Shopping," below). Adjoining that is the **Baumeister's House,** a touristy restaurant with a fine courtyard (see "Eating," below), featuring a famous Renaissance facade with statues of the seven virtues and the seven vices—the former supporting the latter. The statues are copies; the originals are in the Reichsstadt Museum (listed below). The green house below that is the former house of the 15th-century Mayor Toppler (it's now the recommended Greifen Guesthouse); next to it is a famous Scottish restaurant (with arches). Keep circling to the big 17th-century **St. George's fountain.** The long metal gutters slid, routing the water into the villagers' buckets. Rothenburg's many fountains had practical functions beyond providing drinking water. The water was used for fighting fires, and some fountains were stocked with fish during times of siege. Two fine buildings behind the fountain show the old-time lofts with warehouse doors and pulleys on top for hoisting. All over town, lofts were filled with grain and corn. A year's supply was required by the city so they could survive any siege. The building behind the fountain is an art gallery (free, usually daily 11:00–17:00) showing off the work of Rothenburg's top artists. To the right is an old-time pharmacy mixing old and new in typical Rothenburg style.

The broad street running under the town hall tower is **Herrngasse.** The town originated with its castle (built in 1142 but now long gone; only the castle garden remains). Herrngasse connected the castle to Market Square. The last leg of this circular walking tour will take you from the castle garden up Herrngasse to where you now stand. For now, walk a few steps down Herrngasse to the arch under the town hall tower (between the new and old town halls). On the left wall are the town's measuring rods—a reminder that medieval Germany was made of 300 independent little countries, each with its own weights and measures. Merchants and shoppers knew that these were the local standards: the rod (4.3 yards), the *Schuh* (or shoe, roughly a foot), and the ell (from elbow to fingertip—4 inches longer than mine...try it). Notice the protruding cornerstone. These are all over town—originally to protect buildings from reckless horse carts (and vice versa). Under the arch, you'll find the...

▲**Historical Town Hall Vaults**—This museum gives a waxy but good look at Rothenburg during the Catholics-vs.-Protestants Thirty Years' War. With fine English descriptions, it offers a look at "the fateful year 1631," a replica of the famous Meistertrunk tankard, and a dungeon complete with three dank cells and some torture lore (€2, May–Oct daily 9:30–17:30, less off-season).

From the museum, walk toward St. Jakob's Church (just northwest of Market Square). You'll pass the public WC (on your left) and the recommended **Friese shop** (see "Shopping," below) tucked into the small square on your right.

Outside the church, you'll see a scene of Jesus praying at Gethsemane, a common feature of Gothic churches. Downhill, notice the nub of a sandstone statue—a rare original, looking pretty bad after 500 years of weather and, more recently, pollution. Original statues are now in the city museum. Better-preserved statues you see on the church are copies. If it's your wedding day, take the first entrance. Otherwise, use the second (downhill) door to enter...

▲▲**St. Jakob's Church**—Built in the 14th century, this church has been Lutheran since 1544. Take a close look at the Twelve Apostles altar in front (from 1546, left permanently in its open festival-day position). Below Christ are statues of six saints. St. James (Jakob in German, pronounced YAH-kohp) is the one with the shell. He's the saint of pilgrims, and this church was a stop on the medieval pilgrimage route to Santiago (St. James in Spanish) de Compostela in Spain. Study the painted panels—ever see Peter with spectacles? Around the back of the altarpiece (upper left) is a great painting of Rothenburg's Market Square in the 15th century—looking like it does today. Before leaving the front of the church, notice the old medallions above the carved choir stalls featuring the coats of arms of Rothenburg's leading families and portraits of city and church leaders.

Stairs in the back of the church, behind the pipe organ, lead to the artistic highlight of Rothenburg and perhaps the most wonderful wood carving in all of Germany: the glorious 500-year-old, 35-foot-high *Altar of the Holy Blood*. Tilman Riemenschneider, the Michelangelo of German woodcarvers, carved this from 1499 to 1504 to hold a precious rock-crystal capsule, set in a cross that contains a scrap of tablecloth miraculously stained in the shape of a cross by a drop of communion wine. Below, in the scene of the Last Supper, Jesus gives Judas a piece of bread, marking him as the traitor, while John lays his head on Christ's lap. Everything is portrayed exactly as described in the Bible. On the left: Jesus enters Jerusalem. On the right: Jesus prays in the Garden of Gethsemane. Notice how Judas, with his big bag of cash, could be removed from the scene—illustrated by photos on the wall nearby—as was the tradition for the four days leading up to Easter (€1.50, April–Oct Mon–Sat 9:00–17:15, Sun 10:45–17:15, Nov–March daily 10:00–12:00 & 14:00–16:00, free helpful English info sheet).

For an interesting walk to the nearby Reichsstadt Museum (listed below), leave the church and from its outside steps, walk around the corner to the right and under the chapel. Go two blocks down **Klingengasse** and stop at **Klosterhof street.** (I've marked your spot with a small circular plaque in the middle of the road.) Looking down Klingengasse, you see the Klingentor (cliff tower). This tower was Rothenburg's water cistern. From 1595 until 1910, a copper cistern high in the tower provided clean spring drinking water to the privileged. To the right of Klingentor is a good stretch of wall rampart to walk. To the left, the wall is low and simple, lacking a rampart because it guards only a cliff. Now find the shell decorating a building on the street corner next to you. That's the symbol of St. James (pilgrims commemorated their visit to Santiago de Compostela with a shell), indicating that this building is associated with the church. Walk under the shell, down Klosterhof (passing the colorful Altfränkische Weinstube; see "Eating," below) to the city history museum, housed in the former Dominican convent. Cloistered nuns used the lazy Susan embedded in the wall (to the right of museum door) to give food to the poor without being seen.

▲▲**Museum of the Imperial City (Reichsstadt Museum)**—You'll get a scholarly sweep through Rothenburg's history here. Highlights include *The Rothenburg Passion,* a 12-panel series of paintings from 1492 showing scenes leading up to Christ's crucifixion (in the *Konventsaal*); an exhibit of Jewish culture through the ages in Rothenburg *(Judaika);* a 14th-century convent kitchen *(Klosterküche);* romantic paintings of the town *(Gemäldegalerie);* and the fine Baumann collection of weapons and armor. Follow the *Rundgang Tour* signs (€3, €6 combo-ticket that includes Medieval Crime and Punishment Museum saves a whopping €0.20, April–Oct daily 9:30–17:30, Nov–March daily 13:00–16:00, English info sheet and descriptions, no photos, tel. 09861/939-043, www.reichsstadtmuseum.rothenburg.de).

Leaving the museum for the Castle Garden (listed below), go around to the right and into the **convent garden** (free, same hours as museum)—a peaceful place to work on your tan...or mix a poison potion. Angle left through the nun's garden (site of the now-gone Dominican church), eventually leaving via an arch at the far end. But enjoy the herb garden first. Monks and nuns, who were responsible for concocting herbal cures in the olden days, often tended herb gardens. Smell (but don't pick) the *Pfefferminze*, *Juniper* (gin), *Chamomilla* (disinfectant), and *Origanum*. Don't smell the plants in the poison corner (potency indicated by the number of crosses...like spiciness stars in a Chinese restaurant).

Exiting opposite where you entered, you see the back end of an original barn (behind a mansion fronting Herrngasse). Go downhill to the town wall (view through bars). This part of the wall takes advantage of the natural fortification provided by the cliff and is therefore much smaller than the ramparts. Angle left along the wall to Herrngasse, then right under the tower *(Burgtor)*. Notice the tiny "eye of the needle" door cut into the big door. If trying to get into town after curfew, you could bribe the guard to let you through this door (which was small enough to keep out any fully armed attackers).

Step through the gate and outside the wall. Look around and imagine being locked out in the year 1400. This was a wooden drawbridge (see the chain slits above). Notice the "pitch nose" mask—designed to pour boiling Nutella on anyone attacking. High above is the town coat of arms: a red castle *(roten Burg)*.

Castle Garden—The garden before you was once that red castle (destroyed in the 14th century). Today it's a picnic-friendly park with a viewpoint at the far end (considered the best place to kiss by romantic local teenagers). But the views of the lush Tauber River Valley below (a.k.a. Tauber Riviera) are just as good from either side of the tower on this near end of the park. To the right, a path leads down to the village of Detwang (you can see the church spire below)—a town even older than Rothenburg. To the left is a fine view of the fortified Rothenburg. Return to the tower, cross carefully under the pitch nose, and hike back up Herrngasse to your starting point.

Herrngasse—Many towns have a Herrngasse—where the richest patricians and merchants (the *Herren*) lived. Predictably, it's your best chance to see the town's finest old mansions. Strolling back to Market Square, you'll pass the old-time puppet theater (German only, on left), the Franciscan church (from 1285, oldest in town, on right), and the Eisenhut Hotel (Rothenburg's fanciest, worth a peek inside, on right). The shop next door at #11 retains the original old courtyard. The Käthe Wohlfahrt Christmas shop (at Herrngasse 1, see "Shopping," below) is your last, and perhaps greatest, temptation before reaching your starting—and ending—point: Market Square.

Museums within a Block of Market Square

▲▲**Medieval Crime and Punishment Museum**—This museum is the best of its kind, full of fascinating old legal bits and *Kriminal* pieces, instruments of punishment and torture—even a special cage complete with a metal gag for nags. As a bonus, you get exhibits on marriage traditions and witches. Follow the yellow arrows. Exhibits are tenderly described in English (€3.20, €6 combo-ticket includes €3 Imperial City Museum, April–Oct daily 9:30–18:00, Nov and Jan–Feb daily 14:00–16:00, Dec and March daily 10:00–16:00, last entry 45 min before closing, fun cards and posters, tel. 09861/5359, www.kriminalmuseum .rothenburg.de).

▲Dolls and Toy Museum—Two floors of historic *Kinder* cuteness is a hit with many. Pick up the free English binder for an extensive description of the exhibits (€4, family ticket-€10, daily March–Dec 9:30–18:00, Jan–Feb 11:00–17:00, just off Market Square, downhill from the fountain at Hofbronneng 13).

▲German Christmas Museum—Herr Wohlfahrt's passion is collecting and sharing historic Christmas decorations. This excellent museum, upstairs in the giant Käthe Wohlfahrt Christmas shop, features a unique and thoughtfully described collection of Christmas-tree stands, mini-trees sent in boxes to WWI soldiers at the front, early Advent calendars, old-time Christmas cards, 450 clever ways to crack a nut, and a look at tree decorations through the ages—including the Nazi era and when you were a kid (€4, April–Dec daily 10:00–18:00, Jan–March only Sat–Sun 10:00–18:00, hours often change off-season, Herrngasse 1).

More Sights in Rothenburg

▲▲Walk the Wall—Just over a mile and a half around, providing great views and a good orientation, this walk can be done by those under six feet tall and without a camera in less than an hour. The hike requires no special sense of balance. Photographers go through lots of film, especially before breakfast or at sunset, when the lighting is best and the crowds are fewest. The best fortifications are in the Spitaltor (south end). Walk from there counterclockwise to the "forehead." Climb the Rödertor en route. The names you see along the way are people who donated money to rebuild the wall after World War II and those who've recently donated €1,000 per meter for the maintenance of Rothenburg's heritage.

▲Rödertor—The wall tower nearest the train station is the only one you can climb. It's worth the 135 steps for the view and a fascinating rundown on the bombing of Rothenburg in the last weeks of World War II, when the east part of the city was destroyed (€1, unreliable hours, usually open daily but closed for lunch April–Oct, closed Nov–March, photos of WWII damage with English translations). If you climb this, you can skip the city hall tower.

Sightseeing Lowlights—St. Wolfgang's Church is a fortified Gothic church built into the medieval wall at Klingentor. Its dungeon-like passages and shepherd's dance exhibit are pretty lame (€1.50, April–Sept daily 11:00–13:00 & 14:00–17:00, Oct until 16:00, closed Nov–March). The cute-looking Farming Museum (Bäuerliches Museum) next door is even worse. The 700-year-old Tradesman's House (Rothenburger

Handwerkerhaus) shows the everyday life of a Rothenburger in the town's heyday (€2.20, April–Oct daily 9:00–18:00, Nov–Dec Mon–Fri 14:00–16:00, Sat–Sun 10:00–16:00, closed Jan–March, Alter Stadtgraben 26, near Markus Tower, tel. 09861/94280).

SHOPPING

Be warned...Rothenburg is one of Germany's best shopping towns. Do it here and be done with it. Lovely prints, carvings, wineglasses, Christmas-tree ornaments, and beer steins are popular.

The Käthe Wohlfahrt Christmas trinkets phenomenon is spreading across the half-timbered reaches of Europe. In Rothenburg, tourists flock to two **Käthe Wohlfahrt Christmas Villages** (on either side of Herrngasse, just off Market Square). This Christmas wonderland is filled with enough twinkling lights to require a special electric hookup, instant Christmas mood music (best appreciated on a hot day in July), and American and Japanese tourists hungrily filling little woven shopping baskets with €5–8 goodies to hang on their trees. Let the spinning flocked tree whisk you in, but pause at the wall of Steiffs, jerking uncontrollably and mesmerizing little kids. (OK, I admit it, my Christmas tree sports a few KW ornaments.) Note: Prices are padded with tour-guide incentives (Mon–Fri 9:00–18:00, Sat 9:00–16:00, Sun 10:00–18:00, tel. 09861/4090, www.wohlfahrt.de). The new **Christmas Museum** upstairs (see "Museums within a Block of Market Square," above) is very good but dumps you back in the store, compelled now by the fascinating history to buy even more. Factor this likely extra expense into the museum's already steep €4 admission fee.

The **Friese shop** offers a charming contrast (just off Market Square, west of TI, on corner across from public WC). Cuckoo with friendliness, trinkets, and souvenirs, it gives shoppers with this book tremendous service: a 10 percent discount, 16 percent tax deducted if you have it mailed, and a free map (normally €1.50). Anneliese, who runs the place with her sons Frankie and Berni and grandson Rene (who played American football), charges only her cost for shipping and money exchange, and lets tired travelers leave their bags in her back room for free. For fewer crowds and better service, visit after 14:00 (Mon–Sat 8:00–17:00, Sun 9:30–17:00, tel. & fax 09861/7166).

The Ernst Geissendörfer **print shop** sells fine prints, etchings, and paintings. Show this book for 10 percent off marked prices on all cash purchases (or minimum €50 credit-card purchases) and a free shot of German brandy to sip while you browse (Mon–Sat 10:00–18:00, Sun 10:00–17:00, late Dec–April closed Sun, enter through bear shop on corner where Market Square hits Schmiedgasse, go up 1 floor, tel. 09861/2005).

For characteristic wineglasses, oenology gear, and local wine from the town's oldest wine-makers, drop by the **Weinladen am Plönlein** (daily 8:30–18:00, Plönlein 27—see "Evening Fun," below, for info on wine-tasting).

Shoppers who mail their goodies home can get handy €1.50 boxes at the **post office** in the shopping center across from the train station (Mon–Fri 9:00–17:30, Sat 9:00–12:00).

Those who prefer to eat their souvenirs shop the *Bäckereien* (bakeries). Their succulent pastries, pies, and cakes are pleasantly distracting...but skip the bad-tasting Rothenburger *Schneebälle.*

SLEEPING

In the Old Town

$$$ **Gasthof Greifen,** once the home of Mayor Toppler, is a big, traditional, 600-year-old place with large rooms and all the comforts. It's run by a fine family staff and creaks with rustic splendor (small Sb-€38, Sb-€48, Db-€60–82, Tb-€97–102, Qb-€105–122, 10 percent off for 3-night stay, self- or full-service laundry, free and easy parking, half a block downhill from Market Square at Obere Schmiedgasse 5, tel. 09861/2281, fax 09861/86374, www.gasthof-greifen.rothenburg.de, info@gasthof-greifen.rothenburg.de, Brigitte and Klingler family). The family also runs a restaurant, serving basic meals in the garden or dining room.

$$$ **Hotel Gerberhaus,** a classy new hotel in an old building, is warmly run by Inge and Kurt, who mix modern comforts into 20 bright and airy rooms while maintaining a sense of half-timbered elegance. Enjoy the pleasant garden in back (Sb-€48–56, Db-€56–79, Tb-€94–99, Qb-€104–114, prices depend on room size, 2-room apartment with kitchen-€89/2 people, €120/4 people, 5 percent off and a free *Schneeball* if you stay 2 nights and pay cash, some non-smoking rooms, some rooms with canopied 4-poster *Himmel* beds, free Internet access, laundry-€4/load, Spitalgasse 25, tel. 09861/94900, fax 09861/86555, www.gerberhaus.rothenburg.de, gerberhaus@t-online.de). The downstairs café serves good soups, salads, and light lunches.

$$$ **Hotel Kloster-Stüble,** deep in the old town near the castle garden, is my classiest listing. Jutta greets her guests while husband Rudolf does the cooking, and Erika (SE) is the fun and energetic first mate who really runs the show (Sb-€50, Db-€75–90, Tb-€110, family rooms-€110–155, luxurious apartment with kitchen and balcony-€105 for 2 or up to €200 for 6, €3 extra on weekends, family deals, Heringsbronnengasse 5, tel. 09861/6774, fax 09861/6474, www.klosterstueble.de, hotel@klosterstueble.de).

$$ **Gasthof zur Goldenen Rose** is a classic family-run place—simple, traditional, comfortable, and a great value—where scurrying Karin serves breakfast and stately Henni (SE) keeps everything in good

SLEEP CODE

(€1 = about $1.10, country code: 49, area code: 09861)

Sleep Code: **S** = Single, **D** = Double/Twin, **T** = Triple, **Q** = Quad, **b** = bathroom, **s** = shower only, **no CC** = Credit Cards not accepted, **SE** = Speaks English, **NSE** = No English. Unless otherwise noted, credit cards are accepted, English is spoken, and breakfast is included.

To help you sort easily through these listings, I've divided the rooms into three categories, based on the price for a standard double room with bath:

$$$ **Higher Priced**—Most rooms €65 or more.
$$ **Moderately Priced**—Most rooms between €40–65.
$ **Lower Priced**—Most rooms €40 or less.

Rothenburg is crowded with visitors, but most are day-trippers. Except for the rare Saturday night and festivals (see "Festivals," page 415), finding a room is easy throughout the year.

Many hotels and guest houses will pick up tired heavy-packers at the station. You may be greeted at the station by *Zimmer* skimmers who have rooms to rent. If you have reservations, resist them and honor your reservation. But if you haven't booked ahead, try talking yourself into one of these more desperate bed-and-breakfast rooms for a youth-hostel price. Be warned: These people are notorious for taking you to distant hotels and then charging you for the ride back if you decline a room.

If you're driving and unable to find your place, stop and give them a call. They will likely rescue you.

order. The hotel has one shower per floor, but the rooms are clean, and you're surrounded by cobbles, flowers, and red-tiled roofs (S-€21, D-€36, Ds-€46, Db-€49, some triples, spacious family apartment-€107/4 people, €128/5 people, kid-friendly, streetside rooms can be noisy, closed Jan–Feb, Spitalgasse 28, tel. 09861/4638, fax 09861/86417, www.thegoldenrose.de, info@thegoldenrose.de). The Favetta family also serves good, reasonably priced meals (restaurant closed Wed). Keep your key to get in after hours (side gate in alley).

$$ Hotel Altfränkische Weinstube am Klosterhof is the place for well-heeled bohemians. Mario and lovely Hanne rent six cozy rooms above their dark and smoky pub in a 600-year-old building. It's an

Rothenburg Hotels

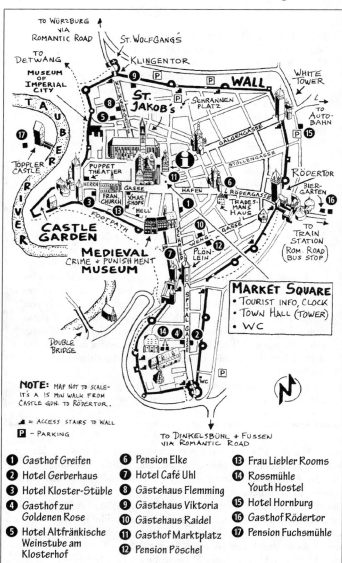

1 Gasthof Greifen
2 Hotel Gerberhaus
3 Hotel Kloster-Stüble
4 Gasthof zur Goldenen Rose
5 Hotel Altfränkische Weinstube am Klosterhof
6 Pension Elke
7 Hotel Café Uhl
8 Gästehaus Flemming
9 Gästehaus Viktoria
10 Gästehaus Raidel
11 Gasthof Marktplatz
12 Pension Pöschel
13 Frau Liebler Rooms
14 Rossmühle Youth Hostel
15 Hotel Hornburg
16 Gasthof Rödertor
17 Pension Fuchsmühle

upscale Monty Python atmosphere, with TVs, modern showers, open-beam ceilings, and *Himmel* beds—canopied four-poster "heaven" beds (Sb-€45, Db-€50–60, Db suite-€70, Tb-€70, prefer cash, kid-friendly, off Klingengasse at Klosterhof 7, tel. 09861/6404, fax 09861/6410, www .romanticroad.com/altfraenkische-weinstube). Their pub is a candlelit classic, serving hot food until 22:30 and closing at 1:00. Drop by on Wednesday evening (19:30–24:00) for the English Conversation Club (see "Meet the Locals," below).

$$ Pension Elke, run by the spry Erich Endress and his son Klaus, rents 10 bright, airy, and comfy rooms above the family grocery store (S-€25, Sb-€35, D-€38–46, Db-€58–62, prices depend on size, extra bed-€15, 10 percent discount with this book when you stay at least 2 nights, no CC, reception in grocery store until 19:00, otherwise go around corner onto Alter Stadtgraben to first door on left and ring bell at top of stairs, near Markus Tower at Rodergasse 6, tel. 09861/2331, fax 09861/935-355, www.pension-elke-rotherburg.de).

$$ Hotel Café Uhl offers 10 fine rooms over a bakery (Sb-€30–35, Db-€50–65, prices depend on size, third person-€18, fourth person-€13, 10 percent discount with this book and cash, non-smoking rooms, parking-€3/day, reception in café, closed Jan, Plönlein 8, tel. 09861/4895, fax 09861/92820, www.hotel-uhl.de, info@hotel-uhl.de, Paul and Robert the baker SE).

$$ Gästehaus Flemming has seven tastefully modern, fresh, and comfortable rooms and a peaceful garden behind St. Jakob's Church (Sb-€45, Db-€55, Tb-€75, no CC, Klingengasse 21, tel. 09861/92380, fax 09861/976-384, Regina SE).

$$ Gästehaus Viktoria is a cheery little place right next to the town wall. Its three rooms overflow with furniture, ribbons, and silk flowers, and lovely gardens surround the house (Db-€45–50, Tb-€60, no CC, breakfast served at nearby Hotel Altfränkische Weinstube, a block from Klingentor at Klingenschütt 4, tel. 09861/87682, Hanne SE).

$$ Gästehaus Raidel, a creaky 500-year-old house filled with beds and furniture all hand-made by Herr Raidel himself, rents 14 large rooms with cramped facilities down the hall. The forlorn ambience and staff make me want to sing the *Addams Family* theme song—but it works in a pinch (S-€20, Sb-€35, D-€38, Db-€48, Tb-€71, no CC, Wenggasse 3, tel. 09861/3115, fax 09861/935-255, www.romanticroad .com/raidel, gaestehaus-raidel@t-online.de, Herr Raidel SE).

$$ Gasthof Marktplatz, right on Market Square, rents nine tidy rooms with 1970s-era wallpaper and unenthusiastic staff (S-€21, D-€38, Ds-€43, Db-€48, T-€50, Ts-€57, Tb-€62, no CC, Grüner Markt 10, tel. & fax 09861/6722, www.gasthof-marktplatz.de, Herr Rosner SE). The maddening town hall bells ring throughout the night.

$ Pension Pöschel is friendly, with seven bearskin-cozy rooms in a concrete but pleasant building with an inviting garden out back (S-€20,

D-€35, Db-€45, T-€45, Tb-€55, small kids free, no CC, Wenggasse 22, tel. 09861/3430, pension.poeschel@t-online.de, Bettina SE).

$ Frau Liebler rents two large, modern, ground-floor rooms with kitchenettes and hardwood floors (Db-€40, no CC, breakfast in room, off Market Square behind Christmas shop, Pfaffleinsgasschen 10, tel. 09861/709-215, fax 09861/709-216).

$ Hostel: Here in Bavaria, hostelling is limited to those under 27, except for families traveling with children under 18. The fine **Rossmühle Youth Hostel** has 184 beds in two buildings. The droopy-eyed building (the old town horse mill, used when the town was under siege and the river-powered mill was inaccessible) houses groups and the office. The adjacent hostel is mostly for families and individuals (dorm beds-€17, bunk-bed Db- €40, includes breakfast and sheets, dinner-€5.10, self-serve laundry-€4, Internet access, entrance on Rossmühlgasse, tel. 09861/94160, fax 09861/941-620, www.djh.de, jhrothenburg@djh-bayern.de). Reserve long in advance.

Outside the Wall

The first two places are a hundred yards outside the wall on the train-station side of town (less than a 10-min walk from the center) and are among the nicest rooms I recommend in town. The third is a rustic adventure below the town in what feels like a wilderness.

$$$ Hotel Hornburg, a grand 100-year-old mansion with groomed grounds and 10 spacious, tastefully decorated rooms a two-minute walk outside the wall, is a super value (Sb-€49–64, Db-€69–95, Tb-€90–110, ground-floor rooms, non-smoking rooms, family-friendly, avoid if you're allergic to dogs, parking-€2/day, bikes for guests-€10/day, exit station and go straight on Ludwig-Siebert Strasse, turn left on Mann Strasse until you're 100 yards from town wall, Hornburgweg 28, tel. 09861/8480, fax 09861/5570, www.hotel-hornburg.de, hotelhornburg @t-online.de, friendly Gabriele and Martin SE).

$$$ Gasthof Rödertor offers 15 decent rooms in a quiet setting one block outside the Rödertor. This guesthouse has an inviting breakfast room with a farmhouse flair, a popular beer garden, and a restaurant dedicated to the potato (see "Evening Fun and Beer Drinking," below). Guest rooms in an annex inside the wall are slightly cheaper (Db-€65–80, Tb-€70–105, Qb-€90–125, kids sleep free, 10 percent discount with this book and cash, Ansbacher Strasse 7, tel. 09861/2022, fax 09861/86324, www.roedertor.com, hotel@roedertor.com, Frau Teutscher and her daughter Katie SE).

$$ Pension Fuchsmühle is a B&B in a renovated old mill on the river below the castle end of Rothenburg. The place is a work-in-progress, with kids and a linoleum-floor feel, but if you want a rustic, countryside experience, it's great. Alex and Heidi Molitor rent six rooms and take good care of their guests (Db-€45–55, Tb-€67–75, Qb-€75–85, prices depend on length of stay, non-smoking, healthy farm-fresh breakfasts, piano, free bikes for guests, free pickup at station, across the street from Toppler's little castle at Taubertalweg 103, tel. 09861/92633, www.fuchsmuehle.de, fuchsmuehle@t-online.de). It's a steep but pleasant 15-minute hike from the Fuchsmühle to Market Square. The Molitors provide flashlights for your return after dark.

EATING

Most restaurants serve meals only 11:30–13:30 and 18:00–20:00. All places listed are within a five-minute walk of Market Square. While all survive on tourism, many still feel like local hangouts. Your choices are typical Franconian or ethnic.

Traditional Franconian Restaurants

Restaurant Glocke, a *Weinstube* (wine bar) popular with locals, is run by Rothenburg's oldest wine-makers, the Thürauf family. Their seasonal menu is complemented by their family wine, served under an atmospheric, big-beamed ceiling. The menu is in German only because the friendly staff wants to explain your options in person. Don't miss their €4 deal to sample five Franconian wines (€10–15, Mon–Sat 10:30–23:00, Sun 10:30–14:00, vegetarian options, Plönlein 1, tel. 09861/958-990).

At **Zur Goldenen Rose,** Reno cooks up traditional German fare at good prices, as Henni stokes your appetite (Tue 11:30–14:00, Thu–Mon 11:30–14:00 & 17:30–20:30, closed Wed, Spitalgasse 28; leafy garden terrace out back open in sunny weather).

Extremely picturesque and touristy, **Baumeister Haus,** tucked deep behind a streetside pastry counter and antlered dining room, fills an inviting courtyard with people who don't understand a German menu (€8–15, daily 8:00–23:00, closes earlier off-season and when slow, a few doors below Market Square, Obere Schmiedgasse 3, tel. 09861/94700).

For cellar dining under medieval murals and pointy pikes, consider **Bürgerkeller,** where Herr Terian and his family pride themselves in quality local cuisine and offer a small but inviting menu and reasonable prices (€7–14, daily 12:00–14:00 & 18:00–21:00, near bottom of Herrngasse at #24, tel. 09861/2126).

Reichs-Küchenmeister is a typical big-hotel restaurant, but on a balmy evening, its pleasant tree-shaded terrace overlooking St. Jakob's Church is hard to beat (€8–16, daily 11:00–22:00, non-smoking room, nouveau German menu, some veggie choices, Kirchplatz 8, tel. 09861/9700).

Hotel Restaurant Klosterstüble, deep in the old town near the castle garden, is a classy place for good traditional cuisine. Rudy's food is

Rothenburg Restaurants

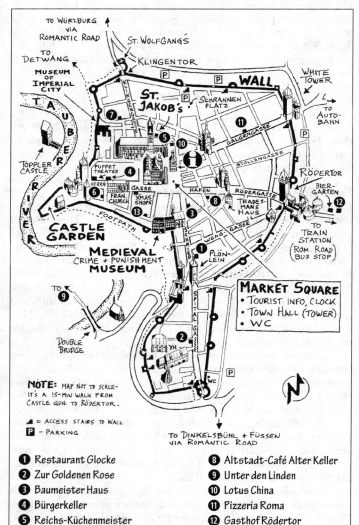

NOTE: MAP NOT TO SCALE—
IT'S A 15-MIN WALK FROM
CASTLE GDN. TO RÖDERTOR.

▪ = ACCESS STAIRS TO WALL
P = PARKING

TO DINKELSBÜHL & FÜSSEN
VIA ROMANTIC ROAD

❶ Restaurant Glocke
❷ Zur Goldenen Rose
❸ Baumeister Haus
❹ Bürgerkeller
❺ Reichs-Küchenmeister
❻ Hotel Restaurant Klosterstüble
❼ Altfränkische Weinstube am Klosterhof

❽ Altstadt-Café Alter Keller
❾ Unter den Linden
❿ Lotus China
⓫ Pizzeria Roma
⓬ Gasthof Rödertor
⓭ Trinkstube zur Hölle ("Hell")

better than his English, but head waitress Erika makes sure communication goes smoothly. The shady terrace is nice on a warm summer evening (€10–15, daily 11:00–14:00 & 18:00–21:00, Heringsbronnengasse 5, tel. 09861/6774).

Bohemians enjoy the **Altfränkische Weinstube am Klosterhof.** This dark and smoky pub is classically candlelit in a 600-year-old building (€5–11, hot food served 18:00–22:30, closes at 1:00, off Klingengasse at Klosterhof 7, tel. 09861/6404). Drop by on Wednesday evening (19:30–24:00) for the English Conversation Club (see "Meet the Locals," below).

For a light meal—indoors or out—try the beautifully restored **Altstadt-Café Alter Keller,** a local favorite, central but without the crazy crowds. Its walls are festooned with old pots and jugs, and Herr Hufnagel, a baker and pastry chef, whips up giant meringue cookies and other treats (Wed–Mon 11:00–20:00, Sun until 18:00, closed Tue, Alter Keller 8, tel. 09861/2268).

In the valley along the river and worth the 20-minute hike is the **Unter den Linden** beer garden (daily in season with decent weather 10:00–22:00 and sometimes later, self-service food and good beer, call first to confirm it's open, tel. 09861/5909).

Ethnic Breaks from Pork and Potatoes

Lotus China is a peaceful world apart, serving good Chinese food (€8 plates, daily 11:30–14:30 & 17:30–23:00, 2 blocks behind TI near church, Eckele 2, tel. 09861/86886).

Pizzeria Roma is smoky because it's the locals' favorite for €6.50 pizza, pastas, and Italian wine. Service can be slow (Thu–Tue 11:30–24:00, closed Wed, also has schnitzel fare, Galgengasse 19, tel. 09861/4540).

You'll find a **Turkish** place on Schrannengasse and a **Greek** restaurant just outside the wall opposite Spitaltor.

A **supermarket** is near Rödertor, just outside the wall (Mon–Fri 8:00–20:00, Sat 8:00–16:00, closed Sun, on left as you exit wall).

Evening Fun and Beer Drinking

Beer Gardens and Discos at Rothenburg's "Bermuda Dreieck": For beer-garden fun on a balmy summer evening (for dinner or beer), Rothenburgers pick **Gasthof Rödertor,** just outside the wall through the Rödertor gate (May–Sept daily 17:00–24:00, look for wood gate). Their *Kartoffeln Stube* inside is dedicated to the potato (€6–10, daily 11:00–23:00, tel. 09861/2022). Two popular **discos** are just down the street: Black Out (Ansbacher 15, in alley next to Sparkasse bank, open Wed and Fri–Sat 22:00–3:00, closed Sun–Tue and Thu) and Club 23 (around corner from bank on Adam Hörber Strasse, open Thu–Sat from 22:00, closed Sun–Mon, tel. 09861/933-045).

Wine Drinking in the Old Center: Trinkstube zur Hölle ("Hell") is dark and foreboding, but they offer thick wine-drinking atmosphere with lots of locals and a short menu until late (a block past Criminal Museum on Burggasse, with devil hanging out front, tel. 09861/4229). Mario's **Altfränkische Weinstube** (see "Traditional Franconian Restaurants," above) is similarly atmospheric. Wine-lovers enjoy **Restaurant Glocke**'s *Weinstube* (recommended above); for €4, you can sample five of their Franconian wines—choose dry or half-dry (Mon–Sat 10:30–23:00, Sun 10:30–14:00, Plönlein 1, tel. 09861/958-990). You're welcome to enjoy just the wine without eating.

Meet the Locals

For a rare chance to mix it up with locals who aren't selling anything, bring your favorite slang and tongue twisters to the **English Conversation Club** at Mario's Altfränkische Weinstube am Klosterhof (Wed 19:30–24:00, Anneliese from Friese shop and Hermann the German are regulars; see restaurant listed under "Traditional Franconian Restaurants," above). This group of intrepid linguists just celebrated their 1,000th meeting in 2003.

TRANSPORTATION CONNECTIONS

By bus: The Romantic Road bus tour takes you in and out of Rothenburg each afternoon (April–Oct), heading to Munich, Frankfurt, or Füssen. See the Romantic Road bus schedule on next page (or check www.euraide.de/ricksteves).

By train: A tiny train line connects Rothenburg to the outside world via **Steinach** (almost hrly, 15 min). If you plan to arrive in Rothenburg by train, note that the last train to Rothenburg departs nightly from Steinach at 20:30 (if you arrive in Steinach after 20:30, call one of the **taxi** services for a €22 ride to Rothenburg; ideally order the taxi at least an hour in advance: tel. 09861/2000, 09861/7227, or 09861/95100). For those leaving Rothenburg by train, the first train to Steinach departs at 6:00, the last train to Steinach at 20:00.

Steinach by train to: Rothenburg (almost hrly, 15 min, last train at 20:30), **Würzburg** (hrly, 1 hr), **Nürnberg** (2/hr, 1–1.5 hr, most change in Ansbach or Neustadt an der Aisch), **Munich** (hrly, 3 hrs, 2 changes), **Frankfurt** (hrly, 2.5 hrs, change in Würzburg). Train connections in Steinach are usually within a few minutes (to Rothenburg generally from track 5). Train info: tel. 01805/996-633.

Romantic Road
(Romantische Strasse)

The Romantic Road winds you past the most beautiful towns and scenery of Germany's medieval heartland. Once Germany's medieval trade route, now it's the best way to connect the dots between Füssen, Munich, and Frankfurt (www.romantischestrasse.de).

Wander through quaint hills and rolling villages, and stop wherever the cows look friendly or a town fountain beckons. My favorite sections are from Füssen to Landsberg and Rothenburg to Weikersheim. (If you're driving with limited time, connect Rothenburg and Munich by autobahn.) Caution: The similarly promoted "Castle Road," which runs between Rothenburg and Mannheim, sounds intriguing but is nowhere near as interesting.

Throughout Bavaria, you'll see colorfully ornamented maypoles decorating town squares. Many are painted in Bavaria's colors, blue and white. The decorations that line each side of the pole symbolize the crafts or businesses of that community. Each May Day, they are festively replaced. Traditionally, rival communities try to steal each other's maypole. Locals will guard their new pole night and day as May Day approaches. Stolen poles are ransomed only with lots of beer for the clever thieves.

Getting around the Romantic Road

By Bus: The Deutsche Touring company runs buses daily between Frankfurt and Füssen in each direction (April–Oct, tel. 069/790-350, www.deutsche-touring.com). A second route goes daily between Munich and Rothenburg (you can transfer at Rothenburg to the other route). Confirm departures and arrivals when you buy your ticket, as special events can temporarily change bus stop locations and schedules.

Buses usually leave from train stations (in towns large enough to have one). The ride (€70 and 11 hrs if you go all the way from Frankfurt to Munich, pay on the bus, add €1.50 per bag) is offered at a 60 percent discount to travelers who have a German railpass, Eurailpass, or Eurail Selectpass (if Germany is one of the selected countries). Buses stop in Rothenburg (about 2 hrs) and Dinkelsbühl (about 1 hr) and too briefly at a few other attractions. The grim drivers usually hand out maps and brochures and play a tape-recorded narration of the journey highlights in English. Bus reservations are almost never necessary. But they are free and easy, and, technically, without one you can lose your seat to someone who has one (call 069/790-350 to reserve). You can start, stop, and switch over where you like. There is no quicker or easier way to travel across Germany and get such a hearty dose of its countryside.

The Romantic Road

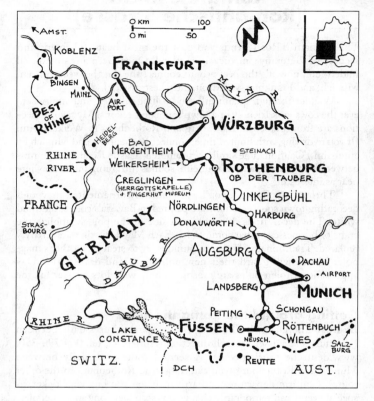

By Car: Follow the brown *Romantische Strasse* signs and the free tourist brochure (available all over the place) that describes the journey.

SIGHTS ALONG THE ROMANTIC ROAD

These sights are listed from north to south.

Frankfurt—The northern terminus of the Romantic Road is in this country's Manhattan (covered in its own chapter).

▲▲**Würzburg**—This historic city, though freshly rebuilt since World War II, is worth a stop for its impressive Prince Bishop's Residenz, the bubbly Baroque chapel (Hofkirche) next door, and the palace's sculpted gardens. The helpful TI is on the Marktplatz (April-Dec Mon–Fri 10:00–18:00, Sat 10:00–14:00, May-Oct also Sun 10:00–14:00; Jan-March Mon-Fri 10:00-16:00, Sat 10:00-13:00, closed Sun, tel.

ROMANTIC ROAD BUS SCHEDULE
(DAILY, APRIL–OCTOBER)

Two different buses run roughly parallel routes (one connecting Rothenburg and Munich, the other linking Frankfurt and
Füssen). You can switch between these buses as you wish at the
stops they have in common (for example, you have to change in
Rothenburg or Dinkelsbühl to get from Frankfurt to Munich).
The following times are based on the 2003 schedule. Check
www.euraide.de/ricksteves for any changes.

North to South

Depart Frankfurt	8:00	—
Depart Würzburg	10:00	—
Arrive Rothenburg	12:50	—
Depart Rothenburg	14:30	14:30
Arrive Dinkelsbühl	15:25	15:25
Depart Dinkelsbühl	15:40	15:45
Arrive Munich	—	19:20
Arrive Füssen	19:55	—

South to North

Depart Füssen	8:00	—
Arrive Wieskirche	8:42	—
Depart Wieskirche	8:55	—
Depart Munich	—	9:00
Arrive Dinkelsbühl	12:45	12:45
Depart Dinkelsbühl	14:00	14:00
Arrive Rothenburg	14:50	14:50
Depart Rothenburg	16:00	—
Depart Würzburg	18:25	—
Arrive Frankfurt	20:00	

0931/372-398, www.wuerzburg.de).
    The Residenz is a Franconian Versailles, with grand rooms, 3-D
art, and a tennis-court-sized fresco by Tiepolo (€4, April-Oct daily
9:00-18:00, summer Thu until 20:00, Nov-March daily 10:00-16:00,
last entry 30 min before closing, no photos, tel. 0931/355-170). English
tours are offered daily at 11:00 and 15:00 (May-Sept, confirm at TI or
call ahead). The elaborate Hofkirche chapel is next door (as you exit the
palace, go left) and the entrance to the picnic-worthy garden is just

beyond. Easy parking is available. Don't confuse the Residenz (a 15-min walk from the train station) with the fortress on the hilltop.

Weikersheim—This untouristy town has a palace with fine Baroque gardens (luxurious picnic spot), a folk museum, and a picturesque town square.

▲**Herrgottskapelle**—This peaceful church is graced with Tilman Riemenschneider's greatest carved altarpiece (Easter–Oct daily 9:15–17:30, less off-season, tel. 07933/508). Across the street is the Fingerhut (thimble, literally "finger hat") museum (€2, April–Oct daily 9:00–18:00, less off-season, tel. 07933/370). The south-bound Romantic Road bus stops here for 15 minutes, long enough to see one or the other. The church and museum are a mile south of Creglingen (TI tel. 07933/631, www.creglingen.de).

▲▲▲**Rothenburg**—See above for information on Germany's best medieval town.

▲**Dinkelsbühl**—Rothenburg's little sister is cute enough to merit a short stop. A moat, towers, gates, and a beautifully preserved medieval wall surround this town. Dinkelsbühl's history museum is meager and without a word of English. The Kinderzeche children's festival turns Dinkelsbühl wonderfully on end for a week at the end of July. The helpful TI on the main street sells maps with a short walking tour and can help find rooms (Mon–Fri 9:00–18:00, Sat 10:00–13:00 & 14:00–16:00, Sun 10:00–13:00, shorter hours off-season, tel. 09851/90240, www.dinkelsbuehl.de).

Rottenbuch—This nondescript village has an impressive church in a lovely setting.

▲▲**Wieskirche**—This is Germany's most glorious Baroque-rococo church, beautifully restored and set in a sweet meadow. Heavenly! Northbound Romantic Road buses from Füssen stop here for 15 minutes. (See the Bavaria and Tirol chapter.)

Füssen—This town, the southern terminus of the Romantic Road, is three miles from the stunning Neuschwanstein Castle, worth a stop on any sightseeing agenda. (See the Bavaria and Tirol chapter for description and accommodations.)

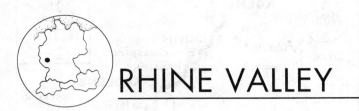

RHINE VALLEY

The Rhine Valley is storybook Germany, a fairy-tale world of legends and robber-baron castles. Cruise the most castle-studded stretch of the romantic Rhine as you listen for the song of the treacherous Loreley. For hands-on castle thrills, climb through the Rhineland's greatest castle, Rheinfels, above the town of St. Goar. Castle connoisseurs will enjoy the fine interior of Marksburg Castle. Spend your nights in a castle-crowned village, either Bacharach or St. Goar. With more time, mosey through the neighboring Mosel Valley (see next chapter).

Planning Your Time

For a good look, cruise in, tour a castle or two, sleep in a genuine medieval town, and take the train out. If you have limited time, cruise less and explore Rheinfels Castle.

Ideally, spend two nights here, sleep in Bacharach, cruise the best hour of the river (from Bacharach to St. Goar), and tour the Rheinfels Castle. Those with more time can ride the riverside bike path. With two days and a car, visit the Rhine and the Mosel.

The Rhine

Ever since Roman times, when this was the empire's northern boundary, the Rhine has been one of the world's busiest shipping rivers. You'll see a steady flow of barges with 1,000- to 2,000-ton loads. Tourist-packed buses, hot train tracks, and highways line both banks.

Many of the castles were "robber-baron" castles, put there by petty rulers (there were 300 independent little countries in medieval Germany) to levy tolls on passing river traffic. A robber baron would put his castle on, or even in, the river. Then, often with the help of chains and a tower on the opposite bank, he'd stop each ship and get his

Rhine Overview

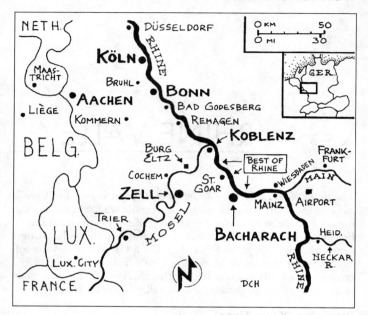

toll. There were 10 customs stops in the 60-mile stretch between Mainz and Koblenz alone (no wonder merchants were early proponents of the creation of larger nation-states).

Some castles were built to control and protect settlements, and others were the residences of kings. As times changed, so did the lifestyles of the rich and feudal. Many castles were abandoned for more comfortable mansions in the towns.

Most Rhine castles date from the 11th, 12th, and 13th centuries. When the pope successfully asserted his power over the German emperor in 1076, local princes ran wild over the rule of their emperor. The castles saw military action in the 1300s and 1400s, as emperors began reasserting their control over Germany's many silly kingdoms.

The castles were also involved in the Reformation wars, in which Europe's Catholic and Protestant dynasties fought it out using a fragmented Germany as their battleground. The Thirty Years' War (1618–1648) devastated Germany. The outcome: Each ruler got the freedom to decide if his people would be Catholic or Protestant, and one-third of Germany was dead. Production of Gummi bears ceased entirely.

The French—who feared a strong Germany and felt the Rhine was the logical border between them and Germany—destroyed most of the castles prophylactically (Louis XIV in the 1680s, the revolutionary army in the 1790s, and Napoleon in 1806). They were often rebuilt in neo-Gothic style in the Romantic age—the late 1800s—and today are enjoyed as restaurants, hotels, hostels, and museums.

For information on Rhine castles, visit www.burgen-am-rhein.de. For more on the Rhine, visit www.loreleytal.com (heavy on hotels but has maps, photos, and a little history).

Getting around the Rhine

While the Rhine flows north from Switzerland to Holland, the scenic stretch from Mainz to Koblenz hoards all the touristic charm. Studded with the crenellated cream of Germany's castles, it bustles with boats, trains, and highway traffic. Have fun exploring with a mix of big steamers, tiny ferries *(Fähre),* trains, and bikes (see "More Rhine Sights," below).

By Boat: While many travelers do the whole trip by boat, the most scenic hour is from St. Goar to Bacharach. Sit on the top deck with your handy Rhine map-guide (or the kilometer-keyed tour in this chapter) and enjoy the parade of castles, towns, boats, and vineyards.

There are several boat companies, but most travelers sail on the bigger, more expensive, and romantic Köln-Düsseldorfer (K-D) line (free with a consecutive-day Eurailpass or with dated Eurail Flexipass, Eurail Selectpass, or German railpass—but it uses up a day of any Flexipass, otherwise about €8.40 for the first hour, then progressively cheaper per hour; the recommended Bacharach–St. Goar trip costs €8.40 one-way, €10.20 round-trip; half-price days: Tue for bicyclists, Mon and Fri for seniors over 60, tel. 06741/1634 in St. Goar, tel. 06743/1322 in Bacharach, www.k-d.com). Boats run daily in both directions from April through October, with no boats off-season. Complete, up-to-date schedules are posted in any station, Rhineland hotel, TI, bank, current Thomas Cook Timetable, or at www.euraide .de/ricksteves. Purchase tickets at the dock up to five minutes before departure. (Confirm times at your hotel the night before.) The boat is rarely full. Romantics will plan to catch the old-time *Goethe,* which sails each direction once a day (see "Rhine Cruise Schedule" in this chapter; confirm time locally).

The smaller Bingen-Rüdesheimer line is slightly cheaper than K-D (railpasses not valid, buy tickets on boat, tel. 06721/14140, www.bingen -ruedesheimer.com), with three two-hour round-trip St. Goar–Bacharach trips daily in summer (about €7.50 one-way, €9.50 round-trip; departing St. Goar at 11:00, 14:10, and 16:10, departing Bacharach at 10:10, 12:00, and 15:00).

Drivers have these options: (1) skip the boat; (2) take a round-trip cruise from St. Goar or Bacharach; (3) draw pretzels and let the loser drive, prepare the picnic, and meet the boat; (4) rent a bike, bring it on the boat for free, and bike back; or (5) take the boat one-way and return by train. When exploring by car, don't hesitate to pop onto one of the many little ferries that shuttle across the bridgeless-around-here river (see below).

By Ferry: While there are no bridges between Koblenz and Mainz, you'll see car-and-passenger ferries (usually family-run for generations) about every three miles. Ferries near St. Goar and Bacharach cross the river every 10 minutes daily in the summer from about 6:00 to 20:00, connecting Bingen–Rüdesheim, Lorch–Niederheimbach, Engelsburg–Kaub, and St. Goar–St.Goarshausen (adult-€1, car and driver-€2.80, pay on the boat).

By Train: Hourly milk-run trains down the Rhine hit every town: St. Goar–Bacharach, 12 min; Bacharach–Mainz, 60 min; Mainz–Frankfurt, 45 min. Some train schedules list St. Goar but not Bacharach as a stop, but any schedule listing St. Goar also stops at Bacharach. Tiny stations are unmanned—buy tickets at the platform machines or on the train. Prices are cheap (for example, €2.60 between St. Goar and Bacharach).

SIGHTS

The Romantic Rhine
These sights are listed from north to south, Koblenz to Bingen.
▲▲▲**Der Romantische Rhein Blitz Zug Fahrt**—One of Europe's great train thrills is zipping along the Rhine in this fast train tour. Here's a quick and easy, from-the-train-window tour (also works for car, bike, or best by boat; you can cut in anywhere) that skips the syrupy myths filling normal Rhine guides. For more information than necessary, buy the handy *Rhine Guide from Mainz to Cologne* (€4.50 book with foldout map, at most shops or TIs). Or for skimpy information and a longer, prettier map, try the *Long Rhine Tour* map (€5.20).

Sit on the left (river) side of the train or boat going south from Koblenz. While nearly all the castles listed are viewed from this side, clear a path to the right window for the times I yell, "Cross over!"

You'll notice large black-and-white kilometer markers along the riverbank. I erected these years ago to make this tour easier to follow. They tell the distance from the Rhinefalls, where the Rhine leaves Switzerland and becomes navigable. Now the river-barge pilots have accepted these as navigational aids as well. We're tackling just 36 miles (58 kilometers) of the 820-mile-long (1,320 kilometer) Rhine. Your Blitz Rhine Tour starts at Koblenz and heads upstream to Bingen. If you're going the other direction, it still works. Just hold the book upside down.

Km 590: Koblenz—This Rhine blitz starts with Romantic Rhine thrills—at Koblenz. Koblenz is not a nice city (it was really hit hard in World War II), but its place as the historic *Deutsche Eck* (German corner)—the tip of land where the Mosel joins the Rhine—gives it a

RHINE CRUISE SCHEDULE

Boats run May through September and on a reduced schedule
for parts of April and October; no boats run November through
March. These times are based on the 2003 schedule. Check
www.euraide.de/ricksteves for any changes.

Koblenz	Boppard	St. Goar	Bacharach
—	9:00	10:15	11:25
*9:00	*11:00	*12:20	*13:35
11:00	13:00	14:15	15:25
14:00	16:00	17:15	18:25
13:10	11:50	10:55	10:15
14:10	12:50	11:55	11:15
—	13:50	12:55	12:15
18:10	16:50	15:55	15:15
*20:10	*18:50	*17:55	*17:15

Riding the "Nostalgic Route," you'll take the 1913 steamer Goethe,
*with working paddle wheel and viewable engine room (departing
Koblenz at 9:00 and Bacharach at 17:15).*

certain historic charm. Koblenz, from the Latin for "confluence," has
Roman origins. Walk through the park, noticing the reconstructed
memorial to the kaiser. Across the river, the yellow Ehrenbreitstein
Castle now houses a hostel. It's a 30-minute hike from the station to
the Koblenz boat dock.

Km 585: Burg Lahneck—Above the modern autobahn bridge over
the Lahn River, this castle *(Burg)* was built in 1240 to defend local silver
mines; the castle was ruined by the French in 1688 and rebuilt in the
1850s in neo-Gothic style. Burg Lahneck faces another Romantic
rebuild, the yellow Schloss Stolzenfels (out of view above the train, a
10-min climb from tiny car park, open for touring, closed Mon).

Km 580: Marksburg—This castle (black and white with the 3
modern chimneys behind it, just after town of Spay) is the best-looking
of all the Rhine castles and the only surviving medieval castle on the
Rhine. Because of its commanding position, it was never attacked. It's
now open as a museum with a medieval interior second only to the
Mosel's Burg Eltz (see self-guided Marksburg tour, below; for all the
details on Burg Eltz, see next chapter). The three modern smokestacks

Best of the Rhine

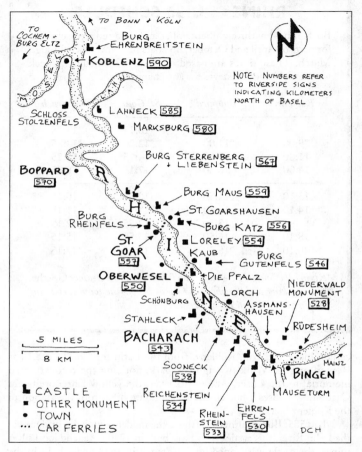

TO COCHEM & BURG ELTZ

↖ TO BONN + KÖLN

BURG EHRENBREITSTEIN

KOBLENZ 590

N

NOTE: NUMBERS REFER TO RIVERSIDE SIGNS INDICATING KILOMETERS NORTH OF BASEL

SCHLOSS STOLZENFELS

LAHNECK 585

MARKSBURG 580

BURG STERRENBERG + LIEBENSTEIN 567

BOPPARD 570

R

H

BURG MAUS 559

ST. GOARSHAUSEN

BURG RHEINFELS →

BURG KATZ 556

ST. GOAR 557

I

LORELEY 554

KAUB

BURG GUTENFELS 546

OBERWESEL 550

→ DIE PFALZ

SCHÖNBURG

LORCH

N

NIEDERWALD MONUMENT 528

STAHLECK →

ASSMANS- HAUSEN

RÜDESHEIM

E

BACHARACH 543

SOONECK 538

MAINZ

BINGEN

REICHENSTEIN 534

MAUSETURM

RHEIN- STEIN 533

EHREN- FELS 530

DCH

5 MILES

8 KM

⌐ CASTLE

■ OTHER MONUMENT

• TOWN

··· CAR FERRIES

vent Europe's biggest car-battery recycling plant just up the valley.

Km 570: Boppard—Once a Roman town, Boppard has some impressive remains of fourth-century walls. Notice the Roman towers and the substantial chunk of Roman wall near the train station, just above the main square.

If you visit Boppard, head to the fascinating church below the main square. Find the carved Romanesque crazies at the doorway. Inside, to the right of the entrance, you'll see Christian symbols from Roman times. Also notice the painted arches and vaults. Originally most Romanesque churches were painted this way. Down by the river, look for the high-water *(Hochwasser)* marks on the arches from various flood years. (You'll find these flood marks throughout the Rhine and Mosel Valleys.)

Km 567: Burg Sterrenberg and Burg Liebenstein—These are the "Hostile Brothers" castles across from Bad Salzig. Take the wall between the castles (actually designed to improve the defenses of both castles), add two greedy and jealous brothers and a fair maiden, and create your own legend. Burg Liebenstein is now a fun, friendly, and affordable family-run hotel (9 rooms, Db-€90, suite-€110, giant king-and-the-family room-€180, easy parking, tel. 06773/308, www.castle-liebenstein .com, hotel-burg-liebenstein@rhinecastles.com, Nickenig family).

Km 560: While you can see nothing from here, a 19th-century lead mine functioned on both sides of the river with a shaft actually tunneling completely under it.

Km 559: Burg Maus—The Maus (mouse) got its name because the next castle was owned by the Katzenelnbogen family. (*Katz* means "cat.") In the 1300s, it was considered a state-of-the-art fortification...until Napoleon had it blown up in 1806 with state-of-the-art explosives. It was rebuilt true to its original plans around 1900. Today, the castle hosts a falconry show (€6.50, daily at 11:00 and 14:30, 20-min walk up, tel. 06771/7669, www.burg-maus.de).

Km 557: St. Goar and Rheinfels Castle—Cross to the other side of the train. The pleasant town of St. Goar was named for a sixth-century hometown monk. It originated in Celtic times (really old) as a place where sailors would stop, catch their breath, send home a postcard, and give thanks after surviving the seductive and treacherous Loreley crossing. St. Goar is worth a stop to explore its mighty Rheinfels Castle. (For information, a guided castle tour, and accommodations, see below.)

Km 556: Burg Katz—Burg Katz (Katzenelnbogen) faces St. Goar from across the river. Together, Burg Katz (built in 1371) and Rheinfels Castle had a clear view up and down the river and effectively controlled traffic. There was absolutely no duty-free shopping on the medieval Rhine. Katz got Napoleoned in 1806 and rebuilt around 1900. Today, it's under a rich and mysterious Japanese ownership. It's technically a hotel—Germany wouldn't allow its foreign purchase for private use—but it's so expensive, nobody's ever stayed there. Below the castle, notice the derelict grape terraces—worked since the eighth century, but abandoned only in the last generation. The Rhine wine is particularly good because the slate absorbs the heat of the sun and stays warm all night, resulting in sweeter grapes. Wine from the flat fields above the Rhine gorge is cheaper and good only as table wine. The wine from the steep side of the Rhine gorge—harder to grow and harvest—is tastier and more expensive.

About Km 555: A statue of the Loreley, the beautiful but deadly nymph (see next listing for legend), combs her hair at the end of a long

spit—built to give barges protection from vicious icebergs that occasionally rage down the river in the winter. The actual Loreley, a cliff, is
just ahead.

Km 554: The Loreley—Steep a big slate rock in centuries of
legend and it becomes a tourist attraction, the ultimate Rhinestone. The
Loreley (flags on top, name painted near shoreline), rising 450 feet over
the narrowest and deepest point of the Rhine, has long been important.
It was a holy site in pre-Roman days. The fine echoes here—thought
to be ghostly voices—fertilized the legendary soil.

Because of the reefs just upstream (at kilometer 552), many ships
never made it to St. Goar. Sailors (after days on the river) blamed their
misfortune on a *wunderbares Fräulein* whose long blonde hair almost
covered her body. Heinrich Heine's *Song of Loreley* (the Cliffs Notes version is on local postcards) tells the story of a count who sent his men to
kill or capture this siren after she distracted his horny son, causing him
to drown. When the soldiers cornered the nymph in her cave, she called
her father (Father Rhine) for help. Huge waves, the likes of which you'll
never see today, rose from the river and carried Loreley to safety. And
she has never been seen since.

But alas, when the moon shines brightly and the tour buses are
parked, a soft, playful Rhine whine can still be heard from the Loreley. As
you pass, listen carefully ("Sailors...sailors...over my bounding mane").

Km 552: Killer reefs, marked by red-and-green buoys, are called
the "Seven Maidens." Okay, one goofy legend: The prince of Schönburg
Castle (*ober* Oberwesel) had seven spoiled daughters who always
dumped men because of their shortcomings. Fed up, he invited seven
of his knights up to the castle and demanded that his daughters each
choose one to marry. But they complained that each man had too big a
nose, was too fat, too stupid, and so on. The rude and teasing girls
escaped into a riverboat. Just downstream, God turned them into the
seven rocks that form this reef. While this story probably isn't entirely
true, there's a lesson in it for medieval children: Don't be hard-hearted.

Km 550: Oberwesel—Cross to the other side of the train.
Oberwesel was a Celtic town in 400 B.C., then a Roman military station.
It now boasts some of the best Roman-wall and medieval-tower remains
on the Rhine, and the commanding Schönburg Castle. Notice how
many of the train tunnels have entrances designed like medieval turrets—they were actually built in the Romantic 19th century. OK, back
to the river side.

**Km 546: Burg Gutenfels and Pfalz Castle: The Classic Rhine
View**—Burg Gutenfels (see white-painted Hotel sign) and the ship-
shape Pfalz Castle (built in the river in the 1300s) worked very effectively to tax medieval river traffic. The town of Kaub grew rich as Pfalz
raised its chains when boats came and lowered them only when the merchants had paid their duty. Those who didn't pay spent time touring its

prison, on a raft at the bottom of its well. In 1504, a pope called for the destruction of Pfalz, but a six-week siege failed. Notice the overhanging outhouse (tiny white room—with faded medieval stains—between two wooden ones). Pfalz is tourable but bare and dull (€2 ferry from Kaub, €2.10 entry, April–Sept Tue–Sun 9:00–13:00 & 14:00–18:00, Oct–March until 17:00, last entry 60 min before closing, closed Mon and Dec, tel. 06774/570 or 0172/262-2800).

In Kaub, a green statue honors the German general Blücher. He was Napoleon's nemesis. In 1813, as Napoleon fought his way back to Paris after his disastrous Russian campaign, he stopped at Mainz—hoping to fend off the Germans and Russians pursuing him by controlling that strategic bridge. Blücher tricked Napoleon. By building the first major pontoon bridge of its kind here at the Pfalz Castle, he crossed the Rhine and outflanked the French. Two years later, Blücher and Wellington teamed up to defeat Napoleon once and for all at Waterloo.

Km 544: "The Raft Busters"—Immediately before Bacharach, at the top of the island, buoys mark a gang of rocks notorious for busting up rafts. The Black Forest is upstream. It was poor, and wood was its best export. Black Foresters would ride log booms down the Rhine to the Ruhr (where their timber fortified coal-mine shafts) or to Holland (where logs were sold to shipbuilders). If they could navigate the sweeping bend just before Bacharach and then survive these "raft busters," they'd come home reckless and romantic, the German folkloric equivalent of American cowboys after payday.

Km 543: Bacharach and Burg Stahleck—Cross to the other side of the train. Bacharach is a great stop (see details and accommodations below). Some of the Rhine's best wine is from this town, whose name means "altar to Bacchus." Local vintners brag that the medieval Pope Pius II ordered Bacharach wine by the cartload. Perched above the town, the 13th-century Burg Stahleck is now a hostel.

Km 540: Lorch—This pathetic stub of a castle is barely visible from the road. Notice the small car ferry (3/hr, 10 min), one of several along the bridgeless stretch between Mainz and Koblenz.

Km 538: Castle Sooneck—Cross back to the other side of the train. Built in the 11th century, this castle was twice destroyed by people sick and tired of robber barons.

Km 534: Burg Reichenstein, and **Km 533: Burg Rheinstein**—Stay on the other side of the train to see two of the first castles to be rebuilt in the Romantic era. Both are privately owned, tourable, and connected by a pleasant trail.

Km 530: Ehrenfels Castle—Opposite Bingerbrück and the Bingen station, you'll see the ghostly Ehrenfels Castle (clobbered by the Swedes in 1636 and by the French in 1689). Since it had no view of the river traffic to the north, the owner built the cute little *Mäuseturm* (mouse tower) on an island (the yellow tower you'll see near the train station today). Rebuilt in the 1800s in neo-Gothic style, it's now used as a Rhine navigation signal station.

Km 528: Niederwald Monument—Across from the Bingen station on a hilltop is the 120-foot-high Niederwald monument, a memorial built with 32 tons of bronze in 1877 to commemorate "the reestablishment of the German Empire." A lift takes tourists to this statue from the famous and extremely touristy wine town of Rüdesheim.

From here, the Romantic Rhine becomes the industrial Rhine, and our tour is over.

More Rhine Sights

▲▲**Marksburg Castle**—Thanks to its formidable defenses, invaders decided to give Marksburg a miss. This best-preserved castle on the Rhine can be toured only with a guide, and tours are generally in German only (4/hr in summer, 1/hr in winter). Still, it's an awesome castle, and my self-guided walking tour (below) fits the 50-minute German-language tour (€4.50, family card-€12.50, daily April–Oct 10:00–18:00, last tour departs at 17:00, Nov–March 11:00–17:00, last tour at 16:00, call ahead to see if a rare English tour is scheduled, tel. 02627/206, www.marksburg.de). Marksburg caps a hill above the Rhine town of Braubach (a short hike or shuttle train from the boat dock). Our tour starts inside the castle's first gate.

1. Inside the First Gate: While the dramatic castles lining the Rhine are generally Romantic rebuilds, Marksburg is the real McCoy—nearly all original construction. It's littered with bits of its medieval past, like the big stone ball that was swung on a rope to be used as a battering ram. Ahead, notice how the inner gate—originally tall enough for knights on horseback to gallop through—was made smaller, therefore safer from enemies on horseback. Climb the Knights' Stairway carved out of slate rock and pass under the murder hole—handy for pouring boiling pitch on invaders. (Germans still say someone with bad luck "has pitch on his head.")

2. Coats of Arms: Colorful coats of arms line the wall just inside the gate. These are from the noble families who have owned the castle since 1283. In 1283, financial troubles drove the first family to sell to the powerful and wealthy Katzenelnbogen family (who made the castle into what you see today). When Napoleon took this region in 1803, an Austrian family who sided with the French got the keys. When Prussia took the region in 1866, control passed to a friend of the Prussians who had a passion for medieval things—typical of this Romantic period. Then it was sold to the German Castles Association in 1900. Its offices are in the main palace at the top of the stairs.

3. Romanesque Palace: White outlines mark where the larger original windows were located, before they were replaced by easier-to-defend smaller ones. On the far right, a bit of the original plaster survives. Slate, which is soft and vulnerable to the elements, needs to be covered—in this case, by plaster. Because this is a protected historic building, restorers can use only the traditional plaster methods...but no one knows how to make plaster that works as well as the 800-year-old surviving bits.

4. Cannons: The oldest cannon here—from 1500—was back-loaded. This was good because many cartridges could be preloaded. But since the seal was leaky, it wasn't very powerful. The bigger, more modern cannons—from 1640—were one piece and therefore airtight, but had to be front-loaded. They could easily hit targets across the river from here. Stone balls were rough, so they let the explosive force leak out. The best cannonballs were stones covered in smooth lead—airtight and therefore more powerful and more accurate.

5. Gothic Garden: Walking along an outer wall, you'll see 160 plants from the Middle Ages—used for cooking, medicine, and witch-craft. The *Schierling* (hemlock, in the first corner) is the same poison that killed Socrates.

6. Inland Rampart: This most vulnerable part of the castle had a triangular construction to better deflect attacks. Notice the factory in the valley. In the 14th century, this was a lead, copper, and silver mine. Today's factory—Europe's largest car-battery recycling plant—uses the old mine shafts as a vent (see the 3 modern smokestacks).

7. Wine Cellar: Since Roman times, wine has been the traditional Rhineland drink. Because castle water was impure, wine—less alcoholic than today's beer—was the way knights got their fluids. The pitchers on the wall were their daily allotment. The bellows were part of the barrel's filtering system. Stairs lead to the...

8. Gothic Hall: This hall is set up as a kitchen, with an oven designed to roast an ox whole. The arms holding the pots have notches to control the heat. To this day, when Germans want someone to hurry up, they say, "give it one tooth more." Medieval windows were thin alabaster or skins. A nearby wall is peeled away to show the wattle-and-daub construction (sticks, straw, clay, mud, then plaster) of a castle's inner walls. The iron plate to the left of the next door enabled servants to stoke the heater without being seen by the noble family.

9. Bedroom: This was the only heated room in the castle. The canopy kept in heat and kept out critters. In medieval times, it was impolite for a lady to argue with her lord in public. She would wait for him in bed to give him what Germans still call "a curtain lecture." The deep window seat caught maximum light for needlework and reading. Women would sit here and chat (or "spin a yarn") while working the spinning wheel.

10. Hall of the Knights: This was the dining hall. The long table is an unattached plank. After each course, servants could replace it with another preset plank. Even today, when a meal is over and Germans are ready for the action to begin, they say, "Let's lift up the table." The "action" back then was traveling minstrels who sang and told of news gleaned from their travels.

The outhouse locked from the outside because any invader knew that the toilet—which simply hung over thin air—was a weak point in the castle's defenses.

11. Chapel: This chapel is still painted in Gothic style with the castle's namesake, St. Mark, and his lion. Even the chapel was designed with defense in mind. The small doorway kept out heavily armed attackers. The staircase spirals clockwise, favoring the sword-wielding defender (assuming he was right-handed).

12. Linen Room: Around 1800, the castle—with diminished military value—housed disabled soldiers. They'd earn a little extra money working raw flax into linen.

13. Two Thousand Years of Armor: Follow the evolution of armor since Celtic times. Because helmets covered the entire head, soldiers identified themselves as friendly by tipping their visor up with their right hand. This evolved into the military salute that is still used around the world today. Armor and the close-range weapons along the back were made obsolete by the invention of the rifle. Armor was replaced with breastplates—pointed (like the castle itself) to deflect enemy fire. This design was used as late as the start of World War I. A medieval lady's armor hangs over the door. While popular fiction has men locking their women up before heading off to battle, chastity belts were actually used by women as protection against rape when traveling.

14. The Keep: This served as an observation tower, a dungeon (with a 22-square-foot cell in the bottom), and a place of last refuge. When all was nearly lost, the defenders would bundle into the keep and burn the wooden bridge, hoping to outwait their enemies.

15. Horse Stable: The stable shows off bits of medieval crime and punishment. Cheaters were attached to stones or pillories. Shame masks punished gossipmongers. A mask with a heavy ball had its victim crawling around with his nose in the mud. The handcuffs with a neck hole were for the transport of prisoners. The pictures on the wall show various medieval capital punishments. Many times the accused was simply taken into a torture dungeon to see all these tools and, guilty or not, confessions spilled out of him. On that cheery note, your tour is over.

The Myth of the Loreley Visitors' Center—This lightweight exhibit reflects on Loreley, traces her myth, and explores the landscape, culture, and people of the Rhine Valley. Displays in English tell the history well, but the highlight for any kid-at-heart are the echo megaphones in the little theater that (with English headphones) tells the legend of the siren (€1, April–Oct daily 10:00–18:00, often closed Nov–March, tel. 06771/9100, www.loreley-touristik.de). From the exhibit, a five-minute walk (marked as 30 minutes) takes you to the impressive viewpoint overlooking the Rhine Valley from atop the famous rock. From there, it's a steep 15-minute hike down to the riverbank.

Biking the Rhine—In Bacharach, you can rent bikes at Pension Malerwinkel if you're a guest (€6/day), or get a free loaner bike if you're staying at Pension Winzerhaus. In St. Goar, Hotel am Markt rents bikes to its guests.

You can bike on either side of the Rhine, but for a designated bike path, stay on the west side, where a 35-mile path runs between Koblenz and Bingen. While the stretch between Bacharach and Bingen hugs the riverside, I'd join the in-line skaters along the fine and more interesting roadside bike lane connecting Bacharach and St. Goar in six miles. In 2004, new sections of the bike path will be finished between Bacharach and Bingen, making the trip completely road-free.

Consider taking a bike on the Rhine boats (free with ticket) and then biking back, or designing a circular trip using the fun and frequent shuttle ferries. A good target might be Kaub (where a tiny boat shuttles sightseers to the better-from-a-distance castle on the island).

Bacharach

Once prosperous from the wine and wood trade, Bacharach (BAHKH-ah-rahkh, with a guttural *kh* sound) is now just a pleasant half-timbered village of a thousand people working hard to keep its tourists happy.

Tourist Information: The TI is on the main street in the Posthof courtyard next to the church (April–Oct Mon–Fri 9:00–17:00, Sat 10:00–16:00, closed Sun, Nov–March Mon–Fri 9:00–12:00, closed Sat–Sun, Internet access-€6/hr, Oberstrasse 45, from train station turn right and walk 5 blocks down main street with castle high on your left, tel. 06743/919-303, www.bacharach.de or www.rhein-nahe-touristik.de, Herr Kuhn and his team SE). The TI stores bags for day-trippers, provides ferry schedules, and sells the handy *Rhine Guide from Mainz to Cologne* (€4.50). For accommodations, see "Sleeping," below.

Shopping: The **Jost** beer-stein stores carry most everything a shopper could want. One shop is across from the church in the main square, the other—which offers more deals—is a block away next to the post office at Rosenstrasse 16 (post office closed 12:30–14:00; Jost store hours: Mon–Fri 8:30–18:00, Sat 8:30–17:00, Sun 10:00–17:00, Rosenstrasse shop closed Sun, ships overseas, 10 percent discount with this book, tel. 06743/1224, www.phil-jost-germany.com). Herr and Frau Jost offer sightseeing advice, send faxes, and reserve German hotels for travelers (reasonable charge for phone and fax fees). **Woodburn House,** which engraves woody signs and knickknacks, lets travelers store bags while they look for a room and gives readers with this book a 10 percent discount (across from Altes Haus, Oberstrasse 60, Frances Geuss SE).

Bacharach

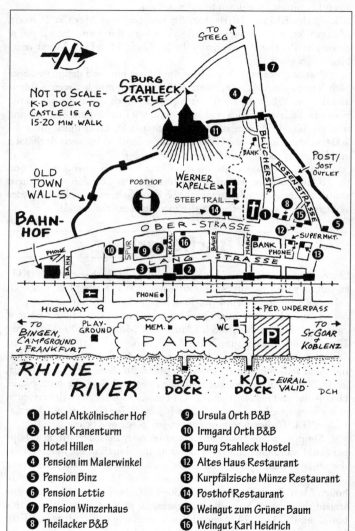

1 Hotel Altkölnischer Hof
2 Hotel Kranenturm
3 Hotel Hillen
4 Pension im Malerwinkel
5 Pension Binz
6 Pension Lettie
7 Pension Winzerhaus
8 Theilacker B&B
9 Ursula Orth B&B
10 Irmgard Orth B&B
11 Burg Stahleck Hostel
12 Altes Haus Restaurant
13 Kurpfälzische Münze Restaurant
14 Posthof Restaurant
15 Weingut zum Grüner Baum
16 Weingut Karl Heidrich

Local Guides: Get acquainted with Bacharach by taking a walking tour. Charming Herr Rolf Jung, retired headmaster of the Bacharach school, is a superb English-speaking guide (€30, 90 min, call to reserve, tel. 06743/1519). If Herr Jung is not available, the TI has a list of other English-speaking guides, or take the self-guided walk, described below.

INTRODUCTORY WALK

Start at the Köln-Düsseldorfer ferry dock (next to a fine picnic park). View the town from the parking lot—a modern landfill. The Rhine used to lap against Bacharach's town wall, just over the present-day highway. Every few years the river floods, covering the highway with several feet of water. The **castle** on the hill is a youth hostel. Two of its original 16 towers are visible from here (up to 5 if you look real hard). The huge roadside wine keg declares this town was built on the wine trade.

Reefs up the river forced boats to unload upriver and reload here. Consequently, Bacharach became the biggest wine trader on the Rhine. A riverfront crane hoisted huge kegs of prestigious "Bacharach" wine (which in practice was from anywhere in the region). The tour buses next to the dock and the flags of the biggest spenders along the highway remind you that today's economy is basically tourism.

At the big town map and public WC (€0.30, daily 9:00–18:00), take the underpass, ascend on the right, make a U-turn, then—if you are less than 2.3 meters tall—walk under the train tracks through the medieval gate (1 out of an original 15 14th-century gates) and to the two-tone Protestant **church,** which marks the town center.

From this intersection, Bacharach's main street (Oberstrasse) goes right to the half-timbered, red-and-white Altes Haus (from 1368, the oldest house in town) and left way down to the train station. To the left (or south) of the church, a golden horn hangs over the old **Posthof** (TI, free WC upstairs in courtyard open from 11:00). The post horn symbolizes the postal service throughout Europe. In olden days, when the postman blew this, traffic stopped and the mail sped through. This post station dates from 1724, when stagecoaches ran from Köln to Frankfurt.

Step into the courtyard—once a carriage house and inn that accommodated Bacharach's first VIP visitors. Notice the fascist eagle (from 1936, on the left as you enter) and the fine view of the church and a ruined chapel above. The Posthof is the home of the **Rhineland Museum,** which hopes to open in 2004 with a cultural landscape exhibit on the Rhine Valley. Manager Bitz's vision even includes wine-tasting (www.mittelrheintal.de).

Two hundred years ago, Bacharach's main drag was the only road along the Rhine. Napoleon widened it to fit his cannon wagons. The steps alongside the church lead to the castle. Return to the church, passing the **Italian Ice Cream** café, where friendly Mimo serves his special invention: Riesling wine–flavored gelato (quite tasty, €0.60 per scoop, opposite Posthof at Oberstrasse 48).

Inside the church (daily 9:00–18:00, English info on table near door), you'll find grotesque capitals, brightly painted in medieval style, and a mix of round Romanesque and pointed Gothic arches. Left of the altar, some medieval frescoes survive where an older Romanesque arch was cut by a pointed Gothic one.

Continue down Oberstrasse past the Altes Haus to the **old mint** *(Münze),* marked by a crude coin in its sign. Across from the mint, the wine garden of Fritz Bastian is the liveliest place in town after dark (see "Eating," below). Above you in the vineyards stands a ghostly black-and-gray tower—your destination.

Take the next left (Rosenstrasse) and wander 30 yards up to the **well.** Notice the sundial and the wall painting of 1632 Bacharach with its walls intact. Climb the tiny-stepped lane behind the well up into the vineyard and to the tower. The slate steps lead to a small path through the vineyard that deposits you at a viewpoint atop the stubby remains of the old town wall (if signs indicate that the path is closed, get as close to the tower base as possible).

A grand medieval town spreads before you. When Frankfurt had 15,000 residents, medieval Bacharach had 4,000. For 300 years (1300–1600), Bacharach was big, rich, and politically powerful.

From this perch you can see the chapel ruins and six surviving **city towers.** Visually trace the wall to the castle. The castle was actually the capital of Germany for a couple of years in the 1200s. When Holy Roman Emperor Frederick Barbarossa went away to fight the Crusades, he left his brother (who lived here) in charge of his vast realm. Bacharach was home of one of seven electors who voted for the Holy Roman Emperor in 1275. To protect their own power, these elector-princes did their best to choose the weakest guy on the ballot. The elector from Bacharach helped select a two-bit prince named Rudolf von Hapsburg (from a no-name castle in Switzerland). The underestimated Rudolf brutally silenced the robber barons along the Rhine and established the mightiest dynasty in European history. His family line, the Hapsburgs, ruled much of Central Europe until 1918.

Plagues, fires, and the Thirty Years' War (1618–1648) finally did Bacharach in. The town, with a population of about a thousand, has slumbered for several centuries. Today, the castle houses commoners—40,000 overnights annually by youth hostelers.

In the mid-19th century, painters such as J. M. W. Turner and writers such as Victor Hugo were charmed by the Rhineland's romantic mix of past glory, present poverty, and rich legend. They put this part of the Rhine on the old "grand tour" map as the "Romantic Rhine." Victor Hugo pondered the ruined 15th-century chapel that you see under the castle. In his 1842 travel book, *Rhein Reise (Rhine Travels),* he wrote,

"No doors, no roof or windows, a magnificent skeleton puts its silhouette against the sky. Above it, the ivy-covered castle ruins provide a fitting crown. This is Bacharach, land of fairy tales, covered with legends and sagas." If you're enjoying the Romantic Rhine, thank Victor Hugo and company.

To get back into town, take the level path that leads along the wall up the valley past the next tower. Then cross the street into the parking lot. Pass Pension Malerwinkel on your right, being careful not to damage the old arch with your head. Follow the creek past a delightful little series of half-timbered homes and cheery gardens known as Painters' Corner *(Malerwinkel)*. Resist looking into some pervert's peep show (on the right) and continue downhill back to the village center. Nice work.

SLEEPING

(country code: 49, area code: 06743)

See map on page 450 for locations. Ignore guest houses and restaurants posting "Recommended by Rick Steves" signs. If they're not listed in the current edition of this book, I do not recommend them.

$$$ **Hotel Altkölnischer Hof,** a grand old building near the church, rents 20 rooms with modern furnishings (and some balconies) over an Old World restaurant. Public rooms are old-time elegant (Sb-€48–70, small or dark Db-€62–65, bright new Db-€72–82, new Db with balcony-€80–105, elevator, closed Nov–March, tel. 06743/1339 or 06743/2186, fax 06743/2793, www.hotel-bacharach-rhein.de, altkoelnischer-hof@t-online.de).

$$ **Hotel Kranenturm** offers castle ambience without the climb—a good combination of hotel comfort with *Zimmer* coziness, a central location, and a medieval atmosphere. Run by hardworking Kurt Engel and his intense but friendly wife, Fatima, this hotel is actually part of the medieval fortification. Its former *Kran* (crane) towers are now round rooms. When the riverbank was higher, cranes on this tower loaded barrels of wine onto Rhine boats. Hotel Kranenturm is 15 feet from the train tracks, but a combination of medieval sturdiness, triple-paned windows, and included earplugs makes the riverside rooms sleepable (Sb-€40–43, Db-€55–60, bigger Db-€60–70, Tb-€75–85, lower price is for off-season or stays of at least 3 nights in high season, family deals, kid-friendly, cash preferred, Rhine views come with ripping train noise, back rooms are quieter, Internet access-€5/hour and laundry service-€12.50/load for guests only, Langstrasse 30, tel. 06743/1308, fax 06743/1021, hotel-kranenturm@t-online.de). Kurt, a good cook, serves €6–18 dinners (guests can have full dinner for €10); try his ice-cream special for dessert. Trade travel stories on the terrace with new friends over dinner, letting screaming trains punctuate your conversation.

SLEEP CODE

(€1 = about $1.10)
Sleep Code: **S** = Single, **D** = Double/Twin, **T** = Triple, **Q** = Quad, **b** = bathroom, **s** = shower only, **no CC** = Credit Cards not accepted, **SE** = Speaks English, **NSE** = No English. All hotels speak some English. Breakfast is included and credit cards are accepted unless otherwise noted.

To help you sort easily through these listings, I've divided the rooms into three categories, based on the price for a standard double room with bath:

   $$$ Higher Priced—Most rooms €70 or more.
    $$ Moderately Priced—Most rooms between €50–70.
     $ Lower Priced—Most rooms €50 or less.

The Rhine is an easy place for cheap sleeps. *Zimmer* and *Gasthäuser* with €20 beds abound (and *Zimmer* normally discount their prices for longer stays). Rhine-area hostels offer €14 beds to travelers of any age. Each town's TI is eager to set you up, and finding a room should be easy any time of year (except for winefest weekends in September and October). Bacharach and St. Goar, the best towns for an overnight stop, are 10 miles apart, connected by milk-run trains, riverboats, and a riverside bike path. Bacharach is a much more interesting town, but St. Goar has the famous castle (see "St. Goar," above). Parking in Bacharach is simple along the highway next to the tracks (3-hr daytime limit is generally not enforced) or in the boat parking lot. Parking in St. Goar is tighter; ask at your hotel.

Drivers park along the highway at the Kranenturm tower. Eurailers walk down Oberstrasse, then turn right on Kranenstrasse.

   $$ Hotel Hillen, a block south of the Hotel Kranenturm, has less charm and similar train noise, with spacious rooms, friendly owners, and good food. To minimize train noise, ask for *ruhige Seite,* the quiet side (S-€28, Sb-€36, D-€42, Ds-€52, Db-€57, Tb-€75, 10 percent less for 3 nights, 15 percent discount on rooms with this book, closed Nov–March, family rooms, Langstrasse 18, tel. 06743/1287, fax 06743/1037, hotel-hillen@web.de, kind Iris speaks some English).

   $$ Pension im Malerwinkel sits like a grand gingerbread house just outside the wall at the top end of town in a little neighborhood so charming it's called "Painters' Corner" *(Malerwinkel).* The Vollmer family's

20-room place is super-quiet and comes with a sunny garden on a brook and easy parking (Sb-€35, Db-€55–58 for 1 night, €50 for 2 nights, €47 for 3 nights, no CC, some rooms have balconies but most face parking lot, bike rental-€6/day, from town center go uphill and up the valley 5 min until you pass the old town gate and look left to Blücherstrasse 41, tel. 06743/1239, fax 06743/93407, www.im-malerwinkel.de, pension@im-malerwinkel.de).

$$ **Pension Binz** offers four large, bright rooms and a plain apartment in a serene location (Sb-€33, Db-€51, third person-€18, apartment with 2-night minimum-€61, fine breakfast, Koblenzer Strasse 1, tel. 06743/1604, pension.binz@freenet.de, cheery Karla speaks a little English).

$ At **Pension Lettie,** effervescent and eager-to-please Lettie offers four bright rooms. Lettie speaks good English (she worked for the U.S. Army before they withdrew) and does laundry—€10.50 per load (Sb-€34, Db-€45, Tb-€61, family room for 4-€75, for 5-€95, for 6-€105, prices valid with this book, discount for 2-night stays, 6 percent more if paying with plastic, strictly non-smoking, buffet breakfast with waffles and eggs, no train noise, a few doors inland from Hotel Kranenturm, Kranenstrasse 6, tel. & fax 06743/2115, pension.lettie@t-online.de).

$ **Pension Winzerhaus,** a 10-room place run by friendly Sybille and Stefan, is 200 yards up the valley from the town gate, so the location is less charming, and the train noise is replaced by street noise. But the parking is easy, and rooms are simple, clean, and modern (Sb-€26, Db-€45, Tb-€60, Qb-€65, 10 percent off with this book, no CC, free bikes for guests, non-smoking rooms, Blücherstrasse 60, tel. 06743/1294, fax 06743/937-779, winzerhaus@compuserve.de).

$ **Herr und Frau Theilacker** run a cozy, German-feeling *Zimmer* just off the main street with four comfortable rooms, vine-covered trellises, and a breakfast room filled with their family photos. They're likely to have a room when others don't (S-€18, D-€36, no CC, in town center behind Altkölnischer Hof, take short lane between Altkölnischer Hof and Altes Haus straight ahead to Oberstrasse 57, no outside sign, tel. 06743/1248, NSE).

$ **Orth** *Zimmer:* Delightful sisters-in-law run two fine little B&Bs across the lane from each other (from station walk down Oberstrasse, turn right on Spurgasse, look for *Orth* sign). **Ursula Orth** rents five rooms and speaks a smidge of English (Sb-€20, D-€31, Db-€34, Tb-€45, no CC, rooms 4 and 5 on ground floor, Spurgasse 3, tel. 06743/1557). **Irmgard Orth** rents two fresh rooms. She speaks no English but is exuberantly cheery and serves homemade honey with breakfast (Sb-€20, Db-€34, no CC, Spurgasse 2, tel. 06743/1553).

$ **Jugendherberge Stahleck** hostel is a 12th-century castle on the hilltop—500 steps above Bacharach—with a royal Rhine view. Open to travelers of any age, this is a newly redone gem with eight beds and a private modern shower and WC in most rooms. A steep 20-minute climb on the trail from the town church, the hostel is warmly run by Evelyn and Bernhard Falke (FALL-kay), who serve hearty, €6, all-you-can-eat buffet dinners. The hostel pub serves cheap local wine until midnight (€16 dorm beds with breakfast and sheets, €3.10 extra for non-members or in a double, couples can share one of five €37 Db, no smoking in rooms, open all day but 22:00 curfew, laundry machine, beds normally available but call and leave your name, they'll hold a bed until 18:00, tel. 06743/1266, fax 06743/2684, jh-bacharach@djh-info.de). If driving, don't go in the driveway; park on the street and walk 200 yards.

EATING

You can easily find inexpensive (€10–15), atmospheric restaurants offering indoor and outdoor dining. The first three places are neighbors.

Altes Haus, the oldest building in town, serves reliably good food with Bacharach's most romantic atmosphere (€9–15, Thu–Tue 12:00–15:30 & 18:00–21:30, closed Wed and Dec–Easter, dead center by the church, tel. 06743/1209). Find the cozy little dining room with photos of the opera singer who sang about Bacharach, adding to its fame.

Kurpfälzische Münze is more expensive but a popular standby for its sunny terrace and classy candlelit interior (€7–21, daily 10:00–22:00, in the old mint, a half-block down from Altes Haus, tel. 06743/1375).

Posthof Restaurant is a historic carriage house—a stopping place for centuries of guests—newly opened as a restaurant. The menu is trendier, with free German tapas (ask), seasonal specials, and local "as organic as possible" produce. You'll sit in a half-timbered cobbled courtyard (€5–15, good salads and veggie dishes, fun kids' play area, daily 11:00 until late, Oberstrasse 45, tel. 06743/599-663).

Hotel Kranenturm is another good value with hearty meals and good main course salads (restaurant closed Nov–Feb, see hotel listing above).

Wine-Tasting: Drop in on entertaining Fritz Bastian's **Weingut zum Grüner Baum** wine bar (also offers soup and cold cuts, good ambience indoors and out, just past Altes Haus, Mon–Wed and Fri from 13:00, Sat–Sun from 12:00, closed Thu and Feb–mid-March, tel. 06743/1208). As the president of the local vintner's club, Fritz is on a mission to give travelers an understanding of the subtle differences among the Rhine wines. Groups of 2–6 people pay €13.50 for a "carousel" of 15 glasses of 14 different white wines, one lonely red, and a basket of bread. Your mission: Team up with others with this book to rendezvous here after dinner. Spin the lazy Susan, share a common cup, and discuss the taste. Fritz insists, "After each wine, you must talk to each other."

For a fun, family-run wine shop and *Stube* in the town center, visit **Weingut Karl Heidrich** (on Oberstrasse, directly in front of Hotel Kranenturm), where American Susanne and German Markus proudly share their family's wine.

St. Goar

St. Goar is a classic Rhine town—its hulk of a castle overlooking a half-timbered shopping street and leafy riverside park busy with sightseeing ships and contented strollers. From the boat dock, the main drag—a pedestrian mall without history—cuts through town before winding up to the castle. Rheinfels Castle, once the mightiest on the Rhine, is the single best Rhineland ruin to explore.

The helpful St. Goar **TI**, which books rooms and offers a free left-luggage service, is on the pedestrian street, three blocks from the K-D

St. Goar

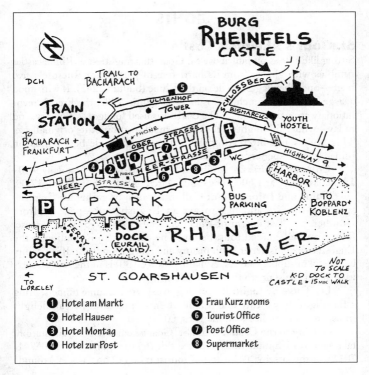

1 Hotel am Markt
2 Hotel Hauser
3 Hotel Montag
4 Hotel zur Post
5 Frau Kurz rooms
6 Tourist Office
7 Post Office
8 Supermarket

boat dock and train station (May–Oct Mon–Fri 8:00–12:30 & 14:00–17:00, Sat 10:00–12:00, closed Sun, Nov–April until 16:30 and closed Sat–Sun, sells *Rhine Guide from Mainz to Cologne;* from train station, go downhill around church and turn left on Heer Strasse; tel. 06741/383).

St. Goar's waterfront park is hungry for a picnic. The small Edeka **supermarket** on the main street is great for picnic fixings (Mon–Fri 8:00–18:30, Sat 8:00–13:00, closed Sun).

The friendly and helpful Montag family runs the Hotel Montag (Michael) and three **shops** (steins—Misha, Steiffs—Maria, and cuckoo clocks—Marion), all at the base of the castle hill road. The stein shop under the hotel has Rhine guides, fine steins, and copies of this year's *Rick Steves' Germany, Austria & Switzerland* guidebook. All three shops offer 10 percent off any of their souvenirs (including Hummels) for travelers with this book (€5 minimum purchase). On-the-spot VAT refunds cover about half your shipping costs (if you're not shipping, they'll give you VAT form to claim refund at airport). The hotel offers expensive coin-op **Internet** access (€8/hr).

SIGHTS

St. Goar's Rheinfels Castle

Sitting like a dead pit bull above St. Goar, this mightiest of Rhine castles rumbles with ghosts from its hard-fought past. Burg Rheinfels *was* huge—once the biggest castle on the Rhine (built in 1245). It withstood a siege of 28,000 French troops in 1692. But in 1797, the French revolutionary army destroyed it. The castle was used for ages as a quarry, and today—while still mighty—it's only a small fraction of its original size. This hollow but interesting shell offers your single best hands-on ruined-castle experience on the river.

Cost and Hours: €4, family card-€10, mid-March–Oct daily 9:00–18:00, last entry at 17:00, Nov–mid-March only Sat–Sun 11:00–17:00.

Tours and Information: Call in advance or gather 10 English-speaking tourists and beg to get an English tour—perhaps from Günther, the "last knight of Rheinfels" (tel. 06741/7753). Otherwise, follow my self-guided tour, below. The castle map is mediocre; the English booklet is better, with history and illustrations (€2). If it's damp, be careful of slippery stones. A handy WC (€0.30) is in the castle courtyard under the stairs to the restaurant entry.

Let There Be Light: If planning to explore the mine tunnels, bring a flashlight, buy a tiny one (€2.60 at entry), or do it by candlelight (museum sells candles with matches, €0.50).

Getting to the Castle: From St. Goar's boat dock or train station, take a steep 15-minute hike, a €5 taxi ride (€6 for a minibus, tel. 06741/7011), or the kitschy "tschu-tschu" tourist train (€2 one-way, €3 round-

St. Goar's Rheinfels Castle

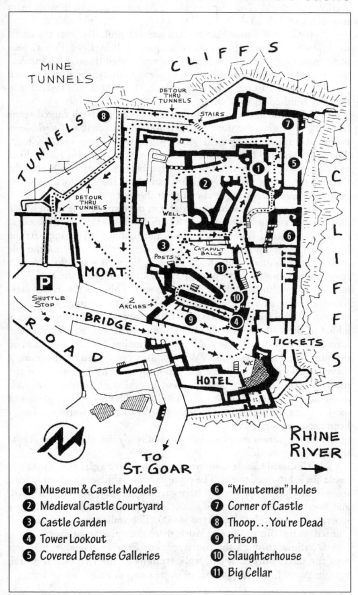

1. Museum & Castle Models
2. Medieval Castle Courtyard
3. Castle Garden
4. Tower Lookout
5. Covered Defense Galleries
6. "Minutemen" Holes
7. Corner of Castle
8. Thoop...You're Dead
9. Prison
10. Slaughterhouse
11. Big Cellar

trip, 7 min to the top, 3/hr, daily 10:00–17:00, runs from square between station and dock, also stops at Hotel Montag, complete with lusty music, tel. 06741/2030).

Self-Guided Tour: Rather than wander aimlessly, visit the castle by following this tour: From the ticket gate, walk straight. Pass *Grosser Keller* on the left (where we'll end this tour), walk through an internal gate past the *zu den gedeckten Wehrgängen* sign on the right (where we'll pass later) uphill to the museum (daily 9:30–12:00 & 13:00–17:30) in the only finished room of the castle.

1. Museum and Castle Model: The seven-foot-tall carved stone immediately inside the door (marked *Keltische Säule von Pfalzfeld)*—a tombstone from a nearby Celtic grave—is from 400 years before Christ. There were people here long before the Romans...and this castle. Find the old wooden library chair near the tombstone. If you smile sweetly, the man behind the desk may demonstrate—pull the back forward and it becomes stairs for getting to the highest shelves.

The sweeping castle history exhibit in the center of the room is well described in English. The massive fortification was the only Rhineland castle to withstand Louis XIV's assault during the 17th century. At the far end of the room is a model reconstruction of the castle (not the one with the toy soldiers) showing how much bigger it was before French revolutionary troops destroyed it in the 18th century. Study this. Find where you are (hint: Look for the tall tower). This was the living quarters of the original castle, which was only the smallest ring of buildings around the tiny central courtyard (13th century). The ramparts were added in the 14th century. By 1650, the fortress was largely complete. Ever since its destruction by the French in the late 18th century, it's had no military value. While no WWII bombs were wasted on this ruin, it served St. Goar as a quarry for generations. The basement of the museum shows the castle pharmacy and an exhibit of Rhine-region odds and ends, including tools and an 1830 loom. Don't miss the photos of ice-breaking on the Rhine—which, thanks to global warming, hasn't been necessary since 1963.

Exit the museum and walk 30 yards directly out, slightly uphill into the castle courtyard.

2. Medieval Castle Courtyard: Five hundred years ago, the entire castle circled this courtyard. The place was self-sufficient and ready for a siege with a bakery, pharmacy, herb garden, brewery, well (top of yard), and livestock. During peacetime, 300–600 people lived here; during a siege, there would be as many as 4,000. The walls were plastered and painted white. Bits of the original 13th-century plaster survive.

Continue through the courtyard, out *Erste Schildmauer,* turn left into the next courtyard, and walk straight to the two old, wooden, upright posts. Find the pyramid of stone catapult balls on your left.

3. Castle Garden: Catapult balls like these were too expensive not to recycle—they'd be retrieved after any battle. Across from the balls is a well—essential for any castle during the age of siegeing. Look in. The old posts are for the ceremonial baptizing of new members of the local trading league. While this guild goes back centuries, it's now a social club that fills this court with a huge wine party the third weekend of each September.

If weary, skip to #5; otherwise, climb the cobbled path up to the castle's best viewpoint—up where the German flag waves.

4. Highest Castle Tower Lookout: Enjoy a great view of the river, castle, and the forest that was once all part of this castle. Remember, the fortress once covered five times the land it does today. Notice how the other castles (across the river) don't poke above the top of the Rhine canyon. That would make them easy for invading armies to see.

Return to the catapult balls, walk down the road, go through the tunnel, veer left through the arch marked *zu den gedeckten Wehrgängen*, go down two flights of stairs, and stop at the top of the next staircase before turning left into the dark covered passageway. From here, we will begin a rectangular walk taking us completely around the perimeter of the castle. But first, take a look at the...

5. Covered Defense Galleries: Soldiers—the castle's "minute-men"—had a short commute: defensive positions on the outside, home in the holes in the wall you see below. Even though these living quarters were padded with straw, life was unpleasant. A peasant was lucky to live beyond age 45.

Now let's walk left through the dark gallery and to the corner of the castle, where you'll see a white painted arrow at eye level. Stand with your back to the arrow on the wall.

6. Corner of Castle: Look up. A three-story, half-timbered build-ing originally rose beyond the highest stone fortification. The two stone tongues near the top just around the corner supported the toilet. (Insert your own joke here.) Turn around and face the wall. The crossbow slits below the white arrow were once steeper. The bigger hole on the river-side was for hot pitch.

Follow that white arrow along the outside to the next corner. Midway you'll pass stairs on the right leading down *zu den Minengängen* (sign on upper left). Adventurers with flashlights can detour here. You may come out around the next corner. Otherwise, stay with me, walking level to the corner. At the corner, turn left.

7. Thoop...You're Dead. Look ahead at the smartly placed cross-bow slit. While you're lying there, notice the stonework. The little round holes were for scaffolds used as they built up. They indicate this stonework is original. Notice also the fine stonework on the chutes. More boiling pitch...now you're toast, too.

Continue along the castle wall around the corner. At the railing, look up the valley and uphill where the sprawling fort stretched. Below, just outside the wall, is land where attackers would gather. The mine tunnels are under there, waiting to blow up any attackers (read below).

Continue along the perimeter, jog left, go down five steps and into an open field, and walk toward the wooden bridge. You may detour here into the passageway (on right) marked *13 Hals Graben*. The "old" wooden bridge is actually modern. Angle left through two arches (before the bridge) and through the rough entry to the *Verliess* (prison) on the left.

8. Prison: This is one of six dungeons. You walked through an entrance prisoners only dreamed of 400 years ago. They came and went through the little square hole in the ceiling. The holes in the walls supported timbers that thoughtfully gave as many as 15 residents something to sit on to keep them out of the filthy slop that gathered on the floor. Twice a day, they were given bread and water. Some prisoners actually survived longer than two years in here. While the town could torture and execute, the castle only had permission to imprison criminals in these dungeons. Consider this: According to town records, the two men who spent the most time down here—2.5 years each—died within three weeks of regaining their freedom. Perhaps after a diet of bread and water, feasting on meat and wine was simply too much.

Continue through the next arch, under the white arrow, and turn left and walk 30 yards to the *Schlachthaus*.

9. Slaughterhouse: Any proper castle was prepared to survive a six-month siege. With 4,000 people, that's a lot of provisions. The cattle that lived within the walls were slaughtered in this room. The castle's mortar was congealed here (by packing all the organic waste from the kitchen into kegs and sealing it). Notice the drainage gutters. "Running water" came through from drains built into the walls (to keep the mortar dry and therefore strong...and less smelly).

Back outside, climb the modern stairs to the left. A skinny, dark passage (yes, that's the one) leads you into the...

10. Big Cellar: This *Grosser Keller* was a big pantry. When the castle was smaller, this was the original moat—you can see the rough lower parts of the wall. The original floor was 13 feet deeper. The draw-bridge rested upon the stone nubs on the left. When the castle expanded, the moat became this cellar. Halfway up the walls on the entrance side of the room, square holes mark spots where timbers made a storage loft, perhaps filled with grain. In the back, an arch leads to the wine cellar (sometimes blocked off) where finer wine was kept. Part of a soldier's pay was wine...table wine. This wine was kept in a single 180,000-liter stone barrel (that's 47,550 gallons), which generally lasted about 18 months.

The count owned the surrounding farmland. Farmers got to keep

20 percent of their production. Later, in more liberal feudal times, the nobility let them keep 40 percent. Today, the German government leaves the workers with 60 percent...and provides a few more services.

You're free. Climb out, turn right, and leave. For coffee on a great view terrace, visit the Rheinfels Castle Hotel, opposite the entrance (WC at base of steps).

Optional Detour—Into the Mine Tunnels: To protect their castle around 1600, the Rheinfellers cleverly booby-trapped the land just outside their walls by building tunnels topped with thin slate roofs and packed with explosives. By detonating the explosives when under attack, they could kill hundreds of invaders. In 1626, a handful of underground Protestant Germans blew 300 Catholic Spaniards to—they figured—hell. You're welcome to wander through a set of never-blown-up tunnels. But be warned: It's 600 feet long, assuming you make no wrong turns; it's pitch-dark, muddy, and claustrophobic, with confusing dead-ends; and you'll never get higher than a deep crouch. It cannot be done without a light (flashlights available at entrance—see above). At stop #6 of the above tour, follow the stairs on the right leading down *zu den Minengängen* (sign on upper left).

The *Fuchsloch* sign welcomes you to the foxhole. Walk level (take no stairs) past the first steel railing (where you hope to emerge later) to the second steel railing. Climb down. The "highway" in this foxhole is three feet high. The ceiling may be painted with a white line indicating the correct path. Don't venture into the narrower side aisles. These were once filled with the gunpowder. After a small decline, take the second right. At the T-intersection, go right (uphill). After about 10 feet, go left. Take the next right and look for a light at the end of the tunnel. Head up a rocky incline under the narrowest part of the tunnel and you'll emerge at that first steel railing. The stairs on the right lead to freedom. Cross the field, walk under the bigger archway, and continue uphill toward the old wooden bridge. Angle left through two arches (before the bridge) and through the rough entry to the *Verliess* (prison) on the left. Rejoin the tour here at stop #8.

SLEEPING

(country code: 49, area code: 06741)

$$$ **Hotel Montag,** with 28 rooms, is on the castle end of town just across the street from the world's largest free-hanging cuckoo clock. Manfred and Maria Montag and their son Mike speak New Yorkish. Even though the hotel gets a lot of bus tours, it's friendly, laid-back, and comfortable (Sb-€35–45, Db-€70–80, Tb-€90–100, coin-op Internet access-€8/hr, Heer Strasse 128, tel. 06741/1629, fax 06741/2086, hotelmontag@01019freenet.de). Check out their adjacent crafts shop (heavy on beer steins).

$$$ Rheinfels Castle Hotel is the town splurge. Actually part of the castle but an entirely new building, this luxury 57-room place is good for those with money and a car (Db-€130–154 depending on river views and balconies, extra bed €34, elevator, free parking, indoor pool and sauna, dress-up restaurant, Schlossberg 47, tel. 06741/8020, fax 06741/802-802, www.schlosshotel-rheinfels.de, info@burgrheinfels.de).

$$ Hotel am Markt, well-run by Herr and Frau Velich, is rustic with all the modern comforts. It features a hint of antler with a pastel flair, 18 bright rooms, and a good restaurant where the son does the cooking. It's a good value and a stone's throw from the boat dock and train station (S-€35, Sb-€43, standard Db-€59, bigger riverview Db-€69, Tb-€82, Qb-€88, 20 percent cheaper off-season, closed Nov–Feb, Am Markt 1, tel. 06741/1689, fax 06741/1721, www.hotelammarkt1.de, hotel.am.markt@gmx.de). Rental bikes are available to guests (€5/day).

$$ Hotel Hauser, facing the boat dock, is another good deal, warmly run by another Frau Velich. Its 12 rooms sit over a fine restaurant (S-€21.50, D-€45, Db-€50, great Db with Rhine-view balconies-€56, show this book and pay cash to get these prices, Db cheaper off-season, costs more with credit card, small bathrooms, restaurant, Heer Strasse 77, tel. 06741/333, fax 06741/1464, www.hotelhauser.de, hotelhauser@t-online.de).

$$ Hotel zur Post, with creaky parquet floors and 12 forgettable, well-worn rooms, is a reasonable value a block off the riverfront (Sb-€37, Db-€62, a block from the station at Bahnhofstrasse 3, tel. 06741/339, fax 06741/2708, www.hotelzurpost-online.de, zurposthotel@gmx.de, family Bergweiler).

$ Frau Kurz offers St. Goar's best *Zimmer* deal, with a breakfast terrace, garden, fine view, and homemade marmalade (S-€22, D-€36–38, Db-€43, showers-€2.60, more for 1-night stays, no CC, free and easy parking, confirm prices, honor your reservation or call to cancel, Ulmenhof 11, tel. & fax 06741/459, some English spoken). It's a steep five-minute hike from the train station (exit left from station, take immediate left at the yellow phone booth, pass under tracks to paved path, go up stairs and follow zigzag path to Ulmenhof, *Zimmer* is just past tower).

$ St. Goar Hostel, the big beige building under the castle (on road to castle, veer right just after railroad bridge) has a 22:00 curfew (but you can borrow the key) and hearty €6 dinners (S-€15, dorm beds-€12, up to 12 beds per room, includes breakfast, no CC, open all day, check-in preferred 17:00–18:00 & 19:00–20:00, Bismarckweg 17, tel. 06741/388, fax 06741/2689, jh-st-goar@djh-info.de).

EATING

Hotel am Markt serves good traditional meals (with plenty of game and fish) at fair prices (€5–16) with good atmosphere and service. For your Rhine splurge, walk, taxi, or drive up to **Rheinfels Castle Hotel** for its incredible view terrace in an elegant setting (€8–15 dinners, daily 18:30–21:15, reserve a table by the window, see hotel listing above).

TRANSPORTATION CONNECTIONS

Milk-run trains stop at all Rhine towns each hour starting as early as 6:00. Koblenz, Boppard, St. Goar, Bacharach, Bingen, and Mainz are each about 15 minutes apart. From Koblenz to Mainz takes 75 minutes. To get a faster big train, go to Mainz (for points east and south) or Koblenz (for points north, west, and along Mosel). Train info: tel. 01805-996-633.

From Mainz to: Bacharach/St. Goar (hrly, 1 hr), **Cochem** (hrly, 2.5 hrs, change in Koblenz), **Köln** (3/hr, 90 min, change in Koblenz), **Baden-Baden** (hrly, 1.5 hrs), **Munich** (hrly, 4 hrs), **Frankfurt** (3/hr, 45 min), **Frankfurt Airport** (4/hr, 25 min).

From Koblenz to: Köln (4/hr, 1 hr), **Berlin** (2/hr, 5.5 hrs, up to 2 changes), **Frankfurt** (3/hr, 1.5 hrs, 1 change), **Cochem** (2/hr, 50 min), **Trier** (2/hr, 2 hrs), **Brussels** (12/day, 4 hrs, change in Köln), **Amsterdam** (12/day, 4.5 hrs, up to 5 changes).

From Frankfurt to: Bacharach (hrly, 1.5 hrs, change in Mainz; first train to Bacharach departs at 6:00, last train at 20:45), **Koblenz** (hrly, 90 min, changes in Mannheim or Wiesbaden), **Rothenburg** (hrly, 3 hrs, transfers in Würzburg and Steinach), **Würzburg** (hrly, 2 hrs), **Nürnberg** (hrly, 2 hrs), **Munich** (hrly, 4 hrs, 1 change), **Amsterdam** (8/day, 5 hrs, up to 3 changes), **Paris** (9/day, 6.5 hrs, up to 3 changes).

From Bacharach to: Frankfurt Airport (hrly, 1.5 hrs, change in Mainz, first train to Frankfurt airport departs about 5:40, last train 21:30).

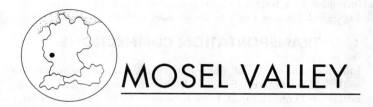

MOSEL VALLEY

The misty Mosel is what some visitors hoped the Rhine would be—peaceful, sleepy, romantic villages slipped between the steep vineyards and the river; fine wine; a sprinkling of castles (Burg Eltz is tops); and lots of friendly *Zimmer*. Boat, train, and car traffic here is a trickle compared to the roaring Rhine. While the swan-speckled Mosel moseys 300 miles from France's Vosges mountains to Koblenz, where it dumps into the Rhine, the most scenic piece of the valley lies between the towns of Bernkastel-Kues and Cochem. I'd savor only this section. Cochem and Trier (see next chapter) are easy day trips from each other (1 hr by train, 55 miles by car). Cochem is the handiest home base unless you want the peace of Beilstein.

Throughout the region on summer weekends and during the fall harvest, wine festivals with oompah bands, dancing, and colorful costumes are powered by good food and wine. You'll find a wine festival in some nearby village any weekend, June through September. The tourist season lasts from April through October. Things close down tight through the winter.

Look for the booklet *The Castles of the Moselle* (€3.80, at local TIs), with information on castles from Koblenz to Trier (including Burg Eltz, Cochem, and Metternich in Beilstein). The booklet not only has historical and structural information, but also some drawings of what the now-ruined castles looked like originally.

Getting around the Mosel Valley

By Train and Bus: The train zips you to Cochem, Bullay, or Trier in a snap. Bullay has bus connections with Zell (nearly hrly, 10 min) and with Beilstein (4/day). Cochem has more frequent bus connections with Beilstein (bus #8060, hrly, less on weekends, 20 min, last bus departs Beilstein about 18:30). A one-way taxi from Cochem to Beilstein costs about €15. Pick up bus schedules at train stations or TIs.

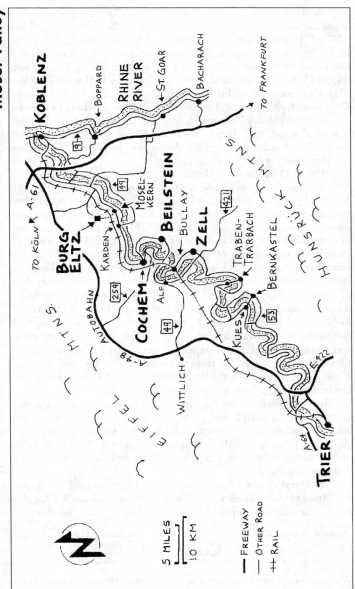

Mosel Valley

KOBLENZ
BOPPARD
RHINE RIVER
ST. GOAR
BACHARACH
TO FRANKFURT

TO KÖLN
A-61
BURG ELTZ
MOSEL-KERN
KARDEN
BEILSTEIN
BULLAY
ZELL
TRABEN-TRARBACH
BERNKASTEL
HUNSRÜCK MTNS.
421

TO KÖLN
AUTOBAHN
259
COCHEM
ALF
49
A-48
WITTLICH
KUES
53
E-422
A-64
TRIER
EIFEL MTNS.
HUNSRÜCK MTNS.

N

5 MILES
10 KM

—— FREEWAY
— OTHER ROAD
++ RAIL

By Boat: Daily departures on the Undine-Kolb Line allow you to cruise the most scenic stretch between Cochem, Beilstein, and Zell (tel. 02673/1515, www.kolb-mosel.de): between **Cochem and Zell** (1–2/day, May–Oct, but none on Fri and Mon May–June, 3 hrs, €14 one-way, €20 round-trip), between **Cochem and Beilstein** (5/day, 1 hr, €8 one-way, €11 round-trip), and between **Zell and Beilstein** (1–2/day May–Oct, but none on Fri and Mon May–June, 2 hrs, €11 one-way, €15 round-trip). You can also take the boat from **Cochem to Karden,** near Burg Eltz (3/day, daily mid-July–mid-Aug; Wed and Sat–Sun only May–mid-July & mid-Aug–Oct, 45 min, €7 one-way, €10 round-trip). To get from Karden to Burg Eltz, choose between a long hike or a taxi ride (see "Getting to Burg Eltz," below).

The K-D (Köln-Düsseldorfer) line sails once a day in each direction, but only between Cochem and Koblenz (mid-June–Sept daily, May–mid-June and most of Oct Fri–Mon only, none in winter, Koblenz to Cochem 9:45–15:00, or Cochem to Koblenz 15:40–20:00, free with consecutive-day Eurailpass or a dated Eurail Flexipass, Eurail Selectpass, or German railpass, uses up a day of a Flexipass, tel. 02671/980-023, www.k-d.com). In early to mid-June, the locks close for 10 days of annual maintenance, and no boats run between Cochem, Koblenz, Beilstein, and Zell. With all the locks, Mosel cruises can be pretty slow.

By Car: The easygoing Mosel Wine Route turns anyone into a relaxed Sunday driver. Pick up a local map at a TI or service station. Koblenz and Trier are linked by two-lane roads that run along both riverbanks. While riverside roads are a delight, the river is very windy and shortcuts overland can save serious time—especially between Burg Eltz and Beilstein (see "Getting to Burg Eltz," below) and from the Mosel to the Rhine (note the Brodenback–Boppard shortcut). Koblenz, Cochem, and Trier have car-rental agencies.

By Bike: Biking along the Mosel is the rage among Germans. You can rent bikes in most Mosel towns (see village listings below). A fine bike path follows the river (with some bits still sharing the road with cars) from Koblenz to Zell. From Cochem, allow an hour to Beilstein and 2.5 hours for the full trip to Zell. Many pedal one way and relax with a return cruise.

By Ferry: About a dozen car-and-passenger ferries *(Fähre)* cross the Mosel between Koblenz and Trier. These are marked AF for auto and PF for pedestrian on the *Moselle Wine Road/Mosellauf* brochure.

Cochem

With a majestic castle and picturesque medieval streets, Cochem is the very touristic hub of this part of the river. For accommodations, see "Sleeping," below.

Tourist Information

The information-packed TI is by the bridge at the main bus stop. Most of the pamphlets (free map with town walk, town history flier) are kept behind the desk—ask. Their thorough 24-hour room listing in the window comes with a free phone connection. The TI also has information on special events, wine-tastings held by local vintners, public transportation to Burg Eltz, area hikes, and the informative €2.60 *Moselle Wine Road (Mosellauf)* brochure. The *Tips and Information from A to Z* brochure (often out of stock) lists everything from car rental agencies to saunas and babysitters (May–Oct Mon–Sat 9:00–17:00, Fri until 18:00, also Sun 10:00–12:00 in July–Oct, off-season closed weekends and at lunch, tel. 02671/60040, www.cochem.de).

Arrival in Cochem

Make a hard right out of the train station (lockers available, €1-2/day, no WC) and walk about 10 minutes to the town center and TI (just past the bus lanes on your left under the bridge).

Drivers can park near the bridge. To get to the main square *(Markt)* and colorful medieval town center, continue under the bridge (€0.30 WC), then angle right and follow Bernstrasse.

Helpful Hints

The Edeka **supermarket** is on Ravenestrasse, a five-minute walk from the TI toward the train station. For **Internet access,** try COCbit-Kommunikation (€5/hr, Mon–Fri 10:00–18:00, Sat 10:00–13:00, closed Sun, on street facing river across from boat ticket booths, Mosel-promenade 7, tel. 02671/211). The only **launderette** in town is across the bridge in a little mall near the youth hostel. Cochem's biggest **wine festival** is held the last weekend in August.

SIGHTS

Cochem Castle—This pointy castle is the work of overly imaginative 19th-century restorers (€4, mid-March–mid-Nov daily 9:00–17:00, closed mid-Nov–mid-Dec & Jan–mid-March, open last half of Dec, 20-min walk from Cochem, follow one of the frequent 40-min German-language tours while reading English explanation sheets or gather 12 English speakers and call a day ahead to schedule an English tour, tel. 02671/255, www.reichsburg-cochem.de). A bus shuttles castle-seekers between the bridge near the TI and the road below the castle (€2 one-way, 2/hr, walk last 10 min uphill to castle).

Town and River Activities—Stroll pleasant paths along the idyllic riverbank, play "life-size chess," or just grab a bench and watch Germany at play.

For great views, you could ride the *Sesselbahn* chairlift (open April–mid-Nov, €4 one-way, €5.50 round-trip, www.cochemer-sesselbahn.de) or **hike** up to the *Aussichtspunkt* (the cross—Pinnerkreuz—on the hill opposite the castle, find trailhead behind train station parking lot).

A little yellow **train** does a sightseeing loop (€2, 2/hour, 30 min).

You can rent **bikes** from the K-D boat kiosk at the dock (€4/4 hrs, €7/full day, May–Oct only) or from Kreutz behind the pumps at the Shell station at Ravenestrasse 42 (Mon–Fri 9:00–18:00, Sat 9:00–13:00, closed Sun, open year-round, €4/4 hrs, €7/full day, includes helmet, no deposit required, just your passport number, tel. 02671/91131). Consider taking a bike on the boat and riding back.

The Tanz Party mit Live Musik **cruise** is popular with German vacationers (€13.40, 20:15–22:30, nightly mid-July–Aug, Tue and Sat May–mid-July, and Tue, Thu, and Sat Sept–Oct, 2-man schmaltzy band, tel. 02671/7387). For Mosel cruises, see "Getting around the Mosel Valley," above.

SLEEPING

$$$ Rustic **Hotel Lohspeicher,** just off the main square on a street with tiny steps, is for those who want a real hotel—high prices—in the thick of things. Its nine high-ceilinged rooms have modern comforts (Sb-€39, Db-€78, about 10 percent higher mid-July–mid-Nov, elevator, breakfast in a fine stone-and-timber room, restaurant, parking-€4.50/day, closed Feb, Obergasse 1, tel. 02671/3976, fax 02671/1772, www.lohspeicher.de, service@lohspeicher.de, Ingo SE).

$$$ **Hotel am Hafen,** across the river, offers views of Cochem (some rooms have balconies; Db-€80–120, €10 extra for 1-night stays, air-con, Uferstrasse 3, tel. 02671/97720, fax 02671/977-227, www.hotel-am-hafen.de, hotel-am-hafen@t-online.de).

$ **Weingut Rademacher** rents six beautiful ground-floor rooms. Wedged between vineyards and train tracks, with a pleasant garden and a big common kitchen, it's a great value. Charming hostess Andrea and her husband Hermann (both SE) give tours of their wine cellar when time permits (earlier is better); guests enter for free. If there's no tour, visitors are welcome to taste the wine (Sb-€26.50, Db on train side-€43, Db on vineyard side-€49, less for 3 nights, family deals, non-smoking, free parking, go right from station on Ravenestrasse, turn right on Pinnerstrasse, walk under tracks and curve right to Pinnerstrasse 10, tel. 02671/4164, fax 02671/91341).

$ **Haus Andreas** has 10 clean, modern rooms at fair prices (Sb-€23, Db-€36–40, Tb-€54, no CC, Schlossstrasse 9, reception is often across the street in shop at #16, tel. 02671/1370 or 02671/5155, fax 02671/1370, Frau Pellny S a little E). From the main square, take

SLEEP CODE

(€1 = about $1.10, country code: 49, area code: 02671)
Sleep Code: **S** = Single, **D** = Double/Twin, **T** = Triple, **Q** = Quad, **b** = bathroom, **s** = shower only, **no CC** = Credit Cards not accepted, **SE** = Speaks English, **NSE** = No English. Unless otherwise noted, credit cards are accepted, English is spoken, and breakfast is included.

To help you sort easily through these listings, I've divided the rooms into three categories based on the price for a standard double room with bath:

   $$$ **Higher Priced**—Most rooms €70 or more.
    $$ **Moderately Priced**—Most rooms between €50–70.
     $ **Lower Priced**—Most rooms €50 or less.

August is very tight, with various festivals and generally inflated prices.

Herrenstrasse; after a block, angle right up the steep hill on Schlossstrasse.

$ Cochem's **hostel,** just opened in 2003, is a huge family-friendly complex with 142 beds, picnic tables, grill pit, playground, game room, bar, restaurant, and a sundeck over the Mosel (dorm bed–€17, Db–€44, more for non-members, includes sheets and breakfast, half- and full-board options available at extra cost, Klottenenstrasse 9, tel. 02671/8633, fax 02671/8568, jh-cochem@djh-info.de).

EATING

Zum Stüffje is a traditional half-timbered *Weinstube* with simple food and veggie options (Wed–Mon 11:30–14:00 & 17:30–21:00, closed Tue, Oberbachstrasse 14, tel. 02671/7260).

    Gaststätte Noss, with fine food served inside or out, is open later than most other restaurants (closed Thu, Moselpromenade 4, tel. 02671/7067).

    Locals go to "Arthur's place," officially named **Alte Gutschänke,** for a glass of wine in a cozy cellar seated at long wooden get-to-know-your-neighbor tables (extensive wine list and basic food, Mon–Fri from 18:00, Sat–Sun from 14:00, open Easter–Oct, closed winter, just up the hill at Schlossstrasse 6, tel. 02671/8950, Arthur SE).

TRANSPORTATION CONNECTIONS

By train to: Koblenz (hrly, 60 min), **Bullay** (near Zell, hrly, 10 min), and **Trier** (hrly, 60 min). Train info: tel. 01805-996-633, Cochem train info: tel. 02671/240. Bus info: tel. 02671/8976.

Burg Eltz

My favorite castle in all of Europe lurks in a mysterious forest. It's been left intact for 700 years and is furnished throughout as it was 500 years ago. Thanks to smart diplomacy and clever marriages, Burg Eltz was never destroyed. (It survived one 5-year siege.) It's been in the Eltz family for 820 years.

Eltz means stream. The first *Burg* on the *Eltz* (castle on the stream) appeared in the 12th century to protect a trade route. By 1472, the castle looked like it does today, with the homes of three big land-lord families gathered around a tiny courtyard within one formidable fortification. Today, the excellent 45-minute tour winds you through two of those homes, while the third remains the fortified quarters of the Eltz family. The elderly countess of Eltz—whose family goes back 33 generations here (you'll see a photo of her family)—enjoys flowers. Each week for 40 years, she's had grand arrangements adorn the public castle rooms.

It was a comfortable castle for its day: 80 rooms made cozy by 40 fireplaces and wall-hanging tapestries. Its 20 toilets were automatically flushed by a rain drain. The delightful chapel is on a lower floor. Even though "no one should live above God," this chapel's placement was acceptable because it fills a bay window—which floods the delicate Gothic space with light. The three families met—working out common problems as if sharing a condo—in the large "conference room." A carved jester and a rose look down on the big table, reminding those who gathered that they were free to discuss anything ("fool's freedom"— jesters could say anything to the king), but nothing discussed could leave the room (the "rose of silence"). In the bedroom, have fun with the sug-gestive decor: the jousting relief carved into the canopy, and the fertile and phallic figures hiding in the lusty green wall paintings.

Near the exit, the €2.50 treasury fills the four higgledy-piggledy floors of a cellar with the precious, eccentric, and historic mementos of this family that once helped elect the Holy Roman Emperor and, later, owned a sizable chunk of Croatia (Hapsburg favors).

Cost, Hours, Information: €6 castle entry, plus €2.50 for treasury, April–Oct daily from 9:30 with the last tour departing at 17:30, closed Nov–March, tel. 02672/950-500, www.burg-eltz.de.

Burg Eltz Area

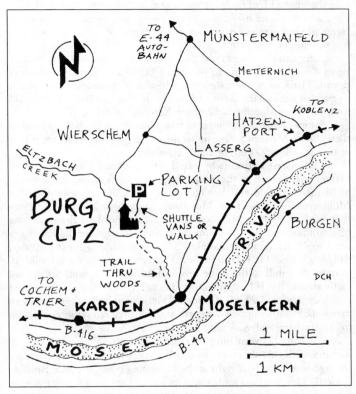

Tours: The only way to see the castle is with a 45-minute tour (included in entry price). German tours go constantly (with helpful English fact sheets, €0.50). Guides speak English and thoughtfully collect English speakers into their own tours—well worth waiting for (never more than 20 minutes). It doesn't hurt to call ahead to see if an English tour is scheduled—or organize your own by corralling 20 English speakers in the inner courtyard, then push the red button on the white porch and politely beg for an English guide.

Getting to Burg Eltz: By **train,** Get off at the Moselkern station midway between Cochem and Koblenz (hrly trains, no lockers at station, but if you ask kindly, clerk will store luggage in office—ring at the window if necessary). Leaving the station, exit right and follow Burg Eltz signs for about 20 minutes up, down, and inland along a residential street (signs are sparse, but have faith and stay on the main road). Then take the marked trail (slippery when wet, slightly steep near end). It's a pleasant 60-minute hike between the station and castle through a pine forest where sparrows carry crossbows, and maidens, disguised as falling leaves, whisper "watch out."

Alternatively, you can **taxi** from Cochem (30 min, €40 one-way for up to 4 people, Cochem taxi tel. 02671/8080) and then enjoy the hike downhill back to the train station in Moselkern. A cheaper taxi option is to train to either Moselkern or Karden, then call a cab from there (15 min, €18 from Moselkern, €23 from Karden, taxi tel. 02672/1407).

A more romantic option is to take a **boat** from Cochem to Karden, then choose between a hike up to the castle (ask boat crew for hiking directions, allow 90 min) or a taxi (see above).

The easiest option is by **car:** From Koblenz, leave the river at Hatzenport following the white Burg Eltz signs through the towns of Münstermaifeld and Wierschem. From Cochem, following the Münstermaifeld signs from Moselkern saves about 10 minutes. (Note that the Eltz signs at Moselkern lead to a trailhead for the hour-long hike to the castle. To drive directly to the castle, ignore the Eltz signs until you reach Münstermaifeld.) The castle parking lot (€1.50/day, daily 9:00–18:00) is 1.25 miles past Wierschem. From the lot, hike 10 minutes downhill to the castle or wait (maximum 10 min) for the red castle shuttle bus (€1.50 one-way). There are three Burg Eltz parking lots; only this lot (1.25 miles south of Wierschem) is close enough for an easy walk. Another option is to park at the Moselkern station (free) and follow the park-and-walk signs (see above).

If driving between Burg Eltz and Beilstein or Zell, you'll save 30 minutes with this **shortcut:** from Eltz, cross the river at Karden, go through town, and bear right at the swimming pool (direction Bruttig-Fankel). This overland route deposits you in Bruttig, a scenic riverside three-mile drive from Beilstein (21 miles from Zell).

Beilstein

Upstream from Cochem is the quaintest of all Mosel towns. Beilstein (BILE-shtine) is Cinderella-land—extremely peaceful except for its territorial swans. Its 180 residents run 30 or so hotels and eateries. Herr Nahlen rents bikes for pleasant riverside rides (ring bell at Bachstrasse 47, €6/day, tel. 02673/1840). Parking is free in any space along the riverside road you can find. For accommodations, see "Sleeping," below.

Beilstein has no real tourist office, but several cafés advertise that they have town info. Buses go about hourly from Beilstein to Cochem (see "Getting around the Mosel Valley," above).

INTRODUCTORY WALK

Explore the narrow lanes, ancient wine cellar, resident swans, and ruined castle by following this short walk.

1. Beilstein's Riverfront: Stand where the village hits the river. In 1963, the big road and the Mosel locks were built, making the river so peaceful today. Before then, access to Beilstein was limited to a tiny one-way lane and the small ferry. The cables that tether the ferry once allowed the motorless craft to go back and forth powered only by the current and an angled rudder. Today, it shuttles people (€1), bikes, and cars constantly from 9:00 to 18:00. The campground across the river is typical of German campgrounds—80 percent of its customers set up their trailers and tents at Easter and use them as summer homes until October, when the regular floods chase them away for the winter. If you stood where you are now through the winter, you'd have cold water up to your crotch five times. Look inland. The Earl of Beilstein—who ruled from his castle above town—built the Altes Zollhaus in 1634 to levy tolls from river traffic. Today, the castle is a ruin, the once-mighty monastery (see the big church high on the left) is down to one monk, and the town's economy is based only on wine and tourists.

Beilstein's tranquility is thanks to Germany's WWI loss. This war cost Germany the region of Alsace (now part of France). Before World War I, the Koblenz–Trier train line—which connects Alsace to Germany—was the busiest in Germany. It tunnels through the grape-laden hill across the river in what was the longest train tunnel in Germany. The construction of a supplemental line destined to follow the riverbank (like the lines that crank up the volume on the Rhine) was stopped in 1914 and, since Alsace went to France in 1918, the plans were scuttled.

Follow Bachstrasse into town. You'll notice blue plaques on the left marking the high-water *(Hochwasser)* points of historic floods.

At the first corner, Furst-Metternich Strasse leads left to the monastery (climb stairs marked the *Klostertreppe*). While its population is down to one Carmelite, Rome maintains an oversized-for-this-little-town church that runs a view restaurant.

Bachstrasse—literally "creek street"—continues straight through Beilstein, covering up the brook that once flowed through town providing a handy disposal service 24/7. Today, Bachstrasse is lined by wine cellars. The only way for a small local vintner to make any decent money these days is to sell his wine directly to customers in inviting little places like these. Your first right leads to the...

2. Market Square: For centuries, neighboring farmers sold their goods on Marktplatz. The *Zehnthaus* (tithe house) was the village IRS, where locals would pay one-tenth *(Zehnte)* of their produce to their landlord (either the Church or the earl). Pop into the Zehnthauskeller.

Packed with peasants' offerings 400 years ago, it's now packed with vaulted medieval ambience. It's fun at night for candlelit wine-tasting, soup and cold cuts, and schmaltzy music (live Fri and Sat). The Bürgerhaus (above the fountain) had nothing to do with medieval fast food. First the village church, then the *Bürger*'s (like a mayor) residence, today it's *the* place for a town party or wedding. Haus Lipmann (on the riverside, now a recommended hotel and restaurant—see "Sleeping," below) dates from 1727. It was built by the earl's family as a residence after the French destroyed his castle. Haus Lipmann's main dining hall was once the knights' hall. The stepped lane leads uphill (past the Zehnthaus, follow signs for Burgruine Metternich) to...

3. Beilstein's Castle: Beilstein once rivaled Cochem as the most powerful town on this part of the Mosel. Its castle (Burg Metternich) is a sorry ruin today, but those who hike up are rewarded with a postcard Mosel view and a chance to hike even higher to the top of its lone surviving tower (€2, daily 9:00–18:00, July-Aug until 19:00, closes earlier off-season, view café/restaurant).

For more exercise and an even better view, continue up behind the castle and follow the road that leads uphill. A hundred yards above the castle (take the left fork), you'll find the ultimate "castle–river bend–carpets of vineyards" photo stop. The derelict roadside vineyard is a sign of recent times—the younger generation is abandoning the family plots, opting out of all that hard winemaking work. A surprising sight—the most evocative Jewish cemetery this side of Prague (*Judenfriedhof*)—is 200 yards farther up the road.

During the 700 years leading up to 1942, Beilstein hosted a Jewish community. As in the rest of Europe, wealthy Jews could buy citizenship and enjoy all the protections afforded to residents. These *Schutzjuden*, or "protected Jews," were shielded from the often crude and brutal "justice" of the Middle Ages. In 1840, 25 percent of Beilstein's 300 inhabitants were Jewish. But no payment could shield this community from Hitler—so there are no Jews in today's Beilstein. (A small Jewish community in Koblenz maintains this lovely cemetery.)

From here, you can return to the castle gate, ring the bell (*Klingel*) and show your ticket to get back in and retrace your steps, or continue on the road, which curves and leads downhill (a gravel path at the next bend on the left leads back into town).

SLEEPING

(country code: 49, area code: 02673)

Between Cochem and Zell, cozier Beilstein is very small and quiet (no train; hourly buses to nearby Cochem, fewer buses on weekends, 15 min; taxi to Cochem-€15). Many hotels shut down from mid-November through March.

$$$ **Hotel Haus Lipmann** is your chance to live in a medieval mansion with hot showers and TVs. A prizewinner for atmosphere, it's been in the Lipmann family for 200 years. The creaky wooden staircase and the elegant dining hall, with long wooden tables surrounded by antlers, chandeliers, and feudal weapons, will get you in the mood for your castle sightseeing, but the riverside terrace may mace your momentum (Sb-€75, Db-€85, no CC, 5 rooms, closed Nov–April, Marktplatz 3, tel. 02673/1573, fax 02673/1521, www.hotel-haus-lipmann.com, hotel.haus.lipmann@t-online.de). The entire Lipmann family—Marion and Jonas, their hardworking son David, and his wife Anja (all SE)—hustles for their guests.

Marion's brother Joachim Lipmann (SE) runs two hotels of his own: The half-timbered, riverfront $$$ **Altes Zollhaus Gästezimmer** packs all the comforts into eight tight, bright, and modern rooms (Sb-€45, Db-€60, deluxe Db-€80, no CC, closed Nov–March, tel. 02673/1850, fax 02673/1287, www.hotel-lipmann.de, lipmann@t-online.de). $$$ **Hotel Am Klosterberg** is a big modern place at the extremely quiet top of town (up the main street 200 yards inland) with 16 comfortable rooms (Db-€60–80, Auf dem Teich 8, same contact info as Altes Zollhaus).

$$ **Hotel Gute Quelle** offers half-timbers, a good restaurant, and 13 comfortable rooms, plus seven in an annex across the street (Sb-€35, D-€52, Db-€60, less for longer stays, closed Dec–March, Marktplatz 34, tel. 02673/1437, fax 02673/1399, www.hotel-gute-quelle.de, helpful Susan speaks Irish).

$ The comfortable **Gasthaus Winzerschenke an der Klostertreppe** is a great value, right in the tiny heart of town (5 rooms, Sb-€26, Db-€44, bigger Db-€54, no CC, discount for 2-night stays, closed Nov–Easter, go up main street and take second left onto Furst-Metternich-Strasse, reception in restaurant, tel. 02673/1354, fax 02673/962-371, www.winzerschenke-beilstein.de, Frau Sausen NSE, her son Christian SE).

EATING

You'll have no problem finding a characteristic dining room or a relaxing riverview terrace. **Restaurant Haus Lipmann** serves good fresh food with daily specials on a glorious leafy riverside terrace (daily 10:00–23:00). The **Zehnthauskeller** on the Marktplatz is *the* place for wine-tasting with soup, cold plates, and lively *Schlager* (kitschy German folk-pop) while old locals on holiday sit under a dark medieval vault (Tue–Sun 11:00–23:00, closed Mon, off-season until 18:00).

Zell

Peaceful, with a fine riverside promenade, a pedestrian bridge over the water, and plenty of *Zimmer*, Zell makes a good overnight stop. Zell has a long pedestrian zone filled with colorful shops, restaurants, and *Weinstuben* (wine bars). A fun oompah folk band plays on weekend evenings on the main square, making evenings here a delight.

The **TI** is on the pedestrian street, four blocks downriver from the pedestrian bridge (Mon–Fri 8:00–12:30 & 13:30–17:00, Sat 10:00–13:00, closed Sun, off-season also closed Sat, tel. 06542/4031, www.zell-mosel .de). The little **Wein und Heimatmuseum** features Mosel history (same building as TI, Wed and Sat 15:00–17:00). For a village **view,** walk up to the medieval wall's gatehouse and through the cemetery to the old munitions tower. Frau Klaus rents **bikes** (€10/day, 1.25 miles out of town, downstream at Hauptstrasse 5, tel. 06542/2589, NSE). Berliner Kaffe-Kännchen offers **Internet access** (2 terminals, €6.80/hr, Mon–Tue and Thu–Fri 8:00–18:30, Sat until 18:00, Sun 14:00–18:00, closed Wed, across pedestrian bridge opposite bus stop at Baldninen Strasse 107, tel. 06542/5450).

Locals know Zell for its Schwarze Katze (Black Cat) wine. Peter Weis (SE) runs the F. J. Weis winery and gives an entertaining and free tour of his 40,000-bottle-per-year **wine cellar.** The clever 20-minute tour starts at 17:00 (call ahead to reserve, open daily April–Nov 10:30–19:00, closed Dec–March but call and they might fit you in for a tasting, tel. 06542/41398); buy a bottle or two to keep this fine tour going. A blue flag marks his *Weinkeller* south of town, 200 yards past the bridge toward Bernkastel, riverside at Notenau 30.

SLEEPING

(country code: 49, area code: 06542)

Zell's hotels are a disappointment, but its private homes are a fine value. The owners speak almost no English and discount their rates if you stay more than one night. They don't take reservations long in advance for one-night stays; just call a day ahead.

Trains go hourly from Cochem or Trier to Bullay, where the bus takes you to little Zell (€1.50, 2/hr, 10 min; bus stop is across street from Bullay train station, check yellow MB schedule for times, last bus at about 19:00). The central Zell stop is called Lindenplatz.

$$$ **Hotel zum Grünen Kranz** is the place if you're looking for room service, a sauna, a pool, and an elevator (32 rooms, Sb-€45–60, Db-€86–120, non-smoking rooms, Balduinstrasse 13, tel. 06542/98610, fax 06542/986-180, www.zum-gruenen-kranz.de). In the annex across the street, they rent 10 immense apartments (prices on request).

$$ Hotel Ratskeller, just off the main square on a pedestrian street, rents 14 sharp rooms with tile flooring and fair rates (Sb-€42, Db-€72, cheaper Nov–mid-April, above a pizzeria, Balduinstrasse 36, tel. 06542/ 98620, fax 06542/986-244, ratskeller-zellmosel@web.de, Gardi SE).

$$ Weinhaus Mayer, a stressed-out old pension, is perfectly central with Mosel-view rooms (12 rooms, Db-€70–72, Balduinstrasse 15, tel. 06542/4530, fax 06542/61160, NSE). They have 16 newly renovated rooms with top comforts, many with riverview balconies, at their *Neues Gästehaus* (Db-€82, no CC, tel. 06542/61169, fax same as above).

$$ Peter Weis Apartments, of the F. J. Weis winery (recommended above), rents two luxurious apartments (Db-€55, less for 2 or more nights, extra person-€7, he'll get breakfast for you-€6, or you can walk to bakery and buy it yourself, 200 yards beyond bridge on Bernkastel road, riverside at Notenau 30, tel. 06542/41398, fax 06542/961-178, f.j.weis@t-online.de).

$ Gasthaus Gertrud Thiesen is classy, with a TV-living-breakfast room and a river view. The Thiesen house has four big, bright rooms and is on the town's first corner overlooking the Mosel from a great terrace (D-€41, no CC, closed Nov–Feb, Balduinstrasse 1, tel. 06542/4453).

$ Weinhaus zum Fröhlichen Weinberg offers four cheap, basic rooms (D-€36, no CC, family *Zimmer*, Mittelstrasse 6, tel. & fax 06542/4308) above a *Weinstube* restaurant (can be noisy, especially weekends; jolly Jürgen SE).

$ Homey Gästehaus am Römerbad, near the church, rents six cheap and sleepable rooms (Sb-€21, Db-€41, no CC, Am Römerbad 5, tel. 06542/41602, Elizabeth Münster SE).

$ Gästezimmer Rosa Mesenich is a little place facing the river (Db-€40, no CC, Brandenburg 48, tel. 06542/4297, NSE).

$ Nearby, the vine-strewn doorway of **Gastehaus Eberhard** leads to gregarious owners, cushy rooms, and potential wine-tastings (Db-€38, no CC, Brandenburg 42, tel. 06542/41216, NSE).

BERLIN

No tour of Germany is complete without a look at its historic and reunited capital, a construction zone called Berlin. Stand over ripped-up tracks and under a canopy of cranes and watch the rebirth of a European capital. Enjoy the thrill of walking over what was the Wall and through Brandenburg Gate.

Berlin has had a tumultuous recent history. After the city was devastated in World War II, it was divided by the Allied powers: The American, British, and French sectors became West Berlin, and the Russian sector, East Berlin. The division was set in stone when the East built the Berlin Wall in 1961. The Berlin Wall lasted 28 years. In 1990, less than a year after the Wall fell, the two Germanys officially became one. When the dust settled, Berliners from both sides of the once-divided city faced the monumental challenge of reunification.

The last decade has taken Berlin through a frenzy of rebuilding. And while there's still plenty of work to be done, a new Berlin is emerging. Berliners joke they don't need to go anywhere, because the city's always changing. Spin a postcard rack to see what's new. A five-year-old guidebook on Berlin covers a different city.

Reunification has had its negative side, and locals are fond of saying "the Wall survives in the minds of some people." Some "Ossies" (impolite slang for Easterners) miss their security. Some "Wessies" miss their easy ride (military deferrals, subsidized rent, and tax breaks). For free spirits, walled-in West Berlin was a citadel of freedom within the East.

The city government has been eager to charge forward with little nostalgia for anything that was Eastern. Big corporations and the national government have moved in, and the dreary swath of land that was the Wall has been transformed. City planners are boldly taking Berlin's reunification and the return of the national government as a good opportunity to make Berlin a great capital once again.

ORIENTATION

(area code: 030)

Berlin is huge, with nearly four million people. But the tourist's Berlin can be broken into four digestible chunks:

1. The area around Bahnhof Zoo and the grand Kurfürstendamm Boulevard, nicknamed "Ku'damm" (transportation, tours, information, hotel, shopping hub).

2. Former downtown East Berlin (Brandenburg Gate, Unter den Linden boulevard, Museum Island (Pergamon), the area around Oranienburger Strasse, and Alexanderplatz).

3. The new city center: Kulturforum museums, Potsdamer Platz, the Jewish Museum, and Wall-related sights.

4. Charlottenburg Palace and museums, on the outskirts of the city.

Planning Your Time

Because of the city's location, try to enter and/or leave by either night train or plane. I'd give Berlin two days and spend them this way:

Day 1: 10:00-Take a guided walking tour (offered by Original Berlin Walks, see "Tours," below). After lunch, take my Do-It-Yourself Orientation Tour (described on page 486), stopping midway to scale the new dome of the Reichstag building, then finishing with a walk through eastern Berlin. End your day at the Pergamon Museum.

Day 2: Spend the morning lost in the painted art of the Gemäldegalerie. After lunch, hike or taxi via Potsdamer Platz to the Topography of Terror exhibit and along the surviving Zimmerstrasse stretch of Wall to the Museum of the Wall at Checkpoint Charlie. With extra time, consider visiting the Jewish Museum.

If you are maximizing your sightseeing, you could squeeze a hop-off, hop-on bus tour into Day 1 and start Day 2 with a visit to the Egyptian and Picasso museums at Charlottenburg. Remember that the Museum of the Wall is open late and most museums are closed on Monday.

Tourist Information

Berlin's TIs are run by a for-profit agency working for the city's big hotels, which colors the information they provide. The main TI is five minutes from the Bahnhof Zoo, in the Europa Center (with Mercedes symbol on top, enter outside to left at Budapester Strasse 45, April–Oct Mon–Sat 8:30–20:30, Sun 10:00–18:30, Nov–March Mon–Sat 10:00–19:00, Sun 10:00–18:00; call toll tel. 0190/016-316 €1/min; tel. from U.S.: 011-49-700/8623-7546, www.berlin-tourism.de). Smaller TIs are in the Brandenburg Gate (daily April–Oct 9:30–19:00, Nov–March 10:00–18:00) and at the bottom of the TV Tower at Alexanderplatz (April–Oct daily 9:00–20:00, Nov–March daily 10:00–18:00).

Berlin Sightseeing Modules

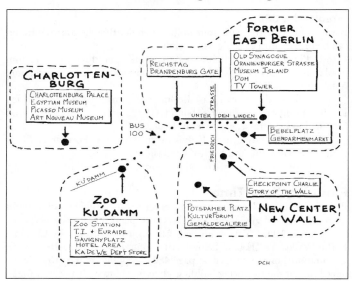

The TIs sell a good city map (€0.50—get it), the *Berlin Programm* (a €1.60 comprehensive German-language monthly that lists upcoming events and museum hours, www.berlin-programm.de), the Museumspass (a.k.a. *Schaulust,* €10, 3-day pass to several museums, including many of the biggies, see "Helpful Hints," below), and the German-English bimonthly *Berlin Calendar* magazine (€1.20, with timely features on Berlin and a partial calendar of events). The TIs also offer a €3 room-finding service (but only to hotels that give them kickbacks—many don't). Most hotels have free city maps.

EurAide's information office, in the Bahnhof Zoo, provides a great service. They have answers to all your questions about Berlin or train travel around Europe. It's staffed by Americans (so communication is simple), and they have a knack for predicting your needs, then publishing free fliers to serve them (Mon–Fri 8:30–12:00 & 13:00–16:30, Sat 8:30–12:00, closed Sun, closed Sat–Sun Oct–March, closed Jan, located in the train station *Reisezentrum,* great opportunity to get future *couchette* reservations nailed down ahead of time, Prague Excursion passes available—see "Transportation Connections" on page 524, www.euraide.de). EurAide also sells all public transit tickets, including the one-day bus/Metro pass (€6.10), the Welcome Card (see "Getting around Berlin" below), and city maps—making a trip to the TI probably unnecessary. To get the most out of EurAide, organize your questions and needs before your visit.

Arrival in Berlin

By Train at Bahnhof Zoo: Berlin's central station is called Bahnhof Zoologischer Garten (because it's near Berlin's famous zoo), or "Zoo" for short (rhymes with "toe"). Coming from Western Europe, you'll probably land at Zoo. It's small, well organized, and handy (lockers and baggage check available in back of station).

Upon arrival by train, orient yourself like this: Inside the station, follow signs to Hardenbergplatz. Step into this busy square filled with city buses, taxis, the transit office, and derelicts. The Original Berlin Walks start from the curb immediately outside the station at the top of the taxi stand (see "Tours," below). Between you and the McDonald's across the street is the stop for bus #100 (departing to the right for the Do-It-Yourself Orientation Tour, described below). Turn right and tiptoe through the riffraff to the eight-lane highway, Hardenbergstrasse. Walk to the median strip and stand with your back to the tracks. Ahead you'll see the black, bombed-out hulk of the Kaiser Wilhelm Memorial Church and the Europa Center (Mercedes symbol spinning on roof), which houses the main TI. Just ahead on the left, amid the traffic, is the BVG transport information kiosk (buy a €6.10 day pass covering the subway and buses, and pick up a free subway map). If you're facing the church, my recommended hotels are behind you to your right.

If you arrive at Berlin's other train stations (trains from most of Eastern Europe arrive at Ostbahnhof), no problem: Ride another train (fastest option) or the S-Bahn or U-Bahn (runs every few min) to Bahnhof Zoo and pretend you arrived here.

By Plane: See "Transportation Connections," page 524.

Getting around Berlin

Berlin's sights spread far and wide. Right from the start, commit yourself to the fine public transit system.

By Subway and Bus: The U-Bahn (*Untergrund-Bahn,* Berlin's subway), S-Bahn (*Schnell-Bahn,* or fast train, mostly above ground and with fewer stops), *Strassenbahn* (streetcars), and all buses are consolidated into one "BVG" system that uses the same tickets. Here are your options:

• Basic ticket *(Einzel Fahrschein)* for two hours of travel on buses or subways (€2.10; *Erwachsener* means adult—anyone 14 or older).

• A day pass *(Tageskarte)* covering zones A and B—the city proper—€6.10, good until 3:00 the morning after. To get out to Potsdam, you need a ticket covering zone C for €6.30. (For longer stays, a 7-day *Tageskarte* is also available—€22, or €28 including zone C; or buy two WelcomeCards, see below.)

• A cheap short-ride ticket *(Kurzstrecke Erwachsener)* for a single short ride of six bus stops or three subway stations, with one transfer (€1.20).

• The Berlin/Potsdam **WelcomeCard** gives you three days of transportation in zones A, B, and C, and those same three days of minor discounts on lots of minor and a few major museums (including Checkpoint Charlie), sightseeing tours (including the recommended Berlin Walks), and music and theater events (€19, valid for an adult and up to 3 kids younger than 14). The WelcomeCard is a good deal for a three-day trip (since three one-day transit cards alone cost only €0.70 less than the WelcomeCard) and worth considering for a two-day trip.

Buy your tickets or cards from machines at U- or S-Bahn stations or at the BVG pavilion in front of Bahnhof Zoo (English instructions). To use the machine, first select the type of ticket you want, then load in the coins or paper. Punch your ticket in a red or yellow clock machine to validate it (or risk a €40 fine). The double-decker buses are a joy (can buy ticket on bus), and the subway is a snap. The S-Bahn (but not U-Bahn) is free with a validated Eurailpass (but it uses a Flexipass day).

Sections of the U- or S-Bahn sometimes close temporarily for repairs. In this situation, a bus route replaces the train (*Ersatzverkehr*, or "replacement transportation").

By Taxi: Taxis are easy to flag down, and taxi stands are common. A typical ride within town costs €5–8, and a cross-town trip (for example, Zoo to Alexanderplatz) will cost you around €14. A local law designed to help people get safely and affordably home from their subway station late at night is handy for tourists any time of day: A short ride of no more than two kilometers (1.25 miles) is a flat €3. (Ask for "*Kurzstrecke, drei euro, bitte.*") To get this cheap price, you must hail a cabbie on the street rather than go to a taxi stand (from a stand, it's a minimum €5 charge). Cabbies aren't crazy about the law, so insist on the price and be sure to keep the ride short.

By Bike: Be careful: In Berlin, motorists don't brake for bikers (and bikers don't brake for pedestrians). Fortunately, some roads and sidewalks have special red-painted bike lanes. Just don't ride on the regular sidewalk—it's *nicht erlaubt* (not allowed—that's *verboten* to you and me).

In western Berlin, you can rent good bikes at the **Bahnhof Zoo** left-luggage counter (in back of station, next to lockers; they come with lock, airpump, and mounted basket, €10/day, €23/3 days, €35/7 days, daily 6:15–21:00, passport required, €50 cash deposit); in the east, go to **Fahrradstation** at Hackesche Höfe (€15/day, Mon–Fri 8:00–20:00, Sat–Sun 10:00–16:00, Rosenthaler Strasse 40, tel. 030/2045-4500).

Helpful Hints

Monday Activities: Most museums are closed on Monday. Save Monday for Berlin Wall sights, the Reichstag building, the Do-It-Yourself Orientation Tour (see below), walking/bus tours, the Jewish Museum, churches, the zoo, or shopping along Kurfürstendamm (Ku'damm) Boulevard or at the Kaufhaus des Westens

(KaDeWe) department store. (When Monday is a holiday—as it is several times a year—museums are open then and closed Tuesday.)

Museums: All **state museums,** including the Pergamon Museum and Gemäldegalerie (plus others as noted in "Sights," below), are free on the first Sunday of each month. There are two different types of discount passes for Berlin's state museums (www.smpk.de, different from the mostly private museums and sights covered by the WelcomeCard—"Getting around Berlin," above). The state museums are covered by a **one-day ticket** (*Tageskarte*, €6, not valid for special exhibitions, purchase at participating museums, not sold at TI). Entry at most of these museums costs €6, so admission to one essentially includes all of the others on the same day. For longer stays, consider the three-day *"Schaulust"* **Museumspass,** which covers most of the state museums as well as several others (including the Jewish Museum). Only €4 more than the day ticket, it's valid for three times as long and is an excellent value if you'll be doing more than two days of museum-hopping (€10, not valid for special exhibitions, purchase at TI or at participating museums). Note that if a museum is closed on one of the days of your Museumspass, you have access to that museum on the fourth day to make up for lost time.

Addresses: Many Berlin streets are numbered with odd and even numbers on the same side of the street, often with no connection to the other side (for example, Ku'damm #212 can be across the street from #14). To save steps, check the white street signs on curb corners; many list the street numbers covered on that side of the block.

Travel Agency: Last Minute Flugbörse can help you find a flight in a hurry (next to TI in Europa Center, tel. 030/2655-1050, www .lastminuteflugboerse.de).

Internet Access: You'll find cheap, fast Internet access at easyInternetnetcafé (daily 24 hrs, Ku'damm 224, 10-min walk from Bahnhof Zoo and near recommended hotels, buy ticket at self-service machines, instructions in English).

Laundry: Schnell und Sauber Waschcenter is a handy launderette near my recommended hotels (daily 6:00–23:00, €5–9 wash and dry, Leibnizstrasse 72, four blocks west of Savignyplatz, near intersection with Kantstrasse).

TOURS

▲▲▲**City Walking Tours**—The Original Berlin Walks offers a variety of worthwhile tours led by enthusiastic guides who are native English speakers. The company, run by Englishman Nick Gay, offers a three-hour **Discover Berlin** introductory walk daily year-round at 10:00 and also at 14:30 from April through October for €12 (€9 if you're under 26 or with WelcomeCard). Just show up at the taxi rank in front of Bahnhof Zoo (or 20 min later in eastern Berlin, at the Kilkenny Irish Pub entrance inside Hackescher Markt S-Bahn station). Their high-quality, high-energy guides also offer other tours: **Infamous Third Reich Sites** (€10, €7.50 with WelcomeCard, at 10:00 May–Sept Wed, Fri, and Sat–Sun; March–April and Oct Sat–Sun only), **Jewish Life in Berlin** (€10, €7.50 with WelcomeCard, Mon at 10:00 May–Sept), and **Potsdam** (€15, €11.20 with WelcomeCard, see "Sights—Near Berlin," below). Many of the Third Reich and Jewish history sights are difficult to pin down without these excellent walks. Also consider their six-hour trip to the **Sachsenhausen** Concentration Camp, intended "to challenge preconceptions," according to Nick (€15, €11.20 with WelcomeCard, at 10:15 May–Sept Tue, Thu, and Sat–Sun; March–April and Oct Tue and Sat; requires transit day ticket with zone C—or buy from guide, call office for tour specifics). Confirm tour schedules at EurAide or by phone with Nick or his wife and partner, Serena (private tours also available, tel. 030/301-9194, www .berlinwalks.com, berlinwalks@snafu.de).

▲**City Bus Tours**—For bus tours, you have two choices:

1. Full-blown, three-hour bus tours. Contact Severin & Kühn (€22, daily 10:00 and 14:00, live guides in 2 languages, from Ku'damm 216, tel. 030/880-4190) or take BVG buses from Ku'damm 18 (€20, 2.5 hrs, leave every 30–60 min daily 10:00–17:00, tel. 030/885-9880).

2. Hop-on, hop-off circle tours. Several companies make a circuit of the city (City-Circle Sightseeing is good, offered by Severin & Kühn). The TI has all the brochures. The tour offers unlimited hop-on, hop-off privileges for its 14-stop route with a good English narration (€18, 10:00–18:00, last bus leaves from Ku-damn at 16:00, 2–4/hr, 2-hr loop, taped commentary). Just hop on where you like and pay the driver. On a sunny day when some double-decker buses go topless, these are a photographer's delight, cruising slowly by just about every top sight in town.

Do-It-Yourself Orientation Tour

Here's an easy ▲▲▲ introduction to Berlin. Half the tour is by bus, the other half is on foot. Berlin's bus #100 (direction Mollstrasse and Prenzlauer Allee) is a sightseer's dream, stopping at Bahnhof Zoo, Europa Center/Hotel Palace, Siegessäule, Reichstag, Brandenburg Gate, Unter den Linden, Pergamon Museum, and ending at Alexanderplatz. If you have the €18 and two hours for a hop-on, hop-off bus tour (described above), take that instead. But this short €2.10 bus ride is a fine city introduction. Buses leave from Hardenbergplatz in front of the Bahnhof Zoo (and nearly next door to the Europa Center TI, in front of Hotel Palace). Buses come every 10 minutes, and single tickets are good for two hours—so take advantage of hop-on-and-off privileges. Climb aboard, stamp your ticket (giving it a time), and grab a seat on top. You could ride the bus all the way, but I'd get out at the Reichstag and walk to Alexanderplatz.

Part 1: By Bus #100 from Bahnhof Zoo to the Reichstag

(This is about a 10-min ride. Note: The upcoming stop will light up on the reader board inside the bus.)

☞ On your left and then straight ahead, before descending into the tunnel, you'll see the bombed-out hulk of the **Kaiser Wilhelm Memorial Church,** with its postwar sister church (described below) and the **Europa Center.** This is the west-end shopping district, a bustling people zone with big department stores nearby. When the Wall came down, East Berliners flocked to this area's department stores (especially KaDeWe, described below). Soon after, the biggest, swankiest new stores were built in the East. Now the West is trying to win those shoppers back by building even bigger and better shopping centers around Europaplatz. Across from the Zoo station, the under-construction Zoofenster tower will be taller than all the buildings you see here.

Emerging from the tunnel, on your immediate right you'll see the Berlin tourist information office.

☞ At the stop in front of Hotel Palace: on the left, the elephant gates mark the entrance to the **Berlin Zoo** and its aquarium (described below).

☞ Driving down Kurfürstenstrasse, you'll pass several Asian restaurants—a reminder that, for most, the best food in Berlin is not German. Turning left, with the huge Tiergarten in the distance ahead, you'll cross a canal and see the famous **Bauhaus Archive** (an off-white, blocky building) on the right. The Bauhaus movement ushered in a new age of modern architecture that emphasized function over beauty, giving rise to the blocky steel-and-glass skyscrapers in big cities around the world. On the left is Berlin's new embassy row. The big turquoise wall marks the communal home of all five Nordic embassies.

☞ The bus enters a 400-acre park called the **Tiergarten,** packed with cycle paths, joggers, and nude sunbathers. The Victory Column (Siegessäule, with the gilded angel, described below) towers above this vast city park that was once a royal hunting grounds, now nicknamed the "green lungs of Berlin."

☞ On the left, a block after leaving the Siegessäule: The 18th-century, late-rococo **Bellevue Palace** is the German White House. Formerly a Nazi VIP guest house, it's now the residence of the federal president (whose power is mostly ceremonial). If the flag's out, he's in.

☞ Driving along the Spree River: This park area was a residential district before World War II. Now, on the left-hand side, it's filled with the buildings of the **new national government.** The huge brick "brown snake" complex was built to house government workers—but it didn't sell—so now its apartments are available to anyone. A Henry Moore

BERLIN AT A GLANCE

▲▲▲**Reichstag** Germany's historic Parliament building, topped with a striking dome you can ascend. **Hours:** Daily 8:00–24:00, last entry 22:00.

▲▲▲**Museum of the Wall at Checkpoint Charlie** Moving museum near the former site of the famous border checkpoint between the American and Soviet sectors, with stories of brave escapes during the Cold War and the gleeful days when the wall fell. **Hours:** Daily 9:00–22:00.

▲▲▲**Gemäldegalerie** Germany's top collection of 13th- through 18th-century European paintings, featuring Dürer, Van Eyck, Rubens, Titian, Raphael, Caravaggio, and more. **Hours:** Tue–Sun 10:00–18:00, Thu until 22:00, closed Mon.

▲▲**Brandenburg Gate** One of Berlin's most famous landmarks, a multi-arched gateway, at the former border of East and West. **Hours:** Always open.

▲▲**Unter den Linden** Leafy boulevard through the heart of former East Berlin, lined with some of the city's top sights. **Hours:** Always open.

▲▲**Pergamon Museum** The only essential museum on Museum Island (just off Unter den Linden), featuring the fantastic second-century B.C. Greek Pergamon Altar. **Hours:** Tue–Sun 10:00–18:00, Thu until 22:00, closed Mon.

▲▲**Berlin Wall** Mostly gone, but parts of the wall are still visible, including the East Side Gallery and a chunk near the Topography of Terror (former SS and Gestapo headquarters). **Hours:** Always open.

▲▲**Jewish Museum Berlin** User-friendly museum celebrating Jewish culture, in a highly conceptual building. **Hours:** Daily 10:00–20:00, Mon until 22:00.

▲▲**Gendarmenmarkt** Inviting square bounded by twin churches, a chocolate shop, and the concert hall. **Hours:** Always open.

▲▲**New Synagogue** Largest prewar synagogue in Berlin, destroyed by Nazis, with a facade that has since been rebuilt. **Hours:** Sun–Thu 10:00–18:00, Fri 10:00–14:00, closed Sat, May-Aug Sun-Mon until 20:00 and Fri until 17:00.

▲▲Egyptian Museum Proud home of the exquisite 3,000-year-old bust of Queen Nefertiti. **Hours:** Tue–Sun 10:00–18:00, closed Mon.

▲Kaiser Wilhelm Memorial Church Evocative destroyed church in the heart of the former West Berlin, with a modern annex. **Hours:** Church open Mon–Sat 10:00–16:00, closed Sun, annex open daily 9:00–19:00.

▲Kurfürstendamm West Berlin's main boulevard (nicknamed Ku'damm), packed with tourists and upscale shops. **Hours:** Always open.

▲Käthe Kollwitz Museum Features the black-and-white art of the local artist who conveyed the suffering of Berlin's stormiest century. **Hours:** Wed–Mon 11:00–18:00, closed Tue.

▲Kaufhaus des Westens (KaDeWe) The "department store of the West"—the biggest on the Continent—where East Berliners flocked when the wall came down. **Hours:** Mon–Fri 9:30–20:00, Sat 9:00–16:00, closed Sun.

▲Potsdamer Platz The Times Square of old Berlin, long a postwar wasteland, now rebuilt with huge glass skyscrapers (can ascend 300-foot-tall Kollhoff tower), an underground train station, and—covered with a huge canopy—the Sony Center mall with eateries. **Hours:** Always open.

▲Music Instruments Museum Impressive collection of historic instruments. **Hours:** Tue–Fri 9:00–17:00, Sat–Sun 10:00–17:00, closed Mon.

▲Berggruen Collection Notable works by Picasso, Matisse, van Gogh, Cézanne, and Paul Klee. **Hours:** Tue–Fri 10:00–18:00, Sat–Sun 11:00–18:00, closed Mon.

▲Bröhan Museum Collection of Art Nouveau and art deco furnishings. **Hours:** Tue–Sun 10:00–18:00, closed Mon.

▲Charlottenburg Palace Skippable Baroque Hohenzollern palace on the edge of town, across street from Egyptian Museum. **Hours:** Tue–Sun 10:00–17:00, closed Mon.

Berlin

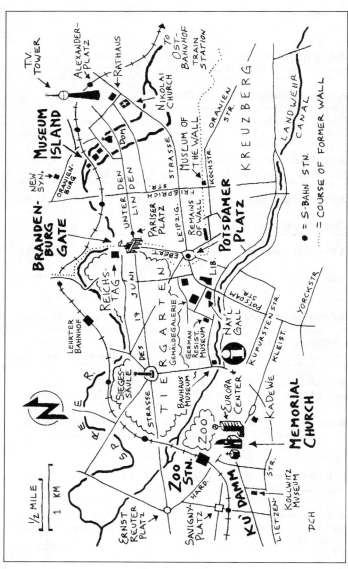

sculpture entitled *Butterfly* floats in front of the slope-roofed House of World Cultures (Berliners have nicknamed this building "the pregnant oyster"). The modern tower (next on left) is a carillon with 68 bells (1987). ☛ While you could continue on bus #100, it's better on foot from here. Leap out at the Platz der Republik. Through the trees on the left you'll see Germany's new and sprawling chancellery. Started during the more imperial rule of Helmut Kohl, it's now considered overly grand. The big park is the Platz der Republik, where the Siegessäule stood until Hitler moved it. The gardens were recently dug up to build underground train tracks to serve Berlin's new main train station (the Lehrter Bahnhof, across the field). Watch your step—excavators found a 250-pound undetonated American bomb.

☛ Just down the street stands the **Reichstag.** As you approach the old building with the new dome, look for the row of slate slabs imbedded in the ground (looks like a fancy slate bicycle rack). This is a memorial to the 96 politicians who were murdered and persecuted because their politics didn't agree with Chancellor Hitler's. Each slab is marked with a name and the party that politician belonged to—mostly KPD (Communists) and SPD (Socialists).

Throughout Berlin, you'll see posters advertising a play called *Ich bin's nicht, Adolf Hitler es gewesen* (It wasn't me, Adolf Hitler did it). The photo is of a model by Hitler's architect Albert Speer of what Berlin was to look like when the Nazis controlled the planet. Hitler planned to rename his capital city "Germania Metropolis." The enormous dome is the Great Hall of the People. Below it and to the right is the tiny Reichstag. Imagine this huge 950-foot-high dome dwarfing everything in Berlin (in the field to your left as you face the Reichstag).

Now visit the Reichstag (open late, no lines in evening) and continue the walk below.

▲▲▲**Reichstag Building**—The Parliament building—the heart of German democracy—has a short but complicated and emotional history. When it was inaugurated in the 1890s, the last emperor, Kaiser Wilhelm, disdainfully called it the "house for chatting." It was from here that the German Republic was proclaimed in 1918. In 1933, this symbol of democracy nearly burned down. While the Nazis blamed a Communist plot, some believe that Hitler himself planned the fire, using it as a handy excuse to frame the Communists and grab power. As World War II drew to a close, Stalin ordered his troops to take the Reichstag from the Nazis by May 1 (the workers' holiday). More than 1,500 Nazis made their last stand here—extending World War II by two days. On April 30, 1945, it fell to the Allies. It was hardly used from 1933 to 1999. For its 101st birthday, in 1995, the Bulgarian-American artist Christo wrapped it in silvery-gold cloth. It was then wrapped again in scaffolding, rebuilt by British architect Lord Norman Foster, and turned into the new parliamentary home of the Bundestag (Germany's lower house). To many Germans, the proud resurrection of the Reichstag—which no longer has a hint of Hitler—symbolizes the end of a terrible chapter in German history.

The **glass cupola** rises 155 feet above the ground, and a double staircase winds 755 feet to the top for a grand view. Inside the dome, a cone of 360 mirrors reflects natural light into the legislative chamber below. Lit from inside at night, this gives Berlin a memorable nightlight. The environmentally friendly cone also helps with air circulation, drawing hot air out of the legislative chamber and pulling in cool air from below.

Hours: Free, daily 8:00–24:00, last entry 22:00, most crowded 10:00–16:00 (wait in line to go up—good street musicians, metal detectors, no big luggage allowed, some hour-long English tours when parliament is not sitting, tel. 030/2273-2152, www.bundestag.de).

Line-Beating Tip: Those with table reservations at the Dachgarten rooftop restaurant don't wait in the long lines. Go straight to the front and tell them you have a reservation. Reserve in advance by phone or e-mail (Dachgarten, €15–26 entrées with a view, daily 9:00–16:30 & 18:30–24:00, tel. 030/2262-9933, kaeferreservierung.berlin@feinkost-kaefer.de).

Self-Guided Tour: As you approach the building, look above the door, surrounded by stone patches from WWII bomb damage, to see the motto and promise: *Dem Deutschen Volke* (to the German people). The open and airy lobby towers 100 feet high with 65-foot-tall colors of the German flag. Glass doors show the **central legislative chamber.** The message: There will be no secrets in government. Look inside. The seats are "Reichstag blue," a lilac-blue color designed by the architect to brighten the otherwise gray interior. The German eagle (a.k.a. the "fat hen") spreads his wings behind the podium. Notice the doors marked "Yes," "No," and "Abstain"...the Bundestag's traditional "sheep jump" way of counting votes (for critical and close votes, all 669 members leave and vote by walking through the door of their choice).

Ride the elevator to the base of the glass **dome.** Take time to study the photos and read the circle of captions—an excellent exhibit telling the Reichstag story. Then study the surrounding architecture: a broken collage of old on new, like Germany's history. Notice the dome's giant and unobtrusive sunscreen that moves as necessary with the sun. Peer down through the skylight to look over the shoulders of the elected representatives at work. For Germans, the best view is down—keeping a close eye on their government.

Start at the ramp nearest the elevator and wind up to the top of the **double ramp.** Take a 360-degree survey of the city as you hike: First, the big park is the **Tiergarten,** the "green lungs" of Berlin. Beyond that is the **Teufelsberg,** or Devil's Hill (built of rubble from the bombed city in the late 1940s and famous during the Cold War as a powerful ear of the West—notice the telecommunications tower on top). Given the violent and tragic history of Berlin, a city blown apart by bombs and covered over by bulldozers, locals say, "You have to be suspicious when you see the nice green park." Find the **Seigessäule,** the Victory Column (moved by Hitler in the 1930s from in front of the Reichstag to its present position in the Tiergarten). Next, scenes of the new Berlin spiral into your view—**Potsdamer Platz,** marked by the conical glass tower that houses Sony's European headquarters. The yellow building to the right is the Berlin Philharmonic Concert Hall. Continue circling left, and find the green chariot atop the **Brandenburg Gate.** A monument to the Gypsy Holocaust will be built between the Reichstag and Brandenburg Gate. (Gypsies, as disdained by the Nazis as the Jews, lost the same percentage of their population to Hitler.) Another Holocaust memorial will be built just south of Brandenburg Gate. Next, you'll see **former East Berlin** and the city's next huge construction zone, with a forest of 300-foot-tall skyscrapers in the works. Notice the TV tower (with the Pope's Revenge—explained below), the Berlin Cathedral's massive dome, the red tower of the city hall, the golden dome of the New Synagogue, and the Reichstag's **roof garden restaurant** (see above). Follow the train tracks in the distance to the left toward a huge construction zone marking the future central Berlin train station, Lehrter Bahnhof. Just in front of it, alone in a field, is the Swiss Embassy. This used to be surrounded by buildings, but now it's the only one left. Complete your spin tour with the blocky **Chancellery,** nicknamed by locals "the washing machine." It may look like a pharaoh's tomb, but it's the office and home of Germany's most powerful person, the chancellor and his team.

Let's continue our walk and cross what was the Berlin Wall. Leaving the Reichstag, turn left around the building. You'll see the Brandenburg Gate ahead on your right.

Part 2: Walking Tour from Brandenburg Gate up Unter den Linden to Alexanderplatz

Allow a comfortable hour for this walk through eastern Berlin, including time for dawdling (but not including museum stops).

▲▲**Brandenburg Gate**—The historic Brandenburg Gate (1791, the last survivor of 14 gates in Berlin's old city wall—this one led to the city of Brandenburg), crowned by a majestic four-horse chariot with the Goddess of Peace at the reins, was the symbol of Prussian Berlin...and later the symbol of a divided Berlin. Napoleon took the statue to the Louvre in Paris in 1806. When the Prussians got it back, she was renamed the Goddess of Victory. The gate sat unused, part of a sad circle dance called the Wall, for more than 25 years. Now postcards all over town show the ecstatic day—November 9, 1989—when the world enjoyed the sight of happy Berliners jamming the gate like flowers on a parade float. Pause a minute and think about struggles for freedom—

past and present. (There's actually a "quiet room" built into the gate for this purpose, daily 11:00–18:00.) Around the gate, look at the information boards with pictures of how much this area changed throughout the 20th century. The latest chapter: The shiny white gate was completely restored in 2002 (financed mostly by Deutsche Telekom). The TI within the gate is open daily (April–Oct 9:30–19:00, Nov–March 10:00–18:00).

▲**Pariser Platz**—From in front of Brandenburg Gate, face Pariser Platz (toward the east). Unter den Linden leads to the TV tower in the distance (the end of this walk). The space used to be filled with important government buildings—all bombed to smithereens. Today, Pariser Platz is unrecognizable as the deserted no-man's-land it became under the Communist regime. Sparkling new banks, embassies (the French Embassy rebuilt where it was before World War II), and a swanky hotel have filled in the void.

Crossing through the gate, look to your right to a construction site—formerly the "death strip." The **U.S. Embassy** once stood here, and a new one will stand in the same spot (due to be completed in 2006). This new embassy has been controversial; for safety's sake, Uncle Sam wanted it away from other buildings, but the Germans preferred it in its original location. A compromise was reached, building the embassy by the gate—but rerouting several major roads to reduce the security risk. The new **Holocaust memorial,** consisting of more than 2,500 gravestone-like pillars, will be completed in 2004 and will stand behind the new embassy.

The **DZ Bank building** (next to the old-new site of the U.S. Embassy) is by Frank Gehry, the unconventional American architect famous for Bilbao's golden Guggenheim, Prague's Dancing House, and Seattle's EMP. Gehry fans might be surprised at the DZ Bank building's low profile. Structures on Pariser Platz are expected to be bland so as not to draw attention away from the Brandenburg Gate. (The glassy facade of the Academy of Arts, next to Gehry's building, is controversial for that very reason.) For your fix of the good old Gehry, step into the lobby and check out its undulating interior.

Brandenburg Gate, the center of old Berlin, sits on a major boulevard, running east–west through Berlin. The western segment, called Strasse des 17. Juni, stretches for four miles from the Siegessäule (past the flea market—see below) to the Olympic Stadium. For our walk, we'll follow this city axis in the opposite direction, east, up what is known as Unter den Linden—into the core of old imperial Berlin and past what was once the palace of the Hohenzollern family who ruled Prussia and then Germany. The palace—the reason for just about all you'll see—is a phantom sight, long gone (though some Berliners hope to rebuild it).

▲▲**Unter den Linden**—This is the heart of former East Berlin. In Berlin's good old days, Unter den Linden was one of Europe's grand

Unter den Linden

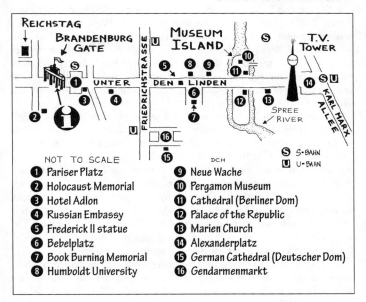

NOT TO SCALE

1 Pariser Platz
2 Holocaust Memorial
3 Hotel Adlon
4 Russian Embassy
5 Frederick II statue
6 Bebelplatz
7 Book Burning Memorial
8 Humboldt University
9 Neue Wache
10 Pergamon Museum
11 Cathedral (Berliner Dom)
12 Palace of the Republic
13 Marien Church
14 Alexanderplatz
15 German Cathedral (Deutscher Dom)
16 Gendarmenmarkt

S S-BAHN
U U-BAHN

boulevards. In the 15th century, this carriageway led from the palace to the hunting grounds (today's big Tiergarten). In the 17th century, Hohenzollern princes and princesses moved in and built their palaces here so they could be near the Prussian emperor.

Named centuries ago for its thousand linden trees, this was the most elegant street of Prussian Berlin before Hitler's time and the main drag of East Berlin after his reign. Hitler replaced the venerable trees—many 250 years old—with Nazi flags. Popular discontent actually drove him to replant linden trees. Today, Unter den Linden is no longer a depressing Cold War cul-de-sac, and its pre-Hitler strolling café ambience is returning.

As you walk toward the giant TV tower, the big building you see jutting out into the street on your right is the **Hotel Adlon.** It hosted such notables as Charlie Chaplin, Albert Einstein, and Greta Garbo. (This was where Garbo said, "I want to be alone," during the filming of *Grand Hotel.*) Destroyed in World War II, the grand Adlon was rebuilt in 1996. See how far you can get inside.

The Unter den Linden S-Bahn station ahead of you is one of Berlin's former **ghost subway stations.** During the Cold War, most underground train tunnels were simply blocked at the border. But a few Western lines looped through the East. To make a little hard Western cash, the Eastern government rented the use of these tracks to the West, but the stations (which happened to be in East Berlin) were strictly off-limits. For 28 years, the stations were unused, as Western trains slowly passed through, seeing only eerie DDR (East German) guards and lots of cobwebs. Literally within days of the fall of the Wall, these stations were reopened, and today they are a time-warp (with dreary old green tiles and original signage). Go down into the station, walk along the track, and exit on the other side, following signs to *Russische Botschaft*...the Russian Embassy.

The **Russian Embassy** was the first big postwar building project in East Berlin. It's built in the powerful, simplified, neoclassical style Stalin liked. While not as important now as it was a few years ago, it's immense as ever. It flies the Russian white, red, and blue. Find the hammer-and-sickle motif decorating the window frames. Continuing past the Aeroflot Airline offices, look across the street to the right to see the back of the **Komische Oper** (comic opera; program and view of ornate interior posted in window). While the exterior is ugly, the fine old theater interior, amazingly missed by WWII bombs, survives. The shop ahead on your right is an amusing mix of antiques, local guide-books, knickknacks, and East Berlin nostalgia souvenirs.

The West lost no time in consuming the East; consequently, some are feeling a wave of nostalgia—*Ost*-algia—for the old days of East Berlin. In recent local elections, nearly half of East Berlin's voters—and 6 percent of West Berliners—voted for the old Communist Party. One symbol of that era has been given a reprieve. As you continue to Friedrichstrasse, look at the DDR–style pedestrian lights, and you'll realize that someone had a sense of humor back then. The perky red and green men—*Ampelmännchen*—were under threat of replacement by the far less jaunty Western signs. Fortunately, the DDR signals will be kept after all.

At **Friedrichstrasse,** look right. Before the war, the Unter den Linden/Friedrichstrasse intersection was the heart of Berlin. In the 1920s, Berlin was famous for its anything-goes love of life. This was the cabaret drag, a springboard to stardom for young and vampy entertain-ers like Marlene Dietrich. (Born in 1901, Dietrich starred in the first German "talkie" and then headed straight to Hollywood.) Today, this boulevard, lined with super department stores (such as Galeries Lafayette, with its cool marble and glass waste-of-space interior, Mon–Fri 9:30–20:00, Sat 9:00–16:00, closed Sun; belly up to its amaz-ing ground floor viewpoint) and big-time hotels (such as the Hilton and Four Seasons), has slowly begun to replace Ku'damm as the grand com-merce and café boulevard of Berlin—though the West is retaliating with some new stores of its own. Across from Galeries Lafayette is American Express (handy for any train ticket needs, Mon–Fri 9:00–19:00, Sat

10:00–13:00, closed Sun, travel agency tel. 030/201-7400, to replace traveler's checks, call 0800/185-3100).

If you continued down Friedrichstrasse, you'd wind up at the Checkpoint Charlie Museum in about 10 minutes (see "Sights—Eastern Berlin," below). But for now, continue along Unter den Linden. You'll notice big, colorful water pipes around here, and throughout Berlin. As long as the city remains a big construction zone, it will be laced with these drainage pipes—key to any building project. Berlin's high water table means any new basement comes with lots of pumping out.

Continue down Unter den Linden a few more blocks, past the large equestrian statue of **Frederick II** ("the Great"), and turn right into the square (Bebelplatz). Stand on the glass window in the center. (Construction of an underground parking lot might prevent you from reaching the glass plate.)

Frederick the Great—who ruled from 1740 to 1786—established Prussia as a military power. This square was the center of the "new Rome" Frederick envisioned. Much of Frederick's palace actually survived World War II but was torn down by the Communists since it symbolized the imperialist past. Now some Berliners want to rebuild the palace, from scratch, exactly as it once was. Other Berliners insist that what's done is done.

Bebelplatz is bounded by great buildings. The German State Opera was bombed in 1941, rebuilt to bolster morale and to celebrate its centennial in 1943, and bombed again in 1945. The former state library is where Lenin studied much of his exile away (climb to the second floor of the library to see a stained glass window depicting his life's work with almost biblical reverence; there's a good café with light food, Tim's Canadian Deli, downstairs). The round Catholic St. Hedwig's Church—nicknamed the "upside-down teacup"—was built to placate the subjects of Catholic lands Frederick added to his empire. (Step inside to see the cheesy DDR government renovation.)

Humboldt University, across Unter den Linden, was one of Europe's greatest. Marx and Lenin (not the brothers or the sisters) studied here as did Grimm (both brothers) and more than two dozen Nobel Prize winners. Einstein—who was Jewish—taught here until taking a spot at Princeton in 1932 (smart guy).

Look down through the glass you're standing on: The room of empty bookshelves is a memorial to the notorious Nazi **book burning.** It was on this square in 1933 that staff and students from the university threw 20,000 newly forbidden books (like Einstein's) into a huge bonfire on the orders of the Nazi propaganda minister Joseph Goebbels.

Continue down Unter den Linden. The next square on your right holds the Opernpalais' restaurants (see "Eating," below). On the university side of Unter den Linden, the Greek temple–like building is the **Neue Wache** (the emperor's New Guardhouse, from 1816). When the

Wall fell, this memorial to the victims of fascism was transformed into a new national memorial. Look inside where a replica of the Käthe Kollwitz statue, *Mother with Her Dead Son*, is surrounded by thought-provoking silence. This marks the tombs of Germany's unknown soldier and the unknown concentration camp victim. The inscription in front reads, "To the victims of war and tyranny." Read the entire statement in English (on wall, right of entrance).

After the Neue Wache, the next building you'll see is the **German History Museum** (Deutsches Historisches Museum im Zeughaus, Thu–Tue 10:00–18:00, Thu until 20:00, closed Wed, tel. 030/203-040, www.dhm.de), but I find its I. M. Pei–designed annex with a spiraling glass staircase more interesting (to find it, go down the street—Hinter dem Giesshaus—to the left of the museum).

Just before the bridge, wander left along the canal through a tiny but colorful arts-and-crafts market (weekends only, a larger flea market is just outside the Pergamon Museum; see below). Canal tour boats leave from here.

Go back out to the main road and cross the bridge to **Museum Island,** home of Germany's first museums and today famous for its Pergamon Museum (see "Sights—Eastern Berlin," below). Eventually, all of the museums on this island will be connected by underground tunnels and consolidate the art collections of East and West Berlin—creating a massive complex intended to rival the Louvre. Today, the museum complex starts with an imposing red neoclassical facade on the left (a musty museum of antiquities; Pergamon is behind it). For 300 years, the square (Lustgarten) has flip-flopped between military parade ground and people-friendly park—depending upon the political tenor of the time. In 1999, it was made into a park again (read history posted in corner opposite church).

The towering church is the 100-year-old **Berlin Cathedral** (Berliner Dom, €4, €5 includes access to dome gallery, Mon–Sat 9:00–20:00, Sun 11:30–18:00, on summer Thu church—but not dome gallery—open until 22:00, www.berliner-dom.de; May–Sept organ concerts offered most Wed,–Fri at 15:00, free with regular admission, for other concerts visit ticket office on Lustgarten side, Mon–Fri 10:00–17:30, closed Sat–Sun, tel. 030/2026-9136). Inside, the great reformers (Luther, Calvin, and company) stand around the brilliantly restored dome like stern saints guarding their theology. Frederick I rests in an ornate tomb (right transept, near entrance to dome). The 270-step climb to the outdoor dome gallery is tough, but offers pleasant, breezy views of the city at the finish line (last entry 30 min before closing, dome closes in bad weather and at 17:00 in winter). The crypt downstairs is not worth a look.

Across the street is the decrepit **Palace of the Republic** (with the copper-tinted windows). A symbol of the Communist days, it was East

Berlin's parliament building and futuristic entertainment complex. Although it officially has a date with the wrecking ball, many Easterners want it saved, and its future is still uncertain.

Before crossing the next bridge (and leaving Museum Island), look right. The pointy twin spires of the 13th-century Nikolai Church mark the center of medieval Berlin. This Nikolai-Viertel (district) was restored by the DDR and was trendy in the last years of socialism. Today, it's dull and, with limited time, not worth a visit. As you cross the bridge, look left in the distance to see the gilded **New Synagogue,** rebuilt after WWII bombing (described below). Across the river to the left of the bridge is the construction site of a new shopping center with a huge aquarium in the center. The elevator will go right through the middle of an undersea world.

Walk toward **Marien Church** (from 1270, interesting but very faded old *Dance of Death* mural inside door) at the base of the TV tower. The big, red-brick building past the trees on the right is the **city hall,** built after the revolution of 1848 and arguably the first democratic building in the city. In the park are grandfatherly statues of Marx and Engels (nicknamed by locals "the old pensioners"). Surrounding them are stainless steel monoliths depicting the struggles of the workers of the world.

The 1,200-foot-tall **Fernsehturm (TV Tower)** offers a fine view from halfway up (€6.50, March–Oct daily 9:00–1:00, Nov–Feb daily 10:00–24:00, tel. 030/242-3333). The tower offers a handy city orientation and an interesting view of the flat, red-roofed sprawl of Berlin—including a peek inside the city's many courtyards *(Höfe)*. Consider a kitschy trip to the observation deck for the view and lunch in its revolving restaurant (reservations smart for dinner, same phone number). Built (with Swedish know-how) in 1969, the tower was meant to show the power of the atheistic state at a time when DDR leaders were having the crosses removed from church domes and spires. But when the sun shined on their tower, the greatest spire in East Berlin, a huge cross, reflected on the mirrored ball. Cynics called it "The Pope's Revenge." East Berliners dubbed the tower "The Big Asparagus." They joked that if it fell over, they'd have an elevator to the West.

Farther east, pass under the train tracks into **Alexanderplatz.** This area—especially the Kaufhof—was the commercial pride and joy of East Berlin. Today, it's still a landmark, with a major U- and S-Bahn station.

For a ride through workaday eastern Berlin, with its Lego-hell apartments (dreary even with their new face-lifts), hop back on bus #100 from here. It loops five minutes to the end of the line and then, after a couple minutes' break, heads on back. (This bus retraces your route, finishing at Bahnhof Zoo.) Consider extending this foray into eastern Berlin to Karl Marx Allee (see "Sights—Eastern Berlin," below).

SIGHTS

Western Berlin

Western travelers still think of Berlin's "West End" as the heart of the city. While it's no longer that, the West End still has the best infrastructure to support your visit and works well as a home base. Here are a few sights within an easy walk of your hotel and the Zoo station.

▲**Kurfürstendamm**—West Berlin's main drag, Kurfürstendamm boulevard (nicknamed "Ku'damm"), starts at Kaiser Wilhelm Memorial Church and does a commercial cancan for two miles. In the 1850s, when Berlin became a wealthy and important capital, her new rich chose Kurfürstendamm as their street. Bismarck made it Berlin's Champs-Elysées. In the 1920s, it became a chic and fashionable drag of cafés and boutiques. During the Third Reich, as home to an international community of diplomats and journalists, it enjoyed more freedom than the rest of Berlin. Throughout the Cold War, economic subsidies from the West made sure that capitalism thrived on Ku'damm. And today, while much of the old charm has been hamburgerized, Ku'damm is still a fine place to feel the pulse of the city and enjoy the elegant shops (around Fasanenstrasse), department stores, and people-watching.

▲**Kaiser Wilhelm Memorial Church (Gedächtniskirche)**—The church was originally a memorial to the first emperor of Germany, who died in 1888. Its bombed-out ruins have been left standing as a memorial to the destruction of Berlin in World War II. Under a fine mosaic ceiling, a small exhibit features interesting photos about the bombing and before-and-after models of the church (free, Mon–Sat 10:00–16:00, closed Sun, www.gedaechtniskirche.com).

After the war, some Berliners wanted to tear the church down and build it anew. Instead, it was decided to keep the ruin as a memorial, and stage a competition to design a modern add-on section. The winning selection—the short, modern building (1961) next to the church—offers a world of 11,000 little blue windows (free, daily 9:00–19:00). The blue glass was given to the church by the French as a reconciliation gift. For more information on both churches, pick up the English booklet (€2.60). The lively square between the churches and the Europa Center (a shiny high-rise shopping center built as a showcase of Western capitalism during the Cold War) usually attracts street musicians.

▲**Käthe Kollwitz Museum**—This local artist (1867–1945), who experienced much of Berlin's stormiest century, conveys some powerful and mostly sad feelings about motherhood, war, and suffering through the black-and-white faces of her art (€5, €1 pamphlet has English explanations of a few major works, Wed–Mon 11:00–18:00, closed Tue, a block off Ku'damm at Fasanenstrasse 24, tel. 030/882-5210, www.kaethe-kollwitz.de).

▲**Kaufhaus des Westens (KaDeWe)**—The "department store of the

Western Berlin

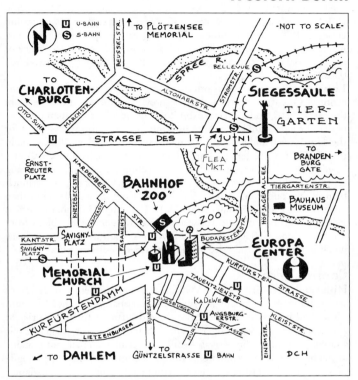

West," with a staff of 2,100 to help you sort through its vast selection of 380,000 items, claims to be the biggest department store on the Continent. You can get everything from a haircut and train ticket (basement) to souvenirs (third floor). The theater and concert box office on the sixth floor charges an 18 percent booking fee, but they know all your options (cash only). The sixth floor is also a world of gourmet taste treats. The biggest selection of deli and exotic food in Germany offers plenty of classy opportunities to sit down and eat. Ride the glass elevator to the seventh floor's glass-domed Winter Garden self-service cafeteria—fun but pricey (Mon–Fri 9:30–20:00, Sat 9:00–16:00, closed Sun, tel. 030/21210, U-Bahn Wittenbergplatz). The Wittenbergplatz U-Bahn station (in front of KaDeWe) is a unique opportunity to see an old-time station. Enjoy its interior.

Berlin Zoo—More than 1,400 different kinds of animals call Berlin's famous zoo home—or so the zookeepers like to think. Germans enjoy seeing the pandas at play (straight in from the entrance). I enjoy seeing the Germans at play (€9 for zoo or world-class aquarium, €14 for both, children half price, daily 9:00–18:30, Nov–Feb until 17:00, aquarium closes at 18:00, feeding times—*Fütterungszeiten*—posted on map just inside entrance, enter near Europa Center in front of Hotel Palace or opposite Bahnhof Zoo on Hardenbergplatz, Budapester Strasse 32, tel. 030/254-010).

Erotic Art Museum—This offers three floors of graphic (mostly 18th-century) Oriental art, a tiny theater showing erotic silent movies from the early 1900s, and a special exhibit on the queen of German pornography, the late Beate Uhse. This amazing woman, a former test pilot for the Third Reich and groundbreaking purveyor of condoms and sex ed in the 1950s, was the female Hugh Hefner of Germany and CEO of a huge chain of porn shops. If you're traveling far and are sightseeing selectively, the sex museums in Amsterdam or Copenhagen are much better. This one, though well described in English, is little more than prints and posters (€5, daily 9:00–24:00, last entry 23:00, hard-to-beat gift shop, at corner of Kantstrasse and Joachimstalerstrasse, a block from Bahnhof Zoo, tel. 030/886-0666). If you just want to see sex, you'll see much more for half the price in a private video booth next door.

Central Berlin

Hitler and the Third Reich—While many come to Berlin to see Hitler sights, these are essentially invisible. The German Resistance Museum (described below) is in German only and difficult for the tourist to appreciate. The Topography of Terror (SS and Gestapo headquarters) is a fascinating exhibit but—again—only in German, and all that remains of the building is its foundation. (Both museums have helpful audioguides in English.) Hitler's bunker is completely gone (near Potsdamer Platz). Your best bet for "Hitler sights" is to take the Infamous Third Reich Sites walking tour offered by Berlin Walks (see "Tours," above). EurAide has a good flier listing and explaining sights related to the Third Reich.

Tiergarten/Siegessäule—Berlin's "Central Park" stretches two miles from Bahnhof Zoo to Brandenburg Gate. Its centerpiece, the Siegessäule (Victory Column), was built to commemorate the Prussian defeat of France in 1870. The pointy-helmeted Germans rubbed it in, decorating the tower with French cannons and paying for it all with francs received as war reparations. The three lower rings commemorate Bismarck's victories. I imagine the statues of Moltke and other German military greats—which lurk in the trees nearby—goose-stepping around the floodlit angel at night. Originally standing at the Reichstag, the immense tower was actually moved to this position by Hitler in 1938 to complement his anticipated victory parades. At the first level, notice how WWII bullets chipped the fine marble columns. Climbing its 285 steps earns you a breathtaking Berlin-wide view and a close-up look at the gilded angel made famous in the U2 video (€2.20, April–Sept Mon–Thu 9:30–18:30, Fri–Sun 9:30–19:00, Oct–March daily 9:30–17:30, closes in the rain, WCs for paying guests only, no elevator, bus #100, 030/8639-8560). From the tower, the grand Strasse des 17. Juni (named for a workers' uprising against the DDR government in the 1950s) leads east to the Brandenburg Gate.

Flea Market—A colorful flea market with great antiques, more than 200 stalls, collector-savvy merchants, and fun German fast-food stands thrives weekends beyond Siegessäule on Strasse des 17 Juni (S-Bahn Tiergarten).

German Resistance Memorial (Gedenkstätte Deutscher Widerstand)— This memorial and museum tells the story of the German resistance to Hitler. The Benderblock was a military headquarters where an ill-fated attempt to assassinate Hitler was plotted (the actual attempt occurred in Rastenburg, eastern Prussia). Stauffenberg and his co-conspirators were shot here in the courtyard. While explanations are in German only, the spirit that haunts the place is multi-lingual (free, Mon–Fri 9:00–18:00, Thu until 20:00, Sat–Sun 10:00–18:00, free and good English audioguide with passport, €3 printed English translation, no crowds, near Kulturforum just south of Tiergarten at Stauffenbergstrasse 13, enter in courtyard, door on left, main exhibit is on third floor, bus #129, tel. 030/2699-5000).

▲**Potsdamer Platz**—The Times Square of Berlin, and possibly the busiest square in Europe before World War II, Potsdamer Platz was cut in two by the Wall and left a deserted no-man's-land for 40 years. This immense commercial/residential/entertainment center (with the European corporate headquarters of Sony and others), sitting on a futuristic transportation hub, was a vision begun in 1991 when it was announced that Berlin would resume its position as capital of Germany. Sony, Daimler-Chrysler, and other huge corporations have turned it once again into a center of Berlin. While most of the complex just feels big (the arcade is like any huge, modern, American mall), the entrance to the complex and Sony Center Platz are worth a visit.

For an overview of the new construction, and a scenic route to Sony Center Platz, go to the east end of Potsdamer Strasse, facing the sky-scrapers (the opposite end from Kulturforum, at main intersection of Potsdamer Strasse/Leipziger Strasse and Ebert Strasse/Stressemanstrasse, U-Bahn: Potsdamer Platz). Find the green hexagonal clock tower with the traffic lights on top. This is a replica of the first automatic **traffic light** in Europe, which once stood at the six-street intersection of Potsdamer Platz. On either side of Potsdamer Strasse, you'll see huge cubical entrances to the brand-new underground Potsdamer Platz train station (due to open in 2005). Near these entrances, notice the **glass cylinders** sticking out of the ground. The mirrors on the tops of the tubes move with the sun to collect the light and send it underground. Now go in one of the train station entrances and follow signs to "Sony Center." (While you're down there, look for the other ends of the big glass tubes.)

You'll come up the escalator into **Sony Center** under a grand canopy. At night, multicolored floodlights play on the underside of this tent. Office workers and tourists eat here by the fountain, enjoying the parade of people. The modern Bavarian Lindenbrau beer hall—the Sony boss wanted a *Bräuhall*—serves good traditional food (big salads, 3-foot-long taster boards of 8 different beers, daily 11:00–24:00, tel. 030/2575-1280). The adjacent Josty Bar is built around a surviving bit of a venerable hotel that was a meeting place for Berlin's rich and famous before the bombs (daily 9:00–1:00, tel. 030/2575-9702). You can browse the futuristic Sony Style Store, visit the Filmhaus (a museum with an exhibit on Marlene Dietrich), and do some surfing at Web Free TV (on the street).

Across Potsdamer Strasse, you can ride what's billed as "the fastest elevator in Europe" to skyscraping rooftop **views.** You'll travel at nearly 30 feet per second to the top of the 300-foot-tall Kollhoff tower (€3.50, Tue–Sun 11:00–20:00, closed Mon, in red brick building at Potsdamer Platz 1, tel. 030/2529-4372, www.panoramapunkt.de).

Kulturforum, in Central Berlin

Just west of Potsdamer Platz, with several top museums and Berlin's concert hall, is the city's cultural heart (admission to all sights covered by €6 day card or 3-day *Schaulust* Museumspass, free on first Sun of month). Of its sprawling museums, only the Gemäldegalerie is a must. The tourist info telephone number for all Kulturforum museums is 030/266-2951. To reach the Kulturforum, take the S- or U-Bahn to Potsdamer Platz, then walk along Potsdamer Platz and Potsdamer Strasse. From the Zoo station, you can also take bus #200 to Philharmonie. Across Potsdamer Strasse from the Kulturforum is the huge National Library (free English periodicals).

▲▲▲Gemäldegalerie—Germany's top collection of 13th- through 18th-century European paintings (more than 1,400 canvases) is beautifully displayed in a building that is a work of art in itself. Follow the excellent free audioguide. The North Wing starts with German paintings of the 13th to 16th centuries, including eight by Dürer. Then come the Dutch and Flemish—Jan Van Eyck, Brueghel, Rubens, Van Dyck, Hals, and Vermeer. The wing finishes with German, English, and French 18th-century art, such as Gainsborough and Watteau. An octagonal hall at the end features a fine stash of Rembrandts. The South Wing is saved for the Italians—Giotto, Botticelli, Titian, Raphael, and Caravaggio (€6, Tue–Sun 10:00–18:00, Thu until 22:00, closed Mon, clever little loaner stools, great salad bar in cafeteria upstairs, Matthäikirchplatz 4).

New National Gallery (Neue Nationalgalerie)—This features 20th-century art, with ever-changing special exhibits (€6, Tue–Fri 10:00–18:00, Thu until 22:00, Sat–Sun 11:00–18:00, closed Mon, café downstairs).

Museum of Arts and Crafts (Kunstgewerbemuseum)—Wander through a thousand years of applied arts—porcelain, fine *Jugendstil* (art nouveau) furniture, Art Deco, and reliquaries. There are no crowds and no English descriptions (€3, Tue–Fri 10:00–18:00, Sat–Sun 11:00–18:00, closed Mon).

▲**Musical Instruments Museum**—This impressive hall is filled with 600 exhibits from the 16th century to modern times. Wander among old keyboard instruments and funny-looking tubas. There's no English, aside from a €0.10 info sheet, but it's fascinating if you're into pianos (€3, Tue–Fri 9:00–17:00, Sat–Sun 10:00–17:00, closed Mon, the low-profile white building east of the big, yellow Philharmonic Concert Hall, tel. 030/254-810).

Poke into the lobby of Berlin's Philharmonic Concert Hall and see if there are tickets available during your stay (ticket office open Mon–Fri 15:00–18:00, Sat–Sun 11:00–14:00, must purchase tickets in person, box office tel. 030/2548-8132).

Eastern Berlin

▲▲**Pergamon Museum**—Of the museums on Museumsinsel (Museum Island), just off Unter den Linden, only the Pergamon is essential. Its highlight is the fantastic Pergamon Altar. From a second-century B.C. Greek temple, it shows the Greeks under Zeus and Athena beating the giants in a dramatic pig pile of mythological mayhem. Check out the action spilling onto the stairs. The Babylonian Ishtar Gate (glazed blue tiles from sixth century B.C.) and many ancient Greek and Mesopotamian treasures are also impressive (€6, covered by Museums-pass, Tue–Sun 10:00–18:00, Thu until 22:00, closed Mon, free on first Sun of month, courtyard café, behind Museum Island's red stone museum of antiquities, Am Kupfergraben, tel. for all sights on Museum Island: 030/2090-5577 or 030/209-050). The excellent audioguide (free with admission) covers the museum's highlights. Don't mind the scaffolding. Renovation projects (due to last until 2008) may cause small sections of the museum to close temporarily in 2004, but the museum will remain open.

Old National Gallery—Also on Museum Island, this gallery shows 19th-century German Romantic art: man against nature, Greek ruins dwarfed in enchanted forests, medieval churches, and powerful mountains (€6, covered by Museumspass, Tue–Sun 10:00–18:00, Thu until 22:00, closed Mon, free on first Sun of month, tel. 030/2090-5801).

▲▲**The Berlin Wall**—The 100-mile "Anti-Fascist Protective Rampart," as it was called by the East German government, was erected almost overnight in 1961 to stop the outward flow of people (3 million leaked

Eastern Berlin

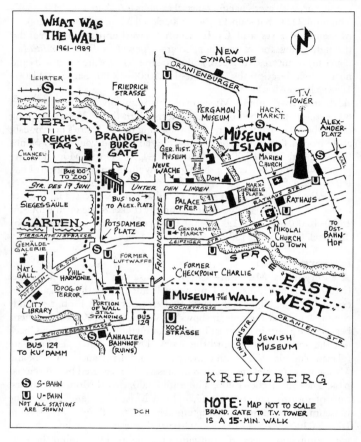

out between 1949 and 1961). The 13-foot-high Wall *(Mauer)* had a 16-foot tank ditch, a no-man's-land that was 30 to 160 feet wide, and 300 sentry towers. During its 28 years, there were 1,693 cases when border guards fired, 3,221 arrests, and 5,043 documented successful escapes (565 of these were East German guards). The carnival atmosphere of those first years after the Wall fell is gone, but hawkers still sell "authentic" pieces of the Wall, DDR (East German) flags, and military paraphernalia to gawking tourists. Pick up the free brochure *Berlin: The Wall,* available at EurAide or the TI, which traces the history of the Wall and helps you find the remaining chunks and other Wall-related sights in Berlin. You can also rent a *Here We Go* audioguide about the Wall, which starts at Checkpoint Charlie, guides you along Zimmerstrasse to Potsdamer Platz, and then brings you back via Leipziger Strasse and Mauerstrasse (€5, 80 min).

▲▲▲**Museum of the Wall at Checkpoint Charlie (Mauermuseum Haus am Checkpoint Charlie)**—While the famous border checkpoint between the American and Soviet sectors is long gone, its memory is preserved by one of Europe's most interesting museums: The House at Checkpoint Charlie. During the Cold War, it stood defiantly—spitting distance from the border guards—showing off all the clever escapes over, under, and through the Wall.

Today, while the drama is over and hunks of the Wall stand like victory scalps at its door, the museum still tells a gripping history of the Wall, recounts the many ingenious escape attempts (early years with a cruder wall saw more escapes), and includes plenty of video and film coverage of those heady days when people-power tore down the Wall (€7.50, assemble 10 tourists and get in for €4.50 each, €3 audioguide, discount with WelcomeCard but not covered by Museumspass, cash only, daily 9:00–22:00, U-6 to Kochstrasse or—better from Zoo—line 2 to Stadtmitte, Friedrichstrasse 43–45, tel. 030/253-7250, www.mauermuseum.de). If you're pressed for time, this is a good after-dinner sight.

Americans—the Cold War victors—have the biggest appetite for Wall-related sights. Where the gate once stood, notice the thought-provoking post with larger-than-life posters of a young American soldier facing east and a young Russian soldier facing west. Around you are reconstructions of the old checkpoint. It's not named for a person, but for Number Three—as in Alpha (at the East–West German border, a hundred miles west of here), Bravo (as you enter Berlin proper), and Charlie (the most famous because it was the only place where foreigners could pass). A few yards away (on Zimmerstrasse), a glass panel describes the former checkpoint. From there, a double row of cobbles in Zimmerstrasse marks where the Wall once stood (these innocuous cobbles run throughout the city, tracing the former Wall's path). Follow it one very long block to Wilhelmstrasse and a surviving stretch of Wall.

When it fell, the Wall was literally carried away by the euphoria. What did manage to survive has been nearly devoured by a decade of persistent "Wall peckers." The park behind the Zimmerstrasse/ Wilhelmstrasse bit of Wall marks the site of the command center of Hitler's Gestapo and SS (explained by English plaques throughout). It's been left undeveloped as a memorial to the tyranny once headquartered here. In the park is...

The Topography of Terror—Because of the horrible things planned here, rubble of the Gestapo and SS buildings will always be left as rubble. The SS, Hitler's personal bodyguards, grew to become a state-within-a-state, with its talons in every corner of German society. Along an excavated foundation of the building, an exhibit tells the story of

National Socialism and its victims in Berlin (free, info booth open May–Sept daily 10:00–20:00, Oct–April daily 10:00–18:00 or until dark, free English audioguide with your passport as a deposit, tel. 030/2548-6703).

Across the street (facing the Wall) is the German Finance Ministry (Bundesministerium der Finanzen). Formerly the headquarters of the Nazi air force, this is the only major Hitler-era government building that survived the war's bombs. The Communists used it to house their—no joke—Ministry of Ministries. Walk up Wilhelmstrasse (to the north) to see an entry gate (on your left) that looks much like it did when Germany occupied nearly all of Europe. On the north side of the building (farther up Wilhelmstrasse, at corner with Leipziger Strasse) is a wonderful example of Communist art. The mural (from the 1950s) is classic Social Realism, showing the entire society—industrial laborers, farmworkers, women, and children—all happily singing the same patriotic song. This was the Communist ideal. For the reality, look at the ground in the courtyard in front of the mural to see an enlarged photograph from a 1953 uprising here against the Communists—quite a contrast.

▲▲Jewish Museum Berlin—This new museum is one of Europe's best Jewish sights. The highly conceptual building is a sight in itself, and the museum inside—an overview of the rich culture and history of Europe's Jewish community—is excellent. The Holocaust is appropriately remembered, but it doesn't overwhelm this celebration of Jewish life.

Designed by the American architect Daniel Libeskind, the zinc-walled building's zigzag shape is pierced by voids symbolic of the irreplaceable cultural loss caused by the Holocaust. Enter the museum through the 18th-century Baroque building next door, then go through an underground tunnel to reach the main exhibit. While underground, you can follow the Axis of Exile to a disorienting slanted garden with 49 pillars, or to the Axis of Holocaust, an eerily empty tower shut off from the outside world.

When you emerge from underground, climb the stairs to the engaging, thought-provoking, and accessible museum. There are many interactive exhibits (spell your name in Hebrew) and pieces of artwork (the *Fallen Leaves* sculpture in the building's largest void is especially powerful), and it's all very kid-friendly (peel the giant garlic and climb through a pomegranate tree). English explanations interpret both the exhibits and the design of the very symbolic building. The museum is in a nondescript residential neighborhood a 10-minute walk from the Checkpoint Charlie museum, but it's well worth the trip (€5, covered by Museumspass, discount with WelcomeCard, daily 10:00–20:00, Mon until 22:00, closed on Jewish holidays, tight security includes bag check and metal detectors, U-Bahn line 1, 6, or 15 to Hallesches Tor, take exit marked Jüdisches Museum, exit straight ahead, then turn right on

Franz-Klühs-Strasse, museum is 5 min ahead on your left at Linden-strasse 9, tel. 030/2599-3300, www.jmberlin.de). The museum has a good café/restaurant (lunch 12:00–16:00, daily special-€9, snacks at other times, tel. 030/2593-9760).

East Side Gallery—The biggest remaining stretch of the Wall is now "the world's longest outdoor art gallery." It stretches for nearly a mile and is covered with murals painted by artists from around the world. The murals are routinely whitewashed, so new ones can be painted. This length of the Wall makes a poignant walk. For a quick look, just go to Ostbahnhof station and look around (exit towards river and turn left on Mühlenstrasse; the freshest and most colorful art is at this end). The gallery only survives until a land ownership dispute can be solved, when it will likely be developed like the rest of the city. (Given the recent history, imagine the complexity of finding rightful owners of all this suddenly very-valuable land.) If you walk the entire length, you'll find a small Wall souvenir shop at the end (they'll stamp your passport with the former East German stamp) and a bridge crossing the river to a subway station at Schlesisches Tor (in Kreuzberg).

Kreuzberg—This district—once abutting the dreary Wall and inhabited mostly by poor Turkish guest laborers and their families—is still run-down, with graffiti-riddled buildings and plenty of student and Turkish street life. It offers a gritty look at melting-pot Berlin in a city where original Berliners are as rare as old buildings. Berlin is the fourth-largest Turkish city in the world, and Kreuzberg is its "downtown." But to call it a "little Istanbul" insults the big one. You'll see *döner kebab* stands, shops decorated with spray paint, and mothers wearing scarves. For a dose of Kreuzberg without getting your fingers dirty, joyride on bus #129 (catch it near Jewish Museum). For a colorful stroll, take U-Bahn to Kottbusser Tor and wander—ideally on Tuesday and Friday between 12:00 and 18:00, when the Turkish Market sprawls along the bank of the Maybachufer Canal.

▲▲**Gendarmenmarkt**—This delightful and historic square is bounded by twin churches, a tasty chocolate shop, and the concert hall (designed by Schinkel, the man who put the neoclassical stamp on Berlin and Dresden) for the Berlin symphony. In summer, it hosts a few outdoor cafés, *Biergartens,* and sometimes concerts. The name of the square—part French and part German—reminds us that in the 17th century, a fifth of all Berliners were French émigrés, Protestant Huguenots fleeing Catholic France. Back then, tolerant Berlin was a magnet for the persecuted. The émigrés vitalized the city with new ideas and know-how.

The Deutscher Dom (German Cathedral, described below) has a history exhibit worthwhile for history buffs. The Franzosischer Dom (French Cathedral) offers a humble museum on the Huguenots (€1.50, Tue–Sun 12:00–17:00, closed Mon) and a chance to climb 254 steps to the top for a grand city view (€1.50, daily 9:00–19:00).

Fassbender & Rausch, on the corner near the Deutscher Dom, is Europe's biggest **chocolate store.** After 150 years of chocolate-making, this family-owned business proudly displays its sweet delights—250 different kinds—on a 55-foot-long buffet. Truffles are sold for about €0.50 each. The shop's evangelical Herr Ostwald (a.k.a. Benny) would love you to try his best-seller: tiramisu (Mon–Fri 10:00–20:00, Sat 10:00–16:00, closed Sun, corner of Mohrenstrasse at Charlottenstrasse 60, tel. 030/2045-8440).

German Cathedral—The Deutscher Dom houses the thought-provoking "Milestones, Setbacks, Sidetracks" (Wege, Irrwege, Umwege) exhibit, which traces the history of the German parliamentary system. The exhibit is well done and more interesting than it sounds. There are no English descriptions, but you can follow a fine and free 90-minute-long audioguide (passport required for deposit; to start, follow the blue arrows downstairs) or buy the detailed €10 guidebook (free, June–Aug Tue–Sun 10:00–19:00, Tue until 22:00, closed Mon, Sept–May Tue–Sun 10:00–18:00, Tue until 22:00, closed Mon, on Gendarmenmarkt just off Friedrichstrasse, tel. 030/2273-0431).

▲▲**New Synagogue**—A shiny gilded dome marks the New Synagogue, now a museum and cultural center on Oranienburger Strasse. Only the dome and facade have been restored, and a window overlooks a vacant field marking what used to be the synagogue. The largest and finest synagogue in Berlin before World War II, it was desecrated by Nazis on Crystal Night in 1938, bombed in 1943, and partially rebuilt in 1990. Inside, past tight security, there's a small but moving exhibit on the Berlin Jewish community through the centuries with some good English descriptions (ground floor and first floor). On its facade, the *Vergesst es nie* message—added by East Berlin Jews in 1966—means "Never forget." East Berlin had only a few hundred Jews, but now that the city is united, the Jewish community numbers about 12,000 (€3, Sun–Thu 10:00–18:00, Fri 10:00–14:00, closed Sat, May–Aug Sun–Mon until 20:00 and Fri until 17:00, last entry 30 min before closing, U-Bahn Oranienburger Tor, Oranienburger Strasse 28/30, tel. 030/8802-8300, www.cjudaicum.de).

Oren, a popular near-kosher café, is next to the synagogue (see "Eating in Eastern Berlin," below). If you're heading for the Pergamon Museum next, take a shortcut by turning left after leaving the synagogue, then right on Monbijoustrasse. Cross the canal and turn left to the museum.

A block from the synagogue, walk 50 yards down Grosse Hamburger Strasse to a little park. This street was known for 200 years as the "street of tolerance" because the Jewish community donated land to Protestants so that they could build a church. Hitler turned it into the "street of death" *(Todes Strasse),* bulldozing 12,000 graves of the city's oldest Jewish cemetery and turning a Jewish old-folks home into a deportation center. Note the two memorials—one erected by the former East Berlin government and one built later by the city's unified government. Somewhere nearby, a plainclothes police officer keeps watch over this park.

▲**Oranienburger Strasse**—Berlin is developing so fast, it's impossible to predict what will be "in" next year. The area around Oranienburger Strasse is definitely trendy (but is being challenged by hip Friedrichshain, farther east).

While the area immediately around the synagogue is dull, 100 yards away things get colorful. The streets behind Grosse Hamburger Strasse flicker with atmospheric cafés, *Kneipen* (pubs), and art galleries.

At night, techno-prostitutes line Oranienburger Strasse. Prostitution is legal here, but there's a big debate about taxation. Since they don't get unemployment insurance, why should they pay taxes?

A block in front of the Hackescher Markt S-Bahn station is **Hackesche Höfe**—with eight courtyards bunny-hopping through a wonderfully restored 1907 *Jugendstil* building. It's full of trendy restaurants, theaters, and cinema (playing movies in their original languages). This is a fine example of how to make huge city blocks livable— Berlin's apartments are organized around courtyard after courtyard off the main roads.

Natural History Museum (Museum für Naturkunde)—This place is worth a visit just to see the largest dinosaur skeleton ever assembled. While you're there, meet "Bobby" the stuffed ape (€3.50, Tue–Fri 9:30–17:00, Sat–Sun 10:00–18:00, closed Mon, last entry 30 min before closing, U-Bahn line 6 to Zinnowitzer Strasse, Invalidenstrasse 43, tel. 030/2093-8591).

Around Charlottenburg Palace

The Charlottenburg district—with a cluster of fine museums across the street from a grand palace—makes a good side-trip from downtown. Ride U-2 to Sophie-Charlotte Platz and walk 10 minutes up the tree-lined boulevard Schlossstrasse (following signs to *Schloss)*, or—much faster—catch bus #145 (direction Spandau) direct from Bahnhof Zoo.

For a Charlottenburg lunch, the **Luisen Bräu** is a comfortable brewpub restaurant with a copper and woody atmosphere, good local "microbeers" (*dunkles* are dark, *helles* light), and traditional German grub (€5–8 meals, daily 9:00–24:00, fun for groups, across from palace at Luisenplatz 1, tel. 030/341-9388).

▲**Charlottenburg Palace (Schloss)**—If you've seen the great palaces of Europe, this Baroque Hohenzollern palace comes in at about number 10 (behind Potsdam, too). It's even more disappointing since the main rooms can be toured only with a German guide (€8 includes 50-min tour, €2 to see just upper floors without tour, €7 to see palace grounds

Charlottenburg Palace Area

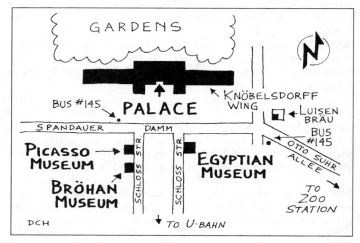

excluding tour areas, last tour 1 hr before closing, cash only, Tue–Sun 10:00–17:00, closed Mon, tel. 030/320-911).

The **Knöbelsdorff Wing** features a few royal apartments. Go upstairs and take a substantial hike through restored-since-the-war, gold-crusted white rooms (€5 depending on special exhibitions, free English audioguide, Tue–Fri 10:00–18:00, Sat–Sun 11:00–18:00, closed Mon, last entry 30 min before closing, when facing the palace walk toward the right wing, tel. 030/3209-1202).

▲▲**Egyptian Museum**—Across the street from the palace, the Egyptian Museum offers one of the great thrills in art appreciation—gazing into the still-young and beautiful face of 3,000-year-old Queen Nefertiti, the wife of King Akhenaton (€6, covered by Museumspass, Tue–Sun 10:00–18:00, closed Mon, free on first Sun of month, free English audioguide, Schlossstrasse 70, tel. 030/343-5730).

This bust of Queen Nefertiti, from 1340 B.C., is perhaps the most famous piece of Egyptian art in Europe. Discovered in 1912, it shows the Marilyn Monroe of the early 20th century, with all the right beauty marks: long neck, symmetrical face, and just the right makeup (she's called "Berlin's most beautiful woman"). The bust never left its studio, but served as a master model for all other portraits of the queen. (That's probably why the left eye was never inlaid.) Buried for over 3,000 years, she was found by a German team who, by agreement with the Egyptian government, got to take home any workshop models they found. Although this bust is not representative of Egyptian art, it has become a symbol for Egyptian art by popular acclaim. Don't overlook the rest of the impressive museum, wonderfully lit and displayed, but with little English aside from the audioguide.

The Egyptian section of the 19th-century Royal Prussian Museum was originally in the Neues Museum on Museum Island. After World War II, the collection was divided between East and West. Plans are in the works to reunite the collection in its original Museum Island building, the Bodesmuseum, which is currently under renovation (due to be completed in 2010).

▲**Berggruen Collection: Picasso and His Time**—This tidy little museum is a pleasant surprise. Climb three floors through a fun and substantial collection of Picasso. Along the way, you'll see plenty of notable work by Matisse, van Gogh, and Cézanne. Enjoy a great chance to meet Paul Klee (€6, covered by Museumspass, Tue–Fri 10:00–18:00, Sat–Sun 11:00–18:00, closed Mon, free the first Sun of month, Schlossstrasse 1, tel. 030/3269-580).

▲**Bröhan Museum**—Wander through a dozen beautifully furnished art nouveau *(Jugendstil)* and art deco living rooms, a curvy organic world of lamps, glass, silver, and posters. English descriptions are posted on the wall of each room on the main floor. While you're there, look for the fine collection of Impressionist paintings by Karl Hagemeister (€4–6 depending on special exhibits, covered by Museumspass excluding special exhibits, Tue–Sun 10:00–18:00, closed Mon, Schlossstrasse 1A, tel. 030/3269-0600, www.broehan-museum.de).

Near Berlin

▲**Sanssouci Palace, New Palace, and Park, Potsdam**—With a lush park strewn with the extravagant whimsies of Frederick the Great, the sleepy town of Potsdam has long been Berlin's holiday retreat. Frederick's super-rococo Sanssouci Palace is one of Germany's most dazzling. His equally extravagant New Palace (Neues Palais), built to disprove rumors that Prussia was running out of money after the costly Seven Years' War, is on the other side of the park (it's a 30-min walk between palaces).

Your best bet for seeing Sanssouci Palace is to take the Potsdam TI's walking tour (see below). Otherwise, to make sense of all the ticket and tour options for the two palaces, stop by the palaces' TI (TI is across the street from windmill near Sanssouci entrance, helpful English-speaking staff, tel. 0331/969-4202).

Sanssouci Palace: Even though *sans souci* means "without a care," it can be a challenge for an English speaker to have an enjoyable visit. The palaces of Vienna, Munich, and even Würzburg offer equal sightseeing thrills with far fewer headaches. While the grounds are impressive, the interior of Sanssouci Palace can be visited only by a one-hour tour in German (with a borrowed English text), and these tours get booked up quickly. The only English option is the Potsdam TI's tour (see below).

Greater Berlin

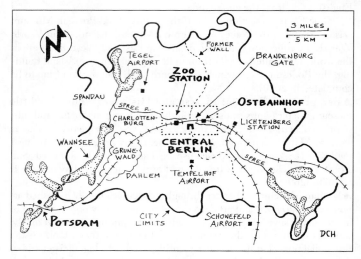

If you take a German tour of Sanssouci, you must be at the palace in person to get your ticket and the appointment time for your tour. In the summer, if you arrive by 9:00, you'll get right in. If you arrive after 10:00, plan on a wait. If you arrive after 12:00, you may not get in at all (€8, April–Oct Tue–Sun 9:00–17:00, closed Mon, Nov–March Tue–Sun 9:00–16:00, closed Mon, tel. 0331/969-4190).

New Palace: Use the English texts to tour Frederick's New Palace (€5, plus €1 for optional live tour in German, May–Oct Sat–Thu 9:00–17:00, closed Fri, Nov–April Sat–Thu 9:00–16:00, closed Fri). If you also want to see the king's apartments, you must take a required 45-minute tour in German (€5, offered May–Oct daily at 11:00 and 14:00). Off-season (Nov–April), the king's apartments are closed, and you can visit the rest of the New Palace only on a German tour (€5); it can take up to an hour for enough people to gather.

Walking Tours: The Potsdam TI's handy walking tour includes Sanssouci Palace, offering the only way to get into the palace with an English-speaking guide (€25 covers walking tour, palace, and park, 11:00 daily except Mon, 3.5 hrs, departs from Film Museum across from TI, reserve by phone, in summer reserve at least 2 days in advance, tel. 0331/275-5850, Potsdam TI hours: April–Oct Mon–Fri 9:00–19:00, Sat–Sun 10:00–16:00, less off-season, 5-min walk from Potsdam S-Bahn station, walk straight out of station and take first right onto An der Orangerie, Friedrich-Ebert Strasse 5, tel. 0331/275-5850).

A "Discover Potsdam" walking tour (which doesn't include

Sanssouci Palace) is offered by "The Original Berlin Walks" and led by a native English-speaking guide. The tour leaves from Berlin at 9:40 on Saturdays May through October (€15, or €11.20 if under age 26 or with WelcomeCard, meet at taxi stand at Zoo Station, public transportation not included but can buy ticket from guide, no booking necessary, tel. 030/301-9194). The guide takes you to Cecilienhof Palace (site of post-war Potsdam conference attended by Churchill, Stalin, and Truman), through pleasant green landscapes to the historic heart of Potsdam for lunch, and to Sanssouci Park.

What to Avoid: Potsdam's much-promoted Wannsee boat rides are torturously dull.

Getting to Potsdam: Potsdam is easy to reach from Berlin (17 min on direct Regional Express/RE trains from Bahnhof Zoo every 30 min, or 30 min direct on S-Bahn #7 from Bahnhof Zoo to Potsdam station; both covered by transit pass with zones A, B, and C). If you're taking the Potsdam TI's tour, walk to the TI from the Potsdam S-Bahn stop (see "Walking Tours," above, for directions). If not taking the TI tour, catch bus #695 from the Potsdam station to the palaces (3/hr, 20 min). Use the same bus #695 to shuttle between the sights in the park. For a more scenic approach, take tram #96 or #X98 from the Potsdam station to Luisenplatz, then walk 15 minutes through the park and enjoy a classic view of Sanssouci Palace.

NIGHTLIFE

For the young and determined sophisticate, *Zitty* and *Tip* are the top guides to alternative culture (in German, sold at kiosks). Also pick up the free schedules *Flyer* and *030* in bars and clubs. *Berlin Programm* lists a nonstop parade of concerts, plays, exhibits, and cultural events (in German, www.berlin-programm.de); the *Ex-Berliner* has less information but is entirely in English (both sold at kiosks and TIs).

Oranienburger Strasse's trendy scene (see "Sights—Eastern Berlin," above) is already being eclipsed by the action at Friedrichshain and Kollwitzplatz farther east. Tourists stroll the Ku'damm after dark.

Visit KaDeWe's ticket office for your music and theater options (sixth floor, 18 percent fee but access to all tickets). Ask about "competitive improvisation" and variety shows.

For jazz (blues and boogie, too) near recommended Savignyplatz hotels, consider **A Trane Jazz Club** (daily, 21:00–2:00, Bleibtreustrasse 1, tel. 030/313-2550) and **Quasimodo Live** (Kantstrasse 12a, under Delphi Cinema, tel. 030/312-8086). For quality blues and New Orleans–style jazz, stop by **Ewige Lampe** (from 21:00, Niebuhrstrasse 11a).

Bar Jeder Vernunft offers modern-day cabaret a short walk from the recommended hotels. This variety show under a classic old tent perched atop a modern parking lot is a hit with German speakers, but can still be worthwhile for non–German speakers (as some of the music shows are in a sort of "Dinglish"). Even some Americans perform here periodically. Tickets are generally around €15, and shows change regularly (shows start at 20:30, closed Sun, seating can be a bit cramped, Schaperstrasse 24, tel. 030/883-1582).

To spend an evening enjoying Europe's largest revue theater, consider **Revue Berlin** at the Friedrichstadt Palast. The show basically depicts the history of Berlin, and is choreographed in a funny and musical way that's popular with the Lawrence Welk–type German crowd. It's even entertaining for your entire English-speaking family (€13–51, Tue–Sat 20:00, also Sat–Sun at 16:00, U-Bahn Oranienburger Tor, tel. 030/284-8830, www.friedrichstadtpalast.de).

SLEEPING

Near Savignyplatz and Bahnhof Zoo

These hotels and pensions are a 5- to 15-minute walk from Bahnhof Zoo (or take S-Bahn to Savignyplatz). Hotels on Kantstrasse have street noise. Ask for a quieter room in back. The area has an artsy charm going back to the cabaret days in the 1920s, when it was the center of Berlin's gay scene. Of the accommodations listed in this area, Pension Peters offers the best value for budget travelers.

$$$ **Pension Savoy** rents 16 comfortable and colorfully decorated rooms with all the amenities. You'll love the cheery old pastel breakfast room and the friendly staff (who speak just enough English). Most rooms overlook a quiet courtyard (Ss-€62, Sb-€73, Db-€102–109, extra person-€34–46, elevator, Meinekestrasse 4, tel. 030/881-3700, fax 030/882-3746, www.hotel-pension-savoy.de).

$$$ **Hotel Astoria** is a friendly, three-star, business-class hotel with 32 comfortably furnished rooms and affordable summer and weekend rates (high season Db-€117–128; prices drop to Sb-€86–97, Db-€94–118 during low season of July–Aug, Nov–Feb, or any 2 weekend nights or if slow; breakfast-€10 extra, rooms with showers are cheaper than rooms with baths, non-smoking floors, elevator, free Internet access, parking-€13/day, around corner from Bahnhof Zoo at Fasanenstrasse 2, tel. 030/312-4067, fax 030/312-5027, www.hotelastoria.de, info@hotelastoria.de).

$$$ **Hecker's Hotel** is an ultramodern, four-star business hotel with 69 rooms and all the sterile Euro-comforts (Sb-€125, Db-€150, breakfast-€15, weekends breakfast included, all rooms-€200 during conferences, non-smoking rooms, elevator, parking-€9/day, between Savignyplatz and Ku'damm at Grolmanstrasse 35, tel. 030/88900, fax 030/889-0260, www.heckers-hotel.com).

$$$ **Hotel Atlanta** has 30 newly renovated rooms in an older building with big leather couches, half a block south of Ku'damm. It's next to

SLEEP CODE

(€1 = about $1.10, country code: 49, area code: 030)
Sleep Code: **S** = Single, **D** = Double/Twin, **T** = Triple, **Q** = Quad, **b** = bathroom, **s** = shower only, **no CC** = Credit Cards not accepted, **SE** = Speaks English, **NSE** = No English. Unless otherwise noted, credit cards are accepted, English is spoken, and breakfast is included.

To help you sort easily through these listings, I've divided the rooms into three categories, based on the price for a standard double room with bath:

$$$ **Higher Priced**—Most rooms €100 or more.
$$ **Moderately Priced**—Most rooms between €80–100.
$ **Lower Priced**—Most rooms €80 or less.

I have concentrated my hotel recommendations around Savignyplatz. While Bahnhof Zoo and Ku'damm are no longer the center of Berlin, the trains, TI, and walking tours are all still handy to Zoo. And the streets around the tree-lined Savignyplatz (a 10-min walk behind the station) have a neighborhood charm. While towering new hotels are being built in the new center, simple, small, and friendly good-value places abound only here. My listings are generally located a couple of flights up in big, run-down buildings. Inside, they are clean, quiet, and spacious enough so that their well-worn character is actually charming. Rooms in back are on quiet courtyards.

The city is packed and hotel prices go up on holidays, including Green Week in mid-January, Easter weekend, the first weekend in May, Ascension weekend in May, the Love Parade (a huge techno-Woodstock, second weekend in July), Germany's national holiday (Oct 2–4), Christmas, and New Year's.

During slow times, the best values are actually business-class rooms on the push list booked through the TI. But as the world learns what a great place Berlin is to visit, a rising tide of tourists will cause these deals to fade away.

Gucci, on an elegant shopping street (Ss-€40–70, Sb-€60–99, Db-€80–120, Tb-€100-140, Qb-€120–160, non-smoking rooms, Fasanen-strasse 74, tel. 030/881-8049, fax 030/881-9872, www.hotelatlanta.de, hatlanta68266759@aol.com).

Berlin's Savignyplatz Neighborhood

S — S-BAHN
U — U-BAHN

❶ Pension Savoy	❽ Hotel Carmer 16
❷ Hotel Astoria	❾ Hotel Imperator
❸ Hecker's Hotel	❿ Pension Peters
❹ Hotel Askanischerhof	⓫ Pension Alexis
❺ Hotel Atlanta	⓬ Hotel Crystal Garni
❻ Hotel-Pension Funk	⓭ Jugendgastehaus am Zoo Hostel
❼ Hotel Bogota	⓮ To Hotels Austriana, Insel Rügen, Bella & Curtis; To Weyers Café Rest.

⓯ Dicke Wirtin Pub	
⓰ Restaurant Die Zwölf Apostel	
⓱ Ristorante San Marino	
⓲ Restaurant Zillemarkt	
⓳ Restaurant Tomasa	
⓴ A Trane Jazz Club	
㉑ Käthe Kollwitz Museum	
㉒ To Launderette	

$$$ Hotel Askanischerhof is the oldest *Zimmer* in Berlin, posh as can be with 16 sprawling antique-furnished rooms. Photos on the walls brag of famous movie-star guests. Frau Glinicke offers Old World service and classic Berlin atmosphere (Sb-€95–110, Db-€117–145, extra bed-€25, free parking, non-smoking rooms, elevator, Ku'damm 53, tel. 030/881-8033, fax 030/881-7206, www.askanischer-hof.de, info @askanischer-hof.de).

$$$ Hotel Carmer 16, with 30 bright, airy rooms, feels like a big, professional hotel with all the comfy extras but with a cold reception staff (Sb-€76–93, Db-€93–122, extra person-€35, some rooms have balconies, elevator and a few stairs, beauty parlor and mini-spa upstairs, Carmerstrasse 16, tel. 030/3110-0500, fax 030/3110-0510, carmer16@t-online.de).

$$ Hotel-Pension Funk, the former home of a 1920s silent-movie star, is delightfully quirky. Kind manager Herr Michael Pfundt offers 14 elegant old rooms with rich art nouveau furnishings (S-€34–57, Ss-€41–72, Sb-€52–82, D-€52–82, Ds-€72–93, Db-€82–113, extra person-€23, prices guaranteed through 2004 with this book, cash preferred, Fasanenstrasse 69, a long block south of Ku'damm, tel. 030/882-7193, fax 030/883-3329, www.hotel-pensionfunk.de, berlin@hotel -pensionfunk.de).

$$ **Hotel Bogota** has 125 unique rooms and several large lounges in a sprawling, drab old maze of a building that once housed the Nazi Chamber of Culture. (After the war, German theater stars were "denazi-fied" here before they could go back to work.) Pieces of the owner's modern art collection lurk around every corner. Take a peek at the bizarre collage in the atrium, with mannequins suspended from the ceiling (S-€44, Ss-€55–57, Sb-€66–72, D-€66–69, Ds-€74–77, Db-€94–98, extra bed-€20, children under 12 free, prices guaranteed through 2004 with this book, non-smoking rooms, elevator, bus #109 from Bahnhof Zoo to Schlüterstrasse 45, tel. 030/881-5001, fax 030/883-5887, www.hotelbogota.de, hotel.bogota@t-online.de).

$$ **Hotel-Pension Imperator** fills a sprawling floor of a grand building with 11 big, quiet, and Old World–elegant rooms and a clientele that includes the occasional actor or musician (S-€42, Ss-€58, Sb-€65, D-€78, Ds-€88–93, Db-€98, Ts-€118, no CC, elevator, Meinekestrasse 5, tel. 030/881-4181, fax 030/885-1919).

$ **Pension Peters,** run by a German-Swedish couple, is sunny and central with a cheery breakfast room. Decorated sleek Scandinavian, with every room renovated, it's a winner (S-€36, Ss-€46, Sb-€58, D-€51, Ds-€67, Db-€66–77, extra bed-€8, kids under 12 free, family room, 3 percent extra if you pay with plastic, prices guaranteed through 2004 with this book, Internet access, 10 yards off Savignyplatz at Kantstrasse 146, tel. 030/3150-3944, fax 030/312-3519, www.pension -peters-berlin.de, penspeters@aol.com, Annika and Christoph SE). The same family also runs a larger hotel just outside of Berlin (see Hotel Pankow under "More Berlin Hotels," below) and rents apartments (ideal for small groups and longer stays).

$ **Pension Alexis** is a classic old-European four-room pension in a stately 19th-century apartment run by Frau and Herr Schwarzer. The shower and toilet facilities are older and cramped, but this, more than any other Berlin listing, has you feeling at home with a faraway aunt (S-€42, D-€65, T-€97, Q-€128, no CC, big rooms, handheld showers, Carmerstrasse 15, tel. 030/312-5144, enough English spoken).

$ **Hotel Crystal Garni** is professional and offers small, well-worn, comfortable rooms and a *vollkorn* breakfast room (S-€36, Sb-€41, D-€47, Ds-€57, Db-€66–77, elevator, a block past Savignyplatz at Kantstrasse 144, tel. 030/312-9047, fax 030/312-6465, run by John and Dorothy Schwarzrock and Herr Vasco Flascher).

$ **Jugendgastehaus am Zoo** is a bare-bones, cash-only youth hostel that takes no reservations and hardly has a reception desk. It's far less comfortable and only marginally cheaper than simple hotels (85 beds, dorm beds-€18, S-€25, D-€44, includes sheets, no breakfast, no CC, Hardenbergstrasse 9a, tel. 030/312-9410, fax 030/312-5430).

South of Ku'damm

Several small hotels are nearby in a charming, café-studded neighborhood 300 yards south of Ku'damm, near the intersection of Sächsische Strasse and Pariser Strasse (bus #109 from Bahnhof Zoo, direction: Airport Tegel). They are less convenient from the station than most of the Savignyplatz listings above.

$$ **Hotel Austriana,** with 25 modern and bright rooms, is warmly and energetically run by Thomas (S-€33–43, Ss-€41–48, Sb-€49–67, Ds-€62–69, Db-€78–89, Ts-€78–96, Qs-€96–104, prices higher for holidays and conferences, half the rooms have balconies, elevator, Pariser Strasse 39, tel. 030/885-7000, fax 030/8857-0088, www.austriana.de, austriana@t-online.de).

$$ **Insel Rügen Hotel,** in the same building as the Austriana, has 31 rooms and ornate, Eastern decor (S-€28, Ss-€39, D-€51, Ds-€61–66, Db-€77–82, elevator, Pariser Strasse 39, tel. 030/884-3940, fax 030/8843-9437, www.insel-ruegen-hotel.de, ir-hotel@t-online.de).

$$ **Hotel-Pension Bella,** a clean, simple, masculine-feeling place with high ceilings, rents nine big, comfortable rooms but is a lesser value (S-€30–45, Ss/Sb-€45–65, D-€50–65, Ds-€70–85, Db-€80–90, extra person-€10, apartment also available, elevator, bus #249 from Zoo, Ludwigkirchstrasse 10a, tel. 030/881-6704, fax 030/8867-9074, www.pension-bella.de, pension.bella@t-online.de).

$ **Hotel-Pension-Curtis,** in the same building as the Austriana and Insel Rügen (recommended above), has 10 hip, piney, basic rooms (S-€32–37, Ss-40–45, Ds-€60–70, Ts-€75–83, Qs-€90–100, no CC, elevator, Pariser Strasse 39, tel. 030/883-4931, fax 030/885-0438).

More Berlin Hotels
Away from the Center

$ **Hotel Pankow** is a new, fresh, colorful 43-room place run by friendly Annika and Christoph (from the Pension Peters, above). It's a 30-minute commute north of downtown but a good value (S-€29, Sb-€44, D-€39, Db-€59, T-€49, Tb-€69, Q-€55, Qb-€75, family rooms, children under 16 free in room with parents, elevator, Internet access, free parking in lot or €3/day in garage, tram station in front of hotel takes you to the center in 30 min, Pasewalker Strasse 14-15, tel. 030/486-2600, fax 030/4862-6060, www.hotel-pankow-berlin.de, hotelpankow@aol.com).

Near Augsburgerstrasse U-Bahn Stop

$$ Consider **Hotel-Pension Nürnberger Eck** (S-€45, Sb-€60, D-€70, Db-€92, Nürnberger Strasse 24a, tel. 030/235-1780, fax 030/2351-7899) or **Hotel Arco** (Sb-€64–75, Db-€82–92, Geisbergerstrasse 30, tel. 030/235-1480, fax 030/2147-5178, www.arco-hotel.de).

Near Güntzelstrasse U-Bahn Stop

$ Choose between **Pension Güntzel** (Ds-€59, Db-€69–79, single rooms €16 less, Güntzelstrasse 62, tel. 030/857-9020, fax 030/853-1108, www.pension-guentzel.de), **Pension Finck** (S-€39, Ss-€42, D-€45, Ds-€59, €3 extra for 1-night stays, no CC, Güntzelstrasse 54, tel. 030/861-2940, fax 030/873-8223), or **Hotel Pension München** (S-€40, Sb-€55, Db-€75, also Güntzelstrasse 62, tel. 030/857-9120, fax 030/8579-1222, www.hotel-pension-muenchen-in-berlin.de).

In Eastern Berlin

$$$ **Hotel Unter den Linden** is ideal for those nostalgic for the days of Soviet rule, although nowadays at least, the management tries to be efficient and helpful. Formerly one of the best hotels in the DDR, this huge, blocky place, right on Unter den Linden in the heart of what was East Berlin, is reasonably comfortable and reasonably priced. Built in 1966, with prison-like corridors, it has 331 modern, plain, and comfy rooms (Sb-€67–87, Db-€109–123, non-smoking rooms, at intersection of Friedrichstrasse, Unter den Linden 14, 10117 Berlin, tel. 030/238-110, fax 030/2381-1100, www.hotel-unter-den-linden.de, reservation@hotel-unter-den-linden.de).

Hostels in Southern and Eastern Berlin

Berlin is known among budget travelers for its fun, hip hostels. Here are four good bets (all prices listed per person): **Studentenhotel Meininger 10** (€23 per person, includes sheets and breakfast, no CC, no curfew, elevator, free parking, near city hall on JFK Platz, Meiningerstrasse 10, U-Bahn: Rathaus Schoneberg, tel. 030/7871-7414, fax 030/7871-7412, www.meininger-hostels.de), **Mitte's Backpacker Hostel** (€15 dorm beds, S-€30, D-€23–28, T-€20, Q-€18, sheets-€2.50, no breakfast, could be cleaner, no curfew, Internet access-€6/hr, laundry, bike rental-€15/day, English newspapers, U-Bahn: Zinnowitzerstrasse, Chausee-strasse 102, tel. 030/2839-0965, fax 030/2839-0935, www.backpacker.de, info@backpacker.de), **Circus** (dorm bed-€13–15, S-€28–32, D-€21–24, T-€18–20, Q-€16–18, 2-person apartment with kitchen-€65–75, 4-person apartment-€115-130, breakfast-€4, sheets-€2, no CC, no curfew, Internet access, 2 locations, U-Bahn: Rosa-Luxemburg Platz, Rosa-Luxemburg Strasse 39, or U-Bahn: Rosenthaler Platz, Weinbergsweg 1a, both tel. 030/2839-1433, fax 030/2839-1484, www.circus-berlin.de, info@circus-berlin.de), or **Clubhouse** (dorm bed-€14, bed in 5- to 7-bed room-€17, S-€32, D-€23, T-€20, breakfast-€3, sheets-€2, no CC, Internet access, on second floor, nightclub below, in hip Oranienburger Strasse area, S- or U-Bahn: Friedrichstrasse, Kalkscheunenstrasse 4-5, tel. 030/2809-7979, fax 030/2809-7977, www.clubhouse-berlin.de, info@clubhouse-berlin.de).

EATING

Don't be too determined to eat "Berlin-style." The city is known only for its mildly spicy sausage. Still, there is a world of restaurants in this ever-changing city to choose from. Your best approach may be to choose a neighborhood, rather than a particular restaurant.

For quick and easy meals, colorful pubs—called *Kneipen*—offer light meals and the fizzy local beer, Berliner Weiss. Ask for it *mit Schuss* for a shot of fruity syrup in your suds. If the kraut is getting *Wurst,* try one of the many Turkish, Italian, or Balkan restaurants. Eat cheap at *Imbiss* snack stands, bakeries (sandwiches), and falafel/kebab places. Bahnhof Zoo has several bright and modern fruit-and-sandwich bars and a grocery (daily 6:00–24:00).

Eating in Western Berlin
Near Savignyplatz
Several good places are on or within 100 yards of Savignyplatz. Take a walk and survey these: **Dicke Wirtin** is a smoky old pub with traditional old-Berlin *Kneipe* atmosphere, famously cheap *Gulaschsuppe,* and salads (daily 12:00–4:00, just off Savignyplatz at Carmerstrasse 9, tel. 030/312-4952). **Die Zwölf Apostel** restaurant is trendy for leafy candlelit ambience and Italian food. A dressy local crowd packs the place for €10 pizzas and €15 to €30 meals. Late-night partygoers appreciate Apostel's great breakfast (daily, 24 hrs, no CC, outside seating in summer until 10:00, immediately across from Savigny S-Bahn entrance, Bleibtreustrasse 49, tel. 030/312-1433). **Ristorante San Marino,** on the square, is another good Italian place, serving cheaper pasta and pizza (daily 11:00–1:00, Savignyplatz 12, tel. 030/313-6086). **Zillemarkt Restaurant,** which feels like an old-time Berlin beer garden, serves traditional Berlin specialties in the garden or in the rustic candlelit interior (€10 meals, daily 10:00–24:00, near the S-Bahn tracks at Bleibtreustrasse 48a, tel. 030/881-7040).

Tomasa is most popular for its weekend breakfast (reservations smart) but also has a nice dinner atmosphere with a completely German crowd (€15 dinner plates, daily 10:00–24:00, a block off Savignyplatz at Knesebackstrasse 22, tel. 030/312-8310).

Weyers Café Restaurant, serving quality international and German cuisine, is a great value and worth a short walk. It's sharp, with white tablecloths, but not stuffy. On a sunny day, its patio is packed with locals (€10 dinner plates, daily 8:00–2:00, seating indoors or outside on the leafy square, Pariser Strasse 16, reservations smart after 20:00, tel. 030/881-9378).

Ullrich Supermarkt is the neighborhood grocery store (Mon–Fri 9:00–20:00, Sat 9:00–16:00, closed Sun, Kantstrasse 7, under the tracks near Bahnhof Zoo). There's plenty of fast food near Bahnhof Zoo and on Ku'damm.

Near Bahnhof Zoo
Self-Service Cafeterias: The top floor of the famous department store, **KaDeWe**, holds the Winter Garden Buffet view cafeteria, and its sixth-floor deli/food department is a picnicker's nirvana. Its arterials are clogged with more than 1,000 kinds of sausage and 1,500 types of cheese (Mon–Fri 9:30–20:00, Sat 9:00–16:00, closed Sun, U-Bahn: Witten-bergplatz). **Wertheim** department store, a half-block from the Memorial Church, has cheap food counters in the basement and a city view from its fine self-service cafeteria, Le Buffet, located up six banks of escalators (Mon–Fri 9:30–20:00, Sat 9:00–16:00, closed Sun, U-Bahn: Ku'damm). **Marche,** a chain that's popped up in big cities all over Germany, is another inexpensive, self-service cafeteria within a half block of the Kaiser Wilhelm church (Mon-Thu 8:00–22:00, Fri–Sat 8:00–24:00, Sun 10:00–22:00, plenty of salads, fruit, made-to-order omelettes, Ku'damm 14, tel. 030/882-7578).

At Bahnhof Zoo: Terrassen am Zoo is a good restaurant right in the station, offering peaceful decency amidst a whirlwind of travel activity (daily 6:00–22:00, upstairs, next to track 1, tel. 030/315-9140).

Eating in Eastern Berlin
Along Unter den Linden
The Opernpalais, preening with fancy prewar elegance, hosts a number of pricey restaurants. Its **Operncafé** has the best desserts and the longest dessert bar in Europe (daily 8:00–24:00, across from university and war memorial at Unter den Linden 5, tel. 030/202-683); sit down and enjoy perhaps the classiest coffee stop in Berlin. The beer and tea garden in front has a cheap food counter (from 10:00, depending on weather). More students and fewer tourists eat in the student facilities at Humboldt University across the street (go through courtyard, enter building through main door, follow signs to cafeteria on right or cheaper, government-subsidized *Mensa* on left, both closed weekends).

Oren Restaurant and Café is a trendy, stylish, near-kosher/vegetarian place next to the New Synagogue. The food is pricey but good, and the ambience is happening (daily 12:00–1:00, Sun open at 10:00, Sat until 3:00, north of Museum Island about 5 blocks away at Oranienburger Strasse 28, tel. 030/282-8228).

Near Pergamon Museum

Try the **Kupfer Keller,** a small basement restaurant, for a short list of traditional German grub, including *Berliner Kartoffelsuppe*—Berlin potato soup (Tue–Sun 11:00–18:00, closed Mon, at corner of Bauhof Strasse and Am Kupfergraben, across from Pergamon).

Deponie3 is a trendy Berlin *Kneipe* usually filled with students from the nearby Humboldt University. Garden seating in the back is nice if you don't mind the noise of the S-Bahn passing directly above you. The interior is a cozy, wooden wonderland of a bar, serving basic sandwiches, salads, and daily specials (sometimes with live music, open Mon–Fri from 9:00, Sat–Sun from 10:00, Georgenstrasse 5, 1 block from Pergamon under S-Bahn tracks, tel. 030/2016-5740).

Near Checkpoint Charlie

Lekkerbek, a busy little bakery and cafeteria, sells inexpensive and tasty salads, soups, pastas, and sandwiches (Mon–Fri 6:00–18:00, Sat 7:00–13:00, closed Sun, a block from Checkpoint Charlie museum at Kochstrasse subway stop, Friedrichstrasse 211, tel. 030/251-7208). For a classier sit-down meal, try **Café Adler,** across the street from the museum (Mon–Sat 10:00–24:00, Sun 10:00–19:00, Friedrichstrasse 20b, tel. 030/251-8965).

TRANSPORTATION CONNECTIONS

Berlin has three train stations (with more on the way). Bahnhof Zoo was the West Berlin train station and still serves Western Europe: Frankfurt, Munich, Hamburg, Paris, and Amsterdam. The Ostbahnhof (former East Berlin's main station) still faces east, serving Prague, Warsaw, Vienna, and Dresden. The Lichtenberg Bahnhof (eastern Berlin's top U- and S-Bahn hub) also handles a few eastbound trains. Expect exceptions. All stations are conveniently connected by subway and even faster by train. Train info: tel. 01805-996-633.

By train to: Frankfurt (14/day, 5 hrs), **Munich** (14/day, 7 hrs, 10 hrs overnight), **Köln** (hrly, 6.5 hrs), **Amsterdam** (4/day, 7 hrs), **Budapest** (2/day, 13 hrs; 1 goes via Czech Republic and Slovakia, so Eurail is not valid), **Copenhagen** (4/day, 8 hrs, change in Hamburg), **London** (4/day, 15 hrs), **Paris** (6/day, 13 hrs, change in Köln, 1 direct night train), **Zürich** (12/day, 10 hrs, 1 direct night train), **Prague** (4/day, 5 hrs, no overnight trains), **Warsaw** (4/day, 8 hrs, 1 night train from Lichtenberg Stn; reservations required on all Warsaw-bound trains), **Kraków** (2/day, 10 hrs), **Vienna** (2/day, 12 hrs via Czech Republic; for second-class ticket, Eurailers pay an extra €23 if under age 26 or €31 if age 26 or above; otherwise, take the Berlin–Vienna via Passau train—nightly at 20:00).

Eurailpasses don't cover the Czech Republic. The **Prague Excursion pass** picks up where Eurail leaves off, getting you from any border into Prague and then back out to Eurail country again within seven days (first class-€50, second class-€40, youth second class-€35, buy from EurAide at Berlin's Bahnhof Zoo or Munich's Hauptbahnhof and get reservations—€3—at the same time).

There are **night trains** from Berlin to Amsterdam, Munich, Köln, Brussels, Paris, Vienna, Budapest, Kraków, Warsaw, Stuttgart, Basel, and Zürich, but there are no night trains from Berlin to anywhere in Italy or Spain. A *Liegeplatz*, or berth (€15–21), is a great deal; inquire at EurAide at Bahnhof Zoo for details. Beds cost the same whether you have a first- or second-class ticket or railpass. Trains are often full, so get your bed reserved a few days in advance from any travel agency or major train station in Europe. Note: Since the Paris–Berlin night train goes through Belgium, railpass holders cannot use a Eurail Selectpass to cover this ride unless they've selected Belgium.

Berlin's Three Airports

Allow €20 for a taxi ride to or from any of Berlin's airports. **Tegel Airport** handles most flights from the United States and Western Europe (4 miles from center, catch the faster bus #X9 to Bahnhof Zoo, or bus #109 to Ku'damm and Bahnhof Zoo for €2; bus TXL goes to Alexanderplatz in East Berlin). Flights from the east and on Buzz Airlines usually arrive at **Schönefeld Airport** (12.5 miles from center, short walk to S-Bahn, catch S-9 to Zoo Station). **Templehof Airport**'s future is uncertain (in Berlin, bus #119 to Ku'damm or U-Bahn 6 or 7). The central telephone number for all three airports is 01805-000-186. For British Air, call 01805-266-522, Delta at 01803-337-880, SAS at 01803-234-023, or Lufthansa at 01803-803-803.

LONDON

London is more than 600 square miles of urban jungle. Teeming with nine million people—who don't all speak English—it's a world in itself and a barrage on all the senses. On my first visit, I felt very, very small. London is much more than its museums and famous landmarks. It's a living, breathing, thriving organism.

London has changed dramatically in recent years, and many visitors are surprised to find how "un-English" it is. Whites are now a minority in major parts of the city that once symbolized white imperialism. Arabs have nearly bought out the area north of Hyde Park. Chinese take-outs outnumber fish-and-chips shops. Many hotels are run by people with foreign accents (who hire English chambermaids), while outlying suburbs are home to huge communities of Indians and Pakistanis. London is learning—sometimes fitfully—to live as a microcosm of its formerly vast empire. Many see the English Channel Tunnel as another foreign threat to the Britishness of Britain.

With just a few days here, you'll get no more than a quick splash in this teeming human tidal pool. But, with a quick orientation, you'll get a good look at its top sights, history, and cultural entertainment, as well as its ever-changing human face.

Have fun in London. Blow through the city on the open deck of a double-decker orientation tour bus, and take a pinch-me-I'm-in-Britain walk through downtown. Ogle the crown jewels at the Tower of London, hear the chimes of Big Ben, and see the Houses of Parliament in action. Hobnob with the tombstones in Westminster Abbey, duck WWII bombs in Churchill's underground Cabinet War Rooms, and brave the earthshaking Imperial War Museum. Visit with Leonardo, Botticelli, and Rembrandt in the National Gallery. Whisper across the dome of St. Paul's Cathedral and rummage through our civilization's attic at the British Museum. Cruise down the Thames River. You'll enjoy some of Europe's best people-watching at Covent Garden, and you'll snap to at Buckingham Palace's Changing of the Guard. Just sit in Victoria Station, at a major Tube station, at Piccadilly Circus, or in Trafalgar Square, and observe. Spend one evening at a theater and the others catching your breath.

Planning Your Time

The sights of London alone could easily fill a trip to Britain. It's a great one-week getaway. On a short tour of Britain I'd give it three busy days. If you're flying in, consider starting your trip in Bath and making London your British finale. Especially if you hope to enjoy a play or concert, a night or two of jet lag is bad news.

Here's a suggested schedule:

Day 1: 9:00-Tower of London (Beefeater tour, crown jewels), 12:00-Munch a sandwich on the Thames while cruising from the Tower to Westminster Bridge, 13:00-Follow the self-guided Westminster Walk (see below) with a quick visit to the Cabinet War Rooms, 15:30-Trafalgar Square and National Gallery, 17:30-Visit the Britain and London Visitors Centre near Piccadilly, planning ahead for your trip, 18:30-Dinner in Soho. Take in a play or 19:30 concert at St. Martin-in-the-Fields.

Day 2: 9:00-Take a hop-on, hop-off bus tour (consider hopping off near the end for the 11:30 Changing of the Guard at Buckingham Palace), 12:30-Covent Garden for lunch and people-watching, 14:00-Tour the British Museum. Have a pub dinner before a play, concert, or evening walking tour.

Days 3 and 4: Choose among these remaining London highlights: Tour Westminster Abbey, British Library, Imperial War Museum, the two Tates (Tate Modern on the south bank for modern art, Tate Britain on the north bank for British art), St. Paul's Cathedral, or the Museum of London; take a spin on the London Eye Ferris Wheel or a cruise to Kew or Greenwich; do some serious shopping at one of London's elegant department stores or open-air markets; or take another historic walking tour.

After considering nearly all of London's tourist sights, I have pruned them down to just the most important (or fun) for a first visit of up to seven days. You won't be able to see all of these, so don't try. You'll keep coming back to London. After 25 visits myself, I still enjoy a healthy list of excuses to return.

ORIENTATION

(area code: 020)

To grasp London comfortably, see it as the old town in the city center, without the modern, congested sprawl. The River Thames runs roughly west to east through the city, with most of the visitor's sights on the north bank. Mentally, maybe even physically, trim down your map to include only the area between the Tower of London (to the east), Hyde Park (west), Regent's Park (north), and the Thames (south). (This is roughly the area bordered by the Tube's Circle Line.) This three-mile stretch between the Tower and Hyde Park (about a 90-min walk) holds 80 percent of the sights mentioned in this chapter.

London is a collection of neighborhoods:

Westminster: This neighborhood includes Big Ben, Parliament, Westminster Abbey, and Buckingham Palace, the grand government buildings from which Britain is ruled.

The City: Shakespeare's London was a walled town clustered around St. Paul's Cathedral. Today it's the modern financial district.

The West End: Lying between Westminster and the City (that is, at the "west end" of the original walled town), this is the center of London cultural life. Trafalgar Square has major museums. Piccadilly Circus and Leicester Square host tourist traps, cinemas, and nighttime glitz. Soho and Covent Garden are thriving people-zones that house theaters, restaurants, pubs, and boutiques.

The South Bank: Until recently, the entire south bank of the Thames River was a run-down, generally ignored area, but now it's the hottest real estate in town, with upscale restaurants, major new sight-seeing attractions, and pedestrian bridges that allow easy access from the rest of London.

Residential neighborhoods to the west: Though they lack major tourist sights, South Kensington, Notting Hill, Chelsea, and Belgravia are home to London's wealthy and trendy, as well as many shopping streets and enticing restaurants.

With this focus and a good orientation, you'll find London manageable and even fun. You'll get a sampling of the city's top sights, history, and cultural entertainment, and a good look at its ever-changing human face.

Tourist Information

The **Britain and London Visitors Centre** is the best tourist information service in town (Mon–Fri 9:00–18:30, Sat–Sun 10:00–16:00, phone not answered after 17:00 Mon–Fri and not at all Sat–Sun, booking service, just off Piccadilly Circus at 1 Lower Regent Street, tel. 020/8846-9000, www.visitbritain.com, www.visitlondon.com). If you're traveling beyond London, take advantage of the Centre's well-equipped England desk. Bring your itinerary and a checklist of questions. Pick up these publications: *London Planner* (a great free monthly that lists all the sights, events, and hours), walking-tour schedule fliers, a theater guide, "Central London Bus Guide," and the Thames River Services brochure.

The Britain and London Visitors Centre sells long-distance bus tickets and passes, train tickets (can also make reservations for you),

British Heritage Passes, and tickets to plays (20 percent booking fee). In addition, they sell **Fast Track tickets** to some of London's attractions (at no extra cost), allowing you to skip the queue at the sights. These can be worthwhile for places that sometimes have long ticket lines, such as the Tower of London, London Eye Ferris Wheel, and Madame Tussaud's Wax Museum. While the Visitors Centre books rooms, you can avoid their £5 booking fee by calling hotels direct.

The **London Pass** provides free entrance to most of the city's sights, but since many museums are free, it's hard to justify the purchase. Still, fervent sightseers can check the list of covered sights and do the arithmetic (1 day -£27, 2 days-£42, 3 days-£52, 6 days-£72, includes 128-page guidebook, tel. 0870-242-9988 for purchase instructions, www.londonpass.com).

Nearby you'll find the **Scottish Tourist Centre** (May–Sept Mon–Fri 9:30–18:30, Sat 10:00–17:00, off-season Mon–Fri 10:00–18:00, Sat 12:00–17:00, Cockspur Street, tel. 0845-225-5121, www.visitscotland.com) and the slick **French National Tourist Office** (Mon–Fri 10:00–18:00, Sat until 17:00, closed Sun, 178 Piccadilly, tel. 0906-824-4123).

Unfortunately, **London's Tourist Information Centres** (which present themselves as TIs at major train and bus stations and airports) are now simply businesses selling advertising space to companies with fliers to distribute.

Local bookstores sell London guides and maps; **Bensons Mapguide** is the best (£2.25, also sold at newsstands).

Helpful Hints

U.S. Embassy: 24 Grosvenor Square (for passport concerns, open Mon–Fri 8:30–11:00 plus Mon and Fri 14:00–16:00, Tube: Bond Street, tel. 020/7499-9000).

Theft Alert: The Artful Dodger is alive and well in London. Be on guard, particularly on public transportation and in places crowded with tourists. Tourists, considered naive and rich, are targeted. Each year, more than 7,500 handbags are stolen at Covent Garden alone.

Pedestrian Safety: Cars drive on the right side of the road, so before crossing a street, I always look right, look left, then look right again just to be sure.

Changing Money: ATMs are the way to go. While regular banks charge several pounds to change traveler's checks, American Express offices offer a fair rate and will change any brand of traveler's checks for no fee. Handy AmEx offices are at Heathrow's Terminal 4 Tube station (daily 7:00–19:00) and near Piccadilly (June–Sept Mon–Sat 9:00–18:00, Sun 10:00–17:00; Oct–May Mon–Sat 9:00–17:30, Sun 10:00–17:00; 30 Haymarket, tel. 020/7484-9610; refund office 24-hr tel. 0800-521-313). Marks & Spencer department stores give good rates with no fees.

Avoid changing money at exchange bureaus. Their latest scam: They advertise very good rates with a same-as-the-banks fee of 2 percent. But the fine print explains that the fee of 2 percent is for buying pounds. The fee for *selling* pounds is 9.5 percent. Ouch!

What's Up: For the best list of what's happening and a look at the trendy London scene, pick up a current copy of *Time Out* (£2.20, www.timeout.com) or *What's On* at any newsstand. The TI's free, monthly *London Planner* covers sights, events, and plays at least as well. For plays, also visit www.officiallondontheatre.co.uk. For a chatty, *People Magazine*-type Web site on London's entertainment, look up www.thisislondon.com.

Sights: Free museums include the British Museum, British Library, National Gallery, National Portrait Gallery, Tate Britain (British art), Tate Modern (modern art), Imperial War Museum, Natural History Museum, Science Museum, Victoria and Albert Museum, and the Royal Air Force Museum Hendon. Special exhibitions cost extra. Telephoning first to check hours and confirm plans is always smart, especially off-season, when hours can shrink.

Internet Access: The astonishing easyInternetcafé offers up to 500 computers per store and is open long hours daily. Depending on the time of day, a £2 ticket buys anywhere from 80 minutes to six hours of computer time. The ticket is valid for four weeks and multiple visits at any of their five branches: Victoria Station (across from front of station, near taxis and buses, long lines), Trafalgar Square (456 Strand), Tottenham Court Road (#9-16), Oxford Street (#358, opposite Bond Street Tube station), and Kensington High Street (#160–166). They also sell 24-hour, seven-day, and 30-day passes (www.easyinternetcafe.com).

Travel Bookstores: Stanfords Travel Bookstore is good and stocks current editions of my books at Covent Garden (Mon–Fri 9:00–19:30, Sat 10:00–19:00, Sun 12:00–18:00, 12 Long Acre, tel. 020/7836-1321). There are two impressive Waterstone's bookstores: the biggest in Europe on Piccadilly (Mon–Sat 10:00–22:00, Sun 12:00–18:00, 203 Piccadilly, tel. 020/7851-2400) and one on the corner of Trafalgar Square (Mon–Sat 9:30–21:00, Sun 12:00–18:00, next to Costa Café, tel. 020/7839-4411).

Left Luggage: As security concerns heighten, train stations have replaced their lockers with left-luggage counters. Each bag must go through a scanner (just like at the airport), so lines can be long. Expect a wait to pick up your bags, too (each item-£5/24 hrs, daily 7:00–24:00). You can also check bags at the airports (£4/day). If leaving London and returning later, you may be able to leave a box or bag at your hotel for free—assuming you'll be staying there again.

Medical Problems: Local hospitals have 24-hour-a-day emergency care centers where any tourist who needs help can drop in and, after a wait, be seen by a doctor. The quality is good and the price is right (free). Your hotel has details. St. Thomas' Hospital, immediately across the river from Big Ben, has a fine reputation.

Arrival in London

By Train: London has eight train stations, all connected by the Tube (subway) and all with exchange offices and luggage storage (see above). From any station, ride the Tube or taxi to your hotel.

By Bus: The bus station is one block southwest of Victoria Station, which has a TI and Tube entrance.

By Plane: For detailed information on getting from London's airports to downtown London, see "Transportation Connections" at the end of this chapter.

Getting Around London

To travel smart in a city this size, you must get comfortable with public transportation. London's excellent taxis, buses, and subway system make a private car unnecessary. In fact, the new "congestion charge" of £5 levied on any private car entering the city center has been effective in cutting down traffic jam delays and bolstering London's public transit. The new revenue subsidizes the buses, which are now cheaper, more frequent, and even more user-friendly than before. Today the vast majority of vehicles in the city center are buses, taxis, and service trucks. (Drivers: For all the details on the congestion charge, see www.cclondon.com.)

By Taxi: London is the best taxi town in Europe. Big, black, carefully regulated cabs are everywhere. I never met a crabby cabbie in London. They love to talk, and they know every nook and cranny in town. I ride in one each day just to get my London questions answered. Rides start at £2 and cost about £1.50 per Tube stop. Connecting downtown sights is quick and easy and will cost you about £4 (e.g., St. Paul's to the Tower of London). For a short ride, three people in a cab travel at Tube prices. Groups of four or five should taxi everywhere. If a cab's top light is on, just wave it down. (Drivers flash lights when they see you.) They have a tiny turning radius, so you can wave at cabs going in either direction. If waving doesn't work, ask someone where you can find a taxi stand. While telephoning a cab gets one in minutes, it's generally not necessary and adds to the cost. London is such a great wave-'em-down taxi town that most cabs don't even have a radio phone.

Don't worry about meter cheating. British cab meters come with a sealed computer chip and clock that ensures you'll get the regular tariff #1 most of the time, tariff #2 during "unsociable hours" (18:00–6:00 and Sat–Sun), and tariff #3 only on holidays. All extra charges are explained in writing on the cab wall. The only way a cabbie can cheat you is to take a needlessly long route. There are alternative cab companies driving normal-looking, non-metered cars that charge fixed rates based on

London

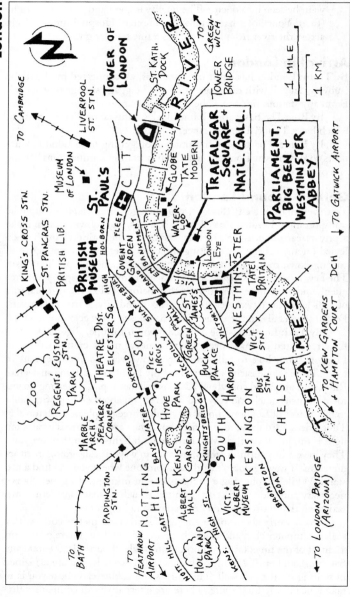

the postal codes of your start and end points. These are generally honest and can actually be cheaper when snarled traffic drives up the cost of a metered cab. Tip a cabbie by rounding up (maximum 10 percent).

By Bus: London's extensive bus system is easy to follow. Just pick up a free "Central London Bus Guide" map from a TI or Tube station. Signs at stops list routes clearly. On most buses (marked on bus stop sign), you'll pay at a machine at the bus stop (exact change only), then show your ticket as you board. On other buses, you pay the conductor (take a seat and he'll come and collect £1). Any ride in downtown London costs £1. (The best views are upstairs.) If you have a Travel Card (see below), get in the habit of hopping buses for quick little straight shots, even just to get to a Tube stop. During bump-and-grind rush hours (8:00–10:00 and 16:00–19:00), you'll go faster by Tube. Consider two special bus deals: all day for £2 and a ticket six-pack for £4 (also see "London Tube and Bus Passes," below).

By Tube: London's subway system (called the Tube or Underground, but never "subway") is one of this planet's great people-movers and the fastest (and cheapest) long-distance transport in town (runs Mon–Sat about 5:00–24:00, Sun about 7:00–23:00).

Survey a Tube map. At the front of this book, you'll find a complete Tube map with color-coded lines and names. You can also pick up a free Tube map at any station window. Each line has a name (such as Circle, Northern, or Bakerloo) and two directions (indicated by the end-of-the-line stop). Find the line that will take you to your destination, and figure out roughly what direction (north, south, east, west) you'll need to go to get there.

In the Tube station, feed your ticket into the turnstile, reclaim it, and hang onto the ticket—you'll need it to get through the turnstile at the end of your journey. Find your train by following signs to your line and the (general) direction it's headed (e.g., Central Line: East).

Since some tracks are shared by several lines, you'll need to double-check before boarding a train: First, make sure your destination is one of the stops listed on the sign at the platform. Also, check the electronic signboards that announce which train is next, and make sure the destination (the end-of-the-line stop) is the one you want. Each train has its final destination above its windshield. When in doubt, ask a local or a blue-vested staff person for help.

Trains run roughly every three to 10 minutes. If one train is absolutely packed and you notice another to the same destination is coming in three minutes, you can wait to avoid the sardine experience. The system can be fraught with construction delays and breakdowns, so pay attention to signs and announcements explaining necessary detours, etc. The Circle Line is notorious for problems. Bring something to do to make your waiting time productive.

You can't leave the system without feeding your ticket to the turn-stile. (The turnstile will either eat your now-expired single-trip ticket, or spit your still-valid pass back out.) Save walking time by choosing the best street exit—check the maps on the walls or ask any station personnel. "Subway" means "pedestrian underpass" in "English." For Tube and bus information 24 hours a day, call 020/7222-1234 (www.transportforlondon .gov.uk). And always...mind the gap.

Cost: Any ride in Zone 1 (on or within the Circle Line, including virtually all my recommended sights and hotels) costs £1.60. Tube tickets are also valid on city buses. You can avoid ticket-window lines in Tube stations by buying tickets from coin-op machines; practice on the punchboard to see how the system works (hit Adult Single and your destination); these tickets are valid only on the day of purchase. Again, nearly every ride will be £1.60. Beware: Overshooting your zone nets you a £10 fine.

Carnet of 10 tickets: If you want to travel a little each day or if you're part of a group, an £11.50 *carnet* (pron. CAR-net) is a great deal: You get 10 separate tickets for Tube travel in Zone 1, paying £1.15 per ride rather than £1.60. Wait for the machine to lay all 10 tickets.

London Tube and Bus Passes: Consider using these passes, valid on both the Tube and buses (all passes are available for more zones, can be purchased as easily as a normal ticket at any station, and can get you a 33 percent discount on most Thames cruises):

One-Day pass: If you figure you'll take three rides in a day, a day pass is a good deal. The One Day Travel Card, covering Zones 1 and 2, gives you unlimited "off-peak" travel for a day, starting after 9:30 on weekdays and anytime on weekends (£4.10). The all-zone version of this card costs £5.10 (and includes Heathrow Airport). The unrestricted version, covering six zones (including Heathrow) at all times, costs £10.70. Families save with the One Day Family Travel Card (price varies depending on number in family). For details, including a handy journey planner, see www.thetube.com.

Weekend pass: The Weekend Travel Card, covering Saturday, Sunday, and Zones 1 and 2 for £6.10, costs 25 percent less than two one-day cards.

Seven-Day pass: The 7-Day Travel Card costs £19.60 and covers Zones 1 and 2.

Group deals: Groups of 10 or more can travel all day on the Tube for £3.10 each (but not on buses).

TOURS

▲▲▲**Hop-on, Hop-off Double-Decker Bus Tours**—Two competitive companies (Original and Big Bus) offer essentially the same tours with buses that have either live (English-only) guides or a tape-recorded, dial-a-language narration. This two-hour, once-over-lightly bus tour drives by all the famous sights, providing a stress-free way to get your bearings and at least see the biggies. You can sit back and enjoy the entire two-hour orientation tour (a good idea if you like the guide and the weather) or hop on and hop off at any of the nearly 30 stops and catch a later bus. Buses run about every 10–15 minutes in summer, every 20 minutes in winter. It's an inexpensive form of transport as well as an informative tour. Buses operate daily (from about 9:00 until early evening in summer, until late afternoon in winter) and stop at Victoria Street (1 block north of Victoria Station), Marble Arch, Piccadilly Circus, Trafalgar Square, and elsewhere.

Each company offers a core two-hour overview tour, two other routes, and a narrated Thames boat tour covered by the same ticket (buy ticket from driver, credit cards accepted at major stops such as Victoria Station, ticket good for 24 hrs, bring a sweater and extra film). Pick up a map from any flier rack or from one of the countless salespeople and study the complex system. Note: If you start at Victoria Station at 9:00, you'll finish near Buckingham Palace in time to see the Changing of the Guard (at 11:30); ask your driver for the best place to hop off. Sunday morning is a fine time for a tour; traffic is light and many museums are closed. The last full loop leaves Victoria at 17:00. Both companies have entertaining as well as boring guides. The narration is important. If you don't like your guide, jump off and find another. If you like your guide, settle in for the entire loop.

Original London Sightseeing Bus Tour: Live guided buses have a Union Jack flag and a yellow triangle on the front of the bus. If the front has many flags or a green or red triangle, it's a tape-recorded multilingual tour—avoid it, unless you have kids who'd enjoy the entertaining tape-recorded kids' tour (£15, £2.50 discount with this book, limit 2 discounts per book, they'll rip off the corner of this page, raise bloody hell if they don't honor this discount, ticket good for 24 hours, tel. 020/8877-1722, www.theoriginaltour.com). Your ticket includes a 50-minute-long round-trip boat tour from Westminster Pier or Waterloo Pier (departs hourly, tape-recorded narration).

Big Bus Hop-on, Hop-off London Tours: These are also good. For £17, you get the same basic tour plus coupons for three different one-hour London walks, as well as the scenic and usually entertainingly guided Thames boat ride (normally £5) between Westminster Pier and the Tower of London. The pass and extras are valid for 24 hours. Buses with live guides are marked in front with a picture of an orange bus; buses with tape-recorded spiels display a picture of a blue bus and headphones. While the price is steeper, Big Bus guides seem more dynamic than the Original guides (daily 8:30–18:00, July–Aug until 18:00, winter until 16:30, from Victoria Station, tel. 020/7233-9533, www.bigbus.co.uk).

At Night: The London by Night Sightseeing Tour runs basically

DAILY REMINDER

Sunday: Some sights don't open until noon. The Tower of London is especially crowded today. Hyde Park Speakers' Corner rants from early afternoon until early evening. These are closed: Banqueting House, Sir John Soane's Museum, and legal sights (Houses of Parliament, Old Bailey, the City is dead). Evensong is at 15:00 at Westminster Abbey (plus organ recital at 17:45 for a fee) and 15:15 at St. Paul's (plus free organ recital at 17:00); both churches are open during the day for worship but closed to sightseers. Many stores and theaters are closed. Street markets flourish: Camden Lock, Spitalfields, Greenwich, and Petticoat Lane.

Monday: Virtually all sights are open except for Apsley House, the Theatre Museum, Sir John Soane's Museum, and a few others. The St. Martin-in-the-Fields church offers a free 13:05 concert. At Somerset House, the Courtauld Gallery is free until 14:00. Vinopolis is open until 21:00.

Tuesday: All sights are open; the British Library is open until 20:00. St. Martin-in-the-Fields has a free 13:05 concert.

Wednesday: All sights are open, plus evening hours at Westminster Abbey (until 19:45), the National Gallery (until 21:00), and Victoria and Albert Museum (until 22:00).

the same circuit as the other companies, but after hours. While the narration is pretty lame (the driver does little more than call out the names of famous places as you roll by), the views at twilight are grand (£9.50, pay driver or buy tickets at Victoria Station or Paddington Station TI, April–Oct only, 2-hr tour with live guide, departs at 19:30, and 21:30 from Victoria Station, Taxi Road, at front of station near end of Wilton Road, tel. 020/8646-1747, www.london-by-night.net).

▲▲**Walking Tours**—Several times a day, top-notch local guides lead (often big) groups through specific slices of London's past. Schedule fliers litter the desks of TIs, hotels, and pubs. *Time Out* lists many scheduled walks, but not all. Simply show up at the announced location, pay £5, and enjoy two chatty hours about Charles Dickens, the Plague, William Shakespeare, Legal London, the Beatles, Jack the Ripper, or whatever is on the agenda. Original London Walks, the dominant company, lists its extensive daily schedule in a beefy, plain, black-and-white *The Original London Walks* brochure—which you'll see at the TI and on racks in every hotel (walks offered year-round—even Christmas, private tours for £90, tel. 020/7624-3978, for a recorded

Thursday: All sights are open, British Museum until 20:30 (selected galleries), National Portrait Gallery until 21:00. St. Martin-in-the-Fields hosts a 19:30 evening concert (for a fee).

Friday: All sights are open, British Museum until 20:30 (selected galleries only), National Portrait Gallery until 21:00, Tate Modern until 22:00. Best street market: Spitalfields. St. Martin-in-the-Fields offers two concerts (13:05-free, 19:30-fee).

Saturday: Most sights are open except legal ones (Old Bailey; Houses of Parliament—open summer Sat for tours only; skip the City). Vinopolis is open until 21:00, Tate Modern until 22:00. Best street markets: Portobello, Camden Lock, Greenwich. Evensong is at 15:00 at Westminster Abbey, 17:00 at St. Paul's. St. Martin-in-the-Fields hosts a concert at 19:30 (fee).

Notes: Evensong occurs daily at St. Paul's (Mon–Sat at 17:00 and Sun at 15:15) and daily except Wednesday at Westminster Abbey (Mon–Tue and Thu–Fri at 17:00, Sat–Sun at 15:00). London by Night Sightseeing Tour buses leave from Victoria Station every evening at 20:00, 21:00, and 22:00. The London Eye Ferris Wheel spins nightly until 22:00 in summer, until 20:00 in winter (closed Jan).

listing of today's walks call 020/7624-9255, www.walks.com). They also run **Explorer day trips,** a good option for those with limited time and transportation (different trip daily: Stonehenge/Salisbury, Oxford/Cotswolds, York, Bath, and so on).

The Beatles: Fans of the still-Fabulous Four can take one of the Beatles walks (5/week, offered by Original London Walks, above), visit the Beatles Shop (daily, 231 Baker Street, next to Sherlock Holmes Museum, Tube: Baker Street, tel. 020/7935-4464), or go to Abbey Road and walk the famous crosswalk (at intersection with Grove End, Tube: St. John's Wood).

Private Guides: Standard rates for London's registered guides are £97 for four hours, £146 for eight hours (tel. 020/7403-2962, www.touristguides.org.uk). Robina Brown leads tours with small groups in her Toyota Previa (£200/3 hrs, £300-450/day, tel. 020/7228-2238, www.driverguidetours.com, robina@driverguidetours.com). Britt Lonsdale, an energetic mother of twins, is another registered London guide (half day-£89, full day-£142, tel. 020/7386-9907, brittl@ntlworld.com).

▲▲Cruises—Boat tours with entertaining commentaries sail regularly from many points along the Thames. It's confusing, since there are several companies offering essentially the same thing. Your basic options are downstream (to the Tower and Greenwich), upstream (to Kew Gardens and Hampton Court), and round-trip scenic tour cruises. Most people depart from the Westminster Pier (at the base of Westminster Bridge under Big Ben). You can catch most of the same boats (with less waiting) from Waterloo Pier at the London Eye Ferris Wheel across the river. For pleasure and efficiency, consider combining a one-way cruise (to Kew, Greenwich, or wherever) with a Tube ride back. While Tube and bus tickets don't work on the boats, a Travel Card can snare you a 33 percent discount on most cruises. Buy boat tickets at the small ticket offices on the docks. Children and seniors get discounts. You can buy drinks and scant, pricey snacks on board. Clever budget travelers pack along a small picnic and munch while they cruise.

Here are some of the most popular cruise options.

To Tower of London: City Cruises boats sail 30 minutes to the Tower from Westminster Pier (one way-£5.20, round-trip-£6.30, one-way included with Big Bus London tour; covered by £8.50 "River Red Rover" ticket that includes Greenwich—see next paragraph; 3/hr during June–Aug daily 10:00–20:40, 2/hr and shorter hours rest of year).

To Greenwich: Two companies head to Greenwich from Westminster Pier. Choose between **City Cruises** (one way-£6.50, round-trip-£8; or get their £8.50 all-day, hop-on, hop-off "River Red Rover" ticket to have option of getting off at London Eye and Tower of London; June–Aug daily 10:00–17:00, fewer off-season, every 40 min, 70 min to Greenwich, usually narrated only downstream—to Greenwich, tel. 020/7740-0400, www.citycruises.com) and **Thames River Services** (one way-£6.50, round-trip-£8, April–Oct daily 10:00–16:00, July–Aug until 17:00, 2/hr, 50 min, has shorter hours and runs every 40 min rest of year, usually narrated only to Greenwich, tel. 020/7930-4097, www.royalriverthames.com).

To Kew Gardens: Westminster Passenger Services Association leaves for Kew Gardens from Westminster Pier (one way-£9, round-trip-£15, 4/day, generally departing 10:30–14:00, 90 min, narrated for 30 min, tel. 020/7930-2062, www.wpsa.co.uk). Some boats continue on to **Hampton Court Palace** for an additional £3 (and 90 min). Because of the river current, you'll save 30 minutes cruising from Hampton Court back into town.

Round-Trip Cruises: Fifty-minute round-trip cruises of the Thames leave hourly from Westminster and Embankment Piers (£7.50, included with Original London Bus tour—listed above, tape-recorded narration, Catamaran Circular Cruises, tel. 020/7987-1185). The London Eye Ferris Wheel operates its own "River Cruise Experience," offering a similar 45-minute circular tour from Waterloo Pier (must be done in combination with Ferris wheel, £20 includes

THAMES BOAT PIERS

While Westminster Pier is the most popular, it's not the only dock in town. Consider all the options:

Westminster Pier, at the base of Big Ben, offers round-trip sightseeing cruises and lots of departures in both directions.

Waterloo Pier, at the base of London Eye Ferris Wheel, is a good, less-crowded alternative to Westminster, with many of the same cruise options.

Embankment Pier is near Covent Garden, Trafalgar Square, and Cleopatra's Needle (the obelisk on the Thames). You can take a round-trip cruise from here, or catch a boat to the Tower of London and Greenwich.

Tower Millennium Pier is at the Tower of London. Boats sail west to Westminster Pier or east to Greenwich.

Bankside Pier (near Tate Modern and Shakespeare's Globe) and **Millbank Millennium Pier** (near Tate Britain) are connected to each other by the new "Tate to Tate" ferry service.

both, reservations recommended and cost 50p, tel. 0870-443-9185, www.ba-londoneye.com).

From Tate to Tate: This new boat service for art-lovers connects the Tate Modern and Tate British galleries in 18 scenic minutes (departing every 40 min from 10:00–17:00, also stops at London Eye Ferris Wheel, £4.50, £10 per family, buy ticket at gallery desk or on board, tel. 020/7887-8008).

On Regent's Canal: Consider exploring London's canals by taking a cruise on historic Regent's Canal in north London. The good ship *Jenny Wren* offers 90-minute guided canal boat cruises from Walker's Quay in Camden Town to Little Venice (£6.50, March–Oct daily 12:30, 14:30, Sat–Sun also 10:30, 16:30, Walker's Quay, 250 Camden High Street, Tube: Camden Town, tel. 020/7485-4433 or 020/7485-6210, www .walkersquay.com). While in Camden Town, stop by the popular Camden Lock Market to browse through trendy arts and crafts (daily 10:00–18:00, busiest on weekends, a block from Walker's Quay).

London Duck Tours—A bright-yellow amphibious vehicle takes a gang of 30 tourists past some famous sights on land (Big Ben, Buckingham Palace, Piccadilly Circus), then splashes into the Thames for a 30-minute cruise (£17, 2/hr, daily 10:00–18:00, 75 min, live commentary, these book up in advance, departs from Chicheley Street behind County Hall near London Eye Ferris Wheel, Tube: Waterloo or Westminster, tel. 020/7928-3132, www.londonducktours.com).

SIGHTS

From Westminster Abbey to Trafalgar Square

▲▲**Westminster Walk**—Just about every visitor to London strolls the historic Whitehall boulevard from Big Ben to Trafalgar Square. Beneath London's modern traffic and big-city bustle lies 2,000 fascinating years of history. This three-quarter-mile, self-guided orientation walk (see map on page 541) gives you a whirlwind tour and connects the sights listed in this section.

Start halfway across **Westminster Bridge** (#1 on map) for that "Wow, I'm really in London!" feeling. Get a close-up view of the **Houses of Parliament** and **Big Ben** (floodlit at night). Downstream you'll see the **London Eye Ferris Wheel.** Down the stairs to Westminster Pier are boats to the Tower of London and Greenwich.

En route to Parliament Square, you'll pass a statue of **Boadicea** (#2), the Celtic queen defeated by Roman invaders in A.D. 60.

To thrill your loved ones (or bug the envious), call home from a pay phone near Big Ben at about three minutes before the hour. You'll find a phone on Great George Street, across from Parliament Square. As Big Ben chimes, stick the receiver outside the booth and prove you're in London: Ding dong ding dong...dong ding ding dong.

Wave hello to Churchill in Parliament Square (#3). To his right is **Westminster Abbey** with its two stubby, elegant towers.

Walk north up Parliament Street (which turns into Whitehall) toward Trafalgar Square. You'll see the thought-provoking **Cenotaph** (#5) in the middle of the street, reminding passersby of Britain's many war dead. To visit the Cabinet War Rooms (see below) take a left before the Cenotaph, on King Charles Street (#4).

Continuing on Whitehall, stop at the barricaded and guarded little **10 Downing Street** to see the British "White House" (#6), home of the prime minister. Break the bobby's boredom and ask him a question.

Nearing Trafalgar Square, look for the **Horse Guards** behind the gated fence (11:00 inspection Mon–Sat, 10:00 on Sun; dismounting ceremony daily at 16:00) and the 17th-century **Banqueting House** across the street (#7; see below).

The column topped by Lord Nelson marks **Trafalgar Square** (#8). The stately domed building on the far side of the square is the **National Gallery** (free), which has a classy café (upstairs in the Sainsbury wing). To the right of the National Gallery is **St. Martin-in-the-Fields Church** and its Café in the Crypt.

To get to Piccadilly from Trafalgar Square, walk up Cockspur Street to Haymarket, then take a short left on Coventry Street to colorful **Piccadilly Circus.**

Near Piccadilly you'll find the **Britain and London Visitors Centre** and piles of theaters. **Leicester Square** (with its half-price ticket booth

Westminster Walk

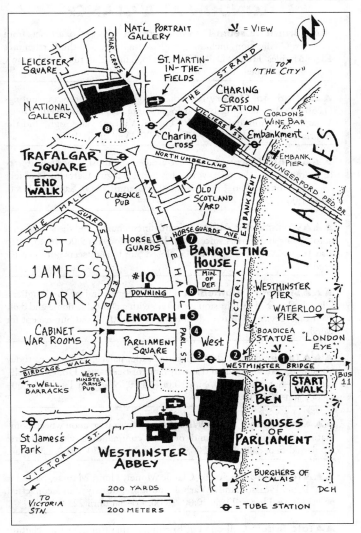

☝ = VIEW

NAT'L PORTRAIT GALLERY

LEICESTER SQUARE

NATIONAL GALLERY

CHAR. CROSS

ST. MARTIN-IN-THE-FIELDS

THE STRAND

TO "THE CITY"

CHARING CROSS STATION

GORDON'S WINE BAR

VILLIERS ST.

Charing Cross

Embankment

EMBANK. PIER

HUNGERFORD PED. BR.

TRAFALGAR SQUARE

NORTHUMBERLAND

END WALK

CLARENCE PUB

OLD SCOTLAND YARD

THE MALL

GUARDS

EMBANKMENT

THAMES

ST JAMES'S PARK

HORSE GUARDS AVE.

Horse Guards

❼

BANQUETING HOUSE

MIN. OF DEF.

WESTMINSTER PIER

WATERLOO PIER

#10 DOWNING

WHITEHALL

❻

VICTORIA

ROAD

CABINET WAR ROOMS

CENOTAPH

❺

❹

West.

BOADICEA STATUE

"LONDON EYE"

PARLIAMENT SQUARE

PARL. ST.

❸

❷

❶

WESTMINSTER BRIDGE

BIRDCAGE WALK

TO WELL. BARRACKS

WEST-MINSTER ARMS PUB

START WALK

BUS 11

BIG BEN

HOUSES OF PARLIAMENT

ST James's Park

VICTORIA ST.

WESTMINSTER ABBEY

BURGHERS OF CALAIS

DCH

TO VICTORIA STN.

200 YARDS

200 METERS

⊖ = TUBE STATION

for plays) thrives just a few blocks away. Walk through gritty **Soho** (north of Shaftesbury Avenue) for its fun pubs (see "Eating," below, for "Food is Fun" Dinner Crawl). From Piccadilly or Oxford Circus, you can taxi, bus, or Tube home.

LONDON AT A GLANCE

▲▲▲**British Museum** The world's greatest collection of artifacts from Western Civilization, including the Rosetta Stone and the Parthenon's Elgin Marbles. **Hours:** Daily 10:00–17:30, Thu–Fri until 20:30, but only a few galleries open after 17:30.

▲▲▲**National Gallery** Remarkable collection of European paintings (1250–1900), including Leonardo da Vinci, Sandro Botticelli, Diego Velázquez, Rembrandt, J.M.W. Turner, Vincent van Gogh, and the Impressionists. **Hours:** Daily 10:00–18:00, Wed until 21:00.

▲▲▲**British Library** Impressive array of the most important literary treasures of the Western world, from the Magna Carta to Handel's *Messiah.* **Hours:** Mon–Fri 9:30–18:00, Tue until 20:00, Sat 9:30–17:00, Sun 11:00–17:00.

▲▲▲**Westminster Abbey** Britain's finest church, and the site of royal coronations and burials since 1066. **Hours:** Mon–Fri 9:00–16:45, Wed also 18:00–19:45, Sat 9:30–14:45, closed Sun to sightseers but open for services.

▲▲▲**St. Paul's Cathedral** The main cathedral of the Anglican Church, designed by Christopher Wren, with a climbable dome and daily evensong services. **Hours:** Mon–Sat 8:30–16:30, closed Sun except for worship.

▲▲▲**Tower of London** Historic castle, palace, and prison, today housing the crown jewels and a witty band of Beefeaters. **Hours:** March–Oct Mon–Sat 9:00–18:00, Sun 10:00–18:00; Nov–Feb Tue–Sat 9:00–17:00, Sun–Mon 10:00–17:00.

▲▲▲**London Eye Ferris Wheel** Enormous observation wheel, dominating London's skyline and offering commanding views. **Hours:** April–mid-Sept daily 9:30–22:00, mid-Sept–March 9:30–20:00, closed Jan.

▲▲▲**Tate Modern** Art by Claude Monet, Henri Matisse, Salvador Dalí, Pablo Picasso, Andy Warhol, and more, displayed in a converted power house. **Hours:** Daily 10:00–18:00, Fri–Sat until 22:00.

▲▲**Tate Britain** Collection of British painting from the 16th century through modern times, including works by William Blake, the Pre-Raphaelites, and Turner. **Hours:** Daily 10:00–17:50.

▲▲**Houses of Parliament** London's famous neo-Gothic landmark, topped by Big Ben and occupied by the Houses of Lords and Commons. **Hours:** House of Commons—Mon 14:30–22:30, Tue–Thu 11:30–19:30, Fri 9:30–15:00; House of Lords—Mon–Wed 14:30–22:30 or until they finish, Thu from 12:00 on, sometimes Fri from 10:00.

▲▲**Imperial War Museum** Examines the military history of the bloody 20th century. **Hours:** Daily 10:00–18:00.

▲▲**Cabinet War Rooms** Underground WWII headquarters of Churchill's war effort. **Hours:** Daily April–Sept 9:30–18:00, Oct–March 10:00–18:00.

▲▲**National Portrait Gallery** A pictorial *Who's Who* of British history, featuring portraits of this nation's most important historical figures. **Hours:** Daily 10:00–18:00, Thu–Fri until 21:00.

▲▲**Buckingham Palace** Britain's royal residence with the famous changing of the guard. **Hours:** Palace—Aug–Sept only, daily 9:30–17:00; Guard—Almost daily in summer at 11:30, every other day all year long.

▲▲**Shakespeare's Globe** Timbered, thatch-roofed reconstruction of the Bard's original wooden "O." **Hours:** Actor-led tours mid-May–Sept Mon–Sat 9:30–12:00, Sun 9:30–11:30; virtual tours daily 12:30–16:00; actor tours also Oct–mid-May daily 10:30–17:00; also regular performances (see "Entertainment and Theater," page 572).

▲▲**Victoria and Albert Museum** The best collection of decorative arts anywhere. **Hours:** Daily 10:00–17:45, Wed until 21:30.

▲▲**Somerset House** Grand 18th-century civic palace housing three fine art museums: Courtauld Gallery (decent painting collection), Hermitage Rooms (rotating exhibits from famous St. Petersburg musuem), and the Gilbert Collection (decorative arts). **Hours:** Daily 10:00–18:00.

▲▲**Old Operating Theatre Museum** 19th-century hall where surgeons performed amputations for an audience of aspiring med students. **Hours:** Daily 10:30–17:00.

▲▲**Vinopolis: City of Wine** Offers a breezy history of wine with plenty of tasting opportunities. **Hours:** Daily 11:00-18:00, Sat and Mon until 21:00.

▲▲▲**Westminster Abbey**—As the greatest church in the English-speaking world, Westminster Abbey has been the place where England's kings and queens have been crowned and buried since 1066. A thousand years of English history—3,000 tombs, the remains of 29 kings and queens, and hundreds of memorials—lie within its walls and under its stone slabs. Like a stony refugee camp huddled outside St. Peter's gates, this place has a story to tell and the best way to enjoy it is with a **tour** (audioguide-£2, live-£3; many prefer the audioguide because it's self-paced, both tours include entry to cloister museums). Experience an **evensong** service—awesome in a nearly empty church (weekdays except Wed at 17:00, Sat–Sun at 15:00). The **organ recital** on Sunday at 17:45 is another highlight (fee, 40 min). Organ concerts here are great and inexpensive; look for signs with schedule details (or visit www.westminster-abbey.org).

Three tiny **museums** ring the cloister (£1 covers all, on top of your abbey ticket; or free with either the audioguide or live tour): the Chapter House (where the monks held their daily meetings, notable for its fine architecture and well-described but faded medieval art), the Pyx Chamber (containing an exhibit on the king's treasury), and the Abbey Museum (which tells of the abbey's history, royal coronations, and burials). Look into the impressively realistic eyes of Henry VII's funeral effigy (one of a fascinating series of wax-and-wood statues that graced royal coffins during funeral processions for three centuries).

Enter the abbey on the Big Ben side (often with a sizable line, visit early to avoid crowds) and then follow a one-way route through this English hall of fame around the church and cloisters (with the three small museums), back through the nave, and out (£6 for abbey entry, Mon–Fri 9:00–16:45, Wed also 18:00–19:45, Sat 9:30–14:45, last admission 60 min before closing, closed Sun to sightseers but open for services and organ recital, photography prohibited, coffee in cloister, Tube: Westminster or St. James's Park, call for tour schedule, tel. 020/7222-7110). Since the church is often closed to the public for special services, it's wise to call first.

For a free peek inside and a quiet sit in the nave, you can tell a guard at the west end (where the tourists exit) that you'd like to pay your respects to Britain's Unknown Soldier. If the guard is nice, he might let you slip in.

▲▲**Houses of Parliament (Palace of Westminster)**—This neo-Gothic icon of London, the royal residence from 1042 to 1547, is now the meeting place of the legislative branch of government. Tourists are welcome to view debates in either the bickering House of Commons or the genteel House of Lords (when in session—indicated by a flag flying atop the Victoria Tower). While the actual debates are generally extremely dull, it is a thrill to be inside and see the British government inaction (House of Commons: Mon 14:30–22:30, Tue, Wed, Thu 11:30–19:30,

Fri 9:30–15:00, generally less action and no lines after 18:00, use St. Stephen's entrance, Tube: Westminster, tel. 020/7219-4272 for schedule, www.parliament.uk). The House of Lords has more pageantry, shorter lines, and less interesting debates (Mon–Wed 14:30–22:30 or until they finish, Thu from 12:00 on, sometimes Fri from 10:00 on, tel. 020/7219-3107 for schedule). If there's only one line outside, it's for the House of Commons. Go to the gate and tell the guard you want the Lords (that's the second "line" with no people in it). You may pop right in—that is, after you've cleared the security gauntlet. Once you've seen the Lords (hide your House of Lords flier), you can often slip directly over to the House of Commons and join the gang waiting in the lobby. Inside the lobby, you'll find an announcement board with the day's line-up for both houses.

Just past security to the left, study the big dark **Westminster Hall,** which survived the 1834 fire. The hall was built in the 11th century, and its famous self-supporting hammer-beam roof was added in 1397. The Houses of Parliament are located in what was once the Palace of Westminster, long the palace of England's medieval kings, until it was largely destroyed by fire in 1834. The palace was rebuilt in Victorian Gothic style (a move away from neo-classicism back to England's Christian and medieval heritage, true to the Romantic Age). It was completed in 1860.

Houses of Parliament tours are offered in August and September (£7; 75 min, roughly Mon, Tue, Fri, and Sat 9:15–16:30; Wed and Thu 13:15–16:30; to avoid waits, book in advance through First Call, tel. 0870-906-3773, www.firstcalltickets.com, no booking fee). Meet your Blue Badge guide (at the Sovereign's Entrance—far south end) for a behind-the-scenes peek at the royal chambers and both Houses.

The **Jewel Tower** is the only other part of the old Palace of Westminster to survive (besides Westminster Hall). It contains a fine little exhibit on Parliament (first floor—history, second floor—Parliament today) with a 25-minute video and lonely, picnic-friendly benches (£2, April–Sept daily 10:00–18:00, Oct daily 10:00–17:00, Nov–March daily 10:00–16:00, across street from St. Stephen's Gate, tel. 020/7222-2219).

Big Ben, the clock tower (315 feet high), is named for its 13-ton bell, Ben. The light above the clock is lit when the House of Commons is sitting. The face of the clock is huge—you can actually see the minute hand moving. For a hip view of it, walk halfway over Westminster Bridge.

▲▲**Cabinet War Rooms**—This is a fascinating walk through the underground headquarters of the British government's fight against the Nazis in the darkest days of the Battle for Britain. The 27-room nerve center of the British war effort was used from 1939 to 1945. Churchill's room, the map room, and other rooms are just as they were in 1945. For

National Gallery Highlights

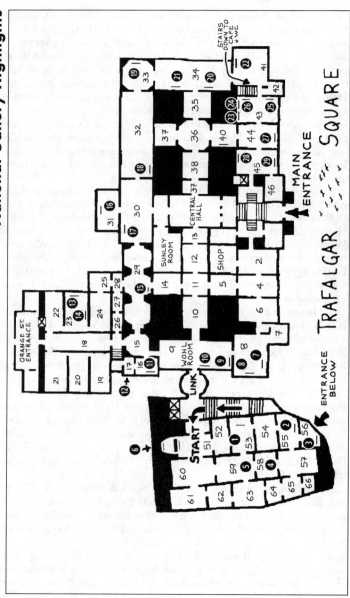

ORANGE ST. ENTRANCE

TRAFALGAR SQUARE

MAIN ENTRANCE

STAIRS DOWN TO CAFÉ + WC

ENTRANCE BELOW

START

LINK

WOHL ROOM

SUNLEY ROOM

CENTRAL HALL

SHOP

MEDIEVAL & EARLY RENAISSANCE

1 Wilton Diptych
2 UCCELLO Battle of San Romano
3 VAN EYCK Arnolfini Marriage
4 BOTTICELLI Venus and Mars
5 CRIVELLI Annunciation with St. Emidius

HIGH RENAISSANCE

6 LEONARDO DA VINCI Virgin and Child (painting and cartoon)

NATIONAL GALLERY MAIN BUILDING – HIGH RENAISSANCE

7 MICHELANGELO Entombment
8 RAPHAEL Pope Julius II

VENETIAN RENAISSANCE

9 TITIAN Bacchus and Ariadne
10 TINTORETTO Origin of the Milky Way

NORTHERN PROTESTANT ART

11 VERMEER Young Woman
12 "A PEEPSHOW"
13 REMBRANDT Belshazzar's Feast
14 REMBRANDT Self-Portrait

BAROQUE & ROCOCO

15 RUBENS The Judgment of Paris
16 VAN DYCK Charles I on Horseback
17 VELAZQUEZ The Rokeby Venus
18 CARAVAGGIO Supper at Emmaus
19 BOUCHER Pan and Syrinx

BRITISH

20 CONSTABLE The Hay Wain
21 TURNER The Fighting Temeraire
22 DELAROCHE The Execution of Lady Jane Grey

IMPRESSIONISM & BEYOND

23 MONET Gare St. Lazare
24 MONET The Water Lily Pond
25 MANET The Waitress (Corner of a Café-Concert)
26 RENOIR Boating on the Seine
27 SEURAT Bathers at Asnières
28 VAN GOGH Sunflowers
29 CEZANNE Bathers

all the blood, sweat, toil, and tears details, pick up an audioguide at the entry and follow the included and excellent 60-minute tour. Be patient—it's worth it (£7, April–Sept daily 9:30–18:00, Oct–March daily 10:00–18:00, last entry 45 min before closing, on King Charles Street 200 yards off Whitehall, follow the signs, Tube: Westminster, tel. 020/7930-6961, www.iwm.org.uk).

For a nearby pub lunch, try the Westminster Arms (food served downstairs, on Storey's Gate, a couple of blocks south of Cabinet War Rooms).

Horse Guards—The Horse Guards change daily at 11:00 (10:00 on Sun), and there's a colorful dismounting ceremony daily at 16:00. The rest of the day, they just stand there—terrible for camcorders (on Whitehall, between Trafalgar Square and #10 Downing Street, Tube: Westminster). While Buckingham Palace pageantry is canceled when it rains, the horse guards change regardless of the weather.

▲**Banqueting House**—England's first Renaissance building was designed by Inigo Jones around 1620. It's one of the few London landmarks spared by the 1666 fire and the only surviving part of the original Palace of Whitehall. Don't miss its Peter Paul Rubens ceiling, which, at Charles I's request, drove home the doctrine of the legitimacy of the divine right of kings. In 1649—divine right ignored—Charles I was beheaded on the balcony of this building by a Cromwellian parliament. Admission includes a restful 20-minute audiovisual history, which shows the place in banqueting action; a 30-minute audio tour—interesting only to history buffs; and a look at the exquisite banqueting hall (£4, Mon–Sat 10:00–17:00, closed Sun, last entry at 16:30, subject to closure for government functions, aristocratic WC, immediately across Whitehall from the Horse Guards, Tube: Westminster, tel. 020/7930-4179). Just up the street is Trafalgar Square.

Trafalgar Square

▲▲**Trafalgar Square**—London's central square, the climax of most marches and demonstrations, is a thrilling place to simply hang out. Lord Nelson stands atop his 185-foot-tall fluted granite column, gazing out to Trafalgar, where he lost his life but defeated the French fleet. Part of this 1842 memorial is made from his victims' melted-down cannons. He's surrounded by giant lions, hordes of people, and—until recently—even more pigeons. London's mayor, Ken Livingstone (nicknamed "Red Ken" for his passion for an activist government), decided that London's "flying rats" were a public nuisance and evicted the venerable seed salesmen (Tube: Charing Cross).

▲▲▲**National Gallery**—Displaying Britain's top collection of European paintings from 1250 to 1900 (works by Leonardo, Botticelli, Velázquez, Rembrandt, Turner, van Gogh, and the Impressionists), this is one of Europe's great galleries. While the collection is huge, following the route suggested on the map (on page 546) will give you my best quick visit. The audioguide tours are the best I've used in Europe (suggested £4 donation). Don't miss the Micro Gallery, a computer room even your dad could have fun in (closes 30 min earlier than museum); you can study any artist, style, or topic in the museum and even print out a tailor-made tour map (free, daily 10:00–18:00, Wed until 21:00, free one-hour overview tours daily at 11:30 and 14:30 plus Wed at 18:30, photography prohibited, on Trafalgar Square, Tube: Charing Cross or Leicester Square, tel. 020/7747-2885, www.nationalgallery .org.uk).

▲▲**National Portrait Gallery**—Put off by halls of 19th-century characters who meant nothing to me, I used to call this "as interesting as someone else's yearbook." But a selective walk through this 500-year-long *Who's Who* of British history is quick and free and puts faces on the story of England. A bonus is the chance to admire some great art by painters such as Hans Holbein, Sir Anthony Van Dyck, William Hogarth, Sir Joshua Reynolds, and Thomas Gainsborough. The collection is well described, not huge, and in historical sequence, from the 16th century on the second floor to today's royal family on the ground floor.

Some highlights: Henry VIII and wives; several fascinating portraits of the "Virgin Queen" Elizabeth I, Sir Francis Drake, and Sir Walter Raleigh; the only real-life portrait of William Shakespeare; Oliver Cromwell and Charles I with his head on; self-portraits and other portraits by Gainsborough and Reynolds; the Romantics (William Blake, Lord Byron, William Wordsworth, and company); Queen Victoria and her era; and the present royal family, including the late Princess Diana.

The excellent audioguide tours (£3 donation requested) describe each room (or era in British history) and more than 300 paintings. You'll learn more about British history from art and actually hear interviews with 20th-century subjects as you stare at their faces (free, daily 10:00–18:00, Thu–Fri until 21:00, entry 100 yards off Trafalgar Square, around corner from National Gallery, opposite Church of St. Martin-in-the-Fields, tel. 020/7306-0055, recorded info tel. 020/7312-2463, www.npg .org.uk). The elegant Portrait Restaurant on the top floor comes with views and high prices (cheaper Portrait Café in basement).

▲**St. Martin-in-the-Fields**—This church, built in the 1720s with a Gothic spire atop a Greek-type temple, is an oasis of peace on the wild and noisy Trafalgar Square (free, donations welcome, open daily, www .stmartin-in-the-fields.org). St. Martin cared for the poor. "In the fields" was where the first church stood on this spot (in the 13th century), between Westminster and the City. Stepping inside, you still feel a compassion for the needs of the people in this community. A free flier provides a brief yet worthwhile self-guided tour. The church is famous for

London's Top Squares

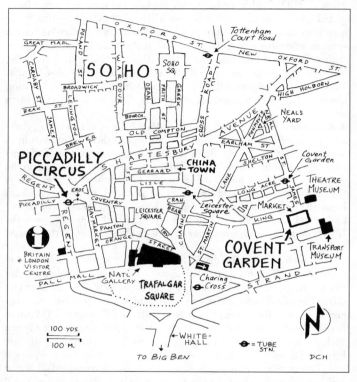

its concerts. Consider a free lunchtime concert (Mon, Tue, and Fri at 13:05) or an evening concert (£6–18, Thu–Sat at 19:30, box office tel. 020/7839-8362, church tel. 020/7766-1100). Downstairs, you'll find a ticket office for concerts, a gift shop, a brass-rubbing center, and a fine support-the-church cafeteria (see "Eating," below).

More Top Squares: Piccadilly, Soho, and Covent Garden

For a "Food Is Fun" dinner crawl from Covent Garden to Soho, see "Eating," below.

▲▲**Piccadilly Circus**—London's most touristy square got its name from the fancy ruffled shirts—*picadils*—made in the neighborhood long ago. Today the square is surrounded by fascinating streets swimming with youth on the rampage. For overstimulation, drop by the extremely trashy **Pepsi Trocadero Center**'s "theme park of the future" for its

Segaworld virtual-reality games, nine-screen cinema, and thundering IMAX theater (admission to Trocadero is free; individual attractions cost £2–8; before paying full price for IMAX, look for a discount ticket at brochure racks at the TI or hotels; located between Coventry Street and Shaftesbury Avenue, just off Piccadilly). Chinatown, to the east, has swollen since Hong Kong lost its independence. Nearby Shaftesbury Avenue and Leicester Square teem with fun-seekers, theaters, Chinese restaurants, and street singers.

Soho—North of Piccadilly, trendy but motley Soho is well worth a gawk. But Soho is also London's red light district, where "friendly models" wait in tiny rooms up dreary stairways and voluptuous con artists sell strip shows. While venturing up a stairway to check out a model is interesting, anyone who goes into any one of the shows will be ripped off. Every time. Even a £5 show in a "licensed bar" comes with a £100 cover or minimum (as it's printed on the drink menu) and a "security man." You may accidentally buy a £200 bottle of bubbly. And suddenly, the door has no handle.

Telephone sex is hard to avoid these days in London. Phone booths are littered with racy fliers of busty ladies "new in town." Some travelers gather six or eight phone booths' worth of fliers and take them home for kinky wallpaper.

▲▲**Covent Garden**—This boutique-ish shopping district is a people-watcher's delight, with cigarette eaters, Punch-and-Judy acts, food that's good for you (but not your wallet), trendy crafts, sweet whiffs of marijuana, two-tone hair (neither natural), and faces that could set off a metal detector (Tube: Covent Garden). For better Covent Garden lunch deals, walk a block or two away from the eye of this touristic hurricane (check out the places north of the Tube station along Endell and Neal streets).

Museums near Covent Garden

▲▲**Somerset House**—This grand 18th-century civic palace offers a marvelous public space, three fine art collections, and a riverside terrace (between the Strand and the Thames). The palace once housed the national registry that records Britain's births, marriages, and deaths ("where they hatched 'em, latched 'em, and dispatched 'em"). Step into the courtyard to enjoy the fountain. Go ahead...walk through it. The 55 jets get playful twice an hour.

Surrounding you are three small and sumptuous sights: the Courtauld Gallery (paintings), the Gilbert Collection (fine arts), and the Hermitage Rooms (the finest art of czarist Russia). All three are open the same hours (daily 10:00–18:00, buy a ticket at one gallery and get a £1 discount off admission to either or both of the other two on the same day, easy bus #6, #9, #11, #13, #15, or #23 from Trafalgar Square, Tube: Temple or Covent Garden, tel. 020/7848-2526 or 020/7845-4600,

Central London

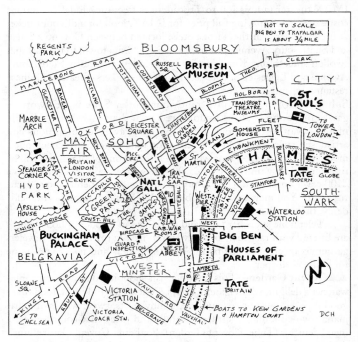

NOT TO SCALE
BIG BEN TO TRAFALGAR
IS ABOUT 3/4 MILE

REGENTS PARK

BLOOMSBURY

MARYLEBONE ROAD

PORTLAND PL.

BAKER ST.

GLOUCESTER PL.

RUSSELL SQ.

BRITISH MUSEUM

TOTTENHAM COURT RD.

BLOOMS. BURY

THEO.

CLERK.

CITY

HOLBORN

HIGH

BLOOMS.

ST PAUL'S

TRANSPORT THEATRE MUSEUMS

MARBLE ARCH

OXFORD

NEW BOND ST.

LEICESTER SQUARE

SHAFTESBURY

COVENT GARDEN

CHARING CROSS RD.

SOMERSET HOUSE

FLEET

STRAND

EMBANKMENT

TO TOWER OF LONDON

MAY FAIR

SOHO

PICC. CIRC.

ST. MARTIN

VICTORIA

WATERLOO

BLACKFRIARS

THAMES

GLOBE

SPEAKER'S CORNER

BRITAIN & LONDON VISITOR CENTRE

NATL GALL.

TRA. FAL. GAR.

LOND. EYE

STAMFORD

TATE MODERN

SOUTH-WARK

HYDE PARK

PICCADILLY

GREEN PARK

THE MALL

WHITEHALL

WEST. PIER.

JUBILEE WALK

YORK

WATERLOO STATION

APSLEY HOUSE

CONST. HILL

ST JAMES PARK

WEST.

KNIGHTSBRIDGE

BUCKINGHAM PALACE

BIRDCAGE

GUARD INSPECTION

CAB. WAR ROOMS

WEST. ABBEY

BIG BEN

HOUSES OF PARLIAMENT

BELGRAVIA

VICTORIA

WEST-MINSTER

LAMBETH

MILLBANK

SLOANE SQ.

KINGS ROAD

EBURY ST.

VICTORIA STATION

VAUX BR RD.

TATE BRITAIN

TO CHELSEA

VICTORIA COACH STN.

BELGRAVE

VAUXHALL

BOATS TO KEW GARDENS & HAMPTON COURT

DCH

www.somerset-house.org.uk). The Web site lists a busy schedule of tours, kids' events, and concerts. The riverside terrace is picnic-friendly (deli inside lobby).

The **Courtauld Gallery** is less impressive than the National Gallery, but its wonderful collection of paintings is still a joy. The gallery is part of the Courtauld Institute of Art, and the thoughtful description of each piece of art reminds visitors that the gallery is still used for teaching. You'll see medieval European paintings and works by Rubens, the Impressionists (Edouard Manet, Claude Monet, Edgar Degas, Georges Seurat), Post-Impressionists (such as Paul Cézanne), and more (£5, free Mon until 14:00, last admission 17:15, downstairs cafeteria, cloak room, lockers, and WC).

The **Hermitage Rooms** offer a taste of Romanov imperial splendor. As Russia struggles and tourists are staying away, someone had the bright idea of sending the best of its art to London to raise some hard cash. These five rooms host a different collection every six months, with a standard intro to the czar's winter palace in St. Petersburg (£6, includes unmissable live video of the square, tel. 020/7420-9410). To see what's on, visit www.hermitagerooms.org.uk.

The **Gilbert Collection** displays 800 pieces of the finest in European decorative arts, from diamond-studded gold snuffboxes to intricate Italian mosaics. Maybe you've seen Raphael paintings and Botticelli frescoes...but this lush collection is refreshingly different (£5, includes free audioguide with a highlights tour and a helpful loaner magnifying glass, free after 16:30, last admission 17:30).

▲**London Transport Museum**—This wonderful museum is a delight for kids. Whether you're cursing or marveling at the buses and Tube, the growth of Europe's biggest city has been made possible by its public transit system. Watch the growth of the Tube, then sit in the simulator to "drive" a train (£6, kids under 16 free, Sat–Thu 10:00–18:00, Fri 11:00–18:00, 30 yards southeast of Covent Garden's marketplace, tel. 020/7565-7299).

Theatre Museum—This earnest museum, worthwhile for theater buffs, traces the development of British theater from Shakespeare to today (free, Tue–Sun 10:00–18:00, closed Mon, free guided tours at 11:00, 12:00, and 16:00, a block east of Covent Garden's marketplace down Russell Street, tel. 020/7943-4700, www.theatremuseum.org).

North London

▲▲▲**British Museum, Great Court, and Reading Room**—Simply put, this is the greatest chronicle of civilization...anywhere. A visit here is like taking a long hike through Encyclopedia Britannica National Park. Entering on Great Russell Street, you'll step into the Great Court, the glass-domed hub of a two-acre cultural complex, containing restaurants, shops, and lecture halls plus the Round Reading Room.

The most popular sections of the museum fill the ground floor: Egyptian, Mesopotamian, and ancient Greek—with the famous Elgin Marbles from the Athenian Parthenon. Huge winged lions (which guarded Assyrian palaces 800 years before Christ) guard these great ancient galleries. For a brief tour, connect these ancient dots:

Start with the **Egyptian.** Wander from the Rosetta Stone past the many statues. At the end of the hall, climb the stairs to mummy land.

Back at the winged lions, wander through the dark, violent, and mysterious **Assyrian** rooms. The Nimrud Gallery is lined with royal propaganda reliefs and wounded lions.

The most modern of the ancient art fills the **Greek** section. Find room 11 behind the winged lions and start your walk through Greek art history with the simple and primitive Cycladic fertility figures. Later, painted vases show a culture really into partying. The finale is the Elgin Marbles. The much-wrangled-over bits of the Athenian Parthenon (from 450 B.C.) are even more impressive than they look. To best appreciate these ancient carvings, take the audioguide tour (available in this gallery).

British Museum

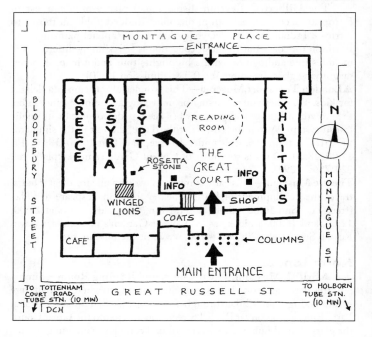

Be sure to venture upstairs to see artifacts from **Roman Britain** (Room 50) that surpass anything you'll see at Hadrian's Wall or elsewhere in Britain. Nearby, the Dark Age Britain exhibits offer a worthwhile peek at that bleak era; look for the Sutton Hoo Ship Burial artifacts from a seventh-century royal burial on the east coast of England (Room 41). A rare Michelangelo cartoon is in Room 90.

The **Queen Elizabeth II Great Court** is Europe's largest covered square—bigger than a football field. This people-friendly court—delightfully out of the London rain—was for 150 years one of London's great lost spaces...closed off and gathering dust. While the vast British Museum wraps around the court, its centerpiece is the stately **Reading Room**—famous as the place where Karl Marx hung out while formulating his ideas on communism and writing *Das Kapital.* The Reading Room—one of the fine cast-iron buildings of the 19th century—is free for you to wander, but there's little to see that you can't see from the doorway.

Hours and Location: The British Museum is free (£2 donation requested, daily 10:00–17:30, Thu–Fri until 20:30—but only a few galleries open after 17:30, least crowded weekday late afternoons, Great Russell Street, Tube: Tottenham Court Road, tel. 020/7323-8000 or recorded information 020/7388-2227, www.thebritishmuseum.ac.uk). The Reading Room is free and open daily 10:00–17:30 (Thu until 20:30). Computer terminals within the Reading Room offer COMPASS, a database of information about selected museum items. The Great Court has longer opening hours than the museum (daily 9:00–18:00, Thu–Sat until 23:00).

Tours: Guided **eyeOpener tours** (free, nearly hrly, 50 min) are each different, focusing on one particular subject within the museum. These leave throughout the day and can make the visit much more meaningful. There are also three types of **audioguide tours:** Top 50 highlights (90 min, pick up at Great Court information desks), the Parthenon Sculptures (60 min, get at desk outside Parthenon Galleries), and the family tour, with themes such as "bodies, boardgames, and beasts" (length varies, pick up at Great Court information desks). To rent an audioguide (£3.50), you'll need to leave a photo ID and £10 for a deposit.

▲▲▲**British Library**—The British Empire built its greatest monuments out of paper. And it's in literature that England made her lasting contribution to civilization and the arts. Britain's national archives has more than 12 million books, 180 miles of shelving, and the deepest

British Library Highlights

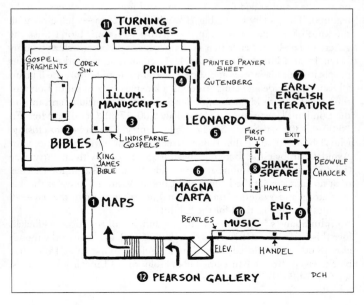

basement in London. But everything that matters for your visit is in one delightful room labeled "The Treasures." This room is filled with literary and historical documents that changed the course of history. You'll trace the evolution of European maps over 800 years. Follow the course of the Bible—from the earliest known gospels (written on scraps of papyrus) to the first complete Bible to the original King James version and the Gutenberg Bible. You'll see Leonardo's doodles, the Magna Carta, Shakespeare's First Folio, the original *Alice in Wonderland* in Lewis Carroll's handwriting, and manuscripts by Ludwig van Beethoven, Wolfgang Amadeus Mozart, John Lennon, and Paul McCartney. Finish in the fascinating *Turning the Pages* exhibit, which lets you actually browse through virtual manuscripts of a few of these treasures on a computer (free, Mon–Fri 9:30–18:00, Tue until 20:00, Sat 9:30–17:00, Sun 11:00–17:00; 60-min tours for £5 usually offered Mon, Wed, and Fri–Sun at 15:00, also Tue 18:30, Sat 10:30, and Sun 11:30; call 020/7412-7332 to confirm schedule and reserve; £3.50 audio-guide, £1 lockers, Tube: King's Cross, turn right out of station and walk a block to 96 Euston Road, library tel. 020/7412-7000, www.bl.uk). The ground-floor café is next to a vast and fun pull-out stamp collection, and the cafeteria upstairs serves good hot meals.

▲**Madame Tussaud's Waxworks**—This is expensive but dang good. The original Madame Tussaud did wax casts of heads lopped off during the French Revolution (such as Marie-Antoinette's). She took her show on the road and ended up in London. And now it's much easier to be featured. The gallery is one big *Who's Who* photo-op—a huge hit with the kind of travelers who skip the British Museum. Don't miss the gallery of has-been heads that no longer merit a body (such as Sammy Davis Jr. and Nikita Khrushchev). After looking a hundred famous people in their glassy eyes and surviving a silly hall of horror, you'll board a Disney-type ride and cruise through a kid-pleasing "Spirit of London" time trip (£20, children-£15, under 5 free, tickets include entrance to the London Planetarium, Jan–Sept daily 9:00–17:30, Oct–Dec Mon–Fri 10:00–17:30, Sat–Sun 9:30–17:30, last entry 30 min before closing, Marylebone Road, Tube: Baker Street). The waxworks are popular. Avoid a wait by either booking ahead to get a ticket with an entry time (tel. 0870-400-3000, online at www.madame-tussauds.com for a £2 fee, or at no extra cost at the Britain and London Visitors Centre or the TIs at Victoria and Waterloo train stations) or arriving late in the day—90 minutes is plenty of time for the exhibit.

Sir John Soane's Museum—Architects and fans of eclectic knickknacks love this quirky place (free, Tue–Sat 10:00–17:00, first Tue of the month also 18:00–21:00, closed Sun–Mon, £3 guided tours Sat at 14:30, five blocks east of British Museum, Tube: Holborn, 13 Lincoln's Inn Fields, tel. 020/7405-2107).

Buckingham Palace

▲**Buckingham Palace**—This lavish home has been Britain's royal residence since 1837. When the queen is at home, the royal standard flies; otherwise the Union Jack flaps in the wind (£12 for state apartments and throne room, open Aug–Sept only, daily 9:30–17:00, only 8,000 visitors a day—to get an entry time, come early or for £1 extra book ahead by phone or online, Tube: Victoria, tel. 020/7321-2233, www.the-royal -collection.com, buckinghampalace@royalcollection.org.uk).

Royal Mews—Actually the queen's working stables, the "mews" are open to visitors to wander, talk to the horse-keeper, and see the well-groomed horses. Marvel at the gilded coaches paraded during royal festivals, see fancy horse gear—all well-described—and learn how skeptical the attendants were when the royals first parked a car in the stables (£5, April–Oct 11:00–16:00, closed Nov–March, Buckingham Palace Road, tel. 020/7321-2233).

▲▲**Changing of the Guard at Buckingham Palace**—The guards change with much fanfare at 11:30 almost daily in the summer and at a minimum, every other day all year long (no band when wet). Each month it's either daily or on odd or even days. Call 020/7321-2233 for the day's plan (or check www.royalresidences.com). Join the mob behind the palace (the front faces a huge and extremely private park). You'll need to be early or tall to see much of the actual Changing of the Guard, but for the pageantry in the street you can pop by at 11:30. Stake out the high ground on the circular Victoria Monument for the best overall view. The marching troops and bands are colorful and even stirring, but the actual Changing of the Guard is a nonevent. It is interesting, however, to see nearly every tourist in London gathered in one place at the same time. Hop into a big black taxi and say, "Buck House, please." The show lasts about 30 minutes: Three troops parade by, the guard changes with much shouting, the band plays a happy little concert, and then they march out. On a balmy day, it's a fun happening.

For all the pomp with none of the crowds, see the colorful **Inspection of the Guard** ceremony at 11:00 in front of the **Wellington Barracks,** 500 yards east of the palace on Birdcage Walk. Afterward, stroll through nearby St. James's Park (Tube: Victoria, St. James's Park, or Green Park).

West London

▲**Hyde Park and Speakers' Corner**—London's "Central Park," originally Henry VIII's hunting grounds, has more than 600 acres of lush greenery, a huge man-made lake, the royal Kensington Palace (not worth touring), and the ornate neo-Gothic Albert Memorial across from the Royal Albert Hall. Early afternoons on Sunday (until early evening), Speakers' Corner offers soapbox oratory at its best (Tube: Marble Arch).

West London

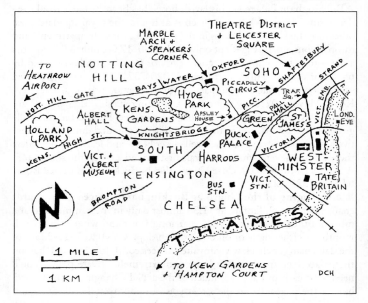

"The grass roots of democracy" is actually a holdover from when the gallows stood here, and the criminal was allowed to say just about anything he wanted to before he swung. I dare you to raise your voice and gather a crowd—it's easy to do.

▲**Apsley House (Wellington Museum)**—Having beaten Napoleon at Waterloo, the Duke of Wellington was once the most famous man in Europe. He was given London's ultimate address, #1 London. His newly refurbished mansion offers one of London's best palace experiences. An 11-foot-tall marble statue (by Antonio Canova) of Napoleon, clad only in a fig leaf, greets you. Downstairs is a small gallery of Wellington memorabilia (including a pair of Wellington boots). The lavish upstairs shows off the duke's fine collection of paintings, including works by Velázquez and Jan Steen (£4.50, Tue–Sun 11:00–17:00, closed Mon, well-described by included audioguide, 20 yards from Hyde Park Corner Tube station, tel. 020/7499-5676, www.apsleyhouse.org.uk). Hyde Park's pleasant and picnic-wonderful rose garden is nearby.

▲▲**Victoria and Albert Museum**—The world's top collection of decorative arts (vases, stained glass, fine furniture, clothing, jewelry, carpets, and more) is a surprisingly interesting assortment of crafts from the West as well as Asian and Islamic cultures.

The V&A, which grew out of the Great Exhibition of 1851—that ultimate festival celebrating the Industrial Revolution and the greatness of Britain—was originally for manufactured art, but fine art sculptures (and copies) were soon added. After much support from Queen Victoria and Prince Albert, it was renamed after the royal couple, and its present building was opened in 1909. The idealistic Victorian notion that anyone can be continually improved by education and example remains the driving force behind this museum.

Cost, Hours, and Location: Free, possible fee for special exhibits, daily 10:00–17:45, Wed until 21:30 (Tube: South Kensington, a long tunnel leads directly from the Tube station to the museum, tel. 020/7942-2000, www.vam.ac.uk).

Museum Overview and Tours: The museum is large and gangly, with 150 rooms and over 12 miles of corridors. While just wandering works well here, consider catching one of the free 60-minute orientation tours (daily, on the half-hour from 10:30–15:30, also daily at 13:00, Wed at 16:30, and a half-hour version at 19:30) or buying the fine £5 *Hundred Highlights* guidebook, or the handy £1 *What to See at the V&A* brochure (outlines five self-guided, speedy tours).

To tour this museum on your own, grab a museum map and start with these ground-floor highlights:

Near the entrance: The **Medieval Treasury** (room 43) has stained glass, bishops' robes, old columns, and good descriptions. Statues by **Antonio Canova** (room 50A)—white, polished, and pretty Greek graces, minotaurs, and nymphs—are rare originals by the neoclassical master.

Southeast corner (to the right of entrance, at the end of the hall): Plaster casts of **Trajan's Column** (room 46A) are a copy of Rome's 140-foot spiral relief telling the story of the conquest of Romania. (The V&A's casts are copies made for the benefit of 19th-century art students who couldn't afford a railpass.) Plaster casts of **Renaissance sculptures** (room 46B) let you compare Michelangelo's monumental *David* with Donatello's girlish *David;* see also Lorenzo Ghiberti's bronze Baptistery doors that inspired the Florentine Renaissance. The hall of **Great Fakes and Forgeries** (room 46) chronicles concocted art and historical objects passed off as originals.

Southwest corner (left of entrance, end of hall): **Raphael's "cartoons"** (room 48A) are seven huge watercolor designs by the Renaissance master for tapestries meant for the Sistine Chapel. The cartoons were sent to Brussels, cut into strips (see the lines), and placed on the looms. Notice that the scenes, the Acts of Peter and Paul, are the reverse of the final product (lots of left-handed saints). The **Dress Gallery** (in room 40) has 400 years of English fashion corseted into 40 display cases. The **Musical Instruments** section displays lutes, harpsichords, early flutes, big violins, and strange, curly horns—some recognizable, some obsolete (room 40A, up the staircase in the center of the Dress Gallery).

The rest of the ground floor: Room 41 has the finest collection of

Indian decorative art outside India. There's medieval **stained glass** in room 28 (and much more upstairs).

Upstairs you can walk through the **British Galleries** for centuries of British furniture, clothing, glass, jewelry, and sculpture.

▲**Natural History Museum**—Across the street from Victoria and Albert, this mammoth museum is housed in a giant and wonderful Victorian, neo-Romanesque building. Built in the 1870s specifically to house the huge collection (50 million specimens), it has two halves: the Life Galleries (creepy-crawlies, human biology, the origin of species, "our place in evolution," and awesome dinosaurs) and the Earth Galleries (meteors, volcanoes, earthquakes, and so on). Exhibits are wonderfully explained, with lots of creative interactive displays. Pop in, if only for the wild collection of dinosaurs and the roaring *Tyrannosaurus rex.* Free 45-minute highlights tours occur daily about every hour from 11:00 to 16:00 (free, possible fee for special exhibits, Mon–Sat 10:00–18:00, Sun 11:00–18:00, last entrance 17:30, a long tunnel leads directly from South Kensington Tube station to museum, tel. 020/7942-5000, exhibit info and reservations tel. 020/7942-5011, www.nhm.ac.uk).

Science Museum—A sister to the Natural History museum, next door, this sprawling wonderland for curious minds is kid-perfect. It offers hands-on fun, from moon walks to deep-sea exploration, with trendy technology exhibits, an IMAX theater, and a kids' zone in the basement (free, daily 10:00–18:00, Exhibition Road, tel. 0870-870-4868).

East London: The City

▲▲**The City of London**—When Londoners say "The City," they mean the one-square-mile business, banking, and journalism center that 2,000 years ago was Roman Londinium. The outline of the Roman city walls can still be seen in the arc of roads from Blackfriars Bridge to Tower Bridge. Within the City are 24 churches designed by Christopher Wren, mostly just ornamentation around St. Paul's Cathedral. Today, while home to only 5,000 residents, the City thrives with over 500,000 office workers coming and going daily. It's a fascinating district to wander on weekdays, but since almost nobody actually lives there, it's dull in the evenings and on Saturday and Sunday.

▲**Old Bailey**—To view the British legal system in action—lawyers in little blond wigs speaking legalese with a British accent—spend a few minutes in the visitors' gallery at the Old Bailey (free, no kids under 14, Mon–Fri 10:30–13:00 & 14:00–16:30 most weeks, closed Sat–Sun, reduced hours in Aug; no bags, mobile phones, or cameras, but small purses OK; you can check your bag at the bagel shop next door—or any other entrepreneurial place nearby—for £1; Tube: St. Paul's, two blocks northwest of St. Paul's on Old Bailey street, follow signs to public entrance, tel. 020/7248-3277).

▲▲▲**St. Paul's Cathedral**—Wren's most famous church is the great

East London: The City

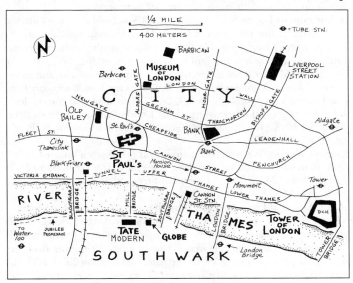

St. Paul's, its elaborate interior capped by a 365-foot dome. The crypt (included with admission) is a world of historic bones and memorials, including Admiral Nelson's tomb and interesting cathedral models. The great West Door is opened only for great occasions, such as the wedding of Prince Charles and the late Princess Diana in 1981. Stand in the back of the church and imagine how Diana felt before making the hike to the altar with the world watching. Sit under the second-largest dome in the world and eavesdrop on guided tours.

Since World War II, St. Paul's has been Britain's symbol of resistance. Despite 57 nights of bombing, the Nazis failed to destroy the cathedral, thanks to the St. Paul's volunteer fire watchmen, who stayed on the dome. Climb the dome for a great city view and some fun in the Whispering Gallery—where the precisely designed barrel of the dome lets sweet nothings circle audibly around to the opposite side (£6, includes church entry and dome climb, Mon–Sat 8:30–16:30, last entry 16:00, closed Sun except for worship and organ recital, no photography allowed, £2.50 for guided 90-min "super tours" of cathedral and crypt Mon–Sat at 11:00, 11:30, 13:30, and 14:00, confirm schedule at church or call 020/7236-4128; £3.50 for audioguide tour available Mon–Sat 8:45–15:00; Tube: St. Paul's). Sunday services are at 8:00, 10:15, 11:30 (sung Eucharist), 15:15 (evensong), and 18:00, with a free organ recital at 17:00. The **evensong** services are free, but nonpaying visitors are not allowed to linger afterward (Mon–Sat at 17:00, Sun at 15:15, 40 min). You'll find an inexpensive and cheery café in the crypt.

▲**Museum of London**—London, a 2,000-year-old city, is so littered with Roman ruins that when a London builder finds Roman antiquities, he doesn't stop work. He simply documents the finds, moves the artifacts to a museum, and builds on. If you're asking, "Why did the Romans build their cities underground?" a trip to the creative and entertaining London Museum is a must. Stroll through London history from pre-Roman times through the 1920s. This regular stop for the local school kids gives the best overview of London history in town (free, Mon–Sat 10:00–18:00, Sun 12:00–18:00, Tube: Barbican or St. Paul's, tel. 020/7600-3699).

Geffrye Decorative Arts Museum—Walk through a dozen English front rooms from 1600 to 1990 (free, Tue–Sat 10:00–17:00, Sun 12:00–17:00, closed Mon, Tube: Liverpool Street, then bus #149 or #242 north, tel. 020/7739-9893).

▲▲▲**Tower of London**—The tower has served as a castle in wartime, a king's residence in peace, and, most notoriously, as the prison and execution site of rebels. This historic fortress is host to more than three million visitors a year. Enjoy the free and entertaining 50-minute Beefeater tour (leaves regularly from inside the gate, first one usually at 9:30, last one usually at 15:30, 14:30 off-season). The crown jewels, dating from the Restoration, are the best on Earth—and come with hour-long lines for most of the day. To avoid the crowds, arrive when the Tower opens and go straight for the jewels, doing the Beefeater tour and White Tower later—or do the jewels after 16:30 (£13.50, one-day combo-ticket with Hampton Court Palace-£18, March–Oct Mon–Sat 9:00–18:00, Sun 10:00–18:00; Nov–Feb Tue–Sat 9:00–17:00, Sun–Mon 10:00–17:00; last entry 60 min before closing, the long but fast-moving ticket line is worst on Sun, no photography allowed of jewels or in chapels, skip the £3 audioguide, Tube: Tower Hill, tel. 0870-751-5177, recorded info: 020/7680-9004, booking: 020/7488-5681). You can avoid the long lines by picking up your ticket at any London TI or the Tower Hill Tube station ticket office.

Ceremony of the Keys—Every night at precisely 21:30, with pageantry-filled ceremony, the Tower of London is locked up, as it has been for the last 700 years. To attend this free 30-minute event (which some find dull and others thrilling), you need to request an invitation at least two months before your visit. Write to Ceremony of the Keys, H.M. Tower of London, London EC3N 4AB. Include your name; the addresses, names, and ages of all people attending (up to 6 people, nontransferable, no kids under age 8 allowed); requested date; alternative dates; and two international reply coupons (buy at U.S. post office—if your post office doesn't have the $1.75 coupons in stock, they can order them; the turn-around time is a few days).

South London, on the South Bank

The South Bank is a thriving arts and cultural center tied together by a riverside path. This popular, pub-crawling walk—called the Jubilee Promenade—stretches from the Tower Bridge past Westminster Bridge, where it offers grand views of the Houses of Parliament. (The promenade hugs the river except just east of London Bridge, where it cuts inland for a couple of blocks.)

▲▲▲London Eye Ferris Wheel—Built by British Airways, the wheel towers above London opposite Big Ben. This is the world's highest observational wheel, giving you a chance to fly British Airways without leaving London. Designed like a giant bicycle wheel, it's a pan-European undertaking: British steel and Dutch engineering, with Czech, German, French, and Italian mechanical parts. It's also very "green," running extremely efficiently and virtually silently. Twenty-five people ride in each of its 32 air-conditioned capsules for the 30-minute rotation (each capsule has a bench, but most people stand). From the top of this 450-foot-high wheel—the highest public viewpoint in the city—Big Ben looks small. You only go around once; save a shot on top for the glass capsule next to yours. Its original five-year lease has been extended to 25 years and it looks like this will become a permanent fixture on the London skyline. Thames boats come and go from here; they use the Waterloo Pier at the foot of the Wheel.

Cost, Hours, Location: £11, April–mid-Sept daily 9:30–22:00, mid-Sept–March 9:30–20:00, closed Jan for maintenance, Tube: Waterloo or Westminster, www.ba-londoneye.com.

Crowd-Beating Tips: While huge lines made advance booking smart in past years, today you can generally just buy your ticket and walk on (never more than a 30-min wait, worst weekends and on school holidays). To book a ticket (with an assigned time) in advance, buy one at a London TI, call, or go online (50p charge, automated booking tel. 0870-500-0600 or www.ba-londoneye.com). Upon arrival, you either pick up your pre-booked ticket (if you've reserved ahead) or wait in the line inside to buy tickets. Then you join the ticket-holders' line at the wheel (starting 10 min before your assigned a half-hour time slot).

Dalí Universe—Cleverly located next to the hugely popular London Eye Ferris Wheel, this exhibit features 500 works of mind-bending art by Salvador Dalí. While pricey, it's entertaining if you like Surrealism and want to learn about Dalí (£8.50, daily 10:00–18:30, generally summer eves until 20:00, last entry 1 hr before closing, tel. 020/7620-2720).

Saatchi Gallery—The new contemporary art gallery at the base of the London Eye features "YBAs"—young British artists. Rather than halls of staid canvases, the collection displays many installations, each in their own room, giving the place a kind of funhouse atmosphere.

Ponder mortality at Damien Hirst's glass case, watching flies breed, feed on a rotting cow's head, then die on the bug zapper (the

The South Bank

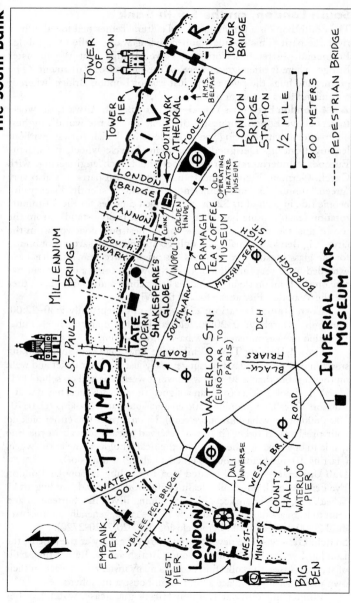

"insectocuter" in Brit-speak). Or gawk at Hirst's (real, dead) cows, pigs, sheep, and sharks sliced into sections and displayed in formaldehyde in glass cases. Ron Mueck's "Dead Dad" is an ultra-realistic (half-size) corpse in silicon and acrylic. Tracey Emin reveals herself by installing her messy bedroom in the main rotunda. And Chris Ofili scandalized New York City with a Virgin Mary splattered with elephant dung.

Much of the Saatchi's art is morbid, and visitors may be off-put or simply grossed out. It's "just conceptual art," but the concepts are realized on a large scale, with big money and ultra-modern technical know-how, and displayed in a wood-paneled Edwardian-era setting. You may not like it, you may be offended, you may find it passé—but it's something to e-mail home about (£8.50, daily 10:00–18:00, Fri–Sat until 22:00, last entry 45 min before closing, located next to London Eye, Tube: Waterloo or Westminster).

▲▲Imperial War Museum—This impressive museum covers the wars of the last century, from heavy weaponry to love notes and Vargas Girls, from Monty's Africa campaign tank to Schwarzkopf's Desert Storm uniform. You can trace the development of the machine gun, watch footage of the first tank battles, see one of more than a thousand V2 rockets Hitler rained on Britain in 1944 (each with more than a ton of explosives), hold your breath through the gruesome WWI trench experience, and buy WWII-era toys in the fun museum shop. The "Secret War" section gives a fascinating peek into the intrigues of espionage in World Wars I and II. The section on the Holocaust is one of the best on the subject anywhere. Rather than glorify war, the museum does its best to shine a light on the powerful human side of one of mankind's most persistent traits (free, daily 10:00–18:00, 90 min is enough time for most visitors, Tube: Lambeth North or bus #12 from Westminster, tel. 020/7416-5000).

The museum is housed in what was the Royal Bethlam Hospital. Also known as "the Bedlam asylum," the place was so wild it gave the world a new word for chaos: "bedlam." Back in Victorian times, locals—without trash-talk shows and cable TV—came here for their entertainment. The asylum was actually open to the paying public on weekends.

▲▲▲Tate Modern—Dedicated in the spring of 2000, this striking museum across the river from St. Paul's opened the new century with art from the old one. Its powerhouse collection of Monet, Matisse, Dalí, Picasso, Warhol, and much more is displayed in a converted power house (free, fee for special exhibitions, daily 10:00–18:00, Fri–Sat until 22:00—a good time to visit, audioguide-£1, free 1-hr guided tours at 11:00 and 14:00, call to confirm schedule, view café on top floor; cross the Millennium Bridge from St. Paul's; or Tube: Southwark plus a 10-min walk; or hop on the new Tate-to-Tate ferry from Tate Britain for £4.50; tel. 020/7887-8008, www.tate.org.uk).

CROSSING THE THAMES ON FOOT

You can cross the Thames on any of the bridges that carry car traffic over the river, but pedestrian bridges are more fun. The **Millennium Bridge,** connecting the sedate St. Paul's Cathedral and the great Tate Modern, is now open, apparently for good. The new **Golden Jubilee Bridge** (consisting of two walkways that flank a railway trestle) connects bustling Trafalgar Square on the North Bank with the London Eye Ferris Wheel and Waterloo Station on the South Bank. Replacing an old, run-down bridge, the Golden Jubilee Bridge—well lit with a sleek, futuristic look—makes this busy route safer and more popular.

▲**Millennium Bridge**—The pedestrian bridge links St. Paul's Cathedral and the Tate Modern across the Thames. This is London's first new bridge in a century. When it first opened, the $25 million bridge wiggled when people walked on it, so it promptly closed for a $7 million stabilization; now it's stable and back open (free). Nicknamed "a blade of light" for its sleek minimalist design—370 yards long, four yards wide, stainless steel with teak planks—it includes clever aerodynamic handrails to deflect wind over the heads of pedestrians.

▲▲**Shakespeare's Globe**—The original Globe Theater has been rebuilt—half-timbered and thatched—as it was in Shakespeare's time. (This is the first thatched roof in London since they were outlawed after the great fire of 1666.) The Globe originally accommodated 2,000 seated and another 1,000 standing. (Today, leaving space for reasonable aisles, the theater holds 900 seated and 600 groundlings.) Its promoters brag that the theater melds "the three A's"—actors, audience, and architecture—with each contributing to the play. Open as a museum and a working theater, it hosts authentic old-time performances of Shakespeare's plays. The theater can be toured when there are no plays. The Globe's exhibition on Shakespeare is the world's largest, with interactive displays and film presentations, a sound lab, a script factory, and costumes (£8, mid-May–Sept Mon–Sat 9:30–12:00, Sun 9:30–11:30, free 30-min actor-led tour offered on the half-hour; also open daily 12:30–16:00 but only for disappointing virtual tours; Oct–mid-May daily 10:30–17:00, free 30-min tour offered on the half-hour, on the South Bank directly across Thames over Southwark Bridge from St. Paul's, Tube: London Bridge plus a 10-min walk, tel. 020/7902-1500, www.shakespeares-globe.org). For details on seeing a play, see "Entertainment and Theater in London," below. The Globe Café is open daily (10:00–18:00, tel. 020/7902-1433).

Bramah Tea and Coffee Museum—Aficionados of tea or coffee will find this small museum fascinating. It tells the story of each drink almost passionately. The owner, Mr. Bramah, comes from a big tea family and wants the world to know how the advent of commercial television, with breaks not long enough to brew a proper pot of tea, required a faster hot drink. In came the horrible English instant coffee. Tea countered with finely chopped leaves in tea bags, and it's gone downhill ever since (£4, daily 10:00–18:00, 40 Southwark Street, Tube: London Bridge plus 3-min walk, tel. 020/7403-5650, www.bramahmuseum.co.uk). Its café, which serves more kinds of coffees and teas than cakes, is open to the public (same hours as museum). The #RV1 bus zips you here scenically from Covent Garden.

▲▲**Old Operating Theatre Museum and Herb Garret**—Climb a tight and creaky wooden spiral staircase to a church attic where you'll find a garret used to dry medicinal herbs, a fascinating exhibit on Victorian surgery, cases of well-described 19th-century medical paraphernalia, and a special look at "anesthesia, the defeat of pain." Then you stumble upon Britain's oldest operating theater, where limbs were sawed off way back in 1821 (£3.75, daily 10:30–17:00, Tube: London Bridge, 9a St. Thomas Street, tel. 020/8806-4325, www.thegarret.org.uk).

▲▲**Vinopolis: City of Wine**—While it seems illogical to have a huge wine museum in London, Vinopolis makes a good case. Built over a Roman wine store and filling the massive vaults of an old wine warehouse, the museum offers an excellent audioguide with a light yet earnest history of wine. Sipping various reds and whites, ports, and champagnes, you're immersed in your headset as you stroll and learn about the libation, such as its Georgian origins and the Chilean industry, as well as a Vespa ride through Chianti country in Tuscany. Allow some time, as the audioguide takes 90 minutes—the sipping can slow things down wonderfully (£11.50 with 5 tastes, £14 with 10 tastes, don't worry...for £2.50 you can buy 5 more tastes inside, daily 11:00–18:00, Sat and Mon until 21:00, last entry 2 hrs before closing, Tube: London Bridge, between the Globe and Southwark Cathedral at 1 Bank End, tel. 0870-241-4040 or 020/7940-8301, www.vinopolis.co.uk).

More South Bank Sights, in Southwark

These sights are mediocre but worth knowing about. The area stretching from the Tate Modern to London Bridge, known as Southwark (pron. SUTH-uck), was for centuries the place Londoners would go to escape the rules and decency of the city and let their hair down. Bear-baiting, brothels, rollicking pubs and theater—you name the dream, and it could be fulfilled just across the Thames. A run-down warehouse district through the 20th century, it's been gentrified with classy restaurants, office parks, pedestrian promenades, major sights (such as the Tate Modern and Shakespeare's Globe), and this colorful collection of lesser sights. The area is easy on foot and a scenic—though circuitous—way to connect the Tower of London with St. Paul's.

Southwark Cathedral—While made a cathedral only in 1905, it's been the neighborhood church since the 13th century and comes with some interesting history (Mon–Sat 10:00–18:00, Sun 11:00–17:00, last admission 30 min before close, evensong services weekdays at 17:30, Sun at 15:00, audioguide-£2.50, tel. 020/7367-6711).

The adjacent church-run **Long View of London Exhibition** tells the story of Southwark (£3, same hours as church).

The Clink Prison—Proudly the "original clink," this was where law-abiding citizens threw Southwark troublemakers until 1780. Today, it's a low-tech torture museum filling grotty old rooms with papier-mâché gore. Unfortunately, there's little to seriously deal with the fascinating problem of law and order in Southwark, where 18th-century Londoners went for a good time (overpriced at £4, daily 10:00–18:00, 1 Clink Street, tel. 020/7378-1558, www.clink.co.uk).

Golden Hinde **Replica**—This is a full-size replica of the 16th-century warship in which Sir Francis Drake circumnavigated the globe from 1577 to 1580. Commanding this ship, Drake earned the reputation as history's most successful pirate. The original is long gone, but this boat has logged more than 100,000 miles, including its own voyage around the world. While the ship is fun to see, its interior is not worth touring (£2.50, daily 9:30–17:30, may be closed if rented out for birthday parties, school groups, or weddings, tel. 0870-011-8700, www.goldenhinde.co.uk).

HMS *Belfast*—"The last big-gun armored warship of World War II" clogs the Thames just upstream from the Tower Bridge. This huge vessel—now manned with wax sailors—thrills kids who always dreamed of sitting in a turret shooting off their imaginary guns. If you're into WWII warships, this is the ultimate...otherwise, it's just lots of exercise with a nice view of the Tower Bridge (£6, March–Oct daily 10:00–18:00, Nov–Feb daily 10:00–17:00, tel. 020/7940-6300).

South London, on the North Bank

▲▲**Tate Britain**—One of Europe's great art houses, Tate Britain specializes in British painting from the 16th century through modern times. The museum has a good representation of William Blake's religious sketches, the Pre-Raphaelites' realistic art, and J. M. W. Turner's swirling works (free, daily 10:00–17:50, last admission 17:00, fine audioguide-£3, free tours: normally Mon–Fri at 11:00—16th, 17th, and 18th centuries; at noon—19th century; at 14:00—Turner; at 15:00—20th century; Sat–Sun at noon and 15:00—highlights; call to confirm schedule; no photography allowed, Tube: Pimlico, then 7-min walk; or arrive directly at museum by taking bus #88 from Oxford Circus or #77A from National Gallery; or catch the Tate-to-Tate ferry from Tate Modern for £4.50, tel. 020/7887-8000, recorded info tel. 020/7887-8008, www.tate.org.uk).

Greater London

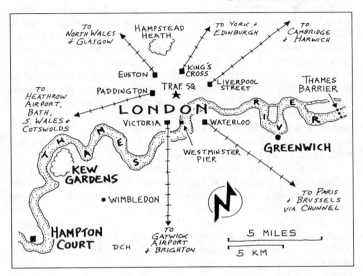

Greater London

▲**Kew Gardens**—For a fine riverside park and a palatial greenhouse jungle to swing through, take the Tube or the boat to every botanist's favorite escape, Kew Gardens. While to most visitors the Royal Botanic Gardens of Kew are simply a delightful opportunity to wander among 33,000 different types of plants, to the hardworking organization that runs the gardens, it's a way to promote understanding and preservation of the botanical diversity of our planet. The Kew Tube station drops you in an little herbal business community a two-block walk from Victoria Gate (the main garden entrance). Pick up a map brochure and check at the gate for a monthly listing of best blooms.

Garden-lovers could spend days exploring Kew's 300 acres. For a quick visit, spend a fragrant hour wandering through three buildings: the Palm House, a humid Victorian world of iron, glass, and tropical plants built in 1844; a Waterlily House that would impress Monet; and the Princess of Wales Conservatory, a modern greenhouse with many different climate zones that grows countless cacti, bug-munching carnivorous plants, and more (£7.50, £5.50 at 16:45 or later, Mon–Fri 9:30–18:30, Sat–Sun 9:30–19:30, until 16:30 or sunset off-season, galleries and conservatories close at 17:30, consider £3 narrated floral 35-min joyride on little train departing on the hour until 16:00 from Victoria Gate, Tube: Kew Gardens, tel. 020/8332-5000). For a sun-dappled lunch, walk 10 minutes from the Palm House to the Orangery (hot meals-£6, daily 10:00–17:30).

▲Hampton Court Palace—Fifteen miles up the Thames from downtown (£15 taxi ride from Kew Gardens) is the 500-year-old palace of Henry VIII. Actually, it was the palace of his minister, Cardinal Wolsey. When Wolsey, a clever man, realized Henry VIII was experiencing a little palace envy, he gave the mansion to his king. The Tudor palace was also home to Elizabeth I and Charles I. Sections were updated by Christopher Wren for William and Mary. The stately palace stands overlooking the Thames and includes some impressive Tudor rooms, including a Great Hall with a magnificent hammer-beam ceiling. The industrial-strength Tudor kitchen was capable of keeping 600 schmoozing courtesans thoroughly—if not well—fed. The sculpted garden features a rare Tudor tennis court and a popular maze.

The palace, fully restored after a 1986 fire, tries hard to please, but it doesn't quite sparkle. From the information center in the main courtyard, visitors book times for tours with tired costumed guides or pick up audioguides for self-guided tours of various wings of the palace (all free). The Tudor Kitchens, Henry VIII's Apartments, and the King's Apartments are most interesting. The Georgian Rooms are pretty dull. The maze in the nearby garden is a curiosity some find fun (maze free with palace ticket, otherwise £3). The train (2/hr, 30 min) from London's Waterloo station drops you just across the river from the palace (£12, 1-day combo-ticket with Tower of London-£18, Mon 10:15–18:00, Tue–Sun 9:30–18:00, Nov–March until 16:30, tel. 020/8781-9500).

Royal Air Force Museum Hendon—A hit with aviation enthusiasts, this huge aerodrome and airfield contain planes from World War II's Battle of Britain up through the Gulf War. You can climb inside some of the planes, try your luck in a cockpit, and fly with the Red Arrows in a flight simulator (free, daily 10:00–18:00, café, shop, parking, Tube: Colindale—top of Northern Line Edgware branch, Grahame Park Way, tel. 020/8205-2266, www.rafmuseum.org.uk).

Disappointments of London

The venerable BBC broadcasts from the Broadcasting House. Of all its productions, its "BBC Experience" tour for visitors is among the worst. On the South Bank, the London Dungeon, a much-visited but amateurish attraction, is just a highly advertised, overpriced haunted house—certainly not worth the £12 admission, much less your valuable London time. It comes with long and rude lines. Wait for Halloween and see one in your hometown to support a better cause. "Winston Churchill's Britain at War Experience" (next to the London Dungeon) wastes your time. The Kensington Palace State Apartments are lifeless and not worth a visit.

SHOPPING

Harrods—Harrods is London's most famous and touristy department store. With a million square feet of retail space on seven floors, it's a place where some shoppers could spend all day. (To me, it's a department store.) Big yet classy, Harrods has everything from elephants to toothbrushes (Mon–Sat 10:00–19:00, closed Sun, mandatory storage for big backpacks-£2.50, on Brompton Road, Tube: Knightsbridge, tel. 020/7730-1234).

Sightseers should pick up the free Store Guide at any info post. Here's what I enjoyed: On the Ground and Lower Ground Floors, find the Food Halls, with their Edwardian tiled walls, creative and exuberant displays, and staff in period costumes—not quite like your local supermarket back home.

Descend to the Lower Ground Floor and follow signs to the Egyptian Escalator, where you'll find a memorial to Dodi Fayed and Princess Diana. Photos and flowers honor the late Princess and her fiancé (the son of Harrods' owner), who both died in a car crash in Paris in 1997. See the wine glass from their last dinner and the engagement ring that Dodi purchased the day before they died.

Ride the Egyptian Escalator—lined with pharaoh-headed sconces, papyrus-plant lamps, and hieroglyphic balconies (Harrods' owner is from Egypt)—to the 4th Floor. From the escalator, make a U-turn left and head to the far corner of the store (toys) to find child-size luxury cars that actually work. A junior Jaguar or Mercedes will set you back about $13,000. The child's Hummer ($30,000) is as big as my car.

Also on the 4th Floor is The Georgian Restaurant. Enjoy a fancy tea under a skylight as a pianist tickles the keys of a Bösendorfer, the world's most expensive piano (tea-£19, includes finger sandwiches and pastries, served after 15:45).

Many of my readers report that Harrods is overpriced (its £1 toilets are the most expensive in Europe), snooty, and teeming with American and Japanese tourists. Still, it's the palace of department stores. The nearby Beauchamp Place is lined with classy and fascinating shops.

Harvey Nichols—Once Princess Diana's favorite, "Harvey Nick's" remains the department store *du jour* (Mon, Tue, Sat 10:00–19:00, Wed–Fri until 20:00, Sun 12:00–18:00, near Harrods, Tube: Knightsbridge, 109 Knightsbridge, www.harveynichols.com). Want to pick up a little £20 scarf for the wife? You won't do it here, where they're more like £200. The store's fifth floor is a veritable food fest, with a gourmet grocery store, a fancy (smoky) restaurant, a Yo! Sushi bar, and a lively café. Consider a take-away tray of sushi to eat on a bench in the Hyde Park rose garden two blocks away.

Toys—The biggest toy store in Britain is **Hamleys,** with seven floors buzzing with 28,000 toys and managed by a staff of 200. At the "Bear

Factory," kids can get a made-to-order teddy bear by picking out a "bear skin" and watch while it's stuffed and sewn (Mon–Fri 10:00–20:00, Sat 9:30–20:00, Sun 12:00–18:00, 188 Regent Street, tel. 0870-333-2455, www.hamleys.com).

Street Markets—Antique buffs, people-watchers, and folks who brake for garage sales love to haggle at London's street markets. There's good early-morning market activity somewhere any day of the week. The best are **Portobello Road** (roughly Mon–Sat 10:00–17:00, closed Sun, go on Sat for antiques—plus the regular junk, clothes, and produce; Tube: Notting Hill Gate, tel. 020/7229-8354) and **Camden Lock Market** (daily 10:00–18:00, arts and crafts, Tube: Camden Town, tel. 020/7284-2084, www.camdenlock.net). The TI has a complete, up-to-date list. Warning: Markets attract two kinds of people—tourists and pickpockets.

Famous Auctions—London's famous auctioneers welcome the curious public for viewing and bidding. For schedules, call **Sotheby's** (Mon–Fri 9:00–16:30, closed Sat–Sun, 34–35 New Bond Street, Tube: Oxford Circus, tel. 020/7293-5000, www.sothebys.com) or **Christie's** (Mon–Fri 9:00–17:00, Tue until 20:00, closed Sat–Sun, 8 King Street, Tube: Green Park, tel. 020/7839-9060, www.christies.com).

ENTERTAINMENT AND THEATER

London bubbles with top-notch entertainment seven days a week. Everything's listed in the weekly entertainment magazines (e.g., *Time Out*), available at newsstands. Choose from classical, jazz, rock, and far-out music, Gilbert and Sullivan, dance, comedy, Baha'i meetings, poetry readings, spectator sports, film, and theater. In Leicester Square, you'll find movies that have yet to be released in the States; if Hugh Grant is attending an opening-night premiere in London, it will likely be at one of the big movie houses here.

London's theater rivals Broadway's in quality and beats it in price. Choose from the Royal Shakespeare Company, top musicals, comedy, thrillers, sex farces, and more. I prefer big, glitzy—even bombastic—musicals over serious chamber dramas, simply because London can deliver the lights, sound, dancers, and multimedia spectacle I rarely get back home. Performances are nightly except Sunday, usually with one matinee a week. Matinees, usually held on Wednesday, Thursday, or Saturday, are cheaper and rarely sell out. Tickets range from about £8 to £40.

Most theaters, marked on tourist maps, are in the Piccadilly/Trafalgar Square area. Box offices, hotels, and TIs offer a handy *Theatre Guide*. To book a seat, simply call the theater box office directly, ask about seats and available dates, and for a £2 fee, buy a ticket with your credit card. (To avoid the fee, buy the ticket in person at the box office.) You can call from the United States as easily as from England; check www.officiallondontheatre.co.uk, the American magazine *Variety*, or photocopy your hometown library's London newspaper theater section. Pick up your ticket 15 minutes before the show.

For a booking fee, you can reserve online (www.ticketmaster.co.uk or www.firstcalltickets.com) or call Global Tickets (U.S. tel. 800/223-6108). While booking through an agency is quick and easy, prices are inflated by a standard 25 percent fee. Ticket agencies (whether in the U.S., at London's TIs, or scattered throughout the city) are scalpers with an address. If you're buying from an agency, look at the ticket carefully (your price should be no more than 30 percent over the printed face value; the 15 percent VAT is already included in the face value) and understand where you're sitting according to the floor plan (if your view is restricted, it will state this on the ticket; for floor plans of the various theaters, see www.theatremonkey.com). Agencies are worthwhile only if a show you've just got to see is sold out at the box office. They scarf up hot tickets, planning to make a killing after the show is sold out. U.S. booking agencies get their tickets from another agency, adding even more to your expense by involving yet another middleman. Many tickets sold on the street are forgeries. Although some theatres have booking agencies handle their advance sales, you'll stand a good chance of saving money and avoiding the middleman by simply calling the box office directly to book your tickets (international phone calls are cheap and credit cards make booking a snap).

Theater Lingo: stalls (ground floor), dress circle (first balcony), upper circle (second balcony), balcony (sky-high third balcony), slips (cheap seats on the fringes). Many cheap seats have a restricted view (behind a pillar).

Cheap Theater Tricks: Most theaters offer cheap returned tickets, standing-room, matinee, and senior or student stand-by deals. These "concessions" are indicated with a "conc" or "s" in the listings. Picking up a late return can get you a great seat at a cheap-seat price. If a show is "sold out," there's usually a way to get a seat. Call the theater box office and ask how.

Half-Price "tkts" Booth at Leicester Square: This famous ticket booth sells discounted tickets for top-price seats to shows on the push list the day of the show only (£2.50 service charge per ticket, Mon–Sat 10:00–19:00, Sun 12:00–15:30, matinee tickets from noon, lines often form early, list of shows available online, www.tkts.co.uk).

Here are some sample prices: A top-notch seat to the long-running *Les Misérables* (which rarely sells out) costs £40 bought directly from the theater, but only £22.50 at Leicester (LESS-ter) Square. The cheapest balcony seat (bought from the theater) is £15.

Half-price tickets can be a good deal, unless you want the cheapest seats or the hottest shows. But check the board; occasionally they sell cheap tickets to good shows. Note that the real half-price booth (with its

WHAT'S ON IN THE WEST END

Here are some of the perennial favorites that you're likely to find among the West End's evening offerings. If spending the time and money for a London play, I like a full-fledged high-energy musical.

Generally you can book tickets for free at the box office or for a £2 fee by telephone or online.

Musicals

Chicago—A chorus-girl-gone-bad forms a nightclub act with another murderess to bring in the bucks (£15-40, Mon–Thu and Sat 20:00, Fri 20:30, matinees Fri 17:00 and Sat 15:00, Adelphi Theatre, Strand, Tube: Covent Garden or Charing Cross, booking tel. 020/7344-0055, www.chicagothemusical.com).

Mamma Mia—This high-energy spandex-and-platform-boots musical weaves together 20 or 30 ABBA hits to tell the story of a bride in search of her real dad as her promiscuous mom plans her Greek Isle wedding. The production has the audience dancing by its happy ending (£19–40, Mon–Thu and Sat 19:30, Fri 20:30, matinees Fri 17:00 and Sat 15:00, Prince Edward Theatre, Old Compton Street, Tube: Leicester Square, booking tel. 020/7447-5400).

Les Misérables—Claude-Michel Schönberg's musical adaptation of Victor Hugo's epic follows the life of Jean Valjean as he struggles with the social and political realities of 19th-century France. This inspiring mega-hit takes you back to the days of France's struggle for a just and modern society (£9–40, Mon–Sat 19:30, matinees Thu and Sat 14:30, Palace Theatre, Cambridge Circus, Tube: Leicester Square, box office tel. 0870-160-2878, www.lesmis.com).

new "tkts" name) is a freestanding kiosk at the edge of the garden in Leicester Square. Several dishonest outfits nearby advertise "official half-price tickets." Avoid these.

Many theaters are so small that there's hardly a bad seat. After the lights go down, scooting up is less than a capital offense. Shakespeare did it.

West End Theaters—The commercial (non-subsidized) theaters cluster around Soho (especially along Shaftesbury Avenue) and Covent Garden. With a centuries-old tradition of pleasing the masses, these present London theater at its glitziest. See the "What's On in the West End" sidebar.

Royal Shakespeare Company—If you'll ever enjoy Shakespeare, it'll be in Britain. The RSC performs at various theaters around London and in

The Phantom of the Opera—A mysterious masked man falls in love with a singer in this haunting Andrew Lloyd Webber musical about life beneath the stage of the Paris Opera (£10–40, Mon–Sat 19:30, matinees Wed and Sat 15:00, Her Majesty's Theatre, Haymarket, Tube: Piccadilly Circus, booking tel. 0870-160-2878, www.thephantomoftheopera.com).

The Lion King—In this Disney extravaganza featuring music by Elton John, Simba the lion learns about the delicately-balanced circle of life on the savanna (£18–43, Mon–Sat 19:30, matinees Wed and Sat 14:00 and Sun 15:00, Lyceum Theatre, Wellington Street, Tube: Charing Cross or Covent Garden, booking tel. 0870-243-9000 or 0161/228-1953, theater info tel. 020/7420-8112, www.thelionking .co.uk).

Thrillers

The Mousetrap—Agatha Christie's whodunit about a murder in a country house continues to stump audiences after 50 years (£11.50–30, Mon–Sat 20:00, matinees Tue 14:45 and Sat 17:00, St. Martin's Theatre, West Street, Tube: Leicester Square, box office tel. 0870-162-2878).

The Woman in Black—The chilling tale of a solicitor who is haunted by what he learns when he closes a reclusive woman's affairs (£10–30, Mon–Sat 20:00, matinees Tue 15:00 and Sat 16:00, Fortune Theatre, Russell Street, Tube: Covent Garden, box office tel. 020/7369-1737, www.thewomaninblack.com).

Stratford year-round. To get a schedule, contact the RSC (Royal Shakespeare Theatre, Stratford-upon-Avon, tel. 01789/403-403, ticket hotline tel. 0870-609-1110, www.rsc.org.uk).

Shakespeare's Globe—To see Shakespeare in a replica of the theater for which he wrote his plays, attend a play at the Globe. This thatch-roofed, open-air round theater does the plays much as Shakespeare intended (with no amplification). The play's the thing from mid-May through September (usually Tue–Sat 14:00 and 19:30, Sun at either 13:00 and 18:30 or 16:00 only, no plays on Mon, tickets can be sold out months in advance). You'll pay £5 to stand and £13–29 to sit (usually on a backless bench; only a few rows and the pricier Gentlemen's Rooms have seats with backs). The £5 "groundling" tickets—while the only ones open to rain—are most fun. Scurry in early to stake out a spot on the stage-edge leaning rail, where the most interaction with the actors occurs. You're a crude peasant. You can lean your elbows on the stage, munch a picnic dinner, or walk around. I've never enjoyed Shakespeare as much as here, performed as it was meant to be in the "wooden O." Plays can be long. Many groundlings leave before the end. If you like, hang out an hour before the finish and beg or buy a ticket from someone leaving early (groundlings are allowed to come and go).

The theater is on the South Bank directly across the Thames over the Millennium Bridge from St. Paul's Cathedral (Tube: Mansion House or London Bridge, tel. 020/7902-1500, box office tel. 020/7401-9919, www.shakespeares-globe.org). The Globe is inconvenient for public transport, but the courtesy phone in the lobby gets a minicab in minutes. (These have set fees—e.g., £8 to South Kensington—but generally cost less than a metered cab and provide fine and honest service.) **Fringe Theatre**—London's rougher evening-entertainment scene is thriving, filling pages in *Time Out.* Choose from a wide range of fringe theater and comedy acts (generally £5).

Music—For easy, cheap, or free concerts in historic churches, check the TIs' listings for lunch concerts (especially Wren's St. Bride's Church; St. James at Piccadilly—free lunch concerts on Mon, Wed, and Fri at 13:10, info tel. 020/7381-0441; and St. Martin-in-the-Fields—free lunch concerts on Mon, Tue, and Fri at 13:05, church tel. 020/7766-1100). St. Martin-in-the-Fields also hosts fine evening concerts by candlelight (£6–18, Thu–Sat at 19:30, box office tel. 020/7839-8362).

At St. Paul's Cathedral, evensong is held Monday through Saturday at 17:00 and on Sunday at 15:15. At Westminster Abbey, it's sung weekdays at 17:00 (but not on Wed) and Saturday and Sunday at 15:00. Organ recitals are held on Sunday at Westminster Abbey (17:45, 40 min, small fee, tel. 020/7798-9055) and at St. Paul's (17:00, 30 min, free, tel. 020/7236-4128).

For a fun classical event (mid-July–early Sept), attend a "Prom Concert" during the annual festival at the Royal Albert Hall. Nightly concerts are offered at give-a-peasant-some-culture prices (standing-room spots sold at the door-£4, restricted-view seats-£7, most seats-£22, depending on performance, Tube: South Kensington, tel. 020/7589-8212, www.royalalberthall.com).

Some of the world's best opera is belted out at the prestigious Royal Opera House, near Covent Garden (box office tel. 020/7304-4000, www.royalopera.org) and at the less-formal Sadler's Wells Theatre (Rosebery Avenue, Islington, Tube: Angel, box office tel. 020/7863-8000, www.sadlers-wells.com). **Walks, Bus Tour, and Cruises**—See "Tours" above for information on walking tours (some are held in the evening), the London by Night bus tour, and Regent's Canal cruise.

A handful of outfits run Thames River evening cruises with four-course meals and dancing. London Showboat offers the best value (£53, April-Oct Wed-Sun, departs 19:00 from Westminster Pier, Thu-Sat evening cruises through the winter, 3.5 hrs, tel. 020/7740-0400, www.citycruises.com). For more on cruising, get the Thames River Services brochure from a London TI.

SLEEPING

Victoria Station Neighborhood, Belgravia

The streets behind Victoria Station teem with budget B&Bs. It's a safe, surprisingly tidy, and decent area without a hint of the trashy, touristy glitz of the streets in front of the station. Here in Belgravia, your neighbors include Andrew Lloyd Webber and Margaret Thatcher (her policeman stands outside 73 Chester Square). Decent eateries abound (see "Eating," below). Cheaper rooms are relatively dumpy. Don't expect £90 cheeriness in a £60 room. Off-season, it's possible to save money by arriving late without a reservation and looking around. Competition softens prices, especially for multinight stays. On hot summer nights, request a quiet back room. All are within a five-minute walk of the Victoria Tube, bus, and train stations. There's a £15-per-day (with a hotel voucher) garage, a nearby **launderette** (daily 8:00–20:30, self-service or full service, past Warwick Square at 3 Westmoreland Terrace, tel. 020/7821-8692), and a little dance club (music from 23:30, Club D'Jan, £8 includes drink, Thu–Sat, 63 Wilton Road).

$$$ **Lime Tree Hotel,** enthusiastically run by David and Marilyn Davies and their daughter Charlotte, comes with spacious and thoughtfully decorated rooms and a fun-loving breakfast room. While priced a bit steep, the place has character and is a good value (30 rooms, Sb-£80, Db-£110–120, Tb-£150, family room-£160, possible discount with cash, all rooms non-smoking, quiet garden, David deals in slow times and is creative at helping travelers in a bind, 135 Ebury Street, tel. 020/7730-8191, fax 020/7730-7865, www.limetreehotel.co.uk, info@limetreehotel.co.uk).

$$$ **Quality Hotel Eccleston** is big, modern (but with tired carpets), well-located, and a fine value for no-nonsense comfort (Db-£130, on slow days drop-ins can ask for "saver prices," if booking in advance check various specials on the Web, breakfast extra or bargained in, non-smoking floor, elevator, 82 Eccleston Square, tel. 020/7834-8042, fax 020/7630-8942, www.qualityinn.com/hotel/gb614, admin@gb614.u-net.com).

$$ **Winchester Hotel** is family-run and perhaps the best value, with 18 fine rooms, no claustrophobia, and a wise and caring management (Db-£85, Tb-£110, Qb-£140, no CC, no groups, no infants, 17 Belgrave Road, tel. 020/7828-2972, fax 020/7828-5191, www.winchester-hotel.net, enquiry@winchester-hotel.net, commanded by Jimmy with

London, Victoria Station Neighborhood

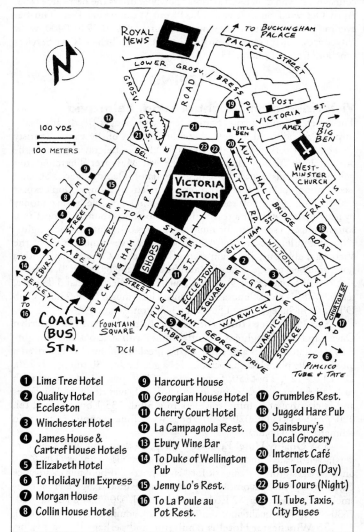

1. Lime Tree Hotel
2. Quality Hotel Eccleston
3. Winchester Hotel
4. James House & Cartref House Hotels
5. Elizabeth Hotel
6. To Holiday Inn Express
7. Morgan House
8. Collin House Hotel
9. Harcourt House
10. Georgian House Hotel
11. Cherry Court Hotel
12. La Campagnola Rest.
13. Ebury Wine Bar
14. To Duke of Wellington Pub
15. Jenny Lo's Rest.
16. To La Poule au Pot Rest.
17. Grumbles Rest.
18. Jugged Hare Pub
19. Sainsbury's Local Grocery
20. Internet Café
21. Bus Tours (Day)
22. Bus Tours (Night)
23. TI, Tube, Taxis, City Buses

SLEEP CODE

(£1 = about $1.60, country code: 44, area code: 020)
Sleep Code: **S** = Single, **D** = Double/Twin, **T** = Triple, **Q** = Quad, **b** = bathroom, **s** = shower only, **no CC** = Credit Cards not accepted. Unless otherwise noted, credit cards are accepted.

To help you sort easily through these listings, I've divided the rooms into three categories based on the price for a standard double room with bath:

$$$ Higher Priced—Most rooms £100 or more.
$$ Moderately Priced—Most rooms between £70–100.
$ Lower Priced—Most rooms £70 or less.

London is expensive. For £70 ($110), you'll get a double with breakfast in a safe, cramped, and dreary place with minimal service and the bathroom down the hall. For £90 ($145), you'll get a basic, clean, reasonably cheery double in a usually cramped, cracked-plaster building with a private bath, or a soulless but comfortable room without breakfast in a huge Motel 6-type place. My London splurges, at £100–150 ($160–240), are spacious, thoughtfully appointed places you'd be happy to entertain or make love in. Hearty English or generous buffet breakfasts are included unless otherwise noted, and TVs are standard in rooms.

Reserve your London room with a phone call or e-mail as soon as you can commit to a date. To call a London hotel from the United States or Canada, dial 011-44-20 (London's area code without the initial zero), then the local eight-digit number. Some hotels will hold a room until 16:00 without a deposit, although most places will ask you for a credit-card number. The pricier ones have expensive cancellation policies (such as no refund if you cancel with less than two weeks' notice). Some fancy £120 rooms rent for a third off if you arrive late on a slow day and ask for a deal.

his able first mates: Juanita, Ian, and Paul). The Winchester also rents apartments—with kitchenettes, sitting rooms, and beds on the quiet back side—around the corner (£125–230).

$$ James House and **Cartref House** are two nearly identical, well-run, smoke-free, 10-room places on either side of Ebury Street (S-£55, Sb-£65, D-£74, Db-£90, T-£100, Tb-£120, family bunk-bed Qb-£140,

5 percent discount with cash, all rooms with fans, no smoking, James House at 108 Ebury Street, tel. 020/7730-7338; Cartref House at 129 Ebury Street, tel. 020/7730-6176, fax for both: 020/7730-7338, www .jamesandcartref.co.uk, jandchouse@aol.com, run by Derek and Sharon).

$$ **Elizabeth Hotel** is a stately old place overlooking Eccleston Square, with fine public spaces and 38 well-worn but spacious and decent rooms (D-£72, small Db-£88, big Db-£99, Tb-£110, Qb-£120, Quint/b-£125, 37 Eccleston Square, tel. 020/7828-6812, fax 020/7828-6814, www.elizabethhotel.com, info@elizabethhotel.com). Be careful not to confuse this hotel with the nearby Elizabeth House. This one is big and comfy, the other small and dumpy.

$$ **Holiday Inn Express** fills an old building with 52 fresh, modern, and efficient rooms (Db-£105, Tb-£120, family rooms, up to 2 kids free, some discounts on Web site, non-smoking floor, elevator, Tube: Pimlico, 106 Belgrave Road, tel. 020/7630-8888 or 0800-897-121, fax 020/7828-0441, www.hiexpressvictoria.co.uk, info@hiexpressvictoria.co.uk).

$ **Morgan House** rents 11 good rooms and is entertainingly run, with lots of travel tips and friendly chat—especially about the local rich and famous—by Rachel Joplin (S-£46, D-£66, Db-£86, T-£86, family suites-£110–122 for 3–4 people, 120 Ebury Street, tel. 020/7730-2384, fax 020/7730-8442, www.morganhouse.co.uk, morganhouse@btclick.com).

$ **Collin House Hotel,** clean, simple and efficiently-run, offers 12 basic rooms with woody, modern furnishings (Sb-£55, D-£68, Db-£82, T-£95, non-smoking rooms, 104 Ebury St, tel.& fax 020/7730-8031, www.collinhouse.co.uk, booking@collinhouse.co.uk, absentee owner).

$ **Harcourt House** rents 10 decent smoke-free rooms (Db-£75, 50 Ebury Street, tel. 020/7730-2722, www.harcourthousehotel.co.uk, harcourthouse@talk21.com, David and Glesni Wood).

$ **Georgian House Hotel** has 50 once-grand, now basic rooms and a cheaper top floor that works well for backpackers (S-£29, tiny D on fourth floor-£45, Db-£69, top floor Db-£59, Tb-£86, Qb-£94, Internet access, 35 St. George's Drive, tel. 020/7834-1438, fax 020/7976-6085, www.georgianhousehotel.co.uk, reception@georgianhousehotel.co.uk).

$ **Cherry Court Hotel,** run by the friendly and industrious Patel family, rents 12 small, basic rooms for good value in a central location (Sb-£42, Db-£48, Tb-£70, Qb-£85, Quint/b-£100, prices promised with this book through 2004, paying with credit card costs 5 percent extra, fruit-basket breakfast in room, non-smoking, free Internet access, peaceful garden patio, 23 Hugh Street, tel. 020/7828-2840, fax 020/7828-0393, www.cherrycourthotel.co.uk, bookings@cherrycourthotel .co.uk).

Big, Cheap, Modern Hotels

These places—popular with budget tour groups—are well-run and offer elevators and all the modern comforts in a no-frills, practical package.

The doubles for £65–94 are a great value for London. Mid-week prices are generally higher than weekend rates.

$$ Jurys Inn rents 200 modern, compact, and comfy rooms near King's Cross station (Db/Tb-£104, 2 adults and 2 kids—under age 12—can share 1 room, breakfast extra, non-smoking floors, 60 Pentonville Road, Tube: Angel, tel. 020/7282-5500, fax 020/7282-5511, www.jurysdoyle.com).

$$ London County Hall Travel Inn, literally down the hall from a $400-a-night Marriott Hotel, fills one end of London's massive former County Hall building. This place is wonderfully located near the base of the London Eye Ferris Wheel and across the Thames from Big Ben. Its 300 slick, no-frills rooms come with all the necessary comforts (Db-£82 for 2 adults and up to 2 kids under age 15, couples can request a bigger family room—same price, breakfast extra, book in advance, no-show rooms are released at 16:00, elevator, some smoke-free and easy-access rooms, 500 yards from Westminster Tube stop and Waterloo Station, Belvedere Road, you can call central reservations at 0870-242-8000 or 0870-238-3300, you can fax 020/7902-1619 but you might not get a response, it's easiest to book online at www.travelinn.co.uk).

Other **$$ London Travel Inns** charging £70-80 per room include **London Euston** (big, blue, Lego-type building on handy but noisy street packed with Benny Hill families on vacation, 141 Euston Road, Tube: Euston, tel. 0870-238-3301), **Tower Bridge** (Tower Bridge Road, Tube: London Bridge, tel. 0870-238-3303), and **London Putney Bridge** (farther out, 3 Putney Bridge Approach, Tube: Putney Bridge, tel. 0870-238-3302). For any of these, call 0870-242-8000, fax 0870-241-9000, or best, book online at www.travelinn.co.uk.

$ Hotel Ibis London Euston, which feels classier than a Travel Inn, is located on a quiet street a block behind Euston Station (380 rooms, Db-£80, breakfast-£5, no family rooms, non-smoking floor, 3 Cardington Street, tel. 020/7388-7777, fax 020/7388-0001, www.ibishotel.com, h0921@accor-hotels.com).

$ Premier Lodge is near Shakespeare's Globe on the South Bank (55 rooms, Db for up to 2 adults and 2 kids-£70, Bankside, 34 Park Street, tel. 0870-700-1456, www.premierlodge.co.uk).

"South Kensington," She Said, Loosening His Cummerbund

To live on a quiet street so classy it doesn't allow hotel signs, surrounded by trendy shops and colorful restaurants, call "South Ken" your London home. Shoppers like being a short walk from Harrods and the designer shops of King's Road and Chelsea. When I splurge, I splurge here. Sumner Place is just off Old Brompton Road, 200 yards from the handy South Kensington Tube station (on Circle Line, 2 stops from Victoria Station, direct Heathrow connection). There's a taxi rank in the median

London, South Kensington Neighborhood

1 Aster House, Five Sumner Place & Sixteen Sumner Place Hotels

2 Jurys Kensington Hotel

3 Claverley Hotel

4 La Bouchee Bistro Café

5 Daquise Restaurant

6 Khyber Pass Tandoori Rest.

7 La Brasserie Restaurant

8 PJ's Bar and Grill

9 Launderette

strip at the end of Harrington Road. The handy Wash & Dry **launderette** is on the corner of Queensberry Place and Harrington Road
(daily 8:00–21:00, bring 20p and £1 coins).

$$\$\$\$ \text{ Aster House,}$$ run by friendly and accommodating Simon and
Leona Tan, has won the "best B&B in London" award for the last two
years. It has a sumptuous lobby, lounge, and breakfast room. Its rooms
are comfy and quiet, with TV, phone, and air-conditioning. Enjoy
breakfast or just lounge in the whisper-elegant Orangery, a Victorian
greenhouse (Sb-£75-99, Db-£135, bigger Db-£150, deluxe four-poster
Db-£180, entirely non-smoking, 3 Sumner Place, tel. 020/7581-5888,
fax 020/7584-4925, www.asterhouse.com, asterhouse@btinternet.com).
Simon and Leona offer free loaner mobile phones to their guests.

$$\$\$\$ \text{ Five Sumner Place Hotel}$$ has received several "best small
hotel in London" awards. The rooms in this 150-year-old building are
tastefully decorated, and the breakfast room is a conservatory/greenhouse

(13 rooms, Sb-£100, Db-£153, third bed-£22, ask for Rick Steves discount; TV, phones, and fridge in rooms by request; non-smoking rooms, elevator, 5 Sumner Place, tel. 020/7584-7586, fax 020/7823-9962, www .sumnerplace.com, reservations@sumnerplace.com, run by John and Barbara Palgan).

$$$ **Sixteen Sumner Place,** for well-heeled travelers, has over-the-top formality and class packed into its 40 rooms, plush lounges, and quiet garden. It's in a labyrinthine building, with modern Italian decor throughout (Db-£165-200—but squishy, breakfast in your room, elevator, 16 Sumner Place, tel. 020/7589-5232, fax 020/7584-8615, U.S. tel. 800/553-6674, www.numbersixteenhotel.co.uk, reservations @numbersixteenhotel.co.uk).

$$$ **Jurys Kensington Hotel** is big, stately, and impersonal, with a greedy pricing scheme (Sb/Db/Tb-£100–220 depending on "availability," ask for a deal, breakfast extra, piano lounge, non-smoking floor, elevator, Queen's Gate, tel. 020/7589-6300, fax 020/7581-1492, www .jurysdoyle.com, kensington@jurysdoyle.com).

$$$ **The Claverley,** two blocks from Harrods, is on a quiet street similar to Sumner Place. The 30 fancy, dark-wood-and-marble rooms come with all the comforts (S-£70, Sb-£85–100, Db-£120–190 depending on size, sofa-bed Tb-£190–215, ask for Rick Steves discount, plush lounge, non-smoking rooms, elevator, 13–14 Beaufort Gardens, Tube: Knightsbridge, tel. 020/7589-8541, fax 020/7584-3410, U.S. tel. 800/747-0398, www.claverleyhotel.co.uk, reservations @claverleyhotel.co.uk).

Notting Hill Gate Neighborhood

Residential Notting Hill Gate has quick bus and Tube access to downtown, is on the A2 Airbus line from Heathrow, and, for London, is very "homely." It has a self-serve launderette on Moscow Road, an artsy theater, a late-hours supermarket, and lots of fun budget eateries (see "Eating," below).

$$$ **Westland Hotel** is comfortable, convenient, and hotelesque, with a fine lounge and spacious rooms. Cheaper rooms are old and simple; others are quite plush (Sb-£80–90, Db-£95–105, cavernous deluxe Db-£110–125, sprawling Tb-£120–140, gargantuan Qb-£135–160, Quint/b-£150–170, 10 percent discount with this book for first visit if claimed upon arrival, elevator, free garage with six spaces, between Notting Hill Gate and Queensway Tube stations, 154 Bayswater Road, tel. 020/7229-9191, fax 020/7727-1054, www.westlandhotel .co.uk, reservations@westlandhotel.co.uk).

$$ **Vicarage Private Hotel,** understandably popular, is family-run and elegantly British in a quiet, classy neighborhood. It has 17 rooms furnished with taste and quality, a TV lounge, and facilities on each floor. Mandy, Richard, and Krassi maintain a homey and caring atmosphere

London, Notting Hill Gate Neighborhood

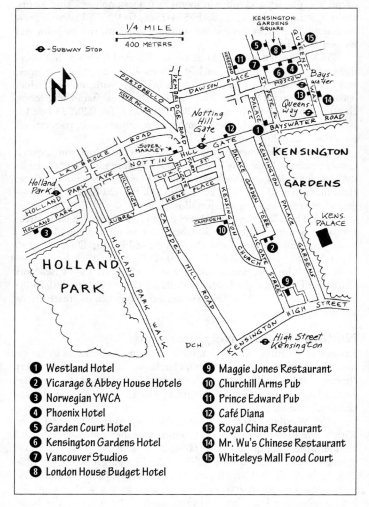

1 Westland Hotel
2 Vicarage & Abbey House Hotels
3 Norwegian YWCA
4 Phoenix Hotel
5 Garden Court Hotel
6 Kensington Gardens Hotel
7 Vancouver Studios
8 London House Budget Hotel

9 Maggie Jones Restaurant
10 Churchill Arms Pub
11 Prince Edward Pub
12 Café Diana
13 Royal China Restaurant
14 Mr. Wu's Chinese Restaurant
15 Whiteleys Mall Food Court

(S-£46, Sb-£75, D-£76, Db-£102, T-£93, Tb-£130, Q-£100, Qb-£140, no CC, 6-min walk from Notting Hill Gate and High Street Kensington Tube stations, near Kensington Palace at 10 Vicarage Gate, tel. 020/7229-4030, fax 020/7792-5989, www.londonvicaragehotel.com, reception@londonvicaragehotel.com).

$$ Abbey House Hotel, next door, has 16 rundown but sleepable rooms—avoid the basement. (16 rooms, S-£45, D-£74, T-£90, Q-£100, Quint-£110, no CC, 11 Vicarage Gate, tel. 020/7727-2594, fax 020/7727-1873, www.abbeyhousekensington.com, abbeyhousedesk@btconnect.com, Rodrigo).

$ Norwegian YWCA (Norsk K.F.U.K.) is for women under 30 only (and men with Norwegian passports). Located on a quiet, stately street, it offers non-smoking rooms, a study, TV room, piano lounge, and an open-face Norwegian ambience. They have mostly quads, so those willing to share with strangers are most likely to get a bed (July–Aug: Ss-£30, shared double-£28/bed, shared triple-£24/bed, shared quad-£21/bed, includes breakfast and sack lunch; Sept–June: same prices also include dinner; 52 Holland Park, tel. 020/7727-9897, fax 020/7727-8718, www.kfuk.dial.pipex.com, kfuk.hjemmet@kfuk-kfum.no). With each visit, I wonder which is easier to get—a sex change or a Norwegian passport?

Near Kensington Gardens

Several big old hotels line the quiet Kensington Gardens, a block off the bustling Queensway shopping street near the Bayswater Tube station. Popular with young international travelers, Queensway is a multicultural festival of commerce and eateries (such as Mr. Wu's Chinese Restaurant and the Whiteleys Mall Food Court—see "Eating," below). These hotels are very quiet for central London. One of several **launderettes** in the neighborhood is Brookford Wash & Dry, at Queensway and Bishop's Bridge Road (daily 7:00–19:30, service from 9:00–17:30, computerized pay point takes all coins).

$$$ Phoenix Hotel, a Best Western modernization of a 125-room hotel, offers American business-class comforts; spacious, plush public spaces; and big, fresh, modern-feeling rooms (Sb-£99, Db-£130, Tb-£165, Qb-£185, flaky "negotiable" pricing list, elevator, 1–8 Kensington Gardens Square, tel. 020/7229-2494, fax 020/7727-1419, U.S. tel. 800/528-1234, www.phoenixhotel.co.uk, info@phoenixhotel.co.uk).

$$ Garden Court rents 34 comfortable, smoke-free rooms and is a fine value. It's friendly and has a garden (S-£39, Sb-£58, D-£58, Db-£88, T-£72, Tb-£99, Q-£82, Qb-£120, 5 percent discount with this book, elevator, 30 Kensington Gardens Square, tel. 020/7229-2553, fax 020/7727-2749, www.gardencourthotel.co.uk, info@gardencourthotel.co.uk).

$$ Kensington Gardens Hotel laces 16 decent rooms together in a tall, skinny place with lots of stairs and no lift (Ss-£45–50, Sb-£50–55, Db-£75, Tb-£95, 9 Kensington Gardens Square, tel. 020/7221-7790, fax 020/7792-8612, www.kensingtongardenshotel.co.uk, info@kensingtongardenshotel.co.uk, charming Rowshanak).

$$ Vancouver Studios offers 45 modern rooms with all the amenities, and gives you a fully-equipped kitchenette (utensils, stove, microwave, and fridge) rather than breakfast (small Sb-£57, big Sb-£77, small Db-£97, big Db-£112, Tb-£132, extra bed-£10, 10 percent discount with week-long stay or more, welcoming staff, homey lounge and private garden, 30 Prince's Square, tel. 020/7243-1270, fax 020/7221-8678, www.vancouverstudios.co.uk, info@vancouverstudios.co.uk).

$ **London House Budget Hotel** is a threadbare, nose-ringed slumber mill renting 240 beds in 93 stark rooms (S-£40, Sb-£45, twin-£54, Db-£68, dorm bed-£15, prices flex downward with demand, includes continental breakfast, lots of school groups, 81 Kensington Gardens Square, tel. 020/7243-1810, fax 020/7243-1723, londonhousehotel@yahoo.co.uk).

Other Neighborhoods

Near Covent Garden: $$$ Fielding House Hotel, located on a charming, quiet, pedestrian street just two blocks east of Covent Garden, offers 24 no-nonsense rooms, bright orange hallways, and lots of stairs (Db-£100–115, Db with sitting room-£130, no smoking, no kids under 13, no breakfast, 4 Broad Court, Bow Street, tel. 020/7836-8305, fax 020/7497-0064, www.the-fielding-hotel.co.uk).

Downtown near Baker Street: $$$ The 22 York Street B&B offers a less hotelesque alternative in the center, renting 18 stark, hardwood, comfortable rooms (Db-£100, Tb-£141, strictly smoke-free, inviting lounge, social breakfast, from Baker Street Tube station walk 2 blocks down Baker Street and take a right, 22 York Street, tel. 020/7224-3990, fax 020/7224-1990, www.22yorkstreet.co.uk, michael @22yorkstreet.co.uk, energetically run by Liz and Michael).

Near Buckingham Palace: $$ Vandon House Hotel, formerly run by the Salvation Army, is now run by the Central University of Iowa. Filled with students most of the year, the 33 rooms are rented to travelers from late May through August at great prices. The rooms, while institutional, are comfy, and the location is excellent (S-£40, D-£62, Db-£80, Tb-£114, Qb-£145, only single beds, non-smoking, elevator, on a tiny road 2 blocks west of St. James's Park Tube station, near east end of Petty France street at 1 Vandon Street, tel. 020/7799-6780, fax 020/7799-1464, www.vandonhouse.com, info@vandonhouse.com).

Euston Station: The $$ Methodist International Centre, a modern, youthful, Christian residence, fills its lower floors with international students and its top floor with travelers. Rooms are modern and simple yet comfortable, with fine bathrooms, phones, and desks. The atmosphere is friendly, safe, clean, and controlled; it also has a spacious lounge and game room (Sb-£48, Db-£74, two-course buffet dinner-£11, non-smoking rooms, elevator, on a quiet street a block west of Euston Station, 81–103 Euston Street—not Euston Road, Tube: Euston, tel. 020/7380-0001, fax 020/7387-5300, www.micentre.com, acc@micentre .com). In June, July, and August, when the students are gone, they rent simple £38 singles.

Near St. Paul's: **$** **The City of London Youth Hostel** is clean, modern, friendly, and well-run. You'll pay £15 per bed in 11-bed dorm, about £25 for a bed in their three- to eight-bed rooms, or £30 for a single room (£2 extra if you have no hostel card, 193 beds, cheap meals, open 24 hrs, Tube: St. Paul's, 36 Carter Lane, tel. 020/7236-4965, fax 020/7236-7681, www.yha.org.uk, city@yha.org.uk).

Near Gatwick and Heathrow Airports

Near Gatwick Airport: The **$** **London Gatwick Airport Travel Inn** rents cheap rooms at the airport (Db-£50, tel. 0870-238-3305, www.travelinn.co.uk). The **$** **Gatwick Travelodge,** also a budget hotel, is two miles from the airport (Db-£50, breakfast extra, Church Road, Lowfield Heath, Crawley, tel. 0870-905-6343, www.travelodge.co.uk).

$ **Barn Cottage,** a converted 16th-century barn, sits in the peaceful countryside, with a tennis court, small swimming pool, and a good pub within walking distance. It has two wood-beamed rooms, antique furniture, and a large garden that makes you forget Gatwick is 10 minutes away (S-£45, D-£55, no CC, can drive you to airport or train station for £8, Leigh, Reigate, Surrey, tel. 01306/611-347, www.barn-cottage.com, bookings@barn-cottage.com, warmly run by Pat and Mike Comer).

$ **Wayside Manor Farm** is another rural alternative to a bland airport hotel. This four-bedroom countryside place is a 10-minute drive from Gatwick (Db-£60, Norwood Hill, near Charlwood, tel. 01293/862-692, www.wayside-manor.com, info@wayside-manor.com).

Near Heathrow Airport: It's so easy to get to Heathrow from central London, I see no reason to sleep there. But for budget beds near the airport, consider **$** **Heathrow Ibis** (Db-£69, Db-£49 on Fri-Sun nights, breakfast extra, cheap shuttle bus to/from terminals except T-4, 112 Bath Road, tel. 020/8759-4888, fax 020/8564-7894, www.ibishotel.com, h0794@accor-hotels.com).

EATING

If you want to dine (as opposed to eat), check out the extensive listings in the weekly entertainment guides sold at London newsstands (or catch a train for Paris). The thought of a £30 meal in Britain generally ruins my appetite, so my London dining is limited mostly to easygoing, fun, but inexpensive alternatives. I've listed places by neighborhood—handy to your sightseeing or hotel.

Pub grub is the most atmospheric budget option. Many of London's 7,000 pubs serve fresh, tasty buffets under ancient timbers, with hearty lunches and dinners for £6-8. (While pubs are going strong, the new phenomenon is coffee shops: Starbucks and its competitors have sprouted up all over town, providing cushy and social watering holes with comfy chairs, easy WCs, £2 lattes, and a nice break between sights.)

Ethnic restaurants—especially Indian and Chinese—are popular, plentiful, and cheap. Most large museums (and many churches) have inexpensive, cheery cafeterias. Of course, picnicking is the fastest and cheapest way to go. Good grocery stores and sandwich shops, fine park benches, and polite pigeons abound in Britain's most expensive city.

Near Trafalgar Square

To locate the following restaurants, see the map on page 591.

St. Martin-in-the-Fields Café in the Crypt is just right for a tasty meal on a monk's budget, sitting on somebody's tomb in an ancient crypt (£6–7 cafeteria plates, cheaper sandwich bar, Mon–Wed 10:00–20:00, Thu–Sat 10:00–23:00, Sun 12:00–20:00, profits go to the church, no CC, underneath St. Martin-in-the-Fields church on Trafalgar Square, tel. 020/7839-4342).

Chandos Pub's Opera Room floats amazingly apart from the tacky crush of tourism around Trafalgar Square. Look for it opposite the National Portrait Gallery (corner of William Street and St. Martin's Lane) and climb the stairs to the Opera Room. This is a fine Trafalgar Square rendezvous point—smoky, but wonderfully local. They serve traditional, plain-tasting, £6-7 pub lunches and dinners (kitchen open 11:00–19:00, until 18:00 on weekends, order and pay at the bar, tel. 020/7836-1401).

The International is a mod complement to Chandos (just across the street), offering a bright and spacious retreat for local office workers oblivious to all the touristic hubbub nearby. The ground-floor bar has two-for-one bar meals daily (noon to 17:00). The classy restaurant upstairs serves modern European cuisine (daily, two-course menu-£10, three courses-£13, 116 St. Martin's Lane, tel. 020/7257-8626).

At **Gordon's Wine Bar,** a simple, steep staircase leads into a candlelit 15th-century wine cellar filled with dusty old bottles, faded British memorabilia, and local nine-to-fivers. At the buffet, choose a hot meal or a fine plate of cheeses and various cold cuts. (One £7 cold plate and a couple of glasses of wine provide a light meal for two economically.) Then step up to the wine bar and consider the many varieties of wine and port available by the glass—at great prices. The low, carbon-crusted vaulting deeper in the back seems to intensify the Hogarth-painting atmosphere. While it's crowded, you can normally corral two chairs and grab the corner of a table (arrive before 17:30 to get a seat, Mon–Sat 11:00–23:00, Sun 12:00–22:00, 2 blocks from Trafalgar Square, bottom of Villiars Street at #47, Tube: Embankment, tel. 020/7930-1408). On hot days, the crowd spills out into a leafy back patio.

The Clarence Pub, down Whitehall, a block south of Trafalgar Square toward Big Ben, is touristy but atmospheric with decent grub (indoor/outdoor seating, meals-£8, daily 11:00–22:00). Nearby are several cheaper cafeterias and pizza joints.

Sherlock Holmes Pub, a block from Trafalgar Square, sounds touristy but is the haunt of government workers and locals awaiting trains at Charing Cross Station. Fans of the fictional detective will appreciate the pub's location in the former Northumberland Hotel (featured in Holmes stories) and the fact that Old Scotland Yard was just across the street. Upstairs in the restaurant area is a replica of 221-B Baker Street (Mon–Sat 11:00–23:00, Sun 12:00–22:30, pub fare downstairs, restaurant meals served upstairs at lunch and dinnertime, 10 Northumberland Street, Tube: Charing Cross or Embankment, tel. 020/7930-2644.)

Crivelli's Garden Restaurant, serving a classy lunch in the National Gallery, is a good place to treat your palate to pricey, light Mediterranean cuisine (lunches-£15, daily 10:00–17:00, first floor of Sainsbury Wing). For something more Dickensian, try Hampton's Wine Bar (Mon–Fri 11:30–23:00, closed Sat–Sun, around the corner at 15 Whitcomb Street, tel. 020-7839-2823).

Near Piccadilly

Hungry and broke in the theater district? Head for Panton Street (off Haymarket, 2 blocks southeast of Piccadilly Circus) for cheap Thai, Chinese, and two famous London eateries. **Stockpot** is a mushy-peas kind of place, famous and rightly popular for its edible, cheap meals (daily 7:00–22:00, 38 Panton Street); see map on page 591. The **West End Kitchen** (across the street at #5, same hours and menu) is a direct competitor that's just as good. Vegetarians prefer the **Woodland South Indian Vegetarian Restaurant,** across from the West End Kitchen. For a £5 Chinese meal, **Mr. Wu's** buffet is on Old Compton Street. And **Pizza Express** has many branches offering a gut busting £5 buffet.

The palatial **Criterion Brasserie** serves a special £15 two-course "Anglo-French" menu (or £18 for three courses) under gilded tiles and chandeliers in a dreamy Byzantine church setting from 1880. It's right on Piccadilly Circus but a world away from the punk junk. The house wine is great and so is the food (specials available Mon–Sat 12:00–14:30 & 17:30–19:00, closed Sun lunch, tel. 020/7930-0488). After 19:00, the menu becomes really expensive. Anyone can drop in for coffee or a drink.

The "Food Is Fun" Dinner Crawl: From Covent Garden to Soho

London has a trendy, Generation-X scene that most Beefeater-seekers miss entirely. For a multicultural, movable feast, consider exploring these. Start around 18:00 to avoid lines, get in on early specials, and find waiters willing to let you split a meal. Prices, while reasonable by London standards, add up. Servings are large enough to share. All are open nightly.

Suggested nibbler's dinner crawl for two: Arrive before 18:00 at **Belgo Centraal** and split the early-bird dinner special: a kilo of mussels, fries, and dark Belgian beer. At **Yo! Sushi,** have beer or sake and a few dishes. Slurp your last course at **Wagamama Noodle Bar.** Then, for dessert, people-watch at Leicester Square, where the serf's always up.

Belgo Centraal serves hearty Belgian specialties. It's a seafood, chips, and beer emporium dressed up as a mod monastic refectory—with noisy acoustics and waiters dressed as Trappist monks. The classy restaurant section requires reservations, but just grabbing a bench in the boisterous beer hall (no reservations possible) is more fun. The same menu and specials work on both sides. Belgians claim they eat as well as the French and as heartily as the Germans. Specialties include mussels, great fries, and a stunning array of dark, blond, and fruity Belgian beers. Belgo actually makes Belgian things trendy—a formidable feat (meals-£10–14; open daily until 23:00; Mon–Fri 17:30–19:00 "beat the clock" meal specials for £5.30–7.00, and you get mussels, fries, and beer; no meal-splitting after 18:30, and you must buy food with beer; daily £6 lunch special 12:00–17:30; 1 block north of Covent Garden Tube station at intersection of Neal and Shelton streets, 50 Earlham Street, tel. 020/7813-2233).

Yo! Sushi is a futuristic Japanese-food-extravaganza experience. With thumping rock, Japanese cable TV, a 195-foot-long conveyor belt, the world's longest sushi bar, a robotic drink trolley, and automated sushi machines, just sipping a sake on a bar stool here is a trip. For £1 each you get unlimited tea, water (from spigot at bar, with or without gas), or miso soup. Grab dishes as they rattle by (priced by color of dish; check the chart: £1.50–3.50 per dish, daily 12:00–24:00, 2 blocks south of Oxford Street, where Lexington Street becomes Poland Street, 52 Poland Street, tel. 020/7287-0443). For more serious drinking on tatami mats, go downstairs into "Yo Below." (If you like Yo, there's a handy branch a block from the London Eye on Belvedere Road.)

Wagamama Noodle Bar is a noisy, pan-Asian, organic slurpathon. As you enter, check out the kitchen and listen to the roar of the basement, where benches rock with happy eaters. Everybody sucks. Stand against the wall to feel the energy of all this "positive eating" (meals-£10, daily 12:00–24:00, crowded after 20:00, non-smoking, 10-A Lexington Street, tel. 020/7292-0990 but no reservations taken). If you like this place, there are now handy branches all over town, including near the British Museum (Streatham Street), High Street Kensington (#26), in Harvey Nichols (109 Knightsbridge), Covent Garden (Tavistock Street), Leicester Square (Irving Street), Piccadilly Circus (Norris Street), Fleet Street (#109), and between St. Paul's and the Tower of London (22 Old Broad Street).

From Covent Garden to Soho: Food is Fun

1. St. Martin-in-the-Fields Café in the Crypt
2. The Chandos Pub
3. The International Pub & Rest.
4. Gordon's Wine Bar
5. The Clarence Pub
6. Crivelli's Garden Rest.
7. Stockpot & West End Kitchen
8. Woodland South Indian Vegetarian Rest.
9. Criterion Brasserie
10. Belgo Centraal
11. Yo! Sushi
12. Wagamama Noodle Bar
13. Soho Spice Indian Rest.
14. Y Ming Chinese Rest.
15. Andrew Edmunds & Mildred's Vegetarian Rest.
16. To Zilly Fish Too Rest.
17. Neal's Yard Rest.
18. Food for Thought Café

Soho Spice Indian is where modern Britain meets Indian tradition—fine cuisine in a trendy, jewel-tone ambience. Unlike many Indian restaurants, when you order an entrée here (£10–15), it comes with side dishes (nan, dal, rice, vegetables). The £15 "tandoori selections" meal is the best "variety" dish and big enough for two (Mon–Sat 11:30–24:00, Sun 12:30–22:30, non-smoking section, 5 blocks north of Piccadilly Circus at 124 Wardour Street, tel. 020/7434-0808).

Y Ming Chinese Restaurant is across Shaftesbury Avenue from the ornate gates, clatter, and dim sum of Chinatown, and it has clean European decor, serious but helpful service, and authentic Northern Chinese cooking (good £10 meal deal offered 12:00–18:00—last order at 18:00, Mon–Sat 12:00–23:30, closed Sun, 35 Greek Street, tel. 020/7734-2721, www.yming.com).

Andrew Edmunds Restaurant is a tiny, candlelit place where you'll want to hide your camera and guidebook and act as local as possible. This great little place—with a jealous and loyal clientele—is the closest I found to Parisian quality in a cozy restaurant in London. The modern European cooking with a creative seasonal menu is worth the splurge (three-course meal-£25, daily 12:30–15:00 & 18:00–22:45, reservations are generally necessary—request ground floor rather than the basement, 46 Lexington Street in Soho, tel. 020/7437-5708).

Mildred's Vegetarian Restaurant, across from Andrew Edmunds, has cheap prices, an enjoyable menu, and a plain-yet-pleasant interior filled with happy eaters (meals-£6, Mon–Sat 12:00–23:00, closed Sun, 45 Lexington Street, tel. 020/7494-1634).

The fun **Zilli Fish Too,** with a modern, bright setting near Covent Garden, serves up fresh seafood with a twist of Italy (two-course meal-£15, three courses-£19, daily 12:00–15:00 & 17:30–23:30, 8 Wild Street, at corner of Great Queen Street, two blocks north of Covent Garden, tel. 020/7240-0011).

Neal's Yard is *the* place for cheap, hip, and healthy eateries near Covent Garden. The neighborhood is a tabbouleh of fun, hippie-type cafés. One of the best is **Food for Thought,** packed with local health nuts (good vegetarian meals-£5, Mon–Sat 12:00–20:30, Sun 12:00–17:00, non-smoking, 2 blocks north of Covent Garden Tube station, 31 Neal Street, tel. 020/7836-0239).

Near Recommended Victoria Station Accommodations

Here are places a couple of blocks southwest of Victoria Station where I've enjoyed eating (see map on page 578).

La Campagnola, small and seriously Italian, is Belgravia's favorite budget Italian restaurant (£8–16, Mon–Sat 12:00–15:00 & 18:00–23:30, closed Sun, 10 Lower Belgrave Street, tel. 020/7730-2057).

Ebury Wine Bar, filled with young professionals, provides a classy atmosphere, delicious meals, and a £13 two-course special from 18:00–19:30 (£15–18, open Mon–Fri 11:00–23:00, Sat 12:00–23:00, Sun 18:00–23:00, 139 Ebury Street, at intersection with Elizabeth Street, near bus station, tel. 020/7730-5447). Several cheap places are around the corner on Elizabeth Street (#23 for take-out or eat-in, super-absorbent fish and chips, and a Spanish tapas place across from that).

Duke of Wellington pub is good, if somewhat smoky, and dominated by local drinkers. It's the neighborhood place for dinner (meals-£6, daily 11:00–15:00 & 18:00–21:00, 63 Eaton Terrace, at intersection with Chester Row, tel. 020/7730-1782).

Jenny Lo's Tea House is a simple, budget place serving up reliably tasty £5–8 eclectic Chinese-style meals to locals in the know (Mon–Fri 11:30–15:00 & 18:00–22:00, Sat 12:00–15:00 & 18:00–22:00, closed Sun, no CC, 14 Eccleston Street, tel. 020/7259-0399).

La Poule au Pot, ideal for a romantic splurge, offers a classy, candlelit ambience with well-dressed patrons and expensive but fine country-style French cuisine (lunch-£15, dinner-£25, daily 12:30–14:30 & 18:45–23:00, Sun until 22:00, leafy patio dining, reservations smart, end of Ebury at intersection with Pimlico, 231 Ebury Street, tel. 020/7730-7763).

Grumbles brags that it's been serving "good food and wine at non-scary prices since 1964." Offering a delicious mix of "modern eclectic French and traditional English," this hip and cozy little place is *the* spot to eat well in this otherwise workaday neighborhood (meals-£12–22, lunch specials-£12, reservations wise, self-serve launderette across the street open evenings, two nice sidewalk tables, daily 12:00–14:30 & 18:00–22:30, half a block north of Belgrave Road at 35 Churton Street, tel. 020/7834-0149).

The Jugged Hare Pub is in a lavish old bank building, its vaults replaced by kegs of beer and a fine kitchen. They have a fun, traditional menu with more fresh veggies than fries, and a plush and vivid pub scene good for a meal or just a drink (meals-£7, daily 12:00–21:00, 172 Vauxhall Bridge Road, tel. 020/7828-1543).

If you miss America, there's a mall-type **food court** at Victoria Place, upstairs in Victoria Station; **Café Rouge** seems to be the most popular here (£8–11 dinners, daily 9:30–22:30).

Groceries in and near Victoria Station: A large grocery, **Sainsbury's Local,** is on Victoria Street in front of the station, just past the buses (daily 6:00–24:00). In the station you'll find another, smaller Sainsbury's (at rear entrance, on Eccleston Street) and a couple other late-hours mini-markets.

Near Recommended Notting Hill Gate B&Bs and Bayswater Hotels

Queensway is lined with lively and inexpensive eateries. See the map on page 584.

Maggie Jones, exuberantly rustic and very English, serves my favorite £20 London dinner. You'll get fun-loving if brash service, solid English cuisine, including huge plates of crunchy vegetables—by candle-light. Avoid the stuffy basement on hot summer nights, and request upstairs seating for the noisy but less-cramped section. If you eat well once in London, eat here—and do it quick, before it burns down (daily 12:30–14:30 & 18:30–23:00, less-expensive lunch menu, reservations recommended, friendly staff, 6 Old Court Place, just east of Kensington Church Street, near High Street Kensington Tube stop, tel. 020/7937-6462).

Churchill Arms pub and **Thai Kitchens** is a local hangout, with good beer and old-English ambience in front and hearty £6 Thai plates in an enclosed patio in the back. You can eat the Thai food in this trop-ical hideaway or in the smoky but wonderfully atmospheric pub section. Arrive by 18:00 to avoid a line (Mon–Sat 12:00–21:30, Sun 12:00–16:00, 119 Kensington Church Street, tel. 020/7792-1246).

Prince Edward Pub serves good pub grub in a quintessential pub setting (meals-£8, Mon–Sat 12:00–14:30 & 18:00–21:00, Sun 12:00–18:00, indoor/outdoor seating, 2 blocks north of Bayswater Road at the corner of Dawson Place and Hereford Road, 73 Prince's Square, tel. 020/7727-2221).

Café Diana is a healthy little eatery serving sandwiches and Middle Eastern food. It's decorated with photos of Princess Diana, who used to drop by for pita sandwiches (daily 8:00–22:30, 5 Wellington Terrace, on Bayswater Road, opposite Kensington Palace Garden Gates—where Di once lived, tel. 020/7792-9606).

Royal China Restaurant is filled with London's Chinese, who consider this one of the city's best eateries. It's dressy in black, white, and chrome, with candles, brisk waiters, and fine food (£7–9 dishes, dim sum until 17:00, Mon–Thu 12:00–23:00, Fri–Sat 12:00–23:30, Sun 11:00–22:00, 13 Queensway, tel. 020/7221-2535).

Mr. Wu's Chinese Restaurant serves a 10-course buffet in a cramped little cafeteria. Just grab a plate and help yourself (£5, daily 12:00–23:00, check quality of buffet—right inside entrance—before committing, pickings can get slim, across from Bayswater Tube station, 54 Queensway, tel. 020/7243-1017).

Whiteleys Mall Food Court offers a fun selection of ethnic and fast-food eateries in a delightful mall (good salads at Café Rouge, second floor, corner of Porchester Gardens and Queensway).

Supermarket: Europa is a half-block from the Notting Hill Gate Tube stop (Mon–Fri 8:00–23:00, Sun 12:00–18:00, 112 Notting Hill Gate, near intersection with Pembridge Road).

Near Recommended Accommodations in South Kensington

Popular eateries line Old Brompton Road and Thurloe Street (Tube: South Kensington). See the map on page 582.

La Bouchee Bistro Café is a classy, hole-in-the-wall touch of France serving early-bird, three-course £12 meals before 19:00 and *plats du jour* for £8 all *jour* (daily 12:00–23:00, Sun until 22:00, 56 Old Brompton Road, tel. 020/7589-1929).

Daquise, a 1930s Polish time-warp, is ideal if you're in the mood for kielbasa and kraut. It's likeably dreary—fast, cheap, family-run, and a part of the neighborhood (meals-£10, daily 11:00–23:00, non-smoking, 20 Thurloe Street, tel. 020/7589-6117).

The **Khyber Pass Tandoori Restaurant** is a nondescript but handy place serving great Indian cuisine. Locals in the know travel to eat here (dinner-£10, daily 12:00–14:30 & 18:00–23:30, 21 Bute Street, tel. 020/7589-7311).

La Brasserie fills a big, plain room painted "nicotine yellow," with ceiling fans, a Parisian ambience, and good, traditional French cooking at reasonable prices (salads and veggie plates-£10, two-course menus-£15–£18, nightly until 23:00, 272 Brompton Road, tel. 020/7581-3089).

PJ's Bar and Grill is lively with the yuppie Chelsea crowd for a good reason. Traditional "New York Brasserie"-style, yet trendy, it has dressy tables surrounding a centerpiece bar. It serves pricey, cosmopolitan cuisine from a menu that changes with the seasons (meals-£20, nightly until 24:00, 52 Fulham Road, at intersection with Sydney Street, tel. 020/7581-0025).

Elsewhere in London

Between St. Paul's and the Tower: The **Counting House,** formerly an elegant old bank, offers great £7 meals, nice homemade meat pies, fish, and fresh vegetables (Mon–Fri 12:00–20:00, closed Sat–Sun, gets really busy with the buttoned-down 9-to-5 crowd after 12:15, near Mansion House in the City, 50 Cornhill, tel. 020/7283-7123).

Near St. Paul's: Degustibus Sandwiches is where a top-notch "artisan bakery" meets the public, offering fresh you-design-it sandwiches, salads, and soups with simple seating or take-out picnic sacks (great parks nearby) just a block below St. Paul's (Mon–Fri 7:00–17:00, closed Sat–Sun, from church steps follow signs to youth hostel a block downhill, 53 Carter Lane, tel. 020/723-60056, Claire).

Near the British Library: Drummond Street (running just west of Euston Station) is famous in London for very cheap and good Indian and vegetarian food. Consider **Chutneys** and **Ravi Shankar** for a good *thali*.

TRANSPORTATION CONNECTIONS

London's Heathrow Airport

Heathrow Airport is the world's fourth busiest. Think about it: 60 million passengers a year on 425,000 flights from 200 destinations riding 90 airlines...some kind of global maypole dance. While many complain about Heathrow, I think it's a great airport. It's user-friendly. Read signs, ask questions. For Heathrow's airport, flight, and transfers information, call the switchboard at 0870-000-0123 (www.baa.co.uk). It has four terminals: T-1 (mostly domestic flights, with some European), T-2 (mainly European flights), T-3 (mostly flights from the United States), and T-4 (British Airways transatlantic flights and BA flights to Paris, Amsterdam, and Athens). Taxis know which terminal you'll need.

Each terminal has an airport information desk, car-rental agencies, exchange bureaus, ATMs, a pharmacy, a **VAT refund desk** (T-4 VAT info tel. 020/8910-3682, you must present the VAT claim form from the retailer here to get your 15 percent tax rebate on items purchased in Britain, see page 6 in this book's Introduction for details), and a £4/day **baggage-check desk** (T-1 and T-2 desks open daily 6:00–23:00, T-3 desk opens at 5:15, and T-4 at 5:30). Heathrow's **Internet Exchange** provides access 24 hours a day (T-3). There are **post offices** in T-2 and T-4. Each terminal has cheap **eateries** (such as the cheery Food Village self-service cafeteria in T-3). The **American Express** desk, in the Tube station at Terminal 4 (daily 7:00–19:00), has rates similar to the exchange bureaus upstairs, but doesn't charge a commission (typically 1.5 percent) for cashing any type of traveler's check.

Heathrow's small **TI**, even though it's a for-profit business, is worth a visit to pick up free information: a simple map, the London Planner, and brochures (daily 8:30–18:00, 5-min walk from Terminal 3 in Tube station, follow signs to Underground; bypass queue for transit info to reach window for London questions). If you're riding the Airbus into London, have your partner stay with the bags at the terminal while you head over to the TI.

If you're taking the Tube into London, buy a one-day Travel Card pass to cover the ride (see below).

Transportation to London from Heathrow Airport

By Tube (Subway): For £3.70, the Tube takes you the 14 miles to downtown London in 50 minutes (6/hr, depending on your destination, may require a change). Even better, buy a £5 one-day Travel Card that covers your trip into London and all your Tube travel for the day (starting at 9:30). Buy it at the ticket window at the Tube. You can hop on the Tube at any terminal.

By Airport Bus: The Airbus, running between the airport and

London's King's Cross station, serves the Notting Hill Gate and Bayswater neighborhoods (£10, round trip-£15, 2/hr, 60 min, runs 5:00–21:15, departs from each terminal, buy ticket from driver, tel. 08705-757-747). The Tube works fine, but with baggage, I prefer the Airbus (assuming it serves my hotel neighborhood) because there are no connections underground and there's a lovely view from the top of the double-decker bus. Ask the driver to remind you when to get off. For people heading to the airport, exact pickup times are clearly posted at each bus stop.

By Taxi: Taxis from the airport cost about £45. For four people traveling together, this can be a deal. Hotels can often line up a cab back to the airport for about £30. For the cheapest taxi to the airport, don't order one from your hotel. Simply flag down a few and ask them for their best "off-meter" rate.

Another good option is Hotelink, a door-to-door airport shuttle (Heathrow-£15 per person, Gatwick-£22 per person, book the day before departure, buy online and save £1–2, tel. 01293/532-244, www .hotelink.co.uk, reservations@hotelink.co.uk).

By Heathrow Express Train: This slick train service zips you between Heathrow Airport and London's Paddington Station. At Paddington Station, you're in the thick of the Tube system, with easy access to any of my recommended neighborhoods—Notting Hill Gate is just two stops away. It's only 15 minutes from downtown from Terminals 1, 2, and 3 and 20 minutes from Terminal 4 (at the airport, you can use the Express as a free transfer between terminals). Buy your ticket to London before you board or pay a £2 surcharge to buy it on the train (£13, but ask about discount promos at Heathrow ticket desk, kids under 16 ride half-price, under 5 ride free, covered by Britrail pass, 4/hr, daily 5:10–23:30, tel. 0845-600-1515, www.heathrowexpress.co.uk). A "Go Further" ticket (£14.60) includes one Tube ride from Paddington to get you to your hotel (valid only on same day and in Zone 1, saves time). For one person on a budget, combining the Heathrow Express with either a Tube or taxi ride (between your hotel and Paddington) is nearly as fast and half the cost of taking a cab directly to (or from) the airport.

Buses from Heathrow to Destinations beyond London

The **National Express Central Bus Station** offers direct Jetlink bus connections to **Gatwick Airport** (2/hr, 70 min or more, depending on traffic), departing just outside arrivals at all terminals (one way-£15, round trip-£20). To **Bath,** direct buses run daily from Heathrow (11/day, 2.5 hrs, £14, tel. 08705-757-747). BritRail passholders may prefer the 2.5-hour Heathrow-Bath bus/train connection via Reading (£9 for bus, rail portion free with pass, otherwise £29.20 total, payable at desk in terminal); first catch the twice-hourly RailAir Link shuttle bus to Reading (RED-ding), then hop on the hourly express train to Bath.

Most Heathrow buses depart from the common area serving Terminals 1, 2, and 3 (a 5-min walk from any of these terminals), although some depart from T-4 (bus tel. 08705-747-777).

London's Gatwick Airport

More and more flights, especially charters, land at Gatwick Airport, halfway between London and the southern coast (recorded airport info tel. 0870-000-2468). Express trains—clearly the best way into London from here—shuttle conveniently between Gatwick and London's Victoria Station (£11, round trip-£21.50, children under 5 free, 4/hr during day, 1–2/hr at night, 30 min, runs 24 hrs daily, can purchase tickets on train at no extra charge, tel. 0845-850-1530, www.gatwickexpress .co.uk). You can save a few pounds by taking South Central rail line's slower and less-frequent shuttle between Victoria Station and Gatwick (£8.20, 3/hr, 1/hr midnight–4:00, 45 min, tel. 08457-484-950, www .southcentraltrains.co.uk).

To get to Bath from Gatwick, you can catch a bus to Heathrow and the bus to Bath from there. By train, the best Gatwick-Bath connection involves a transfer in Reading (2.5 hrs, irregular schedule; avoid transfer in London, where you'll have to change stations).

To make a flight connection between Heathrow and Gatwick (see "Buses," above), allow three hours between your arrival at one airport and departure at the other.

London's Other Airports

If you're flying into or out of **Stansted** (airport tel. 0870-0000-303), you can take the Airbus between the airport and downtown London's Victoria Coach Station (£10, 2/hr, 1.5 hrs, runs 4:00–24:00, picks up and stops throughout London, tel. 0845-850-0150) or take the Stansted Airport Rail Link (£13, departs London's Liverpool Street Station, 40 min, 2–4/hr, 5:00–23:00, tel. 08705-301-530, www.stanstedexpress.com).

For **Luton** (airport tel. 01582/405-100, www.london-luton.com), take Green Line's bus #757, which runs between the airport and London's Victoria Station at Buckingham Palace Road—stop 6 (£8, £7 for easyJet passengers, 2/hr, 1–1.25 hrs depending on time of day, runs 4:30–24:00, tel. 0870-608-7261, www.greenline.co.uk).

Discounted Flights from London

Although bmi british midland has been around the longest, the others generally offer cheaper flights.

With **bmi british midland,** you can fly inexpensively to destinations in the U.K. and beyond (fares start around £30 one-way to Edinburgh, Paris, Brussels, or Amsterdam; or around £50 one-way to Dublin; prices can be higher, but there can also be much cheaper Internet specials—check online). For the latest, call British tel. 0870-

607-0555 or U.S. tel. 800/788-0555 (check www.flybmi.com and their subsidiary, bmibaby, at www.bmibaby.com). Book in advance. Although you can book right up until the flight departs, the cheap seats will have sold out long before, leaving the most expensive seats for latecomers.

With no frills and cheap fares, **easyJet** flies mostly from Luton and Gatwick. Prices are based on demand, so the least popular routes make for the cheapest fares, especially if you book early (tel. 0870-600-0000, www.easyjet.com).

Ryanair is a creative Irish airline that prides itself on offering the lowest fares. It flies from London (mostly Stansted airport) to often obscure airports in Dublin, Glasgow, Frankfurt, Stockholm, Oslo, Venice, Turin, and many others. Sample fares: London-Dublin round trip-£78 (sometimes as low as £25), London-Frankfurt round trip-£67 (Irish tel. 01/609-7881, British tel. 0871-246-0000, www.ryanair.com). Because they offer promotional deals any time of year, it's not essential that you book long in advance to get the best deals.

Virgin Express is a British-owned company with good rates (book by phone and pick up ticket at airport an hour before your flight, tel. 020/7744-0004, www.virgin-express.com). Virgin Express flies from London Heathrow and Brussels. From its hub in Brussels, you can connect cheaply to Barcelona, Madrid, Nice, Malaga, Copenhagen, Rome, or Milan (round trip from Brussels to Rome for as little as £105). Their prices stay the same whether or not you book in advance.

Trains and Buses

London, Britain's major transportation hub, has a different train station for each region. Waterloo handles the Eurostar to Paris. King's Cross covers northeast England and Scotland (tel. 08457-225-225). Paddington covers west and southwest England (Bath) and South Wales (tel. 08457-000-125). For the others, call 08457-484-950. Note that for security reasons, stations offer a left-luggage service (£5/day) rather than lockers.

National Express' excellent bus service is considerably cheaper than trains. (For a busy signal, call 08705-808-080, or visit www.nationalexpress .com or the bus station a block southwest of Victoria Station.)

To Bath by train: Trains leave London's Paddington Station every hour between 7:00 and 19:00 (at :15 after each hour) for the 90-min ride to Bath (costs £33 if you leave after 9:30 any day but Fri, when it's £40).

To Bath by bus via Stonehenge: To get to Bath and see Stonehenge to boot, consider taking a guided bus tour from London to Stonehenge and Bath and abandoning the tour in Bath. Several bus-tour companies take London-based travelers out and back every day. If you're going to Bath and want to stay overnight, consider taking a day tour to Bath and skipping the trip back to London. Depending on the type and

availability of tour, you'll pay about £50, which also includes a visit to
Stonehenge (compare to a £33 one-way second-class train ticket from
London to Bath). Evan Evans' tour is fully guided for £50 (includes
admissions). The tour leaves from Victoria Coach Station, a block from
the Victoria train station, every morning at 8:45 (you can stow your bag
under the bus), stops in Stonehenge (45 min), and then stops in Bath for
lunch and a city tour before returning to London (offered year-round).
You can book the tour at Victoria Coach Station, the Evan Evans' office
(258 Vauxhall Bridge Road, near Victoria Coach Station, tel. 020/7950-
1777, U.S. tel. 866/382-6868, www.evanevans.co.uk, reservations
@evanevanstours.co.uk), or the Green Line Travel Office (4a Fountain
Square, across from Victoria Coach Station, tel. 020/7950-1777). Golden
Tours also runs a fully guided Stonehenge-Bath tour for a similar price
(departs from Fountain Square, located across from Victoria Coach
Station, tel. 020/7233-6668, U.S. tel. 800/456-6303, www.goldentours
.co.uk, reservations@goldentours.co.uk).

   To Points North: Trains run hourly from London's King's Cross
Station, stopping in York (2 hrs), Durham (3 hrs), and Edinburgh (5 hrs).

   To Dublin, Ireland: The boat/bus journey takes between 10 and
11 hours and goes all day or all night (£29–57, 2/day, tel. 08705-143-
219, www.eurolines.com). Consider a cheap 70-minute Ryanair flight
instead (see above).

Crossing the English Channel
Crossing the Channel by Eurostar Train

The fastest and most con-
venient way to get from Big
Ben to the Eiffel Tower is
by rail. In London, advertisements claim "more
businessmen travel from
London to Paris on the
Eurostar than on all airlines
combined."

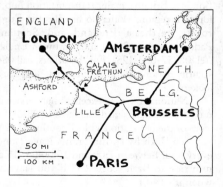

   Eurostar is the speedy
passenger train that zips you
(and up to 800 others in 18
sleek cars) from downtown
London to downtown Paris
(12–15/day, last departure 19:23, 2.5 hrs) or Brussels (8/day, 2.5 hrs)
faster and easier than flying. The actual tunnel crossing is a 20-minute,
black, silent, 100-mile-per-hour non-event. Your ears won't even pop.
You can go direct to Disneyland Paris (1/day, more frequent with transfer at Lille) or change at Lille to catch a TGV to Paris' Charles de
Gaulle Airport.

Channel fares (essentially the same to Paris or Brussels) are reasonable but complicated. Prices vary depending on when you travel; whether you can live with restrictions; and whether you're eligible for any discounts (youth, seniors, and railpass holders all qualify). Rates are lower for round-trip and off-peak (mid-day, mid-week, low-season, and low-interest) travel.

As with airfares, the most expensive and flexible option is a **full-fare ticket** with no restrictions on refundability (even refundable after the departure date; one way in second class-$223, one way in first-class-$312 in first). A first-class ticket comes with a meal (a dinner departure nets you more grub than breakfast)—but it's not worth the extra expense.

Also like the airlines, **cheaper tickets** come with more restrictions—and are limited in number (so they sell out more quickly). Non-full-fare tickets have severe restrictions on refundability (best-case scenario: you'll get 25 percent back, but with many you'll get nothing). But several do allow you to change the specifics of your trip once before departure. For specifics, see "Standard Eurostar Fares," pages 602–603.

Those traveling with a railpass for Britain, France, or Belgium should look first at the **passholder** fare, an especially good value for one-way Eurostar trips. In Britain, passholder tickets can be issued only at the Eurostar office in Waterloo Station or the American Express office in Victoria Station—not at any other stations. You can also order them by phone, then pick them up at Waterloo Station.

Refund and exchange restrictions are serious, so don't reserve until you're sure of your plans. If you are confident of the time and date of your crossing, order ahead from the U.S. Only the most expensive ticket (full fare) is fully refundable, so if you want to have more flexibility, hold off. On the other hand, keep in mind that the longer you wait, the more likely the cheapest tickets will be sold out.

You can check and book fares by phone or online in the United States (order online at www.ricksteves.com/eurostar, prices listed in dollars; order by phone at U.S. tel. 800/EUROSTAR) or in Europe (British tel. 08705-186-186, French tel. 08 92 35 35 39, www.eurostar.com, prices listed in euros). These are different companies, often with slightly different prices and discount deals on similar tickets (see below)—if you order from the United States, check out both. (If you buy from a U.S. company, you'll pay for ticket delivery in the United States; if you book with the British, you'll pick up your ticket at Waterloo Station in London; with the French, at Gare du Nord in Paris.) In Europe, you can get your Eurostar ticket at any major train station in any country or at any travel agency that handles train tickets (expect a booking fee).

Note that Britain's time zone is one hour earlier than the Continent's. Times listed on tickets are local times.

STANDARD EUROSTAR FARES

I've listed only standard (second-class) prices between London and Paris or Brussels. Standard class is comfortable, making first class an unnecessary luxury. Compare one-way fares with cheap round-trip fares (especially the Leisure RT Same Day; you can forget to return).

The following fares are accurate as of mid-2003 and subject to change. Note that the ticket names, restrictions, and prices listed here are for tickets purchased in the U.S. If you buy your ticket in Europe, your options are similar, though rarely identical. Sometimes it's a better deal to buy your ticket in Britain instead of the United States, and sometimes it's not. Compare. For European fares, go to www.eurostar .com and input your travel date and time to see the available rates and restrictions. For U.S. fares (including first-class prices), visit www .ricksteves.com/eurostar. A Premier Train Fee of $7 per order applies.

Standard Class	Major Restrictions	One-Way	Round-Trip
Full Fare	None (fully refundable even after departure date).	$223	$446
Leisure Flexi	One exchange in Europe before departure; 25 percent refund up to three days before departure. Round-trip discount based on seat availability.	$195	$210/300/390
Leisure	No refund or exchange.	$90	$180
Leisure RT	No refund or exchange. Round-trip travel and minimum one-night stay required.	N/A	$150

Crossing the Channel without Eurostar
By bus and boat or by train and boat: The old-fashioned way of crossing the Channel is cheaper than crossing by Eurostar. It's also twice as romantic, complicated, and time-consuming. You'll get better prices arranging your trip in London than you would in the United States. Taking the bus is cheapest, and round-trips are a bargain.

By **bus** to Paris, Brussels, or Amsterdam from Victoria Coach Station (via boat or Chunnel): one way-£35, round trip-£47 for economy fares booked at least two days in advance; 8 hrs to Paris—5/day; 9 hrs to Brussels—5/day; 12 hrs to Amsterdam—4/day; day or overnight, on Eurolines (tel. 08705-143-219, www.eurolines.com).

The **Hoverspeed ferry** runs between Dover, England, and Calais, France (tel. 08705-240-241 or 0870-240-8070, www.hoverspeed.com).

Standard Class	Major Restrictions	One-Way	Round-Trip
Leisure RT Midweek	No refund or exchange. Round-trip travel and minimum one-night stay required. Travel Mon—Thu only. Round-trip discount based on seat availability.	N/A	$90/$120
Leisure RT Same Day	No refund or exchange. Travel round-trip within one day (ideal for Paris day trip from London).	N/A	$94
Passholder	No refund. One exchange in Europe before departure. Trip must occur during the validity period of a railpass including Britain, France, or Belgium.	$75	$150
Senior	Age 60+. No refund. One exchange in Europe before departure.	$90	$180
Youth Peak	Age under 26. No refund, one exchange.	$75	$150
Youth Off-Peak	Age under 26. No refund, one exchange.	$45	$90
Child Age 4-11	No refund, one exchange.	$38	$76

Hoverspeed sells London-Paris rail and ferry packages: one way-£44, round trip with five-day return-£56; and round trip over more than five days-£67. You can buy this package deal in person at Waterloo and Charing Cross stations. If you book by phone (number listed above), you must book at least two weeks in advance, and the ticket will be mailed to you (no ticket pickup at station for bookings by phone).

By **P&O Stena Line ferry** from Dover to Calais: one way or round trip with five-day return-£17, round-trip over more than five days-£34 (tel. 0870-600-0613, www.posl.com). Prices are for the ferry only; you need to book your own train tickets—see P&O's Web site for details.

By Plane: Typical fares are £110 regular, less for student standby. Check with the budget airlines for cheap round-trip fares to Paris (see "Discounted Flights from London," above).

BATH

The best city to visit within easy striking distance of London is Bath—just a 90-minute train ride away. Two hundred years ago, this city of 85,000 was the trendsetting Hollywood of Britain. If ever a city enjoyed looking in the mirror, Bath's the one. It has more "government-listed" or protected historic buildings per capita than any other town in England. The entire city, built of the creamy warm-tone limestone called "Bath stone," beams in its cover-girl complexion. An architectural chorus line, it's a triumph of the Georgian style. Proud locals remind visitors that the town is routinely banned from the "Britain in Bloom" contest to give other towns a chance to win. Bath's narcissism is justified. Even with its mobs of tourists (two million per year), it's a joy to visit.

Long before the Romans arrived in the first century, Bath was known for its hot springs. What became the Roman spa town of Aquae Sulis has always been fueled by the healing allure of its 116-degree mineral hot springs. The town's importance carried through Saxon times, when it had a huge church on the site of the present-day Abbey and was considered the religious capital of Britain. Its influence peaked in 973 with King Edgar's sumptuous coronation in the Abbey. Bath prospered as a wool town.

Bath then declined until the mid-1600s, when it was just a huddle of huts around the Abbey and some hot springs, with 3,000 residents oblivious to the Roman ruins 18 feet below their dirt floors. Then, in 1687, Queen Mary, fighting infertility, bathed here. Within 10 months she gave birth to a son...and a new age of popularity for Bath.

The town boomed as a spa resort. Ninety percent of the buildings you'll see today are from the 18th century. Local architect John Wood was inspired by the Italian architect Andrea Palladio to build a "new Rome." The town bloomed in the neoclassical style, and streets were lined not with scrawny sidewalks but with wide "parades," upon which the women in their stylishly wide dresses could spread their fashionable tails.

Beau Nash (1673–1762) was Bath's "master of ceremonies." He organized both the daily regimen of the aristocratic visitors and the city, lighting and improving street security, banning swords, and opening the Pump Room. Under his fashionable baton, Bath became a city of balls, gaming, and concerts and the place to see and be seen in England. This most civilized place became even more so with the great neoclassical building spree that followed.

With the opening of a new spa tapping Bath's soothing hot springs, the town will once again attract visitors in need of a cure or a soak.

Planning Your Time

Bath needs two nights even on a quick trip. There's plenty to do and it's a joy to do it.

Here's how I'd spend the day in Bath: 9:00-Tour the Roman Baths; 10:30-Catch the free city walking tour; 12:30-Picnic on the open deck of a Bath Bus Tour bus; 14:00-Free time in the shopping center of old Bath or spend an hour soaking at the new spa; 15:30-Tour the Costume Museum. After pub grub or a classy dinner, consider a Bizarre Bath Walking Tour (see "Nightlife," below).

ORIENTATION

(area code: 01225)

Bath's town square, three blocks in front of the bus and train station, is a bouquet of tourist landmarks, including the Abbey, Roman and medieval baths, and the royal Pump Room.

Tourist Information: The TI is in the Abbey churchyard (Mon–Sat 9:30–18:00, Sun 10:00–16:00, Oct–April Mon–Sat until 17:00, tel. 0870-444-6442, www.visitbath.co.uk, tourism@bathnes.gov.uk). Pick up the 50p Bath mini-guide (includes a map) and the free, info-packed *This Month in Bath*. Browse through scads of fliers, books, and maps. Skip their room-finding service (£5) and book direct. If you have a mobile phone and kids along, ask the TI about "Texting Trails," a fun text-message scavenger hunt through Bath.

Arrival in Bath: The Bath **train station** has small-town charm, an international tickets desk, and a privately-run tourism office masquerading as a TI. The **bus station** is immediately in front of the train station. To get to the TI, walk two blocks up Manvers Street from either station and turn left at the triangular "square," by following the small TI arrow on a signpost. My recommended B&Bs are all within a 10- to 15-minute walk or a £3.50 taxi ride from the station.

Helpful Hints

Festivals: The Bath International Music Festival bursts into song from May 21 to June 6 in 2004 (classical, folk, jazz, contemporary; for the line-up, see www.bathmusicfest.org.uk), overlapped by the eclectic Bath Fringe Festival from late May to mid-June (theater, walks, talks, bus trips; www.bathfringe.co.uk). Bath's box office sells tickets for these events and most others, and can tell you exactly what's on tonight (2 Church Street, tel. 01225/463-362, www.bathfestivals.org.uk). Bath's local paper, the *Bath Chronicle*, publishes a "What's On" event listing on Fridays (www.thisisbath.com).

Farmers' Market: It's at Green Park Station on Saturdays (9:00–15:00), with extra days for food stalls in the summer (Wed–Sat 9:00–17:00).

Car Rental: Avis (behind the station and over the river at Unit 4B Riverside Business Park, Lower Bristol Road, tel. 01225/446-680), Enterprise (Lower Bristol Road, tel. 01225/443-311), and Hertz (just outside train station, tel. 01225/442-911) are all trying harder. Sample prices: £39/day, £78/weekend, and £200/week. Most offices are a 10-minute walk from most recommended accommodations. Enterprise will pick you up at your accommodation and bring you down to pick up your car. Most offices close Saturday afternoon and all day Sunday, which complicates weekend pickups.

Internet Access: The Click Café is across from the train station on Manvers Street (£3/hr, daily 10:00–22:00, tel. 01225/481-008). You can also get wired at St. Chrisopher's Inn (Green Street) and Bath Backpackers Hostel (13 Pierrepont Street; coming from train station, you pass hostel on way to TI).

Laundry: The **Spruce Goose Launderette** is around the corner from Brock's Guest House on the pedestrian lane called Margaret's Buildings (self-service or full-service on same day if dropped off at 8:00, Sun–Fri 8:00–20:00, Sat 8:00–21:00, tel. 01225/483-309). Anywhere in town, **"Speedy Wash"** can pick up your laundry for same-day service (£9/bag, Mon–Fri, most hotels work with them, tel. 01225/427-616). East of Pulteney Bridge, the humble **Lovely Wash** is on Daniel Street (daily 9:00–21:00, self-service only).

TOURS

▲▲▲**Walking Tours**—These free two-hour tours, offered by "The Mayor's Corps of Honorary Guides"—volunteers who want to share their love of Bath with its many visitors—are a chatty, historical, gossip-filled joy, essential for your understanding of this town's amazing Georgian social scene. How else will you learn that the old "chair ho" call for your sedan chair evolved into today's "cheerio" farewell? Tours leave from in front of the Pump Room (year-round daily at 10:30 plus Sun–Fri at 14:00; evening walks offered May–Sept at 19:00 on Tue, Fri, and Sat). For Ghost Walks and Bizarre Bath Comedy Walks, see "Nightlife," below. For a private walking tour, call the local guides' bureau (£46/2 hrs, tel. 01225/337-111).

▲▲**City Bus Tours**—The Bath Bus Tour open-top bus (marked "panoramic") makes a 70-minute figure-eight circuit of Bath's main sights with an exhaustingly informative running commentary. For one £8.50 ticket (buy from driver), tourists can stop and go at will for a whole day. The buses cover the city center and the surrounding hills (17 signposted pick-up points, 4/hr spring and fall—runs 9:30–17:00, 6/hr in summer—9:15–18:15, tickets also valid 24 hours on the local First service buses around town and to surrounding areas such as Bradford-on-Avon, Wells, and Glastonbury; tel. 01225/313-222). This is great in sunny weather and a feast for photographers. You can munch a sandwich, work on a tan, and sightsee at the same time. Several competing hop-on, hop-off tour-bus companies, including City Sightseeing, offer similar but less expensive tours that are only 45 minutes and don't include the swing through the countryside. Generally, the Bath Bus Tour guides are better. Note that ticket stubs for any of the bus tours usually get you discounts at some sights. Pick up the various brochures at the TI and see what sights are currently discounted; if you want to see these sights, take the bus tour first.

These tour buses are technically "public service vehicles"—a loophole they use to be able to run the same routes as transit buses. Consequently, tour buses are required to take passengers across town for the normal £1 fare. Nervy tourists have the right to hop on, ask for a "single fare," and pay £1.

Tours from Bath—For bus tours of sights in the countryside, **"Mad Max" Minibus Tours** are best, covering Stonehenge, the Avebury stone circle, and a couple of cute villages (daily, £20 per person, cash only, depart at 8:45—at statue on Cheap Street, next to London Camera Exchange—and return by 16:30, www.madmaxtours.com, reserve by e-mail: maddy@madmax.abel.co.uk or by calling Bath YMCA at 01225/325-900); their Cotswold Discovery tour runs twice weekly. Other companies that'll beam you to Stonehenge and more include **Scarper Tours** (tel. 01225/444-102, www.scarpertours.com), **Heritage City Guided Tour** (runs a Stonehenge Express for £14, mobile 07977-792-9486), and **Celtic Horizons** (tel. 01373/461-784, www.celtichorizons.com, alan@celtichorizons.com).

SIGHTS

▲▲▲**Roman and Medieval Baths**—In ancient Roman times, high society enjoyed the mineral springs at Bath. From Londinium, Romans traveled so often to Aquae Sulis, as the city was called, to "take a bath" that finally it became known simply as Bath. Today a fine museum surrounds the ancient bath. It's a one-way system leading you past well-documented displays, Roman artifacts, mosaics, a temple pediment, and the actual mouth of the spring, piled high with Roman pennies. Enjoy

Bath

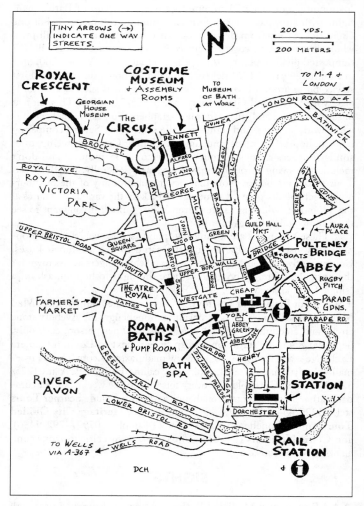

some quality time looking into the eyes of Minerva, goddess of the hot springs. The included self-guided tour audioguide makes the visit easy and plenty informative. For those with a big appetite for Roman history, in-depth 40-minute tours leave from the end of the museum at the edge of the actual bath (included, on the hour, a poolside clock is set for the next departure time). You can revisit the museum after the tour

(£8.50, £11.50 combo-ticket includes Costume Museum at a good savings, family combo-£30, combo-tickets good for 1 week; April–Sept daily 9:00–18:00, July–Aug until 22:00—last entry at 21:00, Oct–March until 17:00, tel. 01225/477-784, www.romanbaths.co.uk). After visiting the Roman Baths, drop by the attached Pump Room for a spot of tea.

▲**Pump Room**—For centuries, Bath was forgotten as a spa. Then, in 1687, the previously barren Queen Mary bathed here, became pregnant, and bore a male heir to the throne. Word of its wonder waters spread, and Bath was back on the aristocratic map. High society soon turned the place into one big pleasure palace. The Pump Room, an elegant Georgian hall just above the Roman baths, offers the visitor's best chance to raise a pinky in this Chippendale elegance. Drop by to sip coffee or tea or enjoy a light meal (daily 9:30–12:00 morning coffee, 12:00–14:30 lunch—£10 two-course menu, 14:30–17:30 traditional high tea—£9.75, £7 tea/coffee and pastry available anytime except during lunch, open for dinner July–Aug only, string trio or live pianist plays sporadically between 10:00 and 17:00, tel. 01225/444-477). Above the newspaper table and sedan chairs, a statue of Beau Nash himself sniffles down at you. Now's your chance to have a famous (but forgettable) "Bath bun" and split (and spit) a 50p drink of the awfully curative water. Convenient public WCs are in the entry hallway that connects the Pump Room with the baths.

Thermae Bath Spa—After simmering unused for a quarter-century, Bath's natural thermal springs will once again offer R&R for the masses. The state-of-the-art leisure and curative spa, housed in a complex combining old buildings with controversial new, blocky architecture, is scheduled to open (after numerous delays) in late 2003. The only natural thermal spa in the United Kingdom will include an open-air rooftop thermal pool and all the "pamper thyself" extras—aromatherapy steam rooms, mud wraps, and various healing-type treatments and classes. Swimwear is required (daily 9:00–22:00, £17/2 hrs, £23/4 hrs, £35/full day; prices do not include treatments, massage, or solarium, which range from £26–68, reservations recommended for these extra services; 100 yards from Roman and medieval baths on Beau Street, tel. 01225/331-234, www.thermaebathspa.com).

▲**Abbey**—Bath town wasn't much in the Middle Ages, but an important church has stood on this spot since Anglo-Saxon times. In 973, Edgar was crowned here. Dominating the town center, the present church—the last great medieval church of England—is 500 years old and a fine example of Late Perpendicular Gothic, with breezy fan vaulting and enough stained glass to earn it the nickname "Lantern of the West" (worth the £2.50 donation, Mon–Sat 9:00–18:00, Sun usually 13:00–14:30 & 15:30–17:30, closes at 16:30 in winter, handy flyer narrates a self-guided 19-stop tour, www.bathabbey.org). The schedule for concerts, services, and **evensong** (Sun at 15:30 year-round, plus most

Sat in Aug at 17:00) is posted on the door. Take a moment to really appreciate the Abbey's architecture from the Abbey Green square.

A small but interesting exhibit, the Abbey's **Heritage Vaults** tell the story of Christianity in Bath since Roman times (£2.50, Mon–Sat 10:00–16:00, last entry 15:30, closed Sun, entrance just outside church, south side).

▲**Pulteney Bridge, Parade Gardens, and Cruises**—Bath is inclined to compare its shop-lined Pulteney Bridge to Florence's Ponte Vecchio. That's pushing it. But to best enjoy a sunny day, pay £1.30 to enter the Parade Gardens below the bridge (April–Sept daily 10:00–19:00, June–Aug until 20:00, shorter hours off-season, includes deck chairs, ask about concerts held some Sun at 15:00 in summer, tel. 01225/394-041).

Across the bridge at Pulteney Weir, tour boats run cruises from under the bridge (£5, up to 7/day if the weather's good, 50 min to Bathampton and back, WCs on board). Just take whatever boat is running. Avon Cruisers stop in Bathampton if you'd like to walk back; Pulteney Cruisers come with a sundeck ideal for picnics.

▲▲**Royal Crescent and the Circus**—If Bath is an architectural cancan, these are the kickers. These first elegant Georgian "condos" by John Wood (the Elder and the Younger) are well explained in the city walking tours. "Georgian" is British for "neoclassical," or dating from the 1770s. As you cruise the Crescent, pretend you're rich. Pretend you're poor. Notice the "ha ha fence," a drop in the front yard offering a barrier, invisible from the windows, to sheep and peasants. The round Circus is a coliseum turned inside out. Its Doric, Ionic, and Corinthian capital decorations pay homage to its Greco-Roman origin.

▲▲**Georgian House at #1 Royal Crescent**—This museum (on the corner of Brock Street and the Royal Crescent) offers your best look into a period house. It's worth the £4 admission to get behind one of those classy exteriors. The volunteers in each room are determined to fill you in on all the fascinating details of Georgian life...like how high-class women shaved their eyebrows and pasted on carefully trimmed strips of furry mouse skin in their place (Tue–Sun 10:30–17:00, closed Mon, closes at 16:00 in Nov, closed Dec–mid-Feb, "no stiletto heels, please," tel. 01225/428-126, www.bath-preservation-trust.org.uk).

▲▲▲**Costume Museum**—One of Europe's great museums, it displays 400 years of fashion—one frilly decade at a time—and is housed within Bath's Assembly Rooms. Follow the included, excellent audioguide tour (£5.50, £11.50 combo-ticket covers Roman Baths, family combo-£30, daily 10:00–17:00, tel. 01225/477-789, www.museumofcostume.co.uk). The Assembly Rooms, which you'll see en route to the museum, are big, elegant, empty rooms where card games, concerts, tea, and dances were held in the 18th century, before the advent of fancy hotels with grand public spaces made them obsolete. They were gutted by WWII bombs, then restored to their original resplendence.

▲▲▲**Museum of Bath at Work**—This is the official title for Mr. Bowler's Business, a 1900s engineer's shop, brass foundry, and fizzy-drink factory with a Dickensian office. It's just a pile of meaningless old gadgets until a volunteer guide lovingly resurrects Mr. Bowler's creative genius. Also featured are various Bath creations through the years, including the versatile plasticine and a 1914 car. Fascinating hour-long tours go regularly; just join the one in session upon arrival (£3.50, April–Oct daily 10:00–17:00, last entry at 16:00, weekends only in winter, 2 blocks up Russell Street from Assembly Rooms, call to be sure a volunteer is available to give a tour, sporadically open café upstairs, tel. 01225/318-348).

Jane Austen Centre—This exhibition focuses on Jane Austen's five years in Bath (around 1800) and the influence Bath had on her writing. While the exhibit is thoughtfully done and a hit with "Jane-ites," there is little of historic substance here. You'll walk through a Georgian town house that she didn't live in and see mostly enlarged reproductions of things associated with her writing. After a live intro explaining how this romantic but down-to-earth girl dealt with the silly, shallow, and arro-gant aristocrat's world where "the doing of nothings all day prevents one from doing anything," you see a 13-minute video and wander through the rest of the exhibit (£4.50, Mon–Sat 10:00–17:30, Sun 10:30–17:30, 40 Gay Street between Queen's Square and the Circus, tel. 01225/443-000, www.janeausten.co.uk). Avid fans gather in mid- to late-September for the annual Bath Jane Austen Festival (readings and lectures, www.janeaustenfestival.co.uk).

The Building of Bath Museum—This offers a fascinating look behind the scenes at how the Georgian city was actually built. It's just a couple rooms of exhibits, but those interested in construction—inside and out—find it worth the £4 (Tue–Sun 10:30–17:00, closed Mon, near the Circus on a street called "The Paragon," tel. 01225/333-895).

Views—For the best views of Bath, try Alexander Park (south of city, 10-min walk from train station), Camden Crescent (10- to 15-min walk north), or Beckfords Tower (steep 45-min walk north up Lansdown Road, www.bath-preservation-trust.org.uk).

▲**American Museum**—I know, you need this in Bath like you need a Big Mac. But this museum offers a fascinating look at colonial and early-American lifestyles. Each of 18 completely furnished rooms (from the 1600s to the 1800s) is hosted by an eager guide waiting to fill you in on the candles, maps, bedpans, and various religious sects that make domestic Yankee history surprisingly interesting. One room is a quil-ter's nirvana (£6, April–Oct Tue–Sun 14:00–17:00, closed Mon and Nov–March, nice arboretum, at Claverton Manor, tel. 01225/460-503, www.americanmuseum.org). The museum is outside of town and a headache to reach if you don't have a car (10-min walk from bus #18).

Shopping—There's great browsing between the Abbey and the Assembly Rooms (Costume Museum). Shops close at 17:30, later on Thursday, and many are open on Sunday (11:00–17:00). Explore the antique shops lining Bartlett Street just below the Assembly Rooms. You'll find the most stalls open on Wednesday. Pick up the local paper (usually out on Fri) and shop with the dealers at estate sales and auctions listed in "What's On" (see "Helpful Hints," above).

NIGHTLIFE

Events are listed in *This Month in Bath* (free, available at TI) and "What's On," appearing Fridays in the local newspaper, the *Bath Chronicle* (www.thisisbath.com).

Plays—The Theatre Royal, newly restored and one of England's loveliest, offers a busy schedule of London West End-type plays, including many "pre-London" dress-rehearsal runs (£11-25, cheaper matinees as low as £5, tel. 01225/448-844, www.theatreroyal.org.uk). Forty standby tickets per evening show go on sale, starting at 12:00 on the day of the performance (either pay cash at box office or call and book with credit card, 2 tickets maximum). Or you can buy a £10 last-minute seat 30 minutes before "curtain up."

Evening Walks—Take your choice: comedy, ghost, or history. For an immensely entertaining walking comedy act "with absolutely no history or culture," follow J. J. or Noel Britten on their creative and entertaining **Bizarre Bath** walk. This 90-minute tour, which plays off local passersby as well as tour members, is a belly laugh a minute (£5, April–Sept nightly at 20:00, smaller groups Mon–Thu, heavy on magic, careful to insult all minorities and sensitivities, just racy enough but still good family fun; leave from Huntsman pub near the Abbey, confirm at TI or call 01225/335-124, www.bizarrebath.co.uk). **Ghost Walks** are another way to pass the after-dark hours (£5, 20:00, 2 hrs, unreliably Mon–Sat April–Oct; in winter Fri only; leave from Garrick's Head pub near Theatre Royal, tel. 01225/463-618, www.ghostwalksofbath.co.uk). The "Mayors Corps of Honorary Guides" offers **free evening walks** in summer (May–Sept at 19:00 on Tue, Fri, and Sat, 2 hrs, leave from Pump Room, confirm at TI); for more information, see "Tours," above.

Summer Nights at the Baths—In July and August, you can stretch your sightseeing day at the Roman Baths, open nightly until 22:00 (last admission 21:00), when they're far less crowded and more atmospheric.

SLEEPING

B&Bs near the Royal Crescent

These listings are all a 15-minute uphill walk or an easy £3.50 taxi ride from the train station. Or take the Bath Bus Tour from the station and

SLEEP CODE

(£1 = about $1.60, country code: 44, area code: 01225)
Sleep Code: **S** = Single, **D** = Double/Twin, **T** = Triple, **Q** = Quad, **b** = bathroom, **s** = shower only, **no CC** = Credit Cards not accepted. Unless otherwise indicated, you can assume credit cards are accepted.

To help you sort easily through these listings, I've divided the rooms into three categories based on the price for a standard double room with bath:

$$$ **Higher Priced**—Most rooms £80 or more.
$$ **Moderately Priced**—Most rooms between £50–80.
$ **Lower Priced**—Most rooms £50 or less.

Bath is a busy tourist town. To get a good B&B, make a telephone reservation in advance. Competition is stiff, and it's worth asking any of these places for a weekday, three-nights-in-a-row, or off-season deal. Friday and Saturday nights are tightest, especially if you're staying only one night, since B&Bs favor those staying longer. If staying only Saturday night, you're very bad news. At B&Bs (and cheaper hotels), expect lots of stairs and no lifts.

get off at the stop nearest your B&B (for Brock's—Assembly Rooms; for Marlborough listings—Royal Avenue; confirm with driver), check in, then finish the tour later in the day. All of these B&Bs are non-smoking.

$$$ Brock's Guest House will put bubbles in your Bath experience. Marion Dodd has redone her Georgian town house (built by John Wood in 1765) in a way that would make the famous architect proud. It's located between the prestigious Royal Crescent and the elegant Circus (Db-£65–78, 1 deluxe Db-£85, Tb-£90–95, Qb-£105–115, reserve with credit card far in advance, little library on top floor, 32 Brock Street, tel. 01225/338-374, fax 01225/334-245, www.brocksguesthouse.co.uk, marion@brocksguesthouse.co.uk).

$$$ Elgin Villa, also thoughtfully run and a fine value, has five comfy, well-maintained rooms (Ss-£34, Sb-£50, Ds-£50, Db-£80, Tb-£90, Qb-£110, more expensive for 1 night, discounted for 3 nights, continental breakfast served in room, non-smoking, parking, 6 Marlborough Lane, tel. & fax 01225/424-557, www.elginvilla.co.uk, stay@elginvilla.co.uk, Alwyn and Carol Landman).

Bath Hotels

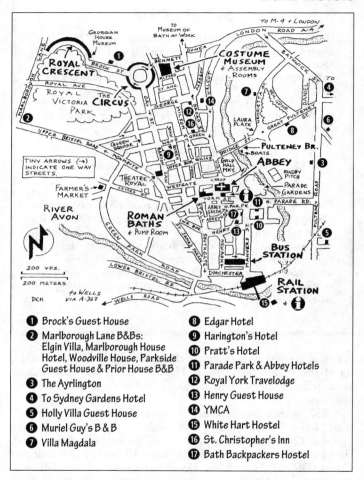

① Brock's Guest House

② Marlborough Lane B&Bs:
Elgin Villa, Marlborough House
Hotel, Woodville House, Parkside
Guest House & Prior House B&B

③ The Ayrlington

④ To Sydney Gardens Hotel

⑤ Holly Villa Guest House

⑥ Muriel Guy's B & B

⑦ Villa Magdala

⑧ Edgar Hotel

⑨ Harington's Hotel

⑩ Pratt's Hotel

⑪ Parade Park & Abbey Hotels

⑫ Royal York Travelodge

⑬ Henry Guest House

⑭ YMCA

⑮ White Hart Hostel

⑯ St. Christopher's Inn

⑰ Bath Backpackers Hostel

$$$ **Marlborough House Hotel** is both Victorian and vegetarian, with seven comfortable rooms—well-furnished with antiques—and organic-veggie dinners available by request (Sb-£45–75, Db-£65–85, Tb-£75–95, price depending on season, varied breakfast menu, room service, 1 Marlborough Lane, tel. 01225/318-175, fax 01225/466-127, www.marlborough-house.net, Americans Laura and Charles).

$$ **Parkside Guest House** has four Edwardian rooms and a spacious back garden (Db-£67, 11 Marlborough Lane, tel. & fax

01225/429-444, www.parksidebandb.co.uk, Erica and Inge Lynall).

$ **Woodville House** is run by Anne and Tom Toalster. This grandmotherly little house has three tidy, charming rooms, one shared shower/WC, an extra WC, and a TV lounge. Breakfast is served at a big, family-style table (D-£40, minimum 2 nights, no CC, strictly non-smoking, some parking, below the Royal Crescent at 4 Marlborough Lane, tel. & fax 01225/319-335, toalster@compuserve.com).

$ **Prior House B&B,** with four well-kept rooms and thoughtful touches such as robes for guests who use the bathroom down the hall, is run by helpful Lynn and Keith Shearn (D-£45, Db-£50, 3 Marlborough Lane, tel. 01225/313-587, fax 01225/443-543, www.greatplaces.co.uk /priorhouse, priorhouse@greatplaces.co.uk).

B&Bs East of the River

These listings are about a 10-minute walk from the city center.

$$$ **The Ayrlington,** next door to a lawn-bowling green, has attractive rooms that hint of a more genteel time. Though this well-maintained hotel fronts a busy street, it feels tranquil inside, with double-paned windows. Rooms in the back have pleasant views of sports greens and Bath beyond. For the best value, request a standard double with a view of Bath (standard Db-£85–120, superior Db-£110–140, deluxe Db with Jacuzzi-£125–160, high prices on Fri, Sat, and Sun, no Sat night only, access to garden in back, easy parking, 24–25 Pulteney Road, tel. 01225/425-495, fax 01225/469-029, Simon and Mee-Ling).

In Sydney Gardens: The $$$ **Sydney Gardens Hotel** is a classy Casablanca-type place with six tastefully decorated rooms, an elegant breakfast room, garden views, and an entrance to Sydney Gardens park (Sb-£65, Db-£85, Tb-£100, Qb-£115, request garden view, easy parking, located on busy road between park and canal, Sydney Road, tel. 01225/464-818, fax 01225/484-347, www.sydneygardens.co.uk, book@ sydneygardens.co.uk, Rory).

Near North Parade Road: The $$ **Holly Villa Guest House,** with a cheery garden, six bright rooms, and a cozy TV lounge, is enthusiastically and thoughtfully run by Jill and Keith McGarrigle (Ds-£50, Db-£50–65, Tb-£75–85, no CC, strictly non-smoking, easy parking, 8-min walk from station and city center: walk over North Parade Bridge, take the first right, and then take the second left, 14 Pulteney Gardens, tel. 01225/310-331, jill@hollyvilla.com).

Near Pulteney Road: $$ **Muriel Guy's B&B** is another good value, mixing Georgian elegance with homey warmth and artistic taste (5 rooms, S-£30, Db-£55, Tb-£65, no CC, serves mostly organic foods, go over bridge on North Parade Road, left on Pulteney Road, cross to church, Raby Place is first row of houses on hill, 14 Raby Place, tel. 01225/465-120, fax 01225/465-283).

East of Pulteney Bridge

These are just a few minutes' walk from the city center.

$$$ **Villa Magdala,** with 18 rooms in a freestanding Victorian town house opposite a park, is formal and hotelesque (Db-£85–140, depending on size and type of bed; in quiet residential area, inviting lounge, parking, Henrietta Road, tel. 01225/466-329, fax 01225/483-207, www.villamagdala.co.uk, office@villamagdala.co.uk, Roy and Lois).

$$ **Edgar Hotel,** with 18 simple rooms and lots of stairs, gives you a budget-hotel option in this elegant neighborhood (Sb-£40–50, Db-£55–75, Tb-£100, Qb-£110, park views from back rooms, smaller rooms on top, avoid #18 on the ground level, pleasant sitting room with old organ and gramophones, 64 Great Pulteney Street, tel. 01225/420-619, fax 01225/466-961, edgar-hotel@pgen.net, Rupert).

The City Center

$$$ **Harington's Hotel,** with 13 newly renovated rooms on a quiet street in the town center, is run by Susan and Desmond Pow (Sb-£78–108, Db-£98–138, prices decrease midweek and increase Fri–Sat, 10 percent discount with this book for 2-night minimum stays Sun–Thu except on public holidays; non-smoking, lots of stairs, attached restaurant-bar serves simple meals and pastries all day, 10 Queen Street, tel. 01225/461-728, fax 01225/444-804, www.haringtonshotel.co.uk).

$$$ **Pratt's Hotel** is as proper and old English as you'll find in Bath. Its creaks and frays are aristocratic. Its public places make you want to sip a brandy, and its 46 rooms are bright, spacious, and come with all the comforts (Sb-£90, Db-£125, advance reservations get highest rate, drop-ins after 16:00 often enjoy substantial discount, dogs-£7.50 but children free, attached restaurant-bar, elevator, 2 blocks immediately in front of the station on South Parade, tel. 01225/460-441, fax 01225/448-807, www.forestdale.com, pratts@forestdale.com).

$$$ **Abbey Hotel** has 60 Best Western-style rooms (some on the ground floor), a super location, and a rare elevator (Sb-£82, standard Db-£128, deluxe Db-£143, attached restaurant, non-smoking rooms, North Parade, tel. 01225/461-603, fax 01225/447-758, www.compasshotels.co.uk, ahres@compasshotels.co.uk).

$$ **Parade Park Hotel,** in a Georgian building, has a central location, helpful owners, and 35 modern, basic rooms (S-£35, D-£50, Db-£60-80, Tb-£90, Qb-£120, non-smoking, *beaucoup* stairs, 10 North Parade, tel. 01225/463-384, fax 01225/442-322, www.paradepark.co.uk, info@paradepark.co.uk).

$$ **Royal York Travelodge**—which offers American-style, characterless, comfortable rooms—worries B&Bs and hotels alike with its reasonable prices (Db-£60, £70 on Fri-Sun, breakfast extra, non-smoking rooms available, 1 York Building, George Street, tel. 0870-191-

1718, central reservation tel. 08700-850-950, www.travelodge.co.uk).

$ **Henry Guest House** is a plain, clean, old, vertical, eight-room, family-run place two blocks in front of the train station on a quiet side street. Nothing matches—not the curtains, wallpaper, carpeting, throw rugs, or bedspreads—but the rooms are pleasant and affordable, and the newly-renovated, cheerful dining room is now open for healthy lunches (S-£25, D-£50, T-£65, no CC, lots of narrow stairs, 3 showers and 2 WCs for all, café open 10:00-17:00, everything on the menu costs £5 or less, 6 Henry Street, tel. 01225/424-052, fax 01225/316-669, www.thehenry.com, enquiries@thehenry.co.uk, helpful Sue and Derek).

Lower-Priced Dorms

The **YMCA,** central on a leafy square down a tiny alley off Broad Street, has 208 beds in industrial-strength rooms with tired carpeting (S-£20–24, D-£32–36, beds in big dorms-£10–12, higher rates on week-ends, includes meager continental breakfast, cheap lunches, lockers, dorms closed 10:00–16:00, Broad Street Place, tel. 01225/460-471, fax 01225/462-065, reservation@ymcabath.co.uk).

White Hart Hostel is a simple, new place offering adults and families good cheap beds in two- to six-bed dorms (£12.50/bed, Db-£50, family rooms, breakfast-£3.50–4.50, smoke-free, kitchen, small café-bar, 5-min walk behind train station at Widcombe—where Widcombe Hill hits Claverton Street, tel. 01225/313-985, www.whitehartbath.co.uk, sue@whitehartinn.freeserve.co.uk, run by Mick and Sue).

St. Christopher's Inn, which opened in 2003 in a prime central Bath location, is part of a chain of low-priced, high-energy hubs for travelers looking for beds and brews (59 beds in 2- to 14-bed rooms-£15–23, deals sometimes available online; lively, affordable restaurant and bar downstairs; Internet access, laundry, lounge with video, 9 Green Street, tel. 020/7407-1856, www.st-christophers.co.uk).

Bath Backpackers Hostel bills itself as a totally fun-packed, mad place to stay. This youthfully run dive/hostel rents bunk beds in 6- to 10-bed rooms (£12/bed, 2 D-£30, T-£45, Internet access for non-guests as well, bar, kitchen, laundry-£2.50/load, a couple of blocks toward city center from train station, 13 Pierrepont Street, tel. 01225/446-787, bath@hostels.co.uk).

EATING

While not a great pub-grub town, Bath is bursting with quaint and stylish eateries. There's something for every appetite and budget—just stroll around the center of town. A picnic dinner of deli food or take-out fish 'n' chips in the Royal Crescent Park is ideal for aristocratic hobos.

Bath Restaurants

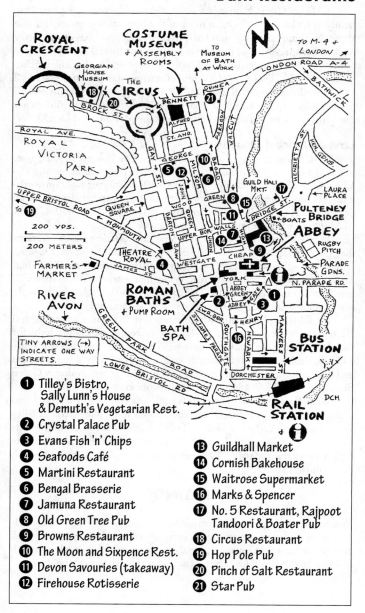

ROYAL CRESCENT

GEORGIAN HOUSE MUSEUM

COSTUME MUSEUM & ASSEMBLY ROOMS

TO MUSEUM OF BATH AT WORK

THE **CIRCUS**

TO MUSEUM OF BATH AT WORK

N

TO M-4 & LONDON

LONDON ROAD A-4

BATHWICK

GUINEA

BENNETT

BROCK ST.

ALFRED

ST. AND.

GAY ST.

GEORGE

MILSOM

JOHN ST.

PASSAGE

WALCOT

BROAD

ROYAL AVE.

ROYAL VICTORIA PARK

UPPER BRISTOL ROAD

TO

QUEEN SQUARE

MONMOUTH

WOOD ST.

QUEEN

BARTON

GREEN

GUILD HALL MKT.

HENRIETTA ST.

HEN. GUNS.

LAURA PLACE

200 YDS.
200 METERS

UPPER BOR

SAW.

UNION

WALLS

BRIDGE ST.

PULTENEY BRIDGE

BOATS

ABBEY

RUGBY PITCH

FARMER'S MARKET

THEATRE ROYAL

JAMES ST.

WESTGATE

CHEAP

LWR. BOR.

YORK

ABBEY GREEN

ABBEY

GATE

N. PARADE RD.

PARADE GDNS.

RIVER AVON

GREEN PARK ROAD

ROMAN BATHS + PUMP ROOM

BATH SPA

ST. JAMES PARADE

SOUTHGATE

HENRY

NEWARK

MANVERS ST.

BUS STATION

TINY ARROWS (→) INDICATE ONE WAY STREETS.

LOWER BRISTOL RD

DORCHESTER

RAIL STATION

DCH

① Tilley's Bistro, Sally Lunn's House & Demuth's Vegetarian Rest.

② Crystal Palace Pub

③ Evans Fish 'n' Chips

④ Seafoods Café

⑤ Martini Restaurant

⑥ Bengal Brasserie

⑦ Jamuna Restaurant

⑧ Old Green Tree Pub

⑨ Browns Restaurant

⑩ The Moon and Sixpence Rest.

⑪ Devon Savouries (takeaway)

⑫ Firehouse Rotisserie

⑬ Guildhall Market

⑭ Cornish Bakehouse

⑮ Waitrose Supermarket

⑯ Marks & Spencer

⑰ No. 5 Restaurant, Rajpoot Tandoori & Boater Pub

⑱ Circus Restaurant

⑲ Hop Pole Pub

⑳ Pinch of Salt Restaurant

㉑ Star Pub

Between the Abbey and the Station

Three fine and popular places share North Parade Passage, a block south of the Abbey:

Tilley's Bistro, popular with locals, serves healthy French, English, and vegetarian meals with candlelit ambience. Their fun menu lets you build your meal, choosing from an interesting array of £7 starters (Mon–Sat 12:00–14:30 & 18:30–23:00, closed Sun, reservations smart, non-smoking, North Parade Passage, tel. 01225/484-200).

Sally Lunn's House is a cutesy, quasi-historic place for expensive doily meals, tea, pink pillows, and lots of lace (£15–20, nightly, smoke-free, 4 North Parade Passage, tel. 01225/461-634). It's fine for tea and buns (£7–10, served until 18:00), and customers get a free peek at the basement Kitchen Museum (otherwise 30p).

Demuth's Vegetarian Restaurant serves good £12 meals (daily 10:00–22:00, vegan options available, reservations wise, tel. 01225/446-059).

Crystal Palace Pub, with typical pub grub under rustic timbers or in the sunny courtyard, is a handy standby (meals-£7, Mon–Fri 11:00–20:00, Sat 11:00–16:00, Sun 12:00–16:00, children welcome on patio until 16:30 but not indoors, 11 Abbey Green, tel. 01225/482-666).

Evans is decent for fish 'n' chips (Mon–Fri 11:30–15:00, Sat 11:30–17:00, closed Sun, on Abbeygate, near Marks & Spencer). Also greasy is **Seafoods** (daily 12:00–23:00, last seating 22:30, last take-out 23:00; try the mushy peas, cup of tea, and fish 'n' chips special for £4; 27 Kingsmead Street, just off Kingsmead Square).

Between the Abbey and the Circus

George Street is lined with cheery eateries: Thai, Italian, wine bars, and so on.

The hopping **Martini Restaurant** is purely Italian, with class and jovial waiters (entrées-£12, pizzas-£7, daily 12:00–14:30 & 18:00–22:30, reservations smart, smoke-free section, 9 George Street, tel. 01225/460-818, Nunzio, Franco, and Luigi).

Bengal Brasserie, a Bangladeshi place specializing in tandoori and curries, is unpretentious with good food at good prices (daily 12:00–14:00 & 18:00–23:00, 32 Milsom Street, tel. 01225/447-906).

Jamuna makes a mean curry (daily until 23:00, 10 percent discount for take-out, Abbey views, 9–10 High Street, tel. 01225/464-631).

The **Old Green Tree Pub** has good grub, locally brewed real ales, and a non-smoking room (lunch only, served 12:00–14:45, no children, Green Street, tel. 01225/448-259).

Browns, a popular, modern chain, offers affordable—though not great—English food throughout the day (Sun–Fri 12:00–23:00, Sat 11:00–23:00, kid-friendly, nice terrace, half-block east of the Abbey, Orange Grove, tel. 01225/461-199).

The Moon and Sixpence, prized by locals, offers "modern English fusion" cuisine, giving British cooking a needed international flair and flavor (two-course lunch-£7.50, three-course dinner menu-£25, daily 12:00–14:30 & 17:30–22:30, indoor/outdoor seating, 6a Broad Street, tel. 01225/460-962).

Devon Savouries serves greasy-but-delicious take-out pasties, sausage rolls, and vegetable pies (Mon–Sat 9:00–17:30, hours vary on Sun, cheaper if you get it to go, on Burton Street, the main walkway between New Bond Street and Upper Borough Walls).

If you're missing California, try the popular **Firehouse Rotisserie** (Mon–Sat 12:00–14:30 & 18:00–23:00, Sun 12:00–14:30, make reservations, near Queen Square on John Street, tel. 01225/482-070).

Guildhall Market, across from Pulteney Bridge, is fun for browsing and picnic shopping, with an inexpensive Market Café if you'd like to sip tea surrounded by stacks of used books, bananas on the push list, and honest-to-goodness old-time locals (Mon–Sat 9:00–17:00, closed Sun, a block north of the Abbey, main entrance on High Street).

The **Cornish Bakehouse,** near the Guildhall Market, has good take-away pasties (open until 17:30, 11a The Corridor, off High Street, tel. 01225/426-635).

Supermarkets: **Waitrose,** at the Podium shopping center, is great for picnics with a good salad bar (Mon–Fri 8:30–20:00, Sat 8:30–19:00, Sun 11:00–17:00, just west of Pulteney Bridge and across from post office on High Street). **Marks & Spencer,** near the train station, has a grocery at the back of its department store (Mon–Sat 9:00–10:00, Sun 11:00–17:00, Stall Street).

East of Pulteney Bridge

For a stylish, intimate setting and "new English" cuisine worth the splurge, dine at **No. 5 Restaurant** (main courses with vegetables-£13–16, Mon–Sat 18:30–22:00, closed Sun, Mon–Tue are "bring your own bottle of wine" nights—no corkage fee, smart to reserve, just over Pulteney Bridge at 5 Argyle Street, tel. 01225/444-499).

Rajpoot Tandoori, next door to No. 5, serves good Indian food. You'll hike down deep into a cellar where the classy Indian atmosphere and award-winning cooking makes paying the extra pounds OK (12:00–14:30 & 18:00–23:00, 4 Argyle Street, tel. 01225/466-833).

Down the street, the popular **Boater Pub** offers a good selection of ales and pub grub and a pleasant beer garden overlooking the river (Mon–Sat 11:00–23:00, Sun 12:00–20:30, 9 Argyle Street, tel. 01225/464-211).

Near the Circus and Royal Crescent

Circus Restaurant is intimate and a good value, with Mozartean ambience and candlelit prices: £18 for a three-course dinner special including great vegetables and a selection of fine desserts (Wed–Sun 12:00–14:00 & 18:30–22:00, closed Tue lunch and all day Mon, reservations smart, 34 Brock Street, tel. 01225/318-918).

The Hop Pole pub, across from Victoria Park and popular with locals, serves up Bath ales and affordable creative cuisine (main courses-£9, open daily for ales, lunch and dinner served Tue–Sat, open courtyard in back, Upper Bristol Road, tel. 01225/446-327).

Pinch of Salt is a splurge with a French accent in a trendy space just off Brock Street (main courses-£14–17, closed Sun, 11 Margaret's Buildings, tel. 01225/421-251).

For real ale (but no food), try the **Star Pub** (daily, top of the Paragon street, tel. 01225/444-437).

TRANSPORTATION CONNECTIONS

Bath's train station is called Bath Spa (train info: tel. 08457-484-950). The National Express bus office (Mon–Sat 8:00–17:30, closed Sun, bus info: tel. 08705-808-080) is one block in front of the train station.

To London: You can catch a **train** to London's Paddington Station (2/hr, 90 min, £33–39 one way after 9:30), or save money but not time by taking the National Express **bus** to Victoria Station (nearly hrly, a little over 3 hrs, one way-£13, round trip-£21, www.nationalexpress .com).

To get *from* London to Bath and see Stonehenge to boot, consider an all-day organized bus tour from London (see page 599 in the London chapter).

To London's Airports: By National Express bus to **Heathrow** and continuing on to London (10/day, 2.5 hrs, £13, tel. 08705-808-080) and to **Gatwick** (approx 2/hr, 4.5 hrs, £20). Trains are faster but more expensive (1/hr, 2.5 hrs, £29.20).

YORK

Historic York is loaded with world-class sights. Marvel at the York Minster, England's finest Gothic church. Ramble through the Shambles, York's wonderfully preserved medieval quarter. Enjoy a walking tour led by an old Yorker. Hop a train at Europe's greatest railway museum, travel to the 1800s in the York Castle Museum, and head back a thousand years to Viking York at the Jorvik exhibit.

York has a rich history. In A.D. 71 it was Eboracum, a Roman provincial capital. Constantine was actually proclaimed emperor here in A.D. 306. In the fifth century, as Rome was toppling, a Roman emperor sent a letter telling England it was on its own, and York became Eoforwic, the capital of the Anglo-Saxon kingdom of Northumbria. A church was built here in 627, and the town became an early Christian center of learning. The Vikings later took the town, and from about 860 to 950 it was a Danish trading center called Jorvik. The invading and conquering Normans destroyed then rebuilt the city, giving it a castle and the walls you see today. Medieval York, with 9,000 inhabitants, grew rich on the wool trade and became England's second city. Henry VIII spared the city's fine minster in order to use York as his Anglican Church's northern capital. The Archbishop of York is second only to the Archbishop of Canterbury in the Anglican Church. In the Industrial Age, York was the railway hub of North England. When it was built, York's train station was the world's largest. Today, York's leading industry is tourism. Its leading drug? Starbucks and Costa are doing their best to turn high tea into high coffee.

Planning Your Time

York rivals Edinburgh as the best sightseeing city in Britain after London. It deserves two nights and a day. For the best 36 hours, follow this plan: Catch the 19:00 city walking tour on the evening of your arrival. The next morning, be at the Castle Museum at 9:30 when it opens—it's worth a good two hours. Then browse and sightsee through the day. Train buffs love the National Railway Museum, and scholars give the Yorkshire Museum three stars. Tour the minster at 16:00 before catching the 17:00 evensong service (at 16:00 Sun). Finish your day with an early evening stroll along the wall and perhaps through the abbey gardens. This schedule assumes you're there in the summer (evening orientation walk) and that there's an evensong on. Confirm your plans with the TI.

ORIENTATION

(area code: 01904)

The sightseer's York is small. Virtually everything is within a few minutes' walk: the sights, train station, TI, and B&Bs. The longest walk a visitor might take (from a B&B across the old town to the Castle Museum) is 15 minutes.

Bootham Bar, a gate in the medieval town wall, is the hub of your York visit. At Bootham Bar (and on Exhibition Square facing it) you'll find the TI, the starting points for most walking tours and bus tours, handy access to the medieval town wall, and Bootham street, which leads to the recommended B&Bs. (In York, a "bar" is a gate and a "gate" is a street. Go ahead, blame the Vikings.) When finding your way, navigate by sighting the tower of the minster or the strategically placed green signposts pointing out all places of interest to tourists.

Tourist Information: The TI at Bootham Bar sells a 90p *York Map and Guide*. Ask for the free monthly *What's On* guide and the *York MiniGuide,* which includes a map and some discounts (April–Oct Mon–Sat 9:00–18:00, Sun 10:00–17:00, likely 10:00–16:00 off-season, WCs next door, tel. 01904/621-756). The TI books rooms for a £4 fee. The train-station TI is smaller but provides all the same information and services (same hours as main TI).

Arrival in York: The train station, which stores luggage for day-trippers (£3, Mon–Sat 8:00–20:30, Sun 9:00–20:30, platform 1), is a five-minute walk from town; turn left down Station Road and follow the crowd toward the Gothic towers of the minster. After the bridge, a block before the minster, signs to the TI send you left on St. Leonard's Place. Recommended B&Bs are a five-minute walk from there. (For a shortcut to B&B area from station, walk 1 block toward the minster, cut through parks to riverside, cross railway bridge/pedestrian walkway, cross parking lot for B&Bs on St. Mary's Street, or duck through pedestrian walkway under tracks to B&Bs on Sycamore and Queen Anne's Road.) **Taxis** zip new arrivals to their B&B for £3.

Helpful Hints

Study Ahead: York has a great Web site: www.visityork.org.
Internet Access: Get online at Internet Exchange (Mon–Sat 9:00–19:00,

Sun 11:00–18:00, 13 Stonegate, tel. 01904/638-808) or Gateway (Mon–Wed 10:00–20:00, Thu–Sat until 23:00, Sun 12:00–16:00, 26 Swinegate, tel. 01904/646-446, fax 01904/670-386).

Festivals: The Viking Festival in late February features lur-blowing, warrior drills, and re-created battles. The Early Music Festival zings its strings in mid-July. And the York Festival of Food and Drink takes a 10-day bite out of the middle of September. Book a room well in advance during festival times and weekends any time of year.

Bike Rental: Trotters, just outside Monk Bar, has free cycling maps. The riverside path is pleasant (£10/day, tandem-£30/day, helmets-£2, Mon–Sat 9:00–17:30, Sun 10:00–16:00, tel. 01904/622-868). Europcar at the train station also rents bikes (£10/day, platform 1, tel. 01904/658-161).

Car Rental: If you're nearing the end of your trip, consider dropping your car upon arrival in York. The money saved by turning it in early nearly pays for the train ticket that whisks you effortlessly to Edinburgh or London. Here are some car-rental agencies in York: Avis (Mon–Sat, closed Sat afternoon and Sun, 3 Layerthorpe, tel. 01904/610-460), Hertz (April–Sept daily, Sat–Sun until 13:00, at train station, tel. 01904/612-586), Sixt (Mon–Sat, closed Sun, inconveniently 3 miles out of town at Clifton Moor Industrial Estate, tel. 01904/479-715), Budget (daily, Sat & Sun until 11:00, 1 mile past recommended B&Bs at Clifton 82, tel. 01904/644-919), and Europcar (Mon–Fri 8:00–18:00, Sat–Sun until 12:00, train station platform 1, tel. 01904/658-161). Beware, car-rental agencies close Saturday afternoon and some close all day Sunday—when drop-offs are OK, but picking up is impossible.

TOURS

▲▲▲**Walking Tours**—Charming local volunteer guides give energetic, entertaining, and free two-hour walks through York (daily 10:15 all year, plus 14:15 April–Oct, plus 18:45 July–Aug, from Exhibition Square across from TI). There are many other commercial York walking tours. YorkWalk Tours, for example, has reliable guides and many themes from which to choose, such as Roman York, City Walls, or Snickleways—small alleys (£5, tel. 01904/622-303, TI has schedule). The ghost tours, all offered after nightfall, are more fun than informative. Haunted Walk relies a bit more on storytelling and history than on masks and surprises (£3, April–Nov nightly at 20:00, 90 min, just show up, depart from Exhibition Square, across street from TI, end in the Shambles, tel. 01904/621-003).

▲**Hop-on, Hop-off Bus Tours**—With one £7.50 ticket, you can jump

York

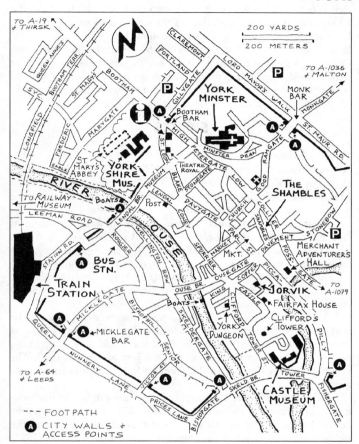

on or off either of the two tours circling York. The tours, run by the same company, generally follow the same route. The main difference is that the Guide Friday York Tour (green bus, 45 min loop) is shorter and has live guides, and the City Sightseeing tour (red bus, 1 hr) has recorded narration and a few extra stops, including the York Racecourse and Rowntree Park. Both tours cover secondary York sights that the city walking tours skip—the workaday perimeter of town (pay driver cash, can also buy from TI with CC, departures every 10 min or more from 9:00 until around 17:00, less frequent off-season, red tours don't run Nov–March, tel. 01904/655-585). While you can hop on and off all day, the tours are of no real value from a transportation-to-the-sights point of view because York is so compact. I'd catch the tour at the Bootham Bar TI and ride it for an orientation all the way around or get off at the Railway Museum, skipping the last five minutes.

Boat Cruise—The York Boat does a lazy 60-minute lap along the River Ouse (£6, Feb–Nov daily from 10:30 on, narrated cruise, leaves from Lendal Bridge and King's Staith landing) and also offers themed evening cruises—ghost, dinner, floodlit, and so on (boat rentals possible, tel. 01904/628-324, www.yorkboat.co.uk).

SIGHTS

York Minster

▲▲▲**Minster**—The pride of York, this largest Gothic church north of the Alps (540 feet long, 200 feet tall) brilliantly shows that the High Middle Ages were far from dark. The word "minster" means a place from which people go out to minister or spread the word of God.

Cost, Hours, and Tours: The cathedral opens daily for worship at 7:00 and for sightseeing Mon–Sat from 9:00 and Sunday from 12:30, when they begin charging £4.50 admission. The closing time flexes with the season (roughly May–Oct at 18:30, earlier off-season—call for details, tel. 01904/557-216). The tower (£2.50) and undercroft (£2.50, or £6 combo-ticket with cathedral entry) have shorter hours, typically opening a half-hour later and closing a half-hour earlier.

When you enter go directly to the welcome desk, pick up the worthwhile "Welcome to the York Minster" flier, and ask when the next free guided **tour** departs (tours go about every half-hour until 15:00, even with just one or two people; you can join one in progress). The helpful minster guides, wearing blue armbands, are happy to answer your questions.

Self-Guided Tour: Your first impression might be the spaciousness and brightness of the nave (built 1280–1350). The nave—from the middle period of Gothic, called "Decorated Gothic"—is one of the widest Gothic naves in Europe. Notice the Great West Window (1338) above the entry. The heart in the tracery is called "the heart of Yorkshire."

Look down the nave. The mysterious gold-and-red dragon's head (in the middle of the nave, sticking out of the side) was probably used as a crane to lift a font cover.

The north and south transepts are the oldest parts of today's church (1220–1270). The oldest complete window in the minster is the entire wall of glass in the north transept (1260). Known as the Five Sisters Window, these 50-foot-high panels were made of modern-looking grisaille (gray-silver) glass. Off the north transept is the **chapter house,** with an elaborately decorated 13th-century Gothic dome—the largest in England without a central supporting pillar—featuring playful details carved in the stonework (pointed out in the flier at the north transept entrance). The south transept has access to the tower and undercroft (see below).

The fanciful choir and the east end (high altar) is from the last stage of Gothic, Perpendicular (1360–1470). The Great East Window (1405), the largest medieval glass window in existence, shows the beginning and the end of the world, with scenes from Genesis and the book of Revelation. A chart (on the right, with a tiny, more helpful chart within) highlights the core Old Testament scenes in this hard-to-read masterpiece. Enjoy the art close up on the chart and then step back and find the real thing.

There are two extra visits to consider, both in the south transept. You can scale the 275-step **tower** for the panoramic view (£2.50). The **undercroft** consists of the crypt, treasury, and foundations (£2.50, or £6 combo-ticket, includes informative audioguide). The crypt is an actual bit of the Romanesque church, featuring 12th-century Romanesque art, excavated in modern times. The foundations give you a chance to climb down—archaeologically and physically—through the centuries to see the roots of the much smaller, but still huge, Norman church (Romanesque, 1100) that stood on this spot and, below that, the Roman excavations. Constantine was proclaimed Roman emperor here in A.D. 306. Peek also at the modern concrete save-the-church foundations.

Evensong and Church Bells: To experience the cathedral in musical and spiritual action, attend an evensong (Mon–Fri 17:00, Sat–Sun 16:00, 45 min). When the choir is off on school break (mid-July–Aug), visiting choirs usually fill in. Arrive 10 minutes early and wait just outside the choir in the center of the church, from where you'll be ushered in and can sit in one of the big wooden stalls. If you're a fan of church bells, Sunday morning (around 10:00) and the Tuesday-evening practice (19:30–21:30) are heavenly.

More Sights

▲**City Walls**—The historic walls of York provide a fine two-mile walk. Walk from Bootham Bar (gate) to Monk Bar for outstanding cathedral views. They're free and open from dawn until dusk (barring attacks).

▲**The Shambles**—This is the most colorful old York street in the half-timbered, traffic-free core of town. Ye olde downtown York, while very touristy, is made for window-shopping, street musicians, and people-watching. The frumpy Newgate Market is fun. For a cheap lunch, consider the cute, tiny **St. Crux Parish Hall.** This medieval church is now used by a medley of charities selling tea, homemade cakes, and light meals. They each book the church for a day, often a year in advance. Chat up the volunteers (Mon–Sat 10:00–16:00, closed Sun, at bottom end of the Shambles, at intersection with Pavement).

▲▲▲**Castle Museum**—Truly one of Europe's top museums, this is a

Victorian home show, the closest thing to a time-tunnel experience England has to offer. It includes the 19th-century Kirkgate (a collection of old shops well stocked exactly as they were 150 years ago), a "From Cradle to Grave" clothing exhibit, and a fine costume collection. The one-way plan allows you to see everything: a working water mill (April–Oct), prison cells, WWII fashions, and old toys. Bring 20p coins to jolt a mechanical Al Jolson into song. The museum's £3 guidebook isn't necessary but makes a fine souvenir (£6, April–Oct daily 9:30–17:00, Nov–March until 16:30, gift shop, parking, cafeteria midway through museum, tel. 01904/687-652).

Clifford's Tower, across from the Castle Museum, is all that's left of York's 13th-century castle, the site of a 1190 massacre of local Jews (read about this at base of hill). If you do climb inside, there are fine city views from the top of the ramparts (not worth the £2.50, April–Sept daily 10:00–18:00, Oct–March until 16:00).

▲**Jorvik**—Sail the "Pirates of the Caribbean" north and back 800 years and you get Jorvik—more a ride than a museum. Innovative 10 years ago, the commercial success of Jorvik (pron. YOR-vik) inspired copycat ride/museums all over England. You'll ride a little Disney-type train car for 13 minutes through the re-created Viking street of Coppergate. It's the year 975, and you're in the village of Jorvik. Next, your little train takes you through the actual excavation site that inspired this. Finally you'll browse through a small gallery of Viking shoes, combs, locks, and other intimate glimpses of that redheaded culture (£7.20, April–Sept opens at 9:30 with last entry at 17:30, Oct–March opens at 10:00, closing varies from 15:30 to 16:30, tel. 01904/643-211, www.vikingjorvik.com).

Midday lines can be an hour long. Avoid the line by going very early or very late in the day or by prebooking (call 01904/543-403, you're given a time slot, booking fee–£1). Some love this "ride"; others call it a gimmicky rip-off. If you're looking for a grown-up museum, the Viking exhibit at the Yorkshire Museum is far better. If you're thinking Disneyland with a splash of history, Jorvik's fun. To me, Jorvik is a commercial venture designed for kids with nearly as much square footage devoted to its shop as to the museum.

▲▲**National Railway Museum**—If you like model railways, this is train-car heaven. The thunderous museum shows 150 fascinating years of British railroad history. Fanning out from a grand roundhouse is an array of historic cars and engines, including Queen Victoria's lavish royal car and the very first "stagecoaches on rails." There's much more, including exhibits on dining cars, post cars, sleeping cars, train posters, and videos. At the "Works" section you can see live train switchboards. And don't miss the English Channel Tunnel video (showing the first handshake at breakthrough). Red-shirted "explainers" are everywhere, eager to talk trains. This biggest and best railroad museum anywhere is interesting even to people who think "Pullman" means "don't push" (free, £3 audioguide with 60 bits of railroad lore—punch in exhibit numbers as you go, daily 10:00–18:00, tel. 01904/621-261).

Cute little "street trains" shuttle you between the minster and the Railway Museum (£1.50 each way, runs Easter–Oct, leaves Railway Museum every 30 min from 12:00 to 17:00 at the top and bottom of the hour; leaves minster—from Duncombe Place—every 30 min, :15 and :45 min after the hour, no trains Nov–Easter).

▲▲Yorkshire Museum—Located in a lush, picnic-perfect park next to the stately ruins of St. Mary's Abbey, Yorkshire Museum is the city's forgotten, serious "archaeology of York" museum. While the hordes line up at Jorvik, the best Viking artifacts are here—with no crowds and a better historical context. A stroll around this museum takes you through Roman (wonderfully described battle-bashed skull in first case), Saxon (great Anglo-Saxon helmet from A.D. 750), Viking, Norman, and Gothic York. Its prize piece is the delicately etched 15th-century pendant called the Middleham Jewel—for which the museum raised $4 million to buy. The 20-minute video about the creation of the abbey is worth a look (£4, various exhibitions can increase price, daily 10:00–17:00, tel. 01904/687-687).

Theatre Royal—A full variety of dramas, comedies, and works by Shakespeare is put on to entertain the locals (£10–17, 19:30 almost nightly, tickets easy to get, closes several weeks during the summer, on St. Leonard's Place next to TI and a 5-min walk from recommended B&Bs, booking tel. 01904/623-568).

Shopping—With its medieval lanes lined with classy as well as tacky little shops, York is a hit with shoppers. I find the **antique malls** interesting. Three places within a few blocks of each other are filled with stalls and cases owned by antique dealers from the countryside. The malls sell the dealers' bygones on commission. Serious shoppers do better heading for the countryside, but York's shops are a fun browse: The Antiques Centre York (daily 9:00–18:00, 41 Stonegate, tel. 01904/635-888), the antique mall at 2 Lendal (Mon–Sat 10:00–17:00, closed Sun, tel. 01904/641-582), and the Red House Antiques Centre (daily 9:30–17:30, as late as 19:00 in summer, a block from the minster at Duncombe Place, tel. 01904/637-000).

SLEEPING

B&Bs near Bootham

These recommendations are in the handiest B&B neighborhood, a quiet residential area just outside the old-town wall's Bootham gate, along the road called Bootham. All are within a five-minute walk of the minster and TI and a 10-minute walk or taxi ride (£3) from the station. If driving, head for the cathedral and follow the medieval wall to the gate called Bootham Bar. Bootham "street" leads away from Bootham Bar.

SLEEP CODE

(£1 = about $1.60, country code: 44, area code: 01904)
Sleep Code: **S** = Single, **D** = Double/Twin, **T** = Triple, **Q** =
Quad, **b** = bathroom, **s** = shower only, **No CC** = Credit Cards
not accepted. You can assume credit cards are accepted unless
otherwise noted.

To help you sort easily through these listings, I've divided
the rooms into three categories based on the price for a standard double room with bath (during high season):

$$$ **Higher Priced**—Most rooms £90 or more.
$$ **Moderately Priced**—Most rooms between £60–90.
$ **Lower Priced**—Most rooms £60 or less.

I've listed peak-season, book-direct prices. Don't use the TI.
Outside of July and August, some prices go soft. B&Bs will
sometimes turn away one-night bookings, particularly for peak-
season Saturdays. (York is worth 2 nights anyway.) Remember
to book ahead during festival times (late Feb, mid-July, middle
of Sept) and weekends year-round.

These B&Bs are all small, non-smoking, and family run. They
come with plenty of steep stairs but no traffic noise. For a good selection, call well in advance. B&B owners will generally hold a room with a
phone call and work hard to help their guests sightsee and eat smartly.
Most have permits for street parking. And most don't take credit cards.

Laundry: Regency Dry Cleaning does small loads (£3.50/kilo-
gram—about 2 lbs, Mon–Fri 8:30–18:00, Sat 9:00–17:00, closed Sun,
drop off by 9:30 for same-day service, 75 Bootham, at intersection with
Queen Anne's Road, tel. 01904/613-311). The next-nearest place is a
long 15-minute walk away (Washeteria Launderette, 124 Haxby Road,
tel. 01904/623-379).

$$$ The Hazelwood, my most hotelesque listing in this neigh-
borhood, is plush, but lacks the intimacy of a B&B. This spacious house
has 13 beautifully decorated rooms with modern furnishings and lots of
thoughtful touches (Db-£80/90/100 depending on room size, 2 ground-
floor rooms, classy breakfast, quiet for being so central, laundry service-
£5; a fridge, ice, and great travel library in the pleasant basement lounge;
24 Portland Street, tel. 01904/626-548, fax 01904/628-032, www
.thehazelwoodyork.com, reservations@thehazelwoodyork.com).

$$ 23 St. Mary's is extravagantly decorated. Chris and Julie

Simpson have done everything super-correctly and offer nine comfy rooms, a classy lounge, and all the doily touches (Sb-£34–40, Db-£64–80 depending on season and size, DVD library and some rooms with DVD players, 23 St. Mary's, tel. 01904/622-738, fax 01904/628-802, www.23stmarys.co.uk).

$$ Crook Lodge B&B, with seven charming, tight rooms, is elegant for a B&B (Db-£64–72, parking, quiet, 26 St. Mary's, tel. 01904/655-614, fax 01904/625-915, www.crooklodge.co.uk, crooklodge@hotmail.com, Brian and Louise Aiken).

$$ The Coach House Hotel is a labyrinthine, funky old place—a little musty, but well-located facing a bowling green and the abbey walls. It offers 12 comfortable old-time rooms and a crackerjack lounge (S-£31, Sb-£34, Db-£68, free parking, 20 Marygate, Bootham, tel. 01904/652-780, fax 01904/679-943, www.coachhousehotel-york.com, info @coachhousehotel-york.com).

$$ Arnot House, run by a hardworking daughter-and-mother team, is homey and lushly decorated with early-1900s memorabilia. The four well-furnished rooms have little libraries and VCRs (Db-£58–62, minimum 2-night stay, video library, 17 Grosvenor Terrace, tel. & fax 01904/641-966, www.arnothouseyork.co.uk, kim.robbins@virgin.net, Kim and Ann Robbins).

$ Airden House, the most central of my Bootham-area listings, has eight spacious rooms, a cozy TV lounge, and brightness and warmth throughout. It's simple, clean, comfortable, and friendly (D-£44–46, Db-£54–56, no CC, 1 St. Mary's, tel. 01904/638-915, www.airdenhouse .co.uk, info@airdenhouse.co.uk, Graham and Lynda Scarisbrick).

$ The Sycamore is a fine value, with seven homey, flowery rooms. It's at the end of a dead end opposite a bowling green that is fun to watch (D-£46, Db-£50–60, family room-£60–69, no CC, 19 Sycamore Place off Bootham Terrace, tel. 01904/624-712, www.thesycamore .co.uk, run by Elizabeth).

$ Abbeyfields Guest House has eight cozy, bright rooms and a quiet lounge. This doily-free place, which lacks the usual clutter, has been designed with care (Sb-£37, Db-£60, no CC, 19 Bootham Terrace, tel. & fax 01904/636-471, www.abbeyfields.co.uk, Richard and Gwen Martin).

$ Queen Anne's Guest House has seven clean, cheery rooms (May–Sept D-£42, Db-£44, Oct–April D-£32, Db-£34, prices good through 2004 with this book, 1 family room, lounge, 24 Queen Anne's Road, tel. 01904/629-389, fax 01904/619-529, www.queen-annes -guesthouse.co.uk, queen.annes@btopenworld.com, Judy and David).

$ Alcuin Lodge has five flowery rooms and solid-wood furnishings (Db-£45–55, 1 small top-floor D-£40, 15 Sycamore Place, tel. 01904/632-222, fax 01904/626-630, alcuinlodg@aol.com, Zoe Collinson and Lea Thomlinson).

B&Bs along the Riverside

Three smoke-free places front the River Ouse midway between the train station and the minster. The Water's Edge B&B is best; the other two places are simpler, a bit worn, and a lesser value. Each faces the same pleasant pedestrian path and comes with a delightful front garden and no traffic noise. Front rooms overlook the river; back rooms watch a sprawling car park.

$ **Water's Edge B&B,** a pastel place with five comfy rooms a teddy bear would like, is well-run by Julie Mett (Db-£55, four-poster riverview Db-£60, 2-room family room, prices through 2004 with this book, CC for 3.5 percent extra, 5 Earlsborough Terrace, tel. 01904/644-625, www.watersedgeyork.co.uk, julie@watersedgeyork.co.uk).

$ **Abbey Guest House** has seven basic rooms (S-£28, Sb-£35, D-£50, Db-£60, Qb-£80, CC for 2.5 percent extra, free parking, Internet access, laundry-£5/load, 14 Earlsborough Terrace, tel. 01904/627-782, fax 01904/671-743, www.bedandbreakfastyork.co.uk, abbey@rsummers.cix.co.uk, Hilary Summers).

$ **Riverside Walk B&B** has 12 small rooms, steep stairs, and narrow hallways (Db-£52–62, CC for 2.5 percent extra, free parking, 8 Earlsborough Terrace, tel. 01904/620-769, fax 01904/671-743, www.bedandbreakfastyork.co.uk, Mr. Summers).

Hotels in the Center

$$$ **Dean Court Hotel,** facing the minster, is a big, stately Best Western hotel with classy lounges and 40 comfortable rooms (small Db-£115, standard Db-£140, superior Db-£155, spacious deluxe Db-£170, some non-smoking rooms, tearoom, restaurant, elevator to most rooms, Duncombe Place, tel. 01904/625-082, fax 01904/620-305, www.deancourt-york.co.uk).

$$ **Galtres Lodge Hotel,** a block from the minster, offers comfy, recently refurbished rooms above a restaurant in the old-town center (S-£30–35, Sb-£35–45, Db-£70–80, non-smoking, Internet access, 54 Low Petergate, tel. 01904/622-478, fax 01904/627-804).

$ **Travelodge** offers 90 identical, affordable rooms near the Castle Museum (Db-£60, kids' bed free, some smoke-free rooms, 90 Piccadilly, central reservations tel. 0870-085-0950, www.travelodge.co.uk).

$ **York Youth Hotel** is a well-run hostel, with a kitchen, launderette, game room, and 120 beds (S-£22, bunk bed D-£32, beds in 4- to 6-bed dorms-£14, beds in larger dorms-£12, less for multi-night stays, family rates, same-sex or coed possible, no breakfast, 10-min walk from station at 11 Bishophill Senior Road, tel. 01904/625-904, fax 01904/612-494, www.yorkyouthhotel.com).

York Hotels and Restaurants

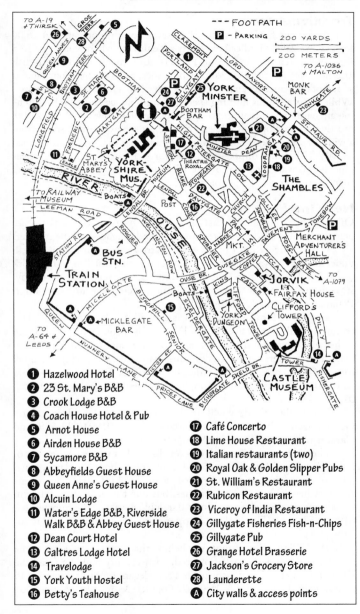

1. Hazelwood Hotel
2. 23 St. Mary's B&B
3. Crook Lodge B&B
4. Coach House Hotel & Pub
5. Arnot House
6. Airden House B&B
7. Sycamore B&B
8. Abbeyfields Guest House
9. Queen Anne's Guest House
10. Alcuin Lodge
11. Water's Edge B&B, Riverside Walk B&B & Abbey Guest House
12. Dean Court Hotel
13. Galtres Lodge Hotel
14. Travelodge
15. York Youth Hostel
16. Betty's Teahouse
17. Café Concerto
18. Lime House Restaurant
19. Italian restaurants (two)
20. Royal Oak & Golden Slipper Pubs
21. St. William's Restaurant
22. Rubicon Restaurant
23. Viceroy of India Restaurant
24. Gillygate Fisheries Fish-n-Chips
25. Gillygate Pub
26. Grange Hotel Brasserie
27. Jackson's Grocery Store
28. Launderette
A. City walls & access points

EATING

Traditional Tea

York is famous for its elegant teahouses. Drop into one around 16:00 for tea and cakes. Ladies love **Betty's Teahouse** where you pay £5.65 for a cream tea (tea and scones) or £10 for a full traditional English afternoon tea (tea, elegant sandwich, scones, and sweets). Your table is so full of doily niceties that the food is served on a little three-tray tower. While Betty's food is nothing special, the ambience and people-watching are hard to beat (daily 9:00–21:00, piano music nightly 18:00–21:00, mostly non-smoking, St. Helen's Square; fine view of street scene from a window seat on the main floor, downstairs near WC is a mirror signed by WWII bomber pilots—read the story). If there's a line, it moves quickly. I'd wait for a seat by the windows on the ground level rather than sit in the much bigger basement.

Near the Minster

Of these listings, the first listing faces the minster, the last two are behind the minster, and the rest are on Goodramgate near the minster.

Café Concerto, a French-style bistro with a fun menu, has an understandably loyal following. Their food is the best I've had in York (great lunch-£8, dinner-£15, daily 10:00–22:00, serves meals all day, smoke-free, smart to reserve for dinner, facing the minster, High Petergate 21, tel. 01904/610-478).

The **Lime House Restaurant** is a small, modern, candlelit place enthusiastically run by chef Adam Fisher. His menu features European dishes revolving with the seasons and always includes a good vegetarian plate. Adam offers a free glass of house wine to anyone with this book (plates-£12, 10 percent off on orders before 19:15, Tue–Sat 12:00–14:00 & 18:00–21:30, closed Sun–Mon, lunch specials, 55 Goodramgate, tel. 01904/632-734).

For Italian food, you'll find a couple popular places along Goodramgate: **Little Italy** (#12, closed Mon, tel. 01904/623-539) and **Caesars** (#27, nightly, tel. 01904/670-914).

There's a pub serving grub on every block. Eat where you see lots of food. The **Royal Oak** offers £5 pub grub throughout the day, a small non-smoking room, and hand-pulled ale (daily 11:00–20:00, Sun opens at noon, heavy meat dishes, fat fries, but don't look in their kitchen, Goodramgate, a block from Monk Bar, a block east of the minster, tel. 01904/653-856). The **Golden Slipper,** next door, is also a classic for basic pub grub and darts (open daily).

St. Williams Restaurant, just behind the great east window of the minster in a wonderful half-timbered, 15th-century building (read the history), serves quick and tasty lunches and elegant candlelit dinners (£15 plates, daily 10:00–17:00 & 18:00–22:00, Oct–March closed Sun–Mon nights, English and Mediterranean, College Street, tel. 01904/634-830).

For vegetarian, try **Rubicon,** a pastel café with dinner specials until 18:30 (£8.50/2 courses, daily, 5 Little Stonegate, tel. 01904/676-076).

The Viceroy of India—just outside Monk Bar and therefore outside the tourist zone—serves great Indian food at good prices to mostly locals. If you've yet to eat Indian on your trip, do it here (plates-£8, Mon–Fri 18:00–24:00, Sat–Sun 12:00–24:00, friendly staff, continue straight through Monk Bar to 26 Monkgate, tel. 01904/622-370).

Near Bootham Bar and Your B&B

Gillygate Fisheries is a wonderfully traditional little fish-and-chips joint where tattooed people eat in and housebound mothers take out (Mel serves £4–5 meals, "eat your mushy peas," Mon–Fri 11:30–13:30 & 17:00–23:30, Sat 11:30–23:30, closed Sun, smoke-free seating, two blocks from the TI at 59 Gillygate).

The **Gillygate** pub has local color and serves decent pub food in a cozy smoke-free room or with the smoking beer drinkers (daily 11:00–19:30, beer garden out back, across from Wackers at 48 Gillygate, tel. 01904/654-103).

The well-worn **Coach House** serves good-quality food with fresh vegetables but can be smoky (£8–11, nightly 18:30–21:00, 20 Marygate, tel. 01904/652-780).

The **Grange Hotel Brasserie,** a couple of blocks from the B&Bs, is classier than a pub and serves a smattering of traditional European dishes. Go downstairs—avoid the pricey main-floor restaurant (£9–13 main dishes, Mon–Sat 12:00–14:00 & 18:00–22:00, Sun 19:00–22:00, 1 Clifton, tel. 01904/644-744).

Jackson's grocery store is open every day 7:00–23:00 (near B&Bs, outside Bootham Bar, on Bootham). For an atmospheric **picnic spot,** try the Museum Gardens (near Bootham Bar) at the evocative 12th-century ruins of St. Mary's Abbey.

TRANSPORTATION CONNECTIONS

By train to: Durham (hrly, 45 min), **Edinburgh** (2/hr, 2.5 hrs), **London** (2/hr, 2 hrs), **Bath** (hrly, 5 hrs, change in Bristol), **Cambridge** (nearly hrly, 2 hrs, change in Peterborough), **Birmingham** (2/hr, 2.5 hrs), **Keswick** (with transfers to Penrith then bus, 4.5 hrs). **Train info:** tel. 08457-484-950.

Connections with London's Airports: Heathrow (hrly, allow 2.5–3 hrs, take Heathrow Express train to London's Paddington Station, tube to King's Cross, train to York—2/hr, 2 hrs), **Gatwick** (from Gatwick catch low-profile Thameslink train to King's Cross-Thameslink station in London; from there, walk 100 yards to King's Cross Station, train to York—2/hr, 2 hrs).

Buses: The **York Bus Information Centre** is at 20 Hudson Street, near the train station (Mon–Fri 8:30–17:00, tel. 01904/551-400, phone answered Mon–Sat 8:00–20:00, Sun 8:00–14:00).

EDINBURGH

Edinburgh, the colorful city of Robert Louis Stevenson, Sir Walter Scott, and Robert Burns, is Scotland's showpiece and one of Europe's most entertaining cities. Historical, monumental, fun, and well organized, it's a tourist's delight.

Promenade down the Royal Mile through Old Town. Historic buildings pack the Royal Mile between the castle (on the top) and Holyrood Palace (on the bottom). Medieval skyscrapers stand shoulder to shoulder, hiding peaceful courtyards connected to High Street by narrow lanes or even tunnels. This colorful jumble is the tourist's Edinburgh.

Edinburgh (ED'n-burah) was once the most crowded city in Europe—famed for its skyscrapers and filth. The rich and poor lived atop one another. In the Age of Enlightenment, a magnificent Georgian city, today's New Town, was laid out to the north, giving the town's upper class a respectable place to promenade. Georgian Edinburgh, like the city of Bath, shines with broad boulevards, straight streets, square squares, circular circuses, and elegant mansions decked out in colonnades, pediments, and sphinxes in the proud, neoclassical style of 200 years ago.

While the Georgian city celebrated the union of Scotland and England (with streets and squares named after English kings and emblems), "devolution" is the latest trend. In a 1998 election, the Scots voted to gain more autonomy and bring their parliament home. Though Edinburgh has been the historic capital of Scotland for centuries, parliament had not met there since 1707. In 2000, Edinburgh resumed its position as home to the Scottish Parliament (although London still calls the strategic shots). A strikingly modern new parliament building, slated to open in 2004, will be one more jewel in Edinburgh's crown.

Planning Your Time

While the major sights can be seen in a day, I'd give Edinburgh two days and three nights.

Day 1: Tour the castle. Then consider catching one of the city bus tours (from a block below the castle at The Hub/Tolbooth church) for a 60-minute loop, returning to the castle. Explore the Royal Mile, going downhill-having lunch, going to museums, shopping, and taking a walking tour (one leaves at 14:00 from Mercat Cross). If you tour Holyrood Palace, do it near the end of the day since it's at the bottom of the Mile. In the evening, take in live music at a pub, a literary pub crawl, or a haunted walk.

Day 2: Tour the Museum of Scotland. After lunch, stroll through the Princes Street Gardens and the National Gallery of Scotland. Then tour the good ship *Britannia.*

ORIENTATION

(area code: 0131)

The center of Edinburgh holds the Princes Street Gardens park and Waverley Bridge, where you'll find the TI, Princes Mall, train station, bus info office (starting point for most city bus tours), National Gallery, and a covered dance-and-music pavilion. Weather blows in and out—bring your sweater.

Tourist Information

The crowded TI is as central as can be atop the Princes Mall and train station (May–June and Sept Mon–Sat 9:00–19:00, Sun 10:00–19:00; July–Aug daily 9:00–20:00; April and Oct Mon–Wed 9:00–17:00, Thu–Sat until 18:00, Sun 10:00–17:00; ATM outside entrance, tel. 0845-225-5121). Unfortunately, all their information—their assessment of museums and even which car-rental companies "exist"—is skewed by tourism payola. Buy a map (£1 if in stock, or the excellent £4 Collins Illustrated Edinburgh map, which comes with opinionated commentary and locates virtually every major shop and sight), and ask for the free monthly entertainment *Gig Guide* if you're interested in late-night music. The *Essential Guide to Edinburgh* (£1), while not essential, lists additional sights and services. Book your room direct without the TI's help (B&Bs charge more for rooms booked through the TI, and you pay the TI a £3 finder's fee). Browse the racks (tucked away in hallway at back of TI) for brochures on the various Scottish folk shows, walking tours, and regional bus tours. Connect@edinburgh, a small Internet café, is beyond the brochure racks (see "Helpful Hints," below). The best monthly entertainment listing, *The List,* sells for £2.20 at newsstands.

Arrival in Edinburgh

Arriving by train at Waverley Station puts you in the city center and below the TI. To get from the train station to the TI and the city bus stop for my recommended B&Bs, either take the many stairs (at the top, TI is to your left; see "Sleeping," below, for directions to B&B neighborhood by bus) or walk up the ramp that surfaces on Waverley Bridge (bus to B&Bs around the block on North Bridge). Luggage storage is near platform 1 (£3.50/6 hrs, £4.50/6–24 hrs, daily 7:00–22:45).

Both Scottish Citylink and National Express buses use the bus station two blocks north of the train station on St. Andrew Square in the New Town.

Edinburgh's slingshot-of-an-airport is 10 miles northwest of the center and well-connected by taxi (£18, 30 min) and by shuttle bus with Waverley Bridge (LRT "Airline" bus #100, £3.30, or £4.20 with all-day "Airsaver" city-bus pass, 6/hr, 30 min, roughly 5:00–24:00). Flight info: tel. 0131/333-1000, bmi british midland tel. 0870-607-0555, British Airways tel. 0845-773-3377, Aer Lingus tel. 0845-084-444.

Helpful Hints

Sunday Activities: Many sights close on Sunday, but there's still a lot to do: You can take a Royal Mile walking tour or a city bus tour; visit Edinburgh Castle, St. Giles Cathedral, Holyrood Palace, or the Royal Botanic Gardens; and climb Arthur's Seat. An open-air market, including antiques, is held every Sunday from 10:00 to 16:00 at New Street Car Park near the train station. The Georgian House and National Gallery are open Sunday afternoon.

Internet Access: It's a cinch to get plugged in. The easyInternetcafé, with 450 terminals, is a block from the National Gallery (daily 7:00–23:00, 58 Rose Street, go through Caffè Nero and upstairs). At the TI, you'll find Connect@edinburgh (Mon–Sat 9:00–19:00, until 20:00 July–Aug, Sun 10:00–17:00, shorter hours off-season, as you enter TI head back to the left down a corridor). The Internet Café is southeast of the castle between Victoria Street and Grassmarket (daily 10:00–23:00, also has cheap phone cards, 98 Westbow, tel. 0131/226-5400).

Late-Night Pharmacy: Try Boots at 48 Shandwick Place (Mon–Fri until 21:00, tel. 0131/225-6757).

Car Rental: Consider Avis (5 West Park Place, tel. 0131/337-6363, airport tel. 0131/344-3900), Europcar (24 East London Street, tel. 0131/557-3456, airport tel. 0131/333-2588), Hertz (10 Picardy Place, tel. 0131/556-8311, airport tel. 0131/333-3494), or Budget (airport tel. 0131/333-1926).

Edinburgh

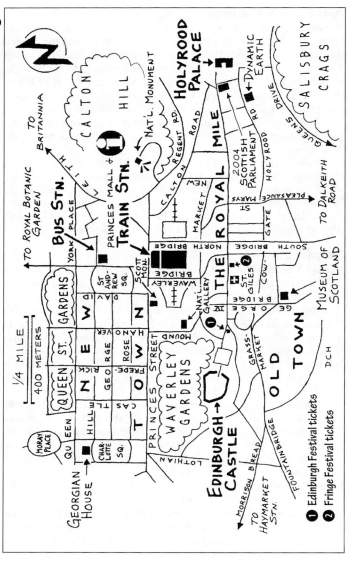

❶ Edinburgh Festival tickets
❷ Fringe Festival tickets

Getting around Edinburgh

Nearly all of Edinburgh's sights are within walking distance of each other.

City **buses** are handy and inexpensive (about 80p/ride, buy tickets on bus, LRT transit office at Old Town end of Waverley Bridge has schedules and route maps, tel. 0131/555-6363). Tell the driver where you're going, have change handy (most buses require exact change; you lose any excess), take your ticket as you board, push the stop button as you near your stop (so your stop isn't skipped), and exit from the middle door. Two companies handle the city routes: LRT (or Lothian) does most of it and First does the rest (e.g., to get from the city center to the recommended B&Bs on Dalkeith Road, you can catch LRT buses #14, #30, and #33 or First bus #86). Day passes sold by each company are valid only on their buses (£2.50, or £1.80 after 9:30 weekdays and all day weekends, buy from driver). Buses run from about 6:00 to 23:00.

Taxis are reasonable and easy to flag down (average ride between downtown and B&B district-£5).

BUS TOURS

Three different 60-minute, hop-on, hop-off bus tours, all operated by Lothian Buses, circle the town center and stop at the biggies—Waverley Bridge, the castle, Royal Mile, Georgian New Town, and Princes Street—with an informative narration and pickups about every 10 to 15 minutes. You can hop on and off with one ticket all day. Hop on at any stop or go to Waverley Bridge to comparison-shop between your bus-tour options.

Two of the tours have live guides: Mac Tours' City Tour and Guide Friday's Edinburgh Tour. Their routes, cost, and frequency are virtually the same—the main difference is that Mac Tours runs vintage buses (£8.50, tickets give 10 percent discount off castle admission, valid 24 hours, buy on bus or on Waverley Bridge, tel. 0131/220-0770). The City Sightseeing Tours have a recorded narration and cost £1 less.

All three tours offer £13 combo-tickets that include their Britannia Tour, a hop-on, hop-off route that stops at the Royal Botanic Garden, docks, and the *Britannia* royal yacht (£8.50, *Britannia* admission extra, departs Waverley Bridge every 15–30 min, live guide, tel. 0131/220-0770). If your main interest is seeing the *Britannia*, you're better off taking a regular bus (see *Britannia*, below).

On sunny days they go topless (the buses), but they also suffer from traffic noise and congestion. Buses run year-round. First and last buses leave Waverley Bridge around 9:15 and continue until 19:00 mid-June through early September (last buses leave earlier off-season).

SIGHTS

Edinburgh

▲▲▲**Edinburgh Castle**—The fortified birthplace of the city 1,300 years ago, this imposing symbol of Edinburgh sits proudly on a rock high above the city. While the castle has been both a fort and a royal residence since the 11th century, most of the buildings today are from its more recent use as a military garrison. This fascinating and multifaceted sight deserves several hours of your time (£8.50, April–Oct daily 9:30–18:00, Nov–March daily 9:30–17:00, last entrance 45 min before closing, cafeteria, tel. 0131/225-9846; consider avoiding the long uphill walk from the nearest city-bus stop by taking a cab to the castle gate).

Entry Gate: Start with the wonderfully droll 20-minute guided introduction tour (free with admission, departs 2-4 times/hr from entry, see clock for next departure; few tours run off-season). The audioguide is excellent, with four hours of quick digital dial descriptions (£3, pay at ticket office, pick up at entry gate before meeting the live guide). The clean WC at the entry annually wins "British Loo of the Year" awards (marvel at the plaques near men's room), but they use a one-way mirror showing the sink area in the women's room (women: pop your head into office near men's room to complain or make sure mirror is curtained).

In the castle there are five essential stops: Crown Jewels, Royal Palace, Scottish National War Memorial, St. Margaret's Chapel (with a city view), and the excellent National War Museum of Scotland. The first four are at the highest and most secure point—on or near the castle square, where your introductory guided tour ends. The War Museum is 50 yards below by the cafeteria and big shop.

1. Crown Jewels: The line of tourists leads from the square directly to the jewels. Skip this line and enter the building around to the left (next to WC), where you'll get to the jewels via a wonderful "Honors of Scotland" exhibition about the crown jewels and how they survived the harrowing centuries.

Scotland's **Crown Jewels** are older than England's. While Oliver Cromwell destroyed England's, the Scots hid theirs successfully. Longtime symbols of Scottish nationalism, they were made in Edinburgh—of Scottish gold, diamonds, and gems—in 1540 for a 1543 coronation. They were last used to crown Charles II in 1651. When the Act of Union, which dissolved Scotland's parliament into England's to create the United Kingdom in 1707, was forced upon the Scots, part of the deal was that they could keep their jewels locked up in Edinburgh. They remained hidden for more than 100 years. In 1818 Walter Scott and a royal commission rediscovered the jewels intact.

The **Stone of Scone** sits plain and strong next to the jewels. This big gray chunk of rock is the coronation stone of Scotland's ancient kings (ninth century). Swiped by the English, it sat under the coronation chair at Westminster Abbey from 1296 until 1996. With major fanfare, Scotland's treasured Stone of Scone returned to Edinburgh on Saint Andrew's Day, November 30, 1996. Talk to the guard for more details.

2. The Royal Palace (facing castle square under the flagpole) has two historic yet unimpressive rooms (through door reading 1566) and the Great Hall (separate entrance from the same castle square). Remember, Scottish royalty lived here only when safety or protocol required. They preferred the **Holyrood Palace** at the bottom of the Royal Mile. Enter the **Mary Queen of Scots room,** where in 1566 the queen gave birth to James VI of Scotland, who later became King James I of England. The **Presence Chamber** leads into **Laich Hall** (Lower Hall), the dining room of the royal family.

The **Great Hall** was the castle's ceremonial meeting place in the 16th and 17th centuries. In modern times it was a barracks and a hospital. While most of what you see is Victorian, two medieval elements survive: the fine hammer-beam roof and the big iron-barred peephole (above fireplace on right). This allowed the king to spy on his partying subjects.

3. The Scottish National War Memorial commemorates the 149,000 Scottish soldiers lost in World War I, the 58,000 lost in World War II, and the 750 lost in British battles since. Each bay is dedicated to a particular Scottish regiment. The main shrine, featuring a green Italian-marble memorial that contains the original WWI rolls of honor, actually sits upon an exposed chunk of the castle rock. Above you, the archangel Michael is busy slaying the dragon. The bronze frieze accurately shows the attire of various wings of Scotland's military. The stained glass starts with Cain and Abel on the left and finishes with a celebration of peace on the right. If the importance of this place is hard to understand, consider that one out of every three adult Scottish men died in World War I.

4. St. Margaret's Chapel, the oldest building in Edinburgh, is dedicated to Queen Margaret, who died here in 1093 and was sainted in 1250. Built in 1130 in the Romanesque style of the Norman invaders, it is wonderfully simple, with classic Norman zigzags decorating the round arch that separates the tiny nave from the sacristy. Used as a powder magazine for 400 years, very little survives. You'll see an 11th-century gospel book of St. Margaret's and small windows featuring St. Margaret, St. Columba (who brought Christianity to Scotland via Iona), and William Wallace (the brave defender of Scotland). The place is popular for weddings and, since it seats only 20, it's particularly popular with brides' fathers.

Mons Meg—a huge and once-upon-a-time frightening 15th-century siege cannon that fired 330-pound stones nearly two miles—stands in front of the church.

Belly up to the banister (outside the chapel below the cannon) to enjoy the great view. Below you are the guns—which fire the one o'clock salute—and a sweet little line of doggie tombstones, the soldiers' pet cemetery. Beyond stretches the Georgian New Town (read the informative plaque).

5. The National War Museum of Scotland thoughtfully covers four centuries of Scottish military history. Instead of the usual musty, dusty displays of endless armor, this museum has an interesting mix of short films, uniforms, weapons, medals, mementos, and eloquent excerpts from soldiers' letters. A pleasant surprise just when you thought your castle visit was about over, this rivals any military museum you'll see in Europe.

When leaving the castle, turn around and look back at the gate. There stand King Robert the Bruce (on the left, 1274–1329) and Sir William Wallace (Braveheart—on the right, 1270–1305). Wallace (recently famous, thanks to Mel Gibson) fought long and hard against English domination before being executed in London—his body cut to pieces and paraded through the far corners of jolly olde England. Bruce beat the English at Bannockburn in 1314. Bruce and Wallace still defend the spirit of Scotland. The Latin inscription above the gate between them reads (basically) "What you do to us...we will do to you."

Along the Royal Mile

These are listed in walking order, from top to bottom. (Bus #35 runs along the Mile, handy for going up after you've hit bottom.)

▲▲▲**Royal Mile**—This is one of Europe's most interesting historic walks. Start at the top and amble down to the palace. The Royal Mile, which consists of a series of four different streets—Castlehill, Lawnmarket, High Street, and Canongate (each with its own set of street numbers)—is actually 200 yards longer than a mile. And every inch is packed with shops, cafés, and lanes leading to tiny squares. As you walk, remember that originally there were two settlements here, divided by a wall: Edinburgh lined the ridge from the castle at the top. The lower end, Canongate, was outside the wall until 1856. By poking down the many side alleys, you'll find a few rough edges of a town well on its way to becoming a touristic mall. See it now. In a few years tourists will be slaloming through the postcard racks on bagpipe skateboards.

Royal Mile Terminology: A "close" is a tiny alley between two buildings (originally with a door that closed it at night). A close usually leads to a "court" or courtyard. A "land" is a tenement block of apartments. A "pend" is an arched gateway. A "wynd" is a narrow winding lane. And "gate" is from an old Scandinavian word for street.

Royal Mile Walking Tours: Mercat Tours offers 90-minute guided walks of the Mile—more entertaining than historic (£6, daily at 10:30, from Mercat Cross on the Royal Mile, tel. 0131/557-6464). The guides, who enjoy making a short story long, ignore the big sights and take you behind the scenes with piles of barely historic gossip, bully-

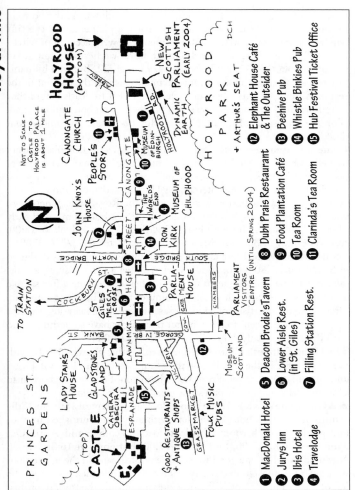

Royal Mile

NOT TO SCALE –
CASTLE TO
HOLYROOD PALACE
IS ABOUT 1 MILE

PRINCES ST. GARDENS

TO TRAIN STATION

HOLYROOD HOUSE (BOTTOM)

NEW SCOTTISH PARLIAMENT (EARLY 2004)

CANONGATE CHURCH

PEOPLE'S STORY

JOHN KNOX'S HOUSE

THE WORLD'S END

MUSEUM OF CHILDHOOD

TRON KIRK

OLD PARLIAMENT HOUSE

ST GILES MERCAT CROSS

LADY STAIR'S HOUSE

GLADSTONE'S LAND

CAMERA OBSCURA

CASTLE (TOP)

ESPLANADE

GOOD RESTAURANTS + ANTIQUE SHOPS

FOLK MUSIC PUBS

GRASSMARKET

MUSEUM OF SCOTLAND

PARLIAMENT VISITORS CENTRE (UNTIL SPRING 2004)

HOLYROOD PARK

ARTHUR'S SEAT

DYNAMIC EARTH

MUSEUM of EDINBURGH

❶ MacDonald Hotel
❷ Jurys Inn
❸ Ibis Hotel
❹ Travelodge
❺ Deacon Brodie's Tavern
❻ Lower Aisle Rest. (in St. Giles)
❼ Filling Station Rest.
❽ Dubh Prais Restaurant
❾ Food Plantation Café
❿ Tea Room
⓫ Clarinda's Tea Room
⓬ Elephant House Café & The Outsider
⓭ Beehive Pub
⓮ Whistle Binkies Pub
⓯ Hub Festival Ticket Office

pulpit Scottish pride, and fun but forgettable trivia. They also offer a variety of other tours. In August only, the Voluntary Guides Association leads free tours of Edinburgh; call for a schedule (tel. 0131/664-7180 or 0131/556-8854).

Castle Esplanade—At the top of the Royal Mile, the big parking lot leading up to the castle was created as a military parade ground in 1816. It's often cluttered with bleachers under construction for the Military Tattoo—a spectacular massing of the bands that fills the square nightly for most of August (see "Edinburgh Festival," below). At the bottom, on the left (where the square hits the road), a plaque above the tiny witch's fountain memorializes 300 women who were accused of witch-craft and burned here. Scotland burned more witches per capita than any other country—17,000 between 1479 and 1722. But in a humanitarian gesture, rather than burning them alive as was the custom in the rest of Europe, Scottish "witches" were strangled to death before they were burned. The plaque shows two witches: one good and one bad. (For 90 minutes of this kind of Royal Mile trivia, take the guided tour described above.)

Camera Obscura—A big deal when built in 1853, this observatory topped with a mirror reflected images onto a disc before the wide eyes of people who had never seen a photograph or captured image. Today you can climb 100 steps for an entertaining 15-minute demonstration (3/hr). At the top enjoy the best view anywhere of the Royal Mile. Then work your way down through three floors of illusions, holograms, and early photos. This is a big hit with kids (£5.95, April–Oct daily 9:30–18:00, July–Aug until 19:30, Nov–March 10:00–17:00, tel. 0131/226-3709).

Scotch Whisky Heritage Centre—This touristy ambush is designed only to distill £7.50 out of your pocket. You get a video history, a short talk, and a little whiskey-keg train-car ride before downing a free sample and finding yourself in the shop 50 minutes later. Those in a hurry are offered the unadvertised quickie—a sample and a whiskey-keg ride for £3.50. People do seem to enjoy it, but that might have something to do with the sample (daily 9:30–17:30, tel. 0131/220-0441).

The Hub (Tolbooth Church)—This neo-Gothic church (1844), with the tallest spire in the city, is now the Hub, Edinburgh's Festival Ticket and Information Centre. From here, Johnston Terrace leads down to Grassmarket street's lively pub scene (see "Nightlife," below).

▲▲**Gladstone's Land**—Take a good look at this typical 16th- to 17th-century merchant's house, complete with a lived-in furnished interior and guides in each room who love to talk (£3.50, mid-April–Oct Mon–Sat 10:00–17:00, Sun 14:00–17:00, last entry at 16:30, closed Nov–mid-April). For a good Royal Mile photo, lean out the upper-floor window (or simply climb the curved stairway outside the museum to the left of the entrance). Notice the snoozing pig outside the front door. Just like every house has a vacuum cleaner today, in the 14th century a snorting rubbish collector was a standard feature of any well-equipped house.

▲**Writers' Museum at Lady Stair's House**—This interesting house, built in 1622, is filled with well-described manuscripts and knickknacks of Scotland's three greatest literary figures: Robert Burns, Sir Walter Scott, and Robert Louis Stevenson. It's worth a few minutes for anyone and is fascinating for fans (free, Mon–Sat 10:00–17:00, closed Sun). Wander around the courtyard here. Edinburgh was a wonder in the 17th and 18th centuries. Tourists came here to see its skyscrapers, which towered 10 stories and higher. No city in Europe was so densely populated as "Auld Reekie."

Deacon Brodie's Pub—This is a decent place for a light meal (see "Eating," page 662). Read the story of its notorious namesake on the wall facing Bank Street. Then check out both sides of the hanging signpost.

Visitors Centre of the Scottish Parliament—Until the new Scottish Parliament building opens, possibly in early 2004 (near Holyrood Palace), this center will show models of the new building and explain how the Scottish Parliament works (free, Mon–Fri 10:00–17:00, Tue–Thu opens at 9:00, closed Sat–Sun, catercorner to Deacon Brodie's on George IV Bridge). You can sign up at the Visitors Centre to witness the Scottish Parliament's debates in their temporary quarters, a few steps north of the Royal Mile, tucked away in Mylnes Court, across from the Hub (debates usually Wed 14:30–17:30, Thu 9:30–12:30 & 14:30–17:30, tel. 0131/348-5411). When the new parliament building opens, this Visitors Centre will close (for updates, see www.scottish.parliament.uk).

Heart of Midlothian—Near the street in front of the cathedral, find the outline of a heart in the brickwork. This marks the spot of a gallows and a prison now long gone. Traditionally, locals stand on the rim of the heart and spit into it. Hitting the middle brings good luck. Go ahead...do as the locals do.

▲▲St. Giles Cathedral—Wander through Scotland's most important church. Stepping inside, find John Knox's statue. Look into his eyes for 10 seconds from 10 inches away. Knox, the great reformer and founder of austere Scottish Presbyterianism, first preached here in 1559. His insistence that every person should be able to read the word of God gave Scotland an educational system 300 years ahead of the rest of Europe. For this reason it was Scottish minds that led the way in math, science, medicine, engineering, and so on. Voltaire called Scotland "the intellectual capital of Europe."

Knox preached Calvinism. Consider that the Dutch and the Scots were about the only nations to embrace this creed of hard work, thrift, and strict ethics. This helps explain why the English and the Scottish are so different (and why the Dutch and the Scots—both famous for their thriftiness and industriousness—are so much alike).

Speaking of intellects, look up at the modern window filling the West Wall celebrating Scotland's favorite poet, Robert Burns. It was made in 1985 by an Icelandic artist (Leifur Breidfjord).

The oldest parts of the cathedral—the four massive central pillars—date from 1120. After the English burnt the cathedral in 1385, it was rebuilt bigger and better than ever, and in 1495 its famous crown spire was completed. During the Reformation—when Knox preached here

(1559–72)—the place was simplified and whitewashed. Before this, with the emphasis on holy services provided by priests, there were lots of little niches. With the new focus on sermons rather than rituals, the floor plan was opened up and the grand pulpit took center stage. The organ (1992, Austrian-built) is one of the best in Europe and comes with a glass panel in the back for peeking into the mechanism.

The neo-Gothic **Chapel of the Knights of the Thistle** (in the far right corner, from 1911), with its intricate wood carving, was built in two years entirely with Scottish material and labor. Find the angel tooting the bagpipes (from inside chapel, above the door to the right). The Scottish crown steeple from 1495 is a proud part of Edinburgh's skyline (Mon–Sat 9:00–17:00, May–Sept Mon–Fri until 19:00, Sat until 17:00, Sun 13:00–17:00 year-round; ask about concerts—some are free, usually Thu at 13:10, especially in the spring; café and WC downstairs; see "Eating," below, tel. 0131/225-9442).

John Knox is buried out back—austerely, under the parking lot, at spot 44. The statue among the cars shows King Charles II riding to a toga party back in 1685.

Parliament House—Stop in to see the grand hall with its fine 1639 hammer-beam ceiling and stained glass. This hall housed the Scottish Parliament until the Act of Union in 1707 (explained in history exhibition under the big stained-glass depiction of the initiation of the first Scottish High Court in 1532). It now holds the law courts and is busy with wigged and robed lawyers hard at work in the old library (peek through the door) or pacing the hall deep in discussion. The friendly doorman is helpful (free, public welcome Mon–Fri 9:00–17:00, best action midmornings Tue–Fri, open-to-the-public trials 10:00–16:00—courtroom has day's docket, entry behind St. Giles Cathedral near parking spot 21).

Mercat Cross—This chunky pedestal, on the downhill side of St. Giles, holds a slender column topped with a white unicorn. Royal proclamations have been read from here since the 14th century. The tradition survives. In 1952, three days (traditionally the time it took for a horse to speed here from London) after the actual event, a town crier heralded the news that England had a new queen. Today Mercat Cross is the meeting point of various walking tours—both historic and ghostly. Pop into the police information center, a few doors downhill, for a little local law-and-order history (free, May–Aug daily 10:00–21:30, less off-season).

Tron Kirk—This fine old building, used as a sales base for a local walking-tour company, sits over an old excavation site and houses a free Old Town history display.

Cockburn Street—Across from Tron Kirk, this street was cut through High Street's dense wall of medieval skyscrapers in the 1860s to give easy access to the Georgian New Town and the train station. Notice how the sliced buildings were thoughtfully capped with facades in a faux-16th-century Scottish baronial style. In medieval times, only tiny lanes (like the Fleshmarket Lane just uphill from Cockburn Street) interrupted the long line of Royal Mile buildings. Continue downhill to the old half-timbered building jutting out (John Knox House). Across the street is the...

▲**Museum of Childhood**—This five-story playground of historical toys and games is rich in nostalgia and history (free, Mon–Sat 10:00–17:00, closed Sun). Just downhill is a fragrant fudge shop offering free samples.

▲**John Knox House**—Fascinating for Reformation buffs, this fine 16th-century house offers a well-explained look at the life of the great reformer (£2.25, Mon–Sat 10:00–17:00, closed Sun, 43 High Street, tel. 0131/556-9579). While some contend Knox never actually lived here, preservationists called it "his house" to save it from the wrecking ball in 1850. All or parts of the museum will be closed for construction period-ically during 2004.

The World's End—For centuries, a wall halfway down the Royal Mile marked the end of Edinburgh and the beginning of Canongate, a com-munity associated with the Holyrood Abbey. Today, where the mile hits St. Mary's and Jeffrey streets, High Street becomes Canongate. Just below John Knox House (at #43) notice the hanging sign showing the old gate. At the intersection, find the brass bricks that trace the gate (demolished in 1764). Look down St. Mary's Street to see a surviving bit of that old wall. Then, entering Canongate, you leave what was Edinburgh...

▲**People's Story**—This interesting exhibition traces the lot of the work-ing class through the 18th, 19th, and 20th centuries (free, Mon–Sat 10:00–17:00, closed Sun, tel. 0131/529-4057). Curiously, while this museum is dedicated to the proletariat, immediately around the back is the tomb of Adam Smith—the author of *Wealth of Nations* and the father of modern capitalism (1723–1790).

▲**Museum of Edinburgh**—Another old house full of old stuff, this one is worth a look for its early Edinburgh history and handy ground-floor WC. Don't miss the original copy of the National Covenant (written in 1638 on an animal skin), sketches of pre-Georgian Edinburgh (which show a lake, later filled in to become Princes Street Gardens when New Town was built), and early golf balls (free, Mon–Sat 10:00–17:00, closed Sun).

White Horse Close—Step into this 17th-century courtyard (bottom of Canongate, on the left, a block before Holyrood Palace). It was from here that the Edinburgh stagecoach left for London. Eight days later, the horse-drawn carriage pulled into its destination: Scotland Yard. Across the street is the new Parliament building.

▲**Scottish Parliament Building**—Scotland's parliament originated in 1293, was dissolved by England in 1707, and returned in 1999. Their extravagant, and therefore controversial, new digs at the base of the Royal Mile next to Holyrood Palace are slated to open in 2004. For a conversation starter, ask a local what he or she thinks about the building's architect, expense, design, and so on.

You can sign up to witness the Scottish Parliament's debates as it creates Scottish history in its temporary quarters off the Royal Mile in Mylnes Court across from the Hub (free, see "Visitors Centre," above), and eventually, in its new building after it opens.

▲**Holyrood Palace**—A palace since the 14th century, this marks the end of the Royal Mile. The queen spends a week in Scotland each summer, during which this is her official residence and office. The abbey—part of a 12th-century Augustinian monastery—stood here first. It was named for a piece of the cross brought here as a relic by queen-then-saint Margaret. Scotland's royalty preferred living here to the blustery castle on the rock, and gradually the palace grew.

The building, rich in history and decor, is filled with elegantly furnished rooms and a few dark older rooms with glass cases of historic bits and Scottish pieces that Scots find fascinating. Bring the palace to life with the included one-hour audioguide. You'll learn which of the kings featured in the 110 portraits lining the Great Gallery are real and which are fictional, what touches were added to the bed chambers to flatter King Charles II, and why the exiled Comte d'Artois took refuge in the palace. You'll also hear a goofy reenactment of the moment when conspirators, dispatched by Mary Queen of Scots' jealous second husband, stormed into the queen's chambers and stabbed her male secretary. You can select the audio you want to hear by punching in the room number (if the rooms aren't yet numbered, ask the docent stationed in the room for the secret code).

The new **Queen's Gallery** features rotating exhibits of drawings from the royal collection (see Cost and Hours, below).

After exiting, you're free to stroll through the ruined abbey and the queen's gardens. Hikers: Note that the palace is near the trail up Arthur's Seat.

Cost and Hours: £7.50 for palace, £4 for Queen's Gallery, £10 joint admission for both, daily 9:30–18:00, Nov–April until 16:30, last admission 45 min before closing (palace guidebook-£4.50, tel. 0131/556-7371). The palace is closed when the queen is at home and whenever a prince drops in.

Dynamic Earth—This immense exhibit tells the story of our planet and fills several underground floors under a vast Gore-Tex tent appropriately pitched at the base of the Salisbury Crags. It's designed for younger kids and does the same thing an American science exhibit would do—but with a charming Scottish accent. Standing in a time tunnel, you watch time rewind from Churchill to dinosaurs to that first big bang. After several short films on stars, tectonic plates, and ice caps, you're free to wander past salty pools, a re-created rain forest, and various TV screens. End your visit with a 12-minute video finale (£8.45, family deals, April–Oct daily 10:00–18:00, Nov–March Wed–Sun 10:00–17:00, last ticket sold 70 min before closing, on Holyrood Road, between the palace and mountain, tel. 0131/550-7800).

▲▲▲**Museum of Scotland**—This huge museum has amassed more historic artifacts than everything I've seen in Scotland combined. It's all wonderfully displayed with fine descriptions offering a best-anywhere hike through the history of Scotland: prehistoric, Roman, Viking, the "birth of Scotland," all the way to life in the 20th century. Free audio-guides offer a pleasant (if slow) description of various rooms and exhibits and even provide mood music for your wanderings (free, Mon–Sat 10:00–17:00, Tue until 20:00, Sun 12:00–17:00, 60-min introduction and highlights tours offered throughout the day, 2 long blocks south of Royal Mile from St. Giles Church, Chambers Street, off George IV Bridge, tel. 0131/247-4422, www.nms.ac.uk).

The **Royal Museum,** next door, fills a fine iron-and-glass Industrial Age building (built to house the museum in 1851) with all the natural sciences as it "presents the world to Scotland." It's great for schoolkids, but of no special interest to foreign visitors (free, same hours as Museum of Scotland). The famous statue of Greyfriars Bobby (Edinburgh's favorite dog—a terrier immortalized by Disney—who stood by his master's grave for 14 years) is across the street. Every business nearby is named for the pooch that put the fidelity into Fido.

More Bonnie Wee Sights

▲**Georgian New Town**—Cross Waverley Bridge and walk through Georgian Edinburgh. According to the 1776 plan, it was three streets (Princes, George, and Queen) flanked by two squares (St. Andrew and Charlotte), woven together by alleys (Thistle and Rose). George Street—20 feet wider than the others (so a four-horse carriage could make a U-turn)—was the main drag. And, while Princes Street has gone down-market, George Street still maintains its old grace. The entire elegantly planned New Town—laid out when George was king—celebrated the hard-to-sell notion that Scotland was an integral part of the United Kingdom. The streets and squares are named after the British royalty (Hanover was the royal family surname). Even Thistle and Rose streets are emblems of the two happily paired nations. Rose Street, mostly pedestrian-only, is famous for its rowdy pubs. Where it hits St. Andrew Square, Rose Street is flanked by the venerable Jenners department store and a Sainsbury supermarket. Sprinkled with popular restaurants and bars, stately New Town is turning trendy.

▲▲**Georgian House**—This refurbished Georgian house, set on Edinburgh's finest Georgian square, is a trip back to 1796. A volunteer guide in each of the five rooms shares stories and trivia. Start your visit with two interesting videos (£5, April–Oct daily 10:00–17:00, March & Nov–Dec 11:00–15:00, closed Jan–Feb, videos total 30 min and cover architecture and Georgian lifestyles, shown in the basement, 7 Charlotte Square, tel. 0131/226-3318). A walk down George Street after your visit here can be fun for the imagination.

▲▲**National Gallery of Scotland**—This elegant neoclassical building has a delightfully small but impressive collection of European masterpieces, from Raphael, Titian, and Peter Paul Rubens to Thomas Gainsborough, Claude Monet, and Vincent van Gogh. And it offers the best look you'll get at Scottish paintings. The gallery's free, but investing £2 in the fine audioguide makes the museum's highlights yours as well (daily 10:00–17:00, Thu until 19:00, tel. 0131/624-6200). After your visit, if the sun's out, enjoy a wander through Princes Street Gardens.

Royal Scottish Academy—Next to the National Gallery, this new museum opened in August 2004 with a major Monet exhibit (generally daily 10:00–17:00, Thu until 19:00, but hours and cost vary per exhibit, tel. 0131/624-6200, www.nationalgalleries.org).

Princes Street Gardens—This grassy park, a former lake bed, separates Edinburgh's New and Old Towns and offers a wonderful escape from the city. Once the private domain of the local wealthy, it was opened to the public in about 1870, not as a democratic gesture, but because it was thought that allowing the public into the park would increase sales for the Princes Street department stores. There are plenty of free concerts and country dances in the summer and the oldest floral clock in the world. Join the local office workers for a picnic lunch break.

▲**Sir Walter Scott Monument**—Built in 1840, this elaborate, neo-Gothic monument honors the great author, one of Edinburgh's many illustrious sons. Scott, who died in 1832, is considered the father of the romantic historical novel. The 200-foot monument shelters a marble statue of Scott and his dog Maida, surrounded by busts of 16 great Scottish poets and 64 characters from his books. Scott was a great dog lover. Of the 30 dogs he had in his lifetime, his favorite was the deerhound Maida. Climb 287 steps for a fine view of the city (£2.50, March–Oct Mon–Sat 9:00–18:00, Sun 10:00–18:00, Nov–Feb daily 10:00–15:00, tel. 0131/529-4068).

Royal Botanic Garden—Britain's second-oldest botanical garden, established in 1670 for medicinal herbs, is now one of Europe's best (free, March and Sept–Oct 9:30–18:00, April–Aug 9:30–19:00, Nov–Feb 9:30–16:00, 90-min "rain forest to desert" tours April–Sept daily at 11:00 and 14:00 for £2.50, 1 mile north of center at Inverleith Row, tel. 0131/552-7171).

Near Edinburgh

▲*Britannia*—This much-revered vessel, which carted around Britain's royal family for more than 40 years and 900 voyages before being retired in 1997, is permanently moored at Edinburgh's Port of Leith. It's open to the public and worth the 15-minute bus or taxi ride from the center.

After watching a video about the ship, wander through the museum filled with fascinating royal-family-afloat history. Then, armed with your included audioguide, hike the stairs to the ship's top deck and begin working your way down. You'll tour the bridge, dining room, and living quarters, and follow in the historic footsteps of such notables as Churchill, Gandhi, and Reagan. It's easy to see how the royals must have loved the privacy this floating retreat offered (£8, April–Sept daily 9:30–18:00, Oct–March daily 10:00–17:00, last ticket sold 1.5 hrs before closing; to get to ship from Edinburgh, catch Lothian bus #22, #34, or #35 at Waverley Bridge—£2.50 round-trip, cheap café on site, tel. 0131/555-5566, www.royalyachtbritannia.co.uk).

Edinburgh Crystal—Blowing, molding, cutting, polishing, and engraving, the Edinburgh Crystal Company glassworks tour smashes anything you'll see in Venice (£3.50, daily 10:00–16:30). There is a shop full of "bargain" second-quality pieces, a video show, and a cafeteria. Take Lothian Bus #37 or #37A from South Bridge, or drive 10 miles south of town on A701 to Penicuik. You can schedule a more expensive VIP tour (£10) where you actually blow and cut glass (tel. 01968/675-128).

ACTIVITIES

▲▲**Arthur's Seat Hike**—A 45-minute hike up the 822-foot volcanic mountain (surrounded by a fine park overlooking Edinburgh) starts from the Holyrood Palace and rewards you with a commanding view. You can drive up most of the way from behind (follow the one-way street from the palace, park by the little lake) or run up like they did in *Chariots of Fire.* Hikers: From the parking lot (immediately south of Holyrood Palace), you'll see two trails going up. For an easier grade, take the wide path to the left and skip the steeper path that begins with steps and skirts the base of the cliffs. You can also hike up to the seat from the Dalkeith B&B neighborhood. Take the road (Holyrood Park Road) that borders the Commonwealth pool, turn right (on Queen's Drive), and continue to a small car park. From here, it's a 20-minute hike.

Brush Skiing—If you'd rather be skiing, the Midlothian Ski Centre in Hillend has a hill on the edge of town with a chairlift, two slopes, a jump slope, and rentable skis, boots, and poles. While you're actually skiing over what seems like a million toothbrushes, it feels like snow skiing on a slushy day. Beware: Local doctors are used to treating an ailment called "Hillend Thumb"—thumbs dislocated when people fall here and get tangled in the brush (£7.50/first hr, then £3/hr, includes gear, Mon–Fri 9:30–21:00, Sat–Sun 9:30–19:00, closed last 2 weeks of June, probably closed if it snows, LRT bus #4 from Princes Street—garden side, tel. 0131/445-4433).

▲**Royal Commonwealth Games Swimming Pool**—This immense pool is open to the public, with a well-equipped fitness center (£6, includes swim), sauna (£6.70 extra), and a coffee shop overlooking the pool (Pool admission only-£3.50, Mon–Fri 6:00–21:30, Sat 6:00–7:45 & 10:00–16:30, Sun 10:00–16:30, closed 9:00–10:00 every Wed, no towels or suit rentals, tel. 0131/667-7211).

Shopping—The streets to browse are Princes Street (the elegant old Jenners department store is nearby on Rose Street, at St. Andrew's Square), Victoria Street (antiques galore), Nicolson Street (south of the Royal Mile for a line of interesting second-hand stores), and the Royal Mile (touristy but competitively priced). Shops are usually open from 9:00 to 17:30 (later on Thu, some closed Sun).

Edinburgh Festival

One of Europe's great cultural events, Edinburgh's annual festival turns the city into a carnival of culture. There are enough music, dance, art, drama, and multicultural events to make even the most jaded traveler drool with excitement. Every day is jammed with formal and sponta-neous fun. A number of festivals—official, fringe, book, film, and jazz and blues—rage simultaneously for about three weeks each August, with the Military Tattoo starting a week earlier (the best overall Web site is www.edinburghfestivals.co.uk). Many city sights run on extended hours, and those that normally close on Sunday (Writers' Museum, Museum of Edinburgh, People's Story, and Museum of Childhood) open in the afternoon. It's a glorious time to be in Edinburgh.

The official festival (Aug 15–Sept 4 in 2004) is the original, more formal, and most likely to get booked up first. Major events sell out well in advance. The ticket office is at the Hub, located in a former church (with café, ATM, and WC) near the top of the Royal Mile (tickets-£4–55, booking from mid-April on, office open Mon–Sat 10:00–17:00 or longer, in Aug until 20:00 plus Sun 10:00–17:00, tel. 0131/473-2000, fax 0131/473-2003). You can also book online at www.eif.co.uk.

The less-formal **Fringe Festival** features "on the edge" comedy and theater (Aug 8–30 in 2004, ticket/info office just below St. Giles Cathedral on the Royal Mile, 180 High Street, tel. 0131/226-0026, bookings tel. 0131/226-0000, can book online from mid-June on, www.edfringe.com). Tickets are usually available at the door, but popular shows can sell out.

Other summer festivals: jazz and blues (tel. 0131/467-5200, www.jazzmusic.co.uk), film (tel. 0131/229-2550, www.edfilmfest.org.uk), and books (tel. 0131/228-5444, www.edbookfest.co.uk).

The **Military Tattoo** is a massing of the bands, drums, and bag-pipes with groups from all over what was the British Empire. Displaying military finesse with a stirring lone-piper finale, this grand spectacle fills the castle esplanade nightly except Sunday, normally from a week before the festival starts until a week before it finishes (Aug 6–28 in 2004). Shows occur Monday through Friday at 21:00 and on Saturdays at 19:30 and 22:30 (£9–30, CC, booking starts in Dec, Fri–Sat shows sell out first; office open Mon–Fri 10:00–16:30, during Tattoo open until show time and Sat 10:00–22:30 and Sun 12:00–17:00; 33 Market Street, behind—and south of—Waverley train station, tel. 0131/225-1188, www.edinburgh-tattoo.co.uk). If nothing else, it is a really big show.

If you do manage to hit Edinburgh during the festival, book a room far in advance and extend your stay by a day or two. While Fringe tickets and most Tattoo tickets are available the day of the show, you may want to book a couple of official events in advance. Do it directly by telephone, leaving your credit-card number. Pick up your ticket at the office the day of the show. Several publications—including the festival's official schedule, the *Edinburgh Festivals Guide Daily*, *The List*, the *Fringe Program,* and the *Daily Diary*—list and evaluate festival events.

NIGHTLIFE

▲**Ghost Walks**—These walks are an entertaining and cheap night out (offered nightly, usually around 19:00 and 21:00, easy socializing for solo travelers). The theatrical and creatively staged **Witchery Tours,** the most established of the ghost tours, offer two different walks: "Ghosts and Gore" and "Murder and Mystery" (£7, 90 min, reservations required, leave from the top of the Royal Mile near castle esplanade, tel. 0131/225-6745, www.witcherytours.com).

▲▲**Literary Pub Tour**—This two-hour walk is interesting even if you think Sir Walter Scott was an arctic explorer. You'll follow the witty dialogue of two actors as they debate whether the great literature of Scotland was the creative recreation of fun-loving louts fueled by a love of whiskey or high art. You'll wander from the Grassmarket, over Old Town to New Town, with stops in three pubs as your guides share their takes on Scotland's literary greats. The tour meets at the Beehive Pub on Grassmarket (£8, book online and save £1, nightly in summer at 19:30, April–May & Oct Thu–Sun, Nov–March Fri; call 0131/226-6665 to confirm, www.scot-lit-tour.co.uk).

▲**Scottish Folk Evenings**—These £35 to £40 dinner shows, generally for tour groups intent on photographing old cultural clichés, are held in huge halls of expensive hotels. (Prices are bloated to include 20 percent commissions.) Your "traditional" meal is followed by a full slate of swirling kilts, blaring bagpipes, and Scottish folk dancing with an "old-time music hall" emcee. If you like Lawrence Welk, you're in for a treat. You can sometimes see the show without dinner for about two-thirds the price. The TI has fliers on all the latest venues.

Prestonfield House offers its Scottish folk evening with or without dinner Sunday to Friday (£21 for show only from 20:00–22:00, £33

includes four-course meal at 19:00, Priestfield Road, a 7-min walk from Dalkeith Road B&Bs, tel. 0131/668-3346, www.prestonfieldhouse.com).
▲▲**Folk Music in Pubs**—Edinburgh used to be a good place for folk music, but in the last few years, pub owners—out of economic necessity—are catering to twenty-somethings more interested in beer drinking than traditional music. Pubs that were regular venues for folk music have gone pop. Especially on weekends, you're unlikely to find much live folk music. The monthly *Gig Guide* (free at TI and various pubs, www.gigguide.co.uk) lists most of the live-music action. **Whistle Binkies** still offers nightly ad-lib traditional music, which can start as early as 19:30 or as late as 24:00 and goes until the wee hours (just off the Royal Mile on South Bridge, another entrance on Niddry Street, tel. 0131/557-5114, for a line-up see www.whistlebinkies.com).

Grassmarket (below the castle) is sloppy with live music and rowdy people spilling out of the pubs and into what was once upon a time a busy market square. It's fun to just wander through Grassmarket late at night. **Finnegan's Wake** has live music—often Irish rock—nightly (starts at 22:00, Sat not very Irish, Sun very Irish, a block off Grassmarket at 9 Victoria Street, tel. 0131/226-3816). Also consider **Biddy Mulligan** (Thu, Fri, Sun, tel. 0131/220-1246) and **White Hart Inn** (Sun, Mon, Thu, tel. 0131/226-2806), among others. By the music and crowds you'll know where to go and where not to. Have a beer and follow your ear.
Theater—Even outside of festival time, Edinburgh is a fine place for lively and affordable theater. Pick up *The List* for a complete rundown of what's on (£2.20 at newsstands).

SLEEPING

Off Dalkeith Road

These recommendations are south of town near the Royal Commonwealth Pool, just off Dalkeith Road. This comfortable and safe neighborhood is a 20-minute walk or 10-minute bus ride from the Royal Mile. All listings are non-smoking, on quiet streets, a two-minute walk from a bus stop, and well-served by city buses. B&Bs are unlikely to accept bookings for one-night stays in August. Some B&Bs offer Internet access, usually for a fee.

Near the B&Bs you'll find plenty of eateries (see "Eating," page 662) and easy free parking.

The Sun Dial **launderette** is along the bus route to the city center at 13 South Clerk Street (open daily, evening hours unpredictable, call to check, last wash 75 min before closing, opposite Queens Hall, tel.0131/667-0549).

To reach the hotel neighborhood from the train station, TI, or Scott Monument, cross Princes Street and wait at the **bus stop** under

SLEEP CODE

(£1 = about $1.60, country code: 44, area code: 0131)
Sleep Code: **S** = Single, **D** = Double/Twin, **T** = Triple, **Q** = Quad, **b** = bathroom, **s** = shower only, **no CC** = Credit Cards not accepted. You can assume credit cards are accepted unless otherwise noted.

To help you sort easily through these listings, I've divided the rooms into three categories based on the price for a standard double room with bath (during high season):

    $$$ **Higher Priced**—Most rooms £80 or more.
      $$ **Moderately Priced**—Most rooms between £50–80.
       $ **Lower Priced**—Most rooms £50 or less.

The advent of big, cheap hotels has made life tough for B&Bs. Still, book ahead, especially in August when the annual festival fills Edinburgh. Conventions, school holidays, and weekends can make finding a room tough at almost any time of year. For the best prices, book directly rather than through the TI, which charges a higher room fee and levies a £3 booking fee. "Standard" rooms, with toilets and showers a tissue-toss away, save you £10 a night.

Room prices in this section are usually listed as a range, from low season (winter) to high season (July–Sept). I have not listed the higher "festival prices," which are limited to August. Prices get soft off-season, for longer visits, and sometimes for midweek stays outside of summer.

the small C&A sign on the department store (80p; LRT buses #14, #30, and #33, or First bus #86; tell driver your destination is "Dalkeith Road;" red bus: exact change or pay more; green bus: makes change; ride 10 min to first or second stop—depending on B&B—after the pool, push the button, exit middle door). These buses also stop at the corner of North Bridge and High Street on the Royal Mile. Buses run from 6:00 to 23:00, and after 9:00 on Sunday morning. **Taxi** fare between the station or Royal Mile and the B&Bs is about £5.

B&Bs off Dalkeith Road

$$ Dunedin Guest House (pron. dun-EE-din)—bright, plush, and elegantly Scottish, with seven huge rooms—is a fine value (S-£25–40, Db-£50–80, family rooms for up to 5, power showers, 8 Priestfield Road, tel.

0131/668-1949, fax 0131/668-3636, reservations@dunedinguesthouse
.co.uk, Marsella Bowen).

$$ Turret Guest House is teddy-on-the-beddy cozy, with a great
bay-windowed family room and a vast breakfast menu that includes
haggis and vegetarian options (8 rooms, S-£23–37, D-£46–56, Db-
£56–74, £2/person discount with this book and cash, Internet access, 8
Kilmaurs Terrace, tel. 0131/667-6704, fax 0131/668-1368, www
.turretguesthouse.co.uk, contact@turretguesthouse.co.uk, Jimmy &
Fiona Mackie).

$$ Amar Agua Guest House, next door to Turret, is an inviting
Victorian home away from home (7 rooms, S-£25–35, Db-£44–70, 3
percent more with CC, Internet access, 10 Kilmaurs Terrace, tel. 0131/
667-6775, fax 0131/667-7687, www.amaragua.co.uk, rickstevesguest
@amaragua.co.uk, run by energetic young couple Dawn-Ann and Tony
Costa).

$$ Dorstan House is more hotelesque, with all the comforts, but
still friendly and relaxed. Several of its 14 thoughtfully decorated rooms are
on the ground floor (S-£20–30, Sb-£30–50, Ds-£40–60, Db-£50–70,
family rooms, self-catering flat, laundry service available, 7 Priestfield Road,
tel. 0131/667-6721, fax 0131/668-4644, www.dorstan-hotel.demon.co.uk,
reservations@dorstan-hotel.demon.co.uk, Richard and Maki Stott).

$$ Kenvie Guest House, well run by Dorothy Vidler, comes with
six pleasant rooms and lots of personal touches (1 small twin-£44, D-
£46, Db-£54, family deals, 3 percent more with CC, 16 Kilmaurs Road,
tel. 0131/668-1964, fax 0131/668-1926, www.kenvie.co.uk, dorothy
@kenvie.co.uk).

$$ Airdenair Guest House, offering views, homemade scones, and
other delicious sweets (made by the owner's mom and dad), has five
attractive rooms with a lofty above-it-all feeling (Sb-£25–35, Db-
£50–60, Tb-£75–90, 2 percent more with CC, 29 Kilmaurs Road, tel.
0131/668-2336, www.airdenair.com, jill@airdenair.com, Jill & Doug
McLennan).

$$ Hotel Ceilidh-Donia is recently refurbished with 14 cheery,
tricked-out rooms—computer hook-ups, strong showers, dimmer
switches—a pleasant back deck, and a fine restaurant (Sb-£25–50, Db-
£45–80, prices with this book through 2004, free Internet access for guests
and diners, laundry service available, 14 Marchhall Crescent, tel. 0131/
667-2743, www.hotelceilidh-donia.co.uk, reservations@hotelceilidh
-donia.co.uk, Max & Annette).

$$ Colquhoun Guest House, in an elegant building, has seven fine
rooms, several on the ground floor (S-£25–28, D-£44, Db-£56, family
room, no CC, 5 Marchhall Road, tel. & fax 0131/667-8481, grace
@colquhounhouse.freeserve.co.uk, run by amazing Grace McAinsh).

$$ Priestville Guest House has all the comforts of home, from
VCRs and a video library to Internet access in the lobby (D-£40–54,

Edinburgh, B&B Neighborhood

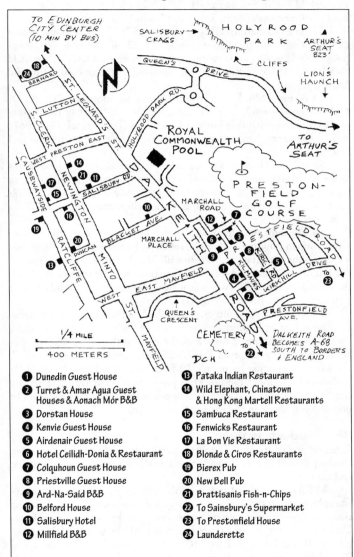

1 Dunedin Guest House
2 Turret & Amar Agua Guest Houses & Aonach Mór B&B
3 Dorstan House
4 Kenvie Guest House
5 Airdenair Guest House
6 Hotel Ceilidh-Donia & Restaurant
7 Colquhoun Guest House
8 Priestville Guest House
9 Ard-Na-Said B&B
10 Belford House
11 Salisbury Hotel
12 Millfield B&B
13 Pataka Indian Restaurant
14 Wild Elephant, Chinatown & Hong Kong Martell Restaurants
15 Sambuca Restaurant
16 Fenwicks Restaurant
17 La Bon Vie Restaurant
18 Blonde & Ciros Restaurants
19 Bierex Pub
20 New Bell Pub
21 Brattisanis Fish-n-Chips
22 To Sainsbury's Supermarket
23 To Prestonfield House
24 Launderette

Db-£44–60, 3 percent more with CC, family rooms available, 10 Priestfield Road, tel. & fax 0131/667-2435, www.priestville.com, bookings@priestville.com, Trina and Colin Warwick).

$$ **Ard-Na-Said B&B** is an elegant 1875 Victorian house with a comfy lounge and five classy rooms (S-£23–40, Db-£46–80, four-poster Db-£56-90, family room, 3 percent more with CC, 5 Priestfield Road, tel. 0131/667-8754, www.ardnasaid.freeserve.co.uk, Jim and Olive Lyons).

$$ **Aonach Mór** has seven simple, pleasant rooms (S-£18–30, D-£40–50, Db-£40–60, family rooms, Internet access, complimentary welcome drink with this book, 14 Kilmaurs Terrace, tel. 0131/667-8694, www.aonachmor.com, info@aonachmor.com, keen Ross and Kathleen Birnie).

$$ **Belford House** is a tidy, homey place offering seven good rooms and a warm welcome (D-£40–44, Db-£50–54, family deals, 5 percent off with cash, 13 Blacket Avenue, tel. 0131/667-2422, fax 0131/667-7508, www.belfordguesthouse.com, tom@belfordguesthouse.com, Tom Borthwick).

$$ **The Salisbury,** more like a hotel than its neighbors, fills a classy old Georgian building with eight rooms, a large lounge, and a dumbwaiter in the breakfast room (Sb-£30–35, D-£50–58, Db-£50–60, 5 percent off with cash and this book, free parking, 45 Salisbury Road, tel. & fax 0131/667-1264, www.salisburyguesthouse.co.uk, brenda-wright@btconnect.com, Brenda Wright).

$ **Millfield B&B,** run graciously by Liz Broomfield, is thoughtfully furnished with antique class, a rare sit-and-chat ambience, and a comfy TV lounge. Since the showers are down the hall, you'll get spacious rooms and great prices (S-£22–25, D-£40–44, T-£50–60, no CC, reconfirm reservation by phone, 12 Marchhall Road, tel. & fax 0131/667-4428). Decipher the breakfast prayer by Robert Burns. Then try the "Taste of Scotland" breakfast option. See how many stone (14 pounds) you weigh in the elegant throne room.

Big, Modern Hotels

The first one's a splurge. The rest are cheap as hotels go and offer more comfort than character. In each case I'd skip the institutional breakfast and eat out.

$$$ **MacDonald Hotel,** my only fancy listing, is an opulent four-star splurge down the street from the new Parliament building. With its classy marble-and-wood decor, fitness center, and pool, it's hard to leave. On a gray winter day in Edinburgh, this could be worth it. Prices can vary wildly (157 rooms, Db-£110, includes breakfast, near bottom of Royal Mile, across from Dynamic Earth, Holyrood Road, tel. 0131/550-4500, fax 0131/550-4545, www.macdonaldhotels.co.uk).

$$$ **Jurys Inn,** a cookie-cutter place with 186 dependably comfortable rooms, is capably run and well-located a short walk from the station (Sb, Db, Tb all £95 Fri–Sat, £75 Sun–Thu, much cheaper in off-season, breakfast-£9, 2 kids sleep free, non-smoking rooms, some views, pub/restaurant, on quiet street just off Royal Mile, 43 Jeffrey Street, tel. 0131/200-3300, fax 0131/200-0400, www.jurys.com).

$$ **Ibis Hotel,** mid-Royal Mile behind Tron Kirk, is well-run and perfectly located. It has 98 soulless but clean and comfy rooms drenched in prefab American charm (Db-£50–70, top price July–Aug, discounted in off-season, lousy continental breakfast-£5, non-smoking rooms, elevator, 6 Hunter Square, tel. 0131/240-7000, fax 0131/240-7007, h2039@accor-hotels.com).

$ **Travelodge,** the cheapest hotel in the center, has 193 no-nonsense, central rooms all decorated in dark blue. All rooms are the same and suitable for two adults with two kids or three adults. While sleepable, it has a cheap feel with a quickly revolving staff (Sb, Db, Tb all £50 except £70 Fri–Sun June–Sept, breakfast-£7, 33 St. Mary's Street, a block off the Royal Mile, tel. 08700-850-950, www.travelodge.co.uk).

Away from the Center

$$ The characterless **Travel Inn,** the biggest hotel in Edinburgh, has a mediocre location a mile west of the Royal Mile, but has a great price. Each of its 280 rooms is modern and comfortable, with a sofa that folds out for two kids if necessary (Db-£53–57 for 2 adults and up to 2 kids under 15, breakfast-£4.50–6.50, elevators, non-smoking rooms, weekends booked long in advance, near Haymarket station west of the castle at 1 Morrison Link, tel. 0131/228-9819, fax 0131/228-9836, www.travelinn.co.uk).

Hostels

Edinburgh's hostels are well-run and open to all, but are scruffy and don't include breakfast. They do offer Internet access, laundry facilities, and £11–13 bunk beds in 8- to 16-bed single-sex dorms (about a £9–12 savings over B&Bs).

$ **Castle Rock Hostel** is hip and easygoing, offering cheap beds, plenty of friends, and a great central location just below the castle and above the pubs with all the folk music (15 Johnston Terrace, tel. 0131/225-9666).

Their sister hostels are nearly across the street from each other: $ **High Street Hostel** (laundry-£2.50, kitchen, 8 Blackfriars Street, just off High Street/Royal Mile, tel. 0131/557-3984) and **Royal Mile Backpackers** (105 High Street, tel. 0131/557-6120).

For more regulations and less color, try the two IYH hostels: $ **Bruntsfield Hostel** (6–12 beds/room, near golf course, 7 Bruntsfield Crescent, buses #11, #15, #16, and #17 from Princes Street, tel.

0131/447-2994) and **Edinburgh Hostel** (4–10 beds/room, 5-min walk from Haymarket station, 18 Eglinton Crescent, tel. 0131/337-1120).

EATING

Along the Royal Mile

Historic pubs and doily cafés with reasonable, unremarkable meals abound. Here are some handy, affordable places for a good bite to eat (listed in downhill order).

Deacon Brodie's Tavern serves soup, sandwiches, and snacks on the ground floor and good £8 meals upstairs in the restaurant. As in all Edinburgh pubs, kids are allowed only in the restaurant section (daily 12:00–22:00, tel. 0131/225-6531). Or munch prayerfully in the **Lower Aisle** restaurant under St. Giles Cathedral (Mon–Fri 9:00–16:30, Sun 10:00–13:30, closed Sat except in Aug).

The **Filling Station,** a big noisy bar decorated with car parts, has an American-type menu, serves good burgers, and rocks at night (daily 12:00–23:30, later on weekends, 235 High Street, near North Bridge, tel. 0131/226-2488).

Dubh Prais Scottish Restaurant—the only serious restaurant on this list—is a dressy little place that fills a cellar 10 steps and a world away from the High Street bustle. The owner-chef promises to serve Scottish fayre at its very best. The only thing not Scottish here is the wine list and some of the guests (£8.50 2-course lunches Tue–Fri 12:00–14:00, £27 dinners Tue–Sat 18:30–22:30, closed Sun–Mon, reservations smart at night, opposite Crowne Plaza at 123b High Street, tel. 0131/557-5732).

Food Plantation has good, inexpensive, fresh sandwiches to eat in or take out (Mon–Fri 8:30–19:00, Sat 9:00–17:00, Sun 11:00–19:00, Internet access, 274 Canongate).

The **Tea Room** serves light lunches, scones, and fine tea in yellow elegance (Thu–Tue 10:30–16:30, off-season closed Wed, next to Museum of Edinburgh at 158 Canongate).

Clarinda's Tea Room, near the bottom of the Royal Mile, is a charming and tasty place to relax after touring the Mile or palace (Mon–Sat 9:00–16:45, Sun 10:00–16:45, 69 Canongate, tel. 0131/557-1888).

For a break from the touristic grind just off the top end of the Royal Mile, consider the **Elephant House,** where locals browse newspapers in the stay-awhile back room, listen to classic rock, and sip coffee or munch a light meal (daily 8:00–23:00, 2 blocks south of Royal Mile near Museum of Scotland at 21 George IV Bridge, tel. 0131/220-5355).

The Outsider, up the block, is a sleek spot serving stuffed pitas and stir-fry dishes (£10–15, daily 12:00–24:00, 15 George IV Bridge, tel. 0131/226-3131).

Grassmarket Street, below the castle, is lined with lots of eateries and noisy pubs. This is the place for live music and absorbent food.

Edinburgh's New Town

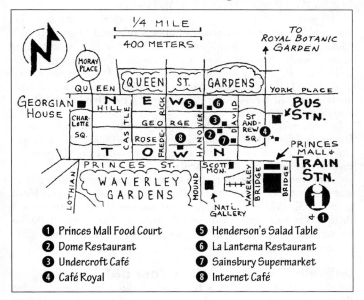

- ❶ Princes Mall Food Court
- ❷ Dome Restaurant
- ❸ Undercroft Café
- ❹ Café Royal
- ❺ Henderson's Salad Table
- ❻ La Lanterna Restaurant
- ❼ Sainsbury Supermarket
- ❽ Internet Café

The New Town

Princes Mall Food Court, below the TI and above the station, is a circus of sticky fast-food joints littered with paper plates and shoppers (Mon–Sat 8:30–18:00, Thu until 19:00, Sun 11:00–17:00). If you'd prefer pubs, browse nearby Rose Street.

The Dome Restaurant serves decent meals around a classy bar and under the elegant 19th-century skylight dome of what was a fancy bank. With soft jazz and dressy, white-tablecloth ambience, it feels a world apart (£12 lunches until 17:00, £17 dinners until 24:00, daily 12:00–24:00, modern cuisine, borderline smoky, open for a drink anytime under the dome or in the adjacent Art Deco bar, 14 George Street, tel. 0131/624-8624). Notice the facade of this former bank building—the various ways to make money fill the pediment with all the nobility of classical gods.

The **Undercroft,** in the basement of St. Andrew's church, is the cheapest place in town for lunch (£1 sandwich or soup and roll, Mon–Fri 12:00–14:00, closed Sat–Sun, on George Street, just off St. Andrew's Square).

Café Royal is a movie producer's dream pub—the perfect fin de siècle setting for a coffee, beer, or light meal (parts of *Chariots of Fire* were filmed in here). Drop in, if only to admire the 1880 tiles featuring famous inventors (daily noon–14:00 & 19:00–late, 2 blocks from Princes Mall on West Register Street, tel. 0131/556-4124).

A generation of New Town vegetarians have munched hearty cuisine and salads at **Henderson's Salad Table and Wine Bar** (£7, Mon–Sat 8:00–22:45, closed Sun, non-smoking section, strictly vegetarian, pleasant live music nightly in Wine Bar, always jazz on weekends, between Queen and George streets at 94 Hanover Street, tel. 0131/225-2131). Henderson's has two different seating areas, but both use the same self-serve cafeteria line. They also run **Henderson's Bistro** upstairs with table service.

Local office workers pile into the friendly and family-run **La Lanterna** for good Italian food (Mon–Sat 12:00–14:00 & 17:15–22:00, closed Sun, dinner reservations wise, 2 blocks off Princes Street, 83 Hanover Street, tel. 0131/226-3090).

Supermarket: The glorious **Sainsbury** supermarket, with a tasty assortment of take-away food and specialty coffees, is just one block from the Sir Walter Scott Monument and the lovely picnic-perfect Princes Street Gardens (Mon–Sat 7:00–22:00, Sun 10:00–20:00, on corner of Rose Street, on St. Andrew Square, across the street from Jenners, the classy department store).

Dalkeith Road Area, Near Your B&B

All these places are within a 10-minute walk of the recommended B&Bs. Most are on or near the intersection of Newington and East Preston Streets. For locations, see map on page 659.

Ethnic Restaurants: **Pataka Indian and Bengali Restaurant,** a 10-table "Indian bistro" with attentive service and great food, is understandably popular with locals. Portions are big, but not overly spicy, and prices are small. This tight little restaurant can be a bit smoky (£7 dishes, daily 12:00–14:00 & 17:30–23:30, also offers take-away, 190 Causewayside, tel. 0131/668-1167).

Wild Elephant serves decent Thai food to locals amid decor imported from Thailand, including a pagoda bar (£6–10, daily 17:00–23:00, also does take-away, 21 Newington Road, tel. 0131/662-8822).

Up the block, you'll find a couple of Chinese-food options: **Chinatown** (£6–9, Tue–Fri 12:00–14:00 & 17:30–23:00, Sat–Sun 17:30–23:30, closed Mon, reservations smart on weekend nights, take-away food 25 percent cheaper, 13 Newington Road, tel. 0131/662-0555) and **Hong Kong Martell** (daily from 12:00, 7 Newington Road, tel. 0131/668-4437).

Sambuca dishes up pizza and pasta in a lively bistro (£8–10 dishes, Mon–Sat 12:30–14:30 & 17:00–late, Sun 17:00–10:00, 103 Causewayside, tel. 0131/667-3307).

Scottish/French Restaurants: Several classy little eight-table places feature "Auld Alliance" cuisine—Scottish cooking with a French flair (seasoned with a joint historic disdain for England). They offer small menus with three or four items per course for two- or three-course meals (about £10 for a 2-course lunch, £20 for a 3-course dinner). These popular places take credit cards, and reservations are smart on weekend evenings. Many offer less-expensive meals outside of weekends.

Fenwicks is cozy and reliable, with tasty food and no French fries (main course-£13–16, daily 12:00–14:00, dinner 18:00–late, 15 Salisbury Place, tel. 0131/667-4265).

La Bon Vie Restaurant is candlelit chic with perhaps the most enticing menu (two-course dinner-£10–18, daily 12:00–14:00 & 18:00–22:00, call ahead to make sure they're open for lunch, 49 Causewayside, tel. 0131/667-1110).

Blonde Restaurant, with a more eclectic and European menu, is less expensive and bigger than the others with no set-price dinners (about £14 for 2 courses, good vegetarian options, Tue–Sun 12:00–14:30 & 18:00–22:00, closed Mon, 75 St. Leonard's Street, tel. 0131/668-2917).

Ciros Restaurant is a hardworking, well-established family affair (£15 2-course dinner, Tue–Sat 18:30–21:30, closed Sun–Mon; 93 St. Leonard's Street, tel. 0131/668-4207, run by Christine, Jean, and Stuart Stevenson).

Hotel Ceilidh-Donia serves well-prepared fish, meat, and vegetarian dishes in a flagstone-floored, high-ceilinged space with a small, friendly adjoining pub (£7–11, Mon–Fri eves plus Sun lunch 13:00–16:00, free Internet access to customers, within a block of most recommended B&Bs at 14 Marchhall Crescent, tel. 0131/667-2743).

Pubs: **Bierex,** a youthful pub, is the neighborhood favorite for modern dishes and camaraderie (£6 plates, daily 10:00–24:00, food served 10:00–21:00, Fri–Sat until 20:00, 132 Causewayside, tel. 0131/667-2335).

The **New Bell** serves up filling classics, from steak and salmon to haggis, in a tidy pub setting (£13 plates, Tue–Sun 17:30–22:30; 2-course £10 special 17:30–18:45; closed Mon, 233 Causewayside, tel. 0131/668-2868).

Cheaper Choices: **Brattisanis** is your basic fish-and-chips joint that serves lousy milk shakes and great haggis. Add a cheap touch of class by bringing in a beer or half bottle of wine from next door (daily 9:30–23:00, 87 Newington Road, tel. 0131/667-5808).

On Dalkeith Road, the huge Commonwealth Pool's noisy **café** has snacks for hungry swimmers and budget travelers alike (Mon–Fri 10:00–18:00, Sat–Sun 11:00–17:00, pass the entry without paying).

Supermarket: The nearest supermarket, **Sainsbury,** is a 10-minute walk or a quick bus ride down Dalkeith Road away from town in the Cameron Toll shopping complex (Mon–Sat 7:30–22:00, Sun 8:00–19:00, tel. 0131/666-5200). There's also a **Tesco** between the Dalkeith

Road B&B neighborhood and the Royal Mile (Mon–Sat 7:00–midnight, Sun 9:00–22:00, 5 long blocks south of the Royal Mile, on Nicolson, just south of intersection with West Richmond Street).

TRANSPORTATION CONNECTIONS

By train to: Inverness (7/day, 4 hrs), **Oban** (3/day, change in Glasgow, 4.5 hrs), **York** (2/hr, 2.5 hrs), **London** (hrly, 5 hrs), **Durham** (hrly, 2 hrs, less frequent in winter), **Newcastle** (hrly, 1.5 hrs), **Keswick,** the Lake District (south past Carlisle to Penrith, then catch bus to Keswick, 6/day, fewer Sun, 40 min), **Birmingham** (6/day, 4.5 hrs), **Crewe** (6/day, 3.5 hrs), **Bristol,** near Bath (hrly, 6–7 hrs). Train info: tel. 08457-225-125, www.gner.co.uk.

By bus to: Oban (4/day, 4 hrs, not on Sun), **Fort William** (1/day, 4 hrs), **Inverness** (hrly, 4 hrs), **Blackpool** (Fri, Sat, Mon only, requires change in Glasgow, 5 hrs), **York** (1/day at 9:45, 5 hrs). For bus info, call Scottish Citylink (tel. 08705-505-050, www.citylink.co.uk) or National Express (tel. 08705-808-080). You can get info and tickets at the bus desk inside the Princes Mall TI.

# DUBLIN

With reminders of its stirring history and rich culture on every corner, Ireland's capital and largest city is a sightseer's delight. Dublin's fair city will have you humming, "Cockles and mussels, alive, alive-O."

Founded as a Viking trading settlement in the ninth century, Dublin grew to be a center of wealth and commerce second only to London in the British Empire. Dublin, the seat of English rule in Ireland for 700 years, was the heart of a "civilized" Anglo-Irish area (eastern Ireland) known as "the Pale." Anything "beyond the Pale" was considered uncultured and almost barbaric...purely Irish.

The Golden Age of English Dublin was the 18th century. The British Empire was on a roll, and Dublin was right there with it. Largely rebuilt during this Georgian era, Dublin—even with its tattered edges—became an elegant and cultured capital.

Then nationalism and human rights got in the way. The ideas of the French Revolution inspired Irish intellectuals to buck British rule and, after the Rebellion of 1798, life in Dublin was never quite the same. But the 18th century left a lasting imprint on the city. Squares and boulevards in the Georgian style (that's British for neoclassical) gave the city an air of grandness. The National Museum, National Gallery, and many government buildings are in the Georgian section of town. Few buildings (notably Christ Church Cathedral and St. Patrick's Cathedral) survive from before this Georgian period.

In the 19th century, with the closing of the Irish Parliament, the famine, and the beginnings of the struggle for independence, Dublin was treated—and felt—more like a colony than a partner. The tension culminated in the Easter Rising of 1916, independence from Britain, and the tragic civil war. With many of its elegant streets left in ruins, Dublin emerged as the capital of the only former colony in Europe.

While bullet-pocked buildings and dramatic statues keep memories of Ireland's recent struggle for independence alive, it's boom time now, and the city is looking to a bright future. Locals are enjoying the "Celtic Tiger" economy—although recently cooled, still the best in Europe—while visitors enjoy a big-town cultural scene wrapped in a small-town smile.

Planning Your Time

Dublin deserves three nights and two days. Consider this aggressive sightseeing plan:

Day 1: 10:15–Trinity College guided walk, 11:00–Book of Kells and Old Library, 12:00–Browse Grafton Street and have lunch there or picnic on Merrion Square, 13:30–Visit Number Twenty-Nine Georgian House, 15:00–National Museum, 17:00–Return to hotel, rest, have dinner—eat well for less during early-bird specials, 19:30–Evening walk (musical or literary), 22:00–Irish music in Temple Bar area.

Day 2: 10:00–Dublin Castle tour, 11:00–Historic town walk, 13:00–Lunch, 14:00–O'Connell Street walk, 16:00–Kilmainham Jail, 18:00–Guinness Brewery tour finishing with view of city, Evening–Catch a play, concert, or Comhaltas traditional music in Dun Laoghaire (DUN-leary).

ORIENTATION

(area code: 01)

Greater Dublin sprawls with over a million people—nearly a third of the country's population. But the center of touristic interest is a tight triangle between O'Connell Bridge, St. Stephen's Green, and Christ Church Cathedral. Within this triangle you'll find Trinity College (Book of Kells), Grafton Street (top pedestrian shopping zone), Temple Bar (trendy and touristy nightlife center), Dublin Castle, and the hub of most city tours and buses. The only major sights outside your easy-to-walk triangle are the Kilmainham Jail and the Guinness Brewery (both west of the center).

The River Liffey cuts the town in two. Focus on the southern half (where nearly all your sightseeing will take place). Dublin's main drag, O'Connell Street, runs from the north side of the river (near the Abbey Theater and outdoor produce market), past the Parnell monument down to the central O'Connell Bridge, then continues south as the major city axis—mostly as Grafton Street—to St. Stephen's Green.

The port suburb of Dun Laoghaire (DUN-leary, covered later in this chapter) lies south of Dublin, 20 minutes away by DART commuter train. Travelers connecting by ferry to Holyhead in Wales or those just looking for a mellow town to sleep in outside of urban Dublin can easily home-base here.

Tourist Information

Dublin's main tourist information office (TI) is a big shop with little to offer other than promotional fliers and long lines (Mon–Sat 9:00–17:30,

Dublin

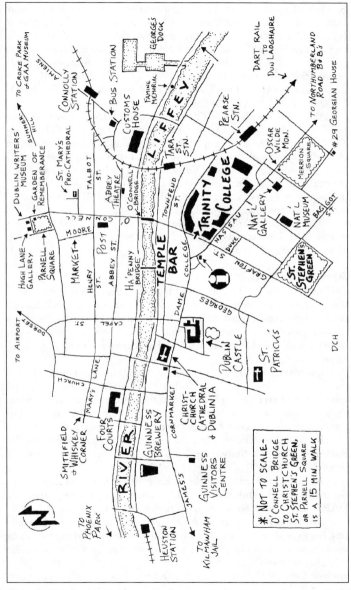

Sun July–Aug only 10:30–15:00, located in a former church on Suffolk Street, 1 block off Grafton Street, tel. 01/605-7700, www.visitdublin.com). It has an American Express office, car-rental agency, bus-info desk, café, and traditional knickknacks. But perhaps its greatest value is the chance to peruse the rack opposite the info counter and pick up brochures for destinations throughout Ireland. There's also a TI at the airport (daily 8:00–22:00) and one at the Dun Laoghaire ferry terminal (Mon–Sat 10:00–13:00 & 14:00–18:00, closed Sun).

While you can buy the TI's lousy map for €0.50, its free newspaper, *The Guide to Dublin,* has the same one on its staple page. The handy *Dublin's Top Visitor Attractions* booklet has a small map and the latest on all of the town's sights—many more than I list here (€3.50, sold at TI bookshop without any wait). For a schedule of happenings in town, check the minimal calendar of events inside *The Guide to Dublin* newspaper (free at TI), or better, buy the informative *In Dublin* at any newsstand (published fortnightly, €2.50).

The excellent *Collins Illustrated Dublin Map* (€8 at TIs and newsstands) is the ultimate city map, listing just about everything of interest, along with helpful opinions.

Arrival in Dublin

By Train: Dublin has two stations. Heuston Station, on the west end of town, serves west and southwest Ireland (30-min walk from O'Connell Bridge; take taxi or bus #90 instead, see below). Connolly Station—which serves the north, northwest, and Rosslare—is closer to the center (10-min walk from O'Connell Bridge). Each station has a luggage-check facility and ATMs.

Bus #90 runs along the river, connecting both train stations, the bus station, and the city center (€0.85, 6/hr). When you're leaving Dublin and you want to reach Heuston Station from the city center, catch bus #90 on the south side of the river; to get to Connolly Station and the Busaras bus station from the city center, catch #90 on the north side of the river.

By Bus: Bus Eireann, Ireland's national bus company, uses the Busaras Central Bus Station next to Connolly Station (10-min walk or short ride on bus #90 to the city center).

By Ferry: Irish Ferries docks at the mouth of the River Liffey (near the town center), while the Stena Line docks at Dun Laoghaire (easy DART train connections into Dublin, at least 3/hr, 20 min).

By Plane: The airport has ATMs, change bureaus, car-rental agencies, baggage check, a café, and a supermarket at the parking lot. Taxis from the airport into Dublin cost about €18, to Dun Laoghaire about €35.

Airport Buses: Consider buying a bus pass that covers the Airlink bus into town (see "Getting Around Dublin," below), but read this first to see if Airlink is best for you. To get to the recommended accommodations in the **city center,** take Airlink bus #748 (not #747) and ask the driver which stop is closest to your hotel (€5, €2.50 with Aer Lingus boarding pass, pay driver, 6/hr, 40 min, connects airport with Heuston train station and Busaras bus station, near Connolly train station). For the **St. Stephen's Green** neighborhood, the Aircoach is your best bet (€5, 4/hr, runs 5:30–22:30; pay driver and confirm best stop for your hotel). If you're staying in **Dun Laoghaire,** take Airlink bus #746 direct to Dun Laoghaire.

City Bus: To get from the airport cheaply to downtown Dublin, take the city bus from the airport; buses marked #16A, #41A, #41B, and #41C go to Marlborough Street, a five-minute walk from O'Connell Bridge (€1.60, exact change required, 3/hr, 40 min).

Helpful Hints

Tourist Victim Support Service: This thoughtful service can be helpful if you run into any problems (Mon–Sat 10:00–18:00, Sun 12:00–18:00, tel. 01/478-5295).

U.S. Embassy: It's on 42 Elgin Road in the Ballsbridge neighborhood (Mon–Fri 8:30–17:00 for passport concerns, tel. 01/668-7122 or 01/668-8777, www.usembassy.ie).

Internet Access: There are Internet cafés on nearly every street. The Net House at the top of Dame Street (facing Kinlay House, near Christ Church Cathedral, tel. 01/679-0977) is fast and open 24 hours a day.

Laundry: Capricorn Launderette, a block southwest of Jurys Inn Christ Church on Patrick Street, is full-service only. Allow four hours and about €8 for a load (Mon–Fri 7:30–20:00, Sat 9:00–18:00, Sun 10:00–16:00, tel. 01/473-1779). The All-American Launderette offers self- and full-service options (Mon–Sat 8:30–19:00, Sun 10:00–18:00, 40 South Great George's Street, tel. 01/677-2779).

Car Rental: For Dublin car-rental information, see the Appendix.

Festivals: St. Patrick's Day is a five-day extravaganza in Dublin (www .stpatricksday.ie). June 16 is Bloomsday, dedicated to the Irish author James Joyce and featuring the Messenger Bike Rally. On rugby weekends (about 4 per year), hotels raise their prices and are packed. Book ahead during festival times and for any weekend.

Getting around Dublin

You'll do most of Dublin on foot. Big green buses are cheap and cover the city thoroughly. Most lines start at the four quays (pron. keys), or piers, nearest O'Connell Bridge. If you're away from the center, nearly any bus takes you back downtown. Tell the driver where you're going, and he'll ask for €0.80, €1.20, €1.40, or €1.60, depending on the number of stops. Bring exact change or lose any excess.

Passes: The bus office at 59 Upper O'Connell Street has free "route network" maps and sells city-bus passes. The three-day Rambler costs €10 (covers Airlink airport bus but not DART trains) and the three-day

Short Hop pass costs €15 (includes DART but not Airlink). Passes are also sold at each TI (bus info tel. 01/873-4222).

DART: Speedy commuter trains connect Dublin with Dun Laoghaire (ferry terminal and recommended B&Bs, at least 3/hr, 20 min, €1.70).

LUAS: The city's new light rail and subway system is scheduled for completion some time in 2004. Ask the TI about prices and routes.

Taxi: Cabbies are honest, plentiful, friendly, and good sources of information (under €7 for most downtown rides, €30 per hour for a guided joyride available from most any cab).

TOURS

While the physical treasures of Dublin are mediocre by European standards, the city has a fine story to tell and people with a natural knack for telling it. It's a good town for walking tours, and the competition is fierce. Pamphlets touting creative walks are posted all over town. There are medieval walks, literary walks, 1916 Easter Rising walks, Georgian Dublin walks, and more. The evening walks are great ways to meet other travelers.

▲▲**Historical Walking Tour**—This is your best introductory walk. A group of hardworking history graduates—many of whom claim to have done more than just kiss the Blarney Stone—enliven Dublin's basic historic strip (Trinity College, Old Parliament House, Dublin Castle, and Christ Church Cathedral). You'll get the story of their city, from its Viking origin to the present. Guides speak at length about the roots of Ireland's struggle with Britain. As you listen to your guide's story, you stand in front of buildings that aren't much to see but are lots to talk about (daily April–Sept at 11:00 and 15:00; Oct–March only Fri, Sat, and Sun at 12:00). From May to September, the same group offers more focused tours at noon (1916 Easter Rising "Terrible Beauty" walks on Tue and Fri; juicy slice-of-old-life Dublin "Sexual History of Ireland" walks on Sat, Sun, and Wed; and gritty "Architecture & Society" walks on Mon and Thu). All walks last two hours and cost €10 (but get the €8 student discount with this book, depart from front gate of Trinity College, private walks also available, tel. 01/878-0227, www.historicalinsights.ie).

The 1916 Rebellion company offers, as you might guess, **1916 Rebellion Walks** (€10, 2 hrs, daily mid-April–Sept Mon–Sat at 11:30 and 14:30, Sun at 13:00, depart from International Bar at 23 Wicklow Street, tel. 01/473-4986, mobile 086-858-3847, www.1916rising.com).

▲**Dublin Literary Pub Crawl**—Two actors take 30 or so tourists on a walk, stopping at four pubs. Half the time is spent enjoying their entertaining banter, which introduces the novice to the high *craic* (conversation) of Joyce, O'Casey, and Yeats. The two-hour tour is punctuated with 20-minute pub breaks (free time). While the beer lubricates the social fun, it dilutes the content of the evening (€10, April–Nov daily at 19:30, plus Sun at noon; Dec–March Thu–Sun only; you can normally just show up, but call ahead in July–Aug when it can fill up, meet upstairs in Duke Pub, off Grafton on Duke Street, tel. 01/670-5602, www.dublinpubcrawl.com).

▲▲Traditional Irish-Music Pub Crawl—This is similar to the Literary Pub Crawl but features music. You meet upstairs at 19:30 at Gogarty's Pub (Temple Bar area, corner of Fleet and Anglesea) and spend 40 minutes each in the upstairs rooms of three pubs listening to two musicians talk about, play, and sing traditional Irish music. While having only two musicians makes the music a bit thin (Irish music aficionados will tell you you're better off just finding a good session), the evening, though touristy, is not gimmicky. It's an education in traditional Irish music. The musicians demonstrate a few instruments and really enjoy introducing rookies to their art (€10, €1 discount with this book, beer extra, April–Oct nightly; Nov and Feb–March Fri–Sat only, allow 2.5 hrs, expect up to 50 tourists, tel. 01/478-0193, www.musicalpubcrawl.com).

▲Hop-on, Hop-off Bus Tours—Two companies (Dublin City Tours and City Sightseeing/Guide Friday) offer hop-on, hop-off bus tours of Dublin, doing virtually identical 90-minute circuits, allowing you to get on or off at your choice of about 16 stops. Buses are mostly topless, with running live commentaries. Both companies go to Guinness Brewery, but only City Sightseeing/Guide Friday stops at Kilmainham Jail. Buy your ticket on board. Each company's map, free with ticket, details various discounts you'll get on Dublin's sights. Your ticket is valid for 24 hours from the time you buy it (daily, 4/hr from 9:30–17:30, until 18:30 in summer, fewer buses Nov–March and only until 15:30). **Dublin City Tour** runs the green-and-cream buses with drivers that do the narration (€14, tel. 01/873-4222). **City Sightseeing/Guide Friday** costs the same but includes Phoenix Park and comes with a guide and a driver, rather than a driver who guides (€14, red buses, tel. 01/872-9010).

▲Viking Splash Tours—If you'd like to ride in a WWII amphibious vehicle—driven by a Viking-costumed guide who's as liable to spout history as he is to growl—this is for you. The tour starts with a group roar from the Viking within us all. At first, the guide talks as if he were a Viking ("When we came here in 841..."), but soon the patriot emerges as he tags Irish history onto the sights you pass. Near the end of the 75-minute tour (punctuated by occasional group roars at passersby), you don a life jacket for a slow spin up and down a boring canal. Kids who expect a Viking splash may feel they've been trapped in a classroom, but historians will enjoy the talk more than the gimmick (€14, Feb–Nov daily 10:30–17:30, sometimes later in summer, none Dec–Jan, depart about hourly from Bull Alley beside St. Patrick's Cathedral; ticket office at 64–65 Patrick Street, on gray days boat is covered but still breezy—dress warmly, tel. 01/707-6000, www.vikingsplashtours.com).

SIGHTS

Trinity College

▲**Trinity College**—Founded in 1592 by Queen Elizabeth I to establish a Protestant way of thinking about God, Trinity has long been Ireland's most prestigious college. Originally the student body was limited to rich Protestant males. Women were admitted in 1903, and Catholics, though

DUBLIN AT A GLANCE

▲▲▲**National Museum** Interesting collection of Irish treasures from the Stone Age to today. **Hours**: Tue–Sat 10:00–17:00, Sun 14:00–17:00, closed Mon.

▲▲▲**Kilmainham Gaol** Historic jail used by the British as a political prison, today a moving museum to the suffering of the Irish people. **Hours**: Daily April–Sept 9:30–18:00, Oct–March 9:30–17:00.

▲▲▲**Trinity Old Library** Contains the exquisite illuminated manuscript, the Book of Kells, the most important piece of art from the Dark Ages. **Hours**: Mon–Sat 9:30–17:00, Sun 9:30–16:30, Oct–May Sun 12:00–16:30.

▲▲**Trinity College** Ireland's most famous school, best visited with a 30-minute tour led by one of its students. **Hours**: Late May–Sept daily 10:30–15:30; late Feb and early May usually weekends only, . weather permitting.

▲▲**Dublin Castle** The city's historic 700-year-old castle, featuring ornate English state apartments, tourable only with a guide. **Hours**: Four tours per hour, Mon–Fri 10:00–17:00, Sat–Sun 14:00–17:00.

▲▲**Number Twenty-Nine Georgian House** Restored 18th-century house provides an intimate glimpse of middle-class Georgian life. **Hours**: Tue–Sat 10:00–17:00, Sun 14:00–17:00, closed Mon.

▲▲**Grafton Street** The city's liveliest pedestrian shopping mall. **Hours**: Always open.

▲▲**O'Connell Bridge** Landmark bridge spanning the River Liffey at the center of Dublin. **Hours**: Always open.

allowed entrance by the school much earlier, were given formal permission to study at Trinity in the 1970s. Today, half of Trinity's 12,500 students are women, and 70 percent are culturally Catholic (although only about 20 percent of Irish youth are churchgoing).

▲▲Trinity College Tour—Inside the gate of Trinity, students organize and lead 30-minute tours of their campus. You'll get a rundown on the mostly Georgian architecture; a peek at student life, both in the early

▲▲O'Connell Street Dublin's grandest promenade and main drag, packed with history and ideal for a stroll. **Hours**: Always open.

▲Dublin Experience Decent but overpriced 45-minute slideshow offering a historic introduction to Dublin. **Hours**: June–Sept daily, showings on the hour 10:00–17:00, closed Oct–May.

▲Chester Beatty Library American expatriate's eclectic collection of mostly non-Western artifacts. **Hours**: Mon–Fri 10:00–17:00, Sat 11:00–17:00, Sun 13:00–17:00, Oct–April closed Mon.

▲National Gallery Fine collection of top Irish painters and European masters. **Hours**: Mon–Sat 9:30–17:30, Thu until 20:30, Sun 12:00–17:30.

▲Guinness Brewery The home of Ireland's national beer, with a museum of beer-making, a gallery of clever ads, and the spectacular Gravity Bar with panoramic city views. **Hours**: Daily 9:30–17:00.

▲Gaelic Athletic Association Museum High-tech museum of traditional Gaelic sports like hurling and Irish football. **Hours**: Mon–Sat 9:30–17:00, Sun 12:00–17:00.

▲St. Stephen's Green Relaxing park surrounded by fine Georgian buildings. **Hours**: Always open.

▲Merrion Square Enjoyable and inviting park with a fun statue of Oscar Wilde. **Hours**: Always open.

▲Temple Bar Dublin's trendiest neighborhood, with shops, cafés, theaters, galleries, pubs, and restaurants—a great spot for live traditional music. **Hours**: Always open.

days and today; and enjoy the company of a witty Irish college kid who talks about the school (late May–Sept daily 10:30–15:30; late Feb and early May usually weekends only, weather permitting; look for small blue kiosk inside gate, €10 tour fee includes the €7.50 fee to see the Book of Kells, where the tour leaves you).

▲▲▲**Book of Kells in the Trinity Old Library**—The only Trinity campus interior welcoming tourists (just follow the signs) is the Old Library, with its precious Book of Kells. The first-class *Turning Darkness into Light* exhibit puts the 680-page illuminated manuscript in its historical and cultural context, preparing you to see the original book and other precious manuscripts in the treasury. The exhibit is a one-way affair leading to the actual treasury, which shows only four books under glass in one display case. Make a point to spend at least half an hour in the exhibit (before reaching the actual Book of Kells). Especially interesting are the video clips showing the exacting care that went into the monk-uscripts and the ancient art of bookbinding.

Written on vellum (baby calfskin) in the eighth or early ninth century—probably by Irish monks in Iona, Scotland—this enthusiastically decorated copy of the four Gospels was taken to the Irish monastery at Kells in A.D. 806 after a series of Viking raids. Arguably the finest piece of art from what is generally called the Dark Ages, the Book of Kells shows that monastic life in this far fringe of Europe was far from dark. It has been bound into four separate volumes, and at any given time, two of the four gospels are on display. The crowd around the one glass case with the treasures can be off-putting, but hold your own and get up close. You'll see four richly decorated, 1,200-year-old pages—two text and two decorated cover pages. The library treasury also displays two other books—likely the Book of Armagh (A.D. 807) and the Book of Durrow (A.D. 680)—neither of which can be checked out.

Next, a stairway leads upstairs to the 200-foot-long main chamber of the Old Library (from 1732), stacked to its towering ceiling with 200,000 of the library's oldest books. Here, you'll find one of a dozen surviving original copies of the Proclamation of the Irish Republic. Patrick Pearse read these words outside the General Post Office on April 24, 1916, starting the Easter Rising that led to Irish independence. Read the entire thing...imagining it was yours. Notice the inclusive opening phrase and the seven signatories (each of whom was executed). Another national icon is nearby: the oldest surviving Irish harp, from the 15th century.

Cost and Hours: €7.50, at Trinity College Library, year-round Mon–Sat 9:30–17:00, Sun 9:30–16:30, Oct–May Sun 12:00–16:30 (tel. 01/608-2308). A long line often snakes out of the building. It's the line to purchase a ticket—not to actually get in. If you take the Trinity College tour or if you buy the combo-ticket at the *Dublin Experience*, you've already bought your Book of Kells ticket and can scoot right past the line and into the exhibit.

▲*Dublin Experience*—This 45-minute fancy slideshow giving a historic introduction to Dublin is one more tourist movie with the sound turned up. It's good—offering a fine, sweeping introduction to the story of Ireland—but pricey, riding on the coattails of the Book of Kells. Considering that the combo-ticket gets you this for half-price and past any Kells line, it's not a bad value (€4.50, included in €10 combo-ticket with Book of Kells/Old Library, June–Sept daily, showings on the hour 10:00–17:00, closed Oct–May, in modern arts building across from Trinity Old Library).

South of the River Liffey

▲▲**Dublin Castle**—Built on the spot of the first Viking fortress, this castle was the seat of British rule in Ireland for 700 years. Located where the Poddle and Liffey Rivers came together, making a black pool ("*dubh linn*" in Irish), Dublin Castle was the official residence of the viceroy who implemented the will of the British royalty. In this stirring setting, in 1922, the Brits handed power over to Michael Collins and the Irish. Today, it's used for fancy state and charity functions. The 45-minute tours offer a room-by-room walk through the lavish state apartments of this most English of Irish palaces. The tour finishes with a look at the foundations of the Norman tower and the best remaining chunk of the 13th-century town wall (€4.50, 4/hr, Mon–Fri 10:00–17:00, Sat–Sun 14:00–17:00, tel. 01/677-7129).

▲**Chester Beatty Library**—Chester Beatty was a rich American mining engineer who retired to Ireland in 1950, later becoming its first honorary citizen. He left his priceless and eclectic collection to his adopted homeland as a public charitable trust.

More an exotic parade of non-Irish treasures than a library, these two floors of rare texts and collectibles sprouted from over 2,000 years of Eastern religions, Islam, and Christianity. You'll see books carved out of jade, ornate snuff bottles, rhino-horn cups, and even the oldest surviving copy of St. Paul's letter to the Romans (A.D. 180). Other highlights include a graceful Burmese book written on palm leaves—bound together to unfold like an accordion—and a densely ornamental sunburst motif from a 500-year-old Iranian Koran (free entry, Mon–Fri 10:00–17:00, Sat 11:00–17:00, Sun 13:00–17:00, Oct–April closed Mon, tel. 01/407-0750, www.cbl.ie). Enter the library via Dublin Castle's pedestrian arch, across Dame Street from the Olympia Theatre; walk straight ahead while crossing the courtyard, turn right behind the old castle turret, walk straight for 50 yards, and enter the walled gardens on the left. It's in the modern addition to the Dublin Castle clock tower building.

Dublin City Hall—The first neoclassical building in this very neoclassical city stands proudly overlooking Dame Street, in front of the gate to Dublin Castle. Built in 1779 as the Royal Exchange, it introduced the neoclassical style (then very popular on the continent) to Ireland. Step

South Dublin

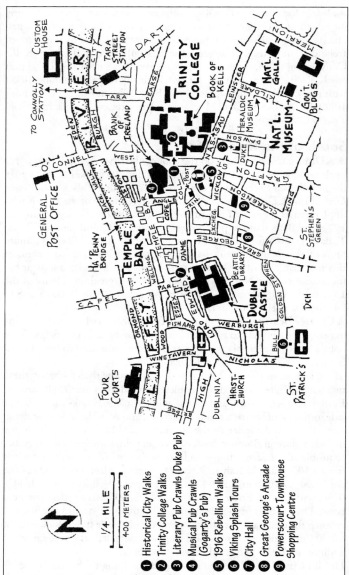

¼ MILE
400 METERS

1 Historical City Walks
2 Trinity College Walks
3 Literary Pub Crawls (Duke Pub)
4 Musical Pub Crawls (Gogarty's Pub)
5 1916 Rebellion Walks
6 Viking Splash Tours
7 City Hall
8 Great George's Arcade
9 Powerscourt Townhouse Shopping Centre

inside (it's free) to feel the prosperity and confidence of Dublin in her 18th-century glory days. In 1852, it became city hall. Under the grand rotunda, a cycle of heroic paintings tells the city's history. Pay your respects to the 18-foot-tall statue of Daniel O'Connell (the great orator and "liberator" who won Catholic emancipation in 1829 from those vile Protestants over in London). The greeter sits like the Maytag repairman at the information desk, eager to give you more information. Downstairs is a simple *Story of the Capital* exhibition—storyboards and video clips of Dublin's history (€4, Mon–Sat 10:00–17:00, Sun 14:00–17:00).

Dublinia—This tries valiantly, but fails, to be a "bridge to Dublin's medieval past." The amateurish look at the medieval town starts with a walk through dim rooms of tableaus, followed by several halls of medieval exhibits, a scale model of old Dublin, and an interesting room devoted to medieval fairs. Then, after piles of stairs, you get a tower-top view of Dublin's skyline of churches and breweries (€5.75, €8.75 includes Christ Church Cathedral, saving you €3; April–Sept daily 10:00–17:00, Oct–March daily 11:00–16:00, brass rubbing, coffee shop open in summer only, across from Christ Church Cathedral, tel. 01/679-4611).

Christ Church Cathedral—The first church on this spot, built of wood in about 1040 by King Sitric, dates back to Viking times. The present structure dates from a mix of periods: Norman and Gothic, but mostly Victorian neo-Gothic (1870s restoration work). The unusually large crypt under the cathedral—actually the oldest building in Dublin—contains stocks, statues, and the cathedral's silver (€5 donation to church, includes downstairs crypt silver exhibition, €8.75 combo-ticket includes Dublinia, free brochure with self-guided tour, daily 10:00–17:00). Because of Dublin's British past, neither of its top two churches is Catholic. Christ Church Cathedral and the nearby St. Patrick's Cathedral are both Church of Ireland. In Catholic Ireland, these sights feel hollow. They're more famous than visit-worthy.

Evensong: At Christ Church, a 45-minute evensong service is sung regularly (less regularly during the summer) several times a week (Wed at 18:00—girls' choir, Thu at 18:00—adult choir, Sat at 17:00–adult choir, and Sun at 15:30—adult choir). The 13th-century St. Patrick's Cathedral, where Jonathan Swift (author of *Gulliver's Travels*) was dean in the 18th century, also offers evensong (Sun at 15:15, Mon–Fri at 17:30, but not Wed July–Aug).

▲▲▲**National Museum**—Showing off the treasures of Ireland from the Stone Age to modern times, this museum is itself a national treasure and wonderfully digestible under one dome. Ireland's Bronze Age gold fills the center. Up four steps, the prehistoric Ireland exhibit rings the gold. In a corner (behind a 2,000-year-old body), you'll find the treasury with the most famous pieces (brooches, chalices, and other examples of

Celtic metalwork) and an 18-minute video (played on request), giving an overview of Irish art through the 13th century. The collection's superstar is the gold, enamel, and amber eighth-century Tara Brooch. Jumping way ahead (and to the opposite side of the hall), a special corridor features *The Road to Independence*, with guns, letters, and death masks recalling the fitful birth of the "Terrible Beauty" (1900–1921, with a focus on the 1916 Easter Rising). The best Viking artifacts in town are upstairs with the medieval collection. If you'll be visiting Cong (in Connemara, near Galway), seek out the original Cross of Cong (free entry, Tue–Sat 10:00–17:00, Sun 14:00–17:00, closed Mon, good café, Kildare Street 2, between Trinity College and St. Stephen's Green). Greatest-hits tours are given several times a day (€2, 40 min, tel. 01/677-7444 in morning for schedule).

▲National Gallery—Along with a hall featuring the work of top Irish painters, this has Ireland's best collection of European masters. It's impressive—although not nearly as extensive as those in London or Paris (free, Mon–Sat 9:30–17:30, Thu until 20:30, Sun 12:00–17:30, call for times of guided tours on weekends, Merrion Square West, tel. 01/661-5133, www.nationalgallery.ie).

▲▲Grafton Street—Once filled with noisy traffic, today Grafton Street is Dublin's liveliest pedestrian shopping mall. A five-minute stroll past street musicians takes you from Trinity College up to St. Stephen's Green (and makes you wonder why American merchants are so terrified of a car-free street). Walking by a buxom statue of "sweet" Molly Malone (known by locals as "the tart with the cart"), you'll soon pass two venerable department stores: the Irish Brown Thomas and the English Marks & Spencer. An alley leads to the Powerscourt Townhouse Shopping Centre, which tastefully fills a converted Georgian mansion. The huge, glass-covered St. Stephen's Green Shopping Centre and the peaceful and green Green itself mark the top of Grafton Street.

▲St. Stephen's Green—This city park, originally a medieval commons, was enclosed in 1664 and gradually surrounded with fine Georgian buildings. Today, it provides 22 acres of grassy refuge for Dubliners. On a sunny afternoon, it's a wonderful world apart from the big city.

▲▲Number Twenty-Nine Georgian House—The carefully restored house at Number 29 Lower Fitzwilliam Street gives an intimate glimpse of middle-class Georgian life—which seems pretty high-class. From the sidewalk, descend the stairs to the basement-level entrance (at the corner of Lower Fitzwilliam and Lower Mount Streets). Start with an interesting 12-minute video (you're welcome to bring in a cup of coffee from the café) before joining your guide, who takes you on a fascinating 35-minute walk through this 1790 Dublin home (€3.50, Tue–Sat 10:00–17:00, Sun 14:00–17:00, closed Mon, tel. 01/702-6165).

▲**Merrion Square**—Laid out in 1762, this square is ringed by elegant Georgian houses decorated with fine doors—a Dublin trademark—with elegant knobs and knockers. The park, once the exclusive domain of the residents, is now a delightful public escape. More inviting than St. Stephen's Green, it's ideal for a picnic. If you want to know what "snogging" is, walk through the park on a sunny day, when it's full of smooching lovers. Oscar Wilde, lounging wittily on the corner nearest the town center and surrounded by his clever quotes, provides a fun photo op.

▲**Temple Bar**—This was a Georgian center of craftsmen and merchants. As it fell on hard times in the 19th century, the lower rents attracted students and artists, giving the neighborhood a bohemian flair. With recent government tax incentives and lots of development money, the Temple Bar district has become a thriving cultural (and beer-drinking) hotspot. Be aware that a pint of beer here costs €1 more here than at less glitzy pubs just a couple blocks away (north of the river or south of Dame Street). Today this much-promoted center of trendy shops, cafés, theaters, galleries, pubs with live music, and restaurants feels like the heart of the city. Dublin's "Left Bank"—which, like Paris', is on the south shore of the river—fills the cobbled streets between Dame Street and the River Liffey. ("Bar" means a walkway along the river.) The central **Meeting House Square** (just off Essex Street) hosts free street theater, as well as a lively organic-produce market and a book market (Sat 10:00–18:00). The square is surrounded by interesting cultural centers.

For a listing of events and galleries, visit the **Temple Bar Properties** office and ask for their free annual TASCQ Guide (18 Eustace Street, www.templebar.ie). Rather than follow particular pub or restaurant recommendations (mine are below, under "Eating"), venture down a few side lanes off the main drag to see what looks good.

The pedestrian-only **Ha' Penny Bridge,** named for the halfpence toll people used to pay to cross it, leads from Temple Bar over the River Liffey to the opposite bank and more sights.

North of the River Liffey
▲▲**O'Connell Bridge**—This bridge spans the River Liffey, which has historically divided the wealthy, cultivated south side from the poorer, cruder north side. While there's plenty of culture north of the river, even today "the north" is considered rougher and less safe.

From the bridge, look upriver (west) as far upstream as you can see. The big concrete building on the left in the distance houses the city planning commission. Maddening to locals, this eyesore is in charge of making sure new buildings in the city are built in good taste. It squats on the still-buried precious artifacts of the first Viking settlement established in Dublin in the ninth century.

North Dublin

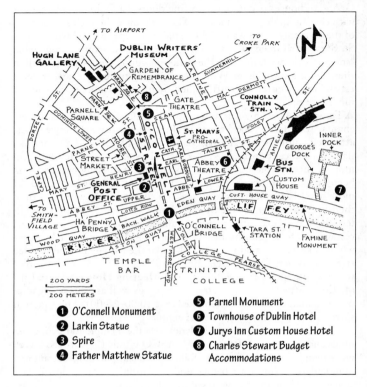

1 O'Connell Monument
2 Larkin Statue
3 Spire
4 Father Matthew Statue
5 Parnell Monument
6 Townhouse of Dublin Hotel
7 Jurys Inn Custom House Hotel
8 Charles Stewart Budget Accommodations

Across the river stands the Four Courts, today's Supreme Court build-ing, shelled and burned in 1922 during the tragic civil war that followed Irish independence. Irreplaceable birth records were lost as the national archives office burned, making it challenging for those with Irish roots to trace their ancestry today. The closest bridge upstream—the elegant iron Ha' Penny Bridge—leads left into the Temple Bar nightlife district. Just beyond that old-fashioned 19th-century bridge is Dublin's pedestrian Millennium Bridge, inaugurated in 2000. (Note that buses leave from O'Connell Bridge—specif-ically Aston Quay—for the Guinness Brewery and the Kilmainham Jail.)

Turn 180 degrees and look downstream to see the tall Liberty Hall union headquarters—for now, the tallest building in the Republic (16 stories tall, some say in honor of the 1916 Easter Uprising)—and lots of cranes. Booming Dublin is developing downstream. The Irish (forever clever tax fiddlers) have subsidized and revitalized this formerly dreary quarter with great success. A short walk downstream along the north bank leads to a powerful series of modern statues memorializing the Potato Famine of 1845–1849.

▲▲O'Connell Street Stroll—Dublin's grandest street leads from O'Connell Bridge through the heart of north Dublin. From the 1740s, it has been a 45-yard-wide promenade. Ever since the first O'Connell Bridge connected it to the Trinity side of town in 1794, it's been Dublin's main drag. (But it was only named O'Connell after independence was won in 1922.) These days, construction reigns as the city makes the street more pedestrian-friendly. The street, though lined with fast-food and souvenir shops, echoes with history. Take the following stroll:

Statues and monuments line O'Connell Street, celebrating great figures in Ireland's fight for independence. At the base of the street stands **Daniel O'Connell** (1775–1847), known as "the Liberator" for founding the Catholic Association and demanding Irish Catholic rights in the British Parliament.

Looking a block east down Abbey Street, you can see the famous **Abbey Theatre**—rebuilt after a fire into a nondescript, modern building. It's still the much-loved home of the Irish National Theatre.

The statue of **James Larkin** honors the founder of the Irish Transport Workers' Union. The one monument that didn't wave an Irish flag—a tall column crowned by a statue of the British hero of Trafalgar, Admiral Nelson—was blown up in 1966...the IRA's contribution to the local celebration of the Easter Rising's 50th anniversary. This spot is now occupied by the 300-foot-tall, stainless steel Millennium Spire that was finally completed in 2003. Dubious Dubliners have nicknamed it "the stiletto in the ghetto."

The **General Post Office** is not just any P.O. It was from here that Patrick Pearse read the Proclamation of Irish Independence in 1916 and kicked off the Easter Rising. The G.P.O. building itself—a kind of Irish Alamo—was the rebel headquarters and scene of a five-day bloody siege that followed the proclamation. Its pillars remain pockmarked with bullet holes. Step inside and trace the battle by studying the well-described cycle of 10 paintings that circle the main hall (open for business and sightseers Mon–Sat 8:00–20:00, Sun 10:00–18:00).

The busy **Moore Street Market** is nearby (Mon–Sat 8:00–18:00, closed Sun). To get there, detour left two blocks after the Post Office down people-filled Henry Street, then wander to the right into the market. Many of its merchants have staffed the same stall for 30 years. Start a conversation. It's a great work-a-day scene. You'll see lots of mums with strollers—a reminder that Ireland is Europe's youngest country, with about 40 percent of the population under the age of 25. An immense glass canopy is planned to eventually cover the street market.

Back on O'Connell Street, cross to the meridian and continue your walk. The lampposts display the colorful three-castle city seal. The Latin motto below the seal states, "Happy the city where citizens obey." Flames rise from the castles, symbolizing the citizens' zeal to defend Dublin.

St. Mary's Pro-Cathedral, a block east of O'Connell down Cathedral Street, is Dublin's leading Catholic church. But, curiously, it's not a cathedral, even though the pope declared Christ Church one in the 12th century—and later, St. Patrick's. (Stubbornly, the Vatican has chosen to ignore the fact that Christ Church and St. Patrick's haven't been Catholic for centuries.) Completed in 1821, it's done in the style of a Greek temple.

Continuing up O'Connell Street, you'll find a statue of **Father Matthew,** a leader of the temperance movement of the 1830s who, some historians claim, was responsible for enough Irish peasants staying sober to enable Daniel O'Connell to organize them into a political force. (Perhaps understanding this dynamic, the U.S.S.R. was careful to keep the price of vodka affordable.) The fancy Gresham Hotel is a good place for an elegant tea or beer.

Charles Stewart Parnell stands boldly at the top of O'Connell Street. The names of the four ancient provinces of Ireland and all 32 Irish counties (North *and* South, since this was erected before Independence) ring the monument, honoring the member of Parliament who nearly won Home Rule for Ireland in the late 1800s. (A sex scandal cost him the support of the Church, which let the air out of any chance for a free Ireland.)

Continue straight up Parnell Square East. At the Gate Theatre (on the left), Orson Welles and James Mason got their professional acting debuts.

The Garden of Remembrance (past Gate Theater, on left) honors the victims of the 1916 Rising. The park was dedicated in 1966 on the 50th anniversary of the uprising that ultimately led to Irish independence. The bottom of the cross-shaped pool is a mosaic of Celtic weapons, symbolic of how the early Irish would proclaim peace by throwing their weapons into a lake or river. The Irish flag flies above the park: green for Catholics, orange for Protestants, and white for the hope that they can live together in peace. Across the street...

The **Dublin Writers' Museum** fills a splendidly restored Georgian mansion. No other country so small has produced such a wealth of literature. As interesting to fans of Irish literature as it is boring to those who aren't, this three-room museum features the lives and works of Dublin's great writers (€6, Mon–Sat 10:00–17:00, Sun 11:00–17:00, June–Aug Mon–Fri until 18:00, helpful audioguide available, 18 Parnell Square North, tel. 01/872-2077). With hometown wits such as Swift, Yeats, Joyce, and Shaw, there is a checklist of residences and memorials to see. Aficionados of James Joyce's work may want to hike 400 yards east to see the James Joyce Centre at 35 North Great George's Street (more Joyce memorabilia is in Dun Laoghaire's James Joyce Museum).

Hugh Lane Gallery (next door to the Dublin Writers' Museum) is a fine little gallery in a grand neoclassical building with a bite-sized selection of Pre-Raphaelite, French Impressionist, and 19th- and 20th-century Irish paintings (free, Tue–Thu 9:30–18:00, Fri–Sat 9:30–17:00, Sun 11:00–17:00, closed Mon, tel. 01/874-1903). Sir Hugh went down on the *Lusitania* in 1915; due to an unclear will, his collection is shared by this gallery and the National Gallery in London.

Tucked in the back of the gallery is the **Francis Bacon Studio,** reconstructed here in its original (messy) state from its London location at the time of the artist's death in 1992. Born in Dublin and inspired by Picasso, Bacon reflected his belief that "chaos breeds energy" in his shocking paintings. This compact space contains touch-screen terminals, display cases of personal items, and a few unfinished works. The 10-minute film interview of Bacon may fascinate like-minded viewers...and disquiet others (€7, same hours as rest of gallery).

Your walk is over. Here on the north end of town, it's convenient to visit the Gaelic Athletic Association Museum at Croke Park (described below, a 30-min walk or short taxi ride away). Otherwise, hop on your skateboard and return to the river.

Dublin's Smithfield Village

Huge investments may make Smithfield Village—until recently a run-down industrial area—the next Temple Bar. It's worth a look for "Cobblestores" (a redeveloped Duck Lane lined with fancy crafts and gift shops), the Old Jameson Distillery whiskey tour, and a chimney observatory with big Dublin views. The sights are clustered close together, two blocks north of the river behind the Four Courts—the Supreme Court building.

The Old Jameson Distillery—Whiskey fans enjoy visiting the old distillery. You get a 10-minute video, 20-minute tour, and a free shot in the pub. Unfortunately, the "distillery" feels fake and put together for tourists. The Bushmills tour in Northern Ireland (in a working factory, see Antrim Coast chapter) and the Midleton tour near Cork (in the huge, original factory, see South Ireland chapter) are better experiences. If you do take this tour, volunteer energetically when offered the chance to take the "whiskey taste test" at the end (€7, daily 9:00–18:00, last tour at 17:30, Bow Street, tel. 01/807-2355).

The Chimney—Built in 1895 for the distillery, the chimney is now an observatory. Ride the elevator 175 feet up for a Dublin panorama not quite as exciting as the view from the Guinness Brewery's Gravity Bar (overpriced at €6, Mon–Fri 10:00–17:00, Sat–Sun 11:00–17:00, tel. 01/817-3838).

Outer Dublin

The jail and the Guinness Brewery are the main sights outside of the old center. Combine them in one visit.

▲▲▲**Kilmainham Gaol (Jail)**—Opened in 1796 as the Dublin County Jail and a debtors' prison and considered a model in its day, this jail was used frequently as a political prison by the British. Many of those who fought for Irish independence were held or executed here, including leaders of the rebellions of 1798, 1803, 1848, 1867, and 1916. National heroes Robert Emmett and Charles Stewart Parnell each did time here. The last prisoner to be held here was Eamon de Valera (later president of Ireland). He was released on July 16, 1924, the day Kilmainham was finally shut down. The buildings, virtually in ruins, were restored in the 1960s. Today, it's a shrine to the Nathan Hales of Ireland.

Start your visit with a guided tour (1 hr, 2/hr, includes 25 min in prison chapel for a rebellion-packed video, spend waiting time in museum). It's touching to tour the cells and places of execution while hearing tales of terrible colonialism and heroic patriotism alongside Irish schoolkids who know these names well. The museum is an excellent exhibit on Victorian prison life and Ireland's fight for independence. Don't miss the museum's dimly-lit Last Words 1916 hall upstairs, which displays the stirring last letters patriots sent to loved ones hours before facing the firing squad (€5, daily April–Sept 9:30–18:00, Oct–March 9:30–17:00, last entry 1 hr before closing; €5 taxi, bus #51b, #78a, or #79 from Aston Quay or Guinness, tel. 01/453-5984). I'd taxi to the jail and then catch the bus from there to Guinness (leaving the prison, take three rights, crossing no streets, to the bus stop and hop bus #51b or #78a). Another option is taking the City Sightseeing/Guide Friday hop-on, hop-off bus, which stops at both the jail and the brewery.

▲Guinness Brewery—A visit to the Guinness Brewery is, for many, a pilgrimage. Arthur Guinness began brewing the famous stout here in 1759. By 1868, it was the biggest brewery in the world. Today the sprawling brewery fills several city blocks. Around the world, Guinness brews more than 10 million pints a day. The home of Ireland's national beer welcomes visitors, for a price, with a sprawling new museum (but there are no tours of the actual working brewery). The museum fills the old fermentation plant, used from 1902 through 1988, vacated, and then opened in 2000 as a huge, shrine-like place. Step into the middle of the ground floor and look up. A tall beer-glass–shaped glass atrium—14 million pints big—leads past four floors of exhibitions and cafés to the skylight. Atop the building, the Gravity Bar provides visitors with a commanding 360-degree view of Dublin—with vistas all the way to the sea—and a free beer. The actual exhibit makes brewing seem more grandiose than it is and treats Arthur like the god of human happiness. Highlights are the cooperage (with old film clips showing the master wood-keg makers plying their now-extinct trade), a display of the brewery's clever ads, and the Gravity Bar, which really is spectacular (€13.50, includes a €4 pint, daily 9:30–17:00, enter on Market Street, bus #78a from Aston Quay near O'Connell Bridge, or bus #123 from Dame Street and O'Connell Street, tel. 01/408-4800). Both hop-on, hop-off bus tours stop here.

▲**Gaelic Athletic Association Museum**—The GAA was founded in 1884 as an expression of an Irish cultural awakening. It was created to foster the development of Gaelic sports, specifically Irish football and hurling, and to ban English sports such as cricket and rugby—but it played an important part in the fight for independence. This museum, at the newly expanded 97,000-seat Croke Park Stadium, offers a high-tech, interactive introduction to Ireland's favorite games. Relive the greatest moments in hurling and Irish-football history. Then get involved. Pick up a stick and try hurling, kick a football, and test your speed and balance. A 15-minute film clarifies the connection between sports and Irish politics (€5, Mon–Sat 9:30–17:00, Sun 12:00–17:00; on game Sundays, museum is open 12:00–17:00 to "new stand" ticket-holders only, as other sections of stands are blocked from museum entry; under the new stand at Croke Park, from O'Connell Street walk 20 min or catch bus #3, #11, #16, #16a, or #123; tel. 01/855-8176).

Hurling or Irish Football at Croke Park—Actually seeing a match here, surrounded by incredibly spirited Irish fans, is a fun experience. Hurling is like airborne hockey with no injury timeouts, and Irish football is a rugged form of soccer. Matches are held on most Sunday afternoons from May to September. Tickets (€15–35) are available at the stadium except during championships (www.gaa.ie).

Greyhound Racing—For an interesting lowbrow look at local life, consider going to the dog races and doing a little gambling (€8, generally Wed, Thu, and Sat at 20:00, Shelbourne Park, tel. 01/668-3502). Greyhounds race on the other days at Harold's Cross Racetrack (Mon, Tue, and Fri at 20:00, tel. 01/497-1081).

SHOPPING

Shops are open roughly Monday to Saturday from 9:00 to 18:00 and until 20:00 on Thursday. They have shorter hours on Sunday (if they're open at all). The best shopping area is Grafton, with its neighboring streets and arcades (such as the fun Great George's Arcade between Great George's and Drury Streets), and nearby shopping centers (Powerscourt and St. Stephen's Green). For antiques, try Francis Street.

For a street market, consider Mother Redcaps (all day Fri–Sun, bric-a-brac, antiques, crafts, Back Lane, Christ Church). For produce, noise, and color, visit Moore Street (Mon–Sat 8:00–18:00, near General Post Office). For raw fish, get a whiff of Michan Street (Tue–Sat 7:00–15:00, behind Four Courts building).

On Saturdays at Temple Bar's Meeting House Square, it's food in the morning (from 9:00) and books in the afternoon (until 18:00). Temple Bar is worth a browse any day for its art, jewelry, new-age paraphernalia, books, music, and gift shops.

ENTERTAINMENT AND THEATER

Ireland has produced some of the finest writers in both English and Irish, and Dublin houses some of Europe's finest theaters. While Handel's *Messiah* was first performed in Dublin (1742), these days Dublin is famous for its rock bands (U2, Thin Lizzie, Sinead O'Connor, and Live Aid founder Bob Geldof's band the Boomtown Rats all got started here).

Abbey Theatre is Ireland's national theater, founded by W. B. Yeats in 1904 to preserve Irish culture during British rule (26 Lower Abbey Street, tel. 01/878-7222, www.abbeytheatre.ie). **Gate Theatre** does foreign plays as well as Irish classics (Cavendish Row, tel. 01/874-4045, www.gate-theatre.ie). **Point Theatre,** once a railway terminus, is now the country's top live-music venue (North Wall Quay, tel. 01/836-3633, www.thepoint.ie). At the **National Concert Hall,** the National Symphony Orchestra performs most Friday evenings (Earlsfort Terrace, off St. Stephen's Green, tickets €11–30, tel. 01/475-1666, www.nch.ie). Street theater takes the stage in Temple Bar on summer evenings.

Pub Action: Folk music fills the pubs and street entertainers are everywhere. For the latest on live theater, music, cultural happenings, restaurant reviews, pubs, and current museum hours, pick up a copy of the twice-monthly *In Dublin* (€2.50, any newsstand).

The Temple Bar area thrives with music—traditional, jazz, and pop. It really is *the* comfortable and fun place for tourists and locals (who come here to watch the tourists). **Gogarty's Pub** (corner of Fleet and Anglesea) has top-notch sessions upstairs nightly from 21:00. Use this as a kick-off for your Temple Bar evening fun.

A 10-minute hike up the river west of Temple Bar takes you to a twosome with a local and less touristy ambience. **The Brazen Head,** famous as Dublin's oldest pub, is a hit for an early dinner and late live music (nightly from 21:30), with smoky, atmospheric rooms and a court-yard made to order for balmy evenings (on Bridge Street, tel. 01/677-9549). **O'Shea's Merchant Pub,** just across the street, is encrusted in memories and filled with locals taking a break from the grind. They have live traditional music nightly (the front half is a restaurant, the magic is in the back half—enter on Bridge Street).

Irish Music in nearby Dun Laoghaire

For an evening of pure Irish music, song, and dance, check out the **Comhaltas Ceoltoiri Eireann,** an association working to preserve this traditional slice of Irish culture. It got started when Elvis and company threatened to steal the musical heart of the new generation. Judging by the pop status of traditional Irish music these days, Comhaltas accomplished its mission. Their "Seisiun" evening is a stage show mixing traditional music, song, and dance (€10, July–Aug Mon–Thu at 21:00, followed by informal music session at 22:30). On Fridays all year long, they have a *ceilidh* (KAY-lee) where everyone does set dances. This style, the forerunner of square dancing, evolved from the French Quadrille dances of 200 years ago with two couples making up a "set" (€7 includes friendly pointers, 21:30–00:30). At 21:00 on Tuesdays and Wednesdays (free) and Saturdays (€3), there are informal sessions by the fireside. All musicians are welcome. Performances are held in Cuturlann na Eireann, near the Seapoint DART stop or a 20-minute walk from Dun Laoghaire, at 32 Belgrave Square, Monkstown (tel. 01/280-0295, www.comhaltas .com). Their bar is free and often filled with music.

SLEEPING

Near Christ Church

These hotels face Christ Church Cathedral, a five-minute walk from the best evening scene at Temple Bar and 10 minutes from the sightseeing center (Trinity College and Grafton Street). The cheap hostels in this neighborhood have some double rooms. Full Irish breakfasts, which cost €9 at the hotels, are half the price at the many small cafés nearby; consider Pilgrims Café (at the corner of Fishamble and Lord Edward Street between Kinlay House and Harding Hotel) or Applewood Café (at 1b Werburgh Street, next to Burdoch's Fish & Chips).

$$ **Harding Hotel** is a hardwood, 21st-century, Viking-style place with 53 institutional-yet-hotelesque rooms. The rooms are simpler than Jurys (below), but they're also more intimate (Sb-€62, Db-€97, Tb-€121, tell them Rick sent you and get 10 percent off, breakfast-€10, Internet access, Copper Alley, across street from Christ Church, tel. 01/679-6500, fax 01/679-6504, www.hardinghotel.ie, harding.hotel@usit.ie).

$$ **Jurys Christ Church Inn** (like its sisters across town, in Galway, and in Belfast) is central and offers business-class comfort in all of its 182 identical rooms. This no-nonsense, modern, American-style hotel chain has a winning keep-it-simple-and-affordable formula. If ye olde is getting old (and you don't mind big tour groups), there's no better value in town. All rooms cost the same: €108 (or €112 Fri–Sat) for one, two, or three adults or two adults and two kids (breakfast extra). Each room has a modern bathroom, direct-dial telephone, and TV. Two floors are strictly non-smoking. Request a room far from the noisy elevator (book long in advance for weekends, parking-€12/day, Christ Church Place, tel. 01/454-0000, fax 01/454-0012, U.S. tel. 800/423-6953, www.jurysdoyle.com, info@jurys doyle.com). Another Jurys is near the Connolly train station (listed below).

$ **Kinlay House,** around the corner from Harding Hotel, is the backpackers' equivalent—definitely the place to go for cheap beds in a central location and an all-ages-welcome atmosphere. This huge, red-brick, 19th-century Victorian building has 149 metal, prison-style beds in spartan, smoke-free rooms. There are singles, doubles, and four- to six-bed coed dorms (good for families), as well as a few giant dorms. It

SLEEP CODE

(€1 = about $1.10, country code: 353, area code: 01)
Sleep Code: **S** = Single, **D** = Double/Twin, **T** = Triple, **Q** = Quad, **b** = bathroom, **s** = shower only, **no CC** = Credit Cards not accepted. Breakfast is included and credit cards are accepted unless otherwise noted. To locate hotels, see map on page 691.

To help you easily sort through these listings, I've divided the rooms into three categories, based on the price for a standard double room with bath:

   $$$ **Higher Priced**—Most rooms €130 or more.
    $$ **Moderately Priced**—Most rooms between €65–130.
     $ **Lower Priced**—Most rooms €65 or less.

Dublin is popular and rooms can be tight. Book ahead for weekends any time of year, particularly in summer and during rugby weekends. Prices are often discounted on weeknights (Mon–Thu) and from November through February.

Big and practical places (both cheap and moderate) are most central at Christ Church on the edge of Temple Bar. For classy, older Dublin accommodations, you'll pay more and stay a bit farther out (east of St. Stephen's Green).

For a small-town escape with the best budget values, take the convenient DART train (at least 3/hr, 20 min) to nearby Dun Laoghaire (see page 694).

fills up most days. Call well in advance, especially for singles, doubles, and summer weekends (S-€42–50, D-€52–62, Db-€56–66, dorm beds-€18-26, includes continental breakfast, kitchen access, launderette-€7.50, Internet access-€4/hr, left luggage, travel desk, TV lounge, small lockers, lots of stairs, Christ Church, 2–12 Lord Edward Street, tel. 01/679-6644, fax 01/679-7437, www.kinlayhouse.ie, kinlay.dublin@usit.ie).

$ Four Courts Hostel is a new, 236-bed hostel beautifully located immediately across the river from the Four Courts, a five-minute walk from Christ Church and Temple Bar. It's bare and institutional (as hostels are) but expansive and well-run, with a focus on security and efficiency (dorm beds from €17–20, bunk D-€60, bunk Db-€66, includes small breakfast, girls' floor and boys' floor, elevator, no smoking, Internet access, game room, laundry service, some parking, left luggage room, 15 Merchant's Quay, tel. 01/672-5839, fax 01/672-5862, www.fourcourtshostel.com, info@four courtshostel.com, bus #748 from airport, #90 from train or bus station).

Dublin Hotels

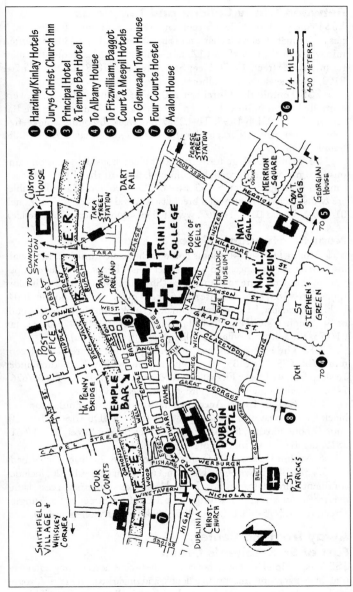

1. Harding/Kinlay Hotels
2. Jurys Christ Church Inn
3. Principal Hotel & Temple Bar Hotel
4. To Albany House
5. To Fitzwilliam, Baggot Court & Mespil Hotels
6. To Glenveagh Town House
7. Four Courts Hostel
8. Avalon House

1/4 MILE
400 METERS

Between Trinity College and Temple Bar

$$$ Principal Hotel Fleet Street rents 70 decent rooms. For its size, it has an intimate feel with character (Sb-€106–127, Db-€130–169, often mid-week deals, breakfast-€12, non-smoking rooms, request a quiet room off the street, 19–20 Fleet Street, tel. 01/670-8122, fax 01/670-8103, www.bewleysprincipalhotel.com).

$$$ Temple Bar Hotel is a 130-room business-class place, very centrally located midway between Trinity College and the Temple Bar action (Sb-€150, Db-€195, Tb-€255, mid-week discounts, smoke-free rooms, Fleet Street, Temple Bar, tel. 01/677-3333, fax 01/677-3088, templeb@iol.ie).

$$ Trinity College turns its 800 student-housing rooms on campus into no-frills, affordable accommodations in the city center each summer (mid-June–Sept, S-€53, Sb-€64, D-€106, Db-€124, all doubles are twins, includes continental breakfast, cooked breakfast-€3 extra, tel. 01/608-1177, fax 01/671-1267, www.tcd.ie/accom, reservations@tcd.ie).

Near St. Stephen's Green

$$$ Albany House's 40 rooms come with classic furniture, high ceilings, Georgian elegance, and some street noise. Request the huge "superior" rooms, which are the same price (Sb-€100, Db-€160, €120 in slow times, Tb-€185, Una promises 10 percent off with this book in 2004, includes breakfast, back rooms are quieter, smoke-free, just 1 block south of St. Stephen's Green at 84 Harcourt Street, tel. 01/475-1092, fax 01/475-1093, http://indigo.ie/~albany, albany@indigo.ie).

$$$ The Fitzwilliam has an inviting lounge and rents 13 decent rooms (Sb-€75, Db-€135, 10 percent discount with cash, children under 16 sleep free, 41 Upper Fitzwilliam Street, tel. 01/662-5155, fax 01/676-7488, fitzwilliamguesthouse@eircom.net, Declan Carney).

$$$ Baggot Court Accommodations rents 11 similar rooms a block farther away and without a lounge (Sb-€90, Db-€150, Tb-€210, entirely non-smoking, free parking, 92 Lower Baggot Street, tel. 01/661-2819, fax 01/661-0253, baggot@indigo.ie).

$ Avalon House, near Grafton Street, rents 281 backpacker beds (S-€32, Sb-€35, D/twin-€56, Db/twin-€60, dorm beds-€15–20, includes continental breakfast, elevator, Ireland bus tickets, Internet access, launderette across street, a few minutes off Grafton Street at 55 Aungier Street, tel. 01/475-0001, fax 01/475-0303, www.avalon-house.ie).

Away from the Center, East of St. Stephen's Green

$$$ Mespil Hotel is a huge, modern, business-class hotel renting 256 identical three-star rooms (most with a double and single bed, phone, TV, voicemail, and modem hookup) at a good price with all the comforts. This is a cut above Jurys Inn, for a little more money (Sb, Db, or Tb-€150, breakfast-

€13, elevator, 3 non-smoking floors, apartments for week-long stays, 10-min walk southeast of St. Stephen's Green or bus #10, Mespil Road, tel. 01/667-1222, fax 01/667-1244, www.leehotels.com, mespil@leehotels.com).

$$ Glenveagh Town House rents 13 rooms—Victorian upstairs and modern downstairs—southeast of the city center, a 15-minute walk from Trinity College (Sb-€75, Db-€100–130, less in slow times, includes breakfast, car park, 31 Northumberland Road, tel. 01/668-4612, fax 01/668-4559, glenveagh@eircom.net). Catch bus #5, #6, #7, #8, or #45 down Northumberland Road into downtown Dublin (every 10 min).

Near Connolly Train Station
For locations, see map on page 682.

$$ Townhouse of Dublin, with 80 small, stylish rooms (some with pleasant views into a central garden courtyard), hides behind a brick Georgian facade one block north of the Customs House (Sb-€70, Db-€115, Tb-€130, small first-come, first-serve parking lot, 47–48 Lower Gardiner Street, tel. 01/878-8808, fax 01/878-8787, www.townhouseofdublin.com, info@townhouse.com)

$$ Jurys Inn Custom House, on Custom House Quay, offers the same value as the Jurys at Christ Church. Bigger (with 234 rooms) and not quite as well-located (in a boring neighborhood, a 10-min riverside hike from O'Connell Bridge), this Jurys is more likely to have rooms available (Db-€108, or €112 Fri–Sat, tel. 01/607-5000, fax 01/829-0400, U.S. tel. 800/423-6953, www.jurysdoyle.com, info@jurysdoyle.com).

$$ Charles Stewart Budget Accommodations is a big, basic place offering lots of forgettable rooms, many long and narrow with head-to-toe twins, in a great location for a good price (S-€32, Sb-€64, D-€76, Db-€89, Tb-€121, Qb-€140, frequent mid-week discounts, includes cooked breakfast, just beyond top end of O'Connell Street at 5–6 Parnell Square, tel. 01/878-0350, fax 01/878-1387, cstuart@iol.ie).

In nearby Dun Laoghaire
(€1 = about $1.10, country code: 353, area code: 01)
Dun Laoghaire (DUN-leary) is seven miles south of Dublin. This beach resort, with the ferry terminal for Wales and easy connections to downtown Dublin, is a great small-town base for the big city.

While buses run between Dublin and Dun Laoghaire, the **DART** commuter train is much faster (6/hr in peak times, at least 3/hr otherwise, 20 min, runs Mon–Sat about 6:30–23:15, Sun from 9:00, €1.70 one-way, €3 round-trips are good same day only, Eurail valid but uses day of flexipass; for a longer stay, consider the €15 Short Hop 3-day bus and rail ticket covering DART and Dublin buses). If you're coming from Dublin, catch a DART train marked "Bray" and get off at the Sandy Cove or Dun Laoghaire stop, depending on which B&B you choose; if

Dun Laoghaire

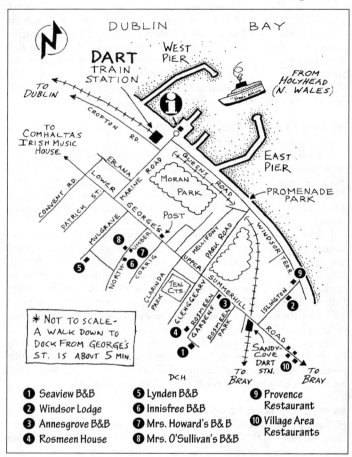

DUBLIN BAY

DART TRAIN STATION

TO DUBLIN

WEST PIER

FROM HOLYHEAD (N. WALES)

TO COMHALTAS IRISH MUSIC HOUSE

CROFTON RD.

EAST PIER

PROMENADE PARK

EBLANA

CONVENT RD.

LOWER

MARINE ROAD

QUEENS ROAD

MORAN PARK

PATRICK ST.

GEORGE'S

POST

MELLIFONT

PARK ROAD

WINDSOR TERR.

MULGRAVE

TIMBER

UPPER

8

NORTH

7

5

6

CORRIG

CLARINDA PARK

TEN. CTS

GLENAGEARY

SUMMERHILL

ISLINGTON

9

ROSMEEN GARDENS

3

2

4

ROSMEEN PARK

1

ROAD

SANDYCOVE DART STN.

DCH

TO BRAY

10

TO BRAY

*NOT TO SCALE — A WALK DOWN TO DOCK FROM GEORGE'S ST. IS ABOUT 5 MIN.

1 Seaview B&B
2 Windsor Lodge
3 Annesgrove B&B
4 Rosmeen House
5 Lynden B&B
6 Innisfree B&B
7 Mrs. Howard's B&B
8 Mrs. O'Sullivan's B&B
9 Provence Restaurant
10 Village Area Restaurants

you're leaving Dun Laoghaire, catch a train marked "Howth" to get to Dublin—get off at the central Tara Street station.

The **taxi** fare from Dun Laoghaire to central Dublin is about €25, to the airport about €35. Try ABC Taxi service (tel. 01/285-5444). With easy free parking and DART access into Dublin, this area is ideal for those with **cars** (which cost €19 a day to park in Dublin).

The **Dun Laoghaire TI** is in the ferry terminal (Mon–Sat 10:00–18:00 year-round, closed Sun). Comhaltas Ceoltoiri Eireann, an association that preserves Irish **folk music**, offers lively shows in Dun Laoghaire (see "Irish Music in nearby Dun Laoghaire," above). The Washerette **laundry** is located in the village of Sandycove (Mon–Sat 8:30–18:00, closed Sun, self- and full-service, 2 Glasthule, across from church). The Net House Café provides a fast **Internet** connection 24 hours a day (28 Upper George's Street, €2.50/30 min). For **restaurants**, see below.

Hike out to the lighthouse at the end of the interesting East Pier. The Dun Laoghaire harbor was strategic enough to merit a line of Martello Towers (built to defend against an expected Napoleonic invasion). By the mid-19th century, the huge breakwaters—reaching like two muscular arms into the Irish Sea—were completed, protecting a huge harbor. Ships sailed regularly from here to Wales (60 miles away), and the first train line in Ireland connected the terminal with Dublin. While still a busy transportation hub, today the nearly mile-long breakwaters are also popular with strollers, bikers, birders, and fishermen.

Near Sandycove DART Station

These listings are within several blocks of the Sandycove DART station and a seven-minute walk to the Dun Laoghaire DART station/ferry landing.

$ Seaview B&B, a modern house run by Mrs. Kane, has three big, cheery rooms and a welcoming guests' lounge. While a few blocks farther out than the others, it's worth the walk for its bright and friendly feeling (Db-€70 through 2004 with this book, no CC, strictly smoke-free, just above Rosmeen Gardens at 2 Granite Hall, tel. & fax 01/280-9105, seaviewbedandbreakfast@hotmail.com).

$ Windsor Lodge rents four fresh, cheery rooms on a quiet street a block off the harbor and a block from the DART station (Db-€60–72, family deals, no CC, non-smoking, 3 Islington Avenue, Sandycove, tel. & fax 01/284-6952, winlodge@eircom.net, Mary O'Farrell).

$ Annesgrove B&B has four tidy rooms decorated in beige and brown (S-€45, D-€60, Db-€70, Tb-€90, no CC, parking, close to park and beach, 28 Rosmeen Gardens, tel. 01/280-9801, Anne D'Alton).

$ Rosmeen House is a similar grandfather-clock kind of place renting four smoke-free rooms (S-€40, Db-€66, no CC, 13 Rosmeen Gardens, tel. 01/280-7613, Joan Murphy).

Near Dun Laoghaire DART Station

$ Lynden B&B, with a classy 150-year-old interior hiding behind a somber front, rents four big rooms (S-€40, Sb-€45, D-€52, Db-€62, 10 percent discount with this book, no CC, past Mulgrave Street to 2 Mulgrave Terrace, tel. 01/280-6404, lynden@iol.ie, Maria Gavin).

$ Innisfree B&B has a fine lounge and six big, bright, and comfy rooms (D-€48, Db-€56, 10 percent discount with this book, from George Street hike up the plain but quiet Northumberland Avenue to #31, tel. 01/280-5598, fax 01/280-3093, inismyth@eircom.net, Brendan and Mary Smyth).

On the same street, you'll find two places renting four big, well-worn rooms each: **$ Mrs. Howard's B&B** (S-€35, Sb-€40, D-€54, Db-€60, no CC, TV lounge, 36 Northumberland Avenue, tel. 01/280-3262, corahoward2003@yahoo.co.uk) and **$ Mrs. O'Sullivan's Duncree B&B** (D-€54, Db-€60, no CC, family room, non-smoking, 16 Northumberland Avenue, tel. 01/280-6118).

EATING

As Dublin does its boom-time jig, fine and creative eateries are popping up all over town. While you can get decent pub grub for €12 on just about any corner, consider saving pub grub for the countryside. And there's no pressing reason to eat Irish in cosmopolitan Dublin. Dublin's good restaurants are packed from 20:00 on, especially on weekends. Eating early (18:00–19:00) saves time and money (as many better places offer an early-bird special).

Eating Quick and Easy around Grafton Street

Cornucopia is a small, earth-mama-with-class, proudly vegetarian, self-serve place two blocks off Grafton. It's friendly and youthful, with hearty €8 lunches and €9.50 dinner specials (Mon–Sat 8:30–20:00, Sun 12:00–19:00, 19 Wicklow Street, tel. 01/677-7583).

O'Neill's offers dependable €9 carvery lunches in a labyrinth of a pub with a handy location across from the main TI (daily 12:00–20:00, Suffolk Street, tel. 01/679-3656).

Graham O'Sullivan Restaurant and Coffee Shop is a cheap, cheery cafeteria serving soup and sandwiches with a salad bar in unpretentious ambience (Mon–Fri 8:00–18:30, Sat 9:00–17:00, closed Sun, smoke-free upstairs, 12 Duke Street). Two pubs on the same street— **The Duke** and **Davy Burns**—serve pub lunches. (The nearby Cathach Rare Books shop at 10 Duke Street displays a rare edition of *Ulysses,* among other treasures, in its window).

Bewley's Café is an old-time local favorite offering light meals from €7 and full meals from €11. Sit on the ground floor among Harry Clarke windows and art deco lamps or upstairs in the bright atrium decorated by local art students (self-service Mon–Sat 7:30–23:00, Sun 8:00–20:00, 78 Grafton Street, tel. 01/635-5470). For a taste of witty Irish lunch theater, check out **Bewley's Café Theatre** upstairs, where you can catch an hour performance with soup and a sandwich for only €10 (daily at 13:00 during a play's run, doors open 12:45, booking info tel. 086-878-4001, best to call ahead to see what's on).

Wagamama Noodle Bar, like its popular sisters in London, is a pan-Asian slurpathon with great and healthy noodle and rice dishes (€10-14) served by walkie-talkie-toting waiters at long communal tables (daily

Dublin Restaurants

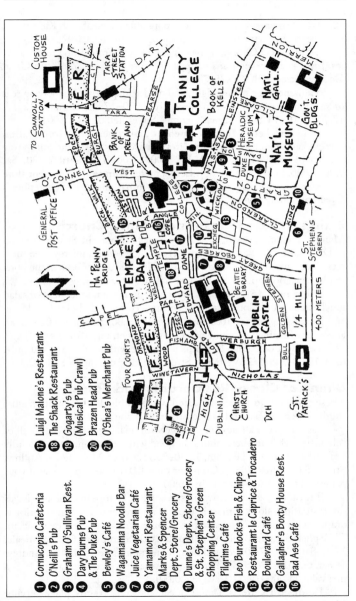

1. Cornucopia Cafeteria
2. O'Neill's Pub
3. Graham O'Sullivan Rest.
4. Davy Burns Pub & The Duke Pub
5. Bewley's Café
6. Wagamama Noodle Bar
7. Juice Vegetarian Café
8. Yamamori Restaurant
9. Marks & Spencer Dept. Store/Grocery
10. Dunne's Dept. Store/Grocery & St. Stephen's Green Shopping Center
11. Pilgrims Café
12. Leo Burdocks Fish & Chips
13. Restaurant le Caprice & Trocadero
14. Boulevard Café
15. Gallagher's Boxty House Rest.
16. Bad Ass Café
17. Luigi Malone's Restaurant
18. The Shack Restaurant
19. Gogarty's Pub (Musical Pub Crawl)
20. Brazen Head Pub
21. O'Shea's Merchant Pub

12:00–23:00, non-smoking, no reservations, often a line, South King Street, underneath St. Stephen's Green Shopping Centre, tel. 01/478-2152).

South Great Georges Street is lined with hardworking little eateries. **Juice** keeps vegetarians happy (daily 11:00–23:00, 73 South Great Georges Street, tel. 01/475-7856).

Yamamori is a plain, bright, and modern Japanese place serving seas of sushi and noodles (€9 lunches daily 12:30–17:30, dinners €12-17, 17:30–23:00, 71 South Great Georges Street, tel. 01/475-5001).

Supermarkets: Marks & Spencer department store (on Grafton Street) has a fancy grocery store in the basement with fine take-away sandwiches and salads (Mon–Fri 9:00–19:00, Thu until 21:00, Sat 9:00–19:00, Sun 11:00–18:30). Locals prefer **Dunne's** department store for its lower prices (same hours, grocery in basement, in St. Stephen's Green Shopping Centre).

Eating Fast and Cheap near Christ Church

Many of Dublin's **late-night grocery stores** (such as the Spar off the top of Dame Street on Parliament Street) sell cheap salads, microwaved meat pies, and made-to-order sandwiches. A €5 picnic dinner back at the hotel might be a good option after a busy day of sightseeing.

Pilgrims Café serves Irish breakfasts and pasta, sandwich, or salad lunches at a handy location between the recommended Harding Hotel and Kinlay House (€6–10, Mon–Fri 7:30–15:00, Sat–Sun 9:00–18:00, at corner of Fishamble and Lord Edward Street, tel. 01/677-0627).

Leo Burdocks Fish & Chips is popular with locals (take-out only, daily 12:00–24:00, 2 Werburgh Street, off Christ Church Square).

Dining at Classy Restaurants and Cafés

These three restaurants are located within a block of each other, just south of Temple Bar and Dame Street, near the main TI.

Le Caprice is a fine Italian place with relaxing ambience, a wall of celebrities-who-ate-here photos, a good wine selection, and a friendly staff (€19–26 meals, Tue–Sun 17:30–23:15, closed Mon, 12 St. Andrew Street, tel. 01/679-4050). Consider their €18 early-bird special if your plans will take you elsewhere by 20:00.

Trocadero, across the street, serves beefy European cuisine to locals interested in a slow, romantic meal. The dressy red-velvet interior is draped with photos of local actors. Come early or make a reservation. This place is a favorite with Dublin's theatergoers (€18-29 meals, Mon–Sat 17:00–24:00, closed Sun, non-smoking section, 3 St. Andrew Street, tel. 01/677-5545). The three-course early-bird special at €19 is a fine value (17:00–19:00, leave by 20:00).

Boulevard Café is a mod, local, likeable, trendy place serving Mediterranean cuisine, heavy on the Italian. They serve salads, pasta, and sandwiches for around €7, three-course lunch specials for €12.50

(Mon–Sat 12:00–16:00), and dinner plates for €13–22 (Mon–Sat 17:30–24:00; closed Sun, 27 Exchequer Street, smart to reserve for dinner, tel. 01/679-2131).

Eating at Temple Bar

Gallagher's Boxty House is touristy and traditional, a good, basic value with creaky floorboards and old Dublin ambience. Its specialty is boxties—the generally bland-tasting Irish potato pancake filled and rolled with various meats, veggies, and sauces. The "Gaelic Boxty" is liveliest (€14–16, also serves stews and corned beef, daily 12:00–23:30, non-smoking section, 20 Temple Bar, tel. 01/677-2762). Popular Gallagher's takes same-day reservations only; to reserve for dinner, stop by between 12:00 and 15:00.

Bad Ass Café is a grunge diner (where Sinead O'Connor was once a waitress) serving cowboy/Mex/veggie/pizzas to old and new hippies. No need to dress up (€7.50 lunch and €17.50 3-course dinner deals, kids' specials, daily 11:30–24:00, Crown Alley, just off Meeting House Square, tel. 01/671-2596).

Luigi Malone's, with its fun atmosphere and varied menu of pizza, ribs, pasta, sandwiches, and fajitas, is just the place to take your high-school date (€10–20, daily 12:00–23:00, corner of Cecila and Fownes Streets, tel. 01/679-2723).

The Shack, while a bit pricey and touristy, has a reputation for good quality and serves traditional Irish, chicken, seafood, and steak dishes (€16–26 entrées, daily 11:00–23:00, in the center of Temple Bar, 24 East Essex Street, tel. 01/679-0043).

Eating in nearby Dun Laoghaire

If staying in Dun Laoghaire, I'd definitely eat here and not in Dublin. Glasthule (called simply "the village" locally, just down the street from the Sandycove DART station) has a stunning array of fun, hardworking little restaurants.

Bistro Vino is the rage lately, with cozy, candlelit, Mediterranean ambience and great food (€12–21 meals, daily 17:00–23:00, nightly €19 early-bird special 17:00–19:00, seafood, pasta, arrive early or have a reservation, 56 Glasthule Road, tel. 01/280-6097).

Café du Journal serves pasta, pizza, or fish in a casual, bookshelved setting opposite the Eagle House pub (€11–15 dinners, daily 8:30–23:00, 57 Glasthule Road, tel. 01/236-5971).

The big **Eagle House** pub serves hearty €10 pub meals (until 21:00) in a wonderful but smoky atmosphere. This is a great local joint for a late drink. The nearby **Daniel's Restaurant and Wine Bar** is less atmospheric but also good (€15–20 meals, Tue–Sun 18:00–23:00, closed Mon, 34 Glasthule Road, tel. 01/284-1027).

Provence, a classy little French restaurant with occasional live piano music, faces the water and serves fine cuisine (€15–25 main courses, Tue–Sat 18:30–22:00, closed Sun–Mon, 1 Martello Terrace, directly down from Sandycove DART station, reservations smart, tel. 01/280-8788).

Walters Public House and Restaurant is a bright, modern place above a pub, offering good food to a dressy crowd (nightly 17:30–22:30, €13–22 meals, 68 Upper George's Street, tel. 01/280-7442).

George's Street, Dun Laoghaire's main drag three blocks inland, has plenty of eateries and pubs, many with live music. A good bet for families is the kid-friendly Bits and Pizza (daily 12:00–24:00, off George's Street at 15 Patrick Street, tel. 01/284-2411).

TRANSPORTATION CONNECTIONS

By bus to: Belfast (6/day, 3 hrs), Trim (10/day, 1 hr), Ennis (13/day, 4.5 hrs), Galway (13/day, 3.5 hrs), Limerick (13/day, 3.5 hrs), Tralee (7/day, 6 hrs), Dingle (4/day, 8 hrs, €23, transfer at Tralee). Bus info: tel. 01/836-6111.

By train from Heuston Station to: Tralee (6/day, 4 hrs, talking timetable tel. 01/805-4266), Ennis (2/day, 4 hrs), Galway (5/day, 3 hrs, talking timetable tel. 01/805-4222).

By train from Connolly Station to: Rosslare (3/day, 3 hrs), Portrush (6/day, 5 hrs, €35 one-way, €47 round-trip, transfer in Belfast or Portadown), Belfast (8/day, 2 hrs, talking timetable tel. 01/836-3333).

Dublin Airport: The airport is well-connected to the city center seven miles away (airport info: tel. 01/814-1111, www.dublin-airport.com, also see "Arrival in Dublin," above). For list of airlines, see below.

Ireland and Britain

Dublin and London: The journey by boat plus train or bus takes 7–12 hours, all day or all night (bus: 4/day, €25–42, British tel. 08705-143-219, www.eurolines.co.uk; train: 4/day, €61–118, Dublin train info: tel. 01/836-6222, British train info: 01/703-1884).

If you're going directly to London, flying is your best bet. Check Ryanair first (€87 round-trip, 90 min, Irish tel. 01/609-7878, www.ryanair.com). Other options include British Airways (Irish tel. 01/814-5201 or toll-free tel. in Ireland 1-800-626-747, in U.S. 800/247-9297, www.britishairways.com), Aer Lingus (tel. 01/886-8888, www.aerlingus.ie), and bmi british midland (Irish tel. 01/407-3036, U.S. tel. 800/788-0555, www.flybmi.com). To get the lowest fares, ask about round-trip ticket prices and book months in advance (though Ryanair offers deals nearly all of the time).

Dublin and Holyhead: Irish Ferries sails between Dublin and Holyhead in North Wales (dock is a mile east of O'Connell Bridge, 5/day: 2 slow, 3 fast; slow boats: 3.25 hrs, €30 one-way walk-on fare; fast boats: 1.75 hrs, €40; Dublin tel. 01/638-3333, Holyhead tel. 08705-329-129, www.irishferries.com).

Dun Laoghaire and Holyhead: Stena Line sails between Dun Laoghaire (near Dublin) and Holyhead in North Wales (3/day, 2 hrs on HSS *Catamaran,* €38–44 one-way walk-on fare, €4 extra if paying with credit card, reserve by phone—they book up long in advance on summer weekends, Dun Laoghaire tel. 01/204-7777, recorded info tel. 01/204-7799, can book online at www.stenaline.ie).

DINGLE PENINSULA

Dingle Peninsula, the westernmost tip of Ireland, offers just the right mix of far-and-away beauty, ancient archaeological wonders, and isolated walks or bike rides—all within convenient reach of its main town. Dingle town is just large enough to have all the necessary tourist services and a steady nocturnal beat of Irish folk music.

Although crowded in summer, Dingle still feels like the fish and the farm really matter. Forty fishing boats sail from Dingle, tractor tracks dirty its main drag, and a faint whiff of peat fills its nighttime streets.

For more than 20 years, my Irish dreams have been set here on this sparse but lush peninsula, where locals are fond of saying, "The next parish is Boston." There's a feeling of closeness to the land on Dingle. When I asked a local if he was born here, he thought for a second and said, "No, it was about six miles down the road." When I told him where I was from, a faraway smile filled his eyes, and he looked out to sea and sighed, "Ah, the shores of Americay." I asked his friend if he'd lived here all his life. He said, "Not yet."

Dingle feels so traditionally Irish because it's a *Gaeltacht,* a region where the government subsidizes the survival of the Irish language and culture. While English is always there, the signs, menus, and songs come in Gaelic. Children carry hurling sticks to class, and even the local preschool brags "ALL Gaelic."

Of the peninsula's 10,000 residents, 1,500 live in Dingle town. Its few streets, lined with ramshackle but gaily painted shops and pubs, run up from a rain-stung harbor always busy with fishing boats and yachts. Traditionally, the buildings were drab gray or whitewashed. Thirty years ago, Ireland's "tidy town" competition prompted everyone to paint their buildings in playful pastels.

It's a peaceful town. The courthouse (1832) is open one hour a month. The judge does his best to wrap up business within a half hour. During the day you'll see teenagers—already working on ruddy beer-

Dingle Peninsula

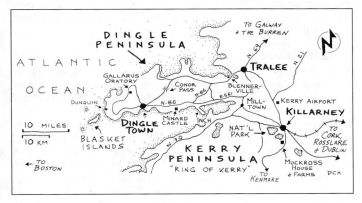

glow cheeks—roll kegs up the streets and into the pubs in preparation for another night of music and *craic* (fun conversation and atmosphere).

Dingle Town

Planning Your Time

For the shortest visit, give Dingle two nights and a day. It takes six to eight hours to get there from Dublin. I like two nights because you feel more like a local on your second evening in the pubs. You'll need the better part of a day to explore the 30-mile loop around the peninsula by bike, car, or tour bus (see "Circular Tour" on page 716). To do any serious walking or relaxing, you'll need two or three days. It's not uncommon to find Americans slowing way, way down in Dingle town.

ORIENTATION

(area code: 066)

Dingle—extremely comfortable on foot—hangs on a medieval grid of streets between the harborfront (where the Tralee bus stops) and Main Street (3 blocks inland). Nothing in town is more than a five-minute walk away. Street numbers are used only when more than one place is run by a family of the same name. Most locals know most locals, and people on the street are fine sources of information. Remember, locals love their soda bread, and tourism provides the butter. You'll find a warm and sincere welcome.

Tourist Information: The TI is a privately owned, for-profit business—little more than a glorified shop with a green staff who are disinclined to really know the town (July–Aug daily 9:00–19:00, June & Sept–Oct daily

9:30–17:30, Nov–May Mon–Tue and Thu–Sat 10:00–17:00, closed Sun and Wed; on Strand Street by the water, tel. 066/915-1188). For more knowledgeable help, drop by the Mountain Man shop (on Strand Street, see "Dingle Activities," below) or talk to your B&B host.

Helpful Hints

Before You Go: The local Web site (www.dingle-peninsula.ie) lists festivals and events. For the peninsula's culture and history, look up these old issues of *National Geographic*: April 1976 and Sept 1994.

Crowds: Crowds trample Dingle's charm throughout July and August. The absolute craziest are the Dingle Races (2nd weekend in Aug), Dingle Regatta (3rd weekend in Aug), and the Blessing of the Boats (end of Aug, beginning of Sept). The first Mondays in May, June, and August are bank holidays, giving Ireland's workers three-day weekends—and ample time to fill up Dingle. The town's metabolism (prices, schedules, activities) rises and falls with the tourist crowds—October through April is sleepy.

Banking: Two banks in town, both on Main Street, offer the same rates (Mon 10:00–17:00, Tue–Fri 10:00–16:00, closed Sat–Sun) and have cash machines. The TI happily changes cash and traveler's checks at mediocre rates. Expect to use cash (rather than credit cards) to pay for most peninsula activities.

Post Office: It's on Main Street near Benners Hotel (Mon–Fri 9:00–17:30, Sat 9:00–13:00, closed Sun).

Laundry: Dingle Cleaners is full-service only—drop off before 10:00 and pick up dried and folded late that afternoon (€8–15 depending on load size, Mon–Sat 9:30–18:00, closed Sun, beside Moran's Market and gas station, tel. 066/915-0680, mobile 087-793-5621).

Internet Access: Dingle Internet Café is on Main Street (€2.60/30 min, April–Sept Mon–Fri 9:00–22:00, Sat 10:00–18:00, Sun 13:00–18:00, shorter hours Oct–March, tel. 066/915-2478).

Bike Rental: Bike-rental shops abound. The best is Paddy's Bike Hire (€10/day or €1 more for 24 hrs, €12 for better bikes, daily 9:00–19:00, on Dykegate next to Grapevine Hostel, tel. 066/915-2311). Foxy John's (Main Street), Mountain Man (no helmets), and the Ballintaggert Hostel also rent bikes. If you're biking the peninsula, get a bike with skinny street tires, not slow and fat mountain-bike tires. Plan on leaving €10 plus a driver's license or passport as a security deposit.

Dingle Activities: The Mountain Man, a hiking shop run by a local guide, Mike Shea, is a clearinghouse for information, local tours, and excursions (July–Sept daily 9:00–21:00, Oct–June 9:00–18:00, just off harbor at Strand Street, tel. 066/915-2400, irasc@eir com.net). Stop by for ideas on biking, hiking, horseback riding,

Dingle Hotels and Services

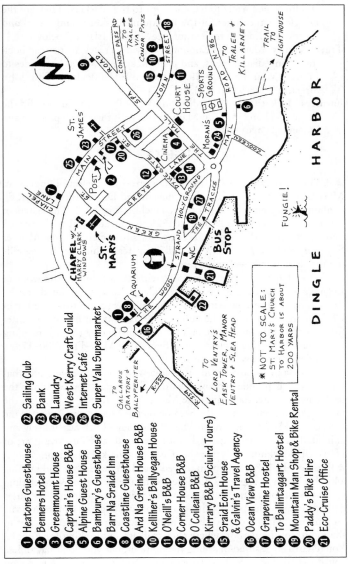

1. Heatons Guesthouse
2. Benners Hotel
3. Greenmount House
4. Captain's House B&B
5. Alpine Guest House
6. Bambury's Guesthouse
7. Barr Na Sraide Inn
8. Coastline Guesthouse
9. Ard Na Greine House B&B
10. Kelliher's Ballyegan House
11. O'Neill's B&B
12. Corner House B&B
13. O Coileain B&B
14. Kirrary B&B (Sciuird Tours)
15. Sraid Eoin House
    & Galvin's Travel Agency
16. Ocean View B&B
17. Grapevine Hostel
18. To Ballintaggart Hostel
19. Mountain Man Shop & Bike Rental
20. Paddy's Bike Hire
21. Eco-Cruise Office

22. Sailing Club
23. Bank
24. Laundry
25. West Kerry Craft Guild
26. Internet Café
27. Super Valu Supermarket

climbing, peninsula tours, and trips to the Blaskets. They are the Dingle town contact for the Dunquin–Blasket Islands boats and shuttle-bus rides to the harbor (see "Blasket Islands," below).

Travel Agency: Maurice O'Connor at Galvin's Travel Agency can book train, long-distance bus, and plane tickets, as well as boat rides to France (Mon–Fri 9:30–18:00, Sat 9:30–17:00, closed Sun, John Street, tel. 066/915-1409).

Farmers Market: Most Saturdays (10:00–14:00), local farmers fill the St. James churchyard (on Main Street) with their fresh produce and homemade marmalade.

SIGHTS

▲▲**The Harry Clark Windows of Diseart**—Just behind Dingle's St. Mary Church stands St. Joseph's Convent and Diseart (dee-ZHART), containing a beautiful neo-Gothic chapel built in 1884. The sisters of this order, who came to Dingle in 1829 to educate local girls, worked heroically during the famine. During Mass in the chapel, the Mother Superior would sit in the covered stall in the rear, while the sisters—filling the carved stalls—chanted responsively.

The chapel was graced in 1922 with 12 windows—the work of Ireland's top stained-glass man, Harry Clark. Long appreciated only by the sisters, these special windows—showing six scenes from the life of Christ—are now open to the public. The convent has become a center for sharing Christian Celtic culture and spirituality (free, June–Aug Mon–Sat 10:00–17:00, closed Sun, Sept–May Mon–Fri 10:00–17:00, closed Sat–Sun, www.diseart.ie).

Enjoy a meditative 15 minutes following the free audioguide that explains the chapel one window at a time. The scenes (clockwise from the back entrance) are: the visit of the Magi, the Baptism of Jesus, "Let the little children come to me," the Sermon on the Mount, the Agony in the Garden, and Jesus appearing to Mary Magdalene. Each face is lively and animated in the imaginative, devout, medieval, and fun-loving art of Harry Clark, whom locals talk about as if he's the kid next door.

▲**Fungie**—In 1983, a dolphin moved into Dingle Harbor and became a local celebrity. Fungie (FOON-gee, with a hard *g*) is now the darling of the town's tourist trade and one reason you'll find so many tour buses parked along the harbor. With a close look at Fungie as bait, tour boats are thriving. The hardy little boats motor seven to 40 passengers out to the mouth of the harbor, where they troll around looking for Fungie. You're virtually assured of seeing the dolphin, but you don't pay unless you do (€10, kids-€5, 1-hr trips depart 10:00–19:00 depending on demand, book a day in advance, behind TI at Dolphin Trips office, tel. 066/915-2626). To actually swim with Fungie, rent wetsuits at Bresnan's B&B (Cooleen Street, tel. 066/915-1967) and catch the early-morning

THE VOYAGE OF ST. BRENDAN

It has long been part of Irish lore that St. Brendan the Navigator (A.D. 484–577) and 12 followers sailed from the southwest of Ireland to the "Land of Promise" (what is now North America) in a currach—a wood-frame boat covered with ox hide and tar. According to a 10th-century monk who poetically wrote of the journey, St. Brendan and his crew encountered a paradise of birds, were attacked by a whale, and suffered the smoke of a smelly island in the north before finally reaching their Land of Promise.

The legend and its precisely described locations still fascinate modern readers. A British scholar of navigation, Tim Severin, re-created the entire journey from 1976 to 1977. He and his crew set out from Brendan Creek in County Kerry in a currach. The prevailing winds blew them to the Hebrides, the Faeroe Islands, Iceland, and finally to Newfoundland. While this didn't successfully prove that St. Brendan sailed to North America, it did prove that he could have.

St. Brendan fans have been heartened by an intriguing archaeological find in Connecticut. Called the "Gungywamp," the site includes a double circle of stones and a beehive-like chamber built in the same manner as the stone *clochans* huts on the Dingle Peninsula. The Gungywamp beehive chamber has been carbon-dated to approximately A.D. 600. Outside the chamber, a stone slab is inscribed with a cross that resembles the unique style of the Irish cross.

According to his 10th-century biographer, "St. Brendan sailed from the Land of Promise home to Ireland. And from that time on, Brendan acted as if he did not belong to this world at all. His mind and his joy were in the delight of heaven."

8:00–10:00 trip (€35 includes wetsuits—unless you've packed your own). ▲Oceanworld—The only place charging admission in Dingle is worth considering. This aquarium offers a little peninsula history, 300 different species of local fish in thoughtfully described tanks, and the easiest way to see Fungie the dolphin...on video. Walk through the tunnel while fish swim overhead. The only creatures not local—other than you—are the sharks. The aquarium's mission is to teach, and you're welcome to ask questions. The petting pool is fun. Splashing attracts the rays, which are unplugged (€8, families-€22, daily July–Aug 10:00–20:30, May–June and Sept 10:00–18:00, Oct–April 10:00–17:00, cafeteria, just past harbor on west edge of town, tel. 066/915-2111).

▲**Short Harbor Walk from Dingle**—For an easy stroll along the harbor out of town (and a chance to see Fungie, 90 min round-trip), head east from the roundabout past the Esso station. Just after Bambury's B&B, take a right, following signs to Skelligs Hotel. At the beach, climb the steps over the wall and follow the seashore path to the mouth of Dingle Harbor (marked by a tower —some 19th-century fat cat's folly). Ten minutes beyond that is a lighthouse. This is Fungie's neighborhood. If you see tourist boats out, you're likely to see the dolphin. The trail continues to a dramatic cliff.

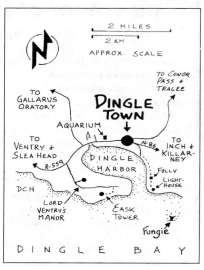

Dingle Area

The Harbor: The harbor was built on land reclaimed (with imported Dutch expertise) in 1992. The string of old stone shops facing the harbor was the loading station for the narrow-gauge railway that hauled the fish from Dingle to Tralee (1891–1953). Make a point to walk out to the end of the breakwater—newly paved and lit at night. The Eask Tower on the distant hill is a marker that was built in 1847 during the famine as a make-work project. In pre-radar days, it helped ships locate Dingle's hidden harbor. The fancy mansion across the harbor is Lord Ventry's 17th-century manorhouse (see "Circular Tour," page 716).

Sailing—The Dingle Marina Centre offers diving, sailing, traditional currach rowing, and a salty little restaurant. Sailors can join the club for a day to sail (€22, July–Aug, tel. 066/915-1984). Currachs—stacked behind the building—are Ireland's traditional lightweight fishing boats, easy to haul and easy to make. Cover a wooden frame with canvas (originally cowhide) and paint with tar—presto.

Dingle Pitch & Putt—For 18 scenic holes and a driving range, hike 10 minutes past Oceanworld (€5 includes gear, driving range €5 for 100 balls, April–Oct daily 10:00–20:00, closed Nov–March, over bridge take first left and follow signs, Milltown, tel. 066/915-2020).

Horseback Riding—Dingle Horse Riding takes out beginners (€26/hr with instruction) and experienced riders on four-hour (€95) and longer six-hour (€130) excursions. Bob along beaches or mountains on an

English-style ride. Book at Greenlane Gallery (Green Street, tel. 066/915-2018, www.dinglehorseriding.com).

Shopping—Dingle is filled with shops showing off local craftsmanship. The **West Kerry Craft Guild**—a co-op selling the work of 15 local artists—is a delight even if you're just browsing. The prices here are very good since you're buying directly from the artists (18 Main Street). The **Niamh Utsch Jewelry** shop next door is much respected for its unique work. **Lisbeth Mulcahy Weaver,** filled with traditional but stylish woven wear, is also the Dingle sales outlet of the well-known potter from out on Slea Head (Green Street, tel. 066/915-1688).

NIGHTLIFE

▲▲▲**Folk Music in Dingle Pubs**—Even if you're not into pubs, take a nap and then give these a whirl. Dingle is renowned among traditional musicians as a place to get work ("€40 a day, tax-free, plus drink"). The town has piles of pubs. There's music every night and rarely a cover charge. The scene is a decent mix of locals, Americans, and Germans. Music normally starts around 21:30, and the last call for drinks is "half eleven" (23:30), sometimes later on weekends. For a seat near the music, arrive early. If the place is chockablock, power in and find breathing room in the back. By midnight, the door is usually closed and the chairs are stacked.

While two pubs, the Small Bridge Bar (An Droichead Beag) and O'Flaherty's, are the most famous for their good beer and folk music, make a point to wander the town and follow your ear. Smaller pubs may feel a bit foreboding to a tourist, but people—locals as well as travelers—are out for the *craic*. Irish culture is very accessible in the pubs; they're like highly interactive museums waiting to be explored. But if you sit at a table, you'll be left alone. Stand or sit at the bar and you'll be engulfed in conversation with new friends. Have a glass in an empty, no-name pub and chat up the publican. Pubs are smoky (pending a possible new no-smoking-in-pubs law) and hot, so leave your coat home. The more offbeat pubs are more likely to erupt into leprechaun karaoke.

Pub crawl: The best pub crawl is along Strand Street to O'Flaherty's. Murphy's is lively, offering rock as well as ballads and traditional music. O'Flaherty's has a high ceiling and less smoke, and is dripping in old-time photos and town memorabilia—it's touristy but lots of fun, with nightly music in the summer. John Benny Moriarty's has dependably good traditional music sessions, with John himself joining in on accordion when he's not pouring pints.

Then head up Green Street. Dick Mack, across from the church, is nicknamed "the last pew." This is a tiny leather shop by day, expanding into a pub at night, with several rooms, a fine snug (private booth, originally designed to allow women to drink discreetly), reliably good beer, and a smoky and strangely fascinating ambience. Notice the Hollywood-type stars on the sidewalk recalling famous visitors. Established in 1899, the grandson of the original Dick Mack now runs the place. A painting in the window shows Dick Mack II with the local gang.

Green Street climbs to Main Street, where two more Dick Mack–type places are filled with smoke and locals deep in conversation (but no music): Foxy John's (a hardware shop by day) and O Currain's (across the street, a small clothing shop by day).

A bit higher up Main Street is McCarthy's Pub, a smoke-stained relic. It's less touristy and has some fine traditional music sessions and occasional plays on its little stage. Wander downhill to the Small Bridge Bar at the bottom. With live music nightly, it's popular for good reason. While the tourists gather around the music, poke around the back and do an end run around the wall, which leads to a window nook actually closest to the musicians. Occasionally musicians sell CDs of their tunes, which can be a nice keepsake of your time in Ireland.

Off-season: From October through April, the bands play on, though at fewer pubs: Small Bridge Bar (live music nightly), John Benny Moriarty's (Mon, Wed, Thu), McCarthy's (Fri, Sat), and Murphy's (Sat).

Music shops: Danlann Gallery sells musical instruments and wood-crafts (Mon–Fri 10:00–18:00, later in summer, "flexible" on weekends, owner makes violins, Green Street). Siopa an Phiobaire, exclusively a music shop, sells traditional wind instruments (Mon–Fri 10:00–17:00, closed Sat–Sun, Craft Centre, on edge of town a few minutes' walk past Oceanworld, tel. 066/915-1778). Dingle Bodhrans sells homemade traditional goatskin drums and gives lessons (1-hour lesson–€25.50–51, rates are on "sliding scale," Mon–Sat 10:30–18:00, closed Sun, Green Street, enter red iron gate of small alley opposite church, tel. 087-245-7689, Andrea).

Folk concerts—Top local musicians offer a quality evening of live, acoustic, classic Irish music in the fine little St. James Church on Main Street (€10, Mon, Wed, and Thu at 19:30, Easter–Sept only, mobile 087-982-9728, see sign on church gate or drop by Murphy's Ice Cream for details).

Dancing—Some pubs host "set dancing" with live music. Your two best possibilities are the Small Bridge Bar or John Benny Moriarty's Pub (see above), but ask at the TI for more suggestions. If you're not a night owl (music in pubs doesn't begin until 21:30) or prefer not to be packed into a pub with the distractions of conversation, then this is your best opportunity to hear Irish traditional music in a more controlled environment.

Theater—Dingle's great little theater is The Phoenix on Dykegate. Its film club (50–60 locals) meets here Tuesdays year-round at 20:30 for coffee and cookies, followed by a film at 21:00 (€6 for film, anyone is welcome). The leader runs it almost like a religion, with a sermon on the film before he rolls it. The regular film schedule for the week is posted on the door.

SLEEPING

$$$ Heatons Guesthouse, big, peaceful, and American in its comforts, is on the water just west of town at the end of Dingle Bay—a five-minute walk past Oceanworld on The Wood. The 16 thoughtfully appointed rooms come with all the amenities (Db-€76–118, suite Db-€130–175, creative breakfasts, parking, The Wood, tel. 066/915-2288, fax 066/915-2324, www.heatonsdingle.com, heatons@iol.ie, Cameron and Nuala Heaton).

$$$ Benners Hotel was the only place in town a hundred years ago. It stands bewildered by the modern world on Main Street, with sprawling public spaces and 52 abundant, overpriced rooms—only its non-smoking rooms smell fresh (Db-€200 July–Aug, €160 May–June, €150 Sept–May, kids under 7-€19 extra, tel. 066/915-1638, fax 066/915-1412, www.dinglebenners.com, info@dinglebenners.com).

$$ Greenmount House sits among chilly palm trees in the countryside at the top of town. A five-minute hike up from the town center, this guest house commands a fine view of the bay and mountains. John and Mary Curran run one of Ireland's best B&Bs, with five superb rooms (Db-€75–90—top price through the summer) and seven sprawling suites (Db-€100–140) in a modern building with lavish public areas and breakfast in a solarium (reserve in advance, no children under 8, most rooms at ground level, parking, top of John Street, tel. 066/915-1414, fax 066/915-1974, www.greenmounthouse.com, greenmount-house@eircom.net).

$$ Captain's House B&B is a shipshape place in the town center, fit for an admiral, with eight classy rooms, peat-fire lounges, a stay-a-while garden, and a magnificent breakfast in the conservatory. Mary,

SLEEP CODE

(€1 = about $1.10, country code: 353, area code: 066)
Sleep Code: **S** = Single, **D** = Double/Twin, **T** = Triple, **Q** = Quad, **b** = bathroom, **s** = shower only, **no CC** = Credit Cards not accepted. Prices vary with the season, with winter cheap and August tops. Breakfast is included and credit cards are accepted unless otherwise noted.

To help you easily sort through these listings, I've divided the rooms into three categories, based on the price for a standard double room with bath:

   $$$ **Higher Priced**—Most rooms €100 or more.
    $$ **Moderately Priced**—Most rooms between €60–100.
     $ **Lower Priced**—Most rooms €60 or less.

whose mother ran a guest house before Dingle was discovered, loves her work and is very good at it (Sb-€50–60, Db-€80–100, great suite-€135–150, The Mall, tel. 066/915-1531, fax 066/915-1079, captigh@eircom.net, Jim and Mary Milhench).

$$ Alpine Guest House looks like a monopoly hotel, but that means comfortable and efficient. Its 13 spacious, bright, and fresh rooms come with wonderful sheep-and-harbor views, a cozy lounge, a great breakfast, and friendly owners (Db-€55–90, Tb-€76–120, prices vary with room size and season, 10 percent discount with this book, parking, Mail Road, tel. 066/915-1250, fax 066/915-1966, www.alpineguesthouse.com, alpinedingle@eircom.net, Paul). Driving into town from Tralee, you'll see this a block uphill from the Dingle roundabout and Esso station.

$$ Bambury's Guesthouse, big and modern with views of grazing sheep and the harbor, rents 12 airy, comfy rooms (Db-€70–100, prices depend on size and season, family deals; coming in from Tralee it's on your left on Mail Road, 2 blocks before Esso station; tel. 066/915-1244, fax 066/915-1786, http://bamburysguesthouse.com, info@bamburysguesthouse.com).

$$ Barr Na Sraide Inn, central and hotelesque, has 22 comfortable rooms (Db-€70–100, family deals, self-service laundry, bar, parking, past McCarthy's pub, Upper Main Street, tel. 066/915-1331, fax 066/915-1446, barrnasraide@eircom.net).

$$ Coastline Guesthouse, on the water next to Heaton's Guesthouse (listed above), is a modern, sterile place with seven bright, spacious rooms (Db-€82, Tb-€120, deals for 3-night stays, non-smoking, parking, The Wood, tel. 066/915-2494, fax 066/915-2493, www.coastlinedingle.com, coastlinedingle@eircom.net, Vivienne O'Shea).

$$ Ard Na Greine House B&B is a charming, windblown, modern house on the edge of town. Mrs. Mary Houlihan rents four well-equipped, comfortable rooms (with fridges) to non-smokers only (Sb-€50, Db-€55–68, Tb-€76, parking, 8-min walk up Spa Road, 3 doors beyond Hillgrove Hotel, tel. 066/915-1113).

$$ Kelliher's Ballyegan House is a big, plain building with six fresh, comfortable rooms on the edge of town and great harbor views (Db-€65, Tb-€95, family deals, 10 percent off through 2004 with this book except June–Aug, no CC, non-smoking, parking, Upper John Street, tel. 066/915-1702, Hannah and James Kelliher).

$ O'Neill's B&B is a homey, friendly place with six decent rooms on a quiet street at the top of town (Db-€60 with this book through 2004, family deals, no CC, strictly non-smoking, parking, John Street, tel. 066/915-1639, Mary O'Neill).

$ Corner House B&B is my longtime Dingle home. It's a simple, traditional place with five large, uncluttered rooms run with a twinkle and a grandmotherly smile by Kathleen Farrell (S-€35, D-€70, T-€85, plenty of plumbing but it's down the hall, no CC, reserve with a phone call and reconfirm a day or 2 ahead, central as can be on Dykegate Street, tel. 066/915-1516). Mrs. Farrell, one of the original three B&B hostesses in a town now filled with them, is a great storyteller.

$ Collins B&Bs: The following two B&Bs, which take up a quiet corner in the town center, are run by the same Collins—Coileain in Gaelic—family that does archaeological tours of the peninsula (below). Both offer pleasant rooms (O Coileain's are a bit bigger), bike rental (€8), identical prices (Db-€70–74), and a homey friendliness. **O Coileain B&B** is run by a young family—Rachel, Michael, and their two cute little girls (tel. 066/915-1937, archeo@eircom.net). **Kirrary B&B,** just over the fence, is grandma's place, with a homey charm (tel. 066/915-1606, collinskirrary@eircom.net, Eileen Collins).

$ Sraid Eoin House offers four modest but pleasant top-floor rooms above Galvin's Travel Agency (Db-€60–70, Tb-€90–100, John Street, tel. 066/915-1409, fax 066/915-2156, sraideoinhouse@hotmail.com, friendly Kathleen and Maurice O'Connor).

$ Ocean View B&B rents three tidy rooms (2 with views) in a humble little waterfront row house overlooking the bay (S-€26, D-€44, welcome treat on arrival, 5-min walk from center, 100 yards past Oceanworld at 133 The Wood, tel. 066/915-1659, thewood@gofree .indigo.ie, Mrs. Brosnan).

Hostels: **$ Grapevine Hostel** is clean and friendly, quietly yet very centrally located, with a cozy fireplace lounge and a fine members' kitchen. Each three- to eight-bed dorm has its own bathroom. Dorms are coed, but there's a girls-only room (29 beds, €13–15 per person, laundry-€5, open all day, Dykegate Lane, tel. 066/915-1434, www.dinglehostel .com, grapevine@dingleweb.com, run by Siobhan—sheh-vahn).

$ Ballintaggart Hostel, a backpacker's complex, is housed in a stylish old manorhouse used by Protestants during the famine as a soup kitchen (for those hungry enough to renounce Catholicism). It comes complete with laundry service (€6), a classy study, a family room with a fireplace, and a resident ghost (130 beds, €13 in 10-bed dorms, €17 beds in Qb, Db-€48, no breakfast but there's a kitchen, a mile east of town on Tralee Road, tel. 066/915-1454, fax 066/915-2207, www .dingleaccommodation.com, info@dingleaccommodation.com). Ask the Tralee bus to drop you here before arriving in Dingle.

EATING

For a rustic little village, Dingle is swimming in good food.

Budget Tips: The Super Valu supermarket/department store, at the base of town, has everything and stays open late (Mon–Sat 8:00–21:00, Sun 8:00–19:00, daily until 22:00 in Aug). Smaller groceries are scattered throughout the town, such as Centra on Main Street (Mon–Sat 8:00–21:00, Sun 8:00–18:00). Consider a grand view picnic

Dingle Restaurants

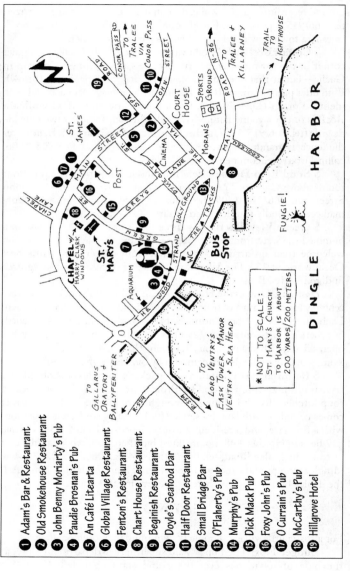

1. Adam's Bar & Restaurant
2. Old Smokehouse Restaurant
3. John Benny Moriarty's Pub
4. Paudie Brosnan's Pub
5. An Café Literarta
6. Global Village Restaurant
7. Fenton's Restaurant
8. Chart House Restaurant
9. Beginish Restaurant
10. Doyle's Seafood Bar
11. Half Door Restaurant
12. Small Bridge Bar
13. O'Flaherty's Pub
14. Murphy's Pub
15. Dick Mack Pub
16. Foxy John's Pub
17. O Currain's Pub
18. McCarthy's Pub
19. Hillgrove Hotel

out on the end of the newer pier (as you face the harbor, it's the plea-sure-boat pier on your right).

Fancy restaurants serve early-bird specials from 18:00 to 19:00. Many "cheap and cheery" places close at 18:00, and pubs do good €12 dinners all over town. Most pubs stop serving food around 21:00 (to make room for their beer drinkers).

Adam's Bar and Restaurant is a tight, old-fashioned place popular with locals for traditional food at great prices. Try their stew, corned beef and cabbage, or lemon-chicken sandwiches (€9 lunches, May–Sept daily 12:00–17:00 & 18:00–21:00, closed Oct–April, Upper Main Street, tel. 066/915-2133).

The Old Smokehouse, serving happy locals in a rustic woody set-ting, offers the best moderate-value meals in town, with fresh Dingle Bay fish and good vegetables (€16–20 dinner plates, Mon–Sat 12:30–14:30 & 18:00–21:30, closed Sun, corner of Main Street & The Mall, tel. 066/915-1061).

John Benny Moriarty's is a waterfront pub dishing up traditional Irish fare (food daily 12:30–21:30, music after 21:30, The Pier). **Paudie Brosnan's** pub, a few doors down, is also popular.

An Café Litearta, a popular eatery hidden behind an inviting book-store, serves tasty soup and sandwiches to a good-natured crowd of Gaelic-speaking smokers (daily 10:00–17:00, Dykegate Street).

The **Global Village Restaurant** is where Martin Bealin concocts his favorite dishes, gleaned from his travels around the world. It's an eclec-tic, healthy, meat-eater's place popular with locals for its interesting cui-sine (€18–22 dinners, good salads and great Thai curry, daily 17:00–22:00, early-bird menus before 19:00, top of Main Street, tel. 066/915-2325).

Dingle's Five Fancy Restaurants

All of these places accept credit cards.

Chart House Restaurant serves contemporary cuisine with a menu dictated by what's fresh and seasonal. Settle back into the sharp, clean, lantern-lit harborside ambience (€28 dinners, Wed–Mon 18:30–22:00, closed Tue, at roundabout at base of town, tel. 066/915-2255).

Beginish Restaurant, serving modern European fare with a fish forte in an elegant Georgian setting, is probably your best dressy splurge meal in town (€25 plates, €30 daily 3-course meal, dinner only, Wed–Sun 18:00–21:30, closed Mon–Tue, you'll be glad you reserved ahead, Green Street, tel. 066/915-1588).

Two of Dingle's long-established top-notch restaurants—**Doyle's Seafood Bar** (more famous, with excellent seafood and service, tel. 066/915-1174) and **The Half Door** (heartier portions; also open for lunch Tue–Sat 12:30–14:00, tel. 066/915-1600)—are neighbors on John Street. They're in the guidebooks for good reason (and therefore filled with tourists), as they serve good food. Both have the same dinner hours

(Mon–Sat 18:00–21:30, closed Sun), offer an early-bird special (3-course meal-€30, 18:00–19:00), and take reservations (wise).

Fenton's is a fine place for seafood meals with a memorable apple cobbler dessert (€18–27 main courses, 3-course meals for €27, Tue–Sun 18:00–21:30, closed Mon, early-bird specials before 19:00, reservations smart, on Green Street down the hill below the church, tel. 066/915-2172).

TRANSPORTATION CONNECTIONS

The nearest train station is in Tralee.

By bus from Dingle to: Galway (4/day, 6.5 hrs), **Dublin** (3/day, 8 hrs), **Rosslare** (2/day, 9 hrs), **Tralee** (4/day, 75 min, €8); fewer departures on Sundays. Most bus trips out of Dingle require at least one or two (easy) transfers. Dingle has no bus station and only one bus stop, on the waterfront behind the Super Valu supermarket (bus info tel. 01/830-2222 or Tralee station at 066/712-3566).

Airports

Kerry Airport, a 45-minute drive from Dingle town, offers direct flights to **Dublin** and **London Stansted** (daily, €31 to London, €70 to Dublin; airport tel. 066/976-4644 or 066/976-4350, Ryanair tel. 0818/303030, Aer Arann Express tel. 1-890-462-726, www.kerryairport.ie).

Shannon Airport, the major airport in Western Ireland, has direct flights to **Dublin** (2–3/day, 30 min) and **London** (6/day, 1 hr). Ryanair (www.ryanair.com) and Aer Lingus (www.aerlingus.ie) fly out of Shannon. Airport info: tel. 061/471-444. Shannon Airport TI: tel. 061/471-664 (daily 6:30–18:00, June–Sept until 19:00). Shannon Airport also has easy bus connections to **Limerick** (nearly hrly, 1 hr, can continue to Tralee—2 hrs, and Dingle—1.25 hrs more), **Ennis** (nearly hrly, 45 min), and **Galway** (every 2 hrs, 2 hrs). Bus info: tel. 061/313-333, www.buseireann.ie.

Dingle Peninsula

CIRCULAR TOUR BY BIKE OR CAR

A sight worth ▲▲▲, the Dingle Peninsula loop trip is about 30 miles long (go in clockwise direction). It's easy by car, or it's a demanding three hours by bike—if you don't stop.

While you can take the basic guided tour of the peninsula (see Dingle Peninsula "Tours," page 722), the route described in this section makes it unnecessary. A fancy map is also unnecessary with my instructions. I've keyed in mileage to help locate points of interest. If you're driving, as you leave Dingle, reset your odometer at Oceanworld. Even if you get off track

Dingle Peninsula Tour

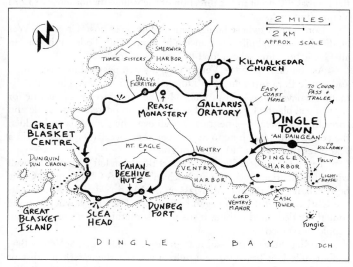

or are biking, derive distances between points from my mileage key. To get the most out of your circle trip, read through this entire section before departing. Then go step by step (staying on R559 and following The Slea Head Drive signs). Roads are very congested in August.

The Dingle Peninsula is 10 miles wide and runs 40 miles from Tralee to Slea Head. The top of its mountainous spine is Mount Brandon—at 3,130 feet, the second-tallest mountain in Ireland. While only tiny villages lie west of Dingle town, the peninsula is home to 500,000 sheep.

Leave Dingle town west along the waterfront (0.0 miles at Ocean-world). There's an eight-foot tide here. The seaweed was used to make formerly worthless land arable. (Seaweed is a natural source of potash—organic farming before that was trendy.) Across the water, the fancy Milltown House B&B (with flags) was Robert Mitchum's home for a year during the filming of *Ryan's Daughter*. Look for the narrow mouth of this blind harbor (where Fungie frolics) and the Ring of Kerry beyond that. Dingle Bay is so hidden, ships needed the tower (1847) on the hill to find its mouth.

0.4 miles: At the roundabout, turn left over the bridge. The hardware store building on the right was a corn-grinding mill in the 18th century.

0.8 miles: The Milestone B&B is named for the stone pillar (*gallaun* in Gaelic) in its front yard. This may have been a prehistoric grave or a boundary marker between two tribes. The stone goes down as far as it sticks up. The peninsula, literally an open-air museum, is dotted with more than 2,000 such monuments dating from the Neolithic Age (4,000

B.C.) through early Christian times. Another stone pillar stands in the field across the street in the direction of the yellow manorhouse of Lord Ventry (in the distance).

Lord Ventry, whose family came to Dingle as post–Cromwell War landlords in 1666, built this mansion in about 1750. Today, it houses an all-Gaelic boarding school for 140 high school girls.

As you drive past the Ventry estate, you'll pass palms, magnolias, and exotic flora introduced to Dingle by Lord Ventry. The mild climate—it never snows—is produced by the Gulf Stream and is fine for subtropical plants. Consequently, fuchsias—imported from Chile and spreading like weeds—line the roads all over the peninsula and redden the countryside from June to September. And over 100 inches of rain a year gives this area its "40 shades of green."

Ten yards past the Tobair Michael B&B (on left) a tiny white wall with a blue marker marks the St. Michael's Well. A Christianized Celtic holy well, it's still the site of a Mass on St. Martin's day. St. Martin was the Christian antidote to pagan holy places. Generally, when you see something dedicated to him, it sits upon something that pre-Christian people worshiped.

3 miles: Stay off the "soft margin" as you enjoy views of Ventry Bay, its four-mile-long beach (to your right as you face the water), and distant Skellig Michael, which you'll see all along this part of the route. Skellig Michael—jutting up like France's Mont St. Michel—contains the rocky remains of an eighth-century monastic settlement. Hermit monks lived here in obscure beehive huts—their main contact with the outside world being trading ships stopping between Spain and Scandinavia. Next to it is a smaller island, Little Skellig—a breeding ground for gannets (seagull-like birds with 6-foot wingspans). In 1866, the first transatlantic cable was laid from nearby Valentia island to Newfoundland. It was in use until 1965. Mount Eagle (1,660 feet), rising across the bay, marks the end of Ireland. In the village of Ventry, Gaelic is the first language. The large hall at the end of the village is used as a classroom by big-city students who come here on field trips to be immersed in the Gaelic language.

4.7 miles: The rushes on either side of the road are the kind used to make the local thatched roofs. Thatching, which nearly died out because of the fire danger, is more popular now that anti-flame treatments are available. Black-and-white magpies fly.

5.3 miles: The Irish football star Paidi O Se (Paddy O'Shea) is a household name in Ireland. He now trains the Kerry team and runs the pub on the left. (Easy beach access from here.)

5.6 miles: The blue house hiding in the trees 100 yards off the road on the left (view through the white gate) was kept cozy by Tom Cruise and Nicole Kidman during the filming of *Far and Away.*

6.6 miles: *Taisteal go Mall* means "go slowly"; there's a peach-colored, two-room schoolhouse on the right (20 students, 2 teachers). On the left is the small Celtic and Prehistoric Museum, a strange private collection of prehistoric artifacts with no real connection to Dingle (overpriced at €5, daily 10:00–17:00).

6.9 miles: The circular mound on the right is a late–Stone Age ring fort. In 500 B.C., it was a petty Celtic chieftain's headquarters, a stone-and-earth stockade filled with little stone houses. These survived untouched through the centuries because of superstitious beliefs that they were "fairy forts." While this is unexcavated, recent digging has shown that people have lived on this peninsula since 4000 B.C.

7.3 miles: Look ahead up Mount Eagle at the patchwork of stone-fenced fields.

7.7 miles: Dunbeg Fort, a series of defensive ramparts and ditches around a central *clochan,* though ready to fall into the sea, is open to tourists. There are no carvings to be seen, but the small (*beg*) fort (*dun*) is dramatic (€2, daily 9:30–20:00, descriptive handout). Forts like this are the most important relics left from Ireland's Iron Age (500 B.C. to A.D. 500). Since erosion will someday take this fort, it has been excavated. Alongside the road, the new stone-roofed house was built to blend in with the landscape and the region's ancient rock-slab architecture (A.D. 2000, tea inside, traditional currach in parking lot). Just 50 yards up the hill is a cottage abandoned by a family named Kavanaugh 150 years ago during the famine (€2, tel. 066/915-6241).

8.2 miles: A group of beehive huts, or *clochans,* is a short walk uphill (€2, daily 9:30–19:00, WC). These mysterious stone igloos, which cluster together within a circular wall, are a better sight than the similar group of beehive huts a mile down the road. Look over the water for more Skellig views.

Farther on, you'll ford a stream. There has never been a bridge here; this bit of road—nicknamed the "upside-down bridge"—was designed as a ford.

9.2 miles: Pull off to the left at this second group of beehive huts. Look downhill at the scant remains of the scant home that was burned as the movie equivalent of Lord Ventry tried to evict the tenants in *Far and Away.* Even without Hollywood, this is a bleak and godforsaken land. Look above at the patches of land slowly made into farmland by the inhabitants of this westernmost piece of Europe. Rocks were cleared and piled into fences. Sand and seaweed were laid on the clay, and in time it was good for grass. The created land, if at all tillable, was generally used for growing potatoes; otherwise it was only good for grazing. Much has fallen out of use now. Look behind at the Ring of Kerry in the distance and ahead at the Blasket Islands.

9.9 miles: At Slea Head, marked by a crucifix, a pullout, and great views of the Blasket Islands (described below), you turn the corner on this tour. On stormy days, the waves are "racing in like white horses."

10.4 miles: Pull into the little parking lot (at Dunchaoin sign) to view the Blaskets and Dunmore Head (the westernmost point in Europe) and to review the roadside map (which traces your route) posted in the parking lot. The scattered village of Dunquin has many ruined rock homes abandoned during the famine. Some are fixed up, as this is a popular place these days for summer homes. You can see more good examples of land reclamation, patch by patch, climbing up the hillside. Mount Eagle was the first bit of land Charles Lindberg saw after crossing the Atlantic on his way to Paris in 1927. Villagers here were as excited as he was—they had never seen anything so big in the air. Ahead, down a road on the left, a plaque celebrates the 30th anniversary of the filming of *Ryan's Daughter.*

11.9 miles: The Blasket Islanders had no church or cemetery on the island. This was their cemetery. The famous Blasket storyteller Peig Sayers (1873–1958) is buried in the center. At the next intersection, drive down the little lane that leads left (100 yards) to a small stone marker commemorating the 1588 shipwreck of the *Santa Maria de la Rosa* of the Spanish Armada. Below that is the often-tempestuous Dunquin Harbor, from which the Blasket ferry departs. Island farmers—who on a calm day could row across in 20 minutes—would dock here and hike 12 miles into Dingle to sell their produce. When transporting sheep, farmers would lash the sheep's pointy little hoofs together and place them carefully upside down in the currach—so they wouldn't puncture the frail little craft's canvas skin.

12 miles: Back on the main road, follow signs to the Great Blasket Centre.

13.5 miles: Leave the Slea Head Road left for the Great Blasket Centre (described below).

13.7 miles: Back at the turnoff, head left (sign to Louis Mulcahy Pottery).

14.5 miles: Passing land that was never reclaimed, think of the work it took to pick out the stones, pile them into fences, and bring up sand and seaweed to nourish the clay and make soil for growing potatoes. Look over the water to the island aptly named the "Sleeping Giant"— see his hand resting happily on his beer belly.

15.1 miles: The view is spectacular. Ahead, on the right, study the top fields, untouched since the planting of 1845, when the potatoes didn't grow, but rotted in the ground. The faint vertical ridges of the potato beds can still be seen—a reminder of the famine (easier to see a bit later). Before the famine, 50,000 people lived on this peninsula. After the famine, the population was so small that there was never again a need to farm so high up. Today, only 10,000 live on the peninsula. Coast downhill. The distant hills are crowned by lookout forts built back when Britain expected Napoleon to invade.

18.3 miles: Ballyferriter (Baile an Fheirtearaigh), established by a Norman family in the 12th century, is the largest town on this side of

Dingle. The pubs serve grub, and the old schoolhouse is a museum (€2, Easter–Sept daily 10:00–16:30, closed off-season). The early-Christian cross next to the schoolhouse looks real. Tap it...it's fiberglass—a prop from *Ryan's Daughter*.

19.1 miles: At the T-junction, signs direct you to Dingle ("An Daingean, 11 km") either way. Go left, via Gallarus (and still following Slea Head Way). Take a right over the bridge, still following signs to Gallarus.

19.5 miles: Just beyond the bridge and a few yards before the sign to Mainistir Riaise (Reasc monastic enclosure), detour right up the lane. After 0.2 miles (the unsigned turnout on your right), you'll find the scant remains of the walled Reasc Monastery (dating from the 6th–12th centuries). The inner wall divided the community into sections for prayer and business (cottage industries helped support the monastery). In 1975, only the stone pillar was visible, as the entire site was buried. The layer of black felt marks where the original rocks stop and the excavators' reconstruction begins. The stone pillar is Celtic (c. 500 B.C.). When the Christians arrived in the fifth century, they didn't throw out the Celtic society. Instead, they carved a Maltese-type cross over the Celtic scrollwork. The square building was an oratory (church—you'll see an intact oratory at the next stop). The round buildings would have been *clochans*—those stone igloo-type dwellings. The monastery ran cottage industries with a double-duty kiln. Just outside the wall (opposite the oratory, past the duplex *clochan*, at the bottom end), find a stone hole with a passage facing the southwest wind. This was the kiln—fanned by the wind, it was used for cooking and drying grain. Locals would bring their grain to be dried and ground, and the monks would keep a tithe. With the arrival of the Normans in the 12th century, these small religious communities were replaced by relatively big-time state and church governments.

20 miles: Return to the main road, continue to the right.

21.1 miles: At the big hotel (Smerwick Harbor), turn left following the sign to Gallarus Oratory.

21.8 miles: At the big building (with camping sign), go right up a lane marked with a sign for the oratory. Another sign directs you to a small tourist center—with a shop, WC, and video theater. For €2 you get a 17-minute video overview of Dingle Peninsula's historic sights. (Bikers and hikers can avoid the entry fee by ignoring the visitors center sign and continuing up the lane 200 yards to a free entrance.)

The Gallarus Oratory, built about 1,300 years ago, is one of Ireland's best-preserved early-Christian churches. Shaped like an upturned boat, its finely fitted drystone walls are still waterproof. Notice the holes once used to secure covering at the door and the fine alternating stonework on the corners.

From the oratory, the little lane leads directly up and over the hill, home to Dingle. To complete this tour, however, you should return to the main road and continue (following sign to An Mhuirioch).

22.9 miles: Turn right at the fork and immediately take a right (at the blue shop sign) at the next fork. Pass a 19th-century church.

24.2 miles: The ruined Kilmalkedar church was the Norman center of worship for this end of the peninsula. It was built when England replaced the old monastic settlements in an attempt to centralize their rule. The 12th-century Irish Romanesque church is surrounded by a densely populated graveyard (which has risen noticeably above the surrounding fields over the centuries). In front of the church, you'll find the oldest medieval tombs, a stately early-Christian cross (substantially buried by the rising graveyard and therefore oddly proportioned), and a much older ogham stone. This stone, which had already stood here 900 years when the church was built, is notched with the mysterious Morris-code–type Ogham script used from the third to seventh centuries. It marked a grave, indicating this was a pre-Christian holy spot. The hole was drilled through here centuries ago as a place where people would come to seal a deal—standing on the graves of their ancestors and in front of the house of God, they'd "swear to God" by touching fingers through this stone. You can still use this to renew your marriage vows (free, B.Y.O. spouse). The church fell into ruin during the Reformation. As Catholic worship went underground until the early 19th century, Kilmalkedar was never rebuilt.

24.6 miles: Continue uphill, overlooking the water. You'll pass another "fairy fort" (Ciher Dorgan) dating back to 1000 B.C. (free, go through the rusty "kissing gate").

25.5 miles: At the crest of the hill, enjoy a three-mile coast back into Dingle town (in the direction of the Eask Tower).

28.3 miles: *Tog Bog E* means "take it easy." At the T-junction, turn left. Then turn right at the roundabout.

29 miles: You're back into Dingle town. Well done.

TOURS

▲▲**Sciuird Archaeology Tours**—Sciuird (SCREW-id) tours are offered by a father-son team with Dingle history—and a knack for sharing it—in their blood. Tim Collins (a retired Dingle police officer) and his son Michael give serious 2.5-hour minibus tours (€15, departing at 10:30 and 14:00, depending upon demand). Drop by the Kirrary B&B (Dykegate and Grey's Lane) or call 066/915-1606 to put your name on the list. Call early. Tours fill quickly in summer. Off-season (Oct–April), you may have to call back to see if the necessary five people signed up to make a bus go. While skipping the folk legends and the famous sights (such as Slea Head), your guide will drive down tiny farm roads (the Gaelic word for road literally means "cow path"), over hedges, and up ridges to hidden Celtic forts, mysterious stone tombs, and forgotten castles with sweeping seaside views. The running commentary gives an intimate peek into the history of Dingle. Sit as close to the driver as possible to get all the information. They do two completely different tours: west (Gallarus Oratory) and east (Minard Castle and a wedge tomb). I enjoyed both. Dress for the weather. In a literal gale with horizontal winds, Tim kept saying, "You'll survive it."

More Minibus Tours—Moran's Tour, which does a quickie minibus tour around the peninsula, offers meager narration and a short stop at the Gallarus Oratory (€16 to Slea Head, normally May–Sept at 10:00 and 14:00 from Dingle TI, 2.5 hrs; Moran's is at Esso station at round-about, tel. 066/915-1155 or mobile 087-275-3333). There are usually enough seats, though it's best to book a day ahead. But if no one shows up, consider a private Moran taxi trip around the peninsula (€60 for 3 people, cabby narrates 2.5-hour ride).

Eco-Cruises—Dingle Marine Eco Tours offers a two-hour birds-and-rocks boat tour of the peninsula. The guided tour sails either east toward Minard Castle or west toward the Blasket Islands (€25, April–Sept, departs 16:00, office around corner from TI, tel. 066/915-0768).

Blasket Islands

This rugged group of six islands off the tip of Dingle Peninsula seems particularly close to the soul of Ireland. The population of Great Blasket Island, home to as many as 160 people, dwindled until the government moved the last handful of residents to the mainland in 1953. Life here was hard. Each family had a cow, a few sheep, and a plot of potatoes. They cut their peat from the high ridge and harvested fish from the sea. There was no priest, pub, or doctor. These people formed the most traditional Irish community of the 20th century—the symbol of antique Gaelic culture.

Their special closeness to their island—combined with their knack for vivid storytelling—is inspirational. From this primitive but proud fishing/farming community came three writers of international repute whose Gaelic work—basically tales of life on Great Blasket—is translated into many languages. You'll find *Peig* (by Peig Sayers), *Twenty Years a-Growing* (Maurice O'Sullivan), and *The Islander* (Thomas O'Crohan) in shops everywhere.

In the summer, there's a café and hostel (mobile 086-852-2321) on Great Blasket Island, but it's little more than a ghost town overrun with rabbits on a peaceful, grassy, three-mile-long poem. The 40-passenger Blasket ferry runs hourly, and in summer, every half hour, depending on weather and demand (€20 round-trip, April–mid-Oct 10:00–19:00, no boats mid-Oct–March). There may be a bus from Dingle town to Dunquin—leaving in the morning and picking up in the late afternoon—coordinated with the ferry schedule (€16 taxi service by Moran, tel.

066/915-1155; Dunquin ferry tel. 066/915-6422). Dunquin has a fine hostel (tel. 066/915-6121).

In summer, a fast 12-passenger boat called the *Peig Sayers* runs between Dingle town and the Blaskets. The ride (which may include a quick look at Fungie) traces the spectacular coastline all the way to Slea Head in a boat designed to slice expertly through the ocean chop. Because of the tricky landing at Great Blasket's primitive, tiny boat ramp, any substantial swell can make actually going ashore impossible (€35 round-trip, departing at 9:00, 11:00, 13:00, and 15:00, includes 40-min ride with free time to explore island; or €70 overnight trip, includes dinner, a bed in the island's hostel, and breakfast; for info, call Mary at 066/915-1344 or mobile 087-672-6100).

▲▲Great Blasket Centre—This state-of-the-art Blasket and Gaelic heritage center gives visitors the best look possible at the language, literature, and way of life of the Blasket Islanders. See the fine 20-minute video (shows on the half hour), hear the sounds, read the poems, browse through old photos, and then gaze out the big windows at those rugged islands and imagine. Even if you never got past limericks, the poetry of these people—so pure and close to each other and nature—will have you dipping your pen into the cry of the birds (€3.50, Easter–Oct daily 10:00–18:00, until 19:00 July–Aug, closed Nov–Easter, cafeteria, on the mainland facing the islands, well-signposted, tel. 066/915-6444). Visit this center before visiting the islands.

ROME

(Roma)

Rome is magnificent and brutal at the same time. Your ears will ring, if you're careless you'll be run down or pickpocketed, and you'll be frustrated by the kind of chaos that only an Italian can understand. You may even come to believe Mussolini was a necessary evil.

But Rome is required, and if your hotel provides a comfortable refuge, if you pace yourself and accept (and even partake in) the siesta plan, if you're well-organized for sightseeing, and if you protect yourself and your valuables with extra caution and discretion, you'll do fine. You'll see the sights and leave satisfied.

Rome at its peak meant civilization itself. Everything was either civilized (part of the Roman Empire, Latin- or Greek-speaking) or barbarian. Today, Rome is Italy's political capital, the capital of Catholicism, and a splendid..."junk pile" is not quite the right term...of Western civilization. As you peel through its fascinating and jumbled layers, you'll find its buildings, cats, laundry, traffic, and 2.6 million people endlessly entertaining. And then, of course, there are the magnificent sights.

Tour St. Peter's, the greatest church on earth, and scale Michelangelo's 330-foot-tall dome, the world's largest. Learn something about eternity by touring the huge Vatican Museum. You'll find the story of Creation, bright as the day it was painted, in the recently restored Sistine Chapel. Do the "Caesar Shuffle" through ancient Rome's Forum and Colosseum. Savor Europe's most sumptuous building—the Borghese Gallery—and take an early evening "Dolce Vita Stroll" down the Via del Corso with Rome's beautiful people. Enjoy an after-dark walk from Campo de' Fiori to the Spanish Steps, lacing together Rome's Baroque and bubbly nightspots.

Rome Area

Planning Your Time

For most travelers, Rome is best done quickly. It's a great city, but it's exhausting. Time is normally short, and Italy is more charming elsewhere. To "do" Rome in a day, consider it as a side trip from Orvieto or Florence, and maybe before the night train to Venice. Crazy as that sounds, if all you have is a day, it's a great one.

Rome in a day: Vatican (2 hours in the museum and Sistine Chapel and 1 hour in St. Peter's), taxi over the river to the Pantheon (picnic on its steps), then hike over Capitol Hill, through the Forum, and to the Colosseum. Have dinner on Campo de' Fiori and dessert on Piazza Navona.

Rome in two to three days: Day one, do the "Caesar Shuffle" from the Colosseum and Forum over Capitol Hill to the Pantheon. After a siesta, join the locals strolling from Piazza del Popolo to the Spanish Steps (see my recommended "Dolce Vita Stroll," page 778). Have dinner near your hotel.

On the second day, see the Vatican City (St. Peter's, climb the dome, and tour the Vatican Museum). Spend the evening walking from Campo de' Fiori—an atmospheric place for dinner—to the Trevi Fountain and Spanish Steps (see "Night Walk Across Rome," page 780). With a third day, add the Borghese Gallery (reservations required) and the National Museum of Rome.

ORIENTATION

Sprawling Rome actually feels manageable once you get to know it. The old core, with most of the tourist sights, sits in a diamond formed by the train station (in the east), Vatican (west), the Borghese Gardens (north) and the Colosseum (south). The Tiber River runs through the diamond from north to south. To give an idea of scale, it takes about an hour-plus to walk from the train station to the Vatican.

Consider Rome in these layers:

The ancient city had a million people. The best of the classical sights stand in a line from the Colosseum to the Pantheon.

Medieval Rome was little more than a hobo camp of 50,000— thieves, mean dogs, and the pope, whose legitimacy required a Roman address. The medieval city, a colorful tangle of lanes, lies between the Pantheon and the river.

Window-shoppers' Rome twinkles with nightlife and ritzy shopping near Rome's main drag, Via del Corso—in the triangle formed by Piazza del Popolo, Piazza Venezia, and the Spanish Steps.

Vatican City is a compact world of its own with two great, huge sights: St. Peter's Basilica and the Vatican Museum.

Trastevere, the seedy, colorful, wrong-side-of-the-river neighborhood/village, is Rome at its crustiest—and perhaps most "Roman."

Baroque Rome is an overleaf that embellishes great squares throughout the town with fountains and church facades.

Since no one is allowed to build taller than St. Peter's dome, the city has no modern skyline. And the Tiber River is ignored. After the last floods (1870), the banks were built up very high and Rome turned its back on its naughty, unnavigable river.

Tourist Information

While Rome has several main tourist information offices, the dozen or so TI kiosks scattered around the town at major tourist centers are handy and just as helpful. If all you need is a map, forget the TI and get one at your hotel.

You'll find helpful tourist offices—especially if they're not too busy—at the airport (daily 9:00–19:00, tel. 06-6595-6074) and at the train station (daily 8:00–21:00, near track 3, accessible from platforms or lobby, marked "Informazioni Turistiche/Tourist Info," crowded, combined with travel agency, tel. 06-4890-6300).

Downtown Rome

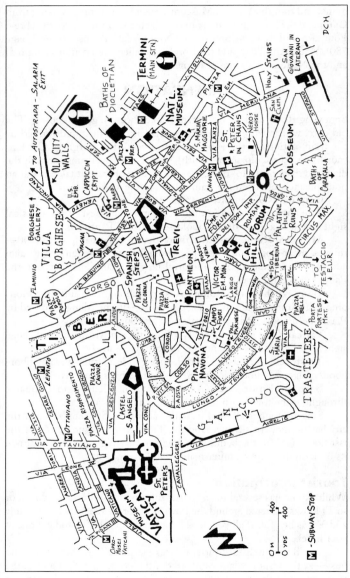

Smaller TIs (daily 9:00–18:00) include kiosks near the Forum (on Piazza del Tempio della Pace), at Via del Corso (on Largo Goldoni), in Trastevere (on Piazza Sonnino), on Via Nazionale (at Palazzo delle Esposizioni), at Castel Sant' Angelo, and at Santa Maria Maggiore. For more information, call 06-3600-4399 (daily 9:00–19:00).

At any TI, ask for a city map, a listing of sights and hours (in the free *Museums of Rome* booklet), and *Passepartout*, the free monthly entertainment guide for evening events and fun. Don't book rooms through a TI; you'll save money by booking direct.

The tourism promotion office, near Piazza della Repubblica's huge fountain, covers the city and the region. It's a five-minute walk out the front of the train station (Mon–Sat 9:00–19:00, Via Parigi 5, free Internet access to Rome tourism sites, www.romaturismo.com, tel. 06-360-64399). It's air-conditioned and less crowded than the TIs but more into promotion than information and therefore less helpful. It does have seats and a study table.

Roma c'è is a cheap little weekly entertainment guide with a helpful English section (at the back) on musical events and the pope's schedule for the week (new edition every Thu, sold at newsstands for €1, www.romace.it, Web site in Italian).

Arrival in Rome

Rome's main train station, **Termini**, is a minefield of tourist services: a TI (daily 8:00–21:00), train info office (daily 7:00–21:45), ATMs, late-hours banks, 24-hour thievery, luggage deposit (near track 24), the main city-bus hub (where you can catch the city orientation tour in front of train station), a subway stop, and the handy, cheery Food Village Chef Express Self-Service Ristorante (daily 11:00–22:30, WC at entrance, near east end of station). In the modern mall downstairs, under the station, you'll find a grocery (oddly named "Drug Store," daily 7:00–24:00) and pharmacy (daily 7:30–22:00, public showers). The station has some sleazy sharks with official-looking business cards. In general, avoid anybody selling anything at the station.

By Bus: Long-distance buses (e.g., from Siena and Assisi) arrive at Rome's small **Tiburtina** station, which is on Metro line B, with easy connections to the main train station (a straight shot 4 stops away) and the entire Metro system.

Most of my hotel listings are easily accessible by foot (those near the Termini train station) or by Metro (those in the Colosseum and Vatican neighborhoods). The train station has its own Metro stop (Termini).

By Plane: If you arrive at the airport, catch a train (hrly, 30 min, €9, credit card accepted) to Rome's train station or take (or share) a taxi to your hotel. For details, see "Transportation Connections" at the end of this chapter.

Dealing with (and Avoiding) Problems

Theft Alert: With sweet-talking con artists meeting you at the station, well-dressed pickpockets on buses, and thieving gangs of children at the ancient sites, Rome is a gauntlet of rip-offs. There's no great physical risk, but green or sloppy tourists will be scammed. Thieves strike when you're distracted. Don't trust kind strangers. Keep nothing important in your pockets. Assume you're being stalked. (Then relax and have fun.) Be most on guard while boarding and leaving buses and subways. Thieves crowd the door, then stop and turn while others crowd and push from behind. The sneakiest thieves are well-dressed businessmen (generally with something in their hands); lately many are posing as tourists with fanny packs and cameras. Scams abound: Don't give your wallet to self-proclaimed "police" who stop you on the street, warn you about counterfeit (or drug) money, and ask to see your wallet. If a bank machine eats your ATM card, see if there's a thin plastic insert with a tongue hanging out that thieves use to extract it.

If you know what to look out for, the gangs of children picking the pockets and handbags of naive tourists are no threat but an interesting, albeit sad, spectacle. Gangs of city-stained children (sometimes as young as 8–10 years old), too young to be prosecuted but old enough to rip you off, troll through the tourist crowds around the Colosseum, Forum, Piazza Repubblica, and train and Metro stations. Watch them target tourists who are overloaded with bags or distracted with a video camera. The kids look like beggars and hold up newspapers or cardboard signs to confuse their victims. They scram like stray cats if you're onto them. A fast-fingered mother with a baby is often nearby. The terrace above the bus stop near the Colosseum Metro stop is a fine place to watch the action and maybe even pick up a few moves of your own.

Reporting Losses: To report lost or stolen passports and documents or to file an insurance claim, you must file a police report (at the train station with Polizia at track 1 or with Carabinieri at track 20, also at Piazza Venezia). To replace a passport, file the police report, then go to your embassy (see below). The following phone numbers, beginning with 800, are Italian (dialed free in Italy). To report stolen or lost credit cards, call the company (Visa—tel. 800-877-232 or 800-819-014, MasterCard—tel. 800-870-866, American Express tel. 800-874-333), then file a police report. To report lost traveler's checks, call your bank (Visa—tel. 800-874-155, Thomas Cook/MasterCard—tel. 800-872-050, American Express—tel. 800-872-000), then file a police report.

Embassies: United States (Mon–Fri 8:30–13:00 & 14:00–17:30, Via Vittorio Veneto 119/A, tel. 06-46741, www.usembassy.it) and Canada (Via Zara 30, tel. 06-445-981, www.canada.it).

Emergency Numbers: Police—tel. 113. Ambulance—tel. 118.

Hit and Run: Walk with extreme caution. Scooters don't need to stop at red lights, and even cars exercise what drivers call the "logical option" of not stopping if they see no oncoming traffic. As noisy scooters are replaced by electric ones, they'll be quieter (hooray) but more dangerous for pedestrians. Follow locals like a shadow when you cross a street (or spend a good part of your visit stranded on curbs).

Staying/Getting Healthy: The siesta is a key to survival in summertime Rome. Lie down and contemplate the extraordinary power of gravity in the eternal city. I drink lots of cold, refreshing water from Rome's many drinking fountains (the Forum has 3). There's a pharmacy (marked by a green cross) in every neighborhood, including a handy one in the train station (daily 7:30–22:00, located downstairs, at west end), and a 24-hour pharmacy on Piazza dei Cinquecento 51 (next to train station on Via Cavour, tel. 06-488-0019). Embassies can recommend English-speaking doctors. Consider MEDline, a 24-hour home medical service (tel. 06-808-0995, doctors speak English). Anyone is entitled to free emergency treatment at public hospitals. The hospital closest to the train station is Policlinico Umberto 1 (entrance for emergency treatment on Via Lancisi, translators available, Metro: Policlinico). The American Hospital is a private hospital on the edge of town accustomed to helping Yankees (tel. 06-225-571).

Helpful Hints

In Rome, get train tickets and railpass-related reservations and supplements at travel agencies, rather than dealing with the congested train station. The cost is either the same or there's a minimal charge. Your hotel can direct you to the nearest travel agency. Quo Vadis, near the Vatican, is helpful (Via della Conciliazione, 22–24, tel. 06-6880-4941, fax 06-6880-3191, qv.viaggi@tiscalinet.it). Or purchase train tickets from the American Express office near the Spanish Steps (Mon–Fri 9:00–17:30, closed Sat–Sun, Piazza di Spagna 38, tel. 06-67641).

Bookstore: Try American Bookstore (Via Torino 136, Metro: Repubblica, tel. 06-474-6877).

Internet Access: The biggest is easyInternetcafe, centrally located on Piazza Barberini (access from €0.50, open 24/7, 350 terminals, www .easyInternetcafe.com). Your hotelier can direct you to an Internet access point near your hotel.

Laundry: Ask your hotelier for the nearest launderette (usually open daily 8:00–22:00, about €6 to wash and dry a 15-pound load). The Bolle Blu chain comes with Internet access (near train station at Via Milazzo 20, Via Palestro 59, and Via Principe Amedeo 70, tel. 06-446-5804).

Web Sites on Rome: www.romaturismo.com (music, exhibitions, and events, in English), www.wantedinrome.com (job openings and real estate, but also festivals and exhibitions, in English), and www .vatican.va (the pope's Web site, in English).

Metropolitana: Rome's Subway

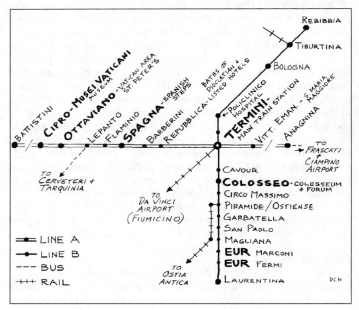

REBIBBIA
TIBURTINA
BOLOGNA
BATTISTINI
CIPRO-MUSEI VATICANI
MUSEUM
OTTAVIANO — VATICAN AREA
ST. PETER'S
LEPANTO
FLAMINIO
SPAGNA — SPANISH STEPS
BARBERINI
REPUBBLICA — LISTED HOTELS
BATHS OF DIOCLETIAN + HOTELS
POLICLINICO HOSPITAL
TERMINI — MAIN TRAIN STATION
VITT. EMAN. — S. MARIA MAGGIORE
ANAGNINA
TO FRASCATI + CIAMPINO AIRPORT
TO CERVETERI + TARQUINIA
TO DA VINCI AIRPORT (FIUMICINO)
CAVOUR
COLOSSEO — COLOSSEUM + FORUM
CIRCO MASSIMO
PIRAMIDE / OSTIENSE
GARBATELLA
SAN PAOLO
MAGLIANA
EUR MARCONI
EUR FERMI
TO OSTIA ANTICA
LAURENTINA

LINE A
LINE B
BUS
RAIL

DCH

Getting around Rome

Sightsee on foot, by city bus, or by taxi. I've grouped your sightseeing into walkable neighborhoods.

Public transportation is efficient, cheap, and part of your Roman experience. It starts running around 5:30 and stops around 23:30, sometimes earlier. After midnight, there are a few very crowded night buses, and taxis become more expensive and hard to get. Don't try to hail one—go to a taxi stand.

Buses and subways use the same ticket. You can buy tickets at newsstands, tobacco shops (*tabacchi*, marked by a black-and-white "T" sign), or at major Metro stations or bus stops, but not on board. Since many Metro stations have no human ticket-sellers and the machines are either broken or require exact change (helps to put in smallest coin first), it's easier to buy a few tickets above ground at newsstands or *tabacchi* (€0.80, good for 75 min, valid for one Metro ride, including transfers, and unlimited buses) or an all-day bus/Metro pass (€3.25, for more info, visit www.atac.roma.it). One-week transit passes cost €12.50. Stamp your ticket before using it (machines are near subway turnstiles and on buses—watch others and imitate).

Buses (especially the touristic #64) and the subway are havens for thieves and pickpockets. Assume any commotion is a thief-created distraction. If one bus is packed, there's likely a second one on its tail with far fewer crowds and thieves.

By Metro: The Roman subway system (Metropolitana) is simple, with two clean, cheap, fast lines that intersect at Termini train station. While much of Rome is not served by its skimpy subway, these stops are helpful:

Termini—train station, National Museum of Rome (at Palazzo Massimo), recommended hotels

Repubblica—Baths of Diocletian/Octagonal Hall, TI, recommended hotels

Barberini—Cappuccin Crypt, Trevi Fountain

Spagna—Spanish Steps, Villa Borghese, classy shopping area

Flaminio—Piazza del Popolo, start of recommended Dolce Vita Stroll down Via del Corso

Ottaviano—St. Peter's and Vatican City

Cipro-Musei Vaticani—Vatican Museum, recommended hotels

Colosseo—Colosseum, Roman Forum, recommended hotels

E.U.R.—Mussolini's futuristic suburb

First and last compartments are generally less crowded.

By Bus: Bus routes are clearly listed at the stops. Ask the TI for a bus map (bus info: tel. 06-4695-2027). Punch your ticket in the orange stamping machine as you board (even if you've already stamped it for the Metro)—or you are cheating. Riding without a stamped ticket on the bus, while relatively safe, is stressful. Inspectors fine even innocent-looking tourists €52. If the validation machine won't work, you can write the date, time, and bus number on the ticket. Ideally, buy a bunch of tickets from a tobacco shop or newsstand first thing so you can hop a bus without first having to search for a tobacco shop that's open.

Here are a few buses worth knowing about:

#64—Termini (train station), Piazza della Repubblica (sights), Via Nazionale (recommended hotels), Piazza Venezia (near Forum), Largo Argentina (near Pantheon), and St. Peter's Basilica. Ride it for a city overview and to watch pickpockets in action (can get horribly crowded).

#40—This express route is especially helpful—it's the same route as #64, but with fewer stops, crowds, and pickpockets.

#8—This tram connects Largo Argentina with Trastevere (get off at Piazza Mastai).

#H—Express connecting Termini train station and Trastevere, with a few stops on Via Nazionale (for Trastevere, get off at Piazza Belli, just over bridge).

By Taxi: I use taxis in Rome more often than in other cities. They're reasonable and useful for efficient sightseeing in a big, hot city. Taxis start at about €2.50 and charge about €1 per kilometer from there

---

DAILY REMINDER

Sunday: These sights are closed: Vatican Museum (except for the last Sunday of the month, when it's free and crowded) and the Catacombs of San Sebastian. The Pantheon and E.U.R.'s Museum of Roman Civilization close early in the afternoon. The old center is delightfully quiet.

Monday: Many sights are closed: National Museum of Rome, Borghese Gallery, Capitol Hill Museum, Octagonal Hall (at Baths of Diocletian), Etruscan Museum, Castel Sant' Angelo, Trajan's Market, Montemartini Museum, Protestant Cemetery, E.U.R.'s Museum of Roman Civilization, and Ostia Antica.

All of the ancient sights (e.g., Colosseum, Forum) and the Vatican Museum, among others, open. The Baths of Caracalla close early in the afternoon.

Tuesday: All sights are open in Rome except for Nero's Golden House. This isn't a good day to side-trip to Naples, because its Archaeological Museum is closed.

Wednesday: All sights are open except for the Catacombs of San Callisto.

Thursday: All sights are open except for the Cappuccin Crypt and Galleria Doria Pamphilj.

Friday: All sights are open in Rome.

(surcharges of €1 on Sun, €2.75 for night hours of 22:00–7:00, €1 surcharge for luggage, €7.25 extra for airport, tip by rounding up to the nearest euro). Sample fares: Train station to Vatican–€9; train station to Colosseum–€6; Colosseum to Trastevere–€7. Three or four companions with more money than time should taxi almost everywhere. It's tough to wave down a taxi in Rome. Find the nearest taxi stand by asking a passerby or a clerk in a shop, *"Dov'è* (doh-vay) *una fermata dei tassi?"* (Some are listed on my maps.) Taxis listing their telephone number on the door have fair meters—use them. To save time and energy, have your hotel call a taxi; the meter starts when the call is received. To call a cab on your own, dial 06-3570, 06-4994, or 06-88177.

When you arrive at the train station or airport, beware of hustlers conning naïve visitors into unmarked rip-off "express taxis." Only use official taxis, with a "taxi" sign and phone number marked on the door. By law, they must display a multilingual official price chart.

By Boat: A new boat service makes stops up and down the Tiber (you'll see the docks, 2/hr, €1/ride, €2.50/day pass, daily 7:30–20:00, until 24:00 in summer). In 2004 they hope to extend the service all the way to Ostia Antica.

TOURS

Scala Reale—Tom Rankin (an American architect in love with Rome and his Roman wife) runs Scala Reale, a company committed to sorting out the rich layers of Rome for small groups with a longer-than-average attention span. Their excellent walking tours vary in length from two to four hours and start at €20 per person. Try to book in advance, since their groups are limited to six and fill up fast. Their fascinating "Rome Orientation" walks lace together lesser-known sights from antiquity to the present (tel. 06-474-5673, 888/467-1986 in the U.S., www.scalareale .org, info@scalareale.org).

If you're interested in weeklong classes on Rome, look into the Institute for Roman Culture, an innovative, educational organization run by Tom Rankin and his colleague, archaeologist Darius Arya (see www.romanculture.org for prices, details, and booking).

Through Eternity—This company, which gets mixed reviews from read-ers, offers four walking tours, all led by native English speakers. The tours include St. Peter's and the Vatican Museum (€35, museum entry not included, 5 hrs, most days); the Colosseum and Roman Forum (€20, 2.5 hrs, daily); Rome at Twilight (€20, nightly); and a Wine Sampling Tour (€35, nightly, includes a glass at 4 or 5 wine bars and dinner). Call or visit their Web site to get the schedule and to book in advance (max of 20 people, tel. 06-700-9336, mobile 347-336-5298, private tours possible, www.througheternity.com, info@througheternity.com, Rob Allen).

Rome Walks—Students working for "Rome Walks" give tours in fluent English to small groups (2–8 people). Sample tours include Colosseum/ Forum/Palatine Walk (€48, includes admission to Colosseum, 3 hrs), Scandal Tour (€30, 2 hrs to dig up the dirt on Roman emperors, royalty, and popes), Vatican City Walk (€55, includes admission to Vatican Museum, 4 hrs), and a Twilight Rome Evening Walk (all the famous squares that offer lively people scenes, €25, 2 hrs). See their Web site for the latest (www.romewalks.com) and book in advance by e-mail (info@romewalks.com) or phone (mobile 347-795-5175, private tours also available, Annie). You'll need to give the name of your hotel and the phone number. Your guide will call or e-mail you to let you know the meeting place.

Roman Odyssey Tours—Another ex-pat tour company, Roman Odyssey, offers various 2-hour, €20 walks. To get folks on board, they often give free 40-minute tours of St. Peters' Square and Basilica (tel. 06-580-9902, mobile 328-912-3720, for a listing of tours see www .romanodyssey.com, Rahul and Jason).

ROME AT A GLANCE

▲▲▲**Vatican Museum** Four miles of the art of Western Civilization, culminating in the Sistine Chapel. **Hours:** March–Oct Mon–Fri 8:45–16:45, Sat 8:45–13:45; Nov–Feb Mon–Sat 8:45–13:45; closed many holidays and Sun except last Sun of the month.

▲▲▲**St. Peter's Basilica** Most impressive church on earth, with Michelangelo's *Pietà* and dome. **Hours:** Daily May–Sept 7:00–19:00, Oct–April 7:00–18:00. Dome: Daily May–Sept 8:30–18:00, Oct–April 8:30–17:00.

▲▲▲**Roman Forum** Ancient Rome's main square, with ruins and grand arches. **Hours:** Daily 9:00–19:00 or until an hour before dark.

▲▲▲**Colosseum** Huge stadium where gladiators fought. **Hours:** Daily 9:00–19:00 or until an hour before dark.

▲▲▲**Pantheon** The defining domed temple. **Hours:** Mon–Sat 8:30–19:30, Sun 9:00–18:00, holidays 9:00-13:00.

▲▲▲**National Museum of Rome** Greatest collection of Roman sculpture anywhere. **Hours:** Tue–Sun 9:00–19:45, closed Mon.

▲▲▲**Borghese Gallery Villa** Bernini sculptures and paintings by Caravaggio, Raphael, and Titian. **Hours:** Tue–Sun 9:00–19:30, Sat maybe until 23:00 June–Sept, closed Mon, reservations mandatory.

▲▲**Catacombs** Layers of tunnels with tombs, mainly Christian, outside the city. **Hours:** Open 8:30–12:00 & 14:30–17:30, until 17:00 in winter (San Callisto closed Wed and Feb, San Sebastian closed Sun and Nov).

▲▲**Capitol Hill Museum** Ancient statues, mosaics, and expansive view of Forum. **Hours:** Tue–Sun 9:00–20:00, closed Mon, Jan 1, May 1, and Dec 25.

▲▲**Capitol Hill** Hilltop square designed by Michelangelo with museum, grand stairway, and Forum overlooks. **Hours:** Always open.

▲**Trajan's Column** Tall column with narrative relief, on Piazza Venezia. **Hours:** Always viewable.

▲**Nero's Golden House** Sparse remains of Emperor Nero's sprawling home. **Hours:** Wed–Mon 9:00–19:45, last entry at 18:40, closed Tue.

▲**Mamertine Prison** Prison that held Saints Peter and Paul. **Hours:** Daily 9:00–12:30 & 14:30–18:00.

▲**Arch of Constantine** Honors Emperor Constantine, who legalized Christianity. **Hours:** Always open.

▲**Palatine Hill** Ruins of emperors' palaces, Circus Maximus view, and museum. **Hours:** Daily 9:00–19:00 or an hour before dark.

▲**Castel Sant' Angelo** Hadrian's Tomb turned castle, prison, papal refuge, now museum. **Hours:** Tue–Sun 9:00–19:00, plus June–Sept Sat 21:00–23:45, closed Mon.

▲**Baths of Diocletian** Once ancient Rome's immense public baths, now a Michelangelo church—Church of Santa Maria degli Angeli—and the Octagonal Hall, a room with minor ancient Roman sculpture. **Hours:** Church open Mon–Sat 7:00–18:30, Sun 8:00–19:30. Octagonal Hall: Tue–Sat 9:00–14:00, Sun 9:00–13:00, closed Mon.

▲**Museum of Roman Civilization** Lifeless museum, but has an interesting 3-D model of ancient Rome. **Hours:** Tue–Sat 9:00–18:45, Sun 9:00–13:30, closed Mon.

▲**Montemartini Museum** 400 Roman statues in a 1932 electric power plant. **Hours:** Tue–Sun 9:30–19:00, closed Mon.

▲**Galleria Doria Pamphilj** Fancy palace packed with art. **Hours:** Fri–Wed 10:00–17:00, closed Thu.

▲**Cappuccin Crypt** Crypt decorated with the bones of 4,000 monks. **Hours:** Fri–Wed 9:00–12:00 & 15:00–18:00, closed Thu.

▲**St. Peter-in-Chains** Church with Michelangelo's *Moses*. **Hours:** Mon–Sat 7:00–12:30 & 15:30–19:00, Sun 7:30–12:30.

▲**Santa Maria della Vittoria** Church with Bernini's swooning *St. Teresa in Ecstasy*. **Hours:** Daily 7:00–12:00 & 15:30–19:00.

▲**St. Paul's Outside the Walls** Huge, Vatican-owned basilica in south Rome, rebuilt in 19th century. **Hours:** Daily 7:00–18:00, cloister closed 13:00–15:00.

▲**Villa Borghese** Central Park of Rome with lake, Borghese Gallery, and Etruscan Museum. **Hours:** Always open.

▲**Trevi Fountain** Baroque hotspot—bring coins. **Hours:** Always flowing.

Private Guides—Consider a personal tour. Any of the tour companies I list can provide a guide. I work with Francesca Caruso, a licensed guide who speaks excellent English and loves to teach and share her apprecia- tion of her city (€100 for 2 hrs or more—she happily stretches the tour to half a day for eager students, individuals, and small groups; chris.fra@mclink.it).

Hop-on, Hop-off Bus Tour—The ATAC city bus tour offers a quick, cheap orientation tour of Rome. In under two hours, you'll have 80 sights pointed out to you (by a live guide in English and maybe one other language). If you've got a little more time and money, you can get out at any of the nine stops and catch a later bus (though stops are poorly marked and the included map is useless). The stops are: Piazza Barberini, Via Veneto, Villa Borghese, Piazza Cavour, St. Peter's Square, Corso Vittorio Emanuele (for Piazza Navona), Piazza Venezia, Colosseum, and Via Nazionale.

While the guide's spiel is limited to simple identification of the sights, this tour provides an efficient and economical orientation to Rome. I'd take the nonstop tour for €7.75; the hop-on, hop-off tour is €13. Bus #110 departs every 30 minutes—at the top and bottom of the hour—from in front of the Termini train station (near platform C, buy tickets at info kiosk there—marked "i bus"—or buy on the bus and pay about 10 percent more, runs March–Sept 9:00–20:00, Oct–Feb 10:00–18:00, tel. 06-4695-2252).

Archeobus—This handy hop-on, hop-off bus runs hourly from the west side of Piazza Venezia way out the Appian Way. By far the easiest way to see the sights down this ancient Roman road, it includes a basic, uninspired two-hour tour (longer if there's traffic) in Italian and English in an air-conditioned minibus (buy €7.75 tickets at green kiosk on Piazza Venezia, hourly departures from 9:00–17:00, tel. 06-4695-4695).

SIGHTS

From the Colosseum Area to Capitol Hill

Beware of gangs of young thieves, particularly between the Colosseum and the Forum; they're harmless if you know their tricks (see Theft Alert, above).

▲**St. Peter-in-Chains Church (San Pietro in Vincoli)**—Built in the fifth century to house the chains that held St. Peter, this church is most famous for its Michelangelo statue. Check out the much-venerated chains under the high altar, then focus on Moses (free, Mon–Sat 7:00–12:30 & 15:30–19:00, Sun 7:30–12:30, modest dress required; the church is a short, uphill, zigzag walk from the Colosseum, or a shorter, simpler walk from the Cavour Metro stop—exiting the Metro stop, go up steep flight of steps, take a right at the top and walk a block to church).

Pope Julius II commissioned Michelangelo to build a massive

Colosseum Area

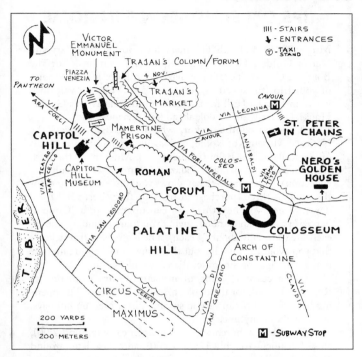

IIII - STAIRS
↓ - ENTRANCES
Ⓣ - TAXI STAND

VICTOR EMMANUEL MONUMENT

TRAJAN'S COLUMN/FORUM

PIAZZA VENEZIA

4 NOV.

TO PANTHEON

VIA ARA COELI

TRAJAN'S MARKET

CAVOUR Ⓜ

VIA LEONINA

ST. PETER IN CHAINS

MAMERTINE PRISON

VIA CAVOUR

CAPITOL HILL

VIA FORI IMPERIALE

COLOS-SEO

VIA ANNIBALDI

VIA TERME TITO

NERO'S GOLDEN HOUSE

VIA TEATRO MARCELLO

CAPITOL HILL MUSEUM

ROMAN

FORUM

Ⓜ

TIBER

VIA SAN TEODORO

PALATINE

HILL

COLOSSEUM

ARCH OF CONSTANTINE

VIA CLAUDIA

CIRCUS

VIA DI SAN GREGORIO

VIA CERCHI

MAXIMUS

200 YARDS

200 METERS

Ⓜ - SUBWAY STOP

tomb, with 48 huge statues, crowned by a grand statue of this egomaniacal pope. The pope had planned to have his tomb placed in the center of St. Peter's Basilica. When Julius died, the work had barely been started, and no one had the money or necessary commitment to Julius to finish the project. Michelangelo finished one statue—Moses—and left a few unfinished statues: Leah and Rachel flanking Moses in this church, the "prisoners" now in Florence's Accademia, and the "slaves" now in Paris' Louvre.

This powerful statue of Moses—mature Michelangelo—is worth studying. The artist worked on it in fits and starts for 30 years. Moses has received the Ten Commandments. As he holds the stone tablets, his eyes show a man determined to stop his tribe from worshiping the golden calf and idols...a man determined to win salvation for the people of Israel. Why the horns? Centuries ago, the Hebrew word for "rays" was mistranslated as "horns."

▲Nero's Golden House (Domus Aurea)—The barren remains of Emperor Nero's "Golden House" were reopened to the public in 1999.

TIPS ON SIGHTSEEING IN ROME

Museums: Plan ahead. The marvelous Borghese Gallery and Nero's Golden House both require reservations. For the Borghese Gallery, it's safest to make reservations well in advance of your trip (for specifics, see page 753). You can wait until you're in Rome to call for a reservation time at Nero's Golden House, but it's wise to book ahead (see previous page).

A special **combo-ticket**, which costs €20, covers the National Museum of Rome, Colosseum, Palatine Hill, Baths of Caracalla, Crypt Balbi (medieval art), Museum of the Bath (Roman inscriptions), and Palazzo Altemps (so–so sculpture collection). The combo–ticket allows you to see seven sights for the price of three (purchase at participating sites, valid for 7 days). When you buy this, you can upgrade to a "Coupon Servizi" pass for an extra €5, giving you tours or audioguides at each site (normally about €4 each). The big plus of this ticket is that you avoid the long lines at the Colosseum (if you purchase it at a participating site other than the Colosseum).

Get a current listing of **museum hours** from one of Rome's TIs—ask for the booklet *Museums of Rome*. The opening hours of sights can vary in summer, in winter, on holidays, and just about anytime.

Churches: Churches generally open early (around 7:00), close for lunch (roughly 12:00–15:00), and close late (around 19:00). Kamikaze tourists maximize their sightseeing hours by visiting churches before 9:00 and seeing the major sights that stay open during the siesta (St. Peter's, Colosseum, Forum, Capitol Hill Museum, National Museum of Rome) while Romans are taking it cool and easy.

A modest dress code is strictly enforced at St. Peter's at the Vatican and St. Paul's Outside the Walls. That means no bare shoulders, miniskirts, or shorts—for men, women, or children. Elsewhere, you'll see many tourists in shorts touring many churches.

This massive house once sprawled across the valley (where the Colosseum now stands) and up the hill—the part you tour today. A colossal, 100-foot-tall bronze statue of Nero towered over everything. The house incorporated an artificial lake (where the Colosseum was later built) and a forest stocked with game.

Nero (ruled A.D. 54–68) was Rome's most notorious emperor. He killed his own mother, kicked his pregnant wife to death, crucified St. Peter, and—most galling to his subjects—was a bad actor. When Rome burned in A.D. 64, Nero was accused of torching it to clear land for an even bigger house. The Romans rebelled and Nero stabbed himself in the neck, crying, "What an artist dies in me!"

While only hints of the splendid, colorful frescoes survive, the towering vaults and the sheer immensity of the place are impressive. As you wander through rooms that are now underground (but originally were not), look up at the holes in the ceiling. Ponder how much of old Rome still hides underground...and why the subway is limited to two lines.

Visits are allowed only with an escort (30 people, about every 30 min) and a reservation (€6, Wed–Mon 9:00–19:45, last entry at 18:40, closed Tue, tour lasts 50 min, audioguide–€2, but listen to the intro before entering or you'll be forever behind, Metro: Colosseo, 200 yards northeast of Colosseum, through a park gate, up a hill, and on the left). If you show up without a reservation, you could luck out and be allowed in (chances are best on a late afternoon on a weekday). Guided tours in English are offered twice daily (€8.50); to reserve a place, call 06-3996-7700 (Mon–Sat 9:00–17:00).

▲▲▲Colosseum—This 2,000-year-old building is *the* great example of Roman engineering. Using concrete, brick, and their trademark round arches, Romans constructed much larger buildings than the Greeks. But in deference to the higher Greek culture, they finished their no-non-sense megastructure by pasting all three orders of Greek columns (Doric, Ionic, and Corinthian) as exterior decorations. The Flavian Amphitheater's popular name, "Colosseum," comes from the colossal statue of Nero that once stood in front of it.

Romans were into "big." By putting two theaters together, they created a circular amphitheater. They could fill and empty its 50,000 numbered seats as quickly and efficiently as we do our superstadiums. Teams of sailors hoisted canvas awnings over the stadium to give fans shade. This was where ancient Romans, whose taste for violence was the equal of modern America's, enjoyed their Dirty Harry and *Terminator*. Gladiators, criminals, and wild animals fought to the death in every conceivable scenario. The floor of the Colosseum is missing, exposing underground passages. Animals were kept in cages here and then lifted up in elevators; they'd pop out from behind blinds into the arena. The gladiator didn't know where, when, or by what he'd be attacked.

Cost, Hours, Location: €8 (includes Palatine Hill visit within 24 hours; also covered by €20 combo-ticket). A dry-but-fact-filled audioguide is available at the ticket office (€4 for 2 hours of use). Guided tours in English depart several times per day and last about one hour (€4). The Colosseum is open daily 9:00–19:00, or until an hour before sunset (tel. 06-3974-9907). Metro: Colosseo.

Colosseum

Outside the entrance of the Colosseum, vendors sell handy little *Rome: Past and Present* books with plastic overlays to un-ruin the ruins (marked €11, price soft). A WC is behind the Colosseum (facing ticket entrance, go right; WC is under stairway). Caution: For a fee, the incredibly crude modern-day gladiators snuff out their cigarettes and pose for photos. They take easy-to-swindle tourists for too much money. Watch out if you tangle with these guys (they're armed...and accustomed to getting as much as €100 from naïve Asian tourists). Also, be on guard as this is traditionally a happy-hunting ground for gangs of child pickpockets.

Avoid Long Lines: Instead of waiting in line (sometimes an hour long) at the Colosseum to purchase a ticket, you have several good alternatives:

1. Buy your ticket at either of the two rarely crowded Palatine Hill entrances near the Colosseum—there's one inside the Forum and another on Via di San Gregorio (facing Forum entry, with Colosseum at

your back, go left on street). This €8 ticket includes entry to both the Colosseum and Palatine (valid for 24 hours).

2. Consider buying a €20 combo-ticket at a less-crowded sight. The combo-ticket—covering the Colosseum, Palatine Hill, National Museum of Rome, Museum of the Bath, Baths of Caracalla, and more—allows you to walk right past the Colosseum ticket line, through the turnstile, and into the Colosseum. Buy it at any of the included sights.

3. You can reserve your ticket in advance for an additional €1.50 fee by calling 06-3996-7700 (automated info in English, pay for ticket at side window of Colosseum's ticket office).

4. You can book a tour on the spot from hustlers who rescue individuals from the line by selling tours that include tickets they already have. This will cost you a few euros (€15 for the tour including the €8 ticket), but can save time and comes with a brief guided tour. Beware—American students working for the guides will tell you that there's a long line, when sometimes, there is none at all. (It can be hard for you to instantly judge the length of the line because it's tucked into the Colosseum arcade.)

▲**Arch of Constantine**—The arch, next to the Colosseum, marks one of the great turning points in history—the military coup that made Christianity mainstream. In A.D. 312, Emperor Constantine defeated his rival Maxentius in one crucial battle. The night before, he had seen a vision of a cross in the sky. Constantine became sole emperor and legalized Christianity. With this one battle, a once-obscure Jewish sect with a handful of followers was now the state religion of the entire Western world. In A.D. 300, you could be killed for being a Christian; later, you could be killed for not being one. Church enrollment boomed.

By the way, don't look too closely at the reliefs decorating this arch. By the fourth century, Rome was on its way down. Rather than struggle with original carvings, the makers of this arch plugged in bits and pieces scavenged from existing monuments. The arch is newly restored and looking great. But any meaning read into the stone will be very jumbled.

▲▲▲**Roman Forum (Foro Romano)**—This is ancient Rome's birthplace and civic center, and the common ground between Rome's famous seven hills (free, daily 9:00–19:00 or an hour before dark, Metro: Colosseo, tel. 06-3974-9907). A €4 audioguide helps decipher the rubble (rent at gift shop at entrance on Via dei Fori Imperiali). Guided tours in English are offered nearly hourly (€4); ask for information at the ticket booth at the Palatine Hill (near Arch of Titus). See "Roman Forum Walk," on page 772.

▲**Palatine Hill**—The hill above the Forum contains scanty remains of the imperial palaces and the foundations of Rome, from Iron Age huts to the legendary house of Romulus (under corrugated tin roof in far corner). We get our word *palace* from this hill, where the emperors chose to live. The Palatine was once so filled with palaces that later emperors had to build out. (Looking up at it from the Forum, you see the sub-structure that supported these long-gone palaces.) The Palatine museum has sculptures and fresco fragments but is nothing special. From the pleasant garden, you'll get an overview of the Forum. On the far side, look down into an emperor's private stadium and then beyond at the dusty Circus Maximus, once a chariot course. Imagine the cheers, jeers, and furious betting. But considering how ruined the ruins are, the heat, the hill to climb, the €8 entry fee, and the relative difficulty in under-standing what you're looking at, the Palatine Hill is a disappointment.

Cost and Hours: €8, includes Colosseum visit within 24 hours, also covered by €20 combo-ticket, daily 9:00–19:00, or one hour before sunset, Metro: Colosseo. The main entrance and ticket office—which also sells Colosseum tickets, enabling smart sightseers to avoid that long line—is near the Arch of Titus and Colosseum. Another Palatine entrance is on Via di San Gregorio.

Audioguides cost €4. Guided tours in English are offered once daily (€3.50); ask for information at the ticket booth.

▲**Mamertine Prison**—This 2,500–year–old, cistern–like prison, which once held Saints Peter and Paul, is worth a look (donation requested, daily 9:00–12:30 & 14:30–18:00, at the foot of Capitol Hill, near Forum's Arch of Septimius Severus). When you step into the room, you'll hit a modern floor. Ignore that and look up at the hole in the ceil-ing, from which prisoners were lowered. Then take the stairs down to the level of the actual prison floor. Downstairs, you'll see the column to which Peter was chained. It's said that a miraculous fountain sprang up in this room so Peter could convert and baptize his jailers, who were subsequently martyred themselves. The upside–down cross commemo-rates Peter's upside–down crucifixion.

Imagine humans, amid fat rats and rotting corpses, awaiting slow deaths. On the walls near the entry are lists of notable prisoners (Christian and non–Christian) and the ways they were executed: *stran-golati*, *decapitato*, *morto di fame* (died of hunger)....

▲**Trajan's Column, Market, and Forum**—This offers the grandest column and best example of "continuous narration" from antiquity. Over 2,500 figures scroll around the 130-foot-high column, telling of Trajan's victorious Dacian campaign (circa A.D. 103, in present-day Romania), from the assembling of the army at the bottom to the victory sacrifice at the top. The ashes of Trajan and his wife were held in the mausoleum at the base while the sun once glinted off a polished bronze statue of Trajan at the top. Today, St. Peter is on top. Study the propaganda that winds up the column like a scroll, trumpeting Trajan's wonderful military exploits. You can see this close up for free (always open and viewable, just off Piazza Venezia, across the street from the Victor Emmanuel Monument). Viewing balconies once stood on either side, but it seems likely Trajan fans came away only with a feeling that the greatness of their emperor and empire was beyond comprehension (for a rolled-out version of the column's story, visit the Museum of Roman Civilization at E.U.R., below). This column marked **Trajan's Forum**, which was built to handle the shopping needs of a wealthy city of over a million. Commercial, political, religious, and social activities all mixed in the forum.

For a fee, you can go inside **Trajan's Market** (boring) and part of Trajan's Forum; the entrance is uphill from the column on Via IV Novembre. The market was once filled with shops selling goods from all over the Roman Empire (€6.20, summer Tue–Sun 9:00–18:30, winter 9:00–16:30, closed Mon, entrance is uphill from the column on Via IV Novembre, tel. 06-679-0048).

Time Elevator Roma—Equipped with headphones, you sit in a comfortable, air-conditioned theater as the history of Rome unfolds before you—from the founding of the city, through its rise and fall, to its impressive Renaissance rebound and up to the present—with special effects en route. Good if it's hot or you're tired (€11, daily 10:00–22:00, 45-min shows every 30 min, no kids under 5, Via dei S.S. Apostoli 20, just off Via del Corso, 3-min walk from Piazza Venezia, tel. 06-699-0053, wwww.time-elevator.it).

Capitol Hill Area

There are several ways to get to the top of Capitol Hill. If you're coming from the north (Piazza Venezia), take Michelangelo's impressive stairway to the right of the big, white Victor Emmanuel Monument (described below). Coming from the south (the Forum), take either the steep staircase or the winding road, which converge near the top of the hill at a great Forum overlook and a refreshing water fountain. Block the spout with your fingers; water spurts up for drinking. Romans, who call this *il nasone* (the big nose), joke that a cheap Roman boy takes his date out for a drink at *il nasone*. Near the *nasone* is a back-door entrance to the Victor Emmanuel Monument (see Monument listing, below).

▲▲**Capitol Hill (Campidoglio)**—This hill was the religious and political center of ancient Rome. It's still the home of the city's government. Michelangelo's Renaissance square is bordered by two fine museums and the mayoral palace. Its centerpiece is a copy of the famous equestrian statue of Marcus Aurelius (the original is behind glass in the adjacent museum).

Michelangelo intended that people approach the square from his grand stairway off Piazza Venezia. From the top of the stairway, you see the new Renaissance face of Rome with its back to the Forum. Notice how Michelangelo gave the buildings the "giant order"—huge pilasters make the existing two–story buildings feel one–storied and more harmonious with the new square. Notice also how the statues atop these buildings welcome you and then draw you in. The terraces just downhill (past either side of the mayor's palace) offer fine views of the Forum.

Capitol Hill Museum

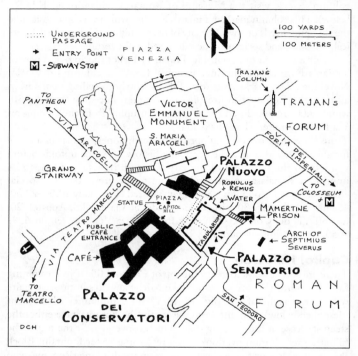

▲▲**Capitol Hill Museum**—This museum encompasses two buildings (Palazzo dei Conservatori and Palazzo Nuovo), connected by an underground passage that leads to the vacant Tabularium and a panoramic overlook of the Forum (€8, Tue–Sun 9:00–20:00, last entry 60 min before closing, closed Mon, audioguide–€4, tel. 06-3996-7800).

For an orientation to the museum's two buildings, face the equestrian statue on Capitol Hill Square (with your back to the grand stairway). The Palazzo Nuovo is on your left and the Palazzo dei Conservatori is on your right (closer to the river). Ahead is the mayor's palace (Palazzo Senatorio); below it and out of sight are the Tabularium and underground passage.

Buy your ticket (and rent the optional audioguide) at Palazzo dei Conservatori.

The **Palazzo dei Conservatori** is one of the world's oldest museums, at 500 years old. Outside the entrance, notice the marriage announcements and, possibly, wedding-party photo ops. Inside the courtyard, have a look at giant chunks of a statue of Emperor

Constantine; when intact, this imposing statue held court in the Basilica of Constantine in the Forum. The museum is worthwhile, with lavish rooms and several great statues. Tops is the original (500 B.C.) Etruscan *Capitoline Wolf* (the little statues of Romulus and Remus were added in the Renaissance). Don't miss the *Boy Extracting a Thorn* or the enchanting *Commodus as Hercules*. The second-floor painting gallery—except for two Caravaggios—is forgettable. The café upstairs, with a splendid patio with city views, is lovely at sunset.

Connect the two museums with the underground passage that leads to the **Tabularium**. Built in the first century A.D., this once held the archives of ancient Rome. The word *Tabularium* comes from tablet, on which the Romans wrote their laws. You won't see any tablets, but you will see a superb head-on view of the Forum from the windows.

The **Palazzo Nuovo** houses mostly portrait busts of forgotten emperors. But it has three must-see statues: the *Dying Gaul*, the *Capitoline Venus* (both on the first floor up), and the original gilded bronze equestrian statue of Marcus Aurelius (behind glass in museum courtyard). This greatest surviving equestrian statue of antiquity was the original centerpiece of the square. While most such pagan statues were destroyed by Dark Age Christians, Marcus was mistaken for Constantine (the first Christian emperor) and therefore spared.

From Capitol Hill to Piazza Venezia—Leaving Capitol Hill, descend the stairs leading to Piazza Venezia. At the bottom of the stairs, look left several blocks down the street to see a condominium actually built around surviving ancient pillars and arches of Teatro Marcello—perhaps the oldest inhabited building in Europe.

Still at the bottom of the stairs, look up the long stairway to your right (which pilgrims climb on their knees) for a good example of the earliest style of Christian church. While pilgrims find it worth the climb, sightseers can skip it. As you walk toward Piazza Venezia, look down into the ditch on your right to see the ruins of an ancient apartment building from the 1st century A.D.; part of it was transformed into a tiny church (faded frescoes and bell tower). Rome was built in layers—almost everywhere there is an earlier version beneath your feet.

Piazza Venezia—This vast square is the focal point of modern Rome. The Via del Corso, which starts here, is the city's axis, surrounded by Rome's classiest shopping district. In the 1930s, Mussolini whipped up Italy's nationalistic fervor here from a balcony above the square (to your left with your back to Victor Emmanuel Monument). Fascist masses filled the square screaming, "Four more years!"—or something like that. Fifteen years later, they hung Mussolini from a meat hook in Milan.

Victor Emmanuel Monument—This oversized monument to Italy's first king—built to celebrate the 50th anniversary of the country's unification—was part of Italy's push to overcome the new country's strong regionalism and to create a national identity. Open to the public, it offers a grand view of the Eternal City (free, long hours, 242 punishing steps to the top).

Romans think of the 200-foot-high, 500-foot-wide monument not as an altar of the fatherland, but as "the wedding cake," "the typewriter," or "the dentures." It wouldn't be so bad if it weren't sitting on a priceless acre of ancient Rome and if they had chosen better marble (this is too in–your–face white and picks up the pollution horribly). Soldiers guard Italy's *Tomb of the Unknown Soldier* as the eternal flame flickers. At the tomb, stand with your back to the flame and see how Via del Corso bisects Rome.

Note: There is a clever little back door access from the top of Capitol Hill, leading directly to the top of the Victor Emmanuel Monument, saving you lots of hiking (go up wide steps in corner near *il nasone* and she-wolf statue, pass through iron gate at top of steps, enter small unmarked door on the right).

Pantheon Area

▲▲▲Pantheon—For the greatest look at the splendor of Rome, antiquity's best-preserved interior is a must (free, Mon–Sat 8:30–19:30, Sun 9:00–18:00, holidays 9:00–13:00, tel. 06-6830-0230). Because the Pantheon became a church dedicated to the martyrs just after the fall of Rome, the barbarians left it alone, and the locals didn't use it as a quarry. The portico is called Rome's umbrella—a fun local gathering in a rainstorm. Walk past its one-piece granite columns (biggest in Italy, shipped from Egypt) and through the original bronze doors. Sit inside under the glorious skylight and enjoy classical architecture at its best.

The dome, 142 feet high and wide, was Europe's biggest until the Renaissance. Michelangelo's dome at St. Peter's, while much higher, is about 3 feet smaller. The brilliance of this dome's construction astounded architects through the ages. During the Renaissance, Brunelleschi was given permission to cut into the dome (see the little square hole above and to the right of the entrance) to analyze the material. The concrete dome gets thinner and lighter with height—the highest part is volcanic pumice.

This wonderfully harmonious architecture greatly inspired Raphael and other artists of the Renaissance. Raphael, along with Italy's first two kings, chose to be buried here.

As you walk around the outside of the Pantheon, notice the "rise of Rome"—about 15 feet since it was built. Nearest WCs are at McDonald's and bars on the square. Great gelato is nearby at **Giolitti's** (Via Uffici del Vicario 40, see "Eating," page 796).

▲▲Churches near the Pantheon—The **Church of San Luigi dei Francesi** has a magnificent chapel painted by Caravaggio (free, Fri–Wed 7:30–12:30 & 15:30–19:00, Thu 7:30–12:30, sightseers should avoid Mass at 7:30 and 19:00).

Pantheon Area

The only Gothic church in Rome is **Santa Maria sopra Minerva**, with a little–known Michelangelo statue, *Christ Bearing the Cross* (the church is on a little square behind the Pantheon, to the east). The **Church of St. Ignazio**, several blocks east of the Pantheon, is a riot of Baroque illusions with a false dome. (Both Sopra Minerva and St. Ignazio churches open early; take a siesta: Sopra Minerva closes at 12:00, St. Ignazio at 12:30; and reopen from around 16:00–19:00). A few blocks away, back across Corso Vittorio Emmanuele, is the rich and Baroque **Gesu Church**, headquarters of the Jesuits in Rome (free, daily 7:00–12:30 & 16:00–19:15). Modest dress is recommended at all churches.

▲**Galleria Doria Pamphilj**—This gallery, filling a palace on Piazza del Collegio Romano, offers a rare chance to wander through a noble family's lavish rooms with the prince who calls this downtown mansion home. Well, almost. Through an audioguide, the prince lovingly narrates his family's story, including how the Doria Pamphilj (pahm-FEEL-yee) family's cozy relationship with the pope inspired the word nepotism. Highlights include paintings by Caravaggio, Titian, and Raphael, and portraits of Pope Innocent X by Velázquez (on canvas) and Bernini (in marble). The fancy rooms of the palace are interesting, with a mini–Versailles–like hall of mirrors and paintings lining the walls to the ceiling in the style typical of 18th–century galleries (€7.30, includes fine audioguide, Fri–Wed 10:00–17:00, closed Thu, from Piazza Venezia walk 2 blocks up Via del Corso and take a left, tel. 06-679-7323, www.doriapamphilj.it).

▲Trevi Fountain—This bubbly Baroque fountain, worth ▲ by day and ▲▲ by night, is a minor sight to art scholars but a major nighttime gathering spot for teens on the make and tourists tossing coins. (For more information, see "Self-Guided Walks in Rome," page 771.)

East Rome, near the Train Station

These sights are within a 10-minute walk of the train station. By Metro, use the Termini stop for the National Museum and the Piazza Repubblica stop for the rest.

▲▲▲National Museum of Rome in Palazzo Massimo—This museum houses the greatest collection of ancient Roman art anywhere, and includes busts of emperors and a Roman copy of the *Greek Discus Thrower*. The ground floor is a historic yearbook of marble statues from the second century B.C. to the second century A.D., with rare Greek originals.

The first floor is peopled by statues from the first through fourth centuries A.D. To see the second-floor collection of frescoes and mosaics that once decorated Roman villas, you must reserve an entry time for a free, 45-minute tour led by an Italian- (and sometimes English-) speaking guide; if interested, book the next available tour when you buy your ticket. Finally, descend into the basement to see fine gold jewelry, dice, an abacus, and vault doors leading into the best coin collection in Europe, with fancy magnifying glasses maneuvering you through cases of coins from ancient Rome to modern times.

Cost and Hours: €6, covered by €20 combo-ticket, Tue–Sun 9:00–19:45, closed Mon, open some summer Saturdays until 23:00, last entry 45 min before closing. An audioguide costs €4 (buy ticket first, then get audioguide at bookshop). The museum is about 100 yards from the Termini train station. As you leave the station, it's the sandstone-brick building on your left. Enter at the far end, at Largo di Villa Peretti (Metro: Termini, tel. 06-481-4144).

Baths of Diocletian—Around A.D. 300, Emperor Diocletian built the largest baths in Rome. This sprawling meeting place, with baths and schmoozing spaces to accommodate 3,000 bathers at a time, was a big deal in ancient Rome. While much of it is still closed, three sections are

East Rome

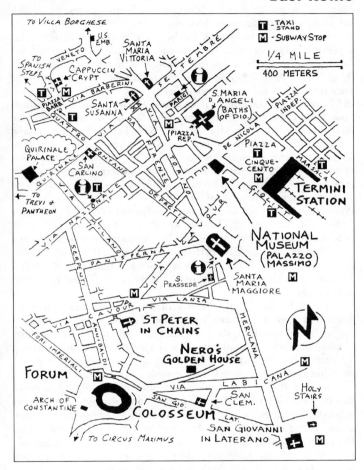

open: the Octagonal Hall, the Church of St. Mary of the Angels and Martyrs (both face Piazza della Repubblica), and the Museum of the Bath (skip it).

▲▲**Octagonal Hall**—The Aula Ottagona, or Rotunda of Diocletian, was a private gymnasium in the Baths of Diocletian. Built around A.D. 300, these functioned until 537, when the barbarians cut Rome's aqueducts. The floor would have been 23 feet lower (look down the window in the center of the room). The graceful iron grid supported the canopy of a 1928 planetarium. Today, the hall's a gallery, showing off fine bronze and marble statues—the kind that would have decorated the baths of imperial Rome. Most are Roman copies of Greek originals...gods, athletes, portrait busts. One merits a close look: the *Boxer at Rest* (first century B.C.). Textbook Hellenistic, this bronze statue is realistic and full of emotion. Slumped over, losing, and exhausted, the boxer gasps for air (free, Tue–Sat 9:00–14:00, Sun 9:00–13:00, closed Mon, borrow the English-description booklet, handy WC hidden in the back corner through an unmarked door).

▲**Church of St. Mary of the Angels and Martyrs (Santa Maria degli Angeli e dei Martiri)**—From Piazza della Repubblica, step through the Roman wall into what was the great central hall of the baths and is now a church (since the 16th century) that was designed by Michelangelo. When the church entrance was moved to Piazza Repubblica, the church was reoriented 90 degrees, turning the nave into long transepts and the transepts into a short nave. The 12 red granite columns still stand in their ancient positions. The classical floor was 15 feet lower. Project the walls down and imagine the soaring shape of the Roman vaults (free, Mon–Sat 7:00–18:30, Sun 8:00–19:30, closed to sightseers during Mass).

▲**Santa Maria della Vittoria**—This church houses Bernini's statue of a swooning *St. Teresa in Ecstasy* (free, daily 7:00–12:00 & 15:30–19:00, on Largo Susanna, about 5 blocks northwest of train station, Metro: Repubblica). Once inside the church, you'll find St. Teresa to the left of the altar.

Teresa has just been stabbed with God's arrow of fire. Now the angel pulls it out and watches her reaction. Teresa swoons, her eyes roll up, her hand goes limp, she parts her lips...and moans. The smiling, Cupid-like angel understands just how she feels. Teresa, a 16th-century Spanish nun, later talked of the "sweetness" of "this intense pain," describing her oneness with God in ecstatic, even erotic, terms.

Bernini, the master of multimedia, pulls out all the stops to make this mystical vision real. Actual sunlight pours through the alabaster windows; bronze sunbeams shine on a marble angel holding a golden arrow. Teresa leans back on a cloud and her robe ripples from within, charged with her spiritual arousal. Bernini has created a little stage setting of heaven. And watching from the "theater boxes" on either side are members of the family that commissioned the work.

Santa Susanna—The home of the American Catholic Church in Rome, Santa Susanna holds Mass in English daily at 18:00 and Sunday at 9:00 and 10:30. Their excellent Web site in English, www.santasusanna.org, contains tips for travelers (Via XX Settembre 15, near recommended Via Firenze hotels, Metro: Repubblica, tel. 06-4201-4554). They arrange papal audiences (see "Vatican City," 756) and have an English library (with my Venice, Florence, and Rome guidebooks).

North Rome: Villa Borghese and nearby Via Veneto

▲Villa Borghese—Rome's scruffy "Central Park" is great for people-watching (plenty of modern-day Romeos and Juliets). Take a row on the lake or visit the park's fine museums.

▲▲▲Borghese Gallery—This private museum, filling a cardinal's mansion in the park, offers one of Europe's most sumptuous art experiences. Because of the gallery's slick mandatory reservation system, you'll enjoy its collection of world-class Baroque sculpture—including Bernini's *David* and his excited statue of Apollo chasing Daphne, as well as paintings by Caravaggio, Raphael, Titian, and Rubens—with manageable crowds.

The essence of the collection is the connection of the Renaissance with the classical world. Notice the second-century Roman reliefs with Michelangelo-designed panels above either end of the portico as you enter. The villa was built in the early 17th century by the great art collector Cardinal Borghese, who wanted to prove that the glories of ancient Rome were matched by the Renaissance.

In the main entry hall, opposite the door, notice the thrilling relief of the horse falling (first century A.D., Greek). Pietro Bernini, father of the famous Bernini, completed the scene by adding the rider.

Each room seems to feature a Baroque masterpiece. The best of all is in Room 3: Bernini's *Apollo Chasing Daphne.* It's the perfect Baroque subject—capturing a thrilling, action-filled moment. In the mythological story, Apollo races after Daphne. Just as he's about to reach her, she turns into a tree. As her toes turn to roots and branches spring from her fingers, Apollo is in for one rude surprise. Walk slowly around. It's more air than stone.

Cost and Hours: €8.50, Tue–Sun 9:00–19:30, sometimes on Sat. until 23:00 June–Sept, closed Mon. No photos are allowed.

Reservations: Reservations are mandatory and easy to get in English over the Internet (www.ticketeria.it) or by phone: call 06-32810 (if you get an Italian recording, press 2 for English; office hours: Mon–Fri 9:00–18:00, Sat 9:00–13:00, closed Sat in Aug and Sun year-round). Reserve a *minimum* of several days in advance for a weekday visit, at least a week ahead for weekends. When you reserve, request a day and time (which you'll be given if available), and you'll get a claim number. While you'll be advised to come 30 minutes before your appointed time, you can arrive a few minutes beforehand. But don't be late, as no-show tickets are sold to standbys.

Visits are strictly limited to two hours. Concentrate on the first floor, but leave yourself 30 minutes for the paintings of the Pinacoteca upstairs; highlights are marked by the audioguide icons. The fine bookshop and cafeteria are best visited outside your two-hour entry window.

North Rome

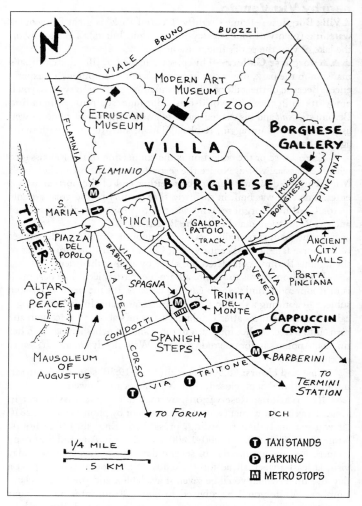

If you don't have a reservation, just show up (or call first and ask if there are openings; a late afternoon on a weekday is usually your best bet). Reservations are tightest at 11:00 and on weekends. No-shows are released a few minutes after the top of the hour. Generally, out of 360 reservation-holders, a few will fail to show (but more than a few may be waiting to grab their slots).

Tours: Guided English tours are offered at 9:10 and 11:10 for €5; reserve with entry reservation (or consider the excellent audioguide tour for €4).

Location: The museum is in the Villa Borghese park. A taxi (tell the cabbie your destination: gah-leh-REE-ah bor-GAY-zay) can get you within 330 feet of the museum. Otherwise, Metro to Spagna and take a 15-minute walk through the park.

Etruscan Museum (Villa Giulia Museo Nazionale Etrusco)—The Etruscan civilization thrived in this part of Italy around 600 B.C., when Rome was an Etruscan town. The Etruscan civilization is fascinating, but the Villa Giulia Museum is extremely low–tech and in a state of disarray. I don't like it, and fans will prefer the Vatican Museum's Etruscan section. Still, the Villa Giulia does have the famous "husband and wife sarcophagus" (a dead couple seeming to enjoy an everlasting banquet from atop their tomb—sixth century B.C. from Cerveteri); the *Apollo from Veii* statue (of textbook fame); and an impressive room filled with gold sheets of Etruscan printing and temple statuary from the Sanctuary of Pyrgi (€4.20, Tue–Sun 8:30–19:30, closes earlier off–season, closed Mon, Piazzale di Villa Giulia 9, tel. 06-322-6571).

▲**Cappuccin Crypt**—If you want bones, this is it. The crypt is below the church of Santa Maria della Immacolata Concezione on Via Veneto, just up from Piazza Barberini. The bones of more than 4,000 monks who died between 1528 and 1870 are in the basement, all artistically arranged for the delight—or disgust—of the always–wide–eyed visitor. The soil in the crypt was brought from Jerusalem 400 years ago, and the monastic message on the wall explains that this is more than just a macabre exercise. Pick up a few of Rome's most interesting postcards (donation, Fri–Wed 9:00–12:00 & 15:00–18:00, closed Thu, Metro: Barberini, tel. 06-487-1185). A painting of St. Francis by Caravaggio is upstairs. Just up the street you'll find the American Embassy, Federal Express, and fancy Via Veneto cafés filled with the poor and envious looking for the rich and famous.

Ara Pacis (Altar of Peace)—Now surrounded by a high fence, this may reopen in 2005 after restoration. In 9 B.C., after victories in Gaul and Spain, Emperor Augustus celebrated the beginning of the Pax Romana by building this altar of peace. Peace is almost worshiped here. The north and south walls show a procession with realistic portraits of the imperial family in Greek Hellenistic style. It's a fine combination of Roman grandeur and Greek elegance. Even during restoration, the altar can sometimes be seen through the windows (a long block west of Via del Corso on Via di Ara Pacis, on east bank of river near Ponte Cavour, nearest Metro: Spagna).

West Rome: Vatican City Area

▲▲▲**St. Peter's Basilica**—There is no doubt: This is the richest and most impressive church on earth. To call it vast is like calling God smart. Marks on the floor show where the next-largest churches would fit if they were put inside. The ornamental cherubs would dwarf a large man. Birds roost inside, and thousands of people wander about, heads craned heavenward, hardly noticing each other. Don't miss Michelangelo's *Pietà* (behind bulletproof glass) to the right of the entrance. Bernini's altar work and seven-story-tall bronze canopy *(baldacchino)* are brilliant.

For a quick walk through the basilica, follow these points (see map on next page):

1. The atrium is larger than most churches. Notice the historic doors (the Holy Door, on the right, won't be opened until the next Jubilee Year, in 2025—see point 13 below).

2. The purple, circular porphyry stone marks the site of Charlemagne's coronation in A.D. 800 (in the first St. Peter's church that stood on this site). From here, get a sense of the immensity of the church, which can accommodate 95,000 worshipers standing on its six acres.

3. Michelangelo planned a Greek-cross floor plan rather than the Latin-cross standard in medieval churches. A Greek cross, symbolizing the perfection of God, and by association the goodness of man, was important to the humanist Michelangelo. But accommodating large crowds was important to the Church in the fancy Baroque age, which followed Michelangelo, so the original nave length was doubled. Stand halfway up the nave and imagine the stubbier design Michelangelo had in mind.

4. View the magnificent dome from the statue of St. Andrew. See the vision of heaven above the windows: Jesus, Mary, a ring of saints, rings of angels, and, on the very top, God the Father.

5. The main altar sits directly over St. Peter's tomb and under Bernini's 70-foot-tall bronze canopy.

6. The stairs lead down to the crypt to the foundation, chapels, and tombs of popes. (Do this last, since it leads you out of the church.)

7. The statue of St. Peter, with an irresistibly kissable toe, is one of the few pieces of art that predate this church. It adorned the first St. Peter's church.

8. St. Peter's throne and Bernini's starburst dove window is the site of a daily Mass (Mon–Sat at 17:00, Sun at 17:30).

9. St. Peter was crucified here when this location was simply "the Vatican Hill." The obelisk now standing in the center of St. Peter's square marked the center of a Roman racecourse long before a church stood here.

10. For most, the treasury (in the sacristy) is not worth the admission.

11. The church is filled with mosaics, not paintings. Notice the mosaic version of Raphael's *Transfiguration.*

12. Blessed Sacrament Chapel.

St. Peter's Basilica

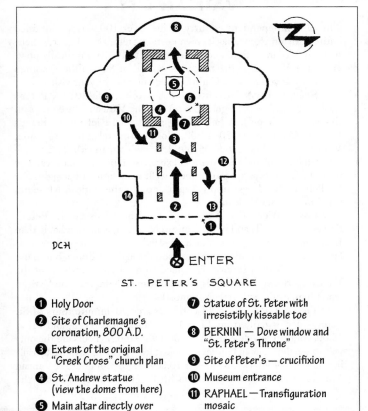

ST. PETER'S SQUARE

❶ Holy Door

❷ Site of Charlemagne's coronation, 800 A.D.

❸ Extent of the original "Greek Cross" church plan

❹ St. Andrew statue (view the dome from here)

❺ Main altar directly over Peter's tomb

❻ Stairs down to the crypt — the foundation of old St. Peter's, chapels and tombs of popes (the entrance moves around)

❼ Statue of St. Peter with irresistibly kissable toe

❽ BERNINI — Dove window and "St. Peter's Throne"

❾ Site of Peter's — crucifixion

❿ Museum entrance

⓫ RAPHAEL — Transfiguration mosaic

⓬ Blessed Sacrament Chapel

⓭ MICHELANGELO — Pietà

⓮ Elevator to roof and dome climb (this entrance moves around, sometimes it is even outside)

13. Michelangelo sculpted his *Pietà* when he was 24 years old. A *pietà* is a work showing Mary with the dead body of Christ taken down from the cross. Michelangelo's mastery of the body is obvious in this powerfully beautiful masterpiece. Jesus is believably dead, and Mary, the eternally youthful "handmaiden" of the Lord, still accepts God's will...even if it means giving up her son.

VATICAN CITY

This tiny independent country of just over 100 acres, contained entirely within Rome, has its own postal system, armed guards, helipad, mini-train station, and radio station (KPOP). Politically powerful, the Vatican is the religious capital of 800 million Roman Catholics. If you're not a Catholic, become one for your visit.

Small as it is, Vatican City has two huge sights: St. Peter's Basilica (with Michelangelo's *Pietà*) and the Vatican Museum (with the Sistine Chapel). A helpful TI is just to the left of St. Peter's Basilica (Mon–Sat 8:30–19:00, closed Sun, tel. 06-6988-1662; Vatican switchboard tel. 06-6982, www.vatican.va). The thief-infested bus #64 and the safer #40 express stop near the basilica. The nearest Metro stops are a 10-minute walk away from either sight: For St. Peter's, the closest stop is Ottaviano; for the Vatican Museum, it's Cipro-Musei Vaticani.

Post Office: The Vatican post, with offices on St. Peter's Square (next to TI) and in the Vatican Museum, is more reliable than Italy's mail service (Mon–Sat 8:30–19:00). The stamps are a collectible bonus. Vatican stamps are good throughout Rome, but to use the Vatican's mail service, you need to mail your cards from the Vatican; write your postcards ahead of time. (Note that the Vatican won't mail cards with Italian stamps.)

Tours: The Vatican TI conducts free 90-minute tours of St. Peter's (depart daily from TI at 14:15, also Mon, Wed, and Fri at 15:00, confirm schedule at TI, tel. 06-6988-1662). Tours are the only way to see the Vatican Gardens; book at least a day in advance by calling 06-6988-4466 (€9, Mon–Sat 10:00–12:00, tours start at Vatican Museum tour desk and finish on St. Peter's Square). To tour the

The Holy Door (just to the right of the *Pietà*) was bricked shut at the end of the Jubilee Year 2000 and won't be opened until 2025. Every 25 years, the Church celebrates an especially festive year derived from the Old Testament idea of the Jubilee Year (originally every 50 years), which encourages new beginnings and the forgiveness of sins and debts. In the Jubilee Year 2000, the pope tirelessly—and with significant success—promoted debt relief for the world's poorest countries.

14. An elevator leads to the roof and the stairway up the dome (€5, allow an hour to go up and down). The dome, Michelangelo's last work, is (you guessed it) the biggest anywhere. Taller than a football field is long, it's well worth the sweaty climb for a great view of Rome, the Vatican grounds, and the inside of the basilica—particularly heavenly

necropolis of St. Peter's and the saint's tomb, call the Excavations Office at 06-6988-5318(€8, 2 hrs, office open Mon–Fri 9:00–17:00).

Seeing the Pope: Your best chances for a sighting are on Sunday and Wednesday. The pope usually gives a blessing at noon on Sunday from his apartment on St. Peter's Square (except summer, when he speaks at his summer residence at Castel Gandolfo 25 miles from Rome; train leaves Rome's Termini station). St. Peter's is easiest (just show up) and, for most, enough of a "visit."

Those interested in a more formal appearance (but not more intimate), can get a ticket for the Wednesday blessing (at 10:30) when the pope, arriving in his bulletproof Popemobile, greets and blesses the crowds at St. Peter's from a balcony or canopied platform on the square (except in winter, when he speaks at 10:30 in the 7,000-seat Aula Paola VI Auditorium, next to St. Peter's Basilica). This requires a ticket—arrange it in advance through your hotel or the Santa Susanna Church (they get it and you pick it up the day before at their church between 17:00 and 18:45; Via XX Settembre 15, near recommended Via Firenze hotels, Metro: Repubblica; tel. 06-4201-4554, www.santasusanna.org).

To find out the pope's schedule or to book a free spot for the Wednesday blessing (either for a seat on the square or in the auditorium), call 06-6988-4631. The weekly entertainment guide *Roma c'è* always has a "Seeing the Pope" section. If you only want to see the Vatican—but not the pope—minimize crowd problems by avoiding these times.

while there is singing. Look around—Rome has no modern skyline. No building is allowed to exceed the height of St. Peter's. The elevator takes you to the rooftop of the nave. From there, a few steps take you to a balcony at the base of the dome looking down into the church interior. After that, the one-way, 300-step climb (for some people claustrophobic) to the cupola begins. The rooftop level (below the dome) has a gift shop, WC, drinking fountain, and a commanding view.

Dress Code: The church strictly enforces its dress code: no shorts or bare shoulders (men and women); no miniskirts. You might be required to check any bags at a free cloakroom near the entry.

Hours of Church: Daily May–Sept 7:00–19:00, Oct–April 7:00–18:00. All are welcome to join in the hour-long Mass at the front

IS THE POPE CATHOLIC?

Rome's tour guides, who introduce tourists to the city's great art and Christian history, field a lot of interesting questions and comments from their groups. Here are a few of their favorites:

Is John Paul II the son of John Paul I?
Who's the guy on the cross?
Oh, to be here in Rome…where our Lord Jesus walked.
Is this where Christ fought the lions?
This guy who made so many nice things, Rene Sance, who
   is he? (Say it fast, and you'll get the gist.)
What's the Sistine Chapel worth in U.S. dollars?
How did Michelangelo get Moses to pose for him?
What's Michelangelo doing now?

altar (Mon–Sat at 8:30, 10:00, 11:00, 12:00, & 17:00; Sun and holidays 9:00, 10:30, 12:10, 13:00, 16:00, & 17:30). The church is particularly moving at 7:00, while tourism is still sleeping. Volunteers who want you to understand and appreciate St. Peter's give free 90-minute tours (depart from TI daily at 14:15; also Mon, Wed, and Fri at 15:00; confirm schedule at TI, tel. 06-6988-1662); the tours are generally excellent but non-Christians can find them preachy. Seeing the *Pietà* is neat; understanding it is divine.

Cost and Hours of Dome: The view from the dome is worth the climb (€5 elevator plus 300-step climb, allow an hour to go up and down, May–Sept daily 8:30–18:00, Oct–April daily 8:30–17:00).

▲▲▲**Vatican Museum**—The four miles of displays in this immense museum—from ancient statues to Christian frescoes to modern paintings—are topped by the Raphael Rooms and Michelangelo's glorious Sistine Chapel. (If you have binoculars, bring them.)

Even without the Sistine, this is one of Europe's top three or four houses of art. It can be exhausting, so plan your visit carefully, focusing on a few themes. Allow two hours for a quick visit, three or four for time to enjoy it. The museum has a nearly impossible-not-to-follow, one-way system (although, for the rushed visitor, the museum does clearly mark out four color-coded visits of different lengths—A is shortest, D longest). Tip: The Sistine Chapel has an exit (optional) that leads directly to St. Peter's Basilica, saving you the 10-minute walk back to the Vatican Museum exit; if you want to squirt out at the Sistine, see the Pinacoteca painting gallery first (described below) and don't get an audioguide (which needs to be returned at the entry/exit).

Start, as civilization did, in Egypt and Mesopotamia. Next, the Pio Clementino collection features **Greek and Roman statues**. Decorating its courtyard are some of the best Greek and Roman statues in captivity, including the *Laocoön* group (first century B.C., Hellenistic) and the *Apollo Belvedere* (a second-century Roman copy of a Greek original). The centerpiece of the next hall is the *Belvedere Torso* (just a 2,000-year-old torso, but one that had a great impact on the art of Michelangelo). Finishing off the classical statuary are two fine fourth-century porphyry sarcophagi; these royal purple tombs were made (though not used) for the Roman emperor Constantine's mother and daughter. They were Christians—and therefore outlaws—until Constantine made Christianity legal (A.D. 312). The tombs, crafted in Egypt at a time when a declining Rome was unable to do such fine work, have details that are fun to study.

After long halls of tapestries, old maps, broken penises, and fig leaves, you'll come to what most people are looking for: The Raphael Rooms (or *stanza*) and Michelangelo's Sistine Chapel.

These outstanding works are frescoes. A fresco (meaning "fresh" in Italian) is technically not a painting. The color is mixed into wet plaster, and, when the plaster dries, the painting is actually part of the wall. This is a durable but difficult medium, requiring speed and accuracy, as the work is built slowly, one patch at a time.

After fancy rooms illustrating the "Immaculate Conception of Mary" (in the 19th century, the Vatican codified this hard-to-sell doctrine, making it a formal part of the Catholic faith) and the triumph of Constantine (with divine guidance, which led to his conversion to Christianity), you enter the first room completely done by **Raphael** and find the newly restored *School of Athens*. This is remarkable for its blatant pre-Christian classical orientation, especially since it originally wallpapered the apartments of Pope Julius II. Raphael honors the great pre-Christian thinkers—Aristotle, Plato, and company—who are portrayed as the leading artists of Raphael's day. The bearded figure of Plato is Leonardo da Vinci. Diogenes, history's first hippie, sprawls alone in bright blue on the stairs, while Michelangelo broods in the foreground—supposedly added late. Apparently, Raphael snuck a peek at the Sistine Chapel and decided that his arch-competitor was so good he had to put their personal differences aside and include him in this tribute to the artists of his generation. Today's St. Peter's was under construction as Raphael was working. In the *School of Athens*, he gives us a sneak preview of the unfinished church.

Next (unless you detour through the refreshingly modern Catholic art section) is the brilliantly restored **Sistine Chapel**. The Sistine Chapel, the pope's personal chapel, is where, upon the death of the ruling pope, a new pope is elected. The College of Cardinals meets here and votes four times a day until a two-thirds-plus-one majority is reached and a new pope is elected.

The Sistine is famous for Michelangelo's pictorial culmination of the Renaissance, showing the story of Creation, with a powerful God weaving in and out of each scene through that busy first week. This is an optimistic and positive expression of the High Renaissance and a stirring example of the artistic and theological maturity of the 33-year-old Michelangelo, who spent four years on this work.

Later, after the Reformation wars had begun and after the Catholic army of Spain had sacked the Vatican, the reeling Church began to fight back. As part of its Counter-Reformation, a much older Michelangelo was commissioned to paint the *Last Judgment* (behind the altar). Brilliantly restored, the message is as clear as the day Michelangelo finished it: Christ is returning, some will go to hell and some to heaven, and some will be saved by the power of the rosary.

In the recent and controversial restoration project, no paint was added. Centuries of dust, soot (from candles used for lighting and Mass), and glue (added to make the art shine) were removed, revealing the bright original colors of Michelangelo. Photos are allowed (without a flash) elsewhere in the museum, but as part of the deal with the company who did the restoration, no photos are allowed in the Sistine Chapel.

For a shortcut, a small door at the rear of the Sistine Chapel allows groups and individuals (without an audioguide) to escape directly to St. Peter's Basilica. If you exit here, you're done with the museum. The Pinacoteca is the only important part left. Consider doing it at the start. Otherwise it's a 10-minute, heel-to-toe slalom through tourists from the Sistine Chapel to the entry/exit.

After this long march, you'll find the **Pinacoteca** (the Vatican's small but fine collection of paintings, with Raphael's *Transfiguration*, Leonardo's unfinished *St. Jerome*, and Caravaggio's *Deposition*), a cafeteria (long lines, mediocre food), and the underrated early-Christian art section, before you exit via the souvenir shop.

Cost and Hours: €10, March–Oct Mon–Fri 8:45–16:45, Sat 8:45–13:45; Nov–Feb Mon–Sat 8:45–13:45; closed Sun except last Sun of the month (when it's free, crowded, and open 8:45–13:45). Last entry is about 90 minutes before the closing time. The Sistine Chapel sometimes shuts down 30 minutes early.

The museum is generally hot and crowded. Saturday, the last Sunday of the month, and Monday are the worst; afternoons are best.

The museum is closed on many holidays (mainly religious ones), including—for 2004: Jan 1 and 6, Feb 11, March 19, Easter and Easter Monday (April 11 and 12), May 1 and 20, June 10 and 29, Aug 14 and 15, Nov 1, and Dec 8 and 25–26.

Modest dress (no short shorts or bare shoulders for men or women) is appropriate and often required. Museum tel. 06-6988-4947.

Vatican City

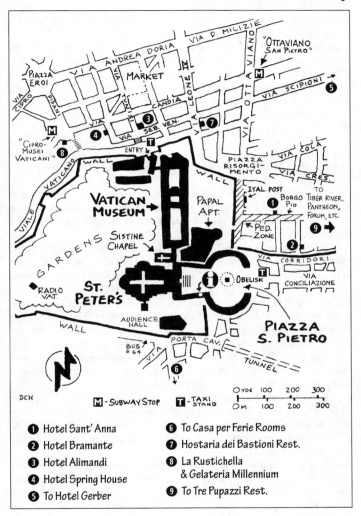

DCH

🅼 - SUBWAY STOP   🆃 - TAXI STAND

| 0 YDS | 100 | 200 | 300 |
| 0 M | 100 | 200 | 300 |

❶ Hotel Sant' Anna
❷ Hotel Bramante
❸ Hotel Alimandi
❹ Hotel Spring House
❺ To Hotel Gerber

❻ To Casa per Ferie Rooms
❼ Hostaria dei Bastioni Rest.
❽ La Rustichella
    & Gelateria Millennium
❾ To Tre Pupazzi Rest.

Tours: A tour in English is offered once daily at 11:00 (€16.50, 2 hrs, call 06-6988-4466 to reserve). You can rent a €5 audioguide (but if you do, you lose the option of taking the shortcut from the Sistine Chapel to St. Peter's, because the audioguide must be returned at the Vatican Museum entrance).

▲**Castel Sant' Angelo**—Built as a tomb for the emperor; used through the Middle Ages as a castle, prison, and place of last refuge for popes under attack; and today, as a museum, this giant pile of ancient bricks is packed with history.

Ancient Rome allowed no tombs, not even the emperor's, within its walls. So Hadrian grabbed the most commanding position just outside the walls and built a towering tomb (circa A.D. 139) well within view of the city. His mausoleum was a huge cylinder (210 by 70 feet) topped by a cypress grove and crowned by a huge statue of Hadrian himself riding a chariot. For nearly a hundred years, Roman emperors (from Hadrian to Caracalla in A.D. 217) were buried here.

In the year 590, the Archangel Michael—signaling the end of a plague by sheathing his sword—appeared above the mausoleum to Pope Gregory the Great. The mausoleum eventually became a fortified palace, renamed for the "holy angel."

In 1277, the pope built the elevated corridor connecting Castel Sant' Angelo with the Vatican. Since Rome was repeatedly plundered by invaders, Castel Sant' Angelo was a handy place of last refuge for threatened popes.

After you walk around the entire base of the castle, take the small staircase down to the original Roman floor. In the atrium, study the model of the castle in Roman times and imagine the niche in the wall filled with a towering "welcome to my tomb" statue of Hadrian. From here, a ramp leads to the right, spiraling 410 feet. At the end of the ramp, stairs climb to the room where the ashes of the emperors were kept. These stairs continue to the top, where you'll find the papal apartments. Don't miss the Sala del Tesoro (treasury), where the wealth of the Vatican was locked up in a huge chest. Do miss the 58 rooms of the military museum. The views from the top are great—pick out landmarks as you stroll around—and a restful coffee with a view of St. Peter's is worth the price.

Cost, Hours, Tours: €5, Tue–Sun 9:00–19:00, plus June–Sept Sat 21:00–23:45, closed Mon. You can take an English–language tour with an audioguide (€4) or live guide (€5, Tue–Fri at 15:00, Sat at 12:15 & 16:30, confirm tour times, tel. 06-3996-7600; Metro: Lepanto or bus #64, near Vatican City).

Ponte Sant' Angelo—The bridge leading to Castel Sant' Angelo was built by Hadrian for quick and regal access from downtown to his tomb. The three middle arches are actually Roman originals and a fine example of the empire's engineering expertise. The angels were designed by Bernini and finished by his students.

Southwest Rome: Trastevere

Trastevere is the colorful neighborhood across *(tras)* the Tiber *(tevere)* River. Trastevere (trahs-TAY-veh-ray) offers the best look at medieval–village Rome. The action unwinds to the chime of the church bells. Go there

Trastavere

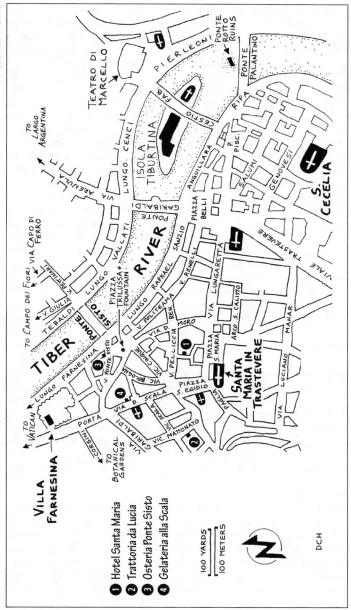

VILLA FARNESINA

SANTA MARIA IN TRASTEVERE

S. CECELIA

TIBER RIVER

ISOLA TIBURTINA

TEATRO DI MARCELLO

PIERLEONI

PONTE ROTTO RUINS

PONTE PALANTINO

TO VATICAN

TO LARGO ARGENTINA

TO CAMPO DEI FIORI

TO BOTANICAL GARDENS

1 Hotel Santa Maria
2 Trattoria da Lucia
3 Osteria Ponte Sisto
4 Gelateria alla Scala

100 YARDS
100 METERS

DCH

and wander. Wonder. Be a poet. This is Rome's Left Bank.

This proud neighborhood was long a working–class area. Now that it's becoming trendy, high rents are driving out the source of so much color. Still, it's a great people scene, especially at night. Stroll the back streets (for restaurant recommendations, see "Eating," page 796).

To get to Trastevere, taxi or ride the bus (from Vatican area—#23; or from Via Nazionale hotels—catch #64, #70, #115, or #640 to Largo Argentina, then transfer to tram #8 and get off at Piazza Mastai).

St. Maria in Trastevere Church—One of Rome's oldest churches, this was made a basilica in the fourth century, when Christianity was legalized (free, daily 7:30–13:00 & 15:00–19:00). It was the first church dedicated to the Virgin Mary. The portico (covered area just outside the door) is decorated with fascinating ancient fragments filled with early Christian symbolism. Most of what you see today dates from around the 12th century, but the granite columns come from an ancient Roman temple, and the ancient basilica floor plan (and ambience) survive. The 12th–century mosaics behind the altar are striking and notable for their portrayal of Mary—the first to show her at the throne with Jesus in Heaven. Look below the scenes from the life of Mary to see ahead–of–their–time mosaics (by Cavallini, from 1300), predating the Renaissance by 100 years.

The church is on Piazza di Santa Maria. While today's fountain is from the 17th century, there has been a fountain here since Roman times.

Linking Trastevere with "Night Walk Across Rome"—You can easily walk from Trastevere to Campo de' Fiori to link up with the beginning of the Night Walk Across Rome (see page 780): From Trastevere's church square (Piazza di Santa Maria), take Via del Moro to the river and cross at Ponte Sisto, a pedestrian bridge with a good view of St. Peter's dome. Continue straight ahead for one block. Take the first left, which leads down Via di Capo di Ferro through the scary and narrow darkness to Piazza Farnese, with the imposing Palazzo Farnese. Michelangelo contributed to the facade of this palace, now the French Embassy. The fountains on the square feature huge, one–piece granite hot tubs from the ancient Roman Baths of Caracalla. One block from there (opposite the palace) is the atmospheric square of Campo de' Fiori.

South Rome

▲**St. Paul's Outside the Walls (Basilica San Paolo Fuori le Mura)**— One of the greatest churches in Christendom, St. Paul's was originally built in 324, then destroyed by fire in the 1820s. Today it's mammoth and pristine, rebuilt true to the ancient basilica plan. It feels sterile, but in a good way—like you're already in heaven. Along with St. Peter's Basilica, San Giovanni in Laterano, and Santa Maria Maggiore, this church is part of the Vatican rather than Italy. St. Paul is supposed to be buried under the altar (without his head, which San Giovanni in

Laterano has). Alabaster windows light the vast interior, fifth–century mosaics decorate the triumphal arch leading to the altar, and mosaic portraits of all 264 popes, from St. Peter to John Paul II, ring the place—with blank spots ready for future popes. Find John Paul II (to right of the high altar: Jo Paulus II, no date) and John Paul I (to his right, with a reign of one month and three days). Wander the ornate yet peaceful cloister (closed 13:00–15:00). The courtyard leading up to the church is typical of early Christian churches; even the first St. Peter's had this kind of welcoming zone (free, daily 7:00–18:00, modest dress code enforced, Via Ostiense 186, Metro: San Paolo).

If you visit Ostia Antica (see below), you can maximize sightseeing efficiency by visiting this sight on your return.

Baths of Caracalla (Terme di Caracalla)—Today it's just a shell—a huge shell—with all of its sculptures and most of its mosaics moved to museums. Inaugurated by Emperor Caracalla in A.D. 216, this massive complex could accommodate 1,600 visitors at a time. Today you'll see a two–story, roofless brick building surrounded by a garden, bordered by ruined walls. The two large rooms at either end of the building were used for exercise. In between the exercise rooms was a pool flanked by two small mosaic–floored dressing rooms. Niches in the walls once held statues. In its day, this was a remarkable place to hang out. For ancient Romans, the baths were a social experience.

The Baths of Caracalla functioned until Goths severed the aqueducts in the sixth century. In modern times, operas were performed here from 1938 to 1993. To keep the ruins from becoming more ruined, the performances were discontinued (€5, covered by €20 combo–ticket, Mon 9:00–17:30, Tue–Sun 9:00–19:30, last entry 1 hour before closing, audioguide-€4, fine €8 guidebook—can read in shaded garden while sitting on a chunk of column, Metro: Circus Maximus, and a 5–min walk south along Via delle Terme di Caracalla, tel. 06-575-8628). Several of the baths' statues are now in Rome's Octagonal Hall; the immense *Toro Farnese* (a marble sculpture of a bull surrounded by people) snorts in Naples' Archaeological Museum.

Ancient Appian Way (Via Appia Antica)

Since the fourth century B.C., this has been Rome's gateway to the East. The first section was perfectly straight. It was the largest, widest, fastest road ever, the wonder of its day, called the "Queen of Roads." Eventually, this most important of Roman roads stretched 430 miles to the port of Brindisi—where boats sailed for Greece and Egypt. Twenty–nine such roads fanned out from Rome. Just as Hitler built the autobahn system in anticipation of empire maintenance, the emperors realized the military and political value of a good road system. A central strip accommodated animal–powered vehicles, and elevated sidewalks served pedestrians. As it left Rome, the road was lined with tombs and funerary monuments. Imagine a funeral procession passing under the pines and cypress and past a long line of pyramids, private mini–temples, altars, and tombs.

Hollywood created the famous image of the Appian Way lined with Spartacus and his gang of defeated and crucified slave rebels. This image is only partially accurate. Spartacus was killed in battle.

Tourist's Appian Way: The road starts less than two miles south of the Colosseum at the massive San Sebastian Gate. The Museum of the Walls, located at the gate, offers an interesting look at Roman defense and (when open) a chance to scramble along a stretch of the ramparts (€2.60, Tue–Sun 9:00–19:00, closed Mon, tel. 06-7047-5284). Half a mile down the road are the two most historic and popular catacombs, those of San Callisto and San Sebastian (described below). Beyond that, the road becomes pristine and traffic–free, popular for biking and hiking.

To reach the Appian Way, take the Archeobus from Piazza Venezia (see "Tours," page 735) or take the Metro to the Colli Albani stop, then catch bus #660 to Via Appia Antica—its last stop and the start of an interesting stretch of the ancient road (the segment between the 3rd and 11th milestones is best). At the bus stop, you'll find Caffe dell' Appia Antica (Via Appia Antica 175), which serves light lunches and rents bikes (lots of fun). From here you can walk 15 minutes (or bike) to the Catacombs of San Callisto.

▲▲**Catacombs**—The catacombs are burial places for (mostly) Christians who died in ancient Roman times. By law, no one was allowed to be buried within the walls of Rome. While pagan Romans were into cremation, Christians preferred to be buried. But land was expensive and most Christians were poor. A few wealthy, landowning Christians allowed their property to be used as burial places.

The 40 or so known catacombs circle Rome about three miles from its center. From the first through the fifth centuries, Christians dug an estimated 375 miles of tomb–lined tunnels, with networks of galleries as many as five layers deep. The tufa—soft and easy to cut, but becoming very hard when exposed to air—was perfect for the job. The Christians burrowed many layers deep for two reasons: to get more mileage out of the donated land and to be near martyrs and saints already buried there. Bodies were wrapped in linen (like Christ's). Since they figured the Second Coming was imminent, there was no interest in embalming the body.

When Emperor Constantine legalized Christianity in 313, Christians had a new, interesting problem. There would be no more persecuted martyrs to bind them and inspire them. Thus the early martyrs and popes assumed more importance, and Christians began making pilgrimages to their burial places in the catacombs.

In the 800s, when barbarian invaders started ransacking the tombs, Christians moved the relics of saints and martyrs to the safety of churches in the city center. For a thousand years, the catacombs were forgotten. Around 1850, they were excavated and became part of the romantic Grand Tour of Europe.

Finding abandoned plates and utensils from ritual meals in the candlelit galleries led 18th– and 19th–century Romantics to guess that persecuted Christians hid out and lived in these catacombs. This Romantic legend grew. But catacombs were not used for hiding out. They are simply early Christian burial grounds. With a million people in Rome, the easiest way for the 10,000 or so early Christians to hide out was not to camp in the catacombs (which everyone, including the government, knew about), but to melt into the city.

The underground tunnels, while empty of bones, are rich in early Christian symbolism, which functioned as a secret language. The dove symbolized the soul. You'll see it quenching its thirst (worshiping), with an olive branch (at rest), or happily perched (in paradise). Peacocks, known for their "incorruptible flesh," symbolized immortality. The shepherd with a lamb on his shoulders was the "good shepherd," the first portrayal of Christ as a kindly leader of his flock. The fish was used because the first letters of these words—"Jesus Christ, Son of God, Savior"—spelled "fish" in Greek. And the anchor is a cross in disguise. A second–century bishop had written on his tomb: "All who understand these things, pray for me." You'll see pictures of people praying with their hands raised up—the custom at the time.

Catacomb tours are essentially the same. Which one you take is not important. The **Catacombs of San Callisto** (a.k.a. Callixtus), the official cemetery for the Christians of Rome and burial place of third–century popes, is the most historic. Sixteen bishops (early popes) were buried here. Buy your €5 ticket and wait for your language to be called. They move lots of people quickly. If one group seems ridiculously large (over 50 people), wait for the next tour in English (Thu–Tue 8:30–12:00 & 14:30–17:30, closed Wed and Feb, closes at 17:00 in winter, Via Appia Antica 110, tel. 06-5130-1580). Dig this: The catacombs have a Web site—www.catacombe.roma.it—that focuses mainly on San Callisto, featuring photos, site info, and a history.

The **Catacombs of San Sebastian** (Sebastiano) are 300 yards farther down the road (€5, Mon–Sat 8:30–12:00 & 14:30–17:30, closed Sun and Nov, closes at 17:00 in winter, Via Appia Antica 136, tel. 06-5130-1580).

E.U.R.

In the late 1930s, Italy's dictator, Benito Mussolini, planned an international exhibition to show off the wonders of his fascist society. But these wonders brought us World War II, and Il Duce's celebration never

E.U.R.

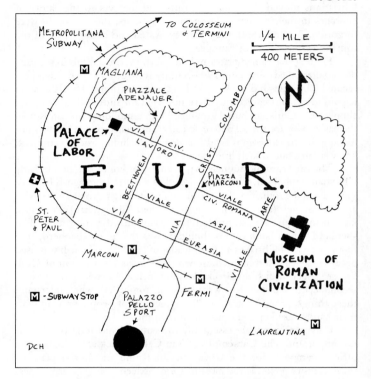

METROPOLITANA SUBWAY

TO COLOSSEUM & TERMINI

1/4 MILE

400 METERS

N

MAGLIANA

PIAZZALE ADENAUER

COLOMBO

PALACE OF LABOR

VIA LAVORO

CIV.

CRISI.

E. U. R.

BEETHOVEN

PIAZZA MARCONI

VIALE

VIALE CIV. ROMANA

ARTE

ST. PETER & PAUL

VIALE

VIA

ASIA

D

MARCONI

EURASIA

VIALE

MUSEUM OF ROMAN CIVILIZATION

M - SUBWAY STOP

PALAZZO DELLO SPORT

FERMI

LAURENTINA

DCH

happened. The unfinished mega–project was completed in the 1950s and now houses government offices and big, obscure museums.

If Hitler and Mussolini won the war, our world might look like E.U.R. (ay-OOR). Hike down E.U.R.'s wide, pedestrian–mean boulevards. Patriotic murals, aren't–you–proud–to–be–an–extreme–right–winger pillars, and stern squares decorate the soulless, planned grid and stark office blocks. Boulevards named for Astronomy, Electronics, Social Security, and Beethoven are more exhausting than inspirational. Today E.U.R. is worth a trip for its Museum of Roman Civilization (described below).

The Metro skirts E.U.R. with three stops (10 min from the Colosseum). Use E.U.R. Magliana for the "Square Colosseum" and E.U.R. Fermi for the Museum of Roman Civilization (both described below). Consider walking 30 minutes from the palace to the museum through the center of E.U.R.

From the Magliana subway stop, stairs lead uphill to the **Palace of the Civilization of Labor (Palazzo della Civilta del Lavoro)**, the essence of fascist architecture. With its giant, no–questions–asked, patriotic statues and its black–and–white simplicity, this is E.U.R.'s tallest building and landmark. It's understandably nicknamed the "Square Colosseum." Around the corner, Café Palombini is still decorated in a 1930s style and is quite popular with young Romans (daily 7:00–24:00, good gelato, pastries, and snacks, Piazzale Adenauer 12, tel. 06-591-1700).

▲Museum of Roman Civilization (Museo della Civilta Romana)— With 59 rooms of plaster casts and models illustrating the greatness of classical Rome, this vast and heavy museum gives a strangely lifeless, close–up look at Rome. Each room has a theme, from military tricks to musical instruments. One long hall is filled with casts of the reliefs of Trajan's Column. The highlight is the 1:250–scale model of Constantine's Rome—circa A.D. 300 (€6.20; Tue–Sat 9:00–18:45, Sun 9:00–13:30, closed Mon; Piazza G. Agnelli, from Metro: E.U.R. Fermi, walk 10 min up Via dell' Arte, you'll see its colonnade on the right; tel. 06-592-6041).

Near Rome

▲▲Ostia Antica—For an exciting day trip less than an hour from downtown Rome, pop down to the ancient Roman port of Ostia Antica. It's similar to Pompeii, but a lot closer and, in some ways, more interesting. Because Ostia was a working port town, it shows a more complete and gritty look at Roman life than does wealthy Pompeii. Wandering around today, you'll see the remains of the docks, warehouses, apartment flats, mansions, shopping arcades, and baths that served a once thriving port of 60,000 people. Later, Ostia became a ghost town, and is now excavated. Start at the 2,000-year-old theater, buy a map, explore the town, and finish with its fine little museum.

Getting There: To get there, take the Metro's B Line to the Piramide stop (consider popping out to see the ancient Roman pyramid tomb). From the Piramide stop, catch the Lido train to Ostia Antica (2/hr, use a Metro ticket). From the train station, cross the road via the blue sky-bridge and walk straight down Via della Stazione di Ostia Antica, following signs to *Scavi di Ostia Antica*, about 400 yards to the gate.

Cost and Hours: €4, Tue–Sun 8:30–18:00 in summer, 9:00–16:00 in winter, closed Mon. The well-done audioguide costs €5 (tel. 06-5635-8099).

SELF-GUIDED WALKS IN ROME

Here are three walks that give you a moving picture of Rome, an ancient yet modern city. You'll walk through history (Roman Forum), take a refreshing early evening stroll (Dolce Vita Stroll), and enjoy the thriving night scene (Night Walk Across Rome).

Roman Forum Walk

The Forum was the political, religious, and commercial center of the city. Rome's most important temples and halls of justice were here. This was the place for religious processions, elections, political demonstrations, important speeches, and parades by conquering generals. As Rome's Empire expanded, these few acres of land became the center of the civilized world.

Cost, Hours, Location: Free, daily 9:00–19:00 or until an hour before dark, Metro: Colosseo, tel. 06-3974-9907. You can rent a €4 audioguide at the gift shop at the entrance on Via dei Fori Imperiali. Tours in English are offered almost hourly (€4); ask at the ticket booth at Palatine Hill (near Arch of Titus). Just like at the Colosseum, street vendors sell small *Rome: Past and Present* books with plastic overlays that restore the ruins (marked €11, offer less).

The Tour Begins: Walk through the entrance nearest the Colosseum, hiking up the ramp marked "Via Sacra." Stand next to the triumphal...

1. Arch of Titus *(Arco di Tito)*: The arch commemorated the Roman victory over the province of Judea (Israel) in A.D. 70. The Romans had a reputation as benevolent conquerors who tolerated the local customs and rulers. All they required was allegiance to the empire, which could be shown by worshiping the emperor as a god. No problem for most conquered people, who already had half a dozen gods on their prayer lists anyway. But the Israelites' god was jealous and refused to let his people worship the emperor. Israel revolted. After a short but bitter war, the Romans defeated the rebels, took Jerusalem, sacked their temple, and brought home 50,000 Jewish slaves...who were forced to build this arch.

Start down the Via Sacra into the Forum. After just a few yards, turn right and follow a path uphill to the three huge arches of the...

2. Basilica of Constantine *(a.k.a. Basilica Maxentius)*: These gigantic arches represent only one third of the original Basilica of Constantine, a mammoth hall of justice. The arches were matched by a similar set along the Via Sacra side (only a few squat brick piers remain). Between them ran the central hall, which was spanned by a roof 130 feet high—about 55 feet higher than the side arches you see. (The stub of brick you see sticking up began an arch that once spanned the central hall.) The hall itself was as long as a football field, lavishly furnished with colorful inlaid marble, a gilded bronze ceiling, fountains, and statues, and filled with strolling Romans. At the far (west) end was an enormous marble statue of Emperor Constantine on a throne. (Pieces of this statue, including a hand the size of a man, are on display in Rome's Capitol Hill Museum.)

This basilica was begun by the emperor Maxentius, but after he was trounced in battle, the victor—Constantine—completed the massive building.

Roman Forum Walk

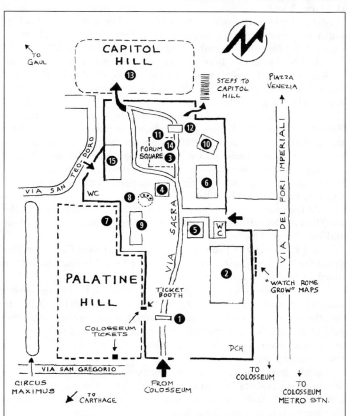

1. Arch of Titus
2. Basilica of Constantine
3. Forum's Main Square
4. Temple of Julius Caesar
5. Temple of Antoninus and Faustina
6. Basilica Aemilia
7. Caligula's Palace
8. Temple of Vesta
9. House of the Vestal Virgins
10. Curia (Senate House)
11. Rostrum
12. Arch of Septimius Severus
13. Temple of Saturn
14. Column of Phocas
15. Basilica Julia

Now stroll deeper into the Forum, down the Via Sacra. Many of the large basalt stones under your feet were walked on by Caesar Augustus 2,000 years ago. Pass the only original bronze door still swinging on its ancient hinges (green, on right) through the trees and between ruined buildings until the path opens up to a flat, grassy area.

3. The Forum's Main Square: The original Forum, or main square, was this flat patch about the size of a football field, stretching to the foot of Capitol Hill. Surrounding it were temples, law courts, government buildings, and triumphal arches.

Rome was born right here. According to legend, twin brothers Romulus (Rome) and Remus were orphaned in infancy and raised by a she-wolf on top of Palatine Hill. Growing up, they found it hard to get dates. So they and their cohorts attacked the nearby Sabine tribe and kidnapped their women. After they made peace, this marshy valley became the meeting place and then the trading center for the scattered tribes on the surrounding hillsides.

At the near (east) end of the main square (the Colosseum is to the east) find the foundations of a temple now capped with a peaked wood-and-metal roof. This is...

4. The Temple of Julius Caesar *(Tempio del Divo Giulio,* or *"Ara di Cesare")*: Julius Caesar's body was burned on this spot (under the metal roof) after his assassination.

Caesar (100–44 B.C.) changed Rome—and the Forum—dramatically. He cleared out many of the wooden market stalls and began to ring the square with even grander buildings. Caesar's house was located behind the temple, near that clump of trees. He walked right by here on the day he was assassinated ("Beware the Ides of March!" warned a street-corner Etruscan preacher).

Though popular with the masses, not everyone liked Caesar's urban design or his politics. When he assumed dictatorial powers, he was ambushed and stabbed to death by a conspiracy of senators, including his adopted son, Brutus *(Et tu, Brute?)*.

The funeral was held here, facing the main square. The citizens gathered and speeches were made. Mark Antony stood up to say (in Shakespeare's words), "Friends, Romans, countrymen, lend me your ears. I come to bury Caesar, not to praise him." When Caesar's body was burned, the citizens who still loved him threw anything at hand on the fire, requiring the fire department to come put it out. Later, Emperor Augustus dedicated this temple in his name, making Caesar the first Roman to become a god.

Behind and to the left of the Temple of Julius Caesar are the eight tall columns of the...

5. Temple of Antoninus and Faustina: The respected Emperor Antoninus (A.D. 138–161) built this temple—originally called the Temple of Faustina—in honor of his late beloved wife. After the

ROME—REPUBLIC AND EMPIRE
(500 B.C.–A.D. 500)

Ancient Rome spanned about a thousand years, from 500 B.C. to A.D. 500. During that time, Rome expanded from a small tribe of barbarians to a vast empire, then dwindled slowly to city size again. For the first 500 years, when Rome's armies made her ruler of the Italian peninsula and beyond, Rome was a republic governed by elected senators. Over the next 500 years, a time of world conquest and eventual decline, Rome was an empire ruled by a military-backed dictator.

Julius Caesar bridged the gap between republic and empire. This ambitious general and politician, popular with the people because of his military victories and charisma, suspended the Roman constitution and assumed dictatorial powers around 50 B.C., then he was assassinated by a conspiracy of senators. His adopted son, Augustus, succeeded him, and soon "Caesar" was not just a name but a title.

Emperor Augustus ushered in the Pax Romana, or Roman peace (from A.D. 1–200), a time when Rome reached her peak and controlled an empire that stretched even beyond Eurail— from Scotland to Egypt, from Turkey to Morocco.

emperor's death, the temple became a monument to them both.

The 56-foot-tall Corinthian (leafy) columns must have been awe-inspiring to out-of-towners who grew up in thatched huts. Although the temple has been reconstructed as a church, you can still see the basic layout—a staircase led to a shaded porch (the columns), which admitted you to the main building (now a church) where the statue of the god sat.

Picture the Forum covered with dirt as high as the green door—as it was until excavated in the 1800s.

There's a ramp next to the Temple of A. and F. Walk halfway up it and look to the left to view the...

6. Basilica Aemilia: A basilica was a Roman hall of justice. In a society that was as legal-minded as America is today, you needed a lot of lawyers and a big place to put them. Citizens came here to work out matters such as inheritances and building permits, or to sue somebody.

Notice the layout. It was a long, rectangular building. The stubby columns all in a row form one long, central hall flanked by two side aisles. Medieval Christians required a larger meeting hall for their worship services than Roman temples provided, so they used the spacious

Roman basilica (hall of justice) as the model for their churches. Cathedrals from France to Spain to England, from Romanesque to Gothic to Renaissance, all have the same basic floor plan as a Roman basilica.

Return again to the Temple of Julius Caesar. Notice the ruts in the stone street in front of the temple—carved by chariot wheels. To the right of the temple are the three tall Corinthian columns of the Temple of Castor and Pollux. Beyond that is Palatine Hill—the corner of which may be...

7. Caligula's Palace (a.k.a. the Palace of Tiberius): Emperor Caligula (ruled A.D. 37–41) had a huge palace on Palatine Hill overlooking the Forum. It actually sprawled down the hill into the Forum (some supporting arches remain in the hillside), with an entrance by the Temple of Castor and Pollux.

Caligula tortured enemies, stole senators' wives, and parked his chariot in handicap spaces. But Rome's luxury-loving emperors only added to the glory of the Forum, with each one trying to make his mark on history.

To the left of the Temple of Castor and Pollux, find the remains of a small white circular temple...

8. The Temple of Vesta: This was Rome's most sacred spot. Rome considered itself one big family, and this temple represented a circular hut, like the kind Rome's first families lived in. Inside, a fire burned, just as in a Roman home. And back in the days before lighters and matches, you never wanted your fire to go out. As long as the sacred flame burned, Rome would stand. The flame was tended by priestesses known as Vestal Virgins.

Around the back of the Temple of Vesta you'll find two rectangular brick pools. These stood in the courtyard of...

9. The House of the Vestal Virgins: The Vestal Virgins lived in a two-story building surrounding a central courtyard with these two pools at one end. Rows of statues to the left and right marked the long sides of the building. This place was the model—both architecturally and sexually—for medieval convents and monasteries.

The six Vestal Virgins, chosen from noble families before they reached the age of 10, served a 30-year term. Honored and revered by the Romans, the Vestals even had their own box opposite the emperor in the Colosseum.

As the name implies, a Vestal took a vow of chastity. If she served her term faithfully—abstaining for 30 years—she was given a huge dowry, honored with a statue (like the ones at left), and allowed to marry (life begins at 40?). But if the Romans found any Virgin who wasn't, she was strapped to a funeral car, paraded through the streets of the Forum, taken to a crypt, given a loaf of bread and a lamp...and buried alive. Many women suffered the latter fate.

ROME FALLS

Again, Rome lasted 1,000 years—500 years of growth, 200 years of peak power, and 300 years of gradual decay. The fall had many causes, among them the barbarians who pecked away at Rome's borders. Christians blamed the fall on moral decay. Pagans blamed it on Christians. Socialists blamed it on a shallow economy based on spoils of war. (George W. Bush blamed it on the Democrats.) Whatever the reasons, the far-flung empire could no longer keep its grip on conquered lands, and it pulled back. Barbarian tribes from Germany and Asia attacked the Italian peninsula and even looted Rome itself in A.D. 410, leveling many of the buildings in the Forum. In 476, when the last emperor checked out and switched off the lights, Europe plunged into centuries of ignorance, poverty, and weak government—the Dark Ages.

But Rome lived on in the Catholic Church. Christianity was the state religion of Rome's last generations. Emperors became popes (both called themselves Pontifex Maximus), senators became bishops, orators became priests, and basilicas became churches. And remember that the goal for the greatest church building project ever—that of St. Peter's—was to "put the dome of the Pantheon atop the Basilica of Constantine." The glory of Rome remains eternal.

Head to the Forum's west end (opposite the Colosseum). Stop at the big, reconstructed brick building (on right) with the triangular roof. If the door's open, look in.

10. The Curia: The Senate House (Curia) was the most important political building in the Forum. Though this current building is a 1930s reconstruction, this was the site of Rome's official center of government since the birth of the republic. Three hundred senators, elected by the citizens of Rome, met here to debate and create the laws of the land. Their wooden seats once circled the building in three tiers; the Senate president's podium sat at the far end. The marble floor is from ancient times. Listen to the echoes in this vast room—the acoustics are great.

(Note: Although Julius Caesar was assassinated in "the Senate," it wasn't here—the Senate was temporarily meeting across town.)

Go back down the Senate steps to the metal guardrail and look right to a 10-foot-high wall at the base of Capitol Hill marked...

11. Rostrum *(Rostri)*: Nowhere was Roman freedom more apparent than at this "Speaker's Corner." The Rostrum was a raised platform,

10 feet high and 80 feet long, decorated with statues, columns, and the prows of ships *(rostra)*.

Rome's orators, great and small, came here trying to draw a crowd and sway public opinion. Mark Antony rose to offer Caesar the laurel-leaf crown of kingship, which Caesar publicly (and hypocritically) refused while privately becoming a dictator. Men such as Cicero railed against the corruption and decadence that came with the city's newfound wealth. In later years, daring citizens even spoke out against the emperors, reminding them that Rome was once free.

The big arch to the right of the Rostrum is...

12. Arch of Septimius Severus: In imperial times, the Rostrum's voices of democracy would have been dwarfed by images of empire such as the huge, six-story-high Arch of Septimius Severus (A.D. 203). The reliefs commemorate the African-born emperor's battles in Mesopotamia. Near ground level, see curly haired Severus marching captured barbarians back to Rome for the victory parade. Despite Severus' efficient rule, Rome's empire was crumbling under the weight of its own corruption, disease, decaying infrastructure, and the constant attacks by foreign "barbarians."

Pass underneath the Arch of Septimius Severus and turn left. On the slope of Capitol Hill are the eight remaining columns of the..

13. Temple of Saturn: These columns framed the entrance to the Forum's oldest temple (497 B.C.). Inside was a humble, very old wooden statue of the god Saturn. But the statue's pedestal held the gold bars, coins, and jewels of Rome's state treasury, the booty collected by conquering generals.

Standing here, at one of the Forum's first buildings, look east at the lone, tall...

14. Column of Phocas: This is the Forum's last great monument (A.D. 608), a gift from the powerful Byzantine Empire to a fallen empire—Rome. After Rome's 1,000-year reign, the city was looted by Vandals, the population of a million-plus shrank to 10,000, and the once-grand city center—the Forum—was abandoned, slowly covered up by centuries of silt and dirt. In the 1700s, an English historian named Edward Gibbon stood here. Hearing Christian monks singing at these pagan ruins, he looked out at the few columns poking up from the ground, pondered the "Decline and Fall of the Roman Empire," and thought, "Hmm, that's a catchy title...."

The Dolce Vita Stroll down Via del Corso

This is the city's chic and hip "cruise," from Piazza del Popolo (Metro: Flaminio) down a wonderfully traffic-free section of Via del Corso, and up Via Condotti to the Spanish Steps each evening around 18:00 (Sat and Sun are best). Strollers, shoppers, and flirts on the prowl fill this

Dolce Vita Stroll

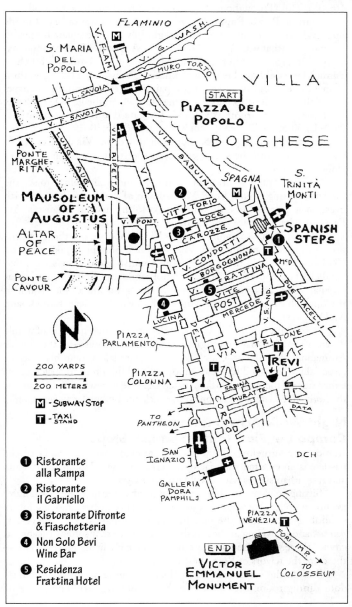

neighborhood of Rome's most fashionable stores (open after siesta 16:30–19:30). Throughout Italy, early evening is the time to stroll.

Start on **Piazza Popolo**. Historians: This area was once just inside medieval Rome's main entry. The delightfully car-free square is marked by an obelisk that was brought to Rome by Augustus after he conquered Egypt. (It once stood in the Circus Maximus.) The Baroque church of **Santa Maria del Popolo**—with Raphael's Chigi Chapel (kee-gee, third chapel on left) and two Caravaggio paintings (side paintings in chapel left of altar)—is next to the gate in the old wall, on the far side of Piazza del Popolo, to the right as you face the gate (church open Mon–Sat 7:00–12:00 & 16:00–19:00, Sun 8:00–13:30 & 16:30–19:30).

From Piazza del Popolo, shop your way down **Via del Corso**. To rest your feet, join the locals sitting on the steps of various churches along the street.

At Via Pontefici, historians turn right and walk a block to see the massive, rotting, round brick **Mausoleum of Augustus**, topped with overgrown cypress trees. Beyond it, next to the river, is Augustus' Ara Pacis, or Altar of Peace (which should reopen in 2005).

From the mausoleum, return to Via del Corso and the 21st century, continuing straight until **Via Condotti**. Shoppers, take a left on Via Condotti to join the parade to the **Spanish Steps**. The streets that parallel Via Condotti to the south (Borgogno and Frattini) are just as popular. You can catch a taxi home at the taxi stand a block south of the Spanish Steps (at Piazza Mignonelli, near American Express and McDonald's).

Historians: Ignore Via Condotti. Continue three-quarters of a mile down Via del Corso—straight since Roman times—to the Victor Emmanuel Monument. Climb Michelangelo's stairway to his glorious (especially when floodlit) square atop Capitol Hill. From the balconies at either side of the mayor's palace, catch the lovely views of the Forum as the horizon reddens and cats prowl the unclaimed rubble of ancient Rome.

Night Walk Across Rome: Campo de' Fiori to the Spanish Steps

Rome can be grueling. But a fine way to enjoy this historian's rite of passage is an evening walk lacing together Rome's floodlit night spots and fine urban spaces with real-life theater vignettes.

Sitting so close to a Bernini fountain that traffic noises evaporate; jostling with local teenagers to see all the gelato flavors; enjoying lovers straddling more than the bench; jaywalking past flak-proof-vested *polizia;* and marveling at the ramshackle elegance that softens this brutal city for those who were born here and can imagine living nowhere else—these are the flavors of Rome best tasted after dark.

Start at the **Campo de' Fiori** (Field of Flowers), my favorite outdoor dining room after dark (see the Eating, below). The statue of

Night Walk Across Rome

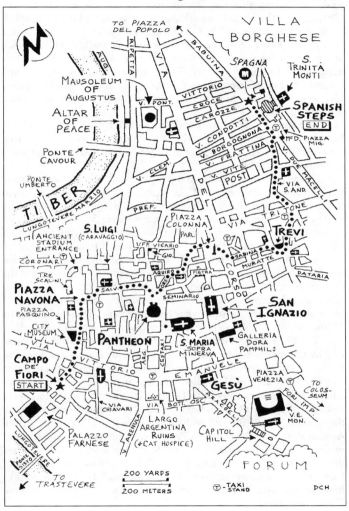

Giordano Bruno, a heretic who was burned in 1600 for believing the world was round and not the center of the universe, marks the center of this great and colorful square. Bruno overlooks a busy produce market in the morning and strollers after sundown. This neighborhood is still known for its free spirit and occasional demonstrations. When the statue of Bruno was erected in 1889, local riots overcame Vatican protests against honoring a heretic. Bruno faces his executioner, the Vatican Chancellory (the big white building in the corner a bit to his right), while his pedestal reads: "And the flames rose up."

At the east end of the square (behind Bruno), the ramshackle apartments are built right into the old outer wall of ancient Rome's mammoth Theater of Pompey. This entertainment complex covered several city blocks, stretching from here to Largo Argentina. Julius Caesar was assassinated in the Theater of Pompey, where the Senate was renting space.

The square is lined with and surrounded by fun eateries. Bruno faces La Carbonara, the only real restaurant on the square. The Forno, next door to the left, is a popular place for hot and tasty take-out *pizza bianco* (plain pizza bread).

If Bruno did a hop, step, and jump forward, then turned right on Via dei Baullari and marched 200 yards, he'd cross the busy Corso Vittorio Emanuele and find **Piazza Navona.** Rome's most interesting night scene features street music, artists, fire-eaters, local Casanovas, ice cream, fountains by Bernini, and outdoor cafés (worthy of a splurge if you've got time to sit and enjoy the human river of Italy).

This oblong square retains the shape of the original racetrack that was built by the emperor Domitian. (If you want to see the ruins of the original entrance, exit the square at the north end, take an immediate left, and look down to the left 25 feet below the current street level.) Since ancient times, the square has been a center of Roman life. In the 1800s, the city would flood the square to cool off the neighborhood.

The **Four Rivers fountain** in the center is the most famous fountain by the man who remade Rome in Baroque style, Gian Lorenzo Bernini. Four burly river gods (representing four continents known in 1650) support an obelisk, while the water of the world gushes everywhere. The Nile has his head covered (since the headwaters were unknown then). The Ganges holds an oar. The Danube turns to admire the obelisk, which Bernini had moved here from a stadium on the Appian Way. And the Rio de la Plata from Uruguay tumbles backward in shock, wondering how he ever made the top four. Bernini enlivens the fountain with horses plunging through the rocks and exotic flora and fauna from these newly discovered lands. Homesick Texans may want to find the armadillo. (It's the big, weird armor-plated creature behind the Plata river statue.)

The Plata river god is gazing upward at the church of Saint Agnes, worked on by Bernini's former student turned rival, Borromini. Borromini's concave facade helps reveal the dome and epitomizes the curved symmetry of Baroque. Tour guides say that Bernini designed his river god to look horrified at Borromini's work. Or he may be shielding his eyes from St. Agnes' nakedness, as she was stripped before being martyred. But the fountain was completed two years before Borromini even started work on the church.

At the **Tre Scalini** café (near the fountain), sample some *tartufo* "death-by-chocolate" ice cream, world-famous among connoisseurs of ice cream and chocolate alike (€3.50 to go, €7 at a table, closed Wed). Seriously admire a painting by a struggling artist. Request "Country Roads" from an Italian guitar player, and don't be surprised when he knows it. Listen to the white noise of gushing water and exuberant humans.

Leave Piazza Navona directly across from Tre Scalini café, go east past rose peddlers and palm readers, jog left around the guarded building, and follow the brown sign to the Pantheon. The Pantheon is straight down Via del Salvatore (cheap pizza place on left just before the Pantheon, WC at McDonald's).

Sit for a while under the floodlit and moonlit **Pantheon's** portico. The 40-foot single-piece granite columns of the Pantheon's entrance show the scale the ancient Romans built on. The columns support a triangular, Greek-style roof with an inscription that says that "M. Agrippa" built it. In fact, it was built *("fecit")* by Emperor Hadrian (A.D. 120), who gave credit to the builder of an earlier structure. This impressive entranceway gives no clue that the greatest wonder of the building is inside—a domed room that inspired later domes, including Michelangelo's St. Peter's and Brunelleschi's Duomo (in Florence). Notice how the pavement slants down from McDonald's to the Pantheon, showing how high modern Rome has built on ancient rubble.

With your back to the Pantheon, veer to the right down Via Orfani. After passing Bar Pantheon, you'll see **Tazza d'Oro Casa del Caffè**, one of Rome's top coffee shops, dating back to the days when this area was licensed to roast coffee beans. Locals come here for its fine *granita di caffè con panna*. Look back at the fine view of the Pantheon from here. Then take Via Orfani to Piazza Capranica.

Piazza Capranica is home to the big, plain, Florentine Renaissance–style Palazzo Capranica. Big shots, like the Capranica family, built stubby towers on their palaces—not for any military use, but just to show off. Leave the piazza to the right of the palace, between the palace and the church. Via in Aquiro leads to a sixth-century B.C. **Egyptian obelisk** (taken as a trophy by Augustus after his victory in Egypt over Mark Antony and Cleopatra). Walk into the guarded square past the obelisk and face the huge parliament building.

A short detour to the left (past Albergo National) brings you to Rome's most famous gelateria. **Gelateria Caffè Pasticceria Giolitti** is cheap to go or elegant and splurge-worthy for a sit among classy locals (open daily until very late, Via Uffici del Vicario 40); get your gelato in a cone *(cono)* or cup *(coppetta)*.

Piazza Colonna features a huge second-century column honoring Marcus Aurelius. The big, important-looking palace—headquarters of the deputies (or cabinet) of the prime minister. The **Via del Corso** is named for the Berber horse races—without riders—that took place here during Carnevale until the 1800s when a horse trampled a man to death in front of a horrified queen. Historically the street was filled with meat shops. When it became Rome's first gas lit street in the 1800s, "nastier" shops were banned and replaced by classier boutiques, jewelers, and antique dealers. Today, every evening most of Via del Corso is closed to traffic and it becomes a wonderful parade of Romans out for an evening stroll. Cross Via del Corso, Rome's noisy main drag, jog right (around the Y-shaped shopping gallery from 1928), and head down Via dei Sabini to the roar of the water, light, and people of the Trevi Fountain.

The **Trevi Fountain** shows how Rome took full advantage of the abundance of water brought into the city by its great aqueducts. This watery Baroque avalanche was built in 1762 by Nicola Salvi, hired by a pope celebrating the reopening of the ancient aqueduct that powers it. Salvi used the palace behind the fountain as a theatrical backdrop for the figure of "Ocean" who represents water in every form. The statue surfs through his wet kingdom—with water gushing from 24 spouts and tumbling over 30 different kinds of plants—while Tritone blows his conch shell. (From here, the water goes underground, then bubbles up again at Bernini's Four Rivers Fountain in Piazza Navona.)

The magic of the square is enhanced by the fact that no streets directly approach it. You can hear the excitement as you approach and then, bam, you're there. The scene is always lively, with lucky Romeos clutching dates while unlucky ones clutch beers. Romantics toss a coin over their shoulder, thinking it will give them a wish and assure their return to Rome. That may sound silly, but every year I go through this touristic ritual...and it actually seems to work.

Take some time to people-watch (whisper a few breathy *bellos* or *bellas*) before leaving. Face the fountain, then go past it on the right down Via delle Stamperia to Via del Triton. Cross the busy street and continue to the Spanish Steps (ask, *"Dov'è Piazza di Spagna?"*—Spagna rhymes with "lasagna,") a few blocks and thousands of dollars of shopping opportunities away.

The Piazza di Spagna, with the very popular **Spanish Steps**, is named for the Spanish Embassy to the Vatican, which has been here for 300 years. It's been the hangout of many Romantics over the years (Keats, Wagner, Openshaw, Goethe, and others). The British poet John Keats pondered his mortality, then died in the pink building on the right side of the steps. Fellow Romantic Lord Byron lived across the square at #66.

The Sinking Boat Fountain at the foot of the steps, which was done by Bernini or his father, Pietro, is powered by an aqueduct. All of Rome's fountains are aqueduct-powered; their spurts are determined by the water pressure provided by the various aqueducts. This one, for instance, is much weaker than Trevi's gush.

The piazza is a thriving night scene. Window-shop along Via Condotti, which stretches away from the steps. This is where Gucci and other big names cater to the trendsetting jet set. Facing the Spanish Steps, you can walk right about a block to tour one of the world's biggest and most lavish McDonald's (salad bar, WC). There's a taxi stand in the courtyard outside McDonald's; or, if you'd prefer, the Spagna Metro stop (usually open until 23:30) is just to the left of the Spanish Steps, ready to zip you home.

SLEEPING

On Via Firenze

I generally stay on Via Firenze because it's safe, handy, central, and relatively quiet. It's a 10-minute walk from the central train station and airport shuttle, and two blocks beyond Piazza della Repubblica and the TI. The Defense Ministry is nearby, and you've got heavily armed guards watching over you all night.

The neighorhood is well connected by public transportation (with the Repubblica Metro stop nearby). Virtually all the city buses that rumble down Via Nazionale (#64, #70, #115, #640, and the #40 express) take you to Piazza Venezia (Forum) and Largo Argentina (Pantheon). From Largo Argentina, electric trolley #8 goes to Trastevere (first stop after crossing the river) and #64 (jammed with people and thieves) and the #40 express continue to St. Peter's.

A 24-hour pharmacy near the recommended hotels is Farmacia Piram (Via Nazionale 228, tel. 06-488-4437). Neighborhood garages charge €24 per day.

$$$ **Residenza Cellini** is a gorgeous six-room place that feels like the guest wing of a neoclassical palace. It offers "ortho/anti-allergy beds" and four-star comforts and service (Db-€165, larger Db-€185, extra bed-€25, €30 discount in off-season—Aug plus mid-Nov–March, these prices good with this book and payment in cash through 2004, elevator, air-con, Via Modena 5, tel. 06-4782-5204, fax 06-4788-1806, www.residenzacellini.it, residenzacellini@tin.it, Barbara, Gaetano, and Donato SE).

$$ **Hotel Oceania** is a peaceful slice of air-conditioned heaven. This 15-room, manor house–type hotel is spacious and quiet, with spotless tastefully-decorated rooms, run by a pleasant father-and-son team. While Armando (the dad) serves world-famous coffee, Stefano (the son) works to give their hotel all the extra touches. He just added a plasma TV with surround sound to his lounge for guests to watch classic movies set in Rome...and Italy episodes from my TV series (Sb-€108, Db-€138, Tb-€168, Qb-€195, these prices promised through 2004 with this book and cash only, additional 25 percent off in Aug and winter; large roof terrace, family suite; Via Firenze 38, 3rd floor; tel. 06-482-4696,

SLEEP CODE

(€1 = about $1.10, country code: 39)
Sleep Code: **S** = Single, **D** = Double/Twin, **T** = Triple, **Q** = Quad, **b** = bathroom, **s** = shower only, **no CC** = Credit Cards not accepted, **SE** = Speaks English, **NSE** = No English. Breakfast is included in all but the cheapest places. You can assume a hotel takes credit cards unless you see "no CC" in the listing

To help you sort easily through these listings, I've divided the rooms into three categories based on the price for a standard double room with bath:

$$$ **Higher Priced**—Most rooms €180 or more.
$$ **Moderately Priced**—Most rooms between €115-180.
$ **Lower Priced**—Most rooms €115 or less.

The absolute cheapest beds (dorms or some cramped doubles) in Rome are €18 in small, backpacker-filled hostels. A nicer hotel (around €130 with a bathroom and air-con) provides an oasis and refuge, making it easier to enjoy this intense and grinding city. If you're going door to door, prices are soft—so bargain. Built into a hotel's official price list is a kickback for a room-finding service or agency; if you're coming direct, they pay no kickback and may lower the price for you. Many hotels have high-season (mid-March–June,

fax 06-488-5586, www.hoteloceania.it, info@hoteloceania.it, Anna and Stefano SE).

$$ Hotel Aberdeen, while a more formal place, offers a particularly great value, with minibars, phones, and showers in its 36 modern, air-conditioned, and smoke-free rooms. It's warmly run by Annamaria, with support from her cousins Sabrina, Laura, and Cinzia. Their inviting lounge, sleek business-class rooms, frescoed breakfast room, and cheery thoughtful staff make this place another winner (Sb-€82, Db-€125, Tb-€145, Qb-€160, these very special "dollar relief program" prices are promised through 2004 with this book only, 30 percent less in Aug and winter, Via Firenze 48, tel. 06-482-3920, fax 06-482-1092, check for deals online at www.travel.it/roma/aberdeen, hotel.aberdeen@travel.it, Fabio, Alessio and Sabrina SE).

$ Residence Adler offers breakfast on a garden patio, wide halls, and eight quiet, simple and air-conditioned rooms in a superb location. A fine value, it's run the old-fashioned way by a charming family (Db-€115, Tb-€150, Qb-€180, Quint/b-€195, prices through 2004 with this book only, additional 5 percent off with cash, 15 percent off in Aug and

Sept–Oct) and low-season prices. If traveling outside of peak times, ask about a discount. Room rates are lowest in sweltering August. Easter, September, and Christmas are most crowded and expensive. On Easter (April 11 in 2004), the entire city gets booked up.

English works in all but the cheapest places. Traffic in Rome roars. My challenge: To find friendly places on quiet streets. With the recent arrival of double-paned windows and air-conditioning, night noise is not the problem it was. Even so, light sleepers should always ask for a *tranquillo* room. Many prices here are promised only to people who show this book and reserve directly, without using a room-finding service. And many places prefer hard cash.

Bed-and-breakfasts are booming in Rome, offering comfy doubles in the old center for around €80. The Beehive hostel is a good contact for booking B&Bs in Rome (www.cross-pollinate.com, see "Sleeping Cheap, Northeast of the Train Station," page 790).

Most hotels are eager to connect you with a shuttle service to the airport. It's reasonable and easy for leaving, but upon arrival I think it's easiest to simply catch a cab or the shuttle train (covered in "Transportation Connections," page 805).

Almost no hotels have parking, but nearly all have a line on spots in a nearby garage (about €21/day).

winter; elevator; Via Modena 5, 2nd floor; tel. 06-484-466, fax 06-488-0940, www.hoteladler-roma.com, info@hoteladler-roma.com, gracious Sr. Brando Massini NSE but tries).

$ **Hotel Nardizzi Americana** offers 18 simple, pleasant, air-conditioned rooms and a delightful rooftop terrace. While loosely run, it's a fine value (Sb-€90, Db-€110, Tb-€135, Qb-€150, prices through 2004 with this book only, 10 percent discounts for off-season and long stays, additional 10 percent off with cash; elevator; Via Firenze 38, 4th floor; tel. 06-488-0368, fax 06-488-0035, www.hotelnardizzi.it, info@hotelnardizzi.it, SE).

Between Via Nazionale and Basilica Santa Maria Maggiore

$$ **Hotel Sonya** is a small, family-run, but impersonal place with 23 comfortable, well-equipped rooms, a central location, and decent prices (Db-€119, Tb-€134, Qb-€155, Quint/b-€170, these special prices guaranteed through 2004 with this book; air-con, elevator; facing the opera at Via Viminale 58, Metro: Repubblica or Termini; tel. 06-481-9911,

Hotels in East Rome

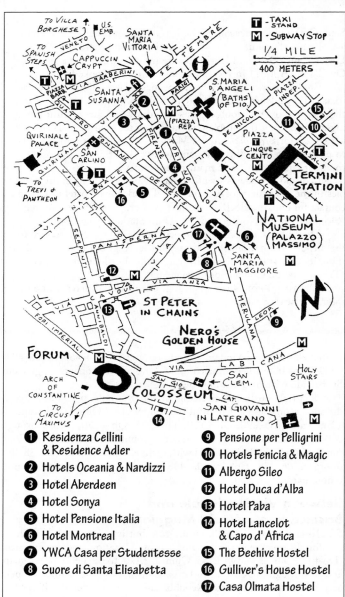

1. Residenza Cellini & Residence Adler
2. Hotels Oceania & Nardizzi
3. Hotel Aberdeen
4. Hotel Sonya
5. Hotel Pensione Italia
6. Hotel Montreal
7. YWCA Casa per Studentesse
8. Suore di Santa Elisabetta
9. Pensione per Pelligrini
10. Hotels Fenicia & Magic
11. Albergo Sileo
12. Hotel Duca d'Alba
13. Hotel Paba
14. Hotel Lancelot & Capo d' Africa
15. The Beehive Hostel
16. Gulliver's House Hostel
17. Casa Olmata Hostel

fax 06-488-5678, www.hotelsonya.it, hotelsonyaroma@katamail.com, Francesca SE).

$ Hotel Pensione Italia, in a busy, interesting, and handy locale, is placed safely on a quiet street next to the Ministry of the Interior. Thoughtfully run by Andrea, Nadine, and Francesca, it has 31 comfortable, airy, clean, and bright rooms (Sb-€75, Db-€100, Tb-€145, Qb-€165, prices through 2004 with this book and cash only, all rooms 30 percent off mid-July–Aug and Nov–March; air-con for €8 extra per day, most rooms have fans, elevator; Via Venezia 18, just off Via Nazionale, Metro: Repubblica or Termini; tel. 06-482-8355, fax 06-474-5550, www.hotelitaliaroma.com, hitalia@nettuno.it, SE). They have eight decent annex rooms across the street.

$ Hotel Montreal, run with care, is a bright, solid, business-class place on a big street a block southeast of Santa Maria Maggiore (soft prices, these are the max: Db-€115 but €90 in July–Aug, Tb-€140 but €120 in July–Aug, mention this book; air-con, elevator, good security; 1 block from Metro: Vittorio, 3 blocks west of train station, Via Carlo Alberto 4, Metro: Termini or Vittorio Emanuele; tel. 06-445-7797, fax 06-446-5522, www.hotelmontrealroma.com, info@hotelmontrealroma.com, SE).

YWCA and Convents

$ YWCA Casa per Studentesse accepts men and women. It's an institutional place, filled with white-uniformed maids, colorful Third-World travelers, and 75 single beds (€26 per person in 3- and 4-bed rooms, S-€37, Sb-€47, D-€62, Db-€74, includes breakfast except on Sun; elevator; Via C. Albo 4, Metro: Repubblica or Termini; tel. 06-488-0460, fax 06-487-1028, www.ywca-ucdg.it, segreteria@ywca-ucdg.it, a little reluctant English spoken). The YWCA faces a great little street market.

$ Suore di Santa Elisabetta is a heavenly Polish-run convent. While often booked long in advance and a challenge in communication, it's a super value (S-€34, Sb-€41, D-€55, Db-€71, Tb-€91, Qb-€110; 23:00 curfew, elevator, fine view roof terrace; a block southwest of Basilica Santa Maria Maggiore at Via dell' Omata 9, Metro: Termini or Vittorio Emanuele; tel. 06-488-8271, fax 06-488-4066, ist.it.s .elisabetta@libero.it, NSE).

$ Pensione per Pelligrini—which might close in 2004—is another nun-run place with 39 big, simple rooms and lots of twin beds. There's a language barrier, but the price is right (S-€35, Sb-€45, D-€65, Db-€84, Tb-€95, breakfast-€5; closed Aug, peaceful garden, elevator; just off Piazza Vittorio Emmanuele II, Istituto Buon Salvatore, Via Leopardi 17, no sign, from station take bus #714, #649, or #360 or Metro: Vittorio Emanuele; tel. 06-446-7147 or 06-446-7225, fax 06-446-1382, Sister Anna Maria SE).

Sleeping Cheap, Northeast of the Train Station

The cheapest hotels in town are northeast of the station (Metro: Termini). Some travelers feel this area is weird and spooky after dark, but these hotels feel plenty safe. With your back to the train tracks, turn right and walk two blocks out of the station.

$ **Hotel Fenicia** rents 13 decent rooms at a fine price (Sb-€53, Db-€80, Tb-€103, bigger and fancier Db-€93, prices through 2004 with this book only, air-con-€5/day, breakfast-€4, 5 percent off with cash, Via Milazzo 20, tel. & fax 06-490-342, www.hotelfenicia.it, info@hotelfenicia.it, Georgio and Anna SE).

$ **The Beehive** gives vagabonds—old and young—a cheap, clean, and comfy home in Rome. Its double rooms are a great value (D-€60, Db-€80, T-€90, Tb-€120, Q-€120, Qb-€160, no CC) and it has an 8-bed dorm (€18 beds). It's thoughtfully run by a friendly young American couple, Steve and Linda (2 blocks north of the train station at Via Marghera 8, tel. 06-447-04553, www.the-beehive.com). They also run a B&B booking service (private rooms in the old center of Rome, Florence, and Venice, offering comparable quality for €70–110—cheaper than the cost of a hotel, www.cross-pollinate.com).

$ **Hotel Magic** has 10 tidy, marbled rooms, up lots of stairs. It's family-run, though not with much warmth (Db-€85, Tb-€110, Qb-€120, air-con-€5/day, prices through 2004 with this book only, confirm rates, 25 percent cheaper in Aug and winter, no CC; thin walls, midnight curfew; Via Milazzo 20, 3rd floor, tel. 06-495-9880, www.hotel-magic-rome.com, info@hotel-magic-rome.com Carmela, Rosanna, and Caesarina NSE).

$ **Albergo Sileo** is a shiny-chandeliered, 10-room place. It has a contract to house train conductors who work the night shift, so its simple, pleasant rooms are rented from 19:00 to 9:00 only. If you can handle this, it's a wonderful value. During the day, they store your luggage, and though you won't have access to a room, you're welcome to shower or hang out in the lobby or bar (D-€45, Db-€55, Tb-€60, Db for 24 hours-€62 when available, elevator, Via Magenta 39, tel. & fax 06-445-0246, www.hotelsileo.com, info@hotelsileo.com, friendly Alessandro and Maria Savioli NSE, daughter Anna SE).

Near the Colosseum

These places are buried in a Roman world of exhaust-stained, medieval ambience. For Alba and Paba, take the subway one stop from the train station to the Cavour Metro stop. The *electrico* bus line #117 (San Giovanni in Laterano, Colosseo, Trevi Fountain, Piazza di Spagna, and Piazza del Popolo) connects you with the sights.

$$$ **Hotel Capo d'Africa** is a new (2002) sleek, business-class place next to recommended Hotel Lancelot and San Clemente Church. It offers 65 of the best rooms I list with plush and sprawling public

spaces, top-end fine points, and all the extras (Db-€200–225 depending on season, promised with this book in 2004 by manager Angelo Battistini, air-con, elevator, sprawling roof terrace, smoke-free floor, gym, Via Capo d'Africa 54, tel. 06-772-801, fax 06-772-80801, www .hotelcapodafrica.com, info@hotelcapodafrica.com, SE).

$$ **Hotel Duca d'Alba**, a tight and modern pastel/marble/hardwood place, is more professional than homey (30 rooms, Sb-€134, Db-€120–160 but higher in Sept and Oct, extra bed-€20, air-con, elevator, Via Leonina 14, tel. 06-484-471, fax 06-488-4840, check Web site for deals, www.hotelducadalba.com, info@hotelducadalba.com, Angelo SE).

$$ **Hotel Paba** has six rooms, chocolate box–tidy and lovingly cared for by Alberta and Pasquale Castelli. While overlooking busy Via Cavour just two blocks from the Colosseum, it's quiet enough (Db-€125, extra bed-€35, show this book for 5 percent discount, breakfast served in room, air-con, elevator, Via Cavour 266, tel. 06-4782-4902, fax 06-4788-1225, www.hotelpaba.com, info@hotelpaba.com, SE).

$$ **Hotel Lancelot**, a favorite among United Nations workers, is big, with 60 rooms, a shady courtyard, rooftop terrace, bar, and restaurant. It's quiet, safe, well-run by Faris and Lubna Khan, and popular with returning guests (Sb-€96–113, Db-€150, Tb-€170, Qb-€185, add €15 for balcony, air-con, elevator, parking-€11/day, behind Colosseum near San Clemente Church at Via Capo d'Africa 47, tel. 06-7045-0615, fax 06-7045-0640, www.lancelothotel.com, info@lancelothotel.com, Lubna S the queen's E).

$ **Hotel Casa Kolbe**, located in a former monastery, rents out 63 monkish, spartan rooms with no fans or air-conditioning. With vast public spaces and a peaceful garden, it's popular with groups. But the location is tranquil: it's on the river side of the Palatine ruins, on a quiet side street about a block from a little-used entrance to the Forum (Sb-€62, Db-€80, Tb-€100, Qb-€110, breakfast-€6, elevator, garden, courtyard, institutional and cheap meals served, not handy to public transit so taxi from the station, Via S. Teodoro 44, tel. 06-679-4974 or 06-679-8866, fax 06-6994-1550, Fortunato and Antonio SE).

Near Campo de' Fiori

While you pay a premium to stay in the old center (and endure a little extra night noise), each of these places is romantically set deep in the tangled back streets near the idyllic Campo de' Fiori and, for many, worth the extra money.

$$ **Casa di Santa Brigida** overlooks the elegant Piazza Farnese. With soft-spoken sisters gliding down polished hallways, and pearly gates instead of doors, this lavish 23-room convent makes exhaust-stained Roman tourists feel like they've died and gone to heaven. If you don't need a double bed, this is worth the splurge (Sb-€95, Db-€170, 3 percent extra with credit card, tasty €15 dinners, roof garden, plush

Hotels in the Heart of Rome

① Casa di Santa Brigida   ⑤ Albergo Santa Chiara
② Hotel Smeraldo   ⑥ Hotel Due Torri
③ To Hotel Arenula   ⑦ To Residenza Frattina
④ Hotel Nazionale   ⑧ Hotel Giardino

library, air-con, Monserrato 54, tel. 06-6889-2596, fax 06-6889-1573, www.brigidine.org, brigida@mclink.it, many of the sisters are from India and speak English). If you get no response to your fax or e-mail within three days, consider that a "no." Groups are welcome here.

$$ Hotel Smeraldo, with 50 rooms, is well-run, clean and a great deal (Sb-€90, Db-€120—this special price through 2004 with this book, Tb-€140, breakfast-€7; flowery roof terrace, centrally-controlled air-con, elevator; Civolo dei Chiodaroli 9, midway between Campo de' Fiori and Largo Argentina; tel. 06-687-5929, fax 06-6880-5495, www .smeraldoroma.com, albergosmeraldoroma@tin.it, Massimo SE).

$$ Hotel Arenula is the only hotel in Rome's old Jewish quarter. While it has the ambience of a gym, it's a fine value in the thick of old Rome with 50 comfy rooms (Sb-€92, Db-€121, Tb-€134, €26 less in July, Aug, and winter, air-con, just off Via Arenula at Via Santa Maria de' Calderari 47, tel. 06-687-9454, fax 06-689-6188, www.hotelarenula .com, hotel.arenula@flashnet.it, SE).

Near the Pantheon

These places are buried in the pedestrian-friendly heart of ancient Rome, each within a four-minute walk of the Pantheon. You'll pay more here—but you'll save time and money by being exactly where you want to be for your early and late wandering.

$$$ Hotel Nazionale, a four-star landmark, is a 16th-century palace sharing a well-policed square with the national Parliament. Its 90 rooms are served by lush public spaces, fancy bars, and a uniformed staff. It's a big hotel with a revolving front door, but it's a worthy splurge if you want security, comfort, and the heart of old Rome at your doorstep (Sb-€188, Db-€292—this special price guaranteed in 2004 with this book, extra person-€62, less in Aug and winter, air-con, elevator, Piazza Montecitorio 131, tel. 06-695-001, fax 06-678-6677, see Web site for discounts in summer and weekends, www.nazionaleroma.it, hotel @nazionaleroma.it, SE).

$$$ Albergo Santa Chiara is big, solid, and hotelesque, offering marbled elegance in the old center at an affordable price. Its ample public lounges are dressy and professional and its 100 rooms are quiet and spacious (Sb-€145, Db-€217, Tb-€250, elevator, all the big hotel services, behind the Pantheon at Via di Santa Chiara 21, tel. 06-687-2979, fax 06-687-3144, www.albergosantachiara.com, stchiara@tin.it).

$$$ Hotel Due Torri, hiding out on a tiny, quiet street, is a little over-priced but beautifully located. It feels professional yet homey, with an accommodating staff, generous public spaces, and 26 comfortable-if-tight rooms—four with balconies (Sb-€118, Db-€190, family apart-ment-€250 for 3 and €275 for 4; air-con; Vicolo del Leonetto 23, a block off Via della Scrofa; tel. 06-6880-6956, fax 06-686-5442, www .hotelduetorriroma.com, hotelduetorri@interfree.it, SE).

Between the Spanish Steps and Piazza Venezia

$$ Residenza Frattina is a pink palace—with 10 high-ceilinged rooms and a panforte-plush living room—in a posh locale. It has an old-fash-ioned feel and an unbeatable location on a main pedestrian shopping drag near Piazza di Spagna and the Spanish Steps (Db-€140–180, Tb-€160–220, prices change with season and are soft, 5 percent cash dis-count, air-con, Via Frattina 104, tel. 06-679-5509, fax 06-678-3701, www.residenzafrattinacorso.com, residenza.frattina@flashnet.it, owner Cesare SE; to locate hotel, see Dolce Vita Stroll map page 779).

$$ Hotel Giardino, thoughtfully run by Englishwoman Kate, offers 11 pleasant rooms in a central location three blocks northeast of Piazza Venezia (Easter–June and Sept–Oct: Sb-€80, Db-€120, other times: Sb-€60, Db-€90, these special prices are promised through 2004 with cash and this book; air-con, double-paned windows; busy street off Piazza di Quirinale, Via XXIV Maggio 51; tel. 06-679-4584, fax 06-679-5155, www.hotel-giardino-roma.com, hotel_giardino@libero.it).

Trastevere
To locate hotel, see map on page 765.

$$ Hotel Santa Maria sits like a lazy hacienda in the midst of Trastevere. Surrounded by a medieval skyline, you'll feel as if you're on some romantic stage set. Its 19 small but well-equipped, air-conditioned rooms—former cells in a cloister—are all on the ground floor, circling a gravelly courtyard of orange trees and stay-awhile patio furniture. Because this is the only hotel in Trastevere, it isn't cheap—but for well-heeled poets, it's a deal (Db-€155, Tb-€191, Qb-€217, family room for 6-€270, for this 20–25 percent discount it's cash only and a 3-night min, good with this book through 2004, smaller discounts also available with this book for shorter stays and credit cards and off-season, a block north of Piazza Maria Trastevere at Vicolo del Piede 2, tel. 06-589-4626, fax 06-589-4815, www.htlsantamaria.com, hotelsantamaria@libero.it, Stefano SE).

Near the Vatican Museum
To locate hotels, see map on page 765.

$$$ Hotel Sant' Anna is pricey, but located on a charming-for-Rome pedestrian street that fills up with restaurant tables at dinnertime. Its 20 comfy rooms, decorated with classical themes, are somewhere between tasteful and too much (Sb-€145, Db-€190, Db discounted to €145 July–Aug, winter, and slow times—any time of year, ask for a Rick Steves' discount; air-con, elevator, courtyard; Borgo Pio 133, near intersection with Mascherino, a couple blocks from entrance to St. Peter's; tel. 06-6880-1602, fax 06-6830-8717, www.hotelsantanna.com, santanna @travel.it, Viscardo SE).

$$$ Hotel Bramante sits like a grand medieval lodge in the shadow of the fortified escape wall that runs from the Vatican to Castel Sant' Angelo. The public spaces and the 16 thoughtfully-appointed rooms are generously sized, with rough wood beams and high ceilings (Sb-€133, Db-€190, Tb-€220, Qb-€230, these special prices promised with this book through 2004, air-con, no elevator, Vicolo delle Palline 24, tel. 06-6880-6426, fax 06-681-33339, www.hotelbramante.com, hotelbramante@libero.it, Maurizio and Loredana SE).

$$ Hotel Alimandi is a good value, run by the friendly and entrepreneurial Alimandi brothers—Paolo, Enrico, and Luigi—and the next generation, Marta, Irene, and Germano. Their 35 rooms are air-conditioned, modern, and marbled in white (Sb-€90, Db-€150, Tb-€175, 5 percent discount with this book and cash; closed Jan–mid Feb, elevator, grand buffet breakfast served in great roof garden, small gym, pool table, piano lounge, free parking; down stairs directly in front of Vatican Museum, Via Tunisi 8, near Metro: Cipro-Musei Vaticani; reserve by phone, no reply to fax means they are full; tel. 06-3972-6300, toll-free in Italy tel. 800-122-121, fax 06-3972-3943, www.alimandi.org, alimandi@tin.it, SE). They offer free airport pickup and drop-off, though you must reserve when you book your room and wait for a scheduled shuttle (every 2 hrs, see their Web site or lobby schedule).

$$ **Hotel Spring House**, with a hotelesque feel (it's a Best Western), offers 51 attractive rooms—some with balconies or terraces (standard Db-€135, superior Db-€180, Tb-€155–195, Qb-€175–210, mention this book for a 15 percent discount July–Aug and Jan–Feb; air-con, elevator, free loaner bikes; Metro: Cipro-Musei Vaticani, Via Mocenigo 7, 2 blocks from Vatican Museum; tel. 06-3972-0948, fax 06-3972-1047, www.hotelspringhouse.com, info@hotelspringhouse .com, Stefano Gabbani SE).

$$ **Hotel Gerber** is modern and air-conditioned, with 27 well-polished businesslike rooms, set in a quiet residential area (two S without air-con-€57, Sb-€100, Db-€130, Tb-€150, Qb-€170, 10 percent discount beyond their best price with this book in high season, 15 percent discount in low season, Via degli Scipioni 241, a block from Metro: Lepanto, at intersection with Ezio, tel. 06-321-6485, fax 06-321-7048, www.hotelgerber.it, info@hotelgerber.it, friendly dog Kira, Peter and Simonetta SE).

Sleeping Cheaply near the Vatican
$ **Casa per Ferie Santa Maria alle Fornaci dei Padri Trinitari** houses pilgrims and secular tourists with simple class just a short walk south of the Vatican in 54 stark utilitarian mostly twin-bedded rooms. This is the only user-friendly convent-type place I found (Sb-€60, Db-€80, Tb-€110; groups welcome, generally booked solid Easter, May, and Oct, fans, elevator; bus #64 from train station to St. Peters Station, then walk 100 yards to Piazza S. Maria alle Fornaci 27; tel. 06-393-67632, fax 06-393-66795, www.trinitariematha.it, cffornaci@tin.it, SE).

Hostels and Dorms
For easy communication with young, friendly entrepreneurs, cheap dorm beds, and some inexpensive doubles—within a 10-minute hike of the train station—consider the following places:

$ **The Beehive,** listed above in "Sleeping Cheap, Northeast of the Train Station," offers €18 dorm beds (in an 8-bed room) in addition to affordable doubles.

$ **Gulliver's House Rome** is a fun little hostel in a safe and handy locale, run by helpful Simon and Sara. Its 24 beds in cramped quarters work fine for backpackers. They host English movie evenings (warm up with my TV shows on Rome) in their lounge nightly (€20 per bunk bed in 8-bed dorm, one D-€70, no CC, closed 12:00–16:00, 1:00 curfew, small kitchen, Via Palermo 36, tel. 06-481-7680, www.gullivershouse .com, stay@gullivershouse.com). Gulliver's also runs a five-room place a 10-minute walk north of the station offering simple, air-con doubles (D-€70, Db-€80, Tb-€100, Via Castro Pretorio 25).

$ **Casa Olmata** is a ramshackle, laid-back backpackers' place midway between the Termini train station and Colosseum (dorm beds-€20, S-€38, bunk bed D-€44, one queen-size D-€55; lots of stairs, laundry service, free Internet access, video rentals, games, rooftop terrace with views and nearly free dinner parties, dinners twice weekly, communal kitchen; a block southwest of Basilica Santa Maria Maggiore, Via dell' Omata 36, 3rd floor, Metro: Vittorio Emaneule; tel. 06-483-019, fax 06-486819, www.casaolmata.com, info@casaolmata.com, Mirella and Marco).

EATING

Romans spend their evenings eating rather than drinking, and the preferred activity is simply to enjoy a fine, slow meal, buried deep in the old city. Rome's a fun and cheap place to eat, with countless little eateries serving memorable €20 meals.

Although I've listed a number of restaurants, I recommend that you just head for a scenic area and explore. Piazza Navona, the Pantheon area, Campo de' Fiori, and Trastevere are neighborhoods packed with characteristic eateries. Sitting with tourists on a famous square enjoying the scene works fine. But for places more out of the way, consider my recommendations.

For Rome's best gelato, see "Near the Pantheon," below.

Trastevere

Colorful Trastevere is now pretty touristy. Still, Romans join the tourists to eat on the rustic side of the Tiber River. Start at the central square (Piazza Santa Maria). Then choose: Eat with tourists enjoying the ambience of the famous square, or wander the back streets in search of a mom-and-pop place with barely a menu. Look over these two places (between Piazza Santa Maria Trastevere and Ponte Sisto) before making a choice. See map on page 765.

Trattoria da Lucia lets you enjoy simple traditional food at a good price in a great scene (Tue–Sun 12:30–15:30 & 19:30–24:00, closed Mon, homey indoor or evocative outdoor seating, Vicolo del Mattonato 2, tel. 06-580-3601, NSE).

Osteria Ponte Sisto, a rough-and-tumble little place, specializes in traditional Roman cuisine with a menu that changes often. Since it's just outside of the tourist zone, it offers the best value and caters mostly to Romans. It's also easy to find: Crossing Ponte Sisto (pedestrian bridge), continue across the little square (Piazza Trilussa) and you'll see it on the right (daily 12:30–15:00 & 19:30–24:00, Via Ponte Sisto 80, tel. 06-588-3411, SE).

The fine little **Gelateria alla Scala** (across from the church on Piazza della Scala) dishes up delightful cinnamon *(cannella)* and oh-wow pistachio (daily 12:30–24:00). Seek this place out.

On and near Campo de' Fiori

While it is touristy, Campo de' Fiori offers a classic and romantic square setting. And, since it is so close to the collective heart of Rome, it remains popular with locals. For greater atmosphere than food value, circle the square, considering each place. Bars and pizzerias seem to overwhelm the square. The **Taverna** and **Vineria** (#16 and #15) offer good perches from which to people-watch and nurse a glass of wine. The only real restaurant is **La Carbonara**. While famous and atmospheric with reasonable prices, it gets mixed reviews (closed Tue, Campo de' Fiori 23, tel. 06-686-4783). Although meals on small surrounding streets are a better value, they lack that Campo de' Fiori magic.

Ostaria da Giovanni ar Galletto—nearby, on the more elegant and peaceful Piazza Farnese—has a dressier local crowd, pleasant outdoor seating, and reasonable prices. Say hi to Angelo, who's committed to serving fine food (closed Sun, tucked in corner of Piazza Farnese at #102, tel. 06-686-1714). Of all my listings, this place offers perhaps the best alfresco dining experience.

Osteria Enoteca al Bric is a mod bistro-type place run by a man who loves to cook and serve good wine. Wine-case lids decorate the wall like happy memories. With candlelit grace and no tourists, it's perfect for the wine snob in the mood for pasta and fine cheese. Aficionados choose their bottle from the huge selection lining the walls as they enter. Beginners order wine with help from the waiter after they order their meal (open from 19:30, closed Mon, reserve after 20:30, 100 yards off Campo de' Fiori at Via del Pellegrino 51, tel. 06-687-9533). Al Bric offers my readers a special "Taste of Italy for Two" deal (fine plate of mixed cheese and meat with two glasses of full-bodied red wine and a pitcher of water) for €20 from 19:30, but you may need to finish by 20:30. This could be a light meal if you're kicking off an evening stroll, a substantial appetizer, or a way to check this place out for a serious meal later.

Filetti de Baccala, a tradition for many Romans, is basically a fish bar with paper tablecloths and cheap prices. Its grease-stained, hurried waiters serve old-time favorites—fried cod fillets, a strange bitter *puntarelle* salad, and their antipasto (delightful anchovies with butter)— to nostalgic locals (no CC; Mon–Sat 17:30–23:00, closed Sun; a block east of Campo de' Fiori tumbling onto a tiny and atmospheric square, Largo dei Librari 88; tel. 06-686-4018). Study what others are eating and order by pointing. Nothing is expensive (see the menu on wall). Urchins can get a cod stick to go and sit on the barnacle church doorsteps just outside.

Trattoria der Pallaro has no menu but plenty of return eaters. Paola Fazi—with a towel wrapped around her head turban-style—and her family serve up a five-course festival of typically Roman food for €19, including wine, coffee, and a wonderful mandarin liqueur. Their slogan: "Here, you'll eat what we want to feed you." Make like Oliver Twist asking for more soup and get seconds on the mandarin liqueur (Tue–Sun 12:00–15:00 & 19:00–24:00, closed Mon; indoor/outdoor seating on quiet square; a block south of Corso Vittorio Emmanuele, down Largo del Chiavari to Largo del Pallaro 15; tel. 06-6880-1488).

Ristorante Grotte del Teatro di Pompeo, sitting atop an ancient theater, serves good food at fair prices, perfect if you want to dine on a characteristic cobbled street busy with strolling people and musicians (closed Mon, Via del Biscione 73, tel. 06-6880-3686).

Between Campo de' Fiori and Piazza Navona: **Cul de Sac** is packed with happy locals cobbling together fun meals from the Italian dim sum-type menu of traditional dishes (often crowded, daily 12:00–16:00 & 19:00–24:00, a block southwest of Piazza Navona on Piazza Pasquino). **L'Insalata Ricca**, next door, is a popular chain that specializes in hearty and healthy €7 salads (daily 12:00–15:45 & 18:45–22:00, Piazza Pasquino 72, tel. 06-6830-7881). Another branch is nearby with more spacious outdoor seating (just off Corso Vittorio Emanuele on Largo del Chiavari).

Near the Pantheon

Ristorante da Fortunato is an Italian classic—with fresh flowers on the tables, and white-coated black-tie waiters politely serving good meat and fish to local politicians, foreign dignitaries, and tourists with good taste. Don't leave without perusing the photos of their famous visitors—everyone from Tariq Aziz to Bill Clinton. The outdoor seating is fine for watching the river of Rome flow by. The air-conditioned interior has a smoke-free room—but I prefer the ambience of the main room. For a dressy night out, this is my choice (surprisingly reasonable, plan to spend €30, Mon–Sat 12:30–15:30 & 19:30–23:30, closed Sun, a block in front of the Pantheon at Via del Pantheon 55, tel. 06-679-2788).

Ristorante Myosotis di Marsili, an elegant place with black-tie waiters and a coat check, is popular with local politicians and diners smart enough to look into the fish locker and make a knowledgeable choice. Secluded and private, it has a traditional yet imaginative menu with a good wine list. Everything here is made on the premises (€40 dinners, Mon–Sat 12:30–15:30 & 19:30–23:30, closed Sun, reservations

Restaurants in the Heart of Rome

1. Taverna, Vineria & La Carbonara Rest.

2. Ostaria da Giovanni ar Galletto

3. Osteria Enoteca al Bric

4. Filetti de Baccala & Trattoria der Pallaro

5. Ristorante Grotte del Teatro di Pompeo

6. Cul de Sac Bar & L'Insalata Ricca Rest.

7. Ristorante da Fortunato

8. Ost. da Mario, Rist. Myosotis di Marsili, & Tav. Le Coppele

9. Miscellanea Restaurant & Ristorante Due Colonne

10. Brek Cafeteria

11. To Non Solo Bevi & Vini e Buffet

12. Giolitti's Gelateria

13. To Rist. alla Rampa, Rist. il Gabriello, Rist. Difronte, & Fiaschetteria

14. Ristorante Pizzeria Sacro e Profano

15. Gelateria San Crispino

wise, behind Osteria da Mario—see directions below—at Vicolo Della Vaccarella 3, tel. 06-686-5554).

Eating Cheap and Colorful near the Pantheon

Eating on the square facing the Pantheon is a temptation (there's even a McDonald's offering some of the best outdoor seating in town) and I'd consider it just to relax and enjoy the classic Roman scene. But if you walk a block or two away you'll get less view and better food. Here are some suggestions:

Miscellanea is run by much-loved Michelangelo, who's on a mission to keep foreign students well-fed. You'll find cheap pasta, hearty €3 sandwiches, and a long list of €5 salads. "Mikki" often tosses in a fun little extra (daily 11:00–24:00, indoor/outdoor seating, a block toward Via del Corso from the Pantheon at Via delle Paste 110).

Osteria da Mario, a homey little mom-and-pop joint with a no-stress menu, serves delicious traditional favorites. The pop (Mario), who passed away—you'll see his photo on the wall—would be happy with the way his wife and kids are carrying on (Mon–Sat 13:00–15:00 & 19:30–23:00, closed Sun; indoor/outdoor; from Pantheon walk 2 blocks up Via Pantheon, go left on Via della Coppelle, take first right to Piazza delle Coppelle 51; tel. 06-6880-6349).

Two other places within a block or so of the Pantheon to consider for inexpensive eating: **Taverna Le Coppele** is good—especially for pizza—with checkered table cloth ambience (closed Tue, Via delle Coppelle 39, tel. 06-688-06557). **Ristorante Due Colonne** serves daily homemade specials and great salads in a simple rustic setting (daily 11:30–15:30 & 18:30–23:30, air-con, indoors only, Via del Seminario 122, tel. 06-6781-449).

Cafeteria Brek, on Largo Argentina just south of the Pantheon, is an appealing, self-service restaurant with a modern, efficient atmosphere and really cheap prices (daily 12:00–15:30 & 19:00–22:15; skip the sandwiches and pizza slices downstairs and go to the cafeteria upstairs, northwest corner of square, Largo Argentina 1; tel. 06-6821-0353).

The classic **Antica Salumeria** is an old-time *alimentari* (grocery store, daily 9:00–19:00) on the Pantheon square. While they sell meager ready-made sandwiches, it's better and more fun to have one made to your specs—ideal for a temple-porch picnic. Sit at the base of a column in the shade and munch lunch.

Non Solo Bevi *enoteca* is a trendy bar several blocks north, tucked into a distant corner of the pedestrian square, Piazza San Lorenzo. Francesco and Lamberto serve fine wine and toothpick munchies free with a glass. Sit at a table (€5 for wine) and enjoy the scene or stand at the bar (€3.50 for wine) and be part of the commotion (open daily, Via in Lucina 15, tel. 06-687-1683; for location, see Dolce Vita Stroll map on page 779). A block off the square, at **Vini e Buffet**, Vittorio serves salads, *bruschette*, and wine by the glass (Mon–Sat 12:30–15:00 & 19:30–23:00, closed Sun, Piazza della Torretta 60, tel. 06-687-1445).

Gelato: Rome's most famous and venerable ice-cream joint is a minute's walk in front of the Pantheon. **Giolitti's** is good, with cheap take-away prices and elegant Old World seating (just off Piazza Colonna and Piazza Monte Citorio at Via Uffici del Vicario 40, tel. 06-699-1243).

Near the Spanish Steps

To locate these restaurants, see the Dolce Vita Stroll map on page 779.

Ristorante alla Rampa is a classic old restaurant just around the corner from the touristy crush of the Spanish Steps. You'll get quality Roman cooking here with appealing indoor/outdoor ambience for a moderate price. They take no reservations, so arrive by 19:30 or be prepared to wait. For a simple meal, go with the €9 *piatto misto all' ortolana*—a self-service trip to their magnificent antipasto spread with meat, fish, and veggies (closed Sun, 100 yards east of Spanish Steps at Piazza Mignanelli 18, tel. 06-678-2621).

Ristorante il Gabriello is inviting and small—mod under medieval arches—offering a peaceful and local-feeling respite from all the top-end fashion shops in the area. Claudio serves with charisma while his brother cooks creative Roman cuisine using fresh, organic products from his wife's farm. Simply close your eyes and point to anything on the menu (pastas-€7, *secondi*-€10; dinner only, Mon–Sat 19:00–24:00, closed Sun; air-con, reservations smart; Via Vittoria 51, 3 blocks from Spanish Steps; tel. 06-6994-0810).

Ristorante Difronte, with a fresh, stylish ambience, serves big fun salads (Tue–Sun 12:00–15:30 & 17:30–24:00, closed Mon, Via della Croce 38, tel. 06-678-0355). Stepping next door takes you back about 100 years to the bustling **Fiaschetteria,** serving quality traditional Italian cuisine (closed Sun, Via della Croce 39). Both places serve €7 plates and offer indoor and outdoor seating.

Near the Trevi Fountain

Ristorante Pizzeria Sacro e Profano fills an old church with spicy south Italian (Calabrian) cuisine and some pricey exotic dishes. Run by Pasquale and friends, this is just far enough away from the Trevi mobs. Their hearty €13 antipasto plate offers a fun montage of Calabrian taste treats—plenty of food for a light meal (daily 12:00–15:00 & 19:00–22:00, a block off Via del Tritone at Via dei Maroniti 29, tel. 06-6791-836).

Gelateria San Crispino, around the corner, serves particularly tasty gelato using creative ingredients such as balsamic vinegar, pear, and cinnamon (daily until 24:00, Via della Panetteria 42, tel. 06-679-3924).

Eating Cheap between the Colosseum and St. Peter-in-Chains Church

You'll find good views but poor value in the restaurants directly behind the Colosseum. To get your money's worth, eat at least a block away. Here are two handy eateries at the top of Terme Di Tito (a block uphill from the Colosseum, near St. Peter-in-Chains church—of Michelangelo's *Moses* fame) and a good mom-and-pop place beyond that.

Caffè dello Studente is a lively spot popular with local engineering students attending the nearby U of Rome. Pina, Mauro, and their daughter Simona (SE) serve typical *bar gastronomia* fare (pick a toasted sandwich at the bar, pizza, drinks). You can get your food to go; stand up and eat at the crowded bar; sit at an outdoor table and wait for a menu; or—if it's not busy—show this book when you order at the bar and sit without paying extra at a table (Mon–Sat 7:30–21:30, closed Sun, tel. 06-488-3240).

Ostaria da Nerone, next door, is less friendly and more aggressive, but still a good bet for a meal in the area—especially their €7 antipasti plate (Mon–Sat 12:00–15:00 & 19:00–23:00, closed Sun, indoor/outdoor seating, Via delle Terme di Tito 96, tel. 06-481-7952).

Ristorante al Cardello di Angelo e Lidia is a characteristic hole-in-the-wall on a scenic corner tucked in a colorful neighborhood (*secondi*–€7, full menu–€15, Mon–Sat from 12:30 and from 19:30, closed Sun, indoor/outdoor seating, near the Forum just off Via Cavour on the corner of Via Frangipani and Via del Cardello, tel. 06-474-5259).

Near Via Firenze and Via Nazionale Hotels

Munching on Via Firenze: You have plenty of eating options near my recommended hotels on Via Firenze.

Snack Bar Gastronomia is a local joint with one table and a booming take-out business—especially popular for its Greek-style yogurt with fruit and honey (€2–4, confirm price of various options; fresh meat or veggie sandwiches, freshly-squeezed juices, daily 7:00–24:00, Via Firenze 34). An old-fashioned *alimentari* (grocery) is across the street (7:00–19:30), just uphill from the McDonald's.

Pasticceria Dagnino, a block away, is popular for its top-quality Sicilian specialties, especially pastries and ice cream (daily 7:00–22:00, in Galleria Esedra off Via Torino, tel. 06-481-8660). Their *arancino*—a rice, cheese, and ham ball—is a greasy Sicilian favorite, and their cannoli is sweet. Direct the construction of your meal at the bar, pay for your trayful at the cashier, and climb upstairs where you'll find the dancing Sicilian girls (free).

Hostaria Romana is a great place for traditional Roman cuisine served by a fun-loving gang who seems to really enjoy their work. For an air-conditioned, classy, local favorite, eat here (closed Sun; reservations generally not needed; midway between Trevi Fountain and Piazza

Restaurants in East Rome

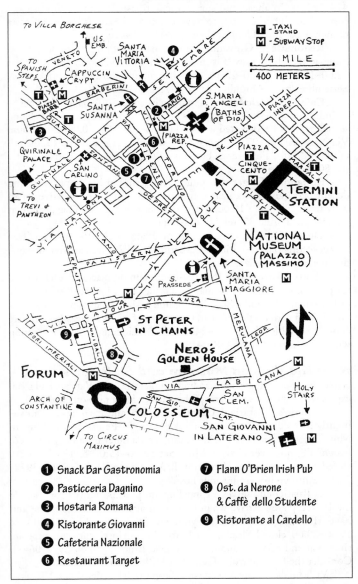

1. Snack Bar Gastronomia
2. Pasticceria Dagnino
3. Hostaria Romana
4. Ristorante Giovanni
5. Cafeteria Nazionale
6. Restaurant Target
7. Flann O'Brien Irish Pub
8. Ost. da Nerone
   & Caffè dello Studente
9. Ristorante al Cardello

Barberini, Via del Boccaccio 1, at intersection with Via Rasella; tel. 06-474-5284). Go ahead and survey the antipasto bar in person (a plate costs €7.50). They're happy to serve an *antipasti misto della casa* and pasta dinner. Take a hard look at their *Specialita Romane* list.

Ristorante da Giovanni is a reasonable option feeding locals and hungry travelers now for 50 years (tired €13 *menu*, Mon–Sat 12:00–15:00 & 19:00–22:30, closed Sun and in Aug, just off Via XX Settembre at Via Antonio Salandra 1, tel. 06-485-950).

Cafeteria Nazionale, with woody elegance, offers light lunches—including salads—at fair prices. It's noisy with local office workers being served by frantic red-vested waitstaff (Mon–Sat 7:00–20:00, closed Sun; Via Nazionale 26–27, at intersection with Via Agostino de Pretis; tel. 06-4899-1716). Their lunch buffet is a delight but gets picked over early (€7.50, 12:00–15:00).

Restaurant Target is a soulless, modern, but handy place serving decent pizza and pasta near recommended hotels (inexpensive, open daily from 12:00 and 19:00, indoor/outdoor seating, don't expect great service, Via Torino 33, tel. 06-474-0066).

The **McDonald's** restaurants on Piazza della Repubblica (free piazza seating outside), Piazza Barberini, and Via Firenze offer air-conditioned interiors and salad bars.

Flann O'Brien Irish Pub is an entertaining place for a light meal (of pasta or something *other* than pasta, such as grilled beef, served early or late when other places are closed), fine Irish beer, live sporting events on TV, and perhaps the most Italian crowd of all. Walk way back before choosing a table (daily 7:30–24:00; Via Nazionale 17, at intersection with Via Napoli; tel. 06-488-0418).

Near the Vatican Museum and St. Peter's

Avoid the restaurant pushers handing out fliers near the Vatican: bad food, expensive menu tricks. Try any of these instead (see map on page 763).

Antonio's Hostaria dei Bastioni is tasty and friendly. It's conveniently located midway on your hike from St. Peters' to the Vatican Museum, with noisy street-side seating and a quiet interior (pastas-€6, *secondi*-€8, no cover charge; Mon–Sat 12:00–15:00 & 19:00–23:30, closed Sun; at corner of Vatican wall, Via Leone IV 29; tel. 06-3972-3034). Antonio is your gracious host.

La Rustichella serves a sprawling antipasti buffet (€7 for a single meal-sized plate). Arrive when they open at 19:30 to avoid a line and have the pristine buffet to yourself (Tue–Sun 12:30–15:00 & 19:30–23:00, closed Mon; near Metro: Cipro-Musei Vaticani, opposite church at end of Via Candia, Via Angelo Emo 1; tel. 06-3972-0649). Consider the fun and fruity **Gelateria Millennium** next door.

Viale Giulio Cesare is lined with cheap **Pizza Rustica** shops, self-serve places, and fun eateries. Restaurants such as **Tre Pupazzi** (closed Sun, tel. 06-686-8371), which line the pedestrian-only Borgo Pio—a block from Piazza San Pietro—are worth a look.

Turn your nose loose in the wonderful **Via Andrea Doria** open-air market, three blocks north of the Vatican Museum (Mon–Sat roughly 7:00–13:30, until 16:30 Tue and Fri except summer, corner of Via Tunisi and Via Andrea Doria). If the market is closed, try the nearby **IN's supermarket** (Mon–Sat 8:30–13:30 & 16:00–20:00, closed Thu eve and Sun; a half block straight out from Via Tunisi entrance of open-air market, Via Francesco 18).

TRANSPORTATION CONNECTIONS

Termini is the central station (see "Arrival in Rome" near beginning of chapter; Metro: Termini). Tiburtina is the bus station (4 Metro stops away from train station; Metro: Tiburtina).

By train from Rome to: Venice (6/day, 5–8 hrs, overnight possible), **Florence** (12/day, 2 hrs, most stop at Orvieto en route), **Pisa** (8/day, 3–4 hrs), **Genoa** (7/day, 6 hrs, overnight option), **Milan** (12/day, 5 hrs, overnight possible), **Naples** (6/day, 2 hrs), **Brindisi** (2/day, 9 hrs, overnight available), **Amsterdam** (2/day, 20 hrs, overnight unavoidable), **Bern** (5/day, 10 hrs, overnight possible), **Frankfurt** (4/day, 14 hrs, overnight available), **Munich** (5/day, 12 hrs, overnight option), **Nice** (2/day, 10 hrs, overnight possible), **Paris** (5/day, 16 hrs, overnight available), **Vienna** (3/day, 13–15 hrs, overnight option).

By bus to: Assisi (3/day, 3 hrs), **Siena** (7/day, 3 hrs).

Rome's Airports
Rome's two airports—Fiumicino (a.k.a. Leonardo da Vinci) and the small Ciampino—share the same Web site (www.adr.it).

Fiumicino Airport: Rome's major airport has a TI (daily 8:00–19:00, tel. 06-6595-4471), ATMs, banks, luggage storage, shops, and bars.

A slick, direct **train** connects the airport and Rome's central Termini train station in 30 minutes. Trains run twice hourly in both directions from roughly 6:00 to 23:00. From the airport, trains depart at :07 and :37 past the hour. From the airport's arrival gate, follow signs to "Stazione/Railway Station." Buy your ticket from a machine or the Biglietteria office (€9, CC). Make sure the train you board is going to "Roma Termini," not "Roma Orte" or others.

Going from the Termini train station to the airport, trains depart at :20 and :50 past the hour, usually from track 25 or 26; to reach these tracks, take a 10-minute walk along track 24 to the end of the station (moving walkways are inside the building to the right on the lower level). Check the departure boards for "Fiumicino Aeroporto"—the local name for the airport—and confirm with an official or a local on the platform that the train is indeed going to the airport (€9, buy ticket from computerized yellow ticket machines, any *tabacchi* shop in station, or at the desk near entrance to track 26). Read your ticket: If it requires validation, stamp it in the yellow machine near the platform before boarding.

Your hotel can arrange a **taxi** to the airport at any hour for about €40. To get from the airport into town cheaply by taxi, try teaming up with any tourist also just arriving (most are heading for hotels near yours in the center). Be sure to wait at the taxi stand. Avoid unmarked, unmetered taxis; these guys will try to tempt you away from the taxi stand line-up by offering an immediate (rip-off) ride.

For **airport information,** call 06-65951. To inquire about flights, call 06-6595-3640 (Alitalia: tel. 06-65643, British Air: toll-free tel. 848-812-266, Delta: toll-free tel. 800-864-114, KLM/Northwest: tel. 06-6501-1441, Lufthansa: tel. 06-6595-4156, SAS: tel. 06-954-070, Swiss Air: tel. 06-847-0555, United: tel. 848-800-692, Air Europa: tel. 06-6595-5854).

Ciampino Airport: Rome's smaller airport (tel. 06-794-941) handles budget and charter flights. To get to downtown Rome from the airport, take the LILA/Cotral bus (2/hr) to the Anagnina Metro stop, where you can connect by Metro to the stop nearest your hotel.

VENICE

(Venezia)

Soak all day in this puddle of elegant decay. Venice is Europe's best-pre-served big city. This car-free urban wonderland of a hundred islands—laced together by 400 bridges and 2,000 alleys—survives on the artificial respirator of tourism.

Born in a lagoon 1,500 years ago as a refuge from barbarians, Venice is overloaded with tourists and is slowly sinking (unrelated facts). In the Middle Ages, the Venetians, becoming Europe's clever middlemen for East-West trade, created a great trading empire. By smuggling in the bones of St. Mark (San Marco, A.D. 828), Venice gained religious impor-tance as well. With the discovery of America and new trading routes to the Orient, Venetian power ebbed. But as Venice fell, her appetite for decadence grew. Through the 17th and 18th centuries, Venice partied on the wealth accumulated through earlier centuries as a trading power.

Today, Venice is home to about 65,000 people in its old city, down from a peak population of nearly 200,000. While there are about 500,000 in greater Venice (counting the mainland, not counting tourists), the old town has a small-town feel. Locals seem to know everyone. To see small-town Venice away from the touristic flak, escape the Rialto–San Marco tourist zone and savor the town early and late without the hordes of vacationers day-tripping in from cruise ships and nearby beach resorts. A 10-minute walk from the madness puts you in an idyllic Venice few tourists see.

Planning Your Time

Venice is worth at least a day on even the speediest tour. Hyperefficient train travelers take the night train in and/or out. Sleep in the old center to experience Venice at its best: early and late. For a one-day visit, cruise the Grand Canal, do the major sights on St. Mark's Square (the square itself, Doge's Palace, and St. Mark's Basilica), see the Church of the Frari (Chiesa dei Frari) for art, and wander the backstreets on a pub crawl (described in "Eating," below). Venice's greatest sight is the city itself. Make time to simply wander. While doable in a day, Venice is worth two. It's a medieval cookie jar, and nobody's looking.

ORIENTATION

The island city of Venice is shaped like a fish. Its major thoroughfares are canals. The Grand Canal winds through the middle of the fish, starting at the mouth where all the people and food enter, passing under the Rialto Bridge, and ending at St. Mark's Square (Piazza San Marco). Park your 21st-century perspective at the mouth and let Venice swallow you whole.

Venice is a car-less kaleidoscope of people, bridges, and odorless canals. The city has no real streets, and addresses are hopelessly confusing. There are six districts: San Marco (most touristy), Castello (behind San Marco), Cannaregio (from the train station to the Rialto), San Polo (other side of the Rialto), Santa Croce, and Dorsoduro. Each district has about 6,000 address numbers.

To find your way, navigate by landmarks, not streets. Many street corners have a sign pointing you to *(per)* the nearest major landmark, such as San Marco, Accademia, Rialto, and Ferrovia (train station). Obedient visitors stick to the main thoroughfares as directed by these signs and miss the charm of backstreet Venice.

Tourist Information

There are three main TIs: at the train station (daily 8:00–18:30, crowded and surly); at St. Mark's Square (Mon–Sat 9:00–15:30, closed Sun; with your back to St. Mark's Basilica, it's in far left corner of square); and near St. Mark's Square vaporetto boat stop on the lagoon (daily 10:00–18:00, sells vaporetto tickets, rents audioguides at €3.65/hr for self-guided walking tours). Smaller offices are at Piazzale Roma and the airport (daily 9:30–19:30). For a quick question, save time by phoning 041-522-5150 or 041-541-5887. The TI's offical Web site is www.turismovenezia.it.

At any TI, pick up a free city map and the free *Leo* bimonthly magazine, which comes with an insert, *Leo Bussola*, listing museum hours, exhibitions, and musical events (in Italian and English). Confirm your sightseeing plans. Ask for the fine brochures outlining three offbeat Venice walks. The free periodical entertainment guide *Un' Ospite di Venezia* (a monthly listing of events, nightlife, museum hours, train and vaporetto schedules, emergency telephone numbers, and so on) is available at the TI or fancy hotel reception desks (www.aguestinvenice.com).

Maps: The cheap Venice map on sale at postcard racks has much more detail than the TI's free map, but the "Illustrated Venice Map" by Magnetic North is by far the best ever (€6, listing nearly every shop, hotel, and restaurant). Also consider the little guidebook (sold alongside

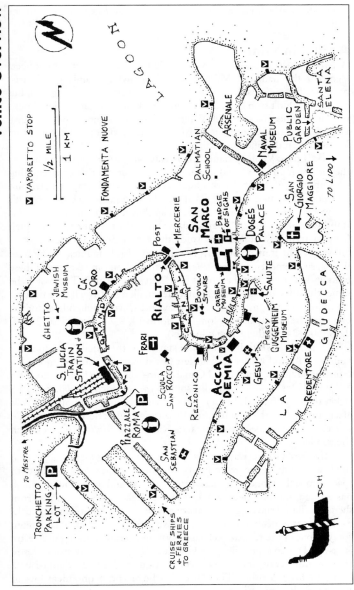

Venice Overview

☑ VAPORETTO STOP

½ MILE

1 KM

LAGOON

N

FONDAMENTA NUOVE

DALMATIAN SCHOOL

ARSENALE

SANTA ELENA

PUBLIC GARDEN

NAVAL MUSEUM

TO LIDO

SAN GIORGIO MAGGIORE

BRIDGE OF SIGHS

SAN MARCO

DOGE'S PALACE

MERCERIE

POST

CA' D'ORO

GHETTO

JEWISH MUSEUM

GRAND

RIALTO

BOVOLO STAIRS

CORRER MUSEUM

CANAL

SALUTE

PEGGY GUGGENHEIM MUSEUM

GIUDECCA

S. LUCIA TRAIN STATION

FRARI

SCUOLA SAN ROCCO

CA' REZZONICO

ACCA-DEMIA

GESÙ

LA

REDENTORE

PIAZZALE ROMA

P

SAN SEBASTIAN

TO MESTRE

TRONCHETTO PARKING LOT

P

CRUISE SHIPS + FERRIES TO GREECE

DCH

the postcards), which comes with a city map and explanations of the major sights.

Arrival in Venice

A two-mile-long causeway (with highway and train lines) connects Venice to the mainland. Mestre, Venice's sprawling mainland industrial base, has fewer crowds, cheaper hotels, and plenty of parking lots, but no charm. Don't stop here, unless you're parking your car in a lot. Trains regularly connect Mestre with Venice's Santa Lucia station (6/hr, 5 min). Don't leave your train at Venezia-Mestre—the next stop is Venezia Santa Lucia (end of the line for Venice).

By Train: Venice's **Santa Lucia train station** plops you right into the old town on the Grand Canal, an easy vaporetto ride or fascinating 40-minute walk to St. Mark's Square. Upon arrival, skip the station's crowded TI because the two TIs at St. Mark's Square are better, and it's not worth a long wait for a minimal map (buy a good one from a newsstand with no wait; see "Maps," above). Confirm your departure plan (stop by train info desk or just study the *partenze*—departure—posters on walls). The train station can be crowded with long lines to buy train tickets, supplements, and *couchette* reservations. You can take care of these tasks at downtown travel agencies (see "Services," below). The cost is the same, the lines and language barrier are smaller, and you'll save time.

Consider storing unnecessary heavy bags, even though lines for the **baggage check** may be very long (platform 14, €3/12 hrs, €5.20/24 hrs, daily 6:00–24:00; there are no lockers).

Then walk straight out of the station to the canal. The dock for **vaporetti** #1 and #82 is on your left (for downtown Venice, most recommended hotels, and Grand Canal Tour—see page 819); the dock for #51 and #52 is on your right (for some recommended hotels). Buy a €5 ticket (or €10.50 all-day pass) at the ticket window and hop on a boat after confirming that it's heading downtown (direction: Rialto or San Marco). Some boats only go as far as Rialto *(solo Rialto)*, so check with the conductor.

By Car: The freeway ends at Venice in a parking lot on the edge of the island. Follow the green lights directing you to a parking lot with space, probably Tronchetto (across the causeway and on the right), which has a huge, multistoried garage (€18/day, tel. 041-520-7555). From there, you'll find travel agencies masquerading as TIs and vaporetto docks for the boat connection (#82) to the town center. Don't let taxi boatmen con you out of the relatively cheap €5 vaporetto ride. Parking in Mestre is easy and cheap (open-air lots €4/day, €5/day garage across from Mestre train station, easy shuttle-train connections to Venice's Santa Lucia Station—6/hr, 5 min). There are also huge and economical lots in Verona, Padua, and Vicenza.

By Plane: Venice's sleek, modern Marco Polo Airport on the mainland, six miles north of the city, has a brand-new wood-beam-and-glass terminal, with a TI, cash machines, car-rental agencies, a few shops and eateries, and easy connections by bus and speedboat to the city center. Airport info: tel. 041-260-611, flight info: tel. 041-260-9240.

Romantics can jet to St. Mark's Square by Alilaguna **speedboat** (easiest transportation to historical center, €10, 2/hr, 70 min, runs 6:15–24:00 from airport; 6:00–22:50 from St. Mark's Square, generally departing airport 10 min after the hour, www.alilaguna.com). A **water taxi** zips you directly to your hotel in 30 minutes for €80. **Buses** connect the airport and the Piazzale Roma vaporetto stop: Catch either the blue ATVO shuttle bus (€3, 2/hr, 20 min, 5:30–20:40 to airport, 8:30–23:30 from airport, www.atvo.it) or the cheaper orange ACTV bus #5 (€1, 2/hr, 20–40 min, 4:40–1:00).

Passes for Venice

To help control (and confuse?) its flood of visitors, Venice now offers cards and passes that cover some museums and/or transportation. For most visitors, the simple Museum Card (the combo Doge's Palace/Correr Museum ticket) or Museum Pass will do.

The **Museum Card** covers the museums of St. Mark's Square: Doge's Palace, Correr Museum, and the two museums accessed from within the Correr—the National Archaeological Museum and the Monumental Rooms of Marciana National Library (€11, called "*Museum Card per i Musei di Piazza San Marco*," valid for 3 months; purchase it at the Correr Museum, then use your card at the Doge's Palace to bypass the long line).

The pricier **Museum Pass** includes the St. Mark's Square museums listed above, plus Ca' Rezzonico (Museum of 18th-Century Venice), Mocenigo Palace museum (textiles and costumes), Casa Goldoni (home of the Italian playwright), and museums on the islands—Murano's Glass Museum and Burano's Lace Museum (€15.50, valid for 3 months).

Venice also (pointlessly) offers two other Museum Cards: €8 for the museums of the 18th century (called "*Museum Card per area del Settecento*"; the museums are Ca' Rezzonico, Casa Goldoni, and Palazzo Mocenigo) and €6 for the island museums (called "*Museum Card per i musei delle isole*," covering Murano's Glass Museum and Burano's Lace Museum).

No cards or passes cover these top attractions: The sights within St. Mark's Basilica, the Campanile, Accademia, Peggy Guggenheim Museum, Scuola Grande di San Rocco, and the Frari Church.

Venice Cards: Personally, I'd skip these, but here's the information. These cards include Venice's public transportation, public toilets, and, if you get the "orange" version, some sights.

The **Blue Venice Card** covers all your vaporetto rides—plus entry to public toilets: 1 day–€11, 3 days–€23, 7 days–€41; cheaper for

DAILY REMINDER

Sunday: The Church of San Giorgio Maggiore (on an island near St. Mark's Square) hosts a Gregorian Mass at 11:00. The Rialto open-air market consists mainly of souvenir stalls today (fish and produce sections closed). These sights are open only in the afternoon: Frari Church (13:00–18:00, closed Sun in Aug) and St. Mark's Basilica (14:00–17:00). It's a bad day for a pub crawl, as most pubs are closed.

Monday: All sights are open except for the Rialto fish market, Dalmatian School, the skippable Palazzo Mocenigo (textiles), and Torcello Museum (on Torcello island). The Accademia and Ca d'Oro (House of Gold) close at 14:00. Don't side-trip to Verona or Vicenza today; most sights are closed.

Tuesday: All sights are open except the Peggy Guggenheim Museum, Ca' Rezzonico (Museum of 18th-Century Venice), and the Lace Museum (on Burano island).

Wednesday: All sights are open except the Glass Museum (on Murano island).

Thursday/Friday: All sights are open.

Saturday: All sights are open (Peggy Guggenheim Museum until 22:00 April–Oct) except the Jewish Museum.

"Juniors" under 30. (If all you want is a vaporetto pass, you can get a 24-hour pass for €10.50 at any vaporetto dock; described under "Getting around Venice," below.)

The **Orange Venice Card**, which also includes transportation and toilets, gets you into the museums covered by the Museum Pass. It's like getting a Blue Venice Card and a Museum Pass (1 day–€26, 3 days–€43, and 7 days–€58; cheaper for "Juniors" under 30).

"Rolling Venice" Youth Discount Pass: This worthwhile €2.60 pass gives those under 26 discounts on sights and transportation, plus information on cheap eating and sleeping. It is sold at major vaporetto kiosks (tel. 041-271-4747, press 2 for English).

Helpful Hints

Cost: Venice is expensive for locals as well as tourists. The demand is huge, supply is limited, and running a business is costly. Things just cost more here; everything must be shipped in and hand-trucked to its destination. Perhaps the best way to enjoy Venice is to just succumb to its charms and blow a lot of money.

Get Lost: Accept the fact that Venice was a tourist town 400 years ago. It was, is, and always will be crowded. While 80 percent of Venice is, in fact, not touristy, 80 percent of the tourists never notice. Hit the backstreets.

Venice is the ideal town to explore on foot. Walk and walk to the far reaches of the town. Don't worry about getting lost. Get as lost as possible. Keep reminding yourself, "I'm on an island, and I can't get off." When it comes time to find your way, just follow the directional arrows on building corners or simply ask a local, "*Dov'è San Marco?*" ("Where is St. Mark's?") People in the tourist business (that's most Venetians) speak some English. If they don't, listen politely, watching where their hands point, say "*Grazie*," and head off in that direction. If you're lost, pop into a hotel and ask for their business card—it comes with a map and a prominent "you are here."

Take Breaks: Venice's endless pavement, crowds, and tight spaces are hard on the tourist. Schedule breaks in your sightseeing. Grab a cool place to sit down, relax, and recoup—meditate on a pew in an uncrowded church or buy a cappuccino and a fruit cup in a café.

Etiquette: Walk on the right and don't loiter on bridges. Picnicking is technically forbidden (keep a low profile). Dress modestly. Men should keep their shirts on. When visiting St. Mark's Basilica or other major churches, men, women, and even children should cover their knees and shoulders (or risk being turned away).

Pigeon Poop: If bombed by a pigeon, resist the initial response to wipe it off immediately—it'll just smear into your hair. Wait until it dries and flake it off cleanly.

Public Toilets: There are handy public WCs near St. Mark's Square and the Accademia Bridge (see map on page 825). You'll find public pay toilets near most major landmarks. Use free toilets—in a museum you're visiting or a café you're eating in—when you can.

Water: Venetians pride themselves on having pure, safe, and tasty tap water piped in from the foothills of the Alps; you can actually see the mountains from Venice bell towers on crisp, clear winter days.

Lingo: *Campo* means square, *calle* is street, *fondamenta* is the road running along a canal, and *rio* is a small canal.

Services

Money: ATMs are plentiful and the easiest way to go. Bank rates vary. The American Express change desk is just off St. Mark's Square (see "Travel Agencies," below). Non-bank exchange bureaus, such as Exacto, will cost you $10 more than a bank for a $200 exchange.

Travel Agencies: If you need to get train tickets, pay supplements, make reservations, or arrange a *couchette*, avoid the time-consuming trip to the crowded train station by using a downtown travel agency. While American Express charges railpass holders a €5 service fee for reservations, the other agencies do basically everything the train station does for the same price with no fee. All can give advice on cheap flights. Remember, you'll get a far better price if you're able to book at least a week in advance. Consider booking flights for later in your trip while you're here (and remember that in Europe, you don't have to buy a round-trip ticket to get the best price).

Kele & Teo Viaggi e Turismo is good and handy (accepts credit cards for train tickets only, Mon–Fri 8:30–19:00, Sat 9:00–12:00, closed Sun, at Ponte dei Bareteri on the Mercerie midway between Rialto and St. Mark's Square, tel. 041-520-8722, incoming@keleteo.com).

American Express books flights, sells train tickets, and makes train reservations (travel agency: Mon–Fri 9:00–17:30, closed Sat–Sun; about 2 blocks off St. Mark's Square at 1471 San Marco, en route to Accademia, tel. 041-520-0844).

Rip-offs, Theft, and Help: While pickpockets work the crowded main streets, docks, and vaporetti (wear your money belt and carry your daybag in front), the dark, late-night streets of Venice are safe. A service called Venezia No Problem tries to help tourists who've been mistreated by any Venetian business (toll-free tel. 800-355-920, for complaints only, not for information).

Church Services: The **San Zulian Church** (the only church in Venice that you can actually walk around) offers a Mass in English at 9:30 on Sunday (May–Sept, 2 blocks toward Rialto off St. Mark's Square). Gregorians would enjoy the sung Gregorian Mass on Sundays at 11:00 (plus Mon–Sat at 8:00) at the Church of **San Giorgio Maggiore** (on island of San Giorgio Maggiore, visible from Doge's Palace, see "Venice Lagoon," below). Call 041-522-7827 to confirm times.

Laundry: I list several below, but your hotelier can direct you to one near your hotel.

A modern self-serve *lavanderia* is near St. Mark's Square on Ruga Giuffa at #4826 (€11 per load, daily 9:00–22:00, next to Hotel al Piave, see "Sleeping," below; tel. 041-241-1223, Massimo).

At either of the following full-service laundries, you can get a nine-pound load washed and dried for €16—confirm price carefully. Drop it off in the morning and pick it up that afternoon. (Call to be sure they're open.) Don't expect to get your clothes back ironed, folded, or even entirely dry. **Lavanderia Gabriella** is near St. Mark's Square (Mon–Fri 8:00–12:30, closed Sat–Sun, 985 Rio Terra Colonne, from San Zulian Church go over Ponte dei Ferali, then take first right down Calle dei Armeni, tel. 041-522-1758). **Lavanderia S.S. Apostoli** is close to the Rialto Bridge on the St. Mark's side (Mon–Fri 9:00–12:00 & 15:30–19:00, closed Sat–Sun, just off Campo S.S. Apostoli on Salizada del Pistor, tel. 041-522-6650).

Post Office: A large post office is just outside the far end of St. Mark's Square (farthest from the basilica, Mon–Sat 8:10–18:00, closed

Sun, shorter hours off-season). A branch is near the Rialto Bridge (on St. Mark's side, Mon–Fri 8:10–13:30, Sat 8:10–12:30, closed Sun).

Internet Access: The **Net House** has dozens of terminals and is open 24 hours most days (on Campo San Stefano, just north of Accademia Bridge, photocopy of your passport required before you start surfing, not cheap as Internet cafés go). **Rialtonet** is near the Rialto fish market (daily 9:30–24:00, San Polo 278, tel. 041-241-3862).

Haircuts: I've been getting my hair cut at Coiffeur Benito for 15 years. Benito has been keeping local men and women trim for 25 years. He's an artist—actually a "hair sculptor"—and a cut here is a fun diversion from the tourist grind (€19.50 for women, €16.50 for men, Tue–Sat 8:30–13:00 & 15:30–19:30, closed Sun–Mon, behind San Zulian Church near St. Mark's Square, Calle S. Zulian Gia del Strazzanol 592A, tel. 041-528-6221).

Getting around Venice

By Vaporetto: The public transit system is a fleet of motorized bus-boats called vaporetti. They work like city buses except that they never get a flat, the stops are docks, and if you get off between stops, you may drown.

For most travelers, only two lines matter: #1 is the slow boat, taking 45 minutes to make every stop along the entire length of the Grand Canal; #82 is the fast boat that zips down the Grand Canal in 25 minutes, stopping mainly at Tronchetto (car park), Piazzale Roma (bus station), Ferrovia (train station), Rialto Bridge, San Tomà (Frari Church), the Accademia Bridge, and St. Mark's Square (specifically, the San Marco/Vallaresso dock). Some #82 boats go only as far as Rialto ("*solo Rialto*")—confirm with the conductor before boarding.

Since boats going both directions often share the same dock, check the direction (e.g., San Marco, Piazzale Roma). Buy a €5 ticket ideally before boarding (at the booth at the dock) or from a conductor on board (before you sit down or you risk being fined). Tickets for non-Grand Canal rides cost €3.50. The €5 Grand Canal tickets are good for 90 minutes. To avoid a fine, be sure your ticket is stamped with a time before boarding. Some tickets come stamped but to be safe, I stick mine into a time-stamping yellow machine before boarding.

A 24-hour pass (€10.50) saves money after two trips. The cheaper "Laguna Tour" covers only stops on the Grand Canal and Murano, Burano, and Torcello (€8.50, valid for 12 hrs). Also consider the 72-hour (€22) pass. It's fun to be able to hop on and off spontaneously. Technically, luggage costs the same as dogs—€3.50—but I've never been charged. Riding free? There's a 1-in-10 chance a conductor will fine you €23.

For vaporetto fun, take the Grand Canal Tour (see page 819); avoid rush hour, when boats are packed heading to St. Mark's Square early in the day and packed heading to the train station late in the day.

If you like joyriding on vaporetti, ride a boat around the city and out into the lagoon and back. Ask for the circular route—*circulare* (cheer-koo-LAH-ray). It's usually the #51 or #52, leaving from the San Zaccaria vaporetto stop (near the Doge's Palace) and from all the stops along the perimeter of Venice.

By *Traghetto*: Only three bridges cross the Grand Canal, but *traghetti* (gondolas) shuttle locals and in-the-know tourists across the Grand Canal at several handy locations (see map on page 820; routes also marked on pricier maps sold in Venice). Take advantage of these time-savers. They can also save money. For instance, while most tourists take the €5 vaporetto to connect St. Mark's with La Salute Church, a €0.40 *traghetto* does the job just as well. Most people stand while riding. *Traghetti* generally run from 6:00 until 20:00, sometimes until 23:00.

By Water Taxi: Venetian taxis, like speedboat limos, hang out at most busy points along the Grand Canal. Prices, which average €40 (about €80 to the airport), are a bit soft. Negotiate and settle before stepping in. For travelers with lots of luggage or small groups who can split the cost, taxi rides can be a worthwhile and time-saving convenience—and skipping across the lagoon in a classic wooden motorboat is a cool indulgence.

By Gondola: To hire a gondolier for your own private cruise, see "Gondola Rides," below.

TOURS

Walking Tours

Audioguide Tours—At the Campanile bell tower and the TI (on the lagoon side of St. Mark's Square), you can rent audioguides for self-guided walking tours of Venice (2 hrs-€5, 24 hrs-€10, just punch the number of what you'd like described—exteriors only). The commentary is boring and—if you're reading this book—unnecessary.

Venice Walks and Tours—This company offers a selection of historic and entertaining walks, including the basic St. Mark's Square introduction, Cannaregio and the Jewish Ghetto, San Polo and Dorsoduro, Ghosts and Legends, Casanova, and secret gardens (€20 per person, cheaper for returnees and students, €5 off if you say "Rick sent me," small groups, English language only, 2 hours each, rain or shine, also day trips into the mainland, www.venicewalksandtours.com, tel. 041-520-8616, mobile 340-050-2444, Monica and Jonathan).

Classic Venice Bars Tour—Debonair local guide Alessandro Schezzini is a connoisseur of Venetian *bacaros*—classic old bars serving traditional *cicchetti* (local munchies). He offers evening tours that involve stopping and sampling a snack and a glass of wine at three of these (Sat and Wed April–Sept at 18:00, other evenings by request and with demand, meet at top of Rialto). The fee—about €30 per person—includes wine,

Venice

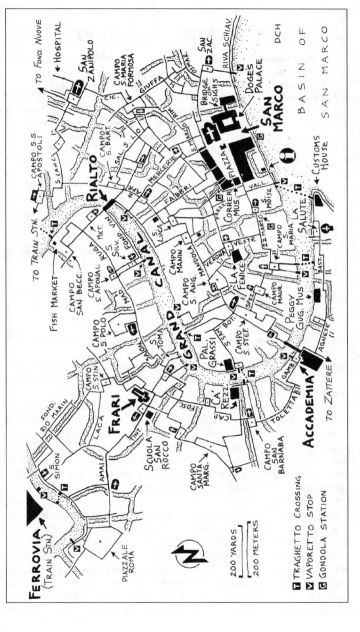

TIPS ON SIGHTSEEING IN VENICE

Crowd Control: Crowds can be a serious problem only at the Accademia (to minimize crowds, go early or late); St. Mark's Basilica (try going early or late); Campanile bell tower (go late—it's open until 21:00 in the summer); and the Doge's Palace. For the Doge's Palace, you have three options for avoiding the ticket-sales line: Buy your Museum Card or Museum Pass at the Correr Museum (then step right up to the Doge's Palace turnstile, skipping the long line); visit the Doge's Palace at 17:00 (if it's April–Oct) when lines disappear; or book a "Secret Itineraries" tour (see page 829).

Hours: The Accademia is open earlier (daily at 8:15) and closes later (19:15 Tue–Sun) than most sights in Venice. Some sights close earlier off-season (e.g., Doge's Palace; Correr Museum; the Campanile bell tower; and St. Mark's Museum, Treasury, and Golden Altarpiece).

Churches: Modest dress is recommended at churches and required at St. Mark's Basilica—no bare shoulders, shorts, or short skirts. Some churches are closed to sightseers on Sunday morning (e.g., St. Mark's Basilica and Frari Church) and many are closed from roughly 12:00 to 15:00 Monday through Saturday (e.g., La Salute and San Giorgio Maggiore).

cicchetti, and a great insight into this local tradition (tel. & fax 041-534-5367, mobile 335-530-9024, venische@tiscalinet.it). He also does Ghost Tours for spooky evening fun (€20, 90 min).

Venicescapes—Michael Broderick's private theme tours of Venice are intellectually demanding and beyond the attention span of most mortal tourists, but for the curious with stamina, he can be enthralling. Michael's challenge: To help visitors gain a more solid understanding of Venice. For a description of his various itineraries, see www.venicescapes.org (book well in advance, 4–6 hour tour: €275 for 2, €50 per person after that, plus admissions and transportation, tel. 041-520-6361, info@venicescapes.org).

Local Guides—Licensed guides are carefully trained and love explaining Venice to visitors. The following companies and guides give excellent tours to individuals, families, and small groups. If you organize a small group from your hotel at breakfast to split the cost (€65/hour with 2-hour minimum), the fee becomes quite reasonable. **Walks Inside Venice** is a group of three women enthusiastic about their teaching (Roberta Curiel, tel. 041-524-1706, mobile 347-253-0560, www.walksinsidevenice.com, info@walksinsidevenice.com). **Venice With**

A Guide is a co-op of 10 equally good guides (see www.venicewith-aguide.com). **Elisabetta Morelli** is also reliable (tel. 041-526-7816, mobile 328-753-5220, bettamorelli@inwind.it).

Alessandro Schezzini (while not a licensed guide and therefore unable to take you into actual sights) does a great job getting you beyond the clichés and into off-beat Venice (€90, 2.5 hrs, listed above in "Classic Venice Bars Tour").

Grand Canal Tour

For a ▲▲▲ joyride, introduce yourself to Venice by boat. Cruise the Canal Grande from Tronchetto (car park) or Ferrovia (Santa Lucia train station) all the way to San Marco. You can ride boat #1 (slow and ideal, 45 min) or #82 (too fast to comfortably follow this tour, 25 min). When catching either boat, confirm that you're on a "San Marco via Rialto" boat (some boats finish at the Rialto Bridge and others take a non-scenic outside route). The conductor announces "Solo Rialto!" for boats going only as far as Rialto. You do not want boats heading for Piazzale Roma.

If you can't snag a front seat, lurk nearby and take one when it becomes available or find an outside seat in the stern. This ride has the best light and fewest crowds early or late. Twilight is magic. After dark, chandeliers light up the building interiors. While Venice is a barrage on the senses that hardly needs a narration, these notes give the cruise a little meaning and help orient you to this great city. Some city maps (on sale at postcard racks) have a handy Grand Canal map on the back.

Overview: The Grand Canal is Venice's "Main Street." At over two miles long, nearly 150 feet wide, and nearly 15 feet deep, it's the biggest canal with the most impressive palaces. The canal is the remnant of a river that once spilled from the mainland into the Adriatic. The sediment it carried formed a delta that was eventually swallowed up by the sea, becoming a lagoon.

Venice is a city of **palaces**, dating from the days when Venice was the world's richest city. The most lavish formed a grand chorus line along the Grand Canal. Once painted in reds and blues, with black-and-white borders and gold-leaf trim, they made Venice a city of dazzling color. This cruise is the only way to really appreciate the palaces, approaching them at water level, where their main entrance were located. Today, strict laws prohibit any changes in these buildings, so while landowners gnash their teeth, we can enjoy Europe's best-preserved medieval city—slowly rotting.

Start at the **train station** or **Tronchetto** car park. We'll orient by the vaporetto stops.

Venice's main thoroughfare is busy with all kinds of **boats:** taxis, police boats, garbage boats, ambulances, construction cranes, and even brown-and-white UPS boats. Venice's sleek, black, graceful **gondolas** are a symbol of the city. While used gondolas cost around €10,000, new

Venice's Grand Canal

ones run up to €65,000 apiece. Today, with over 400 gondoliers joyriding amid the churning vaporetti, there's a lot of congestion on the Grand Canal. Watch your vaporetto driver curse the better-paid gondoliers.

Ferrovia: The **Santa Lucia train station** (on the left bank of the canal), one of the few modern buildings in town, was built in 1954. It's been the gateway into Venice since 1860, when the first station was built. "F.S." stands for "Ferrovie dello Stato," the Italian state railway system. The **bridge** at the station is the first of only three that cross the Canal Grande.

Opposite the train station, atop the green dome of **San Simeone Piccolo** church, Saint Simon waves *ciao* to whoever enters or leaves the "old" city.

Riva di Biasio: Just past the Riva di Biasio stop, look left down the broad **Cannaregio Canal**. The twin pale-pink six-story "skyscrapers" are a reminder of how densely populated the world's original **ghetto** was. Set aside as the local Jewish quarter in 1516, the area (located behind the San Marcuola stop) became extremely crowded. This urban island developed into one of the most closely knit business and cultural quarters of all the

Jewish communities in Italy, and gave us our word ghetto (from the copper foundry located here). For more information, visit the Jewish Museum in this neighborhood (listed under "Cannaregio District," below).

San Marcuola: The gray **Turkish Exchange** (right side, opposite the vaporetto stop), is considered the oldest house in Venice. Its horseshoe arches and roofline of triangles-and-dingleballs is Byzantine. Turkish traders in turbans docked here, unloaded their goods into the warehouse on the bottom story, then went upstairs for a home-style meal and a place to sleep. Venice in the 1500s was very cosmopolitan, welcoming every people of religion and ethnicity, so long as they carried cash.

Venice's **Casino** (left-hand side) is housed in the palace where German composer Richard *(The Ring)* Wagner died in 1883. See his distinct, strong-jawed profile in the white plaque on the brick wall. In the 1700s, Venice was Europe's Vegas, with casinos and prostitutes everywhere. Today, this elegant Casino welcomes men in ties and ladies in dresses.

San Stae: Opposite the San Stae stop, look for the **faded frescoes** (left bank, on lower story). Imagine the facades of the Grand Canal at their finest. As colorful as the city is today, it's still only a sepia-toned snapshot of a Technicolor era.

Ca' d'Oro: The lacy **Ca' d'Oro**, or "House of Gold," (left bank, next to the vaporetto stop) is the best example of "Venetian Gothic" on the canal. Its three stories offer different variations on balcony design, topped with a spiny white roofline. Venetian Gothic mixes traditional Gothic (pointed arches and round medallions stamped with a four-leaf clover) with Byzantine styles (tall, narrow arches atop thin columns), filled in with Islamic frills. Like all the palaces, this was originally painted and gilded to make it even more glorious than it is now. Today the Ca' d'Oro is a museum but, other than temporary exhibits, there's little to see inside.

Farther along, on the right, the outdoor arcade of the **fish and produce market** bustles with people in the morning but is quiet the rest of the day. This is a great scene to wander through—even though new European hygiene standards recently required a less-colorful remodeling job. Find the *traghetto* gondola ferrying shoppers—standing like Washington crossing the Delaware—back and forth.

The huge **post office** (left side, just before the Rialto Bridge), with *servizio postale* boats moored at its blue posts, was once the German Exchange, the trading center for German metal merchants. Rising above the post office, you can see in the distance the golden angel of the Campanile bell tower at St. Mark's Square, where this tour will end.

As the canal bends, we pass beneath the impressive Rialto Bridge. Singing gondoliers love the acoustics here: "*O sole mio...*"

Rialto: A major landmark of Venice, the **Rialto Bridge** is lined with shops and tourists. Constructed in 1588, it's the third bridge built on this spot. With a span of 160 feet and foundations stretching 650 feet on either side, the Rialto was an impressive engineering feat in its day. Earlier Rialto Bridges could open to let in big ships, but not this one. When this new bridge was completed, much of the Grand Canal was closed to shipping and became a canal of palaces. Locals call the summit of this bridge the "icebox of Venice" for its cool breeze. Tourists call it a great place to kiss.

Rialto, a separate town in the early days of Venice, has always been the commercial district, while San Marco was the religious and governmental center. Today, a winding street called the Mercerie connects the two, providing travelers with human traffic jams and a mesmerizing gauntlet of shopping temptations. The restaurants that line the canal feature great views, midrange prices, and low quality.

San Silvestro: On the left side, opposite the vaporetto stop, **two palaces stand side by side**, with stories the same height, creating the effect of one long balcony.

We now enter a long stretch of important **merchants' palaces**, each with proud and different facades. Since ships couldn't navigate beyond the Rialto Bridge (to reach the section of the Grand Canal you just came from), the biggest palaces—with the major shipping needs—lie ahead. Many feature the Roman country villa design of twin towers flanking a huge set of central windows. These were showrooms designed to let in maximum sunlight.

Just after the San Silvestro stop, you'll see (on the right) the palace of a 15th-century **"captain general of the sea."** The Venetian equivalents of five-star admirals were honored with twin obelisks decorating their palaces. This palace flies three flags: those of Italy (green-white-red), the European Union (blue with ring of stars), and Venice (the lion).

Sant' Angelo: Notice how many buildings have a foundation of waterproof white stone *(pietra d'Istria)* upon which the bricks sit high and dry. Many canal-level floors are abandoned; the rising water level takes its toll. The **posts**—historically painted with the gaily-colored equivalent of family coats of arms—don't rot under water. But the wood at the waterline does rot.

Take a deep whiff of Venice. What's all this nonsense about stinky canals? All I smell is my shirt. By the way, how's your captain? Smooth dockings? To get to know him, stand up in the bow and block his view.

San Tomà: After the San Tomà stop, look down the side canal (on the right, before the bridge) to see the traffic light, the **fire station**, and the fireboats ready to go.

We now prepare to round the corner and double back toward St. Mark's. The impressive **Ca' Foscari** (right side) dominates the bend in the canal. Its four stories get increasingly ornate as they rise from the water—from simple Gothic arches at water level, to Gothic with a point, to Venetian Gothic arches topped with four-leaf clovers, to still more medallions and laciness that look almost Moorish. Wow.

Ca' Rezzonico: The grand, heavy, white **Ca' Rezzonico**, directly at the stop of the same name, houses the Museum of 18th-Century Venice. Across the canal is the cleaner and leaner **Palazzo Grassi**, which often showcases special exhibitions.

These days, when buildings are being renovated, huge murals with images of the building mask the ugly scaffolding. Corporations hide the scaffolding for the goodwill—and the publicity.

Accademia: The wooden **Accademia Bridge** crosses the Grand Canal and leads to the **Accademia Gallery** (right side), filled with the best Venetian paintings. The bridge was put up in 1932 as a temporary one. Locals liked it, so it stayed. Cruising under the bridge, you'll get a classic view of the domed La Salute Church ahead.

The low white building among greenery (on the right, between the bridge and the church) is the **Peggy Guggenheim Museum**. The American heiress "retired" here, sprucing up the palace that had been abandoned in mid-construction; the locals call it the "palazzo non finito." Peggy willed the city her fine collection of modern art (described under "Dorsoduro District," below).

Salute: A crown-shaped dome supported by scrolls stands atop **La Salute Church**. This Church of Saint Mary of Good Health was built to coax God into delivering Venice from the devastating plague of 1630 (which eventually killed about a third of the city's population).

Across the canal (left side), several **fancy hotels** have painted facades that hint at the canal's former glory.

As the Grand Canal opens up into the lagoon, the last building on the right with the golden ball is the 16th-century **Customs House** (Dogana da Mar, not open to the public). Its two bronze Atlases hold a statue of Fortune riding the ball. Arriving ships stopped here to pay their tolls.

As you prepare to disembark at the San Marco/Vallaresso stop, look from left to right out over the lagoon. On the left, a wide harborfront walk leads past the town's most elegant hotels to the green area in the distance. This is the public garden, the largest of Venice's few parks, which hosts the Biennale art show. Farther in the distance is the **Lido**, the island with Venice's beach. It's tempting, with sand and casinos, but its car traffic breaks into the medieval charm of Venice.

The ghostly white church that seems to float is the architect Palladio's **San Giorgio Maggiore**. It's just a vaporetto ride away (#82 from the "San Zaccaria Jolanda" stop, just past the Bridge of Sighs; see "Venice Lagoon," below). Across the lagoon (to your right) is a residential island called **Giudecca**.

San Marco/Vallaresso: Get off at the San Marco/Vallaresso stop. Directly ahead is **Harry's Bar**. Hemingway drank here when it was a characteristic no-name *osteria* and the gondoliers' hangout. Today, of course, it's the overpriced hangout of well-dressed Americans who don't mind paying triple for their Bellinis (peach juice with Prosecco wine) to make the scene. St. Mark's Square is just around the corner.

SIGHTS

St. Mark's Square

For information on Venice's Museum Card and Museum Pass, see page 811.

▲▲▲**St. Mark's Square (Piazza San Marco)**—Surrounded by splashy and historic buildings, Piazza San Marco is filled with music, lovers, pigeons, and tourists by day and is your private rendezvous with the Middle Ages late at night. Europe's greatest dance floor is the romantic place to be. St. Mark's Square is about the first place in Venice to flood (you might see stacked wooden benches; when the square floods, these are put end to end to make elevated sidewalks).

With your back to the church, survey one of Europe's great urban spaces, and the only square in Venice to merit the title "Piazza." Nearly two football fields long, it's surrounded by the offices of the republic. On the right are the "old offices" (16th-century Renaissance). On the left are the "new offices" (17th-century Baroque). Napoleon, after enclosing the square with the more simple and austere neoclassical wing across the far end, called this "the most beautiful drawing room in Europe."

The clock tower, a Renaissance tower built in 1496, marks the entry to the Mercerie, the main shopping drag, which connects St. Mark's Square with the Rialto. From the piazza, you can see the bronze men (Moors) swing their huge clappers at the top of each hour. In the 17th century, one of them knocked an unsuspecting worker off the top and to his death—probably the first-ever killing by a robot. Notice the world's first "digital" clock on the tower facing the square (with dramatic flips every 5 minutes).

For a slow and pricey evening thrill, invest €6.20 (plus €4 if the orchestra plays) in a beer or coffee at one of the elegant cafés with the dueling orchestras (see Caffè Florian, described in "Nightlife," below.) If you're going to sit awhile and savor the scene, it's worth the splurge. If all you have is €1, buy a bag of pigeon feed and become popular in a flurry. To get everything airborne, toss your sweater in the air.

Venice's best TI is in the far left corner of the square (Mon–Sat 9:00–15:30, closed Sun; a €0.50 WC is nearby, located a few steps beyond St. Mark's Square en route to the American Express office and the Accademia—see *Albergo Diorno* sign marked on pavement, open daily 9:00–20:00). The other TI is on the lagoon (daily 9:00–18:00, walk toward the water by the Doge's Palace, go right; pay WCs nearby open daily 9:00–19:00).

St. Mark's Square

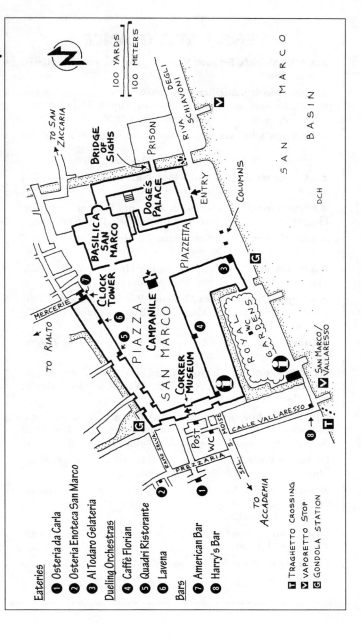

Eateries
1 Osteria da Carla
2 Osteria Enoteca San Marco
3 Al Todaro Gelateria

Dueling Orchestras
4 Caffè Florian
5 Quadri Ristorante
6 Lavena

Bars
7 American Bar
8 Harry's Bar

◘ TRAGHETTO CROSSING
◪ VAPORETTO STOP
Ｇ GONDOLA STATION

VENICE AT A GLANCE

▲▲▲**St. Mark's Square** Venice's grand main square. **Hours:** Always open.

▲▲▲**St. Mark's Basilica** Cathedral with mosaics, saint's bones, treasury, museum, and viewpoint of square. **Hours:** Mon–Sat 9:45–17:00, Sun 14:00–17:00, some areas close at 16:30 in winter.

▲▲▲**Doge's Palace** Art-splashed palace of former rulers, with prison accessed through Bridge of Sighs. **Hours:** April–Oct daily 9:00–19:00, Nov–March daily 9:00–17:00.

▲▲**Correr Museum** Venetian history and art. **Hours:** April–Oct daily 9:00–19:00, Nov–March 9:00–17:00.

▲▲**Frari Church** Franciscan church featuring Renaissance masters. **Hours:** Mon–Sat 9:00–18:00, Sun 13:00–18:00, closed Sun in Aug.

▲▲**Scuola Grande di San Rocco** Tintoretto's "Sistine Chapel." **Hours:** Daily 9:00–17:30, Nov-March 10:00-16:00.

▲▲**Accademia** Venice's top art museum. **Hours:** Mon 8:15–14:00, Tue–Sun 8:15–19:15, shorter hours off-season.

▲▲**Peggy Guggenheim Museum** Popular collection of 20th-century art. **Hours:** Wed–Mon 10:00–18:00, Sat until 22:00 April-Oct, closed Tue.

▲**Campanile** Dramatic bell tower with elevator to top. **Hours:** Daily June–Sept 9:00–21:00, Oct–May 9:00-19:00.

▲**Ca' Rezzonico** Posh Grand Canal palazzo with 18th-century Venetian art. **Hours:** April–Oct Wed–Mon 10:00–18:00, Nov–March 10:00-17:00, closed Tue.

San Giorgio Maggiore Island across the lagoon featuring church with worth-the-trip view from bell tower. **Hours:** Daily 9:30–12:30 & 14:00–18:30, closed for sightseeing during Mass on Sun.

La Salute Church Striking church dedicated to the Virgin Mary. **Hours:** Daily 9:00–12:00 & 15:00–18:00.

Jewish Ghetto Neighborhood and Jewish Museum. **Hours:** Museum: June–Sept Sun–Fri 10:00–19:00, Oct–May Sun–Fri 10:00–17:30, closed Sat.

Dalmatian School Exquisite Renaissance meeting house. **Hours:** Tue–Sat 9:30–12:30 & 15:30–18:30, Sun 9:30–12:30, closed Mon.

Santa Elena 100-year-old neighborhood with few tourists. **Hours:** Always open.

▲▲**St. Mark's Basilica**—Built in the 11th century to replace an earlier church, the basilica has a distinctly Eastern-style of architecture to underscore Venice's connection with Byzantium (thus protecting it from the ambition of Charlemagne and his Holy Roman Empire). It's decorated with booty from returning sea captains—a kind of architectural Venetian trophy chest.

Since about A.D. 830, the saint's bones have been housed on this site. The mosaic above the door at the far left of the church shows two guys carrying Mark's coffin into the church. Mark looks pretty grumpy after the long voyage from Egypt.

To enter the church, modest dress is required even of kids (no shorts or bare shoulders). In peak season, there can be long lines of people waiting to get into the church. People who ignore the dress code hold up the line while they plead fruitlessly with—or put on extra clothes under the watchful eyes of—the dress code police.

The church has 43,000 square feet of Byzantine mosaics, the best and oldest of which are in the atrium (turn right as you enter and stop under the last dome—this may be roped off, but dome is still visible). Facing the church, gape up (it's OK, no pigeons), and read clockwise the story of Adam and Eve that rings the bottom of the dome. Now, facing the piazza, look domeward for the story of Noah, the ark, and the flood (two by two, the wicked being drowned, Noah sending out the dove, a happy rainbow, and a sacrifice of thanks).

Step inside the church (the stairs on the right lead to the bronze horses—save these for later). The interior glows mysteriously with gold mosaics and colored marble. Notice the marble floor richly decorated in mosaics. As in many Venetian buildings, because the best foundation pilings were made around the perimeter, the floor rolls. As you shuffle under the central dome, look up for the Ascension (free, Mon–Sat 9:30–17:00, Sun 14:00–17:00, no photos, tel. 041-522-5205). See the schedule board in the atrium, listing free English guided tours (schedules vary but May–Oct generally Wed and Thu at 11:00). The church is particularly beautiful when lit (unpredictable schedule but worth trying to see, often weekdays 11:30–12:30, Sat–Sun all day). During peak times, the line can be very long.

In the **Galleria and Museum** upstairs, you can see an up-close mosaic exhibition, a fine view of the church interior, a view of the square from the balcony with bronze horses, and (inside, in their own room) the newly restored original horses. These well-traveled horses, made during the days of Alexander the Great (4th century B.C.), were taken to Rome by Nero, to Constantinople/Istanbul by Constantine, to Venice by crusaders, to Paris by Napoleon, back "home" to Venice when Napoleon fell, and finally indoors and out of the acidic air (€1.60, daily 9:45–17:00, 9:45–16:30 in winter, enter from atrium either before or after you tour church).

San Marco's **treasury** (with included and informative audioguide free for the asking) and **altarpiece** (€2 each, daily 9:45–17:00, 9:45–16:30 in winter) give you the best chance outside of Istanbul or Ravenna to see the glories of Byzantium. Venetian crusaders looted the Christian city of Constantinople and brought home piles of lavish loot (until the advent of TV evangelism, perhaps the lowest point in Christian history). Much of this plunder is stored in the treasury *(tesoro)* of San Marco. As you view these treasures, remember that most were made around A.D. 500, while western Europe was still rutting in the mud. Beneath the high altar lies the body of St. Mark ("Marxus") and the Pala d'Oro, a golden altarpiece made with 80 Byzantine enamels (A.D. 1000–1300). Each shows a religious scene set in gold and precious stones. Both of these sights are interesting and historic, but neither is as much fun as two bags of pigeon feed.

▲▲▲**Doge's Palace (Palazzo Ducale)**—The seat of the Venetian government and home of its ruling duke, or doge, this was the most powerful half-acre in Europe for 400 years.

The Doge's Palace was built to show off the power and wealth of the republic and remind all visitors that Venice was number one. In typical Venetian Gothic style, the bottom has pointy arches, and the top has an Eastern or Islamic flavor. Its columns sat on pedestals, but in the thousand years since they were erected, the palace has settled into the mud, and the bases have vanished.

Enjoy the newly restored facades from the courtyard. Notice a grand staircase (with nearly naked Moses and Paul Newman at the top). Even the most powerful visitors climbed this to meet the doge. This was the beginning of an architectural power trip. The doge, the elected-for-life duke or leader of this "dictatorship of the aristocracy," lived with his family on the first floor near the halls of power. From his living quarters (once lavish, now sparsely furnished), you'll follow the one-way route through the public rooms of the top floor, finishing with the Bridge of Sighs and the prison. The place is wallpapered with masterpieces by Veronese and Tintoretto. Don't worry much about the great art. Enjoy the building.

In room 12, the Senate Room, the 200 senators met, debated, and passed laws. From the center of the ceiling, Tintoretto's *Triumph of Venice* shows the city in all her glory. Lady Venice, in heaven with the Greek gods, stands high above the lesser nations, who swirl respectfully at her feet with gifts.

The Armory—a dazzling display originally assembled to intimidate potential adversaries—shows remnants of the military might that the empire employed to keep the East-West trade lines open (and the local economy booming). Squint out the window at the far end for a fine view of Palladio's San Giorgio Maggiore Church and the *lido* (cars, casinos, crowded beaches) in the distance.

The giant Hall of the Grand Council (180 feet long, capacity 2,000) is where the entire nobility met to elect the senate and doge. Ringing the room are portraits of 76 doges (in chronological order). One, a doge who opposed the will of the Grand Council, is blacked out. Behind the doge's throne, you can't miss Tintoretto's monsterpiece, *Paradise*. At 1,700 square feet, this is the world's largest oil painting. Christ and Mary are surrounded by a heavenly host of 500 saints. Its message to electors who met here: Make wise decisions and you'll ultimately join that holy crowd.

Walking over the Bridge of Sighs, you'll enter the prisons. In the privacy of his own home, a doge could sentence, torture, and jail his opponents secretly. As you walk back over the bridge, squeeze your arm through the marble lattice window and wave to the gang of tourists gawking at you.

Cost: €11 (combo-ticket includes admission to the Correr Museum). If the line is very long at the Doge's Palace, buy your ticket at the Correr Museum across the square. With that, you can go directly through the Doge's Palace turnstile without waiting in the long line.

Hours: April–Oct daily 9:00–19:00, Nov–March daily 9:00–17:00, last entry 90 minutes before closing.

Tours: Consider the €5.50 audioguide or the "Secret Itineraries Tour," which takes you into palace rooms otherwise not open to the public (€12.50, at 10:00 and 11:30 in English, 75 min; to make reservation for tour, call 041-291-5911 or 041-520-9070 several days in advance). While the tour skips the main halls inside, it finishes inside the palace and you're welcome to visit the halls on your own.

▲▲**Correr Museum (Museo Civico Correr)**—The city history museum is now included (whether you like it or not) with the admission to the Doge's Palace. In the Napoleon Wing, you'll see fine neoclassical sculpture by Canova. Then peruse armor, banners, and paintings re-creating festive days of the Venetian republic. The top floor lays out a good overview of Venetian art, including several paintings by the Bellini family. And just before the cafeteria is a room filled with traditional games. There are English descriptions and great Piazza San Marco views throughout (€11 on the combo-ticket that includes the Doge's Palace, April–Oct daily 9:00–19:00, Nov–March 9:00–17:00, last entry 70 min before closing, enter at far end of square directly opposite church, tel. 041-240-5211 or 041-522-4951).

▲**Campanile (Campanile di San Marco)**—This dramatic bell tower replaced a shorter lighthouse, once part of the original fortress/palace that guarded the entry of the Grand Canal. The lighthouse crumbled into a pile of bricks in 1902, a thousand years after it was built. Ride the elevator 300 feet to the top of the reconstructed bell tower for the best view in Venice. For an ear-shattering experience, be on top when the bells ring (€6, June–Sept daily 9:00–21:00, Oct–May 9:00–19:00). The golden angel at its top always faces into the wind. Beat the crowds and enjoy crisp morning air at 9:00.

Dorsoduro District

▲▲**Accademia (Galleria dell' Accademia)**—Venice's top art museum, packed with highlights of the Venetian Renaissance, features paintings by the Bellini family, Titian, Tintoretto, Veronese, Tiepolo, Giorgione, Testosterone, and Canaletto. It's just over the wooden Accademia Bridge. Expect long lines in the late morning because they allow only 300 visitors in at a time; visit early or late to miss crowds (€6.50 entry, Mon 8:15–14:00, Tue–Sun 8:15–19:15, shorter hours off-season, ticket window closes 45 min early, no photos allowed, tel. 041-522-2247). The dull audioguides (€4, €6 with 2 earphones, or €6 for a Palm Pilot) don't let you fast-forward to works you want to hear about; you have to listen to the whole spiel for each room.

At the Accademia Bridge, there's a decent pizzeria canalside (Pizzeria Accademia Foscarini; see "Eating," below); a public WC under it; and usually a classic shell game being played on top (study the system as partners in the crowd win big money, inspiring suckers to lose the same). Nearby sights include the Peggy Guggenheim Museum and La Salute Church.

▲▲**Peggy Guggenheim Museum**—This popular collection of far-out art, housed in the American heiress' former retirement palazzo, offers one of Europe's best reviews of the art of the first half of the 20th century. Stroll through styles represented by artists whom Peggy knew personally—cubism (Picasso, Braque), surrealism (Dalí, Ernst), futurism (Boccione), American abstract expressionism (Pollock), and a sprinkling of Klee, Calder, and Chagall (€8, Wed–Mon 10:00–18:00, plus Sat 10:00–22:00 April–Oct, closed Tue, audioguide-€4, guidebook-€18, free and mandatory baggage check, pricey café, photos allowed only in garden and terrace—a fine and relaxing perch overlooking Grand Canal, near Accademia, tel. 041-240-5411). The place is run (cheaply) by American interns working on art history degrees.

La Salute Church (Santa Maria delle Salute)—This impressive church with a crown-shaped dome was built and dedicated to the Virgin Mary by grateful survivors of the 1630 plague (free, daily 9:00–12:00 & 15:00–18:00, tel. 041-522-5558 to confirm). It's a 10-minute walk from Accademia Bridge, or vaporetto ride (stop: Salute), or inexpensive *traghetto* crossing from near St. Mark's Square—catch it on the lagoon next to the TI and Harry's Bar.

▲**Ca' Rezzonico (Museum of 18th-Century Venice)**—This grand Grand Canal palazzo offers the best look in town at the life of Venice's rich and famous in the 1700s. Wander under ceilings by Tiepolo, among furnishings from that most decadent century, enjoying views of the canal and paintings by Guardi, Canaletto, and Longhi (€6.70, April–Oct Wed–Mon 10:00–18:00, Nov–March 10:00-17:00, closed Tue , ticket office closes 1 hour early, audioguide-€5.50, located at Ca' Rezzonico vaporetto stop, tel. 041-241-0100).

San Polo District

▲▲**Frari Church (Chiesa dei Frari)**—My favorite art experience in Venice is seeing art *in situ*—the setting for which it was designed—and my favorite example is the Chiesa dei Frari. The Franciscan "church of the friars" and the art that decorates it are warmed by the spirit of St. Francis. It features the work of three great Renaissance masters: Donatello, Bellini, and Titian, each showing worshipers the glory of God in human terms.

In Donatello's wood carving of St. John the Baptist (just to the right of the high altar), the prophet of the desert—dressed in animal skins and almost anorexic from his diet of bugs 'n' honey—announces the coming of the Messiah. Donatello was a Florentine working at the dawn of the Renaissance.

Bellini's *Madonna and the Saints* painting (in the chapel farther to the right) came later, done by a Venetian in a more Venetian style—soft focus without Donatello's harsh realism. While Renaissance humanism demanded Madonnas and saints that were accessible and human, Bellini places them in a physical setting so beautiful it creates its own mood of serene holiness. The genius of Bellini, perhaps the greatest Venetian painter, is obvious in the pristine clarity, rich colors (notice Mary's clothing), believable depth, and reassuring calm of this three-paneled altarpiece. It's so good to see a painting in its natural setting.

Finally, glowing red and gold like a stained-glass window over the high altar, Titian's *Assumption* sets the tone of exuberant beauty found in the otherwise sparse church. Titian the Venetian—a student of Bellini—painted steadily for 60 years...you'll see a lot of his art. As stunned apostles look up past the swirl of arms and legs, the complex composition of this painting draws you right to the radiant face of the once dying, now triumphant Mary as she joins God in heaven.

Be comfortable discreetly freeloading off passing tours. For many, these three pieces of art make a visit to the Accademia Gallery unnecessary (or they may whet your appetite for more). Before leaving, check out the neoclassical, pyramid-shaped tomb of Canova and (opposite that) the grandiose tomb of Titian. Compare the carved marble Assumption behind Titian's tombstone portrait with the painted original above the high altar.

Cost and Hours: €2, Mon–Sat 9:00–18:00, Sun 13:00–18:00, closed Sun in Aug, last entry 15 min before closing, audioguides-€1.60/person or €2.60/double set (tel. 041-523-4864). Modest dress is recommended.

▲▲**Scuola Grande di San Rocco**—Sometimes called "Tintoretto's Sistine Chapel," this lavish meeting hall (next to the Frari Church) has some 50 large, colorful Tintoretto paintings plastered to the walls and ceilings. The best paintings are upstairs, especially the *Crucifixion* in the smaller room. View the neck-breaking splendor with one of the mirrors (*specchio*) available at the entrance (€5.50, includes free and informative audioguide, daily April–Oct 9:00–17:30, Nov–March 10:00–16:00, or see a concert here and enjoy the art as an evening bonus—see "Nightlife," page 837).

Cannaregio District

Jewish Ghetto—The word "ghetto" is Venetian for foundry, and was inherited by Venice's Jewish community when it was confined to the site of Venice's former copper foundries in 1516. Notice how an island—dominated by the Campo del Ghetto Nuovo square and connected with the rest of Venice by only two bridges—would be easy to isolate. While little survives from that time, in its day the square was densely populated, lined with proto-skyscrapers seven to nine stories high.

This original ghetto becomes most interesting after touring the **Jewish Museum** (€3, June–Sept Sun–Fri 10:00–19:00, Oct–May Sun–Fri 10:00–17:30, closed Sat, Campo di Ghetto Nuovo, tel. 041-715-359). The synagogues are open only by tour (€8, hourly 10:30–16:30, later in summer, in English, contact museum to arrange tour).

Castello District

Dalmatian School (Scuola Dalmata dei San Giorgio)—This "school" (which means "meeting place") is a reminder that Venice was Europe's most cosmopolitan place in its heyday. It was here that the Dalmatians (from the present-day region of Croatia) worshiped in their own way, held neighborhood meetings, and worked to preserve their culture. The chapel on the ground floor happens to have the most exquisite Renaissance interior in Venice, with a cycle painted by Carpaccio ringing the room (€3, Tue–Sat 9:30–12:30 & 15:30–18:30, Sun 9:30–12:30, closed Mon; between St. Mark's Square and Arsenale, on Calle dei Furlani, 3 blocks southeast of Campo San Lorenzo; tel. 041-522-8828).

Santa Elena—For a pleasant peek into a completely non-touristy, residential side of Venice, walk or catch vaporetto #1 or #82 from St. Mark's Square to the neighborhood of Santa Elena (at the fish's tail). This 100-year-old suburb lives as if there were no tourism. You'll find a kid-friendly park, a few lazy restaurants, and beautiful sunsets over San Marco.

Venice Lagoon

The island of Venice sits in a lagoon—a calm section of the Adriatic protected from wind and waves by the neutral breakwater of the *lido*. Four interesting islands hide out in the lagoon.

San Giorgio Maggiore is the dreamy island you can see from the waterfront by St. Mark's Square. The striking church, designed by Palladio, features art by Tintoretto and a bell tower with oh-wow views of Venice (free entry to church, daily 9:30–12:30 & 14:00–18:30, closed Sun to sightseers during Mass, Gregorian Mass sung on Sun at 11:00,

Venice Lagoon

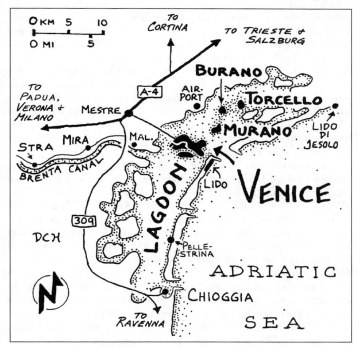

Mon–Sat at 8:00; €3 for bell tower lift, stops 30 min before church's closing time). To reach the island from St. Mark's Square, take the five-minute vaporetto ride on #82 from the San Zaccaria Jolanda stop, just past the Bridge of Sighs, closest to the big statue. (Note: This is not the same vaporetto stop as San Marco/Vallaresso.)

The islands of **Murano, Burano,** and **Torcello** are reached easily, cheaply, and slowly by vaporetto. Pick up a free map of the islands from any TI. Depart from San Zaccaria dock nearest the Bridge of Sighs and Doge's Palace. **Vaporetto line #12** connects all three islands, or take #41 to Murano (get off at the Murano Colonna stop), then #12 to the other islands. If you plan to visit even two of these islands, get a 24-hour €10.50 vaporetto pass or a 12-hour €8.50 "Laguna Tour" pass for convenience. **Speedboat tours** (3–5 hrs) of these three lagoon destinations leave twice a day from the dock past the Doge's Palace near the Cipriani Hotel shuttle dock—look for the signs and booth (€20, usually at 9:30 and 14:30; Nov–March 14:30 only, tel. 041-523-8835); the tours are speedy indeed, stopping for roughly 35 minutes at each island.

Murano, famous for its glass factories, has the Glass Museum, which displays the very best of 700 years of Venetian glassmaking and exhibits of ancient and modern glass art (Museo Vetrario, €4, covered by €15.50 Museum Pass, Thu–Tue 10:00–17:00, Nov–March 10:00–16:00, last entry 30 min before closing, closed Wed, tel. 041-739-586). You'll be tempted by salesmen offering free speedboat shuttles from St. Mark's Square to Murano. If you're interested in glass, it's handy. You must watch the 20-minute glassmaking show, but then you're free to buy or escape and see the rest of the island. Numerous glass factories (*fabbrica* or *fornace*) offer demonstrations all over the island—check one out. When you're ready to go, head to the Faro vaporetto stop and take the #12 to either Burano or Torcello or the #41 back to San Zaccaria.

Burano, famous for its lace, is a sleepy island with a sleepy community—village Venice without the glitz. Lace fans enjoy the Lace Museum (Scuola di Merletti, €4, covered by €15.50 Museum Pass, Wed–Mon 10:00–17:00, Nov–March 10:00–16:00, closed Tue, tel. 041-730-034). The park next to Burano's only vaporetto dock is perfect for a waterfront picnic. While the main drag leading from the vaporetto stop into town is packed with tourists and lined with shops (some sell Burano's locally-produced white wine), simply wander to the far, peaceful side of the island.

Torcello is the least-developed island (pop. 20), with little for the tourist to see except the church (a 10-min walk from the dock), claiming to be the oldest in Venice. It's impressive for its mosaics, but not worth a look on a short visit unless you really love mosaics and can't make it to Ravenna. The complex consists of the church itself, the bell tower (behind the church, climb a ramped stairway for great lagoon views), a sacristy, and a small museum (facing the church, in 2 separate buildings) that displays Roman sculpture and medieval sculpture and manuscripts. A €5.20 combination ticket gets you into all the sights (most open daily 10:30–17:30, museum closed Mon, tel. 041-730-761; pay WC between museum's two buildings).

Gondola Rides

A rip-off for some, this is a traditional must for romantics. Gondoliers charge about €62 for a 50-minute ride during the day; from 20:00 on, figure on €77–105 (for *musica*—singer and accordionist—it's an additional €88 during day, €98 after 20:00). You can divide the cost—and the romance—among up to six people per boat. Note that only two seats (the ones in back) are next to each other. If you want to haggle, you'll find softer prices on back lanes where single gondoliers hang out than at the bigger departure points.

Though they cost nearly double after dark, gondolas are triply romantic and relaxing under the moon. Glide through nighttime Venice with your head on someone's shoulder. Follow the moon as it sails past otherwise unseen buildings. Silhouettes gaze down from bridges while window glitter spills onto the black water. You're anonymous in the city of masks as the rhythmic thrust of your striped-shirted gondolier turns old crows into songbirds. This is extremely relaxing. Since you might get a narration plus conversation with your gondolier, talk with several and choose one you like who speaks English well. Women, beware...while gondoliers can be extremely charming, local women say anyone who falls for one of these Romeos "has slices of ham over her eyes."

For cheap gondola thrills during the day, stick to the €0.40 one-minute ferry ride on a Grand Canal *traghetto*. At night, vaporettos are nearly empty, and it's a great time to cruise the Grand Canal on the slow boat #1. Or hang out on a bridge along the gondola route and wave at— or drop leftover pigeon feed on—romantics.

Festivals

Venice's most famous festival is **Carnevale**, the celebration Americans call Mardi Gras (Feb 14–24 in 2004; www.carnivalofvenice.com). Carnevale, which means "farewell to meat," originated centuries ago as a wild two-month-long party leading up to the austerity of Lent. In Carnevale's heyday—the 1600s and 1700s—you could do pretty much anything with anybody from any social class if you were wearing a mask. These days it's a tamer 10-day celebration, culminating in a huge dance lit with fireworks on St. Mark's Square. Sporting masks and costumes, Venetians from kids to businessmen join in the fun. Drawing the biggest crowds of the year, Carnevale has nearly been a victim of its own success, driving away many Venetians (who skip out on the craziness to go ski in the Dolomites).

Other typically Venetian festival days filling the city's hotels with visitors and its canals with decked-out boats are: **Feast of the Ascension Day** (mid-May), **Feast and Regatta of the Redeemer** (parade and fireworks, July 17–18, 2004), and the **Historical Regatta** (old-time boats and pageantry, first weekend in September). Smaller regattas include the **Murano Regatta** (early July) and the **Burano Regatta** (in September).

Venice's patron saint, **St. Mark**, is commemorated every April 25. Venetian men celebrate the day by presenting roses to the women in their lives (mothers, wives, and lovers).

Every November 21 is the **Feast of Our Lady of Good Health**. On this local "Thanksgiving," a bridge is built over the Grand Canal so the city can pile into the Salute Church and remember how Venice survived the gruesome plague of 1630. On this day, Venetians eat smoked lamb from Dalmatia (which was the cargo of the first ship admitted when the plague lifted).

Every odd year, the city hosts the **Venice Biennale International Art Exhibition**, a world-class contemporary fair spread over the sprawling Castello Gardens (generally March–Nov, vaporetto stop: Giardini/Biennale, www.labiennale.org).

Venice is always busy with special musical and artistic events. The free monthly *Un Ospite de Venezia* lists all the latest in English (free at TI or from fancy hotels). For a comprehensive list of festivals, contact the Italian tourist information office in the United States (see the appendix) and visit www.whatsonwhen.com, www.festivals.com, and www.hostetler.net.

SHOPPING

Shoppers like Murano glass, Burano lace (fun lace umbrellas for little girls), Carnevale masks (fine shops and local artisans all over town), art reproductions (posters, postcards, and books), prints of Venice scenes, traditional stationery (pens and marbled paper products of all kinds), calendars with Venice scenes, silk ties, scarves, and plenty of goofy knick-knacks (Titian mousepads, gondolier T-shirts, and little plastic gondolas).

If you're buying a substantial amount from nearly any shop, bargain. It's accepted and almost expected. Offer less and offer to pay cash; merchants are very conscious of the bite taken by credit-card companies.

Popular **Venetian glass** is available in many forms: vases, tea sets, decanters, glasses, jewelry, lamps, mod sculptures (such as solid-glass aquariums), and on and on. Shops will ship it home for you (snap a photo of it before it's packed up). For a cheap, packable souvenir, consider the glass-bead necklaces sold at vendors' stalls throughout Venice.

If you're serious about glass, visit the small shops on **Murano Island**. Murano's glass-blowing demonstrations are fun; you'll usually see a vase and a "leetle 'orse" made from molten glass.

Various companies offer glass-blowing demos for tour groups around St. Mark's Square. **Galleria San Marco**, a tour-group staple, offers great demos just off St. Mark's Square every few minutes. They have agreed to let individual travelers flashing this book sneak in with tour groups to see the show (and sales pitch). And, if you buy anything, show this book and they'll take 20 percent off the listed price. The gallery faces the square behind the orchestra nearest the church; at #139, go through the shop and climb the stairs (daily 9:30–12:30 & 13:30–17:00, manager Walter Brunello, tel. 041-271-8650).

Along Venice's many shopping streets, you'll notice fly-by-night vendors selling knockoffs of famous-maker handbags (Louis Vuitton, Gucci, etc.). These vendors are willing to bargain. I bought a genuine $1,000 Rolex for $10. Buyer beware.

NIGHTLIFE

Venice is quiet at night, as tour groups are back in the cheaper hotels of Mestre on the mainland, and the masses of day-trippers return to their beach resorts. **Gondolas** can cost nearly double, but are worth the extra expense. Vaporettos are uncrowded, and it's a great time to cruise the Grand Canal on slow boat #1.

Take your pick of traditional Vivaldi **concerts** in churches throughout town. Homegrown Vivaldi is as trendy here as Strauss in Vienna and Mozart in Salzburg. In fact, you'll find frilly young Vivaldis all over town hawking concert tickets. The TI has a list of this week's Baroque concerts (tickets from €18, shows start at 21:00 and generally last 90 min). There's music most nights at Scuola San Teodoro (east side of Rialto Bridge) and San Vitale Church (north end of Accademia Bridge), among others. If you see a concert at Scuola di San Rocco (tickets €15–30), you can enjoy the art (which you're likely to pay €5.50 for during the day) for free during the intermission. Another unique music experience is a Rondo Veneziano concert—classically inspired music with a modern electronic sound. The general rule of thumb: musicians in wigs and tights offer better spectacle, and musicians in black-and-white suits are better performers. Consider the venue carefully. For the latest on church concerts, see www.musicinvenice.com or call 041-962-9999.

On St. Mark's Square, the dueling **café orchestras** entertain at Caffè Florian (listed below), Quadri Ristorante, and Lavena (see map on page 825). Every night, enthusiastic musicians play the same songs, creating the same irresistible magic. Hang out for free behind the tables (which allows you to easily move on to the next orchestra when the musicians take a break) or spring for a seat and enjoy a fun and gorgeously set concert. If you sit a while, it can be €10.20 well spent (€6.20 drink plus a one-time €4 fee for entertainment). Dancing on the square is free (and encouraged).

Caffè Florian, on St. Mark's Square, is the most famous Venetian café and one of the first places in Europe to serve coffee. It has been a popular spot for a discreet rendezvous in Venice since 1720. Today, it's most famous for its outdoor seating and orchestra (see above), but do walk inside through the richly decorated, 18th-century rooms where Casanova, Lord Byron, Charles Dickens, and Woody Allen have all paid too much for a drink (reasonable prices at bar in back, tel. 041-520-5641). A cheaper late-night spot is the stand-up **American Bar,** under the clock tower on St. Mark's Square.

You're not a tourist, you're a living part of a soft Venetian night...an alley cat with money. Streetlamp halos, live music, floodlit history, and a ceiling of stars make St. Mark's magic at midnight. In the misty light, the moon has a golden hue. Shine with the old lanterns on the gondola piers where the sloppy Grand Canal splashes at the Doge's Palace...reminiscing. Comfort the small statues of the four frightened Byzantine emperors where the Doge's Palace hits the basilica. Cuddle history.

SLEEPING

Between St. Mark's Square and Campo Santa Maria di Formosa

$$ **Hotel al Piave**, with 27 fine, air-conditioned rooms above a bright and classy lobby, is fresh, modern, and comfortable (Db-€145, Tb-€190, family suites-€250 for 4, €280 for 5–6, prices good through 2004 with this book, accepts CC but gives discount for cash; take vaporetto to Rialto, find your way to Campo Santa Maria Formosa and it's straight down Ruga Giuffa to #4838/40, Castello; tel. 041-528-5174, fax 041-523-8512, www.hotelalpiave.com, hotel.alpiave@iol.it, Mirella, Paolo, and Ilaria SE, faithful Molly NSE).

$$ **Locanda Correr** is a tight and tiny five-room place buried in the old center and up a long stairway. Newly-opened and proudly-run by Roberto, it features open-beamed ceilings and Venetian-style furnishings along with air-conditioning and modern comforts (Db-€135 with cash and this book promised through 2004, from Campo San Filippo e Giacomo, walk north up Calle Drio la Chiesa, take first left onto Calle

SLEEP CODE

(€1 = about $1.10, country code: 33)

Sleep Code: **S** = Single, **D** = Double/Twin, **T** = Triple, **Q** = Quad, **b** = bathroom, **s** = shower only, **no CC** = Credit Cards not accepted, **SE** = Speaks English, **NSE** = No English. Breakfast is included and credit cards are accepted unless otherwise noted. Air-conditioning, when available, is usually only turned on in summer.

To help you sort easily through these listings, I've divided the rooms into three categories based on the price for a standard double room with bath:

$$$ **Higher Priced**—Most rooms €180 or more.
$$ **Moderately Priced**—Most rooms between €130-180.
$ **Lower Priced**—Most rooms €130 or less.

Hotels in Venice are usually booked up on Carnevale (Feb 14–24 in 2004), Easter (April 11 in 2004), April 25, May 1, in August, Nov 1, and on Fridays and Saturdays year-round.

del Figher and it's hiding just past the well-signed Hotel Castello, Castello 4370, tel. 041-277-7847, fax 041-277-5939, www.locandacorrer.it, info @locandacorrer.com).

$$ Locanda Casa Querini has 11 plush rooms on a quiet square tucked away behind St. Mark's (Db-€140 with cash and this book through 2004, €10 more during festivals, air-con, exactly halfway between San Zaccaria vaporetto stop and Campo Santa Maria Formosa at Campo San Giovanni in Oleo 4388, Castello, tel. 041-241-1294, fax 041-241-4231, www.locandaquerini.com, casaquerini@hotmail.com, Silvia).

$ Hotel Riva, with gleaming marble hallways and bright modern rooms, is romantically situated on a canal along the gondola serenade route. You could actually dunk your breakfast rolls in the canal (but don't). Sandro may hold a corner *(angolo)* room if you ask, and there are also a few rooms overlooking the canal. Confirm prices and reconfirm reservations, as readers have had trouble with both (32 rooms, Sb-€88, 2 D with adjacent showers-€95, Db-€120, Tb-€170, Qb-€210, €10 extra for view; Ponte dell' Angelo—also spelled Anzolo, Castello 5310; tel. 041-522-7034, fax 041-528-5551). Face St. Mark's Basilica, walk behind it on the left along Calle de la Canonica, take the first left (at blue "Pauly & C" mosaic in street), continue straight, go over the bridge, and angle right to the hotel.

Reserve a room as soon as you know when you'll be in town. Book direct—not through any tourist agency. Most places take a credit card number for a deposit. If everything's full, don't despair. Call a day or two in advance and fill in a cancellation. If you arrive on an overnight train, your room may not be ready. Drop your bag at the hotel and dive right into Venice.

I've listed prices for peak season: April, May, June, September, and October. Prices can get soft in July, August, and winter. Hotels sometimes give discounts if you stay at least three nights and/or pay cash. If on a budget, ask for a cheaper room or a discount. Always ask.

Virtually all of these hotels are central. See the map on page 841 for hotel locations. I've listed rooms mainly in two neighborhoods: in the Rialto–San Marco action and in a quiet Dorsoduro area behind the Accademia Gallery. If a hotel has a Web site, check it. Hotel Web sites are particularly valuable for Venice, because they often come with a map that at least gives you the illusion you can easily find the place.

$ **Corte Campana** rents four comfy, quiet rooms just behind St. Mark's Square (Db-€80–130, Tb-€105–150, Qb-€140–180; facing St. Mark's Basilica, take Calle Canonica—to the far left of the church—turn left before canal on Calle dell' Anzolo, take first right on Calle del Remedio, cross the bridge and follow signs to Locanda Remedio and enter little courtyard to your right, go up three flights of steps and ring bell at Calle del Remedio 4410, Castello; tel. 041-523-3603, mobile 389-272-6500, www.cortecampana.com, info@cortecampana.com, enthusiastic Riccardo SE).

On or near the Waterfront, East of St. Mark's Square

These places, about one canal down from the Bridge of Sighs, on or just off the Riva degli Schiavoni waterfront promenade, rub drainpipes with Venice's most palatial five-star hotels. The first two, while a bit pricey because of their location, are professional and comfortable. Ride the vaporetto to San Zaccaria (#51 from train station, #82 from Tronchetto car park).

$$ **Hotel Campiello**, a lacy and bright little 16-room, air-conditioned place, was once part of a 19th-century convent. It's ideally located 50 yards off the waterfront (Sb-€110–120, Db-€120–180, 8 percent discount with cash, cancellation fee; elevator; behind Hotel Savoia, up Calle del Vin off the waterfront street—Riva degli Schiavoni 4647, San Zaccaria; tel. 041-520-5764, fax 041-520-5798, www.hcampiello.it, campiello@hcampiello.it; family-run for 4 generations, sisters Monica and Nicoletta, and Thomas).

$$ **Albergo Paganelli** is right on the waterfront—on Riva degli Schiavoni—and has a few incredible view rooms (S-€100, Sb-€125, Db-€150–181, Db with view-€200, 5 percent discount with cash, prices often soft; request *con vista* for view, air-con; at San Zaccaria vaporetto stop, Riva degli Schiavoni 4182, Castello; tel. 041-522-4324, fax 041-523-9267, www.hotelpaganelli.com, hotelpag@tin.it). With spacious rooms, carved and gilded headboards, and chandeliers, this elegant place is a good value. Seven of their 22 rooms are in a less interesting but equally comfortable *dipendenza* (annex), a block off the canal.

$$ **Hotel Fontana** is a two-star, family-run place with 14 rooms and lots of stairs on a touristy square two bridges behind St. Mark's Square (Sb-€55–110, Db-€90–170 depending on season and length of stay, 10 percent discount with cash, see Web site for off-season deals; air-con, family rooms, quieter rooms on canal side, piazza views can be noisy, 2 rooms have terraces; vaporetto #51 to San Zaccaria, find Calle de le Rasse—to left of Hotel Danieli—take it, turn right at end, continue to first square, Campo San Provolo 4701, Castello; tel. 041-522-0579, fax 041-523-1040, www.hotelfontana.it, htlcasa@gpnet.it).

Hotels near St. Mark's Square

200 YARDS
200 METERS

☑ TRAGHETTO CROSSING
🚉 VAPORETTO STOP

RIALTO
POST
CAMPO S.M. FORMOSA
CANAL
CAMPO S.LUCA
CAMPO MANIN
LA FENICE
CAMP.
POST
WC
DOGE'S PALACE
S. ZAC.
SAN ZAC.
S. MOISE
CAMPO S.MARIA ZOBENIGO
SAN MARCO/VALLARESSO
S. MARIA DEL GIGLIO
SAN MARCO

❶ Hotel Riva
❷ Hotel al Piave
❸ Locanda Casa Querini & Locanda Correr
❹ Hotel Campiello
❺ Albergo Paganelli
❻ Albergo Doni
❼ Hotel Fontana
❽ Corte Campana
❾ Hotel Astoria
❿ Locanda Gambero
⓫ Hotel Bel Sito
⓬ Alloggi alla Scala

$ **Albergo Doni** is a dark, hardwood, clean, and quiet place—a bit of a time-warp—with 13 dim but classy rooms run by a likable smart aleck named Gina (D-€90, Db-€115, T-€120, Tb-€153, secure telephone reservations with CC but must pay in cash; ceiling fans; Riva degli Schiavoni, Calle del Vin 4656, San Zaccaria N.; tel. & fax 041-522-4267, www.albergodoni.it, albergodoni@libero.it, Nicolo, Tessa, and Gina SE). Leave Riva degli Schiavoni on Calle del Vin and go 100 yards with a left jog.

North of St. Mark's Square

$$ **Locanda Gambero**, with 26 rooms, is a comfortable and very central three-star hotel run by Sandro (Sb-€50–130, Db-€90–190, Tb-€150–240, Internet access, air-con, 5 percent discount for payment in cash; from Rialto vaporetto dock walk away from the Rialto bridge, cross one bridge, take first left down skinny Calle le Bembo/Calle del Fabbri; or from St. Mark's Square go through Sotoportego dei Dai then down Calle dei Fabbri to #4687; tel. 041-522-4384, fax 041-520-0431, www.locandaalgambero.com, hotelgambero@tin.it, cheery Gianni covers the night shift, all SE). Gambero runs the pleasant, Art Deco–style La Bistrot on the corner, which serves old-time Venetian cuisine.

$$ **Hotel Astoria** has 24 simple rooms tucked away a few blocks off St. Mark's Square (S-€80–90, Sb-€100, Db-€125, cheaper off-season; some air-con suites available; 2 blocks from San Zulian Church at Calle Fiubera 951; from Rialto vaporetto #1 dock, go straight inland on Calle le Bembo, which becomes Calle dei Fabbri, turn left on Calle Fiubera; tel. 041-522-5381, fax 041-528-8981, www.hotelastoriavenezia.it, info@hotelastoriavenezia.it, Giorgia and Giovanni SE).

West of St. Mark's Square

$$$ **Hotel Bel Sito**, friendly for a three-star hotel, has Old World character and a picturesque location—facing a church on a small square between St. Mark's Square and the Accademia. With solid wood furniture, its 38 rooms feel elegant. Those on the back side are more charming (Sb-€100–130, Db-€170–200, air-con, elevator, some rooms with canal or church views; vaporetto #1 to Santa Maria del Giglio stop, take narrow alley to square, hotel at far end to your right, Santa Maria del Giglio 2517, San Marco, tel. 041-522-3365, fax 041-520-4083, belsito@iol.it).

$ **Alloggi alla Scala**, a seven-room place run by Signora Andreina della Fiorentina, is homey, central, and hidden away on a quiet square that features a famous spiral stairway called Scala Contarini del Bovolo (small Db-€80, big Db-€90, extra bed-€26, breakfast-€9, reserve by CC, 6 percent discount for payment in cash; Campo Manin 4306, San Marco; tel. 041-521-0629, fax 041-522-6451, daughter Emma SE). To find the hotel from Campo Manin, follow signs to (on statue's left) "Scala Contarini del Bovolo."

Near the Rialto Bridge

The first three hotels are on the west side of the Rialto Bridge (away from St. Mark's Square) and the last three are on the east side of the bridge (on St. Mark's side). Vaporetto #82 quickly connects the Rialto with both the train station and the Tronchetto car park.

Hotels near the Rialto Bridge

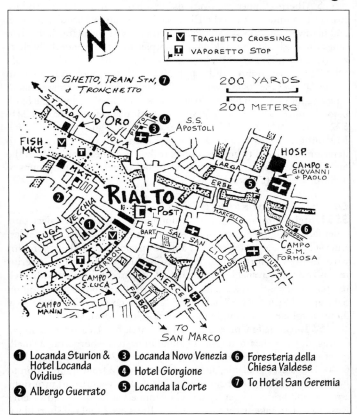

On West Side of Rialto Bridge

$$$ **Hotel Locanda Ovidius**, with an elegant Grand Canal view terrace, a breakfast room with a wood-beamed ceiling, and nine bright, comfortable rooms, is on the Grand Canal (Sb-€77–190, Db-€130–230, Db with view-€185–280, check Web site for special offers, air-con, Calle del Sturion 677a, tel. 041-523-7970, fax 041-520-4101, www .hotelovidius.com, info@hotelovidius.com).

$$$ **Locanda Sturion**, with air-conditioning and all the modern comforts, is pricey because it overlooks the Grand Canal (Db-€150–200, Tb-€180–230, family deals, canal-view rooms cost €25 extra; piles of stairs; 100 yards from Rialto Bridge, opposite vaporetto dock, Calle Sturion 679, San Polo, Rialto; tel. 041-523-6243, fax 041-522-8378,

www.locandasturion.com, info@locandasturion.com, SE).

$ **Albergo Guerrato**, overlooking a handy and colorful produce market two minutes from the Rialto action, is run by friendly, creative, and hardworking Roberto and Piero. Giorgio takes the night shift. Their 800-year-old building is Old World simple, airy, and wonderfully characteristic (D-€85, Db-€110, big top floor Db-€130, T-€105, Tb-€135, Qb-€155, prices promised through 2004 with this book in hand, cash only; walk over the Rialto away from St. Mark's Square, go straight about 3 blocks, turn right on Calle drio la Scimia—not simply Scimia, the block before—and you'll see the hotel sign, Calle drio la Scimia 240a; tel. 041-522-7131 or 041-528-5927, fax 041-241-1408, hguerrat@tin.it, SE). My tour groups book this place for 50 nights each year. Sorry. Call to determine availability before you fax (otherwise, they won't return the fax). They rent family apartments in the old center (great for groups of 4–8) for around €55 per person.

On East Side of Rialto Bridge

$$$ **Hotel Giorgione**, a four-star hotel in a 15th-century palace on a quiet lane, is super-professional, with plush public spaces, pool tables, Internet access, a garden terrace, and 76 spacious, over-the-top rooms with all the comforts (Sb-€90–173, Db-€130–265, pricier superior rooms and suites available, extra bed-€60, 10 percent discount with Web reservations, elevator, air-con, 200 yards off Campo S.S. Apostoli on Salizada del Pistor, #4587, tel. 041-522-5810, fax 041-523-9092, www.hotelgiorgione.com, giorgione@hotelgiorgione.com).

$$ **Locanda la Corte**, a three-star hotel, has 18 attractive, high-ceilinged, wood-beamed rooms—done in pastels—bordering a small, quiet courtyard (Sb-€90–120, standard Db-€120–150, superior Db-€140–170, suites available, air-con; vaporetto #52 from train station to Fondamente Nove, exit boat to your left, follow waterfront, turn right after second bridge to get to S.S. Giovanni e Paolo square, and facing Rosa Salva bar, take street to left—Calle Bressana, hotel is a short block away at #6317 bridge; Castello, tel. 041-241-1300, fax 041-241-5982, www.locandalacorte.it, info@locandalacorte.it).

$ **Locanda Novo Venezia**, a charming eight-room place in a 15th-century palazzo run by industrious Claudio and Ivan, is just off a super square—Campo dei S.S. Apostoli, north of the Rialto Bridge (Db-€130 with this book, family deals for up to 6 in a room; air-con; from Campo dei S.S. Apostoli head down Salizada del Pistor, take first right on Calle dei Preti to #4529, Cannaregio; tel. 041-241-1496, fax 041-241-5989, www.locandanovo.it, locandanovo@tin.it).

Near the Accademia Bridge

When you step over the Accademia Bridge, the commotion of touristy Venice is replaced by a sleepy village laced with canals. This quiet area, next to the best painting gallery in town, is a 15-minute walk from St. Mark's Square and the Rialto. The fast vaporetto #82 connects the Accademia Bridge with both the train station (15 min) and St. Mark's Square (5 min).

On South Side of Accademia Bridge

$$$ Hotel Belle Arti is a good bet if you want to be in the old center without the tourist hordes. With a grand entry and all the American hotel comforts, it's a big, 67-room, modern, three-star place sitting on a former schoolyard (Sb-€114–150, Db-€145–210, Tb-€186–255, ask for the "Rick Steves" discount, then get 5 percent more off for cash; plush public areas, air-con, elevator; 100 yards behind Accademia art museum—facing museum, take left, then forced right, Via Dorsoduro 912; tel. 041-522-6230, fax 041-528-0043, www.hotelbellearti.com, info@hotelbellearti.com, SE).

$$ Pensione Accademia fills the 17th-century Villa Maravege. While its 27 comfortable and air-conditioned rooms are nothing extraordinary, you'll feel aristocratic gliding through its grand public spaces and lounging in its breezy garden (Sb-€83–123, standard Db-€160–180, bigger "superior" Db-€180–230, family deals; facing Accademia art museum, take first right, cross first bridge, go right, Dorsoduro 1058; tel. 041-523-7846, fax 041-523-9152, www.pensioneaccademia.it, info @pensioneaccademia.it).

$$ Hotel Galleria has nine tight, velvety rooms, most with views of the Grand Canal. Some rooms are quite narrow; ask for a larger room (S-€66–90, D-€90–97, Db-€110–145, big canal-view rooms #8 and #10 Db-from €135, includes scant breakfast in room; fans; near Accademia art museum, and next to recommended Foscarini pizzeria, Dorsoduro 878a; tel. 041-523-2489, tel. & fax 041-520-4172, www.hotelgalleria.it, galleria@tin.it).

$$ Hotel Agli Alboretti is a cozy, family-run, 24-room place in a quiet neighborhood a block behind the Accademia art museum. With red carpeting and wood-beamed ceilings, it feels elegant (Sb-€104, Db-€180, Tb-€210, Qb-€240; air-con; 100 yards from the Accademia vaporetto stop on Rio Terra a Foscarini at Accademia 884—facing Accademia art museum, go left, then forced right; tel. 041-523-0058, fax 041-521-0158, www.aglialboretti.com, alborett@gpnet.it, SE).

$$ Pensione La Calcina, the home of English writer John Ruskin in 1876, comes with all the three-star comforts in a professional yet intimate package. Its 29 rooms are squeaky clean, with good wood furniture, hardwood floors, and a peaceful canalside setting facing Giudecca island (S-€75, Sb-€96, Sb with view-€110, Db-€130–145, Db with view-€160–185, prices vary with room size and season; air-con, rooftop terrace, killer sundeck on canal and canalside buffet-breakfast terrace; Dorsoduro 780, at south end of Rio di San Vio; tel. 041-520-6466, fax

Hotels near the Accademia Bridge

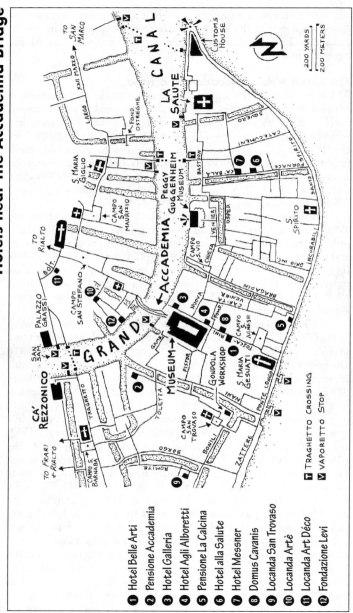

1 Hotel Belle Arti
2 Pensione Accademia
3 Hotel Galleria
4 Hotel Agli Alboretti
5 Pensione La Calcina
6 Hotel alla Salute
7 Hotel Messner
8 Domus Cavanis
9 Locanda San Trovaso
10 Locanda Artè
11 Locanda Art Déco
12 Fondazione Levi

⧉ TRAGHETTO CROSSING
🚤 VAPORETTO STOP

041-522-7045, www.lacalcina.com, la.calcina@libero.it). They also rent apartments nearby (max 2 people, €140–240, air-con). From the Tronchetto car park or station, catch vaporetto #51 or #82 to Zattere (at vaporetto stop, exit right and walk along canal to hotel). Guests get a fine dinner at their La Piscina restaurant discounted to €20.

$$ **Hotel alla Salute**, a basic retreat buried deep in Dorsoduro, is ideal for those wanting a quiet Venice residence (Db-€140, cash discount, plans air-con for 2004, facing the canal Rio delle Fornace near La Salute church, tel. 041-523-5404, fax 041-522-2271, www.hotelsalute .com, info@hotelsalute.com).

$$ **Hotel Messner,** a sprawling place popular with groups, rents 40 nondescript rooms in a peaceful canal-side neighborhood near La Salute Church. While remote, it has cheap and handy *traghetto* access to St. Mark's Square (Sb-€90–110, Db with air-con-€120–150, Db without air-con in simpler annex-€100–120, Tb-€145–180, Qb-€160–200, peaceful garden, midway between lagoon and Grand Canal on Rio delle Fornace canal, tel. 041-522-7443, fax 041-522-7266, www.hotelmessner .it, messnerinfo@tin.it).

$ **Domus Cavanis**, across the street from—and owned by—Hotel Belle Arti, is a big, practical, stark place with a garden, renting 30 quiet, simple, and spacious rooms (Db-€103, Tb-€150, family rooms, includes breakfast at Hotel Belle Arti, air-con, elevator, Dorsoduro 895, tel. 041-528-7374, fax 041-522-8505, www.hotelbellearti.com, info @hotelbellearti.com).

$ **Locanda San Trovaso** is sparkling new, with seven classy, spacious rooms and a peaceful location on a small canal (Sb-€90, Db-€115–130, Tb-€145; breakfast in your room, fans, small roof terrace; Dorsoduro 1351, take vaporetto #82 from Tronchetto or #51 from Piazzale Roma or train station, get off at Zattere, exit left, turn right at tiny Calle Trevisan, cross bridge, cross adjacent bridge, take immediate right, then first left; tel. 041-277-1146, fax 041-277-7190, www.locandasantrovaso .com, s.trovaso@tin.it, Mark and his son Alessandro SE).

On North Side of Accademia Bridge

$ **Locanda Artè** has eight homey rooms with high ceilings, old-style Venetian furnishings, air-conditioning, and thoughtful touches (Db-€90–120, 10 percent cash discount, family room sleeps up to 6, just north of Accademia Bridge, 100 yards west of Campo San Stefano on Calle de Frutariol, San Marco 2900, tel. 041-520-0882, fax 041-277-8395, www .locandaarte.com, info@locandaarte.com, Alberto SE).

$ **Locanda Art Déco** is a charming place run by accommodating and equally charming Judith. While the art deco theme is pretty scant, a wrought-iron staircase leads from her inviting lobby to seven thoughtfully decorated rooms. Confirm that your booking is for this hotel (Db-€100–160, min 3 nights on weekends, 10 percent discount with this book and cash, 2 family rooms, air-con, just north of the Accademia Bridge off Campo Santo Stefano at 2966 Calle delle Botteghe, tel. 041-277-0558, fax 041-270-2891, www.locandaartdeco.com, info@locandaartdeco.com).

$ **Fondazione Levi**, a dorm run by a foundation that promotes research on Venetian music, offers 21 quiet, institutional yet comfortable and spacious rooms (Sb-€65, Db-€108, Tb-€124, Qb-€145, twin beds only, elevator; 80 yards from base of Accademia Bridge on St. Mark's side—from Accademia vaporetto stop, cross Accademia Bridge, take immediate left—, cross the bridge Ponte Giustinian, go down Calle Giustinian directly to the Fondazione, buzz the "Foresteria" door to the right, San Vidal 2893; tel. 041-786-711, fax 041-786-766, foresterialevi@libero.it, SE).

Near the Train Station
$$ **Hotel San Geremia**, a three-minute walk from the station, offers 20 clean and simple rooms at decent prices near a self-service laundry, Internet café, and the Ferrovia vaporetto stop. Head left outside the station and follow Lista di Spagna to Campo San Geremia #290/A (small Db-€75, Db-€110–145, the higher price is for weekends, tel. 041-716-245, fax 041-524-2342, sangeremia@yahoo.it, Claudio SE).

Cheap Dormitory Accommodations
$ **Foresteria della Chiesa Valdese**, warmly run by the Methodist church, offers 33 beds in dorms and doubles, halfway between St. Mark's Square and the Rialto Bridge. This run-down but charming old place has elegant ceiling paintings (dorm bed-€22, D-€56, Db-€74, family apartment-€155 for 5, must check in and out when office is open: 9:00–13:00 & 18:00–20:00, from Campo Santa Maria Formosa, walk past Bar all' Orologio to end of Calle Lunga and cross bridge, Castello 5170, reservation by phone only, tel. & fax 041-528-6797, fax 041-241-6238, foresteriavenezia@diaconiavaldese.org).

$ Venice's **youth hostel** on Giudecca Island is crowded and inexpensive (€16 beds with sheets and breakfast in 10- to 16-bed rooms, membership required, office open daily 7:00–9:30 & 13:30–23:00, catch vaporetto #82 from station to Zittele, tel. 041-523-8211). The budget cafeteria welcomes non-hostelers (nightly 17:00–23:30).

EATING

While touristy restaurants are the scourge of Venice, and most restaurateurs believe you can't survive in Venice without catering to tourists, there are plenty of places that are still popular with locals and respect the tourists who happen in. First trick: Walk away from triple-language menus. Second trick: Order the daily special. Third trick: Most seafood dishes are the local catch-of-the-day.

For romantic—and usually pricey—meals along the water, see "Eating with a Romantic Canalside Setting," below. For dessert, it's gelato (see end of this chapter).

Between Campo Santi Apostoli and Campo S.S. Giovanni e Paolo

For locations, see map on page 850.

Trattoria da Bepi is a classy family-run place where mama scours the market for just the best ingredients and son, Loris, takes good care of the hungry clientele (€30 meals; Fri–Wed 19:00–22:00, closed Thu; near Rialto, half a block north of Campo Santi Apostoli on Calle Pistor; tel. 041-528-5031).

Antiche Cantine Ardenghi de Lucia e Michael is a leap of local faith and an excellent splurge. Effervescent Michael and his wife, Lucia, proudly cook Venetian for a handful of people each night by reservation only. You must call first. You pay €50 per person and trust them to wine, dine, and serenade you with Venetian class. (The €50 price—promised for 2004—includes absolutely everything...including a "reasonable" amount of wine.) The evening can be quiet or raucous depending on who and how many are eating. While Michael's menu is very heavy on crustaceans, he promises to complement the seafood with plenty of veggies and fruit as well (but *only* if you request this—be forceful with your needs—when you reserve). Find #6369. There's no sign, the door's locked, and the place looks closed. But knock, say the password *(La Repubblica Serenissima),* and you'll be admitted. From Campo S.S. Giovanni e Paolo, pass the church-like hospital (notice the illusions painted on its facade), go over the bridge to the left, and take the first right on Calle della Testa to #6369 (you must reserve the day before, Tue–Sat 20:00–24:00, closed Sun–Mon, tel. 041-523-7691, mobile 389-523-7691).

The following colorful *osterias* are good for *cicchetti* (munchies), wine-tasting, or a simple, rustic, sit-down meal surrounded by a boisterous local ambience:

Osteria da Alberto serves *cicchetti* (18:15–19:30) and great €20 dinners (Mon–Sat 19:30–23:00, closed Sun; midway between Campo Santi Apostoli and Campo S.S. Giovanni e Paolo, next to Ponte de la Panada on Calle Larga Giacinto Gallina; tel. 041-523-8153).

Osteria ai Promessi Sposi does *cicchetti* with gusto—the best selection I found—and offers a little garden for sit-down meals. The ambience is Venetian shipwreck (Thu–Tue 9:00–23:00, closed Wed, a block off Campo S.S. Apostoli and a block inland from Strada Nova at Calle dell' Oca, tel. 041-522-8609).

Osteria al Bomba is run attentively by Sr. Filippi and his two sons. Ask for the menu and stand or sit at the very long table. The place is less ye olde and has a fun list of Bollicine—the local champagne (Tue–Sun from 18:00, closed Mon, near Campo SS Apostoli a block off the Strada

Venice Restaurants

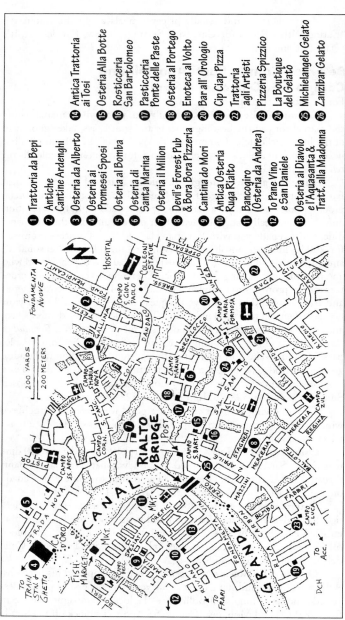

1. Trattoria da Bepi
2. Antiche Cantine Ardenghi
3. Osteria da Alberto
4. Osteria ai Promessi Sposi
5. Osteria al Bomba
6. Osteria di Santa Marina
7. Osteria il Milion
8. Devil's Forest Pub & Bora Bora Pizzeria
9. Cantina do Mori
10. Antica Osteria Ruga Rialto
11. Bancogiro (Osteria da Andrea)
12. To Pane Vino e San Daniele
13. Osteria al Diavolo e l'Aquasanta & Tratt. alla Madonna
14. Antica Trattoria ai Tosi
15. Osteria Alla Botte
16. Rosticceria San Bartolomeo
17. Pasticceria Ponte delle Paste
18. Osteria al Portego
19. Enoteca al Volto
20. Bar all' Orologio
21. Cip Ciap Pizza
22. Trattoria agli Artisti
23. Pizzeria Spizzico
24. La Boutique del Gelato
25. Michielangelo Gelato
26. Zanzibar Gelato

Nuova on Calle Oca, tel. 041-520-5175). You'll find more pubs nearby, in the side streets opposite Campo St. Sofia across Strada Nova.

East of the Rialto Bridge, near Campo San Bartolomeo

Osteria di Santa Marina is a dressy new place rapidly gaining fame for its mission to reinvent traditional dishes with a creative twist. They serve only the finest seasonal produce (fun-if-pricey menu with €14 pastas and €20 *secondi*, Mon–Sat 12:30–14:30 & 19:30–23:00, closed Sun, eat indoors or outdoors on pleasant little square, midway between Rialto and Campo Santa Maria Formosa on Campo Marina, tel. 041-528-5239).

Osteria il Milion, with bow-tied waiters and dressy candle-lit tables indoors and out, is quietly situated next to Marco Polo's home. It serves traditional Italian meals for around €25 (Thu–Tue 12:00–15:00 & 18:30–23:00, closed Wed; near Rialto, head north from Campo San Bartolomeo, over one bridge, take first right off San Giovanni Grisostomo, at #5841; tel. 041-522-9302).

The **Devil's Forest Pub**, an air-conditioned bit of England tucked away a block from the crowds, is—strangely—more Venetian these days than the *tipico* places. Locals come here for good English and Irish beer on tap, big salads (€7.50, lunch only), hot bar snacks, and an easygoing ambience (daily 8:00–24:00, meals 12:00–15:30, bar snacks all the time, closed Sun in Aug, no cover or service charge, fine prices, backgammon and chess boards available-€2.50, a block off Campo San Bartolomeo on Calle dei Stagneri, tel. 041-520-0623). Across the street, **Bora Bora Pizzeria** serves pizza and salads from an entertaining menu (Thu–Tue 12:00–15:00 & 19:15–22:30, closed Wed, tel. 041-523-6583).

The Stand-Up Progressive Venetian Pub-Crawl Dinner

My favorite Venetian dinner is a pub crawl. A *giro di ombra* (pub crawl) is a tradition unique to Venice—ideal in a city with no cars. (*Ombra*—slang for a glass of wine—means shade, from the old days when a portable wine bar scooted with the shadow of the Campanile bell tower across St. Mark's Square.)

Venice's residential back streets hide plenty of characteristic bars (*baccaros*) with countless trays of interesting toothpick munchies *(cicchetti)* and blackboards listing which wines are uncorked and served by the glass. This is a great way to mingle and have fun with the Venetians.

Cicchetti **bars** have a social stand-up zone and a cozy gaggle of tables where you can generally sit down with your *cicchetti* or order from a simple menu. Food generally costs the same price whether you stand or sit.

I've listed plenty of pubs in walking order for a quick or extended crawl below. If you've crawled enough, most of these bars make a fine one-stop, sit-down dinner.

Try fried mozzarella cheese, gorgonzola, calamari, artichoke hearts, and anything ugly on a toothpick. Meat and fish *(pesce;* PESH-shay) munchies can be expensive; veggies *(verdure)* are cheap, around €3 for a meal-sized plate. In many places, there's a set price per food item (e.g., €1.50). To get a plate of assorted appetizers for €8 (or more, depending on how hungry you are), ask for: *"Un piatto classico di cicchetti misti da* €8" (oon pee-AH-toh KLAH-see-koh dee cheh-KET-tee MEE-stee da OH-toh ay-OO-roh). Bread sticks *(grissini)* are free for the asking.

Drink the house wines. A small glass of house red or white wine *(ombra rosso* or *ombra bianco)* or a small beer *(birrino)* costs about €1. The house keg wine is cheap—€1 per glass, around €4 per liter. *Vin bon,* Venetian for fine wine, may run you from €1.50 to €6 per little glass. *Corposo* means full-bodied. A good last drink is *fragolino,* the local sweet wine—*bianco* or *rosso.* It often comes with a little cookie *(biscotti)* for dipping.

Bars don't stay open very late, and the *cicchetti* selection is best early, so start your evening by 18:00. Most bars are closed on Sunday.

Cicchetterie and Light Meals West of the Rialto Bridge

Cantina do Mori is famous with locals (since 1462) and savvy travelers (since 1982) as a classy place for fine wine and *francobollo* (a spicy selection of 20 tiny mayo-soaked sandwiches nick-named "stamps"). Choose from the featured wines. Order carefully or they'll rip you off. From Rialto Bridge, walk 200 yards down Ruga degli Orefici away from St. Mark's Square—then ask a local for directions (Mon–Sat 17:00–20:30, closed Sun, arrive early before the *cicchetti* are gone, stand-up only, San Polo 429, tel. 041-522-5401).

Antica Osteria Ruga Rialto, "the Ruga," is a local fixture where Marco serves great bar snacks and wine to his devoted clientele (daily 11:00–14:30 & 19:00–24:00, easy to find, just past Chinese Restaurant on Ruga Vecchia S Giovanni).

Bancogiro (Osteria da Andrea), a simple bar behind the Rialto market, has stark yet powerfully atmospheric outdoor seating overlooking the Grand Canal. Peruse their wine list and basic menu at the bar (strong local cheeses are a forte), order, and grab a table—worth the reasonable cover charge (Tue–Sat 10:30–15:00 & 18:30–22:00, closed Sun—Mon; less than 200 yards from Rialto Bridge on Campo San Giacometto, San Polo 122; tel. 041-523-2061).

Pane Vino e San Daniele means bread, wine and the very best ham. While its tables are rustic, the jazz and decor give the bar a trendy feel. They offer free little bruschetti, a rich cheese plate, refreshing and substantial *spritzes,* fine trios of explosive little ham sandwiches, a helpful menu and a blackboard of great wine by the glass (Tue–Sun 10:30–16:00 & 18:00–24:00, closed Mon, from Rialto it's a quarter of the way to the train station on Calle dei Boteri 1544—worth the walk, mobile 380-410-8446).

Osteria al Diavolo e l'Aquasanta, three blocks west of the Rialto, serves good—if pricey—pasta and makes a handy lunch stop for sight-seers (Mon 12:00–15:00, Wed–Sun 12:00–15:00 & 19:00–23:00, closed Tue; hiding on a quiet street just off Rua Vecchia S. Giovanni, on Calle della Madonna; tel. 041-277-0307). While they list *cicchetti* and wine by the glass on the wall, I'd come here for a light meal rather than tapas.

Trattoria alla Madonna, also on Calle della Madonna, serves Venetian fare informally at lunch—on long tables—and formally at din-ner, with private tables and a more varied menu (tel. 041-522-3824).

Antica Trattoria ai Tosi, a small, classy place near the Rialto fish market, offers simple €15, two-course *menus* for *turisticos*—the seafood one is great. Add wine/water and you'll get out for about €20–25 per per-son. With its pleasant stay-awhile atmosphere, it's good for a quiet, romantic dinner (closed Mon, near Sora al Ponte, Rialto San Polo 1586, tel. 041-524-1086).

Cicchetterie and Light Meals East of the Rialto Bridge, near Campo San Bartolomeo

Osteria "Alla Botte" Cicchetteria is an atmospheric place packed with a young, local, bohemian-jazz clientele. It's good for a *cicchetti* snack with wine at the bar (see the posted, enticing selection of wines by the glass) or for a light meal in the small back room (Fri–Tue 10:00–15:00 & 18:00–23:00, closed Thu and Sun, 2 short blocks off Campo San Bartolomeo in the corner behind the statue—down Calle de la Bissa, notice the "day after" photo showing a debris-covered Venice after the notorious 1989 Pink Floyd open-air concert, tel. 041-520-9775).

If the statue on the Campo San Bartolomeo walked backward 20 yards, turned left, and went under a passageway, he'd hit **Rosticceria San Bartolomeo**. This cheap—if confusing—self-service restaurant has a likeably surly staff (good €6–7 pasta, great fried *mozzarella al prosciutto* for €1.40, delightful fruit salad, and €2 glasses of wine, prices listed on wall behind counter, no cover or service charge, daily 9:30–21:30, tel. 041-522-3569). Take out, grab a table, or munch at the bar.

From Rosticceria San Bartolomeo, continue over a bridge to Campo San Lio. Here, turn left, passing Hotel Canada and following Calle Carminati straight about 50 yards over another bridge. On the right is the pastry shop *(pasticceria)* and straight ahead is Osteria Al Portego (at #6015). Both are listed below:

Pasticceria Ponte delle Paste is a feminine and pastel *salon de tè*, popular for its pastries and aperitifs. Italians love taking 15-minute breaks to sip a *spritz* aperitif with friends after a long day's work, before head-ing home. Ask sprightly Monica for a *spritz al bitter* (white wine, *amaro*, and soda water, €1.50; or choose from the menu on the wall) and munch some of the free goodies at the bar around 18:00 (daily 7:00–20:30, Ponte delle Paste).

Osteria al Portego is a friendly, local-style bar serving great *cicchetti* and good meals (Mon–Fri 9:00–22:00, closed Sat–Sun, tel. 041-522-9038). The *cicchetti* here can make a great meal, but you should also consider sitting down for an actual dinner. They have a fine menu.

Enoteca al Volto offers a vast assortment of Italian wines by the glass and comes with a commitment to good *cicchetti* (the best selection of munchies is 17:00–20:00, closed Sun; from Rialto vaporetto stop walk along the canal away from the bridge, take last left before road ends, on Calle Cavalli; tel. 041-522-8945, Andrea).

On or near Campo Santa Maria di Formosa

Campo Santa Maria Formosa is just plain atmospheric (as most squares with a Socialist Party office seem to be). For a balmy outdoor meal, have a pizza with wine on the square. **Bar all' Orologio** has a good setting and friendly service but mediocre "freezer" pizza (they're happy to let you split a pizza, Mon–Sat 6:00–23:00, closed Sun and in winter at 18:00). To have a great pizza picnic on the square, cross the bridge behind the canalside *gelateria* and grab a slice to go from **Cip Ciap Pizza** (Wed–Mon 9:00–21:00, closed Tue; facing *gelateria*, take bridge to the right, Calle del Mondo Novo).

Trattoria agli Artisti is efficient and friendly, with good food, especially the spaghetti *frutti di mare* (dinner from 18:00, closed Wed, half block off square down Ruga Giuffa, tel. 041-277-0029).

Pub-crawlers get a salad course at the fruit-and-vegetable stand next to the water fountain (Mon–Sat, closes about 19:30 and on Sun). The **Zanzibar** *gelateria* on the canal at Campo Santa Maria Formosa seems to wish the tourists would go away...but is very well-situated (open 8:00–24:00).

In Dorsoduro, Near the Accademia Bridge

Restaurant/Pizzeria Accademia Foscarini, next to the Accademia Bridge and Galleria, offers decent €7–8 pizzas in a great canalside setting (Wed–Mon 7:00–22:00 in summer, until 21:00 in winter, closed Tue, Dorsoduro 878C, tel. 041-522-7281).

Enoteca Cantine del Vino Gia Schiavi—much loved for its *cicchetti*—is a good place for a glass of wine and appetizers (Mon–Sat 8:00–14:30 & 15:30–20:00, closed Sun; 100 yards from Accademia Gallery on San Trovaso canal—facing Accademia, take a right and then a forced left at canal to the second bridge—S. Trovaso 992; tel. 041-523-0034). You're welcome to enjoy your wine and finger-food while sitting on the bridge.

Ai Gondolieri is considered one of the best restaurants for meat—not fish—in Venice. Its sauces are heavy and prices are high, but carnivores love it (Wed–Mon 12:00–13:00 & 19:00–22:00, closed Tue and for lunch July–Aug, reservations smart, Dorsoduro 366 San Vio, behind

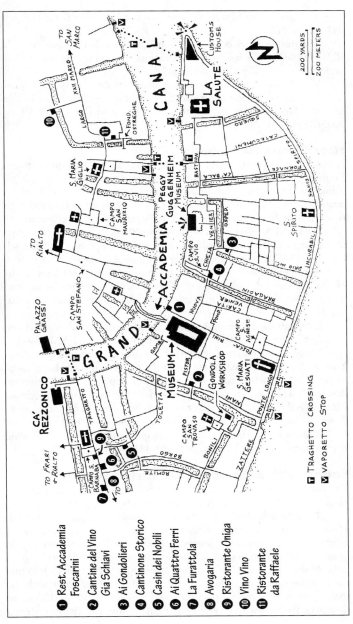

Restaurants near the Accademia Bridge

1. Rest. Accademia Foscarini
2. Cantine del Vino Gia Schiavi
3. Ai Gondolieri
4. Cantinone Storico
5. Casin dei Nobili
6. Ai Quattro Ferri
7. La Furattola
8. Avogaria
9. Ristorante Oniga
10. Vino Vino
11. Ristorante da Raffaele

Peggy Guggenheim Museum on west end of Rio delle Torreselle, tel. 041-528-6396).

Cantinone Storico, also in this neighborhood, and Ristorante da Raffaele (on St. Mark's side of Accademia Bridge) is described below under "Romantic Canalside Settings."

Vino Vino is a small, simple place that seats about 25 (pasta-€5, *secondi*-€9–125, open long hours, closed Tue; between Accademia Bridge and St. Mark's Square, just south of La Fenice on Ponte delle Veste, 2007/A; tel. 041-241-7688).

Near Campo San Barnaba

A number of less-touristed restaurants cluster around this small square. From the Accademia, head northwest, following the curve of the Grand Canal. In five minutes, you'll spill out onto Campo San Barnaba (and the nearby Campo Santa Margherita). Follow the straight and narrow path (Calle Lunga di San Barnaba) west of the square for more restaurants.

Casin dei Nobili has a diverse, reasonably-priced menu in an informal setting (closed Mon, a half-block south of Campo San Barnaba, tel. 041-241-1841). The name means pleasure-palace (Casino) of the nobles.

Ai Quattro Ferri is a trattoria-style noisy, bustling place for catch-of-the-day seafood, with excellent grilled fish, but very few non-seafood items (closed Sun, just off the square on Calle Lunga di San Barnaba, tel. 041-520-6978).

La Furattola is more upscale, with an extensive seafood menu (closed Thu, farther west on Calle Lunga di San Barnaba, tel. 041-520-8594).

Avogaria is a hip, modern, goateed-waiter wine bar and restaurant. You can have a full meal, or just sit at the tiny bar and drink a glass of Soave Classico while you build a meal of appetizers and delicious desserts. The small outside terrace was made for warm evenings (closed Mon; several hundred yards west of Campo San Barnaba on Calle Lunga San Barnaba, near San Sebastian church; tel. 041-296-0491).

Ristorante Oniga, right on Campo San Barnaba, is a wine bar/restaurant (closed Tue, tel. 041-522-4410).

Eating with a Romantic Canalside Setting

Of course, if you want a canal view, it comes with lower quality or a higher price. But the memory is sometimes most important.

Ristorante da Raffaele is *the* place for classy food on a quiet canal. It's filled with top-end tourists sent by the fancy hotels. The place was a haunt of the avant-garde a few generations ago. Today it's on a main gondolier thoroughfare—in fact, many guests arrive or depart by gondola. Make a reservation if you want a canalside table (you do). While the multilingual menu is designed for the tourists, locals stick with the daily specials (expensive—plan on €60, Fri–Wed 18:30–22:30, closed Thu, exactly halfway between Piazza San Marco and the Accademia

Bridge at Ponte delle Ostreghe, tel. 041-523-2317). Before leaving, wander around inside to see the owner's intriguing old weapons collection.

Ristorante Cantinone Storico sits on a peaceful canal in Dorsoduro between the Accademia Bridge and the Peggy Guggenheim Museum. It's dressy, specializes in fish, has six or eight tables on the canal, and is worth the splurge (Mon–Sat 12:30–14:30 & 19:30–21:30, closed Sun, reservations wise, on the canal Rio de S. Vio, tel. 041-523-9577).

Rialto Bridge Tourist Traps: Locals are embarrassed by the lousy food and aggressive "service" of the string of joints dominating the best romantic Grand Canal real estate in town. Still, if you want to linger over dinner with a view of the most famous bridge and the romantic song of gondoliers oaring by (and don't mind eating with other tourists), this can be enjoyable. Don't trust the waiter's recommendations for special meals. Just get a simple pizza or pasta and a drink, and you'll savor the ambience without being ripped off.

Near St. Mark's Square
For the location of these restaurants, see the map on page 825.

Osteria da Carla, two blocks west of St. Mark's Square, is a fun and very local hole-in-the-wall where the food is good and the price is right (€8–12 dishes). They have hearty tuna salads and a daily pasta special along with traditional antipasti, polenta, and decent wine by the glass (see blackboard). Seafood-lovers might try their "triple fish and polenta" plate (sardine, squid and cod, €10). While you can eat outside, table #3 comes with a flushing soundtrack (Mon–Sat 8:00–22:00, closed Sun; from American Express head toward St. Mark's Square, first left down Frezzeria, first left again through "Contarina" tunnel, at Sotoportego e Corte Contarina, sign over door says "Pietro Panizzolo"—it's historic and can't be removed; tel. 041-523-7855, Michela SE).

Osteria Enoteca San Marco offers beautifully-presented "creative new Italian" cuisine with a mod ambience in a classic medieval shell. They proudly offer fine wine by the glass (€20 meals, Mon–Sat 12:30–3:00 & 19:30–23:00, closed Sun, a long block west of St. Mark's Square at #1610 Frezzeria, tel. 041-528-5242, Carlo and his hard-working staff SE).

Near the Train Station
For fast, cheap food near the station, consider **Brek**, a popular self-service cafeteria (after serving breakfast, it's open 11:30–22:00; with back to station, facing canal, go left on Rio Terra—it becomes Lista di Spagna in 2 short blocks, Lista di Spagna 124; tel. 041-244-0158).

Eating Elsewhere
Ristorante Aqua Pazza (literally, "crazy water") provides good pizza in a wonderful setting on Campo San Angelo (check out the leaning tower

over your shoulder) midway between the Rialto, Accademia, and St. Mark's. The owner is from Naples and he delights locals with Amalfi/Naples cuisine. That means perhaps the best—and most expensive—pizza in Venice (Tue–Sun 12:00–15:00 & 19:00–23:00, closed Mon, Campo S. Angelo 3809, tel. 041-277-0688).

Osteria al Bacco, far beyond the crowds in a rustic Venetian setting, is worth the hike for its local cuisine (€35 for 3 courses and wine; Tue–Sun 19:00–22:00, closed Mon; reservations recommended; halfway between train station and northernmost tip of Venice, Fondamenta Cappuccine, Cannaregio 3054; tel. 041-717-493).

Osteria la Zucca is a hardworking, homey place on the Rio del Megio canal away from the crowds. You'll get good, typical Venetian cuisine at a moderate price (€20 meals, Mon–Sat 12:30–14:30 & 19:00–22:30, closed Sun; mostly indoors, reserve for canal windows, a few outdoor tables with one on the canal; midway between train station and Rialto Bridge at San Giacomo dell'Orio, Calle Larga, Santa Croce 1762; tel. 041-524-1570). A short block away is the square called San Giacomo dell'Orio—a breezy scene with trees, families at play, and a couple of simple trattorias offering basic food and classic non-touristy outdoor seating.

Cheap Meals

A key to cheap eating in Venice is **bar snacks,** especially stand-up mini-meals in out-of-the-way bars. Order by pointing. *Panini* (sandwiches) are sold fast and cheap at bars everywhere. Basic reliable ham-and-cheese sandwiches (white bread, crusts trimmed) come toasted—simply ask for "toast"; these make a great supplement to Venice's skimpy hotel breakfasts.

For budget eating, I like small *cicchetti* **bars** (see "Pub-Crawl Dinner," above); for speed, value, and ambience, you can get a filling plate of local appetizers at nearly any of the bars.

Pizzerias are cheap and easy—try for a sidewalk table at a scenic location. If you want a fast-food pizza place, try **Spizzico** on Campo San Luca (roughly between St. Mark's Square and the Rialto Bridge).

The **produce market** that sprawls for a few blocks just past the Rialto Bridge is a great place to assemble a picnic (best 8:00–13:00, closed Sun). The adjacent fish market is wonderfully slimy. Side lanes in this area are speckled with fine little hole-in-the-wall munchie bars, bakeries, and cheese shops.

Gelato

La Boutique del Gelato is considered the best *gelateria* in Venice (daily 10:00–20:30, closed Dec–Jan; 2 blocks off Campo Santa Maria di Formosa on corner of Salizada San Lio and Calle Paradiso, next to Hotel Bruno, #5727—just look for the crowd).

Late-night Gelato: At the Rialto, try **Michielangelo**, just off Campo San Bartolomeo, on the St. Mark's side of the Rialto Bridge on Salizada Pio X (Thu–Tue 10:00–22:00, closed Wed). At St. Mark's Square, the **Al Todaro** *gelateria* opposite the Doge's Palace is open late (daily 8:00–22:00, closes at 20:00 and on Mon in winter).

TRANSPORTATION CONNECTIONS

By train to: Padua (hrly, 30 min), **Vicenza** (hrly, 1 hr), **Verona** (hrly, 90 min), **Ravenna** (hrly, 3–4 hrs, transfer in Ferrara or Bologna), **Florence** (7/day, 3 hrs), **Dolomites** (8/day to Bolzano, about hourly, 4 hrs with 1 transfer; catch bus from Bolzano into mountains), **Milan** (1/hr, 3–4 hrs), **Monterosso/La Spezia/Cinque Terre** (2/day, 6 hrs, departs Venice at 10:00 and 15:00), **Rome** (7/day, 5 hrs, slower overnight), **Naples** (change in Rome, plus 2–3 hrs), **Brindisi** (3/day, 11 hrs, change in Bologna), **Bern** (3/day, change in Milan, 8 hrs), **Munich** (2/day, 8 hrs), **Paris** (4/day, 11 hrs), and **Vienna** (4/day, 9 hrs). Train and *couchette* reservations (about €18) are easily made at a downtown travel agency.

FLORENCE

(Firenze)

Florence, the home of the Renaissance and birthplace of our modern world, is a "supermarket sweep," and the groceries are the best Renaissance art in Europe.

Get your bearings with a Renaissance walk. Florentine art goes beyond paintings and statues—there's food, fashion, and handicrafts. You can lick Italy's best gelato while enjoying some of Europe's best people-watching.

Planning Your Time

If you're in Europe for three weeks, Florence deserves a well-organized day. Make reservations in advance for the Uffizi Gallery (best Italian paintings anywhere) and Accademia (Michelangelo's *David*). For a day in Florence, see the Accademia, tour the Uffizi Gallery, visit the underrated Bargello (best statues), and do the Renaissance ramble (explained below).

Art-lovers will want to chisel out another day of their itinerary for the many other Florentine cultural treasures. Shoppers and ice cream-lovers may need to do the same.

Plan your sightseeing carefully. Some sights close Mondays and afternoons. While many spend several hours a day in lines, thoughtful travelers avoid this by making reservations or going late in the day. Places open at night are virtually empty.

Connoisseurs of smaller towns should consider taking the bus to Siena for a day or evening trip (75-min one-way, confirm when last bus returns). Siena is magic after dark. For more information, see the Siena chapter.

ORIENTATION

The Florence that we're interested in lies mostly on the north bank of the Arno River. The main historical sights cluster around the red-brick dome of the cathedral (Duomo). Everything is within a 20-minute walk of the train station, cathedral, or Ponte Vecchio (Old Bridge). The less impressive but more characteristic Oltrarno (south bank) area is just over the bridge. Though small, Florence is intense. Prepare for scorching summer heat, kamikaze Vespa moterscooters, slick pickpockets, few WCs, and erratic museum hours.

Tourist Information

There are three TIs in Florence: across from the train station, near Santa Croce Church, and on Via Cavour.

The TI across the square from the train station is most crowded—expect long lines (Mon–Sat 8:30–19:00, Sun 8:30–14:00; with your back to tracks, exit the station—it's across the square in wall near corner of church, Piazza Stazione; tel. 055-212-245). Note: In the train station, avoid the Hotel Reservations "Tourist Information" window (marked *Informazioni Turistiche Alberghiere*) near the McDonald's; it's not a real TI but a hotel reservation business.

The TI near Santa Croce Church is pleasant, helpful, and uncrowded (Mon–Sat 9:00–19:00, Sun 9:00–14:00, shorter hours off-season, Borgo Santa Croce 29 red, tel. 055-234-0444).

Another winner is the TI three blocks north of the Duomo (Mon–Sat 8:15–19:15, Sun 8:30–13:30, closed Sun in winter, Via Cavour 1 red, tel. 055-290-832 or 055-290-833, international bookstore across street).

At any TI, pick up a map, a current museum-hours listing (extremely important, since no guidebook—including this one—has ever been able to accurately predict the hours of Florence's sights), and any information on entertainment. The free monthly *Florence Concierge Information* magazine lists museums, plus lots that I don't: concerts and events, markets, sporting events, church services, shopping ideas, bus and train connections, and an entire similar section on Siena. Get yours at the TI or from any expensive hotel (pick one up, as if you're staying there).

Arrival in Florence

By Train: The station soaks up time and generates dazed and sweaty crowds. If you arrive by train, there's no need to linger at the station. Extremely user-friendly, coin-operated gray-and-yellow machines can display schedules, issue tickets, and even make reservations for railpass holders. Otherwise, get onward tickets and train information at travel agencies away from the congested station (e.g., American Express, listed in "Helpful Hints," below). The fake "Tourist Information" office in the station (next to McDonald's) is actually a room-booking service funded by the hotels. The real TI is across the square from the station (see above).

FLORENCE AT A GLANCE

▲▲▲**Uffizi Gallery** Greatest collection of Italian paintings anywhere—reserve ahead. **Hours:** Tue–Sun 8:15–18:50, 8:15–22:00 on holidays and maybe on summer Sat, closed Mon.

▲▲▲**Accademia** Michelangelo's *David* and powerful (unfinished) *Prisoners*—reserve ahead. **Hours:** Tue–Sun 8:15–18:50, 8:15–22:00 on holidays and maybe on summer Sat, closed Mon.

▲▲▲**Bargello** Underappreciated sculpture museum (Michelangelo, Donatello, Medici treasures). **Hours:** Daily 8:15–13:50; closed first, third, and fifth Sun and second and fourth Mon of each month.

▲▲**Museum of San Marco** Best collection anywhere of frescoes and paintings by the early Renaissance master Fra Angelico. **Hours:** Weekdays 8:15–13:50, Sat–Sun 8:15–19:00; closed first, third, and fifth Sun and second and fourth Mon of each month.

▲▲**Medici Chapels** Tombs of Florence's great ruling family, designed and carved by Michelangelo. **Hours:** Daily 8:15–17:00; closed the second and fourth Sun and the first, third, and fifth Mon of each month.

▲▲**Church of Santa Maria Novella** 13th-century Dominican church with Masaccio's famous 3-D painting. **Hours:** Mon–Thu and Sat 9:30–17:00, Fri and Sun 13:00–17:00.

▲▲**Santa Croce Church** 14th-century Franciscan church with precious art, tombs of famous Florentines, and Brunelleschi's Pazzi Chapel. **Hours:** Mon–Sat 9:30–17:30, Sun 15:00–17:30; off-season Mon–Sat 9:30–12:30 & 15:00–17:30, Sun 15:00–17:30.

▲▲**Science Museum** Fascinating collection of old clocks, telescopes, maps, and Galileo's finger. **Hours:** Mon and Wed–Fri 9:30–17:00, Tue and Sat 9:30–13:00, closed Sun.

▲▲**Pitti Palace** Three museums in lavish palace: Palatine Gallery (Raphael art), Modern Art Gallery, Grand Ducal Treasures (Medici treasure chest), plus sprawling Boboli Gardens. **Hours:** Palatine: Tue–Sun 8:15–18:50, closed Mon; Modern Art and Treasures: daily 8:15–13:50; closed second and fourth Sun and first, third, and fifth Mon; Boboli: daily 9:00–18:30, 9:00–19:30 June–Aug, 9:00–16:30 in winter, closed first and last Mon of month.

▲▲**Brancacci Chapel** Works of Masaccio, early Renaissance master who re-invented perspective. **Hours:** Mon and Wed–Sat 10:00–17:00, Sun 13:00–17:00, closed Tue.

▲▲**Duomo Gothic** Cathedral with colorful facade, long nave, and the first dome built since ancient Roman times. **Hours:** Mon–Wed and Fri–Sat 10:00–17:00 except first Sat of month 10:00–15:30, Thu 10:00–15:30, Sun 13:30–16:45.

▲▲**Duomo Museum** Underrated cathedral museum with great sculpture. **Hours:** Mon–Sat 9:00–19:30, Sun 9:00–13:40, closed on holidays.

▲**Climbing Duomo's Dome** Grand view into the cathedral, close-up of dome architecture, and, after 463 steps, a glorious Florence vista. **Hours:** Mon–Fri 8:30–19:00, Sat 8:30–17:40 except first Sat of month 8:30–16:00, closed Sun.

▲**Giotto's Tower** Bell tower with views equaling Duomo's, 50 fewer steps, and fewer lines. **Hours:** Daily 8:30–19:30.

▲**Baptistery** Bronze doors fit to be the gates of Paradise Doors always viewable; Baptistery open. **Hours:** Mon–Sat 12:00–19:00, Sun 8:30–14:00.

▲**Orsanmichele Church** Church made from walled-in loggia, with glorious tabernacle inside and niche statuary outside. **Hours:** Unreliably open 9:00–12:00 & 16:00–18:00, closed first and last Mon of month.

▲**Palazzo Vecchio** Fortified palace once the home of the Medici family, wallpapered with mediocre art. **Hours:** Fri–Wed 9:00–19:00, Thu 9:00–14:00, in summer maybe 9:00–23:00 on Mon and Fri.

▲**Ponte Vecchio** Famous bridge lined with gold and silver shops. **Hours:** Bridge always open.

▲**Mercato Nuovo** Bustling market in loggia. **Hours:** Open daily.

▲**Michelangelo's House** Museum featuring early, lesser-known works of the master. **Hours:** Wed–Mon 9:30–14:00, closed Tue.

▲**Piazzale Michelangelo** Hilltop square in south Florence offering stunning view of city and Duomo. **Hours:** Always open.

With your back to the tracks, to your left are most of my recommended hotels, a 24-hour pharmacy (*Farmacia Comunale*, near McDonald's), city buses, and the entrance to the underground mall/passage that goes across the square to the Church of Santa Maria Novella. (Note: This tunnel is frequented by pickpockets, especially the surface point near the church.) Baggage check is near track 16. The taxi stand in front of the train station often has a line. To catch a cab without the line, wander deeper into the city.

By Car: If you're taking the autostrada (north or south) to Florence, get off at the Certosa exit and follow signs to *Centro;* at Porta Romana, go to the left of the arch and down Via Francesco Petrarca. After driving and trying to park in Florence, you'll understand why Leonardo never invented the car. Cars flatten the charm of Florence. Don't drive in Florence and don't risk parking illegally (fines up to €150).

Non-residents are not allowed to park on the streets anywhere near or in the old center. The city has plenty of **parking lots.** For a short stay, park underground at the train station (€2/hr). The Fortezza da Basso is clearly marked in the center (€20/24 hrs). The least expensive lots are Parcheggio Parterre (Firenze Parcheggi, €16/24 hrs, perhaps cheaper with hotel reservation) and Parcheggio Oltrarno (near Porta Romana—pass through gate and on left, €15 per day). For parking information, ask at your hotel or call 055-500-1994.

By Plane: Florence has its own airport and Pisa's is nearby. See "Transportation Connections," near the end of this chapter, for details.

Helpful Hints

Theft Alert: Florence has particularly hardworking thief gangs. They specialize in tourists and hang out where you do: near the train station, the station's underpass (especially where the tunnel surfaces), and major sights. Also be on guard at two squares frequented by drug pushers (Santa Maria Novella and Santo Spirito). American tourists—especially older ones—are considered easy targets.

Medical Help: To track down a doctor who speaks English, call 055-475-411 (reasonable hotel calls, cheaper if you go to the clinic at Via L. Magnifico 59) or get a list of English-speaking doctors from the TI. There are 24-hour pharmacies at the train station and near the Duomo on Borgo San Lorenzo.

Addresses: Street addresses list businesses in red and residences in black or blue (color-coded on the actual street number and indicated by a letter following the number in printed addresses: r = red, no indication = black). *Pensioni* are usually black but can be either. The red and black numbers each appear in roughly consecutive order on streets but bear no apparent connection with each other. I'm lazy and don't concern myself with the distinction (if one number's wrong, I look for the other) and find my way around fine.

DAILY REMINDER

Sunday: Today the Duomo's dome, the Science Museum, and the Museum of Precious Stones are closed. These sights close early: the Duomo Museum (at 13:40) and the Baptistery's interior (at 14:00). A few sights are open only in the afternoon: Duomo (13:30–16:45), Santa Croce Church (15:00–17:30), and the Brancacci Chapel and Church of Santa Maria Novella (both 13:00–17:00).

   The Museum of San Marco, which is open on the second and fourth Sunday of the month until 19:00, closes entirely—as does the Bargello—on the first, third, and fifth Sunday. The Medici Chapels and the Modern Art Gallery (in the Pitti Palace) close on the second and fourth Sunday. (Need a calendar? Look in the appendix.)

Monday: The biggies are closed—Accademia (David) and Uffizi Gallery and the Palatine Gallery/Royal Apartments (in the Pitti Palace).

   The Medici Chapels and the Modern Art Gallery (in the Pitti Palace) close on the first, third, and fifth Monday of the month. The Museum of San Marco and the Bargello close on the second and fourth Monday. The Orsanmichele Church and Boboli Gardens close on the first and last Monday. The Palazzo Vecchio may stay open until 23:00 in summer.

   Target these sights on Mondays: Duomo Museum, Giotto's Tower, Brancacci Chapel, Michelangelo's House, Science Museum, Palazzo Vecchio, and churches. Or take a walking tour.

Tuesday: All sights are open except for Michelangelo's House and the Brancacci Chapel. The Science Museum closes early (13:00).

Wednesday: All sights are open except for the Medici Riccardi Palace.

Thursday: All sights are open. The Museum of Precious Stones stays open late (19:00) while these sights close early: Duomo (15:30) and Palazzo Vecchio (14:00).

Friday: All sights are open. The Church of Santa Maria Novella opens late (13:00–17:00) and Palazzo Vecchio closes late (maybe until 23:00 in summer).

Saturday: All sights are open, but the Science Museum closes at 13:00. These sights close early on the first Saturday of the month: Duomo (15:30) and the Duomo's dome (16:00). The Museum of San Marco stays open until 19:00. The Accademia, Uffizi, and Palatine Gallery/Royal Apartments may stay open until 22:00 in summer.

TIPS ON SIGHTSEEING IN FLORENCE

Make Reservations to Avoid Lines: Florence has a great reservation system for its top five sights—Uffizi, Accademia, Bargello, Medici Chapels, and the Pitti Palace. Two of these sights nearly always have long lines: the Accademia (Michelangelo's *David*) and the Uffizi (Renaissance paintings). To avoid long waits—up to two hours at the Uffizi on busy days—simply make a reservation by phone. Frankly, it's stupid not to.

While you can generally make a reservation a day in advance (upon arrival in Florence), you'll have a wider selection of entry times by calling a few days ahead. You dial 055-294-883 (busy signals common—be persistent, Mon–Fri 8:30–18:30, Sat 8:30–12:30, closed Sun), an English-speaking operator walks you through the process, and two minutes later you say *grazie,* with appointments (15-minute entry window) and six-digit confirmation numbers for each of the top museums and galleries. The ticket phone number is often busy. If you call months in advance (during off-season) or request your hotel to make the appointment for you (when you confirm your hotel room), you may save some frustration. Some booking agencies offer reservations online for a fee (such as www.weekendafirenze.it).

If you haven't booked ahead, you can make reservations for the top sights at the minor, less-crowded sights (such as the Museum of San Marco or Museum of Precious Stones). Clerks at the ticket booths at these sleepy sights can reserve and sell tickets to the major sights—often for admission the same day—allowing you to skip right past the dreary mob scene.

There is occasionally even a line at the Uffizi for those with reservations who are waiting to pick up tickets. If you have reservations, consider picking up your Uffizi ticket at a less-crowded sight (any ticket office can issue reserved tickets).

Hours of Sights Can Change Suddenly: Because of labor demands, hours of sights change without warning. Pick up the latest listing of museum hours at a TI, or you'll miss out on something you came to see. Don't put off seeing a must-see sight such as *David;* you never know when a place will close unexpectedly for a holiday, strike, or restoration.

More Tips: The biggies (Uffizi and Accademia) close on Monday. Several museums are closed alternating Sundays and Mondays (e.g., closed first, third, and fifth Sun and second and fourth Mon of each month); use the calendar in the appendix to figure out which day they're closed during your trip. Churches usually close from 12:30 to 15:00 or 16:00. Some museums close at 14:00 and stop selling tickets 30 minutes before that.

American Express: American Express offers all the normal services, but is most helpful as an easy place to get your train tickets, reservations, supplements (all the same price as at the station), or even just information on train schedules (Mon–Fri 9:00–17:30, Sat money exchange only 9:00–12:30, 3 short blocks north of Palazzo Vecchio on Via Dante Alighieri 22 red, tel. 055-50981).

Long-Distance Telephoning: Small newsstand kiosks sell PIN phone cards that give you cheap international rates (10 minutes/€1).

Books: Feltrinelli International, a fine bookstore that sells fiction and guidebooks in English, is a few blocks north of the Duomo and across the street from the TI on Via Cavour (Mon–Sat 9:00–19:30, closed Sun, Via Cavour 20 red, tel. 055-219-524). Edison Bookstore sells CDs and novels on the Renaissance (daily 9:00–24:00, facing Piazza della Repubblica, tel. 055-213-110). Paperback Exchange also sells fiction and guidebooks (cheaper but smaller selection; Mon–Fri 9:00–19:30, Sat 10:00–13:00 & 15:30–19:30, closed Sun, shorter hours in Aug; Via Fiesolana 31 red, at corner of Via Fiesolana and Via dei Pilastri, 6 blocks east of Duomo; tel. 055-247-8154).

Laundry: The Wash & Dry Lavarapido chain offers long hours and efficient, self-service launderettes at several locations (about €6.20 for wash and dry, daily 8:00–22:00, tel. 055-580-480). These are close to recommended hotels: Via dei Servi 105 (and a rival launderette at Via Guelfa 22 red, off Via Cavour; both near *David*), Via del Sole 29 red and Via della Scala 52 red (between train station and river), and Via dei Serragli 87 red (across the river in Oltrarno neighborhood).

Getting around Florence

I organize my sightseeing geographically and do it all on foot. A €1 ticket gives you one hour on the buses, €1.80 gives you three hours, and €4 gets you 24 hours (tickets not sold on bus—buy in *tabacchi* shops or newsstands before 21:00, validate on bus; after 21:00 buy tickets on bus, route map available at TI). Multi-day passes are also available.

The minimum cost for a taxi ride is €4, or, after 22:00, €5 (rides in the center of town should be charged as tariff #1). A taxi ride from the train station to Ponte Vecchio costs about €8. Taxi fares and supplements (e.g., €2 extra if you telephone a cab) are clearly explained on signs in each taxi.

TOURS

Walking Tours of Florence—This company offers a variety of tours (up to 4 per day Mon–Sat year-round plus summer Sundays) featuring downtown Florence, Uffizi highlights, or Tuscany (countryside, Siena, San Gimignano, Pisa, or the Cinque Terre), presented by informative,

Florence Overview

entertaining, native English–speaking guides. The "Original Florence" walk hits the main sights but gets off-beat to weave a picture of Florentine life in medieval and Renaissance times. You can expect lots of talking, which is great if you like history. Tours, offered throughout the year regardless of the weather, start at their office and are limited to a maximum of 22 but will go with as few as two participants. Extra guides are available if more people show up (€25 for 3-hr Original Florence walk; office open Mon–Sat 8:30–18:00, closed for lunch off-season; Piazza Santo Stefano 2 black, a short block north of Ponte Vecchio; go east on tiny Vicolo San Stefano, in Piazza Santo Stefano at #2, see map on page 884; booking necessary for Uffizi tour, private tours available; tel. 055-264-5033, mobile 329-613-2730, www.artviva.com). For all the schedule details, pick up their extensive brochure in your hotel lobby.

Florentia—These top-notch, historical walking tours of Florence and Tuscany are led by local scholars. The tours, ranging from introductory city walks to in-depth visits of museums and lesser-known destinations, are geared for thoughtful, well-heeled travelers with longer-than-normal attention spans (semi-private tours start at $45 per person, max 8 per group; private tours start at $180 for half-day tour, reserve in advance, tel. 055-225-535, U.S. tel. 510-549-1707, www.florentia.org, info@florentia.org).

Local Guide—**Paola Migliorini** offers museum tours, city walking tours, and Tuscan excursions by van. You (and your group) can tailor tours as you like. The van allows slow walkers to enjoy the city nearly sweat-free (€50/hr, or €65/hr with 8-seat van, Via S. Gallo 120, tel. 055-472-448, mobile 347-657-2611, www.florencetour.com, info@florencetour.com).

Note that big bus companies offer tours of Florence but for most the city is really best on foot.

A Renaissance Walk through Florence

Even during the Dark Ages, people knew they were in a "middle time." It was especially obvious to the people of Italy—sitting on the rubble of Rome—that there was a brighter age before them. The long-awaited rebirth, or Renaissance, began in Florence for good reason. Wealthy because of its cloth industry, trade, and banking; powered by a fierce city-state pride (locals would pee into the Arno with gusto, knowing rival city-state Pisa was downstream); and fertile with more than its share of artistic genius (imagine guys like Michelangelo and Leonardo attending the same high school)—Florence was a natural home for this cultural explosion.

Take a walk through the core of Renaissance Florence by starting at the Accademia (home of Michelangelo's *David*) and cutting through the heart of the city to Ponte Vecchio on the Arno River. (A 13-page, self-guided tour of this walk is outlined in my museum guidebook, *Rick Steves' Mona Winks*, and in *Rick Steves' Florence;* otherwise, you'll find brief descriptions below.)

At the Accademia, you'll look into the eyes of Renaissance man—humanism at its confident peak. Then walk to the cathedral (Duomo) to see the dome that kicked off the architectural Renaissance. Step inside the baptistery to view a ceiling covered with preachy, flat, 2-D, medieval mosaic art. Then, to learn what happened when art met math, check out the realistic 3-D reliefs on the doors. The painter, Giotto, also designed the bell tower—an early example of a Renaissance genius excelling in many areas. Continue toward the river on Florence's great pedestrian mall, Via de' Calzaiuoli (or "Via Calz")—part of the original grid plan given to the city by the ancient Romans. Down a few blocks, compare medieval and Renaissance statues on the exterior of the Orsanmichele Church. Via Calz connects the cathedral with the central square (Piazza della Signoria), the city palace (Palazzo Vecchio), and the Uffizi Gallery, which contains the greatest collection of Italian Renaissance paintings in captivity. Finally, walk through the Uffizi courtyard—a statuary think tank of Renaissance greats—to the Arno River and Ponte Vecchio.

Sights on the Renaissance Walk

▲▲▲**Accademia (Galleria dell' Accademia)**—This museum houses Michelangelo's *David* and powerful (unfinished) *Prisoners.* Eavesdrop as tour guides explain these masterpieces. More than with any other work of art, when you look into the eyes of *David,* you're looking into the eyes of Renaissance man. This was a radical break with the past. Hello, humanism. Man was now a confident individual, no longer a plaything of the supernatural. And life was now more than just a preparation for what happened after you died.

The Renaissance was the merging of art, science, and humanism. In a humanist vein, *David* is looking at the crude giant of medieval darkness and thinking, "I can take this guy." (David was an apt mascot for a town surrounded by big bully city-states.) Back on a religious track, notice *David*'s large and overdeveloped right hand. This is symbolic of the hand of God that powered David to slay the giant...and enabled Florence to rise above its crude neighboring city-states.

Beyond the magic marble are two floors of interesting pre-Renaissance and Renaissance paintings, including a couple of lighter-than-air Botticellis.

Cost, Hours, Location: €6.50 (plus €3 reservation fee), Tue–Sun 8:15–18:50, until 22:00 on holidays and maybe on summer Sat, closed Mon (last entry 45 min before closing, Via Ricasoli 60, tel. 055-238-8609). No photos or videos are allowed. The museum is most crowded on Sun, Tue, and the first thing in the morning. It's easy to reserve ahead; see page 866 for details.

Nearby: Piazza Santissima Annunziata, behind the Accademia, displays lovely Renaissance harmony. Facing the square are two fine buildings: the 15th-century Santissima Annunziata church (worth a peek) and Brunelleschi's Hospital of the Innocents (*Spedale degli Innocenti,* not worth going inside), with terra-cotta medallions by Luca della Robbia. Built in the 1420s, the hospital is considered the first Renaissance building.

▲▲**Duomo**—Florence's Gothic Santa Maria del Fiori cathedral has the third-longest nave in Christendom (free, Mon–Wed and Fri–Sat 10:00–17:00 except first Sat of month 10:00–15:30, Thu 10:00–15:30, Sun 13:30–16:45, modest dress code enforced, tel. 055-230-2885). Note: The massive crowds that overwhelm the entrance in the morning clear out by afternoon.

The church's noisy neo-Gothic facade from the 1870s is covered with pink, green, and white Tuscan marble. Since nearly all of its great art is stored in the Museo dell' Opera del Duomo (behind the church), the best thing about the interior is the shade. The inside of the dome is decorated by one of the largest paintings of the Renaissance, a huge (and newly restored) *Last Judgment* by Vasari and Zucarri.

Think of the confidence of the age: The Duomo was built with a hole awaiting a dome in its roof. This was before the technology to span it with a dome was available. No matter. They knew that someone soon could handle the challenge...and the local architect Brunelleschi did. The cathedral's claim to artistic fame is Brunelleschi's magnificent dome— the first Renaissance dome and the model for domes to follow.

▲**Climbing the Cathedral's Dome**—For a grand view into the cathedral from the base of the dome, a peek at some of the tools used in the dome's construction, a chance to see Brunelleschi's "dome-within-a-dome" construction, a glorious Florence view from the top, and the equivalent of 463 plunges on a Stairmaster, climb the dome. To avoid

Florence Sights

the long, dreadfully slow-moving line, arrive by 8:30 (€6, Mon–Fri 8:30–19:00, Sat 8:30–17:40 except first Sat of month 8:30–16:00, closed Sun, enter from outside church on south/river side, tel. 055-230-2885). When planning St. Peter's in Rome, Michelangelo rhymed (not in English), "I can build its sister—bigger, but not more beautiful, than the dome of Florence."

▲**Giotto's Tower (Campanile)**—If you're not interested in experiencing dome-within-a-dome architecture, you'll likely feel that climbing Giotto's 270-foot bell tower beats scaling the neighboring Duomo's dome because it's 50 fewer steps, faster, and offers the same view plus the dome (€6, daily 8:30–19:30, last entry 40 min before closing).

▲▲**Duomo Museum (Museo dell' Opera del Duomo)**—The underrated cathedral museum, behind the church at #9, is great if you like sculpture. It has masterpieces by Donatello (a gruesome wood carving of Mary Magdalene clothed in her matted hair, and the *cantoria,* a delightful choir loft bursting with happy children) and by Luca della Robbia (another choir loft, lined with the dreamy faces of musicians praising the Lord). Look for a late Michelangelo *pietà* (Nicodemus, on top, is a self-portrait), Brunelleschi's models for his dome, and the original restored panels of Ghiberti's doors to the baptistery. This is one of the few museums in Florence open on Monday (€6, Mon–Sat 9:00–19:30, Sun 9:00–13:40, closed on holidays, tel. 055-230-2885). If you find all this church art intriguing, look through the open doorway of the Duomo art studio, which has been making and restoring church art since the days of Brunelleschi (a block toward the river from the Duomo at 23a Via dello Studio).

▲**Baptistery**—Michelangelo said its bronze doors were fit to be the gates of Paradise. Check out the gleaming copies of Ghiberti's bronze doors facing the Duomo. Making a breakthrough in perspective, Ghiberti used mathematical laws to create the illusion of receding distance on a basically flat surface. The earlier, famous competition doors are around to the right (north); Ghiberti, who beat Brunelleschi, got the job of designing these doors.

Inside, sit and savor the medieval mosaic ceiling where it's Judgment Day, and Jesus is giving the ultimate thumbs up and thumbs down (€3; interior open Mon–Sat 12:00–19:00, Sun 8:30–14:00, bronze doors are on the outside, so always "open"; original panels are in the Duomo Museum).

▲**Orsanmichele Church**—In the ninth century, this loggia (a covered courtyard) was a market used for selling grain (stored upstairs). Later, it was closed in to make a church. Notice the grain spouts on the pillars inside. The glorious tabernacle (1359) by Orcagna takes you back.

Study the sculpture in the niches outside. You can see man stepping out of the literal and figurative shadow of the Church in the great Renaissance sculptor Donatello's *St. George.* Look into George's face; he's a sensitive new-age guy (SNAG). The predella (panels) at the base of this statue shows St. George slaying the dragon to protect the wispy, melodramatic maiden. This was groundbreaking Renaissance emotion and perspective (free; unreliably open 9:00–12:00 & 16:00–18:00, closed first and last Mon of month, often closed due to staffing problems; on Via Calzaiuoli, enter through back door). The iron bars spanning the vaults were the Italian Gothic answer to the French Gothic external buttresses.

A block away, you'll find the...

▲**Mercato Nuovo (a.k.a. the Straw Market)**—This market loggia is how Orsanmichele looked before it became a church. Originally a silk and straw market, Mercato Nuovo still functions as a rustic market today (at the intersection of Via Calimala and Via Porta Rossa). Prices are soft.

Notice the circled *X* in the center, marking the spot where people hit after being hoisted up to the top of the market and dropped as punishment for bankruptcy. You'll also find *Porcellino* (a statue of a wild boar nicknamed "little pig"), which people rub and give coins to in order to ensure their return to Florence. Nearby, a wagon sells tripe (cow innards) sandwiches.

▲**Palazzo Vecchio**—With its distinctive castle turret, this fortified palace, once the home of the Medici family, is a Florentine landmark. But if you're visiting only one palace interior in town, the Pitti Palace is better. The Palazzo Vecchio interior is wallpapered with mediocre magnificence, worthwhile only if you're a real Florentine art and history fan. The museum's most famous statues are Michelangelo's *Genius of Victory,* Donatello's static *Judith and Holerfernes,* and Verrocchio's *Winged Cherub* (a copy tops the fountain in the free courtyard at entrance, original inside).

Scattered throughout the museum are a dozen computer terminals with information in English on the Medici family, Palazzo Vecchio, and the building's architecture and art, including an animated clip showing how Michelangelo's *David* was moved from the square to the Accademia (€5.70, Fri–Wed 9:00–19:00, Thu 9:00–14:00, in summer maybe open until 23:00 on Mon and Fri, ticket office closes 1 hour earlier, tel. 055-276-8465).

Even if you don't go to the museum, do step into the free courtyard (behind the fake *David*) just to feel the essence of the Medicis. Until 1873, Michelangelo's *David* stood at the entrance, where the copy is today. While the huge statues in the square are important only as the whipping boys of art critics and rest stops for pigeons, the nearby Loggia dei Lanzi has several important statues. Look for Cellini's bronze statue of Perseus holding the head of Medusa. The plaque on the pavement in front of the fountain marks the spot where the monk Savonarola was burned in MCDXCVIII (for more on the monk, see "Museum of San Marco" listing, below).

Uffizi Gallery

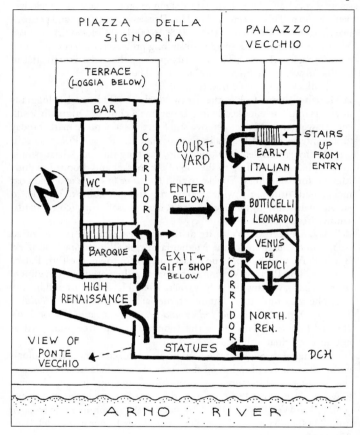

▲▲▲**Uffizi Gallery**—The greatest collection of Italian paintings anywhere is a must, with plenty of works by Giotto, Leonardo, Raphael, Caravaggio, Rubens, Titian, and Michelangelo and a roomful of Botticellis, including his *Birth of Venus*. Make a reservation to avoid the long line (see page 866). Because only 780 visitors are allowed inside the building at any one time, there's generally a very long wait during the day. The good news: No Louvre-style mob scenes. The museum is nowhere near as big as it is great: Few tourists spend more than two hours inside. The paintings are displayed on one comfortable floor in chronological order, from the 13th through 17th centuries.

Essential stops are (in this order): Gothic altarpieces (narrative, pre-Realism, no real concern for believable depth) including Giotto's altarpiece, which progressed beyond "totem-pole angels"; Uccello's *Battle of San Romano,* an early study in perspective (with a few obvious flubs); Fra Filippo Lippi's cuddly Madonnas; the Botticelli room, filled with masterpieces, including a pantheon of classical fleshiness and the small *La Calumnia,* showing the glasnost of Renaissance free-thinking being clubbed back into the darker age of Savonarola; two minor works by Leonardo; the octagonal classical sculpture room with an early painting of Bob Hope and a copy of Praxiteles' *Venus de Medici*—considered the epitome of beauty in Elizabethan Europe; a view through the window of Ponte Vecchio—dreamy at sunset; Michelangelo's only surviving easel painting, the round *Holy Family;* Raphael's noble *Madonna of the Goldfinch;* Titian's voluptuous *Venus of Urbino;* and Duomo views from the café terrace at the end (WC near café).

Cost, Hours, Reservations: €8.50, plus €3 for recommended reservation, Tue–Sun 8:15–18:50, until 22:00 on holidays and maybe on summer Sat, closed Mon, last entry 45 min before closing, after entering take elevator or climb 4 long flights of stairs.

Avoid the two-hour peak-season midday wait by making a telephone reservation. It's easy, slick, and costs only €3 (tel. 055-294-883, explained on page 866). At the Uffizi, walk briskly past the 200-yard-long line—pondering the IQ of this gang—to the special entrance for those with reservations (labeled in English "Entrance for Reservations Only"), give your number, pay (cash only), and scoot right in.

If you haven't called ahead, there are other ways to make an Uffizi reservation—sometimes for the same day, depending on luck and availability: (1) buy Uffizi tickets with reservations at the Museum of San Marco, the Museum of Precious Stones, or another Florence sight; (2) try booking directly at the Uffizi (ask the clerk who stands at the reservations entrance if you can reserve in person—he may direct you to the ticket office); or (3) take a tour of the museum with Walking Tours of Florence (booking required, see "Tours," above).

In Courtyard of Uffizi: Enjoy the Uffizi's courtyard (free), full of artists and souvenir stalls. The surrounding statues honor earthshaking Florentines: artists (Michelangelo), philosophers (Machiavelli), scientists (Galileo), writers (Dante), and explorers (Amerigo Vespucci), and the great patron of so much Renaissance thinking, Lorenzo "the Magnificent" de Medici.

▲**Ponte Vecchio**—Florence's most famous bridge is lined with shops that have traditionally sold gold and silver. A statue of Cellini, the master goldsmith of the Renaissance, stands in the center, ignored by the flood of tacky tourism. This is a romantic spot late at night. In fact, hanging over the edge of the bridge (on either side of the Cellini bust) are piles of padlocks. Guys demonstrate the enduring quality of their love by ceremonially taking their girls here, locking a lock, and throwing the key into the Arno. (But what's with the combination lock?)

Notice the "prince's passageway" above the bridge. In less secure times, the city leaders had a fortified passageway connecting the Vecchio Palace and Uffizi with the mighty Pitti Palace, to which they could flee in times of attack. This passageway, called the **Vasari Corridor,** is technically open to the public, but good luck getting an appointment (tel. 055-265-4321).

SIGHTS

Near the Accademia

▲▲**Museum of San Marco (Museo di San Marco)**—One block north of the Accademia on Piazza San Marco, this museum houses the greatest collection anywhere of frescoes and paintings by the early Renaissance master Fra Angelico. You'll see why he thought of painting as a form of prayer, and couldn't paint a crucifix without shedding tears. Each of the monks' cells has a Fra Angelico fresco. Don't miss the cell of Savonarola, the charismatic monk who rode in from the Christian right, threw out the Medicis, turned Florence into a theocracy, sponsored "bonfires of the vanities" (burning books, paintings, and so on), and was finally burned himself when Florence decided to change channels (€6, daily 8:15–13:50, Sat–Sun 8:15–19:00, but closed first, third, and fifth Sun and second and fourth Mon of each month, tel. 055-238-8608). The ticket office can issue reserved tickets, and even sell tickets (often with immediate reservation) to the Uffizi and Accademia.

Museum of Precious Stones (Museo dell' Opificio delle Pietre Dure)—This unusual gem of a museum features mosaics of inlaid marble and semiprecious stones. You'll see remnants of the Medici workshop from 1588, including 500 different semiprecious stones, the tools used to cut and inlay them, and room after room of the sumptuous finished product. The fine loaner booklet describes it all in English (€2; Mon–Sat 8:15–14:00, Thu until 19:00, closed Sun; Via degli Alfani 78, around corner from Accademia). This ticket booth can also sell tickets with reservations (often for the same day) to the Uffizi and Accademia.

Heart of Florence

▲▲▲**Bargello (Museo Nazionale)**—This under-appreciated sculpture museum is in a former prison that looks like a mini–Palazzo Vecchio. It has Donatello's painfully beautiful *David* (the very influential first male nude to be sculpted in a thousand years), works by Michelangelo, and rooms of Medici treasures cruelly explained in Italian only—mention that English descriptions would be wonderful (€4, daily 8:15–13:50 but closed first, third, and fifth Sun and second and fourth Mon of each month, last entry 40 min before closing, Via del Proconsolo 4, tel. 055-238-8606).

▲▲**Medici Chapels (Cappelle dei Medici)**—The chapel, containing two Medici tombs, is drenched in lavish High Renaissance architecture and sculpture. The highlight is a chapel with interior decoration by Michelangelo, including the brooding Night, Day, Dawn, and Dusk statues (€6, daily 8:15–17:00 but closed the second and fourth Sun and the first, third, and fifth Mon of each month, tel. 055-238-8602).

Nearby: Behind the chapels on Piazza Madonna di degli Aldobrandini is a lively market scene that I find just as interesting. Take a stroll through the huge double-decker Mercato Centrale (central food market) one block north.

Medici Riccardi Palace (Palazzo Medici Riccardi)—Lorenzo the Magnificent's home is worth a look for its art. The tiny Chapel of the Magi contains colorful Renaissance gems—the *Procession of the Magi* frescoes by Benozzo Gozzoli. Another room has a High Baroque ceiling fresco by Luca Giordano, a prolific artist from Naples known as Fast Luke (*Luca fa presto*) for his ambidextrous painting abilities (€4, Thu–Tue 9:00–19:00, closed Wed, Via Cavour 3, kitty-corner from San Lorenzo Church, 1 long block north of Baptistery).

▲**Piazza della Repubblica**—This large square sits on the site of Florence's original Roman Forum. The lone column—nicknamed the belly-button of Florence—is the only remaining bit of Roman Florence except for its grid street plan. Look at the map (by the benches—where the old boys hang out to talk sports and politics) to see the ghost of Rome. Roman Florence was a garrison town—a rectangular fort with this square marking the intersection of the two main roads (Via Corso and Via Roma).

Today's piazza, framed by a triumphal arch, is really a nationalistic statement celebrating the unification of Italy. Florence, the capital of the country (1865–1870) until Rome was liberated, lacked a square worthy of this grand new country. So the neighborhood here was razed to open up a grand modern forum surrounded by grand circa-1890 buildings.

Between here and the river you'll find characteristic parts of the medieval city that give a sense of what this neighborhood felt like before it was bulldozed. Back then, writers described Florence as so densely built up that when it rained, pedestrians didn't get wet. Torches were used to light the lanes in midday. The city was prickly with noble family towers (like San Gimignano) and had Romeo-and-Juliet-type family feuds. But with the rise of the Medicis (c. 1300), no noble family was allowed to have an architectural ego trip taller then theirs, and nearly all other towers were taken down.

The fancy La Rinascente department store, facing the Piazza della Repubblica, is one of the city's finest (WC on 4th floor, view terrace in small pricey bar above that).

▲▲**Science Museum (Museo di Storia della Scienza)**—This is a fascinating collection of Renaissance and later clocks, telescopes, maps, and ingenious gadgets. One of the most talked-about bottles in Florence is the one here containing Galileo's finger. Loaner English guidebooklets are available. It's friendly, comfortably cool, never crowded, and just a block east of the Uffizi on the Arno River (€6.50, Mon and Wed–Fri 9:30–17:00, Tue and Sat 9:30–13:00, closed Sun, Piazza dei Giudici 1, tel. 055-265-311).

▲▲**Church of Santa Maria Novella**—This 13th-century Dominican church, just south of the train station, is rich in art. Along with crucifixes by Giotto and Brunelleschi, there's every textbook's example of the early Renaissance mastery of perspective: *The Holy Trinity* by Masaccio; it's opposite the side entrance (€2.50, Mon–Thu and Sat 9:30–17:00, Fri and Sun 13:00–17:00)

Nearby: A palatial **perfumery** is around the corner 100 yards down Via della Scala at #16 (free but shopping encouraged, Mon–Sat 9:30–19:30, closed Sun, tel. 055-216-276). Thick with the lingering aroma of centuries of spritzes, it started as the herb garden of the Santa Maria Novella monks. Well-known even today for its top-quality products, it is extremely Florentine. Pick up the history sheet at the desk and wander deep into the shop. From the back room, you can peek at Santa Maria Novella's cloister with its dreamy frescoes and imagine a time before Vespas and tourists.

Santa Croce and Nearby

▲▲**Santa Croce Church**—This 14th-century Franciscan church, decorated with centuries of precious art, holds the tombs of great Florentines (€4, Mon–Sat 9:30–17:30, Sun 15:00–17:30, in winter Mon–Sat 9:30–12:30 & 15:00–17:30, Sun 15:00–17:30, modest dress code enforced, tel. 055-244-619). The loud 19th-century Victorian Gothic facade faces a huge square ringed with tempting shops and littered with tired tourists. Escape into the church.

On your right as you enter you'll see the tomb of Galileo (allowed in by the Church only long after his death). Directly opposite (across the back end of the nave) find the tomb of Michelangelo (with the allegorical figures of painting, architecture, and sculpture); a memorial to Dante (no body...he was banished by his hometown because of political differences); the tomb of Machiavelli (who wrote the book on hardball politics); a relief by Donatello of the Annunciation; and the tomb of the composer of the *William Tell* Overture (a.k.a. the *Lone Ranger* theme), Rossini.

To the right of the altar, step into the sacristy where you'll find a bit of St. Francis' cowl and old sheets of music. In the bookshop, notice the photos of the devastating flood of 1966 high on the wall. Beyond that is a touristy—but mildly interesting—"leather school." The chapels lining the front of the church are richly frescoed. The chapel to the right of the main altar is a masterpiece by Giotto featuring scenes from the life of St. Francis. Exit between the Rossini and Machiavelli tombs into the cloisters. On the left enter Brunelleschi's **Pazzi Chapel,** considered one of the finest pieces of Florentine Renaissance architecture.

▲**Michelangelo's House (Casa Buonarroti)**—Fans enjoy a house owned by Michelangelo that he gave to his nephew, who turned it into a little museum honoring his famous uncle. You'll see some of Michelangelo's early, much-less-monumental statues and sketches (€6.50, Wed–Mon 9:30–14:00, closed Tue, English descriptions, Via Ghibellina 70, tel. 055-241-752).

South of the Arno River

▲▲**Pitti Palace**—From the Uffizi, follow the course of the elevated passageway (closed to non-Medicis) across the Ponte Vecchio to the gargantuan Pitti Palace, which has several separate museums.

The **Palatine Gallery/Royal Apartments (Galleria Palatina)** is the biggie, featuring palatial room after chandeliered room, its walls sagging with masterpieces by minor artists and minor pieces by masters. Its Raphael collection is the biggest anywhere (first floor, €6.50, Tue–Sun 8:15–18:50, closed Mon, buy tickets on right-hand side of courtyard, tel. 055-238-8614).

The **Modern Art Gallery** features Romanticism, neoclassicism, and Impressionism by 19th- and 20th-century Tuscan painters (second floor, €5, daily 8:15–13:50 but closed second and fourth Sun and first, third, and fifth Mon).

The **Grand Ducal Treasures (Museo degli Argenti)** is the Medici treasure chest, with jeweled crucifixes, exotic porcelain, gilded ostrich eggs, and so on to entertain fans of applied arts (ground floor, €4, virtually the same hours as Modern Art Gallery).

Behind the palace, the huge landscaped **Boboli Gardens** offer a shady refuge from the city heat (€4, daily 9:00–18:30 in fall and spring, until 19:30 June–Aug, until 16:30 in winter, but closed first and last Mon of month).

▲▲**Brancacci Chapel**—For the best look at Masaccio's works (he's the early Renaissance master who re-invented perspective), see his restored frescoes here. Since only a few tourists are let in at a time, seeing the chapel often involves a wait (€3.10, Mon and Wed–Sat 10:00–17:00, Sun 13:00–17:00, closed Tue, cross Ponte Vecchio and turn right and hike to Piazza del Carmine).

The neighborhoods around the church are considered the last surviving bits of old Florence.

Santo Spirito Church—This has a classic Brunelleschi interior and a very early Michelangelo crucifix, painted on carved wood, given by the sculptor to the monastery in appreciation for the opportunity that they gave him to dissect and learn about bodies. Pop in here for a delightful Renaissance space and a chance to marvel at a Michelangelo all alone (free, most days 10:00–12:00 & 16:00–17:30, Sat–Sun only 16:00–17:30, closed Wed, Piazza Santo Spirito, tel. 055-210-030).

▲**Piazzale Michelangelo**—Overlooking the city from across the river (look for the huge statue of David), this square is worth the 30-minute hike, drive, or bus ride (either #12 or #13 from the train station) for the view of Florence and the stunning dome of the Duomo. After dark, it's packed with local schoolkids feeding their dates slices of watermelon and then licking them clean. Just beyond it is the stark and beautiful, crowd-free, Romanesque San Miniato Church.

EXPERIENCES

▲▲**Gelato**—Gelato is an edible art form. Italy's best ice cream is in Florence—one souvenir that can't break and won't clutter your luggage. But beware of scams at touristy joints on busy streets that turn a simple request for a cone into a €10 "tourist special." A key to gelato-appreciation is sampling liberally and choosing flavors that go well together. Ask, as the locals do, for *"Un assaggio, per favore?" (*A taste, please?) and *"Que si sposano bene?"* (What marries well?).

Gelateria Carrozze is very good (daily 11:00–24:00, closes at 21:00 in winter; on riverfront 30 yards from Ponte Vecchio toward the Uffizi, Via del Pesce 3; also has decent sandwiches to go). **Gelateria dei Neri** is another local favorite worth tracking down (daily in summer 12:00–23:00, closed Wed in winter, 2 blocks east of Palazzo Vecchio at Via Dei Neri 20 red).

Vivoli's, which serves "only today's production" is the most famous (Tue–Sun 8:00–1:00; closed Mon, the last 3 weeks in Aug, and winter; opposite the Church of Santa Croce, go down Via Torta a block, turn right on Via Stinche). Before ordering, try a free sample of their *riso* flavor—rice.

If you want an excuse to check out the little village-like neighborhood across the river from Santa Croce, enjoy a gelato at the tiny **no-name gelateria** at Via San Miniato 5 red (just before Porta San Miniato).

SHOPPING

Florence is a great shopping town. Busy street scenes and markets abound, especially near San Lorenzo, near Santa Croce, on Ponte Vecchio, and at Mercato Nuovo (a covered market square 3 blocks north of Ponte Vecchio, listed above in "Sights"). Leather (often better quality for less than the U.S. price), gold, silver, art prints, and tacky plaster mini-*David*s are most popular. Shops usually have promotional stalls in the market squares. Prices are soft in markets. Many visitors spend entire days shopping.

For ritzy Italian fashions, browse along Via de Tornabuoni, Via della Vigna Nuova, and Via Strozzi. Typical chain department stores are **Coin,** the local Macy's (Mon–Sat 9:30–20:00, Sun 11:00–20:00, on Via Calzaiuoli, near Orsanmichele Church); **Oviesse,** the local J.C. Penney's, a discount clothing/grocery store (Mon–Sat 9:00–19:55, closed Sun; at intersection of Via Panzani and Via del Giglio, near train station); and **La Rinascente,** the local Nordstroms (Mon–Sat 9:00–21:00, Sun 10:30–20:00, on Piazza della Repubblica).

For shopping ideas, ads, and a list of markets, see the *Florence Concierge Information* magazine described under "Tourist Information," above (free from TI and many hotels).

SLEEPING

Between the Station and Duomo

$$$ **Palazzo Castiglioni** offers 16 grand rooms with all the conveniences and a peaceful, *palazzo* decor. Most rooms are spacious, several have frescoes, and all make a fine splurge (Db-€170, Db suite-€200, Tb-€210, 5 percent discount with cash and this book in 2004, air-con, elevator, Via del Giglio 8, tel. 055-214-886, fax 055-274-0521, pal.cast@flashnet.it, Laura SE).

$$ **Hotel Accademia** is an elegant two-star place with marble stairs, parquet floors, attractive public areas, 21 pleasant rooms, and a floor plan that defies logic (Sb-€87, Db-€140, Tb-€170, prices promised through 2004 with this book, 5 percent additional discount with cash, air-con, tiny courtyard, Via Faenza 7, tel. 055-293-451, fax 055-219-771, www .accademiahotel.net, info@accademiahotel.net, Tea SE).

$$ **Hotel Bellettini** rents 30 bright, cool, well-cared-for rooms with inviting lounges (S-€78, Sb-€100, D-€105, Db-€135, Tb-€165, Qb-€210, 5 percent discount with this book if claimed upon arrival, aircon, Via de' Conti 7, tel. 055-213-561, fax 055-283-551, hotel.bellettini @dada.it, frisky Gina SE). Be warned, they rent much higher-priced rooms in a nearby annex.

$$ **Residenza dei Pucci,** a block north of the Duomo, has 12 tastefully decorated rooms—in soothing earth tones—with aristocratic furniture and tweed carpeting. It's fresh and bright (Sb-€130, Db-€145, Db in Aug and much of winter-€105, Tb-€165, suite with grand Duomo view-€207 for 2 people, €233 for 4, claim a 10 percent discount through 2004 with cash and this book, breakfast served in room, Via dei Pucci 9, tel. 055-281-886, fax 055-264-314, http://residenzapucci.interfree.it, residenzapucci@interfree.it, SE).

$ **Hotel Aldobrandini,** a good budget choice, has 15 basic, clean rooms, with the San Lorenzo market at its doorstep and the entrance to the Medici Chapel a few steps away (Ss-€40, Sb-€50, D-€65, Db-€80 with this book, lots of night noise but has double-paned windows, fans, hiding behind market stalls and mopeds at Piazza Madonna Degli Aldobrandini 8, tel. 055-211-866, fax 055-267-6281, Ignazio SE).

$ **Pensione Centrale** is a traditional, yet institutional-feeling place with a creaky, elegant living room and 18 spacious rooms (D-€85, Db-€109, quiet, air-con, often filled with American students, elevator, Via de' Conti 3, tel. 055-215-761, fax 055-215-216, www.hotelcentralefirenze .it, info@hotelcentralefirenze.it).

Near the Central Market

$$ **Hotel Basilea** offers predictable three-star, air-conditioned comfort in its 38 modern rooms (Sb-€80–110, Db-€110–150, Tb-€150–210, low prices Aug and Nov–March, elevator, terrace, Via Guelfa 41, at intersection with Nazionale—a busy street, ask for a room in the back, tel. 055-214-587, fax 055-268-350, www.florenceitaly.net/basilea, basilea @dada.it, SE).

$ **Casa Rabatti** is the ultimate if you always wanted to be a part of a Florentine family. Its four simple, clean rooms are run with motherly warmth by Marcella and her husband Celestino, who speak minimal English. Seeing 10 years of my family Christmas cards on their walls, I'm reminded of how long they've been keeping budget travelers happy (D-€50, Db-€60, €25 per bed in shared quad or quint, prices

---

SLEEP CODE

(€1 = about $1.10, country code: 39)
Sleep Code: **S** = Single, **D** = Double/Twin, **T** = Triple, **Q** = Quad, **b** = bathroom, **s** = shower only, **no CC** = Credit Cards not accepted, **SE** = Speaks English, **NSE** = No English. Unless otherwise noted, breakfast is included (but usually optional) and credit cards are accepted. English is generally spoken.

To help you sort easily through these listings, I've divided the rooms into three categories based on the price for a standard double room with bath:

$$$ **Higher Priced**—Most rooms €160 or more.
$$ **Moderately Priced**—Most rooms between €110-160
$ **Lower Priced**—Most rooms €110 or less.

The accommodations scene varies wildly with the season. Spring and fall are very tight and expensive, while mid-July through August is wide open and discounted. November through February is also generally empty. I've listed prices for peak season: April, May, June, September, and October. If a price range is listed, the lower end

good with this book, no CC; no breakfast, fans; no sign other than on doorbell, 5 blocks from station, Via San Zanobi 48 black; tel. 055-212-393, casarabatti@inwind.it).

$ Affitacamere Freda Lucia is basic, clean, and cheap. Its four ground floor-yet-quiet rooms share two bathrooms, a kitchenette, and a leafy garden terrace (S-€45, D-€55, T-€70, €5 less for 3 or more days, discounts in winter, cash only; no breakfast; Via San Zanobi 76, but ring at #31; tel. 055-487533, luciafreda@libero.it, kind Lucia and son Claudio).

$ Soggiorno Magliani, central and humble with seven rooms, feels and smells like a great-grandmother's place (S-€36, D-€46, T-€64, cash only but secure reservation with credit card, no breakfast, double-paned windows, near Via Guelfa at Via Reparata 1, tel. 055-287-378, hotel -magliani@libero.it, run by friendly family duo Vincenza and English-speaking daughter Cristina).

East of the Duomo

$$$ Hotel Loggiato dei Serviti, at the most prestigious address in Florence on the most Renaissance square in town, gives you Old World romance with hair dryers. Stone stairways lead you under open-beam ceilings through this 16th-century monastery's classy public rooms. The

reflects off-season (Aug, Nov–March) and the higher end, peak season.

With good information and an e-mail or phone call beforehand, you can find a stark, clean, and comfortable double with breakfast and a shower down the hall for about €70 (for the room, not per person). A typical room with a private bath costs around €100 (less at the smaller places, such as the *soggiornos*). You get elegance in peak season for €150. Some places listed are old and rickety, and described as such. Virtually all of the accommodations are central, within minutes of the great sights. Few hotels escape Vespa noise at night.

Contact the hotels directly—not through a tourist agency. Tourist information room-finding services cannot give opinions on quality. If you're traveling off-season, you can show up without reservations and find huge discounts. Ask if you'll get a discount for paying in cash, for staying for three or more nights (or both), or for using this book. And ask if you can skip breakfast (the overpriced breakfasts are legally optional, though some hotels pretend otherwise).

Book ahead. I repeat, book ahead (by e-mail, fax, or phone). Places will hold a room until early afternoon. If they say they're full, mention that you're using this book.

Hotels in Florence

1. Palazzo Castiglioni & Hotel Aldobrandini
2. Hotel Accademia
3. Hotel Bellettini
4. Residenza dei Pucci
5. Pensione Centrale
6. Hotel Basilea
7. Casa Rabatti
8. Affitacamere Freda Lucia
9. Soggiorno Magliani
10. Hotel Loggiato dei Serviti
11. Hotel Morandi alla Crocetta
12. Hotel Le Due Fontane
13. Oblate Sisters of the Assumption
14. Hotel Pendini
15. Residenza Giotto
16. Pensione Maxim
17. Soggiorno Battistero
18. Albergo Firenze
19. Hotel Beatrice
20. Hotel Pensione Elite
21. Bellevue House
22. Hotel Sole
23. Hotel Torre Guelfa & Hotel Pensione Alessandra
24. In Piazza della Signoria B&B
25. Florence Walking Tours

34 cells, with air-conditioning, TVs, mini-bars, and telephones, would-n't be recognized by their original inhabitants. The hotel staff is both professional and friendly (Sb-€146, Db-€210, family suites from €263, 30 percent discounts in Aug and late Nov–Feb, 5 elegant rooms in 17th-century annex, elevator, Piazza S.S. Annuziata 3, tel. 055-289-592, fax 055-289-595, www.loggiatodeiservitihotel.it, info@loggiatodeiservitihotel .it, Simonetta, Francesca, and Andrea SE). Ask for a backside room to avoid piazza night noise.

$$$ **Hotel Morandi alla Crocetta,** another former convent, envelops you in a 16th-century cocoon. Located on a quiet street, with period furnishings, parquet floors, and wood-beamed ceilings, it takes you back (10 rooms, Sb-€110, Db-€170, breakfast-€11, a block off Piazza S.S. Annunziata at Via Laura 50, tel. 055-234-4747, fax 055-248-0954, www.hotelmorandi.it, welcome@hotelmorandi.it, Claudio SE).

$$ **Hotel Le Due Fontane** faces the Renaissance Piazza S.S. Annunziata but fills its old building with a smoky, 1970s, business-class ambience. Its 57 air-conditioned rooms are big and comfortable (Sb-€110, Db-€160, Tb-€200, prices promised through 2004 only if you claim them upon reserving, elevator, Piazza S.S. Annunziata 14, tel. 055-210-185, fax 055-294-461, www.leduefontane.it, info@leduefontane.it, SE).

$ **Oblate Sisters of the Assumption** run an institutional 20-room hotel in a Renaissance building with a dreamy garden and a quiet, nice-place-to-relax-after-you-die feel. Not a hint of English spoken here (S-€35, Db-€70, elevator, no CC, Borgo Pinti 15, 50121 Firenze, tel. 055-248-0582, fax 055-234-6291).

Near Piazza Repubblica

These are the most central of my accommodations recommendations (and therefore a little overpriced). While worth the extra for many, given Florence's walkable core, nearly every hotel can be considered central.

$$ **Hotel Pendini,** a well-run and well-worn three-star hotel with Old World tiles, chandeliers, and 42 rooms, is popular and central, over-looking the grand Piazza Repubblica (Sb-€86–110, Db-€110–150 depending on season, elevator, fine lounge and breakfast room, air-con, Via Strozzi 2, tel. 055-211-170, fax 055-281-807, www.florenceitaly.net, pendini@dada.it, Barbara SE).

$$ **Residenza Giotto** has six bright and modern rooms, and a ter-race so close to the Duomo you can almost touch it (Sb-€120, Db-€130, Tb-€145, 10 percent discount for cash with this book if claimed at time of reservation; breakfast served in room, elevator; Via Roma 6, 4th floor; tel. 055-214-593, fax 055-264-8568, www.residenzagiotto.it, residenzagiotto @tin.it, SE).

$$ **Pensione Maxim,** right on Via dei Calzaiuoli, is a big, institu-tional-feeling place as close to the sights as possible. Its halls are nar-row, but the 29 rooms are comfortable and well-maintained (Sb-€83,

Db-€113, Tb-€148, Qb-€173, takes CC but pay first night in cash, air-con, elevator, Via dei Calzaiuoli 11, tel. 055-217-474, fax 055-283-729, www.hotelmaximfirenze.it, hotmaxim@tin.it, Paolo Maioli SE).

$ **Soggiorno Battistero,** next door to the Baptistery, has seven simple, airy rooms, most with great views, overlooking the Baptistery and square. You're in the heart of Florence (Sb-€73, Db-€95, Tb-€130, Qb-€140, these prices good with this book, 5 percent additional discount with cash; breakfast served in room, ceiling fans, double-paned windows, no elevator; Piazza San Giovanni 1, 3rd floor; tel. 055-295-143, fax 055-268-189, www.soggiornobattistero.it, battistero@dada.it, lovingly run by Italian Luca and his American wife, Kelly).

$ **Albergo Firenze,** a big, efficient place, offers 58 good, basic rooms in a wonderfully central, reasonably quiet locale two blocks behind the Duomo (Sb-€73, Db-€94, Tb-€132, Qb-€162, cash only, prepay first night with a bank draft or traveler's check, elevator, air-con, off Via del Corso at Piazza Donati 4, tel. 055-214-203, fax 055-212-370, www.hotelfirenze-fi.it, firenze.albergo@tiscali.it, Manuela SE).

Near Piazza della Signoria and Ponte Vecchio

$$$ **Hotel Torre Guelfa** is topped by a fun medieval tower with a panoramic rooftop terrace and a huge living room. Its 29 rooms vary wildly in size (Sb-€110, small Db-€145, standard Db-€180, Db junior suite-€220, family deals, 5 percent discount with cash and this book). Room #15, with a private terrace—€210—is worth reserving several months in advance (elevator, air-con; a couple blocks northwest of Ponte Vecchio, Borgo S.S. Apostoli 8; tel. 055-239-6338, fax 055-239-8577, www.hoteltorreguelfa.com, torreguelfa@flashnet.it, Sabina, Giancarlo, Carlo, and Sandro all SE).

$$$ **In Piazza della Signoria B&B** is peaceful, classy, and homey at the same time and overlooks Piazza della Signoria. It comes with all the special touches—much like a top-end American B&B. Each of its eight rooms has a huge and lavish bathroom (Sb-€130–190, Db-€190–240, Tb-€220–270, lower prices without view, family apartments, tiny elevator, air-con, Via dei Magazzini 2, tel. 055-239-9546, fax 055-267-6616, mobile 348-321-0565, www.inpiazzadellasignoria.it, info@inpiazzadellasignoria.it, Silka SE).

$$ **Hotel Pensione Alessandra** is a 16th-century, tranquil place with 27 big, modern rooms (S-€67, Sb-€108, D-€108, Db-€145, T-€145, Tb-€191, Q-€160, Qb-€212, 5 percent discount with cash, air-con, Borgo S.S. Apostoli 17, tel. 055-283-438, fax 055-210-619, www.hotelalessandra.com, info@hotelalessandra.com, SE).

Near the Train Station

Note: As with any big Italian city, the area around the train station is a magnet for hardworking pickpockets on the alert for lost, vulnerable tourists with bulging moneybelts hanging out of their khakis.

$$ Hotel Beatrice, a three-star hotel popular with tour groups, is well-located—especially if you've packed heavy. It's a block north of the train and bus stations (20 rooms, Sb-€75–90, Db-€95–142, Tb-€120-190, 5 percent discount with cash and this book, most rooms air-con—request one as you reserve, elevator, Via Fiume 11, tel. 055-216-790, fax 055-280-711, www.hotelbeatrice.it, info@hotelbeatrice.it, Constantino SE).

$ Hotel Pensione Elite, run warmly by sunny Nadia, is a fine value. It has 10 comfortable—if plainly furnished—rooms and a charm rare in this price range (Ss-€60, Sb-€75, Ds-€75, Db-€90, breakfast-€6; air-con, fans; Via della Scala 12, 2nd floor; tel. & fax 055-215-395, easy reservations by phone, SE).

$ Bellevue House is a fourth-floor oasis (no elevator) with six spacious rooms flanking a long, mellow yellow lobby. It's a peaceful time-warp run by Suzanna and Antonio Di Grazia (Db-maximum €100 in May, June, Sept, and Oct, Db-maximum €80 off-season, prices promised through 2004, 5 percent cash discount, includes breakfast in a street level bar; over-sized modern bathrooms; Via della Scala 21, 50123 Florence; tel. 055-260-8932, fax 055-265-5315, mobile 333-612-5973, www .bellevuehouse.it, info@bellevuehouse.it).

$ Hotel Sole, a clean, cozy, family-run place with eight bright, modern rooms, is just off Santa Maria Novella square toward the river. Friendly Anna makes you feel like a guest of the family (Sb-€47, Db-€78, Tb-€105, no CC; no breakfast, air-con, elevator, 1:00 curfew; Via del Sole 8, 3rd floor; tel. & fax 055-239-6094, NSE).

Oltrarno, South of the River

Across the river in the Oltrarno area, between the Pitti Palace and Ponte Vecchio, you'll still find small traditional crafts shops, neighborly piazzas, and family eateries. The following places are an easy walk from the Ponte Vecchio.

$$$ Hotel Lungarno is *the* place to stay if money is no object. This deluxe, four-star hotel with 74 rooms strains anything stressful or rough out of Italy, and gives you only service with a salute, physical elegance everywhere you look, and fine views over the Arno and Ponte Vecchio (Sb-€225, Db-€385, Db facing river-€484, fancier suites, great riverside public spaces, air-con, elevator, 100 yards from Ponte Vecchio at Borgo San Jacopo 14, tel. 055-27261, fax 055-268-437, www.lungarnohotels .com, bookings@lungarnohotels.com, SE).

$$$ Hotel Silla, a classic three-star hotel with 36 cheery, spacious, pastel, and modern rooms, is a fine value. It faces the river and overlooks a park opposite the Santa Croce Church (Db-€170, Tb-€210, mention this book for a discount, elevator, air-con, Via dei Renai 5, tel. 055-234-2888, fax 055-234-1437, www.hotelsilla.it, hotelsilla@tin.it, Laura and Stefano SE).

Florence's Oltrarno Neighborhood

1. Hotel La Scaletta
2. To Hotel Silla
3. Pensione Sorelle Bandini
4. Hotel Lungarno
5. Soggiorno Althea
6. Istituto Gould
7. Ostello Santa Monaca

$$ Hotel La Scaletta, ramshackle and reeking in character, is a dark, cool place with a labyrinthine floor plan, senseless stairs, loose tiles, lots of Old World lounges, and a romantic, panoramic roof terrace (16 rooms, S-€50, Sb-€95, D-€110, Db-€115–130, Tb-€130–150, Qb-€150–170, higher price is for quieter rooms in back, €5–10 discount for cash; mostly air-con, elevator, bar with fine wine at good prices; Via Guicciardini 13 black, 150 yards south of Ponte Vecchio; tel. 055-283-028, fax 055-289-562, www.lascaletta.com, info@lascaletta.com, Barbara and her son Manfredo SE). Manfredo loves to cook and offers a fine family-style dinner. He also serves a €15 "Taste of Tuscany for Two" deal (plate of quality Tuscan meats and cheeses with bread and 4 glasses of robust Chianti)—ideal for a light lunch or dinner on the roof terrace.

$$ Pensione Sorelle Bandini is a rickety 500-year-old palace on a perfectly Florentine square, with cavernous rooms, museum-warehouse interiors, a musty youthfulness, cats, a balcony lounge-loggia with a view, and an ambience that, for romantic bohemians, can be a highlight of Florence. Mimmo or Sr. Romeo will hold a room until 16:00 with a phone call (D-€109, Db-€130, T-€148, Tb-€178, includes optional €9 breakfast, no CC, elevator, Piazza Santo Spirito 9, tel. 055-215-308, fax 055-282-761, pensionebandini@tiscali.it, SE). This square can attract drug pushers; just don't invite them to your room.

$ **Soggiorno Althea** is a small guesthouse run by Antonio deep in the Oltrarno. While it's on a noisy street, half its rooms are on the back (Db-€71, Tb-€80, prices special with this book; air-con, no breakfast, no reception desk, a couple blocks beyond Piazza San Spirito on corner of Via delle Caldaie and Via del Campuccio, at Via delle Caldaie 25; tel. 055-233-5341, mobile 388-233-5341, info@florencealthea.it).

$ **Istituto Gould** is a Protestant Church–run place with 41 clean but drab rooms with twin beds and modern facilities (S-€32, Sb-€38, D-€40, Db-€50, Tb-€66, €21 per person in quads, no breakfast, quieter rooms in back, Via dei Serragli 49, tel. 055-212-576, fax 055-280-274, gould.reception@dada.it). You must arrive when the office is open (Mon–Fri 9:00–13:00 & 15:00–19:00, Sat 9:00–13:00, no check-in Sun or holidays, SE).

$ **Ostello Santa Monaca,** a cheap hostel, is a few blocks south of Ponte Alla Carraia, one of the bridges over the Arno (€15.50 beds, 4- to 20-bed rooms, 1:00 curfew, Via Santa Monaca 6, tel. 055-268-338, fax 055-280-185, www.ostello.it, info@ostello.it).

EATING

To save money and time for sights, you can keep lunches fast and simple, eating in one of the countless self-service places and pizzerias or just picnicking (try juice, yogurt, cheese, and a roll for €5). For good sit-down meals, consider the following. Remember, restaurants like to serve what's fresh. If you're into flavor, go for the seasonal best bets—featured in the *Piatti del Giorno* ("special of the day") sections of the menus.

North Of The River
Near Santa Maria Novella and the Train Station
Osteria Belledonne feels like eating dinner in a crowded terrarium. I loved the meal but had to correct the bill—read it carefully. They take only a few reservations; arrive early or wait (Mon–Fri 12:00–14:30 & 19:00–22:30, closed Sat–Sun, Via delle Belledonne 16 red, tel. 055-238-2609).

Ristorante La Spada is another fine local favorite serving typical Tuscan cuisine with less atmosphere and more menu. Order the €19 "Spada's Fantasy" for an unending parade of food (€11 lunch special, daily 12:00–15:00 & 19:00–22:30, air-con, near Via della Spada at Via del Moro 66 red, evening reservations smart, tel. 055-218-757). Their take-out *rosticcería* (at their Via della Spada entrance) serves the same food for picnic prices.

Trattoria Marione serves good home-cooked-style meals to a local crowd in a happy, food-loving, and steamy ambience (dinners run about €15 plus wine, open daily, Via della Spada 27 red, tel. 055-214-756).

Trattoria Sostanza-Troia is a characteristic and well-established place with shared tables and a loyal local following. Whirling ceiling fans and walls strewn with old photos create a time-warp ambience. They offer two seatings, requiring reservations: one at 19:30 and one at 21:00 (dinners for about €15 plus wine, great steaks, lunch 12:00–14:00, closed Sat, Via del Porcellana 25 red, tel. 055-212-691).

Ristorante il Latini is a hugely popular institution packed with Florentines and tourists munching cheap Tuscan cuisine noisily under pendulous hamhocks. Arrive right at 12:30 or 19:30 or you'll wait for a table (€6 pastas, €12 *secondis*, each table has a bottle of Chianti—you pay €1 per glass, closed Mon, off Via d. Vigna Nuova at Via Palchetti 6, tel. 055-210-916).

Near the Central and San Lorenzo Markets

For piles of picnic produce, people-watching, or just a rustic sandwich, try the huge Central Market—**Mercato Centrale** (Mon–Sat 7:00–14:00, a block north of San Lorenzo street market).

Trattoria la Burrasca is a Flintstone-chic, family-run place ideal for Tuscan home cooking. It's small—10 tables—and often filled with our readers. Anna and Antonio Genzano have cooked and served here with passion since 1982. If Andy Capp were Italian, he'd eat here for special nights out. Everything is homemade except the desserts. And if you want good wine cheap, order it here (Fri–Wed 12:00–15:00 & 19:00–22:00, closed Thu, Via Panicale 6b, at north corner of Central Market, tel. 055-215-827, NSE).

Osteria la Congrega brags it's "a Tuscan wine bar designed to help you lose track of time." In a fresh and romantic two-level setting, chef/owner Mahyar takes pride in his fun, easy menu featuring modern Tuscan cuisine, with top-notch meat and seasonal produce. He offers quality vegetarian dishes, creative salads, and an inexpensive but excellent house wine. With just 10 uncrowded tables, reservations are required for dinner (€5–6 pasta, €11 nightly specials, daily 12:00–15:00 & 19:00–23:00, Via Panicale 43 red, tel. 055-264-5027).

For a cheap lunch, try **Trattoria San Zanobi's** €5 Pasta Break Lunch (open daily, Via San Zanobi 33 red, a couple blocks northeast of Central Market, tel. 055-475-286).

Near the Accademia and Museum of San Marco

Gran Caffè San Marco, conveniently located on Piazza San Marco, churns out cheap but tired cafeteria fare to cheap but tired tourists (no cover charge, self-service and restaurant; door to cafeteria hides near

Restaurants in Florence

1. Osteria Belledonne
2. Ristorante La Spada
3. Trattoria Marione
4. Trattoria Sostanza-Troia
5. Ristorante il Latini
6. Mercato Centrale (Market)
7. Trattoria la Burrasca & Osteria la Congrega
8. Trattoria San Zanobi
9. Gran Caffè San Marco
10. Self-Service Ristorante Leonardo
11. Antico Ristorante il Sasso di Dante
12. Ristorante il Ritrovo
13. Ristorante il Cavallino
14. Osteria Vini e Vecchi Sapori
15. Cantinetta dei Verrazzano & Ristorante Paoli
16. I Fratellini Wine & Sandwich Shop
17. Trattoria Icche C'è C'è
18. Osteria del Porcellino
19. Trattoria Nella
20. Gelateria Carrozze
21. Gelateria dei Neri
22. Vivoli's Gelateria

Piazza San Marco 11 red, across square from Museum of San Marco entrance; tel. 055-215-833).

Near the Duomo (Cathedral)

Self-Service Ristorante Leonardo is fast, cheap, air-conditioned, and handy, just a block from the Duomo, southwest of the Baptistery (€3 pastas, €4 main courses, Sun–Fri 11:45–14:45 & 18:45–21:45, closed Sat, upstairs at Via Pecori 5, tel. 055-284-446). Luciano (like Pavarotti) runs the place with enthusiasm.

Antico Ristorante il Sasso di Dante serves standard Tuscan fare in a surprisingly pleasant indoor/outdoor setting in the shadow of the Duomo (€20 meals, always good vegetarian dishes and special menu of the day, daily 12:00–14:30 & 19:00–22:30, come early to snare the front-row view seats, Piazza delle Pallottole 6, tel. 055-282-113).

Cavernous **Ristorante il Ritrovo** offers a bright, dressy ambience and meaty Tuscan cuisine cooked with family pride. They serve a good two-course €10 lunch special for hurried office workers (€25 meals, 12 tables, air-con, Tue–Sun 12:30–15:00 & 19:00–23:00, closed Mon, a long block north of the Duomo at Via dei Pucci 4, tel. 055-281-688, Marco SE).

Near Palazzo Vecchio

Piazza della Signoria, the square facing Palazzo Vecchio, is ringed by beautifully situated yet touristic eateries. Any will do for a reasonably-priced pizza. Perhaps the least of these evils is **Ristorante il Cavallino** with its glum crowd of tourists, dumbed-down menu, and great outdoor seating in the shadow of the palace (€11 fixed-price lunch *menu*, €16 fixed-price dinner *menu*, open daily, tel. 055-215-818).

Osteria Vini e Vecchi Sapori, half a block north of Palazzo Vecchio, is a colorful hole-in-the-wall serving traditional food, including plates of mixed *crostini* (€1 each—step right up and choose at the bar) and €10 daily specials (Tue–Sun 11:00–22:00, closed Mon; Via dei Magazzini 3 red, facing the bronze equestrian statue in Piazza della Signoria, go behind its tail into the corner and to your left; gruff Giorgio SE).

Cantinetta dei Verrazzano is a long-established bakery/café/wine bar, serving delightful sandwich plates in an elegant old-time setting, and hot focaccia sandwiches to go. The *Specialita Verrazzano* is a fine plate of four little *crostini* (like mini *bruschetta*) featuring different local breads, cheeses, and meats (€7). The *Tagliere di Focacce,* a sampler plate of mini–focaccia sandwiches, is also fun. Either of these dishes with a glass of Chianti makes a fine light meal. Paolo describes things to make eating educational. As office workers pop in for a quick bite, it's traditional to share tables at lunchtime (Mon–Sat 12:30–21:00, closed Sun, just off Via Calzaiuoli on a side street across from Orsanmichele Church at Via dei Tavolini 18, tel. 055-268-590).

I Fratellini is a rustic little place where the "little brothers" have served peasants 27 different kinds of sandwiches and cheap glasses of Chianti wine (see list on wall) since 1875. Join the local crowd, then sit on a nearby curb or windowsill to munch, placing your glass on the wall rack before you leave (€4 for sandwich and wine, daily 8:00–20:00, 20 yards in front of Orsanmichele church on Via dei Cimatori).

Ristorante Paoli serves great local cuisine to piles of happy eaters under a richly frescoed Gothic vault. Because of its fame and central location, it's filled mostly with tourists, but for a dressy, traditional splurge meal, this is my choice (€20 tourist menu, à la carte is pricier, Wed–Mon 12:00–14:00 & 19:00–22:00, closed Tue, reserve for dinner, midway between old square and Duomo at Via de Tavolini 12 red, tel. 055-216-215). Salads are flamboyantly cut and mixed from a trolley right at your table.

Trattoria Icche C'è C'è (dialect for "whatever is, is"; ee-kay chay chay) is a small, family-style eatery where fun-loving Gino serves good traditional meals (3-course €11 meals, not too touristy, Tue–Sun 12:30–14:30 & 19:30–22:30, closed Mon, midway between Bargello and river at Via Magalotti 11 red, tel. 055-216-589).

Osteria del Porcellino is a rare place that serves late. This dark, dense, candlelit place is packed with a mix of locals and tourists and run with style and enthusiasm by friendly chef Enzo (daily 19:00–1:00, summer lunches; reserve for dinner, indoor/outdoor; Via Val di Lamona 7 red, half a block behind Mercato Nuovo; tel. 055-264-148).

Trattoria Nella serves good, typical Tuscan cuisine at affordable prices, including melt-in-your-mouth gnocchi. Arrive early or be disappointed—it's understandably popular (€20 meals, Mon–Sat 12:00–14:30 & 19:00–22:00, closed Sun; 3 blocks northwest of Ponte Vecchio, Via delle Terme 19 red; tel. 055-218-925).

Oltrarno, South of the River
Near Ponte Vecchio

Ristorante Bibo serves *"cucina tipica Fiorentina"* with a pink-tablecloth-and-black-bowties dressiness and a leafy, candlelit outdoor seating (good €15 three-course meal, leave this book face up on the table for a 15 percent discount, reserve for outdoor seating, Wed–Mon 12:00–14:30 & 19:00–22:30, closed Tue, Piazza Santa Felicita 6 red, tel. 055-239-8554, Tonino SE).

Trattoria Bordino, just up the street and actually built into the old town wall (c. 1170), serves tasty and beautifully presented Florentine cuisine in a brooding, candlelit atmosphere (Mon–Sat 12:00–14:30 & 19:30–22:30, closed Sun, Via Stracciatella 9 red, tel. 055-213-048).

Golden View Open Bar is a lively, trendy place good for a salad, pizza, or pasta with a view of Ponte Vecchio and the Arno River. Reservations for window tables are limited to 19:30 and 21:30 seatings

Restaurants in Oltrarno

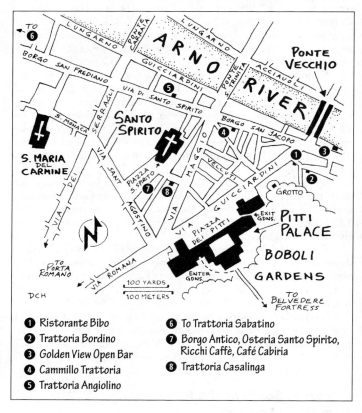

1 Ristorante Bibo
2 Trattoria Bordino
3 Golden View Open Bar
4 Cammillo Trattoria
5 Trattoria Angiolino

6 To Trattoria Sabatino
7 Borgo Antico, Osteria Santo Spirito, Ricchi Caffè, Café Cabiria
8 Trattoria Casalinga

(reasonable prices, daily 11:30–24:00, impressive wine bar, Internet access, 50 yards upstream from Ponte Vecchio at Via dei Bardi 58, tel. 055-214-502). They have live jazz Mondays and Wednesdays at 21:00.

Via Santo Spirito and Borgo San Jacopo

Several good and colorful restaurants line this multinamed street a block off the river in Oltrarno. I'd survey the scene before making a choice.

Cammillo Trattoria was formerly run by Cammillo, who is now is slurping spaghetti in heaven. But his granddaughter Chiara carries on the tradition, mixing traditional Tuscan and creative, modern cuisine. With a charcoal grill and a team of white-aproned waiters cranking out wonderful food in a fun, dressy-but-down-to-earth ambience, this place is a hit (full dinners about €36 plus wine, Thu–Tue 12:00–14:30 &

19:30–22:30, closed Wed, reservations smart, Borgo San Jacopo 57 red, tel. 055-212-427).

Trattoria Angiolino serves good, old-fashioned local cuisine. Sit in the main hall rather than the stuffy side rooms (€20 for dinner plus wine, Tue–Sun 12:00–14:30 & 19:30–22:30, closed Mon, Via di Santo Spirito 36 red, tel. 055-239-8976).

Trattoria Sabatino, farthest away and least touristy, is spacious and disturbingly cheap, with family character, red-checkered tablecloths, and a simple menu. A wonderful place to watch locals munch, it's just outside the Porta San Frediano (medieval gate), a 15-minute walk from Ponte Vecchio (Mon–Fri 12:00–14:30 & 19:20–22:00, closed Sat–Sun, Via Pisana 2 red, tel. 055-225-955, NSE).

Piazza Santo Spirito

This classic Florentine square (lately a hangout for drug pushers, therefore a bit seedy-feeling and plagued by bag-snatchers on mopeds) has several popular little restaurants and bars that are open nightly. They offer good local cuisine, moderate prices, and impersonal service, with a choice of indoor or romantic on-the-square seating (reservations smart): lively **Borgo Antico** (Piazza Santo Spirito 6 red, tel. 055-210-437) and the quieter yet more bohemian **Osteria Santo Spirito** (entrée salads, Piazza Santo Spirito 16 red, tel. 055-238-2383).

Ricchi Caffè, next to Borgo Antico, has fine gelato and shaded outdoor tables. After noting the plain facade of the Brunelleschi church facing the square, step inside the café, and pick your favorite of the many ways it might be finished. **Café Cabiria,** next door, is a trendy local hangout with good light meals and a cozy Florentine funky room in back. If you're a scene crasher, try it here.

Trattoria Casalinga, an inexpensive standby, comes with aproned women bustling around the kitchen. You'll find more tourists than locals, but all seem to leave full, happy, and with euros to spare for gelato (Mon–Sat 12:00–14:30 & 19:00–21:45, after 20:00 reserve or wait, closed Sun and all of Aug; just off Piazza Santo Spirito, near the church at Via dei Michelozzi 9 red; tel. 055-218-624).

TRANSPORTATION CONNECTIONS

By train to: Pisa (2/hr, 1.25 hrs), **Lucca** (9/day, 1.5 hrs), **Siena** (9/day, 1.75 hrs, more with transfer in Empoli; bus is better), **La Spezia** (for the Cinque Terre, 2/day direct, 2 hrs, or change in Pisa), **Milan** (12/day, 3–5 hrs), **Venice** (7/day, 3 hrs), **Assisi** (3/day, 2 hrs, more frequent with transfers, direction: Foligno), **Orvieto** (6/day, 2 hrs), **Rome** (hrly, 2.5 hrs), **Naples** (10/day, 4 hrs), **Brindisi** (3/day, 11 hrs with change in Bologna), **Frankfurt** (3/day, 12 hrs), **Paris** (1/day, 12 hrs overnight), **Vienna** (4/day, 9–10 hrs).

Buses: The SITA bus station, a block west of the Florence train station, is user-friendly. Schedules are posted everywhere, with TV monitors indicating imminent departures. Bus service drops dramatically on Sunday. You'll find buses to: **San Gimignano** (€6, hrly, 1.75 hrs), **Siena** (€6.50, hrly, 75-min *corse rapide* fast buses are faster than the train, avoid the 2-hr *diretta* slow buses), and the **airport** (€4, hrly, 15 min). Bus info: tel. 800-373760 or 055-214-721 from 9:30 to 12:30; some schedules are in the *Florence Concierge Information* magazine.

Taxi to Siena: For around €100, you can arrange a ride directly from your Florence hotel to your Siena hotel. For a small group or for people with more money than time, this can be a good value.

Airports

The **Amerigo Vespucci Airport** (www.safnet.it), several miles northwest of Florence, has a TI, cash machines, car rental agencies, and easy connections by airport shuttle bus with Florence's bus station, a block west of the train station (€4, 2/hr, 30 min, from Florence runs 5:30–23:00, from airport 6:00–23:30). Airport info: 055-306-1300, flight info: 055-306-1700 (domestic), 055-306-1702 (international). Allow about €16–20 for a taxi.

International flights often land at Pisa's **Galileo Galilei Airport** (also has TI and car rental agencies, www.pisa-airport.com), an hour from Florence by train (runs hourly; if you're leaving Florence for this airport, catch the train at Florence's train station at platform #5). Flight info: 050-849-300.

SIENA

Siena was medieval Florence's archrival. And while Florence ultimately won the battle, Siena still competes for the tourists. Sure, Florence has the most heavyweight sights. But Siena seems to be every Italy connoisseur's pet town. In my office, whenever Siena is mentioned, someone moans, "Siena? I looove Siena!"

Seven hundred years ago (from about 1260–1348), Siena was a major banking and trade center, and a military power in a class with Florence, Venice, and Genoa. With a population of 60,000, it was even bigger than Paris. Situated on the north-south road to Rome (the "Via Francigena"), Siena traded with all Europe. Then in 1348, the Black Plague that swept through Europe hit Siena and cut the population by a third. Siena never recovered. In the 1550s, her bitter rival, Florence, really "salted" her, forever making Siena a nonthreatening backwater. Siena's loss became our sightseeing gain, as its political and economic irrelevance pickled it purely medieval. Today, Siena's population is still 60,000, compared to Florence's 420,000.

Siena's thriving historic center, with red-brick lanes cascading every which way, offers Italy's best medieval city experience. Most people do Siena, just 30 miles south of Florence, as a day trip, but it's best experienced at twilight. While Florence has the blockbuster museums, Siena has an easy-to-enjoy soul: Courtyards sport flower-decked wells, alleys dead-end at rooftop views, and the sky is a rich blue dome. Right off the bat, Siena becomes an old friend.

For those who dream of a Fiat-free Italy, pedestrians rule in the old center of Siena. Sit at a café on the red-brick main square. Wander narrow streets lined with colorful flags and iron rings to tether horses. Take time to savor the first European city to eliminate automobile traffic from its main square (1966) and then, just to be silly, wonder what would happen if they did it in your city.

Planning Your Time

On a quick trip, consider spending three nights in Siena (with a whole-day side trip into Florence and a day to relax and enjoy Siena). Whatever you do, enjoy a sleepy medieval evening in Siena. After an evening in Siena, you can see its major sights in half a day.

ORIENTATION

Siena lounges atop a hill, stretching its three legs out from Il Campo. This main square, the historic meeting point of Siena's neighborhoods, is pedestrian-only. And most of those pedestrians are students from the local university.

Everything I mention is within a 15-minute walk of the square. Navigate by three major landmarks (Campo, Duomo, and church of San Domenico), following the excellent system of street-corner signs. The typical visitor sticks to the San Domenico–Il Campo axis.

Siena itself is one big sight. Its individual sights come in two little clusters: the square (Civic Museum and City Tower) and the cathedral (Baptistery and Duomo Museum with its surprise viewpoint). Check these sights off, and you're free to wander.

Tourist Information: Pick up a free town map from the main TI at #56 on Il Campo (Mon–Sat 8:30–19:30, tel. 0577-280-551, www .terresiena.it, info@terresiena.it). The helpful booklet *Terre di Siena* lists current hours and prices for sights in Siena and outlying towns. The little TI at San Domenico is for hotel promotion only and sells a Siena map for €0.50.

Arrival in Siena

By Train: The small train station, located on the edge of town, has a bar and bus office (baggage check and lockers closed indefinitely).

To get from the station to the city center, take a taxi or a city bus. The **taxi stand** is to your far right as you exit the station; allow about €8 to Il Campo, the main square (to call a taxi from the station, dial 0577-44504; for taxis at Piazza Matteotti in the center, call 0577-49222). For the **city bus,** buy a €0.75 ticket from the Bus Ticket Office in the station lobby (daily 6:15–19:30, ask for a city map—it's free and just a bus route map but helps get you started). You can also buy a bus ticket from the blue machine in the lobby (touch screen for English and select "urban" for type of ticket). Then cross the parking lot and the street to reach the sheltered bus stop. Catch orange city bus #3, #9 or #10 to get into town (punch ticket in machine on bus to validate it). You'll end up at one of three stops—Piazza Gramsci/Lizza, Piazza Sale, or Via Stufa Secca—all within several blocks of each other (buses run about every 15 min, fewer on Sun). If you get off at Via Stufa Secca's tiny square, you're soon faced with two uphill roads—take the one to the right for one block to reach the main drag, Banchi di Sopra.

To get to Siena's train station from the center of Siena, catch the city bus at Piazza Gramsci, Piazza del Sale, or Via Stufa Secca; note that bus stops are rarely marked with a "bus stop" sign but instead with a posted schedule and sometimes with yellow lines painted on the pavement, showing a bus-sized rectangle and the word "bus." Confirm with the driver that the bus is going to the *stazione* (stat-zee-OH-nay). Remember to purchase your ticket in advance from a *tabacchi* shop.

By Bus: Some buses arrive in Siena at the train station (see "Arrival by Train," above), others at Piazza Gramsci (a few blocks from city center), and some stop at both. The main bus companies are Sena and the confusingly named Tra-in (pronounced TRAAH-in). You can store baggage underneath Piazza Gramsci in Sotopassaggio la Lizza (€3.50, daily 7:00–19:45, no overnight).

By Car: Drivers coming from the autostrada take the Porta San Marco exit and follow signs for *Centro*, then *Stadio* (stadium, soccer ball). The soccer-ball signs take you to the stadium lot (Parcheggio Stadio, €1.50/hr, €12.50/day) at the huge, bare-brick San Domenico Church. The Fortezza lot nearby charges the same. Or park in the lot under the train station. You can drive into the pedestrian zone (a pretty ballsy thing to do) only to drop bags at your hotel. You can park free in the lot below the Albergo Lea, in white-striped spots behind Hotel Villa Liberty, behind the Fortezza, and overnight in most city lots from 20:00 to 8:00. (The signs showing a street cleaner and a day of the week indicate which day the street is cleaned; there's a €105 tow-fee incentive to learn the days of the week in Italian.)

Helpful Hints

Local Guide: Roberto Bechi, a hardworking Sienese guide, specializes in off-the-beaten-path tours of the city and the surrounding countryside. Married to an American (Patti) and having run restaurants in Siena and the United States, Roberto communicates well with Americans. His passions are Sienese culture, Tuscan history, and local cuisine. Book well in advance (full-day tours from €65–95 per person, half-day tours from €30–60 per person, mobile 328-727-3186 or 328-425-5648, www.toursbyroberto.com, tourrob@tin.it; for U.S. contact, fax Greg Evans at 540/434-4532).

Internet Access: In this university town, there are lots of places to get plugged in. **Internet Point** is just off Piazza Matteotti, on Via Paradiso (across street from McDonald's) and **Internet Train** is near Il Campo, at Via di Città 121 (tel. 0577-226-366).

Launderettes: Two modern, self-service places are Lavarapido Wash and Dry (daily 8:00–22:00; Via di Pantaneto 38, near Logge del Papa) and Onda Blu (daily 8:00–21:00; Via del Casato di Sotto 17, 50 yards from Il Campo).

Markets: The produce market is held on Piazza del Marcato, behind Il Campo (Mon–Sat mornings). On Wednesday morning, the weekly market—consisting mainly of clothes and some food—sprawls between the Fortress and Piazza Gramsci along Viale Cesare Maccabi and the adjacent Viale XXV Aprile.

SIGHTS

Siena's Main Square

▲▲▲ **Il Campo**—Siena's great central piazza is urban harmony at its best. Like a people-friendly stage set, its gently tilted floor fans out from the tower and city hall backdrop. It's the perfect invitation to loiter. Think of it as a trip to the beach without sand or water.

Il Campo was located at the historic junction of Siena's various competing districts, or *contrade,* on the old marketplace. The brick surface is divided into nine sections, representing the council of nine merchants and city bigwigs who ruled medieval Siena.

The square is dominated by the City Hall (Palazzo Pubblico), with its 330-foot tower. In medieval Siena, this secular City Hall was the center of the city, and the whole focus of the Campo flows down to it. Its crenellated roofline and three-bay windows are echoed around the city.

At the square's high point, look for the *Fountain of Joy,* the two naked guys about to be tossed in, and the pigeons politely waiting their turn to gingerly tightrope down slippery spouts to slurp a drink. (You can see parts of the original fountain, of which this is a copy, in an interesting exhibit at Siena's Santa Maria della Scala museum, listed below in "Sights") At the square's low point is the City Hall and tower. The chapel located at the base of the tower was built in 1348 as thanks to God for ending the Black Plague (after it killed more than a third of the population).

To say Siena and Florence have always been competitive is an understatement. In medieval times, a statue of Venus stood on Il Campo (where the *Fountain of Joy* is today). After the plague hit Siena, the monks blamed this pagan statue. The people cut it to pieces and buried it along the walls of Florence.

Picture the Campo at Palio time, when the famous horse races are held (July 2 and Aug 16); see sidebar on page 902. Ten horses and riders race hell-for-leather three times around the perimeter (the gray pavement), which is covered with dirt, with mattresses padding the sharpest turns. Spectators waving the banners of their neighborhoods cram (for free) into the center of the square or watch from temporary bleachers, or if they're lucky, from the balconies of their friends.

The market area behind the city hall, a wide-open expanse since the Middle Ages, originated as a farming area within the city walls to feed the citizens in times of siege. Now the morning produce market is held here Monday through Saturday. (The closest public WCs to Il Campo

Siena Sights

TO HOSTEL

TO TRAIN STATION

FORTEZZA

V. GARI.

VIALE FRANCHI

PIAZZA SALE

VIALE MACCARI

VIA STUFA-SECCA

PIAZZA GRAMSCI

P – PARKING

25 APR.

VIA MONT.

BUSES TO FLORENCE

ENOTECA ITALIA

P

VIA TOZZI

PIAZZA MATTEOTTI

PIAZZA SALIMBENI

100 YDS.
100 m

STADIO

POST

PIAZZA TOLOMEI

V. DEI MILLE

VIA CURTATONE

PARADISIO

McD

VIA DI SAPIENZA

BANCHI DI SOPRA

ROSSI

i

WC

CAMPOREGIO

S. PITTORI

S. CAT.

TERME

CECCO

CIVIC MUSEUM,

SAN DOMENICO

SANCT. S. CAT.

ANT. GALLUZZA

TERMINI

P. IND.

BANCHI

CITY HALL & TOWER

ESTERINA FONT.

COSTONE

V. FONT.

DIACETO

WC

BANCHI DI SOTTO

IL CAMPO

BAPT.

FRANC.

VIA PELL.

VIA DI CITTÀ

VIA DI OSLO

PANT.

PORRIONE

DUOMO

PIAZZA DUOMO

CASTORO

GIO. DUPRE

SALICOTTO

SANTA MARIA DELLA SCALA

WC

CAPITANO

CAS. DI

PIAZZA MERCATO

DUOMO MUSEUM

STALLOREGGI

S. PIETRO

100 YDS.
100 m

PINACOTECA –PICTURE GALL.–

① Sottopassaggio La Lizza   **②** Palio Movie

are each about a block away: at Via Beccheria—a few steps off Via de Città—and on Casato di Sotto; €0.60.)

▲**Civic Museum (Museo Civico)**—At the base of the tower is Siena's City Hall (Palazzo Pubblico), the spot where secular government got its start in early Renaissance Europe. There, you'll find city government still at work, along with a sampling of local art.

SIENA'S PALIO

In the Palio, the feisty spirit of Siena's 17 *contrade* (neighborhoods) lives on. These neighborhoods celebrate, worship, and compete together. Each even has its own historical museum. *Contrada* pride is evident any time of year in the colorful neighborhood banners and parades. (If you hear distant drumming, run to it for some medieval action, often featuring flag-throwers.) But *contrada* passion is most visible twice a year—on July 2 and August 16—when they have their world-famous horse race, the Palio di Siena. Ten of the 17 neighborhoods compete (chosen by lot), hurling themselves with medieval abandon into several days of trial races and traditional revelry. On the big day, jockeys and horses go into their *contrada*'s church to be blessed ("Go and win," says the priest). It's considered a sign of luck if a horse leaves droppings in the church.

On the evening of the big day, Il Campo is stuffed to the brim with locals and tourists, as the horses charge wildly around the square in this literally no-holds-barred race. A horse can win even if its rider has fallen off. Of course, the winning neighborhood is the scene of grand celebrations afterward. Winners receive a *palio* (banner), typically painted by a local artist and always featuring the Virgin Mary. But the true prize is simply proving your *contrada* is numero uno. All over town, sketches and posters depict the Palio. This is not some folkloristic event. It's a real medieval moment. If you're packed onto the square with 15,000 people who each really want to win, you won't see much, but you'll feel it. While the actual Palio packs the city, you could side-trip in from Florence to see horse-race trials each of the three days before the big day (usually at 9:00 and around 19:30).

▲**Palio al Cinema**—This 20-minute film, *Siena, the Palio, and its History,* helps recreate the craziness. See it at the Cinema Moderno in Piazza Tolomei, two blocks from Il Campo (€5.25, with this book pay €4.25, or €8 for 2; runs May–Oct only, Mon–Sat 9:30–17:30, English showings generally hourly at :30 past the hour, schedule posted on door, closed Sun; air-con, tel. 0577-289-201). Call or drop by to confirm when the next English showing is scheduled—there are usually nine a day. At the ticket desk, you can buy the same show on video or DVD (video-€10.50, DVD-€11.50, discount only with this book, video must be labeled "NTSC American System" or it'll be a doorstop at your home).

In the following order, you'll see: the Sala Risorgimento, with dramatic scenes of Victor Emmanuel's unification of Italy (surrounded by statues that don't seem to care); the chapel, with impressive inlaid wood chairs in the choir; and the Sala del Mappamondo, with Siena's first fresco, Simone Martini's *Maestà* (Enthroned Virgin—a groundbreaking, down-to-earth Madonna), facing the faded *Guidoriccio da Fogliano* (a mercenary providing a more concrete form of protection).

Next is the *Sala della Pace*—where the city's fat cats met. Looking down on the oligarchy during their meetings were two interesting frescoes showing the effects of good and bad government. Notice the whistle-while-you-work happiness of the utopian community ruled by the utopian government (in the better-preserved fresco) and the fate of a community ruled by politicians with more typical values (in a terrible state of repair). The message: Without justice, there can be no prosperity.

Take a moment to savor one of those to-sigh-for rural panoramas out the window of the *Sala della Pace*. The view out the window is essentially the same as that from the top of the big stairs (€6.50, €9.50 combo-ticket includes tower, daily March–Oct 10:00–19:00, July–Sept until 23:00, Nov–Feb 10:00–16:00, last entry 45 min before closing, audio-guide €3.75 for 1 person, €5.25 for 2, tel. 0577-292-111).

▲City Tower (Torre del Mangia)—Siena gathers around its City Hall, not its church. It was a proud republic; its "declaration of independence" is the tallest secular medieval tower in Italy. The 330-foot-tall Torre del Mangia was named after a hedonistic watchman who consumed his earnings like a glutton consumes food (his chewed-up statue is in the courtyard, to the left as you enter). Its 300 steps get pretty skinny at the top, but the reward is one of Italy's best views (€5.50, €9.50 combo-ticket with Civic Museum, daily 10:00–19:00, mid-July–mid-Sept until 23:00, Nov–March 10:00–16:00, closed in rain, sometimes long lines, avoid midday crowd, limit of 30 tourists at a time, often sold out).

▲National Picture Gallery (Pinacoteca)—Siena was a power in Gothic art. But the average tourist, wrapped up in a love affair with the Renaissance, hardly notices. This museum takes you on a walk through Siena's art, chronologically from the 12th through the 15th centuries. For the casual sightseer, the Sienese art in the Civic and Duomo Museums is adequate. But art fans enjoy this opportunity to trace the evolution of Siena's delicate and elegant works, from stiff, gold-backed icon-like Madonnas to curvy, graceful Madonnas to Italian Renaissance. Concentrate on pieces by Duccio (artist of the *Maestà* in the Duomo Museum), Simone Martini (who did the *Maestà* in the Civic Museum), the brothers Ambrogio and Pietro Lorenzetti (Ambrogio did the *Allegory of Good and Bad Government* in the Civic Museum), Pinturicchio (who did the Piccolomini Library in the Duomo), and Domenico Beccafumi (who inlaid pavement in the Duomo). To reach the museum from Il Campo, walk out Via di Città and go left on Via San Pietro (€4, Sun–Mon 8:30–13:15, Tue–Sat 8:15–19:15, audioguide-€4, tel. 0577-281-161).

Siena's Cathedral Area

▲▲▲Duomo—Siena's 13th-century cathedral is as Baroque as Gothic gets. This cathedral, with its six-story striped bell tower—Siena's ultimate tribute to the Virgin Mary—is heaped with statues, plastered with frescoes, and paved with art. The striped facade is piled with statues and ornamentation, and the interior is decorated from top to bottom. The heads of 172 popes peer down from the ceiling, over the fine inlaid art on the floor. This is one busy interior. (Modest dress is required for entry.)

To orient yourself in this *panforte* of Italian churches, stand under the dome and think of the church floor as a big clock. You're the middle, and the altar is high noon: You'll find the *Slaughter of the Innocents* roped off on the floor at 10:00, Pisano's pulpit between two pillars at 11:00, Duccio's round stained glass window at high noon, Bernini's chapel at 3:00, two Michelangelo statues (next to doorway leading to a shop, snacks, and WC) at 7:00, the Piccolomini Library at 8:00, and a Donatello statue at 9:00.

Take some time with the floor mosaics in the front. Nicola Pisano's wonderful pulpit is crowded with delicate Gothic storytelling from 1268. To understand why Bernini is considered the greatest Baroque sculptor, step into his sumptuous *Cappella della Madonna del Voto*. This last work in the cathedral, from 1659, is enough to make a Lutheran light a candle. Move up to the altar and look back at the two Bernini statues: Mary Magdalene in a state of spiritual ecstasy, and St. Jerome playing the crucifix like a violinist lost in beautiful music.

The Piccolomini altar is most interesting for its two Michelangelo statues (the lower big ones). Paul, on the left, may be a self-portrait. Peter, on the right, resembles Michelangelo's more famous statue of Moses. Originally contracted to do 15 statues, Michelangelo left the project early (1504) to do his great *David* in Florence.

The Piccolomini Library—worth the €1.50 entry—is brilliantly frescoed with scenes glorifying the works of a pope from 500 years ago. It contains intricately decorated, illuminated music scores and a statue (a Roman copy of a Greek original) of the Three Graces. Donatello's bronze statue of St. John the Baptist, in his famous rags, is in a chapel to the right of the library.

Cost and Hours: Entrance is generally free, although you'll pay €3 to visit from September to mid-October (for *pavimento Cattedrale*, when much of the elaborate mosaic floor is uncovered for the annual viewing) and €1.50 to visit the Piccolomini Library. The church and library are open mid-March–Oct daily 7:30–19:30, worship only Sun 10:15–14:00; Nov–mid-March Mon–Sat 7:30–17:00, Sun 14:30–17:30. Modest dress is required to enter.

Audioguides: There's a daunting number of audioguides. An audioguide for just the church costs €3.50; to add the library, it's €4; and to add the Cathedral Museum (Museo dell' Opera de Panorama), it's €5.50. For the church and museum only, it's €4.50. Two headphones are available at a price break.

▲▲**Duomo Museum (Museo dell' Opera e Panorama)**—Siena's most enjoyable museum, on the Campo side of the church (look for the yellow signs), was built to house the cathedral's art. The ground floor is filled with the cathedral's original Gothic sculpture by Giovanni Pisano (who spent 10 years in the late 1200s carving and orchestrating the decoration of the cathedral) and a fine Donatello *Madonna and Child.* Upstairs to the left awaits a private audience with Duccio's *Maestà (Enthroned Virgin,* 1311*).* Pull up a chair and study one of the great pieces of medieval art. The flip side of the *Maestà* (displayed on the opposite wall), with 26 panels—the medieval equivalent of pages—shows scenes from the Passion of Christ.

Climb onto the "Panorama dal Facciatone." From the first landing, take the skinnier second spiral for Siena's surprise view. Look back over the Duomo and consider this: When rival republic Florence began its grand cathedral, proud Siena decided to build the biggest church in all Christendom. The existing cathedral would be used as a transept. You're atop what would have been the entry. The wall below you, connecting the Duomo with the museum of the cathedral, was as far as Siena got before a plague killed the city's ability to finish the project. Were it completed, you'd be looking straight down the nave—white stones mark where columns would have stood (€5.50, worthwhile 40-minute audioguide-€3, daily mid-March–Sept 9:00–19:30, Oct 9:00–18:00, Nov–mid-March 9:00–13:30, tel. 0577-283-048).

▲**Baptistery**—Siena is so hilly that there wasn't enough flat ground on which to build a big church. What to do? Build a big church and prop up the overhanging edge with the Baptistery. This dark and quietly tucked-away cave of art is worth a look (and €2.50) for its cool tranquility and the bronze panels and angels—by Ghiberti, Donatello, and others—adorning the pedestal of the baptismal font (daily mid-March–Sept 9:00–19:30, Oct 9:00–18:00, Nov–mid-March 10:00–13:00 & 14:00–17:00).

▲**Santa Maria della Scala**—This museum (opposite the Duomo entrance) was used as a hospital as recently as the 1980s. Now it displays a lavishly frescoed hall, a worthwhile exhibit on Quercia's *Fountain of Joy* (downstairs), and a so-so archaeological museum (subterranean, in labyrinthine tunnels). The entire museum is a maze, with various exhibitions and paintings plugged in to fill the gaps.

The frescoes in the **Pellegrinaio Hall** show medieval Siena's innovative health care and social welfare system in action (c. 1442, wonderfully described in English). The hospital was functioning as early as the 11th century, nursing the sick and caring for abandoned children (see frescoes). The good work paid off, as bequests and donations poured in, creating the wealth that's evident in the chapels elsewhere on this floor. The Old Sacristy was built to house precious relics, including a Holy Nail thought to be from Jesus' cross.

Downstairs, the engaging exhibit on Jacopo della Quercia's early 15th-century *Fountain of Joy* doesn't need much English description, fortunately, because there isn't much. In the 19th century, the *Fountain of Joy* in Il Campo was deteriorating. It was dismantled and plaster casts were made of the originals. The *Fountain of Joy* that stands in Il Campo today is a replica. In this exhibit, you'll see the plaster casts of the original, eroded panels paired with their restored twins, along with the statues that originally stood on the edges of the fountain. In general, the pieces at the beginning and end of the exhibit are original. If there's a piece in a dim room near the exit of the exhibit, it's likely an original chunk awaiting cleaning.

The **Archaeological Museum,** way downstairs, consists mainly of pottery fragments in cases lining tunnel after tunnel. It's like being lost in a wine cellar without the wine. Unless there's a special exhibit, it's not worth the trip.

Cost and Hours: €5.25, daily 10:00–18:00, off-season 10:30–16:30. The chapel just inside the door to your left is free (English description inside chapel entrance—also pick up a copy of *Il Giornale di Santa Maria della Scala* for a list of upcoming events, such as concerts and guided tours).

Siena's San Domenico Area

Church of San Domenico—This huge brick church is worth a quick look. The bland interior fits the austere philosophy of the Dominicans. Walk up the steps in the rear for a look at various paintings from the life of Saint Catherine, patron saint of Siena. Halfway up the church on the right, you'll see a metal bust of Saint Catherine and a small case containing her finger (sometimes loaned out to other churches). In the chapel surrounded with candles, you'll see her actual head (free, daily March–Oct 7:00–13:00 & 14:30–18:30, Nov–Feb 9:00–13:00 & 15:00–18:00; WC for €0.50 at far end of parking lot—facing church entrance, it's to your right).

Sanctuary of Saint Catherine—Step into Catherine's cool and peaceful home. Siena remembers its favorite hometown gal, a simple, unschooled, but mystically devout soul who, in the mid-1300s, helped convince the pope to return from France to Rome. Pilgrims have come here since 1464. Since then, architects and artists have greatly embellished what was probably a humble home (her family worked as wool-dyers). Enter through the courtyard and walk to the far end. The chapel on your right contains the wooden crucifix upon which Catherine was meditating when she received the stigmata in Pisa. The chapel on your left used to be the kitchen. Go down the stairs to the left of the chapel/kitchen to reach the saint's room. Catherine's bare cell is behind see-through doors. Much of the art throughout the sanctuary depicts scenes from her life (free, daily 9:00–12:30 & 15:00–18:30, Via Tiratoio). It's a few downhill blocks toward the center from San Domenico (follow signs to Santuario di Santa Caterina).

SHOPPING AND NIGHTLIFE

Shopping—Shops line Via Banchi di Sopra, the *passeggiata* route. For a budget department store, try Upim on Piazza Matteotti (Mon–Sat 9:30–19:50, closed Sun). The Feltrinelli bookstore closest to the Campo sells books and magazines in English (daily 9:00–19:30, Banchi di Sopra 52). The large, colorful scarves/flags, each depicting the symbol of one of Siena's 17 different neighborhoods (such as the wolf, the turtle, and the snail), are easy-to-pack souvenirs, fun for decorating your home (€7 apiece for large size, sold at souvenir stands).

Nightlife—Join the evening *passeggiata* (peak strolling time is 19:00) along Via Banchi di Sopra with gelato in hand. **Nannini's** at Piazza Salimbeni has fine gelato (daily 11:00–24:00).

The **Enoteca Italiana** is a good wine bar in a cellar in the Fortezza/Fortress (sample glasses in 3 different price ranges: €2, €3, €5.50; Mon 12:00–20:00, Tue–Sat 12:00–01:00, closed Sun; bottles and snacks available; cross bridge and enter fortress, go left down ramp, not to be confused with Enoteca Toscana—same location but not as nice; tel. 0577-288-497).

Museums are often open late on summer Fridays and Saturdays; check with the TI for current hours.

SLEEPING

Near Il Campo

Each of these listings is forgettable but inexpensive, and just a horse wreck away from one of Italy's most wonderful civic spaces.

$ **Piccolo Hotel Etruria,** a good bet for a hotel with 19 decent rooms but not much soul, is just off the square (S-€43, Sb-€48, Db-€78, Tb-€105, Qb-€127, breakfast-€5; curfew at 00:30; with your back to the tower, leave Il Campo to the right at 2:00, Via Donzelle 1—3; tel. 0577-288-088, fax 0577-288-461, hetruria@tin.it, Fattorini family SE).

$ **Albergo Tre Donzelle** has 28 plain, institutional rooms next door to Piccolo Hotel Etruria that make sense only if you think of Il Campo as your terrace (S-€36, D-€50, Db-€63, Via Donzelle 5, tel. 0577-280-358, fax 0577-223-933, Signora Iannini SE).

$ **Locanda Garibaldi** is a modest, very Sienese restaurant/*albergo*. Gentle Marcello wears two hats, as he runs a busy restaurant downstairs and seven pleasant rooms up a funky, artsy staircase (Db-€70, Tb-€89,

SLEEP CODE

(€1 = about $1.10, country code: 39)
Sleep Code: **S** = Single, **D** = Double/Twin, **T** = Triple, **Q** = Quad, **b** = bathroom, **s** = shower only, **no CC** = Credit Cards not accepted, **SE** = Speaks English, **NSE** = No English. Breakfast is generally not included. Have breakfast on Il Campo or in a nearby bar.

To help you sort easily through these listings, I've divided the rooms into three categories based on the price for a standard double room with bath:

   $$$ **Higher Priced**—Most rooms €120 or more.
   $$ **Moderately Priced**—Most rooms between €90-120.
   $ **Lower Priced**—Most rooms €90 or less.

Finding a room is tough during Easter or the Palio in early July and mid-August. Call ahead any time of year, as Siena's few budget places are listed in all the budget guidebooks. While day-tripping tour groups turn the town into a Gothic amusement park in midsummer, Siena is basically yours in the evenings and off-season.

Most of the listed hotels lie between Il Campo and the Church of San Domenico. Part of Siena's charm is its lively, festive character—this means that all hotels can be plagued with noise, even (and sometimes especially) the hotels in the pedestrian-only zone. If tranquility is important for your sanity, ask for a room that's off the street or consider staying at the recommended places outside the center.

Credit cards are accepted unless otherwise noted. A handful of the listings don't take credit cards, no matter how earnestly you ask. Cash machines are plentiful on the main streets.

family deals, no CC, takes reservations only a week in advance, half a block downhill off the square at Via Giovanni Dupre 18, tel. 0577-284-204, NSE).

$ Hotel Cannon d'Oro, a few blocks up Via Banchi di Sopra, is spacious, comfortable, and group-friendly (30 rooms, Sb-€69, Db-€86, Tb-€109, Qb-€128, these discounted prices promised through 2004 with this book, family deals, breakfast-€6, Via Montanini 28, tel. 0577-44321, fax 0577-280-868, cannondoro@libero.it, Maurizio and Debora SE).

Sleeping Fancy, Southwest of Il Campo

These two places are a 10-minute walk from Il Campo.

$$$ Hotel Duomo is a classy place with 23 spacious rooms and a bizarre floor plan (Sb-€110, Db-€150, Tb-€175, Qb-€200, includes breakfast; air-con, elevator, picnic-friendly roof terrace, free parking; follow Via di Città, which becomes Via Stalloreggi, to Via Stalloreggi 38; tel. 0577-289-088, fax 0577-43043, www.hotelduomo.it, booking @hotelduomo.it, Stefania SE). If you arrive by train, take a taxi (€8); if you drive, go to Porta San Marco and follow the signs to the hotel, drop off your bags, and then park in nearby "Il Campo" lot.

$$$ Pensione Palazzo Ravizza, elegant and friendly, with an aristocratic feel and a peaceful garden, is a worthwhile splurge (Sb-€130, Db-€120–270, Tb-€220–310, suites available, includes breakfast, cheaper mid-Nov–Feb, air-con, elevator, back rooms face open country, good restaurant, free parking, Via Pian dei Mantellini 34, tel. 0577-280-462, fax 0577-221-597, www.palazzoravizza.it, bureau@palazzoravizza.it, SE).

Near San Domenico Church

These hotels are within a 10-minute walk northeast of Il Campo. Albergo Bernini and Alma Domus, which enjoy views of the old town and cathedral, are the best values in town.

$$$ Hotel Villa Liberty has 18 big, bright, comfortable rooms (S-€75, Db-€130, includes breakfast, only one room with twin beds; elevator, bar, air-con, TVs, courtyard, facing fortress at Viale V. Veneto 11, tel. 0577-44966, fax 0577-44770, www.villaliberty.it, info@villaliberty.it, SE).

$$ Hotel Chiusarelli, a proper hotel in a beautiful building with a handy location, comes with traffic noise at night—ask for a quieter room in the back (49 rooms, S-€63, Sb-€79, Db-€118, Tb-€160, includes buffet breakfast, suites available, air-con, pleasant garden terrace, across from San Domenico at Viale Curtatone 15, tel. 0577-280-562, fax 0577-271-177, www.chiusarelli.com, info@chiusarelli.com, SE).

$ Alma Domus is ideal—unless nuns make you nervous, you need a double bed, or you plan on staying out past the 23:30 curfew (no mercy given). This quasi-hotel (not a convent) is run with firm but angelic smiles by sisters who offer clean and quiet rooms for a steal and save the best views for foreigners. Bright lamps, quaint balconies, fine views, grand public rooms, top security, and a friendly atmosphere make this a great value. The checkout time is strictly 10:00, but they will store your luggage in their secure courtyard (Db-€60, Tb-€70, Qb-€90, no CC; ask for view room—*con vista,* elevator; from San Domenico walk downhill with the church on your right toward the view, turn left down Via Camporegio, make a U-turn at the little chapel down the brick steps to Via Camporegio 37; tel. 0577-44177 and 0577-44487, fax 0577-47601, NSE).

$ Albergo Bernini makes you part of a Sienese family in a modest, clean home with nine fine rooms. Friendly Nadia and Mauro welcome you to their spectacular view terrace for breakfast and picnic lunches and dinners. Outside of breakfast and checkout time, Mauro, an accomplished accordionist, might play a song for you if you ask (Sb-€77, D-€62, Db-€82, breakfast-€7, less in winter, no CC, midnight curfew, on the main San Domenico–Il Campo drag at Via Sapienza 15, tel. & fax 0577-289-047, www.albergobernini.com, hbernin@tin.it, son Alessandro SE).

$ **Albergo Lea** is a creaky, old-fashioned place in a residential neighborhood a few blocks away from the center (past San Domenico) with 11 rooms and easy parking (S-€50, Db-€87, Tb-€110, cheaper in winter, includes breakfast, yard and rooftop terrace, Viale XXIV Maggio 10, tel. & fax 0577-283-207, SE).

Southeast of Il Campo
These two places are near each other, in the direction of Porta Romana city gate.

$$$ **Antica Torre** rents eight rooms in an atmospheric medieval tower a 10-minute walk from Il Campo (Sb-€95, Db-€110, Tb-€115, breakfast-€7, Via Fieravecchia 7, tel. & fax 0577-222-255, anticatorre@email.it, SE).

$ **Casa Laura** has five clean, charming, well-maintained rooms, some of which have brick-and-beam ceilings (Db-€83 with breakfast, €73 without, cheaper for 3 nights or more; Via Roma 3, about a 10-min walk from Il Campo toward Porta Romana; tel. 0577-226-061, fax 0577-225-240, www.turismoverde.com/ospiti/casalaura, labenci@tin.it, NSE).

Farther from the Center
$$$ **Hotel Santa Caterina** is a three-star, 18th-century place, best for drivers who need air-conditioning. Professionally run with real attention to quality, it has 22 comfortable rooms with a delightful garden (Sb-€105, small Db-€105, Db-€140, Tb-€190, these prices only when you mention this book, includes buffet breakfast, elevator, garden side is quieter but street side—with multi-paned windows—isn't bad, fridge in room, parking-€15/day—request when you reserve, 100 yards outside Porta Romana at Via E.S. Piccolomini 7, tel. 0577-221-105, fax 0577-271-087, www.hscsiena.it, info@hscsiena.it, SE). A city bus runs frequently (Mon–Sat 4/hr, Sun 2/hr) to the town center. A taxi to/from the station runs around €8.

$$$ **Palazzo di Valli,** with 11 spacious rooms and a garden, is a seven-minute walk beyond Porta Romana (the Roman gate) and feels like it's in the country. Catch the city bus into town (Sb-€105, Db-€140, Tb-€170, includes breakfast; parking; Via E.S. Piccolomini 135, bus to center Mon–Sat 4/hr, Sun 2/hr; tel. 0577-226-102, fax 0577-222-255, Camarda family SE). From the autostrada, exit at Siena Sud in the direction of Porta Romana.

EATING

Sienese restaurants are reasonable by Florentine and Venetian standards.
Antica Osteria Da Divo is the place for a fine €40 meal. The
kitchen is creative, the ambience is candlelit, and the food is fresh and
top-notch. The lamb goes baaa in your mouth. They offer a basket of
exotic fresh breads and excellent seasonal dishes. And the chef is understandably proud of his desserts (daily 12:00–14:30 & 19:00–22:00,
reserve for summer eves; Via Franciosa 29, facing baptistery door, take
the far right and walk one long curving block; tel. 0577-286-054).

Trattoria La Tellina has patient waiters and great Mediterranean
food, including excellent homemade tiramisu. Arrive early to get a seat
(Sun–Fri 11:30–15:00 & 18:00–22:00, closed Sat; Via dell Terme 52,
between St. Catherine's House and Piazza Tolomei—where Palio film
is shown; tel. 0577-283-133).

Taverna San Giuseppe, a local favorite, offers modern Tuscan cuisine in a dressy grotto atmosphere. Check the posters tacked around the
entry for daily specials. Reserve or arrive early to get a table (Mon–Sat
12:15–14:30 & 19:15–22:00, closed Sun; 7-min walk up street to the
right of the City Hall, Via Giovanni Dupre 132; tel. 0577-42286).

Osteria il Tamburino is friendly, small, popular, and serves up tasty
meals (Mon–Sat 12:00–14:30 & 19:00–21:30, closed Sun; follow Via di
Città off Il Campo, becomes Stalloreggi, Via Stalloreggi 11; tel. 0577-
280-306).

Ristorante Gallo Nero is a friendly "grotto" for Tuscan cuisine.
Popular with groups, this "black rooster" serves *ribollita* (hearty Tuscan
bean soup) and offers a €23 "medieval menu," as well as several Tuscan
menus, starting at €16 (daily 12:00–15:30 & 19:00–24:00, 3 blocks down
Via del Porrione from Il Campo at #65, tel. 0577-284-356).

Il Verrochio, a block away—tucked between a church and loggia—
serves a decent €13 *menu* in a cozy, wood-beamed setting (daily
12:00–14:30 & 19:00–22:00, closed Wed in winter, Logge del Papa 1,
tel. 0577-284-062).

Le Campane, two blocks off Il Campo, is classy. Run by the same
family for 25 years, it features modern Tuscan fare (daily 12:15–14:30 &
19:15–22:00, closed Mon in winter, indoor/outdoor seating, a few steps
off Via di Città at Via delle Campane 6, tel. 0577-284-035).

Osteria Nonna Gina wins praise from locals for its good quality
and prices (Tue–Sun 12:30–14:30 & 19:30–22:30, closed Mon, Piano
dei Mantellini 2, 10-min walk from Il Campo, near Hotel Duomo, tel.
0577-287-247).

Osteria la Chiacchera is an atmospheric, tasty, and affordable hole-
in-the-brick-wall serving "peasant food" (daily 11:00–24:00, reservations
wise, skip the *trippa*—tripe, 2 rooms, below Pension Bernini at Costa di
San Antonio 4, tel. 0577-280-631).

Siena Hotels and Restaurants

1. Piccolo Hotel Etruria
2. Albergo Tre Donzelle
3. Locanda Garibaldi
4. Hotel Cannon d'Oro
5. To Hotel Duomo, Pen. Pal. Ravizza, & Ost. Nonna Gina
6. To Hotel Villa Liberty & Albergo Lea
7. Hotel Chiusarelli
8. Alma Domus
9. Albergo Bernini & Ost. la Chiacchera

10. To Casa Laura, Antica Torre, Hotel Sta. Caterina, & Palazzo di Valli
11. To Hostel
12. Antica Osteria Da Divo
13. Trattoria La Tellina
14. To Taverna San Giuseppe
15. Osteria il Tamburino
16. Ristorante Gallo Nero
17. Il Verrochio Rest.

18. Le Campane Rest.
19. Pizzeria Spadaforte
20. Gelateria Artigiana
21. Ciao Cafeteria & Spizzico
22. Consorzio Agrario Siena (grocery)
23. Lavarapido Launderette
24. Onda Blu Launderette

For authentic Sienese dining at a fair price, eat at **Locanda Garibaldi,** down Via Giovanni Dupre at #18, within a block of Il Campo (€15 menu, Sun–Fri opens at 12:00–14:00 for lunch and 19:00–21:00 for dinner, arrive early to get a table, closed Sat). Marcello does a little *piatto misto dolce* for €4, featuring several local desserts with sweet wine.

Even with higher prices, lousy service, and lower-quality food, consider eating on Il Campo—a classic European experience. **Pizzeria Spadaforte,** at the edge of Il Campo, has a decent setting, mediocre pizza, and tables steeper than its prices (daily 12:00–16:00 & 19:30–22:30, to far right of city tower as you face it, tel. 0577-281-123).

Cheap Meals, Snacks, and Picnics

Snack with a view from a small balcony overlooking Il Campo. Survey these three places from Il Campo to see which has a free table. On Via di Città, you'll find **Gelateria Artigiana,** which has perhaps Siena's best ice cream, and **Barbero d'Oro,** which serves cappuccino and *panforte* (€1.75/100 grams, balcony with 2 tables, closed Sun). **Bar Paninoteca** is on Vicolo di S. Paolo, on the stairs leading down to Il Campo (sandwiches, has a row of chairs on balcony, closed Mon).

At the bottom of Il Campo, a **Ciao** cafeteria offers easy self-service meals, no ambience, and no views. The crowded **Spizzico,** a pizza counter in the front half of Ciao, serves huge, inexpensive quarter pizzas; on sunny days, people take the pizza, trays and all, out on Il Campo for a picnic (CC only in cafeteria, daily 11:00–22:00, non-smoking section—*non fumatori*—in back, to left of city tower as you face it).

Budget eaters look for *pizza al taglio* shops, scattered throughout Siena, selling pizza by the slice. Picnickers enjoy the market held mornings (except Sun) behind Il Campo, on Piazza del Mercato. Of the grocery shops scattered throughout town, the biggest is **Consorzio Agrario Siena;** it's one block off Piazza Matteotti, toward Il Campo. Their pesto is the besto (Mon–Sat 8:00–19:30, Via Pianigiani 5).

Sienese Sweets

All over town, **Prodotti Tipici** shops sell Sienese specialties. Siena's claim to caloric fame is its *panforte,* a rich, chewy concoction of nuts, honey, and candied fruits that impresses even fruitcake-haters. There are a few varieties to try: *margherita,* dusted in powdered sugar, is more fruity, *panepatto* has a spicy, peppery crust. Locals prefer a chewy white macaroon-and-almond cookie called *ricciarelli.* All this and more can be found at **Bini,** where women in aprons box your sweets like precious gifts (Tue–Sun 9:00–13:30 & 16:30–20:00, closed Mon, Via dei Fusari 13).

TRANSPORTATION CONNECTIONS

Siena has sparse trains connections, but is a great hub for buses to the hill towns.

By train to: Florence (9/day, 1.75 hrs, more with transfer in Empoli).

By bus to: Florence (2/hr, 1.25–2 hrs, by Tra-in bus, last bus at 20:45), **San Gimignano** (6/day, 1.25 hrs, by Tra-in bus, more frequent with transfer in Poggibonsi), **Assisi** (2/day, 2 hrs, by Sena bus; the morning bus goes direct to Assisi, the afternoon bus might terminate at Santa Maria degli Angeli, from here catch a local bus to Assisi, 2/hr, 20 min), **Rome** (7/day, 3 hrs, by Sena bus, arrives at Rome's Tiburtina station), **Milan** (4/day, 5 hr). Schedules get sparse on Sundays and holidays.

Buses depart Siena from Piazza Gramsci, the train station, or both; confirm when you purchase your ticket. You can get tickets for Tra-in buses or Sena buses at the train station (Tra-in bus office: Mon–Sat 5:50–20:00; for Sena, buy tickets at *tabacchi* shop unless they've opened a separate office in the station), or easier and more central, under Piazza Gramsci at Sottopassaggio La Lizza (Tra-in bus office: daily 5:50–20:00, tel. 0577-204-246, toll-free tel. 800-570-530, www.trainspa.it; Sena bus office: Mon–Sat 7:45–19:45, closed Sun, tel. 800-930-960, www.senabus.it).

Sottopassaggio La Lizza, under Piazza Gramsci, has a cash machine (neither bus office accepts credit cards), luggage storage (€3.50/day, daily 7:00–19:45, no overnight storage), posted bus schedules, TV monitors (listing imminent departures), an elevator, and expensive WCs (€0.55). If you decide to depart Siena after the bus offices close, you can buy the ticket directly from the driver (and get charged a supplement). You can also get tickets—and help sorting through schedules—from Palio Viaggi on Piazza Gramsci (La Lizza 12, tel. 0577-280-828, info@palioviaggi.it).

On schedules, the fastest buses are marked *corse rapide*. Note that if a schedule lists your departure point as Via Tozzi or La Lizza, you catch the bus at Piazza Gramsci (Via Tozzi is the street that runs alongside Piazza Gramsci and La Lizza is the name of the bus station).

ASSISI

Assisi is famous for its hometown boy, St. Francis, who made very good.

Around the year 1200, a simple friar from Assisi challenged the decadence of Church government and society in general with a powerful message of non-materialism, simplicity, and a "slow down and smell God's roses" lifestyle. Like Jesus, Francis taught by example. A huge monastic order grew out of his teachings, which were gradually embraced (some would say co-opted) by the Church. Clare, St. Francis' partner in poverty, founded the Order of the Poor Clares. Catholicism's purest example of simplicity is now glorified in beautiful churches. In 1939, Italy made Francis and Clare its patron saints.

Francis' message of love and sensitivity to the environment has a broad and timeless appeal. But any pilgrimage site will be commercialized, and the legacy of St. Francis is Assisi's basic industry. In summer, this Umbrian town bursts with flash-in-the-pan Francis fans and Franciscan knickknacks. Those able to see past the tacky friar mementos can actually have a "travel on purpose" experience.

Planning Your Time

Assisi is worth a day and a night. The town has a half-day of sightseeing and another half-day of wonder. The essential sight is the Basilica of St. Francis. For a good visit, take the Assisi Welcome Walk (below), ending at the basilica. Schedule time to linger on the main square. Hikers enjoy sunset at the castle.

Most visitors are day-trippers. While the town's a zoo by day, it's a delight at night. Assisi after dark is closer to a place Francis could call home.

ORIENTATION

Crowned by a ruined castle at the top, Assisi spills downhill to its famous Basilica of St. Francis. The town is beautifully preserved and rich in history. The 1997 earthquake did more damage to the tourist industry than to the local buildings. Fortunately, tourists have returned—whether art-lovers, pilgrims, or both—drawn by Assisi's powerful sights.

Tourist Information: The TI is in the center of town on Piazza del Comune (summer Mon–Sat 8:00–18:30, Sun 10:00–13:00 & 14:00–17:00; winter Mon–Sat 8:00–14:00 & 15:00–18:00, Sun 9:00–13:00; tel. 075-812-534, info@iat.assisi.pg.it; visit www.umbria2000.it for info on Umbria).

Also on (or just off) Piazza del Comune, you'll find the Roman temple of Minerva, a Romanesque tower, banks, a finely frescoed pharmacy, and an underground Roman Forum.

A combo-ticket *(biglietto cumulativo*, €5.25/1 day) covers three sights: Rocca Maggiore (castle), Pinacoteca (paintings), and the Roman Forum; you'd need to see all three to save money (sold at participating sights).

Market day is Saturday on Piazza Matteotti (which has a good parking garage). Your hotel may give you an Assisi Card, which offers discounts on parking and some affiliated restaurants and shops.

Arrival in Assisi

By Train and Bus: City buses connect Assisi's train station with the old town of Assisi on the hilltop (€0.80, 2/hr, about 15–20 min), stopping at Piazza Unita d'Italia (near Basilica of St. Francis), then Largo Properzio (near Basilica of St. Clare), and finally Piazza Matteotti (top of old town). Going to the old town, buses usually leave from the train station at :16 and :46 past the hour. Going to the train station from the old town, buses usually run from Piazza Matteotti at :10 and :40 past the hour, and from Piazza Unita d'Italia at :17 and :47 past the hour. At Piazza Unita d'Italia, there are two bus stops *(fermata bus):* one sign reads "*per f.s. S.M. Angeli*" (to the train station), and the other reads "*per P. Matteotti*" (to the top of the old town). Note that you can take this bus within Assisi to save a long walk uphill (e.g., visit basilica, walk down to bus stop, then catch bus up to the middle or top of town).

By Taxi: Taxis from the station to the old town run about €10–12. There are legitimate extra charges for luggage, night service, and each person above four passengers, but beware: Many taxis rip off tourists by using tariff #2 (Sunday and holiday fare); the meter should be set on tariff #1 (€2.85 drop). You can check bags at the train station (€2.60/12 hrs, daily 6:30–19:30), but not in the old town. When departing the old town of Assisi, you'll find taxi stands at Piazza Unita d'Italia, the Basilica of St. Clare, and Piazza del Comune (or have your hotel call for you, tel. 075-812-600).

By Car: Drivers just coming in for the day should follow the signs to Piazza Matteotti's wonderful underground parking garage at the top of the town (which comes with bits of ancient Rome in the walls,

€1.10/hr, €11/day with Assisi Card—offered by many hotels, €15.75 without, €0.05/hour and €2/day more on Sun and holidays; open 7:00–21:00, until 23:00 in summer).

Helpful Hints

Travel Agency: You can get train tickets and most bus tickets (but not for Siena) at Agenzia Viaggi Stoppini, between Piazza del Comune and the Basilica of St. Clare (Mon–Fri 9:00–12:30 & 15:30–18:30, Sat 9:00–12:30, closed Sun, Corso Mazzini 31, tel. 075-812-597). For Siena, you buy tickets on the bus (see "Transportation Connections," below).

Internet Access: Internet World has several computers at exorbitant rates (€2.50/10 min, non-smoking, Mon–Sat 11:00–13:00 & 15:00–21:00, Sun 16:00–21:00, Via San Gabriele 25, a long block off Piazza del Comune, tel. 347-528-2062).

Local Guide: Anne Robichaud, an American who has lived here since 1975, gives informative tours of the town and the countryside with the aim of connecting tourists to locals and their customs and culture. Set your own itinerary, or use one of her suggestions, including day trips to neighboring hill towns and tours during local festivals (half-day from €66 per person, full day from €99, cooking lessons, can combine small groups for price reduction, tel. 075-802-334, fax 075-813-698, www.annesitaly.com). Thanks to Anne for her help with the following self-guided walk.

Assisi Welcome Walk

There's much more to Assisi than St. Francis and what all the blitz tour groups see.

This walk, rated ▲▲, covers the town from Piazza Matteotti at the top, down to the Basilica of St. Francis at the bottom. To get to Piazza Matteotti, ride the bus from the train station (or from Piazza Unita d'Italia) to the last stop, or drive there (underground parking with Roman ruins).

The Roman Arena: Start 50 yards beyond Piazza Matteotti (at intersection at far end of parking lot, away from city center—see map). A lane named Via Anfiteatro Romano leads to a cozy circular neighborhood built around a Roman arena. Assisi was an important Roman town. Circle the arena counterclockwise (the chain stretched across the road is to keep cars out, not you). Imagine how colorful the town laundry must have been in the last generation, when the women of Assisi gathered here to do their wash. Adjacent to the laundry is a small rectangular pool filled with water; above it are the coats of arms of the town's leading families. A few steps farther, hike up the stairs to the top of the hill for an aerial view of the oval arena. The Roman stones have

Assisi

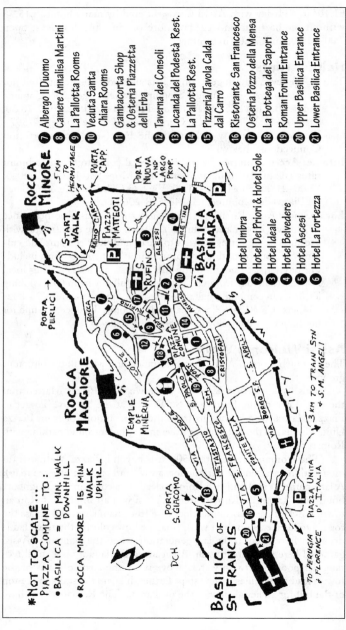

*Not to scale...
- PIAZZA COMUNE TO:
  - BASILICA = 10 MIN. WALK DOWNHILL
  - ROCCA MINORE = 15 MIN. WALK UPHILL

ROCCA MINORE

ROCCA MAGGIORE

START WALK

5 KM TO HERMITAGE

PORTA PERLICI

PORTA CAPP.

PIAZZA MATTEOTI

EREMO CARC.

PORTA NUOVA AND LARGO PROP.

S. RUFINO

ALESSI

ARETINO

BASILICA S. CHIARA

VIA S. AGNESE

VIA PORT.

PIAZZA COMUNE

CRISTOFANI

S. PAOLO

SEM.

VIA S. APOLL.

TEMPLE OF MINERVA

VIA METASTASIO

VIA S. CROCE

VIA S. FRANCESCO

PONTE BELLA

BORGO S.P.

CITY

3 KM TO TRAIN STN & S.M. ANGELI

PORTA S. GIACOMO

PIAZZA UNITA D'ITALIA

TO PERUGIA & FLORENCE

BASILICA of ST FRANCIS

DCH

- 1 Hotel Umbra
- 2 Hotel Dei Priori & Hotel Sole
- 3 Hotel Ideale
- 4 Hotel Belvedere
- 5 Hotel Ascesi
- 6 Hotel La Fortezza
- 7 Albergo Il Duomo
- 8 Camere Annalisa Martini
- 9 La Pallotta Rooms
- 10 Veduta Santa Chiara Rooms
- 11 Gambacorta Shop & Osteria Piazzetta dell'Erba
- 12 Taverna dei Consoli
- 13 Locanda del Podestà Rest.
- 14 La Pallotta Rest.
- 15 Pizzeria/Tavola Calda dal Carro
- 16 Ristorante San Francesco
- 17 Osteria Pozzo della Mensa
- 18 La Bottega dei Sapori
- 19 Roman Forum Entrance
- 20 Upper Basilica Entrance
- 21 Lower Basilica Entrance

long been absorbed into the medieval architecture. It was Roman tradition to locate the arena outside of town...which this was. Continue on. The lane leads down to a city gate.

Umbrian view: Leave Assisi at the Porta Perlici for a commanding view. Umbria, called the "green heart of Italy," is the country's geographical center and only landlocked state. Enjoy the greens: silver green on the valley floor (olives), emerald green 10 yards below you (grapevines), and deep green on the hillsides (evergreen oak trees). Also notice Rocca Maggiore (big castle), a fortress providing townsfolk a refuge in times of attack, and, behind you atop the hill, Rocca Minore (little castle). Now walk back to Piazza Matteotti. Go to the opposite end of this piazza, to the corner with the blobby stone tower. As you walk down the lane next to this tower, you'll see the big dome of the Church of San Rufino. Walk to the courtyard of the church; its big bell tower is on your left.

Church of San Rufino: While Francis is Italy's patron saint, Rufino is Assisi's—the town's first bishop (martyred and buried here in the third century). The church is 12th-century Romanesque with a neoclassical interior. Enter the church (daily 7:00–13:00 & 15:00–19:00). To your right (in the back corner of the church with the black, iron grate) is the font where Francis and Clare were baptized. Traditionally, the children of Assisi are still baptized here.

The striking glass panels in the church floor reveal a recent discovery: ancient foundations dating from Roman times. You're walking on history. After the 1997 earthquake, the church was checked from ceiling to floor by structural inspectors. When they looked under the paving stones, they discovered bodies (it used to be a common practice to bury people in church, until Napoleon decreed otherwise) and underneath the graves, Roman foundations and some animal bones (suggesting the possibility of animal sacrifice). There might have been a Roman temple here; churches were often built on the sites of ruined Roman temples. Standing at the back of the church (facing the altar), look left to the Roman cistern (inside the great stone archway). This was once the town's water source when under attack.

Underneath the church, alongside the Roman ruins, are the foundations of an earlier Church of San Rufino, now the crypt. When it's open, you can go below to see the saint's sarcophagus (€3, mid-March–mid-Oct daily 10:00–13:00 & 15:00–18:00). With your back to the crypt entrance, you'll see the door to the museum of the church (entry included with crypt ticket, same hours as above except 10:00–18:00 in Aug). An archaeology museum may open here in 2004.

Medieval Architecture: When you leave the church, take a sharp left (on Via Dono Doni—say it fast three times), following the sign to Santa Chiara. Take the first right, down the stairway. At the bottom, notice the pink limestone pavement. The medieval town survives. The arches built over doorways indicate that the buildings date from the 12th through the 14th century. The vaults that turn lanes into tunnels are reminders of medieval urban expansion (mostly 15th century). While the population grew, people wanted to live within its protective walls, so Assisi became more dense. Medieval Assisi had five times the population density of today's Assisi.

Notice the floating gardens. Assisi has a flowering balcony competition each June. When you arrive at a street, turn left, going slightly uphill for a block, then jog right. Pause at Via Sermei 6b (on your left) to check out Signore Silvano Giombolini's display of mechanized figures petting sheep, sawing wood, and drawing well water. Look for the nativity scene, featuring an adoring baby Jesus captioned with scriptures and Franciscan-style admonitions to love one another and appreciate life's simple pleasures (free but donations appreciated). Continue ahead, following the "S. Chiara" sign down to the Basilica of St. Clare.

Basilica of St. Clare (Santa Chiara): For a description of this stark, impressive church built to honor St. Clare, see "More Sights," page 926.

Another Umbrian View: Belly up to the viewpoint in front of the basilica. On the left is the convent of St. Clare; below you, the olive grove of the Poor Clares since the 13th century; and, in the distance, a grand Umbrian view. Assisi overlooks the richest and biggest valley in otherwise hilly and mountainous Umbria. The municipality of Assisi has a population of 29,000, but only 1,000 people live in the old town. The lower town grew up with the coming of the railway in the 19th century. In the haze, the blue-domed church is St. Mary of the Angels (Santa Maria degli Angeli, see description below), the cradle of the Franciscan order, marking the place St. Francis lived and worked. This church, a popular pilgrimage sight today, is the first Los Angeles. Franciscans settled in California, naming L.A. (after this church), San Francisco, and even Santa Clara.

Arches and Artisans: From Via Santa Chiara, you can see two arches over the street. The arch at the back of the church dates from 1265. (Beyond it but out of view, the 1316 Porta Nuova marks the final expansion of Assisi.) Toward the city center (on Via Santa Chiara, the high road), an arch indicates the site of the Roman wall.

About 40 yards before this arch, pop into the souvenir shop at #1b. The plaque over the door explains that the old printing press (a national monument now, just inside the door) was used to make fake documents for Jews escaping the Nazis in 1943 and 1944. The shop is run by a couple of artisans: The man makes frames out of medieval Assisi timbers; the woman makes the traditional Assisi, or Franciscan, cross-stitch.

Just past the gate and on your left is the La Pasteria natural products shop (Corso Mazzini 18b, across from entrance of Hotel Sole). Cooks love to peruse Umbrian wines, herbs, pâtés, and truffles, and sample an aromatic "fruit infusion." The Lisa Assisi clothing shop

(Corso Mazzini 25b, across the street and to your right) has a delightful basement, with surviving bits of a 2,000-year-old mortarless Roman wall. Ahead at Corso Mazzini 14d, the small shop (Poiesis) sells olive-wood carvings. Drop in. It's said that St. Francis made the first nativity scene to help teach the Christmas message, which is why you'll see so many in Assisi. Even today, nearby villages are enthusiastic about their "living" manger scenes. Ahead of you, the columns of the Temple of Minerva mark the Piazza del Comune (described below). Sit at the fountain on the square for a few minutes of people-watching—don't you love Italy? Within 200 yards of this square, on either side, were the medieval walls. Imagine a commotion of 5,000 people confined within these walls. No wonder St. Francis needed an escape for some peace and quiet. I'll meet you over at the temple on the square.

Roman Temple/Christian Church: Assisi has always been a spiritual center. The Romans went to great lengths to make this Temple of Minerva a centerpiece of their city. Notice the columns cutting into the stairway. It was a tight fit here on the hilltop. The stairs probably went down triple the distance you see today. The church of Santa Maria sopra (over) Minerva was added in the ninth century. The bell tower is 13th-century. Pop inside the temple/church (Mon–Sat 7:00–19:00, Sun 8:00–19:00, closes at sunset and midday in winter). Today's interior is 17th-century Baroque. Flanking the altar are the original Roman temple floor stones. You can even see the drains for the bloody sacrifices that took place here. Behind the statues of Peter and Paul, the original Roman embankment peeks through.

A few doors back toward the fountain, step into the 16th-century vaults from the old fish market. Notice the Italian flair for design. Even this smelly fish market was once finely decorated. The art style was "grotesque"—literally, a painting in a grotto. This was painted in the early 1500s, a few years after Columbus brought turkeys back from the New World. The turkeys painted here may have been that bird's European debut. (Public WCs are a few steps off Piazza del Comune; near the fountain, go through Via dell' Arco dei Priori, then down the street on the left.)

Church of Santo Stefano: From the main square, hike past the temple up the high road, Via San Paolo. After 200 yards, a sign directs you down a lane to Santo Stefano, which used to be outside the town walls in the days of St. Francis. Legend is that its bells miraculously rang on October 3, 1226, the day St. Francis died. Surrounded by cypress, fig, and walnut trees, it's a delightful bit of offbeat Assisi. Step inside. This is the typical rural Italian Romanesque church—no architect, just built by simple stonemasons who put together the most basic design (daily 8:30–21:30). The lane zigzags down to Via San Francesco. Turn right and walk under the arch toward the Basilica of St. Francis.

Via San Francesco: This was the main drag leading from the town to the basilica holding the body of St. Francis. Francis was a big deal even in his own day. He died in 1226 and was made a saint in 1228—the same year the basilica's foundations were laid—and his body was moved in by 1230. Assisi was a big-time pilgrimage center, and this street was a booming place. Notice the fine medieval balcony just below the arch. A few yards farther down (on the left), cool yourself at the fountain. The hospice next door was built in 1237 to house pilgrims. Notice the three surviving faces of its fresco: Jesus, Francis, and Clare.

SIGHTS

Basilica of St. Francis

A ▲▲▲ sight, the Basilica de San Francesco is one of the artistic and religious highlights of Europe. In 1226, St. Francis was buried (with the outcasts he had stood by) outside of his town on the "Hill of the Damned"—now called the "Hill of Paradise." The basilica is frescoed from top to bottom by the leading artists of the day: Cimabue, Giotto, Simone Martini, and Pietro Lorenzetti. A 13th-century historian wrote, "No more exquisite monument to the Lord has been built."

From a distance, you see the huge arcades "supporting" the basilica. These were 15th-century quarters for the monks. The arcades lining the square leading to the church housed medieval pilgrims.

Orientation: There are three parts to the church: the upper basilica, the lower basilica, and the saint's tomb (below the lower basilica). In the 1997 earthquake, the lower basilica—with walls nearly nine feet thick—was unscathed. The upper basilica, with bigger windows and walls only three feet thick, was damaged. After restoration was completed, the entire church was reopened to visitors in late 1999.

To get oriented, stand at the lower entrance in the courtyard. Opposite the entry to the lower basilica is the information center. You'll find two different WCs within a half-block (up the road in a squat building and halfway down the big piazza on the left).

Cost, Hours, and Information: Free entry, lower basilica daily 6:15–18:45, relic chapel in lower basilica supposedly 8:00–18:30 but often closed, upper basilica daily 8:30–18:30 (Tel. 075-819-0084, www .sanfrancescoassisi.org). Modest dress is required to enter the church—no sleeveless tops or shorts for men, women, or children. The info center sells an excellent guidebook, *The Basilica of Saint Francis—A Spiritual Pilgrimage* (€2.50, by Goulet, McInally, and Wood), which I used as a source for my self-guided tour (below).

Tours: At the info center, ask about tours in English—or better yet, call or e-mail in advance (tours Mon–Sat 9:00–12:30 & 14:30–17:30, no tours Sun, tel. 075-819-0084, assisisanfrancesco@libero.it). Tours are free, but a €25 donation per group is appropriate. The new 75-minute audioguide is also good (€5/person).

Self-Guided Tour: The Basilica of St. Francis, a theological work of genius, can be difficult for the 21st-century tourist/pilgrim to appreciate. Since the basilica is the reason most people visit Assisi, and the message of St. Francis has even the least devout blessing the town Vespas, I've designed this self-guided tour with an emphasis on the place's theology (rather than art history).

Enter through the grand doorway of the lower basilica. Just inside, decorating the top of the first arch, look up and see St. Francis, who greets you with a Latin inscription. Sounding a bit like John Wayne, he says the equivalent of "Slow down and be joyful, pilgrim. You've reached the Hill of Paradise, and this church will knock your spiritual socks off." Start with the tomb (turn left into the nave; midway down the nave to your right, follow signs and go downstairs to the tomb).

The message: Francis' message caused a stir. He traded a life of power and riches for one of obedience, poverty, and chastity. The Franciscan existence (Brother Sun, Sister Moon, and so on) is a space where God, man, and the natural world frolic harmoniously. Franciscan friars, known as the "Jugglers of God," were a joyful part of the community. In an Italy torn by fighting between towns and families, Francis promoted peace and the restoration of order. (He set an example by reconstructing a crumbled chapel.) While the Church was waging bloody Crusades, Francis pushed ecumenism and understanding. Even today the leaders of the world's great religions meet here for summits.

This rich building seems to contradict the teachings of the poor monk it honors, but it was built as an act of religious and civic pride to remember the hometown saint. It was also designed, and still functions, as a pilgrimage center and a splendid classroom.

The tomb: In medieval times, pilgrims came to Assisi because St. Francis was buried here. Holy relics were the "ruby slippers" of medieval Europe. They gave you power—got your prayers answered and helped you win wars—and ultimately helped you get back to your eternal Kansas. Assisi made no bones about promoting the saint's relics, but hid his tomb for obvious reasons of security. Not until 1818 was the tomb opened to the public. The saint's remains are above the altar in the stone box with the iron ties. His four closest friends and first followers are buried in the corners of the room. Opposite the altar, up four steps in between the entrance and exit, notice the small gold box behind the metal grill; this contains the remains of Francis' rich Roman patron, Jacopa dei Settesoli. Climb back to the lower nave.

Lower basilica nave: Appropriately Franciscan, subdued and Romanesque, its nave was frescoed with parallel scenes from the lives of Christ and Francis—connected by a ceiling of stars. Unfortunately, after the church was built and decorated, the popularity of the Franciscans meant side chapels needed to be built. Huge arches were cut out of some scenes, but others survive. In the fresco directly above the entry to the tomb, Christ is being taken down from the cross (just the bottom half of his body can be seen, to the left), and it looks like the story is over. Defeat. But in the opposite fresco (above the tomb's exit), we see Francis preaching to the birds, reminding the faithful that the message of the Gospel survives.

These stories directed the attention of the medieval pilgrim to the altar, where he could meet God through the sacraments. The church was thought of as a community of believers sailing toward God. The prayers coming out of the nave (*navis,* or ship) fill the triangular sections of the ceiling—called *vele,* or sails—with spiritual wind. With a priest for a navigator and the altar for a helm, faith propels the ship.

Stand behind the altar (toes to the bottom step) and look up. The three scenes in front of you are, to the right, "Obedience" (Francis wearing a rope harness); to the left, "Chastity" (in a tower of purity held up by two angels); and straight ahead, "Poverty." Here Jesus blesses the marriage as Francis slips a ring on Lady Poverty. In the foreground, two "self-sufficient" merchants (the new rich of a thriving North Italy) are throwing sticks and stones at the bride. But Poverty, in her patched wedding dress, is fertile and strong, and even those brambles blossom into a rosebush crown.

Putting your heels to the altar and bending back like a drum major, look up at Francis on a heavenly throne, who traded a life of earthly simplicity for glory in heaven. Now, turn to the right and march to the corner, where steps lead down into the...

Relic chapel: This chapel is often unexpectedly closed, it's but worth a look if open. Circle the room clockwise. You'll see the silver chalice and plate that Francis used for the bread and wine of the Eucharist (in small, dark, windowed case set into wall, marked *Calice con Patena).* Francis believed that his personal possessions should be simple, but the items used for worship should be made of the finest materials. In the corner display case is a small section of the haircloth worn by Francis as penitence. In the next corner are the tunic and slippers that Francis wore during his last days. Next, find a prayer (in a fancy silver stand) that St. Francis wrote for Brother Leo, signed with his tau cross. Tav ("tau" in Greek), the last letter in the Hebrew alphabet, is symbolic of faithfulness to the end. Francis signed his name with this simple character. Next is a papal document (1223) legitimizing the Franciscan order and assuring his followers that they were not risking a (deadly) heresy charge. Finally, see the tunic lovingly patched and stitched by followers of the five-foot, four-inch-tall St. Francis.

Return up the stairs to the...

Lower basilica transept: This church brought together the greatest Sienese (Martini and Lorenzetti) and Florentine (Cimabue and Giotto) artists of the day. Look around at the painted scenes. In 1300, this was radical art—believable homespun scenes, landscapes, trees, real people. Study the crucifix (by Giotto) with the eight sparrowlike angels. For the first time, holy people are expressing emotion: One angel turns her head sadly at the sight of Jesus, and another scratches her hands down her cheeks, drawing blood. Mary (lower left), previously in control, has fainted in despair. The Franciscans, with their goal of bringing God to the people, found a natural partner in Europe's first modern painter, Giotto.

To see the Renaissance leap, look at the painting to the right. This is by Cimabue—it's Gothic, without the 3-D architecture, natural back-drop, and slice-of-life reality of the Giotto work. Cimabue's St. Francis (far right with stigmata—the marks of the cross—for easy identification) is considered by some to be the earliest existing portrait of the saint. To the left, at eye level, enjoy the Martini saints and their exquisite halos.

Francis' friend, "Sister Death," was really not all that terrible. In fact, Francis would like to introduce you to her now (above and to the right of the door leading into the relic chapel). Go ahead, block the light and meet her. Then cross the transept to the other side of the altar for the staircase going up. By the way, monks in robes are not my idea of easy-to-approach people, but the Franciscans are still God's jugglers (and most of them speak English).

Courtyard: The treasury to the left of the bookstore is free (dona-tion requested) and features ornately-decorated chalices, reliquaries, vestments, and altarpieces. There's a free, clean WC two-thirds of the way down the great hall on your right.

From the courtyard, climb the stairs to the...

Upper basilica: Built later than the lower, the upper basilica is brighter, Gothic (the first Gothic church in Italy, 1228), and practically wallpapered by Giotto. This gallery of frescoes by Giotto and his assis-tants shows 28 scenes from the life of St. Francis.

Look for these scenes:

• **A common man spreads his cape before Francis** (immediately to right of altar, as you face altar) out of honor and recognition to a man who will do great things. Symbolized by the rose window, God looks over the 20-year-old Francis, a dandy imprisoned in his selfishness. A medieval pilgrim fluent in symbolism would understand this because the Temple of Minerva (which you saw today on Assisi's Piazza del Comune) was a prison at that time. The rose window, which never existed, is symbolic of God's eye.

• **Francis offers his cape to a needy stranger** (next panel). Prior to this act of kindness, Francis had been captured in battle, held as a pris-oner of war, and then released by his father's ransom.

• **Francis is visited by the Lord in a dream** (next panel) and told to leave the army and go home to wait for a non-military assignment: "Go and repair my house, which you see is in ruins." This marks the true beginning of Francis' conversion.

Francis prays to the crucifix in San Damiano church (next panel), which admonishes him to give up his life of wealth and privilege and follow Jesus.

• **Francis relinquishes his possessions** (next panel), giving his dad his clothes, his credit cards, and even his time-share condo on Capri. Naked Francis is covered by the bishop, symbolizing his transition from a man of the world to a man of the Church. Notice the disbelief and concern on the bishop's advisors' faces; subtle expressions like these wouldn't have made it into a medieval fresco of this scene.

• **The pope has a vision** (next panel) of a simple man propping up his teetering Church. This led to the papal acceptance of the Franciscan order.

• **Christ appears to Francis** being carried by a seraph—a six-winged angel (other side of church, fourth panel from the door). For the strength of his faith, Francis is given the marks of his master, the "battle scars of love"...the stigmata. Throughout his life, Francis was interested in chivalry; now he's joined the spiritual knighthood.

• **Francis preaches to the birds** (to the right of the exit). Francis was more than a nature-lover. The birds, of different species, represent the diverse flock of humanity and nature, all created and beloved by God and worthy of each other's love.

Before you leave, look at the ceiling above the altar and front entrance to see large tan patches; these careful repairs were made after the basilica was damaged in the 1997 earthquake. It's a blessing that so many of the frescoes remain.

Near the outside of the upper basilica are the Latin pax (peace) and the Franciscan tau cross in the grass. Tau and pax. For more pax, take the high lane back to town, up to the castle, or into the countryside.

More Sights

▲**Basilica of Saint Clare (Basilica di Santa Chiara)**—Dedicated to the founder of the order of the Poor Clares, this Umbrian Gothic church is simple, in keeping with the Poor Clares' dedication to a life of contemplation. The church was built in 1265, and the huge buttresses were added in the next century. The interior's fine frescoes were whitewashed in Baroque times. The Chapel of the Crucifix of San Damiano, on the right (actually an earlier church incorporated into this one), has the crucifix that supposedly spoke to St. Francis, leading to his conversion in 1206. Stairs lead from the nave down to the tomb of Saint Clare. Her tomb is at the far end. The walls depict scenes from Clare's life and death (1193–1253). The saint's robes, hair, and an enormous tunic she made—along with relics of Saint Francis (including a shoe that he was wearing when he received the stigmata)—are in a large case between the stairs. The attached cloistered community of the Poor Clares has flourished for 700 years (church open daily 6:30–12:00 & 14:00–19:00, until 18:00 in winter).

Roman Forum (Foro Romano)—For a look at Assisi's Roman roots, tour the Roman Forum, which is actually under Piazza del Comune. The floor plan is sparse, the odd bits and pieces obscure, but it's well-explained in English (a 10-page booklet is loaned to you when you enter) and you can actually walk on an ancient Roman road. For an orientation, look at the poster for sale at the entry to get an idea of the original setting of forum and temple (€2.50 entry, or included in €5.20 combo-ticket, daily 10:00–13:00 & 14:00–18:00, closes at 17:00 in winter; from Piazza del Comune, go one-half block down Via San Francesco—it's on your right).

Pinacoteca—This small museum attractively displays its 13th- to 17th-century art (mainly frescoes), with general English information in nearly every room. There's a damaged Giotto Madonna and a rare secular fresco (to right of Giotto), but it's mainly a peaceful walk through a pastel world, best for art-lovers (€2.20, or included in €5.20 combo-ticket: daily 10:00–13:00 & 14:00–18:00: Via San Francesco, no building number, look for banner above entryway, on main drag between Piazza del Comune and Basilica of St. Francis: tel. 075-812-033).

▲**Rocca Maggiore**—The "big castle" offers a good look at a 14th-century fortification and a fine view of Assisi and the Umbrian countryside (€2.20, or included in €5.20 combo-ticket, daily from 10:00 until an hour before sunset, opens at 9:00 July–Aug). If you're pinching your euros, the view is just as good from outside the castle, and the interior is pretty bare.

Commune with Nature—For a picnic with the same birdsong and views that inspired St. Francis, leave all the tourists and hike to the Rocca Minore (small private castle, not tourable) above Piazza Matteotti.

Santa Maria degli Angeli

This flat, modern part of Assisi has one major sight: The basilica that marks the spot where Francis lived, worked, and died.

▲▲**St. Mary of the Angels (Basilica di Santa Maria degli Angeli)**—This huge basilica, towering above the buildings below Assisi, was built around the tiny but historic Porziuncola Chapel (now directly under the dome). When the pope gave Francis his blessing, he was given this *porziuncola*, or "small portion"—a little land with a fixer-upper chapel. Francis lived here after he founded the Franciscan Order in 1208, and this was where he consecrated St. Clare as the Bride of Christ. A chapel called Cappella del Transito marks the place where Francis died (behind and to the right of the Porziuncola Chapel). Follow signs to the Roseta (Rose Garden). Francis, fighting off a temptation that he never named, threw himself onto roses. As the story goes, the thorns immediately dropped off the roses. Ever since, thornless roses have grown here. Look through the window at the rose garden (to the right of the statue of

Francis petting a sheep). The Rose Chapel (Cappella delle Rose) is built over the place where Francis lived. The bookshop has some books in English and the free *museo* has a few monastic cells interesting to pilgrims (museum open April–Oct Mon–Fri 9:00–12:00 & 15:00–18:00, Sat–Sun 8:30–12:30 & 15:00–18:00, closed Wed and Nov–March).

Hours: The basilica is open daily 7:00–19:00. There's a little TI to your right as you face the church (supposedly open daily 9:00–12:00 & 15:00–18:00 but may be closed, tel. 075-812-534). A WC is 40 yards to the right of the TI, behind the hedge.

Getting There: To get to Basilica di Santa Maria degli Angeli from Assisi's train station, it's a five-minute **walk** (exit station left, take first left at McDonald's). When you're leaving the basilica, you can catch a bus directly to the station and on to the old town of Assisi (as you leave church, stop is to your right, next to basilica). The orange city buses run twice hourly (buses to the old town depart the basilica at :10 and :40 after the hour; tickets cost €0.80 if you buy at *tabacchi* or newsstand, €1.50 if you buy from driver; 20-min ride up to old town).

It's efficient to visit this basilica either on your way to the old town of Assisi or when you leave. You can easily walk to the basilica from the station (baggage check available, €2.60/12 hrs, access through shop). If you're heading to Siena next, visit the basilica right before you leave, because that's where you'll catch the bus to Siena (as you leave basilica, stop is to your right, across the street, buy ticket on bus); see "Transportation Connections," below.

SLEEPING

$$$ **Hotel Umbra,** the best splurge in the center, feels like a quiet villa in the middle of town (25 rooms, Sb-€77, Db-€95–120, Tb-€135, includes breakfast, air-con, peaceful garden and view sun terrace, most rooms have views, good restaurant, dinner only, go downhill in Piazza del Comune, take left fork towards Basilica of Saint Francis and turn immediately left under the arch at Via degli Archi 6, tel. 075-812-240, fax 075-813-653, www.hotelumbra.it, humbra@mail.caribusiness.it, family Laudenzi SE).

$$$ **Hotel Dei Priori** is a three-star palatial place in the old center, with big, quiet, posh rooms that have all the comforts (Db-€100–125, superior Db-€140–160, includes breakfast, elevator, air-con, Corso Mazzini 15, tel. 075-812-237, fax 075-816-804, www.assisi-hotel.com, hpriori@tiscali.net, SE).

$$ **Hotel Ideale,** on the top edge of town overlooking the valley, offers 12 bright, modern rooms (all with view, 10 with balconies), a peaceful garden, free parking, and a warm welcome (Sb-€47, Db-€80, includes big-for-Italy breakfast, confirm your arrival time, especially if

SLEEP CODE

(€1 = about $1.10, country code: 39)
Sleep Code: **S** = Single, **D** = Double/Twin, **T** = Triple, **Q** = Quad, **b** = bathroom, **s** = shower only, **no CC** = Credit Cards not accepted, **SE** = Speaks English, **NSE** = No English. Unless otherwise noted, credit cards are accepted.

To help you sort easily through these listings, I've divided the rooms into three categories based on the price for a standard double room with bath:

$$$ **Higher Priced**—Most rooms €90 or more.
$$ **Moderately Priced**—Most rooms between €55-90.
$ **Lower Priced**—Most rooms €55 or less.

The town accommodates large numbers of pilgrims on religious holidays. Finding a room at any other time should be easy. See the map on page 918 for hotel locations.

arriving after 17:00, Piazza Matteotti 1, tel. 075-813-570, fax 075-813-020, www.hotelideale.it, info@hotelideale.it, sisters Lara and Ilaria SE). This hotel, at the top of the old town, is close to the bus stop (and parking lot) at Piazza Matteotti, easy to reach by public transportation.

$$ Hotel Sole is well-located, with 35 spacious, comfortable rooms in a 15th-century building (Sb-€42, Db-€64, Tb-€85, breakfast-€6; half its rooms are in newer annex across the street, some rooms have views and balconies, elevator in annex; Corso Mazzini 35, 100 yards before Basilica of St. Clare; tel. 075-812-373, fax 075-813-706, www.assisihotelsole .com, info@assisihotelsole.com, SE).

$$ Hotel Belvedere, which offers good views and 16 basic rooms (9 with views), is run by Enrico and his American wife, Mary (Db-€75, breakfast-€5, elevator, large communal view terrace, 2 blocks past Basilica of St. Clare at Via Borgo Aretino 13, tel. 075-812-460, fax 075-816-812, assisihotelbelvedere@hotmail.com, SE). Their attached restaurant is good (open by request and reservation only).

$ Hotel Ascesi has an inviting little lobby, nine pleasant rooms, and a tiny terrace, all within a block of the Basilica of St. Francis. They may close temporarily in 2004—if you get no response, try somewhere else (Sb-€36, Db-€52, breakfast-€4; air-con; Via Frate Elia 5, walk up from Piazza Unita d'Italia, turn left at Piazzetta Ruggero Bonghi, see sign on right; tel. & fax 075-812-420, hotelascesi@libero.it). This hotel is near the bus stop and parking lot at the bottom of town (Piazza Unita d'Italia), handy if you're packing lots of luggage.

$ Hotel La Fortezza is a simple, modern, and quiet place with seven rooms (Db-€52, Tb-€70, Qb-€80, a short block above Piazza del Comune at Vicolo della Fortezza 19b, tel. 075-812-993, fax 075-819-8035, www .lafortezzahotel.com, lafortezza@lafortezzahotel.com, Lorenzo SE).

$ Albergo Il Duomo is tidy and *tranquillo*, with nine rooms on a stair-step lane one block up from San Rufino. Check in at Hotel Rufino, just before you head up the lane (Sb-€33, Db-€44, breakfast-€5; Vicolo S. Lorenzo 2, from Church of San Rufino follow sign, then turn left on stair-stepped alley; tel. & fax 075-812-742, www.hotelsanrufino.it, info@sanrufino.it, SE).

$ Camere Annalisa Martini is a cheery home swimming in vines and roses in the town's medieval core. Annalisa speaks English and enthusiastically accommodates her guests with a picnic garden, a washing machine (€5 per small load, including drying and ironing), a communal refrigerator, and six homey rooms (S-€23, Sb-€25, D-€32, Db-€36, Tb-€50, Qb-€60, no CC; 3 rooms share 2 bathrooms, no breakfast, you can use her computer to check your e-mail, €10/day parking nearby with her business card; 1 block from Piazza del Comune, go downhill toward basilica, turn left on Via S. Gregorio to #6; tel. & fax 075-813-536, cameremartini@libero.it).

$ La Pallotta, a recommended restaurant (see "Eating," below), offers seven clean, bright rooms (rooms and restaurant are in different locations). Rooms #12 and #18 have views (Db-€47; view terrace and view sitting room on top floor; Via San Rufino 6, go up short flight of stairs outside building to reach entrance, a block off Piazza del Comune; tel. & fax 075-812-307, www.pallottaassisi.it, pallotta @pallottaassisi.it, SE).

$ Veduta Santa Chiara offers 10 newly remodeled, comfortable rooms near the Basilica of Saint Clare. The two ground-floor rooms have part of the city's Roman foundations incorporated into their decor, and four rooms have basilica views (politely decline the cramped attic room). Staying here is like staying with family, Italian-style—Mamma Nadia and her daughter Annamaria take good care of their guests (Sb-€32, Db-€45, Tb-€65, Vicolo San Antonio 1, tel. & fax 075-815-220). At Piazza del Comune, face the fountain and go through the archway on your right. Jog left around the building and continue downhill past Ristorante Medioevo. At the bottom of that street, jog left again with the road and look for the sign at the bottom of the hill on your right.

$ The Gambacorta family rents several decent rooms and has a roof terrace on a quiet lane (Via Sermei 9) just above St. Chiara. There is no sign or reception desk, so you'll need to check in at their shop a half-block east of Piazza del Comune at San Gabriele 17; look for sign

"Bottega del Buongustaio" on a raised piazzetta (S-€20 Db-€40, Tb-€50; 2-night stays preferred, no breakfast but has kitchen, bag transport available; store open Mon–Wed and Fri–Sat 8:00–13:00 & 16:30–20:00, Thu 8:00–13:00, closed Sun; if you can't arrive when store is open, call when you arrive, tel. 075-812-454, fax 075-813-186, www .ilbongustaio.com, geo@umbrars.com, SE a little). She also has two apartments for stays of at least four nights (3 rooms-€90/day, 5 rooms-€200/day, kitchen, no breakfast).

EATING

For a fine Assisian perch, good regional cooking, and snappy service, relax on a terrace overlooking Piazza del Comune at the third-generation **Taverna dei Consoli** (€14 4-course *menu*, also à la carte, Thu–Tue 12:00–14:30 & 19:00–21:30, closed Wed and Jan, tel. 075-812-516). Friendly owner Moreno, who speaks a leetle English, recommends the *bruschetta, filet al tartufo, cinghiale* (boar), and *stringozzi* (noodles named for the cords that poor people used to strangle priests who extorted sky-high tithes).

At **Locanda del Podestà,** chef Selvio serves up tasty grilled Umbrian sausages, *gnocchi alla sacrantina* (cooked in local wine), and all manner of truffles while English-speaking Romina graciously serves happy diners. Try the tasty *scottadita* ("burn your fingers") lamb chops—as in "they're so good, you can't wait for them to cool before you dive in" (open Thu–Tue 12:00–15:00 & 19:00–22:00, closed Wed; 5-min walk uphill from St Francis' basilica, San Giacomo 6c; tel. 075-813-034).

La Pallotta, a local favorite run by a friendly, hardworking family, offers regional specialties, such as *piccione* (squab, a.k.a. pigeon), *coniglio* (rabbit), and several tasting *menus* of Umbrian cuisine (€15–€24, including vegetarian; Wed–Mon 12:15–14:30 & 19:15–21:30, closed Tue; also rents rooms—see listing above; a few steps off Piazza del Comune, through gate across from temple/church, Vicolo della Volta Pinta 2; tel. 075-812-649).

Osteria Piazzetta dell Erba is a fun, little, family-run place a block above Piazza del Comune, serving good, basic Umbrian specialties next to the Gambacorta grocery (Tue–Sun 12:00–14:00 & 19:00–21:45, closed Mon, Via San Gabriele 15b, tel. 075-815-352).

Pizzeria/Tavola Calda dal Carro is popular, affordable, and friendly (good pizzas and €13 *menu*; watch them grill up your steak or Umbrian sausages over the fire in their open kitchen; Thu–Tue 12:00–15:00 & 19:00–22:00, closed Wed; Vicolo di Nepis 2b, leave Piazza del Comune on Via San Gabriele, then take first right—down a stepped lane; tel. 075-815-249).

Ristorante San Francesco is the place to splurge for dinner (€12–14 *primi*) with a view on the Basilica of Saint Francis (Thu–Tue 12:00–14:30 & 19:30–22:00, closed Wed, facing Basilica at Via San Francesco 52, tel. 075-812-329).

Osteria Pozzo della Mensa offers up organic salads and lots of other typical Umbrian vegetarian choices, as well as locally-produced *salumi* and cheeses (Thu–Tue 12:00–15:00 & 19:00–22:00, closed Wed; Via del Pozzo della Mensa 11b; head up Via San Rufino from Piazza del Comune and take first right, then straight ahead 50 yards; tel. 347-344-0644).

For a picnic of Umbrian treats, try **La Bottega dei Sapori** for its good prosciutto sandwiches and specialty items, including truffle paste. Friendly Fabrizio may give you a taste (daily 9:00–20:00, closed Tue in winter, Piazza del Comune 34, tel. 075-812-294).

TRANSPORTATION CONNECTIONS

By train to: Rome (5/day, 1.75–2.5 hrs), **Florence** (5/day, 2–2.75 hrs, more with transfers at Terontola and Cortona), **Orvieto** (7/day, 2 hrs, transfer in Terontola), **Siena** (6/day, 3.25 hrs, transfers in Chiusi and Terontola; bus is more efficient). Train station: tel. 075-804-0272.

Several different bus companies offer service by **bus** to: **Rome** (3/day, 3 hrs, €16.50, pay driver, departs Assisi's Piazza Unita d'Italia, arrives at Rome's Tiburtina station), **Siena** (2/day, 2 hrs, €9, pay driver, departs from Basilica di Santa Maria degli Angeli near Assisi train station; to get from station to basilica, exit station left, take first left at McDonald's—as you face basilica, bus stop is to your left across street). Don't take the bus to **Florence** (1/day, departs Piazza Unita d'Italia at 6:45 a.m., 2.75 hrs); the train is better.

HILL TOWNS
OF CENTRAL
ITALY

Sun-dried tomatoes, homemade pasta, wispy cypress-lined driveways following desolate ridges to fortified 16th-century farmhouses, and dusty old-timers warming the same bench day after day while soccer balls buzz around them like innocuous flies. The sun-soaked hill towns of Central Italy offer what to many is the quintessential Italian experience.

Italy's hill towns retain their medieval charm, and are best enjoyed by adapting to the pace of the countryside. So...slow...down...and enjoy the delights that these villages offer. Spend the night if you can, as many hill towns are mobbed by day-trippers.

Planning Your Time

How in Dante's name does a traveler choose from the literally hundreds of Central Italy's hill towns? I cover some of the best towns in this chapter (listed roughly from north to south). The one(s) you visit will depend on your time, interests, and mode of transportation. There's no hard-and-fast best plan. Go where you want, stay as long as you want.

Multi-towered San Gimignano is a classic, but peak-season crowds can overwhelm the town's charms. Wine aficionados won't want to miss Montalcino or Montepulciano. Art-lovers and those eager to trace Frances Mayes' footsteps under the Tuscan sun will make the pilgrimage to Cortona. The grand, classic town of Orvieto is famous for its wine, ceramics, and colorful cathedral. But my longtime favorite is the tiny, obscure, and (to be honest) dying hill town of Civita.

Getting Around the Hill Towns

Bigger destinations (like Cortona, Orvieto, and Civita) are doable by public transportation. Smaller hill towns are easier to visit by car.

By Bus or Train: Traveling by public transportation is an economical way to see the countryside and rub elbows with the locals. While trains connect some of the smaller towns like Cortona, the train stations

Hill Towns

are likely to be in the valley several miles from the town center, usually connected by a local bus.

Buses are most often the better, if not the only, choice to connect destinations. Siena is a great hub of local bus lines. You can find schedules at local TIs and buy tickets at newsstands or tobacco shops (look for the black sign with a big white T on it). Confirm the departure point (*Dov'è la fermata?*). Some piazzas have more than one bus stop, so double-check that the posted schedule lists your destination and departure time. In general, orange buses are local city buses and blue buses are for long distances.

Once the bus arrives, confirm the destination with the driver. You are expected to stow big packs underneath the bus (open the luggage compartment if it's closed). Sundays and holidays are problematic. Buses, even from large cities like Siena, have sparse schedules and the few departing ones are usually jam-packed. Bus ticket offices are often closed on Sundays, so make plans and buy your ticket ahead of time. If you must

Hill Towns: Public Transportation

travel on a day when there are few choices (like Easter), drop into a travel agency and ask for help. Most agencies book bus and train tickets with little or no commission.

By Car: A car is the best way to maximize your time in Italy's hill towns. Since a car is a headache in big cities (such as Florence and Siena), pick up your car in the last big city you visit, then head to the countryside. Get a big, detailed regional road map at a newsstand. Although roads are numbered on the map, you will not find any numbers referenced on the actual road signs. Roads are indicated by blue signs with a city name on them

If you are staying overnight, ask your hotelier for parking suggestions. Keep all valuables out of sight and locked in the trunk of the car.

San Gimignano

The epitome of a Tuscan hill town, with 14 medieval towers still standing (out of an original 72!), San Gimignano is a perfectly preserved
tourist trap, so easy to visit and visually pleasing that it's a good stop.

In the 13th century, back in the days of Romeo and Juliet, towns
were run by feuding noble families. They'd periodically battle things out
from the protection of their respective family towers. Pointy skylines were
the norm in medieval Tuscany. But in San Gimignano, fabric was big
business, and many of its towers were built simply to hang dyed fabric
out to dry.

While the basic three-star sight here is the town of San Gimignano
itself, there are a few worthwhile stops. From the town gate, shop
straight up the traffic-free town's cobbled main drag to Piazza del
Cisterna (with its 13th-century well). The town sights cluster around the
adjoining Piazza del Duomo. Thursday is market day (on Piazza
Duomo), but for local merchants, every day is a sales frenzy.

Tourist Information: The helpful TI is in the old center on Piazza
Duomo (daily March–Oct 9:00–13:00 & 15:00–19:00, Nov–Feb 9:00–
13:00 & 14:00–18:00, free maps, sells bus tickets, books rooms, tel.
0577-940-008, www.sangimignano.com, prolocsg@tin.it, SE). A public WC is just off Piazza della Cisterna (€.50).

SIGHTS

Collegiata—This Romanesque church, with round windows and wide
steps, is filled with fine Renaissance frescoes, some painted by Domenico
Ghirlandaio (€3.50, €5.50 combo-ticket includes mediocre Religious Art
Museum, Mon–Fri 9:30–19:30, Sat 9:30–17:00, Sun 13:00–17:00).
Civic Museum (Museo Civico)—This is a small, fun museum inside
the City Hall (Palazzo Comunale). As you enter, head right, into the
room called Sala di Consiglio. It's *molto* medieval and covered in festive
frescoes, including the *Maesta* by Lippo Memmi. This virtual copy of
Simone Martini's *Maesta* in Siena proves that Memmi doesn't have quite
the same talent as his famous brother-in-law. Upstairs the Pinacoteca
displays a classy little painting collection, with a 1422 altarpiece by
Taddeo di Bartolo honoring Saint Gimignano. You can see the saint
with the town in his hands surrounded by events from his life. As you
exit, be sure to stop by the Camera del Podesta to check out the medieval
dating scene (€5, includes Torre Grossa, daily 9:30–19:30, Nov–Feb
10:00–17:00, includes Torre Grossa).
Torre Grossa—The city's tallest tower, at 200 feet, can be scaled (€5,
includes Civic Museum, same hours as museum).

San Gimignano

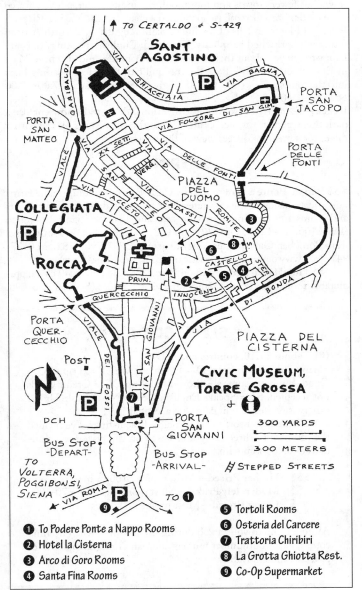

↑ TO CERTALDO & S-429

SANT' AGOSTINO

PORTA SAN JACOPO

VIA GARIBALDI

VIA GHIACCIAIA

VIA BAGNAIA

VIA FOLGORE DI SAN GIM.

PORTA SAN MATTEO

VIALE

PORTA DELLE FONTI

EX SETT.

VIA

VIA S. MATTEO

VIA VERG.

VIA DELLE FONTI

VIA D'ACETO

VIA CADASSI

PIAZZA DEL DUOMO

ROMITE

S. STEF.

COLLEGIATA

ROCCA

PRUN.

QUERCECCHIO

INNOCENTI

CASTELLO

VIA DI BONDA

PORTA QUER-CECCHIO

VIALE DEI FOSSI

VIA SAN GIOVANNI

VIA

PIAZZA DEL CISTERNA

Post

CIVIC MUSEUM, TORRE GROSSA

N

DCH

PORTA SAN GIOVANNI

300 YARDS

300 METERS

⑦

Bus Stop -Depart-

Bus Stop -Arrival-

⑨ STEPPED STREETS

TO VOLTERRA, POGGIBONSI, SIENA

VIA ROMA

TO ❶

❶ To Podere Ponte a Nappo Rooms
❷ Hotel la Cisterna
❸ Arco di Goro Rooms
❹ Santa Fina Rooms

❺ Tortoli Rooms
❻ Osteria del Carcere
❼ Trattoria Chiribiri
❽ La Grotta Ghiotta Rest.
❾ Co-Op Supermarket

Sant' Agostino Church—This peaceful church, at the opposite end of town, has fewer crowds and more soul. Behind the altar, a lovely fresco cycle by Benozzo Gozzoli (who painted a chapel in the Medici-Riccardi Palace in Florence) tells of the life of Saint Augustine, a North African monk who preached simplicity. The kind, English-speaking friars are happy to tell you about their church and way of life, and also have Mass in English on Sundays. Pace the tranquil cloister before heading back into the tourist mobs (free, but €.50 lights the frescoes, daily 7:00–12:00 & 15:00–19:00).

Rocca—Formerly Florentine fortifications, these walls now enclose a park that's perfect for picnicking. Climb the steep stairs on the corner tower for a great (and free) view of the towers.

SLEEPING

$$$ Podere Ponte a Nappo, run by Carla Rossi, is a comfortable farmhouse just outside of the city gates. The tastefully decorated apartments and rooms are surrounded by vineyards and a view of San Gimignano (Db-€100, Tb-€115, Qb-€130, no CC, 15-min walk or 5-min drive from Porta San Giovanni, parking, air-con, tel. 0577-907-282, fax 0577-941-268, www.appartamentirossicarla.com, cabusini@tin.it).

$$ Hotel la Cisterna, right on Piazza Cisterna, offers 49 clean, predictable rooms, some with panoramic view terraces (Sb-€70, Db-€90,

SLEEP CODE

(€1 = about $1.10, country code: 39)

Sleep Code: **S** = Single, **D** = Double/Twin, **T** = Triple, **Q** = Quad, **b** = bathroom, **s** = shower only, **no CC** = Credit Cards not accepted, **SE** = Speaks English, **NSE** = No English. Unless otherwise noted, credit cards are accepted.

To help you sort easily through these listings, I've divided the rooms into three categories based on the price for a standard double room with bath:

$$$ **Higher Priced**—Most rooms €100 or more.
$$ **Moderately Priced**—Most rooms between €70-100.
$ **Lower Priced**—Most rooms €70 or less.

Although the town is a zoo during the daytime, when evening comes, locals outnumber tourists and San Gimignano becomes peaceful and enjoyable.

Db with view-€103, Db with terrace-€115, buffet breakfast, elevator, good restaurant with great view, discounts off-season, closed Jan–Feb, Piazza della Cisterna 24, tel. 0577-940-328, fax 0577-942-080, www .hotelcisterna.it, info@hotelcisterna.it, Alessio SE).

$$ Enterprising **Carla Rossi,** who runs Poldere Ponte a Nappo above, also rents rooms and apartments—most with views—throughout the town. You could rent rooms in the charming little houses of **Arco di Goro** and **Santa Fina**, while **Tortoli** has elegant rooms in a medieval tower overlooking Piazza Cisterna (Db-from €60, most around €100, Tb & Qb around €110–150, no CC, no breakfast, Via di Cellole 81, tel. & fax 0577-955-041, mobile 349-882-1565, www .appartamentirossicarla.com, cabusini@tin.it, son Francesco SE).

$ **Associazione Strutture Extralberghiere** is a clearinghouse for reasonably-priced private rooms around the city (Db-€60, no CC, no breakfast, Piazza della Cisterna, tel. 0577-943-190).

EATING

Osteria del Carcere has good food and prices (12:30–15:00 & 19:30–22:00, closed Wed and lunch Thu; Via del Castello 13, just off Piazza della Cisterna; tel. 0577-941-905).

The tiny **Trattoria Chiribiri,** just inside Porta San Giovanni, serves homemade pasta and desserts at a remarkably fair price (daily 11:00–23:00, Piazza della Madonna 1, tel. 0577-941-948).

La Grotta Ghiotta makes good soup and sandwiches that can be packed up *portare via*—to go (daily 10:00–20:00, Via Santo Stefano 10, tel. 0577-942-074)

Picnics: Co-Op sells all you need for a nice spread (Mon–Sat 8:30–20:00, closed Sun, at parking lot below Porta San Giovanni). Or browse the shops guarded by wild boar statues to buy boar by the gram. Pick up some boar (*cinghiale;* cheeng-gee-AH-lay), cheese, bread, and wine and enjoy a picnic in the garden at the Rocca or the park outside Porta San Giovanni.

TRANSPORTATION CONNECTIONS

By bus to: Florence (hrly, 75 min, change in Poggibonsi), **Siena** (5/day, 1.25 hrs, more with change in Poggibonsi). Sunday buses are few, far between, and crowded. In San Gimignano, bus tickets are sold at the bar just inside the town gate or at the TI. The town has no baggage-check service.

Drivers: You can't drive within the walled town of San Gimignano, but a car park awaits just a few steps outside.

Montalcino

On a hill overlooking vineyards and valleys below, Montalcino—famous for its delicious and pricey Brunello di Montalcino red wines—is a must-sip for wine lovers.

In the Middle Ages, Montalcino (mohn-tahl-CHEE-noh) was considered Siena's biggest ally. Originally allied with Florence, the town switched sides after the Sienese beat up Florence in the battle of Monteaperti in 1260. The Sienese persuaded the Montalcini to their views by forcing them to sleep one night in the bloody, Florentine-strewn battlefield.

Montalcino prospered under Siena, but like its ally, waned after the Medici family took control of the region. The village regained fame when, in the late 19th century, the Biondi Santi family created a fine, dark red wine, calling it "the brunette."

Non–wine-lovers may find Montalcino a bit too focused on *vino*, but one sip of Brunello makes even wine skeptics believe that Bacchus was on to something. Note that the Rosso di Montalcino wine is also good at half the price. Those with sweet tooths will enjoy munching Ossi di Morta ("bones of the dead"), a crunchy cookie with almonds.

Tourist Information: The TI is just off Piazza Garibaldi, in the city hall (daily 10:00–13:00, 14:00–17:50, closed Mon in winter, tel. & fax 0577-849331, www.prolocomontalcino.it, info@prolocomontalcino.it, some English).

SIGHTS

Fortezza—The 14th-century fort, built under the rule of Siena, now houses an *enoteca* wine bar (see below). Climb the ramparts to enjoy a panoramic view of the Asso and Orcia valleys, or enjoy a picnic in the park surrounding the fort (€3.50 for rampart walk, daily 9:00–20:00, closed Monday off-season).

Museo Civico—Gothic art is the star of this museum, with works from Montalcino's heyday, the 13th- to 16th-centuries. Wooden sculptures and religious objects round out the collection (€4.50, €6 combo-ticket includes fort, Tue–Sun 10:00–13:00, 14:00–17:50, closed Mon, Via Ricasoli, tel. 0577-846-014).

Wineries—While there are plenty of *enotecas*, there are no real wineries inside the city. The countryside, however, is littered with them, and most wineries will give tastings, but require an appointment. Banfi is the most touristy and produces well-respected wines (tours Mon–Fri 16:00, 10 min south of Montalcino in Sant' Angelo Scalo, reserve in advance, tel. 0577-840111, www.castellobanfi.com, reservations@banfi.it).

The TI can give you the list of more than 150 others to choose from (www.consorziobrunellodimontalcino.it, consbrun@tin.it).

SLEEPING

(€1 = about $1.10, country code: 39)

$$ Albergo il Giglio, although lacking in warmth, has 12 comfortable rooms, some with vaulted ceilings. Ask for a room with a view (Sb-€53, Db-€80, Tb-€85, breakfast-€6.50, Via Saloni 5, tel. & fax 0577-848-167, hotelgiglio@tin.it).

$ Ristorante il Moro rents four pleasant, modern rooms around the corner from their restaurant. The two upper rooms have views, the lower have terraces, and they all share a cozy common room with a kitchen (Db-€50, no breakfast, Via Mazzini 4, tel. 0577-849-384, Alessandro & Julia SE).

$ Affittacamere Mariuccia is basic and drab, but central and cheap (Sb-€35, Db-€44, no breakfast, air-con, check-in at Enoteca Pierangioli, Piazza del Popolo 16, tel. & fax 0577-849-113, www.enotecapierangioli.com, enotecapierangioli@hotmail.com, Stefania NSE).

Eating in Montalcino

Taverna Il Grappolo Blu is dressy yet friendly, serving local specialties and vegetarian options (Sat–Thu 12:00–15:30 & 19:00–22:00, closed Fri, Scale di Via Moglio 1, tel. 0577-847-150, Luciano SE).

Trattoria Sciame, a family-run hole-in-the-wall, has nine small tables and homemade desserts (pasta-€7, meat-€8, Wed–Mon 12:00–14:30 & 19:00–21:30, closed Tue, Via Ricasoli 9, tel. 0577-848-017).

Gather ingredients for a picnic at the **Co-Op supermarket** on Via Ricasoli, then enjoy your feast in front of the Fortezza. **Market day** is Friday, in Viale della Liberta (7:00–13:00).

Wine Tasting in Montalcino

The medieval setting inside Montalcino's fort at **Enoteca La Fortezza** makes this a fun place for a glass or three of local wine. Spoil yourself with Brunello in the cozy enoteca or at outdoor tables (3 tastes for €12, snacks for two-€8, daily 9:00–20:00, closes at 18:00 and on Mon off-season, inside the Fortezza, tel. 0577-849-211, www.enotecalafortezza.it).

Ferruccio Biondi-Santi, the founder of the café, **Fiaschetteria Italiana**, was also the creator of the famous Brunello wine. The wine library in the back boasts many choices of local wine, including a prized bottle from 1955, a vintage year. A meeting place since 1888, this grand café also serves light lunches and espresso to tourists and locals alike (€8–10 for glass of Brunello and plate of snacks, daily 7:30–24:00, Piazza del Popolo 6, tel. 0577-849-043).

TRANSPORTATION CONNECTIONS

To: Siena (10 buses/day, 90 min), **Montepulciano** (10 buses/day, change to line #114 in Torrenieri, 60 min plus transfer time). Bus tickets are sold at tobacco shops or on board. The town has no baggage-check service.

Montepulciano

Curving its way along a ridge, Montepulciano (mohn-tay-PULL-chee-ah-noh) delights visitors with *vino* and views. Alternately under Sienese and Florentine rule, the city still retains its medieval *contrade* districts, each with a mascot and flag. The neighborhoods compete the last Sunday of August in the *Bravio delle Botti*, where teams of men push large wine casks uphill from Piazza Marzocco to Piazza Grande, all hoping to win a banner and bragging rights.

The city is a collage of architectural styles, but the elegant San Biagio Church, at the base of the hill, is the most impressive Renaissance building. Most ignore the architecture and focus more on the city's other creative accomplishment, the tasty Vino Nobile di Montepulciano red wine.

The action in Montepulciano centers on two streets, the steep Via di Gracciano nel Corso, and Via Ricci, but the quiet back streets are well worth a visit.

Tourist Information: The TI is on Via Gracciano nel Corso 26, not to be confused with the more central and less helpful "Strada del Vino" office on Piazza Grande (daily March–Oct 9:30–13:00 & 15:00–18:30, closed Tue, tel. 0578-717-242, www.comune.montepulciano.si.it, prolocomp@bccmp.com).

Helpful Hints: Market day is Thursday, and a larger market takes place at the bus station on Saturday (8:00–14:00). Public WCs are located next to Palazzo del Comune and the church of St. Augustine.

SIGHTS

Piazza Grande—This pleasant, lively piazza is surrounded by an architectural grab-bag. The medieval Palazzo del Comune has a Florentine-style **clock tower;** you can climb to the top for a windy, panoramic view (€1.55, daily 10:00–18:00). The Palazzo de' Nobili-Tarugi is a Renaissance arcaded confection, while the unfinished Duomo glumly looks on, wishing the city hadn't run out of money for the facade. Dream up a way to finish it while you enjoy a cappuccino at the café on the square.

Civic Museum (Museo Civico)—Small and eclectic, this well-presented museum is worthwhile if only for its colorful Della Robbia ceramic altarpieces (€4.13, Tue–Sat 10:00–13:00 & 15:00–18:00, Sun 10:00–18:00, closed Mon, Via Ricci, tel. 0578-715-322).

San Biagio Church—Down a picturesque driveway lined with cypress, this church—designed by Antonio da Sangallo—is Renaissance perfection. The proportions of the Greek cross plan give the building a pleasing rhythmic quality. The lone tower was supposed to have a twin, but it was never built. The soaring interior is impressive, with a high dome and lantern (daily 9:00–13:00 & 15:00–19:00). The street Via di San Biagio, leading from the church up into town, makes for an enjoyable, if challenging walk.

Cantinas—Montepulciano's most popular attraction is its Vino Nobile. This robust red wine can be tasted in any of the cantinas lining Via Ricci and Via nel Corso, but **Contucci** is the most famous. Lively Adamo has been making wine since 1953 and welcomes tourists into his cellar with warmth and wisecracks (€5.50 for guided visit and 4 tastes, no reservation necessary, Piazza Grande 7, tel. 0578-717-484). The information office for the "Strada del Vino" on Piazza Grande may not give out much city information, but it does organize **wine tours** in the city (€13, Wed 17:30) and minibus winery tours farther afield (€21, Thu 13:30, call for current days and times, tel. 0578-717-484, www .stradavinonobile.it, info@stradavinonobile.it).

SLEEPING

(€1 = about $1.10, country code: 39)

$$ **Mueble il Riccio** (hedgehog in Italian) is medieval-elegant, with modern rooms, a view terrace, and friendly owners. When Giorgio isn't manning the desk, he's out giving country tours in one of his classic Italian cars (Sb-€75, Db-€85, Tb-€105, breakfast-€8, Via Talosa 21, tel. & fax 0578-757-713, www.ilriccio.net, info@ilriccio.net, *poco* English).

$ **Camere Bellavista** has simple rooms with views, and nicer rooms without. Room 6 has a view terrace worth reserving (standard Db-€55, nicer Db-€65, no CC, no breakfast, no elevator, Via Ricci 25, tel. 0347-823-2314, fax 0578-716-341, bellavista@bccmp.com, NSE).

EATING

Ai Quattro Venti is fresh, flavorful, fun, and right on Piazza Grande. Mushroom fans should try anything with the word *bosco* in it (pasta-€7, Fri–Wed 12:00–14:00 & 19:00–22:00, closed Thu, next to city hall on Piazza Grande, tel. 0578-717-231).

Osteria dell'Aquacheta serves pasta and salads at reasonable prices, with a mix of locals and tourists (€5 pasta and salads, Wed–Mon 12:30–15:00 & 19:30–22:30, closed Tue, Via del Teatro 22, tel. 0578-717-086).

TRANSPORTATION CONNECTIONS

To: Siena (8 buses/day, 1.25 hrs, few in afternoon, none on Sun), **Pienza** (8 buses/day, 30 min). The town has no baggage-check service.

Cortona

Cortona clings by its fingernails to the top of a mountain (1,700 feet), dangling above views of the Tuscan and Umbrian landscape below. Frances Mayes' books, such as *Under the Tuscan Sun,* have placed this town in the touristic limelight, just as Peter Mayle's books popularized (and populated) the Luberon region in France. But even before Mayes ever published a book, Cortona was considered one of the classic Tuscan hill towns.

The city began as one of the largest Etruscan settlements, the remains of which can be seen at the base of the city walls, as well as in the nearby tombs. It grew to its present size in the 13th to 15th centuries, when it was a colorful and crowded city, eventually allied with Florence.

The farmland that fills almost every view from the city was marshy and uninhabitable until about 300 years ago, when it was drained and turned into some of the most fertile land in Tuscany.

Bring good walking shoes; the streets here can be steep and unforgiving. Mercifully, most of Cortona's sights and shops cluster around the level streets on the Piazza Garibaldi-to-Piazza del Duomo axis.

Art-lovers will know Cortona as the home of Renaissance painter Luca Signorelli, Baroque master Pietro della Cortona (Berretini), and the 20th-century Futurist artist Gino Severini. Cortona's museums and churches reveal many of the works of these native sons.

Tourist Information: The helpful TI is on the main drag, Via Nazionale 42 (daily March–Oct 9:00–13:00 & 15:00–19:00, cash machine, also sells train tickets, tel. 0575-630-352, info@cortonantiquaria.com, SE). **Market day** is Saturday (early–14:00, Piazza Signorelli).

Arrival in Cortona: You'll probably arrive at Piazza Garibaldi, where the bus stop is located outside the massive town walls. From here it is a level five-minute walk down bustling shop-lined Via Nazionale (stop by the TI) to Piazza della Reppublica, the heart of the town, dominated by the City Hall (Palazzo della Comune). From this square it's a five-minute level walk past the interesting Etruscan Museum and theater to Piazza Duomo, where you'll find the recommended Diocesan Museum. Steep streets, many of them stepped, lead from Piazza della Repubblica up to the San Nicolo and Santa Margherita churces and the Medici Fortress (30 min).

Cortona

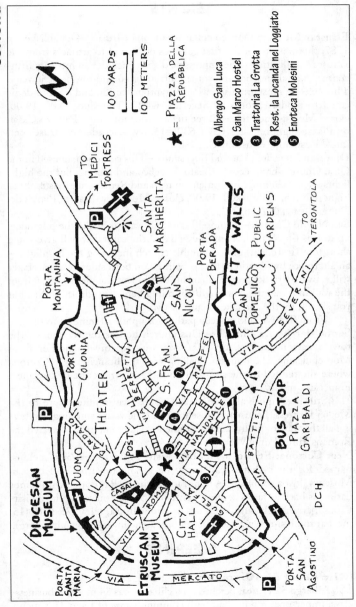

100 YARDS
100 METERS

★ = PIAZZA DELLA REPUBBLICA

❶ Albergo San Luca
❷ San Marco Hostel
❸ Trattoria La Grotta
❹ Rest. la Locanda nel Loggiato
❺ Enoteca Molesini

SIGHTS

Etruscan Museum (Museo della Accademia Etrusca)—Established in 1787, this was one of the first galleries dedicated to artifacts from the Etruscan civilization. The impressive display includes an intricate fifth-century B.C. chandelier and some fantastic gold and turquoise jewelry. This eclectic museum also has an Egyptian section and a room dedicated to modern works by Severini (€4.20, Tue–Sun 10:00–19:00, closed Mon, guided tour–€7, see ticket office for times, Palazzo Casali on Piazza Signorelli, tel. 0575-630-415, www.accademia-etrusca.net, info@accademia-etrusca.net).

Diocesan Museum (Museo Diocesano)—This collection, housed in the Gesu Church, has pieces by Beato Angelico and Duccio, but the highlights are the paintings by hometown hero and Renaissance master, Luca Signorelli (€5, daily 10:00–19:00, closed Mon Nov–March, Piazza del Duomo 1, tel. 0575-637-235).

San Nicolo Church—Signorelli fans will want to make the pilgimage up to this tiny church. Ring the bell and the caretaker will give you a short tour (in Italian) of this humble church including the highlight—an altarpiece by Signorelli that is painted on both sides. The caretaker will activate a tricky arm mechanism that moves the picture away from the wall to reveal the painting behind it. There's no admission fee, but you should tip the caretaker a euro or two.

From San Niccolo, a steep path leads uphill 10 minutes to the...

Santa Margherita Church—This church houses the remains of the town's patron saint. Saint Margaret was an unwed mother from Montepulciano who found her calling with the Franciscans in Cortona where she tended to the sick and poor. Her son eventually became a Franciscan monk.

Still need more altitude? Head uphill five minutes more to the Medici Fortress. It's usually closed, but the views are stunning, stretching all the way to distant Lake Trasimeno, where Hannibal defeated the Romans in the Punic Wars.

Near Cortona: Etruscan Tombs—Visits to nearby *melone* (melons, named for their shape) can easily be arranged with the Etruscan Museum. Just a couple miles out of town, the road is dotted with tombs dating as back as far as seventh-century B.C. (compulsory guided visit–€10.50, arrange through museum or Aioncultura, tel. 0575-630-415, meet at tomb site, www.aioncultura.org, aioncultura@aioncultura.org).

SLEEPING

(€1 = about $1.10, country code: 39)
$$$ **Albergo San Luca,** perched on a cliffside, has 54 modern, business-class, impersonal rooms, half with stunning views of Lago Trasimeno.

Right at the bus stop, it's perfect if you want to avoid dragging your bags up the hill (Sb-€70, Db-€100, popular with Americans and groups, reserve view rooms ASAP, Piazza Garibaldi 1, tel. 0575-630-460, fax 0575-630-105, www.sanlucacortona.com, info@sanlucacortona.com, SE).

$ **San Marco Hostel**, at the top of town, housed in a remodeled 13th-century palace, is one of Italy's best (€10.50, in rooms with 2, 4 or 8 beds, lockout 11:00–17:00, Via Maffei 57, tel. 0575-601-392, SE).

Near Cortona

$$$ **Casa San Martino**, 12 miles east of Cortona near the isolated village of Lisciano Niccone, is a 250-year-old countryside farmhouse run as a B&B by American Italophile Lois Martin. While Lois reserves the summer (June–Aug) for one-week stays, she'll take guests staying a minimum of three nights for the rest of the year (Db-€160, 10 percent discount for my readers—mention this book when you reserve, includes breakfast, pool, washer/dryer, house rental available, Casa San Martino 19, Lisciano Niccone, tel. 075-844-288, fax 075-844-422). Lois' neighbors, Ernestine and Gisbert Schwanke, run the tidy **La Villetta di San Martino B&B** (Db-€110 includes breakfast, 2-night min, common kitchen and sitting room, San Martino 36, tel. & fax 075-844-309, erni@netemedia.net, SE).

$$ **Castello di Montegualandro** is a well-preserved castle on a hill opposite Cortona, overlooking the lake and countryside. Christina and dad, Claudio, rent four charming medieval apartments, formerly peasants' quarters, inside the peaceful castle walls. Each one is unique and named for its former use—the Fornaio's sunken living room used to be a kiln. The castle's chapel is a popular spot for weddings (3–4 person apartment-€100, 3-night min, mention this book for a 7 percent discount, discounts for longer stays, no CC; 10 min drive southeast of Cortona, Tuoro sul Trasimeno; tel. & fax 075-8230-267, montegualandro @iol.it, SE).

EATING

Trattoria la Grotta, just off Piazza Repubblica, is a traditional, cave-like place with daily specials and a fun outdoor seating area (pasta-€7, meat-€8, Wed–Mon 12:00–15:00 & 19:00–22:00, closed Tue, Piazza Baldelli 3, tel. 0575-630-271).

La Locanda nel Loggiato, run by Lara and Marco, serves up big portions of Tuscan cuisine (pasta-€7, meat-€7–15, Thu–Tue 12:00–15:00 & 19:00–23:00, closed Wed, Piazza Pescheria 3, tel. 0575-630-575).

Put together a **picnic** at the ultra-touristy Enoteca Molesini (Piazza della Repubblica 23) and munch with a million-euro view from Piazza Garibaldi or the public gardens behind San Domenico Church.

TRANSPORTATION CONNECTIONS

To: Rome (10 trains/day, 2.25 hrs), **Florence** (hrly, 1.5 hrs), **Montepulciano** (8/day, 1.25 hrs, change in Chiusi).

Most trains stop at Cortona's Camucia train station (tel. 0575-603-018), but fast trains from Rome and Florence stop at Terontola, 10 miles away (tel. 0575-670-034). From both Terontala and Camucia, orange buses depart for Piazza Garibaldi twice hourly (€1.60, buy tickets at newsstand).

Drivers: Some free parking is available inside the town walls—if you can find it. The best bets are Piazzale del Mercato and Piazzale di Santa Margherita.

Orvieto

Umbria's grand hill town, just off the freeway, is no secret, but worth a quick look. The town sits majestically on a big chunk of *tufa*, volcanic soil from Lake Bolsena. Locals will tell you that tufa is actually Swiss cheese because it's sturdy and riddled with holes (you can dig into it with bare hands). Since the Etruscan era, city dwellers have created a honeycomb of tunnels and catacombs underneath its streets.

Orvieto, which has three popular claims to fame (cathedral, Classico wine, and ceramics)—is loaded with tourists by day and quiet by night. Drinking a shot of wine in a ceramic cup as you gaze up at the cathedral lets you experience Orvieto all at once. (What I like best about Orvieto is its easy bus connection with my favorite hill town, Civita—covered below.)

Piazza Cahen is a key transportation hub at the entry to the hilltop town. As you exit the funicular, the town center and cathedral are straight ahead.

Tourist Information: The TI is at Piazza Duomo 24 on the cathedral square (Mon–Fri 8:15–13:30 & 16:00–19:00, Sat 10:00–13:00 & 15:00–19:00, Sun 10:00–12:00 & 16:00–18:00, tel. 0763-341-772). Pick up the free city map and ask about train and bus schedules. The TI sells a €3 admission ticket for the Chapel of St. Brizio (within the cathedral). For a longer visit, consider buying the €12.50 **Carta Unica** combo-ticket, which covers entry to the chapel, Archaeological Museum (Museo Claudio Faina e Museo Civico), Underground Orvieto Tours, and Torre del Moro (tower), plus your public transportation (bus and funicular) for one day or five hours of parking (at *parcheggio* Campo della Fiera).

Market Days: Drop by Piazza del Popolo with your cloth shopping bag on Tuesday and Saturday mornings.

Orvieto

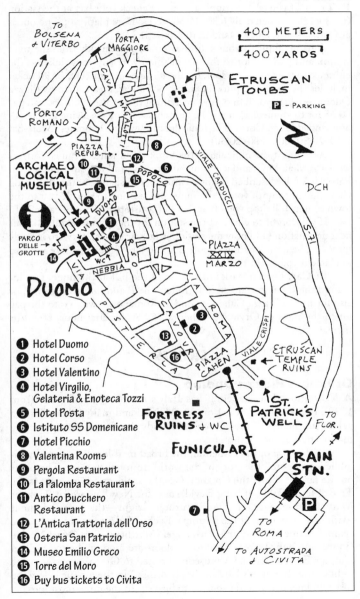

400 METERS
400 YARDS

P – PARKING

TO BOLSENA & VITERBO

PORTA MAGGIORE

ETRUSCAN TOMBS

PORTO ROMANO

PIAZZA REPUB.

VIALE CARDUCCI

DCH

ARCHAEO LOGICAL MUSEUM

PIAZZA XXIX MARZO

PARCO DELLE GROTTE

WC

VIA DUOMO

VIA COSTA

VIA NEBBIA

VIA POSTIERLA

VIA DELLA CAVA

VIA ROMA

DUOMO

VIALE CRISPI

ETRUSCAN TEMPLE RUINS

PIAZZA CAHEN

ST. PATRICK'S WELL

TO FLOR.

FORTRESS RUINS & WC

FUNICULAR

TRAIN STN.

P

TO ROMA

TO AUTOSTRADA & CIVITA

1 Hotel Duomo
2 Hotel Corso
3 Hotel Valentino
4 Hotel Virgilio, Gelateria & Enoteca Tozzi
5 Hotel Posta
6 Istituto SS Domenicane
7 Hotel Picchio
8 Valentina Rooms
9 Pergola Restaurant
10 La Palomba Restaurant
11 Antico Bucchero Restaurant
12 L'Antica Trattoria dell'Orso
13 Osteria San Patrizio
14 Museo Emilio Greco
15 Torre del Moro
16 Buy bus tickets to Civita

Arrival in Orvieto

By Train: If you're day-tripping, you can check your bag at the station (€2.80/12 hrs, open daily 6:30–19:30, access from platform; if no one is around, ask at the newsstand in the station).

A handy funicular/bus shuttle will take you quickly from the train station and parking lot to the top of the town. Buy your ticket at the entrance to the *funiculare;* look for the *biglietteria* sign. The €0.90 ticket includes the funicular plus the minibus from Piazza Cahen to Piazza Duomo—where you'll find most everything that matters. Or you can pay €0.65 for the funicular only—the best choice if you're staying at the recommended Hotel Corso. The funicular runs every 10 minutes (Mon–Sat 7:20–20:30, Sun 8:00–20:30).

As you exit the funicular at the top, to your left is a ruined fortress with a garden, WC, and a commanding view, and to your right are St. Patrick's Well (described below), Etruscan ruins, and another sweeping view. Just in front of you is an orange bus waiting to shuttle you to the town center. It'll drop you off at the TI (last stop, in front of cathedral).

If you forgot to check at the station for the train schedule to your next destination (and now the station is far, far below), Orvieto is ready for you. The train schedule is posted at the top of the *funiculare* and also available if you ask at the TI.

By Car: Drivers park at the base of the hill at the huge, free lot behind the Orvieto train station (follow the P and *funiculare* signs), or also for free in Piazza Cahen, or on Via Roma; otherwise go to the pay lot to the right of Orvieto's cathedral (€0.80 for first hour, €0.60/hr thereafter).

SIGHTS

Orvieto's Piazza Duomo

▲▲**Duomo**—The cathedral has Italy's most striking facade (from 1330), thanks to architect Lorenzo Maitani and many others. Grab a gelato (to the left of the church) and study this fascinating, gleaming mass of mosaics and sculpture.

At the base of the cathedral, the broad marble pillars carved with biblical scenes tell the story of the world from left to right. The pillar on the far left shows the Creation (see the snake and Eve), next is the Tree of Jesse (father of King David), next the New Testament (look for Mary and a manger, etc.), and on the far right—the Last Judgment (with hell, of course, at the bottom). Each pillar is topped by a bronze symbol of one of the evangelists: angel (Matthew), lion (Mark), eagle (John), and bull (Luke). The bronze doors are modern, by the Sicilian sculptor Emilio Greco. (A museum devoted to Greco's work is to the right of the church; it's labeled simply *Museo.*) In the mosaic below the rose window, Mary is transported to heaven. In the uppermost mosaic,

Mary is crowned.

Why such an impressive church in a little *tufa* town? Because of a blood-stained cloth. In the 1260s, a Bohemian priest—who doubted that the bread used in Communion was really the body of Christ—went to Rome on a pilgrimage. On his return journey, he worshiped in Bolsena, near Orvieto. During Mass, the bread bled, staining a linen cloth. The cloth was brought to the pope, who was visiting Orvieto at the time. Such a miraculous relic required a magnificent church. You can see the actual cloth from the Miracle of Bolsena displayed in the chapel to the left of the altar.

Hours of Cathedral: April–Sept daily 7:30–12:45 & 14:30–19:15; March and Oct closes at 18:15, Nov–Feb at 17:15. Admission is free, but there is a charge for the Chapel of St. Brizio.

Cost and Hours of Chapel: Visitors' hours are Mon–Sat 10:00–12:45 & 14:30–19:15, Sun 14:30–17:45 (closes 1 hour earlier in winter). Buy the €3 ticket at the TI or the shop across the square from the facade of the church; it's included in the €12.50 Carta Unica combo-ticket. Only 25 people are allowed in the chapel at a time. The chapel is also open (and free, no ticket required) daily 7:30–10:00, but it's technically only for worshippers (keep a low profile and be respectful of those who are praying).

Chapel of St. Brizio: This chapel, to the right of the altar, features Luca Signorelli's brilliantly-lit frescoes of the Apocalypse (1449–1451). Step into the chapel and you're surrounded by vivid scenes, including the *Preaching of the Antichrist* (to your left as you enter—the figure standing on far left is a self-portrait of Signorelli, next to Fra Angelico, who worked on the ceiling); the *Calling of the Elect to Heaven* (left of altar—hear that celestial band); the *Damned in Hell* (right of altar—the scariest mosh pit ever); and the *Resurrection of the Bodies* (to your right as you enter; people dreamily climb out of the earth as skeletons chatter in the corner, wondering where to snare some skin). On the same wall is a gripping *pietà*. Fra Angelico started the ceiling and Signorelli finished it, turning the entire room into Orvieto's artistic, must-see sight.

After leaving the cathedral, if you want a break at a viewpoint park, exit left and pass the small parking lot. The nearest WCs are in the opposite direction (exit cathedral to the right), down the stairs from the left transept.

Archaeological Museum (Museo Claudio Faina e Museo Civico)— Across from the entrance to the cathedral is a fine Etruscan art museum (2 upper floors) combined with a miniscule city history museum on the ground floor that features a sarcophagus and temple bits. The Faina art—consisting largely of Etruscan vases, plates, and coins, with some jewelry and bronze dishes—was collected by Mauro Faina and his nephew starting in the late 19th century. They bought some of the art, and dug up the rest in haphazardly conducted excavations. Many of the vases came from the Etruscan necropolis (Crocifisso del Tufo) just outside Orvieto. The English placards in most rooms offer some information, especially on the Faina family (€4.50, included in €12.50 Carta Unica combo-ticket, April–Sept Tue–Sun 9:30–18:00, Oct–March Tue–Sun 10:00–17:00, closed Mon, audioguide, WC after ticket desk and on top floor, tel. 0763-341-511). Look out the windows at the Duomo's glittering facade.

▲Museo Emilo Greco—This museum displays the work of Emilio Greco (1913–1995), the Sicilian artist who designed the doors of Orvieto's cathedral. His sketches and bronze statues show his absorption with gently twisting and turning nudes. In the back left corner of the museum, look for the sketchy outlines of women—simply beautiful. The artful installation of his work in this palazzo, with walkways and even a spiral staircase up to the ceiling, allows you to view his sculptures from different directions (€2.50, €4.50 includes St. Patrick's Well, April–Sept daily 10:30–13:00 & 14:30–18:30, Oct–March closes 1 hour earlier, no English but not essential: next to Duomo, marked *Museo*, tel. 0763-344-605).

Underground Orvieto Tours (Parco delle Grotte)—Guides weave a good archaeological history into an hour-long look at about 100 yards of caves (€5.50, included in €12.50 Carta Unica combo-ticket, 1-hr English tours daily at 12:15 and 17:15, confirm times by calling 335-733-2764 or checking with TI). Orvieto is honeycombed with Etruscan and medieval caves. You'll see the remains of an old olive press, two impressive 130-foot-deep Etruscan well shafts, and the remains of a primitive cement quarry. If you want underground Orvieto, this is the place to get it.

More Sights in Orvieto

Torre del Moro—For yet another viewpoint, this distinctive square tower comes with 250 steps and an elevator. The elevator goes only partway to the top, leaving you with a mere 173 steps to scurry up (€2.70, included in €12.50 Carta Unica combo-ticket, April–Oct daily 10:00–19:00, May–Aug until 20:00, Nov–March 10:30–13:00 & 14:30–17:00, terrace on top, at intersection of Corso Cavour and Via Duomo).

St. Patrick's Well (Posso de S. Patrizio)—Engineers are impressed by this deep well—175 feet deep and 45 feet wide—designed in the 16th century with a double-helix pattern. The two spiral stairways allow an efficient one-way traffic flow; intriguing now, but critical then. Imagine if donkeys and people, balancing jugs of water, had to go up and down the same stairway. At the bottom is a bridge that people could walk on to scoop up water.

The well was built because a pope got nervous. After Rome was sacked in 1527 by renegade troops of the Holy Roman Empire, the pope fled to Orvieto. He feared that even this little town (with no water source on top) would be besieged. He commissioned a well, which was started in 1527 and finished 10 years later. It was a huge project. Even today, when a local is faced with a difficult task, people say, "It's like digging St. Patrick's Well." The unusual name came from the well's supposed resemblance to the Irish saint's cave. It's not worth climbing up and down a total of 495 steps; a quick look is painless but pricey (€3.50, €4.50 includes Museo Emilio Greco, April–Sept daily 10:00–18:45, Oct–March 10:00–17:45; the well is to your right as you exit *funiculare*). Bring a sweater if you descend to the chilly depths.

View Walks—For short, pleasant walks, climb the medieval wall (access at western end of town, between Piazza S. Gionvenale and Via Garibaldi) or stroll the promenade park on the northern edge of town (along Viale Carducci, which becomes Gonfaloniera).

Sights near Orvieto

Wine-Tasting—Orvieto Classico wine is justly famous. For a short tour of a local winery with Etruscan cellars, visit Tenuta Le Velette, where English-speaking Corrado and Cecilia (cheh-CHEEL-yah) Bottai will welcome you—if you've called ahead to set up an appointment (€8 for tour and tasting, Mon–Fri 8:30–12:00 & 14:00–17:00, Sat 8:30–12:00, closed Sun, tel. 0763-29144, fax 0763-29114). From their sign (5 min past Orvieto at top of switchbacks just before Canale, on Bagnoregio road), cruise down a long, tree-lined drive, then park at the striped gate (must call ahead; no drop-ins).

SLEEPING

(€1 = about $1.10, country code: 39)
All of the recommended hotels are in the old town except Hotel Picchio, which is in a more modern neighborhood near the station.

   $$$ Hotel Duomo, centrally located, is super-duper modern, with splashy art and 17 sleek rooms named after artists who worked on the Duomo (Sb-€70, Db-€100, Db suite-€120, Tb-€130, includes breakfast; elevator, air-con, double-paned windows keep out noise, sunny terrace out front; a block from Duomo, behind *gelateria* at Via di Maurizio 7; tel. 0763-341-887, fax 0763-394-973, www.orvietohotelduomo.com, hotelduomo@tiscalinet.it, SE).

   $$ Hotel Corso is friendly and clean, with 18 comfy, modern rooms, some with balconies and views (Sb-€60, Db-€82, 10 percent discount with this book, buffet breakfast-€6.50, elevator, air-con, garage or free parking nearby, on main street up from funicular toward Duomo at Via Cavour 339, tel. & fax 0763-342-020, www.argoweb.it/hotel_corso, hotelcorso@libero.it, SE).

   $$ Hotel Valentino offers 19 simple, quiet rooms in a modern hotel 200 yards off Corso Cavour (Db-€80, elevator, air-con, Via Angelo da Orvieto 30/32, tel. & fax 0763-342-464, hotelvalentino@libero.it).

$$ Hotel Virgilio has modern but faded and overpriced rooms shoehorned into an old building, ideally located on the main square facing the cathedral (Sb-€62, Db-€85, breakfast-€6, send personal or traveler's check for first night's deposit; elevator, noisy church bells every 15 min; Piazza Duomo 5, 05018 Orvieto; tel. 0763-341-882, fax 0763-343-797, www.hotelvirgilio.com, info@hotel.virgilio.com, SE). They also have a cheaper *dependencia*—a double and quad in a one-star hotel a few doors away (Db-€57, Qb-€103).

$ Hotel Posta is a five-minute walk from the cathedral into the medieval core. It's a big, old, formerly elegant but well-cared-for-in-its-decline building with a breezy garden, an elevator, and a grand old lobby. 20 spacious, clean, plain rooms hold vintage rickety furniture and good mattresses (S-€31, Sb-€37, D-€43, Db-€56, breakfast-€6, no CC, Via Luca Signorelli 18, tel. & fax 0763-341-909, NSE).

$ The sisters of the **Istituto SS Domenicane** rent 15 spotless twin rooms in their heavenly convent with a peaceful terrace (Sb-€41, Db-€52, 2-night min, breakfast-€3, no CC, elevator, parking, just off Piazza del Popolo at Via del Popolo 1, tel. & fax 0763-342-910, www.argoweb.it/istituto_sansalvatore/istituto.it.html, NSE).

$ Hotel Picchio, with 27 newly-remodeled rooms, is a wood-and-marble place, more comfortable but with less character than others in the area. It's in the lower, plain part of town, 300 yards from the train station (Sb-€36, Db-€48, Tb-€59, ask for the Rick Steves 5 percent discount; only some rooms are air-con and cost extra; Via G. Salvatori 17, tel. & fax 0763-301-144, dan_test@libero.it, family-run by Marco and Picchio, SE). A trail leads from here up to the old town.

$ Valentina rents six clean and airy, well-appointed rooms and a studio apartment (all with air-con) in the heart of Orvieto behind the grand staircase in Piazza del Popolo. Facing the stairs, head right around the Gothic palazzo and then left down Via Vivaria about 50 yards. She rents another 2-room apartment near the Duomo as well (Db-€60, Tb-€75, includes breakfast; also studio with kitchen-€80, apartment for up to 5-€130; Via Vivaria 7, tel. 0763-341-607, mobile 347-652-7779, valentina.z@tiscalinet.it, SE).

$ Franco Sala, who runs the Antico Forno restaurant and a B&B in Civita, also rents a comfortable, centrally-located one-bedroom apartment with a hand-carved stone spiral staircase and a curvy kitchen in a renovated 14th-century palazzo in Orvieto (€70–100, sleeps up to 5 people, 2-night min, tel. 0761-760-016).

EATING

Near the Duomo, consider **Pergola**—its affordable menu is popular with locals (Thu–Tue 12:30–15:00 & 19:15–22:00, closed Mon, Via dei Magoni 9, tel. 0763-343-065).

Orvieto and Civita Area

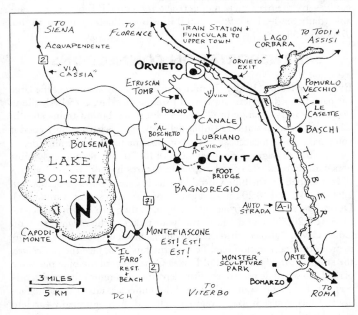

La Palomba, also a good bet, features game and truffle specialties (Thu–Tue 12:30–14:15 & 19:30–22:00, closed Wed; Via Cipriano Manente 16, just off Piazza della Repubblica; tel. 0763-343-395).

For a bit of a splurge, try **Antico Bucchero** for its classy candlelit ambience and fine food (Thu–Tue 12:00–15:00 & 19:00–24:00, closed Wed; indoor/outdoor seating; Via de Cartari 4, a half-block south of Corso Cavour, between Torre del Moro and Piazza della Repubblica; tel. 0763-341-725).

L'Antica Trattoria dell'Orso offers well-prepared Umbrian cuisine paired with fine wines in a cozy atmosphere. Ciro and chef Gabriele will steer you towards the freshest seasonal plates (Wed–Sun 12:30–14:00 & 19:30–22:00, closed Mon–Tue, Via della Misericordia 18–20, just off Piazza della Repubblica, tel. 0763-341-642).

Osteria San Patrizio, near the funicular, creatively presents traditional Umbrian specialties (12:00–15:00 & 19:00–23:00, closed Sun eve and Mon, Corso Cavour 312, tel. 0763-341-245).

For dessert, try the deservedly popular *gelateria* **Pasqualetti** (daily 12:30–24:00, closed in winter; Piazza Duomo 14, next to left transept of church; another branch is at Corso Cavour 56, open until 20:30 during winter).

Enoteca Tozzi, to the left of the Duomo, serves up rustic *panini*—try the roast suckling pig (*porchetta*, por-KET-tah) if it's available (daily 8:30–21:00, 9:00–20:00 in winter, Piazza Duomo 13, tel. 0763-344-393).

TRANSPORTATION CONNECTIONS

By train to: Rome (19/day, 75 min, consider leaving your car at the large car park behind Orvieto station), **Florence** (14/day, 2.25 hrs), **Siena** (8/day, 2–3 hrs, change in Chiusi; all Florence-bound trains stop in Chiusi). The train station's Buffet della Stazione is surprisingly good if you need a quick focaccia sandwich or pizza picnic for the train ride.

By bus to Bagnoregio (near Civita): It's 70 minutes going, 40 minutes coming back (€2 round-trip). Departures in 2003 from Orvieto's Piazza Cahen on the blue Cotral bus, daily except Sunday: 6:20, 9:10, 12:45, 15:45, and 18:20 (buses stop at Orvieto's train station 5 min later). During the school year (roughly Sept–June), there are additional departures at 7:20, 7:50, and 13:55. Buy your ticket at the *tabacchi* stop on Corso Cavour (also confirm the schedule) a block up from the *funiculare* or from the train station bar. To find the bus stop, face the *funiculare;* the stop is at the far left end of Piazza Cahen where the blue buses are parked (no schedule posted; confirm departure and return times with driver). At the station, wait at the left of the funicular station as you're facing it. Once you're in Bagnoregio, you'll find the Bagnoregio–Orvieto bus schedule posted at the bus stop.

Civita di Bagnoregio

Perched on a pinnacle in a grand canyon, the traffic-free village of Civita is Italy's ultimate hill town. Curl your toes around its Etruscan roots.

Civita is terminally ill. Only 15 residents remain as, bit by bit, the town is being purchased by rich big-city Italians who come here to escape. The University of Washington architecture program that once brought American students here is a thing of the past.

Civita is connected to the world and the town of Bagnoregio by a long pedestrian bridge—and a Web site (www.civitadibagnoregio.it). While Bagnoregio lacks the pinnacle-town romance of Civita, it's actually a healthy, vibrant community (unlike Civita, the suburb that it calls "the dead city"). In Bagnoregio, get a haircut, sip a coffee on the square, and walk down to the old laundry (ask, *"Dov'è la lavanderia vecchia?"*). A Grand Spesa supermarket is 300 yards from the bus stop (Mon–Sat 8:30–13:00 & 17:00–20:00, closed Sun; take main drag from town gate—away from Civita, angle right at pyramid monument). A lively market fills the bus parking lot each Monday.

Civita

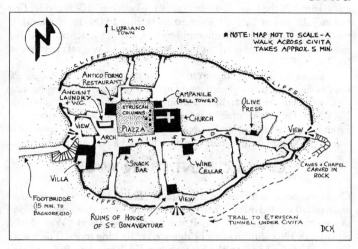

From Bagnoregio, yellow signs direct you along its long, skinny spine to its older neighbor, Civita. Enjoy the view as you walk up the bridge to Civita. Be prepared for the little old ladies of Civita, who can be aggressive at getting money out of visitors—tourists are their only source of support. Off-season, Civita, Bagnoregio, and Al Boschetto (see "Sleeping," below) are all deadly quiet—and cold. I'd side-trip in quickly from Orvieto or skip the area altogether.

Arrival in Bagnoregio, near Civita

If you're arriving by bus from Orvieto, you'll get off at the bus stop in Bagnoregio. Look at the posted bus schedule and write down the return times to Orvieto.

Baggage Check: While there's no official baggage-check service in Bagnoregio, I've arranged with Mauro Laurenti, who runs the Bar/Enoteca/Caffè Gianfu, to let you leave your bags there (€1/bag, daily 7:00–24:00 with a 13:00–13:30 lunch break, closed Thu Oct–March; to get to café from Orvieto bus stop where you got off, go back in the direction that the Orvieto bus just came from and go right around corner).

From Bagnoregio to Civita: From Bagnoregio, you can walk or take a little orange shuttle bus to the base of the bridge to Civita. From here, you have to walk the rest of the way. It's a 10-minute hike up a pedestrian bridge that gets steeper near the end. There's no bus—only you and your profound regret that you didn't get in better shape before your trip.

The little shuttle **bus** runs from Bagnoregio (catch bus across from gas station) to the base of the bridge (€1, pay driver, 10-min ride, first bus at 7:39, last at 18:20, 1–2/hr except during 13:00–15:30 siesta). If you'll want to return to Bagnoregio by bus, check the schedule posted near the bridge (at edge of car park, where bus let you off) before you head up to Civita.

To **walk** from Bagnoregio to the base of Civita's bridge (about 20 min, fairly level), take the road going uphill (overlooking the big parking lot), then take the first right and an immediate left onto the main drag, Via Roma. Follow this straight out to the belvedere for a superb viewpoint. From the viewpoint, backtrack a few steps (staircase at end of viewpoint is a dead end), and take the stairs down to the road leading to the bridge.

CIVITA ORIENTATION WALK

Civita was once connected to Bagnoregio. The saddle between the separate towns eroded away. Photographs around town show the old donkey path, the original bridge. It was bombed in World War II and replaced in 1965 with the new **bridge** you're climbing today. The town's hearty old folks hang on the bridge's hand railing when fierce winter weather rolls through.

Entering the town, you'll pass through a cut in the rock (made by Etruscans 2,500 years ago) and under a 12th-century Romanesque **arch**. This was the main Etruscan road leading to the Tiber Valley and Rome.

Inside the town gate, on your left is the old **laundry** (in front of the WC). On your right, a fancy wooden door and windows (above the door) lead to thin air. This was the facade of a Renaissance palace—one of five that once graced Civita. It fell into the valley riding a chunk of the ever-eroding rock pinnacle. Today, the door leads to a remaining chunk of the palace—complete with Civita's first hot tub—owned by the "Marchesa," a countess who married into Italy's biggest industrialist family.

Peek into the museum next door if it's open (Wed and Sat–Sun 10:00–13:00, marked *Benvenuti a Civita*) and check out the **viewpoint** a few steps away. Nearby is the site of the long-gone home of Civita's one famous son, Saint Bonaventure, known as the "second founder of the Franciscans."

Now wander to the **town square** in front of the church, where you'll find Civita's only public phone, bar, and restaurant—and a wild donkey race on the first Sunday of June and the second Sunday of September. The church marks the spot where an Etruscan temple, and then a Roman temple, once stood. The pillars that stand like giants' bar stools are ancient—Roman or Etruscan.

Go into the **church**. You'll see frescoes and statues from "the school of Giotto" and "the school of Donatello," a portrait of the patron saint of your teeth (notice the scary-looking pincers), and an altar dedicated to Marlon Brando (or St. Ildebrando).

The basic grid street plan of the ancient town survives. Just around the corner from the church, on the main street, is Rossana and Antonio's cool and friendly **wine cellar** (their sign reads *bruschette con prodotti locali*). Pull up a stump and let them or their children, Arianna and Antonella, serve you *panini* (sandwiches), *bruschetta* (garlic toast with optional tomato topping), wine, and a local cake called *ciambella*. Climb down into the cellar and note the traditional wine-making gear and the provisions for rolling huge kegs up the stairs. Tap on the kegs in the cool bottom level to see which are full (April–Oct daily 10:00–21:00, even later in Aug, Nov–March Sat–Sun only, 10:00–18:00).

The rock below Civita is honeycombed with ancient cellars (for keeping wine at the same temperature all year) and cisterns (for collecting rainwater, since there was no well in town). Many of these date from Etruscan times.

Explore further down the street, but remember—nothing is abandoned. Everything is still privately owned. After passing an ancient Roman tombstone on your left, you'll come to Vittoria's **Antico Mulino**, an atmospheric collection of old olive presses. The huge press in the entry is about 1,500 years old and was in use as recently as the 1960s (donation requested, give about €1). Vittoria's sons, Sandro and Felice, and her grandson Fabrizio (with his American wife, Heather) run the local equivalent of a lemonade stand, toasting delicious *bruschetta* on weekends and holidays (roughly 10:00–20:00 in summer, winter Sat–Sun only, tel. 0176-793-179). Choose your topping (chopped tomato is super) and get a glass of wine for a fun, affordable snack.

Farther down the way and to your left, Maria (for a donation of about €1) will show you through her **garden** with a grand view (Maria's Giardino) and share historical misinformation (she says Civita and Lubriano were once connected). Maria's husband, Peppone, used to carry goods on a donkey back and forth on the path between the old town and Bagnoregio.

At the end of town, the main drag winds downhill past small **Etruscan caves** to your right. The first two were used as stables until last year. The third cave is an unusual chapel, cut deep into the rock, with a barred door—this is the **Chapel of the Incarcerated** (Cappella del Carcere). In Etruscan times, the chapel may have originally been a tomb, and in medieval times, it was used as a jail. When Civita's few residents have a religious procession, they come here, in honor of the Madonna of the Incarcerated.

After the chapel, the paving-stone path peters out into a dirt trail leading down and around to the right to a **tunnel**. Dating from the Etruscan era, the tunnel may have served as a shortcut to the river below. It was widened in the 1930s so farmers could get between their scattered fields more easily, and now the residents use it as a shortcut in fall to collect chestnuts from the trees that cover the hillside. Backtrack to the town square.

Evenings on the town square are a bite of Italy. The same people sit on the same church steps under the same moon, night after night, year after year. I love my cool, late evenings in Civita. If you visit in the morning, have cappuccino and rolls at the small café on the town square.

Whenever you visit, stop halfway up the donkey path and listen to the sounds of rural Italy. Reach out and touch one of the Monopoly houses. If you know how to turn the volume up on the crickets, do so.

SLEEPING

(€1 = about $1.10, country code: 39)
In Civita

$$$ **Carol Watts** rents a furnished two-bedroom Civita apartment with a terrace and cliffside garden ($900/week, 1-week minimum Sat to Sat, personal checks OK). Give her a call in Kansas (785/539-0815, evenings or weekends, http://homepage.mac.com/cmwatts/civita.html, cmwatts @mac.com).

$ **Civita B&B**, run by Franco Sala, who also owns the Antico Forno restaurant, has three comfortable rooms overlooking Civita's main square. Call a minimum of one day in advance to reserve (D-€62, Db-€68, €14 more for optional half-pension, Piazza del Duomo Vecchio, tel. 0761-760-016, mobile 347-611-5426, www.civitadibagnoregio.it, fsala@pelagus.it).

In Bagnoregio

$ **Romantica Pucci B&B** is a haven for city-weary travelers. Its five spacious rooms are indeed romantic with canopied beds and flowing veils, and Pucci and Lamberto take special care of their guests (Sb-€39, Db-€65, Piazza Cavour 1, tel. 0761-792-121, www.hotelromanticapucci.it, lacasadipucci@libero.it, SE). It's on the road to Civita from Bagnoregio at Piazza Cavour (from Civita bus stop, walk up stairs, turn left on the main street, continue 150 yards to square, B&B on left).

$ **Hotel Fidanza**, near the bus stop in Bagnoregio, is tired but decent and the only hotel in town. Of its 25 rooms, #206 and #207 have views of Civita (Sb-€52, Db-€62, breakfast-€5.50, no CC; attached restaurant; Via Fidanza 25, Bagnoregio/Viterbo; tel. & fax 0761-793-444).

Just outside Bagnoregio is $ **Al Boschetto.** The Catarcia family speaks no English, so have an English-speaking Italian call for you (Sb-€34, D-€40, Db-€50, breakfast-€3; Strada Monterado, Bagnoregio/Viterbo; tel. 0761-792-369). Most of the 12 rooms, while very basic, have private showers. The Catarcia family (Angelino, his wife Perina, sons Gianfranco and Domenico, daughter-in-law Giuseppina, and the grandchildren) offers a candid look at rural Italian life. Meals are uneven in quality, and the men are often tipsy (which can pose a problem for women). If the men invite you down deep into the gooey, fragrant bowels of the cantina, be warned: The theme song is *"Trinka Trinka Trinka,"* and there are no rules unless the female participants set them. The Orvieto bus drops you at the town gate (no bus on Sun). The hotel is a 15-minute walk out of town past the old arch (follow *Viterbo* signs); turn left at the pyramid monument and right at the first fork (follow *Montefiascone* sign). Civita is a pleasant 45-minute walk (back through Bagnoregio) from Al Boschetto.

EATING

In and near Civita

In Civita, try **Trattoria Antico Forno**, which serves up pasta at affordable prices (daily for lunch 12:30–15:30 and sporadically for dinner 19:30–22:00, on main square, also rents rooms—see above, tel. 0761-760-016). At **Da Peppone**, the small café/bar on the square, you can get simple treats (daily 9:30–12:30 & 14:00–19:00, closed 17:00 and Mon or Tue in winter, tel. 0761-79320).

Hostaria del Ponte offers light, creative cuisine with a great view terrace at the parking lot at the base of the bridge to Civita (Tue–Sun 12:30–14:30 & 19:30–21:30, closed Mon; Nov–April closed Sun, tel. 0761-793-565).

In Bagnoregio, check out **Il Fumatore di Pizzo Ornelio**'s traditional Italian cuisine (Fri–Wed 12:30–15:00 & 19:00–22:00, closed Thu, on Piazza Marconi 5, 0761-792-642). At **Al Boschetto,** you'll get country cooking, such as bunny (just outside Bagnoregio; see "Sleeping," above, daily 12:30–14:30 & 20:00–22:00).

TRANSPORTATION CONNECTIONS

To Orvieto: Public buses (7/day, 40 min, €2 round-trip) connect Bagnoregio to the rest of the world via Orvieto. Departures in 2003 from Bagnoregio, daily except Sunday: 5:30, 6:50, 9:50, 10:10, 13:00, 14:25, and 17:20. During the school year (roughly Sept–June), buses also run at 6:35, 13:35, and 16:40 (for info on Orvieto, see "Transportation—Orvieto," page 956).

THE CINQUE TERRE

The Cinque Terre (CHINK-weh TAY-reh), a remote chunk of the Italian Riviera, is the traffic-free, lowbrow, underappreciated alternative to the French Riviera. There's not a museum in sight. Just sun, sea, sand (well, pebbles), wine, and pure unadulterated Italy. Enjoy the villages, swimming, hiking, and evening romance of one of God's great gifts to tourism. For a home base, choose among five villages, each of which fills a ravine with a lazy hive of human activity—calloused locals, sunburned travelers, and no Vespas. Vernazza is my favorite home base. While the Cinque Terre is now well-discovered (www.cinqueterre.it), I've never seen happier, more relaxed tourists.

The chunk of coast was first described in medieval times as "the five lands." Tiny communities grew up in the protective shadows of the castles (in feudal times, the land was the property of the castles), ready to run inside at the first hint of a Turkish "Saracen" pirate raid. Many locals were kidnapped and ransomed or sold into slavery somewhere far to the east. As the threat of pirates faded, the villages grew, with economies based on fish and grapes. Until the advent of tourism in this generation, the towns were remote. Even today, traditions survive, and each of the five villages comes with a distinct dialect and proud heritage. The region has become a national park, and its natural and cultural wonders will be carefully preserved.

Over the next decade, Italy has quiet plans for the Cinque Terre. For the sake of tranquility, a new train line will be built inland for the noisy fast trains, leaving the Cinque Terre tracks for just the pokey milk-run trains.

Sadly, a few ugly, noisy Americans are giving tourism a bad name here. Even hip young locals are put off by loud, drunken tourists. They say (and I agree) that the Cinque Terre is a special place. It deserves a special dignity. Party in Viareggio or Portofino, but be mellow in the

Cinque Terre. Talk softly. Help keep it clean. In spite of the tourist crowds, it's still a real community, and we are guests.

In this chapter, I cover Vernazza first (my favorite), then Riomaggiore (more of a workaday town), Manarola (picturesque), Corniglia (on a hilltop), and Monterosso (a resort).

Planning Your Time

The ideal minimum stay is two nights and a completely uninterrupted day. The Cinque Terre is served by the milk-run train from Genoa and La Spezia. Speed demons arrive in the morning, check their bags in La Spezia, take the five-hour hike through all five towns, laze away the afternoon on the beach or rock of their choice, and zoom away on the overnight train to somewhere back in the real world. But be warned: The Cinque Terre has a strange way of messing up your momentum.

The towns are each just a few minutes apart by hourly train or boat. There's no checklist of sights or experiences; just a hike, the towns themselves, and your fondest vacation desires. Study this chapter in advance and piece together your best day, mixing hiking, swimming, trains, and a boat ride. For the best light and coolest temperatures, start your hike early.

Market days perk up the towns from 8:00 to 13:00 on Tuesday in Vernazza, Wednesday in Levanto, Thursday in Monterosso, and Friday in La Spezia.

ORIENTATION

Cinque Terre Cards and Passes

Now that the Cinque Terre is a national park (www.parconazionale5terre .it), visitors hiking between the towns need to pay a **park entrance fee**. You have two options: the Hiking Pass or Cinque Terre Card. The **Hiking Pass** costs €3 (kids under 4 free, comes with map) and is valid for one day (until midnight). The Hiking Pass, which does not need to be validated, can be purchased at trailheads and usually at train stations. The pricier **Cinque Terre Card** covers the park entrance fee and your transportation on the local trains (from Levanto to La Spezia, including all Cinque Terre towns), plus the shuttle buses that run about twice an hour within each Cinque Terre town (€5.40/1 day, €13/3 days, €20.60/week, kids 4–12 half-price, under 4 free; includes map, brochure, and train schedule). A new one-day **Cinque Terre Card Plus Boats** includes all of the above, plus unlimited passage on Cinque Terre boats (€13.60). Cinque Terre Cards, valid until midnight of the day they expire, are sold at train stations (but not at trailheads). Validate your Cinque Terre Card at a train station by punching it into the yellow machine.

Cinque Terre

Getting around the Cinque Terre

By Train: At La Spezia, the gateway to the Cinque Terre, you'll transfer to the milk-run Cinque Terre train. There might be a TI at the station in summer. But if not, skip the 20-minute hike to La Spezia's main
TI at Viale Mazzini 47 near the waterfront (daily in summer 9:30–13:00
& 15:30–18:00; winter Mon–Sat 9:30–13:00 & 14:00–17:00, Sun
9:30–13:00; tel. 0187-718-997).

At the station, buy your train ticket (€1.05 weekdays, €1.10 weekends) or Cinque Terre Card, and take the half-hour train ride into the
Cinque Terre town of your choice. Once in the Cinque Terre, you'll get
around the villages more cheaply by train but more scenically by boat.

Cinque Terre Train Schedule: Since the train is the Cinque Terre

EVENTS ON THE CINQUE TERRE

late May	Monterosso: Lemon Festival
June 13	Monterosso: Corpus Domini (procession on carpet of flowers at 18:00)
June 24	Riomaggiore and Monterosso: Festival in honor of St. John the Baptist (procession and fireworks; big fire on old town beach the day before)
June 29	Corniglia: Festival of St. Peter and St. Paul
July 20	Vernazza: Festival for patron saint, St. Margaret
Aug 10	Manarola: Festival for patron saint, St. Lawrence
Aug 15	All towns: Ascension of Mary
Sept 8	Monterosso: Maria Nascente, or "Rising Mary" (fair with handicrafts)

lifeline, many shops and restaurants post the current schedule. Try to get a photocopied schedule—it'll come in handy (comes with Cinque Terre Card).

Trains leave La Spezia for the Cinque Terre villages at 7:12, 8:17, 10:08, 11:20, 12:23, 13:20, 14:27, 15:08, 16:20, 17:24, 18:25, 19:18, 20:25, 21:20, and 22:38 (last year's schedule, only daily trains listed—there are others that run only weekdays or only Sundays as well).

Trains leave Monterosso al Mare for La Spezia at 6:32, 8:12, 10:18, 12:11, 13:03, 14:12, 15:16, 16:17, 17:13, 18:40, 19:14, 20:28, 22:32, 23:24, and 0:02 (same trains depart Vernazza about 4 min later, last year's schedule).

Do not rely on these train times. Check the current posted schedule and then count on half the trains being 15 minutes or so late (unless you're late, in which case they are right on time).

To orient yourself, remember that directions are "*per* (to) Genova" or "*per* La Spezia." Note that many trains leaving La Spezia skip all of the towns or stop only in Monterosso. The five towns are just minutes apart by train. Know your stop. After the train leaves the town before your destination, go to the door to slip out before mobs pack in. Since the stations are small and the trains are long, you might get off the train deep in a tunnel, and you might need to flip open the handle of the door yourself.

The train stations should be staffed at all five Cinque Terre towns. Stations sell train tickets, the Cinque Terre Card, the Cinque Terre Card Plus Boats, and maybe the Hiking Pass. The Cinque Terre Card, which includes the national park entry fee, is convenient, but if you're on a tight budget, you can save a bit of money by buying a one-day Hiking Pass (€3) and paying separately for your train travel. For more on all of these passes, see "By Foot," below.

It's cheap to buy individual train tickets to travel between the towns. Since a one-town hop costs the same as a five-town hop (around €1.10) and every ticket is good for six hours with stopovers, save money and explore the region in one direction on one ticket. Stamp the ticket at the station machine before you board.

If you have a Eurailpass, don't spend one of your valuable flexi-days on the cheap Cinque Terre.

By Boat: From Easter to late October (through Nov if weather is good), a daily boat service connects Monterosso, Vernazza, Manarola, Riomaggiore, and Portovenere (on Sat and Sun, a boat also makes an afternoon run to Portofino). Boats provide a scenic way to get from town to town and survey what you just hiked. It's also the only efficient way to visit the nearby resort of Portovenere; the alternative is a tedious train/bus connection via La Spezia. In peaceful weather, the boats are more reliable than the trains, but if sea is rough, they often don't run at all.

Boats go about hourly, from 10:30 until 18:00 from Monterosso and stop at the Cinque Terre towns (note that boats do not stop at Corniglia), ending in Portovenere. Boats coming from Portovenere to Monterosso run from 9:00 until 17:10. Single hops cost about €3. An all-day pass covering the Cinque Terre towns costs up to €22—less off-season and weekdays (you can save money by getting the €15 afternoon pass that kicks in at 14:30 and ends when boats quit for the evening). Also consider new Cinque Terre Card Plus Boats (see above). You can buy tickets at little stands at each town's harbor (tel. 0187-732-987 and 0187-818-440). Schedules are posted at docks, harbor bars, Cinque Terre Park offices, and hotels.

Hiking the Cinque Terre

All five towns are connected by good trails. You'll experience the area's best by hiking from one end to the other. The entire seven-mile hike can be done in about four hours, but allow five for dawdling. While you can detour to dramatic hilltop sanctuaries (one trail leads from Vernazza's cemetery uphill), I'd keep it simple by following the easy red-and-white-marked low trails between the villages. Good hiking maps (about €5–6, sold everywhere, not necessary for this described walk) cover the expanded version of this hike, from Portovenere through all five Cinque Terre towns to Levanto, and more serious hikes in the high country. Sometimes severe rains can wash out trails, especially in winter. Ask around whether the trails are open, particularly in spring. Remember that hikers need to pay a fee to enter the trails (see "Cinque Terre Cards and Passes," above).

Since I still get the names of the Cinque Terre towns mixed up, I think of the towns by number: Riomaggiore (town #1), Manarola (#2), Corniglia (#3), Vernazza (#4), and resorty Monterosso (#5).

Riomaggiore–Manarola (20 min): Facing the front of the train station in Riomaggiore (town #1), go up the stairs to the right, following signs for the Via dell' Amore. The film-gobbling promenade—wide enough for baby strollers—leads down the coast to Manarola. While there's no beach here, stairs lead down to sunbathing rocks.

Manarola–Corniglia (45 min): The walk from Manarola (#2) to Corniglia (#3) is a little longer and a little more rugged than that from #1 to #2.

Ask locally about the more difficult six-mile inland hike to Volastra (shuttle buses run hrly to Volastra from Manarola and Corniglia, €2.50 or free with Cinque Terre Card). This tiny village, perched between Manarola and Corniglia, hosts the Five-Terre wine co-op; stop by the Cantina Sociale. If you take this high road between Manarola and Corniglia, allow two hours; in return, you'll get sweeping views and a closer look at the vineyards.

Corniglia–Vernazza (90 min): The hike from Corniglia (#3) to Vernazza (#4)—the wildest and greenest of the coast—is most rewarding. From the Corniglia station and beach, zigzag up to the town (taking the steeper corkscrew stairs, the longer road, or the shuttle bus). Ten minutes past Corniglia toward Vernazza, you'll see the nude Guvano beach far beneath you (see "Corniglia," below). The trail leads past a bar and picnic tables, through lots of fragrant and flowery vegetation, and scenically into Vernazza.

Vernazza–Monterosso (90 min): The trail from Vernazza (#4) to Monterosso (#5) is a scenic up-and-down-a-lot trek. Trails are rough (and some readers report "very dangerous") and narrow but easy to follow. Camping at the picnic tables midway is frowned upon. The views just out of Vernazza are spectacular.

Swimming and Kayaking

Every town has a beach. Monterosso has the biggest and sandiest, with paddle boats, beach umbrellas, and beach-use fees (free where there are no umbrellas). Of Corniglia's two beaches, the Guvano beach is nude. Riomaggiore has a fine beach just outside town. Vernazza's is tiny—better for sunning than swimming. Manarola has the worst beach (no sand), but offers the best deep-water swimming.

Wear your walking shoes and pack your swim gear. Several of the beaches have showers (no shampoo, please) that may work better than your hotel's. Underwater sightseeing is full of fish—goggles are sold in local shops. Sea urchins can be a problem if you walk on the rocks; consider using Aquasocks or fins.

You can rent kayaks in Vernazza, Monterosso, and Riomaggiore (details listed below per town).

TOURS

Hiking Tour—For a guided tour, consider spending a day with a hard-working and likable American student, Sean Risatti, who liked the Cinque Terre so much he moved in (€45, almost daily April–Oct, departing Monterosso at 10:00 or Vernazza at 10:45; book at cinqueterretrek @hotmail.com, tel. 320-047-6865, or ask for Sean in Monterosso at The Net or at Kate's Fishnet Travel Services). The day—which is a great way to meet other travelers—includes a hike from Vernazza to Manarola, lots of information, special glimpses of the area, and a dinner that evening.

Kayak Tour—An alternative to the often-crowded trails are Sean Risatti's kayak tours (half- and full-day itineraries, includes equipment, €40–80/person, also does boat tours, see contact information above).

Vernazza (Town #4)

With the closest thing to a natural harbor—overseen by a ruined castle and an old church—and only the occasional noisy slurping up of the train by the mountain to remind you of the modern world, Vernazza is my Cinque Terre home.

The action is at the harbor, where you'll find outdoor restaurants, a bar hanging on the edge of the castle (great for evening drinks), a break-water with a promenade, and a tailgate-party street market every Tuesday morning. In the summer, the beach becomes a soccer field, where teams fielded by local bars and restaurants provide late-night entertainment. In the dark, locals fish off the promontory, using glowing bobs that shine in the waves.

The town's 500 residents, proud of their Vernazzan heritage, brag that "Vernazza is locally owned. Portofino has sold out." Fearing the change it would bring, keep-Vernazza-small proponents stopped the construction of a major road into the town and region. Families are tight and go back centuries; several generations stay together. Leisure time is devoted to the *passeggiata*—strolling lazily together up and down the main street. Sit on a bench and study the passersby. Then explore the characteristic alleys, called *carugi*. In October, the cantinas are draped with drying grapes. In the winter, the population shrinks as many people move to more comfortable big-city apartments.

A steep five-minute hike in either direction from Vernazza gives you a classic village photo op (for the best light, head toward Corniglia in the morning, toward Monterosso in the evening). Franco's Bar (a.k.a.

Vernazza

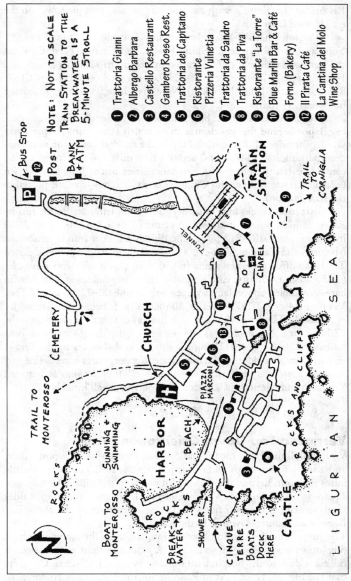

NOTE: Not to scale
TRAIN STATION TO THE
BREAKWATER IS A
5-MINUTE STROLL

1 Trattoria Gianni
2 Albergo Barbara
3 Castello Restaurant
4 Gambero Rosso Rest.
5 Trattoria del Capitano
6 Ristorante Pizzeria Vulnetia
7 Trattoria da Sandro
8 Trattoria da Piva
9 Ristorante "La Torre"
10 Blue Marlin Bar & Café
11 Forno (Bakery)
12 Il Pirata Café
13 La Cantina del Molo Wine Shop

BUS STOP
POST
BANK + ATM
TRAIN STATION
TRAIL TO CORNIGLIA
TUNNEL
VIA ROMA
CHAPEL
CHURCH
CEMETERY
TRAIL TO MONTEROSSO
PIAZZA MARCONI
ROCKS
SUNNING + SWIMMING
HARBOR
BEACH
BOAT TO MONTEROSSO
BREAK-WATER
ROCKS
SHOWER
CINQUE TERRE BOATS DOCK HERE
CASTLE
ROCKS AND CLIFFS
LIGURIAN SEA

Ristorante "La Torre"), with a panoramic terrace, is at the tower on the trail toward Corniglia.

The town has ATMs and two banks (in center and top of town). You can buy train tickets, Hiking Passes, and Cinque Terre Cards at the Vernazza train station/TI, staffed by helpful trio Eliano, Diego, and Francesco (daily in summer 6:30–22:00, in winter 8:00–20:00, tel. 0187-812-533, a little English spoken). Note that there is no luggage storage in Vernazza's train station.

Bus Service: A shuttle bus, generally with friendly English-speaking Beppe behind the wheel, runs twice hourly (free with Cinque Terre Card, otherwise €1.50) from the top of the main street to the non-resident parking lot (€11/24 hrs) about a half-mile above Vernazza. You can also catch the bus to the two sanctuaries in the hills above town (€2.50 each way or free with Cinque Terre Card, bus schedule posted in the train station).

Internet Access and Laundry: The slick Internet Point, run by Alberto and Isabella, is in the village center (daily 9:30–20:00, until 23:00 in summer, tel. 0187-812-949). The Blue Marlin bar (run by exuberant Massimo and Carmen, 7ish–24:00, open daily in Aug, otherwise closed Thu) also offers Internet access (€0.10/min) plus a self-service laundry (€4.50 wash, €4.50 dry, English instructions, buy tokens at Blue Marlin bar—note hours above, laundry open Fri–Wed 8:00–22:00, closed Thu, Via Roma 49, tel. 0187-821-149, 30 meters yards below train station).

Beach: The harbor's sandy cove has kayak rentals (June–Sept only, €7/hour for a 2-person kayak, €4 for single, also dinghy and taxi boat rentals, tel. 0187-920-011), sunning rocks, and showers by the breakwater. There's a ladder on the breakwater for deepwater access. The tiny *acque pendente* (waterfall) cove which locals call their *laguna blu*, between Vernazza and Monterosso, is accessible only by small hired boat.

TOURS

Vernazza Top-Down Orientation Walk

Walk uphill until you hit the parking lot—with a bank, a post office, and a barrier that keeps all but service vehicles out. Vernazza's shuttle buses run from here to the parking lot and into the hills. The tidy new square is called Fontana Vecchia, after a long-gone fountain. Older locals remember the river filled with townswomen doing their washing. Begin your saunter downhill to the harbor.

Just before the Pension Sorriso sign, you'll see the ambulance barn (big brown wood doors) on your right. A group of volunteers is always on call for a dash to the hospital, 30 minutes away in La Spezia. Opposite that is a big empty lot next to Pension Sorriso. Like many landowners, the owner of the Sorriso had plans to expand, but the government said no. The old character of these towns is carefully protected.

Across from Pension Sorriso is the honorary clubhouse for the ANPI (members of the local WWII resistance). Only five ANPI old-timers survive. Cynics consider them less than heroes. After 1943, Hitler called up Italian boys over 15. Rather than die on the front for Hitler, they escaped to the hills. Only to remain free did they become "resistance fighters."

A few steps farther along, you'll see a monument (marble plaque in wall to your left) to those killed in World War II. Not a family was spared. Study this: soldiers *"morti in combattimento"* fought for Mussolini, some were deported to *Germania*, and *Part* (stands for *partigiani* or "partisans") were killed later fighting against Mussolini.

The tiny monorail *trenino* (as you're facing plaque, look up on the wall on your right) is parked quietly here except in September and October, when it's busy helping locals bring down the grapes (sorry, not open to the public). The path to Corniglia leaves from here (it runs above plaque, starting at your left). Behind you is a tiny square playground, decorated with three millstones, which no longer grind local olives into oil. From here, Vernazza's tiny river goes underground.

In the tunnel under the railway tracks, you'll see a door marked "Croce Verde Vernazza" (Green Cross). Posted on the other side of the tunnel is the "P.A. Croce Verde Vernazza" (in a small green display case), the list of volunteers ready for ambulance duty each day of the month.

The train tracks are above you. The second set of tracks (nearer the harbor) was recently renovated to lessen the disruptive noise; locals say it made no difference.

Follow the road downhill. Until the 1950s, Vernazza's river ran open through the center of town from here to the *gelateria*.

Wandering through this main business center, you'll pass many locals doing their *vasca* (laps) past the entrepreneurial Blue Marlin bar and the tiny Chapel of Santa Marta (the small stone building with iron grillwork over the window, across from Il Baretto), where Mass is celebrated only on special Sundays. Next you'll see a grocery, *gelateria*, bakery, pharmacy, another grocery, and another *gelateria*.

On the left, in front of the second *gelateria*, an arch leads to what was a beach where the river used to flow out of town. Continue on down to the harbor square and breakwater. Vernazza, with the only natural harbor of the Cinque Terre, was established as the sole place boats could pick up the fine local wine. (The town is named for a kind of wine.) Peek into the tiny street behind the Vulnetia restaurant with the commotion of arches. Vernazza's most characteristic side streets, called *carugi*, lead up from here. The trail (above the church toward Monterosso) leads to the classic view of Vernazza (best photos just before sunset).

The Burned-Out Sightseer's Visual Tour of Vernazza

Sit at the end of the harbor breakwater (perhaps with a glass of local white wine or something more interesting from Bar Capitano—borrow the glass, they don't mind), face the town, and see...

The harbor: In a moderate storm, you'd be soaked, as waves routinely crash over the *molo* (breakwater, built in 1972). The train line (to your left), constructed 130 years ago to tie a newly united Italy together, linked Turin and Genoa with Rome. A second line (hidden in a tunnel at this point) was built in the 1960s. The yellow building alongside the tracks was Vernazza's first train station. You can see the four bricked-up alcoves where people once waited for trains. Vernazza's fishing fleet is down to three small fishing boats (with the net spools); the town's restaurants buy up everything they catch. Vernazzans are more likely to own a boat than a car. In the '70s, tiny Vernazza had one of the top water polo teams in Italy, and the harbor was their "pool." Later, when a real pool was required, Vernazza dropped out of the league.

The castle: On the far right, the castle, which is now a grassy park with great views, still guards the town (€1, daily 10:00–19:00, from harbor, take stairs by Trattoria Gianni and follow signs to Castello restaurant, tower is a few steps beyond, see the photo and painting gallery rooms). It's called *Belforte*, or "loud screams," for the warnings it made back in pirating days. The highest umbrellas mark the recommended Castello restaurant. The squat tower on the water is great for a glass of wine or a bite to eat (follow the rope to the Belforte Bar; open Wed–Mon 12:00–24:00, kitchen closes between 15:00–19:00 and at 22:30, closed Tue, tel. 0187-812-222; inside the submarine-strength door, a photo of a major storm shows the entire tower under a wave).

The town: Vernazza has two halves. *Sciuiu,* on the left (literally, "flowery"), is the sunny side, and *luvegu,* on the right (literally, "dank"), is the shady side. The houses below the castle were connected by an interior arcade—ideal for fleeing attacks. The pastel colors are regulated by a commissioner of good taste in the community government. The square before you is locally famous for some of the region's finest restaurants. The big, red, central house, the 12th-century site where Genoan warships were built, used to be a kind of guardhouse.

Above the town: The small, round tower above the guardhouse, another part of the city fortifications, reminds us of Vernazza's importance in the Middle Ages, when it was a key ally of Genoa (whose archenemies were the other maritime republics of Pisa, Amalfi, and Venice). Franco's Bar (also called Ristorante "La Torre"), just behind the tower, welcomes hikers finishing, starting, or simply contemplating the Corniglia–Vernazza hike, with great town views (12:00–21:30). Vineyards fill the mountainside beyond the town. Notice the many terraces. Someone calculated that the vineyard terraces of the Cinque Terre have the same amount of stonework as the Great Wall of China. Wine production is down nowadays, as the younger residents choose less physical work. But locals still work their plots and proudly serve their family wines. A single steel train line winds up the gully behind the tower. This is for the vintner's *trenino*, the tiny service train.

The church, school, and city hall: Vernazza's Ligurian Gothic church, built with black stones quarried from Punta Mesco (the distant point behind you), dates from 1318. The gray-and-red house above and to the left of the spire is the local elementary school (which about 25 children attend). High school is in the "big city," La Spezia. The red building to the right of (and below) the schoolhouse is the former monastery and present city hall. Vernazza and Corniglia function as one community. Through most of the 1990s, the local government was communist. In 1999, they elected a coalition of many parties working to rise above ideologies and simply make Vernazza a better place. Finally, on the top of the hill, with the best view of all, is the town cemetery, where most locals plan to end up.

SLEEPING

Pensions
$$ Trattoria Gianni rents 23 small rooms just under the castle. The funky ones are artfully decorated à la shipwreck and are up lots of tight, winding, spiral stairs; and most have tiny balconies and grand views. The new, comfy rooms lack views but have modern bathrooms and a super-scenic, cliff-hanging private garden. Marisa, who rarely smiles at anyone (not just you), requires a two-night minimum and check-in before 16:00 (S-€40, D-€60, or €65 with small balcony, sinks and bathrooms down the hall; Db-€77, Tb-€99, accepts credit cards but offers 10 percent discount for cash; Piazza Marconi 5, closed Jan–Feb, tel. & fax 0187-812-228, tel. 0187-821-003, www.giannifranzi.it, info@giannifranzi.it, a little English spoken). Pick up your keys at Trattoria Gianni's restaurant/reception on the harbor square and hike up dozens of stairs to #41 (funky, *con vista sul mare*) or #47 (new, *nuovo*) at the top. (Note: My tour company books this place 50 nights of the season.) Telephone three days in advance and leave your first name and time of arrival. If you arrive on Wednesday, when the restaurant is closed, pick up your keys at the big *gelateria* by the grotto (they'll give you details when you reserve).

$ Albergo Barbara, on the harbor square, is run by kindly Giuseppe and his Swiss wife, Patricia. Their nine clean, modern rooms share three public showers and WCs (S-€45–€48 depending on season, D without view-€45, D with small view-€48, D with big view-€60, bunky family Q-€75, call to reserve, then fax with credit card information to hold room—but you'll have to pay cash, 2-night stay preferred,

SLEEP CODE

(€1 = about $1.10, country code: 39)

Sleep Code: **S** = Single, **D** = Double/Twin, **T** = Triple, **Q** = Quad, **b** = bathroom, **s** = shower only, **no CC** = Credit Cards not accepted, **SE** = Speaks English, **NSE** = No English. Breakfast is included only in real hotels. Unless otherwise noted, credit cards are accepted.

To help you sort easily through these listings, I've divided the rooms into three categories based on the price for a standard double room with bath:

   $$$ **Higher Priced**—Most rooms €100 or more.
    $$ **Moderately Priced**—Most rooms between €50-100.
     $ **Lower Priced**—Most rooms €50 or less.

Vernazza, the essence of the Cinque Terre, is my top choice for a home base. There are two recommended pensions and piles of private rooms for rent.

If you arrive without a reservation, you can call these places from the pay phone at the bottom of the stairs at the train station. Or drop by the nearest shop or bar; most locals know someone who rents rooms.

Anywhere you stay here will require some climbing. Night noises can be a problem if you're near the station, and rooms on the harbor come with church bells from 7:00–22:00.

A parking lot (€1.50/hr, €11/day, just over a half-mile out of town) and a hardworking shuttle service make driving to Vernazza a reasonable option for drivers with nerves of steel. The little shuttle bus makes the run from the lot to the top of town twice an hour.

Usually, when a price range is listed, the lower price is charged during winter (roughly Nov–March) and the higher price the rest of the year.

confirm before 17:00 on day of arrival or lose your room, loads of stairs, fans, closed Dec–Feb, Piazza Marconi 30 , tel. & fax 0187-812-398, mobile 338-793-3261, SE). The two big doubles on the main floor come with grand harbor views and are the best value (top-floor doubles have small windows and small views). The office is on the top floor of the big, red, vacant-looking building facing the harbor.

Private Rooms (Affitta Camere)

The town is honeycombed year-round with private rooms, offering the best values in Vernazza. The owners are usually reluctant to reserve rooms far in advance. It's easiest to call a day or two ahead or simply show up in the morning and look around. The rooms cost about €45–70 for a double, depending on the view, season, and plumbing. Most places accept only cash. Some have killer views, come with lots of stairs, and cost the same as a small dark place on a back lane over the train tracks. Little or no English is spoken at these places. Any main-street business has a line on rooms for rent. If you call to let them know your arrival time, they'll meet you at the train station.

$$ **Francamaria** rents four sharp, comfortable rooms overlooking the harbor square. One room sleeps 4–6 and comes with a kitchen and small terrace, another is just a few steps up from the harbor—a rarity in vertical Vernazza (Db-€60–100, Qb-€100–140, prices depend on season, rates soft Nov–Feb, Piazza Marconi 30, tel. 0187-812-002, fax 0187-812-956, www.francamaria.com, francamaria@francamaria.com). Son Giovanni has three rooms of his own to rent (same prices but no views, metalgearsolid@inwind.it).

$$ **Martina Callo** rents four fine, lofty rooms overlooking the square, up plenty of steps near the church tower (Db-€50–70, Qb-€103–110; room #1-Qb with harbor view, room #2-Qb huge family room with no view, room #3-Db with grand view terrace, room #4-roomy Db with no view; heating in winter; ring bell at Piazza Marconi 26, tel. & fax 0187-812-365, mobile 329-435-5344, roomartina@supereva.it).

$$ **Elisabetta's Villino Azzurro** rents an apartment and a comfy private room with a sea-view window. Both have big sun terraces overlooking the sea, castle, and town (Db-€45–60, Via Carattino 62, tel. 0187-458-437, mobile 347-451-1834, www.cinqueterreedintorni.it/elisabetta, carroelisabetta@hotmail.com

$$ **Mike and Franca Castiglione**, who speak New Yorkish (and have the attitude to prove it), rent a small double studio with kitchen, great sea view, and a private garden overlooking the sea and castle (Db-€65–75, prices guaranteed with this book through 2004; turn left at pharmacy, climb Via Carattino to #16; tel. 0187-812-374).

$$ **Tilde's** neat and tidy studio apartment has a superb sea view and comes with a kitchen (Db-€70, Via Mazzini 9, mobile 339-298-9323).

$$ **Affitta Camere da Annamaria** offers five pleasant rooms up spiral staircases (Db-€60–83 with sea or town views or terrace—the terrace rooms are best, turn left at pharmacy, climb Via Carattino to #64, tel. 0187-821-082).

$$ **Giuliano Basso** rents three fine rooms that share a large view balcony overlooking the whole town and his own terraced gardens below

SLEEPING ON THE CINQUE TERRE

If you're trying to avoid my readers, stay away from Vernazza. Monterosso is a good choice for the younger crowd (more nightlife) and rich, sun-worshiping softies (who prefer firm reservations for hotels with private bathrooms). Wine-lovers and mountain goats like Corniglia. Sophisticated Italians and Germans choose Manarola. Travelers who show up without reservations enjoy Riomaggiore for its easy room-booking services.

While the Cinque Terre is too rugged for the mobs that ravage the Spanish and French coasts, it's popular with Italians, Germans, and Americans in the know. Hotels charge the most and are packed on Easter, in August, and on summer Fridays and Saturdays. August weekends are worst. But €65 doubles abound throughout the year.

If you'll be here in July or August, or on a weekend, it's smart to book ahead. To reserve ahead, call, fax, or e-mail. At other times, you can land a €65 double room on any day by just arriving in town (ideally by noon) and asking around at bars and restaurants, or simply by approaching locals on the street. This seems scary, but it's true.

Most prevalent in Vernazza, these private rooms—called *affitta camere*—are pleasant rooms in small apartment buildings or in homes (with separate entrances). Some are apartments with kitchens—cheap for families.

For the best value, visit three private rooms and snare the best. Going direct cuts out a middleman and softens prices. Plan on paying cash. Private rooms are generally bigger and more comfortable than those offered by the pensions and they offer the same privacy as a hotel room.

If you want the security of a reservation, make it at a hotel long in advance (small places generally don't take reservations made weeks ahead). If you don't get a reply to your faxed request for a room, assume the place is fully booked. If you do reserve, honor your reservation (or, if you must, cancel as early as possible). Since the owners of private rooms usually don't take deposits, they lose money if you don't show up. Cutthroat room hawkers at the stations might try to lure you away with offers of cheaper rates from a room that you've reserved. Don't do it. You owe it to your hosts to stick with your original reservation.

(Db-€65, €75 with breakfast; open year-round, fridge access; above train station, direction: Corniglia, take a right before Sorriso's, then take left fork, 5-min walk to harbor; mobile 333-341-4792, www.cdh.it/giuliano, giuliano@cdh.it).

$$ Tonino Basso rents four super, clean, modern rooms—each with its own computer for free Internet access—near the post office, in the only building in Vernazza with an elevator. Tranquil rooms come with air-conditioning and a private bath but no views (Sb-€60, Db-€80, Tb-€100, Qb-€130; when you arrive, call Tonino's mobile number from train station—phones at bottom of stairs—and he will meet you; or the Gambero Rosso restaurant at harbor can find him—but then you'll have to backtrack to get to his rooms; tel. 0187-821-264, mobile 335-269-436, fax 0187-821-260, toninobasso@libero.it).

$$ Nicolina rents four decent rooms: a large one with a view, two overlooking Vernazza's main drag (one comes with frescoed ceiling and a washing machine she'll let you use), and one without any view. Inquire at Pizzeria Vulnetia on the harbor square or reserve in advance by phone (Db-€65, Qb with terrace and view-€130, Piazza Marconi 29, tel. & fax 0187-821-193).

$$ Armanda rents a stylish, immaculate one-room apartment without a view near the Castello (€65, Piazza Marconi 15, tel. 0187-812-218, mobile 347-306-4760).

$$ Rosa Vitali rents two apartments overlooking the main street, one for three people (has terrace and fridge), the other (for 4 people) has windows and a full kitchen (€75–124/night, tel. 0187-821-181, mobile 340-267-5009, rosa.vitali@libero.it, SE).

$$ Egi Rooms, run by friendly Egidio Verduschi (SE), offers three rooms right in the center of the main drag. The common area includes a partial kitchen (no stove, but microwave, fridge, and sink), comfy living room, and shared bath (€30–45 per person depending on season, Via Visconti 9, call a day ahead to reserve, leave message at mobile 338-822-3202 or tel. 0187-703-905, egidioverduschi@libero.it).

$$ Memo Rooms offers three newly renovated, immaculate rooms overlooking the main street. This feels more like a hotel than any other private rooms in Vernazza (Db-€65, Via Roma 15, tel. 0187-812-360, mobile 338-285-2385).

$$ Camere Fontana Vecchia has four bright, spacious, quiet rooms near the post office (no view) and may be the only place in Vernazza with almost no stairs to climb (D-€50–60, Db-€60–70, T-€80, Tb-€100, closed Nov–March, Via Gavino 15, tel. 0187-821-130, mobile 333-454-9371, m.annamaria@libero.it, Annamaria SE).

$$ Moggia Manuela rents tranquil rooms at the top of town near the old fountain between the bank and the post office (Db-€70, Qb and kitchen-€110, cheaper Nov–mid-April, Via Gavino 22, tel. 0187-812-397, mobile 333-413-6374).

$$ L'Eremo sur Mare, perched high on the trail to Corniglia, has breathtaking views (literally—it's a hike to get here with your bags; heavy packers should look elsewhere). The three rooms share a garden and sun terrace (Db-€78 with breakfast, tel. 339-2685-617, www .eremosulmare.com).

$$ Mamma Rina was the first in Vernazza to rent out private rooms. Staying here is like staying at Grandma's. Rooms with terraces overlook the hills north of Vernazza (D-€60, D without terrace-€55, each room has a private bath but it's down the hall, Via Ettore 9, tel. 0187-812-025).

$$ Patrizia has a bright, cheery studio apartment with fishnet decor and views (across from grotto on main drag). Their other, smaller twin apartment, closer to the station, looks out onto the street (Db-€65-70, tel. 0187-821-231, mobile 335-653-1563, fax 0187-812-907, bemili@libero.it).

$$ Renaldo Leonardini rents a three-bed room with loft and kitchen overlooking the grotto and lively main street of Vernazza. The full-length window opens to make a little balcony (Db-€60-75, Via Visconti 15, just a few stairs up from street level, tel. 0187-821-065 or leave message in English at tel. 0187-703-905, NSE).

$$ Villa Antonia has two remodeled rooms with a shared bath on the main drag (Db-€75, tel. 0187-821-143).

$ Giuseppina's Villa, a cozy apartment with a low-ceilinged loft and a mountainside forming one of the walls, has one window, no view, and a kitchen. The woman at the grocery store nearest the harbor (with *Salumi e Formaggi* on the awning) can check if it's available (€25 per person, Via S. Giovanni Battista 7, only a short climb from harbor, tel. 0187-812-026). Giuseppina also rents a double room up the street (no view, but has a garden, terrace, and kitchen).

EATING

If you enjoy Italian cuisine, Vernazza's restaurants are worth the splurge. All take pride in their cooking and have similar prices. Wander around at about 20:00 and compare the ambience.

Castello, run by gracious and English-speaking Monica, her husband Massimo, kind Mario, and the rest of her family, serves great seafood and regional specialties with great views, just under the castle (Thu–Tue 12:00–15:00 for lunch, 15:00–19:00 for drinks and snacks on cliff-hugging terrace, 19:30–22:00 for dinner, closed Wed and Nov–April, tel. 0187-812-296).

Four places fill the harborfront with happy eaters: **Gambero Rosso**, considered Vernazza's best restaurant, feels classy and costs only a few euros more than the others (Tue–Sun 12:00–15:00 & 19:00–22:00, closed Mon and Dec–Feb, Piazza Marconi 7, tel. 0187-812-265).

CINQUE TERRE CUISINE 101

Local Specialities: *Accuighe* (ah-CHOO-gay) are anchovies, a local specialty—always served the day they're caught. If you've always hated anchovies (the harsh, cured-in-salt American kind), try them fresh here. *Tegame alla Vernazza* is the most typical main course in Vernazza: anchovies, potatoes, tomatoes, white wine, oil, and herbs. *Pansotti* is ravioli with ricotta and spinach, often served with a hazelnut or walnut sauce...delightful and filling. While antipasto means cheese and salami in Tuscany, here you'll get *antipasti di mare*, a plate of mixed fruits of the sea and a fine way to start a meal. For many, splitting this and a pasta dish is plenty. Try the fun local dessert: *torta della nonna* (grandmother's cake), with a glass of *sciacchetrà* for dunking (see "Wine," below).

Pesto: This region is the birthplace of pesto. Basil, which loves the temperate Ligurian climate, is mixed with cheese (half *Parmigiano* cow cheese and half pecorino sheep cheese), garlic, olive oil, and pine nuts, and then poured over pasta. Try it on spaghetti, *trenette*, or *trofie* (made of flour with a bit of potato, designed specifically for pesto). Many also like pesto lasagna. If you become addicted, small jars of pesto are sold in the local grocery stores (you can take it home or spread it on focaccia here).

Focaccia: This tasty bread also originates from here in Liguria. Locals say the best focaccia is made between the Cinque Terre and Genoa. It's simply bread with olive oil and salt. The baker roughs up the dough with finger holes, then bakes it. Focaccia comes plain or with onions, sage, and olive bits, and is a local favorite for a snack on the beach. Bakeries sell it in rounds or slices by the weight (a portion is about 100 grams, or *un etto*).

Wine: The *vino delle Cinque Terre*, respected throughout Italy, flows cheap and easy throughout the region. It's white—great with the local seafood. *D.O.C.* is the mark of top quality. Red wine is better elsewhere. For a sweet dessert wine, the local *sciacchetrà* wine is worth the splurge (€2.60 per glass, often served with a cookie). While 10 kilos of grapes yield seven liters of local wine, *sciacchetrà* is made from near-raisins, and 10 kilos of grapes make only 1.5 liters of *sciacchetrà*. The word means "push and pull"...push in lots of grapes, pull out the best wine. If your room is up a lot of steps, be warned: *Sciacchetrà* is 18 percent alcohol, while regular wine is only 11 percent. In the cool, calm evening, sit on the Vernazza breakwater with a glass of wine and watch the phosphorescence in the waves.

Trattoria del Capitano might serve the best food for the money (Thu–Tue 12:00–15:00 & 19:00–22:00, closed Wed except in Aug, closed Dec–Jan, tel. 0187-812-201, Paolo and Barbara SE). **Trattoria Gianni** is an old standby for locals and tourists alike, especially for well-prepared seafood (daily 12:00–15:00 & 19:30–22:00 in July–Aug, otherwise closed Wed, tel. 0187-812-228). **Ristorante Pizzeria Vulnetia** serves regional specialties and pizza (Tue–Sun 12:00–15:00 & 18:30–22:00, closed Mon, Piazza Marconi 29, tel. 0187-821-193).

Trattoria da Sandro, on the main drag, mixes Genovese and Ligurian cuisine with friendly service, and can be a peaceful alternative to the harborside scene (Wed–Mon 12:00–15:00 & 19:00–22:00, closed Tue, just below train station, Via Roma 60, tel. 0187-812-223, Gabriella SE). The more offbeat and intimate **Trattoria da Piva** may come with late-night guitar strumming and Piva's songs in local dialect (Tue–Sun 12:00–14:30 & 19:00–22:00, closed Mon; Via Carattino 6, around corner from pharmacy; tel. 0187-812-194).

For basic grub, a grand view, and perfect peace, hike to Franco's **Ristorante "La Torre"** for a dinner at sunset (Wed–Mon 12:00–21:30, kitchen closes from 15:00–19:30 but drinks are served, sometimes closed Tue, on trail toward Corniglia, tel. 0187-821-082).

The main street is creatively determining tourists' needs and filling them. The **Blue Marlin** bar offers a good selection of sandwiches, salads, and *bruschetta*. The **Forno** bakery has good focaccia and veggie tarts, and several bars sell sandwiches and pizza by the slice. Grocery stores make inexpensive sandwiches to order (Mon–Sat 8:00–13:00 & 17:00–19:30, Sun 7:30–13:00). The town's two *gelaterias* are good.

At **Il Pirata delle Cinque Terre,** Sicilian twin brothers Gianluca and Massimo enthusiastically offer a great assortment of handcrafted authentic Sicilian pastries. Gianluca is a pastry artist and hand-paints fanciful sculptured marzipan. Their *granitas* (slushies) are made from fresh fruit garnished with thick whipped cream (daily 6:30–24:00; by the post office at the top of town, Via Gavino 36; tel. 0187-812-047).

La Cantina del Molo, the wine shop, will uncork the bottle you buy and supply cups to go (daily 10:30–20:00, until 22:00 in summer, owner makes 5 of the wines, tasting possible). Most harborside bars will let you take your glass on a breakwater stroll.

Breakfast: Locals take breakfast about as seriously as flossing. A cappuccino and a pastry or a piece of focaccia does it. The two harbor-front bars offer the most ambience (you can walk out with the cup, grab a view picnic bench, and return the cup when you're done). The bakery opens early, offering freshly-made focaccia. **Il Pirata delle Cinque Terre** (listed above) makes pastries every morning. The **Blue Marlin** serves a special €6.20 breakfast: ham and cheese focaccia, an assortment of fresh local pastries, juice, and cappuccino (Fri–Wed 7:00–24:00, closed Thu, open daily in Aug, just below station, tel. 0187-821-149).

Riomaggiore (Town #1)

The most substantial non-resort town of the group, Riomaggiore is a disappointment from the train station. But walk through the tunnel next to the train tracks (or ride the elevator through the hillside to the top of town), and you land in a fascinating tangle of pastel homes leaning on each other as if someone stole their crutches. There's homemade gelato at the Bar Central on main street, and, if Ivo is there, you'll feel right at home. When Ivo closes, the gang goes down to the harborside with a guitar.

Tourist Information: The TI is inside the train station (Mon–Fri 6:30–20:00 in winter, until 22:00 in summer, tel. 0187-920-633). Two Cinque Terre Park offices flank the TI; the one to the right of the TI with your back to the tracks has Internet access (9:00–23:00 daily in summer, until 22:00 in winter).

Bus Service: The bus shuttles locals and tourists up and down Riomaggiore's steep main street and continues to the parking lot outside of town (free with Cinque Terre Card, €1.50 without, 2/hr, just flag it down).

Hikes: Consider the cliff-hanging trail that leads from the beach to a hilltop botanical garden (free with Cinque Terre Card) and old WWII bunkers. Another climbs scenically to the Madonna di Montenero sanctuary high above the town.

Beach: The beach is rocky, but clean and peaceful. It's a two-minute walk from the harbor: face the harbor, then take the path to your left. At the La Conchiglia bar, go down the stairs to the right of the bar. Follow the path to the beach.

Mar Mar Rooms rents kayaks (€8/hr for 2-person kayak) and offers boat excursions (fishing or cruising €30/day per person for up to 8 people, Via Malborghetto 4, tel. & fax 0187-920-932, marmar@5terre.com). The town also has a diving center (scuba, snorkeling, boats, kayaks, Via San Giacomo, tel. 0187-920-011).

Introductory Riomaggiore Walk

Here's an easy loop trip that maximizes views and minimizes uphill walking. Start at the train station (if you arrive by boat, take the tunnel alongside the tracks to get to the station). From the station, walk past the colorful murals glorifying the nameless workers who constructed the nearly 300 million cubic feet of dry stone walls (without cement) throughout the Cinque Terre, giving the region its characteristic *mura secca* terracing for vineyards and olive groves.

At the entrance of the railway tunnel, take the elevator up to the top of town (€0.50, free with Cinque Terre Card). At the top, go right, following the walkway—with spectacular sea views—around the cliff.

Riomaggiore

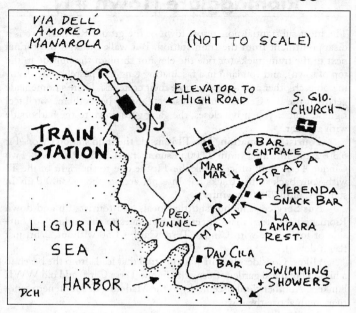

Ignore the steps marked *Marina Seacoast* (harbor). Instead, continue along the path; it's a five-minute, fairly level walk to the church. Continue past the church and then take a right down the stairs to Via Colombo, Riomaggiore's main street.

Stroll down Via Colombo. Just past the WC, you'll see flower boxes on the street, sometimes blocking it; these slide back electronically to let the shuttle bus get past. On your way down the hill, you'll pass colorful, small shops, including a bakery, a couple of grocery shops, and a self-service laundry (€3.50 wash, €3.50 dry, daily 8:00–22:00, next door to Edi Rooms). When Via Colombo dead-ends, on your left you'll find the stairs down to the harbor, boat dock, and a 200-yard trail to the beach *(spiaggia)*. To your right is the tunnel, running alongside the tracks, which takes you directly back to the station. Either take a train or hop a boat (from the harbor) to your next destination.

SLEEPING

Riomaggiore has organized its private room scene better than its neighbors. Several agencies within a few yards of each other on the main drag (with somewhat regular office hours, English-speaking staff, and e-mail addresses) manage a corral of local rooms for rent. Each of these offices can close unexpectedly; it's smart to settle up the day before you leave (in case they're closed when you have to depart). Expect lots of stairs.

Room-Finding Services

$$ Edi's Rooms rents five fine rooms and 12 apartments—half have views (Db-€52–80, Qb-€104 depending on view, season, and number of people, office open daily 9:00–20:00 in summer, otherwise 9:00–13:00 & 15:00–19:00, Via Colombo 111, tel. & fax 0187-920-325, tel. 0187-760-842, www.wel.it/vesignaedi, edi-vesigna@iol.it).

$$ Mar Mar Rooms, run by Mario Franceschetti, has 12 pleasant rooms, 10 apartments, and a mini-hostel (dorm bed-€21, Db apartments-€55–80, bunky family deals-€100–120 for 4 people, can request kitchen and balcony, parking €10/day but reserve in advance, unpredictable hours, Internet access in office, 30 yards above train tracks on main drag next to Lampara restaurant, Via Malborghetto 4, tel. & fax 0187-920-932, marmar@5terre.com). The same people run the recommended Albergo Caribana (below) using the same e-mail address; specify what you're interested in when you write. Mar Mar also rents kayaks and runs fishing trips (see above).

$$ Luciano and Roberto Fazioli loosely run three apartments, nine rooms, and a basic eight-bed mini-hostel (dorm bed-€20–25, D-€50–70, Db-€50–80, apartments-€30–70 per person, open daily 8:00–20:00, Via Colombo 94, tel. 0187-920-904, robertofazioli@libero.it).

$$ La Dolce Vita, across from Edi Rooms, offers five rooms and eight apartments (€20–30 per person; open daily 9:30–19:30, if they're closed, they're full; Via Colombo 120; tel. 0187-760-044, agonatal@tin.it).

Private Rooms and Hotels

$$$ Villa Argentina is worth considering if you want a real hotel. It's on the top ridge of town (15-min walk uphill from "downtown"), with 15 crisply clean, modern rooms, fine balconies (for 9 rooms), and sea views. While this is a good choice for drivers, the little bus that shuttles people (and their luggage) between the top and bottom of town also makes this hotel a possibility for train travelers (Db-€120, includes breakfast, no CC; Via de Gasperi 170, go through tunnel from station, wait for bus or walk 15 min uphill, then take a left at parking booth; tel. 0187-920-213, fax 0187-920-213, villaargentina@libero.it).

$$ Michielini Anna rents four clean, attractive apartments in the center with kitchens and no views (€52/2 people, €93/3 people, €104/4 people mid-April–Sept, less during low season, credit card to reserve but pay cash, cheaper for longer stays, 2 nights preferred June–Sept, across from Bar Centrale at Colombo 143, ring bell to open door; to call friendly Daniela, who speaks good English, dial 0187-920-950 or mobile 328-131-1032; for solo-Italiano-speaking mother, try tel. & fax

0187-920-411; anna.michielini@tin.it or michielinis@yahoo.it).

$$ **Albergo Caribana** has six modern rooms with views and shared terraces. At the edge of town, it's a five-minute walk to the center. The free, easy parking makes this especially appealing to drivers (Db–€64–90, depending on season, includes breakfast, Via Santuario 114, tel. 0187-920-773, tel. & fax 0187-920-932, marmar@5terre.com). The same people run Mar Mar Rooms, a room-finding service (see above), using the same e-mail address; specify what you want when you write.

EATING

Ristorante La Lampara serves a *frutti di mare* pizza, *trenette al pesto,* and the aromatic *spaghetti al cartoccio*—spaghetti with mixed seafood cooked in foil (€15 tourist *menu,* Wed–Mon 12:00–14:30 & 18:00–22:30, closed Tue in winter, on Via Malborghetto 10 just above tracks off Via Colombo, tel. 0187-920-120). Groceries and delis (such as Da Simone) on Via Colombo sell food to go, including pizza slices; have your picnic at the harbor.

Bar Centrale, run by friendly Ivo and Alberto, is a good stop for breakfast, cheeseburgers, Internet access, and live music (sometimes in summer). Ivo lived in San Francisco, fills his bar with only the best San Franciscan rock, parties on the Fourth of July, speaks great English, and can even help you find a room. During the day, Bar Centrale is a shaded place to relax with other travelers. At night, it offers the only action in town (daily 7:30–1:00, closed Mon in winter only, confirm prices, Via Colombo 144, tel. 0187-920-208, barcentr@tin.it). There's prizewinning gelato next door.

While the late-night fun is at Ivo's Bar Centrale, take a walk down to the harborside **Dau Cila** bar (10:30–24:30, closed Tue, tel. 0187-760-032) for jazz, nets, and mellow *limoncino*—a drink of lemon juice, sugar, and pure alcohol (a.k.a. *limoncello* elsewhere in Italy).

For a snack or good takeout, try **Te Do Io La Merenda** ("I'll give you a snack"). Their counter is piled with an assortment of munchies, and they have pastas, roasted chicken, and focaccia to go (daily 8:30–21:30, tel. 0187-920-148, Via Colombo 171).

Manarola (Town #2)

Like Riomaggiore, Manarola is attached to its station by a 200-yard-long tunnel. The town is tiny and picturesque, a tumble of buildings bunny-hopping down its ravine to the fun-loving harbor. Notice how the I-beam crane launches the boats.

Facing the harbor, look at the hillside to your right, dotted with a bar in the middle. It's Punta Bonfiglio, an entertaining park/game area/bar

Manarola

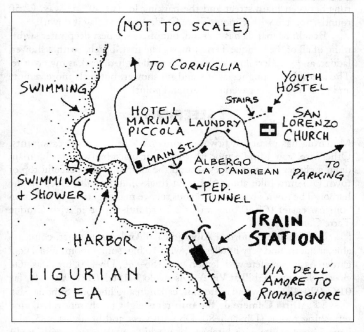

with the best view playground on the coast. The gate farther up the hillside is the entrance to the cemetery. From here you can get poster-perfect views of Manarola (2-min walk from the harbor on path to Corniglia).

In the middle of town, across from the railway tunnel, you'll see Bar Aristide, which sometimes shows outdoor movies on weekends in August by hanging a screen over part of the tunnel entrance (closed Mon, Via Discovolo 290, tel. 0187-920-000). At the top of the town, you'll find great views, the church, and a cluster of accommodations, including a super hostel.

The simple, wooden **religious scenes** that you'll likely see on the hillside are the work of local resident Mario Andreoli. Before his father died, Mario promised him he'd replace the old cross on the family's vineyard. Mario's been adding figures ever since. After recovering from a rare illness, he redoubled his efforts. The scenes, which do change occasionally (a sheep here, an apostle there), are sometimes left up year-round. On religious holidays, everything's lit up: the Nativity, the Last Supper, the Crucifixion, the Resurrection, and more.

Services: You can store baggage in the Cinque Terre Park office in train station (€0.50/hr, up to 6 hours, then €6/up to 24 hrs, daily

7:00–22:00, 8:00–20:00 in winter). Within Manarola, the shuttle bus runs between main street and the parking lot (€1.50 one-way, €2.50 round-trip, free with Cinque Terre Card, 2/hr, just flag it down).

Beach: Manarola has no sand, but offers the best deepwater swimming of all of the Cinque Terre towns. The first "beach," with a shower, ladder, and wonderful rocks (with daredevil high-divers), is my favorite. The second has tougher access and no shower, but feels more remote and pristine (follow paved path around point).

SLEEPING

Manarola has plenty of private rooms. Ask in bars and restaurants. Otherwise, you'll find a modern three-star place halfway up the main drag, a cluster of great values around the church at the peaceful top of town (a 5-min hike above the train tracks), and a salty place on the harbor. The town's handy shuttle bus service makes getting to and from your car easier (€1.50 one-way, €2.50 round-trip, free with Cinque Terre Card).

$$ The utterly normal **Albergo ca' d'Andrean** is quiet, comfortable, modern, and very hotelesque, with 10 big, sunny rooms and a cool garden oasis complete with lemon trees (Sb-€60, Db-€80, breakfast-€6, closed Nov, up the hill at Via A. Discovolo 101, tel. 0187-920-040, fax 0187-920-452, www.cadandrean.it, cadandrean@libero.it, Simone SE).

$$ **Affitta Camere de Baranin** rents eight newly renovated, airy, refreshing rooms (Db-€63–80, Db with view and breakfast-€85, also have 5 apartments with kitchen for weekly rental, reserve with credit card but pay cash, Internet access; reception office open 7:30–13:30 & 15:30–19:30; climb stairway against wall beyond church square—with your back to the church, stairway is at 7:00, follow sign to Trattoria dal Billy, Via Rollandi 29; tel. & fax 0187-920-595, www.baranin.com, Sara, Silvia, and Andrea SE).

$$ **La Torretta** has four compact apartments with kitchens, five doubles, one quad, and a large, shared seaview terrace and sundeck with lounge chairs, all attractively designed by the young English-speaking architect/manager Gabriele Baldini (student Db-€26–38, standard Db-€52–72, Db apartment-€57–77, Qb-€83–124, prices vary with season, reserve with credit card but pay cash, $50 nonrefundable deposit is lost if you cancel, views, big garden; with your back to church, it's at 10:00—look left across the square toward the sea, Piazza della Chiesa, Vico Volto 14; tel. & fax 0187-920-327, www.cinqueterre.net/torretta, torretta@cdh.it, also rents a Tuscan villa).

$$ **Marina Piccola** offers 13 bright, modern rooms on the water—so they figure a warm welcome is unnecessary (Db-€80 for 1-night stays, discounts for longer stays, half-pension available at €72 per person but only for stays of 3 nights or longer, Via allo Scalo 16, tel.

0187-920-103, fax 0187-920-966, www.hotelmarinapiccola.com, info
@hotelmarinapiccola.com).

$ **Casa Capellini** rents four fine rooms; one has a view balcony,
another a 360-degree terrace (Db–€42; the *alta camera* on the top, with
a kitchen, private terrace, and knockout view, costs €57; 2 doors down
the hill from the church, with your back to the church, it's at 2:00, Via
Ettore Cozzani 12, tel. 0187-920-823 or 0187-736-765, casa.capellini
@tin.it, NSE).

$ **Ostello 5-Terre,** Manarola's modern and well-run hostel, stands
like a Monopoly hotel behind the church square. It's smart to reserve at
least two weeks in advance in high season (1 week in off-season). You
book with your credit card number; if you cancel with less than three
days' notice, you'll be charged for one night. This is not a party hostel;
quiet is greatly appreciated (May–Sept: beds–€20, Qb–€80; off-season:
beds–€17, Qb–€64; closed early Jan–mid-Feb; 48 beds in 4- to 6-bed
rooms, not coed except for couples and families; office closed
13:00–17:00; rooms closed 10:00–17:00, curfew–1:00; off-season: office
and rooms closed until 16:00 and curfew at 24:00; open to anyone of
any age, laundry, safes, phone cards, Internet access, book exchange, elevator, optional €3.50 breakfast and €6 dinner, great roof terrace and
sunset views, Via B. Riccobaldi 21, tel. 0187-920-215, fax 0187-920-
218, www.hostel5terre.com, ostello@cdh.it). They also rent bikes,
kayaks, and snorkeling gear.

Corniglia (Town #3)

From the station, a footpath zigzags up nearly 400 stairs to the only town
of the five not on water. Take the bus (€1.50, free with Cinque Terre
Card, 2/hr). Originally settled by a Roman farmer who named it for his
mother, Cornelia (how Corniglia is pronounced), the town and its
ancient residents produced a wine so famous that vases found at Pompeii
touted its virtues. Today, wine is still its lifeblood. Follow the pungent
smell of ripe grapes into an alley cellar and get a local to let you dip a
straw into a keg. Remote and less visited, Corniglia has fewer tourists,
cooler temperatures, a windy belvedere (on its promontory), a few restaurants, and plenty of private rooms for rent (ask at any bar or shop).

Beaches: This hilltop town has a rocky man-made beach below its
station (toward Manarola). It's clean and uncrowded, and the beach bar
has showers, drinks, and snacks.

The nude Guvano (GOO-vah-noh) beach is in the opposite direction (toward Vernazza). This beach made headlines in Italy in the 1970s,
as clothed locals in a makeshift armada of dinghies and fishing boats
retook their town beach. But big-city nudists still work on all-around
tans in this remote setting. From the Corniglia train station, follow the

Corniglia

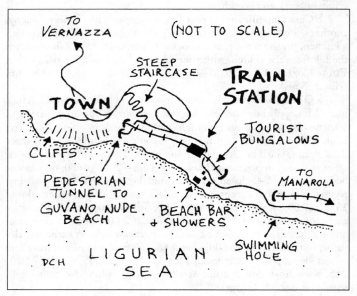

TO VERNAZZA

(NOT TO SCALE)

STEEP STAIRCASE

TRAIN STATION

TOWN

CLIFFS

TOURIST BUNGALOWS

PEDESTRIAN TUNNEL TO GUVANO NUDE BEACH

TO MANAROLA

BEACH BAR & SHOWERS

DCH

SWIMMING HOLE

LIGURIAN SEA

road north, go over the tracks, then zigzag below the tracks, following signs to the tunnel in the cliff (walk past the *proprieta privata* sign). When you buzz the intercom, the hydraulic *Get Smart*–type door is opened from the other end. After a 15-minute hike through a cool, moist, and dimly lit unused old train tunnel, you'll emerge at the Guvano beach—and get charged €3. The beach has drinking water, but no WC. A steep (free) trail leads from the beach up to the Corniglia–Vernazza trail. The crowd is Italian counterculture: pierced nipples, tattooed punks, hippie drummers in dreads, and nude exhibitionist men. The ratio of men to women is about three to two. About half the people on the pebbly beach keep their swimsuits on.

SLEEPING

Perched high above the sea on a hilltop, Corniglia has plenty of private rooms (generally Db-€60). To get to the town from the station, catch the shuttle bus or take a 15-minute uphill hike. If you hike, choose between a long road or lots of stairs. At the top of the stairs, turn left to reach the town (if you've taken the road, just stay on the road). The main drag is Via Fieschi, stretching to the tip of the promontory and its viewpoint park.

$$ **Domenico Spora** has eight apartments scattered throughout town, all with views, terraces, and private bath (Db-€70, Qb-€100, Via alla Stazione 19, tel. 0187-812-293, NSE). Her place is about three-fourths of the way up the hill—if you're walking, take the road, rather than the stairs, up from the station.

$$ **La Lanterna** bar on the main square rents 12 sleepable rooms in town, some with a view (D-€53, Db-€65, also has 6 new rooms in Comeneco a 30-min walk away—better for drivers, tel. 0187-812-291, Via Fieschi 164, www.5terre.com).

$$ **Louisa and Cristiana** rent four rooms (2 with views) and a great apartment (with three doubles, big comfy living room/kitchen, and seaview terrace) on the tiny soccer court near the end of Via Fieschi (rooms are Db-€60, grand apartment for 2 people-€80, for 4 people-€100, for 6 people-€140, cheaper in winter, Via Fieschi 157, call English-speaking daughter Cristiana at tel. 0187-812-236—she works at Bar Matteo on Via Fieschi, below main square; also tel. & fax 0187-812-345; rents small apartment for €70 with no view).

$$ **Villa Cecio,** more like a hotel, has eight breezy, tranquil rooms on the outskirts of town (Db-€60, cash preferred, views, on main road 200 yards toward Vernazza, tel. 0187-812-043).

$ **Pellegrini,** on a quiet side street, offers three comfortable rooms (one with balcony) that share two baths and a terrace (D-€42 with view; going up Via Fieschi, take a left at Via Solferino, then go right, left, and left to find #34; tel. 0187-812-184 or 0187-821-176).

$ **Villa Sandra** has five good doubles (D-€55—2 have terraces, Db-€60) and seven apartments (Db-€62–70, Qb-€120, Via Fieschi 212, tel. & fax 0187-812-384, www.cinqueterre-laposada.com, la_posada @libero.it).

Monterosso al Mare (Town #5)

This is a resort with cars, hotels, rentable beach umbrellas, crowds, and a thriving nightlife. The town is split into the old and new (called Fegina), connected by a tunnel. The train station is in the new town, clustered with the TI and Cinque Terre park office. The statue named *Il Gigante*, which you'll see on the coast in the new town, is 45 feet tall, once held a trident, and looks as if it were hewn from the rocky cliff—but it's made of reinforced concrete and dates from the beginning of the 20th century.

Along the waterfront, whether in the new part of town or the breakwater of the old town, look for all the towns of the Cinque Terre strung out along the coast. Monterosso's old town contains Old World charm, small crooked streets, and Internet access.

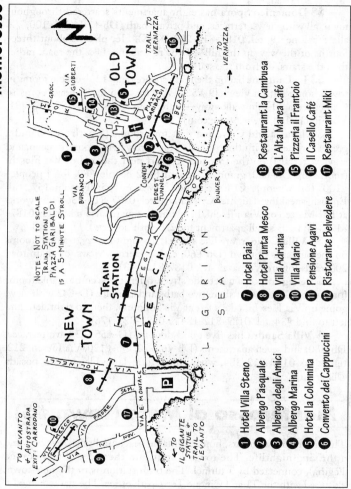

Monterosso

NOTE: NOT TO SCALE
Train Station to
Piazza Garibaldi
is a 5-minute stroll

OLD TOWN

TRAIL TO VERNAZZA

TO VERNAZZA

NEW TOWN

TRAIN STATION

LIGURIAN SEA

TO LEVANTO
& AUTOSTRADA
EXIT: CARRODANO

TO
IL GIGANTE
STATUE &
TRAIL TO
LEVANTO

① Hotel Villa Steno
② Albergo Pasquale
③ Albergo degli Amici
④ Albergo Marina
⑤ Hotel la Colonnina
⑥ Convento dei Cappuccini
⑦ Hotel Baia
⑧ Hotel Punta Mesco
⑨ Villa Adriana
⑩ Villa Mario
⑪ Pensione Agavi
⑫ Ristorante Belvedere
⑬ Restaurant la Cambusa
⑭ L'Alta Marea Café
⑮ Pizzeria il Frantoio
⑯ Il Casello Café
⑰ Restaurant Miki

Monterosso is 30 minutes off the freeway (exit: Carrodano). Parking is easy (except summer weekends and August) in the huge, beachfront guarded lot (€9/day).

Helpful Hints

Tourist Information: The TI Proloco is next to the train station (Mon–Sat 9:30–12:00 & 14:30–18:40, Sun 9:30–12:00, closed Nov–Easter, exit station and go left a few doors, tel. 0187-817-506)

The Cinque Terre park office is in the station (Parco Nazionale delle Cinque Terre, daily 8:00–22:00, until 20:00 in winter, bag check (€0.50/hour up to 6 hrs, then €6/up to 24 hours; in the station, tel. 0187-817-059,www.parconazionale5terre.it, parconazionale5terre@libero.it).

Medical Help: The town's doctor is Dr. Vitone (mobile 338-853-0949).

Internet Access: The Net, a few steps off the main drag Via Roma on Via Vittorio Emanuele, offers 10 high-speed computers, classical music if Renato's on duty, and a free cuppa joe to patrons. Renato and Enzo happily provide information on the Cinque Terre and book accommodations, guides, and scuba diving (Via Vittorio Emanuele 55, tel. 0187-817-288, www.cinqueterrenet.com).

Laundry: A self-service launderette is at Via Mazzini 4 (daily 9:30–13:00 & 15:00–20:00).

Bus Service: There are two shuttle bus routes that run along the waterfront between the station, Piazza Garibaldi (main square in the old town just beyond the tunnel), the parking lot at the end of Via Fegina (stop is called Campo Sportivo), and the hills above Monterosso. Bus line #1 runs from Piazza Garibaldi to the train station (3 min, departs every hour at :30), then on to the parking lot and Colle di Gritta, where you can hike back down to Monterosso via the Sanctuary of Soviore (1 hr, easy), or to Levanto via Punta Mesco (2 hrs, strenuous). Bus line #2 runs in the opposite direction, from the parking lot to the station, Piazza Garibaldi, and up to Colle di Gritta (1/hr departing on the hour, runs daily 8:30–19:00, 10-min ride between old and new towns). Rides costs €1 (free with Cinque Terre Card).

Boats: From the old town harbor, boats run nearly hourly from 10:30–17:00 to Vernazza, Manarola, Riomaggiore and Portovenere. Boats also cruise twice daily to Levanto (June–Sept, otherwise weekends only). Schedules are posted in Cinque Terre park offices near every train station (€3 one-way to Vernazza or Levanto, €4.50 round-trip, €15 for a half-day pass beginning at 14:30, and up to €22 for a weekend all-day pass, pick up flier at any park office or at boat docks, tel. 0187-732-987 or 0187-818-440).

Beaches: The beaches, immediately in front of the train station, are easily the Cinque Terre's best and most crowded. Monterosso is a sandy resort with everything rentable...lounge chairs, umbrellas, paddleboats, and usually even beach access. Beaches are free only where you see no umbrellas.

Tours and Rentals: For hiking tours, boat excursions and rentals, chartered fishing, and other tourist services, check out American expat Kate Little's Fishnet Travel Services (tel. 328-842-6885, www.fishnet.it, kate@fishnet.it). Sean Risatti rents kayaks (€10/hour, €35/day) and offers kayak and hiking tours (see "Tours," near beginning of chapter, tel. 320-047-6865, cinqueterretrek@hot-mail.com, or ask for Sean at The Net or Fishnet Travel Services).

Short Hike Connecting Old and New Towns

You can easily stroll the short tunnel between the new and old towns, but hikers prefer the trail. It's like a mini–Cinque Terre trail, combining scenery and greenery. Heading from the train station to the old town, take the path to the right of the tunnel entrance. The path leads to views of a German WWII bunker below on the rocks (worth seeing from afar, but not worth climbing down to).

Continuing on the path gets you into the old town. Or, at the point where you see the bunker, take the path up to the top of the hill (where you'll see a statue of St. Francis), and up farther still through the woods to reach a gate (marked Convento e Chiesa Cappuccini) leading to a church with a Van Dyck painting of the Crucifixion (accommodations next to church, see "Sleeping," below). You're a world away from the resort town below.

A trail to the right of the church leads up to the cemetery; appreciate its flowers, photos, and your beating heart. Backtrack to the St. Francis statue, and take the trail down into the old town. (Reversing this, if you're going from the old town to the new, take the trail to the right of the tunnel entrance; go right on Zii di Frati to see the church, or continue straight to get to the new town). Allow a total of 30 minutes if you include the church and cemetery.

NIGHTLIFE

Young travelers and night owls gather at Fast Bar on Via Roma in the old town to mix travel tales and beer (sandwiches and snacks served until midnight, closes 1:30, Oct–May closed Mon). For nightlife with a sea view, wander up to Il Casello by the *bocce* courts on the road toward Vernazza; its outdoor tables are sandwiched between the old town beaches (Wed–Mon 10:30–3:00, closed Oct–March, tel. 0187-818-330). Many of the little bars and *enotecas* (wine bars) in the old town stay open late during the summer months—wander the back streets until you find your favorite.

SLEEPING

Monterosso al Mare, the most beach-resorty of the five Cinque Terre towns, offers maximum comfort and ease. The TI (Pro Loco) just outside the train station can give you a list of €30–35-per-person double rooms (pricier for a single) or check with the Net Internet café in town.

Recommended hotels are listed for the old town and the new town (connected by a tunnel), with a convent-run place in between. To locate hotels, see the map on page 990. My favorite is the Hotel Villa Steno in the old town. To get to the old town from the station, exit left, walk along the waterfront, and go through the tunnel.

In the Old Town

$$$ The lovingly managed **Hotel Villa Steno** features great view balconies, private gardens off some rooms, air-conditioning, and the friendly help of English-speaking Matteo. Of his 16 rooms, 12 have view balconies (Sb-€90, Db-€135, Tb-€155, Qb-€175, includes hearty buffet breakfast, €10 discount per room per night if you pay cash and show this book, Internet access, self-service laundry for guests only, 10-min hike from train station to top of old town at Via Roma 109, tel. 0187-817-028 or 0187-818-336, fax 0187-817-354, www.pasini.com, steno@pasini.com). Readers get a free Cinque Terre info packet and a glass of the local sweet wine, *sciacchetrà*, when they check in—ask. The Steno has a tiny parking lot (free, but call to reserve a spot).

$$$ Albergo Pasquale is a modern, comfortable place, run by the same family who owns Hotel Villa Steno (see listing above). It's just a few steps from the beach, boat dock, tunnel entrance (to new town), and train tracks. The air-conditioning minimizes any train noise (Sb-€90, Db-€135, Tb-€155, Qb-€175, includes breakfast, €10 discount per room per night if you pay cash and show this book, readers get a free glass of the local sweet wine-*sciacchetrà*-at check-in, same-day laundry service, Via Fegina 4, tel. 0187-817-550 or 0187-817-477, fax 0187-817-056, pasquale@pasini.com, Felicita and Marco SE).

$$$ The next two places, next door to each other on a quiet street, both require half-pension during peak season: the fancy **Albergo degli Amici** (40 modern rooms; Db-€98–130, breakfast included, Db with half-pension-€136—required July–Aug; no views from rooms, but peaceful above-it-all view garden with "sun beds"—lawn chairs with movable sun shades; Via Buranco 36, tel. 0187-817-544, fax 0187-817-424, www.cinqueterre.it/hotel_amici, amici@cinqueterre.it) and the less-fancy **Albergo Marina** (23 decent rooms, Db-€96–114, credit cards accepted but 5 percent discount with cash, elevator, air-con, garden with lemon trees, next door at Via Buranco 40, tel. & fax 0187-817-242 or 0187-817-613, www.hotelmarinacinqueterre.it, marina@cinqueterre.it). To get to the Amici and Marina from the old town harbor, go to the left of the arcaded building with the bell tower and turn left after a block; for the next listing go to the right of the arcaded building up Via Roma.

$$ Hotel La Colonnina, a comfy, modern place on a sleepy side street, takes reservations in advance only for three-night stays. For a shorter stay, just call a day or two ahead to see if they have space (Db-€80–95, breakfast extra, elevator, garden, rooftop terrace, Via Zuecca 6, tel. 0187-817-439). In the old town by the train tracks, look for the playground and the square with a statue of Garibaldi; Via Zuecca is directly behind him (the hotel is one block up, to the right).

Between the Old and New Towns

$$ The religious **Convento dei Cappuccini** rents 16 spartan rooms on the hill above the tunnel connecting the old and new parts of town. The terrace, overlooking the garden and a long stretch of coastline, has a tremendous panoramic view (S-€35, D-€70, Db-€80, all twins, includes breakfast, dinner €15 and optional; reserve ahead, must send a deposit of 30 percent—personal check OK; €8 parking-reserve in advance; 19016 Monterosso; tel. 0187-817-531, monterosso.convento@libero.it, SE). To hike to the convent from the station (15 min), follow the recommended walk listed in Cinque Terre Towns/Monterosso, above. Or, instead of hiking, you can take a taxi (€8) or shuttle bus (€1) to the cemetery 200 yards away (go around or walk through cemetery to reach convent; its door is to left of church).

In the New Town

Turn right leaving the station for the following listings.

$$$ The central, waterfront **Hotel Baia** has appealing, high-ceilinged rooms, but impersonal staff (Db-€100–140, includes breakfast, slow elevator, some balconies, request view—same price, Via Fegina 88, tel. 0187-817-512, fax 0187-818-322, www.baiahotel.it).

$$$ **Hotel Punta Mesco** has 17 quiet, modern rooms (Db-€110, discount with cash, no views but some rooms have little terraces, free parking, exit right from station, take first right, Via Molinelli 35, tel. 0187-817-495, www.hotelpuntamesco.it, info@hotelpuntamesco.it, SE).

$$$ **Villa Adriana** has 55 decent, clean rooms divided between a 19th-century villa and an adjacent, modern annex. With a lofty setting (up off the street with a tropical garden as its front yard), and a religious, institutional atmosphere, it's peaceful (Sb-€65, Db-€130, half-pension available June–mid-Sept: Sb-€80, Db-€140, doubles and twins available; some views, some balconies, attached chapel, elevator, parking, private beach access-€6/day for umbrella and chair, €7/day for umbrella and lounge; exit right from station, walk along waterfront, turn right at Via IV Novembre, 300 yards off beach, Via IV Novembre 23, reception at back of building; tel. 0187-818-109, fax 0187-818-128, SE).

$$ **Villa Mario**, good for backpackers, has three basic rooms with a view terrace and a squawky bird (Db-€60–80, exit right from station, take second right, walk 5 min uphill, Via Padre Semeria 28, tel. & fax 0187-818-030, villamariomonte@libero.it).

$$ **Pensione Agavi** has 10 bright, airy rooms (Sb-€47, Db-€85, reserve with credit card but pay cash, refrigerators, turn left out of station to Fegina 30, tel. 0187-817-171, mobile 333-697-4071, fax 0187-818-264, www.paginegialle.it/hotelagavi, agavi@libero.it, spunky Hillary SE).

EATING

In the Old Town

Ristorante Belvedere is a good bet for good value. Their *amphora di pesce*—mixed seafood stew (€43/2 people minimum)—is inspiring (Wed–Mon 12:00–14:30 & 19:00–22:00, closed Tue, right on the harbor, across from Albergo Pasquale, tel. 0187-817-033).

La Cambusa serves up traditional Ligurian cuisine to hungry locals and tourists alike (Tue–Sun 12:00–14:30 & 18:45–22:00, closed Mon except July–Aug, Via Roma 6, tel. 0187-817-546).

Lots of shops and bakeries sell pizza and focaccia for an easy picnic at the beach. **L'Alta Marea** offers a specialty fish ravioli, the catch of the day, and huge crocks of fresh, steamed mussels (Thu–Tue 12:00–15:00 & 18:30–22:00, closed Wed, Via Roma 54, tel. 0187-817-170). **Il Frantoio** makes tasty pizza to go (Wed–Fri 9:00–14:00 & 16:00–20:00, closed Thu in winter, Via Gioberti 1, just off Via Roma, tel. 0187-818-333). For a quick salad or sandwich near the beach, try **Il Casello**, next to the *bocce* court on the trail to Vernazza (Wed–Mon 10:30–3:00 in morning, closed Tue Oct–March, tel. 0187-818-330).

In the New Town

Miki is packed with locals who know their seafood and don't want to spend a fortune (Wed–Mon 12:00–15:00 & 19:00–23:00, reservations wise, 100 yards north of train station at Via Fegina 104, tel. 0187-817-608).

TRANSPORTATION CONNECTIONS

Cinque Terre

The five towns of the Cinque Terre are on a milk-run train line described earlier in this chapter. Hourly trains connect each town with the others, La Spezia, and Genoa. While a few of the milk-run trains go to more distant points (Milan or Pisa), it's faster to change in La Spezia or Monterosso to a bigger train. Train info: Monterosso tel. 0187-817-458.

From **La Spezia by train to: Rome** (10/day, 4 hrs), **Pisa** (hrly, 1 hr, direction: Livorno, Rome, Salerno, Naples, etc.), **Florence** (nearly hrly, 2.5 hrs, change at Pisa), **Milan** (hrly, 3 hrs direct or 4 hrs with change in Genoa), **Venice** (2/day, 6 hrs, with change in Pisa and Florence or 2/day change in Milan, 1 direct/day in summer only).

From **Monterosso by train to: Venice** (2/day, 5.5 hrs with change in Florence and Pisa or 2/day 6 hrs with change in Milan), **Milan** (11/day with change in Genova, 3 hrs), **Genoa** (hrly, 1.25 hrs), **Turin** (7/day, 3 hrs), **Pisa** (8/day, 1.5 hrs), **Sestri Levante** (hrly, 15 min, most trains to Genova stop here), **La Spezia** (nearly hrly, 20 min), **Levanto** (nearly hrly, 6 min).

AMSTERDAM

Amsterdam is a progressive way of life housed in Europe's most 17th-century city. Physically, it's built upon millions of pilings. But more than that, it's built on good living, cozy cafés, great art, street-corner jazz, stately history, and a spirit of live-and-let-live. It has more than 700,000 people and about as many bikes. It also has more canals than Venice and about as many tourists.

During its Golden Age in the 1600s, Amsterdam was the world's richest city, an international sea-trading port, and the cradle of capitalism. Wealthy, democratic burghers built a planned city of canals lined with trees and townhouses topped with fancy gables. Immigrants, Jews, outcasts, and political rebels were drawn here by its tolerant atmosphere, while painters like young Rembrandt captured that atmosphere on canvas. But all this history is only the beginning.

Approach the city not as a historian but as an ethnologist observing a strange culture. Stroll through any neighborhood, and see things that are commonplace here but rarely found elsewhere. Carillons chime quaintly in neighborhoods selling sex, as young professionals smoke pot with impunity next to old ladies in bonnets selling flowers. Observe the neighborhood's "social control," where a man feels safe in his home knowing he's being watched by the hookers next door.

The Dutch people are unique. They may be the world's most handsome people—tall, healthy, and with good posture—and the most open, honest, and refreshingly blunt. As connoisseurs of world culture, they appreciate Rembrandt paintings, Indonesian food, and the latest French film—but with an unsnooty, blue-jeans attitude.

Be warned: Amsterdam, a bold experiment in freedom, may box your Puritan ears. Take it all in, then pause to watch the sunset—at 10:00 p.m.—and see the Golden Age reflected in a quiet canal.

Planning Your Time

Amsterdam is worth a full day of sightseeing on even the busiest itinerary. While the city has a couple of must-see museums, its best sight is its own breezy ambience. The city's a joy on foot. It's a breezier and faster joy by bike. Here are the essential stops for a day in Amsterdam:

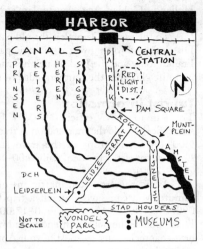

In the morning, see the city's two great art museums: the Van Gogh and the Rijksmuseum (cafeteria lunch). Walk from the museums to the Singel flower market, then take a relaxing hour-long, round-trip canal cruise from the dock at Spui (see "Tours" below). After the cruise, stroll through the peaceful Begijnhof courtyard and tour the nearby Amsterdam History Museum. Visiting the Anne Frank House after 18:00 (it's open until 21:00) will save you an hour in line. Have a memorable dinner: try Dutch pancakes or a *rijsttafel*—an Indonesian smorgasbord.

On a balmy evening, Amsterdam has a Greek-island ambience. Stroll through the Jordaan neighborhood for the idyllic side of town and wander down Leidsestraat to Leidseplein for the roaring café and people scene. Tour the Red Light District while you're at it.

With extra time: With two days in Holland, I'd side-trip by bike, bus, or train to an open-air folk museum and visit Edam or Haarlem. With a third day, I'd do the other great Amsterdam museums. With four days, I'd visit The Hague (for details, see "Netherlands Day Trips" in the next chapter).

ORIENTATION

(area code: 020)

Amsterdam's central train station, on the north edge of the city, is your starting point (TI, bike rental, and trams fanning out to all points). Damrak is the main street axis, connecting the station with Dam Square (people+watching and hangout center) and its Royal Palace. From this spine, the city spreads out like a fan, with 90 islands, hundreds of bridges, and a series of concentric canals (named "Prince's,"

"Gentleman's," and "Emperor's") that were laid out in the 17th century, Holland's Golden Age. Amsterdam's major sights are within walking distance of Dam Square.

To the east of Damrak is the old part of the city (today's Red Light District), and to the west is the new part, where you'll find the Anne Frank House and the Jordaan neighborhood. Museums and Leidseplein nightlife cluster at the southern edge of the city center.

Tourist Information

There are four VVV offices ("VVV" is Dutch for TI—tourist information office): inside the train station at track 2 (Mon–Sat 8:00–20:00, Sun 9:00–17:00), in front of the train station (daily 9:00–17:00), on Leidsestraat (less crowded, daily 9:00–19:00), and at the airport (daily 7:00–22:00).

Avoid the crowded, inefficient offices if you can. For €0.60 a minute, you can save yourself a trip by calling the TI toll line at 0900/400-4040 (Mon–Fri 9:00–17:00). If you're staying in nearby Haarlem, use the helpful, friendly, and rarely crowded Haarlem TI (see next chapter) to answer most of your Amsterdam questions and provide you with the brochures. Consider buying a city map (€2), *Day by Day* entertainment calendar (€1.50), and any of the (€1.50) walking-tour brochures ("Discovery Tour through the Center," "The Former Jewish Quarter," "Walks through Jordaan").

At Amsterdam's Centraal Station, GWK Change has hotel reservation windows whose clerks sell phone cards (local and international) and cheaper city maps (€1.60) and can answer basic tourist questions with shorter lines. (In west tunnel at the right end of station as you leave platform, tel. 020/627-2731.)

Don't use the TI (or GWK) to book a room; you'll pay €5 per person and your host loses 13 percent—meaning you'll likely pay a higher rate. The phone system is easy, everyone speaks English, and the listings in this book are a better value than the potluck booking you'd get from the TI.

Helpful Hints

Theft Alert: Tourists are considered green and rich, and the city has more than its share of hungry thieves—especially on trams and at the many hostels. Wear your money belt.

Street Smarts: Most canals are lined by streets with the same name. When walking around town, beware silent transportation—trams and bicycles. (Don't walk on tram tracks or pink bicycle paths.)

Shop Hours: Many shops close all day Sunday and Monday morning.

Bookstore: For fiction and guidebooks, including mine, try the American Book Center at Kalverstraat 125 (Mon–Sat 10:00–20:00, Sun 11:00–18:30).

Maps: The free and cheap tourist maps can be confusing. Consider paying a bit more (€2) for a top-notch map. I like the Carto Studio Centrumkaart Amsterdam or, better yet, the "Amsterdam: Go where the locals go" map by Amsterdam Anything.

Telephones: Calling the United States from a phone booth is now very cheap—you'll get about three minutes for a euro. Handy telephone cards (€5 or €10) are sold at TIs, the GVB public-transit office (in front of train station), tobacco shops, post offices, and train stations.

Happy Birthday: On the Queen's Birthday, April 30, Amsterdam turns into a gigantic garage sale/street market.

Internet Access: It's easy at cafés all over town. Two huge easy-Internetcafés offer hundreds of terminals with fast and cheap access (€2.50/1hr, daily 9:00–22:00, Damrak 33, a block in front of train station, and at Reguliersbreestraat 22, between Mint Tower and Rembrandtplein). "Coffeeshops," which sell marijuana, also offer Internet access, letting you surf the Net with a special bravado.

Useful Phone Numbers and Web Sites

Amsterdam's Emergency Telephone Number: 112
Schiphol Airport: toll tel. 0900-7244-7465
Taxi: 020/677-7777
Entertainment (AUB Ticket Office): toll tel. 0900-0191
Tourist Information: toll tel. 0900-400-4040
Tourist Information Online: www.amsterdam.nl (City of Amsterdam), www.holland.com (Netherlands Board of Tourism)

Arrival in Amsterdam

By Train: Amsterdam swings, and the hinge that connects it to the world is its perfectly central Centraal Station. You'll find the new international ticket office at track 2 and luggage lockers at the far east end of the building (from €3/24 hrs, daily 7:00–23:00).

Walk out the door of the station, and you're in the heart of the city. You'll nearly trip over trams ready to take you anywhere your feet won't. Straight ahead is Damrak street, leading to Dam Square. With your back to the entrance of the station, the TI and GVB public-transit offices are just ahead and to your left. And on your right is a vast, multistoried bike garage.

By Plane: From Schiphol Airport, take the direct train to Amsterdam (6/hr, 20 min, €3). A taxi from Schiphol to Amsterdam's Centraal Station costs €35. The KLM Hotel Bus departs from lane A7 in front of the airport (2 routes—ask the attendant which is best for you, 3/hr, 20 min, €10). The bus stops in front of the Westerkerk near the Anne Frank House and many recommended hotels.

If you're staying in Haarlem, take a direct express bus to Haarlem (4/hr, 40 min, €3.50, #300 from lane B2 in front of the airport).

Getting around Amsterdam

The helpful GVB transit-information office is in front of the train station and next to the TI. Its free multilingual *Public Transport Amsterdam Tourist Guide* includes a transit map and explains ticket options and tram connections to all the sights.

By Bus, Tram, and Métro: Trams #2 and #5 travel the north-south axis from Centraal Station to Dam Square to Leidseplein to Museumplein. Tram #14 goes east-west (Westerkerk-Dam Square-Muntplein-Waterlooplein- Plantage). If you get lost in Amsterdam, 10 of the city's 17 trams take you back to the central train station.

The Métro (underground train) is used mostly for commuting to the suburbs, but it does connect Centraal Station with some sights east of Damrak (Nieuwmarkt-Waterlooplein-Weesperplein). Individual **tickets** cost €1.70 and give you an hour on the buses, trams, and Métro system (pay as you board on trams and buses; for the Métro, buy tickets from machines).

Strip tickets are cheaper than individual tickets. Any downtown bus or tram ride costs two strips (good for 1 hour of transfers). A card with 15 strips costs €6.50 and can be purchased at the GVB public-transit office, machines at the train station, post offices, airport, or tobacco shops throughout the country. Shorter strip tickets (2, 3, and 8 strips) are also sold on some buses and trams but are more expensive. Strip tickets are good on buses all over the Netherlands (the further you go, the more strips you'll use, such as 6 strips for Haarlem to the airport), and you can share them with your partner.

A €5.80 **Day Card** gives you unlimited transportation on the buses and Métro for a day in Amsterdam; you'll almost break even if you take three trips (valid until 6:00 the following morning; buy as you board or at the GVB public-transit office, which also sells a better-value 2-day version for €9.00; sometimes costs €0.50 more if you buy it on board).

The **Amsterdam Pass** offers unlimited use of the tram, bus, and Métro as well as free or discounted admissions to many city sights and boat rides (€26/24 hrs, €36/48 hrs, €46/72 hrs, sold at GVB public-transit office and TIs). If you'll be using the tram a lot and visiting lots of museums, this pass can save you about a third on your transportation and sightseeing. (It doesn't include the Anne Frank House).

By Foot: The longest walk a tourist would take is 45 minutes from the station to the Rijksmuseum. Watch out for silent but potentially painful bikes, trams, and crotch-high curb posts.

By Bike: Everyone—bank managers, students, pizza delivery boys, and police—uses this mode of transport. It's *the* smart way to travel, where 40 percent of all traffic rolls on two wheels. You'll get around town by bike faster than you can by taxi. On my last visit, I rented a bike for five days, parked it outside my hotel, enjoyed wonderful mobility, and felt pretty smart. I highly encourage this for anyone who wants to get maximum fun per hour in Amsterdam. One-speed bikes, with "brrringing" bells and two locks (use them both; bike thieves are bold and brazen here), rent for about €8 per day (cheaper for longer periods) at any number of places. Hotels can send you to the nearest spot.

MacBike is the bike-rental powerhouse, with a huge and efficient outlet at Centraal Station (daily 9:00–17:45, €4/2 hrs, €7/day, €9/24 hrs, €11.50/2 days, more for 3 gears, €50 deposit plus passport or credit card imprint, at west end of station just before Ibis Hotel, tel. 020/625-3845, can reserve online, www.macbike.nl). MacBike gives out a free basic "Great Waterland Bicycle Tour" brochure (3 hr, 12 miles) and sells several booklets outlining bike tours in and around Amsterdam for €1. For those staying near the Anne Frank House, Frederic Rent-a-Bike is also good (€10/24 hours, cheaper longer, daily 9:00–18:00, Brouwersgracht 78, tel. 020/624-5509 www.frederic.nl).

No one wears helmets. For safety: Use arm signals, stay in the obvious and omnipresent bike lanes, yield to traffic on the right, and fear tram tracks. Cross tram tracks at a perpendicular angle to avoid catching your tire in the rut. You must walk your bike through pedestrian zones. Lock your bike to something immovable—or lose it. Warning: Police are ticketing bikers as drivers. Obey traffic signals.

By Boat: While the city is great on foot or bike, another option is the Museum Boat, which shuttles tourists from sight to sight on an all-day ticket. Tickets cost €13.50 (with sight discounts worth about €2.25). The sales booths in front of the Centraal Station (and the boats) offer handy free brochures with museum times and admission prices. The narrated ride takes 90 minutes if you don't get off (every 30 min in summer, every 45 min off-season, 7 stops, live quadrilingual guide, departures 9:30–17:00, discounted after 13:00 to €11.50, tel. 020/530-1090). A similar Canal Bus is nearby (their €15 ticket is valid until 12:00 the following day). If you're looking for a floating nonstop tour, the regular canal tour boats (without the stops) give more information, cover more ground, and cost less (see "Tours," below).

By Taxi: Amsterdam's taxis are expensive (€2.50 drop and €1.50 for each kilometer). You can wave them down, find a rare taxi stand, or call one (tel. 020/677-7777) for a pick-up. Given the fine tram system, taxis are rarely a good value.

By Car: Forget it—frustrating one-ways, terrible parking, and meter maids with a passion for booting cars wrongly parked.

TOURS

▲▲**Canal Boat Tours**—These long, low, tourist-laden boats leave continually from several docks around the town for a relaxing, if uninspiring, one-hour quadrilingual introduction to the city (€6.50, 2/hr, more frequent in summer). One very central company is at the corner of Spui

Amsterdam

and Rokin streets, about five minutes from Dam Square (daily 10:00–22:00, tel. 020/623-3810). No fishing allowed—but bring your camera. Some prefer to cruise at night, when the bridges are illuminated. **Bike Tours**—The Yellow Bike Tour company offers a three-hour-long city tour (€17, usually at 9:30 and 13:00, Sat at 9:30 and 14:00) and a six-hour tour of the countryside (€23, April–Nov daily at 11:00, 35 km, €100 deposit or credit card imprint, Nieuwezijds Kolk 29, 3 blocks from Centraal Station, tel. 020/620-6940).

Wetlands Safari, Nature Canoe Tours near Amsterdam—If you'd like to get some exercise and a dose of the *polder* country and village life, consider this tour. Majel Tromp, a young villager who speaks great English, takes groups limited to 15 people. The program: Meet at the VVV tourist office outside Centraal Station at 9:30, catch a bus, stop for coffee, take a canoe trip with several stops, tour a village by canoe, munch a rural canal-side picnic lunch (included), then canoe and bus back into the big city by 14:30 (€30, 10 percent off with this book, May–mid-Sept Mon–Fri, reservations required, tel. 020/686-3445 or mobile 06/5355-2669, www.wetlandssafari.nl, info@wetlandssafari.nl).

Adam's Apple Tours—This walking tour offers a 90-minute English-only look at the historic roots of Amsterdam. You'll have a small group and a caring guide starting at Centraal Station, ending at the Dam Square (€15, 10:00, 12:30, and 15:00 most days May–Sept, call 020/616-7867 to check times and book, www.adamsapple.nl).

Private Guide—Ab Walet is a likeable, hard-working, and knowledge-able local guide who enjoys personalizing tours for Americans interested in knowing his city better. He specializes in history and architecture and exudes a passion for Amsterdam (€70/half-day, €120/day, tel. 020/671-2588, mobile 06/2069-7882, abwalet@yahoo.com).

Do-It-Yourself Bike Tour of Amsterdam—A day enjoying the bridges, bike lanes, and sleepy off-the-beaten-path canals on your own one-speed is an essential Amsterdam experience. The real joys of Europe's best-preserved 17th-century city are the countless intimate glimpses it offers: the laid-back locals sunning on their porches under elegant gables, rusted bikes that look as if they've been lashed to the same lamppost since the 1960s, wasted hedonists planted on canal-side benches, and happy sailors permanently moored but still manning the deck.

For a good day, rent a bike at Centraal Station (see "By Bike" on page 1,000). Head west down Haarlemmerstraat, working your wide-eyed way down the Prinsengracht (drop into Café 't Papeneiland at Prinsengracht 2) and detouring through the gentrified small streets of the Jordaan neighborhood before popping out at Westerkerk under the tallest spire in the city.

Pedal out to the lush and peaceful Vondelpark, and then cut back through the center of town (Leidseplein to the Mint Tower, down Rokin street to the Dam Square). From there, cruise the Red Light District, following Oudezijds Voorburgwal past the Oude Kerk (Old Church) to Zeedijk street and return to the train station.

From Centraal Station, you can escape into the countryside by hopping on the free ferry behind the station. In five minutes, Amsterdam will be gone, and you'll be rolling through your very own Dutch painting (get free "Great Waterland Bicycle Tour" brochure from MacBike rental shop, on west side of train station).

AMSTERDAM AT A GLANCE

▲▲▲**Rijksmuseum** Best collection anywhere of the Dutch masters: Rembrandt, Hals, Vermeer, and Steen. **Hours:** Daily 10:00–17:00, sometimes 9:00–21:00.

▲▲▲**Van Gogh Museum** 200 paintings by this angst-ridden artist. **Hours:** Daily 10:00–18:00.

▲▲▲**Anne Frank House** Young Anne's hideaway during the Nazi occupation. **Hours:** Daily April–Aug 9:00–21:00, Sept–March 9:00–19:00.

▲▲**Dutch Resistance Museum** History of the Dutch struggle against the Nazis. **Hours:** Tue–Fri 10:00–17:00, Sat–Mon 12:00–17:00.

▲▲**Amstelkring Museum** Catholic church hidden in the attic of a 17th-century merchant's house. **Hours:** Mon–Sat 10:00–17:00, Sun 13:00–17:00.

▲▲**Red Light District** Women of the world's oldest profession on the job. **Hours:** Best between noon and evening—avoid late night.

▲▲**Vondelpark** City park and concert venue. **Hours:** Always open.

▲**History Museum** Shows city's growth from fishing village to trading capital to today. Includes some Rembrandts and a playable carillon. **Hours:** Mon–Fri 10:00–17:00, Sat–Sun 11:00–17:00.

▲**Rembrandt's House** The master's reconstructed house, displaying

SIGHTS

Southwest Amsterdam

▲▲▲**Rijksmuseum**—Built to house the nation's great art, the Rijksmuseum owns several thousand paintings, including an imcomparable collection of Dutch masters: Rembrandt, Vermeer, Hals, and Steen. The museum has made it easy for you to focus on the highlights, because that's all that is on display while most of the building undergoes several years of renovation (due to be completed in the summer of 2008).

Wander through the Rijksmuseum's Philips Wing for a delightful, concentrated dose of 17th-century Dutch masterpieces (€9, daily 10:00–17:00, sometimes 9:00–21:00, tram #2 or #5 from train station

his etchings. **Hours:** Mon–Sat 10:00–17:00, Sun 13:00–17:00.

▲**Dutch Theater** Moving memorial in former Jewish detention center. **Hours:** Daily 11:00–16:00.

▲**Tropical Museum** Re-creations of tropical-life scenes. **Hours:** Daily 10:00–17:00.

▲**Herengracht Canal Mansion** Elegant 17th-century house. **Hours:** Mon–Fri 10:00–17:00, Sat–Sun 11:00–17:00.

▲**Begijnhof** Quiet courtyard lined with picturesque houses. **Hours:** Daily 10:00–17:00.

▲**Leidseplein** Lively square with cafés and street musicians. **Hours:** Always open, best on sunny afternoons.

▲**Museumplein** Square with art museums, street musicians, crafts, and nearby diamond demos. **Hours:** Always open.

▲**Diamonds** Tours at shops throughout the city. **Hours:** Generally daily 9:00–17:00.

▲**Heineken Brewery** Best beer tour in Europe. **Hours:** Tue–Sun 10:00–18:00, closed Mon.

▲**Marijuana and Hemp Museum** All the dope, from history and science to memorabilia. **Hours:** Daily 11:00–22:00.

to Hobbemastraat, where the entrance of Philips Wing is located, on the south side of the Rijks—the part of the huge building nearest the Van Gogh Museum, tel. 020/674-7000, www.rijksmuseum.nl).

▲▲▲**Van Gogh Museum**—Near the Rijksmuseum, this remarkable museum showcases 200 paintings by the troubled artist whose art seemed to mirror his life. The exhibition hall (usually included with admission) features temporary exhibits of 1840–1920 art (€9, €2.50 if under 18, daily 10:00–18:00, good audioguide-€4, Paulus Potterstraat 7, tel. 020/570-5200, www.vangoghmuseum.nl).

Stedelijk Modern Art Museum—Next to the Van Gogh Museum, this place is fun, far-out, refreshing, and unfortunately closed until 2005. It has mostly post-1945 art but also a sometimes-outstanding collection

Museumplein

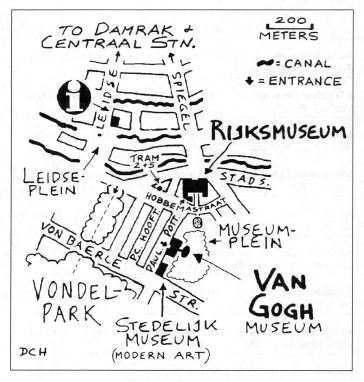

of Monet, van Gogh, Cézanne, Picasso, and Chagall, and a lot of special exhibitions.

▲**Museumplein**—Bordered by the Rijks, Van Gogh, and Stedelijk museums and the Concertgebouw (classical music hall), this square is interesting even to art haters. Amsterdam's best acoustics are found underneath the Rijksmuseum, where street musicians perform everything from chamber music to Mongolian throat singing. Mimes, human statues, and crafts booths dot the square. Coster Diamonds offers tours showing stone cutting and polishing. Skateboarders careen across a concrete tube, while locals enjoy a park bench or a coffee at the Cobra café.

▲**Heineken Brewery**—The leading Dutch beer is no longer brewed here, but this old brewery now welcomes visitors to a slick and entertaining beer-appreciation experience. It's really the most enjoyable beer tour I've encountered in Europe. You'll learn as much as you want, marvel at the huge vats and towering ceilings, see videos, and go on rides. "What's it like to be a Heineken bottle and be filled with one of the best beers in the world? Try it for yourself." An important section recognizes a budding problem of our age—vital to people as well as beer—this planet's scarcity of clean water. With globalization, corporations are well on the way to owning the world's water supplies (€7.50 for self-guided hour-long tour and 3 beers or soft drinks, must be over age 18, Tue–Sun 10:00–18:00, last entry 17:00, closed Mon, tram #16, #24, or #25 to Stadhouderskade 78, an easy walk from Rijksmuseum, tel. 020/523-9666).

▲Leidseplein—Brimming with cafés, this people-watching mecca is an impromptu stage for street artists, accordionists, jugglers, and unicyclists. Sunny afternoons are liveliest. The Boom Chicago theater fronts this square. Stroll nearby Lange Leidse-dwarsstraat (1 block north) for a taste-bud tour of ethnic eateries from Greek to Indonesian.

▲▲Vondelpark—This huge and lively city park is popular with the Dutch—families with little kids, romantic couples, strolling seniors, and hippies sharing blankets and beers. It's a popular venue for free summer concerts. On a sunny afternoon, it's a hedonistic scene that seems to say "parents...relax."

Amsterdam Film Museum—It's actually not a museum but a movie theater. In its three 80-seat theaters, it shows several films a day, from small foreign productions to 70 mm classics drawn from its massive archives (€6.25, always in the original language, often English subtitles, Vondelpark 3, tel. 020/589-1400, www.filmmuseum.nl).

Houseboat Museum Amsterdam—Small sail-powered cargo ships became uneconomical with the advent of modern cargo boats in the 1930s. Almost worthless, they found a new use—as houseboats lining the canals of Amsterdam. Today 2,500 such boats—their cargo holds turned into elegantly cozy living rooms—are called home by locals. For a peek into this *gezellig* (cozy) world, visit this tiny museum. Captain Vincent enjoys showing visitors around the museum, which feels lived in because until 1997 it was (€2.50, March–Oct Wed–Sun 11:00–17:00, closed Mon–Tue, Nov–Feb Fri–Sun 11:00–17:00, closed Mon–Thu, Prinsengracht opposite #296 facing Elandsgracht, tel. 020/427-0750).

Central Amsterdam, near Dam Square

▲▲▲Anne Frank House—A pilgrimage for many, this house offers a fascinating look at the hideaway of young Anne during the Nazi occupation of the Netherlands. Pick up the English pamphlet at the door. The exhibit offers thorough coverage of the Frank family, the diary, the stories of others who hid, and the Holocaust. In summer, skip the hour-long daytime lines by arriving after 18:00 (last entry is 20:30) and visit after dinner (€7.50, April–Aug daily 9:00–21:00, Sept–March daily 9:00–19:00, Prinsengracht 267, near Westerkerk, tel. 020/556-7100, www.annefrank.nl).

Central Amsterdam

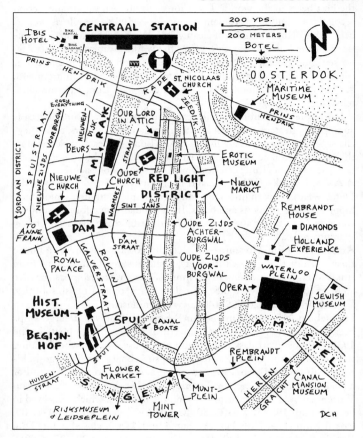

For an interesting glimpse of Holland under the Nazis, rent the powerful movie *Soldier of Orange* before you leave home.

Westerkerk Church—Near the Anne Frank House, this landmark church (generally open April–Sept 11:00–15:00) has a barren interior, Rembrandt's body buried somewhere under the pews, and Amsterdam's tallest steeple. The tower is open by tour only. The mandatory €3 guided tour (in English and Dutch) tells of the church and its carillon and takes you up to see the view (45 min, departures on the hour, April–Sept Mon–Sat 10:00–17:00, last trip at 17:00, closed Sun and in Oct–March).

Royal Palace (Koninklijk Paleis)—The palace, right on Dam Square, was built as a lavish city hall for Amsterdam, when the country was a proud new republic and Amsterdam was awash in profit from trade. When constructed (around 1660), this building was one of Europe's finest. Today it's the official (but not actual) residence of the queen and has a sumptuous interior (while it pretends that it's open to the public, this is rare, tel. 020/620-4060, www.koninklijkhuis.nl).

▲**Begijnhof**—Stepping into this tiny, idyllic courtyard in the city center, you escape into the charm of old Amsterdam. Notice house #34, a 500-year-old wooden structure (rare since repeated fires taught city fathers a trick called brick). Peek into the hidden Catholic church, dating from the time when post-Reformation Dutch Catholics couldn't worship in public. It's opposite the English Reformed church, where the Pilgrims worshiped while waiting for their voyage to the New World (marked by a plaque near the door). Be considerate of the people who live around the courtyard (free, daily 10:00–17:00, on Begijnensteeg lane, just off Kalverstraat between #130 and #132, pick up flier at office near entrance, open weekdays 10:00–16:00).

▲**Amsterdam History Museum**—Follow the city's growth from fishing village to world trader to hippie haven. This creative and hard working museum features Rembrandt's paintings, fine English descriptions, and a carillon loft. The loft comes with push-button recordings of the town bell tower's greatest hits and a self-serve carillon "keyboard" that lets you ring a few bells yourself (€6.50, Mon–Fri 10:00–17:00, Sat–Sun 11:00–17:00, good-value restaurant, next to Begijnhof, Kalverstraat 92, tel. 020/523-1822). The museum's free pedestrian corridor—lined with old-time group portraits—is a powerful teaser.

Southeast Amsterdam

To reach these sights from the train station, take tram #9 or #14. All of these sights except the last two (Tropical Museum and Maritime Museum) are close to each other and could easily be connected into an interesting walk.

Waterlooplein Flea Market—For more than a hundred years, the Jewish Quarter flea market has raged daily except Sunday behind the Rembrandt House. The long narrow park is filled with stalls selling cheap clothes, hippie stuff, old records, tourist knick-knacks, and garage-sale junk.

▲**Rembrandt's House**—Tour the place this way: See the 10-minute introductory video (Dutch and English showings alternate); tour Rembrandt's reconstructed house (filled with exactly what his bankruptcy inventory of 1656 said he owned); imagine him at work in his reconstructed studio; ask the printer to explain the etching process; then, for the finale, enjoy several rooms of original Rembrandt etchings. You'll find no paintings, but the etchings are marvelous and well described (€7, or see combo-ticket deal in Holland Experience listing below, Mon–Sat 10:00–17:00, Sun 13:00–17:00, Jodenbreestraat 4, tel. 020/520-0400).

Holland Experience—Bragging "Experience Holland in 30 minutes," this 3-D movie takes you traveling with three clowns through an idealized montage of Dutch clichés. There are no words but lots of images and special effects as you rock with the boat and get spritzed with perfume while viewing the tulips (€8.50, €2 discount with this book, or show this book and get €1.25 off the €13.50 combo-ticket with Rembrandt's House, daily 10:00–18:00 on the hour, adjacent to Rembrandt's house at Jodenbreestraat 8, tel. 020/422-2233). The men's urinal is a trip to the beach. Plan for it.

▲**Diamonds**—Many shops in the "city of diamonds" offer tours. These tours come with two parts: a chance to see experts behind magnifying glasses polishing the facets of precious diamonds, followed by a visit to an intimate sales room to see (and perhaps buy) a tiny, shiny souvenir. The handy and professional Gassan Diamonds facility fills a huge warehouse a block from Rembrandt's House. You'll get a security sticker and join a tour to see a polisher at work and hear a general explanation of the process (free, 15 min). Then you'll have an opportunity to sit down and have color and clarity described and illustrated with diamonds ranging in value from $100 to $30,000. Afterwards you can bring your free cup of coffee from the café to the Delftware painting exhibit across the parking lot (daily 9:00–17:00, Nieuwe Uilenburgerstraat 173, tel. 020/622-5333, www.gassandiamonds.com).

Jewish History Museum—Four historic synagogues have been joined by steel and glass to make one modern complex telling the story of the Jews in Amsterdam through the centuries (€6.50, daily 11:00–17:00, good kosher café, Jonas Daniel Meijerplein 2, tel. 020/626-9945).

De Hortus Botanical Garden—This is a unique oasis of tranquil-ity within the city (no cell phones allowed because "our collection of plants is a precious community, treat it with respect"). One of the oldest botanical gardens in the world, it dates from 1638, when medicinal herbs were grown here. Today, among its 6,000 different kinds of plants—most of which were collected by the Dutch East India Company in the 17th and 18th centuries—you'll find medicinal herbs, cacti, several greenhouses (one with a fluttery butterfly house—a hit with kids), and a tropical palm house. Much of it is thoughtfully described in English: "A Dutch merchant snuck a coffee plant out of Ethiopia, which ended up in this garden in 1706. This first coffee plant in Europe was the literal grand-daddy of the coffee cultures of Brazil—long the world's biggest coffee producer." (€6, Mon–Fri 9:00–17:00, Sat–Sun 11:00–17:00, until 16:00 in winter, Plantage Middenlaan 2A, tel. 020/625-9021.)

▲**Dutch Theater (Hollandsche Schouwburg)**—This is a moving memorial. Once a lively theater in the Jewish neighborhood, this was used as an assembly hall for local Jews destined for Nazi concentration camps. On the wall, 6,700 family names pay tribute to the 104,000 Jews deported and killed by the Nazis. Upstairs is a small history exhibit on

Waterlooplein Neighborhood

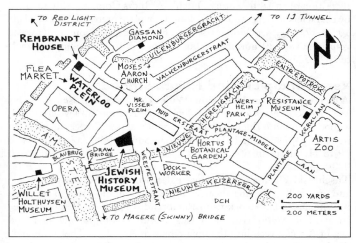

local Jews during World War II. The ruined theater actually offers little to see but plenty to think about—notice the hopeful messages that visiting school groups attach to the wooden tulips (free, daily 11:00–16:00, Plantage Middenlaan 24, tel. 020/626-9945).

▲▲**Dutch Resistance Museum (Verzetsmuseum)**—This is an impressive look at how the Dutch resisted their Nazi occupiers from 1940 to 1945. You'll see propaganda movie clips, study forged ID cards under a magnifying glass, and read of ingenious, clever, and courageous efforts to hide local Jews from the Germans. And at the end of the war, Nazi helmets were turned into bedpans (€5, Tue–Fri 10:00–17:00, Sat–Mon 12:00–17:00, closed April 30, well described in English, recommended café adjacent, tram #9 from station, Plantage Kerklaan 61, tel. 020/620-2535). Amsterdam's famous zoo is just across the street.

▲**Tropical Museum (Tropenmuseum)**—As close to the Third World as you'll get without lots of vaccinations, this imaginative museum offers wonderful re-creations of tropical-life scenes and explanations of Third World problems. Ride the elevator to the top floor, and circle your way down through this immense collection opened in 1926 to give the Dutch a peek at their vast colonial holdings. Don't miss the display case allowing you to see and hear the world's most exotic musical instruments. The Ekeko cafeteria serves tropical food (€7, daily 10:00–17:00, tram #9 to Linnaeusstraat 2, tel. 020/568-8215).

Netherlands Maritime (Scheepvaart) Museum—This huge collection of model ships, maps, and sea-battle paintings fills the 300-year-old Dutch Navy Arsenal. Given the Dutch seafar-ing heritage, I expected a more interesting museum. Sailors may disagree, but—even with its recreation of an 18th-century Dutch East India Company ship manned by characters in old costumes—I found the place pretty lifeless (€7, daily 10:00–17:00, closed Mon off-season, English explanations, don't waste your time with 30-min movie, bus #22 or #32 to Kattenburgerplein 1, tel. 020/523-2222).

Rembrandtplein and Neighborhood

▲**Herengracht Canal Mansion (Willet Holthuysen Museum)**—This 1687 patrician house offers a fine look at old Amsterdam's wealthy, with a good 15-minute English introductory film and a 17th-century garden in back (€4, Mon–Fri 10:00–17:00, Sat–Sun 11:00–17:00, tram #4 or #9 to Herengracht 605, 1 block southeast of Rembrandtplein, tel. 020/523-1870).

Tuschinski Theater—This movie palace from the 1920s glitters inside and out. Still a working theater, it's a delightful old place to see first-run movies (a half-block from Rembrandtplein down Reguliersbree-straat). The exterior is an interesting hybrid of styles, forcing the round peg of Art Nouveau into the square hole of Art Deco. The stone-and-tile facade features stripped-down, functional Art Deco squares and rectangles but is ornamented with Art Nouveau elements—Tiffany-style windows, garlands, curvy iron lamps, Egyptian pharaohs, and exotic gold lettering over the door. Inside, the sumptuous decor features red carpets, nymphs on the walls, and semi-abstract designs. Grab a seat in the lobby and watch the ceiling morph (Reguliersbreestraat 26–28).

Red Light District

▲▲**Our Lord in the Attic (Amstelkring)**—Near the train station, in the Red Light District, you'll find a fascinating hidden Catholic church (from 1663) filling the attic of a 17th-century merchants' house. When hard-line Protestants took power in 1578, Catholics were forbidden to worship openly, so worshippers gathered secretly to say Mass in homes and offices. In 1663, a wealthy merchant built Our Lord in the Attic, one of a handful of such places in Amsterdam serving as a secret parish church until Catholics were allowed in 1795 to once again worship in public. This unique church—embedded within a townhouse in the middle of the Red Light District—comes with a little bonus: a rare glimpse inside an historic Amsterdam home (€4.50, Mon–Sat 10:00–17:00, Sun 13:00–17:00, Oudezijds Voorburgwal 40, tel. 020/624-6604).

▲▲**Red Light District**—Europe's most touristed ladies of the night shiver and shimmy, as they have since 1200, in 450 display-case windows around Oudezijds Achterburgwal and Oudezijds Voorburgwal, surrounding the Oude Kerk (Old Church). Drunks and druggies make the streets uncomfortable late at night, but it's a fascinating walk between noon and nighttime.

The neighborhood, one of Amsterdam's oldest, has had prostitutes since 1200. Prostitution is entirely legal here, and the prostitutes are generally entrepreneurs, renting space and running their own businesses. Popular prostitutes net around €300 a day (S&F, €25–50) and fill out tax returns.

The **Prostitution Information Center,** open to the public, offers a small booklet that answers most of the questions tourists have about the Red Light District (free, Tue, Wed, Fri, and Sat 12:00–19:00, facing Oude Kerk at Enge Kerksteeg 3).

Sex Museums—Amsterdam has two sex museums: one in the Red Light District and one a block in front of the train station on Damrak. While visiting one can be called sightseeing, visiting both is hard to explain. Here's a comparison:

The Erotic Museum in the Red Light District is less offensive; its five floors rely heavily on badly dressed dummies of prostitutes in various acts. It also has a lot of uninspired paintings, videos, phone sex, old photos, and sculpture (€5, daily 11:00–24:00, along the canal at Oudezijds Achterburgwal 54, tel. 020/624-7303).

The Damrak sex museum goes farther, telling the story of pornography from Roman times through 1960. Every sexual deviation is revealed in various displays, and the nude and pornographic art is a cut above that of the other sex museum. Also interesting are the early French pornographic photos and memorabilia from Europe, India, and Asia. You'll find a Marilyn Monroe tribute and some S&M displays, too (€2.50, daily 10:00–23:30, Damrak 18, a block in front of station).

▲**Marijuana and Hemp Museum**—This is a collection of dope facts, history, science, and memorabilia (€6, daily 11:00–22:00, Oudezijds Achterburgwal 148, tel. 020/623-5961). While small, it has a shocking finale: the high-tech grow room in which dozens of varieties of marijuana are cultivated in optimal hydroponic (among other) environments. Some plants stand five feet tall and shine under the intense grow lamps. The view is actually through glass walls into the neighboring Sensi Seed Bank Grow Shop, which sells carefully cultivated seeds and all the gear needed to grow them. It's an interesting neighborhood.

The **Cannabis College Foundation,** "dedicated to ending the global war against the cannabis plant through public education," is a half a block away at #124 (free, daily 11:00–19:00, tel. 020/423-4420, www .cannabiscollege.com).

SHOPPING

Amsterdam brings out the browser even in those who were not born to shop. Ten general markets, open six days a week (closed Sunday), keep folks who brake for garage sales pulling U-turns. Shopping highlights include Waterlooplein (the flea market); the huge Albert Cuyp street market; various flower markets (such as the Singel Canal market near mint tower/*Munttoren,* daily except Sun); diamond dealers (free cutting and polishing demos on Potterstraat behind Rijksmuseum; on Dam Square; and at Gassan Diamonds near Rembrandt's House—see "Sights—Southeast Amsterdam," above); and Kalverstraat, Amsterdam's soul-less but teeming pedestrian/shopping street (parallel to Damrak).

For something a little different, stroll **The Nine Little Streets** (De Negen Straatjes), home to 190 diverse shops mixing festive, creative, nostalgic, practical, and artistic items. The cross streets make a tic-tac-toe with a couple of canals just west of Kalverstraat. (Look for the zone where Hartenstraat, Wolvenstraat, and Huidenstraat cross Keizersgracht and Herrengracht canals.)

To experience a Dutch shopping mall, drop by the **Magna Plaza Shopping Center.** This former main post office in a grand 19th-century building has been transformed into a stylish mall with 40 boutiques. You'll find fashion, luxury goods, and gift shops galore. It's just behind the Royal Palace a block off Dam Square.

NIGHTLIFE

On summer evenings, people flock to the main squares for drinks at outdoor tables. Leidseplein is the glitziest, surrounded by theaters, restaurants, and nightclubs. The slightly quieter Rembrandtplein (with adjoining Thorbeckeplein) is the center of gay discos. Spui features a full city block of bars. And Nieuwmarkt, on the east edge of the Red Light District, is a bit rough, but is probably the most local.

Boom Chicago (in English) and *Uitkrant* (in easy-to-decipher Dutch) are two free publications (available at TIs and many bars) that list festivals and performances of theater, film, dance, cabaret, and live rock, pop, jazz, and classical music. The **AUB ticket office** at Stadsschouwburg Theater (Leidseplein 26, tel. 0900/0191) is the best one-stop-shopping box office for theater, classical music, and major rock shows.

Music—You'll find classical music at the Concertgebouw (free 12:30 lunch concerts on Wed in summer, at the far south end of Museumplein, tel. 020/675-4411) and at the former Beurs (on Damrak, tel. 020/627-0466), and opera and dance at the new opera house on Waterlooplein (tel. 020/551-8100). In the summer, Vondelpark hosts open-air concerts.

Two rock music (and hip-hop) clubs near Leidseplein—Melkweg (Lijnbaansgracht 234a, tel. 020/531-8181, www.melkweg.nl) and Paradiso (Weteringschans 6, tel. 020/626-4521, www.paradiso.nl)—present big-name acts that you might recognize if you're younger than I am.

Jazz has a long tradition at the Bimhuis nightclub, east of the Red Light District (concerts Thu–Sat, Oude Schans 73–77, box office tel. 020/623-1361, www.bimhuis.nl).

Comedy—An R-rated comedy theater act, **Boom Chicago,** was started 10 years ago by a group of Americans on a graduation tour. They have been entertaining tourists and locals alike ever since. The show is a series of rude, clever, and high-powered skits offering a raucous look at Dutch culture and local tourism (€18, Sun–Thu at 20:15, Fri–Sat 19:30 and 22:45, dinner seating early in the 270-seat Leidseplein Theater, Leidseplein 12, tel. 020/423-0101, www.boomchicago.nl). They do four shows: *Best of Boom* (a collection of their greatest hits over the years), a new show for locals and return customers, and two improv shows. Meals are optional and a good value.

Movies—Catch modern movies in the 1920s setting of the classic Tuschinski Theater (between Muntplein and Rembrandtplein; see "Sights—Rembrandtplein," above). It's not unusual for movies at many cinemas to be sold out—consider buying tickets during the day.

Also consider the Amsterdam Film Museum, which shows several films a day, varying from obscure to classic (Vondelstraat 69, near Vondelpark, tel. 020/589-1400, www.filmmuseum.nl, see " Sights—Southwest Amsterdam," above).

SLEEPING

Near the Train Station

$$$ **Ibis Amsterdam Hotel** is a modern and efficient 187-room place towering over the station and a multistory bicycle garage. It offers a central location, comfort, and good value without a hint of charm (Db-€163, family-€189, €5 extra on weekends, skip breakfast and save €13 per person, book long in advance, air-con, smoke-free rooms on request, Stationsplein 49, tel. 020/638-9999, fax 020/620-0156, www.ibishotel .com, H1556-FO@accor-hotels.com).

$$ **Amstel Botel,** the city's only remaining "boat hotel," is a ship-shape, bright, and clean floating hotel with 175 rooms (Sb/Db-€87, Tb-€117, worth the extra €5 per room for canal view, breakfast-€10, elevator, €25/day parking pass, 400 yards from train station, on your left as you leave station, you'll see the sign and the big white boat on Oosterdokskade, tel. 020/626-4247, fax 020/639-1952, www.amstelbotel.com).

$$ **B&B Gelderse Neel,** a three-minute walk from the train station and near the Red Light District, offers rooms in a canal house (D/Db-€90–100, Geldersekade 75, tel. 020/422-3338, fax 020/422-3566, gelneel@hotmail.com, Ruud and Robbert).

Between Dam Square and the Anne Frank House

$$$ **Hotel Toren** is a chandeliered historic mansion in a pleasant, quiet canalside setting in downtown Amsterdam. This splurge, run by Eric and Petra Toren, is classy yet friendly and two blocks northeast of the

SLEEP CODE

(€1 = about $1.10, country code: 31, area code: 020)
Sleep Code: **S** = Single, **D** = Double/Twin, **T** = Triple, **Q** =
Quad, **b** = bathroom, **s** = shower only, **no CC** = Credit Cards
not accepted. Nearly everyone speaks English in the
Netherlands, and prices include breakfast unless noted. Credit
cards are accepted unless otherwise noted.

To help you sort easily through these listings, I've divided
the rooms into three categories based on the price for a standard double room with bath:

  $$$ **Higher Priced**—Most rooms €140 or more.
  $$ **Moderately Priced**—Most rooms between €80–140.
  $ **Lower Priced**—Most rooms €80 or less.

Greeting a new day by descending your steep stairs and stepping into a leafy canalside scene—graceful bridges, historic
gables, and bikes clattering on cobbles—is a fun part of experiencing Amsterdam. But Amsterdam is a tough city for budget
accommodations, and any room under €140 will have its rough
edges. Still, you can sleep well and safely in a great location for
€80 per double.

Amsterdam is jammed during convention periods, the
Queen's Birthday (April 30), and on summer weekends. Many
hotels will not take weekend bookings for people staying less
than three nights.

Parking in Amsterdam is even worse than driving. You'll
pay €32 a day to park safely in a garage—and then hike to your
hotel.

While I prefer sleeping in cozy Haarlem (see next chapter),
those into more urban charms will find that, with the exception
of the times noted above, Amsterdam has plenty of beds.

Anne Frank House. The least expensive four-star in town, it's a great
value (Sb-€100–120, Db-€125–160, deluxe canalside Db-€215, Tb-
€160-185, "bridal suites" for €205–230, prices vary with season, 10 percent discount for cash with this book, breakfast buffet-€12, air-con,
Keizersgracht 164, tel. 020/622-6352, fax 020/626-9705, www.toren.nl).
Bernarda, who runs the bar, is a great source of local advice.

  $$$ Canal House Hotel, a few doors down, offers a rich 17th-
century atmosphere. Above generous and elegant public spaces, tangled

Amsterdam Hotels

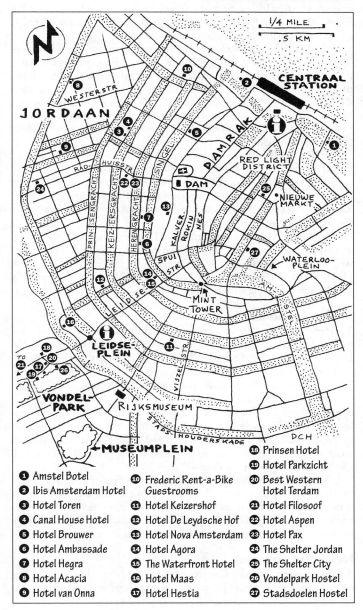

1. Amstel Botel
2. Ibis Amsterdam Hotel
3. Hotel Toren
4. Canal House Hotel
5. Hotel Brouwer
6. Hotel Ambassade
7. Hotel Hegra
8. Hotel Acacia
9. Hotel van Onna
10. Frederic Rent-a-Bike Guestrooms
11. Hotel Keizershof
12. Hotel De Leydsche Hof
13. Hotel Nova Amsterdam
14. Hotel Agora
15. The Waterfront Hotel
16. Hotel Maas
17. Hotel Hestia
18. Prinsen Hotel
19. Hotel Parkzicht
20. Best Western Hotel Terdam
21. Hotel Filosoof
22. Hotel Aspen
23. Hotel Pax
24. The Shelter Jordan
25. The Shelter City
26. Vondelpark Hostel
27. Stadsdoelen Hostel

antique-filled halls lead to 26 spacious, tastefully appointed rooms. Evenings come with candlelight and soft music (Sb-€140, Db-€150, big Db-€190, elevator, Keizersgracht 148, tel. 020/622-5182, fax 020/624-1317, www.canalhouse.nl, info@canalhouse.nl).

$$$ **Hotel Ambassade**—lacing together 60 rooms in 10 houses—is an amazingly elegant and fresh place, sitting aristocratically but daintily on the Herengracht. Its public rooms are palatial, with a library and plush antique furnishings. A family-run hotel this size is unusual (Sb-€158, Db-€188, Db suite-€260, Tb-€220, extra bed-€30, 5 percent tax, breakfast-€15—and actually worth it—elevator, free Internet access, Herengracht 341, tel. 020/555-0222, www.ambassade-hotel.nl, info @ambassade-hotel.nl).

$$ **Hotel Brouwer,** a woody and homey old-time place situated peacefully but centrally on the Singel canal, rents eight basic rooms up lots of very steep stairs (Sb-€50, Db-€85, small elevator, located between train station and Dam Square, near Lijnbaanssteeg at Singel 83, tel. 020/624-6358, fax 020/520-6264, www.hotelbrouwer.nl, akita @hotelbrouwer.nl).

$$ **Hotel Hegra** is a rare, simple, and inexpensive, yet comfy, sedate, and cat-friendly place with 11 rooms run by Robert de Vries. The place is well worn but feels safe (D-€65, Ds-€80, Db-€90, includes breakfast, Herengracht 269, tel. 020/623-7877, fax 020/623-8159). The lack of a Web site is in keeping with the character of Robert's management.

In the Jordaan

$$ **Hotel Acacia's** 20 plain rooms fill a funky cheese-wedge-shaped building on a canal and a great workaday square, buried deep in the Jordaan (Sb-€70, Db-€85, Tb-€105, Qb-€125, Quint/b-€130, 5 percent extra to pay with 3-night minimum for advance reservations, some larger studios, lots of steep stairs, parking, bus #18 from station, Lindengracht 251, tel. 020/622-1460, fax 020/638-0748, www.hotelacacia.nl, acacia.nl @wxs.nl). The Acacia also rents four fine rooms or apartments in two **Acacia Houseboats** moored adjacent to the hotel. This is your best opportunity for that old-time Amsterdam-houseboat experience in a quintessential Amsterdam neighborhood (Db-€100–115, Tb-€120, Qb-€135, see Web site for details).

$$ **Hotel van Onna** is a smoke-free, professional-feeling place renting 41 simple, industrial-strength rooms. Some beds are a bit springy—but the price is unbeatable and the location makes you want to crack out your easel (Sb-€40, Db-€80, Tb-€120, no CC, reserve only by phone, Bloemgracht 104, tel. 020/626-5801, www.vanonna.nl).

Near the Jordaan

$ **Frederic Rent-a-Bike Guestrooms,** with a bike rental shop as the reception, is a collection of private rooms on a gorgeous canal just outside the Jordaan, a five-minute walk from the train station. Frederic has amassed about 100 beds ranging from dumpy €60 doubles to spacious and elegant apartments (from €40 per person). Some places are great for families and groups of up to six. He also rents houseboat apartments. All are displayed in living color on his Web site (bike shop open daily 9:00–18:00, cash only, Brouwersgracht 78, tel. 020/624-5509, www.frederic.nl).

In the Spui and Leidseplein Neighborhoods

The area around Amsterdam's rip-roaring nightlife center (Leidseplein) is colorful, comfortable, and convenient. These canalside places are within a five-minute walk of Leidseplein but in generally quiet and characteristic settings.

$$$ **Hotel Nova Amsterdam,** a bright, spacious place offering professional service and reliability, rents 60 stark yellow and beechwood rooms in a great locale (Sb-€109, Db-€149.50, Tb-€185, Qb-€220, elevator, midway between Dam Square and Spui at Nieuwezijds Voorburgwal 276, tel. 020/623-0066, fax 020/627-2026, www.novahotel.nl, reservations@novahotel.nl).

$$$ **Hotel Maas** is a big, quiet, and hotelesque place. Though it's on a busy street rather than a canal, it's a handy option (S-€80, Sb-€105, one D-€95, Db-€145, suite-€205, prices vary with view and room size, extra person-€20, hearty breakfast, elevator, tram #1, #2, or #5 from station; Leidsekade 91, tel. 020/623-3868, fax 020/622-2613, www.hotelmaas.nl, info@hotelmaas.nl).

$$ **Hotel Keizershof** is wonderfully Dutch, with six bright, airy rooms in a 17th-century canal house. A steep spiral staircase leads to rooms named after old-time Hollywood stars. The enthusiastic hospitality of the de Vries family gives this place a friendly, almost small-town charm (S-€45, D-€65, Ds-€75, Db-€90, 2-night minimum, fine family-style breakfast around a big table, strictly non-smoking, tram #16, #24, or #25 from train station; Keizersgracht 618, where Keizers canal crosses Nieuwe Spiegelstraat, tel. 020/622-2855, fax 020/624-8412, www .hotelkeizershof.nl).

$$ **Wildervanck B & B,** run by Helene and Sjoerd Wildervanck, offer rooms in a great 17th-century canal house (big Db on first floor-€110, Db with twin beds on ground floor-€95, breakfast in their pleasant dining room, family has 3 little girls, Keizersgracht 498, on Keizersgracht canal just west of Leidsestraat, tel. 020/623-3846, fax 020/421-6575, www.wildervanck.com, info@wildervanck.com).

Two well-located places offering mediocre value are side-by-side overlooking the Singel canal where it hits Koningsplein: $$ **Hotel Agora** (16 rooms, Db-€120, view Db-€135, Singel 462, tel. 020/627-2200, fax 020/627-2202, www.hotelagora.nl, info@hotelagora.nl), and $$ **The Waterfront Hotel,** which feels cozier with lots of steep stairs and 10 rustic yet nice rooms (Db-€110, view Db-€135, Singel 458, tel. & fax

020/421-6621, www.waterfront.demon.nl, info@hotelwaterfront.nl).

$ Hotel de Leydsche Hof, canalside with simple, quiet rooms, is open only from Easter through mid-September. Its peaceful demeanor almost allows you to overlook the flimsy cots and old carpets (Ds-€60, Ts-€90, Qs-€110, no breakfast, no CC, 10-min walk from Leidseplein, Leidsegracht 14, near where it hits Keizersgracht, tel. 020/623-2148, run by friendly Mr. Piller).

Near Vondelpark

These options cluster around Vondelpark in a safe neighborhood that lacks the canal flavor but is only a short walk from the action. The first four places are in a pleasant nook between the rollicking Leidseplein and the breezy Vondelpark. They are easily connected with the train station on trams #1, #2, and #5. The last place has more personality but is farther away.

$$$ AMS Hotel Terdam is an 89-room American-style hotel well situated on a quiet street just across the bridge from bustling Leidseplein (Db-€130–170 depending on season and air-con, breakfast likely not included but often used as a bargaining chip, elevator, Tesselschadestraat 23, tel. 020/612-6876, fax 020/683-8313, www.ams.nl).

$$ Hotel Hestia, on a safe and sane street, feels very professional with 18 clean, bright, and generally spacious rooms (Sb-€80, very small Db-€95, Db-€105–130, Tb-€160, Qb-€190, elevator, Roemer Visscherstraat 7, tel. 020/618-0801, fax 020/685-1382, www.hotel-hestia.nl, info@hotel-hestia.nl).

$$ Prinsen Hotel, with 45 nicely appointed but generally cramped rooms, is family-run and has a peaceful garden and a safe, professional feel (small Db on weekdays-€120, small Db on weekends-€131, bigger Db-€138, elevator, Vondelstraat 36, tel. 020/616-2323, fax 020/616-6112, www.prinsenhotel.nl, info@prinsenhotel.nl).

$$ Hotel Parkzicht, an old-fashioned place with extremely steep stairs, rents 13 big, plain rooms on a quiet street bordering Vondelpark (S-€39, Sb-€49, Db-€78-90, Tb-€110-120, Qb-€120-130, closed Nov-March, Roemer Visscherstraat 33, tel. 020/618-1954, fax 020/618-0897, www.parkzicht.nl, hotel@parkzicht.nl).

$$ Hotel Filosoof greets you with Aristotle and Plato in the foyer and classical music in its generous lobby. Its 38 rooms are decorated with themes; the Egyptian room has a frieze of hieroglyphics. Philosophers' sayings hang on the walls, and thoughtful travelers wander down the halls or sit in the garden, rooted in deep discussion. The rooms are small, but the hotel is endearing (Db-€111–130, Tb-€150–185, elevator, 3-min walk from tram line #1, get off at Jan Peter Heierstraat, Anna Vondelstraat 6, tel. 020/683-3013, fax 020/685-3750, www.hotelfilosoof.nl, reservations@hotelfilosoof.nl).

$$ **Tulips B&B,** with three cozy rooms in a shoes-off home, is run by a friendly Englishwoman, Karen, and her Dutch husband, Paul. Rooms are clean, white, and bright, with red carpeting and green plants. The top-floor room is a lovely suite. They also offer similar rooms—one with a rooftop patio—around the corner on the third floor (no reception desk) on busy Zeilstraat 22 (D-€55–75, Db-€85, suite-€110, includes milk and cereal breakfast, no CC, non-smoking, Sloterkade 65, they send directions when you book, tel. 020/679-2753, fax 020/408-3028, www.bedandbreakfastamsterdam.net).

Southwest Amsterdam

$$ At **Rooms & Co.,** Mayke Stribos rents four modern, well-decorated rooms in her recently renovated house, close to the Amstel River and within walking distance of Museumplein (Db-€130, Hemonystraat 1a, tel. 020/671-5247, fax 020/664-8421, www.roomsandco.nl, info @roomsandco.nl).

Lower-Priced Backpacker Hotels and Hostels

Cheap hotels line the convenient but noisy main drag between the town hall and the Anne Frank House. Expect a long, steep, and depressing stairway, noisy rooms in the front, and quieter rooms in the back.

Hotel Aspen, a good value for a budget hotel, is tidy, stark, and well maintained (8 rooms, S-€35, D-€44, Db-€65, Tb-€75, Qb-€90, no breakfast, Raad-huisstraat 31, tel. 020/626-6714, fax 020/620-0866, info@hotelaspen.nl, run by Esam). A few doors away, **Hotel Pax** has large, plain, but airy backpacker-type rooms (S-€25–34, D-€37–57, Db-€55–85, T-€50–68, Tb-€60–100, Q-€55–77, no breakfast, prices vary with size and season, 2 showers and 2 toilets for 6 rooms, Raadhuisstraat 37, tel. 020/624-9735, run by two young brothers: Philip and Peter).

The Shelter Jordan is a scruffy, friendly, Christian-run, 100-bed place in a great neighborhood. While most of Amsterdam's hostels are pretty wild, this place is drug-free and alcohol-free with boys on one floor and girls on another. These are Amsterdam's best budget beds, in 14- to 20-bed dorms (€17.50–19.50, includes sheets and breakfast, maximum age 35, Internet access, non-smoking, 02:00 curfew, near Anne Frank House, Bloemstraat 179, tel. 020/624-4717, www.shelter.nl, jordan@shelter.nl). The Shelter serves hot meals, runs a snack bar, offers lockers, leads nightly Bible studies, and closes the dorms from 10:30 to 13:00. Its sister hostel, **The Shelter City** in the Red Light District, is similar but definitely not preaching to the choir (€17.50–19.50, includes breakfast and sheets, maximum age 35, curfew, Barndesteeg 21, tel. 020/625-3230, fax 020/623-2282, www.shelter.nl, city@shelter.nl).

The city's two official hostels are **Vondelpark,** Amsterdam's top hostel (€18–24 with breakfast, D-€66, nonmembers pay €2.25 extra, no CC, lots of school groups, 4–20 beds per room, right on the park at

Zandpad 5, tel. 020/589-8996, fax 020/589-8955, www.njhc.org /vondelpark) and **Stadsdoelen** (€17 with breakfast, nonmembers pay €2.25 extra, no CC, just past Dam Square, Kloveniersburgwal 97, tel. 020/ 624-6832, fax 020/639-1035, www.njhc.org, stadsdoelen@njhc.org). While these hostels are generally booked long in advance, a few beds open up each day at 11:00.

EATING

Traditional Dutch food is basic and hearty, with lots of bread, cheese, soups, and fish. Lunch and dinner are served at American times (roughly 12:00–14:00 and 18:00–21:00).

Dutch treats include cheese, pancakes *(pannenkoeken)*, gin *(jenever)*, light pilsner-type beer, and "syrup waffles" *(stroopwafel)*.

Experiences you owe your tongue in Holland: trying a raw herring (outdoor herring stands are all over), lingering over coffee in a "brown café," sipping an old *jenever* with a new friend, and consuming an Indonesian feast—a *rijsttafel*.

Budget Tips: Get a sandwich to go, and grab a park bench on a canal. Sandwiches *(broodjes)* of delicious cheese on fresh bread are cheap at snack bars, delis, and *broodje* restaurants. Ethnic fast-food stands abound, offering a variety of meats wrapped in pita bread. Easy to buy at grocery stores, yogurt in the Netherlands (and throughout Northern Europe) is delicious and drinkable right out of its plastic container.

A central supermarket is **Albert Heijn,** at the corner of Koningsplein and Singel Canal near the flower market (Mon–Sat 10:00–20:00, Sun 12:00–18:00).

Restaurants

Of Amsterdam's thousand-plus restaurants, no one knows which are best. I'd pick an area and wander. The rowdy food ghetto thrives around Leidseplein. Wander along Leidsedwarsstraat, Restaurant Row. The area around Spui canal and that end of Spuistraat is also trendy and a bit less rowdy. For fewer crowds and more charm, find something in the Jordaan district. The best advice: your hotelier's. Most keep a reliable eating list for their neighborhood and know which places keep their travelers happy.

Here are some handy places to consider.

Near Spui in the Center

The first four places all cluster along the colorful, student-filled Grimburgwal lane near the intersection of Spui and Rokin (mid-way between Dam Square and the Mint Tower).

The city university's **Atrium** is a great budget cafeteria (€5.50 meals, Mon–Fri 11:00–15:00 & 17:00–19:00, closed Sat–Sun, from

Amsterdam Restaurants

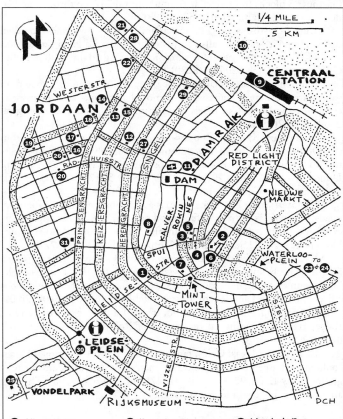

1. Albert Heijn Supermarket
2. Atrium Cafeteria
3. Café 't Gasthuys
4. Pannenkoekenhuis Upstairs
5. Restaurant Kapitein Zeppos
6. De Jaren Café
7. La Place
8. Restaurant Haesje Claes
9. Stationsrestauratie
10. Pier 10

11. Restaurant de Roode Leeuw
12. Restaurant de Luwte
13. Pancake Bakery
14. De Bolhoed
15. Dimitri's
16. De Groene Lantaarn
17. Café Restaurant de Reiger
18. Café 't Smalle
19. Restaurant Vliegende Schotel
20. Long Pura Restaurant

21. Moeder's Pot
22. Café 't Papeneiland
23. To Rest. Plancius
24. To Taman Sari Restaurant
25. Café Vertigo

Coffeeshops:
26. Paradox
27. The Grey Area
28. Coffee Shop Relax
29. Siberia Coffeeshop
30. The Bulldog
31. La Tertulia

Spui, walk west down Landebrug Steeg past the canalside Café 't
Gasthuys 3 blocks to Oudezijds Achterburgwal 237, go through arched
doorway on the right, tel. 020/525-3999).

Café 't Gasthuys, one of Amsterdam's many brown cafés (so called
for their smoke-stained walls), serves light meals and good sandwiches
and offers indoor or peaceful canalside seating (daily 12:00–24:00,
Grimburgwal 7, tel. 020/624-8230).

Pannenkoekenhuis Upstairs is a tiny and characteristic perch up
some extremely steep stairs where Arno Jakobs cooks and serves delicious €7 pancakes to four tables (daily from 12:00–18:00, Grimburgwal
2, tel. 020/626-5603).

Restaurant Kapitein Zeppos—named for a Belgian TV star from
the 1960s—serves French-Dutch food in a relatively big and festive setting. The light lunch specials—soups and sandwiches—cost €5–10.
Dinners go for around €20 (daily 11:00–15:30 & 17:30–23:00, just off
Grimburgwal at Gebed Zonder End 5, tel. 020/624-2057).

De Jaren Café (The Years Café) is a stark and trendy place for soup,
salads, sandwiches, or just coffee over a newspaper. On a sunny day, its
canalside patio is popular with yuppies (daily 10:00–24:00, Nieuwe
Doelenstraat 20–22, just up from Muntplein, tel. 020/625-5771).

La Place, a cafeteria on the ground floor of a department store, is a
festival of fresh, appealing food served cafeteria-style. It has a no-smok-
ing section and a small outdoor terrace upstairs. This thriving place has
a lively market feel and lots of great vegetables (Mon–Sat 10:00–20:00,
Thu until 21:00, Sun 12:00–20:00, it's in La Marché at the end of
Kalverstraat, near Mint Tower, corner of Rokin and Muntplein, tel.
020/622-0171).

Restaurant Haesje Claes, famous as *the* place for traditional Dutch
cooking in the center, is big and fast enough to be a standard for tour
groups (daily 12:00–22:00, Spuistraat 275, tel. 020/624-9998). The area
around it is a huge and festive bar scene.

In and near the Train Station

Stationsrestauratie is a surprisingly classy, budget, self-service option
inside the station on platform 2 (Mon–Sat 7:00–21:30, Sun from 8:00).
The entire platform 2 is lined with eateries, including the tall, venerable,
1920s-style First Class Grand Café.

Pier 10, once an old fishing shack, is now a charmingly simple little
restaurant offering cozy harborfront dining (may be closed during renovation of train station). It's at the end of a dock in the shadow of (but
ignoring) the huge train station. Reserve a place in the tiny five-table
front room (two seatings: 18:30 and 21:30) where it's just you and the
harbor traffic by candlelight (€30 meals, fun but small menu, seafood
and modern European, daily from 17:30, De Ruyterkade Steiger 10, tel.
020/624-8276).

Near Dam Square

Restaurant de Roode Leeuw is a grand place offering a respite from the crush of Damrak. You'll get a menu filled with Dutch traditions, dressy service, and plenty of tourists (€18–22 main dish, 3-course menu with lots of intriguing choices for €30, daily 12:00–22:00, Damrak 93–94, tel. 020/555-0666).

Near the Anne Frank House and in the Jordaan District

All these places except for the last two are within a few scenic blocks of Anne Frank's house, providing handy lunches and atmospheric dinners in Amsterdam's most characteristic neighborhood.

Restaurant de Luwte is painfully romantic on a picturesque street overlooking a canal, with lots of candles, a muted but fresh modern interior, and French Mediterranean cuisine (€18 main courses, €35 for a full meal, big dinner salads for €15, daily 18:00–22:00, Leliegracht 26, tel. 020/625-8548).

The **Pancake Bakery** serves good pancakes in a nothing-special family atmosphere. The menu features a fun selection of ethnic-themed pancakes—including Indonesian, for those who want two experiences in one (€8.50 pancakes, splitting OK, daily 12:00–21:30, Prinsengracht 191, tel. 020/625-1333).

De Bolhoed, across the canal, serves serious vegetarian and vegan food in a colorful setting Buddha would dig (€13 meals, daily 12:00–22:00, Prinsengracht 60, tel. 020/626-1803).

Dimitri's is a nondescript little place serving creative salads, with a few outdoor tables on a street filled with bikes and cobbles (€9 main-course salads, breakfasts too, daily 8:00–22:00, Prinsenstraat 3, tel. 020/627-9393).

De Groene Lantaarn (The Green Lantern) is fun for fondue. The menu offers fish, meat, and cheese (Dutch, not Swiss) with salad and fruit for €17–22 (Thu–Sun from 18:00, closed Mon–Wed, a few blocks into the Jordaan at Bloemgracht 47, tel. 020/620-2088).

Café Restaurant de Reiger must offer the best cooking of any *eet-café* in the Jordaan. It's famous for its fresh ingredients and delightful bistro ambience. In addition to an English menu, ask for a translation of the €15 daily specials on the chalkboard. The café, which is crowded late and on weekends, takes no reservations but you're welcome to have a drink at the bar while you wait (daily 11:00–15:30 & 18:00–22:30, glass of house wine for €2.50, veggie options, non-smoking section, Nieuwe Leliestraat 34, tel. 020/624-7426).

Café 't Smalle is extremely charming with three zones where you can enjoy a light lunch or a drink: canalside, inside around the bar, and up some steep stairs in a quaint little loft. While open daily until midnight, food is served only at lunch from 12:00 to 17:00 (plenty of interesting wines by the glass posted, at Egelantiersgracht 12 where it hits

Prinsengracht, tel. 020/623-9617).

Restaurant Vliegende Schotel is a folksy, unvarnished little Jordaan eatery decorated with children's crayon art that has a cheap and fun meatless menu featuring fish and vegetarian fare. After entering, just choose a table and then order at the counter. Nothing trendy about this place—just locals who like food and don't want to cook (plates €8–11, daily 17:00–23:00, non-smoking section, wine by the glass, Nieuwe Leliestraat 162, tel. 020/625-2041).

Long Pura is a good place for authentic Indonesian. Though pricey, filled with tourists, and on a noisy street, it's conveniently located, friendly, and proudly serves reliably delicious rice-table extravaganzas in a tastefully Indonesian setting (€31 for *rijsttafel,* €37 with appetizer and dessert, daily 18:00–23:00, Rozengracht 46, tel. 020/623-8950).

Moeder's Pot, a six-table neighborhood eatery with great character and charm, is gruff with the smell of fried food and cigarettes. Hearty main courses come with fried potatoes and vegetables, applesauce, and salad. The place is not central but puts you in a charming little neighborhood at the seaside edge of the Jordaan (€7–15, Mon–Sat 17:00–22:00, closed Sun and holidays, Vinkenstraat 119, tel. 020/623-7643).

Café 't Papeneiland is a classic brown café. With Delft tiles, an evocative old stove, and a stay-awhile perch overlooking a canal with welcoming benches, it's been the neighborhood hangout since the 17th century (overlooking northwest end of Prinsengracht at #2, tel. 020/624-1989). Though the café serves light meals, most come here to nurse a drink and chat.

Catering Small World is a cozy sandwich bar with good coffee, the best muffins in town, and only a few seats (€4–10, Mon–Sat 10:30–20:00, Sun 12:00–20:00, Binnen Oranjestraat 14).

Near the Botanical Garden and Dutch Resistance Museum

Restaurant Plancius, adjacent to the Dutch Resistance Museum, is a mod, handy spot for lunch. With good indoor and outdoor seating, it's popular with the broadcasters from the nearby local TV studios (creative breakfasts and light lunches €5–8, daily 10:00–22:00, Plantage Kerklaan 61a, tel. 020/330-9469).

Taman Sari Restaurant is the local choice for Indonesian, serving hearty, quality €9 dinners and *rijsttafel* dinners for €14–18 (daily 17:00–23:00, 32 Plantage Kerklaan, tel. 020/623-7130).

Near Vondelpark

Café Vertigo offers a fun selection of excellent soups and sandwiches. The service can be slow, but if you grab an outdoor table, you can watch the world spin by (daily 11:00–24:00, beneath Film Museum, Vondelpark 3, tel. 020/612-3021).

Drugs and Coffeeshops

Amsterdam, Europe's counterculture mecca, thinks the concept of a "victimless crime" is a contradiction in terms. Heroin and cocaine are strictly illegal in the Netherlands, and the police stringently enforce laws prohibiting their sale and use. But, while hard drugs are definitely out, marijuana causes about as much excitement as a bottle of beer. If tourists call an ambulance after smoking too much pot, medics just say, "Drink something sweet and walk it off."

Throughout the Netherlands you'll see "coffeeshops"—pubs selling marijuana. The minimum age for purchase is 18. Coffeeshops can sell up to five grams of marijuana per person per day. Locals buy marijuana by asking, "Can I see the cannabis menu?" The menu looks like the inventory of a drug bust. Display cases show various joints or baggies for sale. The Dutch include a little tobacco in their prerolled joints. To avoid the tobacco, you either need to roll your own (get cigarette papers free with your baggie, dispensed like toothpicks) or borrow a bong. Baggies of marijuana usually cost €5—smaller contents mean better quality.

Most of downtown Amsterdam's countless coffeeshops feel grungy and foreboding to anyone over thirty. The neighborhood places (and those in small towns throughout the countryside) are much more inviting to people without piercings, tattoos, and favorite techno artists. I've listed a few places with a more pub-like ambience for older Americans wanting to go local but within reason.

Paradox is the most *gezellig* (cozy) coffeeshop I found—a mellow, graceful place. The manager, Ludo, is patient with descriptions and is happy to walk you through all your options. This is a rare coffeeshop that serves light meals. The juice is fresh, the music is easy, and the neighborhood is charming. Colorful murals with bright blue skies are all over the walls, creating a fresh and open feeling (loaner bongs, games, daily 10:00–20:00, 2 blocks from Anne Frank House at 1e Bloemdwarsstraat 2, tel. 020/623-5639).

The Grey Area coffeeshop is a cool, welcoming, and smoky hole-in-the-wall appreciated among local aficionados as a seven-time winner of Amsterdam's Cannabis Cup award. Judging by the proud autographed photos on the wall, many famous Americans have dropped in. You're welcome to just nurse a bottomless cup of coffee (open Tue–Sun high noon to 20:00, closed Mon, between Dam Square and Anne Frank House at Oude Leliestraat 2, tel. 020/420-4301, www.greyarea.nl, run by two friendly Americans, Steven and John).

Coffee Shop Relax is simply the neighborhood pub serving a different drug. It's relaxed and has a helpful staff and homey atmosphere with plants, couches, and bar seating. The great straightforward menu chalked onto the board behind the bar details what it has to offer (daily 10:00–24:00, a bit out of the way, but a pleasant Jordaan walk to Binnen Orangestraat 9).

Siberia Coffeeshop is central but feels cozy, with a friendly canal-side ambience (daily 11:00–23:00, Internet access, helpful staff, fun English menu that explains the personalities of each item, a variety of €4 bags, Brouwersgracht 11).

La Tertulia is a sweet little mother-daughter-run place with pastel décor and a cheery terrarium ambience (Tue–Sat 11:00–19:00, closed Sun–Mon, games, sandwiches, brownies, Prinsengracht 312, www.coffeeshopamsterdam.com).

The Bulldog is the high-profile, leading touristy chain of coffeeshops. They are young but welcoming, with reliable selections. They're pretty comfortable for green tourists wanting to just hang out for a while. The flagship branch, in a former police station right on Leidseplein, is very handy, offering fun outdoor seating where you can watch the world skateboard by (daily 9:00–01:00, Leidseplein 17, tel. 020/625-6278, www.bulldog.nl).

TRANSPORTATION CONNECTIONS

Amsterdam's train-information center requires a long wait. Save lotsof time by getting train tickets and information in a smalltown station, at the airport upon arrival, or from a travel agency. For phone information, dial 0900-9292 for local trains or 0900-9296 for international trains (€0.50/min, daily 7:00–24:00, wait through recording and hold... hold...hold...).

By train to: Schiphol Airport (6/hr, 20 min, €3), **Haarlem** (6/hr, 15 min, €5.50 same-day return), **The Hague** (2/hr, 50 min), **Rotterdam** (4/hr, 1 hr), **Bruges** (hrly, 3.5–4.25 hrs, 1–3 transfers; transfers are timed closely—be alert and check with conductor), **Brussels** (2/hr, 3 hrs, €30), **Ostende** (hrly, 4 hrs, change in Antwerp), **London** (8/day, 6.5 hrs, with transfer to Eurostar Chunnel train in Brussels, Eurostar discounted with railpass, www.eurostar.com), **Copenhagen** (5/day, 10 hrs, transfer in Osnabrück and Hamburg; or 3-hr train to Duisberg and transfer to 11-hr night train), **Frankfurt** (8/day, 5–6 hrs, transfer in Köln or Duisburg), **Munich** (7/day, 9 hrs, transfer in Mannheim, Hanover, or Köln, one 11-hr direct night train), **Bonn** (10/day, 3 hrs, some direct but most transfer in Köln), **Bern** (5/day, 9 hrs, one direct but most transfer in Basel, Köln, or Brussels), **Paris** (5/day, 5 hrs, required fast train from Brussels with €11 supplement). If you don't have a railpass, the cheapest way to get to Paris is by bus (Euroline buses make the 8-hour trip five times daily, about €39 or €60 round-trip compared to €100 second-class by train; bus station in Amsterdam at Julianaplein 5, Amstel Station, 5 stops by Métro from Centraal Station, tel. 020/560-8788, www.eurolines.com).

Schiphol Airport

The airport, like most of Holland, is English-speaking, user-friendly, and below sea level. Its banks offer fair rates (24 hrs daily, in arrival area).

Schiphol (SKIP-pol) Airport has easy connections with **Amsterdam** by train (6/hr, 20 min, €3) and by KLM Hotel Bus (3/hr, 20 min, €10, leaves from lane A7 in front of the airport, 2 routes—ask attendant which comes closest to your hotel, one bus stops at Westerkerk near Anne Frank House and many recommended hotels). Allow about €35 for a taxi to Amsterdam.

Schiphol also has good connections with **Haarlem** by train (4/hr, 40 min, transfer at Amsterdam-Sloterdijk, €4.55) and by bus #300 (6/hr, 40 min, departs from lane B2 in front of the airport, €3.50). Figure about €45 to Haarlem by taxi.

The airport has a train station of its own. You can validate your Eurailpass and hit the rails immediately or, to stretch your train pass, buy an inexpensive ticket into Amsterdam today and start the pass later.

Schiphol flight information (tel. 0900-7244-7465, €0.10/min) can give you flight times and your airline's Amsterdam number for reconfirmation before going home (€0.45/min to climb through its phone tree). To reach the airlines, dial: KLM at 020/649-9123 or 020/474-7747, Northwest is same as KLM, Martinair at 020/601-1222, SAS at 0900-746-63727, American Airlines at 06/022-7844, British Air at 023/554-7555, and easyJet at 023/568-4880.

If you have time to kill at Schiphol, check out the Dutch Masters. The Rijksmuseum loans a dozen or so of its masterpieces from the Golden Age to the Rijksmuseum Schiphol, a free little art gallery behind the passport check between piers E and F.

HAARLEM

Cute, cozy, yet real and handy to the airport, Haarlem is a fine home base, giving you small-town, overnight warmth with easy access (15 min by train) to wild and crazy Amsterdam.

Bustling Haarlem gave America's Harlem its name back when New York was "New Amsterdam," a Dutch colony. For centuries Haarlem has been a market town, buzzing with shoppers heading home with fresh bouquets, nowadays by bike.

Enjoy the market on Monday (clothing) or Saturday (general), when the square bustles like a Brueghel painting with cheese, fish, flowers, and families. Make yourself at home; buy some flowers to brighten your hotel room.

ORIENTATION

(area code: 023)
Tourist Information: Haarlem's TI (VVV), at the train station, is friendlier, more helpful, and less crowded than Amsterdam's. Ask your Amsterdam questions here (Mon–Fri 9:30–17:30, Sat 10:00–14:00, closed Sun, tel. 0900/616-1600, €0.50/min, helpful parking brochure). The €1 *Holiday Magazine* is not necessary, but it's free if you buy the fine €2 town map. The TI also sells a €2 self-guided walking-tour map for over-achievers. The little computer terminal prints out free maps anytime on the curb outside the TI.

Arrival in Haarlem: As you walk out of Haarlem's train station (which has lockers), the TI is on your right and the bus station is across the street. Two parallel streets flank the train station (Kruisweg and Jansweg). Head up either street, and you'll reach the town square and church within 10 minutes. If you need help, ask a local person to point you toward the *Grote Markt* (Main Square).

Parking is expensive on the streets and €1 an hour in several central garages. Two main garages let you park overnight for €1 (at the train station and near Die Raeckse Hotel).

Helpful Hints

Bike Rental: You can rent bikes at the train station (€6.50/day, €50 deposit and passport number, Mon–Sat 6:00–24:00, Sun 7:30–24:00).

Changing Money: The handy GWK change office at the train station offers fair exchange rates (Mon–Fri 8:00–20:00, Sat 9:00–17:00, Sun 10:00–17:00).

Internet Access: Try Internet Café Amadeus (in the Hotel Amadeus overlooking Market Square, €1.20/15 min, 25 percent discount with this book) or nearly any coffeeshop (if you don't mind the marijuana smoke).

Post Office: It's at Ged. Oude Gracht 2 (Mon–Fri 9:00–18:00, Sat 10:00–13:30, closed Sun, has ATM).

Laundry: My Beautiful Launderette is handy and cheap (€5 wash and dry, self-service, bring change, daily 8:30–20:30, €8 full service available Mon–Fri 9:00–17:00, near Vroom & Dreesman department store at Boter Markt 20).

Festival: On April 24, 2004, an all-day Flower Parade of floats wafts through eight towns, including Haarlem.

Local Guide: Consider Walter Schelfhout (€75/2-hr walk, tel. 023/535-5715).

SIGHTS

▲▲**Market Square (Grote Markt)**—Haarlem's market square, where 10 streets converge, is the town's delightful centerpiece...as it has been for 700 years. To enjoy a coffee or beer here, simmering in Dutch good living, is a quintessential European experience. In a recent study, the Dutch were found to be the most content people in Europe. And later, the people of Haarlem were found to be the most content in the Netherlands. Observe. Sit and gaze at the church, appreciating the same scene Dutch artists captured in oil paintings that now hang in museums.

Just a few years ago trolleys ran through the square and cars were parked everywhere. But today it's a people zone, with market stalls filling the square on Mondays and Saturdays and café tables on other days.

This is a great place to build a picnic with Haarlem finger foods—raw herring, local cheese (Gouda and Edam), a *frikandel* (little corn-dog sausage), French fries with mayonnaise, *stroopwafels* (waffles with syrup), and *poffertjes* (little sugar doughnuts).

Haarlem

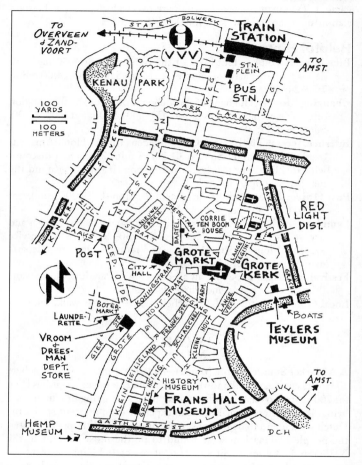

▲**Great Church (Grote Kerk)**—This 15th-century Gothic church (now Protestant) is worth a look, if only for its Oz-like organ (100 feet high, its 5,000 pipes impressed both Handel and Mozart). One of the best-known landmarks in the Netherlands, the Great Church is visible from miles around, rising above the flat plain that surrounds it.

The church was built over a 150-year period (c. 1390–1540) in the late Gothic style of red and gray brick, topped with a lead-covered wood roof and a stacked tower with a golden crown and a rooster weathervane.

To enter, find the small *Entrée* sign behind the church at Oude

Groenmarkt 23 (€1.50, Mon–Sat 10:00–16:00, closed Sun to tourists, tel. 023/532-4399). Consider attending (even part of) a concert to hear Holland's greatest pipe organ (regular free concerts Tue at 20:15 mid-May–mid-Oct, additional concerts Thu at 15:00 July–Aug, confirm schedule at TI or at www.bavo.nl).

▲▲**Frans Hals Museum**—Haarlem is the hometown of Frans Hals (c. 1582–1666), and this refreshing museum, once an almshouse for old men back in 1610, displays many of his greatest paintings. Hals was an articulate visual spokesman for his generation—the generation of the Golden Age. Stand eye-to-eye with life-size, lifelike portraits of Haarlem's citizens—brewers, preachers, workers, bureaucrats, and housewives—and see the people who built the Golden Age, then watched it start to fade.

Along with Frans Hals work, the museum features Pieter Breughel's painting *Proverbs,* illustrating 72 old Dutch proverbs. To peek into old Dutch ways, identify some with the help of the English-language key (€5.40, Tue–Sat 11:00–17:00, Sun 12:00–17:00, closed Mon, Groot Heiligland 62, tel. 023/511-5775, www.franshalsmuseum.nl).

History Museum—This small museum, across the street from the Frans Hals Museum, offers a glimpse of old Haarlem. Request the English version of the 10-minute video. Study the large-scale model of Haarlem in 1822 while its fortifications were still intact, and enjoy the new "time machine" computer and video display that shows you various aspects of life in Haarlem at different points in history (€1, Tue–Sat 12:00–17:00, Sun 13:00–17:00, closed Mon, Groot Heiligland 47, tel. 023/542-2427). The adjacent architecture center (free) may be of interest to architects.

Corrie Ten Boom House—Haarlem is home to Corrie Ten Boom, popularized by *The Hiding Place,* an inspirational book and movie about the Ten Boom family's experience protecting Jews from the Nazis. Corrie Ten Boom gives the other half of the Anne Frank story—the point of view of those who risked their lives to hide Dutch Jews during the Nazi occupation (1940–1945).

The clock shop was the Ten Boom family business. The elderly father and his two daughters—Corrie and Betsy, both in their 50s—lived above the store and in the brick building attached in back (along Schoutensteeg alley). Corrie's bedroom was on the top floor at the back. This room was tiny to start with, but the family built a second, secret room at the very back—the hiding place, where they could hide six or seven Jews at a time.

Devoutly religious, the family had a long tradition of tolerance, having for generations hosted prayer meetings here in their home for both Jews and Christians.

The Gestapo, tipped off that the family was harboring Jews, burst into the Ten Boom house. Finding a suspicious number of ration coupons, the Nazis arrested the family but failed to find the six Jews in the hiding place (who later escaped). Corrie's father and sister died while in prison, but Corrie survived the Ravensbruck concentration camp to tell her story in her memoir.

The Ten Boom House is open for 60-minute English tours; the tours are sometimes mixed with preaching (donation accepted, April–Oct Tue–Sat 10:00–16:00, Nov–March Tue–Sat 11:00–15:00, closed Mon, 50 yards north of Market Square at Barteljorisstraat 19, the clock-shop people get all wound up if you go inside—wait in the little side street at the door, where tour times are posted, tel. 023/531-0823).

▲**Teylers Museum**—Famous as the oldest museum in Holland, Teylers is interesting mainly as a look at a 200-year-old museum—fossils, minerals, and primitive electronic gadgetry. New exhibition halls (with rotating exhibits) have freshened up the place. Stop by if you enjoy mixing, say, Renaissance sketches with pickled extinct fish (€5.50, Tue–Sat 10:00–17:00, Sun 12:00–17:00, Spaarne 16, tel. 023/531-9010).

Canal Cruise—Making a scenic loop through and around Haarlem, these little trips by Woltheus Cruises are more relaxing than informative (€6.50, Tue–Sun 10:00–17:00, closed Mon, 70 min, 4/day, across canal from Teylers Museum at Spaarne 11a, tel. 023/535-7723).

Red Lights—Wander through a little red light district as precious as a Barbie doll—and legal since the 1980s (2 blocks northeast of Market Square, off Lange Begijnestraat, no senior or student discounts). Don't miss the mall marked by the red neon sign reading *t'Steegje*. The nearby *t'Poortje* (office park) costs €6.

NIGHTLIFE

Haarlem's evening scene is great. The bars around the Grote Kerk and Lange Veerstraat are colorful and lively. You'll find plenty of music. The best show in town: the café scene on Market Square. In good weather, café tables tumble happily out of the bars.

For trendy local crowds, sip a drink at **Café Studio** (daily 12:00–4:00, on Market Square, next to Hotel Carillon, tel. 023/531-0033). Tourists gawk at the old-fashioned belt-driven ceiling fans in **Café 1900** across from the Corrie Ten Boom House (daily 9:00–00:30, live music Sun night except in July, Barteljoris Straat 10, tel. 023/531-8283).

SLEEPING

In the Center

$$$ **Hotel Lion D'Or** is a classy, 34-room business hotel with all the professional comforts and a handy location. Don't expect a warm welcome (Sb-€135–155, Db-€165–185, extra bed-€30, elevator, some non-smoking rooms, across the street from train station at Kruisweg 34, tel. 023/532-1750, fax 023/532-9543, www.goldentulip.nl/hotels/gtliondor,

SLEEP CODE

(€1 = about $1.10, country code: 31, area code: 023)
Sleep Code: **S** = Single, **D** = Double/Twin, **T** = Triple, **Q** = Quad, **b** = bathroom, **s** = shower only, **no CC** = Credit Cards not accepted. Unless otherwise noted, credit cards are accepted.

To help you sort easily through these listings, I've divided the rooms into three categories based on the price for a standard double room with bath:

$$$ **Higher Priced**—Most rooms €100 or more.
$$ **Moderately Priced**—Most rooms between €65–100.
$ **Lower Priced**—Most rooms €65 or less.

The helpful Haarlem TI, just outside the train station, can nearly always find you a €20 bed in a private home (for a €4.50-per-person fee plus a cut of your host's money). Avoid this if you can; it's cheaper to reserve calling direct. Nearly every Dutch person you'll encounter speaks English.

Haarlem is most crowded in April and May (especially Easter weekend) and in July and August.

The listed prices include breakfast unless otherwise noted) and usually include the €1.70-per-person-per-day tourist tax. To avoid this town's louder-than-normal street noises, forgo views for a room in the back. Hotels and the TI have a useful parking brochure.

reservations@hotelliondor.nl).

$$ Hotel Amadeus, on Market Square, has 15 small, bright, and basic rooms. Some have views of the square. This characteristic hotel, ideally located above an early 20th-century dinner café, is relatively quiet. Its lush old lounge/breakfast room on the second floor overlooks the square, and Mike and Inez take good care of their guests (Sb-€57.50, Db-€80, Tb-€105, Qb-€110, includes tax, 2-night stay and cash get you a 5 percent discount, 12-min walk from train station, steep climb to lounge, then an elevator, Grote Markt 10, tel. 023/532-4530, fax 023/532-2328, www.amadeus-hotel.com, info@amadeus-hotel.com). The hotel also runs a six-terminal Internet café (€1.20/15 min, 25 percent discount with this book).

$$ Hotel Carillon also overlooks the town square but comes with a little more traffic and bell-tower noise. Many of the 20 well-worn rooms are small, and the stairs are ste-e-e-p. The front rooms come with great town-square views and street noise (tiny loft singles €31.50, Db-€72, Tb-€92, Qb-€97.50, tax extra, includes breakfast, 12-min walk from train station, no elevator, Grote Markt 27, tel. 023/531-0591, fax 023/531-4909, www.hotelcarillon.com, info@hotelcarillon.com).

$$ **Hotel Joops,** with 20 comfortable rooms, is located just behind the church (Db-€90, Tb-€100, Qb-€120, breakfast buffet-€9.50, Internet access, Oude Groenmarkt 20, tel. 023/532-2008, fax 023/532-9549, joops@easynet.nl).

$$ **Die Raeckse Hotel**—family-run and friendly—is not as central as the others and has less character and more traffic noise, but its 21 rooms are decent and comfortable (Sb-€55, Db-€70-80 depending upon the size, Tb-€98, Qb-€110, 10 percent discount for 2-night stay Nov-March, Raaks Straat 1, tel. 023/532-6629, fax 023/531-7937, www.die-raeckse.nl, dieraeckse@zonnet.nl). A big, cheap garage is across the street.

$ **Bed and Breakfast House de Kiefte** is your get-into-a-local-home budget option. Marjet (mar-yet) and Hans, a frank, interesting Dutch couple who speak English well, rent four bright, cheery, non-smoking rooms (includes breakfast and travel advice) in their quiet 1892 home (Ds-€52, T-€73, Qs-€94, no CC, 2-night min, very steep stairs, family loft sleeps up to 5, kids over 4 welcome, Coornhertstraat 3, tel. 023/532-2980, mobile 06-5474-5272). It's a 15-minute walk or €7 taxi ride from the train station and a five-minute walk from the center. From Grote Markt, walk to the right of city hall straight out Zijlstraat and over the bridge and take a left on the fourth street.

Near Haarlem

$$ **Hotel Haarlem Zuid**—with 300 rooms and very American—is sterile but a good value for those interested only in sleeping and eating. It sits in an industrial zone, a 20-minute walk from the center on the road to the airport (Db-€80, breakfast-€12, elevator, free parking, laundry service, fitness center, inexpensive hotel restaurant, Toekanweg 2, tel. 023/536-7500, fax 023/536-7980, www.hotelhaarlemzuid.nl, haarlemzuid@valk.com). Buses #70, #71, and #72 connect the hotel with the train station and Market Square every 10 minutes. Bus #80 makes runs to the beach or Amsterdam. Fast airport bus #300 stops at the hotel.

$ **B&B Koning,** a 15-minute walk north of the train station or a quick jaunt on bus #2 or #71, has five simple rooms in a row house in a residential area (S-€25, D-€50, T-€75, 2-night min, includes breakfast, no CC, Kleverlaan 179, tel. 023/526-1456).

$ **Stayokay Haarlem,** completely renovated and with all the youth-hostel comforts, charges €18–21 for beds in eight-bed dorms (€2.50 extra for nonmembers, includes sheets and breakfast, daily 7:30–24:00, Jan Gijzenpad 3, 2 miles from Haarlem station—take bus #2 from platform A1, or a 5-min walk from Santpoort Zuid train station, tel. 023/537-3793, fax 023/537-1176, www.stayokay.com/haarlem, haarlem@stayokay.com).

EATING

Between Market Square and the Train Station

Pancakes for dinner? **Pannekoekhuis De Smikkel** serves a selection of over 50 dinner (meat, cheese, etc.) and dessert pancakes. The €8 pancakes are filling; smaller sizes are available (daily 12:00–21:00, Sun from 16:00, closed Mon in winter, 2 blocks in front of station, Kruisweg 57, tel. 023/532-0631).

Enjoy a sandwich or coffee surrounded by trains and 1908 architecture in the classy **Foodcourt Haarlem Station** (daily 7:30–20:00, between tracks #3 and #6 at the station).

On or near Zijlstraat

Eko Eet Café is great for a cheery, tasty vegetarian meal (€11 menu, daily 17:30–21:30, Zijlstraat 39, tel. 023/532-6568).

Vincent's Eethuis serves the best cheap, basic Dutch food in town. This former St. Vincent's soup kitchen now feeds more gainfully employed locals than poor (€6, friendly staff, Mon–Fri 16:30–19:30, closed Sat–Sun, Nieuwe Groenmarkt 22).

The cheery **De Buren** offers handlebar-mustache fun, serving happy locals traditional Dutch food such as *draadjesvlees* (beef stew with applesauce). Gerard and Marjo love their work. Enjoy their entertaining and creative menu, made especially for you (€11–16 dinners, "you choose the sauce," Wed–Sun 17:00–22:00, closed Mon–Tue, back garden terrace, outside the tourist area at Brouwersvaart 146, follow Raaks Straat west across the canal from Die Raeckse Hotel, tel. 023/534-3364).

Between the Market Square and
Frans Hals Museum

Jacobus Pieck Eetlokaal is popular with locals for its fine-value "global cuisine" (€9.50 plate of the day, great €5 sandwiches, Mon 10:00–17:00, Tue–Sat 10:00–22:00, closed Sun, Warmoesstraat 18, behind church, tel. 023/532-6144).

Friethuis de Vlaminck is the place for a (€1.55) cone of old-fashioned French fries (Warmoesstraat 3, Tue–Sat until 18:00, closed Sun–Mon, behind church).

La Plume steak house is noisy with a happy, local, and carnivorous crowd (€12–18 meals, daily from 17:30, Lange Veerstraat 1, tel. 023/531-3202).

Bastiaan serves good Mediterranean cuisine in a classy atmosphere (€16 dinners, Tue–Sat from 18:00, closed Sun–Mon, Lange Veerstraat 8, tel. 023/532-6006).

De Lachende Javaan (The Laughing Javanese) serves the best Indonesian food in town. The €18 *rijsttafel* is excellent (Tue–Sun from 17:00, closed Mon, Frankestraat 27, tel. 023/532-8792).

Haarlem Hotels and Restaurants

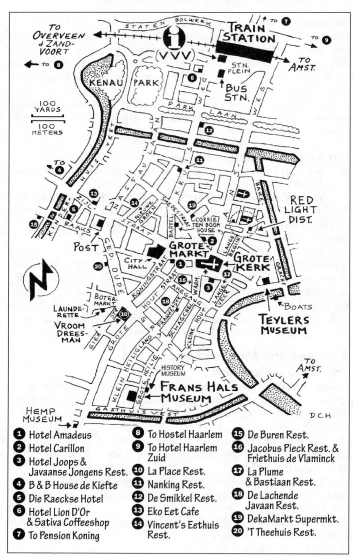

❶ Hotel Amadeus	❽ To Hostel Haarlem	⓯ De Buren Rest.
❷ Hotel Carillon	❾ To Hotel Haarlem Zuid	⓰ Jacobus Pieck Rest. & Friethuis de Vlaminck
❸ Hotel Joops & Javaanse Jongens Rest.	❿ La Place Rest.	⓱ La Plume & Bastiaan Rest.
❹ B & B House de Kiefte	⓫ Nanking Rest.	⓲ De Lachende Javaan Rest.
❺ Die Raeckse Hotel	⓬ De Smikkel Rest.	⓳ DekaMarkt Supermkt.
❻ Hotel Lion D'Or & Sativa Coffeeshop	⓭ Eko Eet Cafe	⓴ 'T Theehuis Rest.
❼ To Pension Koning	⓮ Vincent's Eethuis Rest.	

Fondue Restaurant "in 't goede uur" is a romantic, 10-table place with classical music on the most charming street in Haarlem. Reservations are required (€17 cheese fondue, Tue–Sun 17:00–22:00, closed Mon, no CC, Korte Houtstraat 1, tel. 023/531-1174).

La Place serves a healthy budget lunch with Haarlem's best view. Sit on the top floor or roof garden of the Vroom & Dreesman department store (Mon 11:00–17:30, Tue–Sat 9:30–17:30, Thu until 20:30, closed Sun, on the corner of Grote Houtstraat and Gedempte Oude Gracht.

Picnic shoppers head to the **DekaMarkt supermarket** (Mon 11:00–20:00, Tue–Sat 8:30–20:00, Thu until 21:00, closed Sun, Gedemple Oude Gracht 54, between Vroom & Dreesman department store and post office).

TRANSPORTATION CONNECTIONS

By train to: Amsterdam (6/hr, 15 min, €3.20 one-way, €5.50 same-day return, ticket not valid on "Lovers Train," a misnamed private train that runs hrly), **Delft** (2/hr, 40 min), **Hoorn** (4/hr, 1 hr), **The Hague** (4/hr, 35 min), and **Alkmaar** (2/hr, 30 min).

To **Schiphol Airport:** by **taxi** (about €45), by **train** (4/hr, 40 min, transfer at Amsterdam-Sloterdijk, €4.55); by **bus** (6/hr, 40 min, bus #300 leaves from Haarlem's train station in the "Zuidtangent" lane, €3.50).

Netherlands Day Trips

The Netherlands are tiny. The sights listed below are an easy day trip by bus or train from Amsterdam or Haarlem. Match your interest with the village's specialty: flower auctions, folk museums, cheese, Delft porcelain, beaches, or modern art.

Delft

Peaceful as a Vermeer painting (he was born here) and lovely as its porcelain, Delft is a typically Dutch town with a special soul. Enjoy it best by simply wandering around, watching people, munching local syrup waffles, or daydreaming from the canal bridges.

Tourist Information: The TI is a tourist's dream, offering a good brochure on Delft (which includes an excellent map and a self-guided "Historical Walk through Delft"), and a number of brochures describing self-guided walking tours (Sun–Mon 11:00–15:00, Tue–Fri 9:00–18:00, Sat 9:00–17:00, Hyppolytusbuurt 4, tel. 015/215-401, www.delft.nl).

Arrival in Delft: From the train station (free WCs, ATM on left as you leave), walk across the canal and follow blue-and-white signs to the town center. Drivers take the Delft exit 9 off A13 expressway.

Netherlands Day Trips

Market Days: Multiple all-day markets are held on Thursdays (general on Market Square, flower on Hippolytusbuurt Square) and on Saturdays (general on Brabantse Turfmarkt and Burgwal, flea market at Hippolytusbuurt Square, and sometimes an art market at Heilige Geestkerkhof).

SIGHTS

Royal Dutch Delftware Manufactory—The blue earthenware made at Delft's Koninklijke Porceleyne Fles is famous worldwide and the biggest tourist attraction in town. The Dutch East India Company, headquartered here, had imported many exotic goods, including Chinese porcelain. The Chinese designs became trendy and were copied by many of the local potters. Three centuries later, their descendants are still going strong, and you can see them at work in this factory. Catch an English-language tour (prices vary depending on tour, April–Oct 10:00, 11:00, 14:00, and 15:00) or take a self-guided tour at any time: Watch the short video, follow the small tile arrows, and feel free to stop and chat with any of the artisans (€2.50, April–Oct daily 9:00–17:00, Nov–March daily 9:30–17:00, Rotterdamsweg 196, from train station catch tram #1 or bus #63, #121, or #129 and get off at TU Aula bus stop, 5-min walk from tram or bus stop, tel. 015/251-2030).

SLEEPING

(€1 = about $1.10, country code: 31, area code: 015)
$$ **Herberg de Emauspoort,** a picture-perfect family-run hotel, is relaxed, friendly, and ideally located around the family's 80-year-old bakery. Rooms overlook the canalside or peek into the courtyard. Romantics can stay in one of their gypsy caravans ("Pipo de Clown" or "Mammaloe"). Borrow bikes for free (16 rooms, Sb-€77.50, Db-€87.50, Tb-€115, Qb-€140, taxes extra, includes breakfast, near main square at Vrouwenregt 9–11, tel. 015/219-0219, fax 015/214-8251, www.emauspoort.nl, emauspoort@emauspoort.nl).

$$$ **Hotel Leeuwenbrug,** a former warehouse, has 36 cozy rooms, an Old World atmosphere, and a helpful and friendly staff (Sb-€75–109, Db-€90–125, prices varies seasonally, ask for off-season pricing, includes breakfast, Koornmarkt 16, tel. 015/214-7741, fax 015/215-9759, www.leeuwenbrug.nl, sales@leeuwenbrug.nl).

$ **'T Raedthuys,** located in the heart of Delft on the main square, has 8 tired, basic rooms (S-€40, Ss-€50, D-€50, Ds-€60, Qb-€95, ask for off-season discount, Markt 38–40, tel. 015/212-5115, fax 015/213-6069, www.raedthuys-delft.com).

TRANSPORTATION CONNECTIONS

To: Amsterdam (2 trains/hr, 40 min), **The Hague** (you can take the train, but the tram is easier, catch tram #1—Scheveningen to The Hague's city center, purchase tickets at TI).

Edam

For the ultimate in cuteness and peace, make tiny Edam your home. It's sweet but palatable and 30 minutes by bus from Amsterdam (2/hr).

While Edam is known today for cheese, it was once an industrious shipyard and port. But having a canal to the sea caused such severe flooding in town—cracking walls and spilling into homes—that a frustrated resident even built a floating cellar (now in Edam Museum). To stop the flooding, the harbor was closed off with locked gates (you'll see the gates in Dam Square next to TI). The harbor silted up, forcing the decline of the shipbuilding trade.

Edam's Wednesday market is held year-round, but it's best in July and early August, when the focus is on cheese, and you—along with piles of other tourists—can meet the cheese traders, local farmers, and even the cheese queen.

Tourist Information: The TI, often staffed by volunteers, is on Dam Square. Pick up the free "Edam Holland" brochure and consider the €2 "A Stroll Through Edam" self-guided walking tour (April–Sept Mon–Sat 10:00–17:00, closed Sun, Oct–March Mon–Sat 10:00–15:00, closed Sun, WC, ATM just outside, tel. 0299/315-125, www.vvv-edam.nl, info@vvv-edam.nl). The **TI** (tel. 0299/315-125) has a list of inexpensive rooms in private homes.

Arrival in Edam: To get from the bus station to Dam Square and the TI, it's a five-minute walk: Leaving the station, head for the Station-Zuid Hotel/Restaurant (good place to eat). From there, turn left on Zuidervesting, turn right at the first canal onto Schepenmakersdijk, then left over the first walking bridge onto Lingerzijde; follow this street until you pass the leaning bell tower and take a right onto Kleine Kerkstraat, which leads to Dam Square.

SLEEPING

$$ Hotel de Fortuna—an eccentric canalside place with flowers and duck and bird noises—offers steep stairs and low-ceilinged rooms in several ancient buildings in the old center of Edam (run by the Dekke family for more than 30 years, Db-€90–100, includes breakfast, garden patio, attached restaurant, Spuistraat 3, tel. 0299/371-671, fax 0299/371-469, www.fortuna-edam.nl, fortuna@fortuna-edam.nl).

$$ Damhotel, centrally located on a canal around the corner from the TI, has attractive, comfortable rooms with a plush feel (Sb-€55, Db-€90, Tb-€125, Qb-€170, includes breakfast, attached restaurant, Keizersgracht 1, tel. 0299/371-766, fax 0299/374-031, www.damhotel.nl).

$ De Gravin, an authentic old little house Edam-style, is run by Greetje Reilingh, who'll bring you a picnic basket for breakfast in the morning (Db-€60, tel. 0299/72725, 2-min walk from Dam Square, no CC, Kapsteeg 3, reilingh@wxs.nl).

EATING

Restaurant Tai Wah has take-out Chinese/Indonesian (eat in De Fortuna garden) and indoor seating (€8 take-out plates, Mon and Wed–Sat 16:00–21:00, Sun 13:00–21:00, closed Tue, Lingerzijde 62, tel. 0299/371-088).

Picnickers stock up at the **Toppers grocery** (to the left of the Edam Museum).

TRANSPORTATION CONNECTIONS

From Amsterdam, take direct bus #114 (30 min) or bus #110 for a scenic route through the town of Volendam (45 min).

Arnhem

Arnhem, an hour southeast of Amsterdam, has two fine sights: the Arnhem Open-Air Dutch Folk Museum and the Kröller-Müller Museum, featuring modern art in a huge park.

Arnhem's **TI** is at the train station (Mon 11:00–17:30, Tue–Thu 9:00–17:30, Fri 10:00–16:00, closed Sat–Sun, tel. 026/442-6767).

▲▲**Kröller-Müller Museum and Hoge Veluwe National Park**—Near Arnhem, Hoge Veluwe National Park is the Netherlands' largest (13,000 acres) and is famous for its Kröller-Müller Museum. This huge, striking modern-art collection, including 55 paintings by van Gogh, is set deep in the forest. The park has hundreds of white bikes you're free to use to make your explorations more fun. At the Bezoekerscentrum (visitors' center) you'll find maps, WCs, a cafeteria-style restaurant, and a playground for children. While riding through the vast green woods, make a point to get off your bike and climb an inland sand dune (€5 to enter park, €5 more for museum, museum open Tue–Sun 10:00–17:00, closed Mon, easy €5 parking, tel. 031/859-1041).

To reach the museum from Amsterdam, take the train to Ede-Wageningen, where bus #110 goes directly into the Hoge Veluwe National Park. Ask the driver where to get off for the visitors' center or the art museum.

To get to the park from the Arnhem train station, catch the bus to Otterlo, then switch to bus #110 which will take you into the park (1/hr). At this time there is no direct connection between Arnhem and the Kröller-Müller Museum. Consider a taxi (have the visitors' center call for you).

▲▲**Arnhem Open-Air Dutch Folk Museum**—Arnhem has the Netherlands' first and biggest folk museum. You'll enjoy a huge park of windmills, old farmhouses (gathered from throughout the Netherlands and reassembled here), traditional crafts in action, and a pleasant education-by-immersion in Dutch culture.

Visit the Entrance Pavilion to get a free map or the English guidebook (€4). See the multimedia exhibit, HollandRama. Ask about special events and activities (especially for kids) as you enter (€11, Easter–Oct daily 10:00–17:00, tel. 026/357-6111, www.openluchtmuseum.nl).

Hit the highlights: any farmhouse, the drawbridge, little village (with bakery and old-time toys in the main square), the laundry, paper mill (usually a demo in progress), and the Freia Steam-Dairy Factory (where you can sample free cheese). The park has several good budget restaurants. The rustic Pancake House serves hearty (splittable) Dutch flapjacks and the De Kasteelboerderji Café-Restaurant (with a traditional €8 *dagmenu*, or plate of the day) is a friendly place that can feed 300 visitors at once.

To reach the open-air museum *(openluchtmuseum)* from the Arnhem train station, take bus #3 (direction: Alteveer) or the faster #13 (4/hr, 15 min, runs July–Aug only).

TRANSPORTATION CONNECTIONS

Trains connect Arnhem with **Amsterdam** (2/hr, 70 min, likely transfer in Utrecht).

By car from Amsterdam, take A2 south to Utrecht, then A12 east to Arnhem. Just before Arnhem, take the Arnhem Nord exit Openluchtmuseum (exit #26) and follow signs to the nearby museum. (If driving from Haarlem, skirt Amsterdam to the south on E9, then follow signs to Utrecht).

MORE SIGHTS IN THE NETHERLANDS

Zaanse Schans Open-Air Museum—This 17th-century Dutch village turned open-air folk museum puts Dutch culture—from cheese making to wooden-shoe carving—on a lazy Susan.

Located in the town of Zaandijk, this is your easiest one-stop look at traditional Dutch culture. At the visitors' center, pick up the free brochure/map and ask about the day's scheduled events (bike rentals, lockers, WC, tel. 075/616-8228). The park hosts the Netherlands' best collection of windmills. Take an inspiring climb to the top of a whirring windmill; gather a group and ask for a tour. Visit the bakery, take a boat tour, sample cheese, and see a wooden shoe being made.

Zaanse Schans' museum, with a multimedia presentation and included audioguide, explains Holland's industrial past and present (€4.50, includes audioguide, Tue–Sat 10:00–17:00, Sun 12:00–17:00, closed Mon, tel. 075/616-2862). The Pannenkoeken Restaurant offers delicious and traditional sweet and/or savory pancakes (€4–7, cash only, closes at 18:00).

Cost and Hours: The entrance to the grounds is free, but you must pay a euro or two to go in the windmills and other sights in the park (daily 8:30–17:30, until 17:00 in winter, parking €3.50/first hr, €7 max, tel. 075/616-8218, www.zaanseschans.nl). Zaanse Schans is your typical big-bus tour stop. To avoid the masses, visit early or late.

Getting There: The park is 15 minutes by train north of Amsterdam. Take the Alkmaar-bound train to Station Koog-Zaandijk and then walk, following the teal signs—past a fragrant chocolate factory—for 15 minutes. If driving from Amsterdam, take the A8 (direction: Zaanstad/Purmerend), turn off at Purmerend A7, then follow signs to Zaanse Schans.

▲▲**Enkhuizen Zuiderzee Museum**—This lively, open-air folk museum in the salty old town of Enkhuizen has a "Living on Urk" village (patterned after an old Dutch fishing town), populated by people who do a convincing job of role-playing no-nonsense 1905 Dutch villagers. No one said "Have a nice day" back then. You can eat herring hot out of the old smoker and see barrels and rope made. Children enjoy playing at the dress-up chest, trying out old-time games, and making sailing ships out of old wooden shoes (€9, early April–late Oct daily 10:00–17:00, July–Aug free tours at 13:30, private guide for €40, tel. 0228/351-111, www.zuiderzeemuseum.nl). Take the train from Amsterdam direct to Enkhuizen. To get to the museum from the station, catch a shuttle boat (4/hr) or take a pleasant 15-minute walk.

▲▲**Aalsmeer Flower Auction**—Get a bird's-eye view of the huge Dutch flower industry. Wander on elevated walkways (through what's claimed to be the biggest commercial building on earth) over literally trainloads of freshly cut flowers. About half of all the flowers exported from Holland are auctioned off here in four huge auditoriums. Stop at one of the "listening posts" for on-the-spot information (€4, Mon–Fri 7:30–11:00, closed Sat–Sun, the auction wilts after 9:30 and on Thu, gift shop, cafeteria; bus #172 from Amsterdam's station, 2/hr, 60 min; from Haarlem take bus #198 and transfer to bus #172 in Aalsmeer, 2/hr, 60 min; tel. 0297/392-185). Aalsmeer is close to the airport and a handy last fling before catching a late morning weekday flight out.

▲▲▲**Keukenhof**—This is the greatest bulb-flower garden on earth. Each spring six million flowers, enjoying the sandy soil of the Dutch dunes and *polderland,* conspire to make even a total garden-hater enjoy them. This 100-acre park is packed with tour groups daily (€11.50, open March 25–May 20 in 2004, daily 8:00–19:30, last tickets sold at 18:00, tel. 0252/465-555, www.keukenhof.nl).

To get to Keukenhof from Amsterdam, take the train to Leiden, then catch bus #54 to the garden (allow 75 min total). From Haarlem, go by train to Leiden, then take bus #54 to Keukenhof (allow 45 min total). Go late in the day for the best light and the fewest groups.

Note that Holland's **2004 Flower Parade** will be held on April 24. This all-day parade, featuring floats decorated with blossoms instead of crepe paper, runs through eight towns, including Lisse and Haarlem.

▲**Alkmaar**—Holland's cheese capital is especially fun (and touristy) during its weekly cheese market (April–Aug only, Fri 10:00–12:30, TI tel. 072/511-4284).

▲▲**The Hague (Den Haag)**—Locals say the money is made in Rotterdam, divided in The Hague, and spent in Amsterdam. The Hague is the Netherlands' seat of government and the home of several engaging museums. The Hague's TI is at the train station (Mon–Sat 9:00–17:30, later in summer, Sun 10:00–17:00, tel. 0900-340-3505, €0.45/min).

The **Mauritshuis'** delightful, easy-to-tour art collection stars Vermeer and Rembrandt (€7, Tue–Sat 10:00–17:00, Sun 11:00–17:00, Korte Vijverberg 8, tel. 070/302-3456). Across the pond, the **Torture Museum** (Gevangenpoort) shows the medieval mind at its worst (€3.75, Tue–Fri 11:00–17:00, Sat–Sun 12:00–17:00, closed Mon, required tours on the hour, last one at 16:00, ask ticket-taker if film and talk will be in English before you commit, tel. 070/346-0861).

For a look at the 19th century's attempt at virtual reality, tour **Panorama Mesdag,** a 360-degree painting of nearby Scheveningen in the 1880s with a 3-D sandy-beach foreground (€4, Mon–Sat 10:00–17:00, Sun 12:00–17:00, Zeestraat 65, tel. 070/310-6665). The nearby **Peace Palace,** a gift from Andrew Carnegie, houses the International Court of Justice (€3.40, Mon–Fri, required guided tours at 10:00, 11:00, 14:00, or 15:00, closes without warning—call ahead or check at TI, tram #7 or #8 from station, tel. 070/302-4137).

Scheveningen, the Dutch Coney Island, has a newly renovated pier and is liveliest on sunny summer afternoons (from the Hague train station, take tram #1, #8, or #9 to Gevers Deynootplein/Kurhaus and walk via Palace Promenade to the Boulevard).

Madurodam, a mini-Holland amusement park, is a kid-pleaser (€11, kids 4–11–€8, Sept–mid-March daily 9:00–18:00, mid-March–June until 20:00, July–Aug until 22:00, George Maduroplein 1, tram #1 or #9 from Hague train station, tel. 070/355-3900, www.madurodam.nl).

BARCELONA

Barcelona is Spain's second city and the capital of the proud and distinct region of Catalunya. With Franco's fascism now history, Catalan flags wave once again. Language and culture are on a roll in Spain's most cosmopolitan and European corner.

Barcelona bubbles with life in its narrow Gothic Quarter alleys, along the grand boulevards, and throughout the chic, grid-planned new town. While Barcelona had an illustrious past as a Roman colony, Visigothic capital, 14th-century maritime power, and—in more modern times—a top Mediterranean trading and manufacturing center, it's most enjoyable to throw out the history books and just drift through the city. If you're in the mood to surrender to a city's charms, let it be in Barcelona.

After the 1992 Olympics were held here, Barcelona's mayor promised another multinational event in the city in the upcoming years. That event is Euroforum 2004, a cultural symposium that will liven up the summer, held on three freshly-landscaped acres north of the Olympic Port (May 9–Sept 26, 2004, www.barcelona2004.org).

Planning Your Time

Sandwich Barcelona between flights or overnight train rides. There's little of earth-shaking importance within eight hours by train. It's as easy to fly into Barcelona as into Madrid, Lisbon, or Paris for most travelers from the United States. Those renting a car can cleverly start here, fly to Madrid, see Madrid and Toledo, and pick up the car as they leave Madrid.

On the shortest visit, Barcelona is worth one night, one day, and an overnight train or evening flight out. The Ramblas is two different streets by day and by night. Stroll it from top to bottom at night and again the next morning, grabbing breakfast on a stool in a market café. Wander the Gothic Quarter, see the cathedral, and have lunch in

Barcelona

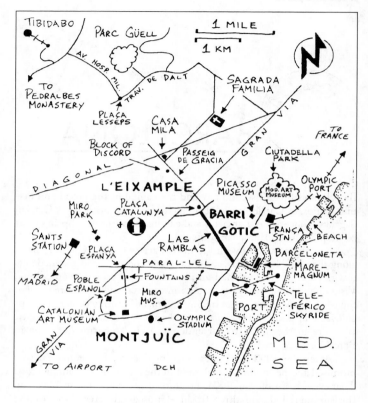

Eixample (eye-SHAM-plah). The top two sights in town, Gaudí's Sacred Family Church and the Picasso Museum, are usually open until 20:00. The illuminated fountains (on Montjuïc) are a good finale for your day.

Of course, Barcelona in a day is insane. To better appreciate the city's ample charm, spread your visit over two or three days.

ORIENTATION

Orient yourself by locating these essentials on the map: Barri Gòtic/Ramblas (old town), Eixample (fashionable modern town), Montjuïc (hill covered with sights and parks), and Sants Station (train to Madrid). The soul of Barcelona is in its compact core—the Barri Gòtic (Gothic Quarter) and the Ramblas (main boulevard). This is your strolling, shopping, and people-watching nucleus. The city's sights are widely scattered, but with a map and a willingness to figure out the sleek subway system (or a few euros for taxis), all is manageable.

Tourist Information

There are several useful **TIs** in Barcelona: at the **airport** (offices in both terminal A and terminal B, free room-finding service, daily 9:00–21:00, tel. 934-784-704); at the **Sants Train Station** (daily 8:00–20:00, near track 6); and **Plaça de Catalunya** (daily 9:00–21:00, on main square near recommended hotels, look for red sign; also has room-finding service).

On weekends, the TI at Plaça de Catalunya offers walking tours in English of the Gothic Quarter (€7, 2 hrs, Sat–Sun at 10:00, meet at TI, call to reserve, toll call tel. 906-301-282—€0.40/minute, www .barcelonaturisme.com) and also has a half-price ticket booth—"Tiquet 3"—where you can drop by in the early evening (3 hrs before showtime) to see what tickets are available.

The all-Catalunya TI offices are at **Passeig de Gràcia** (Mon–Sat 10:00–19:00, Sun 10:00–14:00, #107, tel. 932-384-000) and **Plaça de Sant Jaume** in the city hall Ajuntament building (Mon–Fri 9:00–20:00, Sat 10:00–20:00, Sun 10:00–14:00; last-minute room-finding service, less crowded than other TIs).

At any TI, pick up the free small map or the large city map (€1), the brochure on public transport, and the free quarterly *See Barcelona* guide with practical information on museum hours, restaurants, transportation, history, festivals, and so on.

Throughout the summer, you'll see young red-jacketed tourist info helpers on the streets in the touristed areas of town.

Palau de la Virreina, an arts-and-culture TI, offers information on Barcelona cultural events—music, opera, and theater (Mon–Sat 10:00– 20:00, Sun 10:00–15:00, Ramblas 99).

Arrival in Barcelona

By Train: Although many international trains use the França Station, all domestic (and some international) trains use Sants Station. Both França and Sants have baggage lockers and subway stations: França's station is Barceloneta (2 blocks away), and Sants' is Sants Estacio (under the station). Sants Station has a good TI, a world of handy shops and eateries, and a classy, quiet Sala Euromed lounge for travelers with first-class reservations (TV, free drinks, study tables, and coffee bar). Subway or taxi to your hotel. Most trains to or from France stop at the subway station Passeig de Gràcia, just a short walk from the center (Plaça de Catalunya, TI, hotels).

By Plane: Barcelona's **El Prat de Llobregat Airport,** 8 miles southwest of town, is connected cheaply and quickly by **Aerobus** (immediately in front of arrivals lobby, 4/hr until 24:00, 30 min to Plaça de

"YOU'RE NOT IN SPAIN, YOU'RE IN CATALUNYA!"

This is a popular pro-nationalist refrain you might see on T-shirts or stickers around town. Catalunya is *not* the land of bullfighting and flamenco that many visitors envision when they think of Spain (best to wait until you're in Madrid or Sevilla for those).

The region of Catalunya—with Barcelona as its capital—has its own language, history, and culture, and the people have a proud independent spirit. Historically, Catalunya has often been at odds with the central Spanish government in Madrid. The Catalan language and culture have been repressed or outlawed at various times in Spanish history, most recently during the Franco era. Three of Barcelona's monuments are reminders of that suppression: The Parc de la Ciutadella was originally a much-despised military citadel, constructed in the 18th century to keep locals in line. The Castle of Montjuïc, built for similar reasons, has been the site of numerous political executions, including hundreds during the Franco era. Although rivalry between Barcelona and Madrid has calmed down in recent times, it rages any time the two cities' football clubs meet.

To see real Catalan culture, look for the *sardana* dance (described in "Sights") or an exhibition of castellers. These teams of human-castle builders come together for festivals throughout the year to build towers that can reach over 50 feet high, topped off by the bravest member of the team—a child! The Gràcia festival in August and the Mercè fesitival in September are good times to catch the castellers.

Catalunya, buy €3.45 ticket from driver) or by RENFE **train** (walk through overpass from airport to station, 2/hr at :13 and :43 after the hour, 20 min to Sants Station and Plaça de Catalunya; €2.30, or buy a T-10 transit pass at the airport and use it for this trip—see below. A **taxi** to or from the airport costs under €20. The airport has a post office, pharmacy, left luggage office, and ATMs (avoid the gimmicky machines before the baggage carrousels; instead use the bank-affiliated ATMs at the far-left end of arrival hall as you face the street). Airport info: tel. 932-983-467 or 932-983-465.

Getting around Barcelona

By Subway: Barcelona's Metro, among Europe's best, connects just about every place you'll visit. It has five color-coded lines. Rides cost €1.05. The T-10 Card for €5.80 gives you 10 tickets good for all local bus and Metro lines as well as the separate FGC line and RENFE train

The Catalan language is irrevocably tied to the history and spirit of the people here. Since the end of the Franco era in the mid-1970s, the language has made a huge resurgence. Now most school-age children learn Catalan first and Spanish second. Although Spanish is understood here (and the basic survival words are the same), Barcelona speaks Catalan. Here are the essential Catalan phrases:

Hello	*Hola*	(OH-lah)
Please	*Si us plau*	(see oos plow)
Thank you	*Gracies*	(GRAH-see-es)
Goodbye	*Adeu*	(ah-DAY-oo)
Exit	*Sortida*	(sor-TEE-dah)
Long live Catalunya!	*¡Visca Catalunya!*	(BEE-skah...)

Most place-names in this chapter are listed in Catalan. Here is a pronunciation guide:

Barcelona	bar-sah-LOH-nah
Plaça de Catalunya	PLAS-sah duh cat-ah-LOON-yah
Eixample	eye-SHAM-plah
Passeig de Gràcia	PAH-sage duh grass-EE-ah
Catedral	CAH-tah-dral
Barri Gòtic	BAH-rrree GAH-teek
Montjuïc	MOHN-jew-eek

lines (including the airport). Pick up the TI's guide to public transport. One-, two-, and three-day passes are available (for €4.40, €8, and €11.30).

By Hop-on, Hop-off Bus: The handy Tourist Bus *(Bus Turistic)* offers two multi-stop circuits in colorful double-decker buses (red route covers north Barcelona—most Gaudí sights; blue route covers south—Gothic Quarter, Montjuïc) with multilingual guides (25 stops, 2 hrs per route, 9:00–21:30, buses run every 6–30 min, most frequent in summer, buy tickets on bus or at TI). Ask for a brochure (which has a good city map) at the TI or at a pick-up point. One-day (€15) and two-day (€19) tickets include 10–20 percent discounts on the city's major sights—which will likely reimburse you for half the tour cost over the course of your visit.

By Taxi: Barcelona is one of Europe's best taxi towns. Taxis are plentiful and honest (€1.30 drop charge, €0.88/km, luggage-€0.85/piece, other extras posted in window). Save time by hopping a cab (figure €4 from Ramblas to Sants Station).

Helpful Hints

Theft Alert: You're more likely to be pickpocketed here—especially on the Ramblas—than about anywhere else in Europe. Most of the crime is nonviolent, but muggings do occur. Be on guard. Leave valuables in your hotel, and wear a money belt.

Here are a few common street scams, easy to avoid if you recognize them. Most common is the too-friendly local who tries to engage you in conversation by asking for the time, whether you speak English, and so on. If you suspect the person is more interested in your money than your time, ignore him and move on. A common street gambling scam is the pea-and-carrot game, a variation on the shell game. The people winning are all ringers and you can be sure that you'll lose if you play. Also beware of groups of women aggressively selling carnations, people offering to clean off a stain from your shirt, and people picking things up in front of you on escalators. If you stop for any commotion or show on the Ramblas, put your hands in your pockets before someone else does. Assume any scuffle is simply a distraction by a team of thieves.

U.S. Consulate: Passeig Reina Elisenda 23 (tel. 932-802-227).

Emergency Phone Numbers: Police—092, Emergency—061, directory assistance—010.

24-hour Pharmacy: Near the Boqueria Market at #98 on the Ramblas.

American Express: AmEx offices are at Passeig de Gràcia 101 (with all the travel-agency services, Mon–Fri 9:30–18:00, Sat 10:00–12:00, closed Sun, Metro: Diagonal, tel. 932-170-070) and at La Ramblas 74, opposite the Liceu Metro station (banking services only, daily 9:00–24:00, tel. 933-011-166, toll-free tel. 900-994-426).

Cheap Rental Cars: Consider Easycar.com for its great rates (tel. 902-182-028, www.easycar.com).

Internet Access: When **easyInternetcafé** arrived, prices for Internet access fell all over town. Europe's favorite Internet access—with piles of computers, drinks, and munchies—is open 8:00–24:00 and offers zippy access (€1/30 min) at two central locations: one is half a block west of Plaça de Catalunya on Ronda Universitat, and another near the seedy bottom of the Ramblas at #31. The rival **BBiGG** is at Calle Comtal 9, near Plaça de Catalunya (Mon–Sat 9:00–23:00 Sun 10:00–23:00, 300 terminals, tel. 933-014-020).

TOURS

Barcelona Guided Tours leads walking tours on weekdays (€13, departs from Plaça de Catalunya, Mon–Fri at 10:30 for the Gothic Quarter,

13:00 for Modernism, tel. 653-622-763).

The TI on Plaça de Catalunya runs English-languge walking tours of the Gothic Quarer on weekend mornings (€7, see "Tourist Information," above).

Local Guides: The Barcelona Guide Bureau is a co-op with plenty of excellent local guides who give personalized four-hour tours for €150; Joanna Wilhelm is good (Via Laietana 54, tel. 932-682-422 or 933-107-778, www.bgb.es).

Introductory Walk:
From Plaça de Catalunya down the Ramblas

A ▲▲▲ sight, Barcelona's central square and main drag exert a powerful pull as many visitors spend a major part of their time here doing laps on the Ramblas. Here's a top-to-bottom orientation walk:

Plaça de Catalunya—This vast central square, littered with statues of Catalan heroes, divides old and new Barcelona and is the hub for the Metro, bus, airport shuttle, and both hop-on, hop-off buses (red northern route leaves from El Corte Inglés, blue southern route from west side of Plaça). The grass around its fountain is the best public place in town for serious necking. Overlooking the square, the huge **El Corte Inglés** department store offers everything from bonsai trees to a travel agency, plus one-hour photo developing, haircuts, and cheap souvenirs (Mon–Sat 10:00–22:00, closed Sun, pick up English directory flier, supermarket in basement, 9th-floor terrace cafeteria/restaurant with great city view—take elevator from entrance nearest the TI, tel. 933-063-800).

Four great boulevards start from Plaça de Catalunya: the Ramblas, the fashionable Passeig de Gràcia, the cozier but still fashionable Rambla Catalunya, and the stubby, shop-filled, pedestrian-only Portal de L'Angel. Homesick Americans can even find a Hard Rock Café. Locals traditionally start or end a downtown rendezvous at the venerable Café Zürich.

Cross the street from the café to reach...

Ramblas Walk Stop #1: The top of the Ramblas—Begin your ramble 20 yards down at the ornate fountain (near #129).

More than a Champs-Elysées, this grand boulevard takes you from rich at the top to rough at the port in a one-mile, 20-minute walk. You'll raft the river of Barcelonan life past a grand opera house, elegant cafés, retread prostitutes, pickpockets, power-dressing con men, artists, street mimes, an outdoor bird market, great shopping, and people looking to charge more for a shoeshine than you paid for the shoes.

Grab a bench and watch the scene. Open up your map and read some history into it: You're about to walk right across medieval Barcelona from Plaça de Catalunya to the harbor. Notice how the higgledy-piggledy street plan of the medieval town was contained within

BARCELONA AT A GLANCE

▲▲▲Ramblas Barcelona's colorful, gritty pedestrian thoroughfare. **Hours:** Always open.

▲▲▲Picasso Museum Extensive collection offering insight into the Spanish artist's early years. **Hours:** Tue–Sat 10:00–20:00, Sun 10:00–15:00, closed Mon.

▲▲▲Sagrada Família Gaudí's unfinished cathedral. **Hours:** Daily April–Oct 9:00–20:00, Nov–March 9:00–18:00.

▲▲Casa Milà Barcelona's quintessential modernist building, the famous melting-ice-cream Gaudí creation. **Hours:** Daily 10:00–20:00.

▲▲Catalan Art Museum World-class collection of this region's art, including a substantial Romanesque collection. **Hours:** Tue–Sat 10:00–19:00, Sun 10:00–14:30, closed Mon.

▲▲Catalan Concert Hall Best modernist interior in Barcelona. **Hours:** English tours daily on the hour 10:00–15:00.

▲Cathedral Colossal Gothic cathedral. **Hours:** Daily 8:00–13:30 & 16:30–19:30.

▲City History Museum Tracing Barcelona's history, from Roman times through the Middle Ages to today. **Hours:** June–Sept Tue–Sat

the old town walls—now gone but traced by a series of roads named Ronda (meaning "to go around"). Find the Roman town, occupying about 10 percent of what became the medieval town—with tighter roads yet around the cathedral. The sprawling modern grid plan beyond the Ronda roads is from the 19th century. Breaks in this urban waffle show where a little town was consumed by the growing city. The popular Passeig de Gràcia boulevard was literally the road to Gràcia (once a town, now a characteristic Barcelona neighborhood).

Rambla means "stream" in Arabic. The Ramblas used to be a drainage ditch along the medieval wall that once defined what's now called the Gothic Quarter. "Las Ramblas" is plural, a succession of five separately named segments, but address numbers treat it as a single long street.

You're at Rambla Canaletes, named for the fountain. The black-and-gold Fountain of Canaletes is the beginning point for celebrations and demonstrations. Legend says that one drink from the fountain

10:00–20:00, Sun 10:00–14:00, closed Mon; Oct–May Tue–Sat 10:00–14:00 & 16:00–20:00, Sun 10:00–14:00, closed Mon.

▲*Sardana* **Dances** Patriotic dance where proud Catalans join hands in a circle. **Hours:** Often on Sun at 18:00 in spring and summer, 18:30 in fall and winter.

▲**Palau Güell** Exquisitely curvy Gaudí interior. **Hours:** Mon–Sat 10:00–20:00, closed Sun, closes at 18:00 Nov–April.

▲**The Block of Discord** Noisy block of competing modernist facades by Gaudí and his rivals. **Hours:** Always open.

▲**Park Güell** Colorful park at the center of the unfinished Gaudí-designed housing project. **Hours:** Always open.

▲**Fundació Joan Miró** World's best collection of Catalan native Joan Miró, plus other modern artists. **Hours:** July–Sept Tue–Sat 10:00–20:00, Thu until 21:30, Sun 10:00–14:30, closed Mon, Oct–June closes at 19:00 Tue–Sat.

▲**Monastery of Pedralbes** Historic monastery with fine art gallery. **Hours:** Tue–Sun 10:00–14:00, closed Mon.

ensures that you'll return to Barcelona one day. All along the Ramblas, you'll see newspaper stands (open 24 hrs, selling phone cards) and ONCE booths (selling lottery tickets that support Spain's organization of the blind, a powerful advocate for the needs of people with disabilities).

Got some change? As you wander downhill, drop coins into the cans of the human statues (the money often kicks them into entertaining gear). Warning: Wherever people stop to gawk, pickpockets are at work.

Walk 100 yards downhill to #115 and...

Ramblas Walk Stop #2: Rambla of the Little Birds—Traditionally, kids bring their parents here to buy pets, especially on Sundays. Apartment-dwellers find birds, turtles, and fish easier to handle than dogs and cats. Balconies with flowers are generally living spaces, those with air-conditioning are generally offices. The Academy of Science's clock (at #115) marks official Barcelona time—synchronize. The Champion supermarket (at #113) has cheap groceries and a handy deli

From Plaça de Catalunya down the Ramblas

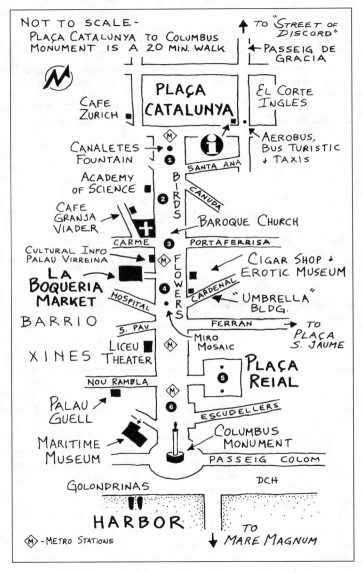

NOT TO SCALE—
PLAÇA CATALUNYA TO COLUMBUS
MONUMENT IS A 20 MIN. WALK

TO "STREET OF DISCORD"
PASSEIG DE GRACIA

PLAÇA CATALUNYA

EL CORTE INGLES

CAFE ZURICH

CANALETES FOUNTAIN

SANTA ANA

AEROBUS, BUS TURISTIC & TAXIS

ACADEMY OF SCIENCE

BIRDS

CANUDA

CAFE GRANJA VIADER

CARME

BAROQUE CHURCH

PORTAFERRISA

CULTURAL INFO PALAU VIRREINA

FLOWERS

CIGAR SHOP & EROTIC MUSEUM

LA BOQUERIA MARKET

CARDENAL

"UMBRELLA" BLDG.

HOSPITAL

BARRIO

S. PAU

FERRAN

TO PLAÇA S. JAUME

XINES

LICEU THEATER

MIRO MOSAIC

PLAÇA REIAL

NOU RAMBLA

PALAU GUELL

ESCUDELLERS

MARITIME MUSEUM

COLUMBUS MONUMENT

PASSEIG COLOM

GOLONDRINAS

DCH

Ⓜ - METRO STATIONS

HARBOR

TO MARE MAGNUM

with cooked food to go. A newly-discovered Roman necropolis is in a park across the street, 50 yards behind the big modern Citadines Hotel (go through the passageway at #122). Local apartment-dwellers blew the whistle on contractors who hoped they could finish their building before anyone noticed the antiquities they had unearthed. Imagine the tomb-lined road leading into the Roman city of Barcino 2,000 years ago.

Another 100 yards takes you to Carrer del Carme (at #2), and...

Ramblas Walk Stop #3: Baroque Church—The big plain church fronting the boulevard is Baroque, unusual in Barcelona. While Barcelona's Gothic age was rich (with buildings to prove it), the Baroque age hardly left a mark (the city's importance dropped when New World discoveries shifted lucrative trade to ports on the Atlantic). The Bagues jewelry shop across Carrer del Carme from the church is known for its Art Nouveau jewelry (exactingly duplicated from the c. 1898 molds of Masriera, displayed in the window; buzz to get inside). At the shop's side entrance, step on the old-fashioned scales (free, in kilos) and head down the lane opposite (behind the church, 30 yards) to a place expert in making you heavier. Café Granja Viader (follow the narrow lane behind the church; see "Eating," below) has specialized in baked and dairy delights since 1870. (For more sweets, follow "A Short, Sweet Walk," listed below in "Eating," below, which begins at the intersection in front of the church.)

Stroll through the Ramblas of Flowers to the subway stop marked by the red M (near #100), and...

Ramblas Walk Stop #4: La Boqueria—This lively produce market is an explosion of chicken legs, bags of live snails, stiff fish, delicious oranges, and sleeping dogs (#91, Mon–Sat 8:00–20:00, best mornings after 9:00, closed Sun). The Conserves shop sells 25 kinds of olives (straight in, near back on right, 100-gram minimum, €0.20–0.40). Full legs of ham *(jamón serrano)* abound; *Paleta Iberica de Bellota* are best and cost about €120 each. Beware: *Huevos de toro* are bull testicles—surprisingly inexpensive...and oh so good. Drop by a cafe for an *espresso con leche* or breakfast *(tortilla española*—potato omelet). For lunch and dinner options, consider La Gardunya, located at the back of the market (see "Eating," below).

The Museum of Erotica is your standard European sex museum—neat if you like nudes and a chance to hear phone sex in four languages (€7.50, daily June–Sept 10:00–24:00, shorter hours Oct–May, across from market at #96).

At #100, Gimeno sells cigars (appreciate the dying art of cigar boxes). Go ahead...buy a Cuban (singles from €1). Tobacco shops sell stamps.

Farther down the Ramblas at #83, the Art Nouveau Escriba Café—an ornate world of pastries, little sandwiches, and fine coffee—still looks like it did on opening day in 1906 (daily 8:30–21:00, indoor/outdoor seating, tel. 933-016-027).

Fifty yards farther, find the much-trod-upon anchor mosaic (a reminder of the city's attachment to the sea, created by noted abstract artist Joan Miró), marking the midpoint of the Ramblas. (The towering statue of Columbus in the distance marks the end of this hike.) From here, walk down to the Liceu Opera House (reopened after a 1994 fire, tickets on sale Mon–Fri 14:00–20:30, tel. 902-332-211; 45-minute €5 tours in English daily at 10:00; 20-min €2.50 version from upper balcony—sometimes with no light—daily at 11:00, 12:00, 13:00; reserve in advance, tel. 934-859-914, www.liceubarcelona.com). From the Opera House, cross the Ramblas to Café de l'Opera for a beverage (#74, tel. 933-177-585). This bustling café, with modernist decor and a historic atmosphere, boasts it's been open since 1929, even during the Spanish Civil War. Continue to #46; turn left down an arcaded lane to a square filled with palm trees...

Ramblas Walk Stop #5: Plaça Reial—This elegant neoclassical square comes complete with old-fashioned taverns, modern bars with patio seating, a Sunday coin and stamp market (10:00–14:00), Gaudí's first public works (the two colorful helmeted lampposts), and characters who don't need the palm trees to be shady. Herbolari Ferran is a fine and aromatic shop of herbs, with fun souvenirs such as top-quality saffron, or *safra* (Mon–Sat 9:30–14:00 & 16:30–20:00, closed Sun, downstairs at Plaça Reial 18). The small streets stretching toward the water from the square are intriguing but less safe.

Back across the Ramblas, **Palau Güell** offers an enjoyable look at a Gaudí interior (€3 for 60-min English/Spanish tour, usually open Mon–Sat 10:00–20:00, closed Sun, closes at 18:00 Nov–April, Carrer Nou de la Rambla 3–5, tel. 933-173-974). If you plan to see Casa Milà, skip the climb to this rooftop.

Farther downhill, on the right-hand side, is...

Ramblas Walk Stop #6: Chinatown (Barri Xines)—This is the world's only Chinatown with nothing even remotely Chinese in or near it. Named for the prejudiced notion that Chinese immigrants go hand in hand with poverty, prostitution, and drug dealing, the actual inhabitants are poor Spanish, Arab, and Gypsy people. At night, the Barri Xines features prostitutes, many of them transvestites, who cater to sailors wandering up from the port. A nighttime visit gets you a street-corner massage—look out. Better yet—stay out.

The Rambla of the Sea—The bottom of the Ramblas is marked by the Columbus Monument. And just beyond that, **La Rambla de Mar** ("Rambla of the Sea") is a modern extension of the boulevard into the harbor. A popular wooden pedestrian bridge—with waves like the sea—leads to Maremagnum, a soulless Spanish mall with a cinema, huge aquarium, restaurants (including the recommended Tapas Maremagnum; see "Eating," below), and piles of people. Late at night, it's a rollicking youth hangout. It's a worthwhile stroll.

SIGHTS

Ramblas Sights at the Harbor

Columbus Monument (Monument a Colóm)—Marking the point where the Ramblas hits the harbor, this 197-foot-tall monument built for an 1888 exposition offers an elevator-assisted view from its top (€2, June–Sept daily 9:00–20:30, Oct–March Mon–Fri 10:00–13:30 & 15:30–18:30, Sat–Sun 10:00–18:30, April–May until 19:30, the harbor cable car offers a better—if less handy—view). It's interesting that Barcelona would so honor the man whose discoveries ultimately led to its downfall as a great trading power. It was here in Barcelona that Ferdinand and Isabel welcomed Columbus home after his first trip to America.

Maritime Museum (Museo Maritim)—Housed in the old royal shipyards, this museum covers the salty history of ships and navigation from the 13th to the 20th century, showing off the Catalan role in the development of maritime technology (for example, the first submarine is claimed to be Catalan). With fleets of seemingly unimportant replicas of old boats explained in Catalan and Spanish, landlubbers may find it dull—but the free audioguide livens it up for sailors (€5.40, daily 10:00–19:00, closed Mon off-season). For just €0.60 more, visit the old-fashioned sailing ship *Santa Eulàlia*, docked in the harbor across the street.

Golondrinas—Little tourist boats at the foot of the Columbus Monument offer 30-minute harbor tours (€3.20, daily 11:00–20:00). A glass-bottom catamaran makes longer tours up the coast (€8 for 75 min, 4/day, daily 11:30–18:30). For a picnic place, consider one of these rides or the harbor steps.

Gondola Lift to Montjuic—You'll see the gondola carrying tourists to the hill of Montjuic, which offers views, a castle, and several museums (military, Catalan art, and Joan Miró's art); see "Sights—Barcelona's Montjuic," below).

Gothic Quarter (Barri Gòtic): The Cathedral and Nearby

The Barri Gòtic is a bustling world of shops, bars, and nightlife packed between hard-to-be-thrilled-about 14th- and 15th-century buildings. The area around the port is seedy. But the area around the cathedral is a tangled yet inviting grab bag of undiscovered courtyards, grand squares, schoolyards, Art Nouveau storefronts, baby flea markets (Thursdays), musty junk shops, classy antique shops (Carrer de la Palla), street musicians strumming Catalan folk songs, and balconies with domestic jungles behind wrought-iron bars. Go on a cultural scavenger hunt. Write a poem.

▲**Cathedral**—As you stand in the square looking at the cathedral, you're facing what was Roman Barcelona. To your right, letters spell out BARCINO—the city's Roman name. The three towers on the building to the right are mostly Roman.

Barcelona's Gothic Quarter Sights

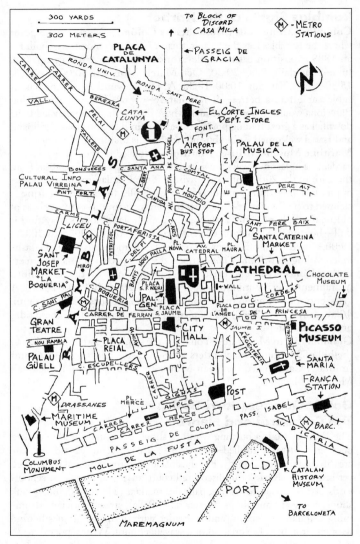

The colossal **cathedral,** started in about 1300, took 600 years to complete. Rather than stretching toward heaven, it makes a point of being simply massive (similar to the Gothic churches of Italy). The west front, though built according to the original plan, is only 100 years old (note the fancy, undulating rose window). The cathedral welcomes visitors daily (8:00–13:30 & 16:30–19:30; cloisters: daily 9:00–13:00 & 17:00–19:00; tel. 933-151-554).

The spacious interior—characteristic of Catalan Gothic—was supported by buttresses. These provided walls for 28 richly ornamented chapels. While the main part of the church is fairly plain, the chapels, sponsored by local guilds, show great wealth. Located in the community's most high-profile space, they provided a kind of advertising to illiterate worshipers. Find the logos and symbols of the various trades represented. The Indians Columbus brought to town were supposedly baptized in the first chapel on the left.

The **chapels** ring a finely carved 15th-century choir *(coro)*. Pay €1 for a close-up look (with the lights on) at the ornately carved stalls and the emblems representing the various knights of the Golden Fleece who once sat here. The chairs were folded up, giving VIPs stools to lean on during the standing parts of the Mass. Each was creatively carved and—since you couldn't sit on sacred things—the artists were free to enjoy some secular fun here. Study the upper tier of carvings.

The **high altar** sits upon the tomb of Barcelona's patron saint, Eulàlia. She was a 13-year-old local girl tortured 13 times by Romans for her faith and finally crucified on an X-shaped cross. Her X symbol is carved on the pews. Climb down the stairs for a close look at her exquisite marble sarcophagus.

Ride the **elevator** to the roof and climb a tight spiral staircase up the spire for a commanding view (€1.40, Mon–Fri 10:30–12:30 & 16:30–18:00, closed Sat–Sun, start from chapel left of high altar).

Enter the **cloister** (through arch, right of high altar). From there, look back at the arch, an impressive mix of Romanesque and Gothic. A tiny statue of St. George slaying the dragon stands in the garden. Jordi (George) is one of the patron saints of Catalunya and by far the most popular boy's name here. Though cloisters are generally found in monasteries, this church added one to accommodate more chapels—good for business. Again, notice the symbols of the trades or guilds. Even the pavement is filled with symbols—similar to Americans getting their name on a brick for helping to pay for something.

Long ago the resident geese—there are always 13 in memory of Eulàlia—functioned as an alarm system. Any commotion would get them honking, alerting the monk in charge.

From St. Jordi, circle to the right (past a WC hidden on the left). The skippable little €0.60 **museum** (far corner) is one plush room with a dozen old religious paintings. In the corner the dark, barrel-vaulted

Barcelona's Cathedral

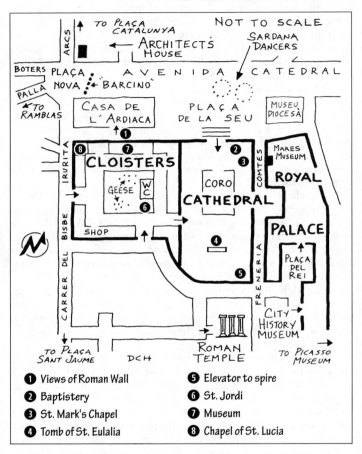

1. Views of Roman Wall
2. Baptistery
3. St. Mark's Chapel
4. Tomb of St. Eulalia
5. Elevator to spire
6. St. Jordi
7. Museum
8. Chapel of St. Lucia

Romanesque Chapel of Santa Lucia was a small church predating the cathedral and built into the cloister. The candles outside were left by people hoping for good eyesight (Santa Lucia's specialty). Farther along, the Chapel of Santa Rita (her forte: impossible causes) usually has the most candles. Complete the circle and exit at the door just before the place you entered.

Walk uphill, following the church. From the end of the apse turn right 50 yards up Carrer del Paradis to the **Roman Temple** (Temple Roma d' August). In the corner a sign above a millstone in the pavement marks "Mont Tabor, 16.9 meters." Step into the courtyard for a peek at a surviving corner of the imposing temple which once stood here on the city's highest hill, keeping a protective watch over Barcino (free, daily 10:00–14:00 & 16:00–20:00).

Plaça del Rei—The Royal Palace sat on King's Square (a block from the cathedral) until Catalunya became part of Spain in the 15th century. Then it was the headquarters of the local Inquisition. Columbus came here to show King Ferdinand souvenirs from what he thought was India.

▲City History Museum—For a walk through the history of the city, take an elevator down 65 feet (and 2,000 years) to stroll the streets of Roman Barcelona. You'll see sewers, models of domestic life, and bits of an early Christian church. Then a new exhibit in the 11th-century count's palace shows you Barcelona through the Middle Ages (€3.50 includes museum, presentation, and visits to Pedralbes Monastery and Verdaguer House Museum, see museum pamphlet for details; June–Sept Tue–Sat 10:00–20:00, Sun 10:00–14:00, closed Mon; Oct–May Tue–Sat 10:00–14:00 & 16:00–20:00, Sun 10:00–14:00, closed Mon, Plaça del Rei, tel. 933-151-111).

Frederic Mares Museum—This classy collection combines medieval religious art with a quirky bundle of more modern artifacts—old pipes, pinups, toys, and so on (Tue–Sat 10:00–15:00, Sun 10:00–14:00, closed Mon, Carrer del Comtes, off Plaça de la Seu, next to cathedral, tel. 933-105-800).

▲*Sardana* Dances—The patriotic *sardana* dances are held at the cathedral (most Sun at 12:00) and at Plaça de Sant Jaume (often on Sun at 18:00 in spring and summer, 18:30 in fall and winter). Locals of all ages seem to spontaneously appear. They gather in circles after putting their things in the center—symbolic of community and sharing (and the ever-present risk of theft). Holding hands, they raise their arms as they hop and sway gracefully to the band. The band *(cobla)* consists of a long flute, tenor and soprano oboes, strange-looking brass instruments, and a tiny bongolike drum *(tambori)*. The rest of Spain mocks this lazy circle dance, but, considering what it takes for a culture to survive within another culture's country, it is a stirring display of local pride and patriotism.

Shoe Museum (Museu del Calçat)—Shoe-lovers enjoy this two-room shoe museum (with a we-try-harder attendant) on the delightful Plaça Sant Felip Neri (€1.20, Tue–Sun 11:00–14:00, closed Mon, 1 block beyond outside door of cathedral cloister, behind Plaça de G. Bachs, tel. 933-014-533). The huge shoe at the entry is designed to fit the foot of the Columbus Monument at the bottom of the Ramblas.

Plaça de Sant Jaume—On this stately central square (pronounced jau-mah) of the Gothic Quarter, two of the top governmental buildings in Catalunya face each other: The Barcelona city hall (Ajuntament, free Sun 10:00–13:30) and the seat of the autonomous government of Catalunya (Palau de la Generalitat). *Sardana* dances take place here many Sundays (see "*Sardana* Dances," above).

▲▲**Catalan Concert Hall (Palau de la Música Catalana)**—This concert hall, finished in 1908, features the best modernist interior in town. Inviting arches lead you into the 2,000-seat hall. A kaleidoscopic skylight features a choir singing around the sun while playful carvings and mosaics celebrate music and Catalan culture. Admission is by tour only and starts with a relaxing 20-minute video (€5, 1 hr, in English, daily on the hour 10:00–15:00, maybe later, about 6 blocks northeast of cathedral, tel. 932-967-200). Ask about concerts (300 per year, inexpensive tickets, www.palaumusica.com).

Gothic Quarter:
The Picasso Museum and Nearby
▲▲▲**Picasso Museum**—This is the best collection of Picasso's (1881–1973) work in Spain, and—since he spent his formative years (age 14–21) in Barcelona—the best collection of his early works anywhere. By seeing his youthful realistic art, you can more fully appreciate the artist's genius and better understand his later, more challenging art. It's scattered through two Gothic palaces, six blocks from the cathedral.

Cost, Hours, and Location: €5, free on first Sun of month, Tue–Sat 10:00–20:00, Sun 10:00–15:00, closed Mon, free and required bag check, Montcada 15–23, ticket office at #21, Metro: Jaume I, tel. 933-196-310. The ground floor offers a handy array of services (bookshop, WC, bag check, and cafeteria). For a good lunch, see "Eating—Near the Picasso Museum," below.

Background: Picasso's personal secretary amassed a huge collection of his work and bequeathed it to the city. Picasso, happy to have a fine museum showing off his work in the city of his youth, added to the collection throughout his life. (Sadly, since Picasso vowed never to set foot in a fascist, Franco-ruled Spain and he died 2 years before Franco, the artist never saw the museum.)

Self-Guided Tour: While the rooms are constantly rearranged, the collection (291 paintings) is always presented chronologically. With the help of thoughtful English descriptions for each stage, it's easy to follow the evolution of Picasso's work. The room numbers in parentheses—though not exact—can help you orient through the museum. You'll see his art evolve in these twelve stages:

Stage 1—Boy wonder, age 12–14, 1895–1897 (Rooms 1, 2, 3): Pablo's earliest art is realistic and serious. A budding genius emerges at age 12 as Pablo moves to Barcelona and gets serious about art. Even this young, his portraits of grizzled peasants show great psychological insight and flawless technique. You'll see portraits of Pablo's first teacher, his father *(Padre del Artista)*. Displays show his art-school work. Every time Pablo starts breaking rules, he's sent back to the standard classic style. The assignment: Sketch nude models to capture human anatomy accurately. Three self-portraits (1896) show the self-awareness of a thoughtful genius blossoming. When Pablo was 13, his father quit painting to nurture his young prodigy. Look closely at the portrait of his mother *(Retrato de la Madre del Artista)*. Pablo, then age 15, is working on the fine details and gradients of white in her blouse and the expression in her cameo-like face. Notice the signature. Spaniards keep both parents' surnames: Pablo Ruiz Picasso. Pablo was closer to his mom than his dad. Eventually he kept just his mom's name.

Stage 2—Málaga, exploration of nature (Rooms 4, 5, 6): During a short trip to Málaga, Picasso dabbles in Impressionism (unknown in Spain at the time).

Stage 3—A sponge, influenced by local painters (Rooms 7, 8): As a 15-year-old, Pablo dutifully enters art-school competitions. His first big painting—while forced to show a religious subject *(First Communion,* Room 7)—is more an excuse to paint his family. Notice his sister Lola's exquisitely painted veil. This painting was heavily influenced by local painters.

Science and Charity (Room 8), which won second prize at a fine-arts exhibition, got Picasso the chance to study in Madrid. Now Picasso conveys real feeling. The doctor (Pablo's father) represents science. The nun represents charity and religion. But nothing can help as the woman is clearly dead (notice her face and lifeless hand). Pablo painted a little perspective trick: Walk back and forth across the room to see the bed stretch and shrink. Four small studies for this painting, hanging in the back of the room, show how this was an exploratory work. The frontier: light.

Picasso travels to Madrid for further study. Finding the stuffy fine-arts school in Madrid stifling, Pablo hangs out in the Prado Gallery and learns by copying the masters. Notice his nearly perfect copy of Felipe IV by Velázquez.

Stage 4—Independence (Rooms 4, 8): Having absorbed the wisdom of the ages, in 1898, Pablo visits Horta, a rural Catalan village, and finds his artistic independence.

Stage 5—Sadness, 1899–1900 (Rooms 9, 10): Pablo's good friend dies. He's poor, and without love. He returns to Barcelona. It's 1900, and Art Nouveau is the rage. Upsetting his dad, Pablo quits art school and falls in with the avant-garde crowd. These bohemians congregate daily at the Four Cats (slang for "a few crazy people"—see "Eating," below). Further establishing his artistic freedom, he paints portraits—no longer of his family...but of his new friends. Still a teenager, Pablo puts on his first one-man show.

Stage 6—Paris, 1900–1901 (Room 10): Nineteen-year-old Picasso arrives in Paris, a city bursting with life, light, and love. Dropping the surname Ruiz, Pablo establishes his commercial brand name: "Picasso." Here the explorer Picasso goes Bohemian, befriending poets, prostitutes, and artists. He paints Impressionist landscapes like Monet, posters like

Toulouse-Lautrec, still-lifes like Cézanne, and bright-colored Fauvist works like Matisse. (*La Espera*—with her bold outline and strong gaze—pops out from the Impressionistic background.) It was Cézanne's technique of "building" a figure with "cubes" of paint that inspired Picasso to soon invent Cubism.

Stage 7—Blue Period, 1901–1904 (Room 11): The bleak weather and poverty Picasso experiences in Paris leads to his "Blue Period." He cranks out piles of blue art just to stay housed and fed. With blue backgrounds (the coldest color) and depressing subjects, this period was revolutionary in art history. Now the artist is painting not what he sees but what he feels. The touching portrait of a mother and child, *Desamparados* (*Despair*, 1903), captures the period well. Painting misfits and street people, Picasso, like Velázquez and Toulouse-Lautrec, sees "the beauty in ugliness." Back home in Barcelona, Picasso paints his hometown at night from rooftops *(Terrats de Barcelona)*. Still blue, here we see proto-Cubism...five years before the first real Cubist painting.

Stage 8—Rose (Room 11): The woman in pink *(Retrato de la Sra. Canals),* painted with classic "Spanish melancholy," finally lifts Picasso out of his funk, moving him out of the blue and into a happier "Rose Period" (of which this museum has only one painting).

Stage 9—Cubism, 1907–1920 (Rooms 12, 13, 14): Pablo's invention in Paris of the shocking Cubist style is well-known—at least I hope so, since this museum has no true Cubist paintings. In the age of the camera, the Cubist gives just the basics (a man with a bowl of fruit) and lets you finish it.

Stage 10—Eclectic, 1920–1950 (Rooms 12, 13, 14): Picasso is a painter of many styles. We see a little post-Impressionistic Pointillism in a portrait that looks like a classical statue. After a trip to Rome, he paints beefy women, inspired by the three-dimensional sturdiness of ancient statues. The expressionist horse symbolizes to Spaniards the innocent victim. In bullfights, the horse—clad with blinders and pummeled by the bull—has nothing to do with the fight. To take the symbolism in a deeper, more human direction, to Picasso the horse was feminine and the bull masculine. Picasso would mix all these styles and symbols—including this image of the horse—in his masterpiece *Guernica* (in Madrid) to show the horror and chaos of modern war.

Stage 11—Picasso and Velázquez, 1957 (Rooms 15, 16, 17): Notice the print of Velázquez's *Las Meninas* (in Madrid's Prado) that introduces this section. Picasso, who had great respect for Velázquez, painted over 50 interpretations of the painting many consider the greatest painting by anyone, ever. These two Spanish geniuses were artistic equals. Picasso seems to enjoy a relationship with Velázquez. Like artistic soulmates, they spar and tease. He dissects Velázquez, and then injects playful uses of light, color, and perspective to horse around with the earlier masterpiece. In the big black-and-white canvas, the king and queen (reflected in the mirror in the back of the room) are hardly seen while the self-portrait of the painter towers above everyone. The two women of the court on the right look like they're in a tomb—but they're wearing party shoes. In these rooms, see the fun Picasso had playing paddleball with Velázquez's masterpiece—filtering Velázquez's realism through the kaleidoscope of Cubism.

Stage 12—Windows, 1957 (Room 17): All his life, Picasso said, "Paintings are like windows open to the world." Here we see the French Riviera—with simple black outlines and Crayola colors, he paints sun-splashed nature and the joys of the beach. He died with brush in hand, still growing. To the end—through his art—he continued exploring and loving life. As a child, Picasso was taught to paint as an adult. Now, as an old man (with little kids of his own and an also-childish artist Chagall for a friend), he paints like a child.

As a wrap-up, notice 41 works in Rooms 18 and 19, representing Picasso's ceramist period during his later years (1947).

Textile and Garment Museum (Museu Textil i de la Indumentaria)— If fabrics from the 12th to 20th centuries leave you cold, have a *café con leche* on the museum's beautiful patio (€3.50, Tue–Sat 10:00–18:00, Sun 10:00–15:00, closed Mon, free entrance to patio—an inviting courtyard with a WC and coffeshop, which is outside museum but within the walls, 30 yards from Picasso Museum at Montcada 12–14).

Chocolate Musuem (Museo de la Xocolata)—This new museum, only a couple of blocks from the Picasso Museum, is a delight for chocolate lovers. It tells the story of chocolate from Aztecs to Europeans via the port of Barcelona, where it was first unloaded and processed. Even if you're into architecture more than calories, don't miss this opportunity to see the Sagrada Família church finished—and ready to eat (€3.80, Wed–Mon 10:00–19:00, Sun until 15:00, closed Tue, Carrer Comerç 36, tel. 932-687-878, www.museuxocolata.com).

Eixample

Uptown Barcelona is a unique variation on the common grid-plan city. Barcelona snipped off the building corners to create light and spacious eight-sided squares at every intersection. Wide sidewalks, hardy shade trees, chic shops, and plenty of Art Nouveau fun make the Eixample a refreshing break from the old town. For the best Eixample example, ramble Rambla Catalunya (unrelated to the more famous Ramblas) and pass through Passeig de Gràcia (described below, Metro: Passeig de Gràcia for Block of Discord or Diagonal for Casa Milà).

The 19th century was a boom time for Barcelona. By 1850 the city was busting out of its medieval walls. A new town was planned to follow a gridlike layout. The intersection of three major thoroughfares—Gran Vía, Diagonal, and Meridiana—would shift the city's focus uptown.

The Eixample, or "Expansion," was a progressive plan in which everything was made accessible to everyone. Each 20-block-square district would have its own hospital and large park, each 10-block-square area would have its own market and general services, and each five-block-square grid would house its own schools and day-care centers. The hollow space found inside each "block" of apartments would form a neighborhood park.

While much of that vision never quite panned out, the Eixample was an urban success. Rich and artsy big shots bought plots along the grid. The richest landowners built as close to the center as possible. For this reason, the best buildings are near the Passeig de Gràcia. While adhering to the height, width, and depth limitations, they built as they pleased—often in the trendy new modernist style.

Gaudí's Art and Architecture

Barcelona is an architectural scrapbook of the galloping gables and organic curves of hometown boy Antonio Gaudí. A devoted Catalan and Catholic, he immersed himself in each project, often living on-site. He called Parc Güell, La Pedrera, and the Sagrada Família all home.

▲▲▲**Sagrada Família (Holy Family) Church**—Gaudí's most famous and persistent work is this unfinished landmark. He worked on the church from 1883 to 1926. Since then, construction has moved forward in fits and starts. Even today, the half-finished church is not expected to be completed for another 50 years. One reason it's taking so long is that the temple is funded exclusively by private donations and entry fees. Your admission helps pay for the ongoing construction (€6, €3 with Modernist Route combo-ticket. Daily April–Oct 9:00–20:00, Nov–March 9:00–18:00; €3 extra for English tours: 4/day April–Oct, usually 2/day Nov–March; audioguide-€3; Metro: Sagrada Família, tel. 932-073-031, www.sagradafamilia.org).

When the church is finished, a dozen 330-foot spires (representing the apostles) will stand in groups of four and mark the three entry facades of the building. The center tower (honoring Jesus) will reach 560 feet up and be flanked by 400-foot-tall towers of Mary and the four evangelists. A unique exterior ambulatory will circle the building like a cloister turned inside out.

1. Passion Facade (on the side where you enter): This shows Gaudí's spiritual drive. Inspired by Gaudí's vision, it's full of symbolism from the Bible (find the stylized alpha and omega over the door; Jesus, hanging on the cross, has an open book for hair; the grid of numbers all add up to 33—Jesus' age at the time of his death). The distinct face of the man on the lower left is a memorial to Gaudí.

Judge for yourself how the recently completed and controversial Passion facade by Josep Maria Subirachs fits with Gaudí's original formulation. Now look high above: The colorful ceramic caps of the

Modernist Sights

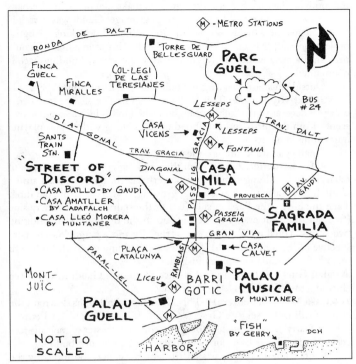

M - METRO STATIONS

RONDA DE DALT

TORRE DE BELLESGUARD

PARC GUELL

FINCA GUELL

COL-LEGI DE LAS TERESIANES

FINCA MIRALLES

BUS #24

LESSEPS

DIAGONAL

CASA VICENS

SANTS TRAIN STN.

TRAV. GRACIA

M LESSEPS

TRAV. DALT

M FONTANA

"STREET OF DISCORD"

DIAGONAL

CASA MILA

• CASA BATLLO-BY GAUDI

• CASA AMATLLER BY CADAFALCH

PROVENCA

AV. GAUDI

• CASA LLEO MORERA BY MUNTANER

M PASSEIG GRACIA

SAGRADA FAMILIA

GRAN VIA

PLAÇA CATALUNYA

M CASA CALVET

MONT-JUIC

PARAL-LEL

LICEU

M BARRI GOTIC

PALAU MUSICA BY MUNTANER

PALAU GUELL

M

"FISH" BY GEHRY

DCH

NOT TO SCALE

HARBOR

columns symbolize the mitres (formal hats) of bishops. This is only a side entrance. The nine-story apartment flat to the right will be torn down to accommodate the grand front entry of this church.

Now walk down to your right to the...

2. Museum (in church basement): The museum displays physical models used for the church's construction. As you wander, you'll see how the church's design is a fusion of nature, architecture, and religion. The columns seem light, with branches springing forth and capitals that look like palm trees. The U-shaped choir hovers above the nave, tethered halfway up the columns. Find the hanging model showing how Gaudí used gravity to calculate the perfect parabolas incorporated into the church design (the mirror above this model shows how the right-side-up church is derived from this).

Gaudí lived on the site for more than a decade and is buried in the crypt. When he died in 1926, only the stubs of four spires stood above the building site. A window allows you to look down into the neo-Gothic 19th-century crypt (which is how the church began) to see the tomb of Gaudí. There's a move afoot to make Gaudí a saint. Perhaps some day, this tomb will be a place of pilgrimage. Gaudí was certainly driven to greatness by his passion for God. When undertaking a lengthy project, he said, "My client"—meaning God—"is not in a hurry." You'll peek into a busy workshop where the slow and steady building pace is maintained.

Outside, just after leaving the building, you'll encounter the...

3. Nativity Facade: This really shows Gaudí's vision. It was the only real decorative part of the church finished in his lifetime, and shows scenes from the birth and childhood of Jesus along with angels playing musical instruments.

Finally you walk through the actual...

4. Construction Zone: With the cranking cranes, rusty forests of rebar, and scaffolding requiring a powerful faith, the Sagrada Família Church offers a fun look at a living, growing, bigger-than-life building. Take the lift on the Passion side (€2) or the stairs on the Nativity side (free but often miserably congested) up to the dizzy lookout bridging two spires. You'll get a great view of the city and a gargoyle's-eye perspective of the loopy church. If there's any building on earth I'd like to see, it's the Sagrada Família...finished.

▲**Palau Güell**—This is a good chance to enjoy a Gaudí interior (see "Introductory Walk," page 1053). Curvy.

▲▲**Casa Milà (La Pedrera)**—This Gaudí exterior laughs down on the crowds filling Passeig de Gràcia. Casa Milà, also called La Pedrera ("The Quarry"), has a much-photographed roller coaster of melting-ice-cream eaves. This is Barcelona's quintessential modernist building.

Visits come in three parts: apartment, attic, and rooftop. Buy the €7 ticket to see all three. Starting with the apartment, an elevator whisks you to the *Life in Barcelona 1905–1929* exhibit (well-described in English). Then you walk through a sumptuously furnished Art Nouveau apartment. Upstairs in the attic, wander under brick arches—enjoying a multimedia exhibit of models, photos, and videos of Gaudí's works. From there a stairway leads to the fanciful rooftop, where chimneys play volleyball with the clouds. From here, you can see Gaudí's other principal works, the Sagrada Família, Casa Batlló, and Parc Güell (daily 10:00–20:00; free tour in English Mon–Fri at 16:00, or rent the €3 audioguide; Passeig de Gràcia 92, Metro: Diagonal, tel. 934-845-530). At ground level of Casa Milà, poke into the dreamily-painted original entrance courtyard (free). The first floor hosts free art exhibits. During the summer, a concert series called "Pedrera by Night" features live music—jazz, flamenco, tango—a glass of champagne, and the chance to see the rooftop illuminated (€10, July–Sept Fri–Sat at 22:00, tel. 934-845-900).

▲**The Block of Discord**—Four blocks from Casa Milà, you can survey a noisy block of competing late-19th-century facades. Several of Barcelona's top modernist mansions line Passeig de Gràcia (Metro: Passeig de Gràcia). Because the structures look as though they are trying to outdo each other in creative twists, locals nicknamed the block between Consell de Cent and Arago the "Block of Discord." First (at #43) and most famous is Gaudí's Casa Batlló, with skull-like balconies and a tile roof that suggests a cresting dragon's back (Gaudí based the work on the popular St. Jordi-slays-the-dragon legend). By the way, if you're tempted to snap your photos from the middle of the street, be careful—Gaudí died under a streetcar.

Next door, at Casa Amatller (#41), check out architect Puig i Cadafalch's creative mix of Moorish, Gothic, and iron grillwork. This is the only place in town to purchase **Modernist Route combo-tickets.** For €3.60, you get a 50 percent discount to 10 of the most important modernist sights in Barcelona (valid for 1 month). Even if you only see Sagrada Família and Casa Milà, you'll save money with this ticket.

On the corner (at #35) is Casa Lleo Morera, by Lluís Domènech i Muntaner, who did the Catalana Concert Hall (you'll see similarities). The perfume shop halfway down the street has a free and interesting little perfume museum in the back. The Hostal de Rita restaurant, just around the corner on Carrer Arago, serves a fine three-course lunch for a great price at 13:00 (see "Eating," below).

▲**Park Güell**—Gaudí fans enjoy the artist's magic in this colorful park (free, daily 9:00–20:00) and small Gaudí Museum (€4, daily 10:00–20:00, closes at 18:00 Oct–March; red Tourist Bus or bus #24 from Plaça de Catalunya; €6 by taxi, tel. 932-130-488). Gaudí intended this garden to be a 60-residence housing project—a kind of gated community—rather than a park. As a high-income housing development, it flopped. As a park, it's a delight, offering another peek into the eccentric genius of Gaudí. From the bus stop, you'll hike uphill three blocks to the main (lower) entry to the park. (Taxis take you right there.) Notice the mosaic medallions that say "park" in English, reminding folks that this is modeled on an English garden.

Imagine living here 100 years ago, when this gated community was filled with Barcelona's wealthy. Stepping past fancy gate houses (which now house a good bookshop and an audiovisual intro), you walk by Gaudí's wrought-iron gas lamps (1900–1914)—his dad was a blacksmith, and he always enjoyed this medium. Climb the grand stairway past the ceramic dragon fountain. At the top, drop by the Hall of 100 Columns, a produce market for the neighborhood's 60 mansions. The fun columns—each different, made from concrete and rebar, topped with colorful ceramic, and studded with broken bottles and bric-a-brac—add to the market's vitality. After shopping, continue up. Look left down the play-ful "pathway of columns" that support a long arcade. Gaudí drew his inspiration from nature, and this arcade is like a surfer's perfect "tube." From here, continue up to the terrace. Sit on a colorful bench—designed to fit your body ergonomically—and enjoy one of Barcelona's best views. Look for the Sagrada Família church in the distance.

When considering the failure of Park Güell, consider also that it was an idea just a hundred years ahead of its time. Back then high-society ladies didn't want to live so far from the cultural action. Today, the surrounding neighborhoods are some of the wealthiest in town and a gated community here would be a big hit.

Barcelona's Montjuïc

The Montjuïc ("Mount of the Jews"), overlooking Barcelona's hazy port, has always been a show-off. Ages ago it had the impressive fortress. In 1929, it hosted an international fair, from which most of today's sights originated. And in 1992, the Summer Olympics directed the world's attention to this pincushion of attractions.

Getting to Montjuïc: You have several options: on the blue Tourist Bus route (see "Getting around Barcelona," above); by bus #50 from the corner of Gran Vía and Passeig de Gràcia (€1, every 10 min); take the Metro to Parallel and catch the funicular (included in transit pass, Mon–Fri 8:00–22:00, Sat–Sun 9:00–20:00); or by taxi (about €7). The first three options leave you at the *teleférico* (cable car), which you can take to the Castle of Montjuïc (€3.40 one-way, €4.80 round-trip, daily 11:15–21:00, less Nov–March, tel. 934-430-859). Alternatively, from the same spot, you can walk uphill 20 minutes through the pleasant park. Only a taxi gets you doorstep delivery. From the port, the fastest and most scenic way to Montjuïc is via the 1929 Transbordador Aereo (at tower in port, ride elevator up to catch dangling gondola, €7.20 round-trip, 4/hr, daily 10:30–19:00, tel. 934-430-859).

Castle of Montjuïc—The castle offers great city views and a military museum (€2.50, €1 for views from fortress only, daily 9:30–20:00). The seemingly endless museum houses a dull collection of guns, swords, and toy soldiers. An interesting section on the Spanish-American War covers Spain's valiant fight against American aggression (from its perspective). Unfortunately, there are no English descriptions. Those interested in Jewish history will find a fascinating collection of ninth-century Jewish tombstones. The castle itself has a fascist past. It was built in the 18th century by the central Spanish government to keep an eye on Barcelona and stifle citizen revolt. When Franco was in power, the castle was the site of hundreds of political assassinations.

▲**Fountains (Font Magica)**—Music, colored lights, and huge amounts of water make an artistic and coordinated splash on summer nights (20-min shows start on the half-hour Fri–Sun 19:00–21:00, also Thu in summer, from Metro: Plaça Espanya, walk toward towering National Palace).

Spanish Village (Poble Espanyol)—This tacky five-acre model village uses fake traditional architecture from all over Spain as a shell to contain gift shops. Craftspeople do their clichéd thing only in the morning (not worth your time or €6). After hours, it's a popular local nightspot.

▲▲Catalan Art Museum (Museo Nacional d'Art de Catalunya)— Often called "the Prado of Romanesque art," this is a rare, world-class collection of art taken mostly from remote Catalan village churches in the Pyrenees (saved from unscrupulous art dealers—many American).

The Romanesque wing features frescoes, painted wooden altar fronts, and ornate statuary. This classic Romanesque art—with flat 2-D scenes, each saint holding his symbol, and Jesus (easy to identify by the cross in his halo)—is impressively displayed on replicas of the original church ceilings.

In the Gothic wing, fresco murals give way to vivid 14th-century paintings of Bible stories on wood. A roomful of paintings by the Catalan master Jaume Huguet (1412–1492) deserves a close look.

Before you leave, ice-skate under the huge dome over to the air-conditioned cafeteria. This was the prime ceremony room and dance hall for the 1929 International Exposition (museum entry-€4.80, free first Thu of month, Tue–Sat 10:00–19:00, Sun 10:00–14:30, closed Mon, tel. 936-220-375). The museum is in the massive National Palace building above the fountains, near Plaça Espanya (Metro: Plaça Espanya, then hike up or ride the bus; blue Tourist Bus and bus #50 stop close by).

▲Fundació Joan Miró—For something more up-to-date, this museum—showcasing the modern-art talents of yet another Catalan artist—has the best collection of Joan Miró art anywhere. You'll also see works by other modern artists (such as Alexander Calder's *Mercury Fountain*). If you don't like abstract art, you'll leave scratching your head, but those who love this place are not faking it...they understand the genius of Miró and the fun of abstract art.

As you wander, consider this: Miró believed that everything in the cosmos is linked—colors, sky, stars, love, time, music, dogs, men, women, dirt, and the void. He mixed these things creatively, as a poet uses words. It's as liberating for the visual artist to be abstract as it is for the poet: Both can use metaphors rather than being confined to concrete explanations. Miró would listen to music and paint. It's interactive, free interpretation. He said, "For me, simplicity is freedom."

To enjoy Miró's art: 1) meditate on it, 2) read the title (for example, *The Smile of a Tear*), 3) meditate on it again. There's no correct answer—it's pure poetry. Devotees of Miró say they fly with him and don't even need drugs. Take advantage of the wonderful audioguide, included with admission (€7.20, July–Sept Tue–Sat 10:00–20:00, Thu until 21:30, Sun 10:00–14:30, closed Mon, Oct–June closes at 19:00 Tue–Sat, tel. 934-439-470).

Citadel Park and Nearby

Citadel Park (Parc de la Ciutadella)—Barcelona's biggest, greenest park, originally the site of a much-hated military citadel, was transformed in 1888 for a World's Fair (Universal Exhibition). The stately Triumphal Arch at the top of the park was built as the main entrance. Inside you'll find wide pathways, plenty of trees and grass, the zoo, the Geology and Zoology Museums, and the Modern Art Museum (see below). In Barcelona, which suffers from a lack of real green space, this park is a haven. Enjoy the ornamental fountain that the young Antonio Gaudí helped design, and consider a jaunt in a rowboat on the lake in the center of the park (€1.20/person for 30 min). Check out the tropical Umbracle greenhouse and the Hivernacle winter garden, which has a pleasant café-bar (daily 8:00–20:00, Metro: Arc de Triomf, east of França train station).

Modern Art Museum (Museu d'Art Modern)—This manageable museum in Citadel Park exhibits Catalan sculpture, painting, glass, and furniture by Gaudí, Casas, Llimona, and more (€3, Tue–Sat 10:00–19:00, Thu until 21:00, Sun 10:00–14:30, closed Mon).

Barcelona's Beach—Take the trek through the charming Barceloneta neighborhood to the tip of this man-made peninsula. The beaches begin here and stretch for 2.5 miles up the coast to the Olympic Port and beyond. Everything you see here—palm trees, cement walkways, and tons of sand—was installed in the mid-1980s in an effort to shape up the city for the 1992 Olympic Games. The beaches are fine for sunbathing (beach chair rental-€3/day), but the water quality is questionable for swimming. Take a lazy stroll down the seafront promenade to the Olympic Port, where you'll find bars, restaurants, and, at night, dance clubs. The Euroform 2004 cultural fair will be held near the Port this summer (May 9–Sept 26, www.barcelona2004.org).

NIGHTLIFE

Refer to the *See Barcelona* guide (free from TI) and find out the latest at a TI. Sights open daily until 20:00 include the Picasso Musuem, Casa Milà, and Gaudí's Sagrada Família and Parc Güell. On Thursday, the Modern Art Museum stays open until 21:00 and the Joan Miró museum until 21:30. On Montjuïc, the fountains on Plaça Espanya make a splash on weekend evenings (Fri–Sun, plus Thu in summer).

For music, consider a performance at Casa Milà ("Pedrera by Night" summer concert series), the Liceu Opera House, or the Catalan Concert Hall (all listed above). Two decent music clubs are La Boite (477 Diagonal, near El Corte Inglés) and Jamboree (on Plaça Reial).

SLEEPING

Eixample

For an uptown, boulevardian neighborhood, sleep in Eixample, a 10-minute walk from the Ramblas action.

$$ Hotel Gran Vía, filling a palatial mansion built in the 1870s, offers Botticelli and chandeliers in the public rooms; a sprawling, peaceful sun garden; and 54 spacious, comfy, air-conditioned rooms. While borderline ramshackle, it's charming and an excellent value (Sb-€75, Db-€110, Tb-€135, prices valid through 2004 but only by reserving direct with this book, elevator, Internet access, quiet, Gran Vía de les Corts Catalanes 642, tel. 933-181-900, fax 933-189-997, www.nnhotels .es, hgranvia@nnhotels.es, Juan Gomez SE).

$$ Hotel Continental Palacete is a new place filling a 100-year-old chandeliered mansion. With flowery wallpaper and cheap but fancy furniture under ornately gilded stucco, it's gaudy in the city of Gaudí. But it's friendly, clean, quiet, and well-located, and the beds are good. Owner Señora Vallet (whose son, José, runs the recommended Hotel Continental—see "Hotels with Personality on or near the Ramblas," below) has a creative vision for this 19-room hotel (Sb-€90–150, Db-€110–150, Tb-€150–180, includes breakfast and free fruit-and-drink buffet all day, air-con, 2 blocks north of Plaça de Catalunya at corner of Carrer Diputacio, Rambla de Catalunya 30, tel. 934-457-657, fax 934-450-050, www.hotelcontinental.com, palacete@hotelcontinental.com).

$ Hotel Residencia Neutral, with a classic Eixample address and 28 very basic rooms, is a family-run time warp (tiny Ss-€29, Ds-€43, Db-€49, extra bed-€9, €5 breakfast in pleasant breakfast room, elevator, fans, thin walls and some street noise, elegantly located 2 blocks north of Gran Vía at Rambla Catalunya 42, tel. 934-876-390, fax 934-876-848, owner Ramón SE). Its sister hotel, **Hotel Universal,** lacks the friendly feel and is stark but well-located (Sb-€45, Db-€60, Tb-€70, no breakfast, Arago 281, tel. 934-879-762, fax 934-874-028).

Business-Class Comfort near Plaça de Catalunya and the Top of the Ramblas

These nine places have sliding glass doors leading to plush reception areas, air-conditioning, and newly-renovated modern rooms. Most are on big streets within two blocks of Barcelona's exuberant central square. Being business hotels, they have hard-to-pin-down prices fluctuating wildly with the demand.

$$$ Hotel Catalonia Albinoni, the best located of all these places, elegantly fills a renovated old palace with wide halls, hardwood floors, and 74 modern rooms with all the comforts. It overlooks a thriving pedestrian boulevard. Front rooms have views; balcony rooms on the

SLEEP CODE

(€1 = about $1.10, country code: 34)

Sleep Code: **S** = Single, **D** = Double/Twin, **T** = Triple, **Q** = Quad, **b** = bathroom, **s** = shower only, **no CC** = Credit Cards not accepted, **SE** = Speaks English, **NSE** = No English. Unless otherwise noted, credit cards are accepted.

To help you sort easily through these listings, I've divided the rooms into three categories based on the price for a standard double room with bath (during high season):

$$$ **Higher Priced**—Most rooms €150 or more.
$$ **Moderately Priced**—Most rooms between €100–150.
$ **Lower Priced**—Most rooms €100 or less.

Book ahead. If necessary, the TI at Plaça de Catalunya has a room-finding service. Barcelona is Spain's most expensive city. Still, it has reasonable rooms. Cheap places are more crowded in summer; fancier business-class places fill up in winter and offer discounts on weekends and in summer. Prices listed do not include the 7 percent tax or breakfast (ranging from simple €3 spreads to €13.25 buffets) unless otherwise noted. While many recommended places are on pedestrian streets, night noise is a problem almost everywhere (especially in cheap places, which have single-pane windows). For a quiet night, ask for *"tranquilo"* rather than *"con vista."*

back are quiet and come with sun terraces (Db-€159, extra bed-€30, family rooms, great buffet breakfast is free when booking direct and showing this book, elevator, air-con, a block down from Plaça de Catalunya at Portal de l'Angel 17, tel. 933-184-141, fax 933-012-631, www.hoteles-catalonia.es, albinoni@hoteles-catalonia.es).

$$$ **Hotel Duques de Bergara** boasts four stars. It has splashy public spaces, slick marble and hardwood floors, 150 comfortable rooms, and a garden courtyard with a pool a world away from the big-city noise (Sb-€149, Db-€186, Tb-€206, elevator, air-con, a half-block off Plaça de Catalunya at Bergara 11, tel. 933-015-151, fax 933-173-442, www.hoteles-catalonia.es, duques@hoteles-catalonia.es).

$$$ **Hotel Occidental Reding,** on a quiet street a five-minute walk west of the Ramblas and Plaça de Catalunya action, rents 44 modern business-class rooms (Db-€118 in low season, €170 in high, extra bed-€51, elevator, air-con, near Metro: University at Gravina 5,

Barcelona's Gothic Quarter Hotels

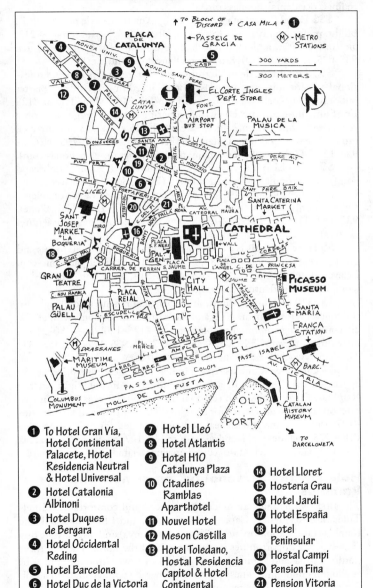

1. To Hotel Gran Vía, Hotel Continental Palacete, Hotel Residencia Neutral & Hotel Universal
2. Hotel Catalonia Albinoni
3. Hotel Duques de Bergara
4. Hotel Occidental Reding
5. Hotel Barcelona
6. Hotel Duc de la Victoria
7. Hotel Lleó
8. Hotel Atlantis
9. Hotel H10 Catalunya Plaza
10. Citadines Ramblas Aparthotel
11. Nouvel Hotel
12. Meson Castilla
13. Hotel Toledano, Hostal Residencia Capitol & Hotel Continental
14. Hotel Lloret
15. Hostería Grau
16. Hotel Jardi
17. Hotel España
18. Hotel Peninsular
19. Hostal Campi
20. Pension Fina
21. Pension Vitoria

tel. 934-121-097, fax 932-683-482, www.occidental-hoteles.com, reding@occidental-hoteles.com).

$$$ Hotel Barcelona is another big, American-style hotel with 72 bright, prefab, comfy rooms (Sb-€143, Db-€170, Db with terrace-€215, air-con, elevator, a block from Plaça de Catalunya at Caspe 1–13, tel. 933-025-858, fax 933-018-674, hotelbarcelona@husa.es).

$$$ Hotel Duc de la Victoria, with 156 rooms, is a new, professional-yet-friendly business-class hotel, buried in the Gothic Quarter but only three blocks off the Ramblas (Sb/Db-€165 Mon–Thu or €128 Fri–Sun, summer rate: Db-€100, superior rooms—bigger and on a corner with windows on 2 sides—are worth €15 extra, elevator, air-con, groups get weekend rate, Duc de la Victoria 15, tel. 932-703-410, fax 934-127-747, www.nh-hotels.com, nhducdelavictoria@nh-hotels.com).

$$ Hotel Lleó is a well-run business hotel with 90 big, bright, and comfortable rooms and a great lounge (Db-€130–160, on weekends-€144, summer Db special-€100, add about €25 for extra person, elevator, air-con, 2 blocks west of Plaça de Catalunya at Pelai 22, tel. 933-181-312, fax 934-122-657, www.hotel-lleo.es, reservas@hotel-lleo.es).

$$ Hotel Atlantis is a solid business-class hotel with 50 rooms and great prices for the area (Sb-€85, Db-€105, Tb-€125, elevator, air-con, Pelayo 20, tel. 933-189-012, fax 934-120-914, www.hotelatlantis-bcn.com, inf@hotelatlantis-bcn.com).

$$ H10 Catalunya Plaza, an impersonal business hotel right on the square, was redone in 2003 and has 47 tight mod rooms with all the air-conditioning and minibar comforts (Sb-€126–180, Db-€150–210 in busy times, elevator, Plaça de Catalunya 7, tel. 933-177-171, fax 933-177-855, www.h10.es, catalunya.plaza@h10.es).

$$ Citadines Ramblas Aparthotel is a clever concept, offering 130 apartments by the day in a bright, modern building right on the Ramblas. Prices range with seasonal demand and rooms come in two categories (studio apartment for 2 with sofa bed or twin and kitchenette-€127–152, apartment with real bed and sofa bed for up to 4 people-€185–225, includes tax, laundry-€9, Ramblas 122, tel. 932-701-111, fax 934-127-421, www.citadines.com, barcelona@citadines.com).

Hotels with "Personality" on or near the Ramblas

The first two listings are moderately-priced and comfortable. Hotels Toledano, Residencia Capitol, Continental, and Lloret overlook the Ramblas (at the top, very near Plaça de Catalunya) and offer classic tiny view-balcony opportunities if you don't mind the noise. The last three (Jardi, España, and Peninsular) are a few blocks away from the boulevard at about its midpoint. These places are generally family-run with ad-lib furnishings, more character, and much lower prices.

$$ **Nouvel Hotel,** an elegant, Victorian-style building on a handy pedestrian street, has royal lounges and 71 comfy rooms (Sb-€88–100, Db-€145–158, includes breakfast, manager Gabriel promises 10 percent discount when booking direct with this book, air-con, Carrer de Santa Ana 18, tel. 933-018-274, fax 933-018-370, www.hotelnouvel.com, info @hotelnouvel.com).

$$ **Meson Castilla** is well-located, with 57 clean rooms, but it's also pricey, a bit sterile (less quirky), and in all the American guidebooks. It's three blocks off the Ramblas in an appealing university neighborhood (Sb-€93, Db-€117, Tb-€156, Qb apartment-€187, includes buffet breakfast, elevator, air-con, Valldoncella 5, tel. 933-182-182, fax 934-124-020, hmesoncastilla@teleline.es).

$ **Hotel Toledano,** overlooking the Ramblas, is suitable for backpackers and popular with dust-bunnies. Small, folksy, and with new furniture, it's warmly run by Albert Sanz, his father Juan, Juanma, and trusty Daniel on the night shift (Sb-€34, Db-€55, Tb-€69, Qb-€77, some with air-con, front rooms have Ramblas-view terraces, back rooms have no noise—request your choice when you call; Internet access; Rambla de Canaletas 138, tel. 933-010-872, fax 934-123-142, www .hoteltoledano.com, reservas@hoteltoledano.com). The Sanz family also runs **Hostal Residencia Capitol** one floor above—quiet, plain, cheaper, and also appropriate for backpackers (S-€26, D-€38, Ds-€43, Q-€56, 5-bed room-€63).

$ **Hotel Continental** has comfortable rooms, double-thick mattresses, and wildly clashing carpets and wallpaper. To celebrate 100 years in the family, José includes a free breakfast and an all-day complimentary coffee bar. Choose a Ramblas-view balcony or quiet back room (Db with double bed-€75, with twin-€85, with balcony-€95, extra bed-€20, includes tax, special family room, fans in rooms, elevator, Internet access, Ramblas 138, tel. 933-012-570, fax 933-027-360, www.hotelcontinental.com, ramblas@hotelcontinental.com).

$ **Hotel Lloret** is a big, dark, Old World place on the Ramblas with plain, neon-lit rooms. A dark, dusty elevator cage fills the stairwell like Darth Vader—but on a hot day, you're glad it's there (Sb-€48, Db-€85, Tb-€95, Qb-€110, choose a noisy Ramblas balcony or *tranquilo* in the back, air-con in summer, Rambla de Canaletas 125, tel. 933-173-366, fax 933-019-283).

$ **Hostería Grau** is a homey, almost alpine place, family-run with 27 clean and woody rooms just far enough off the Ramblas (S-€27, D-€45, Ds-€51, Db-€60, family suites with 2 bedrooms-€120, €6 extra charged July–Sept, fans, Internet access, 200 yards up Calle Tallers from Ramblas at Ramelleres 27, tel. 933-018-135, fax 933-176-825, www .hostalgrau.com, reservas@hostalgrau.com, Monica SE).

$ **Hotel Jardi** offers 40 clean and newly-remodeled rooms on a breezy square in the Gothic Quarter. Rooms with tight little balconies

(€10 extra) overlooking the peaceful leafy square enjoy an almost Parisian ambience and minimal noise (Sb-€65, Db-€75, Sb/Db with square view-€80, extra bed-€10, breakfast-€5, elevator, air-con, halfway between Ramblas and cathedral on Plaça Sant Josep Oriol #1, tel. 933-015-900, fax 933-425-733, hoteljardi@retemail.es).

$ **Hotel España** is a big, creaky, circa-1900 place with lavish public spaces still sweet with Art Nouveau decor by locally popular Modernista architect Domenech i Muntaner. While it's 100 yards off the Ramblas on a borderline seedy street, it feels safe (84 rooms, Sb-€45, Db-€86, Tb-€118, includes tax and breakfast, air-con, elevator, near Metro: Liceu at Sant Pau 9, tel. 933-181-758, fax 933-171-134, www.hotelespanya.com, hotelespanya@hotelespanya.com).

$ **Hotel Peninsular,** farther down the same street, is thoughtfully run and a unique value in the old center. A former convent, the 80 still-basic and thinly-furnished rooms—once nuns' cells—gather prayerfully around a bright, peaceful courtyard (S-€26, Sb-€45, D-€45, Db-€65, Tb-€80, prices include tax and breakfast and are the same year-round, elevator, air-con, Carrer Sant Pau, tel. 933-023-138, fax 934-123-699, Alex and Augustin SE).

Humble Cheaper Places Buried in Gothic Quarter

$ **Hostal Campi**—big, quiet, and ramshackle—is a few doors off the top of the Ramblas. The streets can be noisy, so request a quiet room in the back (24 rooms, D-€42, Db-€49, T-€58, no CC, Canuda 4, tel. & fax 93-301-3545, hcampi@terra.es, friendly Sonia and Margarita SE).

$ **Pension Fina** offers more cheap sleeps (25 rooms, S-€32, D-€48, Db-€54, Portaferrissa 11, tel. & fax 933-179-787).

$ **Pension Vitoria** has loose tile floors and 12 basic, newly-repainted rooms, each with a tiny balcony. It's more dumpy than homey, but consider the price (D-€25, Db-€35, T-€35, cheaper off-season, a block off day-dreamy Plaça dei Pi at Carrer la Palla 8, tel. & fax 933-020-834, Andrés SE).

EATING

Barcelona, the capital of Catalan cuisine, offers a tremendous variety of colorful places to eat. Many restaurants close in August (or July), when the owners vacation.

Eating Simply yet Memorably near the Ramblas and in the Gothic Quarter

Taverna Basca Irati serves 40 kinds of hot and cold Basque *pintxos* for €1.10 each. These are open-faced sandwiches—like Basque sushi but on bread. Muscle in through the hungry local crowd. Get an empty plate from the waiter, then help yourself. It's a Basque honor system: You'll be charged by the number of toothpicks left on your plate when you're done. Wash it down with a €1.20 glass of Rioja (full-bodied red wine), €1.40 Txakoli (spritely Basque white wine), or €1.10 *sidra* (apple wine) poured from on high to add oxygen and bring out the flavor (daily 12:00–24:00, a block off the Ramblas, behind arcade at Carrer Cardenal Casanyes 17, near Metro: Liceu, tel. 933-023-084).

Juicy Jones, next door, is a tutti-frutti vegan/vegetarian place with garish colors, a hip veggie menu (served downstairs), and a stunning array of fresh-squeezed juices served at the bar (lunch and dinner *menu*-€8, daily 10:00–24:30, Carrer Cardenal Casanyes 7). Pop in for a quick €2.50 "juice of the day."

Restaurant Elisabets is a happy little neighborhood eatery packed with antique radios and popular with locals for its "home-cooked" three-course €7 lunch special. Stop by for lunch, survey what those around you are enjoying, and order what looks best (Mon–Sat 13:00–16:00, Fri also 21:00–1:00, closed Sun, tapas only in the evening, 2 blocks west of Ramblas on far corner of Plaça Bonsucces at Carrer Elisabets 2, tel. 933-175-826, run by friendly Pilar).

Café Granja Viader is a quaint time warp, family-run since 1870. They boast to be the first dairy business to bottle and distribute milk in Spain. This feminine place—specializing in baked and dairy delights, toasted sandwiches, and light meals—is ideal for a traditional breakfast (note the "Esmorzars" specials posted). Try a glass of *orxata* (horchata—almond milk, summer only), *llet mallorquina* (Majorca-style milk with cinnamon, lemon, and sugar), or *suis* (literally, "Switzerland"—hot chocolate with a snowcap of whipped cream). Described on the Ramblas walk above, it's a block off the boulevard behind El Carme church (Mon 17:00–20:45, Tue–Sat 9:00–13:45 & 17:00–20:45, closed Sun, Xucla 4, tel. 933-183-486).

Try eating at **La Boqueria market** at least once. Locals fill the market's bars, munching at the counter. The best is **Kiosko Universal** (packed after 13:30, tel. 93-317-8286; as you enter market from Ramblas, it's all the way to the left on the first alley). **La Gardunya,** located at the back of La Boqueria market, offers tasty meat and seafood meals made with fresh ingredients bought directly from the market (€9 lunch *menus* include wine and bread, €12.50 dinner *menus* don't include wine, Mon–Sat 13:00–16:00 & 20:00–24:00, closed Sun, Carrer Jerusalem 18, tel. 933-024-323).

Tired tourists consider **La Poma** for a good pizza, pasta, and salads in a bright modern setting at the top of the Ramblas with comfortable views of all the street action (daily 9:00–24:00, Ramblas 117, tel. 933-019-400).

Homesick tourists flock to **The Bagel Shop** for fresh bagels and brownies (Mon–Sat 9:30–21:30, Sun 11:00–16:00, Carrer Canuda 25, tel. 933-024-161).

Barcelona's Gothic Quarter Restaurants

1. Taverna Basca Irati & Juicy Jones
2. Restaurant Elisabets
3. Café Granja Viader
4. La Gardunya
5. La Poma Rest. & Champion Supermarket
6. The Bagel Shop
7. La Fonda
8. Les Quinze Nits
9. La Crema Canela
10. La Dolca Herminia
11. Els Quatre Gats
12. El Pintor Rest.
13. Restaurante Agut
14. Tapasbar Maremagnum
15. El Xampanyet Tapas Bar
16. Celestial Rest.
17. Self Naturista Veggie Buffet
18. Bio Center Veggie Café
19. Fresc Co Veggie Cafeteria
20. To La Bodegueta, Hostal de Rita & Quasi Queviures
21. To Cova Fumada & Bar Electricitat
22. Carrer Merce tapas bars
23. Casa Coloma Sweet Shop
24. La Pallaresa Granja-Xocolateria
25. Fargas Chocolate Shop

Shoestring tourists buy **groceries** at El Corte Inglés (Mon–Sat 10:00–22:00, closed Sun, supermarket in basement, Plaça de Catalunya) and Champion Supermarket (Mon–Sat 9:00–22:00, closed Sun, Ramblas 113).

Dining in the Gothic Quarter

A chain of five bright, modern restaurants with traditional cuisine in classy bistro settings with great prices has stormed Barcelona. Because of their three-course (with wine) €7 lunches and €15 dinners, all are crowded with locals and tourists in the know. They take no reservations and are marked by long lines at the door. Arrive 30 minutes before opening or be prepared to wait. The first three are within a block of the Plaça Reial, the fourth is near the Catalan Concert Hall, and the fifth (Hostal de Rita) is described in the Eixample section below: **La Fonda** (daily 13:00–15:30 & 20:30–23:30, a block from Plaça Reial at Escudellers 10, tel. 933-017-515); **Les Quinze Nits** (daily 13:00–15:45 & 20:30–23:30, on La Plaça Reial at #6—you'll see the line, tel. 933-173-075); **La Crema Canela** (feels cozier than the others in this chain, daily 13:30–15:45 & 20:00–23:30, Ptge. Madoz 6, 30 yards north of Plaça Reial, tel. 933-182-744); and **La Dolca Herminia** (2 blocks toward Ramblas from Catalan Concert Hall at Magdalenes 27, tel. 933-170-676).

Els Quatre Gats, Picasso's hangout (and the place he first showed off his paintings), still has a bohemian feel in spite of its tourist crowds. Before the place was founded in 1897, the idea of a café for artists was mocked as a place where only *quatre gats*—"four cats," meaning crazies—would go (€10 3-course lunch, daily 8:30–24:00, live piano from 21:00, Montsio 3, tel. 933-024-140).

El Pintor Restaurante serves perhaps the best €30 dinner in town. Under medieval arches and rough brick with candles and friendly service, you'll enjoy Catalan and Mediterranean cuisine (daily 13:30–16:30 & 20:00–24:00, from Plaça de Sant Jaume walk north on Carrer Sant Honorat to #7, reserve for eve, tel. 933-014-065).

Restaurante Agut, buried deep in the Gothic Quarter four blocks off the harbor, is a fine place with an enticing menu (in English) for local-style food in a local-style setting. It's almost dressy, with white tablecloths and candles (Tue–Sun 13:30–16:00 & 21:00–24:00, closed Mon and Aug, Carrer Gignas 16, reservations smart for dinner, tel. 933-151-709).

At **Carrer de Banys Vells** and **Palla Street,** several places offer great coffee, local cheeses, ham, sausage, and *cava* (sparkling wine).

Out at Sea—Maremagnum

Tapasbar Maremagnum is a big, rollicking sports-bar kind of tapas restaurant, great for large groups. It's a fun way to end your Ramblas walk, a 10-minute stroll past the Columbus Monument straight out the

dock, with breezy harbor views and good local food with emphasis on
the sea (daily 11:00–24:00, Moll d'Espanya, tel. 932-258-180, www
.tapasbar.es).

Near the Picasso Museum

El Xampanyet, a fun and characteristic bar, specializes in tapas and
anchovies. A *sortido* (assorted plate) of meat *(carne)* or fish *(pescado)* costs
about €6 with *pan con tomate*—tomato bread (Mon–Sat 12:00–15:30 &
19:00–24:00, closed Sun, half a block beyond Picasso Museum at
Montcada 22, tel. 933-197-003).

 Celestial, close to Santa Maria church, is an easy option with a
lunch and dinner buffet (lunch-€7.60, dinner-€9.65, weekends-€11.60,
daily 12:30–16:00 & 20:00–24:00, Argentaria 53, tel. 933-104-294.

Vegetarian near Plaça de Catalunya
and off the Ramblas

Self Naturista is a quick, no-stress buffet that makes vegetarians and
health-food lovers feel right at home. Others may find a few unidentifi-
able plates and drinks. The food seems tired—pick what you like and
microwave it—but the place is very handy (Mon–Sat 11:30–22:00,
closed Sun, near several recommended hotels, just off the top of
Ramblas at Carrer de Santa Ana 11–17).

 Bio Center, a Catalan soup-and-salad place popular with local vegetarians, is better but not as handy (€8 lunches, Mon–Sat 13:00–17:00,
closed Sun, Pintor Fortuny 25, Metro: Catalunya, tel. 933-014-583).
This street has several other good vegetarian places.

 Fresc Co is a healthy and hearty buffet in a sleek and efficient cafeteria. For one cheap price (€7 for lunch, €9 for dinner and on weekends),
you get a drink and all the salad, pasta, soup, pizza, and dessert you
want. Choose from two locations: west of Plaça de Catalunya at Ronda
Universitat 29 or a block off the Ramblas (near La Boqueria market) at
Carme 16 (daily 12:45–24:00, tel. 914-474-388).

 Juicy Jones is a juice bar with a modern, fun veggie restaurant in
back (just off the Ramblas at midpoint, described above).

Eixample

The people-packed boulevards of the Eixample (Passeig de Gràcia and
Rambla Catalunya) are lined with appetizing places with breezy outdoor
seating. Many trendy and touristic tapas bars offer a cheery welcome and
slam out the appetizers.

 La Bodegueta is an unbelievably atmospheric below-street-level
bodega serving hearty wines, homemade *Vermouth, anchoas* (anchovies),
tapas, and *flautas*—sandwiches made with flute-thin baguettes. Its daily
€8 lunch special (3 courses with wine) is served from 13:00 to 16:00
(Mon–Sat 8:00–24:00, Sun 19:00–24:00, Rambla Catalunya 100, at

intersection with Provenza, Metro: Diagonal, tel. 932-154-894). A long block from Gaudí's Casa Milà, this makes a fine sightseeing break.

Hostal de Rita is a fresh and dressy little place serving Catalan cuisine near the Block of Discord. Their lunches (3 courses with wine–€7, Mon–Fri from 13:00) and dinners (€15, à la carte, daily from 20:30) are a great value (a block from the Passeig de Gracia Metro stop, near corner of Carrer de Pau Claris and Carrer Arago at Arago 279, tel. 934-872-376). Like its four sister restaurants described above, its prices attract long lines, so arrive just before the doors open...or wait.

Quasi Queviures serves upscale tapas, sandwiches, or the whole nine yards—classic food served fast from a fun menu with modern decor and a sports-bar ambience. For €10 you can try three tiny dishes and a glass of wine (daily 7:00–24:00, between Gran Via and Via Diputacio at Passeig de Gràcia 24, tel. 933-174-512).

Sandwich Shops

Bright, clean, and inexpensive sandwich shops are proudly holding the cultural line against the fast-food invasion hamburgerizing the rest of Europe. You'll find great sandwiches at **Pans & Company** and **Bocatta,** two chains with outlets all over town. Catalan sandwiches are made to order with crunchy French bread. Rather than butter, locals prefer *pa amb tomaquet* (pah ahm too-MAH-kaht), a mix of crushed tomato and olive oil. Study the instructive multilingual menu fliers to understand your options.

Near the Harbor in Barceloneta

Barceloneta is a charming beach suburb of the big city with a village ambience. A grid plan of long, narrow, laundry-strewn streets surrounds the central Plaça Poeta Boscan. For an entertaining evening, wander around the perimeter of this slice-of-life square. Plenty of bakeries, pastry shops, and tapas bars ring a colorful covered produce market. Drop by the two places listed here or find your own restaurant (an unpleasant 15-min walk, Metro: Barceloneta, or taxi). During the day, a lively produce market fills one end of the square. At night, kids play soccer and ping-pong.

Cova Fumada, with unmarked wooden doors at #56, is the neighborhood eatery. Josep Maria and his family serve famously fresh fish (Mon–Fri 9:00–15:00 & 18:30–20:30, closed Sat–Sun and Aug, Carrer del Baluarte 56, on corner at Carrer Sant Carles, tel. 932-214-061). Their *sardinas a la plancha* (grilled sardines, €3) are fresh and tasty. *Calamar a la plancha* (sautéed whole calamari, €4.50) and *bombas* (potato croquets with pork, €1.10) are the house specialty. It's macho to eat your *bomba picante* (spicy with chili sauce); gentler taste buds prefer it *alioli,* with garlic cream. Catalan *bruschetta* is *pan tostado* (toast with oil and garlic, €1). Wash it down with *vino tinto* (house red wine, €0.60).

At **Bar Electricitat,** Lozano is the neighborhood source for cheap wine. Drop in. It's €1.05 per liter; the empty plastic water bottles are for takeaway. Try a €0.70 glass of Torroja Tinto, the best local red; Priorato Dulce, a wonderfully sweet red; or the homemade candy-in-heaven Vermouth. Owner Agapito can fix a plate of sheep cheese and almonds for €3.50 (Tue–Sun 8:00–15:00 & 18:00–21:00, closed Mon, across square from Cova Fumada, Plaça del Poeta Bosca 61, tel. 932-215-017, NSE).

The Olympic Port, a swank marina district, is lined with harborside restaurants and people enjoying what locals claim is the freshest fish in town (a short taxi ride past Barceloneta from the center).

Tapas on Carrer Merce in the Gothic Quarter

While tapas aren't as popular in Catalunya as they are in the rest of Spain, Barcelona boasts great tascas—colorful local tapas bars. Get small plates (for maximum sampling) by asking for "tapas," not the bigger *"raciones."* Glasses of *vino tinto* go for about €0.50.

While trendy uptown places are safer, better lit, and come with English menus and less grease, these places will stain your journal.

From the bottom of the Ramblas (near the Columbus Monument), hike east along Carrer Clave. Then follow the small street that runs along the right side of the church (Carrer Merce), stopping at the *tascas* that look fun. For restaurant dining in the area, Restaurante Agut (described above) comes with tablecloths and polite service. But for a montage of edible memories, wander Carrer Merce west to east considering these places and stopping wherever looks most inviting:

La Pulpería serves up fried fish, octopus, and *patatas bravas,* all with Galician Ribeiro wine. A block down the street, at **Casa del Molinero,** you can sauté your chorizo *al diablo* (sausage from hell). It's great with the regional specialty, *pan con tomate.* Across the street, **La Plata** keeps things wonderfully simple, serving extremely cheap plates of sardines (€1.25), little salads (€1.10), and small glasses of keg wine (€0.50). **Tasca el Corral** serves mountain favorites from northern Spain, such as *queso de cabrales* (very moldy cheese) and chorizo (spicy sausage) with *sidra* (apple wine sold by the €4 bottle). **Sidreria Tasca La Socarrena** (at #21), being a *sidreria,* is the only place that serves hard cider by the glass. At the end of Carrer Merce, **Bar Vendimia** serves up tasty clams and mussels (hearty *raciones* for €3 a plate—they don't do smaller portions so order sparingly). Their *pulpo* (octopus) is more expensive and the house specialty. Carrer Ample and Carrer Gignas, the streets paralleling Carrer Merce inland, have more refined barhopping possibilities.

A Short, Sweet Walk

To sample three Barcelona sweets, follow this quick walk. Start at the corner of Carrer Portaferrisa midway down the Ramblas. For the best atmosphere, begin your walk around 18:00.

Walk down Carrer Portaferrisa to #8. **Casa Coloma,** founded in 1908, sells homemade *Turrón*—a variation of nougat made of almond, honey, and sugar, brought to Spain by the Moors 1,200 years ago. Ask them for a sample *(muestra)* of *blando, duro,* and *yema* (soft, hard, and yolk). They sell sizable slabs for €6 (Mon–Sat 10:00–20:30, Sun 12:30–20:30, tel. 93-122-511).

Continue down Carrer Portaferrisa, taking a right at Carrer Petrixol to **La Pallaresa Granja-Xocolateria.** This is where the old ladies gather for the Spanish equivalent of tea-time: *chocolate con churros* (€3.50 for 5 churros and a small chocolate, Mon–Sat 9:00–13:00 & 16:00–21:00, Sun 9:00–13:00 & 17:00–21:00, Petrixol 11, tel. 933-022-036).

For your last stop, head for the ornate **Fargas** chocolate shop (a couple blocks farther toward the cathedral at Calle Pino 16; daily 9:30–13:30 & 16:00–20:00, tel. 933-020-342). Founded in 1827, this is one of the oldest and most traditional chocolate places in Barcelona. Ask if you can see the old chocolate mill *(¿Puedo ver molino?).*

TRANSPORTATION CONNECTIONS

By train to: Lisbon (1/day, 17 hrs with change in Madrid, €113), **Madrid** (7/day, 7–9 hrs, €41–44), **Paris** (1/day, 12 hrs, €127, night train, reservation required), **Sevilla** (3/day, 11 hrs, €49), **Granada** (2/day, 12 hrs, €48), **Málaga** (2/day, 14 hrs, €50), **Nice** (1/day, 12 hrs, €58, change in Cerbère), **Avignon** (5/day, 6–9 hrs, €38). Train info: tel. 902-240-202.

By bus to: Madrid (12/day, 8 hrs, half the price of a train ticket, departs from station Barcelona Nord at Metro: Marina). Sarfa buses serve all the coastal resorts (tel. 902-302-025).

By plane: To avoid 10-hour train trips, check the reasonable flights from Barcelona to Sevilla or Madrid. Iberia Air (tel. 902-400-500) and Air Europa (tel. 902-401-501 or 932-983-907) offer $80 flights to Madrid. Airport info: tel. 932-983-467.

MADRID

Today's Madrid is upbeat and vibrant, still enjoying a post-Franco renaissance. You'll feel it. Even the living-statue beggars have a twinkle in their eyes.

Madrid is the hub of Spain. This modern capital—Europe's highest, at more than 2,000 feet—has a population of more than four million and is young by European standards. Only 400 years ago, King Philip II decided to move the capital of his empire from Toledo to Madrid. One hundred years ago Madrid had only 400,000 people—so 90 percent of the city is modern sprawl surrounding an intact, easy-to-navigate historic core.

Dive headlong into the grandeur and intimate charm of Madrid. The lavish Royal Palace, with its gilded rooms and frescoed ceilings, rivals Versailles. The Prado has Europe's top collection of paintings. The city's huge Retiro Park invites you for a shady siesta and a hopscotch through a mosaic of lovers, families, skateboarders, pets walking their masters, and expert bench-sitters. Save time for Madrid's elegant shops and people-friendly pedestrian zones.

The city's latest plans include the creation of a pedestrian street crossing the city from the Prado to the Royal Palace (the section from the Prado along Huertas street to Plaza Angel, near Plaza Santa Ana, has already been completed), and a new macro-train station in Puerta del Sol (which will keep that subway station under construction until 2008).

Madrid is working hard—installing posts to keep cars off sidewalks, making the streets safer after dark, and restoring old buildings—to make the city more livable...and fun to visit.

On Sundays, cheer for the bull at a bullfight or bargain like mad at a mega-flea market. Lively Madrid has enough street-singing, barhopping, and people-watching vitality to give any visitor a boost of youth.

Planning Your Time

Madrid's top two sights, the Prado and the palace, are each worth a half day. On a Sunday (Easter–Oct), consider allotting extra time for a bull-fight. Ideally, give Madrid two days and spend them this way:

Day 1: Breakfast of *churros* (see "Eating," below) before a brisk, good-morning-Madrid walk for 20 minutes from Puerta del Sol to the Prado (from Puerta del Sol, walk three blocks southeast to Plaza Angel, then take the new pedestrian walkway to the Prado along Huertas street); spend the rest of the morning at the Prado; take an afternoon siesta in Retiro Park or tackle modern art at Centro Reina Sofia *(Guernica)* and/or Thyssen-Bornemisza Museum; dinner at 20:00, with tapas around Plaza Santa Ana.

Day 2: Follow this book's "Puerta del Sol to Royal Palace Walk"; tour the Royal Palace, lunch near Plaza Mayor; afternoon free for other sights, shopping, or side trip to El Escorial (open until 19:00). Be out at the magic hour—before sunset—when beautifully-lit people fill Madrid.

Note that the Prado, Thyssen-Bornemisza Museum, and El Escorial all close on Monday.

ORIENTATION

The historic center is enjoyably covered on foot. No major sight is more than a 20-minute walk or a €3.50 taxi ride from Puerta del Sol, Madrid's central square. Divide your time between the city's top three attractions: the Royal Palace, the Prado, and its barhopping contemporary scene.

The Puerta del Sol marks the center of Madrid. The Royal Palace to the west and the Prado Museum and Retiro Park to the east frame Madrid's historic center. Southwest of Puerta del Sol is a 17th-century district with the slow-down-and-smell-the-cobbles Plaza Mayor and memories of pre-industrial Spain. North of Puerta del Sol runs Gran Vía, and between the two are lively pedestrian shopping streets. Gran Vía, bubbling with expensive shops and cinemas, leads to the modern Plaza de España. North of Gran Vía is the gritty Malasaña quarter (and the flamboyant Chueca area), with its colorful small houses, shoemakers' shops, sleazy-looking hombres, milk vendors, bars, and hip night scene.

Tourist Information

Madrid has five TIs: **Plaza Mayor**at #3 (Mon–Sat 10:00–20:00, Sun 10:00–15:00, tel. 915-881-636); **near the Prado Museum** (Mon–Sat 9:00–19:00, Sun 9:00–15:00, Duque de Medinaceli 2, behind Palace Hotel, tel. 914-293-705); **Chamartin** train station (Mon–Sat 8:00–20:00, Sun 8:00–15:00, tel. 913-159-976); **Atocha** train station (daily 9:00–21:00); and at the **airport** (daily 8:00–20:00, tel. 913-058-656). The general tourist information number is 915-881-636 (www .munimadrid.es). During the summer, small temporary stands with

Madrid

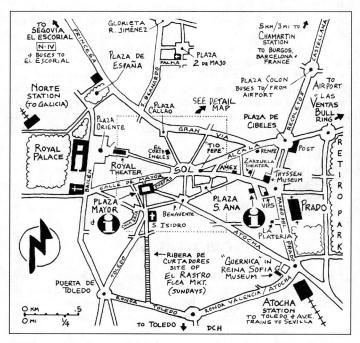

yellow umbrellas pop up at touristed places such as Puerta del Sol, and their yellow-shirted student guides are happy to help out lost tourists. Confirm your sightseeing plans and pick up a city map and the *Enjoy Madrid* publication. The free bus map has the most detailed map of the center. The TI has the latest on bullfights and zarzuela (the local light opera).

For entertainment listings, the TI's free *En Madrid/What's On* is not as good as the easy-to-decipher Spanish-language weekly entertainment guide *Guía del Ocio* (€1, sold at newsstands), which lists events, restaurants, and movies ("v.o." means a movie is in its original language rather than dubbed).

Arrival in Madrid

By Train: Madrid's two train stations, Atocha and Chamartin, are both on subway lines with easy access to downtown Madrid. Each station has all the services. Chamartin handles most international trains. Atocha generally covers southern Spain including the AVE trains to Sevilla. Both stations offer long-distance trains *(largo recorrido)* as well as smaller, local trains *(regionales and cercanias)* to nearby destinations. To travel between Chamartin and Atocha, don't bother with the subway (which involves a transfer)—the *cercanias* trains are faster (6/hr, 12 min, €1.20, free with railpass—show it at ticket window in the middle of the turnstiles, departing from Atocha's track 2 and generally Chamartin's track 2 or 3—but check the *Salidas Immediatas* board for the next departure).

Chamartin Station: The TI is opposite track 19. The impressively large *Centro de Viajes/Travel Center* customer-service office is in the middle of the building. You can use the Club Intercity lounge if you have a first-class railpass and first-class seat or sleeper reservations. The *cercanias* platforms cluster around track 5. The station's Metro stop is Chamartin. (If you arrive by Metro at Chamartin, follow signs to *Información* to get to the lobby rather than signs to *Vias*, which send you directly to the platforms.)

Atocha Station: Atocha is split into two halves, connected by a corridor of shops. On one side are the slick AVE trains, some Talgo trains, and a botanical garden. This side is in the towering old-station building, complete with birds, places to sit, a pharmacy (daily 8:00–23:00), a cafeteria, the good Samarcanda restaurant (Mon–Fri 13:00–20:00, Sat–Sun 11:00–20:00), and—likely for 2004—a TI (see below). On the other side of the station, you'll find the local *cercanias, regionales,* some Talgos, and the Metro stop named Atocha RENFE. (Note that the stop named simply "Atocha" is a different Metro stop in Madrid—not at the train station.)

Each side of the station has separate schedules; this can be confusing if you're in the wrong side of the building. The **TI** handles tourist info only—not train info (daily 9:00–21:00, 50 yards straight ahead of Metro's turnstiles on ground floor—but will likely move to the AVE hall in 2004). For train info, try the customer-service office called *Atención al Cliente* (daily 7:00–23:00); although there's one office for each half of the building, the office on the AVE side (just off the botanical garden) is more likely to speak English.

Atocha's Club AVE is a lounge reserved solely for AVE business-class travelers, and Sala Club is for first-class ticket-holders or Eurailers with a first-class reservation (both upstairs on AVE side of station, free drinks, newspapers, showers, and info service).

To buy tickets at Atocha for the local *cercanias* trains (for example, to Toledo), go to the middle of the *cercanias* side and get your ticket from ticket windows in the small rectangular offices (marked *Venta de Billetes sin reserva*). You can buy AVE and other long-distance train tickets in the bigger ticket offices in either half of the building; the airier *Taquillas* office on the AVE side (next to *Atención al Cliente* off the botanical garden) is more pleasant. Since station ticket offices can get really crowded, it's often quicker to buy your ticket at an

English-speaking travel agency (such as in El Corte Inglés Travel Agency at the bottom of the AVE area, or at the Puerta del Sol Corte Inglés—see "Helpful Hints," below) or at the downtown RENFE office, which offers train information, reservations, tickets, and minimal English (Mon–Fri 9:30–20:00, closed Sat–Sun, credit cards accepted, go in person, 2 blocks north of the Prado at Calle Alcala 44, tel. 902-240-202, www.renfe.es). For train travel to points onward, see "Transportation Connections" at the end of the chapter.

By Bus: Madrid's three key bus stations, all connected by Metro, are Larrea (for Segovia, Metro: Príncipe Pío), Estación Sur Autobuses (for Toledo, Ávila, and Granada, on top of Metro: Méndez Alvaro, tel. 914-684-200), and Estación Intercambiador (for El Escorial, in Metro: Moncloa).

By Plane: For information on Madrid's Barajas Airport, see "Transportation Connections" at the end of this chapter.

Getting around Madrid

By Subway: Madrid's subway is simple, speedy, and cheap (€1.10/ride, runs 6:00–1:30). The €5.20, 10-ride Metrobus ticket can be shared by several travelers and works on both the Metro and buses (sold at kiosks, tobacco shops, and in Metro). The city's broad streets can be hot and exhausting. A subway trip of even a stop or two saves time and energy. Most stations offer free maps (*navegamadrid;* www.metromadrid.es). Navigate by subway stops (shown on city maps). To transfer, follow signs to the next subway line (numbered and color-coded). End stops are used to indicate directions. Insert your ticket in the turnstile, then retrieve it as you pass through. Green *Salida* signs point to the exit. Using neighborhood maps and street signs to exit smartly can save lots of walking.

By Bus: City buses, while not as easy as the Metro, can be useful (bus maps at TI or info booth on Puerta del Sol, €1.10 tickets sold on bus, or €5.20 for a 10-ride Metrobus—see "By Subway," above; buses run 6:00–24:00).

By Taxi: Madrid's 15,000 taxis are easy to hail and reasonable (€1.50 drop, €0.85 per km, more at night and on weekends; €4 supplement for airport, €2 supplement for train/bus stations). These rates are *Tarifa 1* (Mon–Fri 6:00–22:00); rides at other times cost more. If your cabbie uses anything rather than *Tarifa 1* during these times, you're being cheated. Threesomes travel as cheaply by taxi as by subway. A ride from the Royal Palace to the Prado costs about €3.50.

Helpful Hints

Theft Alert: Be wary of pickpockets, anywhere, anytime, but particularly on Puerta del Sol (main square), the subway, and crowded streets. Assume a fight or any commotion is a scam to distract people about to become victims of a pickpocket. Wear your money belt. The small streets north of Gran Vía are particularly dangerous, even before nightfall. Muggings occur, but are rare. Victims of a theft can call 902-102-112 for help (English spoken).

Embassies: The U.S. Embassy is at Serrano 75 (tel. 915-872-200); the Canadian Embassy is at Nuñez de Balboa 35 (tel. 914-233-250).

Travel Agencies and Free Maps: The grand department store, El Corte Inglés, has two travel agencies (on first and seventh floors, Mon–Sat 10:00–22:00, just off Puerta del Sol) and gives out free Madrid maps (at information desk, immediately inside door, just off Puerta del Sol at intersection of Preciados and Tetuán; has post office and supermarket in basement). El Corte Inglés is taking over the entire intersection; the main store is the tallest building, with the biggest sign.

American Express: The AmEx office at Plaza Cortes 2 sells train and plane tickets, and even accepts Visa and MasterCard (Mon–Fri 9:00–19:30, Sat 10:00–14:00, closed Sun, 2 blocks from Metro: Banco de España, opposite Palace Hotel, tel. 913-225-445).

Books: For books in English, try **Fnac Callao** (Calle Preciados 8, tel. 915-956-190), **Casa del Libro** (English on ground floor in back, Gran Vía 29, tel. 915-212-219), and **El Corte Inglés** (guidebooks and some fiction, in its Libreria branch kitty-corner from main store, see listing within "Travel Agencies," above).

Laundry: The new, impeccable **Onda Blue** will wash, dry, and fold your laundry for €7 plus soap (self-service also available, change machines, 5 Internet terminals, daily 9:00–22:30, Leon 3, south of Plaza Santa Ana, tel. 913-695-071). The self-service Lavamatique across the street and half a block up is a less attractive option— older, fewer machines, no Internet—but it'll do in a pinch (Mon–Sat 9:00–20:00, closed Sun, Leon 8).

Internet Access: The popular **easyInternetcafe** offers 250 fast, cheap terminals 24/7 at Calle de la Montera (a block above Puerta del Sol and a block below piles of tattoo shops and prostitutes). **NavegaWeb,** centrally located at Gran Vía 30, is also good (daily 9:00–24:00). **BBiGG** is next to a Starbucks at Calle Alcalá 21 (daily 9:00–02:00, 300 terminals, near Puerta del Sol, tel. 916-647-700). **Zahara's** Internet café is at the corner of Gran Vía and Mesoneros (Mon–Fri 9:00–24:00, Sat–Sun 9:00–24:00).

TOURS

Madrid Vision Hop-On, Hop-Off Bus Tours—Madrid Vision offers three different hop-on, hop-off circuits of the city (historic, modern, and monuments). Buy a ticket (€10/1 day, €12/2 days) and you can hop from sight to sight and route to route as you like, listening to a recorded

MADRID AT A GLANCE

▲▲▲**Prado Museum** One of the world's great museums, loaded with masterpieces by Velázquez, Goya, El Greco, and Bosch. **Hours:** Tue–Sun 9:00–19:00, closed Mon.

▲▲▲**Bullfight** Spain's controversial pastime. **Hours:** Sundays and holidays March–mid-Oct, plus daily May–mid-June.

▲▲**Thyssen-Bornemisza Museum** A great complement to the Prado, with lesser-known yet still impressive works (especially good Impressionist collection). **Hours:** Tue–Sun 10:00–19:00, closed Mon.

▲▲**Centro Reina Sofia** Modern-art museum featuring Picasso's epic masterpiece *Guernica*. **Hours:** Mon and Wed–Sat 10:00–21:00, Sun 10:00–14:30, closed Tue.

▲▲**Royal Palace** Spain's sumptuous national palace, lavishly furnished. **Hours:** April–Sept Mon–Sat 9:00–18:00, Sun 9:30–14:30; Oct–March Mon–Sat 9:30–17:00, Sun 9:00–14:00.

▲▲**Zarzuela** Madrid's delightful light opera. **Hours:** Season roughly Jan–June.

▲**Retiro Park** Festive green escape from the city, with rental rowboats and great people-watching. **Hours:** Always open.

English commentary along the way. Each route has about 15 stops and takes about 75 minutes, with buses departing every 10 or 15 minutes. The three routes intersect at the south side of Puerta del Sol (at #5, daily 10:00–21:00, shorter in winter, tel. 917-791-888).

Walking Tours—British expatriate Stephen Drake-Jones gives entertaining, informative walks of historic old Madrid almost nightly (along with more specialized walks, such as Hemingway, Civil War, and Bloody Madrid). A historian with a passion for the memory of Wellington (the man who stopped Napoleon), Stephen is the founder and chairman of the Wellington Society. For €25 you become a member of the society for one year and get a free two-hour tour that includes stops at two bars for local drinks and tapas. Eccentric Stephen takes you back in time to sort out Madrid's Hapsburg and Bourbon history. Chairman Stephen likes his wine. If that's a problem, skip the tour. Tours start at the statue on Puerta del Sol (maximum 10 people, tel. 609-143-203 to confirm tour and reserve a spot, www.wellsoc.org,

▲El Rastro Europe's biggest flea market. **Hours:** Sun 9:00–15:00, best before 12:00.

Charles III's Botanical Garden A relaxing museum of plants, with specimens from around the world. **Hours:** Daily 10:00–20:00, until 18:00 in winter.

Naval Museum Seafaring history of a country famous for its Armada. **Hours:** Tue–Sun 10:00–13:30, closed Mon.

Chapel San Antonio de la Florida Church with Goya's tomb, plus frescoes by the artist. **Hours:** Tue–Fri 10:00–14:00 & 16:00–20:00, Sat–Sun 10:00–14:00, closed Mon, July and Aug only 10:00–14:00.

Royal Tapestry Factory Watch tapestries being made. **Hours:** Mon–Fri 10:00–13:30, closed Sat–Sun and Aug.

Moncloa Tower Elevator whisks you up to the best view in town. **Hours:** Tue–Fri 10:00–14:00 & 17:00–19:00, Sat–Sun 10:30–18:00, closed Mon.

Teleférico Cable car dangling over Madrid's city park. **Hours:** Daily from 12:00, July and Aug from 11:00.

chairman@wellsoc.org). Members of the Wellington Society can take advantage of Stephen's helpline (if you're in a Spanish jam, call him to translate and intervene) and assistance by e-mail (for questions on Spain, your itinerary, and so on). Stephen also does private tours and day trips to great spots in the countryside for small groups (about €350 per group per day, explained on his Web site).

LeTango Tourist Services—Carlos Galvin, a Spaniard who speaks flawless English (and has led tours for me since 1998), offers private tours when he's in Madrid. If he's out, his American wife, Jennifer, also works as a guide. Carlos mixes a city drive (for the big Madrid picture) with a historic walk (to get intimate with the old center and its ways). This gives a fine three-hour orientation and introduction to Madrid (€70 for individuals and groups up to 3...4 if you'll squeeze). Carlos and Jennifer can also arrange longer tours of both the city and the region (tel. 914-393-790, mobile 661-752-458, www.letango.com, carlos@letango.com).

Typical Big Bus City Sightseeing Tours—Juliatours offers standard, inexpensive guided bus tours departing from Gran Vía 68 (no reservations required—just show up 15 min before, tel. 915-599-605). Consider these tours: a three-hour city tour (€19, daily at 9:45 and 15:00); Madrid by Night (€12.50, a 2-hour floodlit overview, nightly at 20:30); Valley of the Fallen and El Escorial (€43, makes the day trip easy, covering both sights adequately with commentary en route, Tue–Sun at 8:45 and 15:00); and a marathon tour of El Escorial, Valley of the Fallen, and Toledo (€87, Tue–Sun at 8:30). If you want to pick up a rental car in Toledo, you could take this tour, stowing your luggage under the bus, then leave the tour at Toledo.

Introductory Walk: From Madrid's Puerta del Sol to the Royal Palace

Connect the sights with the following walking tour. Allow an hour for this half-mile walk, not including your palace visit.

▲▲**Puerta del Sol**—Named for a long-gone medieval gate with the sun carved onto it, Puerta del Sol is ground zero for Madrid. It's a hub for the Metro, buses, and pickpockets.

Stand by the statue of King Charles III and survey the square. Because of his enlightened urban policies, Charles III (who ruled until 1788) is affectionately called the "best mayor of Madrid." He decorated the city squares with fine fountains, got those meddlesome Jesuits out of city government, established the public school system, made the Retiro a public park rather than a royal retreat, and generally cleaned up Madrid.

Look behind the king. The statue of the bear pawing the strawberry bush and the madrono trees in the big planter boxes are symbols of the city. Bears used to live in the royal hunting grounds outside Madrid. And the madrono trees produce a berry that makes the traditional *madroño* liqueur.

The king faces a red-and-white building with a bell tower. This was Madrid's first post office, established by Charles III in the 1760s. Today it's the governor's office, though it's notorious for having been Franco's police headquarters. An amazing number of those detained and interrogated by the Franco police "tried to escape" by flying out the windows to their deaths. Notice the hats of the civil guardsmen at the entry. It's said the hats have square backsides so the men can lean against the wall while enjoying a cigarette.

Crowds fill the square on New Year's Eve as the rest of Madrid watches the action on TV. As Spain's "Big Ben" atop the governor's office chimes 12 times, Madrileños eat one grape for each ring to bring good luck through the coming year.

Cross Calle Mayor. Look at the curb directly in front of the entrance of the governor's office. The scuffed-up marker is "kilometer zero," marking the center of Spain. To the right of the entrance, the

Heart of Madrid

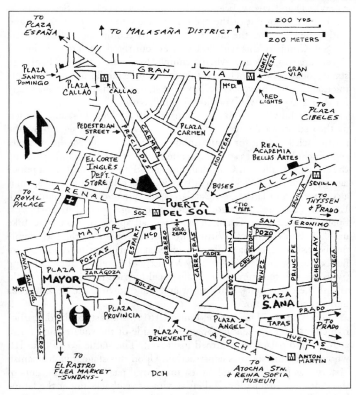

plaque on the wall marks the spot where the war against Napoleon started. Napoleon wanted his brother to be king of Spain. Trying to finagle this, Napoleon brought nearly the entire Spanish royal family to France for negotiations. An anxious crowd gathered outside this building awaiting word of the fate of their royal family. This was just after the French Revolution, and there was a general nervousness between France and Spain. When locals heard that Napoleon had appointed his brother as the new king of Spain, they gathered angrily in the streets. The French guard simply massacred the mob. Goya, who worked just up the street, observed the event and captured the tragedy in his paintings *2nd of May, 1808* and *3rd of May, 1808,* now in the Prado.

Walking from Puerta del Sol to Plaza Mayor: On the corner of Calle Mayor and Puerta del Sol, across from McDonald's, is the busy *confitería* Salon la Mallorquina (daily 9:00–21:00). Cross Calle Mayor to go inside. The shop is famous for its sweet Napolitana cream-filled pastry (€1) and savory, beef-filled *agujas* pastries (€1.50). See the racks with goodies hot out of the oven. Look back toward the entrance and notice the tile above the door with the 18th-century view of the Puerta del Sol. Compare this with today's view out the door. This was before the square was widened, when a church stood where the Tío Pepe sign stands today. The French used this church to detain local patriots awaiting execution. (The venerable Tío Pepe sign, advertising a famous sherry for over 100 years, was Madrid's first billboard.)

Cross busy Calle Mayor (again), round McDonald's, and veer left up the pedestrian alley called Calle de Postas. The street sign shows the post coach heading for that famous first post office. Medieval street signs included pictures so the illiterate could "read" them. Fifty yards up the street, at Calle San Cristobal, drop into Pans & Company, a popular sandwich chain. Pick up their translated flier illustrating that Spain is a country of four languages: Catalan (spoken in and around Barcelona), Euskera (Basque), Galego (a Gaelic language spoken in northwest Spain—Galicia), and Castilian (what we call Spanish). From here, hike up Calle San Cristobal. Within two blocks, you'll pass the local feminist bookshop (Libreria Mujeres) and reach a small square. At the square notice the big, brick 17th-century Ministry of Foreign Affairs building (with the pointed spire)—originally a jail for rich prisoners who could afford the cushy cells. Turn right and walk down Calle de Zaragoza under the arcade into...

▲**Plaza Mayor**—This square, built in 1619, is a vast, cobbled, traffic-free chunk of 17th-century Spain. Each side of the square is uniform, as if a grand palace were turned inside out. The statue is of Philip III, who ordered the square's construction. Upon this stage, much Spanish history was played out: bullfights, fires, royal pageantry, and events of the gruesome Inquisition. Reliefs serving as seatbacks under the lamp-posts tell the story. During the Inquisition, many were tried here. The guilty were paraded around the square (bleachers were built for bigger audiences, the wealthy rented balconies) with billboards listing their many sins. They were then burned. The fortunate were slowly strangled as they held a crucifix, hearing the reassuring words of a priest as this life was squeezed out of them.

The square is painted a democratic shade of burgundy—the result of a citywide vote. Since Franco's death in 1975, there's been a passion for voting here. Three different colors were painted as samples on the walls of this square, and the city voted for its favorite.

A stamp-and-coin market bustles here on Sundays from 10:00 to 14:00, and on any day it's a colorful and affordable place to enjoy a cup of coffee. Throughout Spain, lesser *plazas mayores* provide peaceful pools in the river of Spanish life. The TI is at #3, on the south side of the square. The building decorated with painted figures, on the north side of

From Plaza Mayor to the Royal Palace

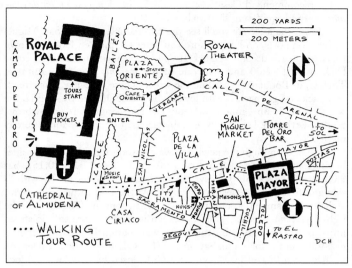

the square, is the Casa de la Panadería, which used to house the Bakers' Guild (interior closed to public).

The Torre del Oro Bar Andalu is a good place for a drink to finish off your Plaza Mayor visit (northwest corner of square, to the left of the Bakers' Guild, daily 8:00–15:00 & 18:00–24:00). This bar is a temple to bullfighting. Warning: They push expensive tapas on tourists. A *caña* (small beer) shouldn't cost more than €1.50. The bar's ambience is "Andalu" (Andalusian). Look under the stuffed head of Barbero the bull. At eye level you'll see a *puntilla*, the knife used to put a bull out of its misery at the arena. This was the knife used to kill Barbero.

Notice the breathtaking action captured in the bar's many photographs. At the end of the bar in a glass case is the "suit of lights" the great El Cordobes wore in his ill-fated 1967 fight. With Franco in attendance, El Cordobes went on and on, long after he could have ended the fight, until finally the bull gored him. El Cordobes survived; the bull didn't. Find Franco with El Cordobes at the far end, to the left of Segador the bull. Under the bull is a photo of El Cordobes' illegitimate son, El Cordobes, kissing a bull. Disowned by El Cordobes and using his dad's famous name after a court battle, El Cordobes is one of this generation's top fighters.

Walking from Plaza Mayor to the Royal Palace: Leave Plaza Mayor on Calle Ciudad Rodrigo (far right corner from where you entered the square, and to your right as you exit Torre del Oro). You'll pass a series of fine turn-of-the-20th-century storefronts and shops such as the recommended Casa Rua, famous for its cheap *bocadillos de calamares*—fried squid-ring sandwiches.

From the archway you'll see the covered Mercado de San Miguel (green iron posts, on left). Before you enter the market, look left down the street Cava de San Miguel. If you like sangria and singing, come back around 22:00 and visit one of the *mesones* (such as Guitarra, Tortilla, or Boquerón) that line the street. These cave-like bars stretch way back and get packed with locals who—emboldened by sangria, the setting, and Spain—might suddenly just start singing. It's a lowbrow, electric-keyboard, karaoke-type ambience, best on Friday and Saturday nights.

Wander through the newly renovated produce market and consider buying some fruit (Mon–Fri 9:00–14:30 & 17:15–20:15, Sat 9:00–14:30, closed Sun). Leave the market on the opposite (downhill) side and follow the pedestrian lane left. At the first corner, turn right, and cross the small plaza to the modern brick convent. The door on the right says *venta de dulces;* to buy inexpensive sweets from the cloistered nuns, buzz the *monjas* button, then wait patiently for the sister to respond over the intercom. Say *"dulces"* (DOOL-thays) and she'll let you in (Mon–Sat 9:30–13:00 & 16:00–18:30, closed Sun). When the lock buzzes, push open the door and follow the sign to *torno,* the lazy Susan that lets the sisters sell their baked goods without being seen (smallest quantities: half, or *medio,* kilo). Of the many choices (all good), consider *pastas de almendra* (crumbly) or *mantecados de yema* (moist and eggy).

Follow Calle del Codo (where those in need of bits of armor shopped—see the street sign) uphill around the convent to Plaza de la Villa, the city-hall square. Ahead, four flags—of city, state, nation, and Europe—grace the city hall building (city government offices are scheduled to move to Plaza de Cibeles sometime in 2004). The statue in the garden is of Don Bazan—mastermind of the Christian victory over the Muslims at the naval battle of Lepanto in 1571. This pivotal battle, fought off the coast of Greece, ended the Muslim threat to Christian Europe.

From here, busy Calle Mayor leads downhill a couple more blocks to the Royal Palace. Halfway down (on the left), there's a tiny square opposite the recommended Casa Ciriaco restaurant (#84). The statue memorializes the 1906 anarchist bombing that killed 23 people as the royal couple paraded by on their wedding day. While the crowd was throwing flowers, an anarchist threw a bouquet lashed to a bomb from a balcony of #84 (the building was a hotel at the time). Photos of the event hang just inside the door of the restaurant.

Continue down Calle Mayor. Within a couple of blocks you'll come to a busy street, Calle de Bailen. (The Garrido-Bailen music store is *the* place to stock up on castanets, unusual flutes, and Galician bagpipes.)

Across the busy street is the **Cathedral of Almudena,** Madrid's new cathedral. Built between 1883 and 1993, its exterior is a contemporary mix and its interior is neo-Gothic, with a colorful ceiling, glittering 5,000-pipe organ, and the 13th-century coffin (empty, painted leather on wood, in a chapel behind the altar) of Madrid's patron saint, Isidoro. Next to the cathedral is the...

▲▲**Royal Palace (Palacio Real)**—Europe's third-greatest palace (after Versailles and Vienna's Schönbrunn), with arguably the most sumptuous original interior, is packed with tourists and royal antiques. After a fortress burned down on this site, King Phillip V commissioned this huge 18th-century palace as a replacement. Though he ruled Spain for 40 years, Phillip V was very French (he was born in Versailles, and spoke French most of the time). He ordered this palace built to be his own Versailles (although his wife's Italian origin had a tremendous impact in the style). It's big—over 2,000 rooms with tons of luxurious tapestries, a king's ransom of chandeliers, priceless porcelain, and bronze decor covered in gold leaf. While the royal family lives in a mansion a few miles away, this place still functions as a royal palace and is used for formal state receptions and tourist daydreams.

   Cost, Hours, and Information: €7 without a tour, €8 with a tour, April–Sept Mon–Sat 9:00–18:00, Sun 9:30–14:30; Oct–March Mon–Sat 9:30–17:00, Sun 9:00–14:00, last tickets sold one hour before closing, palace can close without warning if needed for a royal function (you can call a day ahead to check, tel. 914-548-700). The palace is most crowded on Wednesdays, when it's free for locals. Metro: Opera. (Notice the beer-stein urinals—the rage in Madrid—in the WC just past the ticket booth.)

   Touring the Palace: A simple one-floor, 24-room, one-way circuit is open to the public. You can wander on your own or join an English tour (check time of next tour and decide as you buy your ticket; tours depart about every 20 min). The tour guides, like the museum guidebook, show a passion for meaningless data. Your ticket includes the armory and the pharmacy, both on the courtyard and worth a quick look. The €2 audioguides cover only marginally more of interest than what I describe below (and would never mention beer-stein urinals).

   Self-Guided Tour: If you tour the palace on your own, here are a few details beyond what you'll find on the little English descriptions posted in each room:

   1. The Palace Lobby: In the old days, horse-drawn carriages would drop you off here. Today, a sign divides the visitors waiting for a tour and those going in alone.

   2. The Grand Stairs: Fancy carpets are rolled down (notice the little metal bar-holding hooks) for formal occasions. At the top of the first landing, the blue and red coat of arms is of the current—and popular—constitutional monarch, Juan Carlos. While Franco chose him to be the next dictator, J. C. knew Spain was ripe for democracy. Rather than become "Juan the Brief" (as some were nicknaming him), he turned real power over to the parliament. You'll see his (figure) head on the back of the Spanish euro coin. At the top of the stairs (before entering first room, right of door) is a white marble bust of J.C.'s great-great-g-g-g-great-grandfather Phillip V. The grandson of France's King Louis XIV, he began the Bourbon dynasty in Spain in 1700. That dynasty survives today with Juan Carlos.

3. Guard Room: The guards hung out here. Notice the clocks. Charles IV, a great collector, amassed over 700—the 150 displayed in this palace are all in working order.

4. Hall of Columns: Originally a ballroom, today this room is used for formal ceremonies. (For example, this is the place where Spain formally joined the European Union in 1985—see plaque on far wall.) The tapestries (like most you'll see in the palace) are 17th-century Belgian.

5. Throne Room: Red velvet walls, lions, and frescoes of Spanish scenes symbolize the monarchy in this rococo riot. The chandeliers are the best in the house. The ceiling fresco, the last great work by Tiepolo, celebrates the vast Spanish empire—upon which the sun also never set. Find the American Indian (hint: follow the rainbow to the macho, red-caped conquistador). The throne is only from 1977. This is where ambassadors greet the king before dinner. He receives them relatively informally...standing rather than seated in the throne. Two rooms later you'll find...

6. Charles IV Antechamber: The four paintings are of King Charles IV (looking a bit like a dim-witted George Washington) and his wife (who wore the pants in the palace)—all originals by Goya. Velázquez's masterpiece *Las Meninas* originally hung here. The clock, showing Cronus, god of time, in marble, bronze, and wood, sits on a music box. The gilded decor you see throughout the palace is bronze with gold leaf.

7. Gasparini Room: This room, its painted stucco ceiling and inlaid Spanish marble floor restored in 1992, was the royal dressing room. The Asian influence was trendy at the time. Dressing, for a divine monarch, was a public affair. The court bigwigs would assemble here as the king, standing on a platform—notice the height of the mirrors—would pull on his leotards. In the next room, the silk wallpaper is new; notice the J.C.S. initials of King Juan Carlos and Queen Sofia. Passing through the silk room, you reach the...

8. Charles III Bedroom: Decorated in 19th-century neoclassical style, the bedroom is dominated by a chandelier in the shape of the fleur-de-lis (symbol of the Bourbon family). The thick walls separating each room hide service corridors for servants who scurried about generally unseen.

9. Porcelain Room: The 300 separate plates that line this room were disassembled for safety during the Civil War. (Find the little screws in the greenery that hide the seams.) The Yellow Room leads to the...

10. Gala Dining Room: Up to 12 times a year, the king entertains up to 150 guests at this bowling lane-size table—which can be extended to the length of the room. Find the two royal chairs. (Hint: With the modesty necessary for 21st-century monarchs, they are just a tad higher than the rest.) The parquet floor was the preferred dancing surface when balls were held in this fabulous room. The table in the next room would be lined with an exorbitantly caloric dessert buffet.

11. Cinema Room (Sala de Monedas y Medallas): In the early 20th century the royal family enjoyed "Sunday afternoons at the movies" here. Today it stores glass cases filled with coins and medals.

12. Stradivarius Room: The queen likes classical music. When you perform for her, do it with these precious 300-year-old violins. About 300 Antonius Stradivarius-made instruments survive. This is the only matching quartet: two violins, a viola, and a cello. The next room was the children's room—with kid-sized musical instruments.

13. Royal Chapel: The Royal Chapel is used only for private concerts and funerals. The royal coffin sits here before making the sad trip to El Escorial to join the rest of Spain's past royalty.

14. Queen's Boudoir: The next room was for the ladies, decorated just after Pompeii was excavated and therefore in fanciful ancient-Roman style. You'll exit down the same grand stairway you climbed 24 rooms ago.

15. Billiards and Smoking Rooms: The billiards room and the smoking room were for men only. The porcelain and silk of the smoking room imitates a Chinese opium den, which, in its day, was furnished only with pillows.

Across the courtyard is a fine park view and the **armory** displaying the armor and swords of El Cid, Ferdinand, Charles V, and Phillip II. Near the exit is a cafeteria and a bookstore, which has a variety of books on Spanish history.

As you leave the palace, walk around the corner to the left along the palace exterior to the grand yet people-friendly Plaza de Oriente. Throughout Europe, energetic governments are turning formerly car-congested wastelands into public spaces like this. Madrid's latest mayor is nicknamed "the mole" for all the digging he's doing. Where's all the traffic? Under your feet.

To return to Puerta del Sol: With your back to the palace, face the equestrian statue of Philip IV and (behind the statue) the Royal Theater (*Teatro Real,* neoclassical, rebuilt in 1997, open for visits Tue–Fri at 13:00, Sat–Sun at 11:30, closed Mon, tel. 915-160-660). Walk behind the Royal Theater (on the right, passing Café de Oriente—a favorite with theater-goers) to another square, where you'll find the Opera Metro stop and Calle Arenal—which leads back to Puerta del Sol.

SIGHTS

Madrid's Museum Neighborhood

Three great museums are in east Madrid. From the Prado to the Thyssen-Bornemisza Museum is a five-minute walk; Prado to Centro Reina Sofia is a 10-minute walk.

Museum Pass: If you plan to visit all three museums, you'll save 25 percent by buying the Paseo del Arte combo-ticket (€7.66, sold at each museum, valid for 1 year). Note that the Prado and Centro Reina Sofia museums are free on Saturday afternoon and Sunday (and anytime for those under 18 and over 65); the Prado and Thyssen-Bornemisza are closed Monday; and the Reina Sofia is closed Tuesday.

▲▲▲**Prado Museum**—The Prado holds my favorite collection of paintings anywhere. With more than 3,000 canvases, including entire rooms of masterpieces by Velázquez, Goya, El Greco, and Bosch, it's overwhelming. Pick up the English floor plan as you enter. Take a tour or buy a guidebook (or bring along the Prado chapter from *Rick Steves' Mona Winks*—available without maps and photos for free at www .ricksteves.com/prado). Focus on the Flemish and northern (Bosch, Dürer, Rubens), the Italian (Fra Angelico, Raphael, Titian), and the Spanish art (El Greco, Velázquez, Goya).

Follow Goya through his stages, from cheery *(The Parasol)* to political *(2nd of May, 1808 and 3rd of May, 1808)* to dark ("Negras de Goya": e.g., *Saturn Devouring His Children*). In each stage, Goya asserted his independence from artistic conventions. Even the standard court portraits from his "first" stage reflect his politically liberal viewpoint, subtly showing the vanity and stupidity of his royal patrons by the looks in their goony eyes. His political stage, with paintings such as the *3rd of May, 1808,* depicting a massacre of Spaniards by Napoleon's troops, makes him one of the first artists with a social conscience. Finally, in his gloomy "dark stage," Goya probed the inner world of fears and nightmares, anticipating our modern-day preoccupation with dreams.

Don't miss Velázquez's famous *Las Meninas,* a behind-the-scenes glimpse at royal life, showing Princess Margarita, her two attendants *(meninas),* a jester and a female dwarf, the family dog, and the painter himself—with King Phillip and his wife looking on unobserved.

Seek out Bosch's *The Garden of Earthly Delights*—a three-paneled altarpiece showing creation, the "transparency of earthly pleasures," and the resulting hell. Bosch's self-portrait looks out from hell (with the birds leading naked people around the brim of his hat), surrounded by people suffering eternal punishments appropriate to their primary earthly excesses.

The art is constantly rearranged by the Prado's management, so even the Prado's own maps and guidebooks are out of date. Regardless of the latest location, most art is grouped by painter, and better guards

Madrid's Museum Neighborhood

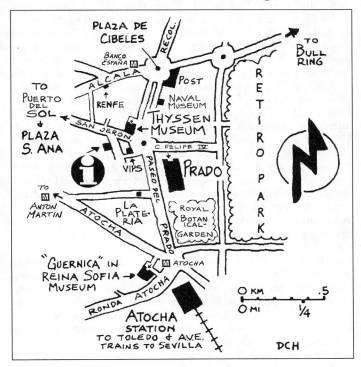

can point you in the right direction if you say, *"¿Dónde está...?"* and the painter's name as Españoled as you can (e.g., Titian is "Ticiano" and Bosch is "El Bosco"). The Murillo entrance—at the end closest to the Atocha train station—often has shorter lines. Lunchtime, from 14:00 to 16:00, is least crowded (€3; free all day Sun and to anyone under 18 and over 65; covered by €7.66 Paseo del Arte combo-ticket; Tue–Sun 9:00–19:00, closed Mon, last entry 30 min before closing; free, mandatory baggage check after your things are scanned just like at the airport; no water bottles inside; photos allowed but no flash; cafeteria in basement at Murillo end; Paseo de Prado, Metro: Banco de España or Atocha—each a 15-min walk from the museum, tel. 913-302-800, http://museoprado.mcu.es). Cabs picking you up at the Prado are likely to overcharge. Insist on the fare meter.

While you're in the neighborhood, consider a visit to the Charles III Botanical Garden (listed under "Near the Prado," below).

▲▲**Thyssen-Bornemisza Museum**—Locals call this stunning museum simply the Thyssen (TEE-sun). It displays the impressive collection that Baron Thyssen (a wealthy German married to a former Miss Spain) sold to Spain for $350 million. It's basically minor works by major artists and major works by minor artists (major works by major artists are in the Prado). But art lovers appreciate how the good baron's art complements the Prado's collection by filling in where the Prado is weak (such as Impressionism). For a delightful walk through art history, ride the elevator to the top floor and do the rooms in numerical order from Primitive Italian (room 1) to Surrealism and Pop Art (room 48). It's kitty-corner from the Prado at Paseo del Prado 8 in Palacio de Villahermosa (€5, or €7 to add current exhibition; covered by €7.66 Paseo del Arte combo-ticket, children under 12 enter free, Tue–Sun 10:00–19:00, closed Mon, ticket office closes at 18:30, audioguide-€3, free baggage check, café, shop, no photos, Metro: Banco de España or Atocha, tel. 914-203-944, www.museothyssen.org). If you're tired, hail a cab at the gate and zip straight to the Centro Reina Sofia.

▲▲**Centro Reina Sofia**—In this exceptional modern-art museum, ride the fancy glass elevator to the second floor and follow the room numbers for art from 1900 to 1950. The fourth floor continues the collection, from 1950 to 1980. The museum is most famous for Picasso's *Guernica* (room 6), an epic painting showing the horror of modern war. Guernica, a village in northern Spain, was the target of the world's first saturation-bombing raid, approved by Franco and carried out by Hitler. Notice the two rooms of studies for *Guernica,* filled with iron-nail tears and screaming mouths. *Guernica* was exiled to America until Franco's death, and now it reigns as Spain's national piece of art.

The museum also houses an easy-to-enjoy collection by other modern artists, including more of Picasso (3 rooms divide his art into pre-civil war, *Guernica,* and post-civil war) and a mind-bending room of Dalís (room 10). Enjoy a break in the shady courtyard before leaving (€3, free Sat afternoon after 14:30 and all day Sun, always free to those under 18 and over 65; covered by €7.66 Paseo del Arte combo-ticket; hardworking audioguide-€2.50, Mon and Wed–Sat 10:00–21:00, Sun 10:00–14:30, closed Tue, good brochure, no photos, no tours in English, free baggage check, Santa Isabel 52, Metro: Atocha, across from Atocha train station, look for exterior glass elevators, tel. 914-675-062, http://museoreinasofia.mcu.es).

Near the Prado

▲**Retiro Park**—Siesta in this 350-acre green and breezy escape from the city. At midday on Saturday and Sunday, the area around the lake becomes a street carnival, with jugglers, puppeteers, and lots of local color. These peaceful gardens offer great picnicking and people-watching. From the Retiro Metro stop, walk to the big lake (El Estanque), where you can cheaply rent a rowboat. Past the lake, a grand boulevard of statues leads to the Prado.

Charles III's Botanical Garden (Real Jardín Botánico)—After your Prado visit, you can take a lush and fragrant break in this sculpted park, wandering among trees from around the world. The flier in English explains that this is actually more than a park—it's a museum of plants (€1.50, daily 10:00–20:00, until 18:00 in winter, entry opposite Prado's Murillo entry, Plaza de Murillo 2).

Naval Museum—This tells the story of Spain's navy from the Armada to today (free, Tue–Sun 10:00–13:30, closed Mon, a block north of the Prado across boulevard from Thyssen-Bornemisza Museum, Paseo del Prado 5, entrance at Calle de Montalbán 2, 913-795-299).

More Madrid Sights

Chapel San Antonio de la Florida—Goya's tomb stares up at a splendid cupola filled with his own frescoes. On June 13, local ladies line up here to ask St. Anthony for a boyfriend, while outside a festival rages, with street musicians, food, and fun (free entry, Tue–Fri 10:00–14:00 & 16:00–20:00, Sat–Sun 10:00–14:00, closed Mon, July and Aug only 10:00–14:00, Glorieta de San Antonio de la Florida, Metro: Príncipe Pío, tel. 915-420-722). This chapel is near the bus station with service to Segovia. If you're day-tripping to Segovia, it's easy to stop by before or after your trip.

Hungry? Next door to the chapel is Restaurante Casa Mingo, popular for its cheap chicken, chorizo, and *cabrales* cheese served with cider. Ask the waiter to pour the cider for you. For dessert, try the *tarta de Santiago* almond cake (daily 11:00–24:00, Paseo de la Florida 34, tel. 915-477-918).

Royal Tapestry Factory (Real Fabrica de Tapices)—Have a look at the traditional making of tapestries (€2.50, some English tours, Mon–Fri 10:00–13:30, closed Sat–Sun and Aug, Calle Fuenterrabia 2, Metro: Menendez Pelayo, take Gutenberg exit, tel. 914-340-551). You can actually order a tailor-made tapestry (starting at $10,000).

Moncloa Tower (Faro de Moncloa)—This tower's elevator zips you up 300 feet to the best skyscraper view in town (€1, Tue–Fri 10:00–14:00 & 17:00–19:00, Sat–Sun 10:30–18:00, closed Mon, Metro: Moncloa, tel. 915-448-104). If you're going to El Escorial by bus, this is a convenient sight near the bus station.

Teleférico—For city views, ride this cable car from downtown over Madrid's sprawling city park to Casa de Campo (€2.85 one-way, €4.10 round-trip, daily from 12:00, July and Aug from 11:00, departs from Paseo del Pintor Rosales, Metro: Arguelles, tel. 915-417-450, www .teleferico.com). Do an immediate round-trip to skip Casa de Campo's strange mix of rental rowboats, prostitutes, a zoo, addicts, and an amusement park.

SHOPPING

Shoppers focus on the colorful pedestrian area between Gran Vía and Puerta del Sol. The giant Spanish department store El Corte Inglés is a block off Puerta del Sol and a handy place to pick up just about anything you need (Mon–Sat 10:00–21:30, closed Sun, free maps at info desk, supermarket in basement).

▲El Rastro—Europe's biggest flea market, held on Sundays and holidays, is a field day for shoppers, people-watchers, and thieves (9:00–15:00, best before 12:00). Thousands of stalls titillate more than a million browsers with mostly new junk. If you brake for garage sales, you'll pull a U-turn for El Rastro. Start at the Plaza Mayor, with its gentle coin-collectors market, and head south or take the subway to Tirso de Molina. Hang on to your wallet. Spin the wheel to try for two cookies for the price of one. Munch on a *pepito* (meat-filled pastry). Europe's biggest stamp market thrives simultaneously on Plaza Mayor.

NIGHTLIFE

▲▲▲Bullfight—Madrid's Plaza de Toros hosts Spain's top bullfights on Sundays and holidays from March through mid-October and nearly every day during the San Isidro festival (May through mid-June—generally sold out long in advance). Fights start between 17:00 and 19:00 (early in spring and fall, late in summer). Tickets range from €3.50 to €100. There are no bad seats at the Plaza de Toros; paying more gets you in the shade and/or closer to the gore. (The action often intentionally occurs in the shade to reward the expensive-ticket holders.) To be close to the bullring, choose areas 8, 9, and 10; for shade: 1, 2, 9, 10; for shade/sun: 3, 8; for the sun and cheapest seats: 4, 5, 6, 7. (Note that fights advertised as "Gran Novillada con Picadores" feature younger bulls and rookie matadors.)

Hotels and booking offices are convenient, but they add 20 percent and don't sell the cheap seats. Telephone both offices before you buy (Plaza Carmen 3—daily 9:30–13:30 & 16:00–19:00, tel. 915-312-732; and Calle Victoria 3—daily 10:00–14:00 & 17:00–19:00, tel. 915-211-213). To save money, stand in the bullring ticket line. About a thousand tickets are held back to be sold on the five days leading up to a fight, including the day of the fight. The bullring is at Calle Alcala 237 (Metro: Ventas, tel. 913-562-200, www.las-ventas.com).

Madrid's **bullfighting museum** is not as good as Sevilla's or Ronda's (Museo Taurino, at the back of bullring, free, Tue–Fri & Sun 9:30–14:30, closed Sat and Mon and early on fight days, tel. 917-251-857).

▲▲Zarzuela—For a delightful look at Spanish light opera that even English speakers can enjoy, try zarzuela. Guitar-strumming Napoleons in red capes; buxom women with masks, fans, and castanets; Spanish-speaking pharaohs; melodramatic spotlights; and aficionados clapping and singing along from the cheap seats where the acoustics are best—this is zarzuela...the people's opera. Originating in Madrid, zarzuela is known for its satiric humor and surprisingly good music. The season, which runs from January through June, features a mix of zarzuela and traditional opera. The rest of the year is devoted to ballet. You can buy tickets at Theater Zarzuela (€8–28, box office open 12:00–18:00 for advance tickets or until showtime for that day, Jovellanos 4, near the Prado, Metro: Banco de España, tel. 915-245-400, http://teatrodelazarzuela.mcu.es). The TI's monthly guide has a special zarzuela listing.

▲**Flamenco**—While Sevilla is the capital of flamenco, Madrid has two easy and affordable options.

Taberna Casa Patas attracts big-name flamenco artists. You'll quickly understand why this intimate (30-table) and smoky venue is called, literally, "the house of legs." Since this is for locals as well as tour groups, the flamenco is contemporary and may be jazzier than your notion—it depends on who's performing (€23 Mon–Thu at 22:00, €28 Fri–Sat at 21:00 and 24:00, closed Sun, 75–90 min, price includes cover and first drink, reservations smart, Canizares 10, tel. 914-298-471 or 913-690-496, www.casapatas.com). Its restaurant is a logical place for dinner before the show (€15–20 dinners, Mon–Sat from 20:00). Or, since this place is three blocks south of the recommended Plaza Santa Ana tapas bars, this could be your post-tapas-crawl entertainment.

Las Carboneras is more downscale—an easygoing, folksy little place a few steps from Plaza Mayor with a nightly 60-minute flamenco show (€20 includes a entry and a drink, €40 gets you a table up front with dinner and unlimited cheap drinks, Mon–Thu at 22:30, Fri–Sat at 23:00, closed Sun, earlier shows possible if a group books, reservations recommended, Plaza del Conde de Miranda 1, tel. 915-428-677, Ronan SE).

Regardless of what your hotel receptionist may want to sell you, other flamenco places like Arco de Cuchilleros (Calle de los Cuchilleros 7), Café de Chinitas (Calle Torija 7, just off Plaza Mayor), Corral de la Morería (Calle de Morería 17) and Torres Bermejas (off Gran Vía) are filled with tourists and pushy waiters.

Mesones—Just west of Plaza Mayor, the lane called Cava de San Miguel is lined with *mesones,* long, skinny cave-like bars famous for drinking and singing late into the night. Toss lowbrow locals, Spanish karaoke, electric keyboards, crass tourists, cheap sangria, and greasy calamari in a late-night blender and turn it on. Probably lively only on Friday and Saturday, but you're welcome to pop in to several and see what you can find.

SLEEPING

In the Pedestrian Zone between Puerta del Sol and Gran Vía

Predictable and away from the seediness, these are good values for those wanting to spend a little more. Their formal prices may be inflated, and some offer weekend and summer discounts whenever it's slow. Use Metro: Sol for all but Hotel Opera (Metro: Opera). See map on page 1,114 for location.

$$$ **Hotel Arosa** charges the same for all of its 134 rooms, whether they're sleekly remodeled Art Deco or just aging gracefully. Ask for a remodeled room with a terrace (Sb-€116, Db-€178, Tb-€240, 20 percent cheaper July–Aug, tax not included, breakfast-€13, air-con, memorably tiny triangular elevator, Calle Salud 21, a block off Plaza del Carmen, tel. 915-321-600, fax 915-313-127, arosa@hotelarosa.com).

$$$ The huge, business-class **Hotel Liabeny** has 222 plush, spacious rooms and all the comforts (Sb-€100, Db-€135, Tb-€155, 25 percent cheaper July–Aug, tax not included, breakfast-€12, air-con, if one room is smoky ask for another, off Plaza Carmen at Salud 3, tel. 915-319-000, fax 915-327-421, www.liabeny.com, liabeny@apunte.es).

$$$ **Hotel Opera,** a serious, modern hotel with 79 classy rooms, is located just off Plaza Isabel II, a four-block walk from Puerta del Sol toward the Royal Palace (Sb-€90, Db-€120, Db with big view terrace-€132, Tb-€156, tax not included, buffet breakfast-€8, air-con, elevator, ask for a higher floor—there are 8—to avoid street noise; consider their "singing dinners" offered nightly at 21:30, average price €42, reservations wise; Cuesta de Santo Domingo 2, Metro: Opera, tel. 915-412-800, fax 915-416-923, www.hotelopera.com, reservas@hotelopera.com). Hotel Opera's cafeteria is understandably popular.

$$$ **Hotel Santo Domingo** has artsy paintings, an inviting lounge, and 120 rooms, each decorated differently (Sb-€127, Db-€184, tax not included, pricier superior rooms are not necessary, air-con, elevator, non-smoking floor, facing Metro: Santo Domingo, Plaza de Santo Domingo 13, tel. 915-479-800, fax 915-475-995, www.hotelsantodomingo.com, reserva@hotelsantodomingo.com). Prices drop €30—and breakfast is included—on weekends (Fri–Sun) and July–Aug.

$$ **Hotel Europa** has red-carpet charm: a royal salon, plush halls with happy muzak, polished wood floors, an attentive staff, and 80 squeaky-clean rooms with balconies overlooking the pedestrian zone or an inner courtyard (Sb-€59, Db-€75, Tb-€105, Qb-€121, Quint/b-€135, tax not included, breakfast-€5.50, easy phone reservations with credit card, fans, elevator, fine lounge on 2nd floor, Calle del Carmen 4, tel. 915-212-900, fax 915-214-696, www.hoteleuropa.net, info@hoteleuropa .net, Antonio and Fernando Garaban and their helpful and jovial staff, Javi and Jim, SE). The convenient Europa cafeteria/restaurant next door

SLEEP CODE

(€1 = about $1.10, country code: 34)
Sleep Code: **S** = Single, **D** = Double/Twin, **T** = Triple, **Q** = Quad, **b** = bathroom, **s** = shower only, **no CC** = Credit Cards not accepted, **SE** = Speaks English, **NSE** = No English. Breakfast is not included unless noted; credit cards are accepted unless otherwise noted. In Madrid, the 7 percent IVA tax is sometimes included in the price.

To help you sort easily through these listings, I've divided the rooms into three categories based on the price for a standard double room with bath during high season:

    $$$ **Higher Priced**—Most rooms €100 or more.
    $$ **Moderately Priced**—Most rooms between €60–100.
    $ **Lower Priced**—Most rooms €60 or less.

Madrid has plenty of centrally located budget hotels and *pensiónes*. You'll have no trouble finding a sleepable double for €30, a good double for €60, and a modern air-conditioned double with all the comforts for €100. Prices are the same throughout the year, and it's almost always easy to find a place. Anticipate full hotels May 15 to May 25 (the festival of Madrid's patron Saint Isidro) and the last week in September (conventions). In July and August prices can be softer—ask about promotional deals. All of the accommodations I've listed are within a few minutes' walk of Puerta del Sol.

is a great scene, fun for breakfast, and a fine value any time of day.

    $$ Hotel Regente is a big and traditional place with 145 tastefully decorated but comfortable air-conditioned rooms, a great location, and a great value (Sb-€58, Db-€97, Tb-€126, tax not included, breakfast-€4.50, midway between Puerta del Sol and Plaza del Callao at Mesonero Romanos 9, tel. 915-212-941, fax 915-323-014, www.hotelregente.com, info@hotelregente.com).

    $$ Euromadrid Hotel—like a cross between a Motel 6 and an old hospital—rents 35 white rooms in a modern but well-worn shell (big Sb-€60, Db-€80, tight Tb-€96, includes buffet breakfast but not tax, air-con, discounted rate for parking-€13/day, Mesonero Romanos 7, tel. 915-217-200, fax 915-214-582, clasit@infonegocio.com).

    $$ The basic **Hotel Anaco** has a drab color scheme and a dreary lobby, but offers 39 quiet, comfortable rooms in a central location

(Sb-€74, Db-€93, Tb-€125, tax not included, breakfast-€4.20, air-con, elevator, non-smoking floor, Tres Cruces 3, a few steps off Plaza del Carmen and its underground parking lot-€12/day, tel. 915-224-604, fax 915-316-484, www.anacohotel.com, info@anacohotel.com).

$$ **Hotel Plaza Mayor,** with 30 newly renovated and solidly out-fitted rooms, is beautifully situated a block off Plaza Mayor (Sb-€48, Db-€70, corner "suite" Db-€85, Tb-€85, air-con, elevator, Calle Atocha 2, tel. 913-600-606, fax 913-600-610, www.h-plazamayor.com, info @h-plazamayor.com, Fedla and Eva SE).

$ **Hostal Acapulco,** overlooking the fine little Plaza del Carmen, rents 16 bright rooms with air-conditioning and all the big hotel gear. The neighborhood is quiet enough that it's smart to request a room with a balcony (Sb-€39, tiny Db-€47, Db-€49, Tb-€65, elevator, Salud 13, 4th floor, tel. 915-311-945, fax 915-322-329, hostal_acapulco@yahoo.es, Marco SE).

$ **Hostal Triana,** at the same address as Acapulco and also a fine deal, is bigger—with 40 rooms—and offers a little less charm for a little less money (Sb-€35, Db-€45, Tb-€60, €3 extra for air-con, taxes included, half the rooms have only fans, elevator, laundry service, Calle de la Salud 13, tel. 915-326-812, fax 915-229-729, www.hostaltriana .com, triana@hostaltriana.com, Victor Gonzalez SE).

$ **Hostales at Gran Vía 44:** The next three are in the same building at Gran Vía 44, overlooking the busy street. All are cheap and work in a jam. **Hostal Helena,** on the top floor, is a homey burgundy-under-heavy-drapes kind of place renting eight fine rooms. Enjoy the great little roof garden (S-€30, Ds-€42, Db-€50, Tb-€60, elevator, fans, Internet access, Gran Vía 44, tel. 915-411-529 or 915-217-585, hostal-helena@hotmail.com, NSE). The next two are well-worn with stark rooms and traffic noise: **Hostal Residencia Valencia** (Sb-€32, Ds-€44, Db-€47, Tb-€62, includes tax, 5th floor, tel. 915-221-115, fax 915-221-113, www.hostal-valencia.com, info@hostal-valencia.com, Antonio SE) and **Hostal Residencia Continental** (Sb-€36, Db-€47, Tb-€63, includes tax, fans, 3rd floor, tel. 915-214-640, fax 915-214-649, www .hostalcontinental.com, continental@mundivia.es, Andres SE).

On or near Plaza Santa Ana

The Plaza Santa Ana area has small, cheap places mixed in with fancy hotels. While the neighborhood is noisy at night, it has a rough but charming ambience, with colorful bars and a central location (3 min from Puerta del Sol's Tío Pepe sign; walk down Calle San Jerónimo and turn right on Príncipe; Metro: Sol). To locate hotels, see map on page 1,116.

$$$ **Suite Prado,** two blocks toward the Prado from Plaza Santa Ana, is a good value, offering 18 sprawling, elegant, air-conditioned

suites with a modern yet homey feel (suites are all the same size, charging €122 for single, €153 double, and €176 triple occupancy; sitting rooms, refrigerators, kitchens, 2nd kid free, breakfast at café next door–€4, elevator, Manuel Fernandez y Gonzalez 10, at intersection with Venture de la Vega, tel. 914-202-318, fax 914-200-559, www.suiteprado.com, hotel@suiteprado.com, Paula and Elena SE).

$ **Residencia Hostal Lisboa,** across the street from Suite Prado (above), is also a good value (25 rooms, Sb-€45, Db-€54, Tb-€75, air-con, elevator, Ventura de la Vega 17, tel. 914-294-676, fax 914-299-894, www.hostallisboa.com, hostallisboa@inves.es, SE).

$ **Hostal R. Veracruz II,** between Plaza Santa Ana and Puerta del Sol, rents 22 decent, quiet rooms (Sb-€36, Db-€50, Tb-€63, no breakfast, elevator, air-con, Victoria 1, 3rd floor, tel. 915-227-635, fax 915-226-749, NSE).

$ *Cheap Hostel Alternatives:* Because of the following two places, I list no Madrid youth hostels. At these cheap hotels, fluent Spanish is spoken, bathrooms are down the hall, and there's no heat during winter. For supercheap beds in a dingy time warp, consider **Hostal Lucense** (13 rooms, S-€15-18, D-€18-25, Db-€28-36, T-€38, €1.20 per shower, no CC, Nuñez de Arce 15, tel. 915-224-888, run by not-so-friendly Sr. and Sra. Michaela Garcia, both interesting characters, Sr. SE) and **Casa Huéspedes Poza** (14 rooms; same prices, street noise, and owners—but Sr. Daniel Muñoz does the cleaning; at Nuñez de Arce 9, tel. 915-224-871).

Near the Prado

$$$ **Hotel Green Lope de Vega** is your best business-class hotel value near the Prado. A four-star place that opened in 2000, it's a "cultural-themed" hotel inspired by the 18th-century writer Lope de Vega. It feels cozy and friendly for a formal business-class hotel (60 rooms, Sb-€102, Db-€128, Tb-€173, 1 child sleeps free, prices about 20 percent lower on weekends and during most of the summer, elevator, air-con, Internet access, parking–€17/day, Calle Lope de Vega 49, tel. 913-600-011, fax 914-292-391, www.hotellopedevega.com, lopedevega@hotellopedevega.com, SE).

$ *At Cervantes 34:* Two fine budget places are at Cervantes 34 (Metro: Anton Martin). **Hostal Gonzalo**—with 15 spotless, newly-painted, comfortable rooms, well run by friendly and helpful Javier—is deservedly in all the guidebooks. Reserve in advance (Sb-€42, Db-€50, Tb-€60, elevator, 3rd floor, tel. 914-292-714, fax 914-202-007). Downstairs, the nearly as polished **Hostal Cervantes,** also with 15 rooms and a fresh coat of paint, is likewise good (Sb-€45, Db-€55, Tb-€65; cheaper on weekdays, in low season, and for longer stays; 2nd floor, tel. 914-298-365, fax 914-292-745, www.hostal-cervantes.com, correo@hostal-cervantes.com, Fabio SE).

Madrid's Center: Hotels and Restaurants

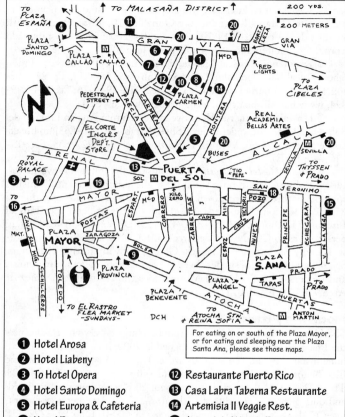

For eating on or south of the Plaza Mayor,
or for eating and sleeping near the Plaza
Santa Ana, please see those maps.

1 Hotel Arosa

2 Hotel Liabeny

3 To Hotel Opera

4 Hotel Santo Domingo

5 Hotel Europa & Cafeteria

6 Hotel Regente

7 Euromadrid Hotel

8 Hotel Anaco

9 Hotel Plaza Mayor

10 Hostals Acapulco & Triana

11 Hostales at Gran Vía 44

12 Restaurante Puerto Rico

13 Casa Labra Taberna Restaurante

14 Artemisia II Veggie Rest.

15 Artemisia I Veggie Rest.

16 To Casa Ciriaco

17 To La Bola Taberna & Café Ricordi

18 Bar Majaderitos

19 Chocolatería San Ginés

20 Internet Cafés (multiple locations)

EATING

In Spain, only Barcelona rivals Madrid for tastebud thrills. You have three dining choices: an atmospheric sit-down meal in a well-chosen restaurant, an unmemorable basic sit-down meal, or a stand-up meal of tapas in a bar or (more likely) several bars. Many restaurants are closed in August (especially through the last half).

Eating Cheaply North of Puerta del Sol

Restaurante Puerto Rico has good meals, great prices, and few tourists (€7.50 3-course *menu*, Mon–Sat 13:00–16:30 & 20:30–24:00, closed Sun, Chinchilla 2, between Puerta del Sol and Gran Vía, tel. 915-322-040).

Hotel Europa Cafeteria is a fun, high-energy scene with a mile-long bar, traditionally clad waiters, great people-watching, local cuisine, and a fines €8 lunch *menu* (daily 7:30–24:00, next to Hotel Europa, 50 yards off Puerta del Sol at Calle del Carmen 4, tel. 915-212-900).

El Corte Inglés' seventh-floor cafeteria is popular with locals (Mon–Sat 10:00–11:30 & 13:00–16:15 & 17:30–20:00, closed Sun, has non-smoking section, just off Puerta del Sol at intersection of Preciados and Tetuán).

Casa Labra Taberna Restaurante is famous among locals as the place where the Spanish Socialist Party was founded in 1879...and where you can get great cod. Packed with locals, it's a wonderful scene with three distinct sections: the stand-up bar (cheapest, 2 different lines for munchies and drinks), a peaceful little sit-down area in back (a little more expensive but still cheap; good €4 salads), and a fancy restaurant (€15 lunches). Their tasty little €1 *bacalao* (cod) dishes put it on the map. The waiters are fun to joke around with (daily 11:00–15:30 & 18:00–23:00, a block off Puerta del Sol at Calle Tetuán 12, tel. 915-310-081).

Vegetarian: Artemisia II is a hit with vegetarians who like good, healthy food in a smoke-free room (great €9 three-course lunch *menu* Mon–Fri only, daily 13:30–16:00 & 21:00–24:00, 2 blocks north of Puerta del Sol at Tres Cruces 4, a few steps off Plaza Carmen, tel. 915-218-721). **Artemisia I** is like its sister (same hours, 4 blocks east of Puerta del Sol at Ventura de la Vega 4 off San Jerónimo, tel. 914-295-092).

Plaza Mayor

Many Americans are drawn to Hemingway's favorite, **Sobrino del Botín** (daily 13:00–16:00 & 20:00–24:00, Cuchilleros 17, a block downhill from Plaza Mayor, tel. 913-664-217). It's touristy, pricey (€24–30 average), and the last place he'd go now...but still, people love it and the food is excellent. If phoning to make a reservation, choose between the downstairs (for dark, medieval-cellar ambience) or upstairs (for a still-traditional but airier and lighter elegance). While this restaurant boasts it's

Plaza Santa Ana Area

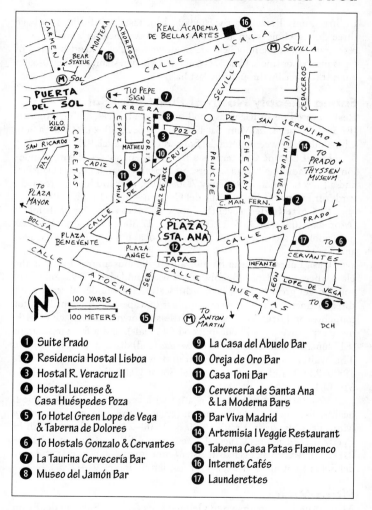

1. Suite Prado
2. Residencia Hostal Lisboa
3. Hostal R. Veracruz II
4. Hostal Lucense & Casa Huéspedes Poza
5. To Hotel Green Lope de Vega & Taberna de Dolores
6. To Hostals Gonzalo & Cervantes
7. La Taurina Cervecería Bar
8. Museo del Jamón Bar
9. La Casa del Abuelo Bar
10. Oreja de Oro Bar
11. Casa Toni Bar
12. Cervecería de Santa Ana & La Moderna Bars
13. Bar Viva Madrid
14. Artemisia I Veggie Restaurant
15. Taberna Casa Patas Flamenco
16. Internet Cafés
17. Launderettes

the oldest in the world (dating from 1725), a nearby restaurant brags, "Hemingway never ate here."

Restaurante los Galayos is less touristy and plenty *típico*, with good local cuisine (daily 8:00–24:00, lunch specials, lunch from 13:00, dinner anytime, arrive early or make a reservation, 30 yards off Plaza Mayor at Botoneras 5, tel. 913-663-028). For many, dinner right on the square at a sidewalk café is worth the premium (consider Cervecería Pulpito, southwest corner of the square at #10).

La Torre del Oro Bar Andalu on Plaza Mayor has soul. Die-hard bullfight aficionados hate the gimmicky Bull Bar listed under "Tapas," below. Here the walls are lined with grisly bullfight photos from annual photo competitions (read the gory description in "Introductory Walk," above). Have a drink but establish all prices first. Don't let the aggressive staff bully you into high-priced tapas you don't want (daily 8:00–15:00 & 18:00–24:00, closed Jan, Plaza Mayor 26, tel. 913-665-016).

Plaza Mayor is famous for its *bocadillos de calamares*. For a cheap and tasty squid-ring sandwich, line up at **Casa Rua** at Plaza Mayor's northwest corner, a few steps up Calle Ciudad Rodrigo (daily 9:00–23:00). Hanging up behind the bar is a photo/ad of Plaza Mayor from the 1950s, when the square contained a park.

Calle Cava Baja, South of Plaza Mayor

Few tourists frequent this traditional neighborhood—Barrio de los Austrias, named for the Hapsburgs. It's three minutes south of Plaza Mayor, or a 10-minute walk from Puerta del Sol. The street, Cava Baja, is lined with a diverse array of restaurants and tapas bars and clogged with locals out in search of a special meal. For a good authentic Madrileño dinner experience, take time to survey the many places along this street between the first and last listings described below and choose your favorite. A key wine-drinking phrase is *mucho cuerpo* (full-bodied).

Posada de la Villa serves Castilian cuisine in a 17th-century posada. Peek into the big oven to see what's cooking (€30 meals, Mon–Sat 13:00–16:00 & 20:00–24:00, closed Sun and Aug, Calle Cava Baja 9, tel. 913-661-860).

El Schotis is less expensive and specializes in meat and fish dishes. Named after a popular local dance, the restaurant retains the traditional character of old Madrid (daily 12:00–17:00 & 20:00–24:00, Calle Cava Baja 11, tel. 913-653-230).

Julian de Tolosa, a classy, pricey, elegantly simple place popular with locals who know good food, offers a small, quality menu of Navarra region cuisine from T-bone steak *(chuletón)* to red *tolosa* beans (Mon–Sat 13:30–16:00 & 21:00–24:00, Sun 13:30–16:00, when having lunch claim your free aperitif with this book, Calle Cava Baja 18, tel. 913-658-210).

Taberna los Lucio has good tapas, salads, *huevos estrellados* (scrambled eggs with potatoes), and wine (Wed–Mon 13:00–16:00 & 20:30–24:00, closed Tue, Calle Cava Baja 30, tel. 913-662-984).

For a splurge, dine with power-dressing locals at **Casa Lucio.** While the king and queen of Spain eat here, it's more stuffy than expensive (daily 13:00–17:00 & 21:00–24:00, Calle Cava Baja 35; unless you're the king or queen, reserve several days in advance, tel. 913-653-252).

South of Plaza Mayor

1 Sobrino del Botín
2 Rest. los Galayos
3 La Torre del Oro Bar Andalu
4 Casa Rua
5 Posada de la Villa
6 El Schotis
7 Julian de Tolosa
8 Taberna los Lucio

9 Casa Lucio
10 Taberna Tempranillo
11 El Madroño
12 Taberna los Austrias
13 Taberna de los 100 Vinos
14 Las Carboneras Flamenco
15 Mesones (cave bars)

Taberna Tempranillo, ideal for hungry wine-lovers, offers tapas and 250 kinds of wine. Use their fascinating English menu to assemble your dream meal. Arrive by 20:00 or wait (daily 13:00–15:30 & 20:00–24:00, closed Aug, Cava Baja 38, tel. 913-641-532).

Tapas-Hopping on Calle del Nuncio (near Calle Cava Baja)

El Madroño ("The Strawberry Tree," a symbol of Madrid) is a fun tapas bar that preserves chunks of old Madrid. A tile copy of Velázquez's famous *Drinkers* grins from its facade. Inside, look above the stairs for photos of 1902 Madrid. Study the coats of arms of Madrid through the centuries as you try a *vermut* on tap and a €2 sandwich, or ask to try the *licor de Madroño* (€7.80 lunch *menu* also available, Tue–Sun 9:00–17:00 & 20:00–24:00, closed Mon, Plaza Puerta Cerrada 7, tel. 913-645-629).

Taberna los Austrias, two blocks away, serves tapas, salads, and light meals on wood-barrel tables (daily 12:00–16:00 & 20:00–24:00, Calle Nuncio 17).

Next door is the very hip and popular **Taberna de los 100 Vinos** ("Tavern of 100 Wines"), a classy wine bar serving top-end tapas and fine wine by the glass—see the chalkboard. Eat delicious €3.25 *pinchos* standing up, or sit down for excellent €10 *raciones* (Tue–Sat 13:00–16:00 & 20:00–24:00, closed Sun–Mon, Calle Nuncio 17).

Near the Royal Palace

Casa Ciriaco is popular with locals who appreciate good traditional cooking (€25 meals, Thu–Tue 13:30–16:00 & 20:30–24:00, closed Wed and Aug, halfway between Puerta del Sol and the Royal Palace at Calle Mayor 84, tel. 915-480-620). It was from this building in 1906 that an anarchist bombed the royal couple on their wedding day (for details, see "Introductory Walk," above). A photo of the carnage is inside the front door.

La Bola Taberna specializes in *cocido Madrileño*—Madrid stew. This is a touristy but tastefully elegant and friendly place stewing various meats, carrots, and garbanzo beans in earthen jugs. The €15 stew, which consists of two courses (first you enjoy the broth as a soup) is big enough to split (weekdays 13:00–16:00 & 20:30–23:00, often closed Sat–Sun, cash only, midway between the Royal Palace and Gran Vía at Calle Bola 5, tel. 915-476-930).

Café Ricordi, just a block from the Royal Theater, is a delightfully romantic little spot, perfect for theatergoers. You can enjoy tiny sandwiches with a glass of wine, coffee, and an elegant sweet, or a full meal in this café/bar/restaurant (Mon–Sat 12:00–24:00, closed Sun, Calle Arrieta 5, tel. 915-479-200).

Near the Prado

Each of the big-three art museums has a decent cafeteria. Or choose from these three places, all within a block of the Prado:

La Plateria Bar Museo is a hardworking little café/wine bar with a good menu for tapas, light meals, and hearty salads (listed as *raciones* and *1/2 raciones* on the chalkboard). Its tables spill onto the leafy little Plaza de Platarías de Matínez (daily 7:30–24:00, directly across busy boulevard Paseo del Prado from Atocha end of Prado, tel. 914-291-722).

Taberna de Dolores, a winning formula since 1908, is a commotion of locals enjoying €2 *canapes* (open-face sandwiches), tasty *almejas* (clams), and *cañas* (small beers) at the bar or at a few tables in the back (daily 13:00–24:00, Plaza de Jesús 4, tel. 914-292-243).

VIPS is where good-looking young tour guides eat cheap and filling salads. This bright, popular chain restaurant is engulfed in a big bookstore (daily 9:00–24:00, across Paseo del Prado boulevard from northern end of Prado in Galería del Prado under Palace Hotel facing Plaza Canovas). Spain's first Starbucks opened in April 2001, just next door.

Fast Food and Picnics

Fast Food: For an easy, light, cheap meal, try Rodilla—a popular sandwich chain with a shop on the northeast corner of Puerta del Sol at #13 (Mon–Fri 9:30–23:00, opens on Sat at 10:00, Sun at 11:00). Pans & Company, with shops throughout Madrid and Spain, offers healthy, tasty sandwiches and chef's salads (daily 9:00–24:00, on Puerta del Sol, Plaza Callão, Gran Vía 30, and many more).

Picnics: The department store El Corte Inglés has a well-stocked deli downstairs (Mon–Sat 10:00–22:00, closed Sun). A perfect place to assemble a cheap picnic is downtown Madrid's neighborhood market, Mercado de San Miguel. How about breakfast surrounded by early-morning shoppers in the market's café? (Mon–Fri 9:00–14:30 & 17:15–20:15, Sat 9:00–14:30, closed Sun; to reach the market from Plaza Mayor, face the colorfully painted building and exit from the upper left-hand corner.) The Museo del Jamón (Museum of Ham) sells cheap picnics to go (see tapas pub-crawl dinner below).

Churros con Chocolate

If you like a Danish and coffee in American greasy-spoon joints, you must try the Spanish equivalent: Greasy *churros* (or the thicker *porras*) dipped in pudding-like hot chocolate. Bar Majaderitos is a good bet (daily 7:00–22:30, Sun from 9:00, best in morning, 2 blocks off Tío Pepe end of Puerta del Sol, south on Espoz y Mina, turn right on Calle de Cadiz). Their tasty grilled cheese sandwich (with ham and/or egg) rounds out your breakfast. With luck, the *churros* machine in the back will be cooking. Notice the expressive WC signs.

The classy Chocolatería San Ginés is much loved by locals for its *churros* and chocolate (Tue–Sun 18:00–7:00, closed Mon). While empty before midnight, it's packed with the disco crowd in the wee hours; the popular Joy disco is next door. Dunk your *churros* into the pudding-like hot chocolate, as locals have done here for over 100 years (from Puerta del Sol, take Calle Arenal 2 blocks west, turn left on book-lined Pasadizo de San Ginés, you'll see the café—it's at #5, tel. 933-656-546).

Tapas: The Madrid Pub-Crawl Dinner

For maximum fun, people, and atmosphere, go mobile and do the "tapa tango," a local tradition of going from one bar to the next, munching, drinking, and socializing. Tapas are the toothpick appetizers, salads, and deep-fried foods served in most bars. Madrid is Spain's tapa capital—tapas just don't get any better. Grab a toothpick and stab something strange, but establish the prices first, especially if you're on a tight budget or at a possible tourist trap. Some items are very pricey, and most bars push larger *raciones* rather than smaller tapas. The real action begins late (around 20:00). But for beginners, an earlier start, with less commotion, can be easier. The litter on the floor is normal; that's where people traditionally toss their trash and shells. Don't worry about paying until you're ready to go. Then ask for *la cuenta* (the bill).

Very important: Before embarking upon this culinary adventure (which could, if done properly, be a highlight of your trip), study and use the "Tasty Tapas Terms" section in this chapter.

Prowl the area between Puerta del Sol and Plaza Santa Ana. There's no ideal route, but the little streets (in this book's map) between Puerta del Sol, San Jerónimo, and Plaza Santa Ana hold tasty surprises. Nearby, the street Jesús de Medinaceli is also lined with popular tapas bars. Below is a five-stop tapa crawl. These places are good, but don't be blind to making discoveries on your own.

1. From Puerta del Sol, walk east a block down Carrera de San Jerónimo to the corner of Calle Victoria. Across from the Museo del Jamón, you'll find **La Taurina Cervecería,** a bullfighters' Planet Hollywood (daily 8:00–24:00). Wander among trophies and historic photographs. Each stuffed bull's head is named, along with its farm, awards, and who killed him. Among the many gory photos study the first post: It's Che Guevara, Orson Welles, and Salvador Dalí, all enjoying a good fight. Around the corner, the Babe Ruth of bullfighters, El Cordobes, lies wounded in bed. The photo below shows him in action. Kick off your pub crawl with a drink here. Inspired, I went for the *rabo de toro* (bull-tail stew, €10.50)—and regretted it. If a fight's on, the place will be packed with aficionados gathered around the TV. Across the street at San Jerónimo 5 is the...

2. Museo del Jamón (Museum of Ham), tastefully decorated—unless you're a pig (or vegetarian). This frenetic, cheap, stand-up bar is an assembly line of fast and simple *bocadillos* and *raciones*. Options are

TASTY TAPAS TERMS

Quanto cuesta una tapa?—
How much does one tapa
cost?
pinchos—bite-size portions
tapas—snack-size portions
raciones—larger portions (half
a meal)
fritos—it's fried
la plancha—it's sauteed
aceitunas—olives
almendras—fried almonds
atun—tuna
bacalao—cod
banderilla—small skewer of
pickled olives, carrots,
and onions (the "mata-
dor's spear")
berenjenas—deep-fried eggplant
bombas—fried meat and potatoes ball
boquerones—fresh anchovies
calamares fritos—fried squid
rings
caracoles—snails (May-Sept)
cazon en adabo—marinated
white fish
champiñones—mushrooms
chorizo—spicy sausage
croquetas de...—greasy breaded
balls of milky flour paste
with...

empanadillas—pastries stuffed
with meat or seafood
ensaladas (rusa)—salads (Russian)
espinacas (con garbanzos)—
spinach (with garbanzo
beans)
gambas (a la plancha, al ajillo)—
shrimp (sauteed, with
garlic)
gazpacho—cold tomato and garlic
soup
guiso—stew
jamón Ibérico—best ham, from
acorn-fed baby pigs
jamón blanco—cheaper "white"
ham
jamón serrano—cured ham
langostinos—prawns
lomo—pork
mejillones—mussels
orejas—pigs' ears
pan—bread
paella—saffron rice dish with fish
(when it appears fresh out of
the kitchen, ask for it)
patatas bravas—fried chunks of
potato with creamy tomato
sauce
pescaditos fritos—assortment of
fried little fish
picos—little breadsticks (free)

shown in photographs with prices. For a small sandwich, ask for a *chiq-uito* (€0.60, unadvertised). The best ham is the pricey *jamón ibérico*—from pigs who led stress-free lives in acorn-strewn valleys. Just point and eat, but be specific; a *jamón blanco* portion costs only €5, while *jamón ibérico* costs €12 (daily 9:00–24:00, sit-down restaurant upstairs). Next, forage halfway up Calle Victoria to the tiny...

   3. La Casa del Abuelo, for seafood-lovers who savor sizzling plates of tasty little *gambas* (shrimp) and *langostinos* (prawns). Try *gambas a la*

pimientos de padron—green peppers

pisto—mixed sautéed vegetables

pulpo—octopus

queso—cheese

queso manchego—sheep's cheese

rabas—squid tentacles

rabo de toro—bull-tail stew

revuelto de...—scrambled with...

salchichon—sausage

setas—wild mushrooms

tortilla de jamon/queso—potato omelet with ham/cheese

Sandwich Sizes

bocadillo—baguette sandwiches, cheap and basic, a tapa on bread

chiquito, montadito—small bocadillo

flauta—sandwich made with flute-thin baguette

canape—tiny open-faced sandwich

sandwich (toast)—Wonder bread (toasted) with meat and/or cheese

con jamón, queso, mixto—with ham, cheese, both

Drinks

aqua con/sin gas—water with/without bubbles

un vaso de aque del grifo—glass of tap water

una jarra de agua—pitcher of tap water

refresco—soft drink

caña—small glass of draft beer

coble—tall glass of beer

tinto de la casa—red wine of the house

un tinto—a small glass of house red wine

chato—small glass of house wine

Rioja—a region known for quality red wine

ribeiro—cloudy Galician-style wine

tinto de verano—a lighter Sangria

mucho cuerpo—full-bodied

afrutado—fruity

seco—dry

dulce—sweet

¡Salud!—cheers!

For quality wine, ask for *crianza* (old), *reserva* (older) or *gran reserva* (oldest).

---

plancha (grilled shrimp, €4.15) or *gambas al ajillo* (ahh-HHEEE-yoh, shrimp version of escargot, cooked in oil and garlic and ideal for bread dipping, €5.80), and a €1.20 glass of red wine (daily 11:30–15:30 & 18:30–23:30, Calle Victoria 12). Across the street is...

4. Oreja de Oro ("Golden Ear"), named for what it sells—sautéed pigs' ears (*oreja*, €2.50). While pigs' ears are a Madrid specialty, this place is Galician, so people also come here for *pulpo* (octopus, €8.50), *pimientos de padron* (green peppers...some sweet and a few hot surprises,

€3), and the distinctive *ribeiro* (ree-BAY-roh) wine, served Galician-style, in characteristic little ceramic bowls (to disguise its lack of clarity). Jaime is a frantic one-man show who somehow gets everything just right. Have fun at this place. For a perfect finale, continue uphill and around the corner to...

5. Casa Toni, for refreshing bowls of gazpacho—the cold tomato-and-garlic soup (€1.50, available all year but only popular when temperatures soar). Their specialties are *berenjena* (deep-fried slices of eggplant, €3.60) and *champiñones* (sautéed mushrooms, €3.70; open daily 11:30–16:00 & 18:00–23:30, closed July, also good for sit-down meal, Calle Cruz 14).

More Options: If you're hungry for more, and want a more trendy, up-to-date tapas scene, head for Plaza Santa Ana. The south side of the square is lined with lively bars offering good tapas, drinks, and a classic setting right on the square. Consider **Cervecería de Santa Ana** (tasty tapas with two zones: rowdy beer-hall and classier sit-down) and **La Moderna** (wine, pâté, and cheese plates).

If you're picking up speed and looking for a place filled with old tiles and young people, power into **Bar Viva Madrid** (Calle Manuel Fernandez y Gonzalez, tel. 914-293-640). The same street has other late-night bars filled with music.

TRANSPORTATION CONNECTIONS

By train to: Toledo (3/day, 1 hr, from Madrid's Atocha station—the *cercanias* (theyr-kah-NEE-ahz) section, not the AVE section; if day-tripping, there's a direct Madrid-Toledo express at 8:34 and a Toledo-Madrid express at 18:56; a proposed Madrid-Toledo AVE train will cut the journey to 15–20 min), **Segovia** (9/day, 2 hrs, both Chamartin and Atocha stations), **Ávila** (8/day, 90 min, from Chamartin and Atocha), **Salamanca** (5/day, 2.5 hrs, from Chamartin), **Barcelona** (7/day, 7–9 hrs, mostly from Chamartin, 2 overnight), **Granada** (2/day, 6 hrs), **Sevilla** (18/day, 2.5 hrs by AVE; 2 slower Talgos/day, 3.5 hrs; both from Atocha), **Córdoba** (18 AVE trains/day, 2 hrs, from Atocha, 12 Talgos/day, 2 hrs), **Málaga** (6/day, 4 hrs, from Atocha), **Lisbon** (1/day departing at 20:45, 10 hrs, pricey overnight Hotel Train from Chamartin), **Paris** (4/day, 12–16 hrs, 1 direct overnight—an expensive Hotel Train, from Chamartin).

By bus to: Ávila (€9.67 round-trip, 8/day, 2 hrs), **Toledo** (2/hr, 60–75 min), and **Granada** (9/day, 5 hrs)—catch bus from Estación sur Autobuses (which sits squarely atop Metro: Méndez Alvaro, with eateries and a small TI—open daily 9:00–20:45, Avenida de Méndez Alvaro, tel. 914-684-200).

Madrid's Barajas Airport

Ten miles east of downtown, Madrid's modern airport has three terminals. You'll likely land at Terminal 1, which has a helpful English-speaking **TI** (marked "Oficina de Información Turística," open Mon–Fri
8:00–20:00, Sat 9:00–13:00, closed Sun, tel. 913-058-656); an **ATM**
(part of the BBVA bank) far busier than the lonely American Express
window; a 24-hour **exchange office** (plus shorter-hour exchange
offices); a **flight info office** (marked simply "Information" in airport
lobby, open 24 hrs/day, tel. 902-353-570); a **post-office** window; a
pharmacy; lots of **phones** (buy a phone card from the machine near the
phones); a few scattered **Internet** terminals (small fee); **eateries;** a
RENFE office (where you can get train info and buy train tickets; daily
8:00–21:00, tel. 913-058-544); and on-the-spot **car-rental agencies** (see
above). The three terminals are connected by long indoor walkways; it's
about an eight-minute walk between terminals (the Metro is in
Terminal 2).

Iberia is Spain's airline, connecting many cities in Spain as well as
international destinations (Velázquez 130, phone answered 24 hrs/day,
tel. 902-400-500, www.iberia.com).

Getting between the Airport and Downtown: By public transport,
consider an affordable, efficient **airport bus/taxi combination.** Take the
airport bus (#89, usually blue) from the airport to Madrid's Plaza Colón
(€2.40, 4/hr, 20–30 min, leaves Madrid 4:30–24:00, leaves airport
5:15–2:00; stops at both Terminals 1 and 2; at the airport the bus stop is
outside Terminal 1's arrivals door—cross the street filled with taxis to
reach stop marked "Bus" on median strip; at Plaza Colón the stop is usually underground, though may be above ground at Calle Serrano). Then,
to reach your hotel from Plaza Colón, catch a taxi (insist on meter, ride
to hotel should be far less than €6; to avoid €2 supplement charge for
rides from a bus station, it's a little cheaper to go upstairs and flag down
a taxi). Or from Plaza Colón, take the subway (from the underground
bus stop, walk up the stairs and face the blue "URBIS" sign high on a
building—the subway stop, M. Serrano, is 50 yards to your right; it takes
one transfer at Bilbao to reach Puerta del Sol). At the airport, remember
it's bus #89 you want; ignore bus #101, a holdover from the time when
the airport didn't have a Metro stop (it runs to the Canillejas Metro stop
on Madrid's outskirts).

Consider the simpler though pricier **AeroCity shuttle bus service,**
which provides door-to-door transport for EUR17 (runs 24 hrs, price
includes one piece of luggage and one carry-on, can book at one of their
desks at the airport: Terminal 1—near arrival gate 2, Terminal 2—
between arrival gates 5 & 6; or reserve in advance online or by phone or
fax; credit card holds reservation, but payment required in cash; tel. 917-
477-570, fax 917-481-114, www.aerocity.com).

You can take the **Metro** all the way between the airport and down-town (with transfers). The airport's futuristic Aeropuerto Metro stop in Terminal 2 provides a cheap way into town (€1.10, or get a shareable 10-pack for €5.20). Access the Metro at the check-in level; to reach the Metro from Terminal 1's arrivals level, stand with your back to the baggage claim, then go to your far right, up the stairs, and follow red-and-blue Metro diamond signs to the station (8-min walk). To get to Puerta del Sol, take line #8 12 minutes to Nuevos Ministerios, then continue on line #10 to Tribunal, then line #1 to Puerto del Sol (30 min more total); or exit at Nuevos Ministerios and take a €5 taxi or bus #150 straight to Puerto del Sol.

For a **taxi** to or from the airport, allow €20 (€4 airport supplement is legal). Cabbies routinely try to get €30—a rip-off. Insist on the meter.

TOLEDO

An hour south of Madrid, Toledo teems with tourists, souvenirs, and great art by day, delicious roast suckling pig, echoes of El Greco, and medieval magic by night. Incredibly well preserved and full of cultural wonder, the entire city has been declared a national monument.

Spain's historic capital is 3,500 years of tangled history—Roman, Visigothic, Moorish, and Christian—crowded onto a high, rocky perch protected on three sides by the Tajo (Tagus) River. It's so well preserved that the Spanish government has forbidden any modern exteriors. The rich mix of Jewish, Moorish, and Christian heritages makes it one of Europe's art capitals.

Perched strategically in the center of Iberia, Toledo was for centuries a Roman transportation hub with a thriving Jewish population. The city was a Visigothic capital back in 554 and—after a period of Moorish rule—Spain's political capital until 1561, when it reached its natural limits of growth as defined by the Tajo River Gorge. During its Golden Age, Toledo was famous for intellectual tolerance—a city for the humanities, where God was known by many names. When the king moved to more spacious Madrid, Toledo was mothballed, only to be rediscovered by 19th-century Romantic travelers who wrote of it as a mystical place.

Today Toledo thrives as a provincial capital and a busy tourist attraction. It remains the historic, artistic, and spiritual center of Spain. In spite of tremendous tourist crowds, Toledo sits enthroned on its history, much as it was when Europe's most powerful king and El Greco called it home.

Planning Your Time
To properly see Toledo's museums (great El Greco), cathedral (best in Spain), and medieval atmosphere (best after dark), you'll need two nights and a day. Plan carefully for lunch closings and note that a few sights are closed Monday.

Toledo is just 60 minutes away from Madrid by bus (2/hr), train (3/day, more when fast AVE train is completed), or taxi (about €65 one-way from Puerta del Sol—negotiate ride without a meter). The new high-speed AVE connection will cut the journey by rail to just 15–20 minutes when it ever gets finished. A car is useless in Toledo. Ideally, see the town outside of car-rental time (pick up or drop your car here—Hertz is at train station, tel. 925-253-890, Avis is on Calle Armac below main square, tel. 925-214-535).

ORIENTATION

Lassoed into a tight tangle of streets by the sharp bend of the Tajo River (called the Tejo where it hits the Atlantic, in Lisbon), Toledo has Spain's most confusing medieval street plan. But it's a small town of 70,000, the major sights are well-signposted, and most locals will politely point you in the right direction.

If driving into town, enjoy a scenic big-picture orientation by following the Ronda de Toledo signs on a big circular drive around the city. The best time for this is the magic hour before sunset when the top viewpoints are busy with tired old folks and frisky young lovers.

Look at the map and take a mental orientation-walk past Toledo's main sights. Starting in the central Plaza Zocódover (zoh-KOH-doh-ver), go southwest along the Calle Comercio. After passing the cathedral on your left, follow the signs to Santo Tomé and the cluster of other sights. The visitor's city lies basically along one small but central street—and most tourists never stray from this axis. Make a point to get lost. It's a small town, bounded on three sides by the river. When it's time to get somewhere, I pull out the map or ask, *"¿Dónde está Plaza Zocódover?"*

Tourist Information

Toledo has three TIs. The one that covers Toledo as well as the region is in a new free-standing brick building just outside the Bisagra Gate (the last surviving gate of the 10th-century fortifications), where those arriving by train or bus enter the old town (Mon–Fri 9:00–18:00, Sat 9:00–19:00, Sun 9:00–15:00, longer hours in summer, tel. 925-220-843).

The second TI is in front of the cathedral on Plaza Ayuntamiento (Mon 10:30–14:30, Tue–Sun 10:30–14:30 & 16:30–19:00, tel. 925-254-030).

A handier, third TI is close to Zocódover square at Silleria 14 (daily 10:30–19:00, closes at 18:00 Oct–March, tel. 925-220-300).

Consider the readable local guidebook, *Toledo: Its Art and Its History* (small version for €5, sold all over town). It explains all of the sights (which generally provide no on-site information) and gives you a photo to point at and say, *"¿Dónde está...?"*

Toledo

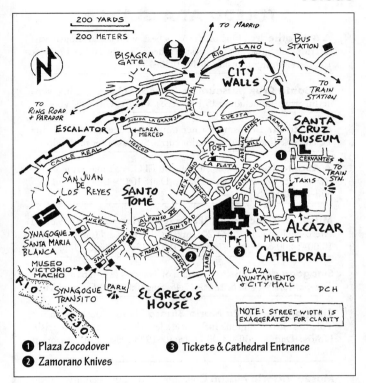

200 YARDS
200 METERS

TO MADRID

BISAGRA GATE

BUS STATION

CITY WALLS

RIO LLANO

TO TRAIN STATION

TO RING ROAD + PARADOR

ESCALATOR

SUBIDA LA GRANJA

PLAZA MERCED

CUESTA

SANTA CRUZ MUSEUM

CALLE REAL

MERCED

POST

LA PLATA

CADENAS NUÑEZ SILL

ARMAS

CERVANTES

TO TRAIN STN.

SAN JUAN DE LOS REYES

SANTO TOMÉ

COMERCIO

TAXIS

ALFONSO XII

NUNCIO

ANGEL

ALFONSO XII

S. TOMÉ

TRINIDAD

SYNAGOGUE SANTA MARIA BLANCA

SAN JUAN DIOS

T. MORO

SALVADOR

S. URSULA

MARKET

ALCÁZAR

MUSEO VICTORIO MACHO

ISABEL

CATHEDRAL

RIO TEJO

SYNAGOGUE TRANSITO

PARK

EL GRECO'S HOUSE

PLAZA AYUNTAMIENTO & CITY HALL

DCH

NOTE: STREET WIDTH IS EXAGGERATED FOR CLARITY

❶ Plaza Zocódover   ❸ Tickets & Cathedral Entrance
❷ Zamorano Knives

Arrival in Toledo

"Arriving" in Toledo means getting uphill to Plaza Zocódover. From the **train station,** that's a 20-minute hike, €3 taxi ride, or easy bus ride (#5 or #6, €0.80, pay on bus, confirm by asking, *"¿Para Plaza Zocódover?"*). You can stow extra baggage in the station's lockers (buy tokens at ticket booth). Consider buying a city map at the kiosk; it's better than the free one at the TI. If you're walking, turn right as you leave the station, cross the bridge, pass the bus station, go straight through the roundabout, and continue uphill to the TI and Bisagra Gate.

If you arrive by **bus,** go upstairs to the station lobby. You'll find lockers and a small bus-information office near the lockers and opposite the cafeteria. Confirm your departure time (probably every half hour on the hour to Madrid). When you buy your return ticket to Madrid—which you can put off until just minutes before you leave—specify you'd

TOLEDO AT A GLANCE

▲▲▲**Cathedral** One of Europe's best, with a marvelously vast interior and great art. **Hours:** Cathedral-daily 10:30–12:00 & 16:00–18:00; sights inside-daily 10:30–18:00.

▲▲**Santa Cruz Museum** Renaissance building housing wonderful artwork, including 15 El Grecos. **Hours:** Unpredictable.

▲▲**Alcázar** Imposing former imperial residence, dominating Toledo's skyline. **Hours:** Interior currently closed for renovation.

▲▲**Santo Tomé** Simple chapel with El Greco's masterpiece, *The Burial of the Count of Orgaz.* **Hours:** Daily 10:00–18:45, until 17:45 mid-Oct–March.

Museo El Greco and "El Greco's House" Replica of El Greco-era home, featuring 20 works by the painter. **Hours:** Tue–Sat 10:00–14:00 & 16:00–17:45, Sun 10:00–13:45, closed Mon.

Sinagoga del Transito Museum of Toledo's Jewish past. **Hours:** Tue–Sat 10:00–14:00 & 16:00–17:45, Sun 10:00–13:45, closed Mon.

Sinagoga de Santa Maria Blanca Harmoniously combines Toledo's three religious influences: Jewish, Christian, Moorish. **Hours:** Daily 10:00–14:00 & 15:30–19:00, closes off-season at 18:00.

Museo Victorio Macho Collection of the 20th-century Toledo sculptor's works, with great river gorge view. **Hours:** Mon–Sat 10:00–19:00, Sun 10:00–15:00.

San Juan de los Reyes Monasterio Church/monastery that was to be the final resting place of Isabel and Ferdinand. **Hours:** Daily 10:00–19:00, until 18:00 in winter.

like a *directo* bus; the *ruta* trip takes longer (60 min vs. 75). From the bus station, Plaza Zocódover is a 15-minute walk (see directions from train station, above), €3 taxi ride, or short bus ride (catch #5 downstairs, underneath the lobby, €0.80, pay on bus).

A series of **escalators** runs near the Bisagra Gate, giving you a free ride up, up, up into town (daily 8:00–22:00). You'll end up near the synagogues and far from Plaza Zocódover (but this doesn't matter). It's great for drivers, who can park free in the streets near the base of the escalator or for a fee (€12/day) in the parking lot across from it. Toledo is no fun to drive in. If you don't park near the escalator, drive into town and park in the Garage Alcázar (opposite the Alcázar in the old town— €1.20/hr, €12/day).

SIGHTS

▲▲▲**Cathedral**—Holy Toledo! Spain's leading Catholic city has a magnificent cathedral. Shoehorned into the old center, its exterior is hard to appreciate. But the interior is so lofty, rich, and vast that it'll have you wandering around like a Pez dispenser stuck open, whispering "Wow."

Cost and Hours: While the basic cathedral is free, seeing the great art—located in four separate places within the cathedral (the choir, chapter house, sacristy, and treasury)—requires a €4.95 ticket sold in the Tienda la Catedral shop opposite the church entrance (shop open Mon–Sat 10:30–18:30, Sun 14:00–18:00; also rents audioguides for €3). The strict dress-code sign covers even your attitude: no shorts, no tank tops...and no slouching.

The cathedral itself is free and open to the public daily (10:30–12:00 & 16:00–18:00, no WC in cathedral or cathedral shop). The four sights inside are open 10:30–18:00. Even though the cathedral closes from 12:00 to 16:00, if you have a ticket you can get in and tour the cathedral as well, with fewer crowds. (Note that the cloister is closed to everyone 13:00–15:30.)

Self-Guided Tour: Holy redwood forest, Batman! Wander among the pillars. Sit under one and imagine a time when the light bulbs were candles and the tourists were pilgrims—before the No Photo signs, when every window provided spiritual as well as physical light. The cathedral is primarily Gothic, but since it took over 250 years to build (1226–1495), you'll see a mix of styles—Gothic, Renaissance, and Baroque. Enjoy the elaborate wrought-iron work, lavish wood carvings, window after colorful window of 500-year-old stained glass, and a sacristy with a collection of paintings that would put any museum on the map.

This confusing collage of great Spanish art deserves a close look. Hire a private guide, freeload on a tour (they come by every few minutes during peak season), or follow this quick tour. Here's a framework for your visit:

1. High Altar: First, walk to the high altar to marvel through the iron grille at one of the most stunning altars in Spain. Real gold on pine wood, by Flemish, French, and local artists, it's one of the country's best pieces of Gothic art. About-face to the...

Toledo's Cathedral

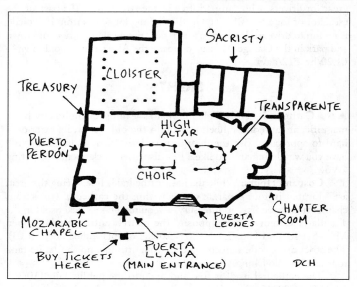

2. Choir: Facing the high altar, the choir is famous for its fine carving and requires a piece of your four-part ticket. The lower wooden stalls are decorated with scenes celebrating the slow one-city-at-a-time Christian victory as the Muslims were pushed back into Africa. Each idealized castle has the reconquered town's name on it, culminating with the final victory at Granada in 1492. The upper stalls (which flank the grand throne of the archbishop) feature Old Testament figures carved out of alabaster. And, as is typical of choir decoration, the carvings on the misericords (the tiny seats allowing tired worshippers to lean while they "stand") feature the frisky, folksy, sexy, profane art of the day. Apparently, since you sat on it, it could never be sacred anyway. There are two fine pipe organs: one 18th-century Baroque and the other 19th-century neoclassical. Note the serene beauty of the 13th-century Madonna and Child at the front, thought to be a gift from the French king to Spain.

The iron grille of the choir is notable for the dedication of the man who built it. Domingo de Cespedes, a Toledo ironworker, accepted the commission to build the grille for 6,000 ducats. The project, which took from 1541 to 1548, was far more costly than he anticipated. The medieval Church didn't accept cost overruns, so to finish it, he sold everything he owned and went into debt. He died a poor—but honorable—man.

3. Chapter House: Face the altar and go around it to your right to the chapter house *(sala capitular).* Its lavish ceiling celebrates Italian Renaissance humanism with a groundbreaking fresco. You're surrounded by interesting Bible-storytelling frescoes and a pictorial review of 1,900 years of Toledo archbishops. Though the upper row of portraits were not painted from life, the lower portraits were, and therefore are of more historic and artistic interest. Imagine sitting down to church business surrounded by all this tradition and theology. As you leave, notice the iron-pumping cupids carved into the pear tree panels lining the walls.

The *transparente,* behind the high altar, is a unique feature of the cathedral. In the 1700s, a hole was cut into the ceiling to let a sunbeam brighten the Mass. Melding this big hole into the Gothic church presented a challenge that resulted in a Baroque masterpiece. Gape up at this riot of angels doing flip-flops, babies breathing thin air, bottoms of feet, and gilded sunbursts. Study the altar, which looks chaotic but is actually thoughtfully structured: the good news of salvation springs from baby Jesus, up past the angel (who knows how to hold a big fish correctly), to the Last Supper high above, and beyond into the light-filled dome. I like it, as did, I guess, the long-dead cardinal whose faded red hat hangs from the edge of the hole. (A perk that only cardinals enjoy is choosing the place in the cathedral where their hat will hang until it rots.)

4. Sacristy: The cathedral's sacristy has 20 El Grecos as well as masterpieces by Goya, Titian, Rubens, Velázquez, Caravaggio, and Bellini. First, notice the fine perspective work on the 18th-century ceiling (frescoed by Lucca Giordano from Naples). Then walk to the end of the room for the most important painting in the collection. El Greco's first masterpiece, from 1579, *The Spoliation* (a.k.a. *The Denuding of Christ*) hangs above the marble altar. This was one of El Greco's first Toledo commissions after arriving from Venice. Notice the parallel contrasts: Jesus' delicate hand before a flaming red tunic and Jesus' noble face among the sinister mob. On the right is a rare religious painting by Goya, the *Betrayal of Christ,* which shows Judas preparing to kiss Jesus, identifying him to the Roman soldiers. Enjoy the many other El Grecos. Find the small but lifelike 17th-century carving of St. Francis by Pedro de Mena (to your right as you entered the door).

5. Treasury: The *tesoro* has plenty to see. The highlight is the 10-foot-high, 430-pound monstrance—the tower designed to hold the Holy Communion bread (the Host) during the festival of Corpus Christi (body of Christ) as it parades through the city. Built in 1517 by a man named Arfe, it's made of 5,000 individual pieces held together by 12,500 screws. There are diamonds, emeralds, rubies, and 400 pounds of gold-plated silver. The inner part is 35 pounds of solid gold. Yeow. The base is a later addition from the Baroque period. Traditionally, it's thought that much of this gold and silver arrived in Columbus' first load home. To the right of the monstrance find the fancy sword of Franco. To the right of that is a gift from St. Louis, the king of France—a 700-year-old Bible printed and beautifully illustrated by French monks. (It's actually a copy, and the precious original is stored elsewhere.) Imagine the exquisite experience for medieval eyes of reading this, with its lavish illustrations. The finely-painted small crucifix on the opposite side—by the great Gothic Florentine painter Fra Angelico—depicts Jesus alive on the back and dead on the front. This was a gift from Mussolini to Franco. Hmmm. There's even a gift in this room from Toledo's sister city, Toledo, Ohio.

If you're at the cathedral between 9:00 and 9:15, you can peek into the otherwise-locked **Mozarabic Chapel** *(Capilla Mozarabe)*. The Visigothic Mass, the oldest surviving Christian ritual in Western Europe, starts at 9:15 (9:45 on Sun). You're welcome to partake in this stirring example of peaceful coexistence of faiths—but once the door closes, you're a Visigoth for 30 minutes.

▲▲**Santa Cruz Museum**—For years, this museum has been in a confused state of renovation—not really open, not really closed. During renovation, the museum's cloister and a room full of its best art will be open and free. If the core of the building is filled with a temporary exhibit, you can generally wander in for a free look. The building's Plateresque facade is worth seeing anytime.

This great Renaissance building was an orphanage and hospital, built from money left by the humanist and diplomat Cardinal Mendoza when he died in 1495. The cardinal, confirmed as Chancellor of Castile by Queen Isabel, was so influential he was called "the third king." The building is in the form of a Greek cross under a Moorish dome. After renovation, the arms of the building—formerly wards—will be filled with 16th-century art, tapestries, furniture, armor, and documents. It'll be a stately, classical, music-filled setting with a cruel lack of English information (Mon–Sat 10:00–18:30, Sun 10:00–14:00, just off Plaza Zocódover, go through arch, Cervantes 3).

The collection includes 15 El Grecos. The highlight: the impressive *Assumption of Mary*—a spiritual poem on canvas (notice old Toledo on the bottom). Painted one year before El Greco's death in 1614, this is considered the culmination of his artistic development.

Find the lavish but faded Astrolabe Tapestry (c. 1480, Belgian) which shows a new world view at the dawn of the Renaissance and the age of discovery: God oversees all, as Atlas spins the Cosmos containing the circular Earth, and the wisdom gang (far right) heralds the new age.

An enormous blue banner hangs like a long, skinny tooth opposite the entry. This flew from the flagship of Don Juan of Austria and recalls the pivotal naval victory over the Muslims at the Battle of Lepanto in 1571 off the coast of Greece. Lepanto was a key victory in the centuries-long struggle of Christian Europe against the Muslim threat.

▲**Alcázar**—This huge former imperial residence—built on the site of Roman, Visigothic, and Moorish fortresses—dominates the Toledo skyline. Currently closed for renovation, it will be the National Military Museum when it reopens. The Alcázar became a kind of right-wing Alamo during Spain's civil war, when a force of Franco's Nationalists (and hundreds of hostages) were besieged for two months. Finally, after many fierce but futile Republican attacks, Franco sent in an army that took Toledo and freed the Alcázar. The place was rebuilt and glorified under Franco.

▲**Tourist Train**—For great city views, hop on the cheesy Tren Imperial Tourist Tram. Crass as it feels, you get a 50-minute putt-putt through Toledo and around the Tajo River Gorge. It's a great way to get a general city overview and for non-drivers to enjoy views of the city from across the Tajo Gorge (€3.60, buy ticket from kiosk opposite pharmacy on Plaza Zocódover or from TI at Silleria 14, daily from 11:00, leaves Plaza Zocódover on the hour, tape-recorded English/Spanish commentary, no photo stops but it goes slow; for the best views of Toledo across the gorge, sit on right side, not behind driver; tel. 925-220-300).

Southwest Toledo

▲**Santo Tomé**—A simple chapel holds El Greco's most-loved painting. *The Burial of the Count of Orgaz* couples heaven and earth in a way only The Greek could. It feels so right to see a painting left in situ where the artist put it 400 years ago. Take this slow. Stay a while—let it perform. The year is 1323. You're at the burial of the good count. After a pious and generous life, he left his estate to the Church. Saints Augustine and Steven have even come down for the burial—to usher the good count directly to heaven. "Such is the reward for those who serve God and his saints."

More than 250 years later, in 1586, a priest hired El Greco to make a painting of the burial to hang over the count's tomb. The painting has two halves divided by a serene line of noble faces. The physical world ends with the line of nobles. Above them a spiritual wind blows, as colors change and shapes stretch. Notice the angel, robe caught up in that wind, "birthing" the soul of the count through the neck of a celestial womb into Heaven—the soul abandoning the physical body to join Christ the Judge. Mary and John the Baptist both intervene on behalf of the arriving soul. This is Counter-Reformation propaganda—notice Jesus pointing to St. Peter, who controls the keys to the pearly gates. Each face is a detailed portrait. El Greco himself (eyeballing you, 7th figure in from the left) is the only one not involved in the burial. The boy in the foreground—pointing to the two saints as if to say, "One's from the first century, the other's from the fourth...it's a miracle!"—is El Greco's son (€1.50, daily 10:00–18:45, until 17:45 mid-Oct–March, free audioguide, tel. 925-256-098).

Museo El Greco and "El Greco's House"—Along with a replica of a house like El Greco's, you'll see about 20 El Greco paintings, including his masterful *View of Toledo* and portraits of the Apostles (€2.40, free Sat afternoon from 14:30 and all day Sun; Tue–Sat 10:00–14:00 & 16:00–17:45, Sun 10:00–13:45, closed Mon, Samuel Levi 3). While many call this El Greco's House, it's actually a traditionally-furnished Renaissance "monument house" built near where he likely lived.

Sinagoga del Transito (Museo Sefardi)—Built in 1366, this is the best surviving slice of Toledo's Jewish past (likely to reopen in 2004 after a long renovation). The museum displays Jewish artifacts, including costumes, menorahs, and books, regrettably without a word of English description (€2.50, free Sat afternoon from 14:30 and all day Sun; Tue–Sat 10:00–14:00 & 16:00–17:45, Sun 10:00–13:45, closed Mon, near Museo El Greco, with same price and hours, on Calle de los Reyes Católicos).

Sinagoga de Santa Maria Blanca—This synagogue-turned-church with Moorish arches is an eclectic but harmonious gem and a vivid reminder of the three cultures that shared this city (€1.50, daily 10:00–14:00 & 15:30–19:00, closes off-season at 18:00, no photos allowed, Calle de los Reyes Católicos 2–4).

Museo Victorio Macho—After *mucho* El Greco, try Macho. Overlooking the gorge, this small, attractive museum—once the home and workshop of the early-20th-century sculptor Victorio Macho—offers several rooms of his bold work interspersed with view terraces. The highlight is *La Madre,* Macho's life-size sculpture of an older woman sitting in a chair. But the big draw for many is the air-conditioned theater featuring a fast-moving nine-minute video sweep through Toledo's history (for more information request the 29-min long version; €3, half-price for young and old, Mon–Sat 10:00–19:00, Sun 10:00–15:00, request video showing in English, Plaza de Victorio Macho 2, between the two *sinagogas* listed above, tel. 925-284-225).

The **river gorge view** from the Museo Vitorio Macho terrace (or free terraces nearby) shows well how the River Tajo served as a formidable moat protecting the city. Imagine trying to attack from this side. The 14th-century bridge on the right and the remains of a bridge on the left connected the town with the region's *cigarrales*—mansions of wealthy families with orchards of figs and apricots that dot the hillside even today.

San Juan de los Reyes Monasterio—St. John of the Monarchs is a grand, generally Flemish-style monastery, church, and cloisters—thought-provoking because the Catholic Monarchs (Isabel and Ferdinand) planned to be buried here. But after the Moors were expelled in 1492 from Granada, their royal bodies were planted there to show Spain's commitment to maintaining a Moor-free peninsula. Today the courtyard is a delightful spot where happy critters carved into the columns seem to chirp with the birds in the trees. Notice the arrows and yoke representing the kingdom's unity achieved by the Royal Monarchs (€1.50, daily 10:00–19:00, until 18:00 in winter, San Juan de los Reyes 2, tel. 925-223-802).

SHOPPING

Toledo probably sells as many souvenirs as any city in Spain. This is the place to buy medieval-looking swords, armor, maces, three-legged stools, and other nouveau antiques. It's also Spain's damascene center, where, for centuries, craftspeople have inlaid black steel with gold, silver, and copper wire.

At the workshop of English-speaking **Mariano Zamorano,** you can see swords and knives being made. Judging by what's left of Mariano's hand, his knives are among the sharpest (Mon–Sat 9:00–14:00 & 16:00–19:00, closed Sat afternoon and Sun, Calle Ciudad 19, near cathedral and Plaza Ayuntamiento, tel. 925-222-634, www.marianozamorano.com).

El Martes, Toledo's colorful outdoor flea market, bustles on Paseo de Marchen, better kown to locals as "La Vega" (near TI at Bisagra Gate) on Tuesdays from 9:00 to 14:00.

SLEEPING

Near Plaza Zocódover

$$ Hotel Las Conchas, a new three-star hotel, gleams with marble and sheer pride. It's so sleek and slick it almost feels more like a hospital than a hotel. Its 35 rooms are plenty comfortable (Sb-€55, Db-€70, Db with terrace-€82, breakfast-€5, includes tax, 5 percent discount with this book, air-con, near the Alcázar at Juan Labrador 8, tel. 925-210-760, fax 925-224-271, www.lasconchas.com, lasconchas@ctv.es, Sole SE).

$ Hotel Imperio is well run, offering 21 basic air-conditioned rooms with marginal beds in a handy old-town location (Sb-€28, Db-€40, Tb-€54, includes tax, 5 percent discount with this book, elevator, cheery café, from Calle Comercio at #38 go a block uphill to Calle Cadenas 5, tel. 925-227-650, fax 925-253-183, www.terra.es/personal/himperio, himperio@teleline.es, friendly Pablo SE).

$ Hostal Centro rents 28 modern, clean, and comfy rooms just around the corner (Sb-€30, Db-€42, Tb-€60, roof garden, 50 yards off Plaza Zocódover, first right off Calle Comercio at Calle Nueva 13, tel. 925-257-091, fax 925-257-848, hostalcentro@telefonica.net, SE).

$ The quiet, modern **Hostal Nuevo Labrador,** with 12 clean, shiny, and spacious rooms, is another good value (Sb-€28, Db-€45, Tb-€55, Qb-€64, includes tax, no breakfast, elevator, Juan Labrador 10, tel. 925-222-620, fax 925-229-399, hostalcentro@telefonica.net, NSE, jointly owned with Hostal Centro, above).

SLEEP CODE

(€1 = about $1.10, country code: 34)
Sleep Code: **S** = Single, **D** = Double/Twin, **T** = Triple, **Q** = Quad, **b** = bathroom, **s** = shower only, **no CC** = Credit Cards not accepted, SE = Speaks English, NSE = No English. Breakfast and the 7 percent IVA tax are not included unless noted. Credit cards are accepted unless otherwise noted.

To help you sort easily through these listings, I've divided the rooms into three categories based on the price for a standard double room with bath during high season:

    $$$ **Higher Priced**—Most rooms €90 or more.
      $$ **Moderately Priced**—Most rooms between €60–90.
       $ **Lower Priced**—Most rooms €60 or less.

Madrid day-trippers darken the sunlit cobbles, but few stay to see Toledo's medieval moonrise. Spend the night. Spring and fall are high season; November through March and July and August are low. There are no private rooms for rent.

$ **Hotel Maravilla,** wonderfully central and convenient, has gloomy, claustrophobic halls and 17 simple rooms (Sb-€28, Db-€44, Tb-€59, Qb-€72, includes tax, back rooms are quieter, air-con, a block behind Plaza Zocódover at Plaza de Barrio Rey 7, tel. 925-228-317, fax 925-228-155, hostalmaravilla@infonegocio.com, Felisa Maria SE).

$ **Pensión Castilla,** a family-run cheapie, has seven very basic rooms (S-€15, Db-€25, extra bed possible, no CC, fans, Calle Recoletos 6, tel. 925-256-318, Teresa NSE).

$ **Pensión Lumbreras** has a tranquil courtyard and 12 simple rooms, some with views, including rooms 3, 6, and 7 (S-€19, D-€33, reception is at Carlo V Hotel around the corner, air-con, Juan Labrador 9, tel. 925-221-571).

Near the Bisagra Gate

$$$ **Hostal del Cardenal,** a 17th-century cardinal's palace built into Toledo's wall, is quiet and elegant with a cool garden and a stuffy restaurant. This poor man's parador, at the dusty old gate of Toledo, is closest to the station but below all the old-town action—however, the new escalator takes the sweat out of getting into town (Sb-€63, Db-€102, Tb-€133, 20 percent cheaper mid-Dec through mid-March, breakfast-€7.28, air-con, nearby parking-€12/day, *serioso* staff, enter

Toledo Plaza Zocódover

* NOT TO SCALE -
PLAZA ZOC. TO
PENSION LUMBRERAS
IS A 5 MIN. WALK

❶ Hotel Las Conchas
❷ Hotel Imperio
❸ Hostal Centro
❹ Hostal Nuevo Labrador
❺ Hotel Maravilla
❻ Pensión Castilla
❼ Pensión Lumbreras
❽ Rincón de Eloy Restaurant
❾ Restaurants Plaza & La Parrilla

through town wall 100 yards below Puerta Bisagra, Paseo de Recaredo 24, tel. 925-224-900, fax 925-222-991, www.hostaldelcardenal.com, cardenal@hostaldelcardenal.com).

$ **Hotel Sol,** with 25 non-smoking, plain, modern, and clean rooms, is a great value on a quiet street halfway between the Bisagra Gate and Plaza Zocódover (Sb-€34, Db-€45, Tb-€58, includes tax,

Toledo Hotels and Restaurants

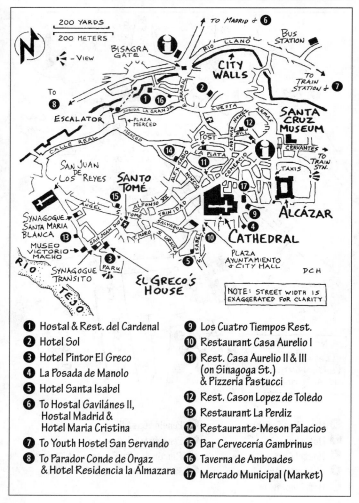

200 YARDS
200 METERS
← - VIEW

N

TO MADRID & **6**

BISAGRA GATE

i

RIO LLANO

BUS STATION

CITY WALLS

To **8**

ESCALATOR

SUBIDA LA GRANJA

1 **16**

ARRABAL

2

CUESTA

TO TRAIN STATION & **7**

PLAZA MERCED

MERCED

NUÑES

ARMAS

12

SILL

SANTA CRUZ MUSEUM

CALLE REAL

POST

CADENAS

CERVANTES

SAN JUAN DE LOS REYES

14

ALEX ARIO

NUNCIO

LA PLATA

11

COMERCIO

TO TRAIN STN.

SANTO TOMÉ

15

ANGEL

S. TOMÉ

ALFONSO XII

TRINIDAD

17

TAXIS

9

ALCÁZAR

SYNAGOGUE SANTA MARIA BLANCA

13

SAN JUAN DIOS

MORO

SALVADOR

S. URSULA

4

CATHEDRAL

MUSEO VICTORIO MACHO

3

PARK

S. ISABEL

10

RIO TEJO

SYNAGOGUE TRANSITO

EL GRECO'S HOUSE

5

PLAZA AYUNTAMIENTO & CITY HALL

DCH

NOTE: STREET WIDTH IS EXAGGERATED FOR CLARITY

1 Hostal & Rest. del Cardenal
2 Hotel Sol
3 Hotel Pintor El Greco
4 La Posada de Manolo
5 Hotel Santa Isabel
6 To Hostal Gavilánes II, Hostal Madrid & Hotel Maria Cristina
7 To Youth Hostel San Servando
8 To Parador Conde de Orgaz & Hotel Residencia la Almazara

9 Los Cuatro Tiempos Rest.
10 Restaurant Casa Aurelio I
11 Rest. Casa Aurelio II & III (on Sinagoga St.) & Pizzeria Pastucci
12 Rest. Cason Lopez de Toledo
13 Restaurant La Perdiz
14 Restaurante-Meson Palacios
15 Bar Cerveceria Gambrinus
16 Taverna de Amboades
17 Mercado Municipal (Market)

breakfast-€3.50, 10 percent discount with this book, air-con, parking-€8/day, 50 yards down lane off busy main drag at Hotel Real, Azacanes 8, tel. 925-213-650, fax 925-216-159, www.fedeto.es/hotel-sol, hotel .sol@to.adade.es, José Carlos SE). Their "Hostal Sol" annex across the street is just as comfortable and a bit cheaper. A handy launderette is next door.

Deep in Toledo

$$$ Hotel Pintor El Greco, at the far end of the old town, has 33 plush and rustic-feeling rooms with all the comforts, yet it's in a historic 17th-century building. A block from Santo Tomé in a Jewish Quarter garden, it's very quiet (Sb-€83, Db-€103, Tb-€122, tax not included, elevator, air-con, Alamillos del Transito 13, tel. 925-285-191, fax 925-215-819, www.hotelpintorelgreco.com, info@hotelpintorelgreco.com).

$$ La Posada de Manolo rents 14 thoughtfully-furnished rooms across from the downhill corner of the cathedral. Manolo Junior recently opened "The House of Manolo" according to his father's vision: a comfortable place with each of its three floors themed a little differently—Moorish, Jewish, and Christian (Sb-€42, Db-€66, big Db-€72, includes breakfast, 10 percent discount when booked directly with this book, no elevator, air-con, 2 nice view terraces, Calle Sixto Ramon Parro 8, tel. 925-282-250, fax 925-282-251, www.laposadademanolo .com, laposadademanolo@wanadoo.es).

$ Hotel Santa Isabel, in a 15th-century building two blocks from the cathedral, has 42 clean, modern, and comfortable rooms and squeaky tile hallways (Sb-€30, Db-€45, Tb-€52, includes tax, breakfast-€4, elevator, air-con, great roof terrace; buried deep in old town so take a taxi instead of the bus; drivers enter from Calle Pozo Amargo, parking-€6; Calle Santa Isabel 24, tel. 925-253-120, fax 925-253-136, www.santa -isabel.com, santa-isabel@arrakis.es, Cesar and Andres SE).

Outside of Town

$$ Hotel Maria Cristina, next to the bullring, is part 15th-century and all modern. This sprawling 74-room hotel has all the comforts under a thin layer of prefab tradition (Sb-€58, Db-€90, Tb-€122, extra bed-€30, €149 suites available, tax not included, breakfast-€5.65, elevator, air-con, attached restaurant, parking-€9/day, Marques de Mendigorria 1, tel. 925-213-202, fax 925-212-650, www.hotelmariacristina.com, informacion@hotelmariacristina.com, SE).

$ On the road to Madrid (near bullring): There's a conspiracy of clean, modern, and hard-working little hotels with comfy rooms a five-minute walk beyond Puerta Bisagra near the bus station and bullring (Plaza de Toros, bullfights only on holidays). Drivers enjoy easy parking here. While it's a 15-minute uphill hike to the old-town action, buses #4 and #6 go from just west of Hostal Madrid directly to Plaza de Zocódover. Two good bets are **Hostal Gavilánes II** (18 just-renovated rooms, Sb-€33, Db-€42, Db suite-€81, Tb-€56, Qb-€65, includes taxes, breakfast-€2.50, parking-€5.50/day, air-con, Marqués de Mendigorría 14, tel. & fax 925-211-628, www.gavilanes.to, hostallosgavilanes2 @hotmail.com, NSE) and **Hostal Madrid** (20 rooms, Sb-€29, Db-€39, Tb-€53, includes tax, breakfast-€2.40, parking-€6/day, air-con, Calle

Marqués de Mendigorría 7, tel. 925-221-114, fax 925-228-113, NSE).
This *hostal* rents nine lesser rooms in an annex across the street.

$ *Hostel:* The **Albergue Juvenil San Servando** youth hostel is
lavish and newly-renovated but cheap, with small rooms for two, three,
or four people; a swimming pool; views; cafeteria; and good management (95 beds, €8.50 per bed if under age 26, €11 if age 26 or older,
hostel membership required—you can buy it here for €18, no CC,
breakfast-€1.50, in 10th-century Arab castle of San Servando, 10-min
walk from train station, 15-min hike from town center, over Puente Viejo
outside town, tel. 925-224-554, reservations tel. 925-267-729, NSE).

Outside of Town with the Grand Toledo View

$$$ Toledo's **Parador Nacional Conde de Orgaz** is one of Spain's best-
known inns, enjoying the same Toledo view El Greco made famous
from across the Tajo Gorge (76 rooms, Sb-€57, Db-€116, Db with
view-€132, Tb with view-€179, breakfast-€9, €24 *menus* in their fine
restaurant overlooking Toledo, 2 windy miles from town at Cerro del
Emperador, tel. 925-221-850, fax 925-225-166, www.parador.es,
toledo@parador.es, SE).

$ **Hotel Residencia La Almazara** was the summer residence of a
16th-century archbishop of Toledo. A friend of the cardinal and fond of
this location's classic Toledo view, El Greco hung out here for inspira-
tion. A lumbering old place with cushy public rooms, 28 simple bed-
rooms, and a sprawling garden, it's truly in the country but just two
miles out of Toledo (Sb-€28, Db-€39, Db with view-€43, Tb-€48, 10
rooms have view, fans, Ctra. de Arges 47, follow signs from circular
Ronda de Toledo road, tel. 925-223-866, fax 925-250-562, www
.hotelalmazara.com, reservas@hotelalmazara.com).

EATING

Dining in Traditional Elegance

A day full of El Greco and the romance of Toledo after dark puts me in
the mood for game. Typical Toledo dishes include partridge *(perdiz),*
venison *(venado),* wild boar *(jabali),* roast suckling pig *(cochinillo asado),*
or baby lamb *(cordero)* similarly roasted after a few weeks of mother's
milk. After dinner, find a *mazapan* place (such as Santo Tomé) for
dessert.

Los Cuatro Tiempos Restaurante offers gamey local specials in a
tasteful and elegant setting with good service (€25 dinners, daily 13:30–
16:00 & 20:30–23:00, at downhill corner of cathedral at Sixto Ramon
Parro 5, tel. 925-223-782).

Toledo's three **Casa Aurelio** restaurants all offer traditional cooking
(soup, game, roast suckling pig) in a classy atmosphere more memorable

than the food (€30 meals, 13:00–16:30 & 20:00–23:30, 2 closed Sun night, each closed either Mon, Tue, or Wed, air-con). All are within three blocks of the cathedral: Plaza Ayuntamiento 4 is festive (tel. 925-227-716), Sinagoga 6 is most *típico* (tel. 925-222-097), and Sinagoga 1 is new and dressiest, with a wine cellar (popular with Toledo's political class, tel. 925-221-392).

Restaurante Cason Lopez de Toledo, a fancy restaurant located in an old noble palace, specializes in Castilian food, particularly venison and partridge. Its character unfolds upstairs (€18 meals, Mon–Sat 13:30–16:00 & 20:30–23:30, closed Sun, Calle Silleria 3, near Plaza Zocódover, tel. 925-254-774).

Hostal del Cardenal Restaurante, a classic hotel restaurant near the Bisagra Gate at the bottom of town, is understandably popular with tourists for its decent traditional roast dishes (daily 13:00–16:00 & 20:30–23:30, Puerto de Recaredo 24, tel. 925-220-862).

For a splurge near the Santa Tomé sights, consider the classy **La Perdiz,** which offers partridge (as the restaurant's name suggests), venison, suckling pig, fish, and more (Tue–Sat 13:00–23:00, closes Sun about 16:00, closed Mon and first half of Aug, Calle de los Reyes Católicos 7, tel. 925-214-658).

Eating Simply but Well

Restaurante-Meson Palacios serves good regional food at cheap prices in a warm and friendly atmosphere. Their *judías con perdiz* (bean soup with partridge) and *pimientos de piquillo rellenos de pescado* (fish-stuffed peppers) are the most popular appetizers among locals (Mon–Sat from 13:00 and from 19:30, closed Sun, Alfonso X 3, near Plaza de San Vicente, tel. 925-215-972, Jesús is appropriately friendly).

Rincón de Eloy is bright, modern, and a cool refuge for lunch on a hot day (€9 *menu*, Mon–Sat 13:00–16:00 & 20:00–22:30, closed Sun night, air-con, Juan Labrador 16, near Alcázar, tel. 925-229-399).

Bar Cervecería Gambrinus is a good tapas bar (*chapatas* are little sandwiches, *tablitas* are "little plates") with restaurant seating in its leafy courtyard or in back (daily 9:00–24:00, near Santa Tomé at Santa Tomé 10, tel. 925-214-440).

Restaurants Plaza and La Parrilla share a tiny square behind Plaza Zocódover (facing the Casa Telesforo on Plaza Zocódover, go left down alley 30 yards to Plaza de Barrio Rey). The bars and cafés on Plaza Zocódover are reasonable, seasoned with some fine people-watching.

At **Taverna de Amboades,** a humble but earnest wine-and-tapas bar near the Bisagra Gate, expert Miguel Angel enjoys explaining the differences among Spanish wines. To try some really good wines with quality local cheese and meat, drop by and let Miguel impress you (2 quality wines and a plate of cheese and meat for €7, Tue–Sun 19:30–24:00, also Thu–Sun 12:30–16:00, closed Mon, Alfonso VI 5, mobile 678-483-749).

Pizzeria Pastucci is the local favorite for pizza (Tue–Sun 12:00–16:00 & 19:00–24:00, closed Mon, near cathedral at Calle de la Sinagoga 10).

Picnics are best assembled at the **Mercado Municipal** on Plaza Mayor (on the Alcázar side of cathedral, with a supermarket inside open Mon–Sat until 9:00–20:00 and stalls open mostly in the mornings until 14:00, closed Sun). This is a fun market to prowl, even if you don't need food. If you feel like munching a paper plate-size Communion wafer, one of the stalls sells crispy bags of *obleas*—a great gift for your favorite pastor.

And for Dessert: *Mazapan*

Toledo's famous almond-fruity-sweet *mazapan* is sold all over town. Locals say the best is made by **Santo Tomé** (several outlets, including a handy one on Plaza Zocódover, daily 9:00–22:22). Browse their tempting window displays. They sell *mazapan* goodies individually (2 for about €1, *sin relleno* is for purists, *de piñon* has pine nuts, *imperiales* is with almonds, others have fruit fillings) or in small mixed boxes. Their *Toledanas* is a crumbly cookie favorite with a subtle thread of pumpkin filling.

For a sweet and romantic evening moment, pick up a few pastries and head down to the cathedral. Sit on the Plaza del Ayuntamiento's benches (or stretch out on the stone wall to the right of the TI). The fountain is on your right, Spain's best-looking city hall is behind you, and her top cathedral, built back when Toledo was Spain's capital, shines brightly against the black night sky before you.

TRANSPORTATION CONNECTIONS

Far more buses than trains connect Toledo with Madrid.

To Madrid: by bus (2/hr, 60–75 min, *directo* is faster than *ruta*, Madrid's Estación sur Autobuses, Metro: Méndez Alvaro, Continental bus company, tel. 925-223-641), **by train** (3/day while they finish new AVE fast train, 50–75 min; new AVE train will do the trip in 15–20 min; Madrid's Atocha station), **by car** (40 miles, 1 hr). Toledo bus info: tel. 925-215-850; train info: tel. 902-240-202.

GIMMELWALD AND THE BERNER OBERLAND

Frolic and hike high above the stress and clouds of the real world. Take a vacation from your busy vacation. Recharge your touristic batteries up here in the Alps, where distant avalanches, cowbells, the fluff of a down comforter, and the crunchy footsteps of happy hikers are the dominant sounds. If the weather's good (and your budget's healthy), ride a gondola from the traffic-free village of Gimmelwald to a hearty breakfast at Schilthorn's 10,000-foot revolving Piz Gloria restaurant. Linger among alpine whitecaps before riding, hiking, or parasailing down 5,000 feet to Mürren and home to Gimmelwald.

Your gateway to the rugged Berner Oberland is the grand old resort town of Interlaken. Near Interlaken is Switzerland's open-air folk museum, Ballenberg, where you can climb through traditional houses from every corner of this diverse country.

Ah, but the weather's fine and the Alps beckon. Head deep into the heart of the Alps and ride the gondola to the stop just this side of heaven—Gimmelwald.

Planning Your Time

Rather than tackle a checklist of famous Swiss mountains and resorts, choose one region to savor: the Berner Oberland. Interlaken is the administrative headquarters and a fine transportation hub. Use it for business (banking, post office, laundry, shopping) and as a springboard for alpine thrills. With decent weather, explore the two areas (south of Interlaken) that tower above either side of the Lauterbrunnen Valley: Kleine Scheidegg/Jungfrau and Mürren/Schilthorn. Ideally, make the village of Gimmelwald your home base for three nights and spend a day on each side of the valley. On a speedy train trip, you can overnight into and out of Interlaken. For the fastest look, consider a night in Gimmelwald, breakfast at the Schilthorn, an afternoon doing the Männlichen–Wengen hike, and an evening or night train out.

What? A nature-lover not spending the night high in the Alps? Alpus interruptus.

Getting around the Berner Oberland

For more than 100 years, this has been the target of nature-worshiping pilgrims. And Swiss engineers and visionaries have made the most exciting alpine perches accessible by lift or train. Part of the fun (and most of the expense) here is riding the many lifts.

Generally, scenic trains and lifts are not covered on train passes, but a Eurailpass or Eurail Selectpass give you a 25 percent **discount** on even the highest lifts (without the loss of a flexi-day). Ask about discounts for early-morning and late-afternoon trips, youths, seniors, families, groups, and those staying awhile. The Junior Card for families pays for itself in the first hour of trains and lifts: Children under 16 travel free with parents (20 SF/1 child, 40 SF/2 or more children; available at Swiss train stations). Get a list of discounts and the free fare and time schedule at any Swiss train station.

Study the "Alpine Lifts in the Berner Oberland" chart on page 1,156. Lifts generally go at least twice hourly, from about 7:00 until about 20:00 (sneak preview: www.jungfrau.ch). **Drivers** can park at the gondola station in Stechelberg (2 SF/2 hrs, 6 SF/day) for the lift to Gimmelwald, Mürren, and the Schilthorn, or at the train station in Lauterbrunnen (2 SF/2 hrs, 9 SF/day) for trains to Wengen and Kleine Scheidegg.

Interlaken

When the 19th-century Romantics redefined mountains as something more than cold and troublesome obstacles, Interlaken became the original alpine resort. Ever since, tourists have flocked to the Alps because they're there. Interlaken's glory days are long gone, its elegant old hotels eclipsed by the new, more jet-setty alpine resorts. Today its shops are filled with chocolate bars, Swiss army knives, and sunburned backpackers.

ORIENTATION

Efficient Interlaken is a good administrative and shopping center. Take care of business, give the town a quick look, and view the live TV coverage of the Jungfrau and Schilthorn weather in the window of the Schilthornbahn office on the main street (at Höheweg 2, Mon–Fri 8:00–12:00 & 13:30–18:00, Sat 8:00–12:00, closed Sun, tel. 033-826-0007, www.schilthorn.ch, also on TV in most hotel lobbies). Then head for the hills. Stay in Interlaken only if you suffer from alptitude sickness (see "Sleeping in Interlaken," at the end of this chapter).

Tourist Information: The TI has good information for the region, advice on alpine lift discounts, and a room-finding service (July–Sept Mon–Fri 8:00–18:30, Sat 8:00–17:00, Sun 10:00–12:00 & 16:00–18:00; Oct–June Mon–Fri 8:00–12:00 & 13:30–18:00, Sat 9:00–12:00, closed Sun, tel. 033-826-5300, www.interlakentourism .ch; attached to Hotel Metropole on the main street between West and East stations, a 10-min walk from either). While the Interlaken/Jungfrau region map costs 2 SF, good mini-versions are included in the many free transportation and hiking brochures. Pick up a Bern map if that's your next destination.

Arrival in Interlaken: Interlaken has two train stations: East (Ost) and West. Most major trains stop at the Interlaken-West station. This station's helpful and friendly train information desk answers tourists' questions (travel center for in-depth rail questions: Mon–Fri 8:00–18:00, Sat–Sun 8:00–12:00 & 14:00–18:00, Nov–March closed Mon–Fri 12:00–14:00; ticket windows: daily 6:00–20:45; tel. 033-826-4750). There's a fair exchange booth next to the ticket windows. Ask at the station about discount passes, special fares, railpass discounts, and schedules for the scenic mountain trains.

It's a pleasant 20-minute walk between the West and East stations, or an easy, frequent train connection (2/hr, 2.60 SF). From the Interlaken-East station, private trains take you deep into the mountainous Jungfrau region (see "Transportation Connections" at the end of this chapter).

Helpful Hints

Telephone: Phone booths cluster outside the post office near the West station. For efficiency, buy a phone card from a newsstand. (Gimmelwald's sole public phone—at the gondola station—takes only cards, not coins.)

Laundry: Friendly Helen Schmocker's *Wäscherei* has a change machine, soap, English instructions, and a pleasant riverside location (open daily 7:00–22:00 for self-service; for full service: Mon–Fri 8:00–12:00 & 13:30–18:00, Sat 8:00–12:00 & 13:30–16:00, closed Sun, drop off in the morning and pick up that afternoon, tel. 033-822-1566; exit left from West station and follow the main street to the post office, turn left and take Marktgasse over 2 bridges to Beatenbergstrasse 5).

Warning: On Sundays and holidays, small-town Switzerland is quiet. Hotels are open, and lifts and trains run, but many restaurants and most stores are closed. If this concerns you, call the Interlaken TI to see if a holiday falls during your visit.

Stores: A brand-new **Migros supermarket** is across the street from Interlaken West train station (Mon–Thu 8:00–18:30, Fri 8:00–21:00, Sat 7:30–16:00, closed Sun). The **Co-op Pronto** mini-market

Interlaken

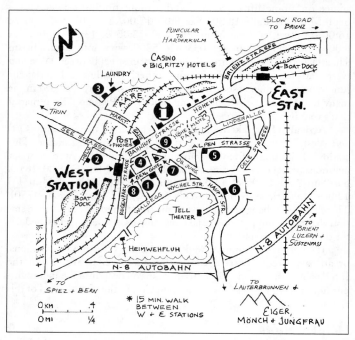

has longer hours (daily 6:00–22:00, across from TI). There's lots of buzz surrounding Interlaken's **Hanf Center,** a small shop selling a wide selection of products made from hemp, including clothes, paper, noodles, and beer (Mon 13:30–18:30, Tue–Fri 10:00–12:00 & 13:30–18:30, Sat 10:00–16:00, closed Sun, Jungfraustrasse 47, near end of Höhematte Park closest to West station, tel. 033-823-1552).

SIGHTS

Boat Trips—*Interlaken* means "between the lakes"—Thun and Brienz, to be exact. You can explore these lakes on a lazy boat trip (8/day mid-June–mid-Sept, fewer off-season, free with Eurail/Eurail Selectpass but uses a flexi-day, schedules at TI or at BLS Travel Center in West station, tel. 033-826-4750 or 033-334-5211). The boats on **Lake Thun** (4 hrs, 40 SF round-trip) stop at the **St. Beatus Höhlen caves** (16 SF, April–mid-Oct daily 10:30–17:00, closed mid-Oct–March, 30-min boat ride from Interlaken, tel. 033-841-1643, www.beatushoehlen.ch) and two visit-worthy towns: Spiez (1 hr from Interlaken) and Thun (1.75 hrs). The boats on **Lake Brienz** (3 hrs, 32 SF round-trip) stop at the super-cute and quiet village of Iseltwald (45 min away) and at Brienz (1.25 hrs away, near Ballenberg Open-Air Folk Museum).

Adventure Trips—For the adventurer with money and little concern for personal safety, several companies offer high-adrenaline trips such as rafting, canyoning (rappelling down watery gorges), bungee jumping, and paragliding. Most adventure trips cost 90–180 SF. Interlaken companies include: Alpin Raft (tel. 033-823-4100, www.alpinraft.ch), Alpin Center (at Wilderswil station and across from Balmer's youth hostel, tel. 033-823-5523, www.alpincenter.ch), Swiss Adventures (tel. 033-773-7373, www.swissadventures.ch), and Outdoor Interlaken (tel. 033-826-7719, www.outdoor-interlaken.ch). For an overview of your options, visit www.interlakenadventure.com.

Recent fatal accidents have understandably hurt the adventure-sport business in the Berner Oberland. In May 2000, an American died bungee jumping from the Stechelberg-Mürren gondola (the operator used a 180-meter rope for a 100-meter jump). Also in 2000, a landslide killed several hikers. In July 1999, 21 tourists died canyoning on the Saxetenbach River, 10 miles from Interlaken; they were battered and drowned by a flash flood filled with debris. Enjoying nature up close comes with risks. Adventure sports increase those risks dramatically. Use good judgment.

Gimmelwald

Saved from developers by its "avalanche zone" classification, Gimmelwald was (before tourism) one of the poorest places in Switzerland. Its traditional economy was stuck in the hay, and its farmers, unable to make it in their disadvantaged trade, survived only by Swiss government subsidies (and working the ski lifts in the winter). For some travelers, there's little to see in the village. Others enjoy a fascinating day sitting on a bench and learning why they say, "If Heaven isn't what it's cracked up to be, send me back to Gimmelwald." The village is my home base in the Berner Oberland (see "Sleeping in Gimmelwald," below).

Take a walk through the town. This place is for real. Most of the 130 residents have the same last name: von Allmen. They are tough and proud. Raising hay in this rugged terrain is labor-intensive. One family harvests enough to feed only 15 or 20 cows. But they'd have it no other way, and, unlike the absentee-landlord town of Mürren, Gimmelwald is locally owned. (When word got out that urban planners wished to develop Gimmelwald into a town of 1,000, locals pulled some strings to secure the town's bogus avalanche-zone building code.)

The huge, sheer cliff face that dominates your mountain views from Gimmelwald (and Mürren) is the Schwarzmönch (Black Monk).

Gimmelwald

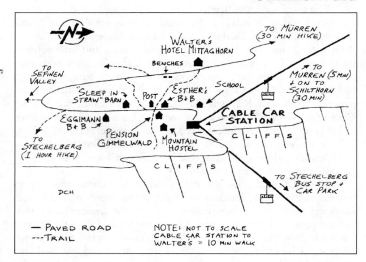

The three peaks above (or behind) it are, left to right, the Eiger, Mönch, and Jungfrau.

Do not confuse obscure Gimmelwald with touristy and commercialized Grindelwald, just over the Kleine Scheidegg ridge.

A WALK THROUGH GIMMELWALD

Gimmelwald, though tiny with one zigzag street, gives a fine look at a traditional mountain Swiss community. Here's a quick walking tour:

Gondola Station: When the lift came in the 1960s, this village's back end became Gimmelwald's front door. This was, and still is, a farm village. Stepping off the gondola, you see a sweet little hut. Set on stilts to keep out mice, the hut was used for storing cheese (the rocks on the rooftop keep the shingles on through wild winter winds). Notice the yellow alpine "street sign" showing where you are, the altitude (4,470 feet), and how many hours *(Std.)* and minutes it takes to walk to nearby points. Behind the cheese hut stands the village schoolhouse. In Catholic Swiss towns, the biggest building is the church. In Protestant towns, it's the school. Gimmelwald's biggest building is the school (2 teachers, 17 students, and a room that doubles as a chapel when the Protestant pastor makes his monthly visit). Don't let Gimmelwald's low-tech look fool you: In this school, each kid has his or her own Web site. In the opposite direction, just beyond the little playground, is Gimmelwald's Mountain Hostel.

Walk up the lane 50 yards, past the shower in the phone booth, to Gimmelwald's...

Times Square: From this tiny intersection, we'll follow the town's main street (away from gondola station, where most yellow arrows are pointing). Most of the buildings used to house two families and are divided vertically right down the middle. The writing on the post office building is a folksy blessing: "Summer brings green, winter brings snow. The sun greets the day, the stars greet the night. This house will keep you warm. May God give us his blessings." The date indicates when it was built or rebuilt (1911).

Main Street: Walk up the road. Notice the announcement board: one side for tourist news, the other for local news. Cross the street and peek into the big new barn, dated 1995. This is part of the Sleep in Straw association, which rents out barn spots to travelers when the cows are in the high country. To the left of the door is a cow scratcher. Swiss cows have legal rights (for example, in the winter, they must be taken out for exercise at least 3 times a week). This big barn is built in a modern style. Traditionally, barns were small (like those on the hillside high above) and closer to the hay. But with trucks and paved roads, hay can be moved easier and farther, and farms need more cows to be viable. Still, even a well-run big farm hopes just to break even. The industry survives only with government subsidies. Go just beyond the next barn and look to your right.

Water Fountain/Trough: This is the site of the town's historic water supply. Local kids love to bathe in this when the cows aren't drinking from it. From here, detour left down a lane about 50 yards (along a wooden fence and past pea-patch gardens) to the next trough and the oldest building in town, Husmättli, from 1658. Study the log-cabin construction. Many are built without nails.

Back on the paved road, continue uphill. Gimmelwald has a strict building code. For instance, shutters can only be natural, green, or white. Notice the cute cheese hut on the right (with stones on the shingles and alpine cheese for sale). It's full of strong cheese—up to three years old. On the left (at B&B sign) is the home of Olle and Maria, the village schoolteachers. Gimmelwald heats with wood and, since the wood needs to age a couple of years to burn well, it's stacked everywhere. Fifty yards farther along is the...

Alpenrose: At the old schoolhouse, notice the big ceremonial cow-bells hanging under the uphill eave. These swing from the necks of cows during the alpine procession from the town to the high Alps (mid-June) and back down (around Sept 20). At the end of town, notice the dramatic Sefinen Valley. The road switches back at the...

Gimmelwald Fire Station: Check out the notices up above on the fire station building. Every Swiss male does a year in the military, then a few days a year in the reserves until about age 40. The 2004 Swiss Army calendar tells the reserves when and where to go. The *Schiessübungen* poster details the shooting exercises required this year. In keeping with the William Tell heritage, each Swiss man does shooting practice annually for the military (or spends 3 days in jail).

High Road: Follow the high road to Hotel Mittaghorn. The resort of Mürren hovers in the distance. And high on the left, notice the hay field with terraces. These are from WWII days, when Switzerland, wanting self-sufficiency, required all farmers to grow potatoes. From Hotel Mittaghorn, you can return to Gimmelwald's Times Square via the stepped path.

Gimmelwald after Dark—Evening fun in Gimmelwald is found at the hostel (offering a pool table, Internet access, lots of young Alp-aholics, and a good chance to share information on the surrounding mountains) or at Pension Gimmelwald's terrace restaurant next door. Walter's bar (in Hotel Mittaghorn) is a local farmers' hangout. When they've made their hay, they come here to play. Although they look like what some people would call hicks, they speak some English and can be fun to get to know. Sit outside (benches just below the rails, 100 yards down the lane from Walter's) and watch the sun tuck the mountaintops into bed as the moon rises over the Jungfrau. If this isn't your idea of nightlife, stay in Interlaken.

BERNER OBERLAND SIGHTS AND ACTIVITIES

Alpine Excursions

There are days of possible hikes from Gimmelwald. Many are a fun combination of trails, mountain trains, and gondola rides. Don't mind the fences (although wires can be solar-powered electric); a hiker has the right of way in Switzerland. However, as late as June, snow can curtail your hiking plans (the Männlichen lift doesn't even open until the first week in June). Before setting out on any hike, get advice from a knowledgeable local to confirm that it is safe, accessible, and doable before dark. Clouds can roll in anytime, but skies are usually clearest in the morning. That means you need rain gear *and* sunscreen, regardless of the current weather. Don't forget a big water bottle and some munchies. Refer to maps (within this chapter) as you read about the following hikes.

▲▲▲**The Schilthorn: Hikes, Lifts, and a 10,000-Foot Breakfast**— The Schilthornbahn carries skiers, hikers, and sightseers effortlessly to the 10,000-foot summit of the Schilthorn, where the Piz Gloria station awaits with a solar-powered revolving restaurant, shop, and panorama terrace. Linger on top. Piz Gloria has a free "touristorama" film room with a multi-screen slide show and explosive highlights from the James Bond thriller that featured the Schilthorn *(On Her Majesty's Secret Service;* if it's not running, press the 007 button on the column in the middle of the room).

Watch hang gliders set up, psych up, and take off, flying 30 minutes with the birds to distant Interlaken. Walk along the ridge out back. This is a great place for a photo of the "mountain-climber you." For another cheap thrill, ask the gondola attendant to crank down the window (easiest on the Mürren–Birg section). Then stick your head out the window...and you're hang gliding.

The early-bird and afternoon-special **gondola tickets** (60 SF round-trip, before 9:00 or after 15:30) take you from Gimmelwald to the Schilthorn and back at a discount (normal rate-80 SF, or 94 SF from the Stechelberg car park; parking-2 SF/2 hrs, 6 SF/day). These same discounted fares are available all day long in the shoulder season (roughly May and Oct). Ask the Schilthorn station for a gondola souvenir decal (Schilthornbahn station in Stechelberg tel. 033-856-2141). For breakfast at 10,000 feet, there's no à la carte—only a fixed meal for 15 SF (rolls and hot chocolate or coffee) or 22.50 SF (add egg, ham, and Champagne; breakfast served 8:00–11:00). If you're going for breakfast before 9:00, consider an early-bird-plus-breakfast combo-ticket to save a few francs (73 SF round-trip from Gimmelwald, 84 SF from Stechelberg). Ask for more hot drinks if necessary. If you're not revolving, ask them to turn it on.

Lifts go twice hourly, and the ride (including 2 transfers) to the Schilthorn takes 30 minutes. Watch the altitude meter in the gondola. (The Gimmelwald–Schilthorn hike is free if you don't mind a 5,000-foot altitude gain.) You can ride up to the Schilthorn and hike down, but it's tough (weather can change; wear good shoes). Youth hostelers scream down the ice fields on plastic-bag sleds from the Schilthorn mountaintop. (English-speaking doctor in Lauterbrunnen.)

Just below Birg is **Schilthornhütte.** Drop in for soup, cocoa, or a coffee schnapps. You can spend the night in the hut's crude loft (dorm bed with breakfast-35 SF, 20 SF more for dinner, open July–Sept Fri–Sun, Dec–April daily, tel. 033-855-5053, schilthornhuette@muerren.ch).

Hard-core hikers could enjoy the **hike** from Birg to Gimmelwald (from Schilthorn summit, ride cable car halfway down, get off at Birg, and hike down from there; buy the round-trip excursion early-bird fare—which is cheaper than the Gimmelwald–Schilthorn–Birg ticket—and decide at Birg if you want to hike or ride down). The most interesting trail from Birg to Gimmelwald is the high one via Grauseeli Lake and Wasenegg Ridge to Brünli, then down to Spielbodenalp and the Sprutz waterfall. Warning: This trail is quite steep and slippery in places and can take four to six hours. Locals take their kindergartners on this hike, but it can seem dangerous to Americans unused to alpine hikes. Do not attempt this hike in snow—which you might find at this altitude even in the peak of summer. From the Birg lift, hike toward the Schilthorn, taking your first left down to the little, newly made Grauseeli Lake. From the lake, a gravelly trail leads down rough switchbacks

Lauterbrunnen Valley: West Side Story

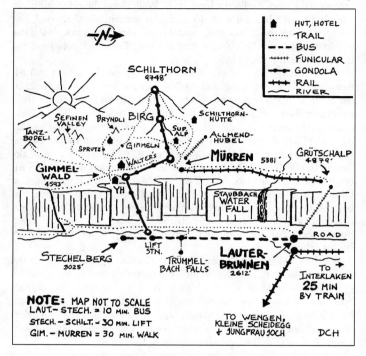

(including a stretch where the path narrows and you can hang onto a guide cable against the cliff face) until it levels out. When you see a rock painted with arrows pointing to Mürren and Rotstockhütte, follow the path to Rotstockhütte, traversing the cow-grazed mountainside. Follow Wasenegg Ridge left and down along the barbed-wire fence to Brünli. (For maximum thrills, stay on the ridge and climb all the way to the knobby little summit, where you'll enjoy an incredible 360-degree view and a chance to sign your name on the register stored in the little wooden box.) A steep trail winds directly down from Brünli toward Gimmelwald and soon hits a bigger, easy trail. The trail bends right (just before the popular restaurant/mountain hut at Spielbodenalp), leading to Sprutz. Walk under the Sprutz waterfall, then follow a steep, wooded trail that will deposit you in a meadow of flowers at the top side of Gimmelwald.

▲▲**North Face Trail from Mürren**—For a pleasant two-hour hike (4 miles, from 6,385 feet to 5,375 feet), ride the Allmendhubel funicular up from Mürren (7.40 SF, cheaper than Schilthorn, good restaurant at top).

Berner Oberland

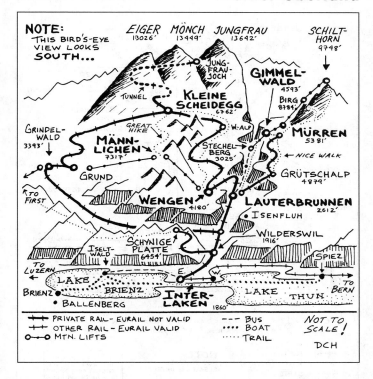

NOTE: THIS BIRD'S-EYE VIEW LOOKS SOUTH...

EIGER 13026' MÖNCH 13449' JUNGFRAU 13642' SCHILT-HORN 9748'

JUNG-FRAU-JOCH

TUNNEL

KLEINE SCHEIDEGG 6762'

GIMMEL-WALD 4593'

BIRG 8784'

W. ALP

GRINDEL-WALD 3393'

GREAT HIKE

MÄNN-LICHEN 7317'

STECHEL-BERG 3025'

MÜRREN 5381'

← NICE WALK

GRUND

GRÜTSCHALP 4879'

↑ TO FIRST

WENGEN 4180'

LAUTERBRUNNEN 2612'

• ISENFLUH

WILDERSWIL 1916'

SCHYNIGE PLATTE 6454'

ISELT-WALD

TO LUZERN ←

LAKE BRIENZ

E.   W.

SPIEZ

TO BERN →

BRIENZ •

• BALLENBERG

INTER-LAKEN 1860'

LAKE THUN

+—+ PRIVATE RAIL - EURAIL NOT VALID
+-+ OTHER RAIL - EURAIL VALID
o—o MTN. LIFTS

--- BUS
•••• BOAT
••••• TRAIL

NOT TO SCALE!

DCH

From there, follow the well-promoted and well-described route circling around to Mürren (or cut off near the end down to Gimmelwald). You'll enjoy great views, flowery meadows, mountain huts, and a dozen information boards along the way describing the climbing history of the great peaks around you.

▲▲▲The Männlichen-Kleine Scheidegg Hike—This is my favorite easy alpine hike. It's entertaining all the way, with glorious Jungfrau, Eiger, and Mönch views. That's the Young Maiden being protected from the Ogre by the Monk. (Note that trails may be snowbound into June; ask about conditions at the lift stations or local TI. If the Männlichen lift is closed, take the train straight from Lauterbrunnen to Kleine Scheidegg.)

If the weather's good, descend from Gimmelwald bright and early to Stechelberg. From here, get to the Lauterbrunnen train station by post bus (3.80 SF, bus is synchronized to depart with the arrival of each lift) or by car (parking at the large multistoried pay lot behind the

Alpine Lifts in the Berner Oberland

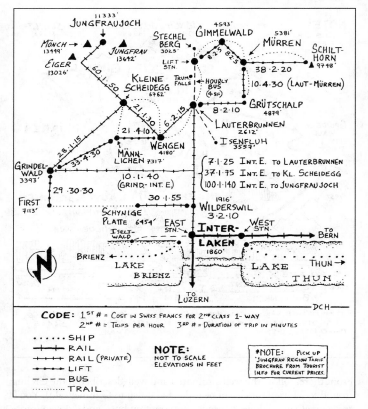

JUNGFRAUJOCH 11333'

MÖNCH 13449' → ▲   ▲ JUNGFRAU 13642'

▲ EIGER 13026'

STECHEL BERG 3025'

GIMMELWALD 4593'

MÜRREN 5381'

SCHILT-HORN 9748' ▲

LIFT STN.

KLEINE SCHEIDEGG 6762'

TRÜM FALLS

HOURLY BUS (4-SF)

38·2·20

10·4·30 (LAUT-MÜRREN)

GRÜTSCHALP 4879'

8·2·10

LAUTERBRUNNEN 2612'

ISENFLUH 3557'

WENGEN 4190'

21·4·10

MÄNN-LICHEN 7317'

GRINDEL-WALD 3393'

28·1·15

33·4·30

10·1·40 (GRIND- INT. E.)

FIRST 7113'

29·30·30

30·1·55

7·1·25 INT. E. TO LAUTERBRUNNEN
37·1·75 INT. E. TO KL. SCHEIDEGG
100·1·140 INT. E. TO JUNGFRAUJOCH

WILDERSWIL 1916'
3·2·10

SCHYNIGE PLATTE 6454'

EAST STN.

ISELT-WALD

INTER-LAKEN 1860'

WEST STN.

TO BERN →

BRIENZ ←

LAKE BRIENZ

LAKE THUN

THUN →

TO LUZERN

DCH

CODE: 1ST # = COST IN SWISS FRANCS FOR 2ND CLASS 1- WAY
2ND # = TRIPS PER HOUR   3RD # = DURATION OF TRIP IN MINUTES

· · · · · · SHIP
—+—+— RAIL
—+++— RAIL (PRIVATE)
—•—•— LIFT
– – – – BUS
· · · · · · · TRAIL

NOTE: NOT TO SCALE ELEVATIONS IN FEET

*NOTE: PICK UP 'JUNGFRAU REGION TARIF' BROCHURE FROM TOURIST INFO FOR CURRENT PRICES.

Lauterbrunnen station-2 SF/2 hrs, 9 SF/day). At Lauterbrunnen, buy a train ticket to Männlichen (28 SF one-way). Sit on the right side of the train for great waterfall views on your way up to Wengen. In Wengen, walk across town (buy a picnic but don't waste time here if it's sunny) and catch the Männlichen lift (departing every 15 min, beginning the first week of June) to the top of the ridge high above you.

From the Wengen-Männlichen lift station, turn left and hike uphill 20 minutes north to the little peak (Männlichen Gipfel) for that king- or queen-of-the-mountain feeling. Then take an easy hour's walk—facing spectacular alpine panorama views—to Kleine Scheidegg for a picnic or restaurant lunch. To start the hike, leave the Wengen-Männlichen lift station to the right. Walk past the second Männlichen lift station (this one leads to Grindelwald, the touristy town in the valley to your left). Ahead of you in the distance, left to right, are the north faces of the Eiger, Mönch, and Jungfrau; in the foreground is the Tschuggen peak, and just behind it, the Lauberhorn. This hike will take you around the left (east) side of this ridge. Simply follow the signs for Kleine (Kl.) Scheidegg, and you'll be there in about an hour—a little more for gawkers, picnickers, and photographers. You might have to tiptoe through streams of melted snow—or some small snow banks, even well into the summer—but the path is well marked, well maintained, and mostly level all the way to Kleine Scheidegg.

About 35 minutes into the hike, you'll reach a bunch of benches and a shelter with incredible unobstructed views of all three peaks—the perfect picnic spot. Fifteen minutes later on the left, you'll see the first sign of civilization: Restaurant Grindelwaldblick, offering a handy terrace lunch stop with tasty, hearty, and reasonable food (daily, closed Dec and May, see "Sleeping and Eating in Kleine Scheidegg," below). After 10 more minutes, you'll be at the Kleine Scheidegg train station, with plenty of other lunch options (including Bahnhof Buffet, see "Sleeping and Eating in Kleine Scheidegg," below).

From Kleine Scheidegg, you can catch the train to "the top of Europe" (see "Jungfraujoch," below). Or head downhill, riding the train or hiking (30 gorgeous min to Wengernalp station; 90 more steep min from there into the town of Wengen). The alpine views might be accompanied by the valley-filling mellow sound of Alp horns and distant avalanches.

If the weather turns bad or you run out of steam, catch the train early at the little Wengernalp station along the way. After Wengernalp, the trail to Wengen is steep and, though not dangerous, requires a good set of knees. Wengen is a good shopping town. (For accommodations, see "Sleeping in Wengen," below.) The boring final descent from Wengen to Lauterbrunnen is knee-killer steep—catch the train.

▲▲▲Jungfraujoch—The literal high point of any trip to the Swiss Alps is a train ride through the Eiger to the Jungfraujoch. At 11,300 feet, it's Europe's highest train station. The ride from Kleine Scheidegg takes about an hour (sit on right side for better views), including two five-minute stops at stations actually halfway up the notorious North Face of the Eiger. You have time to look out windows and marvel at how people could climb the Eiger and how the Swiss built this train more than a hundred years ago. The second half of the ride takes you through a tunnel inside the Eiger (some newer trains run multilingual videos about the history of the train).

Once you reach the top, study the Jungfraujoch chart to see your options (many of them are weather-dependent). There's a restaurant, history exhibit, ice palace (a cavern with a gallery of ice statues), and a continuous 20-minute video. A tunnel leads outside, where you can ski (30 SF for gear and lift ticket), sled (free loaner discs with deposit), ride in a dog sled (6 SF, mornings only), or hike 45 minutes across the ice to

Mönchsjochhütte (a mountain hut with a small restaurant). An elevator leads to the Sphinx observatory for the highest viewing point from which you can see Aletsch Glacier—Europe's longest, at nearly 11 miles—stretch to the south. Remember that your body isn't used to such high altitudes. Signs posted at the top remind you to take it easy.

The first trip of the day to Jungfraujoch is discounted; ask for a Good Morning Ticket and return from the top by noon (Nov–April you can get Good Morning rates for first or second train and stay after noon; train runs all year; round-trip fares to Jungfraujoch: from Kleine Scheidegg-normally 102 SF, 65 SF for first trip of day—about 8:00; from Lauterbrunnen-150 SF, 113 SF for first trip—about 7:05, confirm times and prices, discounts for Eurail/Eurail Selectpass and Swiss rail-pass holders, get leaflet on lifts at a local TI or call 033-828-7233, www.jungfrau.ch). For a trilingual weather forecast, call 033-828-7931; if it's cloudy, skip the trip.

▲▲Hike from Schynige Platte to First—The best day I've had hiking in the Berner Oberland was when I made the demanding six-hour ridge walk high above Lake Brienz on one side, with all that Jungfrau beauty on the other. Start at Wilderswil train station (just above Interlaken) and catch the little train up to Schynige Platte (6,560 feet). Walk through the flower display garden and into the wild alpine yonder. The high point is Faulhorn (8,790 feet, with its famous mountaintop hotel). Hike to a small gondola called "First" (7,110 feet), then descend to Grindelwald and catch a train back to your starting point, Wilderswil. Or, if you have a regional train pass (or no car but endless money), return to Gimmelwald via Lauterbrunnen from Grindelwald over Kleine Scheidegg. For an abbreviated ridge walk, consider the Panoramaweg, a short loop from Schynige Platte to Daub Peak.

▲Mountain Biking—Mountain biking is popular and accepted (as long as you stay on the clearly marked mountain-bike paths). A popular ride is the round-trip Mürren Loop that runs from Mürren to Gimmelwald, down the Sefinen Valley to Stechelberg, Lauterbrunnen (by funicular, bike costs same as person-7.80 SF), Grütschalp, and back to Mürren. You can rent bikes in Mürren (Stäger Sport, 25 SF/4 hrs, 35 SF/day, daily 9:00–17:00, closed May and Nov, across from TI/Sportzentrum, tel. 033-855-2355, www.staegersport.ch) or in Lauterbrunnen (Imboden Bike, 25 SF/4 hrs, 35 SF/day, full-suspension—reserve ahead—45 SF/half-day, 65 SF/full day, daily 8:00-18:30, tel. 033-855-2114).

You can also bike the Lauterbrunnen Valley from Lauterbrunnen to Interlaken. It's a gentle downhill ride via a peaceful bike path across the river from the road. Rent a bike at Lauterbrunnen (see above), bike to Interlaken, and return to Lauterbrunnen by train (to take bike on train, pay 3.30 SF extra from East station or 4.60 SF extra from West station). Or rent a bike at either Interlaken station, take the train to Lauterbrunnen, and ride back.

▲**More Hikes near Gimmelwald**—For a not-too-tough, three-hour walk (but there's a scary 20-minute stretch) with great Jungfrau views and some mountain farm action, ride the funicular from Mürren to Allmendhubel (6,344 feet) and walk to Marchegg, Saustal, and Grütschalp (a drop of about 1,500 feet), where you can catch the panorama train back to Mürren. An easier version is the lower Bergweg from Allmendhubel to Grütschalp via Winteregg. For an easy family stroll with grand views, walk from Mürren just above the train tracks to either Winteregg (40 min, restaurant, playground, train station) or Grütschalp (60 min, train station), then catch the panorama train back to Mürren. An easy, go-as-far-as-you-like trail from Gimmelwald is up the Sefinen Valley. Or you can wind from Gimmelwald down to Stechelberg (60 min).

You can get specifics at the Mürren TI. For a description of six diverse hikes on the west side of Lauterbrunnen, pick up the fine and free *Mürren-Schilthorn Hikes* brochure. This 3-D map of the Mürren mountainside makes a useful and attractive souvenir. For the other side of the valley, get the *Wandern Jungfraubahnen* brochure, also with a handy 3-D map of hiking trails (both brochures free, at stations, hotels, and TIs).

Rainy-Day Options

When it rains here, locals joke that they're washing the mountains. If clouds roll in, don't despair. They can roll out just as quickly, and there are plenty of good bad-weather options.

▲▲**Cloudy-Day Lauterbrunnen Valley Walk**—There are easy trails and pleasant walks along the floor of the Lauterbrunnen Valley. For a smell-the-cows-and-flowers lowland walk—ideal for a cloudy day, weary body, or tight budget—follow the riverside trail from Stechelberg's Schilthornbahn station for three miles to Lauterbrunnen's Staubbach Falls, near the town church (you can reverse the route, but it's a gradual uphill to Stechelberg). Detour to Trümmelbach Falls (below) en route. There's a fine, paved, car-free, riverside path all the way.

If you're staying in Gimmelwald: Take the lift down to Stechelberg (5 min), then walk to Lauterbrunnen, detouring to Trümmelbach Falls shortly after Stechelberg (15 min to falls, another 45 min to Lauterbrunnen). To return to Gimmelwald from Lauterbrunnen, take the funicular up to Grütschalp (10 min), then either walk (90 min to Gimmelwald) or take the panorama train (15 min) to Mürren. From Mürren, it's a downhill walk (30 min) to Gimmelwald. (This loop trip can be reversed.)

▲**Trümmelbach Falls**—If all the waterfalls have you intrigued, sneak a behind-the-scenes look at the valley's most powerful one, Trümmelbach Falls (10 SF, July–Aug daily 8:30–18:00, June 9:00–17:30, Easter–May and Sept–mid-Nov daily 9:00–17:00, closed mid-Nov–Easter, on Lauterbrunnen–Stechelberg road, take postal bus from Lauterbrunnen

TI or Stechelberg gondola station, tel. 033-855-3232). You'll ride an elevator up through the mountain and climb through several caves (wet, with lots of stairs, and—for some—claustrophobic) to see the melt from the Eiger, Mönch, and Jungfrau grinding like God's band saw through the mountain at the rate of up to 5,200 gallons a second (that's 20,000 liters—nearly double the beer consumption at Oktoberfest). The upper area is the best; if your legs ache, skip the lower falls and ride down on the elevator.

Lauterbrunnen Folk Museum—The Heimatmuseum in Lauterbrunnen shows off the local folk culture (free if you're staying in the region, 2 SF if you're staying in Interlaken, 3 SF otherwise, mid-June–mid-Oct Tue, Thu, and Sat–Sun 14:00–17:00, closed off-season, just over bridge and below church at the far end of town, tel. 033-855-3586 or 033-855-1388).

Mürren Activities—This low-key alpine resort town offers a variety of rainy-day activities, from its shops to its slick *Sportzentrum* (sports center) with pools, steam baths, squash, and a fitness center (for details, see "Sleeping in Mürren," below). On Wednesday nights at 20:30 from June through August, Mürren's *Sportzentrum* hosts a lively free cultural night with alpenhorns, folk music, and local wine.

Interlaken Boat Trips—Consider taking a boat trip from Interlaken (see "Interlaken—Sights," above).

▲▲Swiss Open-Air Folk Museum at Ballenberg—Across Lake Brienz from Interlaken, the Swiss Open-Air Museum of Vernacular Architecture, Country Life, and Crafts in the Bernese Oberland is a rich collection of traditional and historic farmhouses from every region of the country. Each house is carefully furnished, and many feature traditional craftspeople at work. The sprawling 50-acre park, laid out roughly as a huge Swiss map, is a natural preserve providing a wonderful setting for this culture-on-a-lazy-Susan look at Switzerland.

The Thurgau house (#621) has an interesting wattle-and-daub (half-timbered construction) display, and house #331 has a fun bread museum. Visit the new chocolate shop. Use the 2 SF map/guide. The more expensive picture book is a better souvenir than guide (entry–16 SF, half-price after 16:00, houses open May–Oct daily 10:00–17:00, park stays open later, craft demonstration schedules are listed just inside entry, tel. 033-952-1030, www.ballenberg.ch).

A reasonable outdoor cafeteria is inside the west entrance, and fresh bread, sausage, mountain cheese, and other goodies are on sale in several houses. Picnic tables and grills with free firewood are scattered throughout the park.

The little wooden village of Brienzwiler (near the east entrance) is a museum in itself, with a lovely little church.

To get from Interlaken to Ballenberg: Take the train from Interlaken to Brienz (hrly, 30 min, 7.20 SF one-way from West station).

From Brienz, catch a bus to Ballenberg (10 min, 3 SF one-way) or hike (45 min, slightly uphill). If you have the time, consider coming back by boat (Brienz boat dock next to train station, one-way to Interlaken-16 SF). Trains also run occasionally from Interlaken to Brienzwiler, a 20-min uphill walk to the museum (every 2 hrs, 30 min, 9.20 SF one-way from West station). A RailAway combo-ticket, available at either Interlaken station, includes transportation to and from Ballenberg and your admission (32 SF from West, 30.40 SF from East, add 9.40 SF to return by boat instead).

SLEEPING AND EATING

Sleeping in Gimmelwald
(4,593 feet, country code: 41)

To inhale the Alps and really hold it in, sleep high in Gimmelwald. Poor but pleasantly stuck in the past, the village has a creaky hotel, happy hostel, decent pension, a couple of B&Bs, and even a Web site (www .gimmelwald.ch). The only bad news is that the lift costs 7.80 SF each way to get there.

$$ **Maria and Olle Eggimann** rent two rooms—Gimmelwald's most comfortable—in their quirky but alpine-sleek chalet. Maria and Olle, who job-share the village's only teaching position and raise three kids of their own, offer visitors a rare, and for some, almost too intimate, peek at this community (D-110 SF, Db with kitchenette-180 SF for 2 or 3 people, optional breakfast-18 SF, no CC, last check-in 19:30, 3-night minimum for advance reservations; from gondola continue straight for 200 yards along the town's only road, B&B on left, tel. 033-855-3575, oeggimann@bluewin.ch, SE fluently).

$$ **Pension Restaurant Gimmelwald** offers 13 basic rooms under low, creaky ceilings (D-110 SF, Db-130 SF, T-150 SF, Q-180 SF, 5 SF per person surcharge for 1-night stays). It also has sheetless backpacker beds (25–35 SF in small dorm rooms). The pension has a scenic terrace overlooking the Jungfrau and the hostel (below), and is the village's only restaurant, offering good meals (closed late Oct–Christmas and mid-April–mid-May, non-smoking rooms but restaurant can get smoky, 50 yards from gondola station; reserve by phone, plus obligatory reconfirmation by phone 2-3 days before arrival; tel. 033-855-1730, fax 033-855-1925, pensiongimmelwald@tcnet.ch, Liesi and Mäni).

$ **Hotel Mittaghorn,** the treasure of Gimmelwald, is run by Walter Mittler, a perfect Swiss gentleman. Walter's hotel is a classic, creaky, alpine-style place with memorable beds, ancient down comforters (short and fat; wear socks and drape the blanket over your feet), and a million-dollar view of the Jungfrau Alps. The loft has a dozen real beds, several sinks, down comforters, and a fire ladder out the back window. The hotel has one shower for 10 rooms (1 SF/5 min). Walter is careful not to let his

SLEEP CODE

(1.40 SF = about $1, country code: 41)
Sleep Code: **S** = Single, **D** = Double/Twin, **T** = Triple, **Q** = Quad, **b** = bathroom, **s** = shower only, **no CC** = Credit Cards not accepted, **SE** = Speaks English, **NSE** = No English. Unless otherwise noted, credit cards are accepted, English is spoken, and breakfast is included.

To help you sort easily through these listings, I've divided the rooms into three categories, based on the price for a standard double room with bath:

$$$ **Higher Priced**—Most rooms 150 SF or more.
$$ **Moderately Priced**—Most rooms between 90–150 SF.
$ **Lower Priced**—Most rooms 90 SF or less.

At higher altitudes, many hotels, restaurants, and shops are closed between Easter and late May. Those traveling by car should note that you can't drive to Gimmelwald, Mürren, Wengen, Kleine Scheidegg, or Obersteinberg—but don't let that stop you from staying up in the mountains (park the car and zip up on a lift; see "Transportation Connections," below). Lauterbrunnen, Stechelberg, Isenfluh, and Interlaken are no problem for drivers.

place get too hectic or big, and he enjoys sensitive Back Door travelers. He runs the hotel with a little help from Rosemarie from the village.

To some, Hotel Mittaghorn is a fire waiting to happen, with a kitchen that would never pass code, lumpy beds, teeny towels, and minimal plumbing, run by an eccentric old grouch. These people enjoy Mürren, Interlaken, or Wengen, and that's where they should sleep. Be warned, you'll see more of my readers than locals here, but it's a fun crowd—an extended family (D-70–80 SF, T-100 SF, Q-125 SF, loft beds-25 SF, 6 SF surcharge per person for 1-night stays except in loft, all with breakfast, no CC, closed Nov–March, tel. 033-855-1658, www.ricksteves.com/mittaghorn). Reserve by telephone only, then reconfirm by phone the day before your arrival. Walter usually offers his guests a simple 15 SF dinner. Hotel Mittaghorn is at the top of Gimmelwald, a five-minute climb up the steps from the village intersection.

$ **Mountain Hostel** is a beehive of activity, as clean as its guests, cheap, and friendly. Phone ahead, or to secure one of its 50 dorm beds the same day, call after 9:30 and leave your name. The hostel has low ceilings, a self-service kitchen, a mini-grocery, a free pool table, and healthy plumbing. It's mostly a college-age crowd; families and older travelers will probably feel more comfortable elsewhere. Petra Brunner has lined the porch with flowers. This relaxed hostel survives with the help of its guests. Read the signs (please clean the kitchen), respect Petra's rules, and leave it tidier than you found it. The place is one of those rare spots where a congenial atmosphere spontaneously combusts, and spaghetti becomes communal as it cooks (20 SF per bed in 6- to 15-bed rooms, sheets included, showers-1 SF, no breakfast, hostel membership not required, no CC, Internet access-12 SF/hour, laundry-5 SF/load, 20 yards from lift station, tel. & fax 033-855-1704, www .mountainhostel.com, mountainhostel@tcnet.ch).

   $ Esther's Guesthouse, overlooking the main intersection of the village, is like an upscale mini-hostel with five clean, basic, and comfortable rooms sharing two bathrooms and a great kitchen (S-40 SF, D-80–95 SF, T-100–120 SF, Q-150 SF, no CC, 2-night stays preferred, make your own breakfast or pay 12 SF and Esther will make it for you, non-smoking, tel. 033-855-5488, fax 033-855-5492, www .esthersguesthouse.ch, info@esthersguesthouse.ch, some English spoken).

   $ Schlaf im Stroh (Sleep in Straw) offers exactly that, in an actual barn. After the cows head for higher ground in the summer, the friendly von Allmen family hoses out their barn and fills it with straw and budget travelers. Blankets are free, but bring your own sheet, sleep sack, or sleeping bag. No beds, no bunks, no mattresses, no kidding (21 SF, 10 SF for kids up to 10, thereafter kids pay their age plus 1 SF, no CC, includes breakfast and a modern bathroom, showers-2 SF, open mid-June–mid-Oct, depending on grass and snow levels, almost never full; from lift, continue straight through intersection, barn marked 1995 on right, run by Esther with same contact info as above).

Eating in Gimmelwald

Pension Gimmelwald, the only restaurant in town, serves a hearty breakfast buffet for 13.50 SF, fine lunches, and good dinners (10–20 SF), featuring cheese fondue, a tasty *Rösti*, local organic produce, homemade pies, and spherical brownies (daily 7:30–23:00). The hostel has a decent members' kitchen, but serves no food. Hotel Mittaghorn serves dinner only to its guests (15 SF). Consider packing in a picnic meal from the larger towns. If you need a few groceries and want to skip the hike to Mürren, you can buy the essentials—noodles, spaghetti sauce, and candy bars—at the Mountain Hostel's reception desk.

   The local farmers sell their produce. Esther (at the main intersection of the village) sells cheese, sausage, bread, and Gimmelwald's best yogurt—but only until the cows go up in June.

Sleeping in Mürren
(5,381 feet, country code: 41)

Mürren—pleasant as an alpine resort can be—is traffic-free and filled with bakeries, cafés, souvenirs, old-timers with walking sticks, GE employees enjoying incentive trips, and Japanese tourists making movies of each other with a Fujichrome backdrop. Its chalets are prefab-rustic. Sitting on a ledge 2,000 feet above the Lauterbrunnen Valley, surrounded by a fortissimo chorus of mountains, the town has all the comforts of home (for a price) without the pretentiousness of more famous resorts. With help from a gondola, train, and funicular, hiking options are endless from Mürren. Mürren has an ATM (by the Co-op grocery), and there are lockers at both the train and gondola stations (located a 10-min walk apart, on opposite ends of town).

Mürren's **TI** can help you find a room, give hiking advice, and change money (July–Sept Mon–Fri 9:00–12:00 & 13:00–18:30, Thu until 20:30, Sat 13:00–18:30, Sun 13:00–17:30, less off-season, above the village, follow signs to Sportzentrum, tel. 033-856-8686, www.wengen-muerren.ch). The slick **Sportzentrum** (sports center) that houses the TI offers a world of indoor activities (13 SF to use pool and whirlpool; 8 SF for Gimmelwald, Lauterbrunnen, and Interlaken hotel guests; free for guests at most Mürren hotels—ask your hotelier for a voucher, pool open Mon–Sat 14:00–18:45, Thu until 20:15, closed Sun, May, and Nov–mid-Dec).

You can rent **mountain bikes** and hiking boots at Stäger Sport (bikes-25 SF/4 hrs, 35 SF/day, boots-12 SF/day, daily 9:00–17:00, closed May and Nov, across from TI/Sportzentrum, tel. 033-855-2355, www.staegersport.ch). You can use the **Internet** at the TI (see above, 5 SF/20 min) or at Eiger Guesthouse (12 SF/hr, daily 8:00–23:00, tel. 033-856-5460, across from train station). Top Apartments will do your **laundry** by request (25 SF per load, unreliable hours: Mon–Sat 9:00–11:00 & 15:00–17:00, closed Sun, behind and across from Hotel Bellevue, look for blue triangle, call first to drop off in morning, tel. 033-855-3706).

Prices for accommodations are often higher during the ski season. Many hotels and restaurants close in spring, roughly from Easter to late May, and any time between late September and mid-December.

$$$ Hotel Alpina is a simple, modern place with 24 comfortable rooms and a concrete feeling—a good thing, given its cliff-edge position (Sb-75–95 SF, Db-140–170 SF, Tb-180–210 SF, Qb-210–240 SF with awesome Jungfrau views and balconies, 4–5 person apartments-250–300 SF, exit left from station, walk 2 min downhill, tel. 033-855-1361, fax 033-855-1049, www.muerren.ch/alpina, alpina@muerren.ch, Taugwalder family).

$$$ Hotel Bellevue has a homey lounge, great view terrace, hunter-themed Jägerstübli restaurant, and 17 good rooms at fair rates,

Mürren

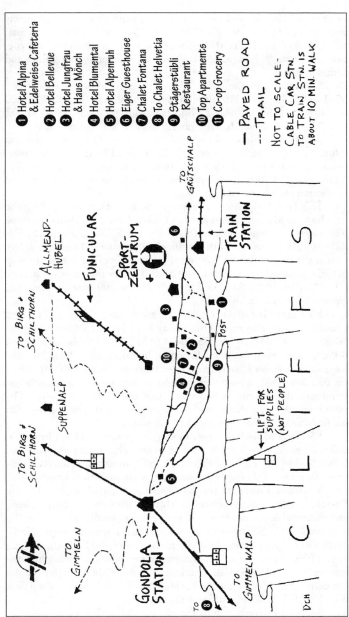

1 Hotel Alpina & Edelweiss Cafeteria
2 Hotel Bellevue
3 Hotel Jungfrau & Haus Mönch
4 Hotel Blumental
5 Hotel Alpenruh
6 Eiger Guesthouse
7 Chalet Fontana
8 To Chalet Helvetia
9 Stägerstübli Restaurant
10 Top Apartments
11 Co-op Grocery

— PAVED ROAD
--- TRAIL

NOT TO SCALE -
CABLE CAR STN.
TO TRAIN STN. IS
ABOUT 10 MIN WALK

FUNICULAR

ALLMEND-HÜBEL

TO BIRG + SCHILTHORN

SPORT-ZENTRUM

TO GRÜTSCHALP

TRAIN STATION

SUPPENALP

TO BIRG + SCHILTHORN

POST

LIFT FOR SUPPLIES
(NOT PEOPLE)

TO GIMMELN

GONDOLA STATION

TO BIRG + SCHILTHORN

TO GIMMELWALD

C L I F F S

DCH

most with balconies and views. The more expensive rooms are newly renovated and larger (Sb-95–125 SF, Db-170–210 SF, Internet access, tel. 033-855-1401, fax 033-855-1490, www.muerren.ch/bellevue, bellevue-crystal@bluewin.ch, run by friendly and hardworking Ruth and Othmar Suter).

$$$ **Hotel Jungfrau** offers 29 modern and comfortable rooms (Sb-95–110 SF, Db-190–210 SF with view, Sb-90–110 SF, Db-170–200 SF without, elevator, near TI/Sportzentrum, tel. 033-855-4545, fax 033-855-4549, www.hoteljungfrau.ch, mail@hoteljungfrau.ch).

$$$ **Hotel Blumental** has 16 older but nicely furnished rooms and a fun, woodsy game/TV lounge (Sb-75–80 SF, Db-150–170 SF, non-smoking rooms but smoky lobby, attached restaurant, tel. 033-855-1826, fax 033-855-3686, www.muerren.ch/blumental, blumental @muerren.ch, von Allmen family).

$$$ **Hotel Alpenruh** is yuppie-rustic and overpriced, but it's the only hotel in Mürren open year-round. The 26 comfortable rooms come with views and some balconies (Sb-105–140 SF, Db-180–260 SF, Tb-225–315 SF, prices vary with season, elevator, attached restaurant, free sauna, tanning bed-10 SF/20 min, free vouchers for breakfast atop Schilthorn, atop Allmendhubel, or at hotel, 10 yards from gondola station, tel. 033-856-8800, fax 033-856-8888, www.muerren.ch/alpenruh, alpenruh@schilthorn.ch).

$$ **Eiger Guesthouse** offers 14 good budget rooms. This is a friendly, creaky, easygoing home away from home (S-60–65 SF, Sb-80–85 SF, D-100–110 SF, Db-130–140 SF, 39–45 SF beds in 2- and 4-bunk rooms, with sheets and breakfast, Internet access, closed Nov and for one month after Easter, across from train station, tel. 033-856-5460, fax 033-856-5461, www.muerren.ch/eigerguesthouse, eigerguesthouse @muerren.ch, well run by Scotsman Alan and Swiss Véronique). The restaurant serves good, reasonably priced dinners. Its poolroom—with public Internet access—is a popular local hangout.

$$ **Haus Mönch,** a basic, blocky lodge run by Hotel Jungfrau, offers 20 woodsy, well-worn but fine rooms, plus good Jungfrau views (Db-140–144 SF, Tb-180 SF, near TI and Sportzentrum, tel. 033-855-4545, fax 033-855-4549, www.hoteljungfrau.ch, mail@hoteljungfrau.ch).

$ **Chalet Fontana,** run by charming Englishwoman Denise Fussell, is a rare budget option in Mürren, with simple, crispy-clean, and comfortable rooms (35–45 SF per person in small doubles or triples with breakfast, 5 SF cheaper without breakfast, 1 apartment with kitchenette-50 SF per person, third and fourth person-10 SF each, no CC, closed Nov–April, across street from Stägerstübli restaurant in town center, tel. 033-855-4385, mobile 078-642-3485, chaletfontana @muerren.ch). If no one's home, check at the Ed Abegglen shop next door (tel. 033-855-1245, off-season only).

$ **Chalet Helvetia,** run by friendly Frau Hunziker, offers a homey, clean two-bedroom apartment with bathroom, kitchen, separate entrance, and balcony for 40 SF per person (up to 5 people, no breakfast, 2-night minimum preferred, higher price for 1-night stays, a few blocks below cable car station on path to Gimmelwald, look for red *Zimmer* sign on right, tel. 033-855-4169, mobile 079-234-7867, kurthunziker105@msn.com).

Eating in Mürren

For a rare bit of ruggedness, eat at the **Stägerstübli** (15–30 SF lunches and dinners, daily 11:30–22:00). **Kandahar Snack Bar** has fun, creative, and inexpensive light meals; a good selection of coffees, teas, and pastries; and impressive views (take-out available, run by lively Canadian Lesley, daily 10:00–18:00, at the **Sportzentrum**). The reasonable **Edelweiss** self-serve restaurant wins the Best View award (daily 10:30–18:00, next to Hotel Alpina). The recommended **Eiger Guesthouse** and **Hotel Bellevue** also have good restaurants (see "Sleeping in Mürren," above). For picnic fixings, shop at **Co-op** (Mon–Fri 8:00–12:00 & 13:45–18:30, Sat until 16:00, closed Sun).

Sleeping in Wengen
(4,180 feet, country code: 41)

Wengen, a bigger, fancier Mürren on the other side of the valley, has plenty of grand hotels, many shops, tennis courts, mini-golf, and terrific views. Minor celebrities (such as Graham Greene) come here to disappear. This traffic-free resort is an easy train ride above Lauterbrunnen and halfway up to Kleine Scheidegg and Männlichen, and offers more activities for those needing distraction from the scenery. Hiking is better from Mürren and Gimmelwald. The **TI** is one block from the station; go up to the main drag, turn left, and look ahead on the left (June–Sept and Dec–mid-April daily 9:00–18:00; mid-April–May and Oct–Nov Mon–Fri 9:00–18:00, closed Sat–Sun; Internet access-5 SF/20 min; tel. 033-855-1414, www.wengen-muerren.ch).

Sleeping above the Station

$$$ Hotel Berghaus, in a quiet area a five-minute walk from the main street, offers 19 rooms above a fine restaurant specializing in fish (Sb-82-117 SF, Db-164-234 SF, 5 percent cheaper with this book and cash, elevator, guests can use pool at Park Hotel for free, call on phone at station hotel board for free pick-up, or walk up street across from Bernerhof Hotel, bear right and then left at fork, 200 yards more past church on the left, tel. 033-855-2151, fax 033-855-3820, www.wengen .com/hotel/berghaus, berghaus@wengen.com, Fontana family).

$$$ Hotel Schönegg is a centrally-located splurge, right on Wengen's main drag (Sb-100-110 SF, Db-200-220 SF; higher July-Aug: Sb-115-125 SF, Db-230-250 SF; non-smoking rooms, all rooms have balconies and great views, cozy family room with fireplace, Internet access, good restaurant with big terrace, look for big yellow hotel on main drag near TI, tel. 033-855-3422, fax 033-855-4233, www.hotel -schoenegg.ch, schoenegg@tcnet.ch, Herr und Frau Berthod).

$$$ Hotel Eiger, next to the train station, is older but clean (Sb-102-125 SF, Db-204-250 SF, all rooms have balconies, tel. 033-856-0505, fax 033-856-0506, www.eiger-wengen.ch, hotel@eiger-wengen.ch).

Sleeping below the Station

The first two listings are bright, cheery, family-friendly, and five minutes below the station: leave the station toward the Co-op store, turn right and go under the rail bridge, bear right (paved path) at the fork, and follow the road down and around.

$$ Bären Hotel, run by friendly Therese and Willy Brunner, offers 14 tidy rooms with perky, bright-orange bathrooms (Sb-60–90 SF, Db-120–160 SF, Tb-180–210 SF, dinner-20 SF more, family rooms, tel. 033-855-1419, fax 033-855-1525, www.baeren-wengen.ch, info@baeren -wengen.ch).

$$ Familienhotel Edelweiss has 25 bright rooms, lots of fun public spaces, a Christian emphasis, and a jittery Chihuahua named Speedy (Sb-65–75 SF, Db-130–150 SF, non-smoking, each room has balcony or TV, great family rooms, elevator, TV lounge, game room, meeting room, kids' playroom, tel. 033-855-2388, fax 033-855-4288, www.vch.ch/edelweiss, edelweiss@vch.ch, Bärtschi family).

$$ Clare and Andy's Chalet (Trogihalten) offers three rustic, low-ceilinged rooms (1-room studio: Sb-52 SF, Db-80 SF; 2-room suite: Sb/Db-98 SF, Tb-131 SF, Qb-172 SF; 4-room flat: Tb-147 SF, Qb-176 SF, breakfast-15 SF, dinner by request-30 SF, 4-night minimum preferred, prices higher for shorter stays, no CC, all rooms with balconies, leave station to the left and follow paved path next to Bernerhof Hotel downhill, soon after path becomes gravel look ahead and to the right, tel. & fax 033-855-1712, http://home.sunrise.ch/aregez, regez .chalet.wengen@spectraweb.ch, Clare's English, Andy's Swiss).

Sleeping and Eating in Kleine Scheidegg
(6,762 feet, country code: 41)

Confirm price and availability before ascending. These two places also serve meals.

$$ Bahnhof Buffet invites you to sleep face-to-face with the Eiger (dorm bed-63 SF, D-156 SF, prices include breakfast and dinner, in the train station building, tel. 033-828-7828, fax 033-828-7830, www .bahnhof-scheidegg.ch).

$ Restaurant Grindelwaldblick, a 10-minute hike from the station, really gets you up into the mountains (38 SF for bed in 12-bed room, includes sheets, closed Nov and May, tel. 033-855-1374, fax 033-855-4205, www.grindelwaldblick.ch).

Sleeping in Stechelberg
(3,025 feet, country code: 41)
Stechelberg is the hamlet at the end of Lauterbrunnen Valley, at the base of the lift to Gimmelwald, Mürren, and the Schilthorn.

$$ Hotel Stechelberg, at road's end, is surrounded by waterfalls and vertical rock, with 20 comfortable, spacious, and quiet rooms and a lovely garden terrace (D-82–104 SF, Db-120–158 SF, T-147 SF, Tb-186 SF, Q-168 SF, Qb-234 SF, post bus stops here, tel. 033-855-2921, fax 033-855-4438, www.stechelberg.ch, hotel@stechelberg.ch).

$ Nelli Beer, renting three rooms in a quiet, scenic, and folksy setting, is your best Stechelberg option (S-35 SF, D-60 SF, 2-night minimum, no CC, over river behind Stechelberg post office at big *Zimmer* sign, get off post bus at post office, tel. 033-855-3930, some English spoken).

$ Naturfreundehaus Alpenhof is a homey, cozy alpine lodge for hikers. New owners Marc (English) and Diane (Australian) have made it a quiet and peaceful place to relax (64 beds, 4–8 people per coed room, 22 SF per bed, less for members, breakfast-9 SF extra, laundry-10 SF, no CC, tel. 033-855-1202, alpenhof@naturfreunde.ch). Behind Hotel Stechelberg (post bus stop), take the path to the right, passing the Hotel's terrace and flowerpots, and cross the river. It's the second house on the left.

Sleeping in Lauterbrunnen
(2,612 feet, country code: 41)
Lauterbrunnen—with a train station, funicular, bank, shops, and lots of hotels—is the valley's commercial center. This is the jumping-off point for Jungfrau and Schilthorn adventures. It's idyllic, in spite of the busy road and big buildings. Stop by the friendly **TI** to check the weather forecast, use the Internet (5 SF/20 min), and to buy any regional train or lift tickets you need (June–Aug Mon–Sat 10:00–12:00 & 15:00–18:30, Sun 15:00–18:30, less off-season, 1 block up from station, tel. 033-856-8568, www.wengen-muerren.ch). You can rent **mountain bikes** at Imboden Bike on the main street (25 SF/4 hrs, 35 SF/day, full-suspension—reserve ahead—45 SF/half-day, 65 SF/full day, daily 8:00-18:30, tel. 033-855-2114). The Valley Hostel on the main street also runs an **Internet café** (12 SF/hr) and a small **launderette** (10 SF/load, don't open dryer door until machine is finished or you'll have to pay another 5 SF to start it again; both daily 8:00–22:00, less Nov–April, tel. 033-855-2008).

$$ Hotel Staubbach, a big Old World place—one of the first hotels in the valley (1890)—is being lovingly restored by hardworking American Craig and his Swiss wife, Corinne. Its 30 plain, comfortable rooms are family-friendly, there's a kids' play area, and the parking is free. Many rooms have great views. They keep their prices down by providing room-cleaning only after every third night (S-50 SF, Ss-60 SF, Sb-90 SF, D-80 SF, Db-110 SF, figure 40 SF per person in family rooms sleeping up to 6, 10 SF extra per room for 1-night stays, elevator, 4 blocks up from station on the left, tel. 033-855-5454, fax 033-855-5484, www.staubbach.ch, hotel@staubbach.ch).

$ **Valley Hostel** is practical, friendly, and comfortable, offering inexpensive beds for quieter travelers of all ages, with a pleasant garden and the welcoming Abegglen family: Martha, Alfred, Stefan, and Fränzi (D with bunk beds-52 SF, twin D-60 SF, beds in larger family-friendly rooms-23 SF each, no breakfast but kitchen is available, no CC, most rooms have balconies, cheese fondue on request for guests 18:00–19:30 —16 SF per person, non-smoking, Internet access, laundry, 2 blocks up from train station, tel. & fax 033-855-2008, www.valleyhostel.ch, info@valleyhostel.ch).

$ **Chalet im Rohr,** a creaky, old, woody place, has oodles of character and 26 SF beds in big one- to four-bed rooms (2 SF discount after second night, no breakfast, common kitchen-0.50 SF per person, no CC, closed for 3 weeks after Easter, below church on main drag, tel. & fax 033-855-2182).

$ **Matratzenlager Stocki** is rustic and humble, with the cheapest beds in town (14 SF with sheets in easygoing little 30-bed coed dorm with kitchen, closed Nov–Dec; across river from station, go below station to parking and take last right before garage, walk on path and then turn left over bridge, walk up and to the right 200 yards; tel. 033-855-1754).

$ **Camping:** Two campgrounds just south of town provide 15–35 SF beds (in dorms and 2-, 4-, and 6-bed bungalows, no sheets, kitchen facilities, no CC, big English-speaking tour groups): **Mountain Holiday Park-Camping Jungfrau,** romantically situated beyond Staubbach Falls, is huge and well organized by Hans (tel. 033-856-2010, fax 033-856-2020, www.camping-jungfrau.ch). It also has fancier cabins (24 SF per person). **Schützenbach Retreat,** on the left just past Lauterbrunnen toward Stechelberg, is simpler (tel. 033-855-1268, www.schutzenbach -retreat.ch).

Eating in Lauterbrunnen

Hotel Restaurant Jungfrau, along the main street on the right-hand side, offers a wide range of specialities served by a friendly staff (daily 12:00–14:00 & 18:00–20:00, tel. 033-855-3434, run by Brigitte Melliger). At **Hotel Restaurant Oberland,** the Nolan family takes pride in serving tasty meals (daily 11:30–16:00 & 17:30–21:00, tel. 033-855-1241). **Hotel Restaurant Schützen** has fine food but impersonal staff (daily 7:15–22:30, tel. 033-855-3026).

Sleeping in Interlaken
(country code: 41)

I'd head for Gimmelwald, or at least Lauterbrunnen (20 min by train or car). Interlaken is not the Alps. But if you must stay...

$$$ Hotel Lotschberg, with a sun terrace and 21 wonderful rooms, is run by English-speaking Susi and Fritz and is the best real hotel value in town. Happy to dispense information, these gregarious folks pride themselves on a personal touch that sets them apart from other hotels. Fritz also organizes guided adventures (Sb-92–110 SF, Db-129–155 SF, big Db-162–190 SF, extra bed-25 SF, family deals, cheaper prices are for Nov–May, non-smoking, elevator, Internet access-14 SF/hr, laundry service-9 SF/load, bike rental, honeymoon/romance decoration-40 SF or 60 SF with champagne, discounted parasailing for guests if you "Fly with Fritz"; 3-min walk from West station: cross the square in front of Migros store, then take first right, and then first left, to General Guisanstrasse 31; tel. 033-822-2545, fax 033-822-2579, www .lotschberg.ch, hotel@lotschberg.ch).

$$ Sunny Days B&B, run by Dave (British) and Brigit (Swiss), has nine colorful, cheery rooms ideal for families. Reserve ahead—this popular place books up early (Sb-98–110 SF, Db-110–155 SF, extra adult in room-45 SF, each additional child under 16 costs 38 SF extra, discounts for longer stays Nov–March, great breakfast, Internet access-16 SF/hr, laundry service-18 SF/load; exit left out of West station and take first bridge to your left, after crossing bridges turn left on peaceful Helvetiastrasse and go 3 blocks to #29; tel. 033-822-8343, fax 033-823-8343, www.sunnydays.ch, mail@sunnydays.ch).

$$ Guest House Susi's B&B is Hotel Lotschberg's no-frills, cash-only annex, run by Fritz and Susi, offering nicely furnished, cozy rooms (Sb-72–90 SF, Db-98–125 SF, apartments with kitchenettes for 2 people-100 SF; for 4–5 people-180 SF, cheaper prices Nov–May, no CC, same phone and fax as Hotel Lotschberg above, www.bnb -interlaken.ch, susis@bnb-interlaken.ch).

$$ Hotel Aarburg offers 13 plain, peaceful rooms in a beautifully located but run-down old building a 10-minute walk from the West station (Sb-80 SF, Db-130 SF, next to launderette at Beatenbergstrasse 1, tel. 033-822-2615, fax 033-822-6397, hotel-aarburg@tcnet.ch).

$ Villa Margaretha, run by perky, English-speaking Frau Kunz-Joerin, offers the best cheap beds in town. It's a big Victorian house with a garden on a quiet residential street. Keep your room tidy and you'll have a friend for life (D-86 SF, T-129 SF, Q-172 SF, the 3 rooms share a big bathroom, 2-night minimum, apartment-156–162 SF with a 1-week minimum, closed Oct–April, no CC, no breakfast served but dishes and kitchenette available, lots of rules to abide by; walk up small street directly in front of West station's parking lot entrance, go 3 blocks and look to your right for Aarmühlestrasse 13, tel. 033-822-1813).

$ **Backpackers' Villa (Sonnenhof) Interlaken** is a creative guest house run by a Methodist church group. It's fun, youthful, and great for families, without the frat-party ambience of Balmer's (below). Rooms are comfortable and half come with Jungfrau-view balconies (D-88 SF, T-120 SF, Q-144 SF, dorm beds in 5- to 7-bed rooms with lockers and sheets-32 SF per person, 5 SF more per person for rooms with toilets and Jungfrau-view balconies, includes breakfast, kitchen, garden, movies, small game room, Internet access-10 SF/hr, laundry-10 SF/load, bike rental, no curfew, open all day, check-in 16:00–22:00, 10-min walk from either station, across big grassy field from TI, Alpenstrasse 16, tel. 033-826-7171, fax 033-826-7172, www.villa.ch, backpackers@villa.ch).

$ **Balmer's Herberge** is many people's idea of backpacker heaven. This Interlaken institution comes with movies, table tennis, a launderette (8 SF/load), bar, restaurant, swapping library, Internet access (20 SF/hr), tiny grocery, bike rental, currency exchange, excursions, a shuttle-bus service (which meets important arriving trains), and a friendly, hardworking staff. This little Nebraska is home for those who miss their fraternity. It can be a mob scene, especially on summer weekends (dorm beds-24 SF, S-40 SF; D, T, or Q-30–34 SF per person, includes sheets and breakfast, non-smoking, open year-round, easy Internet reservations recommended 5 days in advance, Hauptstrasse 23, in Matten, 15-min walk from either Interlaken station, tel. 033-822-1961, fax 033-823-3261, www.balmers.com, balmers@tcnet.ch).

$ **Happy Inn Lodge** has a gruff staff and 16 cheap rooms above a lively, noisy restaurant a five-minute walk from the West station (S-30–40 SF, D-60–80 SF, bunk in 4- to 8-bed dorms-24–30 SF, breakfast-8 SF, Rosenstrasse 17, tel. 033-822-3225, fax 033-822-3268, www.happyinn.com, info@happyinn.com).

TRANSPORTATION CONNECTIONS

From Interlaken by train to: Spiez (2/hr, 20 min), **Brienz** (hrly, 30 min), **Bern** (hrly, 50 min), **Zürich** and **Zürich Airport** (hrly, 2.25 hrs, most direct but some with transfer in Bern). While there are a few long trains from Interlaken, you'll generally connect from Bern. Train info: toll tel. 0900-300-3004.

By train from Bern to: Lausanne (hrly, 70 min), **Zürich** (hrly, 70 min), **Appenzell** (hrly, 4.25 hrs, transfers in Zürich and Gossau or Bern and Gossau, or 5 hrs, change in Luzern and Herisau), **Salzburg** (4/day, 8 hrs, transfers include Zürich), **Munich** (7/day, 5.5–6.5 hrs, transfers in Zürich or Mannheim), **Frankfurt** (hrly, 4.5 hrs, some direct, others transfer in Basel or Mannheim), **Paris** (4/day, 4.5 hrs).

To Gimmelwald from Interlaken

By public transportation: Take the train from the Interlaken East *(Ost)* station to Lauterbrunnen. From here you have two options.

1) The faster, easier way—best in bad weather or at the end of a long day with lots of luggage—is to ride the post bus from Lauterbrunnen station (3.80 SF, hrly bus departure coordinated with arrival of train, stop: Schilthornbahn) to Stechelberg and the base of the Schilthornbahn gondola station, where the gondola will whisk you in five thrilling minutes up to Gimmelwald.

2) The more scenic route is to catch the funicular to Mürren (across the street from the train station). Ride up to Grütschalp, where a special scenic train *(Panorama Fahrt)* will roll you along the cliff into Mürren (total trip from Lauterbrunnen to Mürren: 30 min). From there, either walk a paved 30 minutes downhill to Gimmelwald, or walk 10 minutes across Mürren to catch the gondola (costs 7.80 SF and once in Gimmelwald, you'll have a 2- to 5-min uphill hike to reach accommodations).

By car: You can drive to Lauterbrunnen and to Stechelberg, but not to Gimmelwald (park in Stechelberg, and take the gondola—see below) or to Mürren, Wengen, or Kleine Scheidegg (park in Lauterbrunnen and take the train/funicular). For drivers, the most direct route to Gimmelwald is via the gondola at Stechelberg. It's a 30-minute drive from Interlaken to the Stechelberg gondola station (parking lot: 2 SF/2 hrs, 6 SF/day). Gimmelwald is the first stop above Stechelberg on the Schilthorn gondola (7.80 SF, 2/hr at :25 and :55). Note that for a week in early May and from mid-November through early December, the Schilthornbahn is closed for servicing, so you'll have to park in Lauterbrunnen (lot behind station: 2 SF/2 hrs, 9 SF/day) and go up to Gimmelwald via Mürren (see option #2, above).

APPENDIX

European National Tourist Offices in the United States

Austrian Tourist Office: Box 1142, New York, NY 10108-1142, tel. 212/944-6880, fax 212/730-4568, www.austria-tourism.com, info @oewnyc.com. Ask for their "Vacation Kit" with map. Fine hikes and city information.

Belgian National Tourist Office: 780 Third Ave. #1501, New York, NY 10017, tel. 212/758-8130, fax 212/355-7675, www.visitbelgium .com, info@visitbelgium.com. Hotel and city guides; brochures for ABC lovers—antiques, beer, and chocolates; map of Brussels; and a list of Jewish sights.

Visit Britain: 551 Fifth Ave., #701, New York, NY 10176, tel. 800/462-2748, fax 212/986-1188, www.visitbritain.com, travelinfo @visitbritain.org. Request the Britain Vacation Planner. Free maps of London and Britain. Regional information, garden tour map, and urban cultural activities brochure.

Czech Tourist Authority: 1109 Madison Ave., New York, NY 10028, tel. 212/288-0830, fax 212/288-0971, www.czechcenter.com, travelczech @pop.net. To get a weighty information package (1–2 lbs, no advertising), send a check for $4 to cover postage and specify places of interest. Basic information and map are free.

Denmark (see Scandinavia)

French Government Tourist Office: For questions and brochures (on regions, barging, and the wine country), call 410/286-8310. Ask for the France Guide. Materials delivered in 4 to 6 weeks are free; there's a $4 shipping fee for information delivered in 5 to 10 days.

Their Web site is www.franceguide.com, their e-mail address is info@franceguide.com, and their offices are...

In New York: 444 Madison Ave., 16th floor, New York, NY 10022, fax 212/838-7855.

In California: 9454 Wilshire Blvd. #310, Beverly Hills, CA 90212, fax 310/276-2835.

German National Tourist Office: 122 E. 42nd Street, 52nd floor, New York, NY 10168, tel. 212/661-7200, fax 212/661-7174, www.visits-to -germany.com, gntony@aol.com. Maps, Rhine schedules, castles, biking, and city and regional information.

Tourism Ireland: 345 Park Ave., 17th floor, New York, NY 10154, tel. 800/223-6470 or 212/418-0800, fax 212/371-9052, www.tourismireland .com. Useful "Ireland Magazine," Ireland map, events calendar, golfing, outdoor activities, and historic sights. Tourism Ireland also provides information to travelers who wish to visit Northern Ireland. Learn more about sightseeing opportunities and ask about a vacation planner packet, maps, walking routes, and horseback riding.

Italian Government Tourist Board: Check www.italiantourism.com and contact the nearest office...

In New York: 630 Fifth Ave. #1565, New York, NY 10111, brochure hotline tel. 212/245-4822, tel. 212/245-5618, fax 212/586-9249, enitny@italiantourism.com.

In Illinois: 500 N. Michigan Ave. #2240, Chicago, IL 60611, brochure hotline tel. 312/644-0990, tel. 312/644-0996, fax 312/644-3019, enitch@italiantourism.com.

In California: 12400 Wilshire Blvd. #550, Los Angeles, CA 90025, brochure hotline tel. 310/820-0098, tel. 310/820-1898, fax 310/820-6357, enitla@italiantourism.com.

Netherlands Board of Tourism: 355 Lexington Ave., 19th floor, New York, NY 10017, tel. 888/GO-HOLLAND, fax 212/370-9507, www .holland.com, info@goholland.com. Great country map, events calen-dar, and seasonal brochures; $5 donation requested for mailing (pay on receipt).

Scandinavian Tourism: P.O. Box 4649, Grand Central Station, New York, NY 10163, tel. 212/885-9700, fax 212/885-9710, www .goscandinavia.com, info@goscandinavia.com. Good general booklets on all the Scandinavian countries. Ask for specific country info and city maps.

Tourist Office of Spain: Check their Web sites (www.okspain.org and www.spain.info) and contact their nearest office...

In New York: 666 Fifth Ave., 35th floor, New York, NY 10103, tel. 212/265-8822, fax 212/265-8864, nuevayork@tourspain.es.

In Illinois: 845 N. Michigan Ave. #915E, Chicago, IL 60611, tel. 312/642-1992, fax 312/642-9817, chicago@tourspain.es.

In Florida: 1221 Brickell Ave. #1850, Miami, FL 33131, tel. 305/358- 1992, fax 305/358-8223, miami@tourspain.es.

In California: 8383 Wilshire Blvd. #956, Beverly Hills, CA 90211, tel. 323/658-7188, fax 323/658-1061, losangeles@tourspain.es.

2004

JANUARY						
S	M	T	W	T	F	S
				1	2	3
4	5	6	7	8	9	10
11	12	13	14	15	16	17
18	19	20	21	22	23	24
25	26	27	28	29	30	31

FEBRUARY						
S	M	T	W	T	F	S
1	2	3	4	5	6	7
8	9	10	11	12	13	14
15	16	17	18	19	20	21
22	23	24	25	26	27	28
29						

MARCH						
S	M	T	W	T	F	S
	1	2	3	4	5	6
7	8	9	10	11	12	13
14	15	16	17	18	19	20
21	22	23	24	25	26	27
28	29	30	31			

APRIL						
S	M	T	W	T	F	S
				1	2	3
4	5	6	7	8	9	10
11	12	13	14	15	16	17
18	19	20	21	22	23	24
25	26	27	28	29	30	

MAY						
S	M	T	W	T	F	S
						1
2	3	4	5	6	7	8
9	10	11	12	13	14	15
16	17	18	19	20	21	22
23/30	24/31	25	26	27	28	29

JUNE						
S	M	T	W	T	F	S
		1	2	3	4	5
6	7	8	9	10	11	12
13	14	15	16	17	18	19
20	21	22	23	24	25	26
27	28	29	30			

JULY						
S	M	T	W	T	F	S
				1	2	3
4	5	6	7	8	9	10
11	12	13	14	15	16	17
18	19	20	21	22	23	24
25	26	27	28	29	30	31

AUGUST						
S	M	T	W	T	F	S
1	2	3	4	5	6	7
8	9	10	11	12	13	14
15	16	17	18	19	20	21
22	23	24	25	26	27	28
29	30	31				

SEPTEMBER						
S	M	T	W	T	F	S
			1	2	3	4
5	6	7	8	9	10	11
12	13	14	15	16	17	18
19	20	21	22	23	24	25
26	27	28	29	30		

OCTOBER						
S	M	T	W	T	F	S
					1	2
3	4	5	6	7	8	9
10	11	12	13	14	15	16
17	18	19	20	21	22	23
24/31	25	26	27	28	29	30

NOVEMBER						
S	M	T	W	T	F	S
	1	2	3	4	5	6
7	8	9	10	11	12	13
14	15	16	17	18	19	20
21	22	23	24	25	26	27
28	29	30				

DECEMBER						
S	M	T	W	T	F	S
			1	2	3	4
5	6	7	8	9	10	11
12	13	14	15	16	17	18
19	20	21	22	23	24	25
26	27	28	29	30	31	

Switzerland Tourism: For questions and brochures call 877/794-8037. Comprehensive "Welcome to the Best of Switzerland" brochure, great maps, and hiking material. Or contact 608 Fifth Ave., New York, NY 10020, fax 212/262-6116, www.myswitzerland.com, info.usa@switzerland.com.

U.S. Embassies and Consulates
Austria: U.S. Embassy, Marriott Building 4th floor, Gartenbau-promenade 2, Vienna, tel. 01/313-390, www.usembassy.at
Belgium: U.S. Embassy, Regentlaan 27 Boulevard du Regent, Brussels, tel. 02/508-2111, www.usembassy.be
Britain: U.S. Embassy, 55 Upper Brook Street, London, tel. 020/7499-9000, www.usembassy.org.uk (also see Scotland, below)

Czech Republic: U.S. Embassy, Trziste 15, Prague, tel. 257-530-663, www.usembassy.cz

Denmark: U.S. Embassy, Dag Hammarskjölds Allé 24, Copenhagen, tel. 35 55 31 44, www.usembassy.dk

France: U.S. Embassy, 2 avenue Gabriel, Mo: Concorde, Paris, tel. 01 43 12 22 22, www.amb-usa.fr

Germany: U.S. Embassy, Clayallee 170, Berlin, tel. 030/832-9233, www.usembassy.de

Ireland: U.S. Embassy, 42 Elgin Road, Dublin, tel. 01/668-7122 or 01/668-8777, www.usembassy.ie

Italy: U.S. Embassy, Via Veneto 119, Rome, tel. 06-46741, www .usembassy.it; U.S. Consulate General at Lungarno Vespucci 38, Florence, tel. 055-266-951, www.usembassy.it/florence

The Netherlands: U.S. Embassy at Lange Voorhout 102, The Hague, tel. 070/310-9209, www.usemb.nl; U.S. Consulate at Museumplein 19, Amsterdam (for passport concerns), tel. 020/575-5309, www.usemb.nl /consul.htm

Scotland: U.S. Consulate General, 3 Regent Terrace, Edinburgh, tel. 0131/556-8315, www.usembassy.org.uk/scotland

Spain: U.S. Embassy, Calle Serrano 75, Madrid, tel. 915-872-240, emergency tel. 915-872-200, www.embusa.es/cons/services.html

Switzerland: U.S. Embassy, Jubilaeumsstrasse 93, Bern, tel. 031-357-7234, www.us-embassy.ch

Let's Talk Telephones

To make international calls, you need to break the codes: the international access codes and country codes (see below). For information on making local, long-distance, and international calls, see "Telephones" in this book's introduction.

International Access Codes

When dialing direct, first dial the international access code (011 if you're calling from the U.S.A. or Canada; 00 if you're calling from Europe). All European countries use "00" as their international access code.

Country Codes

After you've dialed the international access code, dial the code of the country you're calling.

Austria—43	Denmark—45
Belgium—32	Estonia—372
Britain—44	Finland—358
Canada—1	France—33
Croatia—385	Germany—49
Czech Rep.—420	Gibraltar—350

European Calling Chart

Just smile and dial, using this key:
AC = Area Code, LN = Local Number.

European Country	Calling long distance within ...	Calling from the U.S.A./ Canada to ...	Calling from a European country to ...
Austria	AC + LN	011 + 43 + AC (without the initial zero) + LN	00 + 43 + AC (without the initial zero) + LN
Belgium	LN	011 + 32 + LN (without initial zero)	00 + 32 + LN (without initial zero)
Britain	AC + LN	011 + 44 + AC (without initial zero) + LN	00 + 44 + AC (without initial zero) + LN
Czech Republic	LN	011 + 420 + LN	00 + 420 + LN
Denmark	LN	011 + 45 + LN	00 + 45 + LN
Estonia	LN	011 + 372 + LN	00 + 372 + LN
Finland	AC + LN	011 + 358 + AC (without initial zero) + LN	00 + 358 + AC (without initial zero) + LN
France	LN	011 + 33 + LN (without initial zero)	00 + 33 + LN (without initial zero)
Germany	AC + LN	011 + 49 + AC (without initial zero) + LN	00 + 49 + AC (without initial zero) + LN
Gibraltar	LN	011 + 350 + LN	00 + 350 + LN From Spain: 9567 + LN
Greece	LN	011 + 30 + LN	00 + 30 + LN

European Country	Calling long distance within...	Calling from the U.S.A./ Canada to...	Calling from a European country to...
Ireland	AC + LN	011 + 353 + AC (without initial zero) + LN	00 + 353 + AC (without initial zero) + LN
Italy	LN	011 + 39 + LN	00 + 39 + LN
Morocco	LN	011 + 212 + LN (without initial zero)	00 + 212 + LN (without initial zero)
Netherlands	AC + LN	011 + 31 + AC (without initial zero) + LN	00 + 31 + AC (without initial zero) + LN
Norway	LN	011 + 47 + LN	00 + 47 + LN
Portugal	LN	011 + 351 + LN	00 + 351 + LN
Spain	LN	011 + 34 + LN	00 + 34 + LN
Sweden	AC + LN	011 + 46 + AC (without initial zero) + LN	00 + 46 + AC (without initial zero) + LN
Switzerland	LN	011 + 41 + LN (without initial zero)	00 + 41 + LN (without initial zero)
Turkey	AC (if no initial zero is included, add one) + LN	011 + 90 + AC (without initial zero) + LN	00 + 90 + AC (without initial zero) + LN

- The instructions above apply whether you're calling a fixed phone or cell phone.

- The international access codes (the first numbers you dial when making an international call) are 011 if you're calling from the U.S.A./Canada, or 00 if you're calling from anywhere in Europe.

- To call the U.S.A. or Canada from Europe, dial 00, then 1 (the country code for the U.S.A. and Canada), then the area code and number. In short, 00 + 1 + AC + LN = Hi, Mom!

Greece—30
Ireland—353
Italy—39
Morocco—212
Netherlands—31
Norway—47
Poland—48

Portugal—351
Slovenia—386
Spain—34
Sweden—46
Switzerland—41
Turkey—90
U.S.A.—1

Numbers and Stumblers

• Europeans write a few of their numbers differently than we do: 1 = $\mathcal{1}$, 4 = $\mathcal{4}$, 7= $\mathcal{7}$. Learn the difference or miss your train.
• Europeans write dates as day/month/year (Christmas is 25/12/04).
• Commas are decimal points, and decimals are commas. A dollar and a half is 1,50. There are 5.280 feet in a mile.
• When counting with fingers, start with your thumb. If you hold up your first finger to request one item, you'll probably get two.
• What we Americans call the second floor of a building is the first floor in Europe.
• Europeans keep the left "lane" open for passing on escalators and moving sidewalks. Keep to the right.

Temperature Conversion: Fahrenheit and Celsius

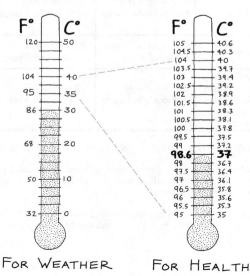

FOR WEATHER   FOR HEALTH

Metric Conversion (approximate)

1 inch = 25 millimeters	32 degrees F = 0 degrees C
1 foot = 0.3 meter	82 degrees F = about 28 degrees C
1 yard = 0.9 meter	1 ounce = 28 grams
1 mile = 1.6 kilometers	1 kilogram = 2.2 pounds
1 centimeter = 0.4 inch	1 quart = 0.95 liter
1 meter = 39.4 inches	1 square yard = 0.8 square meter
1 kilometer = 0.62 mile	1 acre = 0.4 hectare

Climate

Here is a list of average temperatures (first line—average daily low; second line—average daily high; third line—days of no rain). This can be helpful in planning your itinerary, but I have never found European weather to be particularly predictable, and these charts ignore humidity.

J	F	M	A	M	J	J	A	S	O	N	D

AUSTRIA • Vienna

J	F	M	A	M	J	J	A	S	O	N	D
25°	28°	30°	42°	50°	56°	60°	59°	53°	44°	37°	30°
34°	38°	47°	58°	67°	73°	76°	75°	68°	56°	45°	37°
16	17	18	17	18	16	18	18	20	18	16	16

BELGIUM • Brussels

J	F	M	A	M	J	J	A	S	O	N	D
30°	32°	36°	41°	46°	52°	54°	54°	51°	45°	38°	32°
40°	44°	51°	58°	65°	72°	73°	72°	69°	60°	48°	42°
10	11	14	12	15	15	14	13	17	14	10	12

CZECH REPUBLIC • Prague

J	F	M	A	M	J	J	A	S	O	N	D
23°	24°	30°	38°	46°	52°	55°	55°	49°	41°	33°	27°
31°	34°	44°	54°	64°	70°	73°	72°	65°	53°	42°	34°
18	17	21	19	18	18	18	19	20	18	18	18

DENMARK • Copenhagen

J	F	M	A	M	J	J	A	S	O	N	D
29°	28°	31°	37°	45°	51°	56°	56°	51°	44°	38°	33°
37°	37°	42°	51°	60°	66°	70°	69°	64°	55°	46°	41°
14	15	19	18	20	18	17	16	14	14	11	12

FRANCE • Paris

J	F	M	A	M	J	J	A	S	O	N	D
34°	34°	39°	43°	49°	55°	58°	58°	53°	46°	40°	36°
43°	45°	54°	60°	68°	73°	76°	75°	70°	60°	50°	44°
14	14	19	17	19	18	19	18	17	18	15	15

GERMANY • Berlin

J	F	M	A	M	J	J	A	S	O	N	D
23°	23°	30°	38°	45°	51°	55°	54°	48°	40°	33°	26°
35°	38°	48°	56°	64°	70°	74°	73°	67°	56°	44°	36°
15	12	18	15	16	13	15	15	17	18	15	16

	J	F	M	A	M	J	J	A	S	O	N	D
GREAT BRITAIN • London
	36°	36°	38°	42°	47°	53°	56°	56°	52°	46°	42°	38°
	43°	44°	50°	56°	62°	69°	71°	71°	65°	58°	50°	45°
	16	15	20	18	19	19	19	20	17	18	15	16
IRELAND • Dublin
	34°	35°	37°	39°	43°	48°	52°	51°	48°	43°	39°	37°
	46°	47°	51°	55°	60°	65°	67°	67°	63°	57°	51°	47°
	18	18	21	19	21	19	18	19	18	20	18	17
ITALY • Rome
	40°	42°	45°	50°	56°	63°	67°	67°	62°	55°	49°	44°
	52°	55°	59°	66°	74°	82°	87°	86°	79°	71°	61°	55°
	13	19	23	24	26	26	30	29	25	23	19	21
NETHERLANDS • Amsterdam
	31°	31°	34°	40°	46°	51°	55°	55°	50°	44°	38°	33°
	40°	42°	49°	56°	64°	70°	72°	71°	67°	57°	48°	42°
	9	9	15	14	17	16	14	13	11	11	9	10
SPAIN • Madrid
	35°	36°	41°	45°	50°	58°	63°	63°	57°	49°	42°	36°
	47°	52°	59°	65°	70°	80°	87°	85°	77°	65°	55°	48°
	23	21	21	21	21	25	29	28	24	23	21	21
SWITZERLAND • Bern
	29°	30°	36°	42°	49°	55°	58°	58°	53°	44°	37°	31°
	38°	42°	51°	59°	66°	73°	77°	76°	69°	58°	47°	40°
	20	19	22	21	20	19	22	20	20	21	19	21

Faxing Your Hotel Reservation

Use this handy form for your fax or find it online at
www.ricksteves.com/reservation. Photocopy and fax away.

One-Page Fax

To: _____ @ _____
                  hotel   fax

From: _____ @ _____
                   name   fax

Today's date: ____ /_____ /____
                day   month   year

Dear Hotel _____,

Please make this reservation for me:

Name: _____

Total # of people: _____   # of rooms: _____   # of nights: _____

Arriving: ____ /_____ /____   My time of arrival (24-hr clock): _____
            day   month   year   (I will telephone if I will be late)

Departing: ____ /_____ /____
              day   month   year

Room(s): Single___ Double___ Twin___ Triple___ Quad___

With: Toilet___ Shower___ Bath___ Sink only___

Special needs: View___ Quiet___ Cheapest___ Ground Floor___

Credit card: Visa___ MasterCard___ American Express___

Card #: _____

Expiration date:_____

Name on card: _____

After you've confirmed my reservation, you may charge me for the first night
as a deposit. Please fax, e-mail, or mail me confirmation of my reservation,
noting the type of room reserved and the price. Please also inform me of your
cancellation policy. Thank you.

_____
Signature

_____
Name

_____
Address

_____
City   State   Zip Code   Country

_____
E-mail Address

Road Scholar Feedback for
BEST OF EUROPE 2004

We're all in the same travelers' school of hard knocks. Your feedback helps us improve this guidebook for future travelers. Please fill this out (or use the online version at www.ricksteves.com/feedback), attach more info or any tips/favorite discoveries if you like, and send it to us. As thanks for your help, we'll send you our quarterly travel newsletter free for one year. Thanks! **Rick**

Of the recommended accommodations/restaurants used, which was:

Best _____

    Why? _____

Worst _____

    Why? _____

Of the sights/experiences/destinations recommended by this book, which was:

Most overrated _____

    Why? _____

Most underrated _____

    Why? _____

Best ways to improve this book:

_____

_____

I'd like a free newsletter subscription:

_____ Yes   _____ No   _____ Already on list

_____
Name

_____
Address

_____
City, State, Zip

_____
E-mail Address

Please send to: ETBD, Box 2009, Edmonds, WA 98020

INDEX OF SIGHTS

RICK STEVES

 RICK STEVES is on a mission: to help make European travel accessible and meaningful for Americans. Rick has spent 100 days every year since 1973 exploring Europe. He's researched and written 24 travel guidebooks. He writes and hosts the public television series *Rick Steves Europe*, now in its seventh season. With the help of his hardworking staff of 60 at Europe through the Back Door, Rick organizes and leads tours of Europe and offers an information-packed Web site (www.ricksteves.com). Rick, his wife (and favorite travel partner) Anne, and their two teenage children, Andy and Jackie, call Edmonds, just north of Seattle, home.

Rick Steves

COUNTRY GUIDES 2004

Best of Europe
Best of Eastern Europe
France
Germany, Austria & Switzerland
Great Britain
Ireland
Italy
Scandinavia
Spain & Portugal

CITY GUIDES 2004

Amsterdam, Bruges & Brussels
Florence & Tuscany
London
Paris
Provence & The French Riviera
Rome
Venice

MORE EUROPE FROM RICK STEVES

Europe 101
Europe Through the Back Door 2004
Mona Winks
Postcards from Europe

More Savvy. More Surprising. More Fun.

PHRASE BOOKS & DICTIONARIES

French, Italian & German
French
German
Italian
Portuguese
Spanish

VHS RICK STEVES' EUROPE

The Best of Ireland
Bulgaria, Eastern Turkey, Slovenia
    & Croatia
The Heart of Italy
London & Paris
Prague, Amsterdam & the Swiss Alps
Romantic Germany & Berlin
Rome, Caesar's Rome, Sicily
South England, Heart of England & Scotland
Southwest Germany & Portugal
Travel Skills Special
Venice & Veneto 2003

DVD RICK STEVES' EUROPE

Rick Steves' Europe
    All Thirty Shows 2000-2003
Britain & Ireland
Exotic Europe
Germany, the Swiss Alps
    & Travel Skills
Italy